Shifting the Center

Shifting the Center

Understanding Contemporary Families

Fourth Edition

SUSAN J. FERGUSON
Grinnell College

The McGraw·Hill Companies

Connect
Learn
Succeed™

SHIFTING THE CENTER: UNDERSTANDING CONTEMPORARY FAMILIES,
FOURTH EDITION

Published by McGraw-Hill, a business unit of The McGraw-Hill Companies, Inc., 1221 Avenue
of the Americas, New York, NY 10020. Copyright © 2011 by The McGraw-Hill Companies, Inc.
All rights reserved. Previous editions © 2007, 2001, and 1998. No part of this publication may
be reproduced or distributed in any form or by any means, or stored in a database or retrieval
system, without the prior written consent of The McGraw-Hill Companies, Inc., including,
but not limited to, in any network or other electronic storage or transmission, or broadcast for
distance learning.

Some ancillaries, including electronic and print components, may not be available to customers outside the United States.

1 2 3 4 5 6 7 8 9 0 DOC/DOC 10 9 8 7 6 5 4 3 2 1 0

ISBN 978-0-07-340423-3
MHID 0-07-340423-3

Vice President & Editor-in-Chief: *Michael Ryan*
Vice President EDP/Central Publishing Services: *Kimberly Meriwether David*
Senior Sponsoring Editor: *Gina Boedeker*
Executive Marketing Manager: *Pamela S. Cooper*
Managing Editor: *Nicole Bridge*
Project Manager: *Erin Melloy*
Design Coordinator: *Margarite Reynolds*
Cover Designer: *Carole Lawson*
Cover Credit: *Farinaz Taghavi/Getty Images*
Buyer: *Kara Kudronowicz*
Composition: *Laserwords Private Limited*
Typeface: *10/12 Palatino*
Printer: *R.R. Donnelley*

All credits appearing on page or at the end of the book are considered to be an extension of the
copyright page.

Library of Congress Cataloging-in-Publication Data

Shifting the center : understanding contemporary families/[compiled by] Susan J. Ferguson.
— 4th ed.
    p. cm.
  ISBN-13: 978-0-07-340423-3 (alk. paper)
  ISBN-10: 0-07-340423-3
1. Families—United States. 2. Marriage—United States. 3. Kinship—United States. I.
Ferguson, Susan J.
  HQ536.S488 2011
  306.80973—dc22
                                                                    2010009835

www.mhhe.com

With love to my parents Jim and Janet Ferguson

The family is changing, not disappearing. We have to broaden our understanding of it, look for the new metaphors.

—Mary Catherine Bateson

Preface

This anthology originated in the classroom. Over the years, students have challenged me to bring in readings on the family that integrate material on race-ethnicity, social class, gender, and sexual orientation. The lack of fully integrated family texts has been frustrating and puzzling to me; most anthologies on the family "lump" family diversity into one section, which often appears at the end of the book. This placement is problematic because it still marginalizes those families that differ from the idealized traditional family of the dominant culture. Instead, the analysis and discussion of diverse family forms should occur throughout the selected topics of a family course. To achieve an integrated framework, I often have compiled large packets of material to bring diverse family experiences and multicultural and intersectional perspectives into my classroom. After years of teaching family courses this way, I realized that a new anthology could and *should* be created to integrate the voices and experiences of diverse families. This book represents a collection of articles that meets four pedagogical goals: (1) to deconstruct the notion of a universal family over time and across cultures; (2) to reflect cutting-edge scholarship by well-known family scholars; (3) to integrate race-ethnicity, social class, gender, and sexuality in the analysis; and (4) to promote critical reading and thinking.

The title of this anthology, *Shifting the Center: Understanding Contemporary Families*, was inspired by Margaret Andersen and Patricia Hill Collins' essay "Shifting the Center and Reconstructing Knowledge" in *Race, Class, and Gender: An Anthology* (1995). In their essay, Andersen and Collins argue for the need to shift the center of analysis away from the dominant culture to the experiences of all racial-ethnic and social class groups. In her book, *Feminist Theory: From Margin to Center* (1984), bell hooks, too, argues that "much of feminist theory emerges from privileged women who live at the center, whose perspectives on reality rarely include knowledge and awareness of the lives of women and men who live in the margin" (p. x). Thus, hooks argues that in order for us to have an improved understanding of all human lives, we must place the experiences and knowledge of women of color at the center of feminist theorizing and activism. The same argument can be made for any area of scholarship, including the study of families.

In this anthology on families, "shifting the center" means that the research on families of color, gay and lesbian families, working-class families, and other diverse family forms is moved from the margins of analysis to the center of the analytical framework. In many texts, these family forms are often treated as "alternative" or "deviant." By shifting our focus of inquiry away from family structures based only on traditional marriage, students can better understand that numerous family structures coexist. This anthology examines several family forms, including arranged marriages, cohabitation, heterosexual marriage, domestic partnerships, couples living

apart, single-parent households, stepfamilies, multigenerational families, and gay and lesbian families. "Shifting the center" encourages students to compare these diverse family forms to one another. This shift also enables the instructors to deconstruct the idealized, white, middle-class family and enables students to see how present conceptualizations of family have been socially constructed over time and across cultures.

To understand that the family is a social creation, students need to study the family both historically and comparatively. Historical and cross-cultural articles can help shatter the idea that one universal family form is constant across cultures and time. Thus, some of the articles I have selected show how current patterns of family formation and dissolution in the United States differ from those in our past and in other countries. The articles on various racial-ethnic families in the United States, including the selections on immigrant families, also demonstrate how families within a particular cultural group change over time. As family historian Stephanie Coontz argues in her book, *The Way We Never Were* (1992), the study of family history enables students to dispel many myths about families in the United States. As students study family history, they more easily separate nostalgic misconceptions about the family from the realities of contemporary families.

In addition, the articles in this anthology use social science research to show how the institution of the family is related to other social institutions in society and how those institutions affect the intimate center of family lives. Thus, the readings encourage students to discern the relationships between families and society and among individuals within a family. For example, to help students see that family relations are inherently gendered, I have included selections that show how gender is constructed and maintained within the institution of the family, and how gender affects power dynamics, communication, and intimacy between family members. Moreover, by reading articles on families, work, and poverty, students gain a better understanding of how socioeconomic class positions can affect family structure and relations. Reading articles that illuminate either the macrolevel of family structure in society or the microlevel of social interaction within families helps students perceive the multiple linkages between society, families, and individuals. Furthermore, when articles address the intersection of race-ethnicity, gender, social class, and sexual orientation at these two levels of study, students get a fuller picture of contemporary family diversity, including an understanding of how diverse families affect individual identities.

The articles in this anthology should enhance students' abilities to compare social science research findings with the assumptions underlying public debates about family. Students will be better able to utilize research evidence in evaluating images of family life offered in the popular culture, especially in film, on television, and in music lyrics. If students learn to evaluate empirical evidence, they also will be able to make better-informed decisions about public policy issues concerning families and perhaps, in the future, to shape better social policies for *all* families.

Ultimately, it is my hope this anthology will instill a sociological imagination in students. By encouraging students to think critically about what

they are reading, this anthology helps students understand the difference between family concerns that are "public issues" and those that are "private troubles." This anthology contains the most current, innovative work by family scholars that highlights the concepts, theories, and research methodologies currently used to study family. I have tried to choose articles that are accessible, timely, and substantive and which will engage students and promote critical thinking. Thus, my assumption throughout has been not only that students are capable of understanding rigorous social science research on families, but also that the research can inspire students to think more critically about families and our social world.

Changes to the Fourth Edition

With this fourth edition, I maintain my commitment to having the articles meet the four pedagogical goals described earlier: (1) to deconstruct the notion of a universal family over time and across cultures; (2) to reflect cutting-edge scholarship by well-known family scholars; (3) to integrate race-ethnicity, social class, gender, and sexuality in the analysis; and (4) to promote critical reading and thinking. Since I revised the third edition in 2006–2007, there has been an explosion of scholarship in the sociology of the family. Therefore, I have extensively revised this edition to incorporate more of this cutting-edge scholarship. Specifically, I have added 25 new selections that either focus on timely social issues in contemporary family life (i.e., arranged marriages, lesbian coparent families, the college hook-up culture, couples who live apart, foster care, marriage as a "greedy" institution, sperm donation and fatherhood, childcare networks, gender and housework, governmental marriage-promotion policies, the commercialization of childhood, gender and divorce, single mothers and poverty, family policies, fast-track women and "opting out" of work, and the media framing of divorce) or enhance the racial-ethnic diversity of family scholarship already contained in earlier volumes. In particular, I have added eight new articles that examine race and the historical construction of families, transracial adoption, theories and scholarship on black families, Mexican migrants and the work–family balance, gender stratification in different racial-ethnic families, arranged marriages in India, children growing up in Korean and Vietnamese immigrant families, and African American children and alternative caregivers.

Another new feature of the fourth edition is the expansion of several sections to better accommodate the diverse literature on family life and new scholarship. These expanded sections are (1) Historical Changes and Family Variations; (2) Marriage, Cohabitation, and Partnership; (3) Parents and Parenting, Children and Childrearing; (4) Divorce, Remarriage, and Blended Families; and (5) Families, Work, and Carework. This expansion should enable professors and students to examine aspects of family life in greater depth. I also moved the section on motherhood and fatherhood to before the section on parents and children. I think this reorganization will be more clear for professors and students to follow. Of course, for all of the readings, I have

tried to choose selections that are interesting and accessible to students. To that end, I have edited many of the longer readings from the third edition to make them more accessible.

Probably the largest change from the third edition to the fourth edition is the deletion of the part introductions before each section. Several reviewers said they do not assign this as reading in their classes. After much deliberation, I decided to cut these brief summaries in order to make room for a couple more readings that provide a critical new perspective on the family. Note that I also have written an accompanying test manual that contains many examination and discussion questions for each reading. As the editor of this anthology, I developed these items with the goal of helping instructors test students' understanding of key sociological concepts and themes. Please note as well that I welcome feedback from professors and students on this edition of *Shifting the Center: Understanding Contemporary Families.*

Acknowledgments

Several people contributed to the research and development of this anthology on families. My original thinking on the sociology of the family was greatly influenced by my graduate school professors and fellow graduate students at the University of Massachusetts at Amherst. It was there that I worked as a teaching assistant in family courses, began my own research on the never married, and taught my first classes on the family. I especially want to acknowledge and thank professors Naomi Gerstel, Suzanne Model, and Alice Rossi for sharing with me their insights on the family.

At Grinnell College, I am grateful for the ongoing support of both my colleagues and students in the Sociology Department. I particularly want to acknowledge the Grinnell students who have taken my family seminar over the past sixteen years and have suggested new readings or ways of understanding contemporary family life. This anthology was written for them, and they continue to provide insight into how it can be better improved. I also appreciate the labor provided by my student research assistants on the fourth edition: Nichole Baker and Amelia Rudberg.

My special thanks also go to the family scholars who reviewed this edition: Medora W. Barnes, University of Connecticut; Denise A. Copelton, The College at Brockport, State University of New York; Sharon Elise, California State University San Marcos; Amy Holzgang, Cerritos College; E. Brooke Kelly, University of North Carolina at Pembroke; Carolyn Liebler, University of Minnesota; Chadwick L. Menning, Ball State University; and Melanie Moore, University of Northern Colorado.

At McGraw-Hill Publishing, I am appreciative of the work done by Gina Boedeker, Nicole Bridge, and Kate Scheinman. In addition, three other people on the production team need to be acknowledged: Fred Cartwright obtained the permissions in a timely fashion; Margaret Moore did a fine job copy-editing the manuscript; and Vicki Moran kept the book on schedule.

Contents

xi

Part IV MARRIAGE, COHABITATION, AND PARTNERSHIP 174

Part V MOTHERHOOD AND FATHERHOOD 275

Part VI PARENTS AND PARENTING, CHILDREN
         AND CHILDREARING   366

Part VII GRANDPARENTS AND MULTIGENERATIONAL
          RELATIONSHIPS   458

Part IX FAMILIES AND VIOLENCE 572

Part X FAMILIES, WORK, AND CAREWORK 626

About the Editor

Susan Ferguson is a professor of sociology at Grinnell College, where she regularly teaches a seminar on the family. Ferguson also teaches a first-year tutorial, Introduction to Sociology, and courses on the Sociology of Health and Illness, the Sociology of the Body, and research methods. Ferguson has published research in both the areas of medical sociology and the family. Her co-edited book, *Breast Cancer: Society Shapes an Epidemic* (Palgrave, 2000), is highly acclaimed. Ferguson also has an introductory anthology, *Mapping the Social Landscape: Readings in Sociology* (McGraw-Hill, 2010), and she is editor of a series of research monographs on the family, *Families in the 21st Century* (Allyn and Bacon).

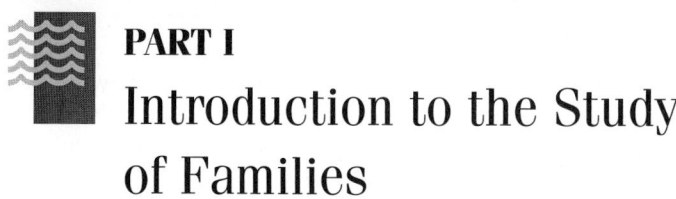

PART I
Introduction to the Study of Families

1

THE FAMILY IN QUESTION
What Is the Family? Is It Universal?

DIANA GITTINS

Until recently, most sociological studies of the family have been dominated by functionalist definitions of what the family is and what "needs" it fulfills in society. Functionalists' theories of the family are treated elsewhere at length (Gittins 1982; Morgan 1975), but it is worth examining some of their main assumptions briefly. Generally, functionalists have argued that the family is a universal institution which performs certain specific functions essential to society's survival. Murdock, for instance, defined the family as a "social group characterised by common residence, economic co-operation, and reproduction. It includes adults of both sexes, at least two of whom maintain a socially approved sexual relationship, and one or more children, own or adopted, of the sexually cohabiting adults."[1] The four basic functions of the family, therefore, are seen as common residence, economic co-operation, reproduction, sexuality. Let us examine each of these in more detail.

Household is the term normally used to refer to co-residence. Murdock's assumption is that it is also a defining characteristic of "the family," and vice versa. It is generally assumed that a married couple, or parent and child(ren), will form a household, and that family implies and presupposes "household." Yet this is by no means always so. Margaret Mead (1971) showed how Samoan children chose the household where they wanted to reside, and often changed their residence again later. Sibling households—or frérèches—were common in parts of Europe, and are a dominant form of household among the Ashanti (Bender 1979:494).

There are numerous examples in contemporary society of families who do not form households, or only form households for periods of time. Families where the husband is in the armed services, is a traveling salesman or travels frequently abroad may only have the husband/father resident for

short periods of time. Families where partners have jobs some distance away from one another may maintain a second household where one of them lives during the week. Children who are sent to boarding school may spend little more than a third of the year residing with their parent(s).

Gutman (1976) found that it was common among black slave families in the USA for a husband and wife to live on different plantations and see one another for a few hours once or twice a week. Soliende de Gonzalez (1965) found this type of household very common in Black Carib society: "there are groupings which I have called 'dispersed families' in which the father, although absent for long periods of time, retains ultimate authority over a household for which he provides the only support, and where affective bonds continue to be important between him and his wife and children" (p. 1544). Obviously people can consider themselves "family" without actually co-residing, and can also co-reside without considering themselves to be "family."

On the other hand, households might be characterised by a shared set of activities such as sleeping, food preparation, eating, sexual relations, and caring for those who cannot care for themselves. Some have argued that a household can be defined to some extent in terms of a range of domestic activities. "Sharing the same pot" has traditionally been the boundary drawn by census enumerators for demarcating one household from another. Yet these activities need not necessarily, and often do not, occur within one household. Some members of a household may eat there all the time, while others only part of the time. Similarly, as mentioned before, some members may not always sleep in the household for a majority of the time. They may well consider themselves notwithstanding to be a family. Conversely, prisoners eat and sleep under the same roof, but do not consider themselves to be a family.

There is no hard-and-fast rule, much less a definition in universal terms, that can be applied to a household in terms of domestic activities. Whether in modern industrial society or in Africa or Asia "there is no basis for assuming that such activities as sleeping, eating, child-rearing and sexual relations must form a complex and must always occur under one roof" (Smith 1978:33). Household is thus in some ways just as nebulous a term as family, although it lacks the ideological implications that "family" carries.

Murdock further posits "economic co-operation" as a defining characteristic of all families. This is a very broad term and can encompass a wide range of activities from cooking to spinning to resources in terms of people and skills. Economic co-operation is something which can, and does, occur throughout all levels of society and is not specific to the family. Economic co-operation frequently occurs *between* households as well as between individuals within households. Undoubtedly households do entail an economic relationship in various ways; in particular, they entail the distribution, production and allocation of resources. Resources include food, drink, material goods, but also service, care, skills, time and space. The notion of "co-operation," moreover, implies an equal distribution of resources, yet this is seldom so. Allocating food, space, time and tasks necessitates some kind of a division of labour; different tasks need doing every day and may vary by week and by season. The number of people living together will be

finite but also changeable—not just in terms of numbers, but also in terms of age, sex, marital status, and physical capacity.

All resources are finite and some may be extremely scarce; some form of allocation therefore has to occur, and this presupposes power relationships. Food, work, and space are rarely distributed equally between co-residing individuals, just as they differ between households and social sectors. Most frequently, the allocation of resources and division of labour is based on differences according to sex and age. Rather than using Murdock's definition of "economic co-operation," it is thus more useful to understand families in terms of the ways in which gender and age define, and are defined by, the division of labour within, and beyond, households. These divisions also presuppose power relationships and inequality—in effect, patriarchy—rather than co-operation and equality.

Power relationships define and inform concepts of sexuality, Murdock's third defining category. His definition of sexuality is *hetero*sexuality, although this is only one of various forms of sexuality. Presumably this is because the final—and perhaps most important—"function" of families as seen by such theorists is reproduction, which necessitates heterosexual relations, at least at times. Sexuality is not something specific to families; rather, the assumption is that heterosexuality *should* be a defining characteristic of families. It also, according to Murdock, presupposes a "socially approved relationship" between two adults.

Social recognition of mating and of parenthood is obviously intimately bound up with social definitions and customs of marriage. It is often assumed that, in spite of a variety of marriage customs and laws, marriage as a binding relationship between a man and a woman is universal. Yet it has been estimated that only 10 per cent of all marriages in the world are actually monogamous; polyandry and polygyny are common in many societies, just as serial monogamy is becoming increasingly common in our own. Marriage is not always a heterosexual relationship; among the Nuer, older women marry younger women. The Nuer also practise a custom known as "ghost marriages," whereby when an unmarried or childless man dies, a relation of his then marries a woman "to his name" and the resulting children of this union are regarded as the dead man's children and bear his name (see Edholm 1982:172).

Marriage customs are not only variable between cultures and over time, but also vary between social classes. Moreover, Jessie Bernard (1973) has shown that the meanings which men and women attribute to the same marriage differ quite markedly. Undoubtedly marriage involves some form of status passage and public avowal of recognizing other(s) as of particular importance in one way or another, yet it does not occur universally between two people, nor between two people of the opposite sex, nor is it always viewed as linked to reproduction. Marriage, in the way in which we think of it, is therefore not universal.

Similarly, definitions of sexuality with regard to incest have not been universal or unchanging. In medieval Europe it was considered incestuous to have sexual relations with anyone less than a seventh cousin, and marriage

between cousins was proscribed. Now it is possible to marry first cousins. In Egypt during the Pharaonic and Ptolemaic period, sibling marriages were permitted, and, in some cases, father–daughter marriages. This was seen as a way of preserving the purity of royalty and was not endorsed for the whole of society—although it was permitted for everyone after the Roman conquest of Egypt.

Incestuous marriages were also permitted among royal families in Hawaii and Peru. The Mormons of Utah allowed incest (and polygamy) as a means of ensuring marriage within their church; this was not banned until 1892 (Renvoize 1982:32). Obviously these examples are more related to marriage customs and inheritance or descent problems, but serve to illustrate that even an incest taboo cannot be taken as a universal defining characteristic of families: "who could Adam's sons marry except their sisters?" (ibid., p. 32). Nevertheless, the almost universal existence of some form of incest taboo is a useful illustration of the fact that all societies do, in a myriad of ways, have some form of social organisation of sexuality, mating and reproduction.

Murdock's definition does not take adequate account of the diversity of ways in which co-residence, economic relations, sexuality and reproduction can be organised. Various theorists have made amendments and refinements to Murdock's definition of the family, but all tend to make similar errors. In particular, they translate contemporary western (and usually middle-class) ideas and ideals of what a family should be into what they assume it is everywhere.

Far more precise attempts at definition and analysis have been made by anthropologists who prefer the term kinship to that of family. A feminist anthropologist defined kinship as "the ties which exist between individuals who are seen as related both through birth (descent) and through mating (marriage). It is thus primarily concerned with the ways in which mating is socially organised and regulated, the ways in which parentage is assigned, attributed and recognised, descent is traced, relatives are classified, rights are transferred across generations and groups are formed" (Edholm 1982:166). This definition of kinship is a vast improvement on functionalist definitions of family because, first, it stresses the fact that kinship is a social construction, and, second, it emphasises the variability of kinship depending on how it is defined. The social nature of kinship has been stressed by many others elsewhere,[2] and yet there remains a strong common-sense belief that kinship is in fact a quite straightforward biological relationship. It is not.

We assume that because we (think we) know who our parents are and how they made us that kinship is therefore a biological fact. Consider, however, stories we have all heard about children who were brought up by parent(s) for perhaps twenty years, who all along believed their parents were their biological parents, but then discovered that they had in fact been adopted. Such people often suffer severe "identity crises" because they no longer know "who they are" or who their parents are. Their suffering is caused by the way in which we define kinship in our society, namely, in strictly biological terms, differentiating clearly between a "biological" and a "social" parent. The biological parent is always seen by our society as the

"real" parent with whom a child should have the strongest ties and bonds. Knowledge of parenthood through families is the central way in which individuals are "located" socially and economically in western society. This, however, is a culturally and historically specific way of defining parenthood and kinship. Other cultures and groups in modern society believe that the person who rears a child is by definition the real parent, regardless of who was involved in the actual reproduction process.

In many poor families in Western Europe and America well into this century it was not uncommon for children to be raised by a grandparent, other kin, or friend, and such children often thought of those who raised them as their parents, even though acknowledging that they also had biological parents who were different. R. T. Smith (1978) found such practises common in Guyana and Jamaica, and reports how "close and imperishable bonds are formed through the act of 'raising' children, irrespective of genetic ties. . . . What is erroneously termed 'fictive kinship' is a widespread phenomenon. . . . While a father may be defined minimally as the person whose genetic material mingled with that of the mother in the formation of the child during one act of sexual intercourse, the father 'role' varies a good deal in any but the most homogeneous societies" (p. 353).

Others have shown the ways in which kinship is a social construction, and how those who are not biologically related to one another come to define themselves as kin: "Liebow, Stack, Ladner and others describe fictive kinship, by which friends are turned into family. Since family is supposed to be more reliable than friendship, 'going for brothers,' 'for sisters,' 'for cousins,' increases the commitment of a relationship, and makes people ideally more responsible for one another. Fictive kinship is a serious relationship" (Rapp 1980:292). It is possible to argue that this is how all kinship began and becomes constructed. Kinship, whether we choose to label it as "biological," "social" or "fictive," is a way of identifying others as in some way special from the rest, people to whom the individual or collectivity feel responsible in certain ways. It is a method of demarcating obligations and responsibility between individuals and groups.

It is thus essential to get away from the idea that kinship is a synonym for "blood" relations—*even though it may often be expressed in those terms*—and to think of it as a social construction which is highly variable and flexible. Some anthropologists recently have argued that kinship is no more and no less than a system of meanings and symbols and that it is "absolutely distinct from a biological system or a system of biological reproduction. Animals reproduce, mate, and undoubtedly form attachments to each other, but they do not have kinship systems" (Smith 1978:351). Indeed, just as Marx argued that it is labour that distinguishes people from animals, it could equally be argued that it is kinship systems that do just that.

This is not to say that many kinship relations do not have some sort of biological base—many do—but the fact that not all of them do, and that the type of base is highly variable, means that it cannot be assumed that there is some universal biological base to kinship. There is not. As Edholm (1982) argues: "notions of blood ties, of biological connection, which to us seem

relatively unequivocal, are highly variable. Some societies of which we have anthropological record recognize only the role of the father or of the mother in conception and procreation. . . . Only one parent is a 'relation,' the other is not. In the Trobriand Islands . . . it is believed that intercourse is not the cause of conception, semen is not seen as essential for conception . . . (but) from the entry of a spirit child into the womb . . . it is the repeated intercourse of the same partner which 'moulds' the child" (p. 168).

Because fatherhood is always potentially unknown, and always potentially contestable, it is therefore also always a social category. Motherhood, on the other hand, is always known. Yet apart from carrying and giving birth to a child, the biological base of motherhood stops there. The rest is socially constructed, although it may be—and often is—attributed to biology or "maternal instinct." Whether or not women breastfeed their children has been historically and culturally variable. Baby bottles are no modern invention, but were used in ancient Egypt and in other cultures since. Historians have noted the number of babies given to "wet nurses" in earlier times in Europe as a sign of lack of love and care for infants on the part of mothers. But we can never really know the emotions felt by people hundreds of years ago or their motivations for their practices. The most we can do is to note that their customs were different. To use our own ideology of motherhood and love and apply it universally to all cultures is a highly ethnocentric and narrow way of trying to understand other societies.

Notions of motherhood and "good mothering" are highly variable:

> In Tahiti young women often have one or two children before they are considered, or consider themselves to be, ready for an approved and stable relationship. It is considered perfectly acceptable for the children of this young woman to be given to her parents or other close kin for adoption. . . . The girl can decide what her relationship to the children will be, but there is no sense in which she is forced into "motherhood" because of having had a baby. (Edholm 1982:170)

Who cares for children and rears them is also variable, although in most cases it is women who do so rather than men. Often those women who rear children may well claim some kinship tie to the biological mother—for example, grandmother or aunt—but this tie may simply be created as a result of rearing another woman's child. Motherhood, therefore, if taken to mean both bearing and rearing children, is not universal and is not a biological "fact."

Nor can it be argued that there is such a thing as maternal "instinct," although it is commonly believed to exist. Women are capable of conceiving children today from the age of 13 or 14, and can continue to bear children approximately every two years until they are 45 or 50. This could mean producing around eighteen or nineteen children (although fecundity declines as women age), and this, of course, seldom occurs. Few women in western society marry before they are 18 or 19, and few women in contemporary society have more than two or three children. Contraceptives control conception, not instincts, and unless it were argued that women are forced to use contraceptives,[3] there is little scope to argue for such a thing as maternal instinct.

Consider further that women who conceive babies now when they are *not* married are not hailed as true followers of their natural instinct, but are considered as "immoral," "loose," "whores," and so on. As Antonis (1981) notes: "maternal instinct is ascribed to *married women* only" (p. 59). That women can conceive and bear children is a universal phenomenon; that they do so by instinct is a fallacy. So is the notion that they always raise them. From the moment of birth, motherhood is a social construction.

Sociological and historical studies of the family have tended to pay most attention to the vertical relationships between parents and children. Less attention is paid to the lateral relationships between siblings. Yet in other cultures, and in Western Europe in earlier times, the sibling tie has often formed the basis of households and may be seen as more important than that between parent and child. Among the poorer sectors of western society until quite recently it was common for the eldest daughter to take responsibility for supervising and caring for younger siblings from quite an early age, thereby freeing her mother to engage in waged or domestic work. This remains common in many contemporary societies. In Morocco, for instance, girls "from the age of about four onwards look after younger siblings, fetch and carry, clean and run errands. The tasks themselves are arranged in a hierarchy of importance and attributed to women and girls according to their authority within the household. . . . Boys tend to be freed from domestic tasks and spend their time in groups of peers who play marbles or trap birds" (Maher 1981:73–74).

The content and importance of sibling ties varies, and this is partly a result of different interpretations of reproduction. In societies where the role of the male is seen as peripheral or unimportant—or even non-existent—in reproduction, then his children by another woman are not seen as having any relation to those of the first mother, or vice versa if the mother's role is seen as unimportant. The salience of sibling ties also depends on the organisation of kinship generally. The relative neglect of studying sibling ties as an important aspect of—or even basis of—kinship betrays our own assumptions about the primacy of parenthood in families and, particularly, the assumption that reproduction is the "essence" of kinship, with the mother and child forming the universal core of kinship. As Yanagisako (1977) points out in writing about Goodenough: "while he is undoubtedly right that in every human society mothers and children can be found, to view their *relationship* as the universal nucleus of the family is to attribute to it a social and cultural significance that is lacking in some cases" (pp. 197–98).

Implicit in definitions of kinship is a way of perceiving the social organisation of reproduction and mating, at the centre of which therefore is an organisation of relations between the sexes. The organisation of, and differentiation between, male and female takes many different forms, but all societies do have a social construction of the sexes into gender. Gender is an inherent part of the manner in which all societies are organised and is also a crucial part of the different ways in which kinship has been constructed and defined. The social, economic and political organisation of societies has been initially at least based on kinship—and thus also on gender. Understanding

society means understanding the ways in which a society organised kinship and gender, and how these influence one another. Gender and kinship are universally present—as are mothers and children—but the content of them, and the meanings ascribed to them, is highly variable.

The most basic divisions of labour within any society, as pointed out by Durkheim (1933) and others, are based on age and sex. While age as a category can eventually be achieved, sex is ascribed, permanent, and immutable. The biological differences between men and women are such that only women can conceive and lactate; only men can impregnate. In spite of these obvious differences, none of them is great enough to be adequate grounds for allocating one kind of work to women and another to men. Indeed, cross-culturally and historically there are very few jobs that can be claimed to be specifically and universally performed by either men or women. Women have ploughed and mined and still do; men have laundered, gathered fruit and minded children. Hunting and warfare have almost always been male activities, while care of the young and sick has usually been a female activity. But allocation of tasks is also strongly based on age, so it is important to remember that it may be *young* men who hunt and *old* men or women who care for children; old women may be responsible for cooking, while both young men and women may work in the fields or mines.

Age is an important factor to consider in trying to understand the organisation of kinship and households. Nobody remains the same age—contrary to contemporary images in the media of the "happy family" where the couple is permanently 30 and the children forever 8 and 6. As individuals age, so the composition and structure of the unit in which they live change. Consider the ways in which the household composition and resources of a couple change as, first, aged 20, they marry and both work; second, aged 25, they have had two children and the wife has left the labour market for a few years to rear the children until they attend school; third, at 30, one partner leaves or dies and one parent is left with total care of the children; fourth, at 35, one or both may remarry someone who perhaps has three children from an earlier marriage, or may take in an elderly parent to care for, and so on. The number of wage earners and dependants changes over a household's cycle, just as it changes for the individuals within the household.

Thinking in terms of "the" family leads to a static vision of how people actually live and age together and what effects this process has on others within the household in which they live. Moreover, the environment and conditions in which any household is situated are always changing, and these changes can and often do have important repercussions on individuals and households. As Tamara Hareven (1982) points out, it is important when analysing families to differentiate between individual time, family time, and historical time. Thus, in considering the structure and meaning of "family" in any society, it is important to understand how definitions of dependency and individual time vary and change, how patterns of interaction between individuals and households change, and how historical developments affect all of these.

The notion of there being such a thing as "the family" is thus highly controversial and full of ambiguities and contradictions. Childbearing,

childrearing, the construction of gender, allocation of resources, mating and marriage, sexuality and ageing all loosely fit into our idea of family, and yet we have seen how all of them are variable over time, between cultures and between social sectors. The claim that "the family" is universal has been especially problematic because of the failure by most to differentiate between how small groups of people live and work together, and what the ideology of appropriate behaviour for men, women and children within families has been.

Imbued in western patriarchal ideology, as discussed previously, are a number of important and culturally specific beliefs about sexuality, reproduction, parenting and the power relationships between age groups and between the sexes. The sum total of these beliefs makes up a strong *symbol-system which is labelled as the family.* Now while it can be argued that all societies have beliefs and rules on mating, sexuality, gender and age relations, the content of rules is culturally and historically specific and variable, and in no way universal. Thus to claim that patriarchy is universal is as meaningless as claiming that the family is universal.

If defining families is so difficult, how do we try to understand how and why people live, work and form relationships together in our own society? First, we need to acknowledge that while what we may think of as families are not universal, there are still trends and patterns specific to our culture which, by careful analysis, we can understand more fully. Second, we can accept that while there can be no perfect definition, it is still possible to discover certain defining characteristics which can help us to understand changing patterns of behaviour and beliefs. Finally, and most important, we can "deconstruct" assumptions usually made about families by questioning what exactly they mean. Before doing this, however, it is useful to attempt some definition of what is meant by "family" in western society.

Problematic though it may be, it is necessary to retain the notion of co-residence, because most people have lived, and do live, with others for much of their lives. Thus "household" is useful as a defining characteristic, while bearing in mind that it does not necessarily imply sexual or intimate relationships, and that, moreover, relationships *between* households are a crucial aspect of social interaction. "Household" should not be interpreted as a homogeneous and undivided unit. Virtually all households will have their own division of labour, generally based on ideals and beliefs, as well as the structure, of age and sex. There will always tend to be power relationships within households, because they will almost invariably be composed of different age and sex groups and thus different individuals will have differential access to various resources.

Because the essence of any society is interaction, a society will always be composed of a myriad of relationships between people, from the most casual to the most intimate. Relationships are formed between people of the same sex, the opposite sex, the same age group, different age groups, the same and different classes, and so on. Some of these relationships will be sexual—and sexual relations can occur in any type of relationship. Some relationships will be affectionate and loving, others will be violent or hostile. They may

be made up of very brief encounters or may extend over the best part of a person's life cycle. Thus while relationships are extremely varied in the ways in which they are formed, their nature and duration, *ideologically* western society has given highest status to long-term relationships between men and women, and between parents and children. Ideologically, such relationships are supposed to be loving and caring, though in reality many are not. They are presented as "natural," but as we have seen, they are not. These ideals have become reified and sanctified in the notion of "family," virtually to the exclusion of all other long-term or intimate relationships.

Ideals of family relationships have become enshrined in our legal, social, religious and economic systems which, in turn, reinforce the ideology and penalise or ostracise those who transgress it. Thus there are very real pressures on people to behave in certain ways, to lead their lives according to acceptable norms and patterns. Patriarchal ideology is embedded in our socioeconomic and political institutions, indeed, in the very language we use, and as such encourages, cajoles and pressures people to follow certain paths. Most of these are presented and defined in terms of "the family," and the family is in turn seen as the bulwark of our culture. The pressures of patriarchal ideology are acted out—and reacted against—in our interpersonal relationships, in marriage and non-marriage, in love and hate, having children and not having children. In short, much of our social behaviour occurs in, and is judged on the basis of, the ideology of "the family."

Relationships are universal, so is some form of co-residence, of intimacy, sexuality and emotional bonds. But the *forms* these can take are infinitely variable and can be changed and challenged as well as embraced. By analysing the ways in which culture has prescribed certain, and proscribed other, forms of behaviour, it should be possible to begin to see the historical and cultural specificity of what is really meant when reference is made to "the family."

ENDNOTES

[1] Murdock quoted in Morgan (1975), p. 20.

[2] Notably B. J. Harris, J. Goody, W. Goode.

[3] For a full discussion of power relationships between men and women with regard to contraceptive practice see Gittins (1982).

REFERENCES

Antonis, B. 1981. "Motherhood and Mothering." In *Women and Society*, edited by Cambridge Women's Study Group. London: Virago.

Bender, D. R. 1979. "A Refinement of the Concept of Household: Families, Co-residence and Domestic Functions." *American Anthropologist* 69.

Bernard, Jessie. 1973. *The Future of Marriage.* London: Souvenir Press.

Durkheim, Émile. 1933. *The Division of Labour in Society.* London: Collier-Macmillan.

Edholm, F. 1982. "The Unnatural Family." In *The Changing Experience of Women*, edited by Whitelegg et al. Oxford: Martin Robertson.

Gittins, Diana. 1982. *Fair Sex: Family Size and Structure, 1900–1939.* London: Hutchinson.

Goode, William J. 1975. "Force and Violence in the Family." In *Violence in the Family*, edited by Steinmetz and Straus. New York: Harper & Row.

Goody, J. 1972. "The Evolution of the Family." In *Household and Family in Past Time*, edited by Laslett and Wall. Cambridge: Cambridge University Press.

———. 1976. "Inheritance, Property and Women: Some Comparative Considerations." In *Family and Inheritance: Rural Society in Western Europe, 1200–1800*, edited by J. Goody, J. Thirsk, and E. P. Thompson. Cambridge: Cambridge University Press.

Goody, J., J. Thirsk, and E. P. Thompson, eds. 1976. *Family and Inheritance: Rural Society in Western Europe, 1200–1800*. Cambridge: Cambridge University Press.

Gutman, Herbert. 1976. *The Black Family in Slavery and Freedom, 1750–1925*. Oxford: Basil Blackwell.

Hareven, Tamara. 1982. *Family Time and Industrial Time*. New York: Cambridge University Press.

Harris, Barbara J. 1976. "Recent Work on the History of the Family: A Review Article." *Feminist Studies* (Spring):159–72.

Ladner, Joyce A. 1971. *Tomorrow's Tomorrow: The Black Woman*. Garden City, NY: Doubleday.

Liebow, Elliott. 1967. *Tally's Corner: A Study of Negro Streetcorner Men*. Boston: Little, Brown.

Maher, V. 1981. "Work, Consumption and Authority within the Household: A Moroccan Case." In *Of Marriage and Market*, edited by Young et al. London: CSE Books.

Mead, Margaret. 1971. *Male and Female*. Harmondsworth: Penguin.

Morgan, D. H. J. 1975. *Social Theory and the Family*. London: Routledge & Kegan Paul.

Murdock, George. 1949. *Social Structure*. New York: Macmillan.

Rapp, Rayna. 1980. "Family and Class in Contemporary America: Notes Towards an Understanding of Ideology." *Science and Society* 42.

Renvoize, J. 1982. *Incest: A Family History*. London: Routledge & Kegan Paul.

Smith, R. T. 1978. "The Family and the Modern World System: Some Observations from the Caribbean." *Journal of Family History* 3.

Soliende de Gonzalez, N. 1965. "The Consanguineal Household and Matrifocality." *American Anthropologist* 67.

Stack, Carol. 1974. *All Our Kin: Strategies for Survival in a Black Community*. New York: Harper & Row.

Yanagisako, Sylvia J. 1977. "Family and Household: The Analysis of Domestic Groups." *Annual Review of Anthropology* 8.

2

FEMINIST RETHINKING FROM RACIAL-ETHNIC FAMILIES

MAXINE BACA ZINN

Understanding diversity remains a pressing challenge for family scholars. Innumerable shortcomings in dominant social science studies render much thinking ill-suited to the task. The growing diversity movement in women's studies, together with new thinking on racial-ethnic groups, holds the promise of a comprehensive understanding of family life.

The Family Transformation in Western Feminism

Two decades of feminist thinking on the family have demystified the idea of the natural and timeless nuclear family. "By taking gender as a basic category of analysis" (Thorne 1992:5), feminist theory has produced new descriptions of family experience, new conceptualizations of family dynamics, and identified new topics for investigation. The following themes show how conventional notions of the family have been transformed:

1. The family is socially constructed. This means that it is not merely a biological arrangement but is a product of specific historical, social, and material conditions. In other words, it is shaped by the social structure.
2. The family is closely connected with other structures and institutions in society. Rather than being a separate sphere, it cannot be understood in isolation from outside factors. As a result, "the family" can be experienced differently by people in different social classes and of different races, and by women and men.
3. Since structural arrangements are abstract and often invisible, family processes can be deceptive or hidden. Many structural conditions make family life problematic. Therefore, families, like other social institutions, require changes in order to meet the needs of women, men, and children.

These themes have made great strides in challenging the myth of the monolithic family, "which has elevated the nuclear family with a breadwinner husband and a full-time wife and mother as the only legitimate family form" (Thorne 1992:4). Viewing family life within wider systems of economic and political structures has uncovered great complexity in family dynamics and important variation among families within particular racial and ethnic groups. Despite these advances, women of color theorists contend that Western feminists have not gone far enough in integrating racial differences into family studies.

Differing Feminist Perspectives on the Family

Issues that are rooted in racial (and class) differences have always produced debates within feminist scholarship. Racial differences have evoked deeply felt differences among feminists about the meaning of family life for women. Rayna Rapp's description of a typical feminist meeting about the family captured well the essence of the debate in the late 1960s and early 1970s:

> Many of us have been at an archetypical meeting in which someone stands up and asserts that the nuclear family ought to be abolished because it is degrading and constraining to women. Usually, someone else (often representing a third world position) follows on her heels, pointing out that the attack on the family represents a white middle-class

position and that other women need their families for support and survival. (Rapp 1982:168)

Women of color feminists have disagreed with several feminist notions about the meaning of family life for women. As Patricia Zavella recounts the differences:

In particular, we had problems with the separatist politics (automatically uncooperative with men) in some early women's organizations, and with the white middle-class focus of Americans' feminism, a focus implicitly and sometimes explicitly racist. . . . Both the lack of race and class consciousness in much 1970s feminist political and scholarly work came in for severe criticism. (Zavella 1991:316)

Western feminism became more contextual in the 1980s. As women of color continued to challenge the notion that gender produced a universal woman's family experience, feminism in general worked to broaden feminist studies beyond issues important to White, middle-class, heterosexual women (Ginsburg and Tsing 1990:3). Although gender remains the basic analytical category, scholars now acknowledge the relationships between families and other social divisions (Thorne 1992). The discovery that families are differentiated by race and class has had limited impact on family theorizing across groups. Feminist social scientists now routinely note the importance of race and class differences in family life. Yet we have been more successful in offering single studies of particular groups of families and women than in providing systematic comparisons of families in the same society. Although Western feminist thought takes great care to underscore race and class differences, it still marginalizes racial-ethnic families as special "cultural" cases. In other words, when it comes to thinking about family patterns, diversity is treated as if it were an intrinsic property of groups that are "different," rather than as being the product of forces that affect all families, but affect them in different ways. Feminism has taken on the challenge of diversity, yet it continues to treat race as epiphenomenal—in other words, to treat racial inequality and the social construction of race as secondary to gender (Zavella 1989:31). So far, mainstream feminism has failed to grapple with race as a power system that affects families throughout society and to apply that understanding to "the family" writ large. As Evelyn Nakano Glenn (1987) says, "Systematically incorporating hierarchies of race and class into the feminist reconstruction of the family remains a challenge, a necessary next step into the development of theories of family that are inclusive" (p. 368).

Inclusive Feminist Perspectives on Race and Family

Families and household groups have changed over time and varied with social conditions. Distinctive political and economic contexts have created similar family histories for people of color. Composite portraits of each group show them to have family arrangements and patterns that differ from those

of White Americans. Although each group is distinguishable from the others, African Americans, Latinos, and Asians share some important commonalities (Glenn with Yap 1993). These include an extended kinship structure and informal support networks spread across multiple households. Racial-ethnic families are distinctive not only because of their ethnic heritage but also because they reside in a society where racial stratification shapes family resources and structures in important ways.

New thinking about racial stratification provides a perspective for examining family diversity as a structural aspect of society. Race is a socially constructed system that assigns different worth and unequal treatment to groups on the basis of its definition of race. While racial definitions and racial meanings are always being transformed (Omi and Winant 1986), racial hierarchies operate as fundamental axes for the social location of groups and individuals and for the unequal distribution of social opportunities. Racial and ethnic groups occupy particular social locations in which family life is constructed out of widely varying social resources. The uneven distribution of social advantages and social costs operates to strengthen some families while simultaneously weakening others.

By looking at family life in the United States across time and in different parts of the social order, we find that social and economic forces in society have produced alternative domestic arrangements. The key to understanding family diversity lies in the relationship between making a living and maintaining life on a daily basis. Feminist scholars call these activities productive and reproductive labor (Brenner and Laslett 1986:117).

Productive Labor

Historically, racial differences in how people made a living had crucial implications for domestic life. In short, they produced different family and household arrangements on the part of slaves, agricultural workers, and industrial workers. European ethnics were incorporated into low-wage industrial economies of the North, while Blacks, Latinos, Chinese, and Japanese filled labor needs in the colonial labor system of the economically backward regions of the West, Southwest and South. These colonial labor systems, while different, created similar hardships for family life. They required women to work outside of the home in order to maintain even minimal levels of family subsistence. Women's placement in the larger political economy profoundly influenced their family lives.

Several women of color theorists have advanced our understanding of the shaping power of racial stratification, not only for families of color but also for family life in general. For example, Bonnie Thornton Dill (1994) uncovers strong connections in the way racial meanings influence family life. In the antebellum United States, women of European descent received a certain level of protection within the confines of the patriarchal family. There is no doubt that they were constrained as individuals, but family life among European settlers was a highly valued aspect of societal development, and women—to the extent that they contributed to the development of families

and to the economic growth of the nation—were provided institutional support for those activities. Unlike White migrants, who came voluntarily, racial-ethnics either were brought to this country or were conquered to meet the need for a cheap and exploitable labor force. Little attention was given to their family and community life. Labor, and not the existence or maintenance of families, was the critical aspect of their role in building the nation.

Women of color experienced the oppression of a patriarchal society (public patriarchy) but were denied the protections and buffering of a patriarchal family (private patriarchy). Thus, they did not have the social structural supports necessary to make their families a vital element in the social order. Family membership was not a key means of access to participation in the wider society. Families of women of color sustained cultural assaults as a direct result of the organization of the labor systems in which their groups participated. The lack of social, legal, and economic support for racial-ethnic families intensified and extended women's reproductive labor, created tensions and strains in family relationships, and set the stage for a variety of creative and adaptive forms of resistance.

Dill's study suggests a different conceptualization of the family, one that is not so bound by the notion of separate spheres of male and female labor or by the notion of the family as an emotional haven, separate and apart from the demands of the economic marketplace. People of color experienced no separation of work and family, no haven of private life, no protected sphere of domesticity. Women's work outside of the home was an extension of their family responsibilities, as family members—women, men, and children—pooled their resources to put food on the table (Du Bois and Ruiz 1990:iii). What we see here are families and women who are buffeted by the demands of the labor force and provided no legal or social protection other than the maintenance of their ability to work. This research on women of color demonstrates that protecting one's family from the demands of the market is strongly related to the distribution of power and privilege in the society. The majority of White settlers had the power to shelter their members from the market (especially their women and children), and to do so with legal and social support. People of color were denied these protections, and their family members were exploited and oppressed in order to maintain the privileges of the powerful. As Leith Mullings (1986) has said, "It was the working class and enslaved men and women whose labor created the wealth that allowed the middle class and upper middle class domestic lifestyles to exist" (p. 50).

Despite the harsh conditions imposed on family life by racial labor systems, families did not break down. Instead, they adapted as best they could. Using cultural forms where possible, and creating new adaptations where necessary, racial-ethnics adapted their families to the conditions thrust upon them. These adaptations were not exceptions to a "standard" family form. They were produced by forces of inequality in the larger society. Although the White middle-class model of the family has long been defined as the rule, it was neither the norm nor the dominant family type. It was, however, the measure against which other families were judged.

Reproductive Labor

Racial divisions in making a living shape families in important ways. They also determine how people maintain life on a daily basis. Reproductive labor is strongly gendered. It includes activities such as purchasing household goods, preparing and serving food, laundering and repairing clothing, maintaining furnishings and appliances, socializing children, providing care and emotional support for adults, and maintaining kin and community ties (Glenn 1992:1). According to Evelyn Nakano Glenn, reproductive labor has divided along racial as well as gender lines. Specific characteristics of the division have varied regionally and changed over time—shifting parts of it from the household to the market:

> In the first half of the century racial-ethnic women were employed as servants to perform reproductive labor in white households, relieving white middle-class women of onerous aspects of that work; in the second half of the century, with the expansion of commodified services (services turned into commercial products or activities), racial-ethnic women are disproportionately employed as service workers in institutional settings to carry out lower-level "public" reproductive labor, while cleaner white collar supervisory and lower professional positions are filled by white women. (Glenn 1992:3)

The activities of racial-ethnic women in "public" reproductive labor suggest new interpretations of family formation. Knowing that reproductive labor has divided along racial lines offers an understanding of why the idealized family has often been a luxury of the privileged.

Family Patterns as Relational

The distinctive place assigned to racial-ethnic women in the organization of reproductive labor has far-reaching implications for thinking about racial patterns in family diversity. Furthermore, insights about racial divisions apply to White families as well as racial-ethnic families. The new research reveals an important *relational* dimension of family formation. "Relational means that race/gender categories are positioned and that they gain meaning in relation to each other" (Glenn 1992:34). As Bonnie Thornton Dill (1986) puts it, when we examine race, class, and gender simultaneously, we have a better understanding of a social order in which the privileges of some people are dependent on the oppression and exploitation of others (p. 16). This allows us to grasp the benefits that some women derive from their race and their class while also understanding the restrictions that result from gender. In other words, such women are subordinated by patriarchal family dynamics. Yet race and class intersect to create for them privileged opportunities, choices, and lifestyles. For example, Judith Rollins (1985) uses the relationships between Black domestics and their White employers to show how one class and race of women escapes some of the consequences of patriarchy by

using the labor of other women. Her study, *Between Women*, highlights the complex linkages among race, class, and gender as they create both privilege and subordination. These are simultaneous processes that enable us to look at women's diversity from a different angle.

The relational themes of privilege and subordination appear frequently in studies of domestic service (Romero 1992). Victoria Byerly (1986) found that White women who worked in the Southern textile mills hired African Americans as domestic workers. The labor of these domestics enabled the White women to engage in formal work. Vicki Ruiz (1988) describes how Mexican American women factory workers in Texas have eased their housework burdens by hiring Mexican domestic workers (Ward 1990:10–11). These studies highlight some of the ways in which race relations penetrate households, intersecting with gender arrangements to produce varied family experiences.

Theorizing across Racial Categories

Historical and contemporary racial divisions of productive and reproductive labor challenge the assumption that family diversity is the outgrowth of different cultural patterns. Racial stratification creates distinctive patterns in the way families are located and embedded in different social environments. It structures social opportunities differently, and it constructs and positions groups in systematic ways. This offers important lessons for examining current economic and social changes that are influencing families, and influencing them differently. Still, the knowledge that family life differs significantly by race does not preclude us from theorizing across racial categories.

The information and service economy continues to reshape family life by altering patterns associated with marriage, divorce, childbearing, and household composition. A growing body of family research shows that although some families are more vulnerable than others to economic marginalization, none are immune from the deep structural changes undermining "traditional" families. Adaptation takes varying forms, such as increased divorce rates, female-headed households, and extended kinship units. Although new patterns of racial formation will affect some families more than others, looking at social contexts will enable us to better understand family life in general.

The study of Black families can generate important insights for White families (Billingsley 1988). Families may respond in a like manner when impacted by larger social forces. To the extent that White families and Black families experience similar pressures, they may respond in similar ways, including the adaptation of their family structures and other behaviors. With respect to single-parent families, teenage parents, working mothers, and a host of other behaviors, Black families serve as barometers of social change and as forerunners of adaptive patterns that will be progressively experienced by the more privileged sectors of U.S. society.

On the other hand, such insights must not eclipse the ways in which racial meanings shape social perceptions of family diversity. As social and economic changes produce new family arrangements, some alternatives become more tolerable. Race plays an important role in the degree to which alternatives are deemed acceptable. When alternatives are associated with subordinate social categories, they are judged against "the traditional family" and found to be deviant. Many alternative lifestyles that appear new to middle-class Americans are actually variant family patterns that have been traditional within Black and other ethnic communities for many generations. Presented as the "new lifestyles of the young mainstream elite, they are the same lifestyles that have in the past been defined as pathological, deviant, or unacceptable when observed in Black families" (Peters and McAdoo 1983:228). As Evelyn Brooks Higginbotham (1992) observes, race often subsumes other sets of social relations, making them "good" or "bad," "correct" or "incorrect" (p. 255). Yet, many of the minority family patterns deemed "incorrect" by journalists, scholars, and policymakers are logical life choices in a society of limited social opportunities.

Growing Racial Diversity and "the Family Crisis"

Despite the proliferation of studies showing that families are shaped by their social context, conservative rhetoric is fueling a "growing social and ideological cleavage between traditional family forms and the emerging alternatives" (Gerson 1991:57). This is complicated further by the profound demographic transformation now occurring in the United States. The unprecedented growth of minority populations is placing a special spotlight on family diversity.

Racial minorities are increasing faster than the majority population. During the 1980s Asians more than doubled, from 3.5 million to 7.3 million, and Hispanics grew from 14.6 to 22.4 million. The Black increase was from 16.5 to 30.0 million. The result of these trends is that whereas Whites in 1980 were 80 percent of the population, they will be only 70 percent by 2000 (Population Reference Bureau 1989:10). Immigration now accounts for a large share of the nation's population growth. The largest ten-year wave of immigration in U.S. history occurred during the 1980s, with the arrival of almost 9 million people. More immigrants were admitted during the 1980s than any decade since 1900–1910. By 2020, immigrants will be more important to the U.S. population growth than natural increase (Waldrop 1990:23). New patterns of immigration are changing the racial composition of society. Among the expanded population of first-generation immigrants, "the Asian-born now outnumber the European-born. Those from Latin America—predominantly Mexican—outnumber both" (Barringer 1992:2). This contrasts sharply with what occurred as recently as the 1950s, when two-thirds of legal immigrants were from Europe and Canada.

Changes in the racial composition of society are creating new polarizations along residential, occupational, educational, and economic lines.

Crucial to these divisions is an ongoing transformation of racial meaning and racial hierarchy. Family scholars must be alert to the effects of these changes because the racial repositioning will touch families throughout the racial order.

New immigration patterns will escalate the rhetoric of family crises as immigrant lifestyles and family forms are measured against a mythical family ideal. Inevitably, some interpretations of diversity will revert to cultural explanations that deflect attention from the social opportunities associated with race. Even though pleas for "culturally sensitive" approaches to non-White families are well-meaning, they can unwittingly keep "the family" ensnared in a White middle-class ideal. We need to find a way to transcend the conflict among the emerging array of "family groups" (Gerson 1991:57). The best way to do this is to abandon all notions that uphold one family form as normal and others as "cultural variations." Immigration will undoubtedly introduce alternative family forms; they will be best understood by treating race as a fundamental structure that situates families differently and thereby produces diversity.

REFERENCES

Barringer, Felicity. 1992. "As American as Apple Pie, Dim Sum or Burritos." *New York Times,* May, sec. 4, p. 2.

Billingsley, Andrew. 1988. "The Impact of Technology on Afro-American Families." *Family Relations* 7:420–25.

Brenner, Johanna and Barbara Laslett. 1986. "Social Reproduction and the Family." In *The Social Reproduction of Organization and Culture,* edited by Ulf Himmelstrand. Newbury Park, CA: Sage.

Byerly, Victoria. 1986. *Hard Times Cotton Mill Girls: Personal Histories of Womanhood and Poverty in the South.* Ithaca, NY: ILR Press.

Dill, Bonnie Thornton. 1986. *Our Mothers' Grief: Racial Ethnic Women and the Maintenance of Families.* Research Paper No. 4. Memphis, TN: Center for Research on Women, Memphis State University.

———. 1994. "Fictive Kin, Paper Sons, and Compadrazgo: Women of Color and the Struggle for Family Survival." In *Women of Color in U.S. Society,* edited by Maxine Baca Zinn and Bonnie Thornton Dill. Philadelphia: Temple University Press.

Du Bois, Ellen Carol and Vicki L. Ruiz, eds. 1990. "Introduction." In *Unequal Sisters: A Multicultural Reader in U.S. Women's History.* New York: Routledge.

Gerson, Kathleen. 1991. "Coping with Commitment: Dilemmas and Conflicts of Family Life." In *America at Century's End,* edited by Alan Wolfe. Berkeley: University of California Press.

Ginsburg, Faye and Anna Lowenhaupt Tsing. 1990. *Uncertain Terms: Negotiating Gender in American Culture.* Boston: Beacon Press.

Glenn, Evelyn Nakano. 1987. "Gender and the Family." In *Analyzing Gender,* edited by Beth B. Hess and Myra Marx Ferree. Newbury Park, CA: Sage.

———. 1992. "From Servitude to Service Work: Historical Continuities in the Racial Division of Paid Reproductive Labor." *Signs: Journal of Women in Culture and Society* 18 (1): 1–43.

Glenn, Evelyn Nakano, with Stacey H. Yap. 1993. "Chinese American Families." In *Minority Families in the United States: Comparative Perspectives,* edited by Ronald L. Taylor. Englewood Cliffs, NJ: Prentice-Hall.

Higginbotham, Evelyn Brooks. 1992. "African-American Women's History and the Metalanguage of Race." *Signs: Journal of Women in Culture and Society* 17 (2): 251–74.

Mullings, Leith. 1986. "Uneven Development: Class, Race, and Gender in the United States Before 1900." In *Women's Work,* edited by Eleanor Leacock and Helen I. Safa. New York: Bergin and Garvey.

Omi, Michael and Howard Winant. 1986. *Racial Formation in the United States.* London: Routledge & Kegan Paul.

Peters, Marie and Harriette P. McAdoo. 1983. "The Present and Future of Alternative Lifestyles in Ethnic American Cultures." In *Contemporary Families and Alternative Lifestyles,* edited by Eleanor D. Macklin and R. H. Rubin. Beverly Hills, CA: Sage.

Population Reference Bureau. 1989. *America in the 21st Century: Human Resource Development.* Washington, DC: Population Reference Bureau.

Rapp, Rayna. 1982. "Family and Class in Contemporary America: Notes toward an Understanding of Ideology." In *Rethinking the Family: Some Feminist Questions,* edited by Barrie Thorne and Marilyn Yalom. New York: Longman.

Rollins, Judith. 1985. *Between Women: Domestics and Their Employers.* Philadelphia: Temple University Press.

Romero, Mary. 1992. *Maid in the U.S.A.* New York: Routledge.

Ruiz, Vicki. 1988. "By the Day or the Week: Mexican Domestic Workers in El Paso." In *Women in the U.S.-Mexico Border,* edited by Vicki Ruiz and Susan Tiano. Boston: Allen & Unwin.

Thorne, Barrie. 1992. "Feminism and the Family: Two Decades of Thought." In *Rethinking the Family: Some Feminist Questions,* 2d ed., edited by Barrie Thorne and Marilyn Yalom. Boston: Northeastern University Press.

Waldrop, Judith. 1990. "You'll Know It's the 21st Century When . . . " *American Demographics* 13 (December): 22–27.

Ward, Kathryn. 1990. *Women Workers and Global Restructuring.* Ithaca, NY: Cornell University Press.

Zavella, Patricia. 1989. "The Problematic Relationship of Feminism and Chicana Studies." *Women's Studies* 17:25–36.

———. 1991. "Mujeres in Factories: Race and Class Perspectives on Women, Work, and Family." In *Gender at the Crossroads of Knowledge,* edited by Micaela di Leonardo. Berkeley: University of California Press.

3

THE EMERGENCE OF LESBIAN-COPARENT FAMILIES IN POSTMODERN SOCIETY

MAUREEN SULLIVAN

The trend toward economic globalization in the last three decades of the twentieth century created social conditions in the industrialized world variously referred to as postmodernity, radicalized modernity, postindustrial society, media or spectacle society, and the information age. These terms try to capture the idea that the international order is changing so rapidly, with the breathless rate of technological innovation and the global movement of capital, that the West is in transition from one epoch to another.

Globalizing capitalist forces produce different effects on national, regional, and local cultures. In the United States the effects often register and

resonate within public discourse as crises of moral leadership and cultural values. The United States' late-century "culture wars" in particular have persistently revolved around sexuality, family, and reproduction, issues that necessarily involve gender relations more broadly. In the context of the culture wars, in which, for some social and political conservatives, nothing less than the "moral bedrock" of American society is at stake, real American families and real communities of diverse sexualities, desires, and politics have pioneered new forms of intimacy. Openly lesbian- and gay-parent families constitute one of these recent formations. Specific to First World consumer societies in the postmodern era, these new families represent a distinct departure from modern conventional families and present a unique opportunity to assess how a substantive change in a social institution such as the family is likely to affect social relations and practices both within these new kin groupings and in the surrounding culture.

One specific variant among these alternative family formations is the lesbian-coparent family in which the partners of a lesbian couple have planned and conceived children through donor insemination and are currently raising them in a nuclear-type family. A plethora of social institutions, norms, practices, and generations of people stand to be affected by the emergence and viability of families headed by two mothers. In particular, the implications of dual-mother families for the social organization of gender and gendered power are significant, since so many facets of gendered power and gender inequality, not to mention historically influential schools of thought such as psychoanalysis and even political liberalism, are founded in assumptions about the immutability of heterosexual-parent families or are constituted by them in connection with other components of social structure, such as occupational sex segregation within the societal division of labor, or institutions, such as schools or the mass media as agents of enculturation.

To illuminate the specific ways in which such a new, perhaps even avant-garde, form of kinship might be affecting social change, the analysis must necessarily consider the social, political, and cultural context within which it has arisen. This [reading] thus traces the historical emergence over the last three decades or so—the beginning of the postmodern era by some accounts—of gay-parent families as alternative families to the modern, nuclear, heterosexual-parent family. Since the politics of "family values" in the United States constitutes the most immediate and contested arena in which alternative families have negotiated the terms of their existence, I turn first to examining how it has played out over the last three decades.

The Politics of Family Values

Some years before the 1992 Democratic presidential campaign soundbite "It's the economy, stupid" temporarily, and successfully, instructed voters that Americans' "family values" were not the problem, right-wing groups in the mid-1970s mobilized to oppose the values of the counterculture, the gains won by second-wave feminists, and the increasing visibility of gay

existence and relationships. What we now think of as various permutations of contemporary family values ideology began as a backlash movement in the immediate wake of such landmark victories for women's reproductive freedom as *Roe v. Wade* and other catalyzing emancipatory events such as the 1969 Stonewall Riot.

In the 1970s and early 1980s in the United States, members of the New Right and so-called profamily movements mobilized antifeminist and anti-gay sentiment, building a mass ideological base, financial infrastructure, and organization at the national level around sexual, reproductive, and family issues. Whether it was Anita Bryant's antigay crusade, Phyllis Schlafly's stop-ERA campaign, or New Right and profamily movement leaders' aggressive organizing of a mass base of "Middle Americans" around "traditional" values, the conservative politics of backlash then, like the family values campaigns and their cavalries of Promise Keepers and Million Man Marchers in the 1990s, worked to reassert patriarchal forms of family structure and male dominance. In her 1982 pamphlet "The New Traditional Woman," profamily movement leader and spokesperson Connie Marshner enjoined the American woman to adhere to traditional values and moral absolutes but also recognized the social and economic tugs of late modernity on her apron strings. The New Traditional Woman, she wrote, "is new because she is of the current era, with all its pressures and fast pace and rapid change. She is traditional because, in the face of unremitting cultural changes, she is oriented around the eternal truths of faith and family. Her values are timeless and true to human nature."

Family values politics in the 1990s conveyed effectively the same message as the backlash to feminism, gay liberation, the counterculture, and sexual revolution in the 1970s and early 1980s in the United States (and in the United Kingdom), which mobilized around reinstating the "traditional" family, resisting the values of secular humanism, and reasserting the legitimacy of male authority and female deference. But in the 1990s, the players expanded to include individuals and groups from across the ideological spectrum and were joined by self-identified "objective" social scientists and academics. The 1990s message emphasized, variously, the pathology of all families not adhering to the structure of the nuclear, heterosexual-parents-and-children family; the specific deviance and pathological effects of single-mother families; the extreme dysfunction of black families headed by women reprehensibly demonized as welfare cheats; and, most recently, the myriad social problems caused by a category of family referred to simply as "fatherless families." In other words, the family values ideology of the 1990s still pronounced as normative a family structure consisting of a heterosexually married couple with children in which the father maintained—or, as some of the rhetoric had it, "reclaimed"—a position of authority and responsibility as the head of household.

Given the almost hysterical moral-panic quality subtending much of the right-wing discourse on family values, it is striking that real, nonconformist families of every imaginable type and practice continue to live in ways that simply do not reflect the story being told about them. Even when

political and academic liberals tone down family values rhetoric by offering amelioration rather than condemnation, the story about the moral and social superiority of two-parent, heterosexual nuclear families does not change. . . . Despite the grand stories being told in family values rhetoric and campaigns, real American families are more diverse than ever; they borrow some elements from the past in configuring their domestic arrangements at the same time that they introduce new practices, especially where procreative methods are concerned; they are fluid, mobile, recombinant, unresolved. In short, they reflect all the features of a postmodern reality that cannot possibly be contained or controlled by the family values mythology. . . .

Gay Identity and Family: A Tale of Two Patterns as Historical Process

No single or coherent path has led to the collective rise of lesbian- and gay-parent families today, but different paths have shared some basic elements: awareness of affective and erotic desire for people of the same gender, intimate practice based on that awareness, and personal and collective definitions of family. I see two patterns that encompass these elements. From historical texts, theoretical and empirical descriptions, and various discourses about the relationship between being gay, on one hand, and living in, growing up in, or wanting families of one's own, on the other, I see a dialectical struggle for self-determination occurring in slightly different, but related, historically contingent patterns. The first pattern involves the separation of sexuality from procreation throughout the larger culture and its correspondence with the formation of gay identity. I characterize this a "revolving-door" pattern, for reasons I clarify in what follows. The second pattern has to do with the politics of gay assimilation versus separation from (or resistance to) mainstream culture. Depending on one's political perspective, either "the gay family" is an undesirable instrument of assimilation into heteronormative culture, or it is desirable precisely because it transgresses heteronormativity.

The Revolving Door of Family and Gay Identity

While several historiographic projects have examined the social process and events that have been implicated in the "making of the modern homosexual," John D'Emilio's *Sexual Politics, Sexual Communities* (1983) stands out for the role he attributes to capitalism and the family in the separation of sexuality from procreation. Building on other sociohistorical accounts of the relationship between families and industrialization, D'Emilio argues that within industrializing regions, the rise of waged labor and the movement of production from household to factory meant that family life became less and less organized around domestic production. Increasingly, as households became primarily agents of consumption rather than production, children became a "liability," since instead of contributing their labor to the domestic economy

they now became burdens, depending on the "family wage" earned by breadwinning fathers. The shift in the family away from production focused it more intensively as a site of affective relations such that the meaning of sexual relations between men and women came under greater scrutiny and reflection. "It became possible," writes D'Emilio, "to release sexuality from the 'imperative' to procreate," since the need for large families had begun to disappear with the family farm.

According to D'Emilio, the overall effect of the shift was that heterosexual intimacy began to be conceived of more in terms of personal pleasure and happiness than in terms of strictly procreative activity. In promoting this disconnection of (hetero)sexuality from reproduction, capitalism allowed for "some men and women to organize a personal life around their erotic/emotional attraction to their own sex" and to discover a way to "survive beyond the confines of the family."

D'Emilio's account of capitalism's liberating effect upon the reproductive function of the family (which had the secondary effect of liberating some individuals to pursue nonheterosexual experiences) complements accounts of modernity that credit urbanization with luring individuals away from traditional, patriarchal rural communities. Cities offered the promise of anonymity and escape from "the surveillance of family, neighbors, priests, . . . all the suffocating pressures of the closed small-town world." Thus the emergence of gay and lesbian subcultures, in these explanations, is a by-product of the growth of industrial capitalism and urbanization, but the relationship to family is what is important here for present purposes.

Taken together, these accounts point to something like a *flight from the family*, an exodus, as a condition of the emergence of gay identity, even though the family itself as an institution had seen dramatic changes, with the gradual reduction of family size being the most important such change for D'Emilio's argument. But even though heterosexual relations within families were no longer oriented toward reproduction as a primary concern, the separation of (hetero)sexuality from prolific procreation and childbearing did not alter the basic heterosexual character or definition of families: the paradigm of family still consisted in heterosexual parenting, intimacy, and sexuality. The shift was more quantitative than qualitative.

For many people facing the emotional and psychological complexities of apprehending their same-sex desire within a larger heterosexually organized family culture, a popular response involved the practice of living in "front" (heterosexual) families and marriages while surreptitiously conducting same-sex erotic and emotional relationships. The historian Lillian Faderman has documented the practice of lesbians and gay men marrying each other and maintaining "heterosexual" households while conducting sexual affairs within their respective gay circles, especially during the 1950s. Other lesbians, Faderman noted, married heterosexual men and conducted a bisexual lifestyle, some in order to live under the protective cover of respectable heterosexuality, others because they were "genuinely" bisexual. A 1983 study summarizing the findings of seven studies of gay men and four studies of lesbians found that 20 percent of the former and about one-third of the latter

had been heterosexually married (Harry 1983). These studies and Faderman's observations, in combination with the above notion of a flight or exodus from the family, suggest a kind of revolving-door dynamic, where some gay people have *exited* heterosexual family life (having come round to understanding their homoerotic desire), while others have *entered* heterosexual marriages and front families for security and protection (and continue to do so).

This dynamic of establishing the gay self in the act of either fleeing or joining the family seemed to take a decisive turn toward the former in the politics and struggle for gay liberation during the late 1960s and 1970s. For lesbians and gay men organizing around liberation and separatism, families clearly embodied some of the most oppressive values from which they sought emancipation. In much the same way that 1960s and 1970s radical feminism, and to a certain extent white liberal feminism, had vigorously criticized the patriarchal family, identifying it as the primary site of women's oppression, theorists of gay liberation did this but took the critique one step further. According to R. W. Connell (1987), gay liberation theorists viewed the family essentially as a "factory" of heterosexuality that served to meet "capital's need for a labour supply and the state's need for subordination" (p. 36). Marriage and family would always be the products and agents of compulsory heterosexuality, as Adrienne Rich famously conceptualized it, since their main function was the repression of homosexual desire. In this view, the family's historical reproduction has depended on the repression of nonheterosexual sexualities. Dennis Altman (1979) perhaps made the point most succinctly: "The homosexual represents the most clear-cut rejection of the nuclear family that exists, and hence is persecuted because of the need to maintain the hegemony of that concept" (p. 47).

Gay and lesbian liberation politics thus coalesced around the separation of sexuality from procreation, asserting the primacy of pleasure, desire, and intimacy over marital love and reproductive duty in sexual practices. This more explicitly antifamily "exodus" stance, of course, would be used against gay liberatory politics by the Supreme Court in its 1986 decision in *Bowers v. Hardwick,* upholding Georgia's antisodomy statute. In the majority opinion, which denied the applicability of privacy laws established in the *Griswold v. Connecticut* case involving marital contraception, the language directly referred to the separation of (gay) sexuality from family, marriage, and procreation: "Accepting the decisions in these cases and the above description of them, we think it evident that none of the rights announced in those cases bears any resemblance to the claimed constitutional right of homosexuals to engage in sodomy that is asserted in this case. No connection between family, marriage, or procreation on the one hand, and homosexual activity has been demonstrated." But as Connell and others noted, gay emancipatory politics also asserted more generally a critical theory of sexuality, echoing Marcuse's thought in *Eros and Civilization* (1995) and to a certain extent reframed by Audre Lorde in her essay "Uses of the Erotic: The Erotic as Power" (1992). According to gay liberation theory and politics, then, the heterosexual family was a primary tool not only of homosexual repression but of oppressive sexual regulation and social control more generally.

At the same time that gay liberation theorists held the heterosexual family in such contempt, some lesbians and gay men in the 1970s had been quietly negotiating the revolving door of gay identity and family: they maintained front families, they entered into heterosexual marriages only to exit them later as they exited the closet, and they struggled to maintain custody of the children from those marriages, as the earliest custody cases starting in the late 1960s attest. And importantly, they began to consider bringing children into their lives as openly gay persons.

In one of the first attempts to grasp the emerging reality of "open" gay and lesbian parenting, Frederick Bozett compiled a collection of writings that presented a number of voices and views on the experience of living as both a self-affirmed gay person and a parent. Most of the writings speak to the experience of parenting children from former heterosexual marriages and relationships. Another work, published in 1993, was one of the first book-length studies of lesbian mothering to document the experiences of women in the 1970s who either had been heterosexually married or were consciously incorporating children into their lives as self-affirmed lesbians. Though published fifteen years after she conducted the first interviews, the study, by the anthropologist Ellen Lewin, reflects the ambivalence of some lesbians negotiating not only the dilemma of how to resolve the apparently contradictory need for gay identity affirmation with the desire for children and family of one's own but also the political dilemma of having family in "contra-indication" of the antifamily stance of liberation politics.

Lewin interpreted the mothers' narratives as highly self-conscious, reflexive negotiations of two identities, "lesbian" and "mother"—identities that liberation politics had constructed as incompatible. In Lewin's account, mothers often felt torn between their loyalties to their children and to the lesbian communities from which they had become increasingly estranged, but ultimately their experience as lesbian mothers served positively (and importantly) to reaffirm their gender identity: motherhood reaffirmed their womanhood. As one-time exiles from normative gender identity, lesbians could, by virtue of their motherhood, "claim membership in the group known as 'women'."

Resistance versus Assimilation

This "redomestication" of lesbian experience and politics fueled concerns about gay parenting and family formation as assimilationist, moving the discourse of gay identity, politics, and family to a framework of resistance versus assimilation, as Lewin (1994) herself observed. This framework, which I see as a new pattern succeeding the revolving-door pattern, reflects the experiences and decisions of the first postliberation generation of gay men and lesbians, who came out (perhaps by means of rejecting and being rejected by their families of origin) and have since wanted to create families of their own. The problem for many in this period, which spanned the 1980s and early 1990s, became one of reconciling the desire for (and actual creation of) families with the unsavory prospect of replicating the heterosexual (and

patriarchal) model of family and compromising gay politics through assimilation into heteronormative culture *via* the family.

It should be noted that this resistance-assimilation tension as mediated by the family would not have arisen had openly gay persons not pursued family formation in the first place, marking an important shift in practice from the antifamily political position toward a profamily one. For some of the women now understood as being responsible for the lesbian baby boom of the late 1970s through the 1980s, "choosing children" proved personally empowering but politically challenging, as the essays in the first anthology on lesbian parenting suggest. Lesbian parents' experiences challenged the opposition of gayness to parenthood, while their writings reflected the tensions of forging some way through the resistance-assimilation dilemma. Family legal theorist and practitioner Nancy Polikoff (1987) summed up the concerns of many lesbian parents faced with this dilemma: "Having a child is a principal indicator of heterosexuality. [Lesbian mothering] . . . does not negate or transform the institution of motherhood. Motherhood, like marriage, is too loaded with this patriarchal history and function to be an entirely different phenomenon just because lesbians are doing it" (pp. 52, 54).

At the same time that thousands of gay people across the country became parents, the worry continued—on both the radical (straight) right and radical (gay) left—that these gay profamily practices would "normalize" same-sex parenting and families. The putative concern on the (straight) right was and always has been that gay parenting would morally corrupt and contaminate the sacredness of heterosexual procreation, marriage, and family. The concern on the (gay) left was that gay parenting would siphon much-needed energy and resources from liberation politics; would "redomesticate" lesbians; and, in line with Polikoff's views above, would serve to replicate existing social relations by means of adherence to and uncritical mimicry of the white, middle-class, heterosexual (patriarchal) family model.

By the early to mid-1990s, the resistance-assimilation problem had crystallized around the issue of legal same-sex marriage. Viewing same-sex marriage as a matter of equal civil rights—like equal protection and non-discrimination—legal practitioners and political activists had generated political momentum and interest in the case *Baehr v. Lewin,* brought before the state Supreme Court in Hawaii in 1993 (Wolfson 1994–95). The prospect of legal same-sex marriage generated a swift and decisive reaction from the political and religious right, as well as the Clinton administration, which signed into law in 1996 the Defense of Marriage Act (DOMA)—a law that, among other things, defined marriage as a union between one man and one woman. The strong reaction from liberals and conservatives alike signaled that gay marriage was supremely threatening to the heterosexual political establishment. In gay community discourse and politics, however, worries were mounting concerning assimilation into and reproduction of inherently unequal, conservative, and repressive institutions, of which legal marriage is crucially emblematic. Nancy Polikoff, again, articulated these concerns in a 1993 article in the *Virginia Law Review.* In that article she wrote: "Advocating lesbian and gay marriage will detract from, and even contradict, efforts

to unhook economic benefits from marriage and make basic health care and other necessities available to all. It will also require a rhetorical strategy that emphasizes similarities between our relationships and heterosexual marriages, and denies the potential of lesbian and gay marriage to transform the gendered nature of marriage for all people" (pp. 1549–50). . . .

In most of these accounts, the view seems to be that the definition and meaning of marriage, while showing some remarkably stable features historically—features that have appeared inexorably to reinforce male authority and control while at the same time repressing alternative forms of marriage and sexuality—are also subject to transformation through concerted, viable social practice and political action. Further, the meaning of marriage thus transformed stands to have some progressive impact on wider societal norms.

Beyond the Resistance-Assimilation Dilemma

In her influential 1991 book, *Families We Choose,* the anthropologist Kath Weston argued that lesbian and gay definitions of family need not be derived from a single position relative to the heterosexual norm. That is, they need not base notions of family in opposition to or agreement with biological or legal definitions of family produced by and serving the interests of a heteropatriarchal order. Instead, Weston proposed that gay and lesbian families be understood as "chosen" families. By incorporating the element of choice, gay and lesbian families may be unbounded, fluid, and permeable groupings based on any combination of a range of intimate, erotic, social, economic, and biological relations. Weston's account of gay families shifts the focus from legal and institutional definitions to a more conceptual and practical level, concentrating on the experiences and practice of gay families as members define them.

Weston's project was and is extremely important for its acute, even prescient, observation that gay families are inherently pluralistic or, more importantly, that they must be understood as such lest the gay community make the same mistakes in creating families as heterosexual society has done with its hierarchies and preferences for unequal authority, its almost fetishistic emphasis on the sexual-conjugal parent unit and putative monogamy, and its formal, instrumentalist treatment of children as the necessary accoutrements of proper bourgeois existence. A fluid, pluralistic notion of gay family life circumvents the resistance-assimilation problem altogether, offering a model of family-defining practices and procedures that is affirmatively non-normative.

Apart from the patterns of the revolving door and resistance-assimilation, which continue today, the sociohistorical emergence of "open" lesbian- and gay-parent families on a collective level over the last two decades in North America and Europe has been facilitated by more mundane activities such as the dissemination of practical information, outreach, education, and support provided within lesbian/gay communities and networks. In the San Francisco Bay Area in the mid- to late 1980s, "considering parenthood" groups formed and met regularly to guide women through the complex of practical,

emotional, and legal issues involved in creating families in the absence of greater societal support and sanction. Educational "how-to" films such as *Choosing Children* began circulating at the same time that parenting support groups formed—many of them organized and sponsored by the beloved Lyon-Martin organization in San Francisco. Out of these earlier pioneering efforts the 1990s witnessed a veritable growth industry explosion of popular and thoughtful advice books, legal aid services, formal gay-parent organizations, and summer camps for children. In short, gay and lesbian communities mobilized to help engineer the gay family revolution that has now secured for gay families an irrevocable, perhaps vanguard position in the increasingly diverse and as yet unsettled array of postmodern kinship arrangements.

Midwives to the Gay Family Revolution: Assisted Reproduction and the Law

While profamily gay/lesbian communities, by their own activism, helped to achieve recognition for gay families worldwide, they were assisted by changes occurring within other institutional domains: the domain of medical, technoscientific knowledge and practice often referred to as "assisted reproduction," as well as that complex of jurisprudence and practice known as family law.

If Weston's idiom of "choice" applies to today's gay- and lesbian-parent families, it does so significantly in the area of family planning. When prospective parents choose to incorporate children into their lives, they make decisions and undertake planning and preparation with considerable deliberateness and self-reflexivity. The formation of gay families with children throughout the 1990s and up to the present has revolved around careful consideration of, and involvement with, institutions and organizations that facilitate the planning and (pro)creation of children and contribute to families' social functioning and legal protection. The historical emergence of lesbian-coparent families as a particular variant of the gay family revolution is thus crucially linked to the evolution of organized reproductive assistance services and to changing juridical attitudes and principles in family law.

Alternative Insemination as a Form of Assisted Reproduction

For lesbian parents who chose or who continue to choose donor insemination, often referred to as alternative or artificial insemination by donor (AID), this path to parenthood was facilitated and made attractive by the increased availability of organized "assisted-reproduction" services to lesbians—namely, donor insemination programs. Nonmedicalized donor insemination has always been available to lesbians and single heterosexual women interested in creating families without men, as the insemination procedure itself is relatively straightforward and does not require "expert" medical intervention. Indeed, self-insemination groups like the London-based Feminist Self-Insemination Group, formed in 1978, pioneered the practices

(and ideology) involved in woman-controlled alternative insemination that would later become incorporated in feminist health centers throughout the United States and northern Europe (Klein 1984).

Today, many of the feminist principles informing these earlier efforts may be found in the organizational philosophy and practices of procreative service organizations that cater specifically to lesbians, gay men, and women who desire biological children outside heterosexual marital and nonmarital relationships. What has changed significantly from the earlier self-insemination movement to the present arrangement of procreative service provision to alternative families is the increased need for organized procurement and "dissemination" of "clean product" and the management of information and risk. Lesbians will continue to self-inseminate "the underground way," as one of my informants put it, and even though there is no way of knowing how many lesbians are opting to self-inseminate versus using a donor insemination program, the need for, at a minimum, the screening of donor semen for transmissible pathogens including HIV makes the coordination and organization of other tasks under one roof attractive. For, ultimately, among a vast array of "enhancements" like sperm washing, treatment, and centrifuging, sperm recipients pay for semen that has been screened, for the task of locating a donor, and, perhaps most important, for the management of information about the donor's identity. Whether prospective parents want a known or anonymous donor, these alternative insemination organizations sell the service of suppressing or releasing—managing—information about the donor, which is of vital importance to the self-determination and sovereignty of alternative families.

Feminist, lesbian, and gay-oriented assisted-reproduction facilities are thus in many ways less techno-medical organizations than procreative service organizations. But unlike impersonal and rationalized financial service or legal service firms, these procreative service organizations aspire to provide more humanistic, socially progressive services than a strictly profit-driven model would suggest. Still, the potential for increased commercialization and the trend toward providing extra services evokes images, as Amy Agigian (1998) has noted, not of "sperm-banking but of a speciality goods model, with product innovation and enhancement, niche marketing, and entrepreneurial middlemen selling their product at a brisk mark-up" (p. 41). Part procreative brokerage firm, part cryo-bank, and part retail outlet, the alternative insemination organization that sees its mission as helping women have children rather than as "treating" a medical condition (infertility) would seem to stand outside male-controlled medical establishment protocols that both assume and dictate heterosexual marital norms among those seeking procreative assistance.

That these services are widely available to lesbians and single heterosexual women throughout the United States—independent of geographic residence, since frozen sperm may be shipped anywhere via overnight delivery—speaks to the growing autonomy of woman-centered family creation. This trend in procreative service provision to lesbians and other women not attached to men thus contributed to the lesbian baby boom(s)

in the 1980s and throughout the 1990s, and it clearly arose in response to the discrimination women experienced when attempting to use (male-controlled) medicalized insemination services.

Now well-established, alternative procreative service organizations facilitate the creation of all types of alternative families, matching gay men longing to become fathers with women who will provide gestational services, matching prospective lesbian mothers with gay sperm donors, and generally offering a wide range of family "brokerage" services.

The Law

Family law powerfully defines which forms of intimate association shall count and which, because they remain outside the dominant conceptual system underlying judicial decision making, remain socially and legally denigrated. In the current complex of federal, state, and local statutes and rulings composing family law in the United States, male-headed, heterosexual-parent families are privileged and protected at the expense of all other family forms, especially single-mother families and gay- and lesbian-parent families.

The very definition of family that most state courts recognize and use in their rulings—persons related by marriage, biology, or adoption—was reinforced most recently at the federal level by the 1996 passage of the Defense of Marriage Act (DOMA), which defined marriage as a union between one man and one woman and exempted states from recognizing marriages granted in other states. Because family law is generally carried out within state and local jurisdictions, DOMA's primary legal effect has been to reinforce the autonomy of states in defining familial rights and responsibilities and granting legal status, as legal scholar Nan Hunter ([1991] 1997) has written:

> Family law has always been a province primarily of state rather than federal regulation, and often has varied from state to state; grounds for divorce, for example, used to differ dramatically depending on geography. What seems likely to occur in the next wave of family cases is the same kind of variability in the legal definition of the family itself. Those very discrepancies may help to denaturalize concepts like "marriage" and "parent," and to expose the utter contingency of the sexual conventions that, in part, construct the family. (P. 299)

Hunter's optimistic view of the potential for variations in the legal definition of family occurring at the state level reflects the complex and contradictory field in which alternative families in general, and lesbian couples with children in particular, have used family law to negotiate some measure of legal protection and legitimacy for their families. However, this same variability that ought to enhance gay couples' chances at winning legal recognition of their familial status has been just as likely to play out more in accordance with the general conservative tendencies of the law, as feminist family law scholars Katherine Bartlett and Rosanne Kennedy (1991) have noted:

> As an institution, law has both helped to implement and constrained feminist agendas. . . . One such constraint is the law's respect for precedent.

Law may be changed, but because law purports to preserve institutional stability and continuity, reform must build from existing legal precedents and doctrines. For feminists, this requirement presents two problems. First, existing precedents are often decidedly androcentric, taking for granted and reinforcing a status quo that is more favorable to male interests than to female ones. Second, arguments that deviate significantly from precedent or accepted doctrine are often considered extreme and thus are less likely to be successful than moderate proposals. (P. 2)

With respect to gay marriage, these conservative ideological tendencies in the law appear to have superseded the progressive potential alluded to in Hunter's assessment of state-level variability and discretion: by midyear 2003, thirty-seven states had enacted laws specifically banning same-sex marriage. . . .

In the United States, the systematic denial of legal recognition of the partnerships of lesbian and gay couples affects real, living families in profoundly pernicious ways, in areas concerning housing, insurance, intestate succession, and, increasingly important as it concerns residence and citizenship, immigration. For example, because couples may not become legal spouses, foreign-born partners who have lived and made their homes with U.S. citizens but whose temporary visas expire are denied the automatic citizenship rights granted to the foreign-born legal spouses of heterosexual people. . . . The contingent, nonuniform patchwork of local, state, and federal statutes and laws pertaining to gay partnerships and families makes it nearly impossible for families easily to do the most ordinary of activities that nongay families and couples take for granted, including the expectation that, when things go wrong in their relationships, they can count on the state to play intermediary with enforcement authority.

How, then, do we understand "the law" as playing midwife to the birthing of lesbian-coparent families? If, despite DOMA, the state-level definitions of family are widely variable, contingent, and prone to promoting an excess of idiosyncratic, judicial discretion, then this contingency may be (and has been) exploited favorably in various cases so as to gradually substitute new precedents for old ones. For instance, functional definitions of family may be used instrumentally for select purposes, as in the ruling by a New York City judge who determined that the surviving partner in a gay couple (who had lived "as spouses" for years before the partner who legally held the couple's long-term tenancy died) could hold onto the tenancy on the grounds that the couple, for all intents and purposes, had lived as and were family.

The same functional arguments provide for the establishment of legal parental status for nonbiological mothers through second-parent adoptions (Fineman 1995). The creation of families through contractual and technologically assisted procreation has given rise to a crisis of meaning concerning parenthood. Courts are increasingly called upon to determine parental status and rights in such situations as the now legendary Baby M. surrogacy case. Lesbian-comother families constitute another case in which the meaning and definition of parenthood must be revised to account for the social

fact of dual motherhood. On a highly idiosyncratic, discretionary basis, then, select county and state judges have recognized nonbiological mothers by granting them second-parent adoptions, and thus lesbian-coparent families have exploited the contingent nature of family law.

Lesbian-parent couples often strategically reside in (or have relocated to) areas where the local jurisdiction has shown a liberal attitude toward gay parenting, granting second-parent adoptions to nonbiological mothers. As of September 2002, nine states, including California, had granted second-parent adoptions at the statewide level, while select counties in these and another fifteen states, including the most populous counties in northern California, had established such precedents. . . .

In sum, the second-parent adoption mechanism for nonbiological parents establishes state sanction and societal recognition of families headed by same-sex parents in a way that is more oblique and therefore less politically inflammatory than legal marriage. Moreover, it is a legal fiction that compensates for the procreative asymmetry between partners in a family system where historically the contributors of genetic material through the (heterosexual) procreative act become, by some other sociojuridical fiction or unexamined cultural axiom, The Parents. Second-parent adoptions have thus provided a way for lesbian-coparent families to achieve some margin of legal protection and familial sovereignty, though these achievements may prove to be Pyrrhic, as the same excess of judicial discretion that engendered them may just as easily overturn them. For now and into the foreseeable future, they remain the best option these families have, a state of affairs pointing to the profound ambivalence, if not outright hypocrisy, of a society that claims to want to strengthen families.

REFERENCES

Agigian, Amy. 1998. "Contradictory Conceptions: Lesbian Alternative Insemination." Ph.D. dissertation, Brandeis University.

Altman, Dennis. 1979. *Coming Out in the Seventies.* Sydney: Wild and Woolley.

Bartlett, Katherine T. and Rosanne Kennedy. 1991. *Feminist Legal Theory: Readings in Law and Gender.* Boulder, CO: Westview Press.

Connell, R. W. 1987. *Gender and Power.* Stanford, CA: Stanford University Press.

D'Emilio, John. 1983. *Sexual Politics, Sexual Communities: The Making of a Homosexual Minority in the United States, 1940–1970.* Chicago: University of Chicago Press.

Fineman, Martha. 1995. *The Neutered Mother, the Sexual Family and Other Twentieth Century Tragedies.* New York: Routledge.

Harry, J. 1983. "Gay Male and Lesbian Relationships." Pp. 216–34 in *Contemporary Families and Alternative Life Styles,* edited by E. D. Macklin and R. H. Rubin. Beverly Hills, CA: Sage.

Hunter, Nan D. [1991] 1997. "Sexual Dissent and the Family: The Sharon Kowalski Case." Pp. 295–99 in *Reconstructing Gender: A Multicultural Anthology,* edited by E. Disch. Mountain View, CA: Mayfield.

Klein, Renate Duelli. 1984. "Doing It Ourselves: Self Inseminations." Pp. 382–90 in *Test Tube Women: What Future for Motherhood?* edited by R. Arditti, R. Duelli Klein, and S. Minden. London: Pandora Press.

Lewin, Ellen. 1994. "Negotiating Lesbian Motherhood: The Dialectics of Resistance and Accommodation." Pp. 335–53 in *Mothering: Ideology, Experience and Agency,* edited by E. Nakano Glenn, G. Chang, and L. R. Forcey. New York: Routledge.

Lorde, Audre. 1992. "Uses of the Erotic: The Erotic as Power." Pp. 53–59 in *Sister Outsider.* New York: Quality Paperback Book Club.

Marcuse, Herbert. 1995. *Eros and Civilization.* Boston: Beacon Press.

Polikoff, Nancy. 1987. "Lesbians Choosing Children: The Personal Is Political." Pp. 47–65 in *Politics of the Heart: A Lesbian Parenting Anthology,* edited by Sandra Pollack and Jeanne Vaughn. Ithaca, NY: Firebrand Books.

Polikoff, Nancy. 1993. "We Will Get What We Ask For: Why Legalizing Gay and Lesbian Marriage Will Not 'Dismantle the Legal Structure of Gender in Every Marriage.'" *Virginia Law Review* 79:1535–50.

Weston, Kath. 1991. *Families We Choose.* New York: Columbia University Press.

Wolfson, Evan. 1994–95. "Crossing the Threshold: Equal Marriage Rights for Lesbians and Gay Men and the Intra-Community Critique." *New York University Review of Law and Social Change* 21:567–615.

4

VALUES, POLICY, AND THE FAMILY

FRANK F. FURSTENBERG

Throughout the past century, especially in the last few decades, marriage practices have been altered in ways that seem either irrevocable, as many authors suggest, or at least very difficult to reinstate, even if we could agree that it were desirable to do so. Moreover, these changes have been widespread, if not universal, throughout the West and there is growing evidence that the weakening of marriage, as a life-long social form, is occurring throughout much of the world.

It seems there is also agreement that this decline of marriage is exacting a cost for children. Although there is not consensus on its size or how much of it can be attributed to family instability, I think no one would argue that family dissolution enhances children's welfare, unless the parents' marriage is highly dysfunctional, in which case everyone agrees that the child is better with one parent than two.

Where marriage survives as a binding contract between individuals, in countries such as Italy, Greece, or even Japan, it is not necessarily fulfilling its traditional function as the institution of social reproduction because birth rates are so low that they endanger the maintenance of the population. Consequently, one might well argue that where marriage has been resistant to change, the consequences for the population have been more adverse than where it has been altered by common practice. So it seems that contemporary societies are damned either way. A sad state of affairs, indeed.

How then can we imagine the renovation of marriage or marriage-like arrangements that provide the stability, security, and nurture that children

need to realize their potential? The central policy question here is how to make marriage more attractive and more viable through shifts in the culture, public policies, or programs designed to shore up marriage. This may not be the right question or at least the most compelling one. Rather, we are likely to address the problem more effectively by addressing the inequities that may be created by growing up in a nonnuclear family than by trying to manufacture more nuclear families as a way of reducing social and economic disadvantage. If this proposition isn't controversial enough, I further claim that we are more likely to improve the state of marriage by adopting the policy of enhancing children's welfare than enhancing marriage directly.

The Problem of Values

The starting point for this thesis is the long-standing uneasiness that Americans have about adopting policies that might seem to undermine marriage and the family. Historians have pointed out that the nuclear family has been enshrined in American culture from the colonial era onward even though the structure of family was more variable in the eighteenth and nineteenth centuries than even today. Nonetheless, the American family, as one social historian observed, was born modern even if a large proportion of children did grow up in nonnuclear families, thanks to the high rates of mortality and separation throughout much of our early history. Apparently, many children survived, then as now, in single-parent or nonparent households, growing up to function well and productively as adults.

De Tocqueville, among other foreign visitors, observed that marriage and family relations were the seedbed of democracy and thus the essential institution in American society. Throughout much of our history, we have privileged the nuclear family as if it almost single-handedly explains children's success as adults and the success of American society. Americans believe that the nuclear family is, as Wade Horn observes, a natural form despite overwhelming evidence by anthropologists that no human family form is universal much less natural. Little wonder that we worry more about the impact of family change than any of our European counterparts. By acting as if families are singularly responsible for children, we have placed huge burdens on parents to shoulder the costs of childrearing and accorded parents the responsibility for their children's fate in life.

Paradoxically, despite these beliefs, we have the highest rate of family instability of any nation in the industrial world, though New Zealand, a country that shares our libertarian ideology, runs a close second in divorce, out-of-wedlock childbearing, and single parenthood. Americans have generally steered clear of many of the social welfare policies that could support children and families despite the lip service typically given by politicians and policy makers to child and family-friendly policies. When Richard Nixon faced the choice of signing a bill greatly expanding child care services for parents, he couldn't overcome the strong objections of many of his advisors that by doing so, he would create incentives for parents to go to work

and hence undermine the family. Similarly, many argue that no-fault divorce ushered in high rates of divorce, that public assistance made out-of-wedlock childbearing more attractive, and that tax policies discourage marriage, and even that marriage among gays will lead to a depreciation of heterosexual marriage. In this triumph of Orwellian logic, policies aimed at supporting the family in fact do just the opposite.

The evidence that family policies have perverse effects on family stability is far from impressive. Few would claim that Nixon's veto of child care legislation kept parents out of the labor force or that promoting contraceptive use increases early and out-of-wedlock parenthood in Europe. Divorce liberalization did not increase divorce beyond a short period of pent-up demand by couples who were already separated or about to separate, and welfare reform has done little if anything to restore marriage. By contrast, there is strong empirical evidence that male joblessness and low earnings produce higher rates of nonmarriage and divorce. Lack of child care forces many parents to stay out of the labor force while its availability seems to reduce stress on marriage. So it seems that many of our objections to supporting the family materially in the form of income supplements and social services have as much to do with our views about the appropriate relationship between the public and private spheres of life as they do with real concerns about undermining marriage and the family.

Impact of Family Structure on Children's Well-Being

Similarly, the evidence on the effects of nonnuclear arrangements on children's well-being is heavily contaminated by an ideological predisposition to believe that parenting is severely compromised when one or both parents are absent from the home. Everyone agrees that children do not fare as well in nonnuclear households, but the explanation for this empirical observation is anything but clear-cut. Wendy Sigle-Rushton and Sara McLanahan's (2004) summary of the most recent literature is somewhat more cautious and circumspect than the message in McLanahan's earlier widely cited collaboration with Gary Sandefur (1994). Researchers have become far more sensitive to the limitations of statistical controls as a means of ruling out unobserved biases than they were a decade or two ago. As Sigle-Rushton and McLanahan observe, the modest to moderate effects attributed to divorce on children's well-being might be greatly attenuated were we able to conduct a random assignment on the impact of marriage and stability.

It is useful to remember that the period of the 1950s and early 1960s, now regarded with such nostalgia as the heyday of the nuclear family, raised the cohort of children who experienced as teenagers a sharp increase in delinquency, drug use, declining academic scores, and, of course, the spectacular rise in sexual activity and nonmarital, teenage childbearing. Conversely, all these behaviors dropped or leveled off in the late 1990s when close to 50 percent of America's children were growing up in single-parent households.

At a macro-level at least, indicators of children's well-being and adult behaviors track changes in the family circumstances very poorly.

Let us suppose, for example, we had a successful way of intervening to promote marriage through family education programs or to deter divorce through counseling unhappily married parents to work through their problems; would we find that the effects of these interventions result in a distinct advantage for children? Probably so, but I am prepared to speculate that the marginal differences of persuading cohabiting parents to wed or discontented couples to remain married might be far less than when parents make these decisions on their own. Many might spend more years in marriage, but would their children be better off as a result? There is no evidence to my knowledge that children spending fifteen years living in a two-biological-parent family fare substantially better than those who spend half or a third of that time doing so. In one English data set, parents who delayed divorce until their children had grown up conferred some advantages for their children compared to those who divorced earlier, but the differences were for the most part confined to the timing of sexual activity and family formation rather than school achievement and earnings (Furstenberg and Kiernan 1998). In sum, there is surely something to be gained by increasing the proportion of children growing up in nuclear families, but even if we designed successful policies to achieve that goal, the alteration of children's life course would be far less dramatic than many imagine.

This leads me to consider several alternative models of how we think about the link between children's well-being, the form of the family, and the general welfare of society (see Figure 1 for a simplified schematic on differing assumptions about these links).

David Ellwood and Christopher Jencks (2004) on the location and sources of marital decline, the comparative perspective on the rise of cohabitation in the West by Kathleen Kiernan, and the summary of marriage and public policies by Daniel Patrick Moynihan, Lee Rainwater, and Timothy Smeeding (2004) are all concerned with the relationship between social and economic change and marriage or its alternatives. Each points to why marriage has become a less obvious choice for young adults. These go a long way towards explaining how younger cohorts have come to think of marriage differently than older and why they may think that it offers fewer advantages to them and their children. The focus is primarily on the changing relationship between society and the family ($S \rightarrow F$).

Sigle-Rushton and McLanahan take up the effects of the family form on children's well-being and social reproduction, showing how and why the offspring of nonnuclear families are disadvantaged and, by implication, the impact reaches the next generation. Their purview is how family forms affect children and the potential problems that form creates for the welfare of society ($F \rightarrow C \rightarrow S$). If this generation of children is less well prepared to enter adulthood, the social costs incurred affect family functioning in the next generation.

This is the starting point for Horn and Nancy Folbre (2004). Both concern themselves with policy alternatives that might be designed to change

Model 1: Ellwood and Jencks; Kiernan; Moynihan, Rainwater, and Smeeding

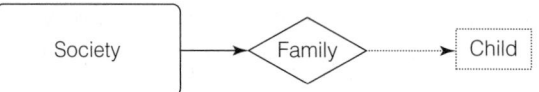

Model 2: Sigle-Rushton and McLanahan; Horn

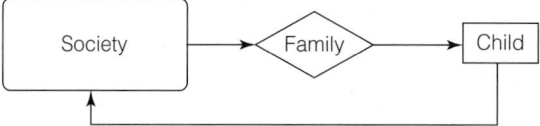

Model 3: Folbre

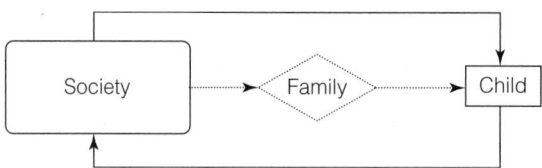

Model 4: Strengthening Marriage Through Family-Neutral Policy

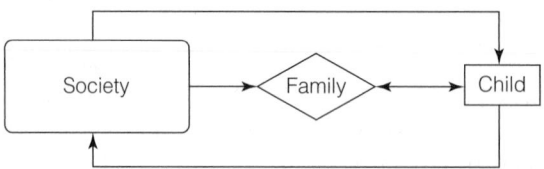

FIGURE 1   Links between Child, Family, and Social Well-Being.

Source: Author's compilation.

the current relationship between family forms and outcomes for children. Horn argues that marriage, if not the only form that promotes children's well-being, is surely the best. He contends that strengthening marriage is the most effective way to improve children's well-being and hence strengthen society (F → C → S). Folbre questions that proposition by posing a series of dilemmas or tradeoffs that might be involved when policy makers address the form of the family. She points to the hidden costs of attempts to restore the institution of marriage, at least as it existed in the heyday of the nuclear family.

Folbre's analysis is provocative, raising as it does interesting questions about the traditional model so widely endorsed by American policy makers: strengthening marriage improves the situation of children and therefore strengthens the larger society. Instead, she points to an alternative model: investing in children directly, in whatever family form they reside, is the best route to effective social reproduction (S → C → S). Her diagnosis of and prescription for managing changes in the institution of marriage, to borrow a

phrase from Moynihan, is to adopt a policy of "benign neglect." Focus on supporting the children and their families rather than worrying about what form of family is most efficient and effective. This appears to be the favored strategy of most European countries whose policies do not explicitly favor one form of the family or another.

Folbre's argument for family neutrality might actually work to strengthen marriage rather than undermine it, as is widely believed by many policy makers. Advocates of a pro-marriage approach argue that life-long marriage is the best form of the family for children. They point to the reasons Horn outlines and Sigle-Rushton and McLanahan review on the effects of marital disruption. I do not dispute the evidence but, like Folbre, I do not think that it necessarily follows from this evidence that the best solution is to privilege the nuclear family in our public policies.

My argument goes a bit further than Folbre's. I would argue that by supporting children and parents regardless of the family form is paradoxically the best way of producing more nuclear families. I think the evidence presented here points to reasons why this seemingly improbable scenario is likely to occur.

First, many of the benefits that are family neutral will help make it easier for parents to contemplate marriage and remain in marriage. We cannot disregard the overwhelming evidence from numerous surveys and qualitative studies that the vast majority of low-income and less-educated young people want to get married. In my study of a cohort of teenage mothers and their children in Baltimore, there was widespread wariness about marriage among the women in the younger generation, but nearly to a person, most wanted and expected to marry someday. Before marrying, they simply wanted to feel more confident about the prospects of the marriage enduring than they did when interviewed in their early twenties. Few felt that the men that they could marry were suitable and reliable partners. They averred that they wanted to wait so that they could have the kind of marriage that their grandparents, rather than their parents, had had. Helping the men whom they might marry return to school, get training, and find and secure remunerative employment would do a lot to make marriage more attractive. So too would efforts to provide support for unmarried couples if they felt that they had access to a range of social services from counseling to child care. Thus there is nothing inconsistent about supporting parents and their children and supporting marriage. Such services could be offered to all low-income parents regardless of their family circumstances; provided with such support, some parents would elect to marry and others might be encouraged to develop more collaborative and mutually supportive care for their children.

A range of economic and social services for low-income married couples might also reduce the incidence of divorce. The vast majority of low-income parents do marry, most often, I suspect, to the father of their first child. But the rates of divorce remain high, as Ellwood and Jencks (2004) observe, for this segment of the population and even for those with modest incomes and some college education. The strains on these families, like those with more

resources, are considerable. Bouts of unemployment, financial crises, conflicting job demands, and time pressures on working parents undermine marital solidarity. People can be taught to manage family strains more effectively, but they apply these lessons more successfully if society does more to relieve some of the material stresses on parents. Holding existing marriages together through a combination of material, social, and psychological support makes good policy sense if we believe that children are better off in stable unions.

Even acknowledging that we can greatly improve our efforts to preserve marriage, I argue that we must accept that for the foreseeable future out-of-wedlock childbearing will occur. In the 1950s, at least 25 percent of all first marriages followed a premarital pregnancy. The majority of those marriages did not survive, helping to produce the huge upsurge in divorce in the following decade. In the Baltimore study, close to half of the women married the father of their child. Four out of five of these marriages did not survive. The children of these abortive marriages did not do better than the children whose mothers elected not to marry the father of the child. This finding suggests that we should be very wary of promoting marriages because we think children are better off if their parents marry. They are not unless their parents marry successfully.

The alternative to promoting marriage exclusively is to support low-income parents so long as they are involved in child care and to support children's material, health, educational, and psychological needs directly. Were we to do so, this family neutral approach would likely produce long-term effects that support marriage as much as an explicit marriage-best policy. To the extent that such provisions reduce the proportion of poorly educated and unskilled youth and those with criminal experience, we would surely increase the pool of marriageable young people. While evidence exists that young people are less inclined to marry or marry successfully when they have grown up in a nonnuclear family, most are still committed to the institution of marriage. In other words, their poorer success rates have less to do with their ideals and aspirations than they do with their skills and abilities. Again, drawing on data from the Baltimore study, the overwhelming majority of offspring of teen mothers wanted to marry and many of them, after achieving their educational goals and entering the labor force, were either married or poised to enter marriage.

Referring again to Figure 1, I advocate a policy approach that supports the child as a means of supporting the family as well as supporting the family as a means of supporting the child ($S \rightarrow C \rightarrow F$ and $S \rightarrow F \rightarrow C \rightarrow F$). Both routes—supporting children through family policies and direct aid for children's educational, health, and social services (such as child care and after school programs)—are likely to produce benefits in the next generation that redound in a favorable way toward strengthening marriage.

While I have not attempted to do so, it is possible to estimate the relative payoff of direct and indirect supports designed to strengthen union stability by examining the intergenerational pattern of marriage practices under different hypothetical policy approaches. Based on my data from Baltimore,

I hypothesize that it may actually be more efficient over time to invest in children directly as a means of increasing union stability than to help children by helping their parents stay together. Let me be clear, I do not see these approaches as competing strategies for increasing union stability because most policies that support children ultimately help the parents. Building stronger child care programs, more effective mental health and counseling services, or, for that matter, better schools in disadvantaged communities, are all services for parents, whether married or unmarried.

It is unfortunate that conservatives, who believe in strengthening marriage, and liberals, who want to see family inequality reduced, cannot agree on a set of family-friendly policies that achieve both ends. The evidence indicates that helping parents—those who live together in wedlock, those who are previously married, those who might marry, and those who have no prospect of marriage—to support and nurture their children and to manage to do so in a collaborative manner is likely to have the highest payoff in producing stable families in the next generation.

REFERENCES

Ellwood, David T. and Christopher Jencks. 2004. "The Spread of Single-Parent Families in the United States since 1960." Pp. 25–65 in *The Future of the Family*, edited by Daniel P. Moynihan, Timothy M. Smeeding, and Lee Rainwater. New York: Russell Sage Foundation.

Folbre, Nancy. 2004. "Disincentives to Care: A Critique of U.S. Family Policy." Pp. 231–262 in *The Future of the Family*, edited by Daniel P. Moynihan, Timothy M. Smeeding, and Lee Rainwater. New York: Russell Sage Foundation.

Furstenberg, Frank and Kathleen Kiernan. 1998. "Delayed Parental Divorce: How Much Do Children Benefit?" *Journal of Marriage and the Family* 63 (2): 446–57.

McLanahan, Sara and Gary Sandefur. 1994. *Growing Up with a Single Parent: What Hurts, What Helps*. Cambridge, MA: Harvard University Press.

Moynihan, Daniel P., Timothy M. Smeeding, and Lee Rainwater, eds. 2004. *The Future of the Family*. New York: Russell Sage.

Sigle-Rushton, Wendy and Sara McLanahan. 2004. "Father Absence and Child Well-Being: A Critical Review." Pp. 116–158 in *The Future of the Family*, edited by Daniel P. Moynihan, Timothy M. Smeeding, and Lee Rainwater. New York: Russell Sage Foundation.

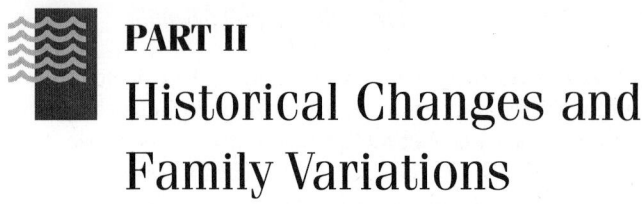

PART II

Historical Changes and Family Variations

5

HISTORICAL PERSPECTIVES ON FAMILY DIVERSITY

STEPHANIE COONTZ

Variability in the European and American Historical Record

In the ancient Mediterranean world, households and kin groupings were so disparate that no single unit of measurement or definition could encompass them. By the late 14th century, however, the English word *family*, derived from the Latin word for a household including servants or slaves, had emerged to designate all those who lived under the authority of a household head. The family might include a joint patrilocal family, with several brothers and their wives residing together under the authority of the eldest, as was common in parts of Italy and France before 1550, as well as in many Eastern European communities into the 19th century. Or it might be a stem family, in which the eldest son brought his bride into his parents' home upon marriage, and they lived as an extended family until the parents' deaths. The son's family then became nuclear in form, until the eldest son reached the age of marriage. Owing to late marriages and early mortality, most such families would be nuclear at any particular census, but most of them would pass through an extended stage at some point in their life cycle (Berkner 1972; Coontz 1988; Hareven 1987).

Until the early 19th century, most middle-class Europeans and North Americans defined *family* on the basis of a common residence under the authority of a household head, rather than on blood relatedness. This definition thus frequently included boarders or servants. Samuel Pepys began his famous 17th-century English diary with the words "I lived in Axe Yard, having my wife, and servant Jane, and no more in family than us three." In 1820

the publisher Everard Peck and his wife, of Rochester, New York, childless newlyweds, wrote home: "We collected our family together which consists of seven persons and we think ourselves pleasantly situated" (Coontz 1988; Hareven 1987).

Among the European nobility, an alternative definition of family referred not to the parent–child grouping, but to the larger descent group from which claims to privilege and property derived. Starting in the late 17th century, other writers used the word to refer exclusively to a man's offspring, as in the phrase *his family* and *wife*. Not until the 19th century did the word *family* commonly describe a married couple with their coresident children, distinguished from household residents or more distant kin. This definition spread widely during the 1800s. By the end of the 19th century, the restriction of the word to the immediate, coresidential family was so prevalent that the adjective *extended* had to be added when people wished to refer to kin beyond the household (Williams 1976).

Diversity in Emotional and Sexual Arrangements

. . . [Family diversity extends] not just to forms and definitions, but to the emotional meanings attached to families and the psychological dynamics within them. Whereas 17th-century Mediterranean families were organized around the principle of honor, which rested largely on the chastity of the family's women, other groups did not traditionally distinguish between "legitimate" and "illegitimate" children. When Jesuit missionaries told a Montagnais-Naskapi Indian that he should keep tighter control over his wife to ensure that the children she bore were "his," the man replied: "Thou hast no sense. You French people love only your own children; but we love all the children of our tribe" (Leacock 1980:31; see also Gutierrez 1991).

What is considered healthy parent–child bonding in our society may be seen as selfishness or pathological isolation by cultures that stress the exchange and fostering of children as ways of cementing social ties. The Zinacantecos of southern Mexico do not even have a word to distinguish the parent–child relationship from the house, suggesting that the emotional saliency of the cooperating household unit is stronger than that of blood ties per se. In Polynesia, eastern Oceania, the Caribbean, and the West Indies (and in 16th-century Europe), to offer your child to friends, neighbors, or other kin for adoption or prolonged coresidence was not considered abandonment but a mark of parental love and community reciprocity (Collier, Rosaldo, and Yanigasako 1982; Peterson 1993; Stack 1993).

Modern Americans stress the need for mother–daughter and father–son identification, but in matrilineal societies, where descent is reckoned in the female line, a man usually has much closer ties with his nephews than with his sons. Among the Trobriand Islanders, for instance, a child's biological father is considered merely a relation by marriage. The strongest legal and emotional bonds are between children and their maternal uncles. Conversely, among the patrilineal Cheyenne, mother–daughter relations were

expected to be tense or even hostile, and girls tended to establish their closest relationships with their paternal aunts (Collier et al. 1982).

What counts as healthy family dynamics or relationships also varies *within* any given society. Research on contemporary families has demonstrated that parenting techniques or marital relationships that are appropriate to middle-class white families are less effective for families that must cope with economic deprivation and racial prejudice (Baumrind 1972; Boyd-Franklin and Garcia-Preto 1994; Knight, Virdin, and Roosa 1994).

Values about the proper roles and concerns of mothers and fathers differ as well. Today women tend to be in charge of family rituals, such as weddings and funerals. In colonial days, however, this was a father's responsibility, while economic activities were far more central to a colonial woman's identity (and occupied much more of her time) than was child rearing. Contemporary American thought posits an inherent conflict between mothering and paid work, but breadwinning is an integral part of the definition of mothering in many cultural traditions. One study found that "traditional" Mexicanas in the United States experience *less* conflict or guilt in integrating the worlds of home and paid employment than do their Chicana counterparts who have internalized the notions of good mothering portrayed in the American mass media (Calvert 1992; Gillis 1996).

Even something as seemingly "natural" as sexual behavior and identity shows amazing variation across time and cultures. Categories of gender and sexuality have not always been so rigidly dichotomous as they are in modern Euro-American culture. Among many Native American societies, for instance, the *berdache* has a spiritual, social, economic, and political role that is distinct from either men's or women's roles. Neither he nor the female counterparts found in other Native American groups can be accurately described by the sexual identity we know as homosexual. Similarly, in traditional African culture, a person's sexual identity was not separable from his or her membership and social role in a family group (Herdt 1994; Jeater 1993; Schnarch 1992; Williams 1986).

Ever since the spread of Freudian psychiatric ideas at the beginning of the 20th century, Europeans and North Americans have tended to see a person's sexual behavior as the wellspring or driving force of his or her identity. The ancient Greeks, in contrast, thought that dreams about sex were "really" about politics. Until comparatively recently in history, a person's sexual acts were assumed to be separate from his or her fundamental character or identity. Indeed, the term *homosexual* did not come into use until the end of the 19th century. A person could commit a sexual act with a person of the same sex without being labeled as having a particular sexual "orientation." This lack of interest in identifying people by their sexual practices extended to heterosexual behavior as well. In mid-17th century New England, Samuel Terry was several times convicted for sexual offenses, such as masturbating, in public, but this behavior did not prevent his fellow townspeople from electing him town constable (D'Emilio and Freedman 1988; Padgug 1989).

Since the early 20th century, most American experts on the family have insisted on the importance of heterosexual intimacy between husband and

wife in modeling healthy development for children, yet in the 19th century, no one saw any harm in the fact that the closest bonds of middle-class women were with other women, rather than with their husbands. Men were often secondary in women's emotional lives, to judge from the silence or nonchalance about them in women's diaries and letters, which were saturated with expressions of passion that would immediately raise eyebrows by modern standards of sexual categorization. Although the acceptability of such passionate bonds may have provided cover for sexual relations between some women, these bonds were also considered compatible with marriage. Men, too, operated in a different sexual framework than today. They talked matter-of-factly about sleeping with their best friends, embracing them, or laying a head on a male friend's bosom—all without any self-consciousness that their wives or fiancées might misinterpret their "sexual orientation" (Duberman, Vicinus, and Chauncey 1989; Faderman 1981; Rotundo 1993; Smith-Rosenberg 1985). . . .

Families in the Cauldron of Colonization

At the time of European exploration of the New World, Native American families in North America orbited around a mode of social reproduction based on kinship ties and obligations. Kinship provided Native Americans with a system of assigning rights and duties on the basis of a commonly accepted criterion—a person's blood relationship (although this relationship might have been fictive) to a particular set of relatives. Kinship rules and marital alliances regulated an individual's place in the overall production and distribution of each group's dominant articles of subsistence and established set patterns in the individual's interactions with others.

Among groups that depended on hunting and gathering, such as those of the northern woods or Great Basin, marriage and residence rules were flexible and informal. In other Native American societies, typically those that had extensive horticulture, people were grouped into different sections, moieties or phratries, and clans, each of which was associated with different territories, resources, skills, duties, or simply personal characteristics. Exogamy, the requirement that an individual marry out of his or her natal group into a different clan or section, ensured the widest possible social cooperation by making each individual a member of intersecting kin groups, with special obligations to and rights in each category of relatives. Marriage and residence rules also organized the division of labor by age and gender (Coontz 1988; Leacock and Lurie 1971; Spicer 1962).

Unlike a state system, which makes sharp distinctions between family duties and civil duties, domestic functions and political ones, North American Native Americans had few institutions (prior to sustained contact with Europeans) that were set up on a basis other than kinship. Some groups, such as the Cherokee, might have had a special governing body for times of war, and the influence of such groups was invariably strengthened once Native Americans engaged in regular conflicts with settlers, but most of

the time village elders made decisions. There was no opposition between domestic or "private" functions and political or public ones. North American Native Americans had no institutionalized courts, police, army, or other agencies to tax or coerce labor. Kin obligations organized production, distributed surplus products, and administered justice. Murder, for example, was an offense not against the state but against the kin group, and, therefore, it was the responsibility and right of kin to punish the perpetrator. To involve strangers in this punishment, as modern state judicial systems deem best, would have escalated the number of groups and individuals involved in the conflict (Anderson 1991; Coontz 1988).

The nuclear family was not a property-holding unit, since resources and land either were available to all or were held by the larger kin corporation, while subsistence tools and their products were made and owned by individuals, rather than families. Its lack of private property meant that the nuclear family had less economic autonomy vis-à-vis other families than did European households. The lack of a state, on the other hand, gave Native American families more political autonomy because people were not bound to follow a leader for any longer than they cared to do so. However, this political autonomy did not seem to create a sense of exclusive attachment to one's "own" nuclear family. The nuclear family was only one of many overlapping ties through which individuals were linked. It had almost no functions that were not shared by other social groupings (Leacock and Lurie 1971; Spicer 1962).

Native American kinship systems created their own characteristic forms of diversity. North American Indians spoke more than 200 languages and lived in some 600 different societies with a wide variety of residence, marital, and genealogical rules. Among nomadic foragers, residence rules were flexible and descent was seldom traced far back. Horizontal ties of marriage and friendship were more important in organizing daily life than were vertical ties of descent. More settled groups tended to have more extensive lineage systems, in which rights and obligations were traced through either the female or the male line of descent. Most of the Great Plains and prairie Indians were patrilineal; matrilineal descent was common among many East Coast groups; the Creeks, Choctaws, and Seminoles of the South; and the Hopi, Acoma, and Zuni groups of the Southwest (Axtell 1981, 1988; Catlin 1973; Coontz 1988; Gutierrez 1991; Leacock and Lurie 1971; Mindel, Habenstein, and Wright 1988; Peters 1995; Snipp 1989).

Native American family systems produced land-use and fertility patterns that helped maintain the abundance of game and forests that made the land so attractive to European settlers. But they also made the Native Americans vulnerable to diseases brought by the Europeans and their animals, as well as to the Europeans' more aggressive and coordinated methods of warfare or political expansion (Axtell 1985, 1988; Cronon 1983).

The impact of European colonization on Native American family systems was devastating. Massive epidemics, sometimes killing 60%–90% of a group's members, devastated kin networks and hence disrupted social continuity. Heightened warfare elevated the role of young male leaders at

the expense of elders and women. In most cases, the influence of traders, colonial political officials, and Christian missionaries fostered the nuclear family's growing independence from the extended household, kinship, and community group in which it had traditionally been embedded. In other instances, as with Handsome Lake's revival movement among the Iroquois, Native Americans attempted to adapt European family systems and religious values to their own needs. Either way, gender and age relations were often transformed, while many Native American groups were either exterminated or driven onto marginal land that did not support traditional methods of social organization and subsistence. Native American collective traditions, however, were surprisingly resilient, and Euro-Americans spent the entire 19th century trying to extinguish them (Adams 1995; Anderson 1991; Calloway 1997; Coontz 1988; Mindel et al. 1988; Peters 1995).

The European families that came to North America were products of an international mercantile system whose organizing principles of production, exchange, ownership, and land use were on a collision course with indigenous patterns of existence. Europeans also had the support of a centralized state apparatus whose claims to political authority and notion of national interests had no counterweight among Native Americans. Colonial families had far more extensive property and inheritance rights than did Native American families, but they were also subjected to far more stringent controls by state and church institutions. The redistribution duties of wealthy families, however, were much more limited than those of Native Americans, so there were substantial differences in wealth and resources among colonial families, with the partial exception of those in the New England colonies right from the beginning (Coontz 1988; Mintz and Kellogg 1988).

These features of colonial society led to a different kind of family diversity than that among Native Americans. In addition to differences connected to the national, class, and religious origins of the settlers, the sex ratio of different colonizing groups, and the type of agriculture or trade they were able to establish, the colonies were also characterized by larger disparities in the wealth and size of households. Poorer colonists tended to concentrate in propertied households as apprentices, servants, or temporary lodgers.

At the same time as European settlers were destroying the Native American kinship system, they were importing an African kinship system, which they also attempted to destroy. But because the colonists depended on African labor, they had to make some accommodations to African culture and to African American adaptations to the requirements of surviving under slavery. The slaves were at once more subject to supervision and manipulation of their families and more able than Native Americans to build new kinship networks and obligations. They adapted African cultural traditions to their new realities, using child-centered, rather than marriage-centered, family systems; fictive kin ties; ritual coparenting or godparenting; and complex naming patterns that were designed to authenticate extended kin connections, all in the service of building kin ties within the interstices of the slave trade and plantation system. But African American families also had their own characteristic forms of diversity, depending on whether they lived in

settlements of free blacks, on large plantations with many fellow slaves, or on isolated small farms in the South (Franklin 1997; Gutman 1976; Stevenson 1996).

Slave families were not passive victims of the traffic in human beings nor organized in imitation of or deference to their masters' values. However, they could never be free of the constraints imposed by their white owners. They emerged out of a complex set of struggles and accommodations between both groups. But slaveowners' families were *also* derived from the dialectic of slavery. Anxieties about social control and racial-sexual hierarchies, fears of alliances between blacks and poor whites, and attempts to legitimate slavery in the face of Northern antislavery sentiment created a high tolerance for sexual hypocrisy; pervasive patterns of violence within white society, as well as against slaves; and elaborate rituals of patriarchy, both in family life and in the community at large (Edwards 1991; Isaacs 1982; McCurry 1995; Mullings 1997; Stevenson 1996).

Families in the Early Commercial and Industrializing Economy

From about the 1820s, a new constellation of family systems emerged in the United States, corresponding to the growth of wage labor, a national market economy, and the specialization of many occupations and professions. Merchants, manufacturers, and even many farmers consolidated production and hired employees to work for a set number of hours, rather than purchased supplies or raw materials from independent producers. Such producers, along with the apprentices and journeymen whom wage workers replaced, lost older routes to self-employment or accession to family farms. At the same time, married women's traditional household production was taken over by unmarried girls working in factories.

In an attempt to avoid becoming wage laborers and to find new professions or sources of self-employment for them and their children, a growing number of middle-class families developed a more private nuclear family orientation, keeping their children at home longer instead of sending them away for training or socialization elsewhere. Meanwhile, immigrants from Europe poured into the growing towns to work in factories or tenement workshops, while westward expansion drew new Mexican and Native American groups into the economy. Such trends in the early development of American capitalism reshaped ethnic traditions and class relations and led to the emergence of "whiteness" as a category that European immigrants could use to differentiate themselves from other groups near the bottom of the economic hierarchy (Johnson 1978; Jones 1997; Roediger 1988; Ryan 1981).

The gravitational force that was pulling families into new orbits in this period was the emergence of wage labor in the context of competing older values and an inadequately developed set of formal supporting institutions for capitalist production—schools, credit associations, unions, and even a developed consumer industry. Families who sought to escape wage labor by

moving west, setting up small businesses, or trying to compete with factory-made goods through household production were just as surely affected by the progress of capitalism as were families who either owned or had to work in the larger workshops and factories that increasingly supplanted apprenticeship arrangements in separate households or farms. At the same time, few families could yet free themselves from some reliance on household production or community sponsorship and social ties.

The gradual separation of work and home—market production and household reproduction—created new tensions between family activities and "economic" ones. Households could no longer get by primarily on things they made, grew, or bartered. However, they could not yet rely on ready-made purchased goods. Even in middle-class homes, the labor required to make purchased goods usable by the families was immense (Strasser 1982).

These competing gravitational pulls produced a new division of labor among middle-class families and many workers. Men (and in working-class families, children as well) began to specialize in paid work outside the home. Wives took greater responsibility for child care and household labor. A new ideology of parenting placed mothers at the emotional center of family life and romanticized the innocence of children, stressing the need to protect them within the family circle. What allowed middle-class white families to keep children at home longer and to divert the bulk of maternal attention from the production of clothes and food to child rearing was the inability of many working-class families to adopt such domestic patterns. The extension of childhood and the redefinition of motherhood among the middle class required the foreshortening of childhood among the slaves or sharecropping families who provided cotton to the new textile mills, the working-class women and children whose long hours in the factory made store-bought clothes and food affordable, and the Irish or free African American mothers and daughters who left their homes to work in what their mistresses insisted in defining as a domestic sanctuary, rather than a workplace. In addition to its class limitations, domesticity (along with its corollary, female purity) was constructed in opposition to the way that women of color were defined (Baca Zinn and Eitzen 1990; Dill 1998; Glenn 1992).

Even as many wives gave up their traditional involvement in production for sale or barter, others followed their domestic tasks out of the household and into the factories or small workshops that made up "the sweated trades." Still, as wage labor increasingly conflicted with domestic responsibilities, most families responded by trying to keep one household member near home. Although most wives of slaves and freed blacks continued to participate in the labor force, wives in most other racial and ethnic groups were increasingly likely to quit paid work outside the home after marriage. After the Civil War, freed slaves also attempted to use new norms of sexually appropriate work to resist gang labor, in a struggle with their former masters and current landlords that helped produce the sharecropping system in the South (Franklin 1997; Hareven 1976; Jones 1985; Lerner 1969; Mullings 1997).

But these superficially similar family values and gender-role behaviors masked profound differences, since working-class families continued

to depend on child labor and support networks of neighbors beyond the family and the work of women within the home or neighborhood varied immensely by class. For example, "unemployed" wives among the working class frequently took in boarders or lodgers, made and sold small articles or foodstuffs, and otherwise kept far too busy with household subsistence tasks to act like the leisured ladies of the upper classes or the hovering mothers of the middle classes (Boydston 1990; Hareven 1987).

Among the wealthy, fluid household membership and extended family ties remained important in mobilizing credit, pooling capital, and gaining political connections. In the working class, family forms diverged. Single-person and single-parent households multiplied among the growing number of transient workers. But the early factory system and its flip side, the sweated trades, reinforced the notion of the family as a productive unit, with all members working under the direction of the family head or turning their wages over to him.

After the Civil War, industrialization and urbanization accelerated. As U.S. families adapted to the demands and tensions of the industrializing society, different groups behaved in distinctive ways, but some trends could be observed. It was during this period that American families took on many of the characteristics associated with "the modern family." They became smaller, with lower fertility rates; they revolved more tightly around the nuclear core, putting greater distance between themselves and servants or boarders; parents became more emotionally involved in child rearing and for a longer period; couples oriented more toward companionate marriage; and the separation between home and work, both physically and conceptually, was sharpened (Coontz 1988; Mintz and Kellogg 1988).

Yet these trends obscure tremendous differences among and within the changing ethnic groups and classes of the industrializing United States. Between 1830 and 1882, more than 10 million immigrants arrived from Europe. After the Civil War, new professions opened up for middle-class and skilled workers, while job insecurity became more pronounced for laborers. Class distinctions in home furnishings, food, and household labor *widened* in the second half of the 19th century. There was also much more variation in family sequencing and form than was to emerge in the 20th century. Young people in the 19th century exhibited fewer uniformities in the age of leaving school and home, marrying, and setting up households than they do today. No close integration between marriage and entry into the workforce existed: Young people's status as children, rather than marriage partners, determined when and where they would start work. Family decisions were far more variable and less tightly coordinated throughout the society than they would become in the 20th century (American Social History Project 1992; Baca Zinn and Eitzen 1990; Graff 1987; Modell 1989).

In addition to this diversity in the life cycle, family forms and household arrangements diverged in new ways. The long-term trend toward nuclearity slowed between 1870 and 1890 when a number of groups experienced an increase in temporary coresidence with other kin, while others took in boarders or lodgers. American fertility fell by nearly 40% between 1855 and

1915, but this average obscures many differences connected to occupation, region, race, and ethnicity. The fertility of some unskilled and semiskilled workers actually *rose* during this period (Coontz 1988; Hareven 1987).

Another form of family and gender-role diversity in the late 19th century stemmed from mounting contradictions and conflicts over sexuality, which was increasingly divorced from fertility. In the middle class, birth control became a fact of life, despite agitated attempts of conservatives, such as Anthony Comstock, to outlaw information on contraceptives. In the working class, fertility diverged from sexuality, in another way—not only in the growth of prostitution in the cities, but with the emergence of a group of single working women who socialized with men outside a family setting. The opportunities for unsupervised sexual behavior in the cities also increased the possibilities for same-sex relationships, and even entire subcultures, to develop (D'Emilio and Freedman 1988).

The changes that helped produce more "modern" family forms, then, started in different classes, meant different things to families who occupied different positions in the industrial order, and did not proceed in a unilinear way. The "modernization" of the family was the result not of some general evolution of "the" family, as early family sociologists originally posited, but of *diverging* and *contradictory* responses that occurred in different areas and classes at various times, eventually interacting to produce the trends we now associate with industrialization. As Katz, Doucet, and Stern (1982) pointed out:

> The five great changes in family organization that have occurred are the separation of home and work place; the increased nuclearity of household structure; the decline in marital fertility; the prolonged residence of children in the home of their parents; and the lengthened period in which husbands and wives live together after their children have left home. The first two began among the working class and among the wage-earning segment of the business class (clerks and kindred workers). The third started among the business class, particularly among its least affluent, most specialized, and most mobile sectors. The fourth began at about the same time in both the working and business class, though the children of the former usually went to work and the latter to school. (P. 317)

The fifth trend did not occur until the 20th century and represented a reversal of 19th-century trends, as did the sixth major change that has cut across older differences among families: the reintegration of women into productive work, especially the entry of mothers into paid work outside the home and the immediate neighborhood.

The Family Consumer Economy

Around the beginning of the 20th century, a new constellation of family forms and arrangements took shape, as a consolidated national industrial system and mass communication network replaced the decentralized production of goods and culture that had prevailed until the 1890s. The standardization of

economic production, spread of mass schooling into the teenage years, abolition of child labor, growth of a consumer economy, and gradual expansion of U.S. international entanglements created new similarities and differences in people's experience of family life.

In the 1920s, for the first time, a bare majority of children came to live in a male-breadwinner, female-homemaker family, in which the children were in school rather than at work. Numerous immigrant families, however, continued to pull their children out of school to go to work, often arousing intense generational conflicts. African American families kept their children in school longer than any immigrant group, but their wives were much more likely than other American women to work outside the home (Hernandez 1993).

A major reorientation of family life occurred in the middle classes and in the dominant ideological portrayals of family life at that time. For the 19th-century middle class, the emotional center of family life had become the mother–child link and the wife's networks of female kin and friends. Now it shifted to the husband–wife bond. Although the "companionate marriage" touted by 1920s sociologists brought new intimacy and sexual satisfaction to married life, it also introduced two trends that disturbed observers. One was increased dissatisfaction with what used to be considered adequate relationships. Great expectations, as the historian May (1980) pointed out, could also generate great disappointments. These disappointments took the form of a jump in divorce rates and a change in the acceptable grounds for divorce (Coontz 1996; May 1980; Mintz and Kellogg 1988; Smith-Rosenberg 1985).

The other was the emergence of an autonomous and increasingly sexualized youth culture, as youths from many different class backgrounds interacted in high schools. The middle-class cult of married bliss and the new romance film industry led young people increasingly to stress the importance of sexual attractiveness and romantic experimentation. At the same time, the model of independent courting activity provided by working-class youths and the newly visible African American urban culture helped spread the new institution of "dating" (Bailey 1989; D'Emilio and Freedman 1988).

Another 20th-century trend was the state's greater intervention into the economy in response to the growth of the union movement, industry's need to regulate competition, the expanding international role of the United States, and other related factors. Families became increasingly dependent on the state and decreasingly dependent on neighborhood institutions for regulating the conditions under which they worked and lived. This change created more zones of privacy for some families but more places for state intervention in others. Sometimes the new state institutions tried to impose nuclear family norms on low-income families, as when zoning and building laws were used to prohibit the coresidence of augmented or extended families or children were taken away from single parents. But in other cases, state agencies imposed a female-headed household on the poor, as when single-parent families were the only model that entitled people to receive governmental subsidies (Gordon 1988; Zaretsky 1982).

Diversity, however, continued to be a hallmark of American family life. Between 1882 and 1930, more than 22 million immigrants came to America, many of them from southern and Eastern Europe, rather than from the traditional Western European suppliers of labor to the United States. They brought a whole range of new customs, religions, and traditions that interacted with their point of entry into the U.S. economy and with the new ethnic prejudices they encountered. By 1910 close to a majority of all workers in heavy industry were foreign born (Baca Zinn and Eitzen 1990).

These immigrants enriched urban life and changed the nature of industrial struggle in the United States. They neither "assimilated" to America nor retained their old ways untouched; rather, they used their cultural resources selectively to adapt to shifting institutional constraints and opportunities. For many groups, migration to America set up patterns of life and interaction with the larger mainstream institutions that forged a new cultural identity that was quite different from their original heritage. But this identity, in turn, changed as the socioeconomic conditions under which they forged their family lives shifted (Baca Zinn and Eitzen 1990; Glenn 1983; Sanchez 1993).

Space does not permit me to develop the history of diversity in 20th-century families, but one of the backdrops to the current debate about family life is that for some years there was a seeming reduction in family diversity, especially after restrictions on immigration in the 1920s began to take effect. For the first two-thirds of the 20th century, there was a growing convergence in the age and order in which young people of all income groups and geographic regions left home, left school, found jobs, and got married. The Great Depression, World War II, and the 1950s contributed to the impression of many Americans, even those in "minority" groups, that family life would become more similar over the course of the 20th century. Most families were hurt by the Great Depression, although the impact differed greatly according to their previous economic status. Marriage and fertility rates fell during the 1930s for all segments of the population; desertion rates and domestic violence increased. World War II spurred a new patriotism that reached across class and racial lines. It also disrupted or reshuffled families from all social and ethnic groups, albeit in different ways, ranging from the removal of Japanese Americans to internment camps to the surge in divorce rates as GIs came home to wives and children they barely knew (American Social History Project 1992; Coontz 1992; Graff 1987; Mintz and Kellogg 1988).

At the end of the 1940s, for the first time in 60 years, the average age of marriage and parenthood fell, the proportion of marriages ending in divorce dropped, and the birth rate soared. The percentage of women remaining single reached a 100-year low. The percentage of children being raised by bread-winner fathers and homemaker mothers and staying in high school until graduation reached an all-time high. The impression that the United States was becoming more homogeneous was fostered by the intense patriotism and anticommunism of the period, by the decline in the percentage of foreign-born persons in the population, and by powerful new media portrayals of the "typical" American family (Coontz 1992; May 1988; Skolnick 1991).

We now know, of course, that the experience of many families was literally "whited out" in the 1950s. Problems, such as battering, alcoholism, and incest, were swept under the rug. So was the discrimination against African Americans and Hispanics, women, elders, gay men, lesbians, political dissidents, religious minorities, and the handicapped. Despite rising real wages, 30% of American children lived in poverty, a higher figure than today. African American married-couple families had a poverty rate of nearly 50%, and there was daily violence in the cities against African American migrants from the South who attempted to move into white neighborhoods or use public parks and swimming areas (Coontz 1992, 1997; May 1988).

Yet poverty rates fell during the 1950s as new jobs opened up for blue-collar workers and the government gave unprecedented subsidies for family formation, home ownership, and education of children. Forty percent of the young men who started families at the end of World War II were eligible for veterans' benefits. Combined with high rates of unionization, heavy corporate investment in manufacturing plants and equipment, and an explosion of housing construction and financing options, these subsidies gave young families a tremendous economic jump start, created predictable paths out of poverty, and led to unprecedented increases in real wages. Sociologists heralded the end of the class society, and the popular media proclaimed that almost everyone was now "middle class." Even dissidents could feel that social and racial differences were decreasing. The heroic struggle of African Americans against Jim Crow laws, for example, finally compelled the federal government to begin to enforce the Supreme Court ruling against "separate but equal" doctrines.

Despite these perceptions, diversity continued to prevail in American families, and it became more visible during the 1960s, when the civil rights and women's liberation movements exposed the complex varieties of family experiences that lay behind the Ozzie and Harriet images of the time. In the 1970s, a new set of divisions and differences began to surface. The prolonged expansion of real wages and social benefits came to an end in the 1970s. By 1973, real wages were falling for young families in particular, and by the late 1970s, tax revolts and service cuts had eroded the effectiveness of the government's antipoverty programs that had proliferated in the late 1960s and brought child poverty to an all-time low by 1970. A new wave of immigrants began to arrive, but this time the majority were from Asian, Latin American, and Caribbean countries, rather than from Europe. By the 1980s, racial and ethnic diversity was higher than it had been since the early days of colonization, while it was obvious to most Americans that the reports of the death of class difference had been greatly exaggerated (Coontz 1992, 1997; Skolnick 1991).

Race relations were also no longer as clear-cut as in earlier times, despite the persistence of racism. They had evolved "from a strictly enforced caste system," in which there was unequivocal subordination of all blacks to whites to a more complex "system of power relations incorporating elements of social status, economics, and race" (Allen and Farley 1986:285). Although long-term residential segregation and discrimination

in employment ensured that the deterioration of the country's inner cities would hit African Americans especially hard, resulting in deepening and concentrated poverty, some professional African Americans made impressive economic progress in the decades after the 1960s, leading to a shift in the coding of racism and often to the rediscovery of white ethnicity by Americans who were seeking to roll back affirmative action (Coontz, Parson, and Raley 1998; Rubin 1994; Wilson 1978, 1996).

In one important way, family life has changed in the same direction among all groups. In 1950 only a quarter of all wives were in the paid labor force, and just 16% of all children had mothers who worked outside the home. By 1991 more than 58% of all married women in the United States, and nearly two-thirds of all married women with children, were in the labor force, and 59% of children, including a majority of preschoolers, had mothers who worked outside the home. Women of color no longer have dramatically higher rates of labor force participation than white women, nor do lower-income and middle-income groups differ substantially in the labor force participation of wives and mothers. Growing numbers of women from all social and racial-ethnic groups now combine motherhood with paid employment, and fewer of them quit work for a prolonged period while their children are young (Spain and Bianchi 1996).

But the convergence in women's participation in the workforce has opened up new areas of divergence in family life. Struggles over the redivision of household labor have created new family conflicts and contributed to rising divorce rates, although they have also led to an increase in egalitarian marriages in which both spouses report they are highly satisfied. Women's new economic independence has combined with other social and cultural trends to produce unprecedented numbers of divorced and unwed parents, cohabiting couples (whether heterosexual, gay, or lesbian), and blended families. Yet each of these family types has different dynamics and consequences, depending on such factors as class, race, and ethnicity (Coontz 1997; Cowan, Cowan, and Kerig 1993; Gottfried and Gottfried 1994; Morales 1990). . . .

Implications of Historical Diversity for Contemporary Families

The amount of diversity in U.S. families today is probably no larger than in most periods of the past. But the ability of so many different family types to demand social recognition and support for their existence is truly unprecedented. Most of the contemporary debate over family forms and values is not occasioned by the *existence* of diversity but by its increasing *legitimation*.

Historical studies of family life can contribute two important points to these debates. First, they make it clear that families have always differed and that no one family form or arrangement can be understood or evaluated outside its particular socioeconomic context and relations with other families. Many different family forms and values have worked (or not worked) for

various groups at different times. There is no reason to assume that family forms and practices that differ from those of the dominant ideal are necessarily destructive.

Second, however, history shows that families have always been fragile, vulnerable to rapid economic change, and needful of economic and emotional support from beyond the nuclear family. *All* families experience internal contradictions and conflicts, as well as external pressures and stresses. Celebrating diversity is no improvement over ignoring it unless we analyze the changing social conditions that affect families and figure out how to help every family draw on its potential resources and minimize its characteristic vulnerabilities.

REFERENCES

Adams, D. 1995. *Education for Extinction: American Indians and the Boarding School Experience, 1877–1928.* Lawrence: University Press of Kansas.

Allen, W. and R. Farley. 1986. "The Shifting Social and Economic Tides of Black America, 1950–1980." *American Review of Sociology* 12:277–306.

American Social History Project. 1992. *Who Built America? Working People and the Nation's Economy, Politics, Culture, and Society.* Vols. 1 and 2. New York: Pantheon.

Anderson, K. 1991. *Chain Her by One Foot: The Subjugation of Women in Seventeenth-Century New France.* New York: Routledge.

Axtell, J. 1981. *The Indian Peoples of Eastern America: A Documentary History of the Sexes.* New York: Oxford University Press.

———. 1985. *The Invasion Within: The Contest of Cultures in Colonial America.* New York: Oxford University Press.

———. 1988. *After Columbus: Essays in the Ethnohistory of Colonial North America.* New York: Oxford University Press.

Baca Zinn, M. and S. Eitzen. 1990. *Diversity in American Families.* New York: HarperCollins.

Bailey, B. 1989. *From Front Porch to Back Seat: Courtship in Twentieth-Century America.* Baltimore: Johns Hopkins University Press.

Berkner, L. 1972. "The Stem Family and the Developmental Cycle of the Peasant Household." *American Historical Review* 77:398–418.

Boyd-Franklin, N. and N. Garcia-Preto. 1994. "Family Therapy: The Cases of African American and Hispanic Women." Pp. 239–64 in *Women of Color: Integrating Ethnic and Gender Identities in Psychotherapy,* edited by L. Lomas-Diaz and B. Greene. New York: Guilford Press.

Boydston, J. 1990. *Home and Work: Housework, Wages, and the Ideology of Love in the Early Republic.* New York: Oxford University Press.

Calloway, C. 1997. *New Worlds for All: Indians, Europeans, and the Remaking of Early America.* Baltimore: Johns Hopkins University Press.

Calvert, K. 1992. *Children in the House.* Boston: Northeastern University Press.

Catlin, G. 1973. *Letters and Notes on the Manners, Customs and Conditions of the North American Indians.* New York: Dover.

Collier, J., M. Rosaldo, and S. Yanigasako. 1982. "Is There a Family? New Anthropological Views." Pp. 25–39 in *Rethinking the Family,* edited by B. Thorne. White Plains, NY: Longman.

Coontz, S. 1988. *The Social Origins of Private Life: A History of American Families, 1600–1900.* London: Verso.

———. 1992. *The Way We Never Were: American Families and the Nostalgia Trap.* New York: Basic Books.

———. 1996. "Where Are the Good Old Days?" *Modern Maturity* 34:36–43.

———. 1997. *The Way We Really Are: Coming to Terms with America's Changing Families.* New York: Basic Books.

Coontz, S., M. Parson, and G. Raley, eds. 1998. *American Families: A Multicultural Reader.* New York: Routledge.

Cowan, P., C. Cowan, and P. Kerig, eds. 1993. *Family, Self, and Society: Toward a New Agenda for Family Research.* Hillsdale, NJ: Lawrence Erlbaum.

Cronon, W. 1983. *Changes in the Land: Indians, Colonists, and the Ecology of New England.* New York: Hill & Wang.

D'Emilio, J. and E. Freedman. 1988. *Intimate Matters: A History of Sexuality in America*. New York: Harper & Row.

Dill, B. T. 1998. "Fictive Kin, Paper Sons, and *Compadrazgo*: Women of Color and the Struggle for Family Survival." Pp. 2–19 in *American Families*, edited by S. Coontz, M. Parson, and G. Raley. New York: Routledge.

Duberman, M., M. Vicinus, and G. Chauncey. 1989. *Hidden from History: Reclaiming the Gay and Lesbian Past*. New York: New American Library.

Edwards, L. 1991. "Sexual Violence, Gender, Reconstruction, and the Extension of Patriarchy in Granville County, North Carolina." *North Carolina Historical Review* 68:237–60.

Faderman, L. 1981. *Surpassing the Love of Men: Romantic Friendship and Love between Women from the Renaissance to the Present*. New York: William Morrow.

Franklin, D. 1997. *Ensuring Inequality: The Structural Transformation of the African-American Family*. New York: Oxford University Press.

Gillis, J. 1996. *A World of Their Own Making: Myth, Ritual, and the Quest for Family Values*. New York: Basic Books.

Glenn, E. N. 1983. "Split Household, Small Producer, and Dual Wage-Earner." *Journal of Marriage and the Family* 45:35–46.

———. 1992. "From Servitude to Service Work: Historical Continuities in Racial Division of Paid Reproductive Labor." *Signs* 18:1–43.

Gordon, L. 1988. *Heroes of Their Own Lives: The Politics and History of Family Violence, Boston 1880–1960*. New York: Viking.

Gottfried, A. and A. Gottfried. 1994. *Redefining Families: Implications for Children's Development*. New York: Plenum.

Graff, H., ed. 1987. *Growing Up in America: Historical Experiences*. Detroit: Wayne State University Press.

Gutierrez, R. 1991. *When Jesus Came, the Corn Mothers Went Away: Marriage, Sexuality, and Power in New Mexico, 1500–1846*. Stanford, CA: Stanford University Press.

Gutman, H. 1976. *The Black Family in Slavery and Freedom, 1750–1925*. New York: Pantheon.

Hareven, T. 1976. "Women and Men: Changing Roles." Pp. 93–118 in *Women and Men: Changing Roles, Relationships and Perceptions Report of a Workshop*, edited by L. A. Cater, A. F. Scott, and W. Martyna. Palo Alto, CA: Aspen Institute for Humanistic Studies.

———. 1987. "Historical Analysis of the Family." In *Handbook of Marriage and the Family*, edited by M. B. Sussman and S. K. Steinmetz. New York: Plenum.

Herdt, G., ed. 1994. *Third Sex, Third Gender: Beyond Sexual Dimorphism in Culture and History*. New York: Zone.

Hernandez, D. 1993. *America's Children: Resources from Family, Government, and the Economy*. New York: Russell Sage Foundation.

Isaacs, R. 1982. *The Transformation of Virginia, 1740–1790*. Chapel Hill: University of North Carolina Press.

Jeater, D. 1993. *Marriage, Perversion, and Power: The Construction of Moral Discourse in Southern Rhodesia, 1894–1930*. New York: Oxford University Press.

Johnson, P. 1978. *A Shopkeeper's Millennium: Society and Revivals in Rochester, New York, 1815–1837*. New York: Hill & Wang.

Jones, J. 1985. *Labor of Love, Labor of Sorrow: Black Women, Work, and the Family from Slavery to the Present*. New York: Basic Books.

———. 1997. *American Work: Four Centuries of Black and White Labor*. New York: W. W. Norton.

Katz, M., M. Doucet, and M. Stern. 1982. *The Social Organization of Industrial Capitalism*. Cambridge, MA: Harvard University Press.

Knight, G. P., L. M. Virdin, and M. Roosa. 1994. "Socialization and Family Correlates of Mental Health Outcomes among Hispanic and Anglo-American Children." *Child Development* 65:212–24.

Leacock, E. 1980. "Montagnais Women and the Program for Jesuit Colonization." In *Women and Colonization: Anthropological Perspectives*, edited by M. Etienne and E. Leacock. New York: Praeger.

Leacock, E. and N. O. Lurie. 1971. *North American Indians in Historical Perspective*. New York: Random House.

Lerner, G. 1969. "The Lady and the Mill Girl: Changes in the Status of Women in the Age of Jackson, 1800–1840." *Midcontinent American Studies Journal* 10:5–14.

May, E. T. 1980. *Great Expectations: Marriage and Divorce in Post-Victorian America*. Chicago: University of Chicago Press.

———. 1988. *Homeward Bound: American Families in the Cold War Era*. New York: Basic Books.

McCurry, S. 1995. *Masters of Small Worlds: Yeoman Households, Gender Relations, and the Political Culture of the Antebellum South Carolina Low Country.* New York: Oxford University Press.

Mindel, C., R. Habenstein, and R. Wright, eds. 1988. *Ethnic Families in America: Patterns and Variations.* New York: Elsevier.

Mintz, S. and S. Kellogg. 1988. *Domestic Revolutions: A Social History of American Family Life.* New York: Free Press.

Modell, J. 1989. *Into One's Own: From Youth to Adulthood in the United States, 1920–1975.* Berkeley: University of California Press.

Morales, E. S. 1990. "Ethnic Minority Families and Minority Gays and Lesbians." Pp. 217–39 in *Homosexuality and Family Relations,* edited by F. W. Bozett and M. B. Sussman. New York: Harrington Park Press.

Mullings, L. 1997. *On Our Own Terms: Race, Class, and Gender in the Lives of African-American Women.* New York: Routledge.

Padgug, R. 1989. "Sexual Matters: Rethinking Sexuality in History." Pp. 54–64 in *Hidden from History: Reclaiming the Gay and Lesbian Past,* edited by M. B. Duberman, M. Vicinus, and G. Chauncey Jr. New York: New American Library.

Peters, V. 1995. *Women of the Earth Lodges: Tribal Life on the Plains.* North Haven, CT: Archon Books.

Peterson, J. 1993. "Generalized Extended Family Exchange: A Case from the Philippines." *Journal of Marriage and the Family* 55:570–84.

Roediger, D. 1988. *The Wages of Whiteness: Race and the Making of the American Working Class.* London: Verso.

Rotundo, A. 1993. *American Manhood.* New York: Basic Books.

Rubin, L. 1994. *Families on the Fault Line.* New York: Basic Books.

Ryan, M. 1981. *Cradle of the Middle Class: The Family in Oneida County, New York.* New York: Cambridge University Press.

Sanchez, G. 1993. *Becoming Mexican-American: Ethnicity, Culture, and Identity in Chicano Los Angeles, 1900–1945.* New York: Oxford University Press.

Schnarch, B. 1992. "Neither Man nor Woman: Berdache—A Case for Non-dichotomous Gender Construction." *Anthropologica* 34:106–21.

Skolnick, A. 1991. *Embattled Paradise: The American Family in an Age of Uncertainty.* New York: Basic Books.

Smith-Rosenberg, C. 1985. *Disorderly Women: Visions of Gender in Victorian America.* New York: Oxford University Press.

Snipp, M. 1989. *American Indians: The First of This Land.* New York: Russell Sage Foundation.

Spain, D. and S. M. Bianchi. 1996. *Balancing Act: Motherhood, Marriage, and Employment among American Women.* New York: Russell Sage Foundation.

Spicer, E. H. 1962. *Cycles of Conquest: The Impact of Spain, Mexico, and the United States on the Indians of the Southwest, 1533–1960.* Tucson: University of Arizona Press.

Stack, C. 1993. "Cultural Perspectives on Child Welfare." Pp. 344–49 in *Family Matters: Readings on Family Lives and the Law,* edited by M. Minow. New York: New Press.

Stevenson, B. E. 1996. *Life in Black and White: Family and Community in the Slave South.* New York: Oxford University Press.

Strasser, S. 1982. *Never Done: A History of American Housework.* New York: Pantheon.

Wilson, W. J. 1978. *The Declining Significance of Race: Blacks and Changing American Institutions.* Chicago: University of Chicago.

———. 1996. *When Work Disappears: The World of the New Urban Poor.* New York: Alfred A. Knopf.

Williams, R. 1976. *Keywords: A Vocabulary of Culture and Society.* New York: Oxford University Press.

Williams, W. L. 1986. *The Spirit and the Flesh: Sexual Diversity in American Indian Culture.* Boston: Beacon Press.

Zaretsky, E. 1982. "The Place of the Family in the Origins of the Welfare State." Pp. 188–224 in *Rethinking the Family,* edited by B. Thorne. White Plains, NY: Longman.

6

FICTIVE KIN, PAPER SONS, AND *COMPADRAZGO*
Women of Color and the Struggle for Family Survival

BONNIE THORNTON DILL

Race has been fundamental to the construction of families in the United States since the country was settled. People of color were incorporated into the country and used to meet the need for cheap and exploitable labor. Little attention was given to their family and community life except as it related to their economic productivity. Upon their founding, the various colonies that ultimately formed the United States initiated legal, economic, political, and social practices designed to promote the growth of family life among European colonists. As the primary laborers in the reproduction and maintenance of families, White[1] women settlers were accorded the privileges and protection considered socially appropriate to their family roles. The structure of family life during this era was strongly patriarchal: denying women many rights, constraining their personal autonomy, and making them subject to the almost unfettered will of the male head of the household. Nevertheless, women were rewarded and protected within patriarchal families because their labor was recognized as essential to the maintenance and sustenance of family life.[2] In addition, families were seen as the cornerstone of an incipient nation, and thus their existence was a matter of national interest.

In contrast, women of color experienced the oppression of a patriarchal society but were denied the protection and buffering of a patriarchal family. Although the presence of women of color was equally important to the growth of the nation, their value was based on their potential as workers, breeders, and entertainers of workers, not as family members. In the eighteenth and nineteenth centuries, labor, and not the existence or maintenance of families, was the critical aspect of their role in building the nation. Thus they were denied the societal supports necessary to make their families a vital element in the social order. For women of color, family membership was not a key means of access to participation in the wider society. In some instances, racial-ethnic families were seen as a threat to the efficiency and exploitability of the work force and were actively prohibited. In other cases,

they were tolerated when it was felt they might help solidify or expand the work force. The lack of social, legal, and economic support for the family life of people of color intensified and extended women's work, created tensions and strains in family relationships, and set the stage for a variety of creative and adaptive forms of resistance.

African American Slaves

Among students of slavery, there has been considerable debate over the relative "harshness" of American slavery, and the degree to which slaves were permitted or encouraged to form families. It is generally acknowledged that many slave owners found it economically advantageous to encourage family formation as a way of reproducing and perpetuating the slave labor force. This became increasingly true after 1807, when the importation of African slaves was explicitly prohibited. The existence of these families and many aspects of their functioning, however, were directly controlled by the master. Slaves married and formed families, but these groupings were completely subject to the master's decision to let them remain intact. One study has estimated that about 32 percent of all recorded slave marriages were disrupted by sale, about 45 percent by death of a spouse, about 10 percent by choice, and only 13 percent were not disrupted (Blassingame 1972). African slaves thus quickly learned that they had a limited degree of control over the formation and maintenance of their marriages and could not be assured of keeping their children with them. The threat of disruption was one of the most direct and pervasive assaults on families that slaves encountered. Yet there were a number of other aspects of the slave system that reinforced the precariousness of slave family life.

In contrast to some African traditions and the Euro-American patterns of the period, slave men were not the main providers or authority figures in the family. The mother–child tie was basic and of greatest interest to the slave owner because it was essential to the reproduction of the labor force.

In addition to the lack of authority and economic autonomy experienced by the husband-father in the slave family, use of rape of women slaves as a weapon of terror and control further undermined the integrity of the slave family.

> It would be a mistake to regard the institutionalized pattern of rape during slavery as an expression of white men's sexual urges, otherwise stifled by the specter of the white womanhood's chastity. . . . Rape was a weapon of domination, a weapon of repression, whose covert goal was to extinguish slave women's will to resist, and in the process, to demoralize their men. (Davis 1981:23–24)

The slave family, therefore, was at the heart of a peculiar tension in the master-slave relationship. On the one hand, slave owners sought to encourage familiarities among slaves because, as Julie Matthaei (1982) states, "These provided the basis of the development of the slave into a self-conscious socialized

human being" (p. 81). They also hoped and believed that this socialization process would help children learn to accept their place in society as slaves. Yet the master's need to control and intervene in the family life of the slaves is indicative of the other side of this tension. Family ties had the potential to become a competing and more potent source of allegiance than the master. Also, kin were as likely to socialize children in forms of resistance as in acts of compliance.

It was within this context of surveillance, assault, and ambivalence that slave women's reproductive labor[3] took place. They and their menfolk had the task of preserving the human and family ties that could ultimately give them a reason for living. They had to socialize their children to believe in the possibility of a life in which they were not enslaved. The slave woman's labor on behalf of the family was, as Angela Davis (1971) has pointed out, the only labor in which the slave engaged that could not be directly used by the slave owner for his own profit. Yet, it was crucial to the reproduction of the slave owner's labor force, and thus a source of strong ambivalence for many slave women. Whereas some mothers murdered their babies to keep them from being slaves, many sought within the family the autonomy and creativity that were denied them in other realms of the society. The maintenance of a distinct African American culture is testimony to the ways in which slaves maintained a degree of cultural autonomy and resisted the creation of a slave family that only served the needs of the master.

Herbert Gutman (1976) gives evidence of the ways in which slaves expressed a unique African American culture through their family practices. He provides data on naming patterns and kinship ties among slaves that fly in the face of the dominant ideology of the period, which argued that slaves were immoral and had little concern for or appreciation of family life. Yet Gutman demonstrates that, within a system that denied the father authority over his family, slave boys were frequently named after their fathers, and many children were named after blood relatives as a way of maintaining family ties. Gutman also suggests that after emancipation a number of slaves took the names of former owners in order to reestablish family ties that had been disrupted earlier. On plantation after plantation, Gutman found considerable evidence of the building and maintenance of extensive kinship ties among slaves. In instances where slave families had been disrupted, slaves in new communities reconstituted the kinds of family and kin ties that came to characterize Black family life throughout the South. The patterns included, but were not limited to, a belief in the importance of marriage as a long-term commitment, rules of exogamy that excluded marriage between first cousins, and acceptance of women who had children outside of marriage. Kinship networks were an important source of resistance to the organization of labor that treated the individual slave, and not the family, as the unit of labor (Caulfield 1974).

Another interesting indicator of the slaves' maintenance of some degree of cultural autonomy has been pointed out by Gwendolyn Wright (1981) in her discussion of slave housing. Until the early 1800s, slaves were often permitted to build their housing according to their own design and taste.

During that period, housing built in an African style was quite common in the slave quarters. By 1830, however, slave owners had begun to control the design and arrangement of slave housing and had introduced a degree of conformity and regularity to it that left little room for the slaves' personalization of the home. Nevertheless, slaves did use some of their own techniques in construction, often hiding them from their masters.

> Even the floors, which usually consisted of only tamped earth, were evidence of a hidden African tradition: slaves cooked clay over a fire, mixing in ox blood or cow dung, and then poured it in place to make hard dirt floors almost like asphalt. . . . In slave houses, in contrast to other crafts, these signs of skill and tradition would then be covered over. (Wright 1981:48)

Housing is important in discussions of family because its design reflects sociocultural attitudes about family life. The housing that slave owners provided for their slaves reflected a view of Black family life consistent with the stereotypes of the period. While the existence of slave families was acknowledged, they certainly were not nurtured. Thus, cabins were crowded, often containing more than one family, and there were no provisions for privacy. Slaves had to create their own.

> Slave couples hung up old clothes or quilts to establish boundaries; others built more substantial partitions from scrap wood. Parents sought to establish sexual privacy from children. A few ex-slaves described modified trundle beds designed to hide parental lovemaking. . . . Even in one room cabins, sexual segregation was carefully organized. (Wright 1981:50)

Perhaps most critical in developing an understanding of slave women's reproductive labor is the gender-based division of labor in the domestic sphere. The organization of slave labor enforced considerable equality among men and women. The ways in which equality in the labor force was translated into the family sphere is somewhat speculative. Davis (1981), for example, suggests that egalitarianism between males and females was a direct result of slavery: "Within the confines of their family and community life, therefore, Black people managed to accomplish a magnificent feat. They transformed that negative equality which emanated from the equal oppression they suffered as slaves into a positive quality; the egalitarianism characterizing their social relations" (p. 18).

It is likely, however, that this transformation was far less direct than Davis implies. We know, for example, that slave women experienced what has been called the "double day" before most other women in this society. Slave narratives (Blassingame 1977; Jones 1985; White 1985) reveal that women had primary responsibility for their family's domestic chores. They cooked (although on some plantations meals were prepared for all the slaves), sewed, cared for their children, and cleaned house after completing a full day of labor for the master. John Blassingame (1972) and others have pointed out that slave men engaged in hunting, trapping, perhaps some

gardening, and furniture making as ways of contributing to the maintenance of their families. Clearly, a gender-based division of labor did exist within the family, and it appears that women bore the larger share of the burden for housekeeping and child care.

In contrast to White families of the period, however, the division of labor in the domestic sphere was reinforced neither in the relationship of slave women to work nor in the social institutions of the slave community. The gender-based division of labor among the slaves existed within a social system that treated men and women as almost equal, independent units of labor.[4] Thus Matthaei (1982) is probably correct in concluding that

> whereas the white homemaker interacted with the public sphere through her husband, and had her work life determined by him, the enslaved Afro-American homemaker was directly subordinated to and determined by her owner. . . . The equal enslavement of husband and wife gave the slave marriage a curious kind of equality, an equality of oppression. (P. 94)

Black men were denied the male resources of a patriarchal society and therefore were unable to turn gender distinctions into female subordination, even if that had been their desire. Black women, on the other hand, were denied support and protection for their roles as mothers and wives, and thus had to modify and structure those roles around the demands of their labor. Reproductive labor for slave women was intensified in several ways: by the demands of slave labor that forced them into the double day of work; by the desire and need to maintain family ties in the face of a system that gave them only limited recognition; by the stresses of building a family with men who were denied the standard social privileges of manhood; and by the struggle to raise children who could survive in a hostile environment.

This intensification of reproductive labor made networks of kin and fictive kin important instruments in carrying out the reproductive tasks of the slave community. Given an African cultural heritage where kinship ties formed the basis of social relations, it is not at all surprising that African American slaves developed an extensive system of kinship ties and obligations (Gutman 1976; Sudarkasa 1981). Research on Black families in slavery provides considerable documentation of participation of extended kin in child rearing, childbirth, and other domestic, social, and economic activities (Blassingame 1972; Genovese and Miller 1974; Gutman 1976).

After slavery, these ties continued to be an important factor linking individual household units in a variety of domestic activities. While kinship ties were also important among native-born Whites and European immigrants, Gutman (1976) has suggested that these ties

> were comparatively more important to Afro-Americans than to lower-class native white and immigrant Americans, the result of their distinctive low economic status, a condition that denied them the advantages of an extensive associational life beyond the kin group and the advantages and disadvantages resulting from mobility opportunities. (P. 213)

His argument is reaffirmed by research on African American families after slavery (Aschenbrenner 1975; Davis 1981; Shimkin, Shimkin, and Frate 1978; Stack 1974). Niara Sudarkasa (1981) takes this argument one step further, linking this pattern to the African cultural heritage.

> Historical realities require that the derivation of this aspect of Black family organization be traced to its African antecedents. Such a view does not deny the adaptive significance of consanguineal networks. In fact, it helps to clarify why these networks had the flexibility they had and why they, rather than conjugal relationships, came to be the stabilizing factor in Black families. (P. 49)

In individual households, the gender-based division of labor experienced some important shifts during emancipation. In their first real opportunity to establish family life beyond the controls and constraints imposed by a slave master, Black sharecroppers' family life changed radically. Most women, at least those who were wives and daughters of able-bodied men, withdrew from field labor and concentrated on their domestic duties in the home. Husbands took primary responsibility for the fieldwork and for relations with the owners, such as signing contracts on behalf of the family. Black women were severely criticized by Whites for removing themselves from field labor because they were seen to be aspiring to a model of womanhood that was considered inappropriate for them. The reorganization of female labor, however, represented an attempt on the part of Blacks to protect women from some of the abuses of the slave system and to thus secure their family life. It was more likely a response to the particular set of circumstances that the newly freed slaves faced than a reaction to the lives of their former masters. Jacqueline Jones (1985) argues that these patterns were "particularly significant" because at a time when industrial development was introducing a labor system that divided male and female labor, the freed Black family was establishing a pattern of joint work and complementarity of tasks between males and females that was reminiscent of preindustrial American families. Unfortunately, these former slaves had to do this without the institutional supports given White farm families and within a sharecropping system that deprived them of economic independence.

Chinese Sojourners

An increase in the African slave population was a desired goal. Therefore, Africans were permitted and even encouraged at times to form families, as long as they were under the direct control of the slave master. By sharp contrast, Chinese people were explicitly denied the right to form families in the United States through both law and social practice. Although male laborers began coming to the United States in sizable numbers in the middle of the nineteenth century, it was more than a century before an appreciable number of children of Chinese parents were born in America. Tom, a respondent in Victor Nee and Brett de Bary Nee's book, *Longtime Californ'* (1973) says:

"One thing about Chinese men in America was you had to be either a merchant or a big gambler, have lot of side money to have a family here. A working man, an ordinary man, just can't!" (p. 80).

Working in the United States was a means of gaining support for one's family with an end of obtaining sufficient capital to return to China and purchase land. This practice of sojourning was reinforced by laws preventing Chinese laborers from becoming citizens, and by restrictions on their entry into this country. Chinese laborers who arrived before 1882 could not bring their wives and were prevented by law from marrying Whites. Thus, it is likely that the number of Chinese American families might have been negligible had it not been for two things: the San Francisco earthquake and fire in 1906, which destroyed all municipal records, and the ingenuity and persistence of the Chinese people, who used the opportunity created by the earthquake to increase their numbers in the United States. Since relatives of citizens were permitted entry, American-born Chinese (real and claimed) would visit China, report the birth of a son, and thus create an entry slot. Years later, since the records were destroyed, the slot could be used by a relative or purchased by someone outside the family. The purchasers were called "paper sons." Paper sons became a major mechanism for increasing the Chinese population, but it was a slow process and the sojourner community remained predominantly male for decades.

The high concentration of males in the Chinese community before 1920 resulted in a split household form of family. As Evelyn Nakano Glenn (1983) observes:

> In the split household family, production is separated from other functions and is carried out by a member living far from the rest of the household. The rest—consumption, reproduction and socialization—are carried out by the wife and other relatives from the home village. . . . The split household form makes possible maximum exploitation of the workers. . . . The labor of prime-age male workers can be bought relatively cheaply, since the cost of reproduction and family maintenance is borne partially by unpaid subsistence work of women and old people in the home village. (Pp. 38–39)

The Chinese women who were in the United States during this period consisted of a small number who were wives and daughters of merchants and a larger percentage who were prostitutes. Lucia Cheng Hirata (1979) has suggested that Chinese prostitution was an important element in helping to maintain the split household family. In conjunction with laws prohibiting intermarriage, it helped men avoid long-term relationships with women in the United States and ensured that the bulk of their meager earnings would continue to support the family at home.

The reproductive labor of Chinese women, therefore, took on two dimensions primarily because of the split household family. Wives who remained in China were forced to raise children and care for in-laws on the meager remittances of their sojourning husbands. Although we know few details about their lives, it is clear that the everyday work of bearing and

maintaining children and running a household fell entirely on their shoulders. Those women who immigrated and worked as prostitutes performed the more nurturant aspects of reproductive labor, that is, providing emotional and sexual companionship for men who were far from home. Yet their role as prostitutes was more likely a means of supporting their families at home in China than a chosen vocation.

The Chinese family system during the nineteenth century was a patriarchal one and girls had little value. In fact, they were considered temporary members of their father's family because when they married, they became members of their husband's family. They also had little social value; girls were sold by some poor parents to work as prostitutes, concubines, or servants. This saved the family the expense of raising them, and their earnings became a source of family income. For most girls, however, marriages were arranged and families sought useful connections through this process. With the development of a sojourning pattern in the United States, some Chinese women in those regions of China where this pattern was more prevalent would be sold to become prostitutes in the United States. Most, however, were married to men whom they saw only once or twice in the twenty- or thirty-year periods during which these men sojourned in the United States. A woman's status as wife ensured that a portion of the meager wages her husband earned would be returned to his family in China. This arrangement required considerable sacrifice and adjustment by wives who remained in China and those who joined their husbands after a long separation.

Maxine Hong Kingston (1977) tells the story of the unhappy meeting of her aunt, Moon Orchid, with her husband, from whom she had been separated for thirty years: "For thirty years she had been receiving money from him from America. But she had never told him that she wanted to come to the United States. She waited for him to suggest it, but he never did" (p. 144). His response to her when she arrived unexpectedly was to say: "'Look at her. She'd never fit into an American household. I have important American guests who come inside my house to eat.' He turned to Moon Orchid, 'You can't talk to them. You can barely talk to me.' Moon Orchid was so ashamed, she held her hands over her face" (1977:178).

Despite these handicaps, Chinese people collaborated to establish the opportunity to form families and settle in the United States. In some cases it took as long as three generations for a child to be born on U.S. soil.

> In one typical history, related by a 21-year-old college student, great-grandfather arrived in the States in the 1890s as a "paper son" and worked for about 20 years as a laborer. He then sent for the grandfather, who worked alongside great-grandfather in a small business for several years. Great-grandfather subsequently returned to China, leaving grandfather to run the business and send remittance. In the 1940s, grandfather sent for father; up to this point, none of the wives had left China. Finally, in the late 1950s father returned to China and brought his wife back with him. Thus, after nearly 70 years, the first child was born in the United States. (Glenn 1981:14)

Chicanos

Africans were uprooted from their native lands and encouraged to have families in order to increase the slave labor force. Chinese people were immigrant laborers whose "permanent" presence in the country was denied. By contrast, Mexican Americans were colonized and their traditional family life was disrupted by war and the imposition of a new set of laws and conditions of labor. The hardships faced by Chicano families, therefore, were the results of the U.S. colonization of the indigenous Mexican population, accompanied by the beginnings of industrial development. The treaty of Guadalupe Hidalgo, signed in 1848, granted American citizenship to Mexicans living in what is now called the Southwest. The American takeover, however, resulted in the gradual displacement of Mexicans from the land and their incorporation into a colonial labor force (Barrera 1979). Mexicans who immigrated into the United States after 1848 were also absorbed into that labor force.

Whether natives of northern Mexico (which became part of the United States after 1848) or immigrants from southern Mexico, Chicanos were a largely peasant population whose lives were defined by a feudal economy and a daily struggle on the land for economic survival. Patriarchal families were important instruments of community life, and nuclear family units were linked through an elaborate system of kinship and godparenting. Traditional life was characterized by hard work and a fairly distinct pattern of sex-role segregation.

> Most Mexican women were valued for their household qualities, men by their ability to work and to provide for a family. Children were taught to get up early, to contribute to their family's labor to prepare themselves for adult life. . . . Such a life demanded discipline, authority, deference— values that cemented the working of a family surrounded and shaped by the requirements of Mexico's distinctive historical pattern of agricultural development, especially its pervasive debt peonage. (Saragoza 1983:8)

As the primary caretakers of hearth and home in a rural environment, Chicanas' labor made a vital and important contribution to family survival. A description of women's reproductive labor in the early twentieth century may be used to gain insight into the work of the nineteenth-century rural women.

> For country women, work was seldom a salaried job. More often it was the work of growing and preparing food, of making adobes and plastering houses with mud, or making their children's clothes for school and teaching them the hymns and prayers of the church, or delivering babies and treating sickness with herbs and patience. In almost every town there were one or two women who, in addition to working in their own homes, served other families in the community as *curanderas* (healers), *parteras* (midwives), and schoolteachers. (Elasser, MacKenzie, and Vigil 1980:10)

Although some scholars have argued that family rituals and community life showed little change before World War I (Saragoza 1983), the American conquest of Mexican lands, the introduction of a new system of labor, the loss of Mexican-owned land through the inability to document ownership, and the transient nature of most of the jobs in which Chicanos were employed resulted in the gradual erosion of this pastoral way of life. Families were uprooted as the economic basis for family life changed. Some people immigrated from Mexico in search of a better standard of living and worked in the mines and railroads. Others, who were native to the Southwest, faced a job market that no longer required their skills. They moved into mining, railroad, and agricultural labor in search of a means of earning a living. According to Albert Camarillo (1979), the influx of Anglo[5] capital into the pastoral economy of Santa Barbara rendered obsolete the skills of many Chicano males who had worked as ranch hands and farmers prior to the urbanization of that economy. While some women and children accompanied their husbands to the railroad and mining camps, many of these camps discouraged or prohibited family settlement.

The American period (after 1848) was characterized by considerable transiency for the Chicano population. Its impact on families is seen in the growth of female-headed households, reflected in the data as early as 1860. Richard Griswold del Castillo (1979) found a sharp increase in female-headed households in Los Angeles, from a low of 13 percent in 1844 to 31 percent in 1880. Camarillo (1979:120) documents a similar increase in Santa Barbara, from 15 percent in 1844 to 30 percent by 1880. These increases appear to be due not so much to divorce, which was infrequent in this Catholic population, as to widowhood and temporary abandonment in search of work. Given the hazardous nature of work in the mines and railroad camps, the death of a husband, father, or son who was laboring in these sites was not uncommon. Griswold del Castillo (1979) reports a higher death rate among men than women in Los Angeles. The rise in female-headed households, therefore, reflects the instabilities and insecurities introduced into women's lives as a result of the changing social organization of work.

One outcome, the increasing participation of women and children in the labor force, was primarily a response to economic factors that required the modification of traditional values. According to Louisa Vigil, who was born in 1890, "The women didn't work at that time. The man was supposed to marry that girl and take care of her. . . . Your grandpa never did let me work for nobody. He always had to work, and we never did have really bad times" (Elasser et al. 1980:14).

Vigil's comments are reinforced in Mario Garcia's (1980) study of El Paso. In the 393 households he examined in the 1900 census, he found 17.1 percent of the women to be employed. The majority of this group were daughters, mothers with no husbands, and single women. In Los Angeles and Santa Barbara, where there were greater work opportunities for women than in El Paso, wives who were heads of household worked in seasonal and part-time jobs, and lived from the earnings of children and relatives in an effort to maintain traditional female roles.

Slowly, entire families were encouraged to go to railroad work camps and were eventually incorporated into the agricultural labor market. This was a response both to the extremely low wages paid to Chicano laborers and to the preferences of employers, who saw family labor as a way of stabilizing the work force. For Chicanos, engaging all family members in agricultural work was a means of increasing their earnings to a level close to subsistence for the entire group and of keeping the family unit together. Camarillo (1979) provides a picture of the interplay of work, family, and migration in the Santa Barbara area in the following observation:

> The time of year when women and children were employed in the fruit cannery and participated in the almond and olive harvest coincided with the seasons when the men were most likely to be engaged in seasonal migratory work. There were seasons, however, especially in the early summer when the entire family migrated from the city to pick fruit. This type of family seasonal harvest was evident in Santa Barbara by the 1890s. As walnuts replaced almonds and as the fruit industry expanded, Chicano family labor became essential. (P. 93)

This arrangement, while bringing families together, did not decrease the hardships that Chicanas had to confront in raising their families. We may infer something about the rigors of that life from Jesse Lopez de la Cruz's description of the workday of migrant farm laborers in the 1940s. Work conditions in the 1890s were as difficult, if not worse.

> We always went to where the women and men were going to work, because if it were just the men working it wasn't worth going out there because we wouldn't earn enough to support a family. . . . We would start around 6:30 a.m. and work for four or five hours, then walk home and eat and rest until about three-thirty in the afternoon when it cooled off. We would go back and work until we couldn't see. Then I'd clean up the kitchen. I was doing the housework and working out in the fields and taking care of two children. (Quoted in Goldman 1981:119–20)

In the towns, women's reproductive labor was intensified by the congested and unsanitary conditions of the barrios in which they lived. Garcia (1980) described the following conditions in El Paso:

> Mexican women had to haul water for washing and cooking from the river or public water pipes. To feed their families, they had to spend time marketing, often in Ciudad Juarez across the border, as well as long, hot hours cooking meals and coping with the burden of desert sand both inside and outside their homes. Besides the problem of raising children, unsanitary living conditions forced Mexican mothers to deal with disease and illness in their families. Diphtheria, tuberculosis, typhus and influenza were never too far away. Some diseases could be directly traced to inferior city services. . . . As a result, Mexican mothers had to devote much energy to caring for sick children, many of whom died. (Pp. 320–21)

While the extended family has remained an important element of Chicano life, it was eroded in the American period in several ways. Griswold del Castillo (1979), for example, points out that in 1845 about 71 percent of Angelenos lived in extended families, whereas by 1880, fewer than half did. This decrease in extended families appears to be a response to the changed economic conditions and the instabilities generated by the new sociopolitical structure. Additionally, the imposition of American law and custom ignored, and ultimately undermined, some aspects of the extended family. The extended family in traditional Mexican life consisted of an important set of family, religious, and community obligations. Women, while valued primarily for their domesticity, had certain legal and property rights that acknowledged the importance of their work, their families of origin, and their children. In California, for example,

> equal ownership of property between husband and wife had been one of the mainstays of the Spanish and Mexican family systems. Community-property laws were written into the civil codes with the intention of strengthening the economic controls of the wife and her relatives. The American government incorporated these Mexican laws into the state constitution, but later court decisions interpreted these statutes so as to undermine the wife's economic rights. In 1861, the legislature passed a law that allowed the deceased wife's property to revert to her husband. Previously it had been inherited by her children and relatives if she died without a will. (Griswold del Castillo 1979:69)

The impact of this and similar court rulings was to "strengthen the property rights of the husband at the expense of his wife and children" (Griswold del Castillo 1979:69).

In the face of the legal, social, and economic changes that occurred during the American period, Chicanas were forced to cope with a series of dislocations in traditional life. They were caught between conflicting pressures to maintain traditional women's roles and family customs, and the need to participate in the economic support of their families by working outside the home. During this period the preservation of traditional customs—such as languages, celebrations, and healing practices—became an important element in maintaining and supporting familial ties.

According to Alex Saragoza (1983), transiency, the effects of racism and segregation, and proximity to Mexico aided in the maintenance of traditional family practices. Garcia has suggested that women were the guardians of Mexican cultural traditions within the family. He cites the work of anthropologist Manuel Gamio, who identified the retention of many Mexican customs among Chicanos in settlements around the United States in the early 1900s.

> These included folklore, songs, and ballads, birthday celebrations, saints' days, baptisms, weddings, and funerals in the traditional style. Because of poverty, a lack of physicians in the barrios, and adherence to traditional customs, Mexicans continued to use medicinal herbs. Gamio

also identified the maintenance of a number of oral traditions, and Mexican-style cooking. (Garcia 1980:322)

Of vital importance to the integrity of traditional culture was the perpetuation of the Spanish language. Factors that aided in the maintenance of other aspects of Mexican culture also helped in sustaining the language. However, entry into English-language public schools introduced the children and their families to systematic efforts to erase their native tongue. Griswold del Castillo reports that in the early 1880s there was considerable pressure against speakers of Spanish in the public schools. He also found that some Chicano parents responded to this kind of discrimination by helping support independent bilingual schools. These efforts, however, were short-lived.

Another key factor in conserving Chicano culture was the extended family network, particularly the system of *compadrazgo* (godparenting). Although the full extent of the impact of the American period on the Chicano extended family is not known, it is generally acknowledged that this family system, though lacking many legal and social sanctions, played an important role in the preservation of the Mexican community (Camarillo 1979). In Mexican society, godparents were an important way of linking family and community through respected friends or authorities. Participants in the important rites of passage in the child's life, such as baptism, first Communion, confirmation, and marriage, godparents had a moral obligation to act as guardians, to provide financial assistance in times of need, and to substitute in case of the death of a parent. Camarillo (1979) points out that in traditional society these bonds cut across class and racial lines.

The rite of baptism established kinship networks between rich and poor, between Spanish, mestizo and American Indian, and often carried with it political loyalty and economic-occupational ties. The leading California patriarchs in the pueblo played important roles in the *compadrazgo* network. They sponsored dozens of children for their workers or poorer relatives. The kindness of the *padrino* and *madrina* was repaid with respect and support from the *pobladores* (Camarillo 1979:12–13).

The extended family network, which included godparents, expanded the support groups for women who were widowed or temporarily abandoned and for those who were in seasonal, part- or full-time work. It suggests, therefore, the potential for an exchange of services among poor people whose income did not provide the basis for family subsistence. Griswold del Castillo (1979) argues that family organization influenced literacy rates and socioeconomic mobility among Chicanos in Los Angeles between 1850 and 1880. His data suggest that children in extended families (defined as those with at least one other relative living in a nuclear family household) had higher literacy rates than those in nuclear families. He also argues that those in larger families fared better economically and experienced less downward mobility. The data here are too limited to generalize to the Chicano experience as a whole, but they do reinforce the actual and potential importance of this family form to the continued cultural autonomy of the Chicano community.

Conclusion

Reproductive labor for African American, Chinese American, and Mexican American women in the nineteenth century centered on the struggle to maintain family units in the face of a variety of assaults. Treated primarily as workers rather than as members of family groups, these women labored to maintain, sustain, stabilize, and reproduce their families while working in both the public (productive) and private (reproductive) spheres. Thus, the concept of reproductive labor, when applied to women of color, must be modified to account for the fact that labor in the productive sphere was required to achieve even minimal levels of family subsistence. Long after industrialization had begun to reshape family roles among middle-class White families, driving White women into a cult of domesticity, women of color were coping with an extended day. This day included subsistence labor outside the family and domestic labor within the family. For slaves, domestics, migrant farm laborers, seasonal factory workers, and prostitutes, the distinctions between labor that reproduced family life and labor that economically sustained it were minimized. The expanded workday was one of the primary ways in which reproductive labor increased.

Racial-ethnic families were sustained and maintained in the face of various forms of disruption. Yet the women and their families paid a high price in the process. High rates of infant mortality, a shortened life span, and the early onset of crippling and debilitating disease give some insight into the costs of survival.

The poor quality of housing and the neglect of communities further increased reproductive labor. Not only did racial-ethnic women work hard outside the home for mere subsistence, they worked very hard inside the home to achieve even minimal standards of privacy and cleanliness. They were continually faced with disease and illness that resulted directly from the absence of basic sanitation. The fact that some African women murdered their children to prevent them from becoming slaves is an indication of the emotional strain associated with bearing and raising children while participating in the colonial labor system.

We have uncovered little information about the use of birth control, the prevalence of infanticide, or the motivations that may have generated these or other behaviors. We can surmise, however, that no matter how much children were accepted, loved, or valued among any of these groups of people, their futures were precarious. Keeping children alive, helping them to understand and participate in a system that exploited them, and working to ensure a measure—no matter how small—of cultural integrity intensified women's reproductive labor.

Being a woman of color in nineteenth-century American society meant having extra work both inside and outside the home. It meant being defined as outside of or deviant from the norms and values about women that were being generated in the dominant White culture. The notion of separate spheres of male and female labor that developed in the nineteenth century had contradictory outcomes for Whites. It was the basis for the confinement

of upper-middle-class White women to the household and for much of the protective legislation that subsequently developed in the workplace. At the same time, it sustained White families by providing social acknowledgment and support to women in the performance of their family roles. For racial-ethnic women, however, the notion of separate spheres served to reinforce their subordinate status and became, in effect, another assault. As they increased their work outside the home, they were forced into a productive labor sphere that was organized for men and "desperate" women who were so unfortunate or immoral that they could not confine their work to the domestic sphere. In the productive sphere, racial-ethnic women faced exploitative jobs and depressed wages. In the reproductive sphere, they were denied the opportunity to embrace the dominant ideological definition of "good" wife or mother. In essence, they were faced with a double-bind situation, one that required their participation in the labor force to sustain family life but damned them as women, wives, and mothers because they did not confine their labor to the home.

Finally, the struggle of women of color to build and maintain families provides vivid testimony to the role of race in structuring family life in the United States. As Maxine Baca Zinn (1990) points out:

> Social categories and groups subordinate in the racial hierarchy are often deprived of access to social institutions that offer supports for family life. Social categories and groups elevated in the racial hierarchy have different and better connections to institutions that can sustain families. Social location and its varied connection with social resources thus have profound consequences for family life. (P. 74)

From the founding of the United States, and throughout its history, race has been a fundamental criterion determining the kind of work people do, the wages they receive, and the kind of legal, economic, political, and social support provided for their families. Women of color have faced limited economic resources, inferior living conditions, alien cultures and languages, and overt hostility in their struggle to create a "place" for families of color in the United States. That place, however, has been a precarious one because the society has not provided supports for these families. Today we see the outcomes of that legacy in statistics showing that people of color, compared with whites, have higher rates of female-headed households, out-of-wedlock births, divorce, and other factors associated with family disruption. Yet the causes of these variations do not lie merely in the higher concentrations of poverty among people of color; they are also due to the ways race has been used as a basis for denying and providing support to families. Women of color have struggled to maintain their families against all of these odds.

ENDNOTES

Acknowledgments: The research in this study was an outgrowth of my participation in a larger collaborative project examining family, community, and work lives of racial-ethnic women in the United States. I am deeply indebted to the scholarship and creativity of members of the group in the development of this study. Appreciation is extended to Elizabeth Higginbotham, Cheryl

Townsend Gilkes, Evelyn Nakano Glenn, and Ruth Zambrana (members of the original working group), and to the Ford Foundation for a grant that supported in part the work of this study.

[1] The term "White" is a global construct used to characterize peoples of European descent who migrated to and helped colonize America. In the seventeenth century, most of these immigrants were from the British Isles. However, during the time period covered by this article, European immigrants became increasingly diverse. It is a limitation of this chapter that time and space do not permit a fuller discussion of the variations in the White European immigrant experience. For the purposes of the argument being made herein and of the contrast it seeks to draw between the experiences of mainstream (European) cultural groups and those of racial-ethnic minorities, the differences among European settlers are joined and the broad similarities emphasized.

[2] For a more detailed discussion of this argument and the kinds of social supports provided these families, see an earlier version of this paper: "Our Mothers' Grief: Racial-Ethnic Women and the Maintenance of Families," *Journal of Family History* 13 (4) (1988): 415–31.

[3] The term "reproductive labor" is used to refer to all of the work of women in the home. This includes, but is not limited to, the buying and preparation of food and clothing, provision of emotional support and nurturance for all family members, bearing children, and planning, organizing, and carrying out a wide variety of tasks associated with socialization. All of these activities are necessary for the growth of patriarchal capitalism because they maintain, sustain, stabilize, and reproduce (both biologically and socially) the labor force.

[4] Recent research suggests that there were some tasks assigned primarily to males and some others to females. Whereas some gender-role distinctions with regard to work may have existed on some plantations, it is clear that slave women were not exempt from strenuous physical labor.

[5] This term is used to refer to White Americans of European ancestry.

REFERENCES

Aschenbrenner, Joyce. 1975. *Lifelines: Black Families in Change.* New York: Holt, Rinehart, and Winston.

Baca Zinn, Maxine. 1990. "Family, Feminism and Race in America." *Gender and Society* 4 (1) (March): 68–82.

Barrera, Mario. 1979. *Race and Class in the Southwest.* Notre Dame, IN: Notre Dame University Press.

Blassingame, John. 1972. *The Slave Community: Plantation Life in the Antebellum South.* New York: Oxford University Press.

———. 1977. *Slave Testimony: Two Centuries of Letters, Speeches, Interviews, and Autobiographies.* Baton Rouge: Louisiana State University Press.

Camarillo, Albert. 1979. *Chicanos in a Changing Society.* Cambridge, MA: Harvard University Press.

Caulfield, Mina Davis. 1974. "Imperialism, the Family, and Cultures of Resistance." *Socialist Review* 4 (2) (October): 67–85.

Davis, Angela. 1971. "Reflections on the Black Woman's Role in the Community of Slaves." *Black Scholar* 3 (4) (December): 2–15.

———. 1981. *Women, Race, and Class.* New York: Random House.

Elasser, Nan, Kyle MacKenzie, and Yvonne Tixier Y. Vigil. 1980. *Las Mujeres.* New York: The Feminist Press.

Garcia, Mario T. 1980. "The Chicano in American History: The Mexican Women of El Paso, 1880–1920—A Case Study." *Pacific Historical Review* 49 (2) (May): 315–58.

Genovese, Eugene D. and Elinor Miller, eds. 1974. *Plantation, Town, and County: Essays on the Local History of American Slave Society.* Urbana: University of Illinois Press.

Glenn, Evelyn Nakano. 1983. "Split Household, Small Producer, and Dual Earner: An Analysis of Chinese-American Family Strategies." *Journal of Marriage and the Family* 45 (1) (February): 35–46.

Goldman, Marion S. 1981. *Gold Diggers and Silver Miners.* Ann Arbor: University of Michigan Press.

Griswold del Castillo, Richard. 1979. *The Los Angeles Barrio: 1850–1890.* Los Angeles: University of California Press.

Gutman, Herbert. 1976. *The Black Family in Slavery and Freedom, 1750–1925.* New York: Pantheon.

Hirata, Lucia Cheng. 1979. "Free, Indentured, Enslaved: Chinese Prostitutes in Nineteenth Century America." *Signs* 5 (Autumn): 3–29.

Jones, Jacqueline. 1985. *Labor of Love, Labor of Sorrow.* New York: Basic Books.

Kingston, Maxine Hong. 1977. *The Woman Warrior.* New York: Vintage Books.

Matthaei, Julie. 1982. *An Economic History of Women in America.* New York: Schocken.

Nee, Victor G. and Brett de Bary Nee. 1973. *Longtime Californ'.* New York: Pantheon.

Saragoza, Alex M. 1983. "The Conceptualization of the History of the Chicano Family: Work, Family, and Migration in Chicanos." In *Research Proceedings of the Symposium on Chicano Research and Public Policy.* Stanford, CA: Stanford University, Center for Chicano Research.

Shimkin, Demetri, E. M. Shimkin, and D. A. Frate, eds. 1978. *The Extended Family in Black Societies.* The Hague: Mouton.

Stack, Carol S. 1974. *All Our Kin: Strategies for Survival in a Black Community.* New York: Harper & Row.

Sudarkasa, Niara. 1981. "Interpreting the African Heritage in Afro-American Family Organization." In *Black Families,* edited by Harriette Pipes McAdoo. Beverly Hills, CA: Sage.

White, Deborah Gray. 1985. *Ar'n't I a Woman? Female Slaves in the Plantation South.* New York: W. W. Norton.

Wright, Gwendolyn. 1981. *Building the Dream: A Social History of Housing in America.* New York: Pantheon.

7

THE POLITICS OF THEORIZING AFRICAN AMERICAN FAMILIES

Old Debates, New Directions

SHIRLEY A. HILL

Twentieth-century family scholars made notable gains in documenting the diversity and functionality of African American families (Allen 1995; Billingsley 1968; McAdoo 1990; Willie and Reddick 2003) and explaining how they are affected by and cope with persistent racial and class inequality (Hill 1972; Jarrett 1994; Stack 1974). The first studies of Black families emerged in the early decades of the 1900s among liberal social scientists challenging research that ignored Black families and/or accepted biological theories that described them as inherently inferior. These scholars attributed the problems of Black families to social forces such as slavery, racial oppression, economic exploitation, and northward migration. E. Franklin Frazier, for example, argued that these social and economic forces had destroyed African cultural traditions, prevented Black people from assimilating into the mainstream culture, and left a significant percentage of them poor and mired in pathological behaviors. But the idea that the African culture had been destroyed by slavery and racial oppression was a matter of some debate

Shirley A. Hill, "The Politics of Theorizing African American Families: Old Directions" (presented at the meeting of the Midwest Sociological Society, Omaha, Nebraska, April 2006). Copyright © 2006 by Shirley A. Hill. Reprinted with the permission of the author.

(Frazier [1939] 1957; Herskovits 1941), and was to meet its strongest rebuttal during the civil rights movement of the 1960s. Revisionist researchers during that era challenged the social deficit perspective spawned by earlier theorists and affirmed the strong cultural traditions of African Americans as important sources of family survival and strength, thus articulating a new perspective on Black families that highlighted their strengths and resiliency.

Revisionist scholars agreed that slavery, racial oppression, segregation, discrimination, and lack of opportunity had adversely affected African American families, but they argued that contemporary racism had done more to undermine the two-parent family structure than slavery (Gutman 1976). But these scholars also rejected the claim that these forces had destroyed African cultural values and traditions, arguing instead that they had been altered, retained, and/or strengthened by the American experience. Their revisionist research broadened notions of what constituted family viability by showing that families need not conform to hegemonic family and gender norms to function well and by arguing that African American families were best described as culturally variant rather than culturally deficient (Allen 1978). They paved the way for the multicultural perspective on race-ethnic families that is now common in the social sciences, where the cultural traditions and coping resources of ethnically diverse families— especially those that are poor—are recognized. In his seminal work, Robert Hill described the cultural strengths of Black families as resilience, religiosity, flexible gender roles, a strong achievement orientation, extended family ties, shared childbearing, and informal adoption (Hill 1972). Garrett R. Fesler traced Black family patterns to African traditions and argued that such traditions continue to shape the worldviews of African Americans, leading them to emphasize the importance of family and community and to be more receptive to polygamy, communal ownership of property, and non-rational causality (Fesler 2004:182).

Understanding the strengths, cultural heritage, and worldviews of poor and/or race-ethnic minority families is an important tool for social workers and family scholars; however, I argue that theorizing African American families as culturally distinct has become increasingly problematic. Although the historic experiences of Black families *do* stand in sharp contrast to those of White families (Billingsley 1968, 1992; Giddings 1984) and may well have been shaped by the retention of African cultural traditions (Burgess 1994; Nobles 1985), the cultural perspective ignores both the historic and contemporary diversity of African American families, especially that based on social class. Too often the concepts of class and culture are conflated, so that what passes for the Black culture is more reflective of the experiences of those who are poor. Cultural theories also walk the fine line of distinguishing between behaviors that are the result of racial oppression and even inimical to the best interests of Black people and those which are actually embedded in their value system. Too often, theorists offer a fairly stagnant rather than dynamic view of culture, one that is lodged in the pre-modern worldviews and practices of Africans, and provide little analysis of the potentially harmful effects of some traditions.

Purpose of Reading

The current [reading] has three distinct but related purposes. First, I highlight how the social construction of African American families is shaped by the political context. Both early theorists and those of the civil rights era agreed that the identities, economic status, and culture of African Americans had been significantly influenced by slavery and racial oppression; indeed, race was a master status that shaped the destiny of Black people regardless of their economic position. Both also engaged in activist research that supported an end to racial oppression, although they made their cases for liberation in different ways. Theorists of the pre–civil rights era, although later described as proffering a "social deficit" perspective, essentially offered a social class analysis of the Black families. They accepted the assimilation framework that was dominant during that era and the logic of structural-functionalism, and their politics pressed for Black assimilation into mainstream society. Their class analysis of African American families served two purposes: (1) to show that Black families could, as seen among those in the middle-class, conform to the family ideals of the dominant society, and (2) to highlight the hardships and pathologies of those that were excluded from full participation in American society. While they did view single-mother families as inherently pathological, their focus on so-called "matriarchal families" was intended more as an indictment of racial oppression than Black families.

Revisionist scholars of the civil rights era also saw slavery and racism as responsible for the plight of poor Black families, but rejected the claim that these families were inherently weak or pathological, or had been deprived of their cultural heritage. Their refusal to describe poor or single-mother families as defective embodied a legitimate demand for new thinking in the study of racial and ethnic minority families and was inspired by the politics of civil rights activism in the 1960s. The major goal of the civil rights movement was to end racial segregation and second-class citizenship for African Americans, but it also inspired themes of pride, unity, and solidarity among Blacks across the globe. Pan-Africanism led many to challenge the assimilation model of race relations, which assumed that European American values were worthy of emulation. This connection with a broader project of racial liberation also helped political activists reject the idea that Blacks were without a culture. Indeed, as Gordon and Anderson (1999) have noted, such a notion reinforced biological definitions of Blacks "as a people without significant history or national or territorial connection; as having nothing cultural or intellectual to offer to 'modernity'; and as racially inferior, marginal, and uncivilized" (p. 285).

Second, I look at how empirical evidence was amassed in support of the class and culture perspectives on Black families. I am not engaging the larger debate on whether a Black culture exists; indeed, the retention and significance of African culture on multiple aspects of American life has been well documented. Rather, I am interested more narrowly in the social construction of African American families during these two distinct eras. Collectively,

Black families differ from White families because they are more likely to live in poverty and be headed by single mothers, more likely to have adult male figures that are absent and/or marginally involved in family life, and more likely to be a part of extended kin networks. Historically, Black women were more likely to work outside of the home than were White women, and some studies have suggested that this produced more egalitarian marriage relationships. The debate centers, of course, on whether these aspects of family life are rooted in social class or cultural traditions.

Finally, I suggest new lines of theorizing and research that move us beyond a simplistic dichotomy or debate over whether Black families are pathological or strong and resilient. Indeed, while racial inequality still shapes the experiences of African American families, the growing pattern of class diversity among Blacks has produced many potentially fruitful research questions.

Black Families in Theoretical and Political Context

Family studies emerged in the late nineteenth century in the context of industrialization, an economic transition that eventually fostered urbanization, an emphasis on upward mobility and economic prosperity, and new family and gender ideologies. Industrialization is often credited with giving rise to the breadwinner–homemaker family, which excluded White women from the labor market and idealized the modern families as a two-parent, marriage-centered, patriarchal unit suited for the demands of the new economy (Parsons and Bales 1955). During that era, few scholars focused on poor and/or racial-ethnic families, and those who did saw only disorder and disorganization. Dominant racist ideologies cast doubt on whether Black people were even biologically or morally capable of creating functional families (Franklin 1997), a theme that grew in prominence once slavery ended and especially as Blacks migrated northward, a move that often shattered the stability of families and made single-mother families more visible. Amid early-twentieth-century studies of race relations among those migrating into urban areas, a few scholars began to look at the specific problems faced by African Americans and their families.

Two theoretical paradigms shaped the work of theorists who were later described as spawning a social deficit perspective on African American families. First, they accepted the premises of the dominant social theory of the era, structural functionalism, which equated the structure of a family with social respectability, socioeconomic mobility, and the ability of the family to function well in modern, industrial society. The ideal family was composed of two married parents and their children and had a breadwinner–homemaker division of labor, that is, men were the wage earners and women took care of domestic work and child care. Conforming to this family structure was challenging for many African Americans, especially in the aftermath of slavery, but they battled myths of their innate inferiority (or that they were reverting to their "primitive ways") by trying to prove that they could

conform to the expectations of the dominant society, especially the norm of two-parent families (Franklin 1997). The second key theoretical focus in the social sciences was assimilation theory. Many scholars, especially those affiliated with the Chicago school, were widely engaged in research on processes of urbanization and assimilation among racial-ethnic minorities (Ross 2004). M. B. Ross (2004) points out that scholars like W. E. B. DuBois, Charles S. Johnson, and E. Franklin Frazier were among those eager to use the tools of social science research to look at "the extent to which the Negro mass [had] adjusted to the moral, social, and economic habits of the dominant culture" (p. 167). Not surprisingly, they found that Black people who moved to urban areas faced major barriers to assimilation and mobility.

The Social Deficit Perspective: A Social Class Analysis of Black Families

Drawing on the theoretical assumptions of structural-functionalism and assimilation theory, Frazier launched a series of studies in the early 1920s aimed at focusing specifically on the problems facing Black families. He argued slavery had practically destroyed Black families by stripping them of their African culture, denying them the right to legal marriage, selling spouses and family members, undermining the traditional family roles for men, and forcing Black women to become overly independent and domineering. The most important legacy of slavery had been the tradition of single-mother families, which Frazier alternately referred to as "maternal" or "matriarchal" families. Frazier claimed that maternal families had often worked well in rural, southern areas, but became weaker and more fragmented under the pressures of urban migration, economic exclusion, and residential segregation (Frazier [1939] 1957). Thus, he initiated the deviancy discourse on single-mother families, which stood and (continues to stand) at the center of the notions of African American families as weak and dysfunctional.

In Frazier's analysis, "the matriarchal" or single-mother family was a key deterrent to the stability and economic mobility of Black families: It symbolized deviance from society's sexual and gender norms, and was associated with poverty and deficient child socialization. His notion of matriarchal families made Frazier the key figure in developing the social deficit perspective on Black families; however, prior to the civil rights era nearly every African American scholar, activist, and institution saw single-mother/male-absent families as the major problem facing Black people (Giddings 1984). Moreover, most attributed the problem to the impact that slavery and racial oppression had on Black families, and they were apt to describe that impact by explaining that they were deprived of their cultural heritage and mired in pathological behaviors. Scholars like Kenneth Stamps claimed that poor Black people were living "cultural chaos," since their own cultural traditions had been destroyed and they experienced the American culture as "meaningless and unintelligible." In a similar vein, W. E. B. DuBois

argued that racial oppression had fostered problems like "shrewd laziness, shameless lewdness, [and] cunning crime" among the poor (quoted in Ross 2004:151).

But despite these dire descriptions of poor families, what is notable is that this research shifted the discourse from biological explanations of Black families to social class or economic explanations, often going to great lengths to draw distinctions between poor and middle-income Blacks. Their work often highlighted the similarities between middle-class Black and White families. One early study comparing childrearing in Black and White families concluded that the most "striking thing about this study is that Negro and white middle-class families are so much alike, and that white and Negro lower-class families are so much alike" (Davis and Havighurst 1946:708). Poverty and racial exclusion, on the other hand, had a corrosive impact on families, producing mothers who were "loveless tyrants" and fathers who were "reclusive, taciturn, violent, punitive, and without interest in their children" (Kardiner and Ovesey 1951). Such was the literature that D. Patrick Moynihan drew on when he offered a social class perspective on Black families. He repeatedly pointed out that his report pertained to low-income, single-mother families, and warned that the success of the growing Black middle-class should not "beguile the nation into supposing that the circumstances of the remainder of the Negro community are equally prosperous" (Moynihan 1965).

The Strength-Resiliency Perspective: Reclaiming the Cultural Heritage of Black Families

During the protests of the 1960s, hegemonic institutions and ideologies, including those pertaining to families, were increasingly under fire for perpetuating gender inequities and maligning the experiences of racial minorities. Thus, the once-accepted premise that families that did not conform to dominant societal norms were inherently defective was being called into question, as were victim-blaming explanations of race and class inequality. The notion that poor Black families were weak and pathological was suddenly out of sync with emerging emphases on family diversity, gender equality, and racial and cultural pride among African Americans. Moreover, although Black women had been key players in the civil rights movement, the increasing prominence of Black men as leaders of the movement (e.g., the politics of Black Power) spawned a new sense of masculinity that did not sit well with the notion of Black men as ruled over or marginalized by their women. The Moynihan Report, thus, served as a catalyst for a new genre of revisionist scholarship on African American families.

Revisionist scholars refuted the idea that African American families were matriarchal and dysfunctional, and that their cultural heritage had been destroyed by slavery and racial oppression. These scholars spawned a strength-resiliency perspective on Black families, in most cases by either integrating the concept of culture into their analyses or by documenting

their survival strategies. In *Black Families in White America,* Billingsley argued that African American families were diverse in structure and class position, but were bound together by common experiences and cultural traditions. Carol Stack's study of Black, low-income, single-mother families highlighted their efficacy, especially their ability to survive through extensive networks of support, reciprocity, and shared childcare. She also challenged hegemonic family definitions by redefining a family as "the smallest, organized, durable network of kin and non-kin who interact daily, providing domestic needs for children and assuring their survival" (1974:31). Joyce Ladner studied African American adolescent girls growing up in a housing project in St. Louis and described them as embracing both mainstream values, such as gendered identities and high aspirations for success, and distinct African-based cultural values, such as the value of strong and economically independent women, a greater acceptance of premarital sex, and a general absence of the concept of illegitimacy.

The Class-Culture Nexus

While revisionist research managed to show that African American families are far from cauldrons of pathology, the concept of culture has remained one of the most contentious issues in the study of African American families. Theorists of the revisionist era often criticized earlier scholars for denying the existence of an African-based Black culture or maligning it as pathological, and even today researchers often start with the premise that Black families are seen from a social deficit perspective. What counts as cultural is often a point of debate, but Boykin and Toms have developed a useful framework for thinking about culture by suggesting that there are three intersecting cultural strands that shape the attitudes and behaviors of African Americans: the mainstream culture, the Black culture, and the minority culture (Boykin and Toms 1985). There is much evidence, for example, that African Americans voice support for the family values and gender ideologies that are espoused by mainstream society, and conform to those values when they have the resources to do so. The debate between the social class and cultural perspectives centers on how to describe behaviors that deviate from those norms.

The Minority Culture: Culture of Poverty Thesis

Poverty, racial exclusion, and economic marginalization are primarily responsible for Boykin and Toms description of the minority culture, which largely intersects with social class position. Being poor and Black is highly correlated with the prevalence of single-mother families, delinquent and criminal behavior, and other socially deviant behaviors. The minority culture is best exemplified by the culture of poverty thesis developed in the 1950s by Oscar Lewis, who argued that poverty and social isolation from mainstream society gave rise to a certain set of values. While these cultural

behaviors initially helped poor people cope with social inequality, they gradually became institutionalized and actually perpetuated poverty, social pathology, welfare dependency, and family instability. Social deficit theorists documented the presence of a culture of poverty among poor Blacks, but they also criticized the thesis as reflecting an "almost total unwillingness of society to admit its complicity in the suffering and exclusion which lower income people experience" (Rainwater and Yancey 1967). Indeed, while the dominant political discourse today invokes the theme of social pathology to describe the family and gender patterns common among poor Blacks, Ann Swidler has argued, the link between what people value and what they do is often tenuous or nonexistent, especially during difficult times. Swidler described cultures as "tool kits" from which people construct "strategies for action," rather than a "style or a set of skills and habits or a set of preferences or wants" (1986:275).

The Black Culture

Revisionist theorists' notion of culture resonates more with what Boykin and Toms described as the Black culture, or a set of positive or distinct values that have emerged out of both African and African American traditions. Afrocentrists believe that is theoretically significant in research on Black people, and insist that African ideals be placed "at the center of any analysis that involved African culture and behavior" (Asante 1987:6). In studying Black families, distinct Afrocentric values include multiple parent figures, interfamilial adoptions, close family networking, an ethos of group survival, and collective responsibility (Nobles 1974).

From Theory to Empirical Research

Although social class (social deficit) and cultural (strength-resilience) theorists differed in their depictions of Black families, especially those that were poor, their methodological strategies were quite similar: They relied on basic descriptive statistics, often drawn from census data, but more saliently they used qualitative research strategies such as participant observation, case studies, and interviews. These research strategies predated analyzing large datasets through sophisticated statistical techniques and were seen as the hallmark of objectivity at institutions like the Chicago school of sociology in the early 1900s (Ross 2004). As Ross points out, scholars of that era wanted to advance the field of sociology by collecting data directly from specific populations, which they saw as enabling them to provide objective analyses of race relations and assimilation. Additionally, he notes that the Chicago school of sociology was an especially ideal setting for studying the impact of social forces on families, as most of its scholars had rejected notions of racial determinism.

The research of revisionist scholars like Stack and Ladner followed the tradition of using qualitative strategies like ethnographies, participant observation, and interviews, yet, unlike quantitative methodologists, they

advanced a portrait of poor Black families as culturally defined, strong, and functional. A key factor in reconceptualizing poor and/or single-mother families has been replacing the dominant structural-functional paradigm with a more culturally relative framework. Walter Allen (2001) has underscored the significance of this theoretical shift by arguing that theory must precede and be seen as more important than one's particular research methods. Still, qualitative research strategies are often seen as best for capturing the lived experiences and perspectives of marginalized racial groups, especially when it comes to understanding their cultural norms (Littlejohn-Blake and Darling 1993) and the resources families draw upon in coping with poverty (Jarrett 1994). Afrocentricity as a research perspective had contended that the experiences of Black people are best understood by cultural and social immersion into their lives (rather than social distance), and commends research that is participatory, committed, and introspective (Asante 1987).

Most contemporary qualitative research has shown that poor families, not surprisingly, have many struggles but manage to cope with them. Single parents (usually mothers) do their best to support their child economically and emotionally, extended kin networks help out, and fathers are often not as absent as they appear to be. Thus most qualitative studies—at least recent ones—tend to embrace the strength-resiliency perspective on Black families, although they do not uniformly describe them in positive terms or stagnant terms. Elijah Anderson, for example, has advanced a more nuanced framework of life in poor Black neighborhoods by noting that they consist of both "decent" and "street" lifestyles. And the notion that non-marital childbearing is widely accepted by African American families (Burton 1990) finds little support in the work of Elaine Bell Kaplan, who found that many Black women saw their unmarried pregnancy in their daughters as diminishing their standing in the community, and usually advised them to get an abortion (Kaplan 1997). Similarly, qualitative studies have begun to document the weakening of extended family ties and support for single mothers among African Americans (Hill 1999, 2005; Willie and Reddick 2003).

Although qualitative studies have provided significant insights and advancements in our knowledge of African American families, they also have several limitations. Many (if not most) have relied on small, racially homogeneous and/or non-representative samples, thus raising questions about the generalizability of their findings. Distinguishing between cultural- and class-based behaviors is difficult since qualitative studies rarely use class and economically diverse samples. And, while there is a tendency to focus on the strengths of poor Black families, the concept of strength is a broad and ambiguous one that does not lend itself well to empirical analysis. That families survive through strategies such as reliance on extended kin for resources and childcare does not tell us much about the long-term costs or consequences of these cultural traditions. For example, Stack's (1974) research on child keeping in low-income Black families noted that children are "transferred back and forth, 'borrowed' or 'loaned'" (p. 66) when mothers start new relationships with men, want to foster kinship ties, or are simply too young or too poor to care for them, yet it offers few insights

on how such arrangements affect the long-term welfare of children. Overall, the focus on survival strategies and strengths may understate the harmful impact of racial and class inequality on poor families.

The last decades of the twentieth century saw a notable increase in the number of quantitative studies that focused explicitly on or included African Americans. While class and culture are mutually interactive and overlapping concepts, drawing on this research can offer some insights on clarifying their respective impact on African American families. Research showing a decline in the strength of extended family resources is especially important since this has been the key linchpin supporting the notion of poor, single-mother families as strong and functional. The work of Ann Roschelle, based on a national survey that included a multi-racial sample, found that extended family support was not the cultural norm for racial minority families; in fact, Whites received more childcare help and household assistance than any other group (Roschelle 1997). Another report noted that while poor single mothers in general receive more assistance from extended kin than do married, middle-class ones, those that are Black receive considerably less support than in the past (Arendell 2000). Regardless of the level of support they receive from their extended kin, quantitative studies increasingly question the premise that children in single-mother families fare as well as those living with both of their biological parents (McLanahan and Schwartz 2002). They also show the impact of poverty on Black children varies based on the psychological characteristics of their mothers (McLoyd et al. 2000).

The notion of African American families as ensconced in supportive, extended family networks seemed almost a mockery by the 1980s, when Black communities were plagued by escalating rates of homicide, violence, child abuse and abandonment, AIDS, and illicit drugs. Federal census data show that the overall rate of non-marriage among Black women more than doubled between 1970 and the mid-1990s, far exceeding the decline found among White women. By the end of that decade the 23 percent of Black families headed by single mothers that had appalled Moynihan in 1960 had grown to nearly 70 percent (Arendell 2000). Single-mother families became a major predictor of poverty and welfare dependency, and poverty rates in Black single-mother families were considerably higher than in White single-mother families (Arendell 2000). By 1995, Black women comprised two-fifths of all welfare recipients; moreover, they stayed on welfare longer and experienced higher rates of welfare recidivism (Edin and Harris 1999).

African American children were still more likely to live with grandmothers, but studies have shown that it is often under the duress of parents mired in drug addiction and unable to care for them (Hill 1994), and grandmothers had become less willing to accept such responsibilities and often did so under the duress of child abandonment and/or drug use by their own children. Even with the assistance of grandparents and other relatives, Black children became significantly overrepresented among those in the foster care system. Indeed, post-revisionist scholars during the 1980s were even questioning the earlier findings of revisionists, painting a much more nuanced historic picture of Black families.

New Directions for Understanding Black Families

Despite notable changes in Black families, many scholars have remained notably wedded to the strength-resilience perspective of the civil rights era, often insisting on a cultural thesis of African American families (Allen 2001). But growing social class diversity makes such a thesis untenable. Many African Americans, especially those whose educational attainments and social class background had placed them in a position to take advantage of civil rights era gains, made remarkable progress during the civil rights era. Between 1960 and the 1990s the rate of high school completion among Blacks quadrupled, those attaining a four-year college degree doubled, and by 2001 almost 23 percent held professional and/or managerial jobs (Hill 2005). Recent census data show the poverty rate among African Americans to have reached an all-time low of less than 25 percent (compared to 75 percent in the pre–civil rights era).

But the overall picture is one of class polarization among African Americans, a pattern similar to that in the dominant society. Frank Furstenberg noted that by the 1980s there was a significant decline in research on African American families (Furstenberg 2007), and I suggest that it had much to do with the demise of Black families in the post–civil rights era, as evidenced by high rates of non-marriage, non-marital childbearing, single-mother families, and welfare dependency—all of which emerged in the context of escalating joblessness and violence in urban areas. In *The Declining Significance of Race,* W. J. Wilson explained these outcomes by citing the devastating impact the loss of industrial jobs was having on young African American men. By the mid-1950s, and for the first time ever, rates of unemployment among African American men were twice as high as those for Whites (Billingsley 1992), and this continued to be the case throughout the twentieth century. In the face of unemployment, menial (and often demeaning) work, and poor wages, African American men were resorting to crime, drugs, and gang violence—all activities that rendered them less eligible for and interested in marriage.

Less attention has been paid to the fact that the earning potential of young Black women, especially those who were college-educated, also declined between 1973 and 1991 due to their overrepresentation in declining industries (Bound and Dresser 1999). Also of significance has been a decline of female-centered support systems for poor mothers and a general loss of the cultural power and authority of African American women. During the 1980s punitive welfare policies left women with less to share, and growing class polarization and a resurgence of Black nationalism and patriarchal thinking curtailed the power of Black women. The fierce rejection of the matriarch thesis created a new determination during the civil rights era to emphasize the leadership roles of Black men, and some theorists claimed that the strong Black woman had outlived her usefulness.

The tenacity of racial ideologies is seen in the fact that, despite decades of research challenging narrow, culturally biased depictions of Black people and their families, research continues to show that Americans endorse a

spate of racist assumptions about African Americans (Bobo, Kluegel, and Smith 1997; Bonilla-Silva 2001). Indeed, the persistence of racial inequality, the ease with which theories of Black inferiority reemerge, and the potential consequences of racist thinking has left many scholars continuing to do battle with the thesis of Black family pathology. Contemporary policymakers, for example, quickly invoked a culture of poverty thesis to explain what they saw as a collapse of morality and family values among African Americans, sometimes even reviving the theme of innate Black inferiority (Murray 1984).

Still, the challenge for researchers today is less to prove the resiliency of Black families but how they are faring in the new post-industrial, class-diversified society. A theoretically astute and plausible analysis of African American families demands a reintegration of the structural and cultural perspectives, and such perspectives must recognize that the cultural behaviors associated with poverty can be adaptive and maladaptive. In her work on welfare reform, for example, Sharon Hays was forced to acknowledge that while most poor people hold mainstream values, a significant minority—perhaps as many as one-third—fit the stereotypical images associated with the culture of poverty (Hays 2003).

The focus on challenging the social deficit perspective and culture of poverty thesis has also deflected attention from other important Black family issues, such as that they are affected by growing class polarization. While social class diversity has always been evident among Black people, the early class analysis of social scientists was supplanted by a focus on racial oppression during the civil rights era. Since then class mobility among Blacks has grown even more sharply, with the most current census data showing poverty among Black people at an all-time low of less than 25 percent. Yet even media depictions of economically affluent African Americans often raise as much angst and ambivalence as adulation, given concern that they suggest hard work can abolish racial barriers and result in full integration (Inniss and Feagin 1995). Most social science studies of middle-class families point to the continuing saliency of race in their lives. For some, their middle-class status is especially precarious, as they face housing segregation, live in marginal neighborhoods, and are more likely to lose ground in economic downturns (Pattillo-McCoy 1999). While the demise of the middle-class has been a major focus in social stratification research since the 1980s, the racial gap in wealth and home ownership also contributes to the fragile grasp of many African Americans on middle-class status.

Beyond the assertion that class mobility does not completely negate the significance of racial inequality, studies have failed to address basic issues, such as how African Americans define middle-class. Some studies suggest that in the past being a porter, headwaiter, barber, preacher, or funeral parlor owner constituted middle-class status for African Americans (Patterson 1997), while others saw that having a steady job, an intact family, and professing allegiance to values such as getting an education made one middle-class. Today, being middle-class often means being able to hold a professional-managerial job usually in an interracial setting. Some research

has shown that Blacks in these positions experience stress-inducing racism (Toliver 1998), yet there seems to be a reluctance to acknowledge it because their lives are qualitatively different from those of poor African Americans. Numerous issues might be explored in terms of how social mobility affects Black families, such as how it affects childrearing values, the quality of marital relationships, and intergenerational family bonds.

The study of intimate relationships among African Americans, especially marriage, has also received short shrift in research on families. More research during the 1980s sought to identify reasons for declining rates of marriage among Blacks, initially concluding that low-paying jobs and high rates of unemployment and criminal incarceration had diminished the supply of marriageable African American men (Wilson 1987). Much less research has been done on how these economic forces have reshaped cultural ideologies, although there is some evidence of a shift in the marital attitudes of Black people (Franklin 2000).

Explicit gender analyses of Black family life are also scarce. White feminists saw capitalism and patriarchal ideologies as responsible for the breadwinner–homemaker family that emerged during the industrial era, and its exclusion of women from the labor market as the linchpin of their secondary status and subordination. Meanwhile, a plethora of research on Black women published during the 1980s described how their historic work, family, and community roles had shaped their gender identities and families in ways that enabled them to evade the narrow boundaries of femininity prescribed for White women. While this work gave further credence to the feminist claim of gender as a social construct, it has also reinforced the myth of gender egalitarianism among Black people. Despite the dismissive attitudes toward gender, the notion that Black couples have achieved equity in the domestic arena is challenged by quantitative analyses using racially diverse samples (John and Shelton 1997), as is the idea that gender matters little in the socialization of Black children (Hill and Zimmerman 1995).

I contend that African American family scholarship must move beyond debates over the viability of poor, single-mother families if it is to become inclusive and viable, and suggest several directions for a broader scope of inquiry. Social class diversity will make conceptualizing Black families increasingly difficult; indeed, in a recent paper Walter Allen concluded that steady overall progress and persistent racial inequalities has made doing so especially difficult (Allen 1995). Ultimately, the broader analysis I suggest here will help us sort one of the central debates in Black family scholarship— whether class or race (culture) account for what has been described as distinctively African American cultural traits. Since research has been built so extensively on the lives of poor, single mothers, will comparative studies including the experiences of those from diverse class backgrounds result in the end of Black family scholarship?

REFERENCES

Allen, Walter R. 1978. "The Search for Applicable Theories of Black Family Life." *Journal of Marriage and the Family* 40:117–129.

———. 1995. "African American Family Life in Societal Context: Crisis and Hope." *Sociological Forum* 10:569–92.

———. 2001. "Whatever Tomorrow Brings: African American Families and Government Social Policies." Pp. 125–43 in *One-Third of a Nation: African American Perspectives,* edited by U. J. O. Bailey and L. Morris. Washington, D.C.: Howard University Press.

Arendell, Terry. 2000. "Conceiving and Investigating Motherhood: The Decade's Scholarship." *Journal of Marriage and the Family* 62:1192–1207.

Asante, M. K. 1987. *The Afrocentric Idea.* Philadelphia: Temple University Press.

Billingsley, Andrew. 1968. *Black Families in White America.* Englewood Cliffs, NJ: Prentice-Hall.

———. 1992. *Climbing Jacob's Ladder: The Enduring Legacy of African-American Families.* New York: Simon & Schuster.

Bobo, Lawrence, James R. Kluegel, and Ryan A. Smith. 1997. "Laissez-faire Racism: The Crystallization of a Kinder, Gentler, Antiblack Ideology." Pp. 15–42 in *Racial Attitudes in the 1990s: Continuity and Change,* edited by S. A. Tuch and J. K. Martin. Westport, CT: Praeger.

Bonilla-Silva, Eduardo. 2001. *White Supremacy and Racism in the Post–Civil Rights Era.* Boulder, CO: Lynne Rienner.

Bound, John and Laura Dresser. 1999. "Losing Ground: The Erosion of the Relative Earnings of African American Women during the 1980s." Pp. 61–104 in *Latinas and African American Women at Work: Race, Gender, and Economic Inequality,* edited by I. Brown. New York: Russell Sage.

Boykin, A. W. and F. D. Toms. 1985. "Black Child Socialization: A Conceptual Framework." Pp. 33–52 in *Black Children: Social, Educational and Parental Environments,* edited by H. P. McAdoo and J. L. McAdoo. Beverly Hill, CA: Sage.

Burgess, Norma J. 1994. "Gender Roles Revisited: The Development of the 'Women's Place' among African American Women in the United States." *Journal of Black Studies* 24:391–401.

Burton, Linda M. 1990. "Teenage Childbearing as an Alternative Life-Course Strategy in Multigeneration Black Families." *Human Nature* 1:123–43.

Davis, A. and R. J. Havighurst. 1946. "Social Class and Color Differences in Child-Rearing." *American Sociological Review* 2:698–710.

Edin, Kathryn and Kathleen Mullan Harris. 1999. "Getting Off and Staying Off: Racial Differences in the Work Route Off Welfare." Pp. 270–300 in *Latinas and African American Women at Work: Race, Gender, and Economic Inequality,* edited by I. Brown. New York: Russell Sage.

Fesler, Garrett R. 2004. "Living Arrangements among Enslaved Women and Men at an Early Eighteenth Century Virginia Quartering Site." Pp. 177–236 in *Engendering African American Archaeology: A Southern Perspective,* edited by J. E. Galle and A. L. Young. Knoxville: University of Tennessee Press.

Franklin, Donna L. 1997. *Ensuring Inequality: The Structural Transformation of the African-American Family.* New York: Oxford University Press.

———. 2000. *What's Love Got to Do with It? Understanding and Healing the Rift between Black Men and Women.* New York: Touchstone.

Frazier, E. Franklin. [1939] 1957. *The Negro in the United States.* New York: Macmillan Company.

Furstenberg, F. F. 2007. "The Making of the Black Family: Race and Class in Qualitative Studies in the Twentieth Century." *Annual Review of Sociology* 33:429–48.

Giddings, Paula. 1984. *When and Where I Enter: The Impact of Black Women on Race and Sex in America.* New York: Bantam.

Gordon, Edmund T. and Mark Anderson. 1999. "The African Diaspora: Toward an Ethnography of Diasporic Identification." *Journal of American Folklore* 112:282–96.

Gutman, Herbert G. 1976. *The Black Family in Slavery and Freedom, 1750–1925.* New York: Pantheon.

Hays, Sharon. 2003. *Flat Broke with Children: Women in the Age of Welfare Reform.* New York: Oxford University Press.

Herskovits, Melville J. 1941. *The Myth of the Negro Past.* New York: Harper & Brothers.

Hill, Robert B. 1972. *The Strengths of Black Families.* New York: Emerson Hall.

Hill, Shirley A. 1994. *Managing Sickle Cell Disease in Low-Income Families.* Philadelphia: Temple University Press.

———. 1999. *African American Children: Socialization and Development in Families.* Thousand Oaks, CA: Sage.

———. 2005. *Black Intimacies: A Gender Perspective on Families and Relationships.* Walnut Creek, CA: AltaMira Press.

Hill, Shirley A. and Mary K. Zimmerman. 1995. "Valiant Girls and Vulnerable Boys: The Impact of Gender and Race on Mothers' Caregiving for Chronically Ill Children." *Journal of Marriage and the Family* 57:43–53.

Inniss, Leslie B. and Joe R. Feagin. 1995. "The Cosby Show: The View from the Black Middle-Class." *Journal of Black Studies* 25:692–711.

Jarrett, Robin L. 1994. "Living Poor: Family Life among Single Parent, African-American Women." *Social Problems* 41:30–50.

John, Daphne and Beth Anne Shelton. 1997. "The Production of Gender among Black and White Women and Men: The Case of Household Labor." *Sex Roles* 36:171–93.

Kaplan, Elaine Bell. 1997. *Not Our Kind of Girl: Unraveling the Myths of Black Teenage Motherhood.* Berkeley and Los Angeles: University of California Press.

Kardiner, Abram and Lionel Ovesey. 1951. *The Mark of Oppression: Explorations in the Personality of the American Negro.* Cleveland and New York: Meridian Books.

Littlejohn-Blake, Sheila M. and Carol Anderson Darling. 1993. "Understanding the Strength of African American Families." *Journal of Black Studies* 23:1993.

McAdoo, H. P. 1990. "A Portrait of African American Families in the United States." Pp. 71–93 in *The American Woman, 1990–1991,* edited by S. E. Rix. New York: Norton.

McLanahan, Sara and Dona Schwartz. 2002. "Life without Father: What Happens to the Children." *Contexts* 1:35–41.

McLoyd, V. C., A. M. Cauce, D. Takeuchi, and L. Wilson. 2000. "Marital Processes and Parental Socialization in Families of Color: A Decade Review." *Journal of Marriage and the Family* 62:1070–93.

Moynihan, Daniel Patrick. 1965. *The Negro Family: The Case for National Action.* Washington, DC: Office of Policy Planning and Research.

Murray, C. 1984. *Losing Ground: American Social Policy 1950–1980.* New York: Basic Books.

Nobles, W. W. 1985. *Africanity and the Black Family.* Oakland, CA: Institute for the Advanced Study of Black Family Life and Culture.

Nobles, Wade W. 1974. "Africanity: Its Role in Black Families." *Black Scholar* 5:10–17.

Parsons, T. and R. Bales. 1955. *Family Socialization and Interaction Processes.* New York: Free Press.

Patterson, Orlando. 1997. *The Ordeal of Integration: Progress and Resentment in America's "Racial" Crisis.* Washington, DC: Civitas/Counterpoint.

Pattillo-McCoy, Mary. 1999. *Black Picket Fences: Privilege and Peril among the Black Middle Class.* Chicago and London: University of Chicago Press.

Rainwater, Lee and William L. Yancey. 1967. *The Moynihan Report and the Politics of Controversy.* Cambridge, MA: MIT Press.

Roschelle, Anne R. 1997. *No More Kin: Exploring Race, Class, and Gender in Family Networks.* Thousand Oaks, CA: Sage.

Ross, Marlon B. 2004. *Manning the Race: Reforming Black Men in the Jim Crow Era.* New York and London: New York University Press.

Stack, Carol. 1974. *All Our Kin: Strategies for Survival in a Black Community.* New York: Harper & Row.

Swidler, Ann. 1986. "Culture in Action: Symbols and Strategies." *American Sociological Review* 51:273–86.

Toliver, Susan D. 1998. *Black Families in Corporate America.* Thousand Oaks, CA: Sage.

Willie, Charles Vert and Richard J. Reddick. 2003. *A New Look at Black Families.* Walnut Creek, CA: AltaMira Press.

Wilson, William Julius. 1978. *The Declining Significance of Race: Blacks and Changing American Institutions.* Chicago: University of Chicago Press.

Wilson, W. J. 1987. *The Truly Disadvantaged.* Chicago: University of Chicago Press.

8

"THE NORMAL AMERICAN FAMILY" AS AN INTERPRETIVE STRUCTURE OF FAMILY LIFE AMONG GROWN CHILDREN OF KOREAN AND VIETNAMESE IMMIGRANTS

KAREN PYKE

The use of monolithic images of the "Normal American Family" as a stick against which all families are measured is pervasive in the family wars currently raging in political and scholarly discourses (Holstein and Gubrium 1995). The hotly contested nature of these images—consisting almost exclusively of White middle-class heterosexuals—attests to their importance as resources in national debates. Many scholars express concern that hegemonic images of the Normal American Family are ethnocentric and that they denigrate the styles and beliefs of racial–ethnic, immigrant, gay–lesbian, and single-parent families while encouraging negative self-images among those who do not come from the ideal family type (Smith 1993; Stacey 1998; Zinn 1994). Yet we still know little about how the Family ideology shapes the consciousness and expectations of those growing up in the margins of the mainstream. This study examines the accounts that grown children of Korean and Vietnamese immigrants provide of their family life and filial obligations. The findings suggest that public images of the Normal American Family constitute an ideological template that shapes respondents' familial perspectives and desires as new racial–ethnic Americans.

Family Ideology as an Interpretive Structure

Images of the Normal American Family (also referred to as the Family) are pervasive in the dominant culture—part of a "'large-scale' public rhetoric" (Holstein and Miller 1993:152). They are found in the discourse of politicians, social commentators, and moral leaders; in the talk of everyday interactions; and in movies, television shows, and books. Smith (1993:63) describes these ubiquitous images as an "ideological code" that subtly "inserts an implicit evaluation into accounts of ways of living together." Such images serve as instruments of control, prescribing how families ought to look and behave (Bernades 1985). Most scholarly concern centers on how this ideology glorifies

Karen Pyke, "'The Normal American Family' as an Interpretive Structure of Family Life among Grown Children of Korean and Vietnamese Immigrants" from *Journal of Marriage and the Family* 62, no. 1 (February 2000). Copyright © 2000. Reprinted with permission.

and presents as normative that family headed by a breadwinning husband with a wife who, even if she works for pay, is devoted primarily to the care of the home and children. The concern is that families of diverse structural forms, most notably divorced and female-headed families, are comparatively viewed as deficient and dysfunctional (Fineman 1995; Kurz 1995; Stacey 1998). Scholars concerned about the impact of such images point to those who blame family structures that deviate from this norm for many of society's problems and who suggest policies that ignore or punish families that don't fit the construct (e.g., Blankenhorn 1995; Popenoe 1993, 1996).

In addition to prescribing the structure of families, the Family ideal contains notions about the appropriate values, norms, and beliefs that guide the way family members relate to one another. The cultural values of "other" families, such as racial–ethnic families, are largely excluded. For example, prevailing family images emphasize sensitivity, open honest communication, flexibility, and forgiveness (Greeley 1987). Such traits are less important in many cultures that stress duty, responsibility, obedience, and a commitment to the family collective that supercedes self-interests (Chung 1992; Freeman 1989). In further contrast to the traditional family systems of many cultures, contemporary American family ideals stress democratic rather than authoritarian relations, individual autonomy, psychological well-being, and emotional expressiveness (Bellah et al. 1985; Bernades 1985; Cancian 1987; Coontz 1992; Skolnick 1991). Family affection, intimacy, and sentimentality have grown in importance in the United States over time (Coontz 1992), as evident in new ideals of fatherhood that stress emotional involvement (Coltrane 1996).

These mainstream family values are evident in the therapeutic ethic, guiding the ways that those who seek professional advice are counseled and creating particular therapeutic barriers in treating immigrant Asian Americans (Bellah et al. 1985; Cancian 1987; Tsui and Schultz 1985). Family values are also widely disseminated and glorified in the popular culture, as in television shows like *Ozzie and Harriet, Leave It To Beaver, The Brady Bunch, Family Ties,* and *The Cosby Show,* many of which are rerun on local stations and cable networks (Coontz 1992). Parents in these middle-class, mostly White, television families are emotionally nurturing and supportive, understanding, and forgiving (Shaner 1982; Skill 1994). Indeed, such shows tend to focus on the successful resolution of relatively minor family problems, which the characters accomplish through open communication and the expression of loving concern. Children in the United States grow up vicariously experiencing life in these television families, including children of immigrants who rely on television to learn about American culture. With 98% of all U.S. households having at least one television set, Rumbaut (1997:949) views TV as an immense "assimilative" force for today's children of immigrants. Yet, he continues, it remains to be studied how their world views are shaped by such "cultural propaganda." The images seen on television serve as powerful symbols of the "normal" family or the "good" parent—and they often eclipse our appreciation of diverse family types. As the authors of one study on media images note, "The seductively realistic portrayals of family life in the media may be the basis for our most common and pervasive conceptions

and beliefs about what is natural and what is right" (Gerbner et al. 1980:3). Family scholars have rarely displayed analytic concern about the emphasis on emotional expressiveness and affective sentimentality that pervades much of the Family ideology, probably because the majority—who as middle-class, well-educated Whites live in the heartland of such values—do not regard them as problematic. As a result, this Western value orientation can seep imperceptibly into the interpretive framework of family research (Bernades 1993; Dilworth-Anderson, Burton, and Turner 1993; Fineman 1995; Smith 1993; Thorne and Yalom, 1992).

The theoretical literature on the social construction of experience is an orienting framework for this study (Berger and Luckmann 1966; Holstein and Gubrium 1995). According to this view, cultural ideologies and symbols are integral components of the way individuals subjectively experience their lives and construct reality. The images we carry in our heads of how family life is supposed to frame our interpretation of our own domestic relations. This is evident in the different ways that Korean and Korean American children perceived their parents' childrearing behavior in a series of studies. In Korea, children were found to associate parental strictness with warmth and concern and its absence as a sign of neglect (Rohner and Pettengill 1985). These children were drawing on Korean family ideology, which emphasizes strong parental control and parental responsibility for children's failings. In this interpretive framework, parental strictness is a positive characteristic of family life and signifies love and concern. Children of Korean immigrants living in the United States, on the other hand, viewed their parents' strictness in negative terms and associated it with a lack of warmth—as did American children in general (Pettengill and Rohner 1985). Korean American children drew on American family ideology, with its emphasis on independence and autonomy, and this cast a negative shadow on their parents' strict practices.

Although pervasive images of the Normal American Family subtly construct Asian family patterns of interaction as "deviant," countervailing images of Asians as a "model minority" are also widely disseminated. News stories and scholarly accounts that profile the tremendous academic success among some immigrant Asian children or describe the upward economic mobility observed among segments of the Asian immigrant population credit the cultural traditions of collectivist family values, hard work, and a strong emphasis on education. Such images exaggerate the success of Asian immigrants and mask intraethnic diversity (Caplan, Choy, and Whitmore 1991; Kibria 1993; Min 1995; Zhou and Bankston 1998). Meanwhile, conservative leaders use model minority images as evidence of the need to return to more traditional family structures and values, and they blame the cultural deficiency of other racial minority groups for their lack of similar success, particularly African Americans and Latinos (Kibria 1993; Min 1995; Zhou and Bankston 1998). The model minority construct thus diverts attention from racism and poverty while reaffirming the Family ideology. In the analysis of the accounts that children of immigrants provided of their family life, references to such cultural images and values emerged repeatedly as a mechanism by which respondents gave meaning to their own family lives.

Korean and Vietnamese Immigrant Families

This study focuses on children of Vietnamese and Korean immigrants because both groups constitute relatively new ethnic groups in the United States. Few Vietnamese and Koreans immigrated to the United States before 1965. However, from 1981 to 1990, Korea and Vietnam were two of the top five countries from which immigrants arrived (*Statistical Yearbook*, 1995, table 2, pp. 29–30). Thus adaptation to the United States is a relatively new process for large groups of Koreans and Vietnamese, one that is unassisted by earlier generations of coethnic immigrants. The children of these immigrants, located at the crossroads of two cultural worlds, offer a good opportunity to examine the familial perspectives and desires of new racial–ethnic Americans. . . .

Method

The data are from an interview study of the family and social experiences of grown children of Korean and Vietnamese immigrants. Respondents either were located at a California university where 47% of all undergraduates are of Asian descent (Maharaj 1997) or were referred by students from that university. In-depth interviews were conducted with 73 respondents consisting of 34 Korean Americans (24 women, 10 men) and 39 Vietnamese Americans (23 women, 16 men). Both parents of each respondent were Korean or Vietnamese, except for one respondent, whose parents were both Sino-Vietnamese. Respondents ranged in age from 18 to 26 and averaged 21 years. Only one respondent was married, and none had children.

Respondents were either born in the United States (second generation) or immigrated prior to the age of 15 (1.5 generation), except for one Vietnamese American woman who immigrated at 17. The foreign born accounted for 77 percent of the sample and immigrated at an average age of 5 years. The remaining 23 percent were born in the United States. Most respondents in this sample spent their entire adolescence in the United States, and a majority lived in the United States for most, if not all, of their childhood. Eight percent of the Vietnamese American respondents were born in the United States, compared to 38 percent of Korean American respondents. All study participants were college graduates or students and all resided in California, where one-third of U.S. legal immigrants arrive and 45 percent of the nation's immigrant student population lives (Zhou 1997). Thus the sample overrepresents those who are academically successful. Because the respondents have endured sustained exposure to assimilation pressures from the educational system, higher levels of assimilation were expected in this sample than in the larger immigrant population. As a result, these respondents were perhaps more likely to invoke American cultural ideals in describing their family life than a more representative sample that included the less educated and those who immigrated at older ages. . . .

This research began with the general goal of learning about the subjective family experiences of children of Asian immigrants. I used a grounded

research approach that emphasized an inductive method of generating explanation from the data (Glaser and Strauss 1967; Strauss and Corbin 1990). Except for the general assumption that respondents are active agents in the construction of their family experiences, I imposed no apriori assumptions, hypotheses, or specific theoretical frames on the research process. . . .

During the analysis, I noted recurring references in one form or another to notions about so-called normal families. Respondents used such references for one purpose only—as a point of contrast to life in their families. Three categorical expressions of this theme emerged in the data: (a) comparisons with television families; (b) comparisons with families of non-Asian friends; and (c) contrasts with specific family behavior or characteristics described as normal or American. I did not anticipate the importance of such family imagery when I devised the interview guide; thus I never asked respondents about family life on TV or among friends, or what they regarded as a normal or ideal family. Rather, this theme emerged unexpectedly in the interviews. The unprompted and recurring nature of these references indicates their importance as resources in respondents' construction of their family experiences. In the following discussion, I present a sample of the qualitative data, in the form of quotes, to illustrate the observed patterns (Ambert et al. 1995). Respondents chose the pseudonyms used here.

Results

I examine two ways in which respondents commonly used the typification of American family life as a contrast structure against which behavior in immigrant Asian families was juxtaposed and interpreted (Gubrium and Holstein 1997). When describing relations with their parents, most respondents provided negative accounts of at least one aspect of their relationship, and they criticized their parents for lacking American values that emphasize psychological well-being and expressive love. Recurring references to a narrow Americanized notion of what families ought to look like were woven throughout many such accounts. However, when respondents described the kinds of filial care they planned to provide for their parents, the respondents switched to an interpretive lens that values ethnic family solidarity. In this context, respondents' references to notions of the Normal American Family became a negative point of comparison that cast their own immigrant families, and Asian families in general, in positive terms.

Viewing Parental Relations through an Americanized Lens

Respondents were asked to fantasize about how they would change their parents if they could change anything about them that they wanted to change. The three areas of desired change that respondents mentioned most often reveal their adoption of many mainstream American values. They wished for parents who (a) were less strict and gave them more freedom; (b) were more liberal, more open-minded, more Americanized, and less traditional; (c) were

emotionally closer, more communicative, more expressive, and more affectionate. These three areas are interrelated. For example, being more Americanized and less traditional translates into being more lenient and expressive. A small minority of respondents presented a striking contrast to the dominant pattern by describing, in terms both positive and grateful, parents who had liberal attitudes or Americanized values and parenting styles.

The communication most respondents described with parents focused on day-to-day practical concerns, such as whether the child had eaten, and about performance in school and college, a major area of concern among parents. Conversations were often limited to parental directives or lectures. For the most part, respondents were critical of the emotional distance and heavy emphasis on obedience that marked their relations with their parents. Chang-Hee, an 18-year-old who immigrated from Korea at 8, provided a typical case. When asked about communication, she disparaged her parents for not talking more openly, which she attributed to their being Asian. Respondents typically linked parental styles with race and not with other factors such as age or personality. Like many other respondents, Chang-Hee constructed an account not only of her family relations, but also of Asian families in general.

> *To tell you the truth, in Asian families you don't have conversations. You just are told to do something and you do it. . . . You never talk about problems, even in the home. You just kind of forget about it and you kind of go on like nothing happened. Problems never really get solved. That's why I think people in my generation, I consider myself 1.5 generation, we have such a hard time because I like to verbalize my emotions. . . . [My parents] never allowed themselves to verbalize their emotions. They've been repressed so much [that] they expect the same out of me, which is the hardest thing to do because I have so many different things to say and I'm just not allowed.*

Some respondents volunteered that their parents never asked them about their well-being, even when their distress was apparent. Chang-Hee observed, "If I'm sad, [my mom] doesn't want to hear it. She doesn't want to know why. . . . She's never asked me, 'So what do you feel?'" This lack of expressed interest in children's emotional well-being, along with the mundane level of communication, was especially upsetting to respondents because, interpreted through the lens of American family ideology, it defined their parents as emotionally uncaring and distant.

Several respondents longed for closer, more caring relationships with their parents that included expressive displays of affection. Thanh, a married 22-year-old college student who left Vietnam when she was 6, said, "I'd probably make them more loving and understanding, showing a bit more affection. . . . A lot of times I just want to go up and hug my parents, but no, you don't do that sort of thing."

Research indicates that the desire for greater intimacy is more common among women than men (Cancian 1987). Thus it was surprising that many male respondents also expressed strong desires for more caring and close

talk—especially from their fathers, who were often described as harsh and judgmental. Ralph, 20, a Korean American man born in the United States, said:

> *My dad, he's not open. He is not the emotional type. So he talks . . . and I would listen and do it. It's a one-way conversation, rather than asking for my opinions. . . . I would think it'd be nicer if he was . . . much more compassionate, caring, because it seems like he doesn't care.*

Similarly, Dat, a 22-year-old biology major who left Vietnam when he was 5, said:

> *I would fantasize about sitting down with my dad and shooting the breeze. Talk about anything and he would smile and he would say, "Okay, that's fine, Dat." Instead of, you know, judge you and tell me I'm a loser. . . .*

A definition of love that emphasizes emotional expression and close talk predominates in U.S. culture (Cancian 1986). Instrumental aspects of love, like practical help, are ignored or devalued in this definition. In Korean and Vietnamese cultures, on the other hand, the predominant definitions of love emphasize instrumental help and support. The great divide between immigrant parents who emphasize instrumental forms of love and children who crave open displays of affection was evident in the following conversation, which occurred between Dat and his father when Dat was 7 or 8 years old. Dat recalled, "I tried saying 'I love you' one time and he looked at me and said, 'Are you American now? You think this is *The Brady Bunch?* You don't love me. You love me when you can support me.'" These different cultural definitions of love contributed to respondents' constructions of immigrant parents as unloving and cold.

The Family as a Contrast Structure in the Negative Accounts of Family Life

Many of the images of normal family life that respondents brought to their descriptions came in the form of references to television families or the families of non–Asian American friends. Although these monolithic images do not reflect the reality of American family life, they nevertheless provided the basis by which respondents learned how to be American, and they served as the interpretive frame of their own family experiences. By contrasting behavior in their immigrant families with mainstream images of normalcy, the respondents interpreted Asian family life as lacking or deficient. Dat referred to images of normal family life in America, as revealed on television and among friends, as the basis for his desire for more affection and closeness with his father:

> *Sometimes when I had problems in school, all I wanted was my dad to listen to me, of all people. I guess that's the American way and I was raised American. . . . That's what I see on TV and in my friends, family. And I expected him to be that way too. But it didn't happen. . . . I would like to talk to him or, you know, say "I love you," and he would look at me and say, "Okay." That's*

my ultimate goal, to say, "I love you." It's real hard. Sometimes when I'm in a good mood, the way I show him love is to put my hands over his shoulders and squeeze it a little bit. That would already irritate him a little. . . . You could tell. He's like, "What the fuck's he doing [sic]?" But I do it because I want to show him love somehow. Affection. I'm an affectionate person.

Similarly, Hoa, a 23-year-old Vietnamese American man who immigrated at age 2, referred to television in describing his own family: "We aren't as close as I would like. . . . We aren't as close as the dream family, you know, what you see on TV. Kind of like . . . *Leave It To Beaver.* You know, stuff I grew up on."

Paul, a 21-year-old Korean American born in the United States, also criticizes his father, and Asian fathers in general, in relation to the fathers of friends and those on television:

I think there is somewhat of a culture clash between myself and my parents. They are very set on rules—at least my father is. He is very strict and demanding and very much falls into that typical Asian father standard. I don't like that too much and I think it is because . . . as a child, I was always watching television and watching other friends' fathers. All the relationships seemed so much different from me and my father's relationship. . . . I guess it's pretty cheesy but I can remember watching The Brady Bunch *reruns and thinking Mike Brady would be a wonderful dad to have. He was always so supportive. He always knew when something was wrong with one of his boys. Whenever one of his sons had a problem, they would have no problem telling their dad anything and the dad would always be nice and give them advice and stuff. Basically I used what I saw on television as a picture of what a typical family should be like in the United States. I only wished that my family could be like that. And friends too—I used to see how my friends in school would be in Little League Baseball and their dad would be like their coaches or go to their games to cheer their sons on and give them support. I could not picture my father to be like that kind of man that I saw on TV, or like my friends' fathers.*

Respondents did not refer to non–Asian American friends who had distant, conflict-ridden family relationships. Yet many respondents likely did have contact with such individuals. It appears as though respondents see only in ways permitted by the Family ideology. That is, as Bernades argued, "the image or idol of 'The Family' rather than the reality of people's lives is taken as the object of attention" (1985:288). Looking at "American" families through this ideological lens determines which families are "seen." Those that do not fit the cultural imagery are not seen or are viewed as atypical. "Atypical" families are not referenced in these accounts, even though, in actuality, they are probably closer to the empirical reality of American family life. Friends whose families do comply, on the other hand, loom large as symbols that verify the existence of the Family ideal.

In comparison to this ideal, even parents who had adopted more American parenting practices fell short. For example, the parents of Mike, 22, who

had immigrated to the United States from Vietnam as an infant, were less strict than the parents of most respondents. Nevertheless, Mike said:

> *My parents were really easy. They let me hang out with my friends, they had no problem with me sleeping over or other people sleeping over. So having friends in high school wasn't hard at all, and going out wasn't a problem at all. It was just, you know, you go over to your friend's house and he just talks to his parents about everything. So I got a little bit jealous. You know, I wished I could talk to my parents about stuff like that but I couldn't.*

Sometimes respondents simply made assumptive references to normal or American families, against which they critically juxtaposed Asian immigrant families. Being American meant that one was a member of the Normal American Family and enjoyed family relations that were warm, close, and harmonious. Being Asian, on the other hand, meant living outside such normality. Thuy, a 20-year-old Vietnamese American woman who had immigrated when 13, said:

> *If I could, I would have a more emotional relationship with my parents. I know they love me, but they never tell me they love me. They also are not very affectionate. This is how I've always grown up. It wasn't really until we came to the United States that I really noticed what a lack of love my parents show. American kids are so lucky. They don't know what it's like to not really feel that you can show emotion with your own parents.*

Similarly, Cora, 20, a Korean American woman born in the United States, remarked:

> *I would probably want [my parents] to be more open, more understanding so I could be more open with them, 'cause there's a lot of things that I can't share with them because they're not as open-minded as American parents. . . . 'Cause I have friends and stuff. They talk to their parents about everything, you know?*

When asked how he was raised, Josh, 21, a Vietnamese American man who immigrated when 2, responded by calling up a construction of the "good" American Family and the "deficient" Asian Family. He said, "I'm sure that for all *Asian* people, if they think back to [their] childhood, they'll remember a time they got hit. *American* people, they don't get hit."

Respondents repeatedly constructed American families as loving, harmonious, egalitarian, and normal. Using this ideal as their measuring stick, Asian families were constructed as distant, overly strict, uncaring, and not normal. In fact, respondents sometimes used the word "normal" in place of "American." For example, Hoa, who previously contrasted his family with the one depicted in *Leave It To Beaver*, said, "I love my dad but we never got to play catch. He didn't teach me how to play football. All the stuff a *normal* dad does for their kids. We missed out on that." Thomas, 20, a Korean American who arrived in the United States at age 8, said, "I always felt like maybe we are not so normal. Like in the real America, like Brady Bunch normal. . . . I always felt like . . . there was something irregular about me." Similarly, after describing a childhood where she spoke very little to her parents,

Van, 24, who immigrated to the United States from Vietnam at 10, began crying and noted, "I guess I didn't have a *normal* childhood." To be a normal parent is to be an American parent. Asian immigrant parents are by this definition deficient. Such constructions ignore diversity within family types, and they selectively bypass the social problems, such as child abuse, that plague many non–Asian American families. It is interesting, for example, that respondents did not refer to the high divorce rate of non–Asian Americans (Sweet and Bumpass 1987) to construct positive images of family stability among Asian Americans. This may be because, applying an Americanized definition of love, many respondents described their parents' marriage as unloving and some thought their parents ought to divorce.

Respondents relied on the Family not only as an interpretive framework, but also as a contrast structure by which to differentiate Asian and American families. This juxtaposition of American and Asian ignores that most of the respondents and the coethnics they describe are Americans. "American" is used to refer to non–Asian Americans, particularly Whites. The words "White" and "Caucasian" were sometimes used interchangeably with "American." Indeed, the Normal American Family *is* White. This Eurocentric imagery excludes from view other racial minority families such as African Americans and Latino Americans. It is therefore not surprising that racial–ethnic families were not referenced as American in these interviews. In fact, respondents appeared to use the term "American" as a code word denoting not only cultural differences but also racial differences. For example, Paul, who was born in the United States, noted, "I look Korean but I think I associate myself more with the *American race.*" The oppositional constructions of Asian and American families as monolithic and without internal variation imply that these family types are racialized. That is, the differences are constructed as not only cultural but also racially essential and therefore immutable (Omi and Winant 1994). By defining American as White, respondents revealed the deep-seated notion that, as Asian Americans, they can never truly be American. Such notions dominate in mainstream depictions of Asian Americans as perpetual foreigners. For example, in a speech about foreign donations, Ross Perot read the names of several Asian American political donors and commented, "So far we haven't found an American name" (Nakao 1996). When respondents centered Whites as a point of reference in these accounts, they reaffirmed the marginalized position of racial–ethnic minorities in the Family ideology and in U.S. culture writ large.

These data illustrate how Eurocentric images of normal family relationships promulgated in the larger society served as an ideological template in the negative accounts that respondents provided of their immigrant parents. However, as described next, when respondents discussed their plans for filial care, they presented positive accounts of their immigrant families.

Maintaining Ethnic Values of Filial Obligation

Respondents were not consistent in their individual constructions of Asian and American families as revealed in their interviews. When discussing

future plans for filial care, most respondents positively evaluated their family's collectivist commitment to care. Such an interpretation is supported by model minority stereotypes in mainstream U.S. culture that attribute the success enjoyed by some Asian immigrants to their strong family values and collectivist practices (Kibria 1993; Zhou and Bankston 1998).

The majority of respondents valued and planned to maintain their ethnic tradition of filial care. For example, Josh, who criticized his parents (and Asian parents in general) for using physical forms of punishment, nonetheless plans to care for his parents in their old age. He said, "I'm the oldest son, and in Vietnamese culture the oldest son cares for the parents. That is one of the things that I carry from my culture. I would not put my parents in a [nursing] home. That's terrible." In contrast to White Americans who condition their level of filial commitment on intergenerational compatibility (Pyke 1999), respondents displayed a strong desire to fulfill their filial obligation and—especially among daughters—were often undeterred by distant and even conflict-ridden relations with parents. For example, after describing a strained relationship with her parents, Kimberly, 20, who came to this country from Vietnam when 7, added, "I would still take care of them whether I could talk to them or not. It doesn't matter as long as I could take care of them." Similarly, in Wolf's study of 22 grown children of Filipino immigrants, respondents who complained of tension and emotional distance with parents nonetheless experienced family ties and responsibilities as a central component of their daily lives and identities (1997).

Most respondents expected to begin financially supporting their parents prior to their elderly years, with parents in their 50s often regarded as old. A few respondents had already begun to help out their parents financially. Many planned on living with parents. Others spoke of living near their parents, often as neighbors, rather than in the same house, as a means of maintaining some autonomy. The tradition of assigning responsibility for the care of parents to the eldest son was not automatically anticipated for many of these families, especially those from Vietnam. Respondents most often indicated that responsibility would be pooled among siblings or would fall exclusively to the daughters. Several said that parents preferred such arrangements, because they felt closer to daughters. Although the tendency for daughters to assume responsibility for aging parents is similar to the pattern of caregiving common in mainstream American families (Pyke and Bengtson 1996), several respondents noted that such patterns are also emerging among relatives in their ethnic homeland.

The Importance of Collectivism as an Expression of Love

Respondents typically attributed their future caregiving to reciprocation for parental care in the past and a cultural emphasis on filial respect and support. Yet the enthusiasm and strong commitment that pervades their accounts suggests that they are motivated by more than obligation. For example, Vinh, 26, a graduate student who immigrated from Vietnam at age 5, said about his parents:

They are my life. They will never be alone. I will always be with them. When I was growing [up] as a child, my parents were always with me. And I believe . . . when you grow up, you should be with them; meaning, I will take care of them, in my house, everything. Your parents didn't abandon you when you were a kid. They did not abandon you when you [were] pooping in your diaper. Then when they do, I will not abandon them. . . . Whatever it takes to make them comfortable, I will provide it. There is no limit.

Unable to express love via open displays of affection and close talk, filial assistance becomes a very important way for adult children to symbolically demonstrate their affection for their parents and to reaffirm family bonds. Blossom, 21, who immigrated to the United States from Korea when 6, described the symbolic value of the financial assistance her father expects. She said, "Money is not really important, but it's more about our heart that [my dad] looks at. Through money, my dad will know how we feel and how we appreciate him." Remember that Dat's father told him, "You love me when you can support me." Because instrumental assistance is the primary venue for expressing love and affection in these immigrant families, adult children often placed no limits on what they were willing to do. For example, John, 20, who immigrated from Vietnam when 3, remarked "I'm willing to do anything (for my parents), that's how much I care."

Parental financial independence was not always welcomed by those children who gave great weight to their role of parental caregivers. For example, it was very important to Sean, 19, an only child, to care for his Sino-Vietnamese parents. Sean, who planned to become a doctor, commuted from his home to a local university. He said, "I want my parents to stay with me. I want to support them. . . . I'll always have room for my parents. . . . When I get my first paycheck, I want to support them financially." As reflected in the following exchange with the interviewer, Sean viewed his parents' retirement plan with some hurt.

Sean: *They have their own retirement plan, and they keep track of it themselves, so they're all prepared for me to be the disobedient son and run away.*

Interviewer: *Is that how you feel?*

Sean: *Yes I do. . . . Or if I don't succeed in life, they'll be taken care of by themselves.*

Interviewer: *So is that how you see their retirement plan, as a kind of symbol that they're . . .?*

Sean: *They're ready for me to mess up.*

The emotional centrality of family ties is also apparent in Sean's description of his hurt when his father—who worries that the time Sean spends away from home studying or at his job is pulling him away from the family—occasionally tests his son's commitment by suggesting that he leave the family home and "fly away." With tear-filled eyes, Sean explained:

It hurts me because I've never had that idea to fly away. . . . I don't want to go and that's what hurts me so bad. I mean, I could cry over things like that. And this is a 19-year-old kid that's crying in front of you. How seldom do you get that?

The Family as a Contrast Structure in the Positive Accounts of Filial Obligation

Many respondents distinguished their ethnic collectivist tradition of filial obligation from practices in mainstream American families, which they described as abandoning elderly parents in retirement or nursing homes. The belief that the elderly are abandoned by their families is widespread in U.S. society and very much a part of everyday discourse. Media accounts of nursing home atrocities bolster such views. Yet most eldercare in this country is not provided in formal caregiving settings but by family members (Abel 1991). Nonetheless, respondents used this tenacious myth as a point of contrast in constructing Asian American families as more instrumentally caring. For example, Thuy, who previously described wanting a "more emotional relationship" with her parents, like "American kids" have, explained:

> With the American culture, it's . . . not much frowned upon to put your parents in a home when they grow old. In our culture, it is a definite no-no. To do anything like that would be disrespectful. . . . If they need help, my brother and I will take care of them, just like my mom is taking care of her parents right now.

Similarly, Hien, 21, a Vietnamese American woman who arrived in this country as an infant, noted, "I know a lot of non-Asians have their parents go to the nursing homes . . . but I personally prefer to find a way of trying to keep them at home."

Mike, who wished he could talk to his parents the way his friends do to theirs, plans to care for his Americanized parents even though they have told him they do not want him to. He was not alone in remaining more committed to filial care than his parents required him to be. He said:

> They tell me to just succeed for yourself and take care of your own family. But [referring to filial care] that's just how the Vietnamese culture is. Here in America, once your parents are old, you put them in a retirement home. But not in my family. When the parents get old, you take care of them. It doesn't matter if they can't walk, if they can't function anymore. You still take care of them.

When discussing relationships with their parents, respondents used the Family as the ideological raw material out of which they negatively constructed their parents as unloving and distant. However, when the topic changed to filial care, respondents switched to an ethnic definition of love that emphasizes instrumental support and that casts a positive and loving light on their families. As Katie, 21, a Korean American woman born in the United States, observed:

> When you say that you are close to your parents here in America, I think most people would take that as you are affectionate with your parents, you hang out with them, you can talk to them about anything . . . more of a friendship thing. But Korean families are not like that. . . . They do not get close to their children like that. They are not friends with them. The kids of Korea do not open up with their parents. Their parents are really their parents. . . . But still, no matter what, they are very close. Here in America . . . Caucasians don't take care of

their parents like we do. They just put them in an old people's home and that's it. It's like they say, "You are too old for me. I don't need you anymore and I'm just going to put you here 'cause it's convenient for me and you'd be in the way anyway. . . ." And in that way, Americans are not *close to their parents. So it really depends on how you define the word "close"—the answer changes. [Note that the words "Caucasian" and "American" are used synonymously here, as previously discussed.]*

In describing their plans for parental care, respondents turned their previous construction of Asian and American families on its head. In this context the Family was constructed as deficient and uncaring, while the families of respondents—and Asian families in general—were described as more instrumentally caring and closer. Respondents' view of American families as uncaring should not be interpreted as a departure from mainstream family ideology. There has been much concern in the public discourse that today's families lack a commitment to the care of their elders and children (e.g., Popenoe 1993; see Coontz 1992:189–91). Indeed, the pervasive criticism that "individualism has gone haywire" in mainstream families—bolstered by references to the solidarity of model minority families—provides ideological support for ethnic traditions of filial care. That is, children of immigrants do not face ideological pressure from the dominant society to alter such practices; rather, they are given an interpretive template by which to view such practices as evidence of love and care in their families. In fact, U.S. legislative attempts to withdraw social services from legal immigrants without citizenship, with the expectation that family sponsors will provide such support, structurally mandate collectivist systems of caregiving in immigrant families (Huber and Espenshade 1997). In other words, the dominant society ideologically endorses and, in some ways, structurally requires ethnic immigrant practices of filial care. Filial obligation thus serves as a site where children of Korean and Vietnamese immigrants can maintain their ethnic identity and family ties without countervailing pressure from the mainstream.

Discussion

Interweaving respondents' accounts with an analysis of the interpretive structure from which those accounts are constructed suggests that the Family ideology subtly yet powerfully influences the children of immigrants, infiltrating their subjective understandings of and desires for family life. Respondents relied on American family images in two ways. When discussing their relations with parents and their upbringing, respondents used the Family ideology as a standard of normal families and good parents, leading them to view their immigrant parents as unloving, deficient, and not normal. However, when respondents discussed filial care, a complete reversal occurred. Respondents referred to negative images of rampant individualism among mainstream American families, specifically in regard to eldercare, to bolster their positive portrayals of the instrumental care and filial

piety associated with their ethnic families. Thus the Family ideology was called upon in contradictory ways in these accounts—in the denigration of traditional ethnic parenting practices and in the glorification of ethnic practices of filial obligation.

Findings from this study illustrate how a narrow, ethnocentric family ideology that is widely promulgated throughout the larger culture and quickly internalized by children of immigrants creates an interpretive framework that derogates many of the ethnic practices of immigrant families. As others have argued, the cultural imposition of dominant group values in this form of "controlling images" can lead minorities to internalize negative self-images (Espiritu 1997). That is, racial–ethnic immigrants can adopt a sense of inferiority and a desire to conform with those values and expectations that are glorified in the mainstream society as normal. Indeed, many respondents explicitly expressed a desire to have families that were like White or so-called American families, and they criticized their own family dynamics for being different. Rather than resist and challenge the ethnocentric family imagery of the mainstream, respondents' accounts reaffirmed the Normal American Family and the centrality of White native-born Americans in this imagery. This research thus reveals a subtle yet powerful mechanism of internalized oppression by which the racial–ethnic power dynamics in the larger society are reproduced. This is a particularly important finding in that racial–ethnic families will soon constitute a majority in several states, causing scholars to ponder the challenge of such a demographic transformation of the cultural and political hegemony of White native-born Americans (Maharidge 1996). This study describes an ideological mechanism that could undermine challenges to that hegemony.

REFERENCES

Abel, E. K. 1991. *Who Cares for the Elderly?* Philadelphia Temple University Press.
Ambert, A., P. Adler, P. Adler, and D. Detzner. 1995. "Understanding and Evaluating Qualitative Research." *Journal of Marriage and the Family* 57:879–93.
Berger, P. L. and T. Luckmann. 1966. *The Social Construction of Reality.* New York: Doubleday.
Bellah, R. N., R. Madsen, W. M. Sullivan, A. Swidler, and S. Tipton. 1985. *Habits of the Heart.* San Francisco: Harper and Row.
Bernades, J. 1985. "'Family Ideology': Identification and Exploration." *Sociological Review* 33:275–97.
Bernades, J. 1993. "Responsibilities in Studying Post-Modern Families." *Journal of Family Issues* 14:35–49.
Blankenhorn, D. 1995. *Fatherless America.* New York: Basic Books.
Cancian, F. M. 1986. "The Feminization of Love." *Signs* 11:692–708.
Cancian, F. M. 1987. *Love in America.* New York: Cambridge University Press.
Caplan, N., M. H. Choy, and J. K. Whitmore. 1991. *Children of the Boat People: A Study of Educational Success.* Ann Arbor: University of Michigan Press.
Chung, D. K. 1992. "Asian Cultural Commonalities: A Comparision with Mainstream American Culture." Pp. 27–44 in *Social Work Practice with Asian Americans,* edited by S. Furuto, R. Biswas, D. Chung, K. Murase, and F. Ross-Sheriff. Newbury Park, CA: Sage.
Coltrane, S. 1996. *Family Man.* New York: Oxford University Press.
Coontz, S. 1992. *The Way We Never Were.* New York: Basic Books.
Dilworth-Anderson, P., L. M. Burton, and W. L. Turner. 1993. "The Importance of Values in the Study of Culturally Diverse Families." *Family Relations* 42:238–242.
Espiritu, Y. L. 1997. *Asian American Women and Men.* Thousand Oaks, CA: Sage.

Fineman, M. A. 1995. *The Neutered Mother, the Sexual Family, and Other Twentieth Century Tragedies.* New York: Routledge.

Freeman, J. M. 1989. *Hearts of Sorrow: Vietnamese-American Lives.* Stanford, CA: Stanford University Press.

Gerbner, G., L. Gross, M. Morgan, and N. Signorielli. 1980. *Media and the Family: Images and Impact.* Washington, DC: White House Conference on the Family, National Research Forum on Family Issues. (ERIC Document Reproduction Service No. ED 198919.)

Glaser, B. G. and A. L. Strauss. 1967. *The Discovery of the Grounded Theory.* New York: Aldine.

Gubrium, J. F. and J. A. Holstein. 1997. *The New Language of Qualitative Method.* New York: Oxford University Press.

Holstein, J. A. and G. Miller. 1993. "Social Constructionism and Social Problems Work." Pp. 151–72 in *Reconsidering Social Constructionism,* edited by J. A. Holstein and G. Miller. New York: Aldine De Gruyter.

Huber, G. A. and T. J. Espenshade. 1997. "Neo-isolationism, Balanced-Budget Conservatism, and the Fiscal Impacts of Immigrants." *International Migration Review* 31:1031–54.

Kibria, N. 1993. *The Family Tightrope: The Changing Lives of Vietnamese Americans.* Princeton, NJ: Princeton University Press.

Kurz, D. 1995. *For Richer, For Poorer.* New York: Routledge.

Maharaj, D. 1997. "E-mail Hate Case Tests Free Speech Protections." *Los Angeles Times,* July 8. p. A1, A16.

Maharidge, D. 1996. *The Coming White Minority: California Eruptions and America's Future.* New York: Basic Books.

Min, P. G. 1995. "Major Issues Relating to Asian American Experiences." Pp. 38–57 in *Asian Americans,* edited by P. G. Min. Thousand Oaks, CA: Sage.

Nakao, A. 1996. "Asians' Political Image Marred: Fund-Raising Probes' Timing 'Unfortunate'." *San Francisco Examiner,* November 17, p. A1.

Omi, M. and H. Winant. 1994. *Racial Formation in the United States.* New York: Routledge.

Pettengill, S. M. and R. P. Rohner. 1985. "Korean-American Adolescents' Perceptions of Parental Control, Parental Acceptance-Rejection and Parent-Adolescent Conflict." Pp. 241–49 in *From a Different Perspective: Studies of Behavior across Culture,* edited by I. R. Lagunes and Y. H. Poortinga. Berwyn, IL: Swets North America.

Popenoe, D. 1993. "American Family Decline, 1960–1990: A Review and Appraisal." *Journal of Marriage and the Family* 55:527–55.

———. 1996. *Life without Father: Compelling New Evidence That Fatherhood and Marriage Are Indispensable and for the Good of the Children and Society.* New York: Free Press.

Pyke, K. D. and V. L. Bengtson. 1996. "Caring More or Less: Individualistic and Collectivist Systems of Family Eldercare." *Journal of Marriage and the Family* 58:379–92.

Pyke, K. D. 1999. "The Micropolitics of Care in Relationships between Aging Parents and Adult Children: Individualism, Collectivism, and Power." *Journal of Marriage and the Family* 61:661–672.

Pyke, K. D. and D. Johnson. 1999. *"Between Two Faces of Gender: The Incongruity of Home and Mainstream Cultures among Sons and Daughters of Asian Immigrants."* Presented at the annual meeting of the National Council of Family Relations, Irvine, CA.

Rohner, R. P. and S. M. Pettingill. 1985. "Perceived Parental Acceptance-Rejection and Parental Control among Korean Adolescents." *Child Development* 56:524–28.

Rumbaut, R. G. 1997. "Assimilation and Its Discontents: Between Rhetoric and Reality." *International Migration Review* 31:923–60.

Shaner, J. 1982. "Parental Empathy and Family Role Interactions as Portrayed on Commercial Television." *Dissertation Abstracts International* 42:3473A.

Skill, T. 1994. "Family Images and Family Actions as Presented in the Media: Where We've Been and What We've Found." Pp. 37–50 in *Media, Children and the Family,* edited by D. Zillman et al. Hillsdale, NJ: Erlbaum.

Smith, D. E. 1993. "The Standard North American Family: SNAF as an Ideological Code." *Journal of Family Issues* 14:50–65.

Stacey, J. 1998. "The Right Family Values." Pp. 859–880 in *Families in the U.S.,* edited by K. Hansen and A. Garey. Philadelphia: Temple University Press.

Strauss, A. and J. Corbin. 1990. *Basics of Qualitative Research.* Newbury Park, CA: Sage.

Sweet, J. A. and L. Bumpass. 1987. *American Families and Households.* New York: Russell Sage Foundation.

Thorne, B. and M. Yalom. 1992. *Rethinking the Family: Some Feminist Questions.* Boston: Northeastern University.

Tsui, P. and G. Shultz. 1985. "Failure of Rapport: Why Psychotherapeutic Engagement Fails in the Treatment of Asian Clients." *American Journal of Orthopsychiatry* 55:561–569.

U.S. Immigration and Naturalization Service. 1997. *Statistical Yearbook of the Immigration and Naturalization Service, 1995.* Washington, DC: U.S. Government Printing Office.

Wolf, D. 1997. "Family Secrets: Transnational Struggles among Children of Filipino Immigrants." *Sociological Perspectives* 40:457–482.

Zhou, M. 1997. "Growing Up American: The Challenge Confronting Immigrant Children and Children of Immigrants." *Annual Review of Sociology* 23:65–95.

Zhou, M. and C. Bankston, III. 1998. *Growing Up American: How Vietnamese Children Adapt to Life in the United States.* New York: Russell Sage Foundation.

Zinn, M. B. 1994. "Feminist Rethinking of Racial-Ethnic Families." Pp. 303–14 in *Women of Color in U.S. Society,* edited by M. B. Zinn and B. T. Dill. Philadelphia: Temple University Press.

9

GENDER, ECONOMY, AND KINSHIP IN COMPLEX HOUSEHOLDS AMONG SIX U.S. ETHNIC GROUPS

RAE LESSER BLUMBERG

In a murder mystery, when the detective assesses the suspects, the big question is, Who benefits? But this question seems less appropriate if we are talking about family and household; culturally, these are supposed to be about love, not material advantage. Yet, the six ethnic groups portrayed in this research—the Navajo living on the vast "Rez" (reservation) in Arizona, the Iñupiat of northern Alaska, the Korean immigrants to New York's Queens, the Hispanic immigrants to central Virginia, the African Americans from urban coastal Virginia, and the white Americans from rural upstate New York—all manage to cobble together a strategy for living that entails residing in complex households very different from the nuclear "Ozzie and Harriet" household that is the implicit basis of the U.S. census. And all do so in a way that combines both caring and material benefits.

Let us begin with a brief overview of the six samples. First, the households of the original Americans, the Navajo and the Iñupiat, are not only complex but also flexible; individuals may shift back and forth between two or more households as part of a strategy of preserving a cherished way of life. Sharing within and between households is widespread, as is informal adoption or fostering of children. Grandparents (particularly grandmothers

among the matrilineal Navajo) are at the heart of this system. And their adult sons and daughters in their prime productive years often voluntarily put their own economic and career advancement in second place in order to support kinfolk's efforts to maintain a beloved subsistence and family system.

Second, the more recent arrivals to our shores, Hispanics in central Virginia and Koreans in the crowded tenements of Queens, have adopted complex household arrangements more out of economic necessity or advantage than for love. Their goal is to get ahead, and part of their definition of the good life, especially among the Hispanics, is moving on up to a nuclear household, where they will not have to live with various and sundry relatives or nonrelatives.

Third, in our samples, urban African Americans in coastal Virginia and rural whites in upstate New York have forged complex households partly to survive structural problems. On the one hand, the African Americans have responded to discrimination, poverty, and their grown children's travails (including drugs) with a highly adaptive matri-oriented system that involves not only complex households but also sharing networks so that children can be raised in loving homes and the worst effects of sometimes dire economic straits kept at the doorstep. On the other hand, the rural white New York sample of aging (average age 54) females (24 of 25 respondents) has adopted complex households to solve the problems of growing old in a region where the population is shrinking and the younger generation is leaving, but the snow still has to be shoveled and the sick succored, no matter what. . . .

In order to analyze gender in all six cases, I turn to my general theory of gender stratification (see, e.g., Blumberg 1978, 1984, 1991). As it turns out, a number of the hypotheses prove useful in illuminating, comparing, and contrasting each group's gender/kinship system. . . . Here, I consider whose kin (his or hers) of which gender are involved in those complex households and what difference this makes to individual and familial strategies of getting by versus getting ahead. . . .

Some Hypotheses from a General Theory of Gender Stratification

My central hypothesis is that the single most important, although far from only, variable affecting the level of gender equality is relative economic power, defined as relative control of economic resources by males and females at a variety of nested levels ranging from the macro (the state) to the micro (the couple or family). . . .

Work in productive activities is necessary, but insufficient, to gain control of economic resources. Factors that help women translate work into economic power include:

1. The extent to which the kinship system provides them with advantages.
   a. The most important advantage is inheritance equal to or greater than that of men.

    b. The second most important advantage is living near or with female kin.
2. A high level of what I term *strategic indispensability* (Blumberg 1984:56–62) as a labor force (e.g., being critical to and irreplaceable in a key activity, controlling technical expertise, being organized, being competed for by more than one group).

But achievement of economic power is complicated by cultural and structural factors, including *macro-* and *micro-level discount factors* (Blumberg 1984, 1991; Blumberg and Coleman 1989). At the level of the state, these involve the extent to which the political, legal, religious, ideological, and economic systems disadvantage women relative to men. The macro-level discount is much smaller in, say, Sweden than in Saudi Arabia, but at present, it is invariably negative worldwide. At the level of the household, however, micro-level discounts can be negative or positive for either males or females—subtracting or adding metaphorical pennies' worth of economic power from and to each dollar brought into the household by a man versus a woman. Micro-level discount factors include male and female members' (1) personal ideologies, including gender ideology, as well as their relative (2) dependence on each others' income, (3) attractiveness, (4) commitment (the less committed have more leverage because the others fear he or she will withdraw), and (5) bargaining assertiveness. . . .

Two kinds of asymmetry also affect economic power: (1) one gets more clout from control of surplus than mere subsistence (because one has more degrees of freedom in allocating surplus), and (2) unless cushioned by strong ideological or kinship organization factors, a woman's position falls rapidly when her economic power drops, whereas increased power leads to a slower, less linear rise.

The consequences of greater economic power, once consolidated, I posit, include the following dependent variables: (1) greater influence over other types of power (e.g., more political clout, less likelihood of being a victim of domestic violence—although the more a man feels threatened by a recent rise in a woman's relative economic power, the more likely a short-term spike in violence), (2) greater self-confidence, and (3) greater control over "life options," aspects of one's destiny known to exist in all human societies, including marriage, divorce, sexuality, fertility, freedom of movement, access to education, and household power. Household power, in turn, includes greater say in decisions involving domestic well-being (e.g., how many years of schooling to give sons versus daughters), economic matters, and fertility control. Finally, greater economic power is linked to having more say in household and community land-use decisions and general influence in community affairs. . . .

The First Arrivals: Navajo and Iñupiat

Viewing the Navajo and the Iñupiat through the lens of gender enriches their stories. We first note that the Navajo and Iñupiat have different

kinship/gender systems. At nearly 300,000 strong, the Navajo are the second-largest U.S. Indian tribe and emphasize mother's side kinship. This is also the case with five more of the eight largest Indian tribes: the Apache, Cherokee (the largest tribe), Choctaw, Iroquois, and Pueblo (including Acoma, Hopi, Laguna, and Zuñi) also have matri-oriented kinship; the other two, Chippewa and Sioux, have male-oriented kinship systems (see Coltrane and Collins 2001:233, for the tribes and Murdock 1967 for the kinship systems).

Technically, the Navajo are matrilineal (they reckon descent mainly through the mother's side) and matrilocal (the young couple traditionally lives with or near the bride's female kin). More importantly, women are the main inheritors of the most important resources (sheep and land-use rights). In short, the traditional Navajo system gives women both economic power and centrality in kinship organization, a very powerful combination in terms of my theory. Further enhancing their power is the fact that "Navajo women very frequently manage the household money regardless of whether the man or the woman earns the most" (Tongue, personal communication).

In contrast, the Iñupiat give about equal weight to maternal and paternal relatives. They have "bilateral" kinship, the same as the U.S. mainstream. In most bilateral kinship systems, women are neither advantaged nor disadvantaged in either inheritance or where they live after marriage, although in some groups' actual practice, inheritance, or marital residence may favor one gender more than the other. Among the Iñupiat, however, women get no extra economic or other power from the kinship system.

The second thing to notice is that both have quite different traditional ways of making a living—ways very different from that of the U.S. mainstream. The Navajo long have lived as nomadic herders on their semi-arid lands, tending sheep (as well as goats, cattle, and horses); they also may do a little farming on rain-fed plots. In contrast, the Iñupiat long have hunted, fished, and, to a limited extent due to climate, gathered.

The resulting gender division of labor is also quite different. On the one hand, Navajo women tend to be the main herders (doing all the work with the sheep aside from the fencing and heavy labor, with even elders walking miles to herd). This remains true, Nancy Tongue writes, even though the Navajo, on average, have not relied on subsistence for more than 35 percent of their diet since the Department of the Interior imposed a drastic stock-reduction program in the 1930s. According to Tongue (personal communication), women keep the sheep not only for tradition's sake but because the wool is the basis of women's "job," as they wash, dye, card, spin, and then weave the wool. They maintain their looms and weaving utensils, which are usually passed down from their grandmothers and treasured. The sale of the resulting rugs, even if only sporadically made, contributes extra income. Many women also have home/cottage industries making jewelry, pottery, or other arts/crafts/handiwork, and this fills in financial gaps for their families.

On the other hand, 18 of 25 (72 percent) in Amy Craver's Iñupiaq sample continue to rely on subsistence resources for over half of their diet; and

the key "culture hero" tasks, hunting and fishing, are done mostly by men (Craver does mention cases of women becoming the hunters for their families, however). Women usually spend more of their time on the less glamorous aspects of hunting and fishing, processing the results, although the seasonal berries and grains gathered mainly by women are appreciated for adding taste and variety to the diet. But recent changes in the division of labor have enhanced the economic power and relative position of Iñupiaq women, while having a less gendered effect among the Navajo.

Specifically, Iñupiaq hunting and fishing are expensive under current conditions: snow machines, guns, ammunition, boats, and the like, are costly. It takes cash income to underwrite the much-valued traditional way of life. These days, young women are more likely than their brothers to provide it. As Craver writes, they are more likely to leave the village for school and get the resulting better jobs than the young men. By voluntarily providing much of the surplus that makes possible the traditional Iñupiaq subsistence strategy, the young women have enhanced their relative position in terms of my theory of gender stratification.

One of my theory's hypotheses (see above) argues that you get more power from allocating surplus than trying to stretch subsistence income (Schmeer 2005:407). The young women decide how much of their disposable income (surplus) to send home and when, which raises their power. In terms of my micro-level discount factors, (1) their families (which, as Craver notes, may be scattered over several dwellings) have become more dependent on the young women's contributions, and (2) the families also may worry about the absent young women's continued commitment, which further enhances the women's relative position. Recall that my theory argues that the person perceived as less committed has more leverage, since he or she is seen as more likely to withdraw.

Nevertheless, although young women's position is rising, they still do not get a full dollar's worth of economic power for every dollar they contribute. This is because of two counterbalancing factors. First, the "cultural ideology" discount factor continues to give greater prestige to (mostly male) hunting and fishing. Second, despite their rising status, young women often pay a different kind of price: leaving their child or children behind with their parents. Such practices are culturally well accepted—adopting a first grandchild is an entrenched custom among the Iñupiat. In this purposive sample study of complex households, 17 of 25 households (68 percent) contain grandparent(s) and grandchild(ren) but are missing the mother of the child(ren). Leaving their kids behind also blunts some of the power these young women could derive from their control of the surplus that they voluntarily contribute to household subsistence hunting and fishing, as well as the leverage they could get from the "relative-commitment" discount factor. The fact that the women's children are in the village helps to ensure that they will continue to send money home for hunting, fishing, and child support, and their families need not fret much about their continuing commitment. Even with these caveats, however, there is no denying that, overall, young women's clout has risen. In contrast, the young men tend to hunt, fish, and

do sporadic odd jobs but live in their parents' house (perhaps sleeping in a nearby shed).

Among today's Navajo, it is common for some, usually men, to have a blue-collar trade that periodically takes them far away from the reservation; women are more likely to stay in school and then get social service jobs on or near the "Rez." Maternal grandmothers' lands and sheep remain the cultural heart of family resources, but the economic heart comes from job income. Yet, even where men's earnings are greater, women's relative position remains strong. "The women are still in charge," according to Tongue (personal communication). They not only continue to have a disproportionate share of the culturally valued and economically significant land and animals, but they also enjoy "solidarity power" with coresident female kin and an ideology that they are central to family and group life.

Even so, the larger U.S. culture has made a few inroads. First, relocation and shrinking landholdings are a continuing problem. Loss of traditional lands is especially disturbing for women who hold the use rights to those lands—it means they have nothing to pass on to their children. Second, women are not always identified as the census "householder." When Tongue asked one woman, who owns her family's home, why she had listed her husband as the primary householder, she laughed. "I just did that because that's how white people do it." Her daughter's husband brings in the money, so the daughter views him as the head of her household. But this is still atypical. Both the Navajo and Iñupiaq cultures remain remarkably resilient and enduring, given the political, legal, economic, and cultural onslaughts of the more powerful dominant group. . . .

Sharing

Both groups practice sharing, although to different extents and in different, gender-differentiated patterns. First, sharing is a "cultural universal" among hunters and gatherers (see Nolan and Lenski 1999; Blumberg 1978): it evens out the ups and downs in finding food and, thus, acts as survival insurance. Accordingly, it remains a crucial part of Iñupiaq survival strategies. Moreover, as noted, the men still dispense the more valued animal and fish protein, which continues to boost their prestige. Navajo sharing involves pooled herds of sheep, shared vehicles and rides, shared subsistence tasks and purchases (e.g., hauling and buying wood and water, installing and repairing fencing), and shared conveniences (one relative's home may have electricity, another's water, and a third may be close to a school; people may move from one household to another as they need these services). Other than sheep, which tend to belong to women, Navajo sharing seems gender neutral and, perhaps, not quite as important as for the Iñupiat.

Informal Adoption and Fostering

Adoption and fostering are very prevalent in the Iñupiaq sample, as in the Navajo sample. Kids may derive special benefits from living with grandparents. For example, they can learn the most interesting and valued aspects

of traditional culture and subsistence: hunting, fishing, and gathering with their grandparents among the Iñupiat, and riding horses and herding sheep on their maternal grandmothers' land among the Navajo. Children may also be fostered with kin closer to school or to help care for an aging relative. In gender terms, adoption and fostering are largely with matrilineal kin among the Navajo. Iñupiaq children, in theory, could go to live with either their mother's or father's parents. But the Iñupiaq "skip-generation" pattern is gendered: it is the children's mother (rather than father) who is likely to be absent, thus tilting child adoption and fostering toward her parents or siblings. In both groups, adoption is formalized only if there's a problem with the state.

Grandparents

Anthropologists recently have come to recognize the benefits that grandparents can provide, even when no formal adoption or fostering is involved. The data tend to show that it is the mother's mother who exerts the most positive influence (Angier 2002), which can include higher rates of infant and child survival. In the Navajo case, the most important grandparent clearly is the maternal grandmother, since she is the source of inherited resources and the "homeland" to which family members return all their lives. Both Iñupiaq grandparents seem important since resources flow from both. But grandfathers get a little extra clout because they are the ones who can teach the most prestigious and important subsistence skills—hunting and fishing.

Spouses

There are distinct patterns in the two groups. The most important difference is that a Navajo man has less formal responsibility to his children if the union breaks up; conversely, mother's brothers are expected to maintain close, loving, and economically supportive ties with their nephews and nieces no matter what. (The relationship with mother's sisters is even closer: they are referred to as mothers and call each other's children sons and daughters, not nephews and nieces.) Navajo do not say "husband" or "wife" but, rather, "spouse," which translates to "the one I make my living with," and they cooperate economically and care for each other. Whether there has been a civil marriage is irrelevant. In contrast, an Iñupiaq husband is closer to his children than are any of his wife's siblings. His obligations to his children continue even if the union ends. In short, we see what we would expect from a matrilineal versus a bilateral kinship system.

This leads to the question, How do Navajo men feel about their kinship/spousal system? The short answer is that they seem to be as emotionally bound by family as women. Tongue's quotes from men are quite eloquent. For example, her cultural liaison, Leo, resides with his wife on land she inherited matrilineally. Her mother resides next door in a traditional *hogan*, her sister's family lives part way down the dirt road, and her single brother

lives "behind the hill next to them." When she asked Leo to describe the people he lives with, he suggested the word *k'é*, which he defined as

> *The people I live with who are part of my family and are my people. They are the ones I shake hands with, and the ones I feel good with above, in front, and behind. They are the ones I have peace with. K'é means family group. It also is our word for peace.* (Tongue 2005)

The Burden on the Middle Generation

This is most visible in the Navajo because of the sheer size of the reservation. A woman will try to see and help her mother as often as possible. Even if she lives a couple hundred miles away and works Monday to Friday, she'll drive long distances every weekend, frequently feeling pressured and exhausted by the effort. Her husband may accompany her, then make long journeys to his own maternal kin. Among the Iñupiat, those who leave also try to return, at minimum for subsistence "high season," when winter does not rule the land. These patterns maintain both caring and traditional economic patterns but at a high price for the "sandwich generation": beyond losing sleep, they may lose chances for career advancement because of their schedule. . . .

The Recent Arrivals: Koreans and Latinos

First, let us note that the complex households encountered among the samples of recent immigrants from South Korea and Latin America (the great majority of the Hispanic households were from Mexico, with most of the rest from El Salvador) are not the typical form in their countries of origin. For example, Patricia Goerman (2004) cites data from Mexico's National Institute of Geography and Informatics that in 1995, 74% of households in Mexico were nuclear families. The situation is similar in South Korea, Tai Kang writes. The country has undergone a dramatic transition from an agrarian to an urbanized, fast-growing nation where gross domestic product has been growing at an average 8% a year for 40 years. Now, the great majority of city folk reside in apartments with nuclear family members only.

The second point to emphasize is that, overwhelmingly, both the Koreans and the Hispanics cited economic reasons in explaining their living arrangements. Also, their current arrangements are not their long-term preference: large majorities of the Latinos Goerman studied named the nuclear household as their ideal and said they would not continue living with their current coresidents permanently. But, for now, as they struggle to establish a toehold on the lower rungs of what they hope will be the ladder of opportunity in the United States, such complex household arrangements provide economic advantages.

The third point to emphasize involves gender differences when we compare Koreans' and Latinos' life in the United States with that in their countries of origin. In preview, the gender stratification and kinship system they left provided more structural advantage to males than is the case here.

Among Koreans, patriarchy is woven into the very fabric of everyday life. As Kang writes, one of the fundamental social and cultural norms (*Oh Rewn*) is "hierarchical role differentiation and separation" between a husband and his wife. In the traditionally patriarchal, patrilineal, patrilocal Korean extended family, the wife is subordinate to her husband, and to her oldest son if she is widowed. In general, females have subordinate and marginal social status, and there is separation of paternal and maternal relatives.

Among the Hispanics, although kinship is formally bilateral, a number of the women reported living with their husband's parents in their home country. Goerman writes,

> Elena told me that in her experience it is quite common for a couple to move in with the husband's parents until they are able to establish their own household. Temporary migration to the United States is often the easiest way to achieve this goal. (Personal communication)

While the traditional systems in Mexico and El Salvador (together, these are the home countries of some 90 percent of the Latino sample) are far less patriarchal than the Koreans', they are near the patriarchal end of the continuum for Latin America and are far more patriarchal than is typical in the United States. Therefore, let us see how these patterns have shifted under the exigencies of surviving—and, hopefully, advancing—in a strange, new land.

Female Labor Force Participation

Though these small, nonrandom samples cannot be generalized to all Korean and Hispanic immigrants, they merit scrutiny. Let us begin with the Hispanic sample, because for reasons of "face," the Koreans were reluctant to discuss whether they were working and at what. (A number were in the underground, informal economy, something they would not admit to an interviewer who, albeit Korean, represented the U.S. Census Bureau.) Of the 49 Hispanic people in two samples discussed by Goerman, 30 were women. Two were older than "prime labor force" age (18–64) and retired, so they are not counted. All but 9 of the 28 other females were working (68 percent). The Mexico and El Salvador data are as follows: in 1995–1997, 39 percent of Mexican and 41% of Salvadoran women aged 15 and older were in the labor force, making up, respectively, 34 percent and 37 percent of the total labor force (United Nations 2000:145).

The 1995–1997 figures for Korea are 50 percent of women aged 15 and older working, making up 41 percent of the total labor force (United Nations 2000:147). It can be inferred, however, that more than 50 percent of all women in his 25 complex households were earning income (Kang personal communication).

Recall that my gender-stratification theory posits that when women control income, they have more economic power and say in household decisions. It also posits that when women's relative income rises, so does their power, although the path to greater clout is not as smooth, fast, and linear

as their drop in power if relative income falls (unless that decline is cushioned by ideological or kinship-structure factors). Here, in the two samples, a larger proportion of Korean and Hispanic women are earning income than in the home country, and in only one case (Kang's description of a 62-year-old widow who gives her paycheck to her son) is there any indication that the woman does not have a say vis-à-vis her own earnings. So, this implies more power for these Korean and Hispanic women.

Whose Kin? Whose Power?

Indeed, in the Korean sample, we find examples of atypical female power. Consider Kang's Case: The grandparents were brought over by their daughter (who has a university degree and a job in Manhattan) to take care of her two children (her husband is a grad student). When Kang asked permission to tape the interview, the old man felt he had to call his daughter for her okay. She refused, and her embarrassed father had to abort the interview. Such a direct exercise of power by a daughter would be heresy in traditional Korean culture. Kang's liaison explained, "You see, the grandmother looks after a few neighborhood Korean children—babysitting work. She gets paid for the work under the table. They do not want people to know about the underground economy that they are a part of."

In fact, Kang looked for three-generation families for his sample, and in 12 of the 25 households, a grandmother (or grandparents) had been brought over to help with the children and chores (Kang personal communication). Intriguingly, this involved another reversal of Korean patriarchal practice:

> [T]he wife's mother was more likely to have moved in, rather than the husband's. In other words, the coresident three-generation families were not a re-creation in Queens of a traditional patriarchal, patrilocal, Korean family. Part of the reason reported by respondents is that sons tend to get along better with their mothers-in-law than their wives do with their mothers-in-law—so, the young couple often sends for the grandmother who will make the most harmonious addition to their tiny, cramped quarters.

Among the Latinos no such dramatic reversals of traditional practices were encountered. Rather, more women were living with husband's male kin than with their own female kin. For this [reading], Goerman and I coded our original census sample of 25 households (Blumberg and Goerman 2000) for side of house. We found the following: of seven households where extended kin were from the woman's side, two included only her female kin; three, both female and male kin; and two, only male kin. In other words, in 5 of 25 households (20 percent), the woman had a kinswoman living with her. But where the kin were from the man's side, six of eight households included only the man's male kin, and two more included both his own male and female kin. In other words, in no household with husband-side kin did a man live with only his own female relatives. All told, in 8 of 25 households (32 percent), the man had a coresident kinsman, compared with the 20 percent

of women living with their own female kin. Using a different subgroup of her purposive sample, Goerman found that 86 percent of 44 households that now or once were complex contained extra men (mean of 2.2 men), whereas only 48 percent contained extra women (mean of 1.2 women). Such patterns may explain why some women cited not having to pick up after husband's male kin as one reason they looked forward to moving up to the preferred nuclear family household once they were better established.

Summing up, women in both the Korean and Hispanic purposive samples have a higher level of labor force participation than do women in their home countries, thereby boosting their power. As an added power bonus, in the United States, these women seem much less likely to have to live with their husband's parents. Further, now they are living in a culture considerably less patriarchal than that of their countries of origin. . . .

Adoption and Fostering

The adoption or fostering of children almost never occurs outside the paternal lineage among Koreans. Latino customs are much more open, with informal adoption and fostering being fairly common in the countries of origin. Such children are viewed as part of the household, and there do not seem to be any strong preferences for fostering maternal versus paternal children.

Cohabitation and "Face"

Hispanics also are much more likely to cohabit and say so (throughout Latin America, up to half of poor people, in particular, live in common-law unions). In most instances, these couples consider themselves spouses, causing a potential recording problem for the census. But Koreans will not admit to being in cohabiting relationships. In Korea, it would be a loss of face in the patriarchal system, as well as unaccepted legally, and the Queens respondents also avoided revealing such ties.

The Balance Sheet

Just reading the description of the Korean family registry is enough to lead most people to conclude that Korean immigrant women living in cramped quarters in Queens have had to swim against a much stronger current of patriarchy but that they have made more *relative* progress than Hispanic women who have lived in a much more moderate system of patriarchy in their home countries. There is evidence, however, that Hispanic women, too, appreciate the greater gender equality afforded them in the United States, as well as the greater opportunities for their children. In fact, other studies have found them to be more reluctant than their husbands to take their savings and return home (see Foner 1978 on Jamaican migrants in London; Pessar 1988 on Dominicans in New York; Hondagneu-Sotelo 1992 on Mexicans in California; and Goerman 2004 for further discussion). This sense of enhanced possibility in the United States may be one of the factors that lead Koreans and Hispanics, female and male, to put up with the negatives in

their complex households. But for women, there is also the bonus of potentially greater autonomy and economic power, with the resulting increased equality in and beyond the household.

Using Complex Households to Solve Complex Issues: African Americans in the South, Rural Whites in the North

Two Commonalities

We found two major commonalities between the samples of African Americans from urban coastal Virginia and rural whites from upstate New York. First, both groups have created nontraditional households that help them solve structural difficulties. The problems and the specific types of complex households that ensue are rather different, but both represent ways that people adapt and use gendered kinship systems to enable them to care for each other and, hopefully, survive and thrive.

Second, both samples had a somewhat defensive attitude about the fact that they are not living in Ozzie-and-Harriet-type nuclear families. . . . The African American sample seemed defensive about how their households are seen by outsiders, and with reason. African Americans have, indeed, been much criticized for a family structure with substantial proportions of households headed by women rather than married couples. *The Negro Family*, better known as the "Moynihan Report" (1965), makes a controversial argument often considered racist, misogynistic, or both, but it has been influential. Daniel Patrick Moynihan saw the rising rates of female-headed families among poor, urban blacks as a growing "social cancer":

> At the center of the tangle of pathology is the weakness of the family structure. Once or twice removed, it will be found to be the principal source of most of the aberrant, inadequate or anti-social behavior that did not establish, *but now serves to perpetuate* the cycle of poverty and deprivation. (Moynihan 1965:30, emphasis added)

The African Americans studied by Bernadette Holmes strongly reject this view. Instead, they point to the fact that blacks have long lived in flexible, adaptive, "extended family networks," rather than in nuclear units, and that the resulting institution has been a source of strength, not weakness, in surviving structural adversity and disadvantage.

In contrast, the rural whites in New York see themselves as generally epitomizing a nonethnic, all-American identity—and traditional values. So, even though this is a purposive, nonrandom sample, it comes as a bit of a surprise that (1) 9 of 25 households (36 percent) involve a cohabiting couple (although 100 percent of the cohabiting rural whites in the sample had previously been married), and (2) 5 of these 9 involve children. According to S. Hewner (2000), who carried out the research, the people in her sample felt a certain stigma that they (of all people!) lived in nontraditional, complex households. For example, only four of the nine cohabiting couples used

the "unmarried partner" terminology favored by the census; the others used alternatives ranging from spouse to girlfriend to "other nonrelative" (in the case of a seemingly gay couple still in the closet). But, like the African Americans, they had structural reasons for living in complex households, whether or not they wanted to publicize the fact. Let us now consider African American patterns in more detail.

Sharing among the African Americans

In general, blacks' postslavery economic history has been marked by more downs than ups, the continuing heritage of discrimination and prejudice. Holmes' sample of 25 households represents a wide range of social classes; this is not an "underclass" group. A good proportion of the complex households came about because of problems where they shoulder the burden of caring for someone (usually a child) who might otherwise fall victim to "the system": 8 of 25 households (32 percent) involved some form of adoption, and 5 (20%) were married grandparents raising a grandchild because of a child's problems (in at least 10 of 25 households, 40 percent, drugs were a factor) (Holmes and Amissah 2002). But all the children were being cared for, and as Holmes' quotes show, extended kin of both sexes contributed love and various kinds of help. There may not have been a village, but a sharing network was involved. . . .

Gender Matters

In order to better understand the relative position of men and women among African Americans, we have to look at the historical big picture. The high labor force participation of African American women goes back to slavery, when women were as expected to work in the fields and do agricultural work as men. Actually, most of these women came from West African horticultural groups where females tended—and still tend—to be the principal farmers (e.g., Boserup 1970; Saito and Weidemann 1990 show that today's sub-Saharan African women raise up to 80% or more of locally grown and traded food crops). Data are rather sketchy, but it appears that since the end of slavery, African American women have generally been more economically active, with a smaller wage gap, than their white counterparts. For example, J. Jones (1995) writes, "African American wives were more likely to work. In the 1870 Census for the cotton belt states, 4 in 10 African American wives had jobs as field workers. In contrast, 98% of white wives said they were keeping house and had no jobs." D. Spain and S. Bianchi (1996) also note that historically, men's and women's work patterns varied by race: black women had higher labor force participation than white women, whereas black men had lower labor force participation than white men.

According to my gender-stratification theory, this would give African American women more power in the household than white women. They would, therefore, be less willing to put up with a bad relationship or one requiring subservience. Also, until the 1996 welfare reform, the United States

maintained a "safety net" system (Aid to Families with Dependent Children, see Hays 2003) for more than two generations; this provided a small, added backup that further reduced African American females' dependence on male income.

Black men themselves often were more economically marginal—or unavailable: The U.S. prison population reached 2 million in 2003, the highest incarceration rate and number in the world, with African American men (especially since the War on Drugs began in 1981) disproportionately likely to be locked up. Given all this, blacks' higher divorce rates and proportions of female-headed households are not surprising.

In short, African American women long have had greater relative economic power and autonomy vis-à-vis their men than white women, but their low overall economic position and social status due to racism did not permit them to "go it alone"; hence, these extended kin networks.

Summing up to this point, it is suggested that because of their (1) historically higher labor force participation rate, (2) apparently smaller wage gap, and (3) long traditions of extended family networks, as well as their (4) lower rates of marriage, black women have proved more likely than white women to be householders, that is, the first person listed on the census form. . . .

In contrast to the black purposive sample, the rural whites participating in this qualitative study had more couple households (19 of 25, or 76 percent) and support systems that were less structured than full-fledged sharing networks. Compared to the black sample, fewer women in Hewner's purposive white sample were in the labor force (after all, they were older), fewer were listed as householders (in part because more were married), and fewer emphasized their own side-of-house relatives. But these whites, too, benefited from kin. Let us now examine their patterns.

Complex Households as Adaptive Strategies among the Rural Whites

By design, the sample's average age was high (54) and almost entirely female (24 of 25, or 96 percent). Most of the respondents earned income (this was primarily a middle-class sample). Why should such people live in nontraditional complex households? In a third of the sample, Childs documents that their complex households came about because someone needed care. In another third, "it just happened." In the last third, respondents said they had chosen it. Most complex households, however, were formed because they addressed the kinds of issues facing an older population that has had to deal with the out-migration of young people, snowy winters, and marital breakups. Creating cooperative arrangements among elderly people was one solution. An example is the woman who tenderly cared for up to five aged women "boarders" for a pittance (about $100 a month per boarder). Indeed, handling elders' sickness and infirmity was a major reason for forming complex households. In sum, the reasons mentioned by the whites varied somewhat from those of the African Americans, but the complex household proved valuable for both groups.

Gender

Not much gender data surfaced in the interviews with the rural whites. But considering that this is an almost all-female group with an average age of 54, the householder's education puts them slightly above the U.S. average: only two had not finished high school, 10 of 25 had finished high school, and the remaining 13 had at least some college. On the one hand, perhaps reflecting their rural background and age more than their level of education, their ideas about gender tended toward the traditional: most saw men as the primary breadwinners, whose chores consist only of outside and heavy-duty work. And they also tended to live in couples (19 of 25, or 76 percent), even though the number of cohabiting couples (9) almost equaled the number of married couples (10). On the other hand, more in keeping with their educational and labor force participation levels, they stretched their notion of women's traditional role to include working for pay outside the home, along with raising the children and maintaining the house.

Gender and Side of House

The rural whites' kinship system is bilateral, which is the U.S. norm. Interestingly, however, in all four households where a married couple lived with a parent, it was the husband's mother. In one case, presented by Childs, in fact, it was both of the husband's mothers—his adoptive mother who raised him and his birth mother with whom he was recently reacquainted (and who was later sent to an assisted living facility because she and the adoptive mother did not get along). In the other three cases, the household was three generational: the couple, their kids, and his mother. The grandmother helped care for the children while the parents were at work, and the parents helped care for the grandmother. This is part of a pattern of forming complex households to care for older kin and has policy relevance in a nation that is "graying" fast.

What Does It All Mean?

The rural New York white sample's complex households are quite flexible. Boundaries have stretched to include a high proportion of cohabiting couples, and the sample households also incorporated a surprisingly high proportion with adopted members (fully 9 of 25, including informal arrangements, 2 cases of fictive kin, and 3 instances of fostering; there were 8 cases among the African American sample, although, again, these are small, nonrandom samples from which inferences cannot be made to the larger population). With such flexibility, the households are able to pool economic resources or carry out necessary services (e.g., shoveling snow) through mutual cooperation. They also can help someone not able to care for him- or herself, while enjoying more companionship than otherwise would have been the case. So, if this rural, "white-bread America" sample is adjusting household patterns, forming unmarried partner relationships, and engaging in informal adoption as shifting structural conditions dictate, we really can invoke Bob Dylan: "the times they are a-changin'."

Conclusion, Commonalities, Contradictions, and Policy Implications

By way of preface, the six ethnic groups in this ethnographic study can be divided into two categories vis-à-vis complex households: those who are committed to a nonnuclear living arrangement (the Navajo, the Iñupiat, and, to a lesser extent, the African Americans) and those who form complex households because of conditions or circumstances (the rural whites, the Hispanics, the Koreans, and, to some extent, the African Americans, who span both categories). . . .

Navajo women started with—and still have—most of the high cards in terms of my theory. Although U.S. government policies led to a drop in women's right to use land and in sheep ownership, enough remains to provide a firm foundation for the matrilineal, matrilocal kinship and inheritance system that provides women with allies, helpers, and valued resources. Considering the micro-level discount factors, (1) gender ideology remains quite egalitarian in most households, (2) women are not shy about bargaining on their own behalf, and (3) both men and women remain committed to their matrikin, especially as embodied in the grandmother and her land. Furthermore, both younger men and women (especially the "sandwich generation") are likely to share earned income with their kin. But women seem likely to remain in more frequent physical contact with their matrikin, even if this involves a never-ending series of long commutes. In short, it is hard to say that women's strategic indispensability or net balance of discount factors is becoming even greater or more favorable, but they do not appear to have eroded, either.

For the other five groups, the strategic indispensability of female labor and income, as well as the net balance of micro-level discount factors, reveal a rising trend for women. The clearest-cut example of increasing gender equality involved young women among the Iñupiat. As discussed above, they were more likely to get schooling and jobs beyond the village, and their families were increasingly beholden to them to send some of their income home so that traditional hunting and fishing activities could be maintained, despite their rising cost. With increased dependence on the young women's voluntarily contributed surplus income comes the worry about their continuing level of commitment. My theory proposes that allocating surplus income is a source of greater economic power than trying to stretch subsistence income to (barely) cover survival needs. . . . In contrast, a rich old person can make younger family members dance to his or her tune lest they be disinherited. But the young women's growing power is dampened slightly by the fact that so many have left children in the village (virtually ensuring continuing contributions and commitment), as well as by the ideology that so highly values (mostly male) hunting and fishing.

Among the other purposive ethnic samples, a higher proportion of both Korean and Hispanic women earned income than is reflected in current statistics for their home countries. Given that most of their households were poor, their contribution would be strongly needed. This might not have

provided as much clout as being able to allocate surplus, but it clearly earned them a plus for the low "dependence on other's income" discount factor. Also, the household's "gender ideology" discount factor probably would be less negative than in the home country due both to the women's income and to the fact that they were now living in a less patriarchal society. Factor in that both Koreans and Latinos were less likely to live with or near the husband's parents than was true among traditional, especially rural, groups in their country of origin, and the women are left with greater autonomy and economic power and fewer constraints on exercising them.

Looking at the northern rural whites and the southern urban blacks in this study, we find the same factors of more income contributed by women, more household dependence on that income, and, for the whites, a more recent de facto acceptance of women working and couples cohabiting. Both female income earning and cohabitation are linked with greater equality for women within the household (Coltrane and Collins 2001; Blumstein and Schwartz 1991). In the New York white sample, however, there was still some awkwardness in admitting nontraditional household arrangements, such as using the term *unmarried partner* for their live-in mate. For the Virginia African American sample, admitting to nontraditional household arrangements was more likely to be edged with sensitivity or pain about how their units, especially those headed by female householders, have been maligned. But these black women were not hesitant about proclaiming their roles as providers.

In recent years, African American women in general have seen their position in the labor market improve more in relative terms than many other race, ethnic, or gender groups. They have moved up the occupational ladder and have shrunk the male–female wage gap (it is now smaller than whites': $.86/$1.00 for blacks working full-time, year-round versus $.76/$1.00 for counterpart whites, per the U.S. Department of Labor 2002). Some of this is due to the fact that African American men have been disproportionately represented among those occupational groups that have fared the worst in recent decades (e.g., blue-collar workers in low-tech manufacturing) as the United States has shed such jobs to lower-wage, Third World countries. Black men also have been disproportionately represented among the incarcerated, even when convicted of the same crime as whites. So, while African American women are doing better, they are forced to shoulder more of the burdens of the continuing legacy of racism, discrimination, and poverty. And some patterns that we used to associate (pejoratively) with black women (e.g., non-marital childbearing, female householding) are now increasingly prevalent throughout our society, as the proportion of women earning and controlling income continues to increase. . . . Clearly, many questions remain unanswered. This [reading] has barely scratched the surface of what is, for now, terra incognita for researchers: exploring the ramifications of simultaneously focusing on ethnicity, household complexity, side of house, and gender. . . .

To complicate matters further, the United States is facing a huge and unprecedented demographic transformation. By 2050, the U.S. non-Hispanic white population is projected to shrink to a bare majority 50%, while the

Latino population is projected to increase from an estimated 13% in 2005 to 24%; concomitantly, Asians listing one race alone are projected to rise from an estimated 4.2% in 2005 to 8% in 2050 (U.S. Census Bureau 2003). Household diversity keeps rising in step with this increasing ethnic diversity, as well as with growing alternative lifestyle diversity (e.g., same-sex couples). In short, we can expect more varied and often complex households. Still, however much they differ from the Ozzie and Harriet nuclear household in composition, all have to set their own balance of caring and coping. Now the trick is measuring, understanding, and, ideally, predicting how different groups of men, women, and children are distributed in households of dizzying and growing diversity.

REFERENCES

Angier, N. 2002. "They're the Real Bond Girls: Maternal Grandmas Are the Link to Family Benefits." *San Diego Union—Tribune/New York Times News Service*, November 20, Pp. F1, F3.

Blumberg, R. L. 1978. *Stratification: Socioeconomic and Sexual Inequality*. Dubuque, IA: William C. Brown.

———. 1984. "A General Theory of Gender Stratification." Pp. 23–101 in *Sociological Theory*, edited by R. Collins. San Francisco: Jossey-Bass.

———. 1991. "Introduction: The 'Triple Overlap' of Gender Stratification, Economy, and Family." Pp. 7–32 in *Gender, Family, and Economy: The Triple Overlap*, edited by R. L. Blumberg. Newbury Park, CA: Sage.

Blumberg, R. L. and M. T. Coleman. 1989. "A Theory Guided Look at the Gender Balance of Power in the American Couple." *Journal of Family Issues* 10:225–49.

Blumberg, R. L. and P. L. Goerman. 2000. "Family Complexity among Latino Immigrants in Virginia: An Ethnographic Study of Their Households Aimed at Improving Census Categories." Final Report to the U.S. Census Bureau.

Blumstein, P. and P. Schwartz. 1991. "Money and Ideology: Their Impact on Power and the Division of Household Labor." Pp. 261–88 in *Gender, Family, and Economy: The Triple Overlap*, edited by R. L. Blumberg. Newbury Park, CA: Sage.

Boserup, E. 1970. *Woman's Role in Economic Development*. New York: St. Martin's Press.

Coltrane, S. and R. Collins. 2001. *Sociology of Marriage and the Family: Gender, Love, and Property*. 5th ed. Belmont, CA: Wadsworth.

Foner, N. 1978. *Jamaica Farewell: Jamaican Migrants in London*. Berkeley: University of California Press.

Goerman, P. 2004. "The Promised Land? The Gendered Experience of New Hispanic 'Proletarian' Immigrants to Central Virginia." Ph.D. dissertation, University of Virginia.

Hays, S. 2003. *Flat Broke with Children: Women in the Age of Welfare Reform*. New York: Oxford.

Hewner, S. 2000. "Ethnic Ambiguity: Changing Perceptions of Rural Caucasians." Report submitted to the U.S. Census Bureau.

Holmes, B. and C. Amissah. 2002. "The Experiences of African American Households: A Kinship Study." Unpublished final report to the Census Bureau for the Complex Households and Relationships in the Decennial Census and in Ethnographic Studies Project.

Hondagneu-Sotelo, P. 1992. "Overcoming Patriarchal Constraints: The Reconstruction of Gender Relations among Mexican Immigrant Women and Men." *Gender & Society* 6:393–415.

Jones, J. 1995. *Labor of Love, Labor of Sorrow: Black Women and the Family from Slavery to the Present*. New York: Basic Books.

Moynihan, Daniel P. 1965. *The Negro Family: The Case for National Action*. Washington, DC: Department of Labor, Office of Policy Planning and Research.

Murdock, George P. 1967. "Ethnographic Atlas: A Summary." *Ethnology* 6:109–236.

Nolan, P. and G. Lenski. 1999. *Human Societies: An Introduction to Macrosociology*. New York: McGraw-Hill.

Pessar, P. R. 1988. "The Constraints on and Release of Female Labor Power: Dominican Migration to the United States." Pp. 195–215 in *A Home Divided: Women and Income in the Third World*, edited by D. Dwyer and J. Bruce. Palo Alto, CA: Stanford University Press.

Saito, K. and J. Weidemann. 1990. "Agricultural Extension for Women Farmers in Africa." Women in Development Working Papers. Washington, DC: World Bank.

Schmeer, K. K. 2005. "Married Women's Resource Position and Household Food Expenditures in Cebu, Philippines." *Journal of Marriage and Family* 67: 399–409.

Spain, D. and S. Bianchi. 1996. *Balancing Act: Motherhood, Marriage and Employment among American Women.* New York: Sage.

Tongue, Nancy E. 2005. "I Live Here and I Stay Here." Pp. 39–93 in *Complex Ethnic Households in America,* edited by Laurel Schwede, Rae Lesser Blumberg, and Anna Y. Chan. UK: Rowman and Littlefield Publishers.

United Nations. 2000. *The World's Women 2000: Trends and Statistics.* New York: United Nations.

U.S. Census Bureau. 2003. "Resident Population by Race and Hispanic Origin Status—Projections: 2005 to 2050." In *Statistical Abstract of the United States: 2003.* Section 1. Population P18, Table 15 at www.census.gov/prod/2004pubs/03statab/pop.pdf.

U.S. Department of Labor. 2002. "Employed Persons by Detailed Occupation, Sex, Race, and Hispanic Origin." Current Population Survey, 2001, at www.dol.gov.

PART III

Courtship, Dating, and Power

10

CHOOSING MATES—THE AMERICAN WAY

MARTIN KING WHYTE

As America's divorce rate has been soaring, popular anxieties about marriage have multiplied. Is it still possible to "live happily ever after," and if so, how can this be accomplished? How can you tell whether a partner who leaves you breathless with yearning will, as your spouse, drive you to distraction? Does "living together" prior to marriage provide a realistic assessment of how compatible you and your partner might be as husband and wife? Questions such as these suggest a need to examine our American way of mate choice. How do we go about selecting the person we marry, and is there something wrong with the entire process?

For most twentieth-century Americans, choosing a mate is the culmination of a process of dating. Examination of how we go about selecting mates thus requires us to consider the American dating culture. Dating is a curious institution. By definition it is an activity that is supposed to be separate from selecting a spouse. Yet, dating is expected to provide valuable experience that will help in making a "wise" choice of a marital partner. Does this combination work?

How well dating "works" may be considered in a number of senses of this term. Is it easy or difficult to find somebody to go out with? Do dates mostly lead to enjoyable or painful evenings? However, these are not the aspects of dating I wish to consider. The issue here is whether dating works in the sense of providing useful experience that helps pave the way for a successful marriage.

Dating is a relatively new institution. The term, and the various practices associated with it, first emerged around the turn of the century. By the 1920s dating had more or less completely displaced earlier patterns of relations among unmarried Americans. Contrary to popular assumptions, even in colonial times marriages were not arranged in America. Parents were expected to give their approval to their children's nuptial plans, a practice captured in our image of a suitor asking his beloved's father for her hand in

Martin King Whyte, "Choosing Mates—The American Way" from *Society* 29, No. 3 (March/April 1992): 71–77. Copyright © 1992 by Transaction Publishers, Inc. Reprinted with permission.

marriage. Parental approval, especially among merchants and other prosperous classes, put some constraint on the marriages of the young. For example, through the eighteenth century, children in such families tended to marry in birth order and marriage to cousins was not uncommon. (Both practices had declined sharply by the nineteenth century.) However, parents rarely directly arranged the marriages of their children. America has always exhibited "youth-driven" patterns of courtship. Eligible males and females took the initiative to get to know each other, and the decision to marry was made by them, even if that decision was to some degree contingent on parental approval. (Of course, substantial proportions of later immigrant groups from Southern and Eastern Europe, Asia, and elsewhere brought with them arranged marriage traditions, and contention for control over marriage decisions was often a great source of tension in such families.)

How did young people get to know one another well enough to decide to marry in the era before dating? A set of customs, dominant for the two centuries, preceded the rise of the dating culture. These activities came to be referred to as "calling" and "keeping company." Young people might meet in a variety of ways—through community and church socials, informally in shops or on the street, on boat and train trips, or through introductions from friends or relatives. (America never developed a system of chaperoning young women in public, and foreign observers often commented on the freedom unmarried women had to travel and mix socially on their own.) Usually young people would go to church fairs, local dances, and other such activities with family, siblings, or friends, rather than paired off with a partner. Most activities would involve a substantial degree of adult and community supervision. Nonetheless, these gatherings did encourage some pairing off and led to hand holding, moonlit walks home, and other romantic exploration.

As relationships developed beyond the platonic level, the suitor would pay visits to the home of the young woman. By the latter part of the nineteenth century, particularly among the middle and upper classes, this activity assumed a formal pattern referred to as "calling." Males would be invited to call on the female at her home, and they were expected to do so only if invited. (A bold male could, however, request an invitation to call.) Invitations might be extended by the mother of a very young woman, but eventually they would come from the young woman herself. Often a woman would designate certain days on which she would receive callers. She might have several suitors at one time, and thus a number of men might be paying such calls. A man might be told that the woman was not at home to receive him, and he would then be expected to leave his calling card. If this happened repeatedly, he was expected to get the message that his visits were no longer welcome.

Initiative and control in regard to calling were in the hands of women (the eligible female and her mother). Although some variety in suitors was possible, even in initial stages the role of calling in examining potential marriage partners was very clear to all involved. The relatively constrained and supervised nature of calling makes it certain that enjoyment cannot have

standard. Men were expected to be the sexual aggressors and to try to achieve as much intimacy as their dates would allow. But women who "went too far" risked harming their reputations and their ability to keep desirable men interested in them for long. Women were expected to set the limits, and they had to walk a careful line between being too unfriendly (and not having males wanting to date them at all) and being too friendly (and being dated for the "wrong reasons").

During the initial decades of the dating era, premarital intimacy increased in comparison with the age of calling, but still a majority of women entered marriage as virgins. In a survey in the greater Detroit metropolitan area, I found that of the oldest women interviewed (those who dated and married prior to 1945), about one in four had lost her virginity prior to marriage. (By the 1980s, according to my survey, the figure was closer to 90 percent.) Escape from parental supervision provided by dating weakened, but did not immediately destroy, the restraints on premarital intimacy.

When Americans began dating, they were primarily concerned with enjoyment, rather than with choosing a spouse. Indeed, "playing the field" was the ideal pursued by many. Dates were not suitors or prospects. Seeing different people on successive nights in a hectic round of dating activity earned one popularity among peers. One of the early students and critics of the dating culture, Willard Waller, coined the term "rating and dating complex" to refer to this pattern. After observing dating among students at Pennsylvania State University in the 1930s, Waller charged that concern for impressing friends and gaining status on campus led to superficial thrill-seeking and competition for popularity, and eliminated genuine romance or sincere communication. However, Waller has been accused of both stereotyping and exaggerating the influence of this pattern. Dating was not always so exploitative and superficial as he charged.

Dating was never viewed as an endless stage or an alternative to courtship. Even if dates were initially seen as quite separate from mate selection, they were always viewed as only the first step in a progression that would lead to marriage. By the 1930s, the stage of "going steady" was clearly recognized, entailing a commitment by both partners to date each other exclusively, if only for the moment. A variety of ritual markers emerged to symbolize the increased commitment of this stage and of further steps toward engagement and marriage, such as wearing the partner's high school ring, being lavaliered, and getting pinned.

Going steady was a way-station between casual dating and engagement. Steadies pledged not to date others, and they were likely to become more deeply involved romantically and physically than casual daters. They were not expected explicitly to contemplate marriage, and the majority of women in our Detroit survey had several steady boyfriends before the relationships that led to their marriages. If a couple was of a "suitable age," though, and if the steady relationship lasted more than a few months, the likelihood increased of explicit talk about marriage. Couples would then symbolize their escalated commitment by getting engaged. Dating arose first among middle and upper middle class students in urban areas, and roughly

simultaneously at the college and high school levels. The practice then spread to other groups—rural young people, working-class youths, to the upper class, and to employed young people. But what triggered the rapid demise of calling and the rise of dating?

One important trend was prolonged school attendance, particularly in public, co-educational high schools and colleges. Schools provided an arena in which females and males could get to know one another informally over many years. Schools also organized athletic, social, and other activities in which adult supervision was minimal. College campuses generally allowed a more total escape from parental supervision than high schools.

Another important influence was growing affluence in America. More and more young people were freed from a need to contribute to the family economy and had more leisure time in which to date. Fewer young people worked under parental supervision, and more and more fathers worked far from home, leaving mothers as the primary monitors of their children's daily activities. These trends also coincided with a rise in part-time and after-school employment for students, employment that provided pocket money that did not have to be turned over to parents and could be spent on clothing, makeup, movie tickets, and other requirements of the dating culture. Rising affluence also fueled the growth of entire new industries designed to entertain and fill leisure time—movies, popular music recording, ice cream parlors, amusement parks, and so on. Increasingly, young people who wanted to escape from supervision of their parents found a range of venues, many of them catering primarily to youth and to dating activities.

Technology also played a role, and some analysts suggest that one particular invention, the automobile, deserves a lion's share of the credit. Automobiles were not only a means to escape the home and reach a wider range of recreation spots. They also provided a semiprivate space with abundant romantic and sexual possibilities. New institutions, such as the drive-in movie theater, arose to take advantage of those possibilities. As decades passed and affluence increased, the borrowed family car was more and more replaced by cars owned by young people, advancing youth autonomy still further.

All this was part of a larger trend: the transformation of America into a mass consumption society. As this happened, people shifted their attention partially from thinking about how to work and earn to pondering how to spend and consume. Marketplace thinking became more and more influential. The image of the individual as *homo economicus* and of modern life typified by the rational application of scientific knowledge to all decisions became pervasive. The new ideological framework undermined previous customs and moral standards and extended to the dating culture.

Dating had several goals. Most obviously and explicitly, dates were expected to lead to pleasure and possibly to romance. It was also important, as Waller and others have observed, in competition for popularity. But a central purpose of dating was to gain valuable learning experience that would be useful later in selecting a spouse. Through dating, young people would learn how to relate to the opposite sex. Dating would increase awareness of

one's own feelings and understanding of which type of partner was appealing and which not. Through crushes and disappointments, one would learn to judge the character of people. And by dating a variety of partners and by increasingly intimate involvement with some of them, one would learn what sort of person one would be happy with as a marital partner. When it came time to marry, one would be in a good position to select "Mr. Right" or "Miss Right." Calling, which limited the possibilities of romantic experimentation, often to only one partner, did not provide an adequate basis for such an informed choice.

What emerged was a "marketplace learning viewpoint." Selecting a spouse is not quite the same as buying a car or breakfast cereal, but the process was seen as analogous. The assumptions involved in shopping around and test driving various cars or buying and tasting Wheaties, Cheerios, and Fruit Loops were transferred to popular thinking about how to select a spouse.

According to this marketplace learning viewpoint, getting married very young and without having acquired much dating experience was risky, in terms of marital happiness. Similarly, marrying your first and only sweetheart was not a good idea. Neither was meeting someone, falling head over heels in love, and marrying, all within the course of a month. While Americans recognized that in some cases such beginnings could lead to good marriages, the rationale of our dating culture was that having had a variety of dating partners and then getting to know one or more serious prospects over a longer period of time and on fairly intimate terms were experiences more likely to lead to marital success.

Eventually, this marketplace psychology helped to undermine America's premarital puritanism, and with it the sexual double standard. The way was paved for acceptance of new customs, and particularly for premarital cohabitation. Parents and other moral guardians found it increasingly difficult to argue against the premise that, if sexual enjoyment and compatibility were central to marital happiness, it was important to test that compatibility before marrying. Similarly, if marriage involved not just hearts and flowers, but also dirty laundry and keeping a budget, did it not make sense for a couple to live together prior to marriage to see how they got along on a day-to-day basis? Such arguments on behalf of premarital sex and cohabitation have swept into popular consciousness in the United States, and it is obvious that they are logical corollaries of the marketplace learning viewpoint.

Our dating culture thus is based upon the premise that dating provides valuable experience that will help individuals select mates and achieve happy marriages. But is this premise correct? Does dating really work? What evidence shows that individuals with longer dating experience, dates with more partners, or longer and more intimate acquaintances with the individuals they intend to marry end up with happier marriages? Surprisingly, social scientists have never systematically addressed this question. Perhaps this is one of those cherished beliefs people would prefer not to examine too closely. When I could find little evidence on the connection between dating and other premarital experiences and marital success in previous studies, I decided to conduct my own inquiry.

My desire to know whether dating experiences affected marriages was the basis for my 1984 survey in the Detroit area. A representative sample of 459 women was interviewed in three counties in the Detroit metropolitan area (a diverse, multi-racial and multi-ethnic area of city and suburbs containing about 4 million people in 1980). The women ranged in ages from 18 to 75, and all had been married at least once. (I was unable to interview their husbands, so unfortunately marriages in this study are viewed only through the eyes of women.) The interviewees had first married over a sixty-year span of time, between 1925 and 1984. They were asked to recall a variety of things about their dating and premarital experiences. They were also asked a range of questions about their marital histories and (if currently married) about the positive and negative features of their relations with their husbands. The questionnaire enabled us to test whether premarital experiences of various types were related to marital success, a concept which in turn was measured in several different ways. (Measures of divorce and of both positive and negative qualities in intact marriages were used.)

The conclusions were a surprise. It appears that dating does not work and that the "marketplace learning viewpoint" is misguided. Marrying very young tended to produce unsuccessful marriages. Premarital pregnancy was associated with problems in marriage. However, once the age of marriage is taken into account, none of the other measures—dating variety, length of dating, length of courtship or engagement, or degree of premarital intimacy with the future husband or others—was clearly related to measures of marital success. A few weak tendencies in the results were contrary to predictions drawn from the marketplace learning viewpoint. Women who had dated more partners or who had engaged in premarital sex or cohabited were slightly less likely to have successful marriages. This might be seen as evidence of quite a different logic.

Perhaps there is a "grass is greener" effect. Women who have led less sheltered and conventional lives prior to marriage may not be as easily satisfied afterward. Several other researchers have found a similar pattern with regard to premarital cohabitation. Individuals who had been living together prior to marriage were significantly less likely to have successful marriages than those who did not.

In the Detroit survey, these "grass is greener" patterns were not consistent or statistically significant. It was not that women with more dating experience and greater premarital intimacy had less successful marriages; rather, the amount and type of dating experience did not make a clear difference one way or the other.

Women who had married their first sweethearts were just as likely to have enduring and satisfying marriages as women who had married only after considering many alternatives. Similarly, women who had married after only a brief acquaintance were no more (nor less) likely to have a successful marriage than those who knew their husbands-to-be for years. And there was no clear difference between the marriages of women who were virgins at marriage and those who had had a variety of sexual partners and who had lived together with their husbands before the wedding.

Dating obviously does not provide useful learning that promotes marital success. Although our dating culture is based upon an analogy with consumer purchases in the marketplace, it is clear that in real life selecting a spouse is quite different from buying a car or breakfast cereal. You cannot actively consider several prospects at the same time without getting your neck broken and being deserted by all of them. Even if you find Ms. Right or Mr. Right, you may be told to drop dead. By the time you are ready to marry, this special someone you were involved with earlier may no longer be available, and you may not see anyone on the horizon who comes close to being as desirable. In addition, someone who is well suited at marriage may grow apart from you or find someone else to be with later. Dating experience might facilitate marital success if deciding whom to marry was like deciding what to eat for breakfast (although even in the latter regard tastes change, and toast and black coffee may replace bacon and eggs). But these realms are quite different, and mate selection looks more like a crap-shoot than a rational choice.

Is there a better way? Traditionalists in some societies would argue that arranged marriages are preferable. However, in addition to the improbability that America's young people will leave this decision to their parents, there is the problem of evidence. The few studies of this topic, including one I have been collaborating on in China, indicate that women who had arranged marriages were less satisfied than women who made the choice themselves. So having Mom and Dad take charge is not the answer. Turning the matter over to computerized matchmaking also does not seem advisable. Despite the growing sophistication of computers, real intelligence seems preferable to artificial intelligence. As the Tin Woodman in *The Wizard of Oz* discovered, to have a brain but no heart is to be missing something important.

Perhaps dating is evolving into new patterns in which premarital experience will contribute to marital success. Critics from Waller onward have claimed that dating promotes artificiality, rather than realistic assessment of compatibility. Some observers suggest that the sort of superficial dating Waller and others wrote about has become less common of late. Dating certainly has changed significantly since the pre–Second World War era. Many of the rigid rules of dating have broken down. The male no longer always takes the initiative; neither does he always pay. The sexual double standard has also weakened substantially, so that increasingly Americans feel that whatever a man can do a woman should be able to do. Some writers even suggest that dating is going out of style, replaced by informal pairing off in larger groups, often without the prearrangement of "asking someone out." Certainly the terminology is changing, with "seeing" and "being with" increasingly preferred to "dating" and "going steady." To many young people the latter terms have the old-fashioned ring that "courting" and "suitor" had when I was young.

My daughter and other young adults argue that current styles are more natural and healthier than the dating experienced by my generation and the generation of my parents. Implicit in this argument is the view that, with formal rules and the "rating and dating" complex in decline, it should be

possible to use dating (or whatever you call it) to realistically assess compatibility and romantic chemistry. These arguments may seem plausible, but I see no evidence that bears them out. The youngest women we interviewed in the Detroit survey should have experienced these more informal styles of romantic exploration. However, for them dating and premarital intimacy were, if anything, less closely related to marital success than was the case for the older women. The changes in premarital relations do not seem to make experience a better teacher.

While these conclusions are for the most part quite negative, my study leads to two more positive observations. First, marital success is not totally unpredictable. A wide range of features of how couples structure their day-to-day marital relations promote success—sharing in power and decision-making, pooling incomes, enjoying similar leisure-time activities, having similar values, having mutual friends and an active social life, and other related qualities. Couples are not "doomed" by their past histories, including their dating histories, and they can increase their mutual happiness through the way they structure their marriages.

Second, there is something else about premarital experience besides dating history that may promote marital success. We have in America not one, but two widely shared, but quite contradictory, theories about how individuals should select a spouse: one based on the marketplace learning viewpoint and another based on love. One viewpoint sees selecting a spouse as a rational process, perhaps even with lists of criteria by which various prospects can be judged. The other, as songwriters tell us, is based on the view that love conquers all and that "all you need is love." Love is a matter of the heart (perhaps with some help from the hormonal system) and not the head, and love may blossom unpredictably, on short notice or more gradually. Might it not be the case, then, that those couples who are most deeply in love at the time of their weddings will have the most successful marriages? We have centuries of poetry and novels, as well as love songs, that tell us that this is the case.

In the Detroit study, we did, in fact, ask women how much they had been in love when they first married. And we did find that those who recalled being "head over heels in love" then, had more successful marriages. However, there is a major problem with this finding. Since we were asking our interviewees to recall their feelings prior to their weddings—in many cases weddings took place years or even decades earlier—it is quite possible and even likely that these answers are biased. Perhaps whether or not their marriage worked out influenced these "love reports" from earlier times, rather than having the level of romantic love then explain marital success later. Without either a time machine or funds to interview couples prior to marriage and then follow them up years later, it is impossible to be sure that more intense feelings of love lead to more successful marriages. Still, the evidence available does not question the wisdom of poets and songwriters when it comes to love. Mate selection may not be a total crap-shoot after all, and even if dating does not work, love perhaps does.

REFERENCES

Bailey, Beth. 1988. *From Front Porch to Back Seat.* Baltimore: Johns Hopkins University Press.

Burgess, Ernest W. and Paul Wallin. 1953. *Engagement and Marriage.* Chicago: Lippincott.

Modell, John. 1983. "Dating Becomes the Way of American Youth." In *Essays on the Family and Historical Change,* edited by Leslie P. Moch and Gary Stark. College Station: Texas A&M University Press.

Rothman, Ellen K. 1984. *Hands and Hearts: A History of Courtship.* New York: Basic Books.

Smith, Daniel S. and Michael Hindus. 1975. "Premarital Pregnancy in America, 1640–1971: An Overview and Interpretation." *Journal of Interdisciplinary History* 4:537–70.

Waller, Willard. 1937. "Rating and Dating Complex." *American Sociological Review* 2:737–39.

Whyte, Martin King. 1990. *Dating, Mating, and Marriage.* New York: Aldine de Gruyter.

11

GENDERED SEXUALITY IN YOUNG ADULTHOOD
Double Binds and Flawed Options

LAURA HAMILTON • ELIZABETH A. ARMSTRONG

As traditional dating has declined on college campuses, hookups—casual sexual encounters often initiated at alcohol-fueled, dance-oriented social events—have become a primary form of intimate heterosexual interaction (England, Shafer, and Fogarty 2007; Paul, McManus, and Hayes 2000). Hookups have attracted attention among social scientists and journalists (Bogle 2008; Glenn and Marquardt 2001; Stepp 2007). To date, however, limitations of both data and theory have obscured the implications for women and the gender system. Most studies examine only the quality of hookups at one point during college and rely, if implicitly, on an individualist, gender-only approach. In contrast, we follow a group of women as they move through college—assessing all of their sexual experiences. We use an interactionist approach and attend to how both gender and class shape college sexuality. Our analyses offer a new interpretation of this important issue, contribute to gender theory, and demonstrate how to conduct an interactionist, intersectional analysis of young adult sexuality.

Gender Theory and College Sexuality

Research on Hooking Up

Paul, McManus, and Hayes (2000) and Glenn and Marquardt (2001) were the first to draw attention to the hookup as a distinct social form. As Glenn and Marquardt (2001:13) explain, most students agree that "a hook up is any-thing 'ranging from kissing to having sex,' and that it takes place outside the context of commitment." Others have similarly found that *hooking up* refers to a broad range of sexual activity and that this ambiguity is part of the appeal of the term (Bogle 2008). Hookups differ from dates in that individu-als typically do not plan to do something together prior to sexual activity. Rather, two people hanging out at a party, bar, or place of residence will begin talking, flirting, and/or dancing. Typically, they have been drinking. At some point, they move to a more private location, where sexual activity occurs (England et al. 2007). While strangers sometimes hook up, more often hookups occur among those who know each other at least slightly (Manning, Giordano, and Longmore 2006).

England has surveyed more than 14,000 students from 19 universities and colleges about their hookup, dating, and relationship experiences. Her Online College Social Life Survey (OCSLS) asks students to report on their recent hookups using "whatever definition of a hookup you and your friends use." Seventy-two percent of both men and women participating in the OCSLS reported at least one hookup by their senior year in college. Of these, roughly 40 percent engaged in three or fewer hookups, 40 percent between four and nine hookups, and 20 percent 10 or more hookups. Only about one-third engaged in intercourse in their most recent hookups, although—among the 80 percent of students who had intercourse by the end of college— 67 percent had done so outside of a relationship.

Ongoing sexual relationships without commitment were common and were labeled "repeat," "regular," or "continuing" hookups and sometimes "friends with benefits" (Armstrong, England, and Fogarty 2009; Bogle 2008; Glenn and Marquardt 2001). Ongoing hookups sometimes became committed relationships and vice versa; generally, the distinction revolved around the level of exclusivity and a willingness to refer to each other as "girlfriend/boyfriend" (Armstrong et al. 2009). Thus, hooking up does not imply interest in a relationship, but it does not preclude such interest. Rela-tionships are also common among students. By their senior year, 69 percent of heterosexual students had been in a college relationship of at least six months.

To date, however, scholars have paid more attention to women's experi-ences with hooking up than relationships and focused primarily on ways that hookups may be less enjoyable for women than for men. Glenn and Marquardt (2001:20) indicate that "hooking up is an activity that women sometimes find rewarding but more often find confusing, hurtful, and awk-ward." Others similarly suggest that more women than men find hooking up to be a negative experience (Bogle 2008:173; Owen et al. 2008) and focus

on ways that hookups may be harmful to women (Eshbaugh and Gute 2008; Grello, Welsh, and Harper 2006).

This work assumes distinct and durable gender differences at the individual level. Authors draw, if implicitly, from evolutionary psychology, socialization, and psychoanalytic approaches to gender—depicting women as more relationally oriented and men as more sexually adventurous. For example, despite only asking about hookup experiences, Bogle (2008:173) describes a "battle of the sexes" in which women want hookups to "evolve into some semblance of a relationship," while men prefer to "hook up with no strings attached."

The battle of the sexes view implies that if women could simply extract commitment from men rather than participating in hookups, gender inequalities in college sexuality would be alleviated. Yet this research—which often fails to examine relationships—ignores the possibility that women might be the losers in both hookups and relationships. Research suggests that young heterosexual women often suffer the most damage from those with whom they are most intimate: Physical battery, emotional abuse, sexual assault, and stalking occur at high rates in youthful heterosexual relationships (Campbell et al. 2007; Dunn 1999). This suggests that gender inequality in college sexuality is systemic, existing across social forms.

Current research also tends to see hooking up as solely about gender, without fully considering the significance of other dimensions of inequality. Some scholars highlight the importance of the college environment and traditional college students' position in the life course (Bogle 2008; Glenn and Marquardt 2001). However, college is treated primarily as a context for individual sexual behavior rather than as a key location for class reproduction. Analyzing the role of social class in sex and relationships may help to illuminate the appeal of hookups for both college women and men.

Gender Beliefs and Social Interaction

Contemporary gender theory provides us with resources to think about gender inequality in college sexuality differently. Gender scholars have developed and refined the notion of gender as a social structure reproduced at multiple levels of society: Gender is embedded not only in individual selves but also in interaction and organizational arrangements (Connell 1987; Glenn 1999; Risman 2004). This [reading] focuses on the interactional level, attending to the power of public gender beliefs in organizing college sexual and romantic relations. . . .

The notion that men and women have distinct sexual interests and needs generates a powerful set of public gender beliefs about women's sexuality. A belief about what women should not do underlies a *sexual double standard:* While men are expected to desire and pursue sexual opportunities regardless of context, women are expected to avoid casual sex—having sex only when in relationships and in love (Crawford and Popp 2003; Risman and Schwartz 2002). Much research on the sexuality of young men focuses on male endorsement of this belief and its consequences (e.g., Bogle 2008; Kimmel 2008;

Martin and Hummer 1989). There is an accompanying and equally powerful belief that normal women should always want love, romance, relationships, and marriage—what we refer to as the *relational imperative* (also see Holland and Eisenhart 1990; Simon, Eder, and Evans 1992). We argue that these twin beliefs are implicated in the (re)production of gender inequality in college sexuality and are at the heart of women's sexual dilemmas with both hook-ups and relationships.

An Intersectional Approach

Gender theory has also moved toward an intersectional approach (Collins 1990; Glenn 1999). Most of this work focuses on the lived experiences of marginalized individuals who are situated at the intersection of several systems of oppression (McCall 2005). More recently, scholars have begun to theorize the ways in which systems of inequality are themselves linked. Beisel and Kay (2004) apply Sewell's (1992) theory of structure to intersectionality, arguing that structures intersect when they share resources or guidelines for action (of which gender beliefs would be one example). Using a similar logic, we argue that gender and class intersect in the sexual arena, as these structures both rely on beliefs about how and with whom individuals should be intimate.

Like gender, class structures beliefs about appropriate sexual and romantic conduct. Privileged young Americans, both men and women, are now expected to defer family formation until the mid-twenties or even early-thirties to focus on education and career investment—what we call the *self-development imperative* (Arnett 2004; Rosenfeld 2007). This imperative makes committed relationships less feasible as the sole contexts for premarital sexuality. Like marriage, relationships can be "greedy," siphoning time and energy away from self-development (Gerstel and Sarkisian 2006; Glenn and Marquardt 2001). In contrast, hookups offer sexual pleasure without derailing investment in human capital and are increasingly viewed as part of life-stage-appropriate sexual experimentation. Self-protection—both physical and emotional—is central to this logic, suggesting the rise of a strategic approach to sex and relationships (Brooks 2002; Illouz 2005). This approach is reflected in the development of erotic marketplaces offering short-term sexual partners, particularly on college campuses (Collins 2004).

In this case, gender and class behavioral rules are in conflict. Gender beliefs suggest that young women should avoid nonromantic sex and, if possible, be in a committed relationship. Class beliefs suggest that women should delay relationships while pursuing educational goals. Hookups are often less threatening to self-development projects, offering sexual activity in a way that better meshes with the demands of college. We see this as a case wherein structures intersect, but in a contradictory way (Friedland and Alford 1991; Sewell 1992). This structural contradiction has experiential consequences: Privileged women find themselves caught between contradictory expectations, while less privileged women confront a foreign sexual culture when they enter college.

After discussing the research design and data, we show how women's experiences are shaped by gender beliefs. We then develop an intersectional analysis of college hookups and relationships, including a discussion of how the experiences of less privileged women differ from those with more class privilege. Finally, we highlight the power of our interactional and intersectional perspective and outline some directions for future research.

Method

The strength of our research strategy lies in its depth: We conducted a longitudinal ethnographic and interview study of a group of women who started college in 2004 at a university in the Midwest, collecting data about their entire sexual and romantic careers. Like McCall (2005), we see an "intercategorical" approach to intersectionality as ideal; however, space and data limitations prevent us from theorizing structural intersection along all axes of inequality and analyzing the experiences of all of the various possible locations in relation to these structures. However, the richness of our data allows us to reveal taken-for-granted gender and class beliefs organizing the college sexual arena. While the data are at the individual level, our goal is to illustrate how the intersection of gender and class as structures creates dilemmas for college women.

Ethnography and Longitudinal Interviews

A research team of nine, including the authors, occupied a room on an all-female floor in a mixed-gender dormitory. When data collection commenced, Laura was a graduate student in her early twenties and Elizabeth an assistant professor in her late thirties. The team also included a male graduate student, an undergraduate sorority member, and an undergraduate with working-class roots. Variation in age, approach, and self-presentation among team members allowed for different relationships with participants and brought multiple perspectives to data analysis—strengths of team ethnography (Erickson and Stull 1998).

Fifty-three 18- to 20-year-old unmarried women (51 freshmen, two sophomores) lived on the floor for at least part of the year. No one opted out of the ethnographic study. All but two identified as heterosexual. All participants were white, a result of low racial diversity on campus overall and racial segregation in campus housing. Sixty-eight percent came from middle-, upper-middle-, or upper-class backgrounds; 32 percent came from working- or lower-middle-class backgrounds. Forty-five percent were from out of state; all of these women were from upper-middle-class or upper-class families. Thirty-six percent, mostly wealthier women, joined sororities in their first year.

Assessment of class background was based on parental education and occupation, student employment during the school year, and receipt of student loans. We refer to those from middle-, upper-middle-, or upper-class

backgrounds as "more privileged" and those from working- or lower-middle-class backgrounds as "less privileged." There were distinct differences between women in these groups. Less privileged women did not have parents with college degrees and struggled to afford college. In contrast, more privileged women had at least one, and more often two, parents with degrees. They received a great deal of parental support, keeping their loans to a minimum and allowing most to avoid working during the year.

The residence hall in which they lived was identified by students and staff as one of several "party dorms." The term refers to the presumed social orientation of the modal resident, not to partying within the dorm itself. Students reported that they requested these dormitories if they were interested in drinking, hooking up, and joining the Greek system. This orientation places them in the thick of American youth culture. Few identified as feminist, and all presented a traditionally feminine appearance (e.g., not one woman had hair shorter than chin length). Most planned to marry and have children. . . .

We conducted interviews with 41 of the 53 women on the floor during their first year, 37 the following year, 35 when they were juniors (two were seniors), and 43 when they were seniors (one had graduated, and one was a fifth-year senior). Forty-six (87 percent) women were interviewed, producing 156 interviews. Most interviews were conducted by Laura, who forged strong ties with a number of the women. Interviews ranged from 45 minutes to two and a half hours and covered partying, sexuality, relationships, friendships, classes, employment, religion, and relationships with parents. This holistic approach enabled us to see how sexual and romantic interactions intersected with the rest of the women's lives. In collecting data over time, we saw women move back and forth among hookups and relationships—expressing dissatisfaction with both. . . .

The Power of Gender Beliefs

A battle of the sexes approach suggests that women have internalized a relational orientation but are unable to establish relationships because hooking up—which men prefer—has come to dominate college sexual culture. Rather than accepting stated individual-level preferences at face value, we focus on the interactional contexts in which preferences are formed and expressed. We show that gender beliefs about what women should and should not do posed problems for our participants in both hookups and relationships.

The "Slut" Stigma

Women did not find hookups to be unproblematic. They complained about a pervasive sexual double standard. As one explained, "Guys can have sex with all the girls and *it makes them more of a man*, but if a girl does then all of a sudden she's a ho, and she's not as quality of a person." Another complained, "Guys, they can go around and have sex with a number of girls

and they're not called anything." Women noted that it was "easy to get a reputation" from "hooking up with a bunch of different guys" or "being wild and drinking too much." Their experiences of being judged were often painful; one woman told us about being called a "slut" two years after the incident because it was so humiliating.

Fear of stigma constrained women's sexual behavior and perhaps even shape their preferences. For example, several indicated that they probably would "make out with more guys" but did not because "I don't want to be a slut." Others wanted to have intercourse on hookups but instead waited until they had boyfriends. A couple hid their sexual activity until the liaison was "official." One said, "I would not spend the night there [at the fraternity] because that does not look good, but now everyone knows we're boyfriend/ girlfriend, so it's like my home now." Another woman, who initially seemed to have a deep aversion to hooking up, explained, "I would rather be a virgin for as much as I can than go out and do God knows who." She later revealed a fear of social stigma, noting that when women engage in nonromantic sex, they "get a bad reputation. I know that I wouldn't want that reputation." Her comments highlight the feedback between social judgment and internalized preference.

Gender beliefs were also at the root of women's other chief complaint about hookups—the disrespect of women in the hookup scene. The notion that hooking up is okay for men but not for women was embedded in the organization of the Greek system, where most parties occurred: Sorority rules prohibited hosting parties or overnight male visitors, reflecting notions about proper feminine behavior. In contrast, fraternities collected social fees to pay for alcohol and viewed hosting parties as a central activity. This disparity gave fraternity men almost complete control over the most desirable parties on campus—particularly for the underage crowd (Boswell and Spade 1996; Martin and Hummer 1989).

Women reported that fraternity men dictated party transportation, the admittance of guests, party themes such as "CEO and secretary ho," the flow of alcohol, and the movement of guests within the party (Armstrong, Hamilton, and Sweeney 2006). Women often indicated that they engaged in strategies such as "travel[ing] in hordes" and not "tak[ing] a drink if I don't know where it came from" to feel safer at fraternity parties. . . . Even those interested in the erotic competition of party scenes tired of it as they realized that the game was rigged.

The sexual double standard also justified the negative treatment of women in the party scene—regardless of whether they chose to hook up. Women explained that men at parties showed a lack of respect for their feelings or interests—treating them solely as "sex objects." This disregard extended to hookups. One told us, "The guy gets off and then it's done and that's all he cares about." Another complained of her efforts to get a recent hookup to call: "That wasn't me implying I wanted a relationship—that was me implying I wanted respect." In her view, casual sex did not mean forgoing all interactional niceties. A third explained, "If you're talking to a boy, you're either going to get into this huge relationship or you are nothing

to them." This either-or situation often frustrated women who wanted men to treat them well regardless of the level of commitment.

The Relationship Imperative

Women also encountered problematic gender beliefs about men's and women's different levels of interest in relationships. As one noted, women fight the "dumb girl idea"—the notion "that every girl wants a boy to sweep her off her feet and fall in love." The expectation that women should want to be in relationships was so pervasive that many found it necessary to justify their single status to us. For example, when asked if she had a boyfriend, one woman with no shortage of admirers apologetically explained, "I know this sounds really pathetic and you probably think I am lying, but there are so many other things going on right now that it's really not something high up on my list. . . . I know that's such a lame-ass excuse, but it's true." Another noted that already having a boyfriend was the only "actual, legitimate excuse" to reject men who expressed interest in a relationship.

Certainly, many women wanted relationships and sought them out. However, women's interest in relationships varied, and almost all experienced periods during which they wanted to be single. Nonetheless, women reported pressure to be in relationships all the time. We found that women, rather than struggling to get into relationships, had to work to avoid them.

The relational imperative was supported by the belief that women's relational opportunities were scarce and should not be wasted. Women described themselves as "lucky" to find a man willing to commit, as "there's not many guys like that in college." This belief persisted despite the fact that most women were in relationships most of the time. As one woman noted, "I don't think anyone really wants to be in a serious relationship, but most, well actually all of us, have boyfriends." Belief in the myth of scarcity also led women to stay in relationships when they were no longer happy. A woman who was "sick of" her conflict-ridden relationship explained why she could not end it: "I feel like I have to meet somebody else. . . . I go out and they're all these asshole frat guys. . . . That's what stops me. . . . Boys are not datable right now because . . . all they're looking for is freshman girls to hook up with. . . . [So] I'm just stuck. I need to do something about it, but I don't know what." It took her another year to extract herself from this relationship. Despite her fears, when she decided she was ready for another relationship, she quickly found a boyfriend. . . .

Gender beliefs may also limit women's control over the terms of interaction within relationships. If women are made to feel lucky to have boyfriends, men are placed in a position of power, as presumably women should be grateful when they commit. Women's reports suggest that men attempted to use this power to regulate their participation in college life. One noted, "When I got here my first semester freshman year, I wanted to go out to the parties . . . and he got pissed off about it. . . . He's like, 'Why do you need to do that? Why can't you just stay with me?'" Boyfriends sometimes tried to limit the time women spent with their friends and the activities in which

they participated. As a woman explained, "There are times when I feel like Steve can get . . . possessive. He'll be like . . . 'I feel like you're always with your friends over me.' He wanted to go out to lunch after our class, and I was like, 'No, I have to come have this interview.' And he got so upset about it." Men's control even extended to women's attire. Another told us about her boyfriend, "He is a very controlling person. . . . He's like, 'What are you wearing tonight?' . . . It's like a joke but serious at the same time." . . .

When women attempted to end relationships, they often reported that men's efforts to control them escalated. We heard 10 accounts of men using abuse to keep women in relationships. One woman spent months dealing with a boyfriend who accused her of cheating on him. When she tried to break up, he cut his wrist in her apartment. Another tried to end a relationship but was forced to flee the state when her car windows were broken and her safety was threatened. Men often drew on romantic repertoires to coerce interaction after relationships had ended. One woman told us that her ex-boyfriend stalked her for months—even showing up at her workplace, showering her with flowers and gifts, and blocking her entry into work until the police arrived.

Intersectionality: Contradictions Between Class and Gender

Existing research about college sexuality focuses almost exclusively on its gendered nature. We contend that sexuality is shaped simultaneously by multiple intersecting structures. In this section, we examine the sexual and romantic implications of class beliefs about how ambitious young people should conduct themselves during college. Although all of our participants contended with class beliefs that contradicted those of gender, experiences of this structural intersection varied by class location. More privileged women struggled to meet gender and class guidelines for sexual behavior, introducing a difficult set of double binds. Because these class beliefs reflected a privileged path to adulthood, less privileged women found them foreign to their own sexual and romantic logics.

More Privileged Women and the Experience of Double Binds

The Self-development Imperative and the Relational Double Bind The four-year university is a classed structural location. One of the primary reasons to attend college is to preserve or enhance economic position. The university culture is thus characterized by the self-development imperative, or the notion that individual achievement and personal growth are paramount. There are also accompanying rules for sex and relationships: Students are expected to postpone marriage and parenthood until after completing an education and establishing a career.

For more privileged women, personal expectations and those of the university culture meshed. Even those who enjoyed relationships experienced phases in college where they preferred to remain single. Almost all privileged

women (94 percent) told us at one point that they did not want a boyfriend. One noted, "All my friends here . . . they're like, 'I don't want to deal with [a boyfriend] right now. I want to be on my own.'" Another eloquently remarked, "I've always looked at college as the only time in your life when you should be a hundred percent selfish. . . . I have the rest of my life to devote to a husband or kids or my job . . . but right now, it's my time.". . .

More privileged women often found committed relationships to be greedy—demanding of time and energy. As one stated, "When it comes to a serious relationship, it's a lot for me to give into that. [What do you feel like you are giving up?] Like my everything. . . . There's just a lot involved in it." These women feared that they would be devoured by relationships and sometimes struggled to keep their self-development projects going when they did get involved. As an upper-class woman told us, "It's hard to have a boyfriend and be really excited about it and still not let it consume you." This situation was exacerbated by the gender beliefs discussed earlier, as women experienced pressure to fully devote themselves to relationships.

Privileged women reported that committed relationships detracted from what they saw as the main tasks of college. They complained, for example, that relationships made it difficult to meet people. As an upper-middle-class woman who had just ended a relationship described, "I'm happy that I'm able to go out and meet new people. . . . I feel like I'm doing what a college student should be doing. I don't need to be tied down to my high school boyfriend for two years when this is the time to be meeting people." A middle-class woman similarly noted that her relationship with her boyfriend made it impossible to make friends on the floor her first year. She explained, "We were together every day. . . . It was the critical time of making friends and meeting people, [and] I wasn't there." Many also complained that committed relationships competed with schoolwork (also see Holland and Eisenhart 1990). An upper-middle-class woman remarked, "[My boyfriend] doesn't understand why I can't pick up and go see him all the time. But I have school. . . . I just want to be a college kid.". . .

For more privileged women, contradictory cultural rules created what we call the *relational double bind*. The relational imperative pushed them to participate in committed relationships; however, relationships did not mesh well with the demands of college, as they inhibited classed self-development strategies. Privileged women struggled to be both "good girls" who limited their sexual activity to relationships and "good students" who did not allow relational commitments to derail their educational and career development.

The Appeal of Hookups and the Sexual Double Bind In contrast, hookups fit well with the self-development imperative of college. They allowed women to be sexual without the demands of relationships. For example, one upper-class woman described hooking up as "fun and nonthreatening." She noted, "So many of us girls, we complain that these guys just want to hook up all the time. I'm going, these guys that I'm attracted to . . . get kind of serious." She saw her last hookup as ideal because "we were physical, and that was it. I never wanted it to go anywhere." Many privileged women understood, if

implicitly, that hooking up was a delay tactic, allowing sex without participation in serious relationships.

As a sexual solution for the demands of college, hooking up became incorporated into notions of what the college experience should be. When asked which kinds of people hook up the most, one woman noted, "All . . . the people who came to college to have a good time and party." With the help of media, alcohol, and spring break industries, hooking up was so institutionalized that many took it for granted. One upper-middle-class woman said, "It just happens. It's natural." They told us that learning about sexuality was something they were supposed to be doing in college. Another described, "I'm glad that I've had my one-night stands and my being in love and having sex. . . . Now I know what it's supposed to feel like when I'm with someone that I want to be with. I feel bad for some of my friends. . . . They're still virgins."

High rates of hooking up suggest genuine interest in the activity rather than simply accommodation to men's interests. Particularly early in college, privileged women actively sought hookups. One noted, "You see a lot of people who are like, 'I just want to hook up with someone tonight.'. . . It's always the girls that try to get the guys." Data from the OCSLS also suggest that college women like hooking up almost as much as men and are not always searching for something more. Nearly as many women as men (85 percent and 89 percent, respectively) report enjoying the sexual activity of their last hookup "very much" or "somewhat," and less than half of women report interest in a relationship with their most recent hookup. . . .

Hookups enabled more privileged women to conduct themselves in accordance with class expectations, but as we demonstrated earlier, the enforcement of gender beliefs placed them at risk of sanction. This conflict gets to the heart of a *sexual double bind:* While hookups protected privileged women from relationships that could derail their ambitions, the double standard gave men greater control over the terms of hooking up, justified the disrespectful treatment of women, supported sexual stigma, and produced feelings of shame.

Less Privileged Women and the Experience of Foreign Sexual Culture

Women's comfort with delaying commitment and participating in the hookup culture was shaped by class location. College culture reflects the beliefs of the more privileged classes. Less privileged women arrived at college with their own orientation to sex and romance, characterized by a faster transition into adulthood. They often attempted to build both relationships and career at the same time. As a result, the third of the participants from less privileged backgrounds often experienced the hookup culture as foreign in ways that made it difficult to persist at the university.

Less privileged women had less exposure to the notion that the college years should be set aside solely for educational and career development. Many did not see serious relationships as incompatible with college life.

Four were married or engaged before graduating—a step that others would not take until later. One reminisced, "I thought I'd get married in college. . . . When I was still in high school, I figured by my senior year, I'd be engaged or married or something. . . . I wanted to have kids before I was 25." Another spoke of her plans to marry her high school sweetheart: "I'll be 21 and I know he's the one I want to spend the rest of my life with. . . . Really, I don't want to date anybody else."

Plans to move into adult roles relatively quickly made less privileged women outsiders among their more privileged peers. One working-class woman saw her friendships dissolve as she revealed her desire to marry and have children in the near future. As one of her former friends described,

> *She would always talk about how she couldn't wait to get married and have babies. . . . It was just like, Whoa. I'm 18. . . . Slow down, you know? Then she just crazy dropped out of school and wouldn't contact any of us. . . . The way I see it is that she's from a really small town, and that's what everyone in her town does . . . get married and have babies. That's all she ever wanted to do maybe? . . . I don't know if she was homesick or didn't fit in.*

This account glosses over the extent to which the working-class woman was pushed out of the university—ostracized by her peers for not acclimating to the self-development imperative and, as noted below, to the campus sexual climate. In fact, 40 percent of less privileged women left the university, compared to 5 percent of more privileged women. In all cases, mismatch between the sexual culture of women's hometowns and that of college was a factor in the decision to leave.

Most of the less privileged women found the hookup culture to be not only foreign but hostile. As the working-class woman described above told us,

> *I tried so hard to fit in with what everybody else was doing here. . . . I think one morning I just woke up and realized that this isn't me at all; I don't like the way I am right now. . . . I didn't feel like I was growing up. I felt like I was actually getting younger the way I was trying to act. Growing up to me isn't going out and getting smashed and sleeping around. . . . That to me is immature.*

She emphasized the value of "growing up" in college. Without the desire to postpone adulthood, less privileged women often could not understand the appeal of hooking up. As a lower-middle-class woman noted, "Who would be interested in just meeting somebody and then doing something that night? And then never talking to them again? . . . I'm supposed to do this; I'm supposed to get drunk every weekend. I'm supposed to go to parties every weekend . . . and I'm supposed to enjoy it like everyone else. But it just doesn't appeal to me." She reveals the extent to which hooking up was a normalized part of college life: For those who were not interested in this, college life could be experienced as mystifying, uncomfortable, and alienating.

The self-development imperative was a resource women could use in resisting the gendered pull of relationships. Less privileged women did not have as much access to this resource and were invested in settling down.

Thus, they found it hard to resist the pull back home of local boyfriends, who—unlike the college men they had met—seemed interested in marrying and having children soon. One woman noted after transferring to a branch campus, "I think if I hadn't been connected with [my fiancé], I think I would have been more strongly connected to [the college town], and I think I probably would have stayed." Another described her hometown boyfriend: "He'll be like, 'I want to see you. Come home.' . . . The stress he was putting me under and me being here my first year. I could not take it." The following year, she moved back home. A third explained about her husband, "He wants me at home. . . . He wants to have control over me and . . . to feel like he's the dominant one in the relationship. . . . The fact that I'm going to school and he knows I'm smart and he knows that I'm capable of doing anything that I want . . . it scares him." While she eventually ended this relationship, it cost her an additional semester of school. . . .

Thus, less privileged women were often caught between two sexual cultures. Staying at the university meant abandoning a familiar logic and adopting a privileged one—investing in human capital while delaying the transition to adulthood. As one explained, attending college led her to revise her "whole plan": "Now I'm like, I don't even need to be getting married yet [or] have kids. . . . All of [my brother's] friends, 17- to 20-year-old girls, have their . . . babies, and I'm like, Oh my God. . . . Now I'll be able to do something else for a couple years before I settle down . . . before I worry about kids." These changes in agendas required them to end relationships with men whose life plans diverged from theirs. For some, this also meant cutting ties with hometown friends. One resolute woman, whose friends back home had turned on her, noted, "I'm just sick of it. There's nothing there for me anymore. There's absolutely nothing there."

Discussion

Public gender beliefs are a key source of gender inequality in college heterosexual interaction. They undergird a sexual double standard and a relational imperative that justify the disrespect of women who hook up and the disempowerment of women in relationships—reinforcing male dominance across social forms. Most of the women we studied cycled back and forth between hookups and relationships, in part because they found both to be problematic. These findings indicate that an individualist, battle of the sexes explanation not only is inadequate but may contribute to gender inequality by naturalizing problematic notions of gender difference. . . .

An intersectional approach sheds light on the ambivalent and contradictory nature of many college women's sexual desires. Class beliefs associated with the appropriate timing of marriage clash with resilient gender beliefs—creating difficult double binds for the more privileged women who strive to meet both. In the case of the relational double bind, relationships fit with gender beliefs but pose problems for the classed self-development imperative. As for the sexual double bind, hookups provide sexual activity with

little cost to career development, but a double standard penalizes women for participating. Less privileged women face an even more complex situation: Much of the appeal of hookups derives from their utility as a delay strategy. Women who do not believe that it is desirable to delay marriage may experience the hookup culture as puzzling and immature.

An intersectional approach also suggests that the way young heterosexuals make decisions about sexuality and relationships underlies the reproduction of social class. These choices are part of women's efforts to, as one privileged participant so eloquently put it, "maintain the lifestyle that I've grown up with." Our participants were not well versed in research demonstrating that college-educated women benefit from their own human capital investments, are more likely to marry than less educated women, and are more likely to have a similarly well-credentialed spouse (DiPrete and Buchmann 2006). Nonetheless, most were aware that completing college and delaying marriage until the mid-to-late twenties made economic sense. Nearly all took access to marriage for granted, instead focusing their attention on when and whom they would marry.

The two-pronged strategy of career investment and delay of family formation has so quickly become naturalized that its historical novelty is now invisible. It is based on the consolidation of class, along with heterosexual, privilege: Heterosexual men and women attempt to maximize their own earning power and that of their spouse—a pattern that is reflected in increased levels of educational homogamy (Schwartz and Mare 2005; Sweeney 2002). Consolidation of privilege is made possible by women's greater parity with men in education and the workforce. In this new marital marketplace, a woman's educational credentials and earning potential are more relevant than her premarital sexual activity, assuming she avoids having a child before marriage. Relationship commitments that block educational and career investments, particularly if they foreclose future opportunities to meet men with elite credentials, are a threat to a woman's upward mobility.

The gender implications of the consolidation of privilege are most visible when contrasted with gender specialization—a marital strategy once assumed to be universal. Marriage was thought to be a system of complementary interdependence in which the man specialized in the market and the woman in domesticity (Becker 1991). Men maximized earning power while women accessed these benefits by marrying those with greater educational or career credentials. Gender specialization does not logically demand chastity of women; however, historically it has often been offered for trade in the marital marketplace. When this occurs, women's sexual reputation and economic welfare are linked. Although this connection has long been attenuated in the United States, it still exists. For example, the term "classy" refers simultaneously to wealth and sexual modesty.

As marriage in the United States has become less guided by gender specialization and more by the consolidation of privilege, gender inequality—at least within the marriages of the privileged—may have decreased. At the same time, class inequality may have intensified. The consolidation of privilege increases economic gaps between the affluent who are married to each

other, the less affluent who are also married to each other, and the poor, who are excluded from marriage altogether (also see Edin and Kefalas 2005; Schwartz and Mare 2005; Sweeney 2002). The hookup culture may contribute in a small way to the intensification of class inequality by facilitating the delay necessary for the consolidation of privilege.

REFERENCES

Armstrong, Elizabeth A., Paula England, and Alison C. K. Fogarty. 2009. "Orgasm in College Hook-ups and Relationships." In *Families as They Really Are*, edited by B. Risman. New York: Norton.

Armstrong, Elizabeth A., Laura Hamilton, and Brian Sweeney. 2006. "Sexual Assault on Campus: A Multilevel, Integrative Approach to Party Rape." *Social Problems* 53:483–99.

Arnett, Jeffrey Jensen. 2004. *Emerging Adulthood: The Winding Road from the Late Teens through the Twenties.* New York: Oxford.

Becker, Gary S. 1991. *A Treatise on the Family.* Cambridge, MA: Harvard University Press.

Beisel, Nicola and Tamara Kay. 2004. "Abortion, Race, and Gender in Nineteenth Century America." *American Sociological Review* 69:498–518.

Bogle, Kathleen A. 2008. *Hooking Up: Sex, Dating, and Relationships on Campus.* New York: New York University Press.

Boswell, A. Ayres and Joan Z. Spade. 1996. "Fraternities and Collegiate Rape Culture: Why Are Some Fraternities More Dangerous Places for Women?" *Gender & Society* 10:133–47.

Brooks, David. 2002. "Making It: Love and Success at America's Finest Universities." *The Weekly Standard,* December 23.

Campbell, Jacquelyn C., Nancy Glass, Phyllis W. Sharps, Kathryn Laughon, and Tina Bloom. 2007. "Intimate Partner Homicide." *Trauma, Violence, and Abuse* 8:246–69.

Collins, Patricia Hill. 1990. *Black Feminist Thought: Knowledge, Consciousness, and the Politics of Empowerment.* Boston: Unwin Hyman.

Collins, Randall. 2004. *Interaction Ritual Chains.* Princeton, NJ: Princeton University Press.

Connell, R. W. 1987. *Gender and Power: Society, the Person, and Sexual Politics.* Stanford, CA: Stanford University Press.

Crawford, Mary and Danielle Popp. 2003. "Sexual Double Standards: A Review and Method-ological Critique of Two Decades of Research." *Journal of Sex Research* 40:13–26.

DiPrete, Thomas A. and Claudia Buchmann. 2006. "Gender-specific Trends in the Value of Education and the Emerging Gender Gap in College Completion." *Demography* 43:1–24.

Dunn, Jennifer L. 1999. "What Love Has to Do with It: The Cultural Construction of Emotion and Sorority Women's Responses to Forcible Interaction." *Social Problems* 46:440–59.

Edin, Kathyrn and Maria Kefalas. 2005. *Promises I Can Keep: Why Poor Women Put Motherhood Before Marriage.* Berkeley: University of California Press.

England, Paula, Emily F. Shafer, and Alison C. K. Fogarty. 2007. "Hooking Up and Forming Romantic Relationships on Today's College Campuses." In *The Gendered Society Reader*, edited by Michael Kimmel. New York: Oxford University Press.

Erickson, Kenneth C. and Donald Stull. 1998. *Doing Team Ethnography: Warnings and Advice.* Thousand Oaks, CA: Sage.

Eshbaugh, Elaine M. and Gary Gute. 2008. "Hookups and Sexual Regret among College Women." *Journal of Social Psychology* 148:77–89.

Friedland, Roger and Robert R. Alford. 1991. "Bringing Society Back In: Symbols, Practices, and Institutional Contradictions." Pp. 232–63 in *The New Institutionalism in Organizational Analysis,* edited by W. W. Powell and P. J. DiMaggio. Chicago: University of Chicago Press.

Gerstel, Naomi and Natalia Sarkisian. 2006. "Marriage: The Good, the Bad, and the Greedy." *Contexts* 5:16–21.

Glenn, Evelyn Nakano. 1999. "The Social Construction and Institutionalization of Gender and Race: An Integrative Framework." Pp. 3–43 in *Revisioning Gender,* edited by M. M. Ferree, J. Lorber, and B. B. Hess. Thousand Oaks, CA: Sage.

Glenn, Norval and Elizabeth Marquardt. 2001. *Hooking Up, Hanging Out, and Hoping for Mr. Right: College Women on Mating and Dating Today.* New York: Institute for American Values.

Grello, Catherine M., Deborah P. Welsh, and Melinda M. Harper. 2006. "No Strings Attached: The Nature of Casual Sex in College Students." *Journal of Sex Research* 43:255–67.

Holland, Dorothy C. and Margaret A. Eisenhart. 1990. *Educated in Romance: Women, Achievement, and College Culture.* Chicago: University of Chicago Press.

Illouz, Eva. 2005. *Cold Intimacies: The Making of Emotional Capitalism.* Cambridge, UK: Polity.

Kimmel, Michael. 2008. *Guyland: The Perilous World Where Boys Become Men.* New York: HarperCollins.

Manning, Wendy D., Peggy C. Giordano, and Monica A. Longmore. 2006. "Hooking Up: The Relationship Contexts of 'Nonrelationship' Sex." *Journal of Adolescent Research* 21:459–83.

Martin, Patricia Yancey and Robert A. Hummer. 1989. "Fraternities and Rape on Campus." *Gender & Society* 3:457–73.

McCall, Leslie. 2005. "The Complexity of Intersectionality." *Signs: Journal of Women in Culture and Society* 30:1771–1800.

Owen, Jesse J., Galena K. Rhoades, Scott M. Stanley, and Frank D. Fincham. 2008. "'Hooking Up' among College Students: Demographic and Psychosocial Correlates." *Archives of Sexual Behavior,* http://www.springerlink.com/content/44j645v7v38013u4/fulltext.html.

Paul, Elizabeth L., Brian McManus, and Allison Hayes. 2000. "'Hookups': Characteristics and Correlates of College Students' Spontaneous and Anonymous Sexual Experiences." *Journal of Sex Research* 37:76–88.

Risman, Barbara J. 2004. "Gender as a Social Structure: Theory Wrestling with Activism." *Gender & Society* 18:429–50.

Risman, Barbara and Pepper Schwartz. 2002. "After the Sexual Revolution: Gender Politics in Teen Dating." *Contexts* 1:16–24.

Rosenfeld, Michael J. 2007. *The Age of Independence: Interracial Unions, Same-Sex Unions and the Changing American Family.* Cambridge, MA: Harvard University Press.

Schwartz, Christine R. and Robert D. Mare. 2005. "Trends in Educational Assortative Marriage from 1940 to 2003." *Demography* 42:621–46.

Sewell, William H. 1992. "A Theory of Structure: Duality, Agency, and Transformation." *American Journal of Sociology* 98:1–29.

Simon, Robin W., Donna Eder, and Cathy Evans. 1992. "The Development of Feeling Norms Underlying Romantic Love among Adolescent Females." *Social Psychology Quarterly* 55:29–46.

Stepp, Laura Sessions. 2007. *Unhooked: How Young Women Pursue Sex, Delay Love, and Lose at Both.* New York: Riverhead.

Sweeney, Megan M. 2002. "Two Decades of Family Change: The Shifting Economic Foundations of Marriage." *American Sociological Review* 67:132–47.

12

DATING AND ROMANTIC RELATIONSHIPS AMONG GAY, LESBIAN, AND BISEXUAL YOUTHS

RITCH C. SAVIN-WILLIAMS

The Importance of Dating and Romance

According to Scarf (1987), the developmental significance of an intimate relationship is to help us "contact archaic, dimly perceived and yet powerfully meaningful aspects of our inner selves" (p. 79). We desire closeness within

the context of a trusting, intimate relationship. Attachment theory posits that humans are prewired for loving and developing strongly felt emotional attachments (Bowlby 1973). When established, we experience safety, security, and nurturance. Early attachments, including those in infancy, are thought to circumscribe an internal blueprint that profoundly affects future relationships, such as the establishment of intimate friendships and romances in adolescence and adulthood (Hazan and Shaver 1987).

Developmentally, dating is a means by which romantic relationships are practiced, pursued, and established. It serves a number of important functions, such as entertainment, recreation, and socialization, that assist participants in developing appropriate means of interacting. It also enhances peer group status and facilitates the selection of a mate (Skipper and Nass 1966). Adolescents who are most confident in their dating abilities begin dating during early adolescence, date frequently, are satisfied with their dating, and are most likely to become involved in a "committed" dating relationship (Herold 1979).

The establishment of romantic relationships is important for youths regardless of sexual orientation. Isay (1989) noted that falling in love was a critical factor in helping his gay clients feel comfortable with their gay identity and that "the self-affirming value of a mutual relationship over time cannot be overemphasized" (p. 50). Browning (1987) regarded lesbian love relationships as an opportunity to enhance

> . . . the development of the individual's adult identity by validating her personhood, reinforcing that she deserves to receive and give love. A relationship can also be a source of tremendous emotional support as the woman explores her goals, values, and relationship to the world. (P. 51)

Because dating experience increases the likelihood that an intimate romantic relationship will evolve, the absence of this opportunity may have long-term repercussions. Malyon (1981) noted some of the reverberations:

> Their most charged sexual desires are usually seen as perverted, and their deepest feelings of psychological attachment are regarded as unacceptable. This social disapproval interferes with the preintimacy involvement that fosters the evolution of maturity and self-respect in the domain of object relations. (P. 326)

Culture's Devaluation of Same-Sex Relationships

Relatively speaking, our culture is far more willing to turn a blind eye to sexual than to romantic relationships among same-sex adolescent partners. Same-sex activity may appear "temporary," an experiment, a phase, or a perverted source of fun. But falling in love with someone of the same gender and maintaining a sustained emotional involvement with that person implies an irreversible deviancy at worst and a bad decision at best. In our homes, schools, religious institutions, and media, we teach that intense relationships

after early adolescence among members of the same sex "should" raise the concern of good parents, good friends, and good teachers. One result is that youths of all sexual orientations may become frightened of developing close friendships with same-sex peers. They fear that these friendships will be viewed as sexually intimate.

It is hardly surprising that a sexual-minority adolescent can easily become "the loneliest person . . . in the typical high school of today" (Norton 1976:376):

> For the homosexual-identified student, high school is often a lonely place where, from every vantage point, there are couples: couples holding hands as they enter school; couples dissolving into an endless wet kiss between school bells; couples exchanging rings with ephemeral vows of devotion and love. (Sears 1991:326–27)

The separation of a youth's homoerotic passion from the socially sanctioned act of heterosexual dating can generate self-doubt, anger, and resentment, and can ultimately retard or distort the development of interpersonal intimacy during the adolescent years. Thus, many youths never consider same-sex dating to be a reasonable option, except in their fantasies. Scientific and clinical writings that ignore same-sex romance and dating among youth contribute to this conspiracy of silence. Sexual-minority youth struggle with issues of identity and intimacy because important impediments rooted in our cultural values and attitudes deter them from dating those they love and instead mandate that they date those they cannot love.

Empirical Studies of Same-Sex Romantic Relationships among Youth

Until the last several years same-sex relationships among sexual-minority youths were seldom recognized in the empirical, scientific literature. With the recent visibility of gay, bisexual, and lesbian youths in the culture at large, social and behavioral scientists are beginning to conduct research focusing on various developmental processes of such youths, including their sexuality and intimacy.

Bisexual, lesbian, and gay youths, whether in Detroit, Minneapolis, Pennsylvania, New York, or the Netherlands, report that they desire to have long-lasting, committed same-sex romantic relationships in their future (D'Augelli 1991; Sanders 1980; Savin-Williams 1990). According to Silverstein (1981), establishing a romantic relationship with a same-sex partner helps one to feel "chosen," to resolve issues of sexual identity, and to feel more complete. Indeed, those who are in a long-term love relationship generally have high levels of self-esteem and self-acceptance.[1]

Although there are few published studies of teens that focus primarily on their same-sex dating or romantic relationships, there are suggestive data that debunk the myth in our culture that gays, lesbians, and bisexuals neither want nor maintain steady, loving same-sex relationships. In two studies of

gay and bisexual male youths, same-sex relationships are regarded as highly desirable. Among 29 Minnesota youths, 10 had a steady male partner at the time of the interview, 11 had been in a same-sex relationship, and, most tellingly, all but 2 hoped for a steady male partner in their future (Remafedi 1987). For these youths, many of whom were living independently with friends or on the street, being in a long-term relationship was considered to be an ideal state. With a college-age sample of 61 males, D'Augelli (1991) reported similar results. One half of his sample was "partnered," and their most troubling mental health concern was termination of a close relationship, ranking just ahead of telling parents about their homosexuality.

The difficulty, however, is to maintain a visible same-sex romance in high school. Sears (1991) interviewed 36 Southern late adolescent and young adult lesbians, gays, and bisexuals. He discovered that although nearly everyone had heterosexually dated in high school, very few dated a member of the same sex during that time. Because of concerns about secrecy and the lack of social support, most same-sex romances involved little emotional commitment and were of short duration. None were overt.

Research with over 300 gay, bisexual, and lesbian youths between the ages of 14 and 23 years (Savin-Williams 1990) supports the finding that sexual-minority youths have romantic relationships during adolescence and young adulthood. Almost 90 percent of the females and two-thirds of the males reported that they have had a romantic relationship. Of the total number of romances listed, 60 percent were with same-sex partners. The male youths were slightly more likely than lesbian and bisexual female youths to begin their romantic career with a same-sex, rather than an opposite-sex, partner.

In the same study, the lesbians and bisexual females who had a high proportion of same-sex romances were most likely to be "out" to others. However, their self-esteem level was essentially the same as those who had a high percentage of heterosexual relationships. If she began same-sex dating early, during adolescence, then a lesbian or bisexual female also tended to be in a current relationship and to experience long-lasting romances. Gay and bisexual male youths who had a large percentage of adolescent romantic relationships with boys had high self-esteem. They were more likely to be publicly "out" to friends and family if they had had a large number of romances. Boys who initiated same-sex romances at an early age were more likely to report that they have had long-term and multiple same-sex relationships.

The findings from these studies are admittedly sparse and do not provide the depth and insight that are needed to help us better understand the experience of being in a same-sex romantic relationship. They do illustrate that youths have same-sex romances while in high school. Where there is desire, some youths will find a way. Sexually active same-sex friendships may evolve into romantic relationships (Savin-Williams 1995), and those most publicly out are most likely to have had adolescent same-sex romances. Certainly, most lesbian, gay, and bisexual youths value the importance of a same-sex, lifelong, committed relationship in their adult years.

Perhaps the primary issue is not the absence of same-sex romances during adolescence, but the hidden nature of the romances. They are seldom recognized and rarely supported or celebrated. The research data offer little information regarding the psychological impact of not being involved in a same-sex romantic relationship or of having to hide such a relationship when it exists. For this, one must turn to stories of the personal struggles of adolescents.

Personal Struggles

Youths who have same-sex romances during their adolescence face a severe struggle to have these relationships acknowledged and supported. Gibson (1989) noted the troubling contradictions:

> The first romantic involvements of lesbian and gay male youth are a source of great joy to them in affirming their sexual identity, providing them with support, and assuring them that they too can experience love. However, society places extreme hardships on these relationships that make them difficult to establish and maintain. (P. 130)

A significant number of youths, perhaps those feeling most insecure regarding their sexual identity, may fantasize about being sexually intimate with a same-sex partner but have little hope that it could in fact become a reality. One youth, Lawrence, reported this feeling in his coming-out story:

> *While growing up, love was something I watched other people experience and enjoy. . . . The countless men I secretly loved and fantasized about were only in private, empty dreams in which love was never returned. I seemed to be the only person in the world with no need for love and companionship. . . . Throughout high school and college I had no way to meet people of the same sex and sexual orientation. These were more years of isolation and secrecy. I saw what other guys my age did, listened to what they said and how they felt. I was expected to be part of a world with which I had nothing in common.* (Curtis 1988:109–110)

A young lesbian, Diane, recalled that "love of women was never a possibility that I even realized could be. You loved your mother and your aunts, and you had girlfriends for a while. Someday, though, you would always meet a man" (Stanley and Wolfe 1980:47). Girls dated boys and not other girls. Because she did not want to date boys, she did not date.

Another youth knew he had homoerotic attractions, but he never fathomed that they could be expressed to the boy that he most admired, his high school soccer teammate. It took alcohol and the right situation:

> *I knew I was checking out the guys in the shower after soccer practice. I thought of myself as hetero who had the urge for males. I fought it, said it was a phase. And then it happened. Derek was my best friend. After soccer practice the fall of our junior year we celebrated both making the "A" team by getting really*

drunk. We were just fooling around and suddenly our pants were off. I was so scared I stayed out of school for three days but we kept being friends and nothing was said until a year later when I came out to everyone and he came up to me with these tears and asked if he made me homosexual. (Savin-Williams 1995)

It is never easy for youths to directly confront the mores of peers whose values and attitudes are routinely supported by the culture. Nearly all youths know implicitly the rules of socially appropriate behavior and the consequences of nonconformity. This single, most influential barrier to same-sex dating, the threat posed by peers, can have severe repercussions. The penalty for crossing the line of "normalcy" can result in emotional and physical pain.

Peer Harassment as a Barrier to Dating

Price (1982) concluded, "Adolescents can be very cruel to others who are different, who do not conform to the expectations of the peer group" (p. 472). Very little has changed in the last decade. For example, 17-year-old actor Ryan Phillippe worried about the consequences on his family and friends if he played a gay teen on ABC's soap opera *One Life to Live* (Gable 1992:3D). David Ruffin, 19, of Ferndale, Michigan, explained why he boycotted his high school senior prom: "The kids could tell I was different from them, and I think I was different because I was gay. And when you're dealing with young people, different means not cool" (Bruni 1992:10A).

Unlike heterosexual dating, little social advantage, such as peer popularity or acceptance, is gained by holding hands and kissing a same-sex peer in school hallways, shopping malls, or synagogues. Lies are spun to protect secrets and to avoid peer harassment. One lesbian youth, Kim, felt that she had to be an actress around her friends. She lied to friends by creating "Andrew" when she was dating "Andrea" over the weekend (Bruni 1992).

To avoid harassment, sexual-minority adolescents may monitor their interpersonal interactions. They may wonder, "Am I standing too close?" or "Do I appear too happy to see him(her)?" (Anderson 1987). Herrick and Martin (1987) found that youths are often apprehensive to show "friendship for a friend of the same sex for fear of being misunderstood or giving away their secretly held sexual orientation" (p. 31). If erotic desires become aroused and threaten expression, youths may seek to terminate same-sex friendships rather than risk revealing their secret. For many adolescents, especially bisexual youths, relationships with the other sex may be easier to develop. The appeal of such relationships is that the youths will be viewed by peers as heterosexual, thus peer acceptance will be enhanced and the threat of harassment and rejection will be reduced. The result is that some sexual-minority youths feel inherently "fake" and they therefore retreat from becoming intimate with others. Although they may meet the implicit and explicit demands of their culture, it is at a cost—their sense of authenticity.

Faking It: Heterosexual Sex and Dating

Retrospective data from gay, bisexual, and lesbian adults reveal the extent to which heterosexual dating and sex are commonplace during the adolescent and young adult years (Bell and Weinberg 1978; Schafer 1976; Troiden and Goode 1980). These might be one-night stands, brief romances, or long-term relationships. Across various studies, nearly two-thirds of gay men and three-quarters of lesbians report having had heterosexual sex in their past. Motivations include fun, curiosity, denial of homoerotic feelings, and pressure to conform to society's insistence on heterosexual norms and behaviors. Even though heterosexual sex often results in a low level of sexual gratification, it is deemed a necessary sacrifice to meet the expectations of peers and, by extension, receive their approval. Only later, as adults, when they have the opportunity to compare these heterosexual relationships with same-sex ones do they fully realize that which they had missed during their younger years.

Several studies with lesbian, bisexual, and gay adolescents document the extent to which they are sexually involved with opposite-sex partners. Few gay and bisexual [male] youth had *extensive* sexual contact with females, even among those who began heterosexual sex at an early age. Sex with one or two girls was usually considered "quite enough." Not infrequently these girls were best friends who expressed a romantic or sexual interest in the gay boys. The male youths liked the girls, but they preferred friendships rather than sexual relations. One youth expressed this dilemma:

> *She was a year older and we had been friends for a long time before beginning dating. It was a date with the full thing: dinner, theater, alcohol, making out, sex at her house and I think we both came during intercourse. I was disappointed because it was such hard work—not physically I mean but emotionally. Later on in my masturbation, my fantasies were never of her. We did it once more in high school and then once more when we were in college. I labeled it love but not sexual love. I really wanted them to occur together. It all ended when I labeled myself gay.* (Savin-Williams 1995)

An even greater percentage of lesbian and bisexual female adolescents engaged in heterosexual sexual experiences—2 of every 3 (Herdt and Boxer 1993), 3 of every 4 (Sears 1991), and 8 of 10 (Savin-Williams 1990). Heterosexual activity began as early as second grade and as late as senior year in high school. Few of these girls, however, had extensive sex with boys—usually with two or three boys within the context of dating. Eighteen-year-old Kimba noted that she went through a heterosexual stage:

> *. . . trying to figure out what was so great about guys sexually. I still don't understand. I guess that, for straights, it is like it is for me when I am with a woman. . . . I experimented in whatever ways I thought would make a difference, but it was no go. My closest friends are guys; there is caring and closeness between us.* (Heron 1983:82)

Georgina also tried to follow a heterosexual script:

> *In sixth and seventh grades you start wearing makeup, you start getting your hair cut, you start liking boys—you start thinking about letting them "French kiss" you. I did all those major things. But, I still didn't feel very satisfied with myself. I remember I never really wanted to be intimate with any guy. I always wanted to be their best friend.* (Sears 1991:327)

One young lesbian, Lisa, found herself "having sex with boys to prove I wasn't gay. Maybe I was even trying to prove it to myself! I didn't enjoy having sex with boys" (Heron 1983:76). These three lesbian youths forfeited a sense of authenticity, intimacy, and love because they were taught that emotional intimacy can only be achieved with members of the other sex.

The reasons sexual-minority adolescents gave as to why they engaged in heterosexual sex were similar to those reported in retrospective studies by adults. The youths needed to test whether their heterosexual attractions were as strong as their homoerotic ones—thus attempting to disconfirm their homosexuality—and to mask their homosexuality so as to win peer- and self-acceptance and to avoid peer rejection. Many youths believed that they could not really know whether they were lesbian, gay, bisexual, or heterosexual without first experiencing heterosexual sex. For many, however, heterosexual activities consisted of sex without feelings that they tried to enjoy without much success (Herdt and Boxer 1993). Heterosexual sex felt unnatural because it lacked the desired emotional intensity. One young gay youth reported:

> *We'd been dating for three months. I was 15 and she, a year or so older. We had petted previously and so she planned this event. We attempted intercourse in her barn, but I was too nervous. I didn't feel good afterwards because it was not successful. We did it every week for a month or so. It was fun but it wasn't a big deal. But then I did not have a great lust or drive. This was just normal I guess. It gave me something to do to tell the other guys who were always bragging.* (Savin-Williams 1995)

Similarly, Kimberly always had a steady heterosexual relationship: "It was like I was just going through the motions. It was expected of me, so I did it. I'd kiss him or embrace him but it was like I was just there. He was probably enjoying it, but I wasn't" (Sears 1991:327).

Jacob, an African American adolescent, dated the prettiest girls in his school in order to maintain his image: "It was more like President Reagan entertaining heads of state. It's expected of you when you're in a certain position" (Sears 1991:126–27). Another Southern male youth, Grant, used "group dates" to reinforce his heterosexual image. Rumors that he was gay were squelched because his jock friends came to his defense: "He's not a fag. He has a girlfriend" (Sears 1991:328).

These and other personal stories of youths vividly recount the use of heterosexual sex and dating as a cover for an emerging same-sex or bisexual identity. Dating provides opportunities to temporarily "pass" as straight

until the meaning of homoerotic feelings are resolved or youths find a safe haven to be lesbian or gay. Heterosexual sex and dating may be less pleasurable than same-sex encounters, but many sexual-minority youths feel that the former are the only safe, acceptable options.

Impediments and Consequences

The difficulties inherent in dating same-sex partners during adolescence are monumental. First is the fundamental difficulty of finding a suitable partner. The vast majority of lesbian, bisexual, and gay youths are closeted, not out to themselves, let alone to others. A second barrier is the consequences of same-sex dating, such as verbal and physical harassment from peers. A third impediment is the lack of public recognition or "celebration" of those who are romantically involved with a member of the same gender. Thus, same-sex dating remains hidden and mysterious, something that is either ridiculed, condemned, or ignored.

The consequences of an exclusively heterosexually oriented atmosphere in the peer social world can be severe and enduring. An adolescent may feel isolated and socially excluded from the world of peers. Sex with others of the same gender may be associated exclusively with anonymous, guilt-ridden encounters, handicapping the ability to develop healthy intimate relationships in adulthood. Denied the opportunity for romantic involvement with someone of the same sex, a youth may suffer impaired self-esteem that reinforces the belief that one is unworthy of love, affection, and intimacy. One youth, Rick, even doubted his ability to love:

> When I started my senior year, I was still unclear about my sexuality. I had dated women with increasing frequency, but never felt love for any of them. I discovered that I could perform sexually with a woman, but heterosexual experiences were not satisfying emotionally. I felt neither love nor emotional oneness with women. Indeed, I had concluded that I was incapable of human love. (Heron 1983:95–96)

If youths are to take advantage of opportunities to explore their erotic sexuality, it is sometimes, at least for males, confined to clandestine sexual encounters, void of romance, affection, and intimacy but replete with misgivings, anonymity, and guilt.

> Ted was 21 and me, 16. It was New Year's Eve and it was a swimming pool party at my rich friend's house. Not sure why Ted was there but he really came on to me, even putting his arm around me in front of everyone. I wasn't ready for that but I liked it. New Year's Day, every time Ted looked at me I looked away because I thought it was obvious that we had had sex. It did clarify things for me. It didn't feel like I was cheating on [my girlfriend] Beth because the sex felt so different, so right. (Savin-Williams 1995)

A gay youth may have genital contact with another boy without ever kissing him because to do so would be too meaningful. Remafedi (1990)

found this escape from intimacy to be very damaging: "Without appropri-ate opportunities for peer dating and socialization, gay youth frequently eschew intimacy altogether and resort to transient and anonymous sexual encounters with adults" (p. 1173). One consequence is the increased risk for contracting sexually transmitted diseases, including HIV. This is particu-larly risky for youths who turn to prostitution to meet their intimacy needs (Coleman 1989).

When youths eventually match their erotic and intimacy needs, they may be surprised with the results. This was Jacob's experience (Sears 1991) when he fell in love with Warren, an African American senior who also sang in the choir. Sex quickly evolved into "an emotional thing." Jacob explained: "He got to the point of telling me he loved me. That was the first time any-body ever said any thing like that. It was kind of hard to believe that even after sex there are really feelings" (p. 127).

Equally common, however, especially among closeted youths, is that lesbian, bisexual, and gay teens may experience a poverty of intimacy in their lives and considerable social and emotional isolation. One youth, Grant, enjoyed occasional sex with a star football player, but he was devastated by the subsequent exclusion the athlete meted out to him: "We would see each other and barely speak but after school we'd see each other a lot. He had his image that he had to keep up and, since it was rumored that I was gay, he didn't want to get a close identity with me" (Sears 1991:330).

Largely because of negative peer prohibitions and the lack of social support and recognition, same-sex romances that are initiated have diffi-culty flourishing. Irwin met Benji in the eighth grade and was immediately attracted to him (Sears 1991). They shared interests in music and academics and enjoyed long conversations, playing music, and riding in the coun-tryside. Eventually, their attractions for each other were expressed and a romantic, sexual relationship began. Although Irwin was in love with Benji, their relationship soon ended because it was no match for the social pres-sures and personal goals that conflicted with Irwin being in a same-sex relationship.

Georgina's relationship with Kay began dramatically with intense feelings that were at times ambivalent for both of them. At one point she overheard Kay praying, "Dear Lord, forgive me for the way I am" (Sears 1991:333). Georgina's parents demanded that she end her "friendship" with Kay. Georgina told classmates they were just "good friends" and began dating boys as a cover. Despite her love for Kay, the relationship ended when Georgina's boyfriend told her that no one liked her because she hung around "that dyke, Kay." In retrospect, Georgina wished: "If everybody would have accepted everybody, I would have stayed with Kay" (p. 334).

Given this situation, lesbian, bisexual, and gay youths in same-sex rela-tionships may place unreasonable and ultimately destructive demands on each other. For example, they may expect that the relationship will resolve all fears of loneliness and isolation and validate all aspects of their personal identity (Browning 1987).

A Success Story

A vivid account of how a same-sex romantic relationship can empower a youth is depicted in the seminal autobiography of Aaron Fricke (1981), *Reflections of a Rock Lobster.* He fell in love with a classmate, Paul:

> With Paul's help, I started to challenge all the prejudice I had encountered during 16 1/2 years of life. Sure, it was scary to think that half my classmates might hate me if they knew my secret, but from Paul's example I knew it was possible to one day be strong and face them without apprehension. (Fricke 1981:44)

Through Paul, Aaron became more resilient and self-confident:

> His strengths were my strengths. . . . I realized that my feelings for him were unlike anything I had felt before. The sense of camaraderie was familiar from other friendships; the deep spiritual love I felt for Paul was new. So was the openness, the sense of communication with another. (Fricke 1981:45)

Life gained significance. He wrote poems. He planned a future. He learned to express both kindness and strength. Aaron was in love, with another boy. But no guidelines or models existed on how best to express these feelings:

> Heterosexuals learn early in life what behavior is expected of them. They get practice in their early teens having crushes, talking to their friends about their feelings, going on first dates and to chaperoned parties, and figuring out their feelings. Paul and I hadn't gotten all that practice; our relationship was formed without much of a model to base it on. It was the first time either of us had been in love like this and we spent much of our time just figuring out what that meant for us. (Fricke 1981:46)

Eventually, after a court case that received national attention, Aaron won the right to take Paul to the senior prom as his date. This victory was relatively minor compared to the self-respect, authenticity, and pride in being gay that their relationship won for each of them.

Final Reflections

As a clinical and developmental psychologist, I find it disheartening to observe our culture ignoring and condemning sexual-minority youth. One consequence is that myths and stereotypes are perpetuated that interfere with or prevent youths from developing intimate same-sex relationships with those to whom they are erotically and emotionally attracted. Separating passion from affection, engaging in sex with strangers in impersonal and sometimes unsafe places, and finding alienation rather than intimacy in those relationships are not conducive to psychological health. In one study the most common reason given for initial suicide attempts by lesbians and gay men was relationship problems (Bell and Weinberg 1978).

A youth's limited ability to meet other bisexual, lesbian, and gay adolescents compounds a sense of isolation and alienation. Crushes may develop

on unknowing friends, teachers, and peers. These are often cases of unrequited love with the youth never revealing their true feelings (Gibson 1989:131).

Sexual-minority youths need the validation of those around them as they attempt to develop a personal integrity and to discover those similar to themselves. How long can gay, bisexual, and lesbian adolescents maintain their charades before they encounter difficulty separating the pretensions from the realities? Many "use" heterosexual dating to blind themselves and others. By so doing they attempt to disconfirm to themselves the growing encroachment of their homoerotic attractions while escaping derogatory name calling and gaining peer status and prestige. The incidence of heterosexual sex and relationships in the adolescence of gay men and lesbians attests to these desires.

Future generations of adolescents will no doubt find it easier to establish same-sex relationships. This is due in part to the dramatic increase in the visibility that adult same-sex relationships have received during the last few years. Domestic partnership ordinances in several cities and counties, victories for spousal equivalency rights in businesses, court cases addressing adoption by lesbian couples and challenges to marriage laws by several male couples, the dramatic story of the life partnership of Karen Thompson and Sharon Kowalski, and the "marriage" of former Mr. Universe Bob Paris to male Supermodel Rod Jackson raise public awareness of same-sex romantic relationships. Even Ann Landers (1992) is spreading the word. In a column, an 18-year-old gay teen from Santa Barbara requested that girls quit hitting on him because, as he explained, "I have a very special friend who is a student at the local university . . . and [we] are very happy with each other" (Landers 1992:2B).

A decade after Aaron Fricke fought for and won the right to take his boyfriend to the prom, a dozen lesbian, gay, and bisexual youths in the Detroit-Ann Arbor area arranged to have their own prom. Most felt excluded from the traditional high school prom, which they considered "a final, bitter postscript to painful years of feeling left out" (Bruni 1992:10A). Seventeen-year-old Brenda said, "I want to feel rich for one moment. I want to feel all glamorous, just for one night" (Bruni 1992:10A). Going to the "Fantasy" prom was a celebration that created a sense of pride, a connection with other sexual-minority teens, and a chance to dance—"two girls together, unguarded and unashamed, in the middle of a room filled with teenagers just like them" (Bruni 1992:10A). One year later, I attended this prom with my life partner and the number of youths in attendance had increased sixfold.

We need to listen to youths such as Aaron, Diane, and Georgina, to hear their concerns, insights, and solutions. Most of all, we need to end the invisibility of same-sex romantic relationships. It is easily within our power to enhance the well-being of millions of youths, including "Billy Joe," a character in a famous Bobbie Gentry song. If Billy Joe had seen an option to a heterosexual life style, he might have considered an alternative to ending his life by jumping off the Tallahatchie Bridge.

ENDNOTE

[1] The causal pathway, however, is unclear (Savin-Williams 1990). That is, being in a same-sex romance may build positive self-regard, but it may also be true that those with high self-esteem are more likely to form love relationships and to stay in them.

REFERENCES

Anderson, D. 1987. "Family and Peer Relations of Gay Adolescents." Pp. 162–78 in *Adolescent Psychiatry: Developmental and Clinical Studies: Vol. 14,* edited by S. C. Geinstein. Chicago: The University of Chicago Press.

Bell, A. P. and M. S. Weinberg. 1978. *Homosexualities: A Study of Diversity among Men and Women.* New York: Simon and Schuster.

Bowlby, J. 1973. *Attachment and Loss.* Vol. 2, *Separation.* New York: Basic Books.

Browning, C. 1987. "Therapeutic Issues and Intervention Strategies with Young Adult Lesbian Clients: A Developmental Approach." *Journal of Homosexuality* 14:45–52.

Bruni, F. 1992. "A Prom Night of Their Own to Dance, Laugh, Reminisce." *Detroit Free Press,* May 22, pp. 1A, 10A.

Coleman, E. 1989. "The Development of Male Prostitution Activity among Gay and Bisexual Adolescents." *Journal of Homosexuality* 17:131–49.

Curtis, W., ed. 1988. *Revelations: A Collection of Gay Male Coming Out Stories.* Boston: Alyson.

D'Augelli, A. R. 1991. "Gay Men in College: Identity Processes and Adaptations." *Journal of College Student Development* 32:140–46.

Fricke, A. 1981. *Reflections of a Rock Lobster: A Story about Growing Up Gay.* Boston: Alyson.

Gable, D. 1992. "'Life' Story Looks at Roots of Homophobia." *USA Today,* June 2, p. 30.

Gibson, P. 1989. "Gay Male and Lesbian Youth Suicide." In *Report of the Secretary's Task Force on Youth Suicide,* vol. 3, *Prevention and Interventions in Youth Suicide (3-110-3-142),* edited by M. R. Feinleib. Rockville, MD: U.S. Department of Health and Human Services.

Hazan, C. and P. Shaver. 1987. "Romantic Love Conceptualized as an Attachment Process." *Journal of Personality and Social Psychology* 52:511–24.

Herdt, G. and A. Boxer. 1993. *Children of Horizons: How Gay and Lesbian Teens Are Leading a New Way Out of the Closet.* Boston: Beacon.

Herold, E. S. 1979. "Variables Influencing the Dating Adjustment of University Students." *Journal of Youth and Adolescence* 8:73–79.

Heron, A., ed. 1983. *One Teenager in Ten.* Boston: Alyson.

Herrick, E. S. and A. D. Martin. 1987. "Developmental Issues and Their Resolution for Gay and Lesbian Adolescents." *Journal of Homosexuality* 14:25–44.

Isay, R. A. 1989. *Being Homosexual: Gay Men and Their Development.* New York: Avon.

Landers, A. 1992. "Gay Teen Tired of Advances from Sexually Aggressive Girls." *Detroit Free Press,* May 26, p. 2B.

Malyon, A. K. 1981. "The Homosexual Adolescent: Developmental Issues and Social Bias." *Child Welfare* 60:321–30.

Norton, J. L. 1976. "The Homosexual and Counseling." *Personnel and Guidance Journal* 54: 374–77.

Price, J. H. 1982. "High School Students' Attitudes toward Homosexuality." *Journal of School Health* 52:469–74.

Remafedi, G. 1987. "Male Homosexuality: The Adolescent's Perspective." *Pediatrics* 79:326–30.

———. 1990. "Fundamental Issues in the Care of Homosexual Youth." *Adolescent Medicine* 74:1169–79.

Sanders, G. 1980. "Homosexualities in the Netherlands." *Alternative Lifestyles* 3:278–311.

Savin-Williams, R. C. 1990. *Gay and Lesbian Youth: Expressions of Identity.* New York: Hemisphere.

———. 1994. "Dating Those You Can't Love and Loving Those You Can't Date." Pp. 196–215 in *Personal Relationships during Adolescence,* vol. 6, *Advances in Adolescent Development,* edited by R. Montemayor, G. R. Adams, and T. P. Gullotta. Newbury Park, CA: Sage.

———. 1995. "Sex and Sexual Identity among Gay and Bisexual Males." Manuscript in preparation, Cornell University, Ithaca, NY.

Scarf, M. 1987. *Intimate Partners: Patterns in Love and Marriage.* New York: Random House.

Schafer, S. 1976. "Sexual and Social Problems of Lesbians." *Journal of Sex Research* 12:50–69.

Sears, J. T. 1991. *Growing Up Gay in the South: Race, Gender, and Journeys of the Spirit.* New York: Harrington Park Press.

Silverstein, C. 1981. *Man to Man: Gay Couples in America.* New York: William Morrow.

Skipper, J. K., Jr., and G. Nass. 1966. "Dating Behavior: Framework for Analysis and an Illustration." *Journal of Marriage and the Family* 27:412–20.

Stanley, J. P. and S. J. Wolfe, eds. 1980. *The Coming Out Stories.* New York: Persephone.

Troiden, R. R. and E. Goode. 1980. "Variables Related to the Acquisition of a Gay Identity." *Journal of Homosexuality* 5:383–92.

13

ARRANGED MARRIAGES
What's Love Got to Do with It?

MONISHA PASUPATHI

In American culture, choice is related to happiness, independence, autonomy, and equality. We do what we choose longer, with more pleasure, and greater ambition (e.g., Cordova and Lepper 1996), and what we choose is to a great extent who we are. Or so it seems, looking both at the world in which we live and at the worlds of social and developmental psychology in which I work. What could be more self-evident, then, than the idea that arranged marriages, which deny the individual the power to make a very important life choice, are an anachronistic and oppressive practice. Further, newspaper and magazine articles (e.g., Lamb 1999) attribute rising rates of female suicide in countries like China and Pakistan partly to arranged marriage practices in these cultures. But a quick count of my own relatives and friends suggests that those whose cultural backgrounds provide them with both alternatives—a marriage of choice and one that is parentally arranged—don't always take the route of choice. The fact that people who are well-acquainted with and open to Western marriage practices do not necessarily adopt those practices suggests that there may be more to arranged marriages than oppression, depression, and suicide. . . .

Toward a Feminist View of Arranged Marriages

The overwhelming majority of people marry or participate in long-term, marriage-equivalent relationships (Hazan and Diamond 2000; Zeifman and Hazan 1997). Within these relationships, people bear and rear children, provide and are given emotional support, companionship, and instrumental support. Arranged marriages represent one class of procedures for forming

such alliances, and by anthropological accounts, they are in widespread use. As many as 80 percent of cultures outside the Western sphere employ arranged marriage practices, although relatively few of these cultures rely exclusively on arranged marriages (Small 1993).

Because the procedures involved in arranging marriages lead to differences in the autonomy with which individual women can choose their spouses, those procedures bear some scrutiny from a feminist standpoint. Do arranged marriages give women an unfair share in their own self-determination? Arranged marriages could pose a particular problem if (1) they are arranged with less input from women than men; (2) they produce inequities of power between women and men; and (3) they are an integral part of a host of other practices reflecting and maintaining women's lower societal status, permitting treatment of women as commodities or property. If arranged marriages mean denying women choice and power and treating them as commodities, then arranged marriages are obviously a feminist nightmare. And if movement toward more choice in marriages would combat clear injustices of other types (less schooling for women, for example), then it is also clear that arranged marriage practices might be a target for feminist reform.

But the evidence, as I note below, suggests a more complex reality for several reasons. First, because of historical changes in arranging marriages and because of the variability of the practices in the modern world, it is difficult to generalize about arranged marriages in terms of their consequences for women's status. Certainly, not all arranged marriages involve less self-determination on the part of the bride as compared to the groom. Even in extreme cases, arranged marriages may simply result in different modes of self-determination and spouse selection than those Western women employ (e.g., Abu-Lughod 1993). Arranged marriage practices are not monolithic rituals with no loopholes that provide the possibility of subversion and resistance. Second, when examined from a psychological perspective, differences between arranged marriages and other marriages are sometimes difficult to demonstrate, whether at the level of what sorts of people are chosen as mates or at the level of what ingredients make up a good marriage. Different procedures for forming alliances may not, in the end, produce different alliances. This similarity makes it difficult to argue that arranged marriages present special difficulties for women. Third, the degree to which arranged marriages produce inequity among men and women, or to which they are an integral part of the oppression of women and control of women's sexuality, is debatable; this is an issue to which I return at the end of the [reading]. . . .

Choice in Love versus Arranged Marriages: How Different?

Are love and arranged marriages fundamentally different in terms of degree of choice and criteria employed? Friends and family often introduce us to the people we eventually marry out of personal choice, and those having an

arranged marriage often exercise some choice in the selection of the future spouse. Such facts complicate this division between arranged and love marriages considerably. Perhaps the most accurate distinction is one between personal and collective choice as methods for selecting spouses.

As seen above, the relative degree of personal choice exercised by individuals in arranged marriages can, in fact, be substantial. But even when the bride and groom have had extensive contact prior to the marriage, they have not usually had the kind of acquaintanceship and dating that leads to romantic love. Given that this is a central criterion for marriage in the United States and other Western industrialized nations (Levine et al. 1995), the logical conclusion is that arranged and love marriages are based on different criteria for selecting spouses (i.e., romantic love versus pragmatic or family concerns). As I demonstrate below, however, even this assumption proves too simplistic.

In fact, the psychological literature suggests that there may be fewer differences between arranged marriages and love marriages than is apparent on the surface. In the remainder of [this section], I focus on two questions: (1) whether arranged marriage practices and love marriages employ different or similar *selection criteria*; and (2) whether arranged marriages and chosen marriages lead to *different outcomes* (e.g., marital satisfaction). The literature reviewed here is by no means exhaustive, and I have concentrated primarily on the relatively sparse psychological literature on arranged marriages rather than on the substantial anthropological literature.

Choosing a "Suitable Boy"

Social psychological views of finding a spouse, based predominantly on Western samples, have shown that the most central factor is proximity, which often comes about by chance (Bandura 1982; Hazan and Diamond 2000). We marry the people we encounter. Still, whether those looking for their own spouse are seeking the same qualities desired by those who select spouses for their children is a different issue. Arguments for cross-cultural variability in the qualities that make for a good mate, as well as arguments for cross-cultural universality, have been advanced. Below, I address these differing arguments in turn and then examine whether comparisons of arranged-marriage cultures and love-marriage cultures support universality or variability.

Different Cultures, Different Goals, Different Practices

It may seem obvious that different cultures will consider different criteria in mate selection, particularly when the cultures differ in marriage practices. Love-marriage selection criteria seem to reflect individuals' personal concerns, such as personal and interpersonal qualities of the prospective mate and compatibility issues, while arranged-marriage selection criteria, not surprisingly, reflect concerns of the total family unit (Blood 1972). These

family concerns include socioeconomic status, health, strength, fertility, temperament, and emotional stability of the prospective spouse. This may be because arranged marriage practices are associated with residence patterns and are more likely in countries where a new couple lives in an extended family dwelling (Fox 1975; Lee and Stone 1980). All of the qualities important to the family not only contribute to collective well-being; they may be particularly important when the new spouse moves in with the extended family.

One Species, Similar Criteria

Alternative perspectives suggest that mating practices may be more similar than different across cultures because of similarity in shared historical pasts or the pressures of evolution upon mating behavior. In fact, some researchers argue that the formation of romantic pair bonds depends on attachment processes exapted from the mother–infant relationship over the course of evolution (Hazan and Diamond 2000; Zeifman and Hazan 1997). Thus, people should report preferences for qualities that enhance or increase the likelihood of secure attachment. The available and relevant data come from two sources: people's preferences about hypothetical mates, and criteria that appear to govern actual mate selection.

Preferences

In a study of thirty-seven cultures, male and female college students reported the qualities of (1) dependability, (2) intelligence, (3) kindness-understanding, and (4) emotional stability as most important in a prospective mate (Buss et al. 1989). Mutual attraction and love were also considered quite important in all cultures sampled. Thus, data on preferences for hypothetical spouses showed few differences across cultures sampled, consistent with shared history or evolutionary arguments. However, in African, Asian, and Middle Eastern countries, where arranged marriage is still practiced, love was ranked somewhat lower than in Western industrialized nations. Similar findings about the importance of romantic love for establishing a marriage in the industrializing Eastern/Asian world were also demonstrated in another study of college students across eleven cultures (Levine et al. 1995). This study bears a closer look because it asked specifically about the role of love as a decision criterion. Respondents from Asian countries (particularly Pakistan, India, and Thailand) reported a willingness to marry a person they did not love, but who possessed all their desired qualities in a mate. They were also unwilling to consider divorce when love is not maintained, in contrast to Western and South American countries. Thus, Eastern/Asian respondents view love as somewhat less important at the beginning of a marriage and regard the absence of love as a less adequate criterion for divorce. One explanation for such findings could be that Eastern/Asian respondents believe that love develops during the course of a marriage, a view that would be consistent with existing evidence (Gupta and Singh 1982). . . .

Choosing a Spouse in India

In Kerala, India, the criteria for marriage partners are multidimensional and include (1) religion/horoscope matching, (2) character, (3) education, (4) dowry, (5) appearance (girls/women), (6) employment, (7) caste/subcaste, (8) geographic distance between families, (9) financial status, and (10) family status, tradition, and reputation. A minimum of five characteristics must be of a suitable nature (i.e., similar across both parties or acceptable given that family's expectations) for a match to be considered by the parents (Yelsma and Athappilly 1988). My own relatives, from the state of Madras, report similar considerations: educational background, social background, and family qualities of the prospective bride and bridegroom are all at issue. These considerations are important in many countries other than India where parental or matchmaker-driven arrangement of marriage is practiced.

The result of these criteria is that arranged-marriage practices tend to pair spouses who are similar in terms of major background characteristics like class, economic status, and education. Arranged-marriage practices also take into consideration character and physical health, perhaps particularly so when the new couple will live with the entire family. On first glance, such criteria seem far removed from romantic love and mutual attraction. However, as discussed earlier, those from cultures where love marriage predominates also consider character when choosing marriage partners. . . .

Love versus Demographics

Despite the prevalence of love as a self-reported reason for marrying, Americans tend to date and marry those who are similar to themselves across a wide range of qualities (Berscheid and Reis 1998). We fall in love with people who are like us in terms of socioeconomic status, education, and age (Houts, Robins, and Huston 1996; Waris 1997), as well as with people who are like us in terms of psychological qualities like personality characteristics, leisure interests, and the complexity with which we think about topics (Keller and Young 1996; Thiessen, Young, and Delgado 1997). Some findings even suggest that we tend to date and marry those who are physically similar to us (Keller and Young 1996; Thiessen et al. 1997). Thus, we who choose our spouses think we choose them for love, but outside observers (who do not hear our professed internal feelings of love and adoration) might think we choose our spouses because they are like us. At this level of analysis, arranged marriages are not, in the end, all that different. . . .

So similarity appears to be a powerful force in marriage making, whether selected by families or by the individuals themselves. If two different selection methods lead to relatively similar pairing outcomes, on average, then why should arranged or love marriages have different outcomes? The assumption of the importance of personal choice in determining happiness has frequently led researchers to question whether partners in arranged marriages will be as happy as those in love marriages.

Is Happily Ever After Equally Happy in Arranged Marriages?

In this section, I focus on marital satisfaction because this has been the outcome variable used in most psychological studies comparing arranged and love marriages, as opposed to divorce rates or other potential indicators. Unlike divorce rates, which are affected by factors such as laws governing who may seek divorce and for what reasons, marital satisfaction indicates the subjective well-being of spouses. Are spouses who choose one another happier together than those who were selected for one another?

Consider some example findings. Israeli couples reported comparably high marital satisfaction regardless of whether their marriage was arranged or self-chosen (Shachar 1991). Perhaps even more surprisingly, the Moonies who entered into arranged marriages also report levels of marital satisfaction typical of community samples (Galanter 1986). Were the Moonies simply representing themselves and their unusual lifestyle positively without actually having similar levels of marital satisfaction? Because their general well-being was lower than that of community samples, a self-presentational bias seems unlikely to account for the findings. Galanter notes the importance of the religious community context in reinforcing and supporting these marriages. Given the right context, choice may not always be the paramount issue in marital satisfaction. In India, in fact, those in arranged marriages sometimes report higher marital satisfaction than their compatriots in love marriages and equivalent marital satisfaction to Western comparison samples (Kumar and Dhyani 1996; Yelsma and Athappilly 1988). . . .

Processes Underlying Marital Satisfaction

Western marital researchers emphasize the processes of communication about conflict areas as the critical factor in marital satisfaction and longevity (e.g., Clements et al. 1998; Gottman 1994). In fact, they suggest that "the positive factors that draw people together—love, attraction, perceived and actual similarities, trust, and commitment—are indicative of marital choice, but not marital success" (Clements et al. 1998:352). So what exactly does it mean to say that the way couples handle conflict is a critical factor in whether they maintain high marital satisfaction over time? For Gottman (1994) it means that couples maintain a relatively high level of positive emotional expression (as compared to negative emotional expression) when discussing conflicts. The *ratio* of positive to negative emotion must be high, regardless of the degree to which a couple is emotionally expressive. . . .

But, as noted, similar levels of marital satisfaction could also mask differences in marital processes that would be very interesting to examine. Even among American couples, there are multiple ways to achieve good (and bad) relationships (Gottman 1994). For example, spouses in instrumental marriages, with an emphasis on the separate roles of the individual partners,

may be satisfied when the husband is a good wage-earner and the wife a competent homemaker (see, e.g., Kamo 1993; Rubin 1976). Spouses oriented toward the expressive socioemotional features of marriage may not be satisfied with the adequate fulfillment of role responsibilities but may require good communication and companionship as well.

There is, in fact, evidence that different processes might be important in other cultures. For example, in Japan, as in the United States, marital satisfaction is related to housework sharing and equality. However, for Japanese spouses, the income of the husband is also an important predictor of marital satisfaction, while in America this is not necessarily the case (Kamo 1993). In India, spouses in arranged marriages show different patterns of adjustment to marriage over time than those in love marriages, although sexual satisfaction contributes similarly to both partners' overall adjustment to marriage in both types of marriage (Kumar and Dhyani 1996).

Another type of difference includes verbal communication. Indian arranged marriages report the lowest level of communication, while Western love marriages report high levels, and Indian love marriages are between these two groups in terms of communication (Yelsma and Athappilly 1988). Relationships of various types of communication (verbal, sexual, and nonverbal) to marital satisfaction were lower in Indian couples. The authors concluded that satisfaction among Indian couples may be better predicted by variables different from those traditionally assessed in the West, where communication about conflictual issues seems critical for marital outcomes (see, e.g., Gottman and Levenson 1988). . . .

Who Is Responsible for Marital Satisfaction?

Gottman and Levenson (1988) have noted that the responsibility for managing the emotional climate of U.S. marriages falls largely on the shoulders of wives; it is wives who must initiate conflict-related discussion and wives who bear the health costs of unhappy marriages. My family members report similar pressure on women in Indian arranged marriages, noting that "the wife is expected to make more adjustments to make the marriage work" and that this pressure arises from family members and the culture as well. In Western love marriages, women maintain satisfaction by initiating discussion of conflicts toward resolution. In arranged marriages, women may do so by suppressing their own needs and desires in order to maintain a good emotional climate, but this remains largely unresearched.

Happily Ever After: Summing Up

Arranged and love marriages do show similar *levels* of marital satisfaction in the few studies available, and it seems that women in both types of marriage assume more responsibility for the emotional quality of the marriage than men. It is not clear whether similarity in levels of marital satisfaction is due to similar factors across cultures, like superior conflict-resolution skills, or to different factors, such as fulfilling culture-specific expectations for a good spouse. . . .

Arranged Marriages: What Can We Conclude?

As suggested above, both social science and personal experience suggest that (1) arranged marriages are heterogeneous across and within cultures in the degree of choice that spouses exert, (2) the factors in selecting spouses may be surprisingly similar regardless of whether marriages are arranged or self-chosen, (3) outcomes like marital satisfaction seem quite similar across marriage type, although it is not clear whether this is driven by underlying similarities (in choices and in the demands of married life) or by underlying differences (in expectations and interaction patterns). Further research may help us understand how the larger cultural context in which a couple lives may determine more everyday facets of their lives, in a relationship that seems to be a human universal in one form or another.

Feminism and Arranged Marriages

Having reviewed some of the empirical work on arranged marriages, it becomes clear that there are few simple perspectives on arranged marriages from a feminist standpoint.

Lack of Choice for Women

First, consider the matter of choice. Though historically, girls/women have had less say in their marriage arrangements than boys/men, that appears to be changing not only in India but also in many other places. In many of the cultures reviewed above, both men and women are denied freedom of personal choice in marriage partners, and the inequity observed revolves around power differentials between children and parents, not between men and women. In fact, Small (1993) found that in 106 societies that practice arranged marriage, only three give prospective grooms more choice than prospective brides. Brides very often (50 percent of the societies examined) had the power to reject a potential marriage. She points out that lack of choice in picking potential candidates doesn't necessarily mean coercion. Further, as suggested above, arranged marriages need not unfold very differently from Western ones once the marriage begins. From some evolutionary standpoints (e.g., Hazan and Diamond 2000), what is required for the formation of attachment bonds between two individuals is the kind of daily physical and psychological interchange that seems part of both types of marriages. Finally, Small problematizes the idea that Western women are totally free to select their own partners—after all, we want our families and friends to like and welcome our new spouses. . . .

Power Inequities in Marriage

There are obviously power inequities in arranged marriages. Are the power inequities observed in India necessarily greater than those in Western marriages? As noted above, wives have been pinpointed as bearing more

of the burden of marriage management in the United States (e.g., Gottman and Levenson 1988); women do more housework, make greater career sacrifices, and ultimately have less negotiating power in the marital relationship (Mahoney 1995). In fact, Mahoney argues that the key factor influencing gender inequity in American marriages is gender-differential educational and career achievement. She suggests that American women who are less well educated and have lower paying jobs than their husbands (which may be true even given equal educational attainment) are at a clear disadvantage when it comes to negotiations about household responsibilities. Are women in arranged marriages likely to experience even larger educational inequity and therefore even less power? In my own family, educational inequities between women and men tend not to be larger than those in the marriages of my Western friends. But stereotypes of cultures that arrange marriages, with images of child brides and of vast numbers of women kept uneducated, suggest that arranged marriage and larger inequity between spouses, in terms of education, go together. Research findings also show that more-educated women appear more likely to have love, rather than arranged, marriages, implying that arranged marriages disproportionately involve less-educated women, vulnerable to greater power inequity in their marriage.

There are several problems with such conclusions. First, it may be that arranged-marriage practices go hand in hand with less education for both spouses. Further, the assumption is that if women were liberated, they would choose their own partners, and thus women who accept an arranged marriage are not liberated women. This is not necessarily true. One of the most obvious confounds is that women who go on to higher education may have more opportunities to meet and fall in love with men of their own choosing. Further, there are many exceptions to the rule—many women are highly educated but still prefer to have some parental involvement in the selection of their spouse. Still, connections between educational attainment and marriage type raise a third issue, which is the role of arranged marriages in upholding sets of inequities within a culture. . . .

Arranged Marriages Perpetuate a Notion of Women as Property

A final critique of arranged marriages is that they open the door for massive abuse of women by setting them up as property (Haider 1995). From the review above, it is clear that arranged-marriage practices do not necessarily treat women as property, although this can be the case. Some modern versions of marriage arranging, however, are better characterized as treating both sons and daughters as parts in a collective whole—that of the family. As parts of a family, sons and daughters should not select their spouses independently of the concerns of the family as a unit.

A second concern is that rates of spouse abuse are difficult to compare across cultures. Stories about battered women in arranged marriages may not be driven strictly by the way that marriages are arranged because spouse abuse occurs in love marriages in the United States and other Western

countries, as well. In some cases, however, arranged marriages may make it easier for women to be abused or treated as property, in part because marriage practices reflect a general societal view of women as possessions. This may be especially true when religious systems and other ideologies within a culture reinforce the idea that women are of a lesser status.

Clearly, arranged marriages can be practiced in ways that demean, demoralize, and mistreat women. And women may be driven to extreme behaviors, such as suicide, to avoid arranged marriages. Whether these darker aspects of arranged-marriage practices are best handled by actively fighting the tradition of arranged marriages or by attempting to place safeguards against such behaviors within existing systems for arranging marriages is not an easy question to answer. Certainly permitting women (and men) to veto marriages seems a workable solution, and is one already implemented in many families. A more collective system of choosing mates may also imply more collective responsibility toward the welfare of the married. Such a perspective does not imply that either women or men are "property" but views the union between two people as collectively chosen and collectively maintained.

Final Words

One of the controversial conclusions of [this reading] is that the practices of arranging marriage do not necessarily lead to the oppression of women. In fact, arranged marriages are but one of many practices that require Western feminism to confront and resolve issues of cultural variability and heterogeneity in their striving for gender equality (see Abu-Lughod 1991). Without such confrontation, Western feminism will remain Western, at best ineffective in achieving its aims for benefiting women worldwide and at worst clumsily harmful. Unlike other culturally particularized rituals involving women (e.g., female circumcision), arranged marriages do not inherently require that women are injured or oppressed. Some of the existing gender inequities I discussed above are not, in the abstract, different from inequities that are part and parcel of modern American culture. The modernization of the arranged marriage occurring at present in India and elsewhere may maximize the benefits of personal and collective choice. Arranged marriages offer some unique benefits in comparison to love marriages; they are embedded in a strongly supportive context and tend not to be related to unrealistic expectations and demands. Combining these benefits while accommodating those who do meet a lifetime partner on their own may produce a very good alternative to the individual choice practiced in other cultures.

REFERENCES

Abu-Lughod, L. 1991. "Writing against Culture." In *Recapturing Anthropology,* edited by R. G. Fox. Santa Fe, NM: School of American Research Press.
Abu-Lughod, L. 1993. "Analyzing Resistance: Bedouin Women's Stories." Pp. 25–38 in *To Speak or Be Silent,* edited by L. B. Ross. Wilmette, Illinois: Chiron Publishers.

Bandura, A. 1982. "The Psychology of Chance Encounters and Life Paths." *American Psychologist* 37:747–55.

Berscheid, E. and H. T. Reis. 1998. "Attraction and Close Relationships." Pp. 193–281 in *The Handbook of Social Psychology,* edited by D. T. Gilbert, S. Fiske, and G. Lindzey. Vol. 2. Boston: McGraw-Hill.

Blood, R. O. 1972. *The Family.* New York: Free Press.

Buss, D. M., et al. 1989. "International Preferences in Selecting Mates: A Study of 37 Cultures." *Journal of Cross-Cultural Psychology* 21:5–47.

Clements, M. L., A. D. Cordova, H. J. Markman, and J. Laurenceau. 1998. "The Erosion of Marital Satisfaction over Time and How to Prevent It." Pp. 335–55 in *Satisfaction in Close Relationships,* edited by R. J. Sternberg and M. Hojjat. New York: Guilford Press.

Cordova, D. I. and M. R. Lepper. 1996. "Intrinsic Motivation and the Process of Learning: Beneficial Effects of Contextualization, Personalization, and Choice." *Journal of Educational Psychology* 88:715–30.

Fox, G. L. 1975. "Love Match and Arranged Marriage in a Modernizing Nation: Mate Selection in Ankara, Turkey." *Journal of Marriage and the Family* 37:180–93.

Galanter, M. 1986. "'Moonies Get Married': A Psychiatric Follow-Up Study of a Charismatic Religious Sect." *American Journal of Psychiatry* 143:1245–49.

Gottman, J. M. 1994. *What Predicts Divorce? The Relationship between Marital Processes and Marital Outcomes.* Hillsdale, NJ: Erlbaum.

Gottman, J. M. and R. W. Levenson. 1988. "The Social Psychophysiology of Marriage." Pp. 192–200 in *Perspective on Marital Interaction,* edited by P. Noller and M. A. Fitzpatrick. Clevedon, England: Multilingual Matters.

Gupta, U. and P. Singh. 1982. "Exploratory Study of Love and Liking and Type of Marriages." *Indian Journal of Applied Psychology* 19:92–97.

Haider, S. 1995. "Lifting the Veil of Silence: Jamuna's Narrative of Pain." *Sociological Bulletin* 44:241–54.

Hazan, C. and L. M. Diamond. 2000. "The Limits of Sexual Strategies Theory and the Promise of Attachment Theory for Explaining Human Mating." *Review of General Psychology: Special Issue on Attachment* 4:186–204.

Houts, R. M., E. Robins, and T. L. Huston. 1996. "Compatibility and the Development of Premarital Relationships." *Journal of Marriage and the Family* 58:7–20.

Kamo, Y. 1993. "Determinants of Marital Satisfaction: A Comparison of the United States and Japan." *Journal of Social and Personal Relationships* 10:551–68.

Keller, M. C. and R. K. Young. 1996. "Mate Assortment in Dating and Married Couples." *Personality and Individual Differences* 21:217–21.

Kumar, P. and J. Dhyani. 1996. "Marital Adjustment: A Study of Some Related Factors." *Indian Journal of Clinical Psychology* 23:112–16.

Lamb, L. 1999. "No Exit Here." *Utne Reader* 95:26–28.

Lee, G. R. and L. H. Stone. 1980. "Mate-Selection Systems and Criteria: Variation According to Family Structure." *Journal of Marriage and the Family* 42:319–26.

Levine, R., S. Sato, T. Hashimoto, and J. Verma. 1995. "Love and Marriage in Eleven Cultures." *Journal of Cross-Cultural Psychology* 26:554–71.

Mahoney, R. 1995. *Kidding Ourselves: Breadwinning, Babies, and Bargaining Power.* New York: Basic Books.

Rubin, L. B. 1976. *Worlds of Pain: Life in the Working-Class Family.* New York: Basic Books.

Shachar, R. 1991. "His and Her Marital Satisfaction: The Double Standard." *Sex Roles* 25:451–67.

Small, M. F. 1993. *Female Choices: Sexual Behavior of Female Primates.* Ithaca, NY: Cornell University Press.

Thiessen, D., R. K. Young, and M. Delgado. 1997. "Social Pressures for Associative Mating." *Personality and Individual Differences* 22:157–64.

Waris, R. G. 1997. "Age and Occupation in Selection of Human Mates." *Psychological Reports* 80:1223–26.

Yelsma, P. and K. Athappilly. 1988. "Marital Satisfaction and Communication Practices: Comparisons among Indian and American Couples." *Journal of Comparative Family Studies* 19:37–54.

Zeifman, D. and C. Hazan. 1997. "Attachment: The Bond in Pair Bonds." Pp. 237–63 in *Evolutionary Social Psychology,* edited by J. A. Simpson and D. T. Kenrick. Mahwah, NJ: Erlbaum.

PART IV

Marriage, Cohabitation, and Partnership

14

THE DEINSTITUTIONALIZATION OF AMERICAN MARRIAGE

ANDREW J. CHERLIN

A quarter century ago, in an article entitled "Remarriage as an Incomplete Institution" (Cherlin 1978), I argued that American society lacked norms about the way that members of stepfamilies should act toward each other. Parents and children in first marriages, in contrast, could rely on well-established norms, such as when it is appropriate to discipline a child. I predicted that, over time, as remarriage after divorce became common, norms would begin to emerge concerning proper behavior in stepfamilies—for example, what kind of relationship a stepfather should have with his stepchildren. In other words, I expected that remarriage would become institutionalized, that it would become more like first marriage. But just the opposite has happened. Remarriage has not become more like first marriage; rather, first marriage has become more like remarriage. Instead of the institutionalization of remarriage, what has occurred over the past few decades is the deinstitutionalization of marriage. Yes, remarriage is an incomplete institution, but now, so is first marriage—and for that matter, cohabitation.

By deinstitutionalization I mean the weakening of the social norms that define people's behavior in a social institution such as marriage. In times of social stability, the taken-for-granted nature of norms allows people to go about their lives without having to question their actions or the actions of others. But when social change produces situations outside the reach of established norms, individuals can no longer rely on shared understandings of how to act. Rather, they must negotiate new ways of acting, a process that is a potential source of conflict and opportunity. On the one hand, the development of new rules is likely to engender disagreement and tension among

the relevant actors. On the other hand, the breakdown of the old rules of a gendered institution such as marriage could lead to the creation of a more egalitarian relationship between wives and husbands. . . .

The Deinstitutionalization of Marriage

Even as I was writing my 1978 article, the changing division of labor in the home and the increase in childbearing outside marriage were undermining the institutionalized basis of marriage. The distinct roles of homemaker and breadwinner were fading as more married women entered the paid labor force. Looking into the future, I thought that perhaps an equitable division of household labor might become institutionalized. But what happened instead was the "stalled revolution," in Hochschild's (1989) well-known phrase. Men do somewhat more home work than they used to do, but there is wide variation, and each couple must work out their own arrangement without clear guidelines. In addition, when I wrote the article, 1 out of 6 births in the United States occurred outside marriage, already a much higher ratio than at midcentury (U.S. National Center for Health Statistics 1982). Today, the comparable figure is 1 out of 3 (U.S. National Center for Health Statistics 2003). . . . Marriage is no longer the nearly universal setting for child-bearing that it was a half century ago.

Both of these developments—the changing division of labor in the home and the increase in childbearing outside marriage—were well under way when I wrote my 1978 article, as was a steep rise in divorce. Here I discuss two more recent changes in family life, both of which have contributed to the deinstitutionalization of marriage after the 1970s: the growth of cohabitation, which began in the 1970s but was not fully appreciated until it accelerated in the 1980s and 1990s, and same-sex marriage, which emerged as an issue in the 1990s and has come to the fore in the current decade.

The Growth of Cohabitation

In the 1970s, neither I nor most other American researchers foresaw the greatly increased role of cohabitation in the adult life course. We thought that, except among the poor, cohabitation would remain a short-term arrangement among childless young adults who would quickly break up or marry. But it has become a more prevalent and more complex phenomenon. For example, cohabitation has created an additional layer of complexity in stepfamilies. When I wrote my article, nearly all stepfamilies were formed by the remarriage of one or both spouses. Now, about one fourth of all stepfamilies in the United States, and one half of all stepfamilies in Canada, are formed by cohabitation rather than marriage (Bumpass, Raley, and Sweet 1995; Statistics Canada 2002). It is not uncommon, especially among the low-income population, for a woman to have a child outside marriage, end her relationship with that partner, and then begin cohabiting with a different partner. This new union is equivalent in structure to a stepfamily but does

not involve marriage. Sometimes the couple later marries, and if neither has been married before, their union creates a first marriage with stepchildren. As a result, we now see an increasing number of stepfamilies that do not involve marriage, and an increasing number of first marriages that involve stepfamilies.

More generally, cohabitation is becoming accepted as an alternative to marriage. British demographer Kathleen Kiernan (2002) writes that the acceptance of cohabitation is occurring in stages in European nations, with some nations further along than others. In stage one, cohabitation is a fringe or avant garde phenomenon; in stage two, it is accepted as a testing ground for marriage; in stage three, it becomes acceptable as an alternative to marriage; and in stage four, it becomes indistinguishable from marriage. Sweden and Denmark, she argues, have made the transition to stage four; in contrast, Mediterranean countries such as Spain, Italy, and Greece remain in stage one. In the early 2000s, the United States appeared to be in transition from stage two to stage three (Smock and Gupta 2002). A number of indicators suggested that the connection between cohabitation and marriage was weakening. The proportion of cohabiting unions that end in marriage within 3 years dropped from 60% in the 1970s to about 33% in the 1990s (Smock and Gupta), suggesting that fewer cohabiting unions were trial marriages (or that fewer trial marriages were succeeding). In fact, Manning and Smock (2003) reported that among 115 cohabiting working-class and lower middle-class adults who were interviewed in depth, none said that he or she was deciding between marriage and cohabitation at the start of the union. Moreover, only 36% of adults in the 2002 United States General Social Survey disagreed with the statement, "It is all right for a couple to live together without intending to get married" (Davis, Smith, and Marsden 2003). And a growing share of births to unmarried women in the United States (about 40% in the 1990s) were to cohabiting couples (Bumpass and Lu 2000). The comparable share was about 60% in Britain (Ermisch 2001). . . .

To be sure, cohabitation is becoming more institutionalized. In the United States, states and municipalities are moving toward granting cohabiting couples some of the rights and responsibilities that married couples have. . . .

The Emergence of Same-Sex Marriage

The most recent development in the deinstitutionalization of marriage is the movement to legalize same-sex marriage. . . .

Lesbian and gay couples who choose to marry must actively construct a marital world with almost no institutional support. Lesbians and gay men already use the term "family" to describe their close relationships, but they usually mean something different from the standard marriage-based family. Rather, they often refer to what sociologists have called a "family of choice": one that is formed largely through voluntary ties among individuals who are not biologically or legally related (Weeks, Heaphy, and Donovan 2001; Weston 1991). Now they face the task of integrating marriages into these

larger networks of friends and kin. The partners will not even have the option of falling back on the gender-differentiated roles of heterosexual marriage. This is not to say that there will be no division of labor; one study of gay and lesbian couples found that in homes where one partner works longer hours and earns substantially more than the other partner, the one with the less demanding, lower paying job did more housework and more of the work of keeping in touch with family and friends. The author suggests that holding a demanding professional or managerial job may make it difficult for a person to invest fully in sharing the work at home, regardless of gender or sexual orientation (Carrington 1999).

We might expect same-sex couples who have children, or who wish to have children through adoption or donor insemination, to be likely to avail themselves of the option of marriage. (According to the United States Census Bureau [2003b], 33% of women in same-sex partnerships and 22% of men in same-sex partnerships had children living with them in 2000.) Basic issues, such as who would care for the children, would have to be resolved family by family. The obligations of the partners to each other following a marital dissolution have also yet to be worked out. In these and many other ways, gay and lesbian couples who marry in the near future would need to create a marriage-centered kin network through discussion, negotiation, and experiment.

Two Transitions in the Meaning of Marriage

In a larger sense, all of these developments—the changing division of labor, childbearing outside of marriage, cohabitation, and gay marriage—are the result of long-term cultural and material trends that altered the meaning of marriage during the 20th century. The cultural trends included, first, an emphasis on emotional satisfaction and romantic love that intensified early in the century. Then, during the last few decades of the century, an ethic of expressive individualism—which Bellah et al. (1985) describe as the belief that "each person has a unique core of feeling and intuition that should unfold or be expressed if individuality is to be realized" (p. 334)—became more important. On the material side, the trends include the decline of agricultural labor and the corresponding increase in wage labor; the decline in child and adult mortality; rising standards of living; and, in the last half of the 20th century, the movement of married women into the paid workforce.

These developments, along with historical events such as the Depression and World War II, produced two great changes in the meaning of marriage during the 20th century. Ernest Burgess famously labeled the first one as a transition "from an institution to a companionship" (Burgess and Locke 1945). In describing the rise of the companionate marriage, Burgess was referring to the single-earner, breadwinner–homemaker marriage that flourished in the 1950s. Although husbands and wives in the companionate marriage usually adhered to a sharp division of labor, they were supposed to be each other's companions—friends, lovers—to an extent not imagined by the spouses in the institutional marriages of the previous era. The increasing

focus on bonds of sentiment within nuclear families constituted an important but limited step in the individualization of family life. Much more so
than in the 19th century, the emotional satisfaction of the spouses became
an important criterion for marital success. However, through the 1950s,
wives and husbands tended to derive satisfaction from their participation
in a marriage-based nuclear family (Roussel 1989). That is to say, they based
their gratification on playing marital roles well: being good providers, good
homemakers, and responsible parents.

During this first change in meaning, marriage remained the only
socially acceptable way to have a sexual relationship and to raise children
in the United States, Canada, and Europe, with the possible exception of the
Nordic countries. In his history of British marriages, Gillis (1985) labeled the
period from 1850 to 1960 the "era of mandatory marriage." In the United
States, marriage and only marriage was one's ticket of admission to a full
family life. . . .

But beginning in the 1960s, marriage's dominance began to diminish,
and the second great change in the meaning of marriage occurred. In the
United States, the median age at marriage returned to and then exceeded
the levels of the early 1900s. In 2000, the median age was 27 for men and
25 for women (U.S. Census Bureau 2003a). Many young adults stayed single into their mid to late 20s, some completing college educations and starting careers. Cohabitation prior to (and after) marriage became much more
acceptable. Childbearing outside marriage became less stigmatized and
more accepted. Birth rates resumed their long-term declines and sunk to
all-time lows in most countries. Divorce rates rose to unprecedented levels.
Same-sex unions found greater acceptance as well.

During this transition, the companionate marriage lost ground not only
as the demographic standard but also as a cultural ideal. It was gradually
overtaken by forms of marriage (and nonmarital families) that Burgess had
not foreseen, particularly marriages in which both the husband and the wife
worked outside the home. Although women continued to do most of the
housework and child care, the roles of wives and husbands became more
flexible and open to negotiation. And an even more individualistic perspective on the rewards of marriage took root. When people evaluated how satisfied they were with their marriages, they began to think more in terms
of the development of their own sense of self and the expression of their
feelings, as opposed to the satisfaction they gained through building a family and playing the roles of spouse and parent. The result was a transition
from the companionate marriage to what we might call the *individualized
marriage*. . . .

During this second change in the meaning of marriage, the role of the
law changed significantly as well. This transformation was most apparent in
divorce law. In the United States and most other developed countries, legal
restrictions on divorce were replaced by statutes that recognized consensual
and even unilateral divorce. The transition to "private ordering" (Mnookin
and Kornhauser 1979) allowed couples to negotiate the details of their
divorce agreements within broad limits. . . .

Sociological theorists of late modernity (or postmodernity) such as Anthony Giddens (1991, 1992) in Britain and Ulrich Beck and Elisabeth Beck-Gernsheim in Germany (1995, 2002) also have written about the growing individualization of personal life. Consistent with the idea of deinstitutionalization, they note the declining power of social norms and laws as regulating mechanisms for family life, and they stress the expanding role of personal choice. They argue that as traditional sources of identity such as class, religion, and community lose influence, one's intimate relationships become central to self-identity. Giddens (1991, 1992) writes of the emergence of the "pure relationship": an intimate partnership entered into for its own sake, which lasts only as long as both partners are satisfied with the rewards (mostly intimacy and love) that they get from it. It is in some ways the logical extension of the increasing individualism and the deinstitutionalization of marriage that occurred in the 20th century. The pure relationship is not tied to an institution such as marriage or to the desire to raise children. Rather, it is "free-floating," independent of social institutions or economic life. Unlike marriage, it is not regulated by law, and its members do not enjoy special legal rights. It exists primarily in the realms of emotion and self-identity.

Although the theorists of late modernity believe that the quest for intimacy is becoming the central focus of personal life, they do not predict that *marriage* will remain distinctive and important. Marriage, they claim, has become a choice rather than a necessity for adults who want intimacy, companionship, and children. . . .

The Current Context of Marriage

Overall, research and writing on the changing meaning of marriage suggest that it is now situated in a very different context than in the past. This is true in at least two senses. First, individuals now experience a vast latitude for choice in their personal lives. More forms of marriage and more alternatives to marriage are socially acceptable. Moreover, one may fit marriage into one's life in many ways: One may first live with a partner, or sequentially with several partners, without an explicit consideration of whether a marriage will occur. One may have children with one's eventual spouse or with someone else before marrying. One may, in some jurisdictions, marry someone of the same gender and build a shared marital world with few guidelines to rely on. Within marriage, roles are more flexible and negotiable, although women still do more than their share of the household work and childrearing.

The second difference is in the nature of the rewards that people seek through marriage and other close relationships. Individuals aim for personal growth and deeper intimacy through more open communication and mutually shared disclosures about feelings with their partners. They may feel justified in insisting on changes in a relationship that no longer provides them with individualized rewards. In contrast, they are less likely than in the past to focus on the rewards to be found in fulfilling socially valued roles such as the good parent or the loyal and supportive spouse. The result of

these changing contexts has been a deinstitutionalization of marriage, in which social norms about family and personal life count for less than they did during the heyday of the companionate marriage, and far less than during the period of the institutional marriage. Instead, personal choice and self-development loom large in people's construction of their marital careers.

Why Do People Still Marry?

There is a puzzle within the story of deinstitutionalization that needs solving. Although fewer Americans are marrying than during the peak years of marriage in the mid-20th century, most—nearly 90%, according to a recent estimate (Goldstein and Kenney 2001)—will eventually marry. A survey of high school seniors conducted annually since 1976 shows no decline in the importance they attach to marriage. The percentage of young women who respond that they expect to marry has stayed constant at roughly 80% (and has increased from 71% to 78% for young men). The percentage who respond that "having a good marriage and family life" is extremely important has also remained constant, at about 80% for young women and 70% for young men (Thornton and Young-DeMarco 2001). What is more, in the 1990s and early 2000s, a strong promarriage movement emerged among gay men and lesbians in the United States, who sought the right to marry with increasing success. Clearly, marriage remains important to many people in the United States. Consequently, I think the interesting question is not why so few people are marrying, but rather, why so *many* people are marrying, or planning to marry, or hoping to marry, when cohabitation and single parenthood are widely acceptable options. . . .

The Gains to Marriage

The dominant theoretical perspectives on marriage in the 20th century do not provide much guidance on the question of why marriage remains so popular. The structural functionalists in social anthropology and sociology in the early- to mid-20th century emphasized the role of marriage in ensuring that a child would have a link to the status of a man, a right to his protection, and a claim to inherit his property (Mair 1971). But as the law began to recognize the rights of children born outside marriage, and as mothers acquired resources by working in the paid workforce, these reasons for marriage become less important.

Nor is evolutionary theory very helpful. Although there may be important evolutionary influences on family behavior, it is unlikely that humans have developed an innate preference for marriage as we know it. The classical account of our evolutionary heritage is that women, whose reproductive capacity is limited by pregnancy and lactation (which delays the return of ovulation), seek stable pair bonds with men, whereas men seek to maximize their fertility by impregnating many women. Rather than being "natural," marriage-centered kinship was described in much early- and mid-20th

century anthropological writing as the social invention that solved the problem of the sexually wandering male (Tiger and Fox 1971). Moreover, when dependable male providers are not available, women may prefer a reproductive strategy of relying on a network of female kin and more than one man (Hrdy 1999). In addition, marriages are increasingly being formed well after a child is born, yet evolutionary theory suggests that the impetus to marry should be greatest when newborn children need support and protection. In the 1950s, half of all unmarried pregnant women in the United States married before the birth of their child, whereas in the 1990s, only one-fourth married (U.S. Census Bureau 1999). Finally, evolutionary theory cannot explain the persistence of the formal wedding style in which people are still marrying. Studies of preindustrial societies have found that although many have elaborate ceremonies, others have little or no ceremony (Stephens 1963). . . .

From a rational choice perspective, what benefits might contemporary marriage offer that would lead cohabiting couples to marry rather than cohabit? I suggest that the major benefit is what we might call *enforceable trust* (Cherlin 2000; Portes and Sensenbrenner 1993). Marriage still requires a public commitment to a long-term, possibly lifelong relationship. This commitment is usually expressed in front of relatives, friends, and religious congregants. Cohabitation, in contrast, requires only a private commitment, which is easier to break. Therefore, marriage, more so than cohabitation, lowers the risk that one's partner will renege on agreements that have been made. In the language of economic theory, marriage lowers the transaction costs of enforcing agreements between the partners (Pollak 1985). It allows individuals to invest in the partnership with less fear of abandonment. For instance, it allows the partners to invest financially in joint long-term purchases such as homes and automobiles. It allows caregivers to make relationship-specific investments (England and Farkas 1986) in the couple's children—investments of time and effort that, unlike strengthening one's job skills, would not be easily portable to another intimate relationship.

Nevertheless, the difference in the amount of enforceable trust that marriage brings, compared with cohabitation, is eroding. Although relatives and friends will view a divorce with disappointment, they will accept it more readily than their counterparts would have two generations ago. As I noted, cohabiting couples are increasingly gaining the rights previously reserved to married couples. It seems likely that over time, the legal differences between cohabitation and marriage will become minimal in the United States, Canada, and many European countries. The advantage of marriage in enhancing trust will then depend on the force of public commitments, both secular and religious, by the partners.

In general, the prevailing theoretical perspectives are of greater value in explaining why marriage has declined than why it persists. With more women working outside the home, the predictions of the specialization model are less relevant. Although the rational choice theorists remind us that marriage still provides enforceable trust, it seems clear that its enforcement power is declining. Recently, evolutionary theorists have argued that women who have difficulty finding men who are reliable providers might choose

a reproductive strategy that involves single parenthood and kin networks, a strategy that is consistent with changes that have occurred in low-income families. And although the insights of the theorists of late modernity help us understand the changing meaning of marriage, they predict that marriage will lose its distinctive status, and indeed may already have become just one lifestyle among others. Why, then, are so many people still marrying?

The Symbolic Significance of Marriage

What has happened is that although the practical importance of being married has declined, its symbolic importance has remained high, and may even have increased. Marriage is at once less dominant and more distinctive than it was. It has evolved from a marker of conformity to a marker of prestige. Marriage is a status one builds up to, often by living with a partner beforehand, by attaining steady employment or starting a career, by putting away some savings, and even by having children. Marriage's place in the life course used to come before those investments were made, but now it often comes afterward. It used to be the foundation of adult personal life; now it is sometimes the capstone. It is something to be achieved through one's own efforts rather than something to which one routinely accedes.

How Low-Income Individuals See Marriage

Paradoxically, it is among the lower social strata in the United States, where marriage rates are lowest, that both the persistent preference for marriage and its changing meaning seem clearest. Although marriage is optional and often foregone, it has by no means faded away among the poor and near poor. Instead, it is a much sought-after but elusive goal. They tell observers that they wish to marry, but will do so only when they are sure they can do it successfully: when their partner has demonstrated the ability to hold a decent job and treat them fairly and without abuse, when they have a security deposit or a down payment for a decent apartment or home, and when they have enough in the bank to pay for a nice wedding party for family and friends. Edin and Kefalas (2005), who studied childbearing and intimate relationships among 165 mothers in 8 low- and moderate-income Philadelphia neighborhoods, wrote, "In some sense, marriage is a form of social bragging about the quality of the couple relationship, a powerfully symbolic way of elevating one's relationship above others in the community, particularly in a community where marriage is rare."

Along with several collaborators, I am conducting a study of low-income families in three United States cities. The ethnographic component of that study is directed by Linda Burton of Pennsylvania State University. A 27-year-old mother told one of our ethnographers:

> *I was poor all my life and so was Reginald. When I got pregnant, we agreed we would marry some day in the future because we loved each other and wanted to raise our child together. But we would not get married until we could afford to get a house and pay all the utility bills on time. I have this thing about utility*

bills. Our gas and electric got turned off all the time when we were growing up and we wanted to make sure that would not happen when we got married. That was our biggest worry. . . . We worked together and built up savings and then we got married. It's forever for us.

Another woman in our study, already living with the man she was engaged to and had children with, told an ethnographer she was not yet ready to marry him:

But I'm not ready to do that yet. I told him, we're not financially ready yet. He knows that. I told him by the end of this year, maybe. I told him that last year. Plus, we both need to learn to control our tempers, you could say. He doesn't understand that bills and kids and [our relationship] come first, not [his] going out and getting new clothes or [his] doing this and that. It's the kids, then us. He gets paid good, about five hundred dollars a week. How hard is it to give me money and help with the bills?

Note that for this woman, more is required of a man than a steady job before he is marriageable. He has to learn to turn over most of his paycheck to his family rather than spending it on his friends and himself. He must put his relationship with his partner ahead of running with his single male friends, a way of saying that a husband must place a priority on providing companionship and intimacy to his wife and on being sexually faithful. And he and his partner have to learn to control their tempers, a vague referent to the possibility that physical abuse exists in the relationship. In sum, the demands low-income women place on men include not just a reliable income, as important as that is, but also a commitment to put family first, provide companionship, be faithful, and avoid abusive behavior. . . .

Alternative Futures

What do these developments suggest about the future of marriage? Social demographers usually predict a continuation of whatever is happening at the moment, and they are usually correct, but sometimes spectacularly wrong. For example, in the 1930s, every demographic expert in the United States confidently predicted a continuation of the low birth rates of the Depression. Not one forecast the baby boom that overtook them after World War II. No less a scholar than Kingsley Davis (1937) wrote that the future of the family as a social institution was in danger because people were not having enough children to replace themselves. Not a single 1950s or 1960s sociologist predicted the rise of cohabitation. Chastened by this unimpressive record, I will tentatively sketch some future directions.

The first alternative is the reinstitutionalization of marriage, a return to a status akin to its dominant position through the mid-20th century. This would entail a rise in the proportion who ever marry, a rise in the proportion of births born to married couples, and a decline in divorce. It would require a reversal of the individualistic orientation toward family and personal life

that has been the major cultural force driving family change over the past several decades. It would probably also require a decrease in women's labor force participation and a return to more gender-typed family roles. I think this alternative is very unlikely—but then again, so was the baby boom.

The second alternative is a continuation of the current situation, in which marriage remains deinstitutionalized but is common and distinctive. It is not just one type of family relationship among many; rather, it is the most prestigious form. People generally desire to be married. But it is an individual choice, and individuals construct marriages through an increasingly long process that often includes cohabitation and childbearing beforehand. It still confers some of its traditional benefits, such as enforceable trust, but it is increasingly a mark of prestige, a display of distinction, an individualistic achievement, a part of what Beck and Beck-Gernsheim (2002) call the "do-it-yourself biography." In this scenario, the proportion of people who ever marry could fall further; in particular, we could see probabilities of marriage among Whites in the United States that are similar to the probabilities shown today by African Americans. Moreover, because of high levels of nonmarital childbearing, cohabitation, and divorce, people will spend a smaller proportion of their adult lives in intact marriages than in the past. Still, marriage would retain its special and highly valued place in the family system.

But I admit to some doubts about whether this alternative will prevail for long in the United States. The privileges and material advantages of marriage, relative to cohabitation, have been declining. The commitment of partners to be trustworthy has been undermined by frequent divorce. If marriage was once a form of cultural capital—one needed to be married to advance one's career, say—that capital has decreased too. What is left, I have argued, is a display of prestige and achievement. But it could be that marriage retains its symbolic aura largely because of its dominant position in social norms until just a half century ago. It could be that this aura is diminishing, like an echo in a canyon. It could be that, despite the efforts of the wedding industry, the need for a highly ritualized ceremony and legalized status will fade. And there is not much else supporting marriage in the early 21st century.

That leads to a third alternative, the fading away of marriage. Here, the argument is that people are still marrying in large numbers because of institutional lag; they have yet to realize that marriage is no longer important. A nonmarital pure relationship, to use Giddens' ideal type, can provide much intimacy and love, can place both partners on an equal footing, and can allow them to develop their independent senses of self. These characteristics are highly valued in late modern societies. However, this alternative also suggests the predominance of fragile relationships that are continually at risk of breaking up because they are held together entirely by the voluntary commitment of each partner. People may still commit morally to a relationship, but they increasingly prefer to commit voluntarily rather than to be obligated to commit by law or social norms. And partners feel free to revoke their commitments at any time.

Therefore, the pure relationship seems most characteristic of a world where commitment does not matter. Consequently, it seems to best fit

middle-class, well-educated, childless adults. They have the resources to be independent actors by themselves or in a democratic partnership, and without childbearing responsibilities, they can be free-floating. The pure relationship seems less applicable to couples who face material constraints (Jamieson 1999). In particular, when children are present—or when they are anticipated anytime soon—issues of commitment and support come into consideration. Giddens (1992) says very little about children in his book on intimacy, and his brief attempts to incorporate children into the pure relationship are unconvincing. Individuals who are, or think they will be, the primary caregivers of children will prefer commitment and will seek material support from their partners. They may be willing to have children and begin cohabiting without commitment, but the relationship probably will not last without it. They will be wary of purely voluntary commitment if they think they can do better. So only if the advantage of marriage in providing trust and commitment disappears relative to cohabitation—and I must admit that this could happen—might we see cohabitation and marriage on an equal footing.

In sum, I see the current state of marriage and its likely future in these terms: At present, marriage is no longer as dominant as it once was, but it remains important on a symbolic level. It has been transformed from a familial and community institution to an individualized, choice-based achievement. It is a marker of prestige and is still somewhat useful in creating enforceable trust. As for the future, I have sketched three alternatives. The first, a return to a more dominant, institutionalized form of marriage, seems unlikely. In the second, the current situation continues; marriage remains important, but not as dominant, and retains its high symbolic status. In the third, marriage fades into just one of many kinds of interpersonal romantic relationships. I think that Giddens' (1992) statement that marriage has already become merely one of many relationships is not true in the United States so far, but it could become true in the future. It is possible that we are living in a transitional phase in which marriage is gradually losing its uniqueness. If Giddens and other modernity theorists are correct, the third alternative will triumph, and marriage will lose its special place in the family system of the United States. If they are not, the second alternative will continue to hold, and marriage—transformed and deinstitutionalized, but recognizable nevertheless—will remain distinctive.

ENDNOTE

Author's Note: I thank Frank Furstenberg, Joshua Goldstein, Kathleen Kiernan, and Céline Le Bourdais for comments on a previous version, and Linda Burton for her collaborative work on the Three-City Study ethnography.

REFERENCES

Beck, U. and E. Beck-Gernsheim. 1995. *The Normal Chaos of Love.* Cambridge, England: Polity Press.
———. 2002. *Individualization: Institutionalized Individualism and Its Social and Political Consequences.* London: Sage.

Bellah, R., R. Marsden, W. M. Sullivan, A. Swidler, and S. M. Tipton. 1985. *Habits of the Heart: Individualism and Commitment in America.* Berkeley: University of California Press.

Bumpass, L. L. and H.-H. Lu. 2000. "Trends in Cohabitation and Implications for Children's Family Contexts in the United States." *Population Studies* 54:19–41.

Bumpass, L. L., K. Raley, and J. A. Sweet. 1995. "The Changing Character of Stepfamilies: Implications of Cohabitation and Nonmarital Childbearing." *Demography* 32:1–12.

Burgess, E. W. and H. J. Locke. 1945. *The Family: From Institution to Companionship.* New York: American Book.

Carrington, C. 1999. *No Place Like Home: Relationships and Family Life among Lesbians and Gay Men.* Chicago: University of Chicago Press.

Cherlin, A. 1978. "Remarriage as an Incomplete Institution." *American Journal of Sociology* 84:634–50.

———. 2000. "Toward a New Home Socioeconomics of Union Formation." Pp. 126–44 in *Ties That Bind: Perspectives on Marriage and Cohabitation,* edited by L. Waite, C. Bachrach, M. Hindin, E. Thomson, and A. Thornton. Hawthorne, NY: Aldine de Gruyter.

Davis, J. A., T. W. Smith, and P. Marsden. 2003. *General Social Surveys, 1972–2002 Cumulative Codebook.* Chicago: National Opinion Research Center, University of Chicago.

Davis, K. 1937. "Reproductive Institutions and the Pressure for Population." *Sociological Review* 29:289–306.

Edin, K. J. and M. J. Kefalas. 2005. *Promises I Can Keep: Why Poor Women Put Motherhood Before Marriage.* Berkeley: University of California Press.

England, P. and G. Farkas. 1986. *Households, Employment, and Gender: A Social, Economic, and Demographic View.* New York: Aldine.

Ermisch, J. 2001. "Cohabitation and Childbearing Outside Marriage in Britain." Pp. 109–39 in *Out of Wedlock: Causes and Consequences of Nonmarital Fertility,* edited by L. L. Wu and B. Wolfe. New York: Russell Sage Foundation.

Giddens, A. 1991. *Modernity and Self-Identity.* Stanford, CA: Stanford University Press.

———. 1992. *The Transformation of Intimacy.* Stanford, CA: Stanford University Press.

Gillis, J. R. 1985. *For Better or Worse: British Marriages, 1600 to the Present.* Oxford, England: Oxford University Press.

Goldstein, J. R. and C. T. Kenney. 2001. "Marriage Delayed or Marriage Forgone? New Cohort Forecasts of First Marriage for U.S. Women." *American Sociological Review* 66:506–19.

Hochschild, A. 1989. *The Second Shift: Working Parents and the Revolution at Home.* New York: Viking.

Hrdy, S. B. 1999. *Mother Nature: Maternal Instincts and How They Shape the Human Species.* New York: Ballantine Books.

Jamieson, L. 1999. "Intimacy Transformed? A Critical Look at the "Pure Relationship." *Sociology* 33:477–94.

Kiernan, K. 2002. "Cohabitation in Western Europe: Trends, Issues, and Implications." Pp. 3–31 in *Just Living Together: Implication of Cohabitation on Families, Children, and Social Policy,* edited by A. Booth and A. C. Crouter. Mahwah, NJ: Erlbaum.

Mair, L. 1971. *Marriage.* Middlesex, England: Penguin Books.

Manning, W. and P. J. Smock. 2003, May. "Measuring and Modeling Cohabitation: New Perspectives from Qualitative Data." Presented at the annual meeting of the Population Association of America, Minneapolis, MN.

Mnookin, R. H. and L. Kornhauser. 1979. "Bargaining in the Shadow of the Law: The Case of Divorce." *Yale Law Journal* 88:950–97.

Pollak, R. A. 1985. "A Transaction Costs Approach to Families and Households." *Journal of Economic Literature* 23:581–608.

Portes, A. and J. Sensenbrenner. 1993. "Embeddedness and Immigration: Notes on the Social Determinants of Economic Action. *American Journal of Sociology* 98:1320–50.

Roussel, L. 1989. *La Famille Incertaine.* Paris: Editions Odile Jacob.

Smock, P. J. 2004. "The Wax and Wane of Marriage: Prospects for Marriage in the 21st Century." *Journal of Marriage and the Family* 66:966–79.

Smock, P. J. and S. Gupta. 2002. "Cohabitation in Contemporary North America." Pp. 53–84 in *Just Living Together: Implications of Cohabitation on Families, Children, and Social Policy,* edited by A. Booth and A. C. Crouter. Mahwah, NJ: Erlbaum.

Statistics Canada. 2002. *Changing Conjugal Life in Canada.* No. 89–576-XIE. Ottawa, Ontario: Statistical Reference Centre.

Stephens, William N. 1963. *The Family in Cross-Cultural Perspective.* New York: Holt, Rinehart and Winston.

Thornton, A. and L. Young-DeMarco. 2001. "Four Decades of Trends in Attitudes toward Family Issues in the United States: The 1960s through the 1990s." *Journal of Marriage and Family* 63:1009–37.

Tiger, L. and R. Fox. 1971. *The Imperial Animal.* New York: Holt, Rinehart and Winston.

U.S. Census Bureau. 1999. "Trends in Premarital Childbearing: 1930–1994." *Current Population Reports,* No. P23-97. Washington, DC: U.S. Government Printing Office.

———. 2003a. "Estimated Median Age at First Marriage, by Sex: 1890 to Present." Retrieved January 11, 2003 (http://www.census.gov/population/www/socdemo/hh-fam.html).

———. 2003b. "Married-Couple and Unmarried-Partner Households: 2000." *Census 2000 Special Reports,* CENSR-5. Washington, DC: U.S. Government Printing Office.

U.S. National Center for Health Statistics. 1982. *Vital Statistics of the United States, 1978.* Vol. I *Natality.* Washington, DC: U.S. Government Printing Office.

———. 2003. "Births: Preliminary Data for 2002." Retrieved December 15, 2003 (http://www. cdc.gov/nchs/data/nvsr/nvsr51/nvsr51_11.pdf).

Weeks, J., B. Heaphy, and C. Donovan. 2001. *Same-Sex Intimacies: Families of Choice and Other Life Experiments.* London: Routledge.

Weston, K. 1991. *Families We Choose: Lesbians, Gays, Kinship.* New York: Columbia University Press.

15

STATE OF OUR UNIONS
Marriage Promotion and the Contested Power of Heterosexuality

MELANIE HEATH

In the 2002 *Frontline* documentary "Let's Get Married," Alex Kotlowitz declared that today "everyone from the government to church leaders to intellectuals—on both the right and the left—are pushing marriage." Kotlowitz is referring to the marriage movement launched in the late 1990s by a coalition of religious and civic leaders, public officials, family therapists, educators, researchers, and others. Advocates support an array of government policies collectively known as "marriage promotion," which seek to reduce the rate of divorce and single parenting. Many of these policies were codified into federal law in the Personal Responsibility and Work Opportunity Reconciliation Act of 1996. Ending more than 60 years of federal welfare benefits to poor families, the Personal Responsibility and Work Opportunity Reconciliation Act created discretionary state block grants under the rubric of Temporary Assistance to Needy Families (TANF) and specifically designated marriage promotion as a sanctioned use of federal funds. Since the

Melanie Heath, "State of Our Unions: Marriage Promotion and the Contested Power of Heterosexuality" from *Gender & Society* 23, no. 1 (February 1, 2009): 27–48. Copyright © 2009 by Sage Publications. Reprinted with the permission of Sage Publications, Inc.

election of President George W. Bush, federal funding for marriage promotion has grown substantially. The Healthy Marriage Initiative has directed federal money to promote marriage and fatherhood programs, and in 2005, Congress passed a federal appropriations act that includes more than $500 million annually for marriage promotion.

This [reading] explores the power dynamics of marriage promotion, particularly in terms of the enforcement of heterosexuality and hierarchies of gender, race, and class. I place the emerging field of critical heterosexuality studies in dialogue with feminist state theory to bring to light the crisis tendencies of institutionalized heterosexuality in relation to the diminishing dominance of the white, nuclear family (Connell 1995; Ingraham 1999). As marriage promotion programs have sprouted across the country, feminist and gay/lesbian scholars have offered criticisms of such policies as a form of discipline and control, particularly for poor women (Cahill 2005; Coltrane 2001; Coontz and Folbre 2002; Hardisty 2007; Mink 2003; Moon and Whitehead 2006; Polikoff 2008). Others embrace the benefits of marriage but caution against it as a panacea for poverty (Lichter, Graefe, and Brown 2003). To date, no study has examined the implementation of marriage promotion policies on the ground. This [reading] draws on data from the first in-depth study of marriage promotion in both state and local contexts. Examining the state's structure as forming a gendered and sexualized national identity, this study reveals the state's polycentric practices that seek to stabilize the norm of the white, middle-class, heterosexual family. At the policy level, state practices seek to secure boundaries of exclusion in the form of rhetoric on "fractured families" and inclusion through the norm of the white, middle-class family. On the ground, marriage workshops teach about gender hierarchy to rehearse an implicit ideology of marital heterosexuality. In contrast to feminist state theories that present a monolithic, top-down model of state control, this [reading] offers a more nuanced examination of the relationship between macro and micro levels of power and their uneven consequences for social change (see Haney 1996).

State Interest in Heterosexual Marriage

Nation-building strategies tied to the white, nuclear family have a long history in the United States. Federal and state law has shaped marriage as a form of inclusion and exclusion by determining who can marry, the rights and obligations involved in marriage, and the conditions under which a marriage can end. Historian Nancy Cott (2000:3) identifies how in the United States the government has promoted a particular model of marriage: "lifelong, faithful monogamy, formed by the mutual consent of a man and a woman, bearing the impress of the Christian religion and the English common law in its expectations for the husband to be the family head and economic provider." The ideal of the nuclear family in the United States evolved by separating "productive labor" from the home, creating a new social category: the "housewife" (Pascale 2001). Domesticity attributed to

wealthy white women became the standard for all women, and the "Cult of True Womanhood" elevated the submissive housewife as morally superior (Brown 1990; Pascale 2001). In contrast, racial ethnic women have systematically been relegated to do the "dirty work" in domestic service and industry (Duffy 2007). Protecting the family and nation has meant maintaining boundaries of racial and sexual purity. In building the nation, the federal and state government sought to "civilize" American Indians by instituting monogamous households, instilling a work ethic among men and domesticity among women (Cott 2000). Slaves were denied the right to marry, signifying their lack of civil rights that would entail the freedom to consent to marriage's obligations. Before and after slaves' emancipation, many states passed laws to ban marriage across the color line, as the specter of sexual relations between white women and African American men created moral panic. Concerns about race and morality also motivated the evolution of immigration law, which largely restricted the entry of Chinese and Japanese women.

Governmental intervention has changed over time in how it envisions protecting "the family," but the thread in this history can be traced to the need to safeguard the boundaries of the nation along the lines of race, class, gender, and sexuality (McClintock 1997). In recent years, federal and state concern has focused on "family breakdown." Sharp rises in female labor force participation, divorce, cohabitation, and single parenting have triggered a "deinstitutionalization" of marriage (Cherlin 2004). These changes, together with the growing movement to legalize same-sex marriage, call into question what constitutes "normal" family life in the United States (Stacey 1996). In the 1960s, President Lyndon Johnson drew on a report from a little-known senator, Patrick Daniel Moynihan, to address the problem of the "breakdown of the Negro family structure" (quoted in Blankenhorn 2007:5). Controversy about the report ultimately led to a new consensus between conservative and liberal policy makers about what they viewed as the bad behavior of impoverished single mothers inherent in "welfare dependency" (Reese 2005). More recently, marriage advocate David Blankenhorn (2007:5) has identified a united policy stance to address "the breakdown of *white* family structure" that he believes has followed the trends purportedly undermining Black families. These concerns now motivate federal and state policy to promote marriage. While race and class are visible in these policies, below the surface are anxieties about changing gender relations and the challenge to heterosexuality presented by the increased visibility of lesbian and gay families. Thus, marriage promotion offers a novel case to contribute to the development of feminist state theory as federal and state actors enact policies to reinstate the heterosexual, nuclear family in American culture.

State Theory and Critical Heterosexuality Studies

Feminist theories of the state are relatively new (Haney 2000). Theories that emerged out of second-wave feminism often envisioned the state as the

perpetuator of patriarchy, offering a monolithic conceptualization of state power over women as a homogeneous group. In recent years, feminist state theory has expanded to analyze the gendered state and its social practices that regulate the gender of its citizens along the lines of race and class (Brown 1992; Mosse 1985; Yuval-Davis 1997). Scholars doing comparative and U.S.-focused research on welfare states have demonstrated the ways that government policy and law concerning welfare, pension, child care/ education, and the labor market shapes and is shaped by ideologies of gender, race, and class while at the same time interacting with norms around family and marriage (Glauber 2008; Gordon 1994; Hays 2003; Misra 1998; Misra, Moller, and Budig 2007; O'Connor, Orloff, and Shaver 1999; Reese 2005). Feminist scholarship on the state, however, has tended to take for granted normative ideas about heterosexuality, including the presumption that heterosexual pairings define social institutions like marriage and the family. As a corrective to this presumption, I put state theory and critical heterosexuality studies in dialogue to examine the relationship of the gendered and sexualized state to normative heterosexuality (Cooper 1995, 2002).

In the 1990s, scholars began to focus a critical lens on the ways that heterosexuality serves as the standard for all "sexual-socio behavior," charting a new theoretical path called critical heterosexuality studies (Ingraham 2005:4). Contemporary theorists of sexuality have elucidated the emergence of "the homosexual" as a category of person distinct from "the heterosexual" in the later part of the nineteenth century and the subsequent amassing of medical, legal, psychological, and literary discourses based on the heterosexual/homosexual binary (Foucault 1981; Katz 1996; Sedgwick 1990). Originating in radical lesbian feminist critiques of heterosexuality as a patriarchal institution, critical heterosexuality scholarship has established heterosexuality and its exclusionary practices vis-à-vis homosexuality as an important topic of inquiry and shed light on its organizational and ritualistic practices as a set of rules and norms for behavior (Ingraham 1999). Marital heterosexuality occupies the largely invisible core of natural and desirable sexuality, and homosexuality the periphery as perverse and unnatural (Roseneil 2002). Legal marriage has consequently been a central mechanism the state has used to regulate institutionalized heterosexuality and the construct of the "natural" (white, middle-class) family.

Critical heterosexuality studies stress the coconstitution of gender and sexuality, contributing to scholarship on the performative aspects within marital heterosexuality (Butler [1990] 1999; Ingraham 1999). Valorizing the "natural" family, U.S. federal and state law attaches a considerable number of benefits to heterosexual marriage: retirement and death benefits, family leave policies, health care decision making and access, taxation, immigration, and numerous others. The power of state practice rests not only in specific law and policy but in its ability to conceal the work involved in maintaining the unitary "nature" of institutionalized heterosexuality. But beyond this, more recent, and more active, efforts to promote marriage have further institutionalized inequalities in the face of growing challenges posed by structural changes in global economies, transformation in family life, and

movements for lesbian and gay rights and gender equality (Ingraham 1999). In this [reading], I examine the uneven outcomes of state policy efforts to implement marriage promotion on the ground.

Studying Marriage Promotion

To study marriage promotion, I conducted ethnographic research for 10 months in 2004 in Oklahoma. Oklahoma is home to the most extensive state-wide marriage initiative in the nation, and consequently its policy "extends out" and is influenced by national marriage promotion politics (Burawoy 1998). In 1999, the governor employed the marriage promotion provisions of the Personal Responsibility and Work Opportunity Reconciliation Act to pioneer the Oklahoma Marriage Initiative at a time when few states opted to exercise this option. The Oklahoma Department of Human Services (OKDHS) committed $10 million from its federal TANF block grant and contracted with Public Strategies, Inc. (a private, for-profit firm) to develop and manage the initiative. The Oklahoma Marriage Initiative trains state employees, community leaders, and other volunteers to offer marriage education workshops throughout the state. The workshops use the Prevention and Relationship Enhancement Program (PREP), a research-based curriculum created by Howard Markman and Scott Stanley that teaches communication skills, conflict management, and problem solving. The initiative also trains volunteers to offer a Christian version of the PREP curriculum in settings that are not state funded. In exchange for receiving free workshop training, volunteers pledge to provide at least four free workshops in their communities.

In addition to its groundbreaking marriage initiative, Oklahoma is also well known for being a Bible Belt state. Nearly 60 percent of registered voters say they attend church regularly, compared to the national average of 40 percent (Campbell 2002). Oklahoma's high religiosity would appear to render it exceptional with respect to wide-ranging marriage promotion activities across the nation. Indeed, Oklahoma's social and cultural environment is likely one reason that the marriage initiative was able to take root in the early years of welfare reform, as a Republican governor initiated it with little political resistance. While there are many unique aspects to the formation of the marriage initiative, Oklahoma has nevertheless served as a model for state and community marriage promotion programs across the nation. In recent years, Alabama, Georgia, North Carolina, New Mexico, New York, Ohio, Texas, and Utah have also designated portions of their TANF block grants for marriage promotion. Texas legislated $7.5 million a year.[1]

The Oklahoma Marriage Initiative blends two models of marriage promotion. On the one hand, it seeks to blanket the state with messages about marriage by providing free marriage workshops to as many Oklahomans as possible. On the other, it targets specific populations, including welfare recipients, low-income parents, high school students, the prison population, the military, and Native Americans. I conducted fieldwork on the workshops

for both the general and target populations and found that the more sustained efforts were the workshops for the general population.

These included large Sweetheart Weekends that occurred every few months and offered the curriculum on a Friday evening and all day Saturday.[2] Advertised on local radio stations and in the newspaper, they drew 50 or more couples on average. Weekly smaller workshops were advertised on the Oklahoma Marriage Initiative's Web site and through local churches. By 2006, the initiative had trained 1,500 volunteers to conduct the workshops and had provided services to 37,500 people. Data for this article include fieldwork on public workshops and in-depth interviews with marriage initiative leaders and participants.

To gain access, I first met with two Oklahoma Marriage Initiative employees at the annual conference of the marriage movement held in Las Vegas in 2003. The Smart Marriages conference features presentations by more than 100 marriage experts and is attended by therapists, counselors, clergy, policy makers, educators, and the public. My two initial contacts expressed enthusiasm about my idea of doing ethnographic research on the initiative's cultural impact. When I arrived in Oklahoma in February of 2004, I contacted them about attending workshops as a single woman. Altogether, I participated in 30 workshops for the general public that were advertised on the marriage initiative's Web site, including three Sweetheart Weekends (six classes), three six-week workshops (15 classes), and 24 weekend workshops (24 classes).[3] At the beginning of each workshop, I introduced myself and my research and took detailed field notes. I also conducted participant observation of a state-sponsored PREP training weekend to discover the method for training volunteers. Finally, I conducted 20 in-depth, semistructured interviews with volunteer participants and leaders from workshops and 15 with the Oklahoma Marriage Initiative leadership and OKDHS staff that lasted between one and two hours.[4] All interviewees were given pseudonyms. The transcribed interviews and field notes were coded using a qualitative software program, Atlas.ti. In this process, I discovered a gap between the Oklahoma Marriage Initiative's stated goals and its on-the-ground practices. This [reading] examines marriage promotion activities targeted to a general population that included predominantly white, middle-class couples.

Rein[State]Ing White, Middle-Class Marriage

In 1999, the former Republican governor of the state of Oklahoma, responding to an economic report that linked Oklahoma's declining economy to its purportedly weakening family structure, announced a goal of reducing the state's divorce rate by one-third by the year 2010. This goal was later restated more nebulously as an initiative to strengthen healthy marriages, an objective that might, at first glance, appear benign. However, when I asked the president and the acting project manager of Public Strategies about the objective, she confirmed that it is specifically aimed to promote marriage—in and of itself—as a special and beneficial type of relationship. She stated,

The goal of the initiative is to strengthen marriage, and we are really unwaver-
ing about that goal. We believe that marriage is a different kind of relationship
with different kinds of outcomes, and so we are not in any way, shape, or form
going to do anything that sells that goal short.

By "outcomes," the project manager evokes the statistical debate about social
scientific research on childhood outcomes. This research has shown that, on
average, children growing up in a one-parent family experience some disadvantage compared to those growing up with two parents. Although scholars
are divided about the causes of these disadvantages (e.g., Blankenhorn 2007;
Cherlin 2003), marriage promotion advocates recite this body of research to
justify the need to promote marriage so that every child can grow up with
her or his biological, married parents.

Fears about the declining significance of the nuclear family have
spurred the Oklahoma Marriage Initiative to offer marriage education to
the public as a mechanism to reinstitutionalize marriage. As one report puts
it, the strategy of the marriage initiative is to provide marriage education
services to all Oklahomans to effect "specific behavior change at the individual level" and to "restore support for the institution of marriage as a
valued social good" (Dion 2006). When I interviewed the OKDHS director, he described being enlightened by reading Barbara Dafoe Whitehead's
(1993:84) *Atlantic Monthly* article "Dan Quayle Was Right," which explains
"family breakup" as breeding behaviors that "damage the social ecology,
threaten the public order, and impose new burdens on core institutions."
Whitehead goes on to express concern that the once isolated breakup of
Black families is now spreading to white ones. This implicit (and sometimes
explicit) racial comparison is a common theme in the discourse of the marriage movement. Kay Hymowitz (2006:78), the author of *Marriage and Caste
in America,* argues that educating the young to be "self-reliant" members
of a democratic society is "The Mission" of white, middle-class families
and that poor Black parents are not "simply middle-class parents *manqué;*
they have their own culture of childrearing, and—not to mince words—
that culture is a recipe for more poverty." This philosophy harks back to
nation-building principles that analogize marriage and the state as a necessary form of governance to produce worthy (white, middle-class) citizens
(Cott 2000).

In the national discussion, the poor Black family remains an invisible
standard of deviancy. As the focus of policy has turned to family breakdown,
the mostly unspoken concern of marriage promotion leaders is the norm of
the white, middle-class family and the harm caused to this norm. During our
interview, the OKDHS director outlined the cost of "fractured families":

Another piece of this, when you sit back and think about it, we spend $40 mil-
lion in this state to run our child support enforcement division. Every one of
those faces is a fractured relationship. So, we are spending $40 million in the
state to do nothing but administer the transfer of cash from non-custodial par-
ents to custodial parents who have experienced fractured relationships. You can
see the high cost of having fractured relationships. It's worth the investment.

The director's words suggest that the "deviancy" of fractured families hurts middle-class families that consist of good citizens who pay taxes and embrace Hymowitz's (2006) "Mission."

The focus on fractured families reinforces a boundary around the normalcy of the white, middle-class, nuclear family. One of the top managers of the marriage initiative, a social worker who maintains a more critical stance, offered this evaluation:

> *The way Governor Keating attached lowering the divorce rate through a poverty-funded program, who are we blaming for the divorce rate? I mean that kind of message is real strong in my mind. I've got an education so I was concerned about people living in poverty being blamed for the divorce rate and the state of families and that kind of thing.*

Attaching marriage promotion to TANF shifts attention away from transformations taking place among white, middle-class families and places it on poor ones. Moreover, the welfare-to-work provisions in TANF, which enforce stringent work requirements and set time limits for receiving aid, help to ensure that poor "dependent" women (most often U.S.-born and immigrant women of color) are bound to low-wage jobs in service industry.

Marriage promotion follows a long history in the United States of defending the ideal gendered family to preserve a bounded space of normalcy against "deviant" others, with attendant social consequences of race and class inequalities. While positioning fractured families as a social problem, the marriage initiative's practices on the ground predominantly focus on white, middle-class couples to promote a bounded heterosexual space to define the ideal family. In the marriage workshops, issues of race and class disappear, and the focus turns on the problematic of gender relations for heterosexual couples. Heterosexuality is the unexamined backdrop to teach about the "opposite sexes" within the ideal family.

Teaching the Importance of Gender (and Heterosexuality)

A dominant ideology of marriage promotion, and its historical presumption in the gendered behavior of the opposite sexes, view it as forming the foundation of a cohesive and stable society. Crisis tendencies, in the form of growing marriage activism by gays and lesbians, are beneath the surface of this ideology, informing the need to strengthen heterosexual relationships. When I asked the OKDHS director, for example, about the goal of the marriage initiative, he confirmed the ideal of marital heterosexuality: "In terms of the marriage initiative, it's relationships between men and women which are committed preferably for life." His use of the words "relationships between men and women" announces the kind of relationships applicable—a declaration that would have been unnecessary 20 years ago—and suggests the prohibition of nonheterosexual love.

With heterosexuality as the unquestioned footing, the marriage workshops for the general population represent a forum to teach the mostly

white, middle-class couples who attend about gender as *the* visible problem. The instruction encourages self-discipline and motivation to do gender in the manner compelled by the ideology of the "natural" family (Hay 2003). PREP, the secular version of the curriculum, engages communication and problem-solving skills. One of its main features is the speaker/listener technique, which instructs the speaker, who holds the "floor"—a tile that lists the rules of communication—to make brief "I" statements and the listener to paraphrase what he or she has heard. Despite the mostly gender-neutral curriculum, the 30 workshops I attended stressed gender relations in marriage.

The three-day, state-sponsored workshop leader training of PREP and its Christian version, taught by its creators—Howard Markman and Scott Stanley—and Vice President Natalie Jenkins, established the importance of gender to an implicit heterosexuality. Volunteers attending the training were predominantly white, many of them counselors and educators receiving continuing education units. Throughout, the three presenters focused on what men versus women do in relationships. Scott Stanley told the audience that he wanted to talk about gender differences and explained how researchers have found a pattern that involves women's pursuing an issue and men's withdrawing. He attributed this to men's tendency to be more physiologically reactive and women to be more emotionally aroused. Stanley acknowledged that these patterns of behavior are complex and that researchers have difficulty deciding what is physiological and what is not. Yet he suggested that the pattern seems to reflect a greater need for men not to argue with their mates. He conveyed that a central goal for teaching PREP is helping couples manage gender differences.

Stanley explained the impact of the decline of marriage on men and women. He argued that today, young people think that cohabiting is a good first step to test marriage but that in reality, practicing serial non-monogamy hurts women because marriage is the only means to ensure a man's commitment. Citing research, Stanley told us that a young man who lives with his girlfriend tends to think she is not the "one," while a young woman thinks just the opposite. He explained, "We have talked young people out of thinking that marriage matters, particularly young women. Women get the worse deal if men don't marry them." Although it is not clear what he meant by the "worse deal," Stanley implied that women are naturally more committed to men, whereas men need the institution of marriage to become self-disciplined practitioners of lifelong monogamy. A dominant script of marital heterosexuality is that men know to settle down—that is, no longer act on their sexual urges—after they marry.

The curriculum includes a number of videos of real couples fighting. One shows a young African American couple who argue over the amount of time the man spends watching sports. During the young man's explanation for why his sport watching is not excessive, Howard Markman stopped the video to point out the way he lifts his hands up and "gazes towards heaven." Markman called this the "beam me up Scotty response." He explained, "This really is an appeal to God. We have a special message to the women in the room. If your partner, husband, son has this response, you might mistakenly

think that he is withdrawing, but he is having a spiritual moment." I laughed along with the audience, but what makes this statement funny is the cultural assumption of an embattled masculinity. Markman implied that women cannot really understand the nature of men, which leads to the kind of exasperation shown in the video. Later, Scott Stanley told us that the young man is asking for his wife to accept this important part of him—the part that lives on sports. Statements like this place the onus on the wife to understand the "nature" of men.

Throughout the training, the presenters performed gender and made jokes that drew on the innate differences between men and women, providing a message about handling gender within heterosexual relationships (Butler [1990] 1999; West and Zimmerman 1987). These performances and dialogue subtly suggest a gender hierarchy compelling women to put up with men's idiosyncrasies since ultimately men are the stronger sex. At one point, Howard Markman told a joke about how many men it takes to change the toilet paper. The punch line: There is no scientific answer because it has not happened. Underneath the humor is the suggestion that men have more important things to do than change toilet paper. Several moments later, he flipped the remote as if he were surfing television channels, distracting from Natalie Jenkins' presentation. She told him to "sit" and informed us that she forgot to take the batteries out of the men's toy. She quickly qualified that she "needed" these guys because she is not the most technologically advanced. As we watched a video of a couple fighting over the way the husband put the laundry soap in the washer, Jenkins asserted that the wife is "missing the miracle. He's doing the laundry!" Later, Jenkins discussed expectations and how, when she was first married, she wanted flowers because all her friends were getting them. She and her husband were having financial difficulties, so she found a 99-cent coupon for a dozen carnations. She put four quarters and the coupon on the fridge with a note saying, "Honey, if this coupon expires so will you."

All of this gender work solidifies the importance of the differences between men and women. Men play with toys (and are technologically advanced); women want flowers (and do laundry). The state's promotion of marriage makes visible the importance of these gendered practices, teaching men and women to monitor and accept the differences between men and women. At heart is a lesson about gender difference as the glue that keeps two people of the opposite sex together. The ideal for white, middle-class families is a configuration of gender hierarchy premised on institutionalized heterosexuality. Tying gender difference to understandings of bodies solidifies marital heterosexuality.

The union of gender differences and bodies together with institutionalized heterosexuality was even more pronounced in the breakout training session of the Christian version of PREP. Scott Stanley discussed how gender differences originate in the Genesis passage of the Bible. He explained,

> *I think it is interesting that it says man [will leave his mother and father] and not man and woman. I have come to believe from science—and this is going to*

sound sexist—why males are called to a higher level of commitment and sacri-fice, biologically and scripturally. Women are inherently made more vulnerable than men because they have babies. Males need to protect. Unfortunately, in our culture, we have gutted that, and women bear the most burden by the lack of a sacrificial ethic.

His statement makes explicit the often implicit instruction on gender differ-ence throughout the training—men are naturally less emotional and better equipped for certain responsibilities in marriage, namely, the need to protect their families. The interaction of gender and heterosexuality is important to position men and women hierarchically as part of a social order that rewards married, heterosexual (and mostly white, middle-class) men as husbands and often as the primary breadwinner.

Linking ideas of gender and heterosexuality directly to bodies, the instructor presented the definition of marriage as a union of male and female. According to Stanley,

God meant something when he specified that there should be male and female and what to do with bodies. I don't just mean sex and physical union, but I mean oneness. They covered up where they are most obviously different. We don't cover up where we are similar. We fear rejection in relationships because of the possibility of difference. Difference symbolizes physical union, which is now apparent to them.

The heterosexual footing implied by the idea of the opposite sexes is also the ground for the performance of gender hierarchy. Through the state-sponsored instruction, potential instructors of PREP and the Christian version of PREP are taught to present ideas about gender and sexuality to encourage self-monitoring in relation to the ideal of the "natural," married family.

Rehearsing the Power of Heterosexuality

Teaching about gender within the confines of marital heterosexuality enables the state to govern indirectly by encouraging self-regulation. However, suc-cess is never guaranteed. While the hierarchical heterosexual/homosexual binary is a systematic presence in modern society, shifts within its organi-zation can render an unproblematic heterosexuality less trouble free. Crisis tendencies motivate efforts like marriage promotion to shore up marriage's boundary while simultaneously undermining these labors. For the marriage initiative, the increasing visibility of same-sex couples troubles efforts to strengthen a clear boundary of marital heterosexuality.

In the 30 marriage promotion workshops I attended, most included heterosexual married or engaged couples and sometimes a single woman or man. In two of the six-week workshops, however, there was one lesbian couple.[5] The first of these included 14 white heterosexual couples, one interra-cial heterosexual couple, and three female coaches, two white and one Black. Tammy and Chris, white lesbians in their fifties, had introduced themselves

as "life partners" on the first day. They had a number of issues with communication. After hearing about the workshop on the radio, Tammy enrolled herself and "a friend." They told me they were relieved they were not asked to leave. The next workshop included Amanda and Jennifer, a white lesbian couple in their late twenties, among the 18 white couples, two white single men, and two female coaches, one white and one Black. Amanda and Jennifer were less talkative, but with their severe communication problems, by their own admission, they monopolized much of the coaches' energy during the practice exercises.

Some of the workshops, especially those targeted to low-income populations, are taught by social workers or other state employees aware of and often committed to the National Association of Social Workers (NASW) code of ethics that takes a strong stand against discrimination on the basis of sexual orientation. In the first workshop, the instructors were volunteers from the community and not social workers: David, a white married professional, and Randy, a white married associate Baptist pastor at a church in town. Randy, joined by Susan, who attended his church, taught the second workshop.

Similar to the training seminar I attended, a central focus of the workshops was on gender differences within marriage. David and Randy often referenced sports to command men's attention. For example, Randy talked about the tendency for one person to withdraw in an argument and said, "This is just what men do, withdraw." He provided the analogy of playing baseball. When you get hit a few times, you tend to give up. He said this is the same with arguing; sometimes it just feels easier to give up or withdraw. Instead of giving up, he encouraged men to practice. David piped in, "Can you do the same analogy with knitting?" and Randy shot back, "I can't, but I'm sure there are those in the audience who can!" In the next six-week workshop, Randy told the participants that having "crappy experiences in marriage is a man thing, not a God thing." This is a "big boy thing," he declared. "God gives me a good picture of how I am supposed to be in a relationship. He calls you to love one person."

The focus on gender within the confines of marital heterosexuality ensured that the same-sex couples' presence remained invisible. This was true even in the case of Tammy and Chris, who were very vocal. The last class of the first six-week session on sensuality/sexuality offered one of the more poignant examples. David asked people to share how their families of origin had discussed sexuality with them when they were young. I was sitting at an end table with Tammy and Chris. David began at the table opposite us and stopped at the table next to ours to talk about his own upbringing, skipping Tammy, Chris, and myself. This omission did not deter the two from participating. When David asked about sensuality and touch, Tammy spoke up: "We assume that what we like, the other person likes." Her words drew attention to the fact that her partner is a woman and not a man. While it is probably true that heterosexuals and nonheterosexuals make this kind of assumption, her statement stood in bold relief to the dominant message of managing difference in heterosexual relationships.

Comments such as this one challenge taken-for-granted assumptions of gender and sexuality.

All the participants I interviewed acknowledged awareness of the lesbian couples without my asking, and most admitted feeling a little uncomfortable due to either their disapproval of or their inexperience dealing with same-sex relationships. Tom, a white man in his mid-twenties who attended with Suzanne, said he was caught off guard by "the two girls who were there together. They were like lesbians. I was surprised, I guess." Becky, a white woman in her thirties who was married and had four children with Martin, an African American man in his early forties, answered my question about whether anything in the workshop made her uncomfortable:

> *Mmm. I did feel uncomfortable with the fact that there were couples in there of the same sex, just because I feel strongly about family values and what the traditional family is. But I know it is something that is happening in the United States, and there is really nothing I can do about it. And, I mean, they are human. They have needs too. It doesn't mean that I agree with them.*

Norm, a white man in his sixties who attended with his third wife, moved from talking about men's responsiveness to his disapproval of homosexuality. He said,

> *At first, the unknown [was uncomfortable]. When you go around and there is more and more interaction, I felt like there was a quality of responses and information given by the men in that class that usually doesn't happen. [Pause] I do consider homosexuality a sin, but I'm not here to judge that. I have a lot of patients that are gay, and they have a lifestyle I do not approve of. But I thought even the gay couple had a lot of good information to toss out.*

Some of the other participants expressed a subtle resentment about dealing with same-sex couples in the marriage workshop but admitted that these couples "have needs too." It is unclear what the reaction would have been if the couples had taken a more in-your-face position, were gay men instead of lesbians, or were not middle class and white. Martin articulated his desire that lesbians and gay men remain in the closet: "Be gay. Don't force it on me."

The invisibility of the same-sex couples confirms the power of heterosexuality to exclude. Nevertheless, same-sex couples in marriage workshops have the effect of troubling dominant gender prescriptions within marital heterosexuality. Bettina, a white woman in her thirties and the only self-identified feminist I interviewed among the heterosexual participants, remarked on the tension that the presence of a lesbian couple brings to gender assumptions: "I was surprised at the lesbian couple who attended. I was shocked every time we came and they were still there! I was very happy to see that, especially because I thought stereotypically everybody is going to be pigeonholed into male–female. I can't imagine what that put on them." Bettina's words reflect the tension that the presence of a same-sex couple created for normative heterosexual gender performance. The environment of these marriage workshops discouraged dealing with gender outside the confines of marital heterosexuality, as doing so might have called into question the institution itself.

One of the lesbians, Jennifer, expressed her exasperation with and resistance to the focus on gender and marital heterosexuality: "So, that was the thing I really found offensive because they kind of gender stereotyped relationships, and I don't think that is completely appropriate if you're teaching gender diverse people." Her words stress the tension of being placed outside the rigid gender binary fundamental to the training. Amanda told me that taking a class with a lesbian was important to change people's perceptions. She said,

> I don't know the personal story of all these people in our class, but if they never met a lesbian before, and now they do, now they see, and hear what I say in class, and don't think we are the devil now, you know, that's a goal in itself. I mean, people are ignorant, and they don't know. So just being open and honest about stuff and talking to people or just being a good person around them and knowing you are gay, it has a positive influence.

Her words rang true. Even though most of the participants I interviewed expressed negative feelings about homosexuality, when faced with a same-sex couple, they tended to soften their stereotypic perceptions. Ultimately, the presence of lesbians in the workshops both strengthened and disrupted the power of heterosexuality; the question of same-sex relationships consistently remained in the background and sometimes came to the foreground when the couples discussed their relationships.

The (in)visibility of the lesbian couples suggests the unevenness of state efforts to reinstate the dominance of the heterosexual, white, middle-class family. On one hand, the teachings on gender and marital heterosexuality inscribe a powerful vision of the "natural" family. On the other, this prevailing image can be interrupted by the increasing diversity of families and prominence of lesbian and gay couples in American society. Even in the face of what appears a monolithic achievement to promote gender and marital heterosexuality, instances of defused power can create small opportunities for social change.

Conclusion

In their annual report, "State of Our Unions: The Social Health of Marriage in America," Barbara Whitehead and David Popenoe (2004:4) remark that "the pathway into marriage is changing. The meaning of marriage is changing. The institutional role of marriage is changing." Fears about the declining significance of the nuclear family have spurred national marriage promotion policies to fund programs to reinstitutionalize heterosexual marriage. For many marriage promotion advocates, concerns about the state of "our unions" center on fears for the white, middle-class (heterosexual) family. In Oklahoma, anxiety about "fractured families" and the use of TANF money to fund marriage promotion focuses attention on single-mother families—coded as women of color and their children. Yet its practices on the ground offer services predominantly to white, middle-class couples.

This research contributes to feminist theories of the state by problematizing the assumption of a male state with unidimensional control of its citizens or subjects. Instead, it reveals polycentric state practices that are structured as gendered and sexualized, and that uphold the dominance of the white, middle-class family and its importance to a cohesive national identity. In the case of marriage promotion, diverse state practices focus policy concerns on "deviant" (coded Black) single-mother families while resources are allocated to teach about gender hierarchy to predominantly white, middle-class couples. Putting feminist state theory and critical heterosexuality studies in dialogue demonstrates the importance of an unspoken heterosexuality to state control. State actors who seek to promote marriage rely on a particular, and conservative, interpretation of social scientific research on families as a noncontroversial way to focus policy concerns on the need to promote "healthy" (heterosexual) families. These policies demonstrate a perceived need on the part of the state to safeguard the health of the nation by strengthening the "mission" of white, middle-class (heterosexual) marriage. The race and class assumptions of this reasoning are largely made invisible as marriage promotion leaders use the rhetoric of health and social capital.

On the ground, marriage education becomes a tool to teach self-monitoring gendered practices within the confines of heterosexual marriage. In the workshops I attended, instruction on the "opposite" sexes signaled heterosexuality to reaffirm the sexual outsider status of same-sex couples as well as that of single-mother families. The on-the-ground practices of promoting heterosexual marriage mirror antigay countermovements, such as the ex-gay movement, which encourages individuals to police their behavior according to scripted gender and heterosexual norms (Robinson and Spivey 2007). This strategy provides states and social movements the ability to govern the behavior of citizens and members from a distance.

Marriage workshops rehearse dominant scripts on gender polarity to reinforce expectations of men's and women's "nature" to make marital heterosexuality appear instinctive and effortless. The decline of marriage and women's increased workforce participation during the past 40 years has challenged traditional norms that created social cohesion through gender hierarchy and implicit heterosexuality. Marriage workshops offer a forum to revisit ideas on hierarchical relationships between men and women. State training for workshop leaders teaches that managing gender differences is essential to a harmonious marriage. The trainers provide examples and offer gendered performances to focus on indisputable differences between men and women that cater to cultural ideas of men as rational (strong) and women as emotional (weak). These performances provide simple answers to complex negotiations that many families face as they juggle tight work schedules along with raising children and try to manage households that often bring children from previous marriages or relationships. The gendered performances teach that wives need to allow "men to be men" and that husbands need to cater to their wives' emotional needs.

State activities to implement self-monitoring practices carry an assumption that "good" citizens will act according to dominant norms; however,

this assumption does not necessarily entail success. In two six-week work-shops, for example, the presence of a lesbian couple challenged the ideology of marital heterosexuality. The performance of gendered binaries intrinsic to institutionalized heterosexuality, a generally seamless aspect of the mar-riage workshops I attended, was rendered more palpable and transparent. Even while the relationships of the lesbians were disregarded, their presence created a disruption. The assumptions underlying the workshops marked these two couples as different from other heterosexual women in the con-text of a marriage class, and the gendered prescriptions made them gender and sexual outsiders. Alternatively, their presence provided a rare opportu-nity to bring together heterosexuals and nonheterosexuals in an equalizing environment to learn communication and problem-solving skills. This was probably one of the few environments in the state, and anywhere else for that matter, that mixed together heterosexual and nonheterosexual couples in an intimate and prolonged setting, specifically in the context of enrich-ing relationships. For heterosexuals, such exposure has the ability to chal-lenge stereotypes about nonheterosexuals and perhaps about gender itself. Thus, while state practices seek to reestablish the hegemony of the white, middle-class, heterosexual family through rhetoric and cultural practice, marriage promotion offers insight into the way these can be destabilized on the ground by the very outsiders whom state policy seeks to outlaw.

ENDNOTES

Author's Note: Many thanks to Shari Dworkin, Celine-Marie Pascale, Kathleen Hull, Cheryl Cooky, Judith Stacey, Michael Messner, Sharon Hays, and Mary Bernstein for their invalu-able feedback on theory and revisions. Also a special thanks to editor Dana Britton and to five anonymous reviewers for their incredibly helpful comments and suggestions. The research this article draws on was funded by a grant from the Center for Religion and Civic Culture at the University of Southern California.

[1] Many of these states, including Texas, have incorporated the "one percent solution," putting 1 percent of their Temporary Assistance to Needy Families money toward marriage promo-tion. From my calculations, Oklahoma designates roughly 5 percent of its Temporary Assis-tance to Needy Families block grant per year.

[2] Recently, the marriage initiative changed the name from "Sweetheart Weekends" to "All about Us."

[3] I was not able to attend every class in the series during the six-week and weekend workshops. Since I acted as a participant in these workshops and determined not to provide any informa-tion that would identify other participants, I did not seek individual consent except in the case of volunteers for in-depth interviews.

[4] In addition to the participant observation and interviews described above, I did fieldwork in 20 marriage workshops for welfare recipients and led three focus groups; attended eight weeks of daily marriage classes for high school students and conducted in-depth interviews with the high school teachers; conducted in-depth interviews with a prisoner and the prison's chaplain; and did participant observation of a marriage workshop for the Chickasaw Nation and interviewed a Chickasaw government official. Finally, I conducted extensive fieldwork on the campaign against the initiative to ban same-sex marriage that was placed on the November ballot in 2004. For analysis of all ethnographic research in this project, see Heath (forthcoming).

[5] One of the initiative leaders told me that she knew of other same-sex couples attending mar-riage workshops. There was no way to find out how many actually did attend since the "All about You" forms that participants fill out at the beginning of the workshops do not ask about sexual orientation or same-sex relationships.

REFERENCES

Blankenhorn, David. 2007. *The Future of Marriage.* New York: Encounter Books.

Brown, Gillian. 1990. *Domestic Individualism: Imagining Self in Nineteenth-Century America.* Berkeley: University of California Press.

Brown, Wendy. 1992. "Finding the Man in the State." *Feminist Studies* 18:7–34.

Burawoy, Michael. 1998. "The Extended Case Method." *Sociological Theory* 16:4–33.

Butler, Judith. [1990] 1999. *Gender Trouble.* New York: Routledge.

Cahill, Sean. 2005. "Welfare Moms and the Two Grooms: The Concurrent Promotion and Restriction of Marriage in US Public Policy." *Sexualities* 8:169–87.

Campbell, Kim. 2002. "Can Marriage Be Taught?" *Christian Science Monitor,* July 18.

Cherlin, Andrew J. 2003. "Should the Government Promote Marriage?" *Contexts* 3:22–29.

———. 2004. "The Deinstitutionalization of American Marriage." *Journal of Marriage and the Family* 66:848–61.

Coltrane, Scott. 2001. "'Marketing the Marriage Solution': Misplaced Simplicity in the Politics of Fatherhood." *Sociological Perspectives* 44:387–418.

Connell, R. W. 1995. *Masculinities.* Berkeley: University of California Press.

Coontz, Stephanie and Nancy Folbre. 2002. "Marriage, Poverty, and Public Policy." Discussion paper from the annual conference of the Council on Contemporary Families, New York, April 26–28.

Cooper, Davina. 1995. *Power in Struggle: Feminism, Sexuality and the State.* London: Open University Press/NYU Press.

———. 2002. "Imagining the Place of the State: Where Governance and Social Power Meet." In *Handbook of Lesbian and Gay Studies,* edited by Diane Richardson and Steven Seidman. London: Sage.

Cott, Nancy. 2000. *Public Vows: A History of Marriage and the Nation.* Cambridge, MA: Harvard University Press.

Dion, Robin. 2006. *The Oklahoma Marriage Initiative: An Overview of the Longest-Running Statewide Marriage Initiative in the U.S.* ASPE research brief. Washington, DC: Office of the Assistant Secretary for Planning and Evaluation, U.S. Department of Health and Human Services.

Duffy, Mignon. 2007. "Doing the Dirty Work: Gender, Race, and Reproductive Labor in Historical Perspective." *Gender & Society* 21:313–36.

Foucault, Michel. 1981. *The History of Sexuality.* Vol. 1, *An Introduction.* Harmondsworth, UK: Penguin.

Glauber, Rebecca. 2008. "Race and Gender in Families and at Work: The Fatherhood Wage Premium." *Gender & Society* 22:8–30.

Gordon, Linda. 1994. *Pitied but Not Entitled.* Cambridge, MA: Harvard University Press.

Haney, Lynne A. 1996. "Homeboys, Babies, Men in Suits: The State and the Reproduction of Male Dominance." *American Sociology Review* 61:759–78.

———. 2000. "Feminist State Theory: Applications to Jurisprudence, Criminology, and the Welfare State." *Annual Review of Sociology* 26:641–66.

Hardisty, Jean. 2007. *Pushed to the Altar: The Right Wing Roots of Marriage Promotion.* Somerville, MA: Political Research Associates and the Women of Color Resource Center.

Hay, James. 2003. "Unaided Virtues: The (Neo)liberalization of the Domestic Sphere and the New Architecture of Community." In *Foucault, Cultural Studies, and Governmentality,* edited by Jack Z. Bratich, Jeremy Packer, and Cameron McCarthy. Albany: State University of New York Press.

Hays, Sharon. 2003. *Flat Broke with Children: Women in the Age of Welfare Reform.* Oxford, UK: Oxford University Press.

Heath, Melanie. Forthcoming. *One Marriage under God: Defense of Marriage Actions in Middle America.* New York: New York University Press.

Hymowitz, Kay S. 2006. *Marriage and Caste in America: Separate and Unequal Families in a Postmarital Age.* Chicago: Ivan R. Dee.

Ingraham, Chrys. 1999. *White Weddings: Romancing Heterosexuality in Popular Culture.* New York: Routledge.

———, ed. 2005. *Thinking Straight: The Power, the Promise, and the Paradox of Heterosexuality.* New York: Routledge.

Katz, Jonathan Ned. 1996. *The Invention of Heterosexuality.* New York: Plume.

Lichter, Daniel, Deborah Roempke Graefe, and J. Brian Brown. 2003. "Is Marriage a Panacea? Union Formation among Economically Disadvantaged Unwed Mothers." *Social Problems* 50:60–86.

McClintock, Ann. 1997. "'No Longer in a Future Heaven': Gender, Race, and Nationalism." In *Dangerous Liaisons: Gender, Nation, and Postcolonial Perspectives,* edited by Anne McClintock, Aamir Mufti, and Ella Shohat. Minneapolis: University of Minnesota Press.

Mink, Gwendolyn. 2003. "From Welfare to Wedlock: Marriage Promotion and Poor Mothers' Inequality." In *Fundamental Differences: Feminists Talk Back to Social Conservatives,* edited by Cynthia Burack and Jyl J. Josephson. Lanham, MD: Rowman & Littlefield.

Misra, Joya. 1998. "Mothers or Workers? The Value of Women's Labor: Women and the Emergence of Family Allowance Policy." *Gender & Society* 12:376–99.

Misra, Joya, Stephanie Moller, and Michelle J. Budig. 2007. "Work-Family Policies and Poverty for Partnered and Single Women in Europe and North America." *Gender & Society* 21:804–27.

Moon, Dawne and Jaye Cee Whitehead. 2006. "Marrying for America." In *Fragile Families and the Marriage Agenda,* edited by Lori Kowaleski-Jones and Nicholas H. Wolfinger. New York: Springer.

Mosse, George L. 1985. *Nationalism and Sexuality.* New York: Howard Fertig.

O'Connor, Julia S., Ann Shola Orloff, and Sheila Shaver. 1999. *States, Markets, Families.* Cambridge, UK: Cambridge University Press.

Pascale, Celine-Marie. 2001. "All in a Day's Work: A Feminist Analysis of Class Formation and Social Identity." *Race, Gender & Class* 8:34–59.

Polikoff, Nancy. 2008. *Beyond (Straight and Gay) Marriage: Valuing All Families under the Law.* Boston: Beacon.

Reese, Ellen. 2005. *Backlash against Welfare Mothers.* Berkeley: University of California Press.

Robinson, Christine M. and Sue E. Spivey. 2007. "The Politics of Masculinity and the Ex-gay Movement." *Gender & Society* 21:650–75.

Roseneil, Sasha. 2002. "The Heterosexual/Homosexual Binary: Past, Present, and Future." In *Handbook of Lesbian and Gay Studies,* edited by Diane Richardson and Steven Seidman. London: Sage.

Sedgwick, Eve Kosofsky. 1990. *Epistemology of the Closet.* Berkeley: University of California Press.

Stacey, Judith. 1996. *In the Name of the Family: Rethinking Family Values in the Postmodern Age.* Boston: Beacon.

West, Candace and Don Zimmerman. 1987. "Doing Gender." *Gender & Society* 1:125–51.

Whitehead, Barbara Dafoe. 1993. "Dan Quayle Was Right." *Atlantic Monthly,* April, 47–84.

Whitehead, Barbara Dafoe and David Popenoe. 2004. *The State of Our Unions: The Social Health of Marriage in America.* Piscataway, NJ: National Marriage Project.

Yuval-Davis, Nira. 1997. *Gender and Nation.* London: Sage.

16

MARRIAGE

The Good, the Bad, and the Greedy

NAOMI GERSTEL • NATALIA SARKISIAN

Few academics and even fewer politicians are critical of marriage today. Instead, they lament the retreat from marriage, emphasizing the poverty and sadness, exhaustion and stress of single and divorced women and men—especially unwed mothers. Often forgotten are the costs that marriage imposes—on individual husbands and wives as well as on wider community ties.

Naomi Gerstel and Natalia Sarkisian, "Marriage: The Good, the Bad, and the Greedy" from *Contexts* 5, no. 4 (November 2006): 16–21. Copyright © 2006 by the American Sociological Association. Reprinted with permission.

Many, bemoaning the retreat from marriage, also mourn the loss of community—imagining Americans who bowl alone. What these nostalgic discussions do not recognize, ironically, is that marriage and community are often at odds with one another. Instead of bolstering community involvement, marriage diminishes ties to relatives, neighbors, and friends.

The Defense

We hear about the benefits of marriage from diverse sources. Welfare reformers, both Republicans and Democrats, emphasize marriage as a way out of poverty for young single mothers and a route to responsibility for young unmarried fathers. The current administration and Congress want to redirect millions of dollars each year to marriage initiatives and incentives, workshops, and classes intended to turn the tide back toward marriage. Likewise, many gay and lesbian groups have placed marriage at the center of their political agenda.

After decades of criticizing marriage, many academics have joined politicians in loud support of it. Advocates such as David Popenoe and Linda Waite assert that marriage is good for one's pocketbook, health, happiness, sex life, and kids. Both men and women who are married tend to have higher incomes, more wealth, better health, and more property than those who are not. More surprisingly, researchers have documented sexual benefits of marriage: Married couples cozying up at home have sex more often than singles who party until dawn. Then there are the physical and mental health benefits of marriage—especially for men but also for women. Marriage, or at least a good marriage with little conflict, protects against everything from cavities to murder and suicide. Some also note that marriage keeps adult men out of crime and their kids out of delinquency. Earlier research suggested that marriage is more beneficial to men than women, but recent advocates insist that the benefits of marriage accrue to both women and men.

Skeptics dismiss these benefits as "selection effects." Marriage itself, they claim, has no salutary effects; those who are healthier, wealthier, sexier, and more law abiding are more likely to find and keep spouses. Men with higher earnings are more likely to marry. Those in trouble with the law are less likely to go to the altar. The sick and the poor are more likely to divorce. Proponents, however, insist that marriage itself creates most of these beneficial effects. As Linda Waite recently suggested, married people's healthier state likely springs from both self-selection into marriage and the protective, stabilizing effects of marriage itself. So what is there to criticize about marriage?

The Critique

Although recent discussions often ignore their critiques, feminists in the 1970s and 1980s insisted on the oppressive character of marriage. Some researchers still identify costs, especially for women. Women's housework increases

(and men's decreases) after marriage. There is the domestic violence—physical, sexual, emotional—that all too many married women endure, and the isolation that violent husbands impose. In addition, according to Barbara Wells and Maxine Baca Zinn, marriage brings fewer benefits to the poor than the affluent. Indeed, sociologists Kathryn Edin and Maria Kefalas find that poor young women do not see many benefits to marriage. They have babies but do not get married because potential husbands impose limits and often cost money but do not make enough even to share the expenses of marriage and parenthood.

Critics point out that only marriages with low levels of hostility and conflict offer the health benefits touted by advocates. In contrast, bad marriages are hazardous to mental and physical health, increasing suicide, stress, cancer, and blood pressure—and even slowing the healing of wounds. Critics point out that lots of marriages involve conflict and hostility, and many deteriorate over time. This debate generally focuses "inward"—both proponents and critics discuss marriage's benefits and costs for the wives, husbands, and children. But the full effects of marriage include social consequences for kin ties and community life.

A few theories of family and kinship suggest that modern marriage competes with, and even undermines, relations in the wider community. Forty years ago, Phillip Slater noted that couples' withdrawal into intimacy reduced group solidarity, although he viewed marriage as a solution to this problem. In contrast, Lewis and Rose Coser described marriage as a "greedy institution" demanding "undivided commitment." In their book *The Anti-Social Family*, feminists Michèle Barrett and Mary McIntosh went further, suggesting that marriage was a "trap" or a "prison"—an exclusive relationship that harmed other relationships. More recently, Vern Bengtson argued that marital instability will increasingly make extended kin ties more central in people's lives. Research on the costs and benefits of contemporary marriages largely ignores these theoretical suggestions.

Is Marriage Greedy?

We used two national surveys, the 1992–94 National Survey of Families and Households (Figure 1) and the 2004 General Social Survey (Figure 2), to compare ties to relatives and friends of those never married, currently married, and formerly married.

Married people—women as well as men—are less involved with their parents and siblings. Not surprisingly, they are much less likely than singles to share a household with their parents or siblings. But the married are also less likely to visit, call, or write these relatives. They are also less likely to give emotional support or advice and less likely to provide practical support such as help with household chores or transportation.

We might expect these differences to result from the different ages or economic positions of married versus unmarried people. Or the number of young children might explain the differences. But this is not the case. These differences in contacts and assistance emerge even if the married, never

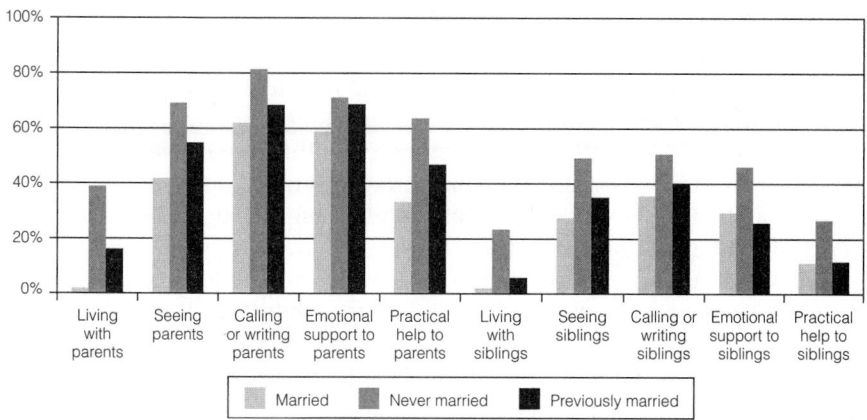

FIGURE 1 **Marital Status and Involvement with Parents and Siblings**
Source: National Survey of Families and Households, 1992–94.

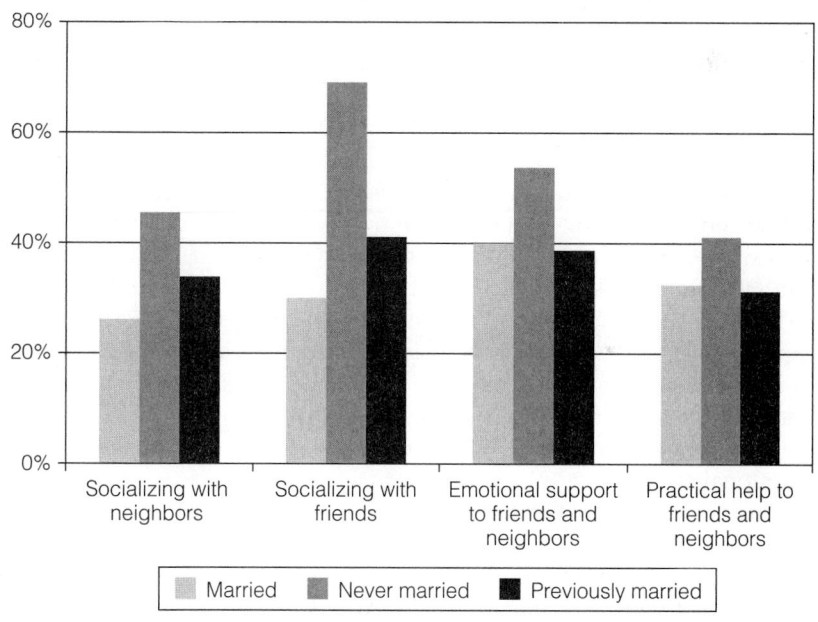

FIGURE 2 **Marital Status and Involvement with Neighbors and Friends**
Source: General Social Survey 2004; National Survey of Families and Households, 1992–94.

married, and previously married are the same age and have the same class position (similar amounts of income and education, and similar employment status). And differences between the married and unmarried exist both among parents of young children and among the childless. They also exist among whites, African Americans, and Hispanics.

Further, these differences exist for both women and men. In some cases, however, the effects of marriage are greater for men than for women. For

example, married women talk on the phone to their parents and siblings less often than those who never got married, or who left or lost a husband. But the difference in phone talk is more dramatic for men: many husbands rely on wives to call their relatives, while men without wives make the connection themselves. For both men and women, the diminished ties to relatives persist even after marriages dissolve; the previously married—on most counts—are less involved with parents and siblings than those never married (but more than the married).

Modern marriage might provide companionship in the form of a spouse, but it deters companionship with relatives other than the spouse. We do not want to overstate. To be sure, most Americans—married or not—still live near extended kin. They want relationships with their elderly parents, siblings, and cousins, see them occasionally, and feel guilty when they cannot visit or help them. They bemoan their inability to maintain stronger ties. Yet today these ties are voluntary and easily lost amid the more pressing demands of marriage.

Other Connections

What about other people in the community, like friends and neighbors? From *The Dick Van Dyke Show* and *Full House* to *Sex and the City, Friends,* and *The OC* to "reality shows" like *Laguna Beach* and even cartoons like *The Simpsons* and *Family Guy,* television offers us images of singles who hang out with their coupled buddies. TV friendships outlast or at least coexist with romantic relationships, even marriage.

The data show the reverse of what television would have us believe. Compared to those never or previously married, married couples disengage from neighbors and friends. They are less likely to socialize with neighbors and less likely to hang out with friends. And the never married are more likely than the married to offer a hand or an ear—to give either practical help or emotional support.

These patterns look the same for women and men. Marriage separates each of them from neighbors and friends. The differences appear especially large when those currently married are compared to those who have never married. The previously married, though still experiencing the effects of marriage, seem to be on the path of returning to their nonmarital state, especially when it comes to socializing. But because friends, like property, are often split when marriages end, it is difficult for the previously married to catch up to those who never got married.

As with relatives, differences in relationships with friends are not due to age, income, education, or employment. The marriage gap in practical help to friends, however, exists only among whites, not among African Americans and Hispanics.

Children help involve the married in networks of friends and neighbors. Married parents provide as much emotional and practical help as single

parents or childless singles; it is the married without children who give less. As Karen Hansen argues in *Not-So-Nuclear Families*, dual-earner parents, searching for ways to make child-rearing feasible, turn to friends, neighbors, and extended kin. And in the case of friends and neighbors, getting help typically means giving it in return. But help is only one kind of interaction. Single and married parents alike "hang out" less with neighbors and friends. Combining these effects, we see a "marriage penalty" on relationships with friends and neighbors, but it is larger for the childless than for those with young children.

To be sure, marriage intensifies social connections in some ways, especially for men. It increases men's (though not women's) participation in church and religious life. It also increases some forms of political engagement—those that are not particularly demanding, such as signing petitions. For women, in contrast, we find no differences in religious involvement between the married and not married. And women are more involved politically when they do not have a mate. Compared to married women, single women are more likely to attend political meetings or rallies, sign petitions, and raise money for political causes.

On balance, marriage weakens both women's and men's ties to those other than the spouse. Why?

Why Is Marriage Greedy?

Marriage is greedy for material, emotional, and cultural reasons. Marriages obviously take time and energy—whether for partners to spend time with each other, or to create and maintain the family home. This detracts from investments in other relationships, especially, perhaps, for dual-earner couples already strapped for time by the demands of two jobs. Some of this time and energy is redirected to children, who also require their parents' time. But it is among the childless that the marriage penalty is particularly large. The married also tend to have more money than the unmarried; as a consequence, the married need less help from family and friends. A norm of reciprocity means they then give less in return.

Marriage can also demand a kind of intense emotional involvement that by itself detracts from collective life. As Phillip Slater wrote, "An intimate dyadic relationship always threatens to short-circuit the libidinal network of the community and drain it of its source of sustenance." This is most obvious with the newly connected couple, all wrapped up in one another with little interest in others. We have all experienced the difficulty of being around such starry-eyed couples. But as our findings suggest, the short-circuiting of community ties characterizes not just oblivious "young" lovers but also stable married couples. Spouses are expected to be confidants and the main source of emotional support, so the married are less likely than singles to call a sibling, parent, or friend to recount their day at work or their problems with kids. The married are also less able to spontaneously get together with friends without worrying that their spouse will feel emotionally deprived.

And friends and family may feel less inclined to just "drop by" due to the risk of "interrupting something."

What's more, marriage today carries cultural expectations of self-sufficiency. Americans believe couples should be able to make it on their own—both practically and emotionally. This does not mean that kin or friends refuse to help the married when asked. It means that, when they get married, couples think they should be able to support and care for themselves. Many even postpone getting married until they know they can "make it on their own," even if that means not getting married at all.

The greed of marriage is hardly universal—it is primarily a contemporary phenomenon. Anthropologists of so-called primitive societies—those hardly touched by industrialization or globalization—find that marriage is often used to expand rather than limit community ties. They observe that rules prohibiting incest and promoting "marrying out" extend to distant relatives. This ensures that family members of married couples can rely economically and politically on a broader array of relatives. Such rules emphasize the communal integration that marriages ensure in such societies. Weddings are clearly community events in this context—they celebrate newly formed kin alliances rather than the special relationship of the marital pair. Banning the withdrawal of husbands and wives, such societies do not have honeymoons—it is not appropriate to leave the community behind to go off on some private adventure.

Modern marriage is different—from the very outset. As a recent Gallup poll finds, 94 percent of unmarried young women and men say their primary goal in marriage is finding a "soul mate" (compare this not only to "primitive societies" but also to the 1950s aspiration of finding a mate who would fit the breadwinner or homemaker mold). Finding a soul mate means turning inward—pushing aside other relationships. In line with these expectations, contemporary weddings place more emphasis on individuals than community. As Andrew Cherlin argues, weddings today celebrate romance—a decidedly private experience. Contemporary wedding rituals promote self-development, individual display, and personal achievement rather than the approval and alliances of kin.

Then comes the honeymoon. Although the wedding may still have elements of a community ritual, the honeymoon is a decidedly private one. Honeymoons, in fact, first developed in the 19th century when the idea of marriage as a private intimate relationship, set off from community life, began to take hold. Today, honeymoons of some kind are a nearly universal experience in the United States. Recent surveys estimate that approximately 85 percent of all weddings, and 99 percent of traditional weddings, culminate in honeymoons. As they go off on their honeymoon adventure, the starry-eyed couple is supposed to leave all the other loved ones behind—the first step toward communal withdrawal. When they return, they are expected to no longer rely on relatives for jobs, education, or welfare assistance. And the expectation for self-sufficiency of married couples in the contemporary United States generates the effect that we observed: namely, marriage threatens ties outside itself.

Communities and Marriages

Political and religious movements have often recognized that marriage can undermine other relationships. Communal societies, like Oneida in the 19th century, rejected marriage and family because they viewed the "marriage spirit" as inimical to community life. If any couple exhibited the marriage spirit, the community worked to break it up. More recently, kibbutzim have emphasized that the strength of the collectivity depends on a weakened marital and family life. Sociologist Jeff Goodwin showed how the Huk rebels in the Philippines imposed limits on marriage to assure that their members would remain committed to the cause. Or take the Catholic Church's stance on the celibacy of monks and nuns; as Coser writes, "[The Church] . . . stressed that ministers should abstain from marriage because the multiplicity of distractions originating in family life rendered it desirable for those in the service of the Church to be relieved from family care and anxiety."

In the recent past, some pointed to the vitality of African American communities—whether on street corners, in churches, households brimming with extended kin, or civil rights movements. In her classic study of poor black families, *All Our Kin,* anthropologist Carol Stack found that the bonds of marriage can be incompatible with other relationships: "Black families and the non-kin they regard as kin have evolved . . . social controls against the formation of marriages that could endanger [them]."

People who are immersed in relationships with relatives and friends may thus be less likely to get married. One reason is that to prevent the weakening of community ties, some communities may discourage marriage. Or those with deep community ties may have less need for marriage because those ties satisfy some of the same needs. Alternatively, intense community ties may reduce the opportunity to meet a marital partner. Someone who hangs out all the time with close relatives and friends may have little chance to meet a new mate. So the reduced community ties of the married likely result both from self-selection into marriage and from the effects of marriage itself.

These reduced ties may even have some favorable effects. Just as we should not romanticize marriage, we should not romanticize community ties. Putnam has recently noted that there can be a "dark side of social capital," including gangs and criminal networks. The reduction of relationships outside marriage may then also be associated with a withdrawal from such dangerous networks. Still, sociologists and politicians agree that community ties are generally a positive force.

What Does Marriage Promotion Do?

Politicians and social commentators talk a lot about the value of the family as well as about its much-lamented decline. But they often assume a very narrow family: married couples and their young children. Many even

blame the decline in community involvement on the decline of that traditional nuclear family. Robert Putnam began with this assumption in his popular book, *Bowling Alone*. But after looking at his data, he dismissed this explanation: "The evidence is not consistent with the thesis that the overall decline in civic engagement and social connectedness is attributable to the decline in the traditional family. On the contrary, to some extent the decline in family obligations ought to have freed up more time for social and community involvement."

Putnam's conclusions, as well as our findings, suggest that the growing advocacy for marriage—from both the right and the left—may unwittingly undermine community. This holds for both the initiatives to promote heterosexual marriages and the movements to allow gay and lesbian marriages. Gays and lesbians, once noted for their vibrant culture and community life, may find themselves behind picket fences with fewer friends dropping by.

But few policymakers today acknowledge that marriage might have detrimental effects. Quite the reverse: pushing marriage, especially on the poor, is popular in mainstream political circles. To be sure, marriage-promotion initiatives often fail. But when they succeed, they have some unanticipated ill effects. They increase domestic violence and marital conflict. As Andrew Cherlin (2003) wrote several years ago, "The problem is that it is hard to support healthy marriages without concurrently supporting unhealthy marriages." But whether they promote healthy or unhealthy unions, marriage initiatives are likely to produce a decline in community engagement. Ties to relatives and friends, like intense political and religious engagement, may depend on an unfettered life.

RECOMMENDED RESOURCES

Michèle Barrett and Mary McIntosh. *The Anti-Social Family* (Verso, 1982). Analyzes the oppressive nature of marriage and the nuclear family and suggests that it cuts off ties to family and friends, especially for women.

Andrew J. Cherlin. "Should the Government Promote Marriage?" *Contexts* 3 (Fall 2003): 22–29. Criticizes governmental marriage-promotion initiatives for their ineffectiveness and unresponsiveness to the realities of family life.

Karen Hansen. *Not-So-Nuclear Families: Class, Gender, and Networks of Care* (Rutgers University Press, 2005). Shows that although mothers and fathers believe in the importance of nuclear family independence, they end up relying on kin, neighbors, and friends for child care.

Robert D. Putnam. *Bowling Alone* (Simon and Schuster, 2000). Over the last 25 years, Americans have become disconnected from family, friends, and social institutions, including the church, recreational clubs, and political parties.

Linda Waite and Maggie Gallagher. *The Case for Marriage: Why Married People Are Happier, Healthier, and Better Off Financially* (Doubleday, 2000). Argues that marriage protects both women and men, making them happier, healthier, and wealthier.

17

CLASHING DREAMS
Highly Educated Overseas Brides
and Low-Wage U.S. Husbands

HUNG CAM THAI

Hours before her husband's plane was due, on a rainy day in July 2000, Thanh Nguyen[1] and about thirty members of her family anxiously waited outside of Tan Son Nhut, Saigon's international airport.[2] Thanh's family was understandably excited. For many families expecting a relative or a close friend from the Vietnamese diaspora, the waiting is an event in itself: they come to the airport long before the plane is due, creating such a commotion outside that it is difficult to follow any one conversation.

I watched and listened, like a waiter at a busy restaurant—intently but discreetly. I could make out only fragments of conversations among people of a culture known for making sure: "Make sure you greet him properly," adults told young children. "Make sure the restaurant knows we are coming," men reminded women. And of course, "Make sure you always show him love and respect," Thanh's parents reminded their thirty-two-year-old daughter.

The Nguyens were prudent people. Although they knew Thanh's husband, Minh, well—he had made the long journey across the Pacific from his home in Quincy, Washington, three times in the last year—they wanted him to feel welcome and important each time he visited. Their instinct was a good one: when I visited him in Quincy, ninety miles from Seattle, the thirty-seven-year-old Minh revealed to me that he often did not feel important or respected in the small suburban town where he lived.

Seattle is one of the most heavily Vietnamese cities outside of Vietnam, and Thanh's husband is one of more than two million *Viet Kieu*, or Vietnamese people living overseas, who make up an aging diaspora that largely began emigrating in the mid-1970s.[3] Thanh will soon join Minh in Quincy as one of more than 200,000 legal marriage migrants who come to the United States each year.[4]

About a quarter of all men and more than 40 percent of all women who currently enter the United States are marriage migrants.[5] Of these marriage migrants, more than 65 percent are women. It is no news that women have

Hung Cam Thai, "Clashing Dreams: Highly Educated Overseas Brides and Low-Wage U.S. Husbands" from *Global Woman: Nannies, Maids, and Sex Workers in the New Economy*, edited by Barbara Ehrenreich and Arlie Russell Hochschild. New York: Metropolitan Books, 2002. Reprinted with the permission of the author.

dominated U.S.-bound migration since the 1930s[6] and that, historically, more women than men have migrated as spouses.[7] However, despite the fact that marriage remains the number one reason people migrate to the United States,[8] we know very little about the specific contemporary marriage migration streams or about why women overwhelmingly dominate them.[9] More familiar is the often sensationalized phenomenon of mail-order brides.[10] Though an important part of the female marriage migration puzzle, such women constitute at most 4 percent of all marriage migrants.[11]

The marriage of Minh and Thanh follows a global trend that has been gathering momentum over the last forty years: immigrant and immigrant-origin men are more and more frequently seeking wives in their countries of origin.[12] An estimated two-thirds of all marriage migrants are of the same ethnicity, and among migrants who come to the United States married to noncitizen permanent residents (presumably immigrants), almost 90 percent are women.[13] Like many international marriages between same-ethnic individuals, especially in Asia, the marriage of Minh and Thanh was arranged. Marriage arrangements come in many forms, and I have addressed these elsewhere.[14] What Minh and Tranh represent is a specific and fairly typical pattern: the marriage of the two "unmarriageables," namely of highly educated women in Vietnam to Vietnamese men who do low-wage work overseas.[15]

The Double Marriage Squeeze

Vietnamese people worldwide are pressed by what demographer Daniel Goodkind calls the "double marriage squeeze."[16] A high male mortality rate during the Vietnam War, combined with the migration of a larger number of men than women during the last quarter of the twentieth century, has produced a low ratio of men to women in Vietnam, as well as an unusually high ratio of men to women in the Vietnamese diaspora, especially in Australia and the United States. Of the fifteen most populous nations in 1989, Vietnam had the lowest ratio of men to women at the peak marrying ages. By 1999, there were approximately 92 men for every 100 women between the ages of 30 and 34 in Vietnam. The reverse situation prevails in the diaspora: in 2000, there were 129 Vietnamese-American men for every 100 women between the ages of 24 and 29. Among Vietnamese-Americans aged 30 to 34, there were about 135 men for every 100 women.[17]

Those who study marriage markets have long documented a nearly universal pattern, called the marriage gradient, whereby women tend to marry men who are older, better educated, and higher earning than they are, while men tend to marry younger women who earn less money and have less education.[18] Men "marry down" economically and socially; women "marry up." Transnational couples like Minh and Thanh, however, seem to reverse the marriage gradient. But depending on the measure one uses, it is often difficult to tell who is really marrying up, and who down.

Thanh belongs to an emerging group of highly educated women in Vietnam who have delayed or avoided marriage with local men. These

women have found that too few men in Vietnam are employed and successful relative to them. More important, in the eyes of many men influenced
by traditional Asian and Confucian hierarchies of gender, age, and class,
a highly educated woman like Thanh is unmarriageable. As with highly
educated African American women in the United States, there is a surfeit
of women like Thanh in Vietnam relative to their educated male counterparts. Minh, on the other hand, belongs to a surfeit group of Viet Kieu men,
many of whom are unable to find marriage partners partly because they are
low-wage workers. Some of these men, though certainly not all, experienced
tremendous downward mobility when they migrated overseas after the
Vietnam War.

In my study of sixty-nine Vietnamese transpacific marriages, 80 percent
of the men were low-wage earners like Minh. These men generally work
for hourly wages, though some work in ethnic enterprises where salaries
are negotiated under the table. For the most part, they work long hours for
low pay. Almost 70 percent of their brides are women like Thanh, who are
college-educated; about 40 percent of these women have advanced degrees,
which permit them to work as doctors, lawyers, computer programmers,
and the like. Of my entire sample about 55 percent were marriages between
these two "unmarriageables."[19]

The double marriage squeeze is one force propelling these transpacific
marriages of the two unmarriageables, but the cultural belief in the marriage gradient is at least as powerful and probably more so. The marriage
gradient is a strict norm in Vietnamese culture. Many Vietnamese, including the unmarriageables themselves, believe that by making these unortho-
dox matches transnational ones, they somehow get around the discomfort
of breaking the marriage gradient norm. It is as though despite their relative incomes and education, if the man is from a First World country, he has
the "up," while a woman from Third World Vietnam has the "down." And
though it is no surprise that the economic divide between the First and Third
Worlds deeply penetrates the private lives of Vietnamese transpacific couples, it is not always clear who has the Third World life in marriages of the
two unmarriageables.

While reaching out overseas seems a perfect solution to the double marriage squeeze, it gives rise to an unanticipated collision of gender ideologies in 90 percent of these couples. The reason is that the dreams that led
both partners into the arrangement often had as much to do with gender
as with economic mobility. Educated women like Thanh hope that a man
living overseas in a modern country will respect women more than men at
home, who may still be in the sway of ancient Vietnamese traditions. Low-
wage working men like Minh, meanwhile, often look to women in Vietnam
precisely because they wish to uphold those ancient traditions, which they
believe have been eroded in modern American life, but which they expect a
woman in Vietnam will maintain.

In their search for spouses, both parties have relied to some extent
on tradition, which leads them to agree to a marriage arranged by family
members. But it is the modern, globalizing culture of Vietnam that makes

the transnational match possible. In 1986, after having had no contact with the outside world for over a decade, the Vietnamese government adopted a new economic policy known as *doi moi*. It did not end state ownership, but it encouraged private enterprise, free markets, and global engagement. In the 1990s, Saigon reemerged as a major international city, first within Asia and then in the world more generally. Vietnam was projected to be one of Asia's next "tigers."[20] Enticed by an emerging labor and consumer market of eighty million people, foreign companies were eager to move their factories there and to make their products known.

Globalization rapidly opened the Vietnamese market for capital, goods, and labor. At the same time, it also opened a more personal exchange of emotions and marriage partners. But while goods and capital tend to flow in two directions, the divide between the First World economy of the West and the Third World economy of Vietnam makes it impossible for women in Vietnam to go abroad to look for grooms but very easy for Viet Kieu men to go to Vietnam for brides. Just as global corporations and factories moved to Vietnam to partake of its large supply of labor, Viet Kieu men go there to choose among its large selection of potential brides. But unlike locals who eagerly take jobs at foreign factories for the pay, Vietnamese transpacific brides have a wide range of reasons for choosing to marry Viet Kieu men.

The Highly Educated Bride

Twenty years ago, Thanh's father was a math teacher at Le Buon Phong, a prestigious high school in Saigon. After the war, Thanh's uncle, her mother's younger brother, and his family were among the several thousand Vietnamese who were airlifted out of Vietnam on April 30, 1975, when Saigon surrendered to the North Vietnamese. They eventually settled in Houston, one of the larger Vietnamese enclaves in the United States, and started a successful restaurant business specializing in *pho*, the popular Vietnamese beef noodle soup. Remittances from Thanh's uncle helped her parents open a small candy factory in the late 1980s; that factory now has more than forty employees. Thanh's parents belong to a small but very visible class of Vietnamese families who enjoy access to overseas resources. They are part of a Viet Kieu economy that has grown from roughly $35 million in 1993 to an estimated $2 billion in 2000.[21]

Thanh was only seven years old when Saigon fell. She is not as old as Minh, whose memory of the war is very strong and formative; nor is she able to put that era completely behind her, like her peers born after the war, who are eager to move forward and to join the global economy. She embraces foreign influences and appreciates the access she has to them. Many of her friends work in foreign companies as translators, or in marketing or sales; some have become local branch supervisors for international corporations such as Citibank and IBM. Nevertheless, Thanh is conscious that her parents

have sustained hidden injuries from accepting remittances from her uncle in Houston, and this saddens her. She observes:

> *My father is a very strong man; nobody ever tells him what to do with his life, like how to raise his children. But I think it is very hard for him when he has to deal with my uncle. My uncle is a very nice man, and he cares a lot for our family. But even though he's younger than my mother, his older sister, he doesn't respect my father. He thinks my father has to listen to him about every-thing, like how to run his business. When he comes back to Vietnam, he always tries to change the ways my dad runs things. And my father always defers to him. He feels that because my uncle helped him financially to open up the candy factory, he has to do everything my uncle says. I know he feels very embarrassed and humiliated inside, but would never tell anyone about it.*

Thanh's family is not alone in its discomfort with receiving money from abroad. Remittances create social inequality and stress between givers and receivers, and even greater inequalities between receivers and nonreceivers in the same community. Nonetheless, Thanh knows that she owes the life-style she enjoys at least partly to her uncle's remittances. After all, the aver-age salary for Saigonese lawyers, according to Thanh, is a little over 2 million Vietnamese *dong* (VND), or US $150 per month, whereas the net profit of her father's candy factory averages close to VND 900 million a year. Thanh earns about VND 2.5 million a month as a part-time lawyer in a small firm that handles legal contracts of all sorts. Although her salary is six times the standard income of the average worker in Saigon, it is still low on a global scale.[22] But the remittances that gave her parents' business a leg up have also allowed Thanh, an only child, to have a greater than average degree of edu-cational and social mobility. She has been able to obtain a good high school education, to study law, and to take lessons at international English schools in Saigon.

Most of Thanh's peers married soon after high school, but Thanh and a small group of her female friends from Le Buon Phong High School decided to continue their schooling instead. Of her seven close female friends from high school, only one did not go to college, choosing instead to marry early. The rest, including Thanh, quietly built professional careers. Most went into fields traditionally reserved for women, including education and nursing. Two pursued advanced degrees. Thanh obtained a law degree, while her friend became a prestigious physician at Vinh Bien, a private hospital cater-ing to Saigon's middle class. Four of the seven, now in their early thirties, remain single. At the time of this writing, there is no available data on the extent of delayed marriages across class and educational levels in Vietnam. But if the paths of Thanh and her four friends who chose singlehood are any indication, a quiet gender revolution is taking place among highly educated Vietnamese women. These women have opted for singlehood in a culture where marriage is not only presumed but often coerced. Women and men who have not yet married at the appropriate age are often dismis-sively referred to as "*e*," or unmarketable. By contrast, women (often young

and beautiful) and men (often educated and financially secure) who fare well on the marriage market are considered *dat,* or scarce goods. As Thanh explained to me,

> *I am already* e *in Vietnam. You know, at thirty-two here, it's hard to find a decent husband. I knew that when I decided to get a good education here that many men would be intimidated by me. But it was important to me to get an education, and I know that for women, marriage is more important. In Asian cultures, but may be in Vietnam especially, the men do not want their wives to be better than them. I think for me it's harder, too, because my parents are successful here, so to the outsider, we seem very successful.*

In truth, Thanh is not completely *e:* several men, sometimes with their families, have come to propose marriage to her. Arranged marriages remain common in Vietnam, although they are more common in villages than in urban areas. Young couples who marry by arrangement are susceptible to significant difficulties if class differences divide their families.[23] Individual and family success can make a Vietnamese woman, particularly if she has passed the socially accepted marriageability age, unmarriageable. Thanh had several proposals for marriage arrangements when she was in her mid-twenties, before she got her law degree, from men who wanted to marry down. Now she is thirty-two and educated; she believes that marrying up is no longer an option, since there are few available men in that category. Although she has many suitors of lesser means and education than herself, Thanh explains that she does not find marrying down to be an appealing prospect. . . .

Thanh's marriage procrastination was partly anchored in her confused class and gender status. Her upward mobility put her at the top locally, but globally, she is at the bottom, since Vietnam has low status among nations. In a traditional marriage, her husband must be the household's provider; but given that she is marrying a low-wage worker, she may end up being the one to seek economic security through her own means. Yet marrying a low-wage worker overseas looks attractive to Thanh because she knows that in Vietnam, her high educational status will not help her escape the gender subordination of marital life. She can think of few men she knows in Vietnam who show respect to their wives.

On our third and final interview, Thanh and I walked along the Saigon River. It was early evening, and the city skyline loomed in the near distance, separated from us by a cacophony of motorcycles, bicycles, and taxis. Disconsolately, Thanh explained:

> *In Vietnam, it is hard being single, female, and old. People will criticize and laugh at you. People always ask me, "Where are your husband and children?" And when I think about that, I realize that I have two choices. I can marry a man in Vietnam who is much less educated and less successful than I whom I will have to support and who will likely abuse me emotionally or physically or dominate me in every possible way. Or I can marry a Viet Kieu man. At least Viet Kieu men live in modern countries where they respect women.*

Ultimately, what Thanh wants in a marriage partner is someone who will respect her, and who will not seek to control her the way she sees so many Vietnamese men control their wives. . . .

The Low-Wage Working Groom

If Thanh's desire for respect stems from her upward mobility, her husband's parallel desire has everything to do with his downward mobility. Minh, whose hands, facial expressions, and graying hair make him seem older than his thirty-seven years, was the only member of his family to leave Vietnam during "Wave II" of the boat exodus that took place after the war.[24] As the eldest son, he was vested with a special status and with a good deal of responsibility for his six siblings. Both of his parents were teachers of philosophy at Le Buon Phong, where they have known Thanh's parents for many years. Today, three of Minh's sisters are teachers and his two brothers are successful merchants in Saigon.

In 1985, at the age of twenty-one, Minh was a man of intellectual ambition and curiosity. He had just completed his third year of engineering school when his parents asked him if he wanted to go to America. They didn't know anyone overseas at the time, but they knew of several people, among the many hundreds of thousands of refugees, who had safely reached a Western country. More than 90 percent of these refugees settled in France, Australia, Canada, or the United States.[25] Minh's parents also knew that as many as half of the refugees on any given boat did not reach their destinations. They died along the way due to starvation, pirate attacks, and often, in the case of women and children, in the combination of rape and murder en route to a refugee camp. Many were also caught by the Vietnamese government and severely punished with long prison sentences.

Nevertheless, Minh's parents were confident that he would survive and find a better life abroad. They spent their entire lives' savings to put him on one of the safest and most reputable boats to leave the Mekong Delta for Western lands of opportunity. These boats and their routes via refugee camps in Southeast Asia were a carefully guarded secret in Vietnam, and they were accessible only to wealthy or well-connected families. Being caught by government officials could lead to severe punishment. Many who were not wealthy, like Minh's family, managed to pool their resources so that one person, usually a son, could go. They saw this as an investment, which they made with the hope it would yield high returns.

Today, Minh considers himself one of the lucky ones who left. After surviving two years in a refugee camp in Malaysia, he was selected in 1987 for entry to the United States. Many people he met at the camp ended up in less desirable places, like Finland, Belgium, or Hungary. Back then, as now, the United States was the top-choice destination, followed by Canada, France, and Australia. Minh arrived in rural Wyoming under the sponsorship of a local Catholic church. Like many of the American churches that sponsored Indochinese refugees from the late 1970s to the mid-1990s, Minh's church

sponsored only one person.[26] He spent the first five years of his new life as the only person of color in a rural town in Wyoming, the name of which he doesn't even want to remember.

Like many Vietnamese refugees in the past three decades, Minh decided to migrate a second time. He wanted to go to Little Saigon, the most highly concentrated Vietnamese enclave outside of Vietnam, located in a seemingly quiet Los Angeles suburb that is today plagued by urban problems.[27] But he had little money and no connections in or around Los Angeles. Then one day, in one of the Vietnamese-produced newspapers that flourished in the United States following the influx of refugees, Minh read about a Chinese restaurant called the Panda Garden that needed dishwashers. Unfortunately, it was not in Los Angeles but in a small town called Quincy, ninety miles from Seattle. Minh heard that Seattle also had many Vietnamese people, and he hoped that moving there would bring him closer to other refugees.

Eleven years later, Minh still lives in Quincy and works at the Panda Garden. He is now a deep fryer and an assistant cook, which is several steps up from the dishwashing position he was first given. Although to him, an assistant cook carries less stigma than a dishwasher, it is far from the engineering career he envisaged in his pre-migration years. His responsibilities include helping the main cook with various kitchen tasks and making sure that the restaurant has a constant supply of egg rolls and wontons. Though known as one of the best and most authentic ethnic restaurants in town, the Panda serves a mainly white American clientele that, according to the restaurant's owners, probably wouldn't know the difference between authentic Chinese food and a Sara Lee frozen dinner.

Quincy is similar to many suburban towns in Middle America: it is not quite rural, but far from urban. People who live here drive to Seattle to shop and eat if they have money, but they stay in town if they want to see a movie. The town has two Chinese restaurants, a dozen other ethnic restaurants, and numerous chain-store franchises. Minh knows five other Vietnamese people in Quincy. They are all men, and three of them work with him at the restaurant. He shares a modest three-bedroom apartment with the barest of furnishings with these coworkers.

Like many Viet Kieu people, Minh sends remittances to Vietnam. But though remittances allow their receivers to enjoy First World consumption, givers often only partake of these fruits when they return to their Third World homes. In the First World settings where they live and work, some givers, like Minh, are able to sustain only a Third World consumption pattern. Minh earns approximately $1,400 a month in Quincy and sends $500 of that back to his family. That amount is much higher than the average of $160 the grooms in my study remit to their wives or families on a monthly basis. At $900, his remaining budget would be considered way below the poverty level anywhere in the United States. But the stream of cash he sends his family permits them to stay connected in the small, though conspicuous, circles of families who have overseas kin networks.

In the meantime, however, Minh finds himself lacking not only in material comforts but in the kind of respect he had come to expect before

he migrated. Minh remembers vividly that in his early twenties, his peers considered him a good catch. He came from a well-respected family, and he was headed for a career in engineering. Young men he knew had not one but several girlfriends at a time, and this was accepted and celebrated during those difficult postwar years. Minh was relatively fortunate: his parents were respected teachers with small but steady incomes. They could afford to spend small amounts of money on leisure activities, and on materials that bought them some status in their pre-remittance circles. When we talked over beer and cigarettes in the hot kitchen where he worked, Minh told me:

> *Life here now is not like life in Vietnam back then. My younger brothers and sisters used to respect me a lot because I was going to college and I was about to get my degree. Many young women I met at the time liked me, too, because I came from a good family and I had status [dia di]. But now, because I don't have a good job here, people don't pay attention to me. That's the way my life has been since I came to the United States. And I don't know if I'm lucky or unlucky, but I think it's hard for a [Vietnamese] man to find a wife here if he doesn't make good money. If you have money, everyone will pay attention [to you], but if you don't, you have to live by yourself.*

For the most part, that's what Minh has done in the sixteen years since he arrived in the United States. Minh believes that money can, and often does, buy love, and that if you don't have much of it, you live by yourself. Although his yearly income puts him just above the poverty level for a single man, I discovered in a budget analysis of his expenditures that after remittances he falls well below the poverty level. The long hours that often accompany low-wage work have made it particularly difficult for him to meet and court marriage partners. If Minh worked long hours for a law firm or a corporation, he would not only get financial rewards but also the status and prestige that men often use as a trade-off in marriage markets. If he were a blue-collar white man in Quincy, he could go to church functions, bowling alleys, or bars to meet and court local women. For Minh, a single, immigrant man who does low-wage work in a low-status job with long hours in Middle America, the prospect of marriage has been, and remains, low. Even under slightly more favorable circumstances, Viet Kieu men complain of a lack of marriage partners. Men I interviewed in ethnic enclaves such as Little Saigon faced difficulties because, as one man told me, "Viet Kieu women know that there are many of us and few of them!"

Low-wage workers like Minh find it especially difficult to compete in intimate markets. Unlike women like Thanh, men like Minh are at the bottom locally, while globally they are at the top, since the United States enjoys high status among nations. That is one reason they turn to Vietnam. After all, men like Minh are in the market for more than just intimacy. They are in it for respect and for a kind of marital life that they believe they cannot obtain locally. For men in general, but especially for working-class men, as sociologist Lillian Rubin has argued in a compelling study, a worthy sense of self is

deeply connected to the ability to provide economically for one's family.[28] As Minh movingly explained to me,

> *I don't know if other men told you this, but I think the main reason why a lot of Viet Kieu men go back to Vietnam for a wife is because the women here [Viet Kieu] do not respect their husbands if the husbands cannot make a lot of money. I think that's why there are a lot of Viet Kieu women who marry white men, because the white men have better jobs than us.[29] Many Viet Kieu women, even though they are not attractive and would not be worth much if there were a lot of them, would not even look at men like me because we can't buy them the fancy house or the nice cars. I need my wife to respect me as her husband. If your wife doesn't respect you, who will?*

How They Meet

Although Minh was upwardly mobile in 1985 and would have become an engineer had he remained in Vietnam, he is now an assistant cook who has spent the bulk of his adult working life confined to a small Chinese restaurant in Middle America. He hasn't read a book in recent memory. In fact, he says little about what he does, except work, or what he owns, except for a used Toyota Tercel he recently bought. Meanwhile, Thanh is a relatively successful lawyer in urban Saigon, where Chanel perfume and Ann Taylor shirts are essential components of her daily life. Thanh speaks very good English, the language we used when she and I met in Vietnam; Minh and I spoke Vietnamese when I interviewed him in Quincy. Thanh is currently working toward an English proficiency degree at an international adult English school, and her reading list includes F. Scott Fitzgerald's *The Great Gatsby*. She often prides herself that she is not as thin as the average woman in Vietnam, nor does she have the stereotypically Vietnamese long, straight black hair. Instead, Thanh has a perm with red highlights, and she spends a large part of her leisure time taking aerobics classes at the Saigonese Women's Union. She likes to joke, "Some people in Vietnam think that I'm a Viet Kieu woman."

Today Minh and Thanh live in seemingly separate worlds. The network of kin and acquaintanceship that unites them was driven by the war, but it still shares the history, memories, and connections of the prewar years. In 1997, when he was nearing his mid-thirties, Minh's family pressed him to find a suitable wife. In Vietnam, there is a strong cultural belief that one should marry in early adulthood, and most certainly before one turns thirty. In 1997, Minh, at thirty-four, was getting old in the eyes of married Vietnamese people. At twenty-eight, Thanh was considered even older as a woman, and both were very old according to Vietnamese notions of fertility. Most people are expected to have a first child, preferably a son, early to ensure patrilineal lineage. Although the average age of marriage has increased in Vietnam in the past few years, as it has worldwide, Vietnamese women are often stigmatized and considered unmarriageable at as young as

twenty-five.[30] In the villages, some women are considered unmarriageable at twenty.

Transpacific marriage arrangements are not always the idea of the grooms or brides involved. More than 55 percent of the grooms I interviewed said the idea of a transpacific marriage did not occur to them until a close friend or family member suggested it. The same was true of only 27 percent of the brides. In other words, more brides than grooms expressed an initial desire for an overseas spouse, while grooms were somewhat hesitant until encouraged. The arrangement for Minh and Thanh started when Minh's siblings expressed concern that their eldest brother appeared lonely and needed a wife (though they never asked him if this was the case). After all, he was the eldest sibling but the only one who remained unmarried and childless. The average age of marriage for his three younger sisters was twenty-one and for his two brothers, twenty-four. While these ages seem lower than the current Vietnamese average of twenty-four years for women and twenty-five years for men, they were not unusual at the time, since all five siblings married in the late 1980s and early 1990.[31] Minh's next brother's eldest child is now in her first year at Le Buon Phong High School. Minh feels old when he thinks of this. He is often embarrassed when his family asks him, "Why didn't you bring your lady friend back to visit us, too?" Minh's long work hours, along with the scarcity of Vietnamese women (relative to men) in the United States in general and Quincy in particular, were among the real reasons why the lady friend was generally "too busy to come home *this time.*"

Both Minh and Thanh faced structural and demographic limitations in their local marriage markets, but in different and reversed ways. Minh knew very few Vietnamese American women, and those he knew usually earned the same amount or more than he did, which made him a less attractive marriage candidate in the United States. Among Asian Americans, especially in California, women tend to get low-wage jobs more easily, to work longer hours, and to earn more money than men.[32] By contrast, Thanh knew many single men in Saigon, but they were far below her in educational status and made much less money than she did. Her economic and educational status made her a less attractive marriage candidate in Vietnam, but the same qualities served her well on the transpacific marriage market. As Thanh explained to me:

> *Any Viet Kieu man can come here to find a wife. And he can surely find a beautiful woman if he wants because there are many beautiful young women willing to marry anyone to go overseas. I think there is something different when you talk about Viet Kieu men coming back here to marry. The women here who marry for money, many of them will marry other foreign men, like Taiwanese and Korean men, but they have sacrificed their lives for their families because they think they can go off to another country and later send money back home. Those [non–Viet Kieu] men seldom check the family backgrounds of the women they marry, because they don't care. They, the women and the men, know it's something like prostitution, like selling oneself, even though they have weddings and everything. But it's not really a marriage. If the brides are lucky,*

*their foreign husbands will love them and take care of them. But when it has to
do with Vietnamese men, they are more selective. They look for a real marriage.
And a marriage that will last forever. So it's important to them to check everything about the woman they will marry and her background. These [Viet Kieu]
men want a woman who is educated and who comes from an educated family,
because that means she comes from a good family. And if her family has money,
he knows she just doesn't want to marry him to go overseas because she already
has a comfortable life in Vietnam.*

News of a split marriage market, one for foreign non–Viet Kieu men
and the other for Viet Kieu men who usually have family connections, has
circulated extensively throughout the Vietnamese diaspora. Men who want
"real" marriages are careful not to meet women on their own, because they
fear they will be used as passes for migration. When I visited Saigon night-
clubs, cafés, and bars where overseas Vietnamese men and local women
converge, I found that both men and women approached public courtship
with a lack of trust. Like women in Taiwan, Thailand, Singapore, Malaysia,
Hong Kong, and other Asian countries I've visited or studied, Vietnamese
women who seek transpacific spouses are so afraid of being seen as prostitutes that they rarely allow themselves to be courted by foreign men in
public. Some Viet Kieu men come back and visit local bars and dance clubs
in search of "one-night stands" either with prostitutes or non-prostitutes, but
they rarely marry women they meet in these public spaces. My sample of
marriages yielded only one couple who met by any means other than kinship introduction or arrangement. That couple had met through an international Vietnamese newspaper based in Sydney. Ninety percent of the couples
had their marriages arranged, and of the remaining 9 percent, the men had
returned to Vietnam to court old school friends or neighbors.

If women are afraid that they will be sexually exploited, Viet Kieu men
are wary of being used as a "bridge" to cross the Pacific.[33] These concerns,
combined with the availability of transnational networks, have propelled
women in Vietnam and Vietnamese men who live overseas to rely on marriage arrangements rather than engaging in individual courtship. As in the
case of arranged marriages among other ethnic groups, marriage candidates
in the Vietnamese diaspora believe that family members make the best judgments in their interests when looking for a spouse.[34] . . .

Minh's parents have known Thanh's family for more than two decades.
Even though Thanh's father taught at Le Buon Phong two decades ago,
and was a friend and colleague of Minh's parents, the current consumption
gap between the two families has created a social distance over the years.
When Minh's siblings convinced him to search for a wife in Vietnam, he was
hesitant at first, but later followed their advice when his parents promised
that they would invest time and care in finding the most suitable spouse.
According to Minh, however, they were surprised to discover that arranging
a marriage for a Viet Kieu was more complicated than they had anticipated:

*I thought that it would be easy for them to find someone. I thought all they had
to do was mention a few things to their friends, and within days they could*

describe a few possible people to me. But my parents told me that they were afraid that women just wanted to use our family to go abroad. We had many people get involved, many people wanted to be matchmakers for the family, and they added so much anxiety and fear about people's intentions. But the first goal for them was to find a woman from a wealthy family so that they were sure she wasn't just interested in money, because if she has money she would already be comfortable in Vietnam. And it would have been best if she had family in the United States already, because we would then know that they already have overseas people who help them out and they would not expect to become dependent on us. In Vietnamese, you know, there is this saying, "When you choose a spouse, you are choosing his or her whole family."

Minh's parents finally contacted Thanh's parents, after the traditional fashion in which the groom's parents represent him to propose, often with rituals and a centuries-old ceremonial language. Like most brides in my study, Thanh relied on an overseas relative—in this case her uncle, Tuan—for advice on Minh's situation in the United States. The family discovered that Minh was a low-wage worker, but a full-time worker nonetheless. During a walk Thanh and I took through the busy Ben Thanh market in the center of Saigon, she revealed that she and her family were already prepared to support a reversed remittance situation:

My father and mother didn't care about how much money Minh has. They figured that they could help us out if Minh doesn't do so well; it sounds strange and hard to believe, but my parents said that they could help us open up a business in the United States later on if Minh wants us to do that. They liked the idea that he is a hardworking man and that he comes from a good family. . . . They know he comes from a good family because he sends money back to his parents. He knows how to take care of them.

Virtually all of the locals I met in Vietnam viewed overseas men as a two-tiered group: the "successful," who were educated or who succeeded in owning ethnic enterprises, and the "indolent," who lacked full-time jobs and were perceived as being welfare-dependent or as participating in underground economies, such as gambling. Some felt that the latter group had taken up valuable spots that others from Vietnam could have filled. "If I had gotten a chance to go, I would be so rich by now," I heard many local men say. Most people, however, could not explain a man like Minh, who is neither lazy nor extremely successful. Thanh's uncle Tuan seemed to know more men in Houston who were not only unemployed but alcoholics and gamblers. Her parents were worried that their daughter was unmarriageable, because there was certainly no shortage of younger women in Vietnam for local men her age to marry. Thanh, too, was already convinced that she was "*e.*" Both her parents and her uncle worried that Thanh was facing a life of permanent singlehood. Finally, they all believed that marrying Thanh to Minh, a Viet Kieu man, would be more desirable than arranging her marriage to a local man in Vietnam. Thanh's parents were confident that Minh's status as a full-time worker who sent remittances back home to his family

spoke well for him as a suitable husband. Most Viet Kieu single men her uncle knew belonged to an underclass of which Minh was not a part. For Thanh, Minh's geographical advantage translated into something socially priceless: a man living in a modern country, she was sure, would respect women.

A Clash of Dreams

Highly educated women like Thanh resist patriarchal arrangements by avoiding marriages with local men. They do not want to "marry down" economically and socially—though this seems to be their only choice—because they believe that marrying local men will only constrain them to domestic roles in a male-dominated culture. As Thanh told me, some women will endure the often painful stigma of singlehood and childlessness over the oppression they could face from dominating husbands. For some of these women, the transpacific marriage market holds out hope for a different kind of marriage—one in which Vietnamese women imagine that their husbands will believe in, and practice, gender equity. Many such women will instead find themselves back in the pre-modern family life they hoped to avoid. As Minh told me, "A woman's place is in the home to take care of her husband and his family."

All but three of the twenty-eight grooms I interviewed shared Minh's view. But this conflict in gender ideology between the two unmarriageables never seemed to come to the fore until it was too late. During the migration period, each expensive phone call and visit is an occasion for love, not for discussing the details of what life will be like when the woman joins the man abroad. Most couples shared only words of joy about being together in the future.

And yet, as I interviewed the couples in their separate countries during this period, I found that the two parties usually held conflicting views of the life they would soon lead together. I did not interview all of the grooms, but I did ask all of the brides about their husbands' ideas about gender relations, and about how they envisioned the organization of their households after they joined their husbands abroad. Among other things, I asked about household division of labor, about whether the couple would live with or without kin, and about whether or not the women expected to work outside the home. Although these concerns address only a fraction of a marriage's potential promise or pitfalls, they can certainly help us understand the interplay between a husband's gender ideology and his wife's.[35]

Nearly 95 percent of the brides in Vietnam wanted to work for a wage when they joined their husbands abroad. Though wanting to work outside the home is not the ultimate measure of a modernized woman in Vietnam, it does indicate these women's unwillingness to be confined to domestic work. Some women who wanted paid jobs were not averse to the idea of doing second shift work as well.[36] However, most of the women, and virtually all of the educated ones—the unmarriageables—wanted and expected to have

egalitarian relationships with their husbands. In general, they objected to traditionally female tasks, although they did not fully embrace what we might call a peer marriage.[37] For the men and women I interviewed, as for mainstream dual-career American couples, marital life consists of much more than just household tasks. But these tasks are important symbols in the economy of gratitude among married people, "for how a person wants to identify himself or herself influences what, in the back and forth of a marriage, will seem like a gift and what will not."[38]. . .

Women like Thanh want a respectful marriage based on principles of gender equality. According to these principles, women expect to work for a wage, to share in making social and economic decisions for their future households, and to have their husbands share in the household division of labor. Above all, they do *not* want to live in multigenerational households, serving as the dutiful daughter-in-law and housewife, the two often inseparable roles historically delegated to women in Vietnam. Many express that reluctance, because they know numerous Viet Kieu men who live with their parents or who plan to do so when their parents are old. In Vietnam, and more generally in Asia, elderly parents often live with their eldest sons. The daily caring work then falls to their sons' wives. Forty percent of the U.S.-based grooms and a third of all Vietnamese grooms live with their parents, most of whom are elderly and require care. Of all low-wage working men married to highly educated women, about 35 percent currently reside with their parents. Virtually all of the men in my study who resided with their parents wanted to continue to do so when their wives joined them abroad.

For Minh, the possibility that a wife will insist on an equal marriage is one of the anxieties of modern life:

Vietnamese women, they care for their husbands and they are more traditional. I think non-Vietnamese women and Viet Kieu women are too modern. They just want to be equal with their husbands, and I don't think that is the way husband and wife should be. . . . I mean that husband and wife should not be equal. The wife should listen to husband most of the time. That is how they will have a happy life together. If the woman tries to be equal they will have problems. . . . I know many Vietnamese men here who abandon their parents because their wives refuse to live with their parents. If my parents were in America, I would definitely plan for them to live with me when they are old. But because they are in Vietnam, they are living with one of my brothers.

Instead of seeking peasant village women or uneducated ones, after the fashion of white men who pursue mail-order brides because they believe such women consent to subordination in marriage, men like Minh seek marriage arrangements with educated women. As Minh explains:

For me, I want to marry an educated woman, because she comes from a good, educated family. It's very hard to find a poor woman or an uneducated woman who comes from an uneducated family to teach their daughters about morals and values, because if they are uneducated they don't know how. I know many

men, Viet Kieu and foreign men, who go to Vietnam to marry beautiful young women, but they don't ask why do those women marry them? Those women only want to use their beauty to go overseas, and they will leave their husbands when they get the chance. They can use their beauty to find other men. I would never marry a beautiful girl from a poor, uneducated family. You see, the educated women, they know it's important to marry and stay married forever. As they say in Vietnam, "Tram nam han phuc [a hundred years of happiness]." Educated women must protect their family's reputation in Vietnam by having a happy marriage, not have it end in divorce.

The Inflated Market of Respect

At first glance, Minh and Thanh seem to come from two vastly different social worlds, assembled only by the complexity of Vietnamese history. But at a closer look, we learn that these two lonely faces of globalization are very much alike. Both of their parents were educated and middle class. Both lack the emotional fulfillment and intimate partnership that adults of their social worlds enjoy. Both long for a kind of marital respect they perceive as scarce in their local marriage markets. Minh has experienced immense, swift downward mobility as a result of migration, and he is eager to regain the respect he has lost. Thanh has practically priced herself out of the local marriage market by acquiring an advanced degree, which she could not have obtained without her uncle's remittances. She wants a husband who respects her as an equal and who accepts that she is a modern woman. He wants to regain something he thinks men like him have lost; she wants to challenge the local marriage norm, including the very preindustrial Vietnamese family life Minh yearns for. Many men in Vietnam do live that life. As Minh told me:

> *My younger brothers have control over their homes. Their wives help them with their shops selling fabrics in Saigon, but their wives don't make any decisions. I think that if they lived in America, and their wives were working, they would not let my brother make all the decisions in the house. . . . And I think that Vietnamese women, when they come to the United States, they are influenced by a lot of different things. That is why there are a lot of divorces in America.*

Minh believes that when he migrated to the United States, he left the respect he now craves behind him in Vietnam. Thanh imagines that the marital respect *she* craves is unobtainable in Vietnam, but awaits her in the United States. Each has inflated the true extent of the respect the other is willing to give. For though there is a quiet feminist revolution of sorts going on among highly educated women in Vietnam, that revolution has not entered the experience or expectations of the less educated, low-wage husbands living overseas. And while many of these Viet Kieu men seek reprieve from modern Western life, the women they marry have washed away those traditions during the long years that the men have been gone.

The Future of Transpacific Marriages

Surely, this clash of dreams and expectations will result in marital conflict when the couple is united overseas. Such conflicts have several potential outcomes. The happiest would have Minh joining the feminist revolution and abandoning his desire for the preindustrial, traditional family life he never had. Some men will go this route, but only a few. In other cases, such marriages may end in divorce—or worse, domestic battery. I believe the latter scenario is an unlikely one for the couples I studied. Many women like Thanh have considered the possibility and are careful to maintain contact with transnational networks that will look out for them. Seventy-five percent of the women in my study have at least one overseas relative. Virtually all the middle-class and college-educated women do.

Most likely, these marriages will resolve themselves with the men getting the respect they want and the women consenting to subordination in the name of family and kinship. Thanh will be going from the patriarchal frying pan to the patriarchal fire, but with one big difference. In the United States, her desire for gender equity will find more support, in a culture where women dare to leave their husbands if they aren't treated equally. But Thanh will still bear the burden of Vietnamese tradition, which will prevent her from leaving her husband. In Vietnam, divorce is stigmatized, and saving face is especially important to educated, middle-class families. If Thanh daringly divorces her husband, she will damage her family's reputation in Vietnam and overseas. She told me she would not be likely to take this risk. If she stays in the marriage, she will probably wind up serving as the traditional wife Minh desires.

Although globalization appears to offer some Vietnamese women an escape from local patriarchal marriages, it may in fact play more to the interests of certain Vietnamese men, offering them the opportunity to create the traditional life they've always wanted within the modern setting where they now live. Strong traditions back in Vietnam protect them against instability in their marriages. But the women they have married don't share their husbands' traditional vision of marital life. The only thing educated women like Thanh have to look forward to is more waiting—waiting for men like their husbands, who live in a modern country, simply to respect women.

ENDNOTES

[1] All names have been changed to protect the privacy of informants. . . .

[2] Although Saigon's name changed to Ho Chi Minh City when the South surrendered to Northern Vietnam in 1975, most people I met in contemporary Vietnam still refer to the city as Saigon, or simply Thanh Pho (the City). I use the name Saigon and Saigonese in deference to local usage.

[3] More than two million people have emigrated from Vietnam since April 1975, which comes to about 3 percent of the country's current population of eighty million. Approximately 60 percent left as boat refugees; the remaining 40 percent went directly to resettlement countries. Ninety-four percent of those who left Vietnam eventually resettled in Western countries. Between 1975 and 1995, the United States accepted 64 percent of that group; 12 percent went to Australia and 12 percent to Canada. . . .

[4] I would like to thank Pierrette Hondagneu-Sotelo for pointing out the complexity and danger of lumping all migrants—legal and illegal—into one category.

[5] These figures refer to individuals aged twenty and over, since aggregate data from the Immigration and Naturalization Service includes in one bracket the ages fifteen through nineteen, thus making it impossible to calculate the legal marriage age of eighteen into the marriage migration figure. Therefore, we can assume that these percentages are slightly lower than the actual numbers of marriage migrants. See United States Immigration and Naturalization Service, "Statistical Yearbook of the Immigration and Naturalization Service, 1997," *Statistics Branch* (1999); United States Immigration and Naturalization Service, "International Matchmaking Organizations: A Report to Congress by the Immigration and Naturalization Service," *A Report to Congress* (1999); and United States Immigration and Naturalization Service, "Annual Report: Legal Immigration, Fiscal Year 1997," *Statistics Branch* (1999), pp. 1–13.

[6] Marion F. Houstoun, Roger G. Kramer, and Joan Mackin Barrett, "Female Predominance in Immigration to the United States since the 1930s: A First Look," *International Migration Review*, vol. 18, no. 4 (1984), pp. 908–63.

[7] Guillermina Jasso, *The New Chosen People: Immigrants in the United States* (New York: Russell Sage Foundation, 1990). In recent years, there has been a lively discussion among feminist scholars about family migration, but no one has specifically looked at processes of marriage migration. See, for example, Alan Booth, Ann C. Crouter, and Nancy Landale, *Immigration and the Family: Research and Policy on U.S. Immigrants* (Mahwah, N.J.: Lawrence Erlbaum Associates Press, 1997); Nancy Foner, "The Immigrant Family: Cultural Legacies and Cultural Changes," *International Migration Review*, vol. 31, no. 4 (1997), pp. 961–74; Yen Le Espiritu, *Asian American Women and Men* (Thousand Oaks, Calif.: Sage Publications, 1997); Pierrette Hondagneu-Sotelo, *Gendered Transitions: Mexican Experiences of Immigration* (Berkeley: University of California Press, 1994); Silvia Pedraza, "Women and Migration: The Social Consequences of Gender," *Annual Review of Sociology*, vol. 17 (1991), pp. 303–25; and Patricia R. Pessar, "Engendering Migration Studies: The Case of Immigrants in the United States," *American Behavioral Scientist*, vol. 42, no. 4 (1999), pp. 577–600.

[8] Ruben G. Rumbaut, "Ties That Bind: Immigration and Immigrant Families in the United States," in *Immigration and the Family: Research and Policy on U.S. Immigrants*, ed. Alan Booth, Ann C. Crouter, and Nancy Landale (Mahwah, N.J.: Lawrence Erlbaum Associates Press, 1997).

[9] Migrants in at least three different streams of marriage migration can obtain, with relative ease, the papers to go abroad. The first is the *commercialized* mail-order bride stream. In their communities of origin, these brides are seen as occupying a continuum that runs from prostitutes (most commonly) to women seeking their dream husbands. Men on the receiving end are usually Caucasians from the United States, Australia, Canada, and Europe who go to "exotic lands" in search of submissive wives. See Mila Glodava and Richard Onizuka, *Mail-Order Brides: Women for Sale* (Colorado: Aleken, 1994). The second stream includes the *non-commercialized* transracial spousal migrant. This has historically included war brides of U.S. servicemen. In contemporary Vietnam and elsewhere, these couples tend to meet by working together in multinational firms, embassies, or universities. The third stream is composed of same-ethnic individuals who live in different countries and have married each other. This third stream is the topic of my research.

[10] See, for example, Eve Tahmincioglu, "For Richer or Poorer: Mail-Order Brides Make for Big Business Online," *Ziff Davis Smart Business for the New Economy*, (Jan. 1, 2001), p. 40.

[11] Although it is difficult to calculate whether or not marriage migrants are in transracial relationships, or how many are part of systems of commercialized mail-order brides, the best estimate we have is that about one-third of all marriage migrant couples are transracial, and that 2.7 to 4.1 percent are mail-order brides. See *Report to Congress, 1999*; Michael C. Thornton, "The Quiet Immigration: Foreign Spouses of U.S. Citizens, 1945–1985," in *Racially Mixed People in America*, ed. Maria P. Root (Newbury Park, Calif.: Sage Publications, 1992), pp. 64–76.

[12] Guillermina Jasso and Mark R. Rosenzweig, "Sponsors, Sponsorship Rates and the Immigration Multiplier," *International Migration Review*, vol. 23, no. 4 (1989), pp. 856–88; Jasso, 1990.

[13] In the United States from 1960 to 1997, the number of marriage migrants multiplied by approximately three times. In the 1960s, only 9 percent of all immigrants were marriage migrants; by 1997, this number jumped to 25 percent. See *Report to Congress, 1999*; Jasso, 1990. Most of those who migrate to marry permanent residents are women. In 1997, for example, a total

of 201,802 individuals came to the United States through legal marriage migration. Of these, 84 percent were marrying U.S. citizens and 16 percent were marrying permanent residents. Of those marrying U.S. citizens, 61 percent were women, whereas 87 percent of those marrying permanent residents were women.

[14] This paper is based on extensive interviews with ninety-eight people (mainly brides and their families) in Vietnam and thirty-one people (mainly grooms) in the United States. I interviewed the brides in their homes in Saigon and in six villages dotted along a main road in the Mekong Delta. I interviewed the grooms in their homes in San Francisco, Los Angeles, Seattle, and Boston. For further details, see Hung Cam Thai, "Marriage Across the Pacific: Family, Gender and Migration in Vietnam and in the Vietnamese Diaspora" (Ph.D. dissertation, University of California, Berkeley).

[15] Except in a few cases, the men who do low-wage work are also less educated than their wives; most of these grooms have barely a grade school education. Education and income are often, but not always, linked. Plumbers, for example, may earn more money than teachers. In this [reading] I refer to the men as both "low-wage workers" and "undereducated" men. The brides I describe here are "highly educated" women compared to most women in Vietnam, meaning that they all have at least a college degree and many have advanced degrees. Most of them, though not all, come from solidly middle-class Vietnamese backgrounds.

[16] Daniel Goodkind, "The Vietnamese Double Marriage Squeeze," *The Center for Migration Studies of New York*, vol. 31, no. 1 (1997), pp. 108–28.

[17] These calculations are based on Goodkind's 1990 data. See Goodkind, 1997. I simply added ten years to each cohort, though mortality for either sex as a whole may have caused a shift in sex ratio since 1990.

[18] Tina Katherine Fitzgerald, "Who Marries Whom? Attitudes in Marital Partner Selection" (Ph.D. dissertation, Department of Sociology, University of Colorado, 1999).

[19] When low-wage men travel to search for spouses abroad, they are unlikely to advertise that they work in low-wage jobs. In my study, however, most men did inform their wives, vis-à-vis matchmakers and go-betweens. Thus, I base my 55 percent figure of low-wage men married to highly educated women on information provided by the brides and their families, as well as interviews with some of the grooms. I did not find that any grooms had misrepresented themselves when I matched their stories to those of their brides. Nonetheless, although I estimate that 80 percent of the grooms in my study are low-wage workers, that number may, in fact, be higher if they misinformed their wives.

[20] Andrew J. Pierre, "Vietnam's Contradictions," *Foreign Affairs*, vol. 79, no. 6 (2000).

[21] Pierre, 2000.

[22] Henry Dietz, "The Rich Get Richer: The Rise of Income Inequality in the United States and the World," *Social Science Quarterly* (Sept. 1991), p. 639; *Saigon: 20 Years After Liberation* (Hanoi, Vietnam: The Gioi Publishers, 1995); Vu Thi Hong, Le Van Thanh, and Troung Si Anh, *Migration, Human Resources, Employment and Urbanization in Ho Chi Minh City* (Hanoi: National Political Publishing House, 1996).

[23] Daniele Belanger and Khuat Thu Hong, "Marriage and Family in Urban North Vietnam, 1965–1993," *Journal of Population*, vol. 2, no. 1 (1996), pp. 83–112; Charles Hirschman and Vu Manh Loi, "Family and Household Structures in Vietnam: Some Glimpses from a Recent Survey," *Pacific Affairs*, vol. 69 (1996), pp. 229–49; Nazli Kibria, *Family Tightrope: The Changing Lives of Vietnamese Americans* (Princeton, N.J.: Princeton University Press, 1993); Dinh Huou Tran, "Traditional Families in Vietnam and the Influence of Confucianism," in *Sociological Studies on the Vietnamese Family*, ed. Rita Lijestrom and Tuong Lai (Hanoi, Vietnam: Social Sciences Publishing House, 1991), pp. 27–53; and Steven K. Wisensale, "Marriage and Family Law in a Changing Vietnam," *Journal of Family Issues*, vol. 20 (1999), pp. 602–16.

[24] Min Zhou and Carl L. Bankston, *Growing Up American: How Vietnamese Children Adapt to Life in the United States* (New York: Russell Sage Foundation, 1998).

[25] Giovanna M. Merli, "Estimation of International Migration for Vietnam 1979–1989" (unpublished paper, Department of Sociology and Center for Studies in Demography and Ecology, University of Washington, Seattle, 1997).

[26] Zhou and Bankston, 1998.

[27] Jack Leonard and Mai Tran, "Probes Take Aim at Organized Crime in Little Saigon; Crackdown: Numerous Agencies Target Gambling, Drug Sales, Counterfeit Labels and Credit

Card Scams," *Los Angeles Times*, Oct. 7, 2000, p. B-7; Richard C. Paddock and Lily Dizon, "3 Vietnamese Brothers in Shoot-out Led Troubled Lives," *Los Angeles Times*, April 15, 1991, p. A3; Richard Marosi and Mai Tran, "Little Saigon Raids Dismantle Crime Ring, Authorities Say," *Los Angeles Times*, Sept. 29, 2000, p. B-3.

[28] Lillian Rubin, *Families on the Fault Line: America's Working Class Speaks about the Family, the Economy, Race and Ethnicity* (New York: HarperCollins, 1994).

[29] Racial and ethnic disparities, including in interethnic and interracial intimate markets, loom large in some of the marriages I studied. For these low-wage working men, categories of class and gender are more internalized, and more to the fore in their reflections on their lived experiences.

[30] Huu Minh Nguyen, "Age at First Marriage in Vietnam: Patterns and Determinants" (unpublished M.A. thesis, Department of Sociology, University of Washington, 1995); *The World's Women, 2000: Trends and Statistics*, 3d ed., Social Statistics and Indicators, series K, no. 16 (New York: United Nations, 2000).

[31] *World's Women*, 2000.

[32] Yen Le Espiritu, "Gender and Labor in Asian Immigrant Families," *American Behavioral Scientist* (1999), pp. 628–47.

[33] Aihwa Ong, *Flexible Citizenship* (London: Duke University Press, 1999). In one highly publicized case that spread throughout the Vietnamese diaspora, a transpacific groom "arrived to meet his bride at Los Angeles International Airport with a dozen red roses only to watch her blithely wave good-bye before she left with friends for San Jose" (Lily Dizon, "Journey Home for a Bride," *Los Angeles Times*, Sept. 19, 1994, p. A1).

[34] Reena Jana, "Arranged Marriages, Minus the Parents; for Some South Asians, Matrimonial Sites Both Honor and Subvert Tradition," *New York Times*, August 17, 2000, p. D1; Molly Moore, "Changing India, Wedded to Tradition; Arranged Marriages Persist with '90's Twists," *Washington Post*, Oct. 8, 1994; Shanthy Nambiar, "Love with the Proper Stranger," *Washington Post*, 1993; Shoba Narayan, "When Life's Partner Comes Pre-Chosen," *New York Times*, 1995; Najma Rizvi, "Do You Take This Man? Pakistani Arranged Marriages," *American Anthropologist* (Sept. 1993), p. 787.

[35] According to sociologist Arlie Russell Hochschild, there are differences between what people say they believe about their marital roles and how they seem to feel about those roles. Furthermore, what they believe and how they feel may also differ from what they actually do. She distinguishes between gender ideologies and gender strategies to point out that ideology has to do with how men and women draw on "beliefs about manhood and womanhood, beliefs that are forged in early childhood and thus anchored to deep emotions." Gender strategies refer to people's plans of action and their emotional preparations for pursuing them. See Arlie Russell Hochschild and Anne Machung, *The Second Shift: Working Parents and the Revolution at Home* (New York: Viking, 1989), p. 15.

[36] Hochschild with Machung, *The Second Shift: Working Parents and the Revolution at Home* (New York: Avon, 1997).

[37] Pepper Schwartz, *Love between Equals: How Peer Marriage Really Works* (New York: Free Press, 1995).

[38] Hochschild with Machung, 1997.

18

FAMILIES FORMED OUTSIDE OF MARRIAGE

JUDITH A. SELTZER

It is a sociological truism that the meaning of cohabitation outside of marriage and other family relationships depends on the social context in which they occur. For example, many Latin American countries have long histories of socially accepted consensual unions, which may substitute for formal unions in some groups (De Vos 1999; Parrado and Tienda 1997). Laws about taxes and housing and child allowances treat unmarried and married couples the same in Sweden, where premarital cohabitation is nearly universal (Hoem 1995). In contrast, in the United States, where cohabitation was uncommon until recently, family law gives cohabitors few of the rights of married couples (Gordon 1998/1999). Similarly, U.S. children born outside of marriage lack some advantages that accrue to children born in marriage, unless the former have legally identified fathers.

As cohabitation and nonmarital childbearing become more common, individuals are less likely to think of them as deviant behaviors. Individuals also have fewer incentives to marry before having a child when children born outside of marriage are eligible for the same benefits and accorded the same social recognition as children born in marriage. In the United States, individuals are marrying and forming nonmarital families in a changing social context. Marriage, as an institution, is increasingly defined as a short-term relationship. Divorce is more acceptable now than in the past. Laws no longer assume that marriage is forever, and celebrations of marriage are less likely to emphasize its permanence. The meaning of cohabitation is shifting, in part because the meaning of marriage has shifted. Marriage offers fewer benefits relative to cohabitation now than in the past. Most young people expect to marry and believe that it is important to have a good marriage and family life, but most do not believe that they must marry to live a good life (Thornton 1995).

The meaning of cohabitation and nonmarital relationships also depends on the expectations of those who form the union and on individuals' own experiences within the relationship. Individuals' attitudes on the appropriate conditions for marriage and childbearing, on whether relationships involve lifetime commitments, and on the different rights and responsibilities of women and men in cohabiting and marital relationships affect how

they understand their personal relationships. Marriage is an economic arrangement, notwithstanding the expressions of love that accompany the formalization of such unions. Economic uncertainty and scarcity of economic resources increase the likelihood of cohabitation compared with marriage, but rates of cohabitation have risen among those with both low and high levels of education, an indicator of likely economic success. Individuals who decide to live together instead of marrying may do so as a way to evaluate whether their partner will end up as a good economic match (Oppenheimer 1988) or an egalitarian partner (Cherlin 2000). Once couples begin living together, they also develop new ties that bring them closer together (Berger and Kellner 1974). Having children together connects cohabiting partners in addition to the symbolic connections adults create. For some couples, these symbolic and child-based sources of solidarity may reinforce their plans to marry. For other couples, these bonds may make the idea of formalizing their union through marriage less important than when they began living together. The secular rise in the public's acceptance of cohabitation and of childbearing outside of marriage contributes to a decline in cohabiting partners' expectations about whether marriage is the "next step" in their own relationship.

The Rise in Cohabitation and Group Differences in Cohabitation

It was clear by the start of this decade that cohabitation was an important aspect of couple relationships in the United States. Between the mid-1970s and 1980s, young adults became more accepting of nonmarital cohabitation, with increasing percentages agreeing that cohabitation was a "worthwhile experiment" and that it was a good idea to live together before marrying (Thornton 1989). Approval of cohabitation is likely to continue to increase in the future through the process of cohort replacement because young adults are more likely than older adults to believe that it is all right for an unmarried couple to live together even if they have no plans to marry (Bumpass and Sweet 1995; Oropesa 1996). British data also show that compared with older persons, young adults are much more likely to say that they would advise a young person to live with a partner before they marry the partner (Kiernan and Estaugh 1993; Thornton 1995). Trends in behavior follow a similar pattern, with each recent birth cohort more likely to cohabit than previous cohorts (Bumpass and Sweet 1989; Chevan 1996). Rates of cohabitation have increased even among older adults, however (Waite 1995). By 1997, there were approximately 4.1 million cohabiting couples of all ages, up from 2.9 million in 1990, an increase of 46% (Casper and Cohen 2000).

The rise in cohabitation is best understood in the context of delayed marriage for recent cohorts compared with cohorts born between the post–World War II period and the mid-1960s. About two-thirds of the decline between 1970 and 1985 in the proportion of young adults married by age 25 can be attributed to the rise in nonmarital cohabitation (Bumpass, Sweet,

and Cherlin 1991, table 1). Although much discussion of cohabitation among young adults considers it a stage in the transition to first marriage, Bumpass and his colleagues showed that cohabiting unions also occur after a marriage dissolves and that rising rates of postmarital cohabitation compensated for the decline in remarriage among couples separated in the early 1980s.

These trends continued for U.S. women in the 1990s. Nearly 40% of women aged 19 to 24 years in 1995 had ever cohabited, compared with just under 30% of women that age in the late 1980s (Bumpass and Lu 2000, table 1). More than half of first unions in the early 1990s began with cohabitation (Bumpass and Lu, table 3). The increase in nonmarital cohabitation occurred for all education groups and for Whites, Blacks, and Hispanics, although the increases were greater for those with a high school degree or less and for non-Hispanic Whites than for other groups (Bumpass and Lu, table 2). Cohabitation continues to offset the decline in marriage for young women.

Cohabitation remains more common among those with less education and for whom economic resources are more constrained (Bumpass and Lu 2000; Clarkberg 1999; Willis and Michael 1994), perhaps because cohabiting unions require less initial commitment to fulfill long-term economic responsibilities (Clarkberg, Stolzenberg, and Waite 1995; Smock and Manning 1997). Because the institution of marriage includes expectations about economic roles, couples may think that they should reach specific financial goals, such as steady employment or housing of a certain quality, before it is appropriate to marry. Those with low incomes may also think that marriage, with its legal rules about marital property and inheritance, is irrelevant for them given their few material assets (Cherlin 1992). Consistent with higher rates of cohabitation among the economically disadvantaged, cohabitors with more financial resources are more likely to expect to marry their partners (Bumpass et al. 1991). They are also more likely to realize their expectations about marriage than cohabiting couples who are economically disadvantaged.

Cohabitation rates have increased at the same time as marriage rates have declined for both Blacks and Whites. By 1998, about two-thirds of White women aged 20 to 24 were never married, nearly doubling the percentage never married in 1970. Marriage is even less common for Black women aged 20 to 24, among whom 85% were never married in 1998 (Cherlin 1992).

Rates of marriage or nonmarriage exaggerate Black–White differences in union formation. When one considers both informal unions (cohabitation) and formal unions (marriages), the race difference in the percentage of young women who have entered a union is reduced by about one half (Raley 1996). Puerto Ricans also enter informal unions at high rates. Compared with non-Hispanic Whites, Puerto Ricans are less likely to marry their cohabiting partners (Landale and Forste 1991). Explanations for race and ethnic differences in cohabitation patterns draw on both cultural and economic factors. Landale and Fennelly (1992), for example, argued that the long history of social recognition of consensual unions in many Latin American countries explains in part why Puerto Rican women, compared to non-Hispanic White

women, are less likely to formalize their unions, even when children are involved.

When men's economic circumstances are precarious, young adults delay marriage (Oppenheimer, Kalmijn, and Lim 1997). Those who are economically insecure, including those still enrolled in school, may choose cohabitation over marriage (Thornton, Axinn, and Teachman 1995; Willis and Michael 1994). Among cohabiting couples, those in which the male partner is more economically secure are more likely to marry than those in which the male partner is economically insecure (Smock and Manning 1997). Economic factors alone, however, do not explain race differences in union formation (Raley 1996), pointing again to the need for explanations that take account of both cultural and economic factors. That men's declining labor market prospects explain some, but not all, of the delay in marriage between 1960 and 1980 for Black and White men reinforces the need to consider both economic and noneconomic factors to account for temporal and cross-sectional differences in union formation (Mare and Winship 1991).

Cohabitation as a Stage before Marriage or as an End in Itself

. . . Not surprisingly, cohabiting women are more similar to married women than to single women in their sexual and contraceptive behavior due to their greater exposure to risk (Bachrach 1987). Although adults in cohabiting relationships report that they have sex more frequently than those who are married, once the younger age of cohabitors is taken into account, the difference diminishes (Laumann et al. 1994). Never-married cohabiting couples are less likely to have a child together than are married couples, but they are significantly more likely to have a child compared with single women (Manning and Landale 1996; Wu, Bumpass, and Musick 1999). However, race and economic characteristics affect the degree to which cohabiting couples' fertility resembles that of married couples (Loomis and Landale 1994; Manning and Landale 1996).

Although cohabitation is often a prelude to marriage, cohabiting unions may be an end in themselves for an increasing percentage of cohabitors. These cohabitors do not necessarily reject marriage. Instead, cohabitors are less likely to see marriage as the defining characteristic of their family lives. Fewer cohabitations end in marriage now than in the past. . . .

Change in the meaning of nonmarital cohabitation comes from the growing importance of cohabitation as a setting in which couples bear and rear children. The percentage of cohabitors who had biological children together increased from 12% in the early 1980s to 15% in the early 1990s (Bumpass, personal communication, 1999). Although these percentages are still low, the change is a 25% increase over a short time. Having a child in the relationship may change how the couple thinks of their union. For example, among Puerto Rican women interviewed in a survey that allowed them to describe their unions as either informal marriages (i.e., they thought of

themselves as married) or cohabitations, women who had borne children outside formal marriage were much more likely to describe their relationship as an informal marriage than women without children (Landale and Fennelly 1992).

At the same time that cohabitors have become more likely to bear children together, the percentage of all children who are born to unmarried parents in the United States increased from about 18% in 1980 to nearly a third in 1997 (Smith, Morgan, and Koropeckyj-Cox 1996; Ventura et al. 1999), a trend I discuss further below. Cohabiting couples are responsible for much of this increase in nonmarital childbearing. In the early 1980s, cohabiting couples had 29% of nonmarital births, compared with 39% a decade later (Bumpass and Lu 2000). About 20% of nonmarital births occur in cohabiting unions after a first marriage has ended in separation or divorce, among women born since 1945 (Brown 2000). Children born to cohabiting parents begin life in a household with both biological parents, but researchers and policy makers often assume that these children live in a single-mother household.

Single women who become pregnant are increasingly likely to move in with rather than marry the father of their child. In the past, many of these pregnancies were "premarital" pregnancies that resulted in marital births; a single woman who became pregnant married the father of their child. (See Parnell, Swicegood, and Stevens 1994 on declines in "legitimation" in the postwar period.) As recently as the early 1980s, about 20% of single noncohabiting women who had a pregnancy that resulted in a live birth married by the time the child was born. By the early 1990s, only 11% did so. Over this same period, the percentage of pregnant single women who began cohabiting by the time their child was born increased from 6% to 9% (Raley 2001). Thus, women are almost as likely to form nonmarital cohabiting unions as marry when they have a child. Cohabiting couples also care for children brought to the union by only one of the partners. Nearly half of cohabiting couples live with children (Bumpass, personal communication, 1999), and cohabiting couples make up one-fourth of all stepfamilies (Bumpass, Raley, and Sweet 1995).

Stability of Cohabiting Unions

Cohabiting unions end quickly because the couple either marries or breaks up. Half end in a year or less for one of these reasons (Bumpass and Lu 2000). Compared with married couples, cohabitors are much more likely to break up. About 29% of cohabitors and only 9% of married couples break up within the first 2 years (Bumpass and Sweet 1989, table 4). Over the past decade, cohabiting unions have become even less stable, but this is mainly because of the decline in the percentage of cohabitors who eventually marry their partners. Within 5 years, more than half of unions begun by cohabitation have ended, regardless of whether the couple formalized the union by marrying (Bumpass and Lu). . . .

Marriages preceded by cohabitation are more likely to end in separation or divorce than marriages in which the couple did not live together previously (Bumpass and Lu 2000; Laumann et al. 1994; Lillard, Brien, and Waite 1995; Sweet and Bumpass 1992). For instance, about 16% of marriages preceded by cohabitation broke up within the first 5 years, compared with about 10% of marriages not preceded by cohabitation among women born in the mid-1930s. For women born a decade later who were marrying during the 1960s when divorce rates were rising, the contrast is 31% compared with 16%, respectively (Schoen 1992, table 1). However, for women born more recently, there is some evidence of convergence in the rates of marital dissolution between those who cohabited and those who did not (Schoen; but see Bumpass and Lu 2000, who reported that the higher disruption rates for marriages preceded by cohabitation persist for a more recent period).

In Britain, premarital cohabitation is also associated with higher rates of marital disruption (Berrington and Diamond 1999). In France, however, Leridon (1990) found that premarital cohabitation does not affect the stability of first marriage. Both cohort and country variation in the association between premarital cohabitation and marital disruption support my earlier claim that the social context affects who cohabits and the meaning and consequences of cohabitation.

In the United States, higher divorce rates for couples who cohabit before marriage may be due to differences in the background, attitudes, and behavior of those who choose premarital cohabitation compared with those who do not. Yet if young adults are correct in their belief that cohabitation is a worthwhile experiment for evaluating the compatibility of a potential spouse, one would expect those who cohabit first to have even more stable marriages than those who marry without cohabiting once preexisting differences between those who cohabit before marriage and those who do not are taken into account. Alternatively, the experience of premarital cohabitation may damage the couple's prospect of having a stable marriage. (See Axinn and Thornton 1992; Sweet and Bumpass 1992.)

Evidence for whether cohabitation *causes* an increase in the chance of divorce is mixed. Young men and women with liberal gender-role attitudes are more likely to cohabit than to marry (Clarkberg et al. 1995). Similarly, those who hold more negative attitudes about marriage and are more accepting of divorce have higher rates of cohabitation and generally lower rates of marriage (Axinn and Thornton 1992). Childhood family characteristics associated with marital disruption also affect whether a person cohabits or marries. Growing up in a single-parent household increases the likelihood of cohabiting in the United States and in Great Britain (Bumpass and Sweet 1989; Thornton 1991). Longitudinal surveys do not measure all of the personality traits and attitudes that distinguish cohabitors from those who marry. Higher rates of marital disruption for those who have previously cohabited disappear when these unobserved differences are taken into account with econometric techniques (Lillard et al. 1995). For German couples, premarital cohabitation actually enhances marital stability after statistical adjustments for unmeasured differences, such as attitudes and the quality of the couple's

relationship, between those who cohabit and those who do not (Brüderl, Diekmann, and Engelhardt 1997). The statistical techniques used in these studies require assumptions that are difficult to meet, but the similarity in findings and their consistency with other longitudinal analyses is reassuring on this point.

Young adults also become more tolerant of divorce as a result of cohabiting, whatever their initial views are (Axinn and Thornton 1992). Cohabitation may expose partners to a wider range of attitudes about family arrangements than those who marry without first living together. In addition, how cohabitors organize their daily lives may carry over into marriage (see below). Women and men in cohabiting couples divide housework somewhat more equally and bring home more similar earnings than married couples (Brines and Joyner 1999; Nock 1995). If these patterns carry over into marriage, they may contribute to higher divorce rates for those who cohabited before marriage because marital solidarity may depend on a specialized division of labor. Couples who cohabited before marriage may find that attempts to pursue a more egalitarian division of labor in marriage, a social institution that promotes a gendered division of labor, creates strain and conflict, which in turn increase the likelihood of divorce (Brines and Joyner). Researchers have done little to address the following questions: How and why do cohabiting couples decide to marry (or not to marry)? And how, if at all, does marriage change their behavior and feelings about the relationship (see Bumpass and Sweet 2001)?

On balance, both the "people who cohabit are different" and "cohabitation changes people" interpretations are supported by recent studies. None of the studies cited above provides definitive evidence on which is the better interpretation of higher divorce rates for those who cohabit before marriage. Much past research focuses on individuals and their attitudes, to the exclusion of partners' attitudes and the characteristics of their union, including how those who cohabit and those who marry organize their lives. Nevertheless, studies using different data and different methods of analysis consistently show that those who live together before marriage come from more "divorce-prone" families and hold more liberal attitudes toward divorce than do those who do not cohabit before marriage. Claims that individuals who cohabit before marriage hurt their chances of a good marriage pay too little attention to this evidence.

Paradoxically, whatever the effect of cohabiting on divorce at the level of the relationship, the instability of individual cohabiting unions stabilizes the rate of divorce. Many relationships that would have been short-term marriages dissolve before couples marry. Living together shows the couple that marriage is not for them, so they break up before formalizing their union. Demographers speculate that this removes some "high-risk" marriages from the pool of marriages that contributes to the formal divorce rate (Bumpass and Lu 2000; Bumpass and Sweet 1989). Recently, however, Goldstein's (1999) simulation provides evidence against this interpretation, suggesting that the rise in cohabitation explains little, if any, of the stabilization in the divorce rate.

How Cohabitors Organize Their Lives:
Work, Couple, and Kin Ties

That couples who cohabit differ in their attitudes about gender roles and family institutions suggests that they may organize their daily lives differently from those who choose to marry. Much of what we know about the organization of cohabiting couples' lives and how their lives compare to the lives of married couples builds on the rich information provided by Blumstein and Schwartz (1983) in their study of couple relationships in the United States. Cohabiting couples have greater flexibility in the degree to which they follow the gender-based division of labor and family responsibilities that is characteristic of formal marriage. Because some couples use cohabitation as a testing ground to evaluate a partner's compatibility, women (and men) who want to marry someone who will share most household and childrearing tasks may be particularly likely to live with a partner before marriage to observe and negotiate these arrangements. Whether the greater similarity in women's and men's roles within cohabitation than in marriage is due to the different goals that cohabitors bring to their relationship or to the lack of institutional supports for a gender-based division of labor is still an open question.

Recent data from large, national probability surveys, such as the National Survey of Families and Households (Sweet and Bumpass 1996), provide similar information on the experiences of heterosexual couples in formal and informal unions. These data show that compared with wives, women in cohabiting couples do fewer hours of housework but more hours of paid work. When differences between married and cohabiting couples in education, paid work, and the presence of children are taken into account, women in cohabiting couples still do about 6 fewer hours of housework than wives do. This is consistent with the finding cited above that compared with those who marry, cohabitors have more liberal gender-role attitudes when they begin their relationship. There are small differences, if any, in housework time for men by whether they are in formal or informal unions (Shelton and John 1993; South and Spitze 1994). In both marriage and cohabitation, women do more housework than men do, but the somewhat greater similarity between women's and men's paid and unpaid work in cohabiting unions suggests that the role responsibilities of female cohabiting partners may differ from those of female marriage partners.

Because cohabiting women perceive their relationships as less secure and as more likely to dissolve than formal marriages, they may be less willing to limit their paid labor force participation or to invest extra effort in housework to the detriment of their participation in the paid labor force. Both women and men may be less committed to their relationships when they cohabit than when they marry. Compared with those who are married, women and men in pre- and post-marital cohabiting unions see fewer costs and more benefits to breaking up (Nock 1995). A study in Norway also showed that a majority of cohabitors, regardless of whether they had a child together, are reluctant to marry because marriages are difficult to dissolve

(Kravdal 1999, table 6). These perceptions of the barriers to breaking up are realistic assessments. Married couples are more likely to pool their financial resources and have other relationship-specific investments, including biological children born to the union, than are cohabiting couples (Blumstein and Schwartz 1983; Loomis and Landale 1994). Another indication that spouses are more committed than are cohabitors to their relationships comes from the U.S. National Health and Social Life Survey of adults, which showed that marriages are more likely to be sexually exclusive than cohabitations, even taking account of cohabitors' more permissive values (Treas and Giesen 2000). We do not know, however, whether partners who invest more in their relationship do so because it is a good relationship or whether the relationship improves and becomes stronger as a result of the partners' investments.

Cohabiting partners may evaluate the success of their union using different criteria than do spouses in formal marriage. For instance, because they hold more egalitarian attitudes, young adult cohabitors may observe how their housework is actually divided to assess whether the relationship is "working." Cohabiting couples in which partners have similar earnings are more stable than those with dissimilar earnings. In contrast, among married couples, a more specialized division of labor, in which wives are not employed but husbands are, increases marital stability, as noted above (Brines and Joyner 1999).

Cohabiting couples face more disapproval of their relationship and receive less social support than do married couples. The lack of support may contribute to higher rates of disruption for cohabiting unions. Although the general public has grown increasingly tolerant of nonmarital cohabitation, parents may prefer that their children marry rather than cohabit. When mothers think marriage is important, their daughters are less likely to cohabit than when mothers hold less favorable attitudes about marriage (Axinn and Thornton 1992). Similarly, data from young adults in the Netherlands show that young adults' intentions to cohabit depend on whether they think that their parents and friends would support their decision (Liefbroer and Gierveld 1993).

Cohabitation may strain relationships between parents and adult children. Members of married couples describe their relationships with parents more positively than do cohabiting couples (Nock 1995). Parents also report closer relationships with married children than with cohabiting children (Aquilino 1997). On the other hand, members of cohabiting couples are almost as likely as members of married couples to have been introduced to each other by a family member, which suggests that spouses and cohabiting partners may be part of similar social circles (Laumann et al. 1994, table 6.1). . . .

Cohabitation, Childbearing, and Childrearing

Do Cohabiting Couples Marry Because They Want Children?

If cohabiting unions are experiments that young couples undertake to decide if they should marry, is there an end to the experiment or some precipitating event that prompts couple members to marry? Cohabiting couples who

decide that they are ready to have children may decide to marry as a first step toward having a child. Cohabiting couples in which the woman becomes pregnant (and does not have an abortion) are more likely to marry than are couples in which the woman is not pregnant (Manning 1995), although this effect is greater for White than for Black women (Manning and Smock 1995). Pregnancy also increases marriage among cohabitors in Sweden, a setting with fewer institutional barriers to childbearing outside of formal marriage than in the United States (Bracher and Santow 1998). Cohabiting couples in the United States who already have children, whether born to the couple or in previous relationships, are more likely to marry than those without children (Manning and Smock 1995). This finding is not consistent across settings, however. In Canada, which has also experienced a rise in cohabitation, couples who have a child in their cohabiting union are less likely to marry than those who have not had a child in their union (Wu and Balakrishnan 1995). Childbearing in cohabitation reduces the chance that a couple will break up, whether or not they formalize their union (Wu and Balakrishnan).

Effects of Cohabitation on Children's Family Experiences

As noted above, much of the recent rise in childbearing outside of marriage can be attributed to childbearing in cohabiting unions. Children in these unions start life in households with both of their biological parents instead of in a single-mother household. For new parents in Oakland, California, and Austin, Texas, about half of unmarried mothers who have just had a child report that they are living with their child's father (McLanahan, Garfinkel, and Padilla 1999a; McLanahan, Garfinkel, and Waller 1999b). . . .

Inferences about children's living arrangements from parents' marital status provide a misleading picture of recent demographic trends, such as the rise of "single"-father families. For instance, Garasky and Meyer (1996) showed that treating cohabitors as two-parent families reduces estimates of the growth in "single"-father families between 1960 and 1990 from about 240% to about 120%. Cohabitation also reduces the amount of time that children will spend in a single-parent household during childhood. Estimates using marital status to infer whether both parents are present have shown that children in recent cohorts will spend a median of nearly 7 years in a single-parent household from the time they first enter it. When cohabiting parents are taken into account, the median duration drops to 3.7 years (Bumpass and Raley 1995).

At first glance, taking cohabitation into account suggests that children's lives have become more stable. Yet because cohabiting unions are usually short-term relationships, taking cohabitation into account increases the number of family disruptions children experience. Just over one-third of children born in either a marital or cohabiting union will experience the break-up of their parents' relationship before the end of their teenage years, and this fraction increased in the decade between the early 1980s and the 1990s (Bumpass and Lu 2000:37). Cohabitation also affects children's experience in stepfamilies, many of which are begun informally when a parent brings

a new partner into the household, rather than by formal marriage. By the early 1980s, almost two-thirds of children who entered a stepfamily did so by cohabitation instead of marriage (Bumpass et al. 1995, table 2). Once children enter a stepfamily, the rates at which they face the dissolution of their stepfamily are similar whether the stepfamily began by cohabitation or by marriage (Bumpass et al. 1995, table 4). The similarity in rates of disruption for cohabiting and remarried stepfamilies suggests that there is less selection into cohabiting unions after a first relationship ends than into premarital cohabiting unions.

Effects of Cohabitation on Children

Adults who live with children share resources with them. A parent's cohabiting partner is likely to contribute toward the economic costs of raising the child(ren). These contributions may occur because the parent and her partner pool their incomes or because the child shares the household's public goods, such as housing, even if the cohabiting partners do not pool all of their incomes. The National Academy of Sciences report on measuring poverty recognizes that cohabiting partners' resources are important for family members' economic well-being. The report recommends that poverty measures treat cohabitors as part of the same family (Citro and Michael 1995). Cohabitors are included in the definition of "family" because of their likely pooling of income, economies of scale, and potential for continued resource sharing for several years. Although we know little about the extent to which cohabiting partners pool their incomes, Bauman (1999) finds that compared with spouses, cohabitors pool less of their income. Partners may be more likely to pool their incomes when they have a child together or have lived together a long time (Winkler 1997).

Income from a parent's cohabiting partner reduces by almost 30% the number of children in cohabiting-couple families who are in poverty (Manning and Lichter 1996). The rise in cohabitation over the past several decades implies that assessments of trends in poverty may overstate poverty in the more recent period relative to poverty rates a few decades ago. In fact, once cohabiting partners are included as family members and contributors to family income, the increase between 1969 and 1989 in child poverty from 13.1% to 18.7%, as measured by official statistics, would have been about 11% less (Carlson and Danziger 1999). Children whose parents cohabit are still more likely to be poor than those in married-couple families because of the age, education, and employment differentials between those who cohabit and those who marry. . . .

Behavioral and Legal Definitions of Family

Cohabitation and childbearing outside of marriage are central features of growth in families formed outside of marriage. Relationships between cohabiting couples and between many parents of babies born outside of

marriage are defined by coresidence and sharing a household. Nonmarital family relationships also cross household boundaries, as when parents and children live apart after divorce. Contact and financial transfers from non-resident parents to minor children help define family ties that may be important for children's welfare (Seltzer 1991, 1994). Cohabitation, childbearing outside of marriage, and relationships between parents and minor children who live apart are all families that exist largely without formal recognition by the state, although state laws about child support are an important exception to the lack of formal recognition. Individual citizens and policy makers seek to formalize relationships between cohabiting couples and fathers and children who live apart to acquire rights and, from the policy makers' side, establish responsibilities.

Two aspects of cohabiting unions may be formalized: rights and responsibilities within the union, including property and inheritance, and rights and responsibilities with respect to the state and other third parties (e.g., Blumberg 1981, 1985). Rights within the union can be formalized by individual contracts and other legal procedures the couple members can initiate. Establishing these legal contracts may be expensive, which means that they are not universally available because cohabitation is more common among the economically disadvantaged.

Rights with respect to third parties, such as social insurance claims, access to health insurance and other "family" benefits, derive from public action, including the passage of state laws, city ordinances establishing domestic partnership licenses, and policies adopted by employers. . . .

Cohabitation and Nonmarital Childbearing: Individual and Social Matters

Families matter for individuals. What happens in our families affects how we live our lives, whether we are rich or poor, the languages we speak, the work that we do, how healthy we are, and how we feel. Families also matter for the larger social group. Family members take care of each other (some better than others) and bear and rear the next generation. Within a society, the work families do depends on what people believe is the right way to treat parents, siblings, children, grandparents, and other kin. A common understanding about the obligations and rights of family members contributes to the institutionalization of family relationships. General consensus in public opinion about who should be counted as a family member and consistent laws also institutionalize relationships. Cohabitation, like remarriage, is still an incomplete institution in the United States (Cherlin 1978; Nock 1995). It takes a long time for new behaviors to become institutionalized.

The rapid increase in cohabitation and nonmarital childbearing over the past few decades suggests that these relationships may become more complete institutions in the future, but it is unlikely that they will have the preferred standing of marriage and childbearing in marriage any time soon. Cohabiting couples are very diverse, in part because they are forming their

relationships under a rapidly changing set of social rules about marriage, cohabitation, and childbearing outside of marriage. The instability of the environment in which individuals make family choices hampers the enforcement of kin obligations and norms about the acceptability of informal families and makes it even more likely that individuals will experiment in their family lives.

Some cohabitors would prefer formal marriage, but their economic circumstances prevent them from achieving this goal. Others seek a different type of relationship, one with greater gender equality, than they expect to find in marriage or than they found in a previous marriage. Yet another group of cohabitors uses their informal relationship as a trial period during which they negotiate and assess whether to formalize their union through marriage. We do not know the relative size of these groups in the population nor do we know how rapidly each group is growing. The heterogeneity of cohabiting couples poses a challenge to researchers who try to understand what cohabitation means.

Adults have more choices today about whether to cohabit and whether to have a child outside of marriage because the social costs, at least to adults, of forming informal families are much less today than just a few decades ago. Choosing one's family is part of a long-term trend toward greater individual autonomy in West Europe and the United States (Lesthaeghe 1995). The ability to choose at the individual level, however, does not mean that all choices will or should have the same standing in the public sphere. Nevertheless, the inclusion of a decade review on families formed outside of marriage in the *Journal of Marriage and the Family* demonstrates the greater legitimacy of individual choice in the contemporary United States and suggests even greater variation in informal families in the near future.

ENDNOTE

Author's Note: This work was supported, in part, by a grant from the Council on Research of the UCLA Academic Senate. The paper benefited from discussion with seminar participants at the University of California, Berkeley; University of Washington; University of California, Riverside; RAND; University of Virginia; University of Wisconsin–Madison; and Notre Dame University. I am grateful to Suzanne Bianchi, Larry Bumpass, Lynne Casper, Wendy Manning, Robert Mare, Kelly Musick, R. Kelly Raley, Christine Schwartz, and Pamela Smock for helpful advice, discussion, and comments on previous versions.

REFERENCES

Aquilino, W. S. 1997. "From Adolescent to Young Adult: A Prospective Study of Parent–Child Relations during the Transition to Adulthood." *Journal of Marriage and the Family* 59:670–86.

Axinn, W. G. and A. Thornton. 1992. "The Relationship between Cohabitation and Divorce: Selectivity or Causal Influence?" *Demography* 29:357–74.

Bachrach, C. A. 1987. "Cohabitation and Reproductive Behavior in the United States." *Demography* 24:623–37.

Bauman, K. J. 1999. "Shifting Family Definitions: The Effect of Cohabitation and Other Nonfamily Household Relationships on Measures of Poverty." *Demography* 36:315–25.

Berger, R. L. and H. Kellner. 1974. "Marriage and the Construction of Reality." Pp. 157–74 in *The Family: Its Structures and Functions*, 2d ed., edited by R. L. Coser. New York: St. Martin's Press.

Berrington, A. and I. Diamond. 1999. "Marital Dissolution among the 1958 British Birth Cohort: The Role of Cohabitation." *Population Studies* 53:19–38.

Blumberg, G. G. 1981. "Cohabitation without Marriage: A Different Perspective." *UCLA Law Review* 28:1125–80.

———. 1985. "New Models of Marriage and Divorce: Significant Legal Developments in the Last Decade." In *Contemporary Marriage: Comparative Perspectives on a Changing Institution*, edited by K. Davis with A. Grossbard-Shechtman. New York: Russell Sage.

Blumstein, R. and R. Schwartz. 1983. *American Couples: Money, Work and Sex.* New York: William Morrow.

Bracher, M. and G. Santow. 1998. "Economic Independence and Union Formation in Sweden." *Population Studies* 52:275–94.

Brines, J. and K. Joyner. 1999. "The Ties That Bind: Principles of Cohesion in Cohabitation and Marriage." *American Sociological Review* 64:333–55.

Brown, S. S. 2000. "Fertility Following Marital Dissolution: The Role of Cohabitation." *Journal of Family Issues* 21:501–24.

Brüderl, J., A. Diekmann, and H. Engelhardt. 1997, August. "Premarital Cohabitation and Marital Stability in West Germany." Paper presented at the annual meeting of the American Sociological Association, Toronto.

Bumpass, L. L. and H. H. Lu. 2000. "Trends in Cohabitation and Implications for Children's Family Contexts in the United States." *Population Studies* 54:29–41.

Bumpass, L. L. and R. K. Raley. 1995. "Redefining Single-Parent Families: Cohabitation and Changing Family Reality." *Demography* 32:97–109.

Bumpass, L. L., R. K. Raley, and J. A. Sweet. 1995. "The Changing Character of Stepfamilies: Implications of Cohabitation and Nonmarital Childbearing." *Demography* 32:425–36.

Bumpass, L. L. and J. A. Sweet. 1989. "National Estimates of Cohabitation." *Demography* 26:615–25.

———. 1995. "Cohabitation, Marriage, and Nonmarital Childbearing and Union Stability: Preliminary Findings from NSFH2." National Survey of Families and Households Working Paper No. 65. Center for Demography and Ecology, University of Wisconsin, Madison.

———. 2001. "Marriage, Divorce, and Intergenerational Relationships." In *The Well-Being of Children and Families*, edited by A. Thornton. Ann Arbor: University of Michigan Press.

Bumpass, L. L., J. A. Sweet, and A. J. Cherlin. 1991. "The Role of Cohabitation in Declining Rates of Marriage." *Journal of Marriage and the Family* 53:913–27.

Carlson, M. and S. Danziger. 1999. "Cohabitation and the Measurement of Child Poverty." *Review of Income and Wealth* 2:179–91.

Casper, L. M. and P. N. Cohen. 2000. "How Does POSSLQ Measure Up? Historical Estimates of Cohabitation." *Demography* 37:237–45.

Cherlin, A. J. 1978. "Remarriage as an Incomplete Institution." *American Journal of Sociology* 84:634–50.

———. 1992. *Marriage, Divorce, Remarriage.* Cambridge, MA: Harvard University Press.

———. 2000. "Toward a New Home Socioeconomics of Union Formation." Pp. 126–44 in *Ties That Bind: Perspectives on Marriage and Cohabitation*, edited by L. J. Waite, C. Bachrach, M. Hindin, E. Thomson, and A. Thornton. Hawthorne, NY: Aldine de Gruyter.

Chevan, A. 1996. "As Cheaply as One: Cohabitation in the Older Population." *Journal of Marriage and the Family* 58:656–67.

Citro, C. F. and R. T. Michael, eds. 1995. *Measuring Poverty: A New Approach.* Washington, DC: National Academy Press.

Clarkberg, J. 1999. "The Price of Partnering: The Role of Economic Well-Being in Young Adults' First Union Experiences." *Social Forces* 77:945–68.

Clarkberg, M., R. M. Stolzenberg, and L. J. Waite. 1995. "Attitudes, Values, and Entrance into Cohabitational versus Marital Unions." *Social Forces* 74:609–34.

De Vos, S. 1999. "Comment of Coding Marital Status in Latin America." *Journal of Comparative Family Studies* 30:79–93.

Garasky, S. and D. R. Meyer. 1996. "Reconsidering the Increase in Father-Only Families." *Demography* 33:385–93.

Goldstein, J. R. 1999. "The Leveling of Divorce in the United States." *Demography* 36:409–14.

Gordon, K. C. 1998/1999. "The Necessity and Enforcement of Cohabitation Agreements: When Strings Will Attach and How to Prevent Them. A State Survey." *University of Louisville Brandeis Law* 37:245–57.

Hoem, B. 1995. "Sweden." Pp. 35–55 in *The New Role of Women: Family Formation in Modern Societies*, edited by H. P. Blossfeld. Boulder, CO: Westview Press.

Kiernan, K. E. and V. Estaugh. 1993. "Cohabitation: Extra-marital Childbearing and Social Policy." Occasional Paper No. 17. London: Family Policy Studies Centre.

Kravdal, O. 1999. "Does Marriage Require a Stronger Economic Underpinning than Informal Cohabitation?" *Population Studies* 53:63–80.

Landale, N. S. and K. Fennelly. 1992. "Informal Unions among Mainland Puerto Ricans: Cohabitation or an Alternative to Legal Marriage?" *Journal of Marriage and the Family* 54:269–80.

Landale, N. S. and R. Forste. 1991. "Patterns of Entry into Cohabitation and Marriage among Mainland Puerto Rican Women." *Demography* 28:587–607.

Laumann, E. O., J. H. Gagnon, R. T. Michael, and S. Michaels. 1994. *The Social Organization of Sexuality: Sexual Practices in the United States.* Chicago: University of Chicago Press.

Leridon, H. 1990. "Cohabitation, Marriage, Separation: An Analysis of Life Histories of French Cohorts from 1968 to 1985." *Population Studies* 44:127–44.

Lesthaeghe, R. 1995. "The Second Demographic Transition in Western Countries: An Interpretation." Pp. 17–82 in *Gender and Family Change in Industrialized Countries,* edited by K. O. Mason and A. M. Jensen. Oxford, UK: Clarendon Press.

Liefbroer, A. C. and J. D. J. Gierveld. 1993. "The Impact of Rational Considerations and Perceived Opinions on Young Adults' Union Formation Intentions." *Journal of Family Issues* 14:213–35.

Lillard, L. A., M. J. Brien, and L. J. Waite. 1995. "Premarital Cohabitation and Subsequent Marital Dissolution: A Matter of Self-Selection." *Demography* 32:437–57.

Loomis, L. S. and N. S. Landale. 1994. "Nonmarital Cohabitation and Childbearing among Black and White American Women." *Journal of Marriage and the Family* 56:949–62.

Manning, W. D. 1995. "Cohabitation, Marriage, and Entry into Motherhood." *Journal of Marriage and the Family* 57:191–200.

Manning, W. D. and N. S. Landale. 1996. "Racial and Ethnic Differences in the Role of Cohabitation in Premarital Childbearing." *Journal of Marriage and the Family* 58:63–77.

Manning, W. D. and D. T. Lichter. 1996. "Parental Cohabitation and Children's Economic Well-Being." *Journal of Marriage and the Family* 58:998–1010.

Manning, W. D. and R. J. Smock. 1995. "Why Marry? Race and the Transition to Marriage among Cohabitors." *Demography* 32:509–20.

Mare, R. D. and C. Winship. 1991. "Socioeconomic Change and the Decline of Marriage for Blacks and Whites." Pp. 175–202 in *The Urban Underclass,* edited by C. Jencks and P. E. Peterson. Washington, DC: Brookings Institute.

McLanahan, S., I. Garfinkel, and Y. Padilla. 1999a. "The Fragile Families and Child Wellbeing Study: Austin, Texas." Baseline report. Center for Research on Child Wellbeing, Princeton University, Princeton, NJ.

McLanahan, S., I. Garfinkel, and M. Waller. 1999b. "The Fragile Families and Child Wellbeing Study: Oakland, California." Baseline report. Center for Research on Child Wellbeing, Princeton University, Princeton, NJ.

Nock, S. L. 1995. "A Comparison of Marriages and Cohabiting Relationships." *Journal of Family Issues* 16:53–76.

Oppenheimer, V. K. 1988. "A Theory of Marriage Timing." *American Journal of Sociology* 94:563–91.

Oppenheimer, V. K., M. Kalmijn, and N. Lim. 1997. "Men's Career Development and Marriage Timing during a Period of Rising Inequality." *Demography* 34:311–30.

Oropesa, R. S. 1996. "Normative Beliefs about Marriage and Cohabitation: A Comparison of Non-Latino Whites, Mexican Americans, and Puerto Ricans." *Journal of Marriage and the Family* 58:49–62.

Parnell, A. M., G. Swicegood, and G. Stevens. 1994. "Nonmarital Pregnancies and Marriage in the United States." *Social Forces* 73:263–87.

Parrado, E. A. and M. Tienda. 1997. "Women's Roles and Family Formation in Venezuela: New Forms of Consensual Unions?" *Social Biology* 44:1–24.

Raley, R. K. 1996. "A Shortage of Marriageable Men? A Note on the Role of Cohabitation in Black–White Differences in Marriage Rates." *American Sociological Review* 61:973–83.

———. 2001. "Increasing Fertility in Cohabiting Unions: Evidence for the Second Demographic Transition in the United States?" *Demography* 38 (1): 59–66.

Schoen, R. 1992. "First Unions and the Stability of First Marriages." *Journal of Marriage and the Family* 54:281–84.

Seltzer, J. A. 1991. "Relationships between Fathers and Children Who Live Apart." *Journal of Marriage and the Family* 53:79–101.

———. 1994. "Consequences of Marital Dissolution for Children." *Annual Review of Sociology* 20:235–66.

Shelton, B. A. and D. John. 1993. "Does Marital Status Make a Difference?" *Journal of Family Issues* 14:401–20.

Smith, H. L., S. P. Morgan, and T. Koropeckyj-Cox. 1996. "A Decomposition of Trends in the Nonmarital Fertility Ratios of Blacks and Whites in the United States, 1960–1992." *Demography* 33:141–51.

Smock, P. J. and W. D. Manning. 1997. "Cohabiting Partners' Economic Circumstances and Marriage." *Demography* 34:331–41.

South, S. J. and G. Spitze. 1994. "Housework in Marital and Nonmarital Households." *Sociological Review* 59:327–47.

Sweet, J. A. and L. L. Bumpass. 1992. "Disruption of Marital and Cohabitation Relationships: A Social Demographic Perspective." Pp. 67–89 in *Close Relationship Loss: Theoretical Approaches,* edited by T. L. Orbuch. New York: Springer-Verlag.

———. 1996. "The National Survey of Families and Households—Waves 1 and 2: Data Description and Documentation." Center for Demography and Ecology, University of Wisconsin, Madison. Retrieved from the World Wide Web (http://www.ssc.wisc.edu/nsfh).

Thornton, A. 1989. "Changing Atitudes toward Family Issues." *Journal of Marriage and the Family* 51:873–93.

———. 1991. "Influence of the Marital History of Parents on the Marital and Cohabitational Experiences of Children." *American Journal of Sociology* 96:868–94.

——— 1995. "Attitudes, Values and Norms Related to Nonmarital Fertility." Pp. 201–15 in *Report to Congress on Out-of-Wedlock Childbearing*. U.S. Department of Health and Human Services (DHHS Pub. No. [PHS] 95-1257). Hyattsville, MD: U.S. Government Printing Office.

Thornton, A., W. C. Axinn, and J. D. Teachman. 1995. "The Influence of School Enrollment and Accumulation on Cohabitation and Marriage in Early Adulthood." *American Sociological Review* 60:762–74.

Treas, J. and D. Giesen. 2000. "Sexual Infidelity among Married and Cohabiting Americans." *Journal of Marriage and the Family* 62:48–60.

Ventura, S. J., J. A. Martin, S. C. Curtin, and T. J. Mathews. 1999. "Births: Final Data for 1997." *National Vital Statistics Reports* 47(18). Hyattsville, MD: National Center for Health Statistics.

Waite, L. J. 1995. "Does Marriage Matter?" *Demography* 32:483–507.

Willis, R. J. and R. T. Michael. 1994. "Innovation in Family Formation: Evidence on Cohabitation in the United States." Pp. 9–45 in *The Family, the Market and the State in Ageing Societies,* edited by J. Ermisch and N. Ogawa. Oxford, UK: Clarendon Press.

Winkler, A. E. 1997. "Economic Decision-Making by Cohabitors: Findings Regarding Income Pooling." *Applied Economics* 29:1079–90.

Wu, L. L., L. L. Bumpass, and K. Musick. 1999, July. "Historical and Life Course Trajectories of Nonmarital Childbearing." Revised version of paper presented at the Conference on Nonmarital Fertility, Institute for Research on Poverty, University of Wisconsin, Madison.

Wu, Z. and T. R. Balakrishnan. 1995. "Dissolution of Premarital Cohabitation in Canada." *Demography* 32:521–32.

19

LIVING APART TOGETHER
A New Family Form

IRENE LEVIN

Susan and Simon are a couple, and have been so for more than 10 years. The difference between Susan and Simon and many other couples is that they do not share their everyday lives together. They have both been married before and have children from these previous relationships.

Susan lives with her children in a neighboring town and meets Simon every weekend and during holidays. Simon lives alone in the same town as his children, who live with their mother. Simon wants to be close to his children so that he can meet them as often as possible. By living in this current arrangement, Simon can have *both* a couple relationship with Susan *and* a parenting relationship with his children. Susan also likes the current situation because she does not have to choose *between* a partner and her children or make her children move away from their friends in order for her to keep her relationship with Simon.

Susan and Simon are living in a living apart together or LAT relationship—a historically new family form. LAT relationships are a result of changes in our living arrangements. These changes have occurred, little by little, during the past 30 years as a result of changing norms. Previously, it was expected that one would be married in order to live together. Only in marriage was a couple considered to be a "real" couple. Now, however, one can choose to live with one's partner without being married—what we call cohabitation (Heimdal and Houseknecht 2003; Kamp Dush, Cohan, and Amato 2003; Trost 1979). Today the ritual of marriage is less important and feelings are what matters. Married and cohabiting couples have, however, a lot in common. They live in the same household and in everyday life there is not a lot of difference in their routines. They share "bed and table." The difference is the marriage ritual—cohabiting couples do not have the status of being married. In many aspects of everyday life this does not matter. Their children may not concern themselves about whether or not their parents are married and their routines are often the same in either case. There may be a difference between married and cohabiting couples with regard to differing consequences of relationship breakdown. Generally speaking, economic consequences differ when one of the couple dies, or when the married couple divorces (Hopper 2001) or the cohabiting couple separates. The exception may be when the cohabiting couple has entered into a special contract.

The question to be considered here is whether two people may be considered to be a couple *without* having a common home. In recent times the answer has become "yes" and a new family form has appeared. To be a couple is no longer dependent upon sharing a common household. It is no longer important for one to be married or to be living in the same household—one can still be a couple, and it is that to which the new term, LAT relationship, refers. Can a LAT relationship be interpreted as a family form? As Levin and Trost (1992) show, family can be defined in a range of different terms. . . . It is argued here that the occurrence of LAT relationships is closely connected to the occurrence of cohabitation and the changes in norms.

Changing Norms

In the 20th century two major changes occurred in the western world that have affected family situations. One was the emergence of cohabitation (Trost 1979) and the other was increase in divorce rates. . . .

At the end of the 1960s and the beginning of the 1970s, marriage rates, in most of the western world, started to decrease. In some countries the changes occurred very rapidly, as in Sweden and Denmark, followed by Norway and Finland. In England, this development was somewhat slower than in the Nordic countries, but not as slow as in, for example, Belgium (Trost 1995). At the same time, the practice of cohabitation began to increase. In the traditional marital system before 1970, four elements were closely connected in time. The prevailing sequence was the marriage ceremony, moving in together, having sexual intercourse together, having the first child about a year later (Levin and Trost 2003; Trost 1993, 1998). The traditional marital system normatively prescribed these four elements, in the given sequence, as the sanctioned practice. With some exceptions, the marriage ceremony and moving in together occurred at the same time, meaning the same day. This seems to have been true for all western societies. . . .

These four elements have lost their normative power and today they are no longer connected to one other. This development is related to the great increase in the rates of cohabitation. It can be argued that cohabitation has become a social institution (Trost 1979). When cohabitation becomes a social institution of the sort we find in, for example, the Scandinavian countries, there is no normative or expected connection between the four elements that traditionally constituted the marital system. In Sweden, more than half of all children, and about two-thirds of all first-born children, have unwed mothers. In Norway, the numbers are slightly fewer, but the changes in norms are more or less the same. . . .

Without a general acceptance of cohabitation and its institutionalization which puts it on an equal footing with marriage, LAT relationships would have remained hidden or "invisible" (Levin and Trost 1999) and they would be much less common than they now are. . . .

Defining LAT Relationships

The definition of a LAT relationship used here is a couple that does not share a home. Each of the two partners lives in his or her own home in which other people might also live. They define themselves as a couple and they perceive that their close surrounding personal network does so as well. The definition requires three conditions: the couple has to agree that they are a couple; others have to see them as such; and they must live in separate homes. This term refers to homosexual as well as heterosexual couples. . . .

The term "LAT" was first used in the Netherlands, where a Dutch journalist, Michel Berkiel, wrote an article in the *Haagse Post,* in 1978, about a phenomenon he had observed, and in which he lived himself with the person he loved. During one of the morning meetings of the newspaper, while he was writing the article, he asked his colleagues to help him choose a title. Someone suggested that he name the article after a recent movie shown in the Netherlands at that time, titled *Eva and Frank: Living Apart Together.* "Living apart together" seemed too long to him and so he chose to use the

acronym LAT or *lat*. Already a word in the Dutch language meaning "stick," this also made its usage easier to accept. The Netherlands is the only country, as far as I know, where the term LAT or *lat* is integrated in everyday speech. In the Scandinavian countries the term *særbo*, in Norwegian, and *särbo*, in Swedish, have now become relatively well-known terms; however, this is more true in Sweden than in Norway.

In France, a different term has been used in a study by Caradec (1996), who uses *cohabitation intermittente* and *cohabitation alternée*. The first term refers to the same phenomenon that is referred to by the phrase LAT relationship—a couple living in separate homes, and looked upon as a couple, by others, and by themselves. The latter term, *cohabitation alternée*, refers to cohabitation where the couple alternates between their two dwellings. Caradec's study claims that nearly 6 percent of the adult population in Paris were living in LAT relationships.

In Germany, Schneider (1996) refers to "partners with different households," or *Partnerschaften mit getrennten Haushalten* in German. Included in his study are only those LAT relationships that have lasted for at least one year. The study is rather special as it contains a majority of "young adults who are in education mainly studying, or who are in their early period of gainful employment" (Schneider 1996:96; my translation). In this study more than 10,000 people, aged 18–61, were interviewed in 1994. He found that 9 percent of the respondents were living in LAT relationships. In the USA, the discussion about LAT relationships is just beginning. There, but also in other places the term "commuting marriage/cohabitation" is used interchangeably with "dual-households" or "dual-residence living" (see Winfield 1985). What marks the distinction between commuting marriage/cohabitation and LAT relationships is closely connected to the issue of one's home or domicile. If the two live in *one home* and one (or both of them) has a second apartment where he or she stays when *away from home*, due to their work or studies, these relationships are defined as commuting marital/cohabitational relationships. In order to be a LAT relationship, each partner must have his or her own home, which means that the partners live apart in *two separate residences*.

Quantitative Study

This research on LAT relationships draws upon data collected by both quantitative and qualitative methods. Most of the quantitative data come from Sweden, where we collected data on three different occasions. . . .

The 1993 Swedish opinion research survey found that 6 percent of those respondents who were neither married nor cohabiting affirmed that they were living in a LAT relationship. The survey suggests that Sweden had about 60,000 couples, or 120,000 persons, living in LAT relationships. The data collected in 1998 found that the relative number of persons living in LAT relationships had increased to 12 percent of those respondents who were neither married nor cohabiting. This suggests that at least 130,000 couples, or

260,000 people, were living in LAT relationships at that time. Some of these couples are same-sex couples but the majority are heterosexual couples.

In the year 2001, a third data collection was undertaken which showed a slight increase in LAT relationships from the survey results in 1998. Fourteen percent of the respondents that were neither married nor cohabiting said that they were living in a LAT relationship in 2001. This suggests that the numbers had risen to about 300,000 people or about 150,000 couples.[1]

At that time we knew very little about how many LAT relationships there were in Norway. However, in 2002, the Norwegian Bureau of Statistics collected data in order to find out how many LAT relationships there were in Norway. Approximately 1000 people, aged 18–74, were interviewed. Eight percent of those who said that they were neither married nor cohabiting saw themselves as living in LAT relationships. The interview study suggests that about 60,000–70,000 people or 30,000–35,000 couples were living in a LAT relationship in Norway, in 2002.

Qualitative Study

In our research we have also interviewed 100 people living in LAT relationships. The interviews were in-depth and structured, but not standardized. The interviews were between one and three hours in length. In order to visualize interviewees' conception of family, a three-step method was used (Levin 1993). First they were asked: "Who is in your family—could you make a list?" Second, "Could you place your family on this sheet of paper according to closeness and distance to you?" Third, they were interviewed about their relationships to their family members and especially their living arrangements.

In some cases we were able to identify people in a LAT relationship but were unable to interview these couples. These people were given a short semi-standardized questionnaire which they answered and sent back to us.

The sample is a convenience sample, and we found our informants in a variety of ways. Sometimes at lectures or presentations, when we had mentioned LAT relationships, people in the audience approached us. We were interviewed in Norwegian and Swedish magazines and newspapers articles in which we solicited people living in LAT relationships to take part in the research. When people asked us about our research and we mentioned the LAT study, some volunteered to be interviewed and others told us about parents, children or friends in LAT relationships. The age range of our informants in the qualitative study is from 20 to 80 years.

The interviewees may be divided into two subgroups:

1. Those who would like to live together but for one reason or another have decided not to do so.
2. Those who would not live together even if they could, and who want to remain a couple *living apart together.*

I start by describing some patterns we found in the first subgroup.

We Would Have Lived Together if It Were Not for One or More Reasons. . .

Responsibility and Care

One reason why some people choose to live in LAT relationships has to do with their feelings of responsibility for other people. This feeling of responsibility is so strong that they do not want a new relationship to another person to impinge upon their deeply felt duties. In particular, it is the responsibility and care for children still living at home and for older parents that are given as reasons for *not living together* with new partners. If another person moves into his or her apartment or if he or she moves away to another apartment, major changes will occur. When it comes to relationships with older parents, people often did not want to leave them alone as this can be a way of forcing them to move into a home for the aged. These are people who do not believe that their children or their parents have appropriated their own decision-making. Rather, they understand their relationship to the new partner as unrelated to the relationship and responsibility they have for their children or for their parents. Here LAT relationships imply that one simply does not have to move *everyone* into the same living arrangement.

People in this situation look upon the new couple relationship as an *addition to* the relationships they already have and not as being *instead of* those other relationships. The new couple relationship is not allowed to threaten or replace already existing relationships. It is simply easier to give each relationship "its due" by not creating a stepfamily household. By keeping the home as it is, it is easier to keep relationships, with children or aged parents, as they are. Even for a parent who is not the custodian of his or her children, to move to another home can be seen as *cheating* one's own children, to leave the child's parental home for the sake of another adult. The following example illustrates such a situation.

Fred and Freda were first an unmarried LAT and they later got married but kept their LAT relationship until all of the children had moved out of their homes. Fred was 56 years old and Freda was 51 at the time of the interview. They met 10 years before when Fred's three children were living at home with him in his custody. At that time, his children were 14, 16, and 20 years old. Freda had two children. They were 10 and 14 years old, and in her custody. Her ex-husband took care of their children every second weekend and during some holidays. Fred and Freda were decided that they would not move in together until their own children had grown up and left home. Both lived in the same city, 15 minutes apart by public transportation. They met and fell in love and felt that they were a couple very quickly, but it took about a year until they were in a LAT relationship, according to their view at the time of the interview. At the beginning of the relationship, they stayed overnight at each other's home during weekends. They did not tell their children about their true relationship at first, but introduced each other to their children as old and good friends. Neither of them wanted to push the other or to be pushed into relationships with one another's children.

After some time, the children on both sides accepted their parent's new relationship.

Two years before the interview took place, Freda and Fred were married. They continued to live in a LAT relationship at the time of the interview. We later learned that they now do live together, after having spent 10 years of their lives in a LAT relationship, both as unmarried and married LATs.

When it comes to caring for elderly parents, LAT relationships can be a solution for those who want to continue to care for their elderly parents and still keep a relationship with a new partner. Often, people in this situation have lived in close contact and proximity to their parents for many years. They might have liked or disliked this arrangement, but they accepted it as a particular feature of their own lives. When the elderly mother or father dies, or becomes severely ill, there are no choices for these people. They dutifully accept the long-term care of their aged or disabled parent.

Taking care of elderly or disabled parents is a strongly felt duty, and a very high priority in the value system and self-understanding of many of those we interviewed that were in this particular situation. If they fail to provide a high level of personal care, they know that they themselves will suffer severely, with feelings of guilt, for not behaving in accordance with their own standards of responsibility and morality. For others in this situation, it is a way of "repaying" the older generation for what it has done for the child in earlier stages of life. Perhaps some respondents had received important help and support with their own children from their parents. All in all, it seems to be preferable for them to remain in their existing surroundings and to continue to care for the elderly parent. It may seem easier, all things considered, to have a LAT relationship, with their partner living in another home. In this way, one can avoid choosing between the aged (and sometimes disabled) parent and the new partner. They can have both.

A strong feeling of responsibility and the duty to care for children and aged parents existed in these people long before they met their new partners. In these examples, the respondents perceive that they are *significant others* for their children and for their parents. If they do not act in accordance with their feelings of responsibility, they know that feelings of guilt will result. The LAT relationship allows them to care for children or aged parents *and* maintain a relationship with a new partner. For these people, the situation is not "either/or" but "both/and." By caring for those others who are so closely related to them they are caring for themselves, too.

They Work or Study in Different Places

In many ways, reconciling the demands created by work or study with a relationship with someone in a different geographic location is tackled by relying upon a similar way of thinking. People in this situation do not want to choose *either* their partner *or* their job. They want both and they decide to keep both. A consequence of this decision requires them to live in separate homes. This might be looked upon as a more temporary condition, in light of their own perceptions, because one's job, at some future date,

may be changed. Their couple relationship and their jobs are important to them and they want to maintain both. If either moved to their partner's domicile, career opportunities would diminish. This might not be solely a question of money. Even if the other person could support him or her, the arrangement would not be acceptable. Being economically independent is a value of high importance for these people. This characteristic is sometimes referred to as the tendency towards individualization. A century ago, and even half a century ago, people were seldom able to think in the same terms as these people now do. Individualization is more pronounced today. There is more acceptance for the idea that couples need to find ways to better accommodate one another's needs for self-realization. Formerly, the matter was framed as a way of showing one's love: "If you love me enough, you will relocate." The job and the partner are seen as being in competition, and one has to choose between them. In particular there would have been social expectations pressuring the woman to relocate. Ordinarily, she was the one who was expected to give up her job and her friends. Today, there is acceptance of the idea that she can keep her job and her friends, as well as her relationship with children, parents and other relatives, and at the same time have a relationship with a man and maintain separate dwellings.

This situation also includes students who study in different places. We were somewhat surprised when we received answers from students defining themselves as LAT partners. We, in our old-fashioned way, saw them more as "going steady." This is a way of seeing their relationship as less serious and uses the traditional marital system as the guiding model (Trost 1979). However, these students told us that if it were not for their studies, they would have been living together as a cohabiting couple. Since their studies are preventing them, they define themselves as LAT partners. . . . For students, the LAT relationship is a temporary one. They expect to live together after graduation and find jobs near their common home.

Given the technological realities of our contemporary lives, the world seems to be getting smaller and smaller. Telephones, faxes, emails, airplanes, all function to make it easier and easier to keep in contact with people living far away. Some of our informants report that they live on different continents. One of the respondents in our study told us that she lives in Norway and he in Malaysia. For some periods in their relationship, she has lived with him in Malaysia, and he with her in Oslo. They define their two homes as theirs in common, but pay the expenses for them separately.

These couples look upon their lives as a process that changes all the time. Their decisions are only made *for the time being*. When their working situation changes, they may also change their living arrangements. At the same time, they are aware that moving to their partner's home might very well mean losing a lot of the friendships and the close quality of their own social network. Moving away will probably lessen one's contacts with children and grandchildren.

The next subgroup we consider is very different from the first one. Whereas people in the first subgroup do not really want to be in a LAT

relationship, for the people in this subgroup the LAT relationship is the *preferred* living arrangement.

Those Who Would Not Wish to Live Together Even if They Could Do So, and Still Want to Remain as a Couple

They Don't Want to Repeat the Same Mistake Twice

People in this situation often choose this way of living in order to avoid creating the same conditions that led to the break-up of a former marriage or cohabitation. For many years, they had all experienced living together with another person in a couple relationship—a living situation that ended in divorce or separation. In order to try being in a new couple relationship, they feel it is important for them to structure the situation so that another break-up will not occur. They believe that living together, in itself, will change the way each of them relates to the other and that those changes could threaten the relationship's survival. Choosing to live apart is a strategy used in order to avoid another painful separation.

The following example illustrates this approach. A woman had been married for 23 years and had three children from that marriage. When her husband asked her for a divorce, because he had started a relationship with his secretary, her whole world fell apart. But somehow, she managed to pull herself together. She bought an apartment and found meaning in her life as a mother, as a grandmother and as a professional woman. Time passed, and she began to like her new situation. She enjoyed the freedom of only being responsible for herself, but did not use this freedom to meet new men. She simply did what she wanted to do whenever she wanted to do so, and she enjoyed the realization that no one expected her to "boil the potatoes" each and every day. She liked being able to join her colleagues for a glass of beer, after work, without inconveniencing anybody else. Eventually, she met a man with whom she fell in love. He was living half an hour's car drive away, and he wanted them to live together like ordinary couples do, in the same home. However, she was worried about making the same mistake twice. Her divorce had been too much of a shock for her, and she would do anything to avoid repeating that experience. She refused his offer to live together, but her refusal was not a sign of her lack of affection and love. On the contrary, she says that she loves him very much, but she does not want to tell him *just how much* she loves him. She says that she would rather live alone during the week and meet him on weekends and spend holidays together. She does not dare to live with him "full-time." The risk is connected to her understanding of her marriage and of its break-up and divorce.

She believes that the break-up of her marriage resulted from the fact that she became less interesting as a woman. She is afraid that she will do the same things that eventually made her boring to her husband. She believes that she knows herself very well, and she is certain that she would begin to perform all the traditional housewife activities. She would prepare food

for him when he came home from work, and she would become the person responsible for all their home comforts. This is the behaviour she would expect from herself and they are related to her own self-esteem and to her identity as a woman. Since she loves him very much, she does not want to risk the good relationship they share, just to live under the same roof, with all of the everyday duties which he (or she) might define as humdrum and boring. She simply does not want to experience another break-up. She has decided to live in a LAT relationship in order to maintain a good couple relationship and to learn the lesson of her past experiences. Her answer to the question "Do you think that you might move in together one day?" is that they probably will do so when she retires, "if he still wants me."

Retired Couples

For retired people, the situation is somewhat different even though the result is the same. These people too do not want to live together even though they are a couple and love one another. Since one or both are not working any more, there is the possibility of moving in together; but deciding to move in together would create difficult practical decisions and necessitate some sacrifices. For instance, who would make the move? Whose furniture would be redundant? Since both might have lived in a one-person home for many years, a lot of the *things* they own are connected to memories of important happenings from their previous lives. The things are *cherished* as symbols of shared experiences. They are reminders of people, and are not just *dead things* as some people may seem to believe—and as such, they are important to them for their own well-being.

Another reason for not wanting to trade two homes for one is their relationship to children and grandchildren. It may be easier to maintain those relationships if they keep their own homes, rather than living together with a partner in one home. One woman told us that she lives 30 km away from her partner and that she sees him every weekend and every Wednesday, and that they go on holiday together. Moving in together is not discussed as a serious possibility because she gets what she wants from their relationship *as it is.* Why would (or should) she change it? When he is ill, she goes over to his home in order to help him. However, he does not do the same when she is ill. When that happens, she gets help from neighbors and from her daughter-in-law. She likes the situation as it is and it has suited her for 18 years. Early on in their relationship they talked of moving in together, but it is not a question they discuss any more. They are quite satisfied with their relationship.

She has been hurt by her partner's criticism of her relationship with her disabled son who lives away. When he comes home her partner feels that she favors him. This criticism was unacceptable for the woman and she gave her partner an ultimatum. Now things have cooled down again and the relationship is back to normal. She is very happy with matters as they stand. One of the things that she most enjoys are their Sunday dinners. She drives them to a neighboring town and he pays for their meal in a nice restaurant.

He is also very generous when it comes to giving her gifts and that is something she greatly appreciates.

From Marriage or Cohabitation to a LAT Relationship

Most of the LAT relationship patterns we found consist of people who begin their LAT relationship without first deciding whether or not their relationship was headed for cohabitation or marriage. For some of our respondents the situation has been the other way around. They started as a married or cohabiting couple and the LAT relationship was a solution to difficulties they experienced in those relationships. They lived together for several years but found that they got on each other's nerves in the course of everyday life together. At the same time, they love each other and feel bound to one another. For that reason, they do not want a divorce or a final end to their relationship. It is not what they want, nor is it what their children want. As a solution, one of the partners moves to a nearby apartment and in so doing an alternative way of living, an arrangement that might better fit their lifestyles, for the time being, is undertaken.

An example of this situation is Paul and Paula, who met about 20 years ago. They soon became a couple and moved in together. A few years later, they had their first child, and a few years after that their second one. For several years their relationship had been deteriorating and it had become boring. They were finding one another irritating. They still loved one another, but a year before our interview, they decided to separate. They sold their house and bought two apartments just a few minutes walk from one another. Their children stay with their mother, but they both spend a lot of time with their father, who also spends a lot of time in his ex-cohabitant's apartment, which is larger than his own. This is their way of saving their couple relationship, which in both their opinions would have ended in a break-up without the LAT relationship.

They are clearly still *significant others* to one another and they both want to maintain their relationship but everyday life together simply became too trying. By having two separate homes they hope to be able to maintain the emotions necessary for them to be a loving couple, for each other, and to be good parents to their children. Here the LAT relationship is an alternative to ending their couple relationship. For some people, this alternative might be a peaceful way to a slow divorce without any abrupt changes for themselves or their children.

Explaining LATs

This [reading] has presented a range of situations where the LAT relationship has been established by couples in ways which differ from marriage or cohabitation. Couples often choose a LAT relationship as their living arrangement in order to avoid choosing between (the felt responsibility to care for) an elderly parent, or their own children, and the new partner, which sharing

a home would present. An alternative arrangement is partly made possible by LAT relationships because the pressure upon couples "to settle down together" in a common dwelling has decreased. More and more people are accepting the "both/and" solution that LAT relationships provide. As Lewis and Meredith (1989) remark, some adult children live together with a parent, not only because of their sense of duty to care for the parent, but also because they enjoy spending time together with the parent.

A question frequently asked is whether or not LAT relationships occur in all classes within society. Is it a decision that only the financially well-off can make? Our findings show that one can find LAT relationships among all sorts of people. This does not imply that being financially well-off does not make the living arrangements easier to manage. Certainly long-distance LAT relationships require the couple to spend more money on telephone calls and travel, and one home is cheaper to maintain than two. There is no argument with these matters of fact. In most cases, however, in our research, where LAT relationships are found to exist, the couple already each have their own home and are used to paying for their own home expenses.

Why is it that the number of LAT relationships has been increasing? Why have we not noticed or registered LAT relationships before? There may be more than one answer to these questions. One factor is the mortality rate. The lower the mortality rate, the greater the likelihood for a person not only to live longer, but also to experience divorce, the death of a spouse, and separation from a non-marital cohabitant, and thus, the greater the likelihood, *ceteris paribus*, for the person to enter into a LAT relationship, or some other new relationship, for that matter. When mortality rates were higher, a greater number of marriages were dissolved by the death of one of the spouses. The need for divorce lessens, therefore, when mortality rates are high. . . .

A second factor that has contributed to the increase in LAT relationships has to do with changes in the labor market. A higher degree of specialization is required, these days, and that means a demand for higher levels of education for most job applicants. Fewer people can simply decide to relocate and assume that they will be able to find a good job. This is true for both men and women. Working women are less able to follow their husbands and find a job when they relocate. The relatively short history of the full-time housewife is almost over, in many countries, and in some others, this role has already become a thing of the past. In order to really understand the new structure of relationships between women and men, including LAT relationships, one has to look into the many processes promoting gender equality and equity in contemporary society.

A third factor has to do with the frequency of travel and with the availability and use of IT communication. People on holiday, or traveling because of their job, meet people living in other places. Some of these meetings result in couples falling in love. Many of these relationships will last, and if one or both cannot or does not want to relocate, they might form a long-distance LAT relationship. Travel for leisure or for work will probably increase, even though advances in IT communication continue apace. Couples are being generated on the Internet. Some of those *virtual* relationships may develop

into long-distance LAT relationships. We will probably see an important increase in LAT relationships in the near future, and the growth will include married and unmarried couples choosing to live in a LAT relationship.

Traditionally, informal social norms prescribed that a couple should live in the same home. Sharing a domicile was the taken-for-granted pattern for couples. In cases where the two could not live together, living arrangements were considered to be merely temporary. With the high divorce rate, the increasing numbers of women who are gainfully employed, and the considerable victories that have been won, by women, in the battle for equity, society and its norms have changed. The move towards greater gender equality and equity has had consequences for intimacy and for couple relationships (see Giddens 1994). Few men, but many women, see advantages in LAT relationships. Therefore the woman is usually the active one in suggesting to move apart.

To summarize, only a few decades ago, marriage was the sole socially approved institution for couples planning to live together. Cohabitation was frowned upon and seen as a deviant phenomenon. There has been a remarkable change in the acceptance of cohabitation. These days, it is more often seen as being a viable option, and it has become an accepted social institution, in its own right, alongside marriage. Without this acceptance of cohabitation, LAT relationships would not have emerged. One might say that cohabitation, as a socially accepted institution, was a prerequisite for the establishment of LAT relationships. The recognition of LAT relationships as a new social phenomenon, in several western societies, and the documented rise in its frequency, as well as the general increasing awareness of the term "LAT relationship," are factors at work today that may some day establish the LAT relationship as a generally recognized and accepted social institution in many more countries. . . .

ENDNOTES

Author's Note: The research reported on in this article was carried out with Professor Jan Trost, Uppsala University, Sweden.

[1] If the percentages in England were the same as in Sweden, there would be, approximately, 750,000 couples living in LAT relationships.

REFERENCES

Caradec, V. 1996. "Les Formes de la vie conjugale des 'jeunes' couple 'âgés'." *Population* 51:897–928.

Giddens, A. 1994. *Intimitetens forandring* [Intimacy in Change]. Copenhagen: Hans Reitzels forlag.

Heimdal, K. R. and S. K. Houseknecht. 2003. "Cohabiting and Married Couples' Income Organisation: Approaches in Sweden and the United States." *Journal of Marriage and Family* 65 (3): 539–49.

Hopper, J. 2001. "The Symbolic Origins of Conflict in Divorce." *Journal of Marriage and Family* 63 (2): 446–57.

Kamp Dush, C. M., C. L. Cohan, and P. R. Amato. 2003. "The Relationship between Cohabitation and Marital Quality and Stability: Change across Cohorts?" *Journal of Marriage and Family* 65 (3): 539–49.

Levin, I. 1993. "Family as Mapped Realities." *Journal of Family Issues* special issue "Rethinking Family as a Social Form" 14 (1): 82–91.

Levin, I. and J. Trost. 1992. "Understanding the Concept of Family." *Family Relations* 41:348–51.

———. 1999. "Living Apart Together." *Community, Work and Family* 2 (3): 279–93.

———. 2003. *Særbo—ett par to hjem*. Oslo: Damm and Søn forlag.

Lewis, J. and B. Meredith. 1989. *Daughters Who Care*. London: Routledge.

Schneider, N. F. 1996. "Partnerschaften mit getrennten Haushalten in den neuen und alten Bundesländern." Pp. 88–97 in *Familie an der Schwelle zum neuen Jahrtausend*, edited by W. Bien. Opladen: Leske und Budrich.

Trost, J. 1979. *Unmarried Cohabitation*. Västerås: International Library.

———. 1993. *Familjen i Sverige* [The Family in Sweden]. Stockholm: Liber.

———. 1995. "Ehen und andere dyadische Beziehungen." Pp. 343–56 in *Familie im Brennpunkt von Wissenschaft und Forschung*, edited by B. Nauck and C. Onnen-Isemann. Berlin: Luchterhand.

Trost, J. 1998. "LAT Relationships Now and in the Future." Pp. 209–20 in *The Family: Contemporary Perspectives and Challenges; Festschrift in Honor of Wilfried Dumon*, edited by K. Matthijs. Leuven: Leuven University Press.

Winfield, F. E. 1985. *Commuter Marriage: Living Together, Apart*. New York: Columbia University Press.

20

FROM THIS DAY FORWARD
Commitment, Marriage, and Family in Lesbian and Gay Relationships

GRETCHEN A. STIERS

I think we wanted to make that level of commitment to each other and we wanted to do it in a way that included friends and family. We really wanted a ritual for ourselves that would provide a marker in terms of where we were in our relationship. We both thought there was no reason that the ritual of marriage had to be an exclusively heterosexual privilege. There was no reason why lesbians couldn't also have their own rituals and ceremonies.

—MARIA SIGGIA

I guess it's not for me. I don't think it makes your relationship more valid if you have a ceremony. It seems like jumping on the bandwagon in a way. Like I can do it too! I'm just as important or as good as you are and I can get a minister, etc. I am resistant to identifying in any way with that sort of lifestyle. I think that's why I rebel a little about joint checking accounts,

*savings, wills, and all that because it's similar to, reminds me of heterosexism
in a way. I think it's their values, what the heterosexual community has said is
important to do to make one's life valid and fulfilled.*

—RICHARD HUDSON

Historical evidence suggests that same-sex ceremonies are not a "new" phenomenon within lesbian and gay communities in the United States. In the past, many same-sex couples said vows, and even may have exchanged rings, to commemorate their unions. In most cases, these ceremonies took place in private without public witnesses or the support of biological family members.[1] Over the past twenty-five years, however, increasing numbers of lesbians and gay men have had "public" ceremonies: rituals in which families and friends are invited to witness the event. While these rituals focus on declaring a couple's love and commitment to each other, one of their central purposes is to garner support and validation for lesbian and gay relationships. Many same-sex ceremonies are rites of passage that not only "create family" but also "build community."

As the two epigraphs to this [reading] suggest, not all lesbians and gay men choose to have ceremonies. Among the ninety people interviewed, thirty-two had or were planning to have a same-sex ceremony. Of the remaining fifty-eight individuals, twenty-eight commented that they might have a ceremony sometime in the future; thirty stated that they did not want to have a ceremony either with their current partner or in a future relationship.

In order to examine motivations for having or not having a same-sex ceremony, this [reading] focuses on three questions: What reasons do lesbians and gay men state for having a commitment or union ceremony? What motivations do other lesbians and gay men have for considering having a ceremony? What reasons do some state for not wanting to have a ceremony? . . .

Same-Sex Ceremonies as Rites of Passage

According to anthropologist Terence Turner (1977), rites of passage are in essence a series of rituals that mark the transition from one social state to another. Although no one accepted definition of "ritual" exists within the anthropological literature, the term generally refers to acts that are conventional and repetitive celebrations or social demarcations of important events (Goody 1977). Therefore, rites of passage involve sequences of customary and standardized behaviors that designate life-changing events, such as birth, marriage, and death. . . .

Even though norms have changed in the United States, marriage remains a significant rite of passage for many heterosexual women and men. It continues to be an important rite of passage for them in part because it signals adulthood, the merging of two distinct kinship networks, the intention to have children, and the formation of a new family unit (Roth 1985).

Traditional marriage rites typically (although not always) take place through a series of rituals: betrothal, engagement party, wedding shower, bachelor party, rehearsal dinner, wedding ceremony, reception, and honeymoon.

For lesbians and gay men, however, no corresponding rites of passage exist to signify important changes in their adult roles or family relationships. In part, this lack of rites and rituals has stemmed from society's long-standing condemnation of homosexuality. Lesbian and gay couples do not receive the same legitimation and support as heterosexual relationships. In sharp contrast to the approval bestowed upon married couples, parents and other relatives of lesbians and gays often invalidate homosexual relationships by acting as if these relationships do not exist, which renders them invisible, or by recognizing the relationships but considering them not genuine (Roth 1985).

Many lesbians and gay men, however, are choosing to create their own rituals and ceremonies to mark their own significant life transitions. Although these ceremonies vary in their content and structure, they are rites of passage; that is, they involve rituals of separation, transition, and integration that demarcate a couple's "partnered" status. As the following section points out, however, respondents' motivations for having a ceremony are both similar to and different from the reasons heterosexuals have weddings.

Motivations for Having a Same-Sex Ceremony

As mentioned, thirty-two respondents either had a ceremony or were planning to have one within a year. Among these respondents, same-sex ceremonies fell into two distinct categories: celebrations of recent commitments and celebrations of existing commitments. Eighteen respondents had ceremonies to acknowledge "recent" commitments—relationships that had lasted less than five years. . . . Most of these respondents used either the phrase "commitment ceremony" or "holy union" to refer to their ceremonies on their invitations. All of these ceremonies took place between six months and four years after the couples had first met. Although their current ages ranged from twenty to forty-four, most respondents were in their twenties or early thirties at the time of the ceremonies.

In addition, five respondents were planning ceremonies to celebrate "recent" commitments within the next year. These respondents had been with their partners for less than two years. Four respondents stated they were planning to have a "wedding," and one woman commented she was planning a "union ceremony." All five respondents were under the age of forty and had never been married legally.

In contrast, five lesbians and two gay men had ceremonies to celebrate their established, long-term relationships. While most of the lesbians called their ceremonies "anniversary celebrations," the gay men used the phrases "holy union" and an "exchange of vows." Regardless of their names, however, all of these ceremonies took place between ten and sixteen years after the couples first met.[2] Unlike the respondents celebrating newer

commitments who were in their twenties and early thirties, these lesbians and gay men were in their thirties, forties, and fifties at the time they had their ceremonies.

Although they cannot marry legally, lesbians and gay men are aware of the purposes weddings serve in the larger community. Correspondingly, respondents who had or were planning a ceremony discussed two main reasons for their decisions: to show their commitment and love to each other and to receive public validation of their commitments from friends and family. Noticeably absent from their accounts, however, were the traditional functions of separating from their families of origin or having children.

According to Patrick Flemming, he and his partner decided to have a ceremony because "we loved each other. We felt committed to each other for our lives and we wanted to let people know that in a very ritualized, public way that they could participate in too." Kathleen O'Brien also commented on the importance of social affirmation.

> I thought that Valerie and I deserved to have some public recognition and support of our commitment. That I deserved the right to hear myself say that I believe we have what it took and that I was willing to commit to that publicly. That our relationship deserved that intangible level of support and recognition.

Similarly, Randall Harris stated, "At the time we started planning to do it we had not yet been living together quite a year but we knew we wanted to make a commitment in a public way with some friends and family there."

In particular, respondents who had "anniversary celebrations" emphasized the need for more "public" support of gay and lesbian relationships. In their accounts, they often used the term "public" to refer to support from friends and family as well as from the larger gay and lesbian community. As Beth Epstein commented, she and her partner wanted to celebrate their twelfth anniversary because

> we really were feeling the need for public support. We had moved to this area just a few years before. We were really still establishing roots here and felt like we just needed some support. We also just really wanted to be able to express publicly to each other our commitment to the relationship, which had undergone some changes once we moved.

Indeed, many respondents stated that it was important to create support since lesbians and gay men have few avenues for gaining social recognition for their relationships. As Melanie Obermeier remarked:

> I think people should have more ritual in their lives. There's not enough. Especially in gay relationships. You get a lot more support if your partner is straight even if you're not religious. You get a lot more ceremonies that give you landmarks and things to remember back to. You don't get those when you are gay. You have to make your own.

For a small minority of respondents, religious recognition and support also were important factors in why they had a ceremony. For Kathleen O'Brien and her partner, Valerie, it was extremely important to have their

"commitment ceremony" in a Unitarian church because of their religious convictions. As Kathleen explained:

> *We had been attending services at the Unitarian church for probably about six months when we realized that the Unitarian Society as a religious institution, not just as a church in Lesbianville,[3] recognized the union of gay and lesbian people as legitimate as straight people. Then we knew that is where we wanted to have our ceremony because we both had a very strong religious upbringing and the power of the symbol of the church was very important to us.*

Similarly, Celeste Davis stated that she and her partner, Grace, had their "holy union" in a Unitarian church because of their religious beliefs. According to Celeste, "We were going to the Unitarian church and were familiar with their dogma. Their perspective reflected our beliefs about religion and having a ceremony."

All five of the respondents who referred to their ceremonies as "holy unions" commented that making a public statement included making a commitment before God. Although Luke Fontaine and his partner, Ben, did not have their "holy union" ceremony in a church, they had strong religious convictions. As Luke recalled:

> *I wanted to make my commitment to Ben public and I wanted him to make his to me public. I think that making a commitment to each other before God and before witnesses is a very important step in making your relationship work. It's not so easy to walk away from something when you've made a public promise that you'll be together till death do us part.*

For these respondents, same-sex ceremonies included religious recognition and support from their religious communities.

Different Motivations from Heterosexual Weddings

Similar to heterosexual weddings, same-sex ceremonies can help lesbian and gay couples integrate into kinship and community networks. For many such couples, however, the functions a ceremony performs often diverge from the heterosexual model. While same-sex ceremonies serve many of the same purposes as traditional heterosexual weddings, they differ in five important respects.

First, lesbian and gay unions do not necessarily begin the process of separating individuals from their families of origin. Since most individuals experience some level of rejection when they come out and identify as gay, typically they already have gone through a process of separation from their families. For this same reason, many same-sex ceremonies are not organized by blood family members and take place outside the traditional context of kin relations. Indeed, . . . a primary purpose of many same-sex ceremonies is to create "chosen" families that include close friends.[4]

Second, although many heterosexual couples marry in order to gain public recognition of their relationships, public support has an additional

significance for lesbians and gay men. For many respondents, the desire for such support from friends and family not only stemmed from wanting affirmation as a "couple" but also acceptance as a "lesbian" or "gay" couple. As Barbara Mercer remarked, "I think having a ceremony is important to show the rest of the world because it can give more validity to the fact that these are real relationships just like straight folks have." Unless heterosexual couples are of mixed races, ethnicities, or religions, they do not automatically face the same level of social rejection as lesbian and gay couples.

The support many same-sex couples who have ceremonies receive not only affirms the couple's relationship but also can be compensation for the lack of acceptance they often feel from biological family members and "the world at large." As Maria Siggia remarked:

> It was important to have that support of friends and family in terms of the kind of isolation that goes along with being part of a subculture or oppressed minority group. It seemed to us that it was very important to have some way to balance out all of the negativeness about being gay or lesbian. That it's really important to affirm our relationship and to ask people to actively support us and help out since the culture doesn't allow for that.

Other respondents also elaborated on the importance of rituals as an avenue for reinforcing the dyadic ties of lesbians and gay men. According to Melanie Obermeier:

> It's a really hard thing to do to have a relationship, and you need all the help you can get. If you're a heterosexual you get incredible support from the community to stay together even when people shouldn't. There is almost a pressure to stay together. And in the gay community there's none. There's none of the baby showers, wedding gifts, anniversaries. None of the "You buy silver on your tenth anniversary and Hallmark cards to my lovely wife" kind of thing. We get nothing, absolutely nothing. I think these types of rituals help maintain relationships.

Third, many respondents discussed how their ceremonies made an important statement to other lesbian and gay couples. This sentiment was articulated especially by couples whose ceremonies celebrated anniversaries. As Margaret Dubek explained:

> We just felt really good about the fact that we were still together after ten years. There aren't too many role models in the community that are able to do that. We wanted to celebrate it for ourselves and invite our friends to help us. I think it is good for our community and our friends to know that there are some successful relationships. That we can survive all the difficulties our society puts on us. We should celebrate that.

Kristen Johnson also remarked that it was important for other couples to have long-term, lesbian relationships as role models.

> The tenth is a milestone and I think that comes from tradition. Even within this community, I think it was important for us and for our friends that a tenth

could be celebrated even in the midst of other long-term relationships breaking up. It was a moment of celebration.

One of the most important purposes of having a same-sex ceremony is the creation of recognition for a relationship within lesbian and gay communities. In the past, couples in long-term, monogamous relationships often received little support from other lesbians and gay men. As sociologists Philip Blumstein and Pepper Schwartz (1983) commented in their study *American Couples:* "There is a general fear in both gay and lesbian circles that relationships are unlikely to last. Long-lasting relationships are seen as quite special. They are unexpected, and therefore newly formed couples are not treated as though they will remain together for fifty years. . . . When a couple is not treated as [sacred], the less likely the partners will see themselves that way" (p. 322).

Similarly, many respondents in this study thought that long-term relationships did not receive enough support from other lesbians and gay men. To quote Melanie Obermeier again: *"Sometimes the gay community doesn't take its own relationships seriously enough and that's part of the reason we have a hard time maintaining relationships. Because even as a community we don't take ourselves seriously and recognize our own relationships."*

Even today there remains a perception among many lesbians and gay men that same-sex couples do not remain together for very long. As authors Berger (1982) and Johnson (1990) have noted, however, many lesbians and gay men do have long-term relationships that last over ten years. Berger (1982) suggests that one reason older lesbian and gay couples seem invisible is that they do not share the same social circles as younger gays and, therefore, remain hidden to them.

Fourth, lesbian and gay ceremonies often are not celebrations of "new" commitments; that is, they may take place at any time during a couple's relationship. For example, Kristen Johnson and her partner decided to have a "tenth-anniversary celebration" instead of a commitment ceremony. According to Kristen:

> *We feel very married and have felt very married right from the year one. Because of our insecurities around our sexuality for the first three or four years we were together, we never had a service. Now we don't think it is really appropriate or necessary to have a commitment ceremony since we have that commitment and have since the year one.*

Similarly, Beth Epstein remarked:

> *We called it a "recommitment celebration." We felt that we couldn't just call it a "commitment celebration." Obviously we had already made some level of commitment to be together for twelve years. Recommitment. Like on this day we publicly recommit to each other. That somehow really captured it for both of us.*

Although heterosexual couples may live together without being married, and thus face a similar decision about publicly acknowledging their commitment, nothing prevents them from marrying. Heterosexual couples have

a choice whether to marry legally; lesbians and gay men do not and, in addition, often face prejudice, which can prevent them from having a commitment ceremony.

Married heterosexual couples may decide to "renew" their vows on a significant anniversary. For such couples, wedding anniversaries are occasions to celebrate the date of their marriages. Since lesbians and gay men do not have the same kind of "formal" date to mark the length of their relationships, often they observe many different relationship anniversaries, including when they first met, had sex, moved in together, or decided to make a commitment. These anniversaries have added significance because they help to validate relationships in a society that discounts them. As a further way to gauge the legitimacy of their relationships, lesbian and gay couples may decide to have some type of ceremony when they reach a significant anniversary. In these instances, the length of the relationship becomes a substitute for conventional forms of societal recognition that heterosexual couples receive (Slater and Mencher 1991).

A few respondents stated that their ceremonies were political acts with political consequences. As Patrick Flemming shouted, "We were saying that we were gay and we were proud. So there!" Similarly, Tom Douglass replied, "I have to admit part of what we were doing was a protest. To say, 'The church says no; the state says no; we say yes!'"

Lesbians' and gay men's political motivations for having a ceremony centered not only on validating gay relationships but affirming gay identity. Ever since politician and gay activist Harvey Milk's admonishments to "come out" in the mid-1970s, being publicly open about one's sexual identity has been considered a political act within lesbian and gay culture.[5] When asked to discuss her reasons for having a ceremony, Melanie Obermeier commented on the importance of taking a stand about one's sexual identity.

> *If we don't do it for ourselves, who's going to do it for us? We're not going to hear anybody in the "het" community saying "hey, you guys, you should all be having ceremonies and celebrations." They're not going to do it for us. If we aren't out for ourselves, they won't be out for us.*

Similarly, Esther Gould remarked:

> *In fact, I think same-sex ceremonies are more legitimate than "weddings." I think they are a much braver thing to do. It's so easy to be heterosexual and get married. It's hard not to, in fact. I think it's a brave and really sort of profoundly creative thing for lesbians to create a ritual like that.*

Given lesbians' and gay men's inability to marry legally, it was surprising that so few respondents specifically mentioned political motivations for having a commitment or union ceremony. In contrast to the political slogan of the 1970s, "the personal is political," most of these respondents did not stress a connection between their personal motivations and larger social change within society. In fact, some specifically commented that their ceremonies were "not political events." Their reasons for having a ceremony focused more on personal aspects of commitment than on social change.

Like heterosexuals, lesbians and gay men clearly have ceremonies because they love their partners and want to acknowledge that bond publicly. Indeed, like heterosexual weddings, lesbian and gay ceremonies serve to integrate a couple into larger kinship and community networks. At their core, same-sex ceremonies are rites of integration as well as rites of passage; their two primary objectives are the creation of family and the building of community. . . . These "family" and "community" networks are very different in form from those generated for heterosexual couples. . . .

Are Same-Sex Ceremonies Acts of Accommodation or Acts of Resistance?

During the last [twenty] years, lesbian and gay scholars have debated whether same-sex ceremonies and the subsequent movement to legalize same-sex "marriages" act to help assimilate gay couples into the mainstream or to break down conventional meanings of marriage (Ettlebrick 1989; Stoddard 1989). Although analyzing same-sex ceremonies as rites of passage implies that they are inherently assimilationist, such ceremonies include both "strategies of accommodation" as well as "strategies of resistance." According to anthropologist Louise Lamphere (1987), strategies of accommodation are activities that help individuals endure oppressive experiences and situations in their daily lives. These strategies, however, often coexist with strategies of resistance that help undermine the coercive practices and institutions the individuals must adapt to.

In her work on immigrant women, Lamphere argues that women who work in the labor force are "active strategists" who utilize accommodative coping strategies in order to survive their specific work situations. In addition, women also use resistance strategies to undermine the authority of management and the control supervisors have over their lives. Thus women do not "passively" accept their working conditions but actively manage their work situations.

In a similar vein, anthropologist Ellen Lewin (1994) described the strategies of resistance and accommodation lesbians use to "manage" motherhood and their dual identities as lesbians and mothers. Lesbians who choose to be mothers face the opposing cultural beliefs that women "naturally" are good mothers and that homosexuality is "unnatural." Lesbians are categorized by default as "unfit" mothers. Motherhood, however, permits "lesbians to be more like other women" while at the same time it empowers them to refute "the equation of homosexuality with unnaturalness . . . allowing the lesbian mother to resist gendered constructions of sexuality" (pp. 348–49).

In creating and having same-sex ceremonies, lesbians and gay men also actively participate in both reinforcing and subverting traditional ideals about gender, sexuality, and marriage. They may utilize accommodation strategies in order to gain the status and recognition accorded married, heterosexual couples. Simultaneously, they may use resistance strategies that question the "abnormality" of homosexuality and the hegemony of traditional gender

relations within marriage. Although some lesbians and gay men frame their ceremonies in the context of traditional marriage norms, others view their ceremonies as contesting these same values. Indeed, many do both. Since same-sex couples cannot marry legally, their motivations for altering the traditional wedding ceremony differ from those of heterosexual couples.

Same-Sex Ceremonies as Acts of Accommodation

Although most of the lesbians and gay men in this study who had or were planning a commitment ceremony stated that they believed their ceremonies were about "creating something new," their personal expectations about being in a committed relationship often echoed more traditional norms. The act of having a commitment ceremony often reinforces traditional marriage norms in two primary ways. First, many same-sex couples uphold a number of conventional expectations about adult relationships. In particular, they endorse the assumptions that couples "should" both make a commitment to having a long-term relationship and be sexually monogamous. Like heterosexual weddings, same-sex ceremonies reinforce the ideology that marriage is the proper site for adult sexual relations. By focusing on commitment and monogamy, they invalidate other forms of sexual expression. As sociologist Émile Durkheim ([1912] 1971) noted, rites of passage convey the "core values" of a society to ritual participants and observers. Like heterosexual weddings, same-sex ceremonies reinforce monogamy as a cultural ideal, if not always the practice of particular individuals.

Second, same-sex ceremonies are one strategy for claiming that being gay or lesbian is not all that different from being heterosexual. For some lesbians and gay men, having a ceremony may help them manage their "spoiled" identities (Goffman 1963). According to sociologist Erving Goffman (1963), all stigmatized individuals struggle with integrating their self-perceptions as being "like" everyone else with society's judgment of them as "others." Same-sex ceremonies can help lesbians and gay men cope with this "other" categorization by stressing the similarities between gay and heterosexual relationships. Indeed, within gay communities, this strategy often is referred to derogatorily as "passing" or attempting to gain "heterosexual privilege." Whether a couple has a ceremony for this reason, same-sex ceremonies are one avenue for trying to become "insiders."

Same-Sex Ceremonies as Acts of Resistance

Although same-sex ceremonies can be interpreted as strategies of accommodation that situate lesbian and gay couples within mainstream heterosexual culture, paradoxically this accommodation is accomplished through strategies of resistance that challenge marriage norms. While same-sex ceremonies reinforce some values about marriage, they simultaneously subvert a number of other conventional ideologies. When two women or two men decide

to celebrate their relationship, they are asserting that marriage does not necessarily entail one man and one woman. In addition, they do not assume that they "must" take on traditional male and female gender roles within their relationships or have children in order to be part of a "family."

As many feminist scholars have noted, resistance takes place on two levels (Abu-Lughod 1990; Lewin 1994). First, direct resistance can occur on the terrain of everyday life through actions that sabotage specific institutions. For example, lesbian and gay organizations, such as the Lambda Legal Defense and Education Fund, that want to legalize same-sex marriages are working to undermine the gendered basis of the institution of marriage. In the United States, state marriage laws explicitly assert or are interpreted to imply that marriage is an act that takes place between a woman and a man. By claiming the legal right to have a commitment or wedding ceremony, lesbians and gay men challenge the gender component of marriage as well as its underlying procreative function.

Second, resistance can take place on the level of consciousness. According to anthropologist Emily Martin (1987), in women's relation to the field of medicine "there are a great many ways that women express consciousness of their position and opposition to oppression" (p. 183). In her definition of resistance, Martin includes "refusing to accept a definition of oneself" and "refusing to act as requested or required" (p. 187).

In having a ceremony, lesbians and gay men participate in both of these types of conscious resistance. They refuse to accept the social construction of homosexuality as "abnormal" by claiming that the desire to marry is a "normal" aspiration for any two adults regardless of sexual identity. In addition, those who have ceremonies question the gendered basis of marriage. Two women or two men who "marry" subvert the belief that women and men take on separate but complementary roles within a marriage and overtly resist the notion that marriage functions to support specifically defined gender roles.

Recently anthropologists have begun to argue that rites of passage do not merely transmit the "core values" of a society, as Durkheim first suggested (Baumann 1994). Rituals are spheres of "contradictory and contestable perspectives—participants having their own reasons, viewpoints, and motives, and in fact, [rituals] are made up as they go along."[6] Although participants and observers expect rituals to follow certain rules, they also have the ability to "reconstruct" rituals by changing the wording or performance of certain procedures. For example, heterosexual couples often decide on the precise wording and procedures for their wedding ceremonies and do not follow a "strict" ritual format. Over time, this process of reconstruction slowly alters the format of wedding rituals, resulting in a moderate form of cultural change.

In creating their ceremonies, however, lesbians and gay men shift the conventional meanings of the wedding ritual more overtly. They consciously seek to reformulate cultural values not only about marriage but about gender and homosexuality as well. As anthropologist Gerd Baumann (1994) notes, rituals may not only "speak to values basic to the culture. . . . They can speak

as clearly and centrally to aspirations towards cultural change . . ." (p. 109). Same-sex ceremonies have a political dimension that is absent from hetero-sexual weddings. They challenge normative ideologies of both gender and homosexuality and "reconstruct" the very meaning of the wedding ritual, contributing to a more radical form of cultural change in marriage norms.

Analyses of same-sex ceremonies need to move beyond framing them in a simple dualistic fashion: as acts of assimilation or as acts of resistance. These ceremonies alter some cultural ideals while supporting other social norms at the same time. "Mixed" strategies of accommodation and resis-tance are commonly part of same-sex ceremonies. One respondent, David Gascon, remarked about the lesbian and gay ceremonies he had been to:

> *To me a wedding is a sexual contract. The gay and lesbian commitment ceremo-nies I've seen have been sexual contracts, companionship contracts, but there also are political statements in them. They are more about, from my perspective, a commitment toward a person than an institution like marriage. Straight peo-ple are expected to be married, whereas the gay culture hasn't expected anybody to do anything. The commitment has more to do with taking control and creat-ing our own world rather than fulfilling someone else's need for us to conform.*

. . . Like heterosexuals, lesbians and gay men make many choices in constructing their ceremonies. Unlike heterosexuals, however, they rarely choose only conventional customs. . . .

Conclusion

Lesbians and gay men are an integral part of the changing landscape of fam-ily life in the United States. Although they always have been part of so-called nuclear families (as spouses, parents, and children), the families they cre-ate with their own partners, children, and friends have become more vis-ible outside of lesbian and gay communities over the last thirty years. This visibility largely has resulted from the political and legal steps they have taken to ensure their unions are accorded the same legal rights as married, heterosexual couples. Over the last twenty years, many lesbians and gay men around the country have fought for increased family, parenting, and marriage rights for same-sex couples.

The accounts in this [reading] highlight four important themes about marriage and family life in the United States today. First, what socially and legally constitutes "family" is continually (albeit slowly) being transformed. Changes in the structure of family are not new to the last few decades but have been in progress for over the last 150 years (Gordon 1988). Clearly, the increasing inclusion of same-sex couples in the social and legal matrix of family life is one important aspect of this evolution.

Second, social definitions of marriage also are changing. In contrast to the breadwinner/homemaker ideal of the 1940s and 1950s, a new "companionate" model of marriage has emerged, which stresses that partners should provide each other with emotional intimacy, companionship, and sexual fulfillment

(Reissman 1990). Indeed, many lesbian and gay couples (although certainly not all) have adopted this model for their own relationships. Their relationships illustrate the potential for self-growth and long-term commitment as well as conflict in this new model of marriage.

Third, although marriage and family norms are changing, marriage remains a primary vehicle through which individuals form intimate relationships. Instead of rejecting marriage as some did in the 1970s and 1980s, today many lesbians and gay men are pushing for the right to be included in this institution. Contrary to the often-stated diatribe by the New Right that same-sex marriages would undermine the institution of marriage, most respondents believed that legal recognition of lesbian and gay unions would further strengthen the social, economic, and legal rights of all married couples (heterosexual, lesbian, or gay) over those of single individuals.

Finally, many individuals hold ambivalent or even contradictory views on the changes occurring in the institutions of marriage and family. Although women have gained more equality within marriage, husbands and wives continue to struggle over money, housework, and child care issues. Not surprisingly, many heterosexuals "remain torn by their reverence for the traditional nuclear family as it was, or seemed to be, and their acceptance of the 'new' forms of family in today's society" (Skolnick 1991:198).

The attitudes of lesbians and gay men toward family and marriage issues highlight the changes taking place in these institutions and the conflicting sentiments individuals have about them. While many respondents were critical of the institutions of marriage and family, the majority valued the ideals of love, commitment, monogamy, and family life. At the same time they were supportive of these so-called traditional values, they also argued that marriage and the family need to be redefined to reflect the families people actually create. Their attitudes both mirrored contemporary beliefs and critiqued these same expectations.

As part of the changing fabric of family life in the United States, lesbians and gay men clearly have a stake in how the institutions of marriage and family will be redefined in the future. Although the views of the people studied cannot be generalized to all lesbians and gay men, they do provide an important critique of modern ideals about intimate relationships. Clearly, the battle over who should and will be included in modern social, religious, and legal definitions of family and marriage will continue into the twenty-first century. Despite some legal setbacks, such as the passage of the Defense of Marriage Act by Congress in 1996, lesbians and gay men will continue to fight for and eventually win the battle for full equality.

ENDNOTES

[1] This does not mean that no lesbians and gay men had "public" ceremonies. In fact, some Black lesbians and gay men in Harlem had highly visible same-sex ceremonies during the 1920s (Ayers and Brown 1994). Same-sex ceremonies that included public witnesses, however, were uncommon until the 1970s and 1980s.

[2] Among the respondents, no ceremonies took place between five and nine years after a couple had gotten together.

[3] The term "Lesbianville" was coined by the *National Enquirer* to refer to the town of Northampton, Massachusetts (Kelliher 1992:1).

[4] The phrase "chosen families" was adopted from Kath Weston, who used it to refer to the families lesbians and gay men create. Members of chosen families can include friends, blood relatives, and children (Weston 1991).

[5] Harvey Milk was the first openly gay city supervisor to be elected to office in San Francisco. He was a city supervisor from June 1977 until his assassination in November 1978 (Adam 1987).

[6] Gerholm quoted in Parkin 1994:13.

REFERENCES

Abu-Lughod, Lila. 1990. "The Romance of Resistance: Tracing Transformations of Power through Bedouin Women." *American Ethnologist* 17 (1): 41–55.

Adam, Barry. 1987. *The Rise of a Gay and Lesbian Movement*. Boston: G. K. Hall.

Ayers, Tess and Paul Brown. 1994. *The Essential Guide to Lesbian and Gay Weddings*. New York: HarperCollins.

Baumann, Gerd. 1994. "Ritual Implicates 'Other': Rereading Durkheim in a Plural Society." Pp. 97–116 in *Understanding Rituals,* edited by Daniel de Copper. New York: Routledge.

Berger, Raymond. 1982. *Gay and Gray: The Older Homosexual Man*. Boston: Alyson.

Blumstein, Philip and Pepper Schwartz. 1983. *American Couples: Money, Work, Sex*. New York: William Morrow.

Durkheim, Émile. [1912] 1971. *The Elementary Forms of Religious Life*. London: George Allen and Unwin.

Ettlebrick, Paula. 1989. "Since When Is Marriage a Path to Liberation?" *OUT/LOOK* 2 (2) (Fall): 14–17.

Goffman, Erving. 1963. *Stigma*. Englewood Cliffs, NJ: Prentice-Hall.

Goody, Jack. 1977. "Against Ritual: Loosely Structured Thoughts on a Loosely Defined Topic." Pp. 25–35 in *Secular Ritual,* edited by Sally Moore and Barbara Myerhoff. Amsterdam: Van Gorcum.

Gordon, Linda, ed. 1988. *Heroes of Their Own Lives*. New York: Penguin.

Johnson, Susan. 1990. *Staying Power: Long-Term Lesbian Couples*. Tallahassee, FL: Naiad Press.

Kelliher, Judith. 1992. "Enquiring Minds Wanted to Know." *Daily Hampshire Gazette,* April 14, p. 1.

Lamphere, Louise. 1987. *From Working Daughters to Working Mothers: Factory Women in Massachusetts*. Albany: State University of New York Press.

Lewin, Ellen. 1994. "Negotiating Lesbian Motherhood: The Dialectics of Resistance and Accommodation." Pp. 333–53 in *Mothering: Ideology, Experience, and Agency,* edited by Evelyn NaKano Glenn, Grace Chang, and Linda Forcey. New York: Routledge.

Martin, Emily. 1987. *The Woman in the Body: A Cultural Analysis of Reproduction*. Boston: Beacon Press.

Parkin, David. 1994. "Ritual as Spatial Direction and Bodily Division." Pp. 9–25 in *Understanding Rituals,* edited by Daniel de Coppet. New York: Routledge.

Reissman, Catherine. 1990. *Divorce Talk: Women and Men Make Sense of Personal Relationships*. New Brunswick, NJ: Rutgers University Press.

Roth, Sally. 1985. "Psychotherapy with Lesbian Couples: Individual Issues, Female Socialization, and the Social Context." *Journal of Marriage and Family Therapy* 11 (3): 273–86.

Skolnick, Arlene. 1991. *Embattled Paradise*. New York: HarperCollins.

Slater, Suzanne and Julie Mencher. 1991. "The Lesbian Family Life Cycle: A Contextual Approach." *American Journal of Orthopsychiatry* 61 (3): 372–82.

Stoddard, Thomas. 1989. "Why Gay People Should Seek the Right to Marry." *OUT/LOOK* 2 (2) (Fall): 9–13.

Turner, Terence. 1977. "Transformation, Hierarchy, and Transcendence: A Reformulation of Van Gennep's Model of the Structure of Rites de Passage." Pp. 53–70 in *Secular Ritual,* edited by Sally Moore and Barbara Myerhoff. Amsterdam: Van Gorcum.

Weston, Kath. 1991. *Families We Choose: Lesbians, Gays, Kinship*. New York: Columbia University Press.

PART V

Motherhood and Fatherhood

21

SHIFTING THE CENTER
Race, Class, and Feminist Theorizing
about Motherhood

PATRICIA HILL COLLINS

I dread to see my children grow, I know not their fate. Where the white boy has every opportunity and protection, mine will have few opportunities and no protection. It does not matter how good or wise my children may be, they are colored.

—An anonymous African American mother in 1904
(reported in LERNER 1972:158)

For Native American, African American, Hispanic, and Asian American women, motherhood cannot be analyzed in isolation from its context. Motherhood occurs in specific historical contexts framed by interlocking structures of race, class, and gender, contexts where the sons of white mothers have "every opportunity and protection," and the "colored" daughters and sons of racial ethnic mothers "know not their fate." Racial domination and economic exploitation profoundly shape the mothering context not only for racial ethnic women in the United States but for all women.[1]

Despite the significance of race and class, feminist theorizing routinely minimizes their importance. In this sense, feminist theorizing about motherhood has not been immune to the decontextualization in Western social thought overall.[2] Although many dimensions of motherhood's context are ignored, the exclusion of race and/or class from feminist theorizing generally and from feminist theorizing about motherhood specifically merits special attention (Spelman 1988).[3]

Much feminist theorizing about motherhood assumes that male domination in the political economy and the household is the driving force in family life and that understanding the struggle for individual autonomy in the face of such domination is central to understanding motherhood (Eisenstein 1983).[4] Several guiding principles frame such analyses. First, such theories posit a dichotomous split between the public sphere of economic and political discourse and the private sphere of family and household responsibilities. This juxtaposition of a public, political economy to a private, noneconomic, and apolitical domestic household allows work and family to be seen as separate institutions. Second, reserving the public sphere for men as a "male" domain leaves the private, domestic sphere as a "female" domain. Gender roles become tied to the dichotomous constructions of these two basic societal institutions—men work and women take care of families. Third, the public/private dichotomy separating the family/household from the paid labor market shapes sex-segregated gender roles within the private sphere of the family. The archetypal white, middle-class, nuclear family divides family life into two oppositional spheres—the "male" sphere of economic providing and the "female" sphere of affective nurturing, mainly mothering. This normative family household ideally consists of a working father who earns enough to allow his spouse and dependent children to forgo participation in the paid labor force. Owing in large part to their superior earning power, men as workers and fathers exert power over women in the labor market and in families. Finally, the struggle for individual autonomy in the face of a controlling, oppressive "public" society or the father as patriarch constitutes the main human enterprise.[5] Successful adult males achieve this autonomy. Women, children, and less successful males—namely, those who are working class or from racial ethnic groups—are seen as dependent persons, as less autonomous, and therefore as fitting objects for elite male domination. Within the nuclear family, this struggle for autonomy takes the form of increasing opposition to the mother, the individual responsible for socializing children by these guiding principles (Chodorow 1978; Flax 1978).

Placing the experiences of women of color in the center of feminist theorizing about motherhood demonstrates how emphasizing the issue of father as patriarch in a decontextualized nuclear family distorts the experiences of women in alternative family structures with quite different political economies. While male domination certainly has been an important theme for racial ethnic women in the United States, gender inequality has long worked in tandem with racial domination and economic exploitation. Since work and family have rarely functioned as dichotomous spheres for women of color, examining racial ethnic women's experiences reveals how these two spheres actually are interwoven (Collins 1990; Dill 1988; Glenn 1985).

For women of color, the subjective experience of mothering/motherhood is inextricably linked to the sociocultural concerns of racial ethnic communities—one does not exist without the other. Whether under conditions of the labor exploitation of African American women during slavery and the ensuing tenant farm system, the political conquest of Native American women during European acquisition of land, or exclusionary

immigration policies applied to Asian Americans and Latinos, women of color have performed motherwork that challenges social constructions of work and family as separate spheres, of male and female gender roles as similarly dichotomized, and of the search for autonomy as the guiding human quest. "Women's reproductive labor—that is, feeding, clothing, and psychologically supporting the male wage earner and nurturing and socializing the next generation—is seen as work on behalf of the family as a whole rather than as work benefiting men in particular," observes Asian American sociologist Evelyn Nakano Glenn (1986:192). The locus of conflict lies outside the household, as women and their families engage in collective effort to create and maintain family life in the face of forces that undermine family integrity. But this "reproductive labor" or "motherwork" goes beyond ensuring the survival of members of one's family. This type of motherwork recognizes that individual survival, empowerment, and identity require group survival, empowerment, and identity. . . .

. . . I use the term *motherwork* to soften the dichotomies in feminist theorizing about motherhood that posit rigid distinctions between private and public, family and work, the individual and the collective, identity as individual autonomy and identity growing from the collective self-determination of one's group. Racial ethnic women's mothering and work experiences occur at the boundaries demarking these dualities. "Work for the day to come" is motherwork, whether it is on behalf of one's own biological children, children of one's racial ethnic community, or children who are yet unborn. Moreover, the space that this motherwork occupies promises to shift our thinking about motherhood itself.

Shifting the Center: Women of Color and Motherwork

What themes might emerge if issues of race and class generally, and understanding racial ethnic women's motherwork specifically, became central to feminist theorizing about motherhood? Centering feminist theorizing on the concerns of white middle-class women leads to two problematic assumptions. The first is that a relative degree of economic security exists for mothers and their children. A second is that all women enjoy the racial privilege that allows them to see themselves primarily as individuals in search of personal autonomy instead of members of racial ethnic groups struggling for power. These assumptions allow feminist theorists to concentrate on themes such as the connections among mothering, aggression, and death, the effects of maternal isolation on mother–child relationships within nuclear family households, maternal sexuality, relations among family members, all-powerful mothers as conduits for gender oppression, and the possibilities of an idealized motherhood freed from patriarchy (Chodorow and Contratto 1982; Eisenstein 1983).

Although these issues merit investigation, centering feminist theorizing about motherhood in the ideas and experiences of African American, Native American, Hispanic, and Asian American women might yield markedly

different themes (Andersen 1988; Brown 1989). This stance is to be distinguished from adding racial ethnic women's experiences to preexisting feminist theories without considering how these experiences challenge those theories (Spelman 1988). Involving much more than consulting existing social science sources, placing the ideas and experiences of women of color in the center of analysis requires invoking a different epistemology concerning what type of knowledge is valid. We must distinguish between what has been said about subordinated groups in the dominant discourse, and what such groups might say about themselves if given the opportunity. Personal narratives, autobiographical statements, poetry, fiction, and other personalized statements have all been used by women of color to express self-defined standpoints on mothering and motherhood. Such knowledge reflects the authentic standpoint of subordinated groups. Placing these sources in the center and supplementing them with statistics, historical material, and other knowledge produced to justify the interests of ruling elites should create new themes and angles of vision (Smith 1990).[6]

Specifying the contours of racial ethnic women's motherwork promises to point the way toward richer feminist theorizing about motherhood. Issues of survival, power, and identity—these three themes form the bedrock of women of color's motherwork. The importance of working for the physical survival of children and community, the dialectical nature of power and powerlessness in structuring mothering patterns, and the significance of self-definition in constructing individual and collective racial identity comprise three core themes characterizing the experiences of Native American, African American, Hispanic, and Asian American women. Examining survival, power, and identity reveals how racial ethnic women in the United States encounter and fashion motherwork. But it also suggests how feminist theorizing about motherhood might be shifted if different voices became central in feminist discourse.

Motherwork and Physical Survival

When we are not physically starving we have the luxury to realize psychic and emotional starvation.

—Moraga 1979:29

Physical survival is assumed for children who are white and middle class. Thus, examining their psychic and emotional well-being and that of their mothers appears rational. The children of women of color, many of whom are "physically starving," have no such assurances. Racial ethnic children's lives have long been held in low regard. African American children face an infant mortality rate twice that for white infants. Approximately one-third of Hispanic children and one-half of African American children who survive infancy live in poverty. Racial ethnic children often live in harsh urban environments where drugs, crime, industrial pollutants, and violence threaten their survival. Children in rural environments often fare no better. Winona

LaDuke reports that Native Americans on reservations frequently must use contaminated water. On the Pine Ridge Sioux Reservation in 1979, for example, 38 percent of all pregnancies resulted in miscarriages before the fifth month or in excessive hemorrhaging. Approximately 65 percent of the children who were born suffered breathing problems caused by underdeveloped lungs and jaundice (LaDuke 1988:63).

Struggles to foster the survival of Native American, Latino, Asian American, and African American families and communities by ensuring the survival of children are a fundamental dimension of racial ethnic women's motherwork. African American women's fiction contains numerous stories of mothers fighting for the physical survival both of their own biological children and of those of the larger African American community.[7] "Don't care how much death it is in the land, I got to make preparations for my baby to live!" proclaims Mariah Upshur, the African American heroine of Sara Wright's 1986 novel *This Child's Gonna Live* (p. 143). The harsh climates that confront racial ethnic children require that their mothers, like Mariah Upshur, "make preparations for their babies to live" as a central feature of their motherwork.

Yet, like all deep cultural themes, the theme of motherwork for physical survival contains contradictory elements. On the one hand, racial ethnic women's motherwork for individuals and the community has been essential for their survival. On the other hand, this work often extracts a high cost for large numbers of women, such as loss of individual autonomy or the submersion of individual growth for the benefit of the group. Although this dimension of motherwork is essential, the question of whether women are doing more than their fair share of such work for community development merits consideration.

Histories of family-based labor have shaped racial ethnic women's motherwork for survival and the types of mothering relationships that ensue. African American, Asian American, Native American, and Hispanic women have all worked and contributed to family economic well-being (Dill 1988; Glenn 1985). Much of these women's experiences with motherwork stems from the work they performed as children. The commodification of children of color—from the enslavement of African children who were legally owned as property to the subsequent treatment of children as units of labor in agricultural work, family businesses, and industry—has been a major theme shaping motherhood for women of color. Beginning in slavery and continuing into the post–World War II period, African American children were put to work at young ages in the fields of southern agriculture. Sara Brooks began full-time work in the fields at age eleven and remembers, "We never was lazy 'cause we used to really work. We used to work like mens. Oh, fight sometime, fuss sometime, but worked on" (Collins 1990:54). Black and Latino children in contemporary migrant farm families make similar contributions to their family's economy. "I musta been almost eight when I started following the crops," remembers Jessie de la Cruz, a Mexican American mother with six grown children. "Every winter, up north. I was on the end of the row of prunes, taking care of my younger brother and sister.

They would help me fill up the cans and put 'em in a box while the rest of the family was picking the whole row" (de la Cruz 1980:168). Asian American children spent long hours working in family businesses, child labor practices that have earned Asian Americans the dubious distinction of being "model minorities." More recently, the family-based labor of undocumented racial ethnic immigrants, often mother–child units doing piecework for the garment industry, recalls the sweatshop conditions confronting turn-of-the-century European immigrants.

A certain degree of maternal isolation from members of the dominant group characterizes the preceding mother–child units. For women of color working along with their children, such isolation is more appropriately seen as reflecting the placement of women of color and their children in racially and class-stratified labor systems than as resulting from patriarchal domination. The unit may be isolated, but the work performed by the mother–child unit closely ties the mothering experiences of women of color to wider political and economic issues. Children learn to see their work and that of their mother not as isolated from the wider society but as essential to their family's survival. Moreover, in the case of family agricultural labor or family businesses, women and children worked alongside men, often performing the same work. If isolation occurred, the family, not the mother–child unit, was the focus.

Children working in close proximity to their mothers received distinctive types of mothering. Asian American children working in urban family businesses report long days filled almost exclusively with work and school. In contrast, the sons and daughters of African American sharecroppers and migrant farm children of all backgrounds did not fare as well. Their placement in rural work settings meant that they had less access to educational opportunities. "I think the longest time I went to school was two months in one place," remembers Jessie de la Cruz. "I attended, I think, about forty-five schools. When my parents or my brothers didn't find any work, we wouldn't attend school because we weren't sure of staying there. So I missed a lot of school" (de la Cruz 1980:167–68). It was only in the 1950s that southern school districts stopped the practice of closing segregated African American schools during certain times of the year so that the children could work.

Work that separated women of color from their children also framed the mothering relationship. Until the 1960s, large numbers of African American, Hispanic, and Asian American women worked in domestic service. Even though women worked long hours to ensure their children's physical survival, that same work ironically denied the mothers access to their children. Different institutional arrangements emerged in African American, Latino, and Asian American communities to resolve the tension between maternal separation due to employment and the needs of dependent children. The extended family structure in African American communities endured as a flexible institution that mitigated some of the effects of maternal separation. Grandmothers are highly revered in African American communities, often because they function as primary caretakers of their daughters' and

daughters-in-law's children (Collins 1990). In contrast, exclusionary immigration policies that mitigated against intergenerational family units in the United States led Chinese American and Japanese American families to make other arrangements (Dill 1988).

Some mothers are clearly defeated by this situation of incessant labor performed to ensure their children's survival. The magnitude of their motherwork overwhelms them. But others, even while appearing to be defeated, manage to pass on the meaning of motherwork for survival to their children. African American feminist thinker June Jordan (1985) remembers her perceptions of her mother's work:

> As a child I noticed the sadness of my mother as she sat alone in the kitchen at night. . . . Her woman's work never won permanent victories of any kind. It never enlarged the universe of her imagination or her power to influence what happened beyond the front door of our house. Her woman's work never tickled her to laugh or shout or dance. (P. 105)

But Jordan also sees her mother's work as being motherwork that is essential to individual and community survival.

> But she did raise me to respect her way of offering love and to believe that hard work is often the irreducible factor for survival, not something to avoid. Her woman's work produced a reliable home base where I could pursue the privileges of books and music. Her woman's work invented the potential for a completely new kind of work for us, the next generation of Black women: huge, rewarding hard work demanded by the huge, different ambitions that her perfect confidence in us engendered.

Motherwork and Power

> *How can I write down how I felt when I was a little child and my grandmother used to cry with us 'cause she didn't have enough food to give us? Because my brother was going barefooted and he was cryin' because he wasn't used to going without shoes? How can I describe that? I can't describe when my little girl died because I didn't have money for a doctor. And never had any teaching on caring for sick babies. Living out in labor camps. How can I describe that?*
>
> —DE LA CRUZ 1980:177

Jessie de la Cruz, a Mexican American woman who grew up as a migrant farm worker, experienced firsthand the struggle for empowerment facing racial ethnic women whose daily motherwork centers on issues of survival. A dialectical relation exists between efforts of racial orders to mold the institution of motherhood to serve the interests of elites, in this case, racial elites, and efforts on the part of subordinated groups to retain power over motherhood so that it serves the legitimate needs of their communities (Collins 1990). African American, Asian American, Hispanic, and Native American

women have long been preoccupied with patterns of maternal power and powerlessness because their mothering experiences have been profoundly affected by this dialectical process. But instead of emphasizing maternal power in dealing either with father as patriarch (Chodorow 1978; Rich 1986) or with male dominance (Ferguson 1989), women of color are concerned with their power and powerlessness within an array of social institutions that frame their lives.

Racial ethnic women's struggles for maternal empowerment have revolved around three main themes. The struggle for control over their own bodies in order to preserve choice over whether to become mothers at all is one fundamental theme. The ambiguous politics of caring for unplanned children has long shaped African American women's motherwork. For example, the widespread institutionalized rape of African American women by white men both during slavery and in the segregated South created countless biracial children who had to be absorbed into African American families and communities (Davis 1981). The range of skin colors and hair textures in contemporary African American communities bears mute testament to the powerlessness of African American women in controlling this dimension of motherhood.

For many women of color, choosing to become a mother challenges institutional policies that encourage white middle-class women to reproduce and discourage low-income racial ethnic women from doing so, even penalizing them (Davis 1981). Rita Silk-Nauni, an incarcerated Native American woman, writes of the difficulties she encountered in trying to have additional children. She loved her son so much that she left him only when she went to work. "I tried having more after him and couldn't," she observes. "I went to a specialist and he thought I had been fixed when I had my Son. He said I would have to have surgery in order to give birth again. The surgery was so expensive but I thought I could make a way even if I had to work 24 hours a day. Now that I'm here, I know I'll never have that chance" (Brant 1988:94). Like Silk-Nauni, Puerto Rican and African American women have long had to struggle with issues of sterilization abuse (Davis 1981). More recently, efforts to manipulate the fertility of poor women dependent on public assistance speaks to the continued salience of this issue in the lives of racial ethnic women.

A second dimension of racial women's struggles for maternal empowerment concerns getting to keep the children that are wanted, whether they were planned for or not. For racial ethnic mothers like Jessie de la Cruz whose "little girl died" because she "didn't have money for a doctor," maternal separation from one's children becomes a much more salient issue than maternal isolation with one's children within an allegedly private nuclear family. Physical or psychological separation of mothers and children designed to disempower racial ethnic individuals forms the basis of a systematic effort to disempower their communities.

For both Native American and African American mothers, situations of conquest introduced this dimension of the struggle for maternal empowerment. In her fictional account of a Native American mother's loss of her

children in 1890, Brant explores the pain of maternal separation. "It has been two days since they came and took the children away. My body is greatly chilled. All our blankets have been used to bring me warmth. The women keep the fire blazing. The men sit. They talk among themselves. We are frightened by this sudden child-stealing. We signed papers, the agent said. This gave them rights to take our babies. It is good for them, the agent said. It will make them civilized" (1988:101). A legacy of conquest has meant that Native American mothers on so-called reservations confront intrusive government institutions such as the Bureau of Indian Affairs in deciding the fate of their children. For example, the long-standing policy of removing Native American children from their homes and housing them in reservation boarding schools can be seen as an effort to disempower their mothers. In the case of African American women under slavery, owners controlled virtually all dimensions of their children's lives—they could be sold at will, whipped, even killed, all with no recourse by their mothers. In such a situation, simply keeping and rearing one's children becomes empowerment.

A third dimension of racial ethnic women's struggles for empowerment concerns the pervasive efforts by the dominant group to control their children's minds. In her short story "A Long Memory," Beth Brant juxtaposes the loss felt in 1890 by a Native American mother whose son and daughter were forcibly removed by white officials to the loss that Brant felt in 1978 when a hearing took away her custody of her daughter. "Why do they want our babies?" queries the turn-of-the-century mother. "They want our power. They take our children to remove the inside of them. Our power" (Brant 1988:105). This mother recognizes that the future of the Native American way of life lies in retaining the power to define that worldview through educating the children. By forbidding children to speak their native languages and in other ways encouraging them to assimilate into Anglo culture, external agencies challenge the power of mothers to raise their children as they see fit.

Schools controlled by the dominant group comprise one important location where this dimension of the struggle for maternal empowerment occurs. In contrast to white middle-class children, whose educational experiences affirm their mothers' middle-class values, culture, and authority, African American, Latino, Asian American, and Native American children typically receive an education that derogates their mothers' perspective. For example, the struggles over bilingual education in Latino communities are about much more than retaining Spanish as a second language. Speaking the language of one's childhood is a way of retaining the entire culture and honoring the mother teaching that culture (Anzaldúa 1987; Moraga 1979).

Jenny Yamoto (1988) describes the stress of ongoing negotiations with schools regarding her part African American and part Japanese sons. "I've noticed that depending on which parent, Black mom or Asian dad, goes to school open house, my oldest son's behavior is interpreted as disruptive and irreverent, or assertive and clever. . . . I resent their behavior being defined and even expected on the basis of racial biases their teachers may struggle

with or hold. . . . I don't have the time or energy to constantly change and challenge their teachers' and friends' misperceptions. I only go after them when the children really seem to be seriously threatened" (p. 24).

In confronting each of these three dimensions of their struggles for empowerment, racial ethnic women are not powerless in the face of racial and class oppression. Being grounded in a strong, dynamic, indigenous culture can be central in racial ethnic women's social constructions of motherhood. Depending on their access to traditional culture, women of color invoke alternative sources of power.[8] "Equality per se may have a different meaning for Indian women and Indian people," suggests Kate Shanley (1988). "That difference begins with personal and tribal sovereignty—the right to be legally recognized as people empowered to determine our own destinies" (p. 214). Personal sovereignty involves the struggle to promote the survival of a social structure whose organizational principles represent notions of family and motherhood different from those of the mainstream. "The nuclear family has little relevance to Indian women," observes Shanley. "In fact, in many ways, mainstream feminists now are striving to redefine family and community in a way that Indian women have long known."

African American mothers can draw upon an Afrocentric tradition where motherhood of varying types, whether bloodmother, othermother, or community othermother, can be invoked as a symbol of power. Many African American women receive respect and recognition within their local communities for innovative and practical approaches to mothering not only their own biological children but also the children in their extended family networks and in the community overall. Black women's involvement in fostering African American community development forms the basis of this community-based power. In local African American communities, community othermothers can become identified as powerful figures through furthering the community's well-being (Collins 1990).

Despite policies of dominant institutions that place racial ethnic mothers in positions where they appear less powerful to their children, mothers and children empower themselves by understanding each other's position and relying on each other's strengths. In many cases, children, especially daughters, bond with their mothers instead of railing against them as symbols of patriarchal power. Cherríe Moraga describes the impact that her mother had on her. Because she was repeatedly removed from school in order to work, Moraga's mother would be considered largely illiterate by prevailing standards. But her mother was also a fine storyteller and found ways to empower herself within dominant institutions. "I would go with my mother to fill out job applications for her, or write checks for her at the supermarket," Moraga (1979) recounts. "We would have the scenario all worked out ahead of time. My mother would sign the check before we'd get to the store. Then, as we'd approach the checkstand, she would say—within earshot of the cashier—'oh honey, you go 'head and make out the check,' as if she couldn't be bothered with such an insignificant detail" (p. 28). Like Cherríe Moraga and her mother, racial ethnic women's motherwork involves collaborating to empower mothers and children within oppressive structures.

Motherwork and Identity

*Please help me find out who I am. My mother was Indian, but we were taken
from her and put in foster homes. They were white and didn't want to tell us
about our mother. I have a name and maybe a place of birth. Do you think you
can help me?*

—Brant 1988:9

Like this excerpt from a letter to an editor, the theme of loss of racial ethnic
identity and the struggle to maintain a sense of self and community per-
vade the remaining stories, poetry, and narratives in Beth Brant's volume,
A Gathering of Spirit. Carol Lee Sanchez offers another view of the impact
of the loss of self. "Radicals look at reservation Indians and get very upset
about their poverty conditions," observes Sanchez. "But poverty to us is not
the same thing as poverty is to you. Our poverty is that we can't be who we
are. We can't hunt or fish or grow our food because our basic resources and
the right to use them in traditional ways are denied us" (Brant 1988:165).
Racial ethnic women's motherwork reflects the tensions inherent in trying
to foster a meaningful racial identity in children within a society that deni-
grates people of color. The racial privilege enjoyed by white middle-class
women makes unnecessary this complicated dimension of the mothering tradition of women of color. Although white children can be prepared
to fight racial oppression, their survival does not depend on gaining these
skills. Their racial identity is validated by their schools, the media, and other
social institutions. White children are socialized into their rightful place in
systems of racial privilege. Racial ethnic women have no such guarantees for
their children. Their children must first be taught to survive in systems that
would oppress them. Moreover, this survival must not come at the expense
of self-esteem. Thus, a dialectical relation exists between systems of racial
oppression designed to strip subordinated groups of a sense of personal
identity and a sense of collective peoplehood, and the cultures of resistance
to that oppression extant in various racial ethnic groups. For women of color,
motherwork for identity occurs at this critical juncture (Collins 1990).

"Through our mothers, the culture gave us mixed messages," observes
Mexican American poet Gloria Anzaldúa (1987). "Which was it to be—strong
or submissive, rebellious or conforming?" (p. 18). Thus women of color's
motherwork requires reconciling two contradictory needs concerning identity. First, preparing children to cope with and survive within systems of
racial oppression is essential. The pressures for these children to assimilate
are pervasive. In order to compel women of color to participate in their children's assimilation, dominant institutions promulgate ideologies that belit-
tle people of color. Negative controlling images infuse the worlds of their
male and female children (Collins 1990; Green 1990; Tajima 1989). Native
American girls are encouraged to see themselves as "Pocahontases" and
"squaws"; Asian American girls as "geisha girls" and "Suzy Wongs"; Hispanic girls as "Madonnas" and "hot-blooded whores"; and African American girls as "mammies," "matriarchs," and "prostitutes." Girls of all groups

are told that their lives cannot be complete without a male partner and that their educational and career aspirations must always be subordinated to their family obligations.

This push toward assimilation is part of a larger effort to socialize racial ethnic children into their proper subordinate places in systems of racial and class oppression. But despite pressures to assimilate, since children of color can never be white, assimilation by becoming white is impossible. Thus, a second dimension of this mothering tradition involves equipping children with skills to challenge the systems of racial oppression. Girls who become women believing that they are capable only of being maids and prostitutes cannot contribute to racial ethnic women's motherwork. Mothers make varying choices in preparing their children to fit into, yet resist, systems of racial domination. Some mothers remain powerless in the face of external forces that foster their children's assimilation and subsequent alienation from their families and communities. . . .

Other mothers become unwitting conduits of the dominant ideology. "How many times have I heard mothers and mothers-in-law tell their sons to beat their wives for not obeying them, for being *hociconas* (big mouths), for being *callajeras* (going to visit and gossip with neighbors), for expecting their husbands to help with the rearing of children and the housework, for wanting to be something other than housewives," asks Gloria Anzaldúa (1987:16).

Some mothers encourage their children to fit in for reasons of survival. . . . To Cherríe Moraga's mother, "on a basic economic level, being Chicana meant being 'less.' It was through my mother's desire to protect her children from poverty and illiteracy that we became 'anglocized'; the more effectively we could pass in the white world, the better guaranteed our future" (Moraga 1979:28). Despite their mothers' good intentions, the costs to children taught to submit to racist and sexist ideologies can be high. Raven, a Native American woman, looks back on her childhood: "I've been raised in white man's world and was forbade more or less to converse with Indian people. As my mother wanted me to be educated and live a good life, free from poverty. I lived a life of loneliness. Today I am desperate to know my people" (Brant 1988:221). Raven's mother did what she thought best to help her daughter avoid poverty. But ultimately, Raven experienced the poverty of not being able to be who she was.

Still other mothers transmit sophisticated skills to their children of how one can appear to submit to yet simultaneously challenge oppression. Willi Coleman's mother used a Saturday-night hair-combing ritual to impart an African American women's standpoint to her daughters:

> Except for special occasions mama came home from work early on Saturdays. She spent six days a week mopping, waxing and dusting other women's houses and keeping out of reach of other women's husbands. Saturday nights were reserved for "taking care of them girls" hair and the telling of stories. Some of which included a recitation of what she had endured and how she had triumphed over "folks that were lower than dirt" and "no-good snakes in the grass." She combed, patted,

twisted and talked, saying things which would have embarrassed or shamed her at other times. (Coleman 1987:34)

Historian Elsa Barkley Brown captures the delicate balance that racial ethnic mothers must achieve. Brown (1989) points out that her mother's behavior demonstrated the "need to teach me to live my life one way and, at the same time, to provide all the tools I would need to live it quite differently" (p. 929).

For women of color, the struggle to maintain an independent racial identity has taken many forms, all revealing varying solutions to the dialectical relation between institutions that would deny their children their humanity and their children's right to exist as self-defined people. Like Willi Coleman's mother, African American women draw upon a long-standing Afrocentric feminist worldview emphasizing the importance of self-definition and self-reliance, and the necessity of demanding respect from others (Collins 1990; Terborg-Penn 1986).

Poet and essayist Gloria Anzaldúa (1987) challenges many of the ideas in Latino cultures concerning women: "Though I'll defend my race and culture when they are attacked by non-mexicanos, . . . I abhor some of my culture's ways, how it cripples its women, *como burras,* our strengths used against us" (p. 21). . . . For Anzaldúa (1987), the Spanish conquest that brought racism and economic subordination to Indian people and created a new mixed-race Latino people simultaneously devalued women:

> No, I do not buy all the myths of the tribe into which I was born. I can understand why the more tinged with Anglo blood, the more adamantly my colored and colorless sisters glorify their colored culture's values— to offset the extreme devaluation of it by the white culture. It's a legitimate reaction. But I will not glorify those aspects of my culture which have injured me and which have injured me in the name of protecting me. (P. 22)

Latino mothers face the complicated task of shepherding their children through the racism of the dominant society and the reactions to that racism framing cultural beliefs internal to Hispanic communities. Many Asian American mothers stress conformity and fitting in as a way to challenge the system. "Our parents are painted as hard workers who were socially uncomfortable and had difficulty expressing even the smallest opinion," observes Japanese American Kesaya Noda in her autobiographical essay "Growing Up Asian in America" (1989:246). Noda questioned this seeming capitulation on the part of her parents: " 'Why did you go into those camps,' I raged at my parents, frightened by my own inner silence and timidity. 'Why didn't you do anything to resist?' " But Noda (1989) later discovers a compelling explanation as to why Asian Americans are so often portrayed as conforming: "I had not been able to imagine before what it must have felt like to be an American—to know absolutely that one is an American—and yet to have almost everyone else deny it. Not only deny it, but challenge that identity with machine guns and troops of white American soldiers. In those circumstances it was difficult to say, 'I'm a Japanese American.' 'American' had to do" (p. 247).

Native American women can draw upon a tradition of motherhood and woman's power inherent in Native American cultures (Allen 1986; Awiakta 1988). . . . Marilou Awiakta (1988) offers a powerful summary of the symbolic meaning of motherhood in Native American cultures: "I feel the Grand-mother's power. She sings of harmony, not dominance. And her song rises from a culture that repeats the wise balance of nature: The gender capable of bearing life is not separated from the power to sustain it" (p. 126). A cul-ture that sees the connectedness between the earth and human survival, and that sees motherhood as symbolic of the earth itself holds motherhood as an institution in high regard.

Concluding Remarks

Survival, power, and identity shape motherhood for all women. But these themes remain muted when the mothering experiences of women of color are marginalized in feminist theorizing about motherhood. The theories reflect a lack of attention to the connection between ideas and the contexts in which they emerge. Although such decontextualization aims to gener-ate universal theories of human behavior, in actuality the theories routinely distort or omit huge categories of human experience.

Placing racial ethnic women's motherwork in the center of analysis recontextualizes motherhood. Whereas the significance of race and class in shaping the context in which motherhood occurs is virtually invisible when white, middle-class women's experiences are the theoretical norm, the effects of race and class stand out in stark relief when women of color are accorded theoretical primacy. Highlighting racial ethnic mothers' struggles concerning their children's right to exist focuses attention on the impor-tance of survival. Exploring the dialectical nature of racial ethnic women's empowerment in structures of racial domination and economic exploitation demonstrates the need to broaden the definition of maternal power. Empha-sizing how the quest for self-definition is mediated by membership in differ-ent racial and social class groups reveals how the issue of identity is crucial to all motherwork.

Existing feminist theories of motherhood have emerged in specific intel-lectual and political contexts. By assuming that social theory will be appli-cable regardless of social context, feminist scholars fail to realize that they themselves are rooted in specific locations, and that the contexts in which they are located provide the thought-models of how they interpret the world. Their theories may appear to be universal and objective, but they actually are only partial perspectives reflecting the white middle-class context in which their creators live. Large segments of experience, those of women who are not white and middle class, have been excluded (Spelman 1988). . . .

Theorizing about motherhood will not be helped, however, by sup-planting one group's theory with that of another—for example, by claim-ing that women of color's experiences are more valid than those of white middle-class women. Just as varying placement in systems of privilege,

whether race, class, sexuality, or age, generates divergent experiences with motherhood, examining motherhood and mother-as-subject from multiple perspectives should uncover rich textures of difference. Shifting the center to accommodate this diversity promises to recontextualize motherhood and point us toward feminist theorizing that embraces difference as an essential part of commonality.

ENDNOTES

[1] In this [reading], I use the terms *racial ethnic women* and *women of color* interchangeably. Grounded in the experiences of groups who have been the targets of racism, the term *racial ethnic* implies more solidarity with men involved in struggles against racism. In contrast, the term *women of color* emerges from a feminist background where racial ethnic women committed to feminist struggle aimed to distinguish their history and issues from those of middle-class white women. Neither term captures the complexity of African American, Native American, Asian American, and Hispanic women's experiences.

[2] Positivist social science exemplifies this type of decontextualization. In order to create scientific descriptions of reality, positivist researchers aim to produce ostensibly objective generalizations. But because researchers have widely differing values, experiences, and emotions, genuine science is thought to be unattainable unless all human characteristics except rationality are eliminated from the research process. By following strict methodological rules, scientists aimed to distance themselves from the values, vested interests, and emotions generated by their class, race, sex, or unique situation. By decontextualizing themselves, they allegedly become detached observers and manipulators of nature. Moreover, this researcher decontextualization is paralleled by comparable efforts to remove the objects of study from their contexts (Jaggar 1983).

[3] Dominant theories are characterized by this decontextualization. Boyd's (1989) helpful survey of literature on the mother–daughter relationship reveals that though much work has been done on motherhood generally, and on the mother–daughter relationship, very little of it tests feminist theories of motherhood. Boyd identifies two prevailing theories—psychoanalytic theory and social learning theory—that she claims form the bulk of feminist theorizing. Both of these approaches minimize the importance of race and class in the context of motherhood.

[4] Psychoanalytic feminist theorizing about motherhood, such as Nancy Chodorow's groundbreaking work *The Reproduction of Mothering* (1978), exemplifies how decontextualization of race and/or class can weaken what is otherwise strong feminist theorizing. Although I realize that other feminist approaches to motherhood exist—see, e.g., Eisenstein's (1983) summary—I have chosen to stress psychoanalytic feminist theory because the work of Chodorow and others has been highly influential in framing the predominant themes in feminist discourse.

[5] The thesis of the atomized individual that underlies Western psychology is rooted in a much larger Western construction concerning the relation of the individual to the community (Hartsock 1983). Theories of motherhood based on the assumption of the atomized human proceed to use this definition of the individual as the unit of analysis and then construct theory from this base. From this grow assumptions that the major process to examine is that between freely choosing rational individuals engaging in bargains (Hartsock 1983).

[6] The narrative tradition in the writings of women of color addresses this effort to recover the history of mothers. Works from African American women's autobiographical tradition such as Ann Moody's *Coming of Age in Mississippi,* Maya Angelou's *I Know Why the Caged Bird Sings,* Linda Brent's *Incidents in the Life of a Slave Girl,* and Marita Golden's *The Heart of a Woman* contain the authentic voices of African American women centered on experiences of motherhood. Works from African American women's fiction include *This Child's Gonna Live,* Alice Walker's *Meridian,* and Toni Morrison's *Sula* and *Beloved.* Asian American women's fiction, such as Amy Tan's *The Joy Luck Club* and Maxine Kingston's *Woman Warrior,* and autobiographies, such as Jean Wakatsuki Houston's *Farewell to Manzanar,* offer a parallel source of authentic voice. Connie Young Yu (1989) entitles her article on the history of Asian American women "The World of Our Grandmothers" and recreates Asian American history with her grandmother as a central figure. Cherríe Moraga (1979) writes a letter to her mother as a way of coming to terms with the contradictions in her racial identity as a Chicana. In *Borderlands/ La Frontera,* Gloria Anzaldúa (1987) weaves autobiography, poetry, and philosophy together in her exploration of women and mothering.

[7] Notable examples include Lutie Johnson's unsuccessful attempt to rescue her son from the harmful effects of an urban environment in Ann Petry's *The Street;* and Meridian's work on behalf of the children of a small southern town after she chooses to relinquish her own child, in Alice Walker's *Meridian.*

[8] Noticeably absent from feminist theories of motherhood is a comprehensive theory of power and an account of how power relations shape any theories actually developed. Firmly rooted in an exchange-based marketplace with its accompanying assumptions of rational economic decision making and white male control of the marketplace, this model of community stresses the rights of individuals, including feminist theorists, to make decisions in their own interest, regardless of the impact on larger society. Composed of a collection of unequal individuals who compete for greater shares of money as the medium of exchange, this model of community legitimates relations of domination either by denying they exist or by treating them as inevitable but unimportant (Hartsock 1983).

REFERENCES

Allen, P. G. 1986. *The Sacred Hoop: Recovering the Feminine in American Indian Traditions.* Boston: Beacon Press.

Andersen, M. 1988. "Moving Our Minds: Studying Women of Color and Reconstructing Sociology." *Teaching Sociology* 16 (2): 123–32.

Anzaldúa, G. 1987. *Borderlands/La Frontera: The New Mestiza.* San Francisco: Spinsters.

Awiakta, M. 1988. "Amazons in Appalachia." Pp. 125–30 in *A Gathering of Spirit,* edited by B. Brant. Ithaca, NY: Firebrand Books.

Boyd, C. J. 1989. "Mothers and Daughters: A Discussion of Theory and Research." *Journal of Marriage and the Family* 51:291–301.

Brant, B., ed. 1988. *A Gathering of Spirit: A Collection by North American Indian Women.* Ithaca, NY: Firebrand Books.

Brown, E. B. 1989. "African-American Women's Quilting: A Framework for Conceptualizing and Teaching African-American Women's History. *Signs* 14 (4): 921–29.

Chodorow, N. 1978. *The Reproduction of Mothering.* Berkeley: University of California Press.

Chodorow, N. and S. Contratto. 1982. "The Fantasy of the Perfect Mother." Pp. 54–74 in *Rethinking the Family: Some Feminist Questions,* edited by B. Thorne and M. Yalom. New York: Longman.

Coleman, W. 1987. "Closets and Keepsakes." *Sage: A Scholarly Journal on Black Women* 4 (2): 34–35.

Collins, P. H. 1990. *Black Feminist Thought: Knowledge, Consciousness and the Politics of Empowerment.* New York: Routledge.

Davis, A. Y. 1981. *Women, Race, and Class.* New York: Random House.

de la Cruz, J. 1980. Interview. In *American Dreams: Lost and Found,* edited by S. Terkel. New York: Ballantine Books.

Dill, B. T. 1988. "Our Mothers' Grief: Racial Ethnic Women and the Maintenance of Families." *Journal of Family History* 13 (4): 415–31.

Eisenstein, H. 1983. *Contemporary Feminist Thought.* Boston: Hall.

Ferguson, A. 1989. *Blood at the Root: Motherhood, Sexuality, and Male Dominance.* New York: Unwin Hyman/Routledge.

Flax, J. 1978. "The Conflict between Nurturance and Autonomy in Mother–Daughter Relationships and within Feminism." *Feminist Studies* 4 (2): 171–89.

Glenn, E. N. 1985. "Racial Ethnic Women's Labor: The Intersection of Race, Gender and Class Oppression." *Review of Radical Political Economics* 17 (3): 86–108.

———. 1986. *Issei, Nisei, War Bride: Three Generations of Japanese American Women in Domestic Service.* Philadelphia: Temple University Press.

Green, R. 1990. "The Pocohontas Perplex: The Image of Indian Women in American Culture." Pp. 15–21 in *Unequal Sisters,* edited by E. C. DuBois and V. Ruiz. New York: Routledge.

Hartsock, N. 1983. *Money, Sex and Power.* Boston: Northeastern University Press.

Jaggar, A. 1983. *Feminist Politics and Human Nature.* Totowa, NJ: Rowman & Allanheld.

Jordan, J. 1985. *On Call.* Boston: South End Press.

LaDuke, W. 1988. "They Always Come Back." Pp. 62–67 in *A Gathering of Spirit,* edited by B. Brant. Ithaca, NY: Firebrand Books.

Lerner, G., ed. 1972. *Black Women in White America: A Documentary History.* New York: Vintage Books.

Moraga, C. 1979. "La Guera." Pp. 27–34 in *This Bridge Called My Back: Writings by Radical Women of Color,* edited by C. Moraga and G. Anzaldúa. Watertown, MA: Persephone Press.

Noda, K. E. 1989. "Growing Up Asian in America." Pp. 243–50 in *Making Waves: An Anthology of Writings by and about Asian American Women,* edited by Asian Women United of California. Boston: Beacon Press.

Rich, A. 1986. *Of Woman Born: Motherhood as Institution and Experience.* New York: Norton.

Shanley, K. 1988. "Thoughts on Indian Feminism." Pp. 213–15 in *A Gathering of Spirit,* edited by B. Brant. Ithaca, NY: Firebrand Books.

Smith, D. E. 1990. *The Conceptual Practices of Power: A Feminist Sociology of Knowledge.* Boston: Northeastern University Press.

Spelman, E. V. 1988. *Inessential Woman: Problems of Exclusion in Feminist Thought.* Boston: Beacon Press.

Tajima, R. E. 1989. "Lotus Blossoms Don't Bleed: Images of Asian Women." Pp. 308–17 in *Making Waves: An Anthology of Writings by and about Asian American Women,* edited by Asian Women United of California. Boston: Beacon Press.

Terborg-Penn, R. 1986. "Black Women in Resistance: A Cross-Cultural Perspective." Pp. 188–209 in *In Resistance: Studies in African, Caribbean and Afro-American History,* edited by G. Y. Okhiro. Amherst: University of Massachusetts Press.

Wright, S. 1986. *This Child's Gonna Live.* Old Westbury, NY: Feminist Press.

Yamoto, J. 1988. "Mixed Bloods, Half Breeds, Mongrels, Hybrids." Pp. 22–24 in *Changing Our Power: An Introduction to Women's Studies,* edited by J. W. Cochran, D. Langston, and C. Woodward. Dubuque, IA: Kendall/Hunt.

Yu, C. Y. 1989. "The World of Our Grandmothers." Pp. 33–41 in *Making Waves: An Anthology of Writings by and about Asian American Women,* edited by Asian Women United of California. Boston: Beacon Press.

22

MOTHERING FROM A DISTANCE
Emotions, Gender, and Intergenerational Relations in Filipino Transnational Families

RHACEL SALAZAR PARREÑAS

An increasing number of Filipina migrants are mothering their children from a distance. In order to provide for their families, they must leave them behind in the Philippines and take advantage of the greater labor market opportunities in other countries of Asia, Europe, and the Americas. One of the largest sources of independent female labor migrants in the world, the Philippines has seen the formation of a growing number of female-headed transnational families.[1] These families are households with core members living in at least two nation-states and in which the mother works in another country while some or all of her dependents reside in the Philippines. This [reading] analyzes the emotional

Rhacel Salazar Parrenas, "Mothering from a Distance: Emotions, Gender, and Intergenerational Relations in Filipino Transnational Families" from *Feminist Studies* 27, no. 2 (Summer 2001). Copyright © 2001 by Feminist Studies, Inc. Reprinted with permission.

consequences of geographical distance in female-headed transnational families and examines the mechanisms by which mothers and children cope with them.

Without a doubt, mothering from a distance has emotional ramifications both for mothers who leave and children who are sent back or left behind. The pain of family separation creates various feelings, including helplessness, regret, and guilt for mothers and loneliness, vulnerability, and insecurity for children. How are these feelings negotiated in the social reproduction of the transnational family?[2] Moreover, how are these feelings influenced by gender ideologies of mothering? The practice of mothering from a distance or "transnational mothering," as Pierrette Hondagneu-Sotelo and Ernestine Avila have called it, ruptures the ideological foundation of the Filipino family.[3] Unlike the "split households" of earlier Chinese, Mexican, and Filipino male migrants in the United States, the traditional division of labor with the father in charge of production and the mother of reproduction is contested in contemporary female-headed transnational households.[4]

This [reading] examines gender and intergenerational relations through the lens of emotion. I show that socialized gender norms in the family aggravate the emotional strains of mothers and children in transnational families and argue that the reconstitution of mothering led by female migrants from the Philippines is stalled by traditional ideologies of family life. I chose emotion as the central analytical principle of this [reading] because emotional strains are prominent characteristics of the family life of migrant Filipina domestic workers. Moreover, these emotional strains beg to be understood systematically. As Arlie Hochschild has shown, emotions do not exist in a vacuum. Instead, they exist in the context of social structures in society. As she states, "Emotion is a sense that tells about the self-relevance of reality. We infer from it what we must have wanted or expected or how we must have been perceiving the world. Emotion is one way to discover a buried perspective on matters." Regulated by "feeling rules," emotions are determined by ideologies,[5] and in the Filipino family, as in many other families, the ideology of woman as nurturer is a central determinant of the emotional needs and expectations of its members.[6] . . .

Methodology

This reading is based primarily on open-ended interviews that I collected with female domestic workers in Rome and Los Angeles: forty-six in Rome and twenty-six in Los Angeles. I tape-recorded and transcribed fully each of my interviews, which were mostly conducted in Tagalog or Taglish (a hybrid of Tagalog and English), and then translated into English. I based my study on these two cities because they are two main destinations of Filipina migrants.

A little less than five months in Rome in 1995 and 1996 gave me ample time to collect forty-six in-depth interviews with Filipina domestic workers. The interviews ranged from one and one-half to three hours in length. I collected an unsystematic sample of research participants by using chain and

snowball referrals. To diversify my sample, I solicited research participants from various sites in the community (e.g., church, parks, and plazas).

In Los Angeles, I collected a smaller sample of twenty-six in-depth interviews with Filipina domestic workers. These interviews range from one and one-half to three hours in length. I collected these interviews between April and September 1996. . . .

Characteristics of Sample

Although there are distinguishing characteristics between my interviewees in Rome and Los Angeles, they also share many social characteristics. Differences between them include regional origin and median age. Interestingly, there are more similarities between them. First, most of them are legal residents of their respective host societies. In Italy, thirty of forty-six interviewees have a *permesso di soggiorno* (permit to stay), which grants them temporary residency for seven years. . . . With the legislation of the Martelli Law in 1990, migrant Filipina domestic workers became eligible to sponsor the migration of their families. Nonetheless, most of my interviewees have chosen not to sponsor the migration of their children.

In Los Angeles, fifteen of twenty-six interviewees have legal documents. Most of the women acquired permanent legal status by marriage or the sponsorship of a wealthy employer. Yet many have not been able to sponsor the migration of dependents, because they have been caught in the legal bind of obtaining legal status only after their children had reached adult age, when they are no longer eligible for immediate family reunification.

Another similarity between my interviewees in Rome and Los Angeles is their high level of educational attainment. Most of them have acquired some years of postsecondary training in the Philippines. . . .

Finally, more than one-half of my interviewees are married women with children. I was surprised to stumble upon this fact, because studies have indicated that Filipina migrants are usually young and single women.[7] . . .

The median age of interviewees suggests that the children of women in Rome are fairly young, and in Los Angeles, the children are older. The median age of my interviewees in Los Angeles is high at fifty-two. . . . In Rome, the median age of interviewees is thirty-one years old, significantly lower than my sample in Los Angeles. . . .

In contrast to the trend for shorter periods of separation among Mexican migrant families, the duration of separation among Filipina migrant domestic workers extends to more than two years for most families, usually encompassing the entire duration of settlement.[8] Significantly, parents with legal documents return to the Philippines sporadically. On average, they visit their children every four years for a period of two months. They attribute the infrequency of their return to the high cost of airfare and to the fact they cannot afford to take time off work. In addition, the fear of losing their jobs prevents them from visiting their families for an extended period of time. As they are limited to short visits to the Philippines, traveling is seen as an

excessive expense of funds that could otherwise be used on meeting the costs of reproducing the family.

The Structural Context of Mothering from a Distance

The globalization of the market economy has triggered a high demand for female workers from developing nations, such as the Philippines, to supply low-wage service labor in more developed nations. In postindustrial nations such as the United States and Italy, their low-wage service labor (e.g., hotel housekeeping and domestic work) is needed by the growing professional population in global cities, meaning new economic centers where special-ized professional services (e.g., legal, financial, accounting, and consult-ing services) are concentrated.[9] In newly industrialized countries, such as Taiwan and Malaysia, globalization and the rise of manufacturing produc-tion has also generated a demand for low-wage service migrant workers. Production activities in these economies have subsumed the traditional proletariat female work force who would otherwise perform low-wage ser-vice jobs such as domestic work. This shift in labor market concentration has generated a need for the lower wage labor of women from neighboring countries in Asia to fill the demand for service employment.[10]

In globalization, even though the "denationalized" economy demands the low-wage service labor of female migrants, the "renationalized" society neither wants the responsibility for the reproductive costs of these workers nor grants them the membership accorded by the contributions of their labor to the economic growth of receiving nations.[11] The entrance of migrant Filipina domestic workers into the global economy is wrought by struc-tural constraints that restrict their incorporation into receiving nations. For example, various countries limit the term of their settlement to temporary labor contracts and deny entry to their spouses and children.[12] As a result, migrant Filipina domestic workers with children are forced to mother from a distance.

Receiving nations curb the integration of migrant Filipina domestic workers so as to guarantee to their economies a secure source of low-wage labor. By containing the costs of reproduction in sending countries, wages of migrant workers can be kept to a minimum. Moreover, by restricting the incorporation of migrants, receiving nations can secure for their economies a supply of low-wage workers who could easily be repatriated if the econ-omy is slow.

Sending the message that only the production and not the reproduction of their labor is desired, nations such as Singapore and Malaysia prohibit the marriage or cohabitation of migrant Filipina domestic workers with native citizens.[13] Pregnancy is furthermore prohibited for Filipina migrants in the Middle East and Asia.[14] The liberal states of the United States and Italy are not exempt from the trend of "renationalization." In the United States, for example, lawmakers are entertaining the promotion of temporary labor migration and the elimination of certain preference categories for family

reunification, including the preference categories for adult children and parents of U.S. citizens and permanent residents—the trend being to continue the labor provided by migrants but to discontinue support for their reproduction. In Italy, the "guest worker" status of migrant Filipinos coupled with their restricted options in the labor market encourages the maintenance of transnational households.

Only in a few countries are migrant Filipina domestic workers eligible for family reunification. They include Canada, the United States, and Italy. However, many structural factors deter migrant Filipina domestic workers in these countries from sponsoring the migration of their children. For instance, the occupational demands of domestic work make it difficult for them to raise their children in these host societies. In Italy, low wages force most day workers to work long hours. In the United States, most of my research informants are live-in domestic workers. As such, their work arrangement limits the time that they can devote to the care of their own families.

Consequently, as I have argued elsewhere, the increasing demand for migrant women to alleviate the reproductive labor of the growing number of working women in postindustrial nations has sparked the formation of an international division of reproductive labor.[15] Under this system, migrant Filipina domestic workers perform the reproductive labor of class-privileged women in industrialized countries and are forced to leave their children behind in the Philippines. Many in turn have had to hire other women in the Philippines to perform their own household work. In fact, many of the women in my study employ paid domestic workers to care for their families in the Philippines. In this sense, we can see the formation of a three-tier chain of the commodification of mothering between middle-class women in the United States and Italy; migrant Filipina domestic workers; and Filipina domestic workers in the Philippines who are too poor to afford the costs of emigration.

Filipina migrants leave or send children back to the Philippines in order to mediate other structural forces of globalization, including the unequal level of economic development between sending and receiving nations and the rise of anti-immigrant sentiments. Negotiating the unequal development of regions in the global economy, migrant Filipina domestic workers mother from a distance to take advantage of the lower costs of reproducing—feeding, housing, clothing, and educating—the family in the Third World. In doing so, they are able to provide their families with a secure middle-class lifestyle. The lesser costs of reproduction in sending countries, such as the Philippines, enable them to provide greater material benefits for their children, including the luxury of paid domestic help and more comfortable housing as opposed to cramped living quarters forced by high rents in global cities. In this way, the family can expedite its goals of accumulating savings and property.

Migrants also form transnational households in response to the pressure of nativism in receiving societies. Nativist grassroots organizations (e.g., Americans for Immigration Control and *Lega* in Northern Italy) aimed at the further restriction and exclusion of immigration have sprouted throughout the United States and Italy.[16] With anti-immigrant sentiments brewing,

migrant parents may not want to expose their children to the racial tensions and anti-immigrant sentiments fostered by the social and cultural construction of low-wage migrants as undesirable citizens. These structural constraints prolong the length of family separation in migration as it may even extend to a span of a life cycle. Among my interviewees, for example, the length of separation between mothers and their now-adult children extends to sixteen years.

The Pain of Mothering from a Distance

When the girl that I take care of calls her mother "Mama," my heart jumps all the time because my children also call me "Mama.". . . I begin thinking that at this hour I should be taking care of my very own children and not someone else's, someone who is not related to me in any way, shape, or form. . . . The work that I do here is done for my family, but the problem is they are not close to me but are far away in the Philippines. Sometimes, you feel the separation and you start to cry. Some days, I just start crying while I am sweeping the floor because I am thinking about my children in the Philippines. Sometimes, when I receive a letter from my children telling me that they are sick, I look up out the window and ask the Lord to look after them and make sure they get better even without me around to care after them. (Starts crying.) **If I had wings, I would fly home to my children. Just for a moment, to see my children and take care of their needs, help them, then fly back over here to continue my work.** *(Author's emphasis.) (Rosemarie Samaniego, widowed, Rome, migrated in 1991, children are ten, twelve, fifteen, eighteen, and nineteen years old.)*[17]

Every day Filipina domestic workers such as Rosemarie Samaniego are overwhelmed by feelings of helplessness: they are trapped in the painful contradiction of feeling the distance from their families and having to depend on the material benefits of their separation. They may long to reunite with their children but cannot, because they need their earnings to sustain their families.

Emotional strains of transnational mothering include feelings of anxiety, helplessness, loss, guilt, and the burden of loneliness. Mothers negotiate these emotional strains in three central ways: the commodification of love; the repression of emotional strains; and the rationalization of distance, that is, they use regulation communication to ease distance. In general, individual women use all three coping mechanisms, although not always consciously. For the most part, they justify their decision to leave their children behind in the Philippines by highlighting the material gains of the family. And they struggle to maintain a semblance of family life by rationalizing distance. Although a few women explicitly deny the emotional strains imposed by separation on their children, most women admit to the emotional difficulties that they themselves feel.

Knowing that they have missed the growing years of children, mothers admit experiencing loss of intimacy in transnational families. In general, a

surreal timelessness is felt during separation that is suddenly catapulted back to reality the moment the family reunites.

> *When I came home, my daughters were teenagers already.* (Starts crying.) *When I saw my family, I dropped my bag and asked who were my daughters. I did not know who they were but they just kept on screaming, "Inay, Inay!" [Mom, Mom!] I asked them who was who and they said, "I'm Sally and I'm Sandra." We were crying. I did not know who was who. Imagine! But they were so small when I left and there they were as teenagers.* . . . (Ermie Contado, widowed, Rome, migrated in 1981, daughters followed her in early 1990s.)

Confronted with the absence of familiarity, transnational mothers often feel an unsurmountable loss over their prolonged separation from their children.

For the women in my study, this pain is usually aggravated by caretaking tasks of domestic work. Taking care of children is not just taking care of children when, in the process of doing so, one cannot take care of one's own children. This contradiction accentuates the pain of domestic work and results in their simultaneous aversion and desire for this job. Ruby Mercado, a domestic worker, states: *"Domestic work is depressing . . . you especially miss your children. I do not like taking care of other children when I could not take care of my own. It hurts too much."* Although a few domestic workers resolve this tension by avoiding childcare, many also resolve it by "pouring love," including Trinidad Borromeo, who states, *"When I take care of an elderly, I treat her like she is my own mother."*

As I have noted, transnational mothers cope with the emotional tensions of mothering from a distance by commodifying love. In the field, I often heard women say: "I buy everything that my children need" or "I give them everything they want." Transnational parents knowingly or unknowingly have the urge to overcompensate for their absence with material goods. Ruby Mercado states:

> *All the things that my children needed I gave to them and even more because I know that I have not fulfilled my motherly duties completely. Because we were apart (since 1983), there have been needs that I have not met. I try to hide that gap by giving them all the material things that they desire and want. I feel guilty because as a mother I have not been able to care for their daily needs. **So, because I am lacking in giving them maternal love, I fill that gap with many material goods.*** . . . (Author's emphasis.)

Unable to provide her four children (now between the ages of eighteen and twenty-six) with daily acts of caregiving, Ruby, not unlike other transnational mothers, feels insecure about the emotional bonds in her family. As a result, she has come to rely on commodities to establish concrete ties of familial dependency.

Transnational parents struggle with and do have regrets over separation, but they are able to withstand these hardships because of the financial gains that they have achieved in migration.

> *I have been lonely here. I have thought about the Philippines while I am scrubbing and mopping that floor. You cannot help but ask yourself what are you doing*

here scrubbing and being apart from your family. Then, you think about the money and know that you have no choice but to be here. (Incarnacion Molina, separated, Rome, migrated in 1991, two daughters in late adolescence.)

By working outside of the Philippines, parents obtain the financial resources that they need to ensure that their children eat daily meals of meat and rice, attend college, and have secure housing.

Although many migrant laborers outside of the Philippines have attained some years of postsecondary education, they have not been able to achieve a "secure" middle-class lifestyle in the Philippines. So, why do they bother to invest in their children's college education? The education of children is a marker of material security for migrant parents. It is a central motivating factor for migration. As a domestic worker states, *"The intelligence of my children would be wasted if they don't attain a college degree, that's why I made up my mind and I prayed a lot that I have a chance to go abroad for the sake of my children's education."*[18] Parents believe that the more educated children there are in their families, the greater the resources of the family and the lesser the dependence of family members on each other, which means there would be less need for a family member to work outside of the Philippines in order to support other members of the family.

Migrant mothers also cope with separation by repressing the emotional tensions in transnational families. Considering that larger structural forces of globalization deny migrant Filipina domestic workers the right to family reunification, they sometimes cannot afford to confront their feelings. As Dorothy Espiritu—a widowed domestic worker in Los Angeles who left her four (now adult) children between the ages of nine and eighteen—explains, lingering over the painful sacrifice of separation only intensifies the emotional hardships of providing the family with material security.

In answer to my question of whether it has been difficult not seeing her children for twelve years, she answered:

If you say it is hard, it is hard. You could easily be overwhelmed by the loneliness you feel as a mother, but then you have to have the foresight to overcome that. Without the foresight for the future of your children, then you have a harder time. If I had not had the foresight, my children would not be as secure as they are now. They would not have had a chance. (Pauses.) *What I did was I put the loneliness aside. I put everything aside. I put the sacrifice aside. Everything. Now, I am happy that all of them have completed college.*

Although mothers usually admit that emotional strains are engendered by geographical distance, they also tend to repress them. In fact, some of my interviewees strategically cope with physical distance by completely denying its emotional costs. It had primarily been mothers who had two sets of children, one in the Philippines and the other abroad, who preferred not to discuss intergenerational relationships at all.

Despite their tendency to downplay the emotional tensions wrought by the formation of transnational households, migrant mothers struggle to amend this loss by regularly keeping in contact with their children in the Philippines.

To fulfill their mothering role from afar, they compress time and space and attempt to counter the physical distance in the family via the telephone and letter writing. Most of my interviewees phone and write their children at least once every two weeks. In doing so, they keep abreast of their children's activities and at the same time achieve a certain level of familiarity and intimacy. As Patricia Baclayon of Los Angeles states: *"There is nothing wrong with our relationship. I pay a lot for the phone bill. Last month, I paid $170 and that's two days of wages. They write too. Last week, I received four letters."*

Ironically, the rationalization of transnational distance in the family, while reassuring for parents, could be stifling for children in the Philippines. At the very least, parents are more likely to consider prolonging separation, as they are reassured that separation is manageable and does not mean the loss of intimacy. The "power geometry" in the process of time-space compression is elucidated by feminist geographer Doreen Massey as having created distinct experiences:

> This point concerns not merely the issue of who moves and who doesn't although that is an important element of it; it is also about power in relation to the flows and the movement. Different social groups [in this case, mothers and children] have distinct relationships to this anyway differentiated mobility: some people are more in charge of it than others; some initiate flows and movement, others don't; some are more on the receiving end of it than others; some are effectively imprisoned by it.[19]

In transnational families, power clearly lies with the parent, in particular the migrant parent. The process of time-space compression is unidirectional with children at the receiving end. Migrant parents initiate calls as children receive them. Migrant parents remit money to children physically immobilized in the Philippines. Children are trapped as time-space compression convinces parents that they have maintained close-knit ties and allows them to keep their children waiting even longer.

From the commodification of love to the "technological" management of distance, my interviewees have found many ways to cope with family separation. Although they ease the barriers that spatial distance has imposed on their families, many still feel that intimacy can only be fully achieved with great investment in time and daily interactions in the family.

The Pain of Growing Up in Transnational Families

Regardless of household structure, whether it is nuclear, single parent, or transnational, intergenerational conflicts frequently arise in the family. As many feminist scholars have argued, the family is not a collective unit. Instead, the family represents an institution with conflicting interests, priorities, and concerns for its members. In transnational households, intergenerational conflicts are engendered by the emotional strains of family life.

Children also suffer from the emotional costs of geographical distance with feelings of loneliness, insecurity, and vulnerability. They also crave

greater intimacy with their migrant parents. For example, the children in Victoria Paz Cruz's survey offer several reasons for their desire to reunite with their migrant parents: "I want them to share with us in our daily life and I want our family to be complete"; "So that they will be there when we need them"; and "We can share our laughters and tears."[20] Denied the intimacy of daily interactions, children struggle to understand the motives behind their mothers' decision to raise them from a distance. Unfortunately, they do not necessarily do so successfully.

Three central conflicts plague intergenerational relationships between migrant mothers and the children whom they have left behind in the Philippines. First, children disagree with their mothers that commodities are sufficient markers of love. Second, they do not believe that their mothers recognize the sacrifices that children have made toward the successful maintenance of the family. Finally, although they appreciate the efforts of migrant mothers to show affection and care, they still question the extent of their efforts. They particularly question mothers for their sporadic visits to the Philippines. As I have noted, most of the mothers whom I interviewed return to the Philippines infrequently, once every four years. . . .

Conclusion

Although enabling the family to maximize its earnings, the formation of female-headed transnational households also involves an emotional upheaval in the lives of transnational mothers and the children whom they have left behind in the Philippines. A central paradox in the maintenance of such households is the achievement of financial security going hand in hand with an increase in emotional insecurity, an impact that could however be softened by an alteration of the traditional gender ideologies in the family.

In mapping out the emotional wounds imposed by geographical distance on mothers and children in transnational households, I do not mean to imply that these wounds can only be healed by the return of migrating mothers. Nor do I mean to suggest that mothers are somehow at fault for deciding to maximize their earning potential by working abroad and leaving children behind in the Philippines. The root causes of these wounds extend beyond the individual female migrant to larger structural inequalities that constrain the options that they have to provide their children with material, emotional, and moral care to the fullest. Various structural inequalities of globalization force them to sacrifice their emotional needs and those of their children for the material needs of the family. These inequalities include legal barriers preventing the migration of dependents; social stratification and the segregation of Filipino migrant workers to informal service employment in most host societies; economic globalization and the unequal level of development among nations; postindustrialization and the demand for female migrant workers; and the rise of anti-immigrant sentiments in receiving nations.

These emotional wounds are telling of the "stalled revolution" faced by women at the beginning of this millennium as they have yet to achieve

full gender parity at home and at work.[21] The ideological foundation of the Filipino family has yet to experience a major rupture even with the high rate of women's labor force participation. The responsibility for emotional care remains with women even in families with fathers who provide a tremendous amount of emotional care to their children and mothers who give a great deal of material care. It is true that feelings of pain in transnational families are fostered by separation; however, they are undoubtedly intensified by the failure in a great number of families to meet the gender-based expectations of children for mothers (and not fathers) to nurture them and also the self-imposed expectations of mothers to follow culturally and ideologically inscribed duties in the family. As shown by the emotional tensions wrought by separation and the greater resentment of children about transnational mothers, rather than fathers, traditional notions of mothering haunt migrant women transnationally. Traditional views still have a deep hold on the most basic values of the youth in the Philippines. However, we can only hope that the "reconstitution of mothering" led by numerous female migrants from the Philippines will eventually seep into and shift the consciousness, values, and ideologies of the general public toward the acceptance of multiple variances of family life.

ENDNOTES

Author's Note: This article benefited from comments and suggestions shared by Arlie Hochschild, Charlotte Chiu, Angela Gallegos, Mimi Motoyoshi, Jennifer Lee, and three anonymous readers. The University of California President's Office, Babilonia Wilner Foundation, and the Graduate School of University of Wisconsin, Madison, provided support during the writing of this article.

[1] See Victoria Paz Cruz, *Seasonal Orphans and Solo Parents: The Impacts of Overseas Migration* (Quezon City, Philippines: Scalabrini Migration Center, 1987); and Maruja Asis, "The Overseas Employment Program," in *Philippine Labor Migration: Impact and Policy,* ed. Graziano Battistella and Anthony Paganoni (Quezon City, Philippines: Scalabrini Migration Center, 1992), 68–112.

[2] By social reproduction, I refer, as defined by Barbara Laslett and Johanna Brenner, to "the activities and attitudes, behaviors and emotions, responsibilities and relationships directly involved in the maintenance of life on a daily basis, and intergenerationally." See Barrie Thorne, "Feminism and the Family: Two Decades of Thought," in *Rethinking the Family: Some Feminist Questions,* ed. Barrie Thorne and Marilyn Yalom, rev. ed. (Boston: Northwestern University Press, 1992), 3–30.

[3] For an excellent article on the reconstitution of mothering in transnational households, see Pierrette Hondagneu-Sotelo and Ernestine Avila, "'I'm Here, but I'm There': The Meanings of Latina Transnational Motherhood," *Gender and Society* 11 (October 1997): 548–71. For a discussion of gender ideologies in the Philippines, see Delia Aguilar, *The Feminist Challenge: Initial Working Principles toward Reconceptualizing the Feminist Movement in the Philippines* (Metro Manila, Philippines: Asian Social Institute, 1988).

[4] Evelyn Nakano Glenn, "Split Household, Small Producer, and Dual Wage Earner: An Analysis of Chinese-American Family Strategies," *Journal of Marriage and the Family* 19 (February 1983): 35–46.

[5] Arlie Hochschild, *The Managed Heart: Commercialization of Human Feeling* (Berkeley: University of California Press, 1983), 85.

[6] See Belinda Medina, *The Filipino Family: A Text with Selected Readings* (Quezon City, Philippines: University of the Philippines Press, 1991).

[7] Examples of such studies include Christine Chin, *In Service and Servitude: Foreign Female Domestic Workers and the Malaysian "Modernity" Project* (New York: Columbia University Press, 1998); and Catholic Institute for International Relations, *The Labour Trade: Filipino Migrant Workers around the Globe* (London: Catholic Institute for International Relations, 1987).

[8] Pierrette Hondagneu-Sotelo, *Gendered Transitions: Mexican Experiences of Migration* (Berkeley: University of California Press, 1994).

[9] For excellent discussions on the labor market incorporation of migrants in urban centers of globalization, see Saskia Sassen, *The Mobility and Flow of Labor and Capital* (New York: Cambridge University Press, 1988), and *Cities in a World Economy* (Thousand Oaks, Calif.: Pine Forge Press, 1994).

[10] See Chin.

[11] For a discussion of the "denationalization" and "renationalization" of societies in globalization, see Saskia Sassen, *Losing Control? Sovereignty in an Age of Globalization* (New York: Columbia University Press, 1996).

[12] For instance, see Chin.

[13] See Abigail Bakan and Daiva Stasiulis, introduction to *Not One of the Family: Foreign Domestic Workers in Canada*, ed. Abigail Bakan and Daiva Stasiulis (Toronto: University of Toronto Press, 1997), 3–27.

[14] See Mary Lou Alcid, "Legal and Organizational Support Mechanisms for Foreign Domestic Workers," in *The Trade in Domestic Workers*, ed. Noeleen Heyzer et al. (London: Zed Books, 1994), 161–77; and Pei-Chia Lan, "Bounded Commodity in a Global Market: Migrant Workers in Taiwan" (paper presented at the Annual Meeting of the Society for the Study of Social Problems, Chicago, 6–8 Aug. 1999).

[15] Rhacel Salazar Parreñas, "Migrant Filipina Domestic Workers and the International Division of Reproductive Labor," *Gender and Society* 14 (August 2000): 560–80.

[16] See the anthology edited by Juan Perea, *Immigrants Out! The New Nativism and the Anti-immigrant Impulse in the United States* (New York: New York University Press, 1997).

[17] I use pseudonyms to protect the anonymity of my informants.

[18] Gloria Acgaoili, "Mother, Behold Your Child," *Tinig Filipino*, May 1995, 14. Italicized sections are translated from Tagalog to English.

[19] Doreen Massey, *Space, Place, and Gender* (Minneapolis: University of Minnesota Press, 1994), 149.

[20] Paz Cruz, 43.

[21] Arlie Hochschild with Anne Machung, *The Second Shift* (New York: Avon Books, 1989).

23

MOTHERING FOR THE STATE
Foster Parenting and the Challenges
of Government-Contracted Carework

TERESA TOGUCHI SWARTZ

We are witnessing a major reorganization of the ways that care is administered in the contemporary United States. Because demographic shifts have escalated care needs at the same time as women, who have traditionally provided care in families, have moved into the labor market, care is becoming more frequently performed by paid

workers. Consequently, one-fifth of the total workforce now works in the "care industries" (Folbre 2001:55). Among the many questions precipitated by this major social transformation, some of the most immediate and controversial revolve around the impact of pay and market rationality on the quality and character of care (Cancian 2000; Folbre and Nelson 2000; Harrington Meyer 2000; Nelson 1999). . . . It is feared that economic incentives and care cannot coincide but are in fact oppositional. My own experience as a researcher of foster care provides a case in point. When I tell people that I am doing research in the area, one question inevitably comes up: "But," someone interjects, "do foster parents do it for the money?"

Informed by such concerns, some policy-minded economists have argued that compensation to careworkers should remain limited so that altruistic motivations remain predominant and workers primarily interested in paychecks are not attracted to the work. Furthermore, there is a concern that financial remuneration will change even those initially inspired by benevolence by crowding out caring feelings and replacing them with self-interested considerations. The worry becomes that caregivers will provide services for money, rather than altruism, ultimately diminishing the quality of care. Such assumptions may have contributed to the "care penalty" charged to wages for occupations that involve carework (England, Budig, and Folbre 2002).

Feminist scholars challenge the necessary dichotomy between altruism and payment, pointing to its gender bias—that this concern about extrinsic rewards undermining intrinsic motivations is applied to caregiving work traditionally performed by women and is not similarly applied to intrinsically rewarding work historically performed by men (Nelson 1999; Ungerson 1990). The social construction that women are naturally suited to be care providers reproduces gender inequalities by burdening women with greater care responsibilities and justifying no or low pay for carework (Abel and Nelson 1990; Harrington Meyer 2000:6; Hooyman and Gonyea 1995). . . . Folbre and Nelson (2000) asserted that pay will not necessarily flatten social relations or make care impersonal but that money flow can be embedded in rich social relationships and is shaped by social norms and policies (see also Nelson 1999). Rather than the mere existence of payment, other features associated with the organization of care in states and markets shape care quality (Abel and Nelson 1990; Cancian 2000; Ungerson 1990). Care can be provided for both love and money, for reasons associated with both the public and private spheres. . . .

Foster care provides a rich setting to examine the ways in which payment and social organization influence the distribution and quality of care. Although the number of children under state protection continues to grow, very little is known about the motivations and experiences of the foster parents who care for them. What we hear from the media about foster families often includes horrific stories about neglectful and even abusive foster parents who take in children for monetary gain, reflecting cultural suspicions of paid care in private families. Despite these portrayals, empirical research finds that nationally, children are not more likely to be abused in foster homes

than in birth homes (Gelles 1996) and that foster children report positive relationships with their foster parents (Barbell 1999). Yet the concern over a foster care crisis is justified given the escalating numbers of foster children, the instability of placements, and the poorer health and well-being of foster children. It is unclear how foster family intentions and the ways these interact with the system contribute to these problems. This [reading] draws on several years of ethnographic research with foster parents in a state-contracted nonprofit agency to investigate foster parents' motives, as well as the effects of compensation and state supervision on foster parents' carework. . . .

Data and Method

. . . Los Angeles County is a particularly important site to investigate foster care in that it is the largest foster care system in the nation, with higher rates of foster child abuse and death than national averages (The Alliance for Children's Rights 2004; Anderson 2003). For 22 months, I engaged in intensive participant observation with the agency, 15 months as a foster care social worker. The ethnography focused on 42 foster families and 25 foster care professionals. My fieldwork was supplemented by observations and interactions with hundreds of other foster families and dozens of professionals associated with the agency during five years of contact. On leaving the field, I conducted semistructured, in-depth interviews with 18 foster parents and 13 professionals averaging 1½ to 2 hours. The agency's and individuals' names have been changed to preserve confidentiality.

The 42 foster families at Hope Children's Services that are the focus of the research reported here were predominantly working-class, high school educated, married couples with children. . . . Half of the foster parents (35) identified as Latino/Hispanic, 26 identified as white, and 9 identified as Black. Hope foster families earned a median annual income of $31,080 in 1995 when the median family income was $45,200 in Los Angeles. Most foster parents who worked outside of their homes labored in blue-collar or service occupations. All of the 28 foster fathers and 14 single foster mothers worked outside of their homes, as did 2 of the married foster mothers. Most of the married Hope foster mothers (26 of 28) stayed home full-time, including 10 who generated income from their homes in addition to foster care stipends through in-home day care or babysitting. Hope foster parents received a stipend of $500 to $600 per month per child for foster care. . . .

Part 1: The Multiple Motivations to Foster Parent

Economic and Family Care Realities of Contemporary Working-Class Foster Families

Most foster parents at Hope Children's Services were from the working class. Generally, they had spent their adult work lives laboring for hourly pay at jobs in factories, restaurants, retail, and other manufacturing and

service positions. The economic restructuring of the late twentieth century and the economic downturn of the early 1990s fostered employment instability and feelings of financial insecurity in these families (Newman 1993). In addition, declining real wages and decreased government benefits combined to require these families to expand the total number of paid work hours. Couples relied on dual earners, while single mother–led families looked for second jobs or other ways to increase income.

Several strategies have been taken up by mothers seeking to balance provider and caregiver responsibilities. Some families purchase childcare and other domestic services, engage in split-shift childcare, or rely on extended family and fictive kin for support (Rubin 1994; Uttal 1996, 1999). Others attempt to work and earn money from home, combining paid labor and unpaid family labor in the same location (Christensen 1987). Many Hope foster mothers attempted this strategy as they dealt with the dilemmas of coordinating work and family. Most Hope foster mothers viewed their participation in foster care as their work, albeit a multifaceted kind of work. Foster parenting was heavily gendered, as foster mothers provided the majority of care to children and bore the daily responsibilities of organizing foster children's lives, interacting with social workers, and managing relations with biological parents. Like other forms of home-based work, foster mothering reflected the class educational and employment experiences of the women who pursued it. Hope foster mothers considered their previous work histories, their current opportunities, their skills, and their competing obligations when they decided to pursue foster care as an option. The ways in which Hope foster families attempted to reconcile economic and family care needs through foster care is illustrated with a few of their stories.

Rosa and Jaime Hernandez were a lower-working-class Latino couple in their mid-forties and the parents of two teenagers. When I met Jaime, he was a dockworker who worked long hours for pay that could not fully support his family of four ($1,000 per month for more than 40 hours per week). Although they both held traditional family ideals and wanted Rosa to remain at home full-time with their children, Rosa had to work throughout their marriage. When their children were young, Rosa worked at McDonald's, scheduling her hours opposite to Jaime's schedule so that one of them could be home with their children. However, Rosa quit when the managers changed and refused to consider her family needs. Given Rosa's education, her skills, and the job market, she was limited to low-paying service-sector work. When her teenaged son was arrested and required to wear an ankle surveillance band, Rosa decided that she had to find some way to stay home. Reflecting her adherence to traditional gender ideologies, Rosa blamed herself for her son's trouble and believed that if she had stayed home, this would not have happened. A friend encouraged Rosa to become a foster mother so that she could earn needed income while at the same time being an at-home mother. Foster care enabled Rosa, and foster mothers like her, to fulfill her perceived maternal obligations while at the same time earning needed income.

Although most of the families in this study were working class, this strategy was used in some middle-class foster families as well. For example,

white middle-class Debbie Watson also aspired to provide around-the-clock mother care to her child. *"Before I started with foster care, I had a career in word processing. But Cassie would cry every day when I left the house for work. . . . I want to stay home and be a mom. . . . I think it's important that I stay home with Cassie. I know she needs me"* (white, married, middle-class woman, 30s). To sustain a middle-class lifestyle, Debbie needed to earn an income, but she also wanted to stay home. Debbie tried home-based medical billing but said she wanted to do something more meaningful. Thus, intrinsic and extrinsic motivations including her preferred traditional family structure, beliefs about her daughter's needs, her need for income, and her desire to make a meaningful contribution led her to foster parenting. . . . These traditional families masked women's economic contribution, as foster mothers' work remained invisible in the private sphere and resembled the work they did daily as mothers.

Working-class single mothers who fostered expressed similar motivations to their married, stay-at-home counterparts. Economic difficulties also forced these women to look for options to augment their income. These single mothers saw foster care as a means to maximize time with their children while increasing their resources. For example, white single mother Tracy Greaves worked as a cashier at a large supermarket. At first, Tracy was very happy with her job, citing the fact that her manager scheduled her hours so that she could be home with her seven-year-old daughter after school. However, a new supervisor refused to consider Tracy's family responsibilities in scheduling, arguing it would not be fair to childless coworkers. Tracy found that she spent more on babysitting than she could afford, and she hated not being able to spend afternoons with her daughter. Tracy took up foster parenting to enable her to be home with her daughter and new foster child some days after school. Like many foster mothers, Tracy also found this work much more meaningful than the kind of paid work she had previously done and appreciated the work–family balance it facilitated.

Both married and single women became foster mothers for the important tangible rewards of simultaneously meeting family financial and care needs. However, a multitude of intangible rewards also motivated these women to become foster mothers.

The Gendered Expertise of Family Carework

One of the worries about paying care providers is that money will attract people who do not care about recipients or who are incompetent at the work, but the evidence from this case study contradicts these presuppositions. Hope foster mothers understood themselves as skilled caregivers. Indeed, this was the area in which they felt most competent because they had years of experience doing this kind of work. They relayed a work history that detailed specific experiences through which they had developed the skills relevant to their informal careers as caregivers. While other occupations may not have valued these skills, they believed that foster care offered them paid work not only in which they were competent but in which they were experts.

Foster mothers developed caregiving skills through gender socialization and the gender modeling of their mothers. As Alisa Ramsey describes, *"I've had a lot of experience with babies and children. When I was growing up, my mother took care of her own kids and foster children. . . . She was so busy, but it was wonderful. I would help my mother take care of the babies. . . . So I wanted to grow up and be a mother, and that's what I did. I grew up and had four children. And now I have foster children too"* (white, working-class, single woman, 50s). Not only did these women watch and identify with their mothers, they learned to provide care through hands-on practice. As they grew up, they helped take care of younger siblings, and babysitting was a regular part of their pre-adolescent and adolescent life. Thus, caregiving was an important aspect of how they learned to do gender. . . . From their perspective, caring for foster children was a continuation of what they had spent their lives doing. Take, for instance, Glenda Frederickson: *"After my mother passed away when I was nine years old, I had to take care of myself and my brothers and sisters. . . . I know how to take care of children and a house; I've been doing it all my life. Then I raised my own eight kids . . . and now I can take care of these kids who need me"* (white, working-class, married woman, 60s).

Hope foster mothers understood their caregiving skills as developed through experiential learning and believed experience made them competent caregivers. Given their class backgrounds and their relationship to formal education, it was not surprising that they considered experience more important than credentials or formal training or that they questioned the legitimacy of advice from childless social workers, like myself at that time.

These foster mothers constructed their sense of self and assessment of their caregiving expertise in relation to their opportunities in the market and social structure. Most of these women had experienced paid employment that was heavily monitored, controlled, and inflexible. They frequently expressed sentiments such as, *"When I'm a mother and watch kids, I'm my own boss. I control what I do and set my own schedule"* (Mindy Lewis, white, working-class, single woman, early 30s). These comments were made in comparison to their previous work experiences in food service, retail, and factory work. Like other domestic workers, they believed this work offered greater flexibility than other occupations available to them (Romero 1992). Within the context of family cultural systems and economic structures, class and gender interacted and prompted these women to seek paid opportunities that allowed them to utilize their well-developed caretaking skills within the home, which they expected would offer greater autonomy and authority than they had experienced in other work environments. . . .

Called to Care: Tangible Successes, Gendered Desires, and Giving to the Community

Cancian and Oliker (2000:87) argued that women are more often drawn to caregiving work than are men because it utilizes skills they learned growing up and because they have learned to view altruistic, emotionally sensitive caregiving as confirming their feminine identity. Foster care enabled Hope

foster mothers to do work that they believed to be highly valuable and that confirmed their gendered identities as caring and other-centered people. *"There are so many children out there now who need a safe and loving place to live. So many parents on drugs, who don't pay any attention to their kids or who abuse them. . . . We can help these kids. We can show them what it is like to have a loving family so that maybe when they grow up they can make a loving family too"* (Diana Ortega, Latina, lower-middle-class, married woman, 20s).

Specific aspects of this work made it meaningful in different ways for different parents. First, foster mothers gained satisfaction from the positive changes they observed in their foster children. Foster parents viewed these changes as resulting from the love and quality care they offered that they believed was missing from the children's biological homes. Debbie Watson discusses how her love changed children: *"We have really helped the children that have stayed in our home. I think we have given life to lifeless children. Like Michael, he came to me as a limp noodle. He was three months old and had no life in him. I just loved him and gave him room to grow. I have so much love to give, and it really changes children's lives when all you do is give them love"* (white, middle-class, married woman, 30s).

Of course, definitions of quality care varied by class and race. Debbie's comments reflected white, middle-class notions of intensive motherhood that emphasized love and attention (Hays 1996). Many Latino and white working-class parents in this sample stressed other elements in their child-rearing, focusing on the discipline and practical skills that had proved valuable in their own lives (Kohn 1969; Lareau 2003). Yet for both working-class and middle-class families, foster care was meaningful work because it changed children in ways perceived to be important.

There were several differences between the cultural perspectives and life situations of the working-class mothers and the few middle-class women without biological children. One particularly noteworthy difference, given the controversial nature of foster family payments, was that the middle-class women without biological children did not need the money. Even so, these women's stories were similarly gendered, involving their desire to mother.

The case of Gina Tilly illustrates the experiences of this group of women. Gina was a single, white, 36-year-old, college-educated woman who constructed a life history oriented around helping others, including a childhood filled with volunteerism and babysitting. Aspiring to go into a helping profession, she was dissuaded by a college counselor who advised her to go into business instead. Gina always assumed she would marry and become a mother but felt that at 36, her chances of getting married and having biological children were fading. Gina became a foster parent to fulfill her life ambition of helping others and mothering:

> *Ever since I was in junior high, I wanted to help people, but a college counselor talked me out of it. . . . I always expected to have a lot of children—I wanted 10 kids. So far, I've had 9 foster children. . . . I had no grand dreams; I just expected to be married and have children . . . but as I got older, it was clear that I was not going to get married. But I still wanted kids. . . . My whole*

life I wanted to hold babies. . . . When I first got into foster care, I thought I'd have just one child. But I didn't realize what it would bring to my life. (white, middle-class, single woman, 30s)

Gina's successful business career brought her several times the income she earned foster parenting, yet her dream was to stop working in business and devote her life to nurturing children. *"If it was possible, I wouldn't work and would take care of these kids full time. . . . My dream is to open a group home. . . . It's in the works. I'm getting a house with my sister that is big enough for us and six kids."*

Like other foster mothers in this study, Gina needed money to do the good work of caring for children, but it did not stand as the primary rationale for fostering. A cynic might suggest that these foster parents used the culturally acceptable rhetoric of care for children but really were driven by financial concerns. I would argue against this perspective. The case is clearest for Gina and other middle-class foster mothers who had more lucrative options for employment. She regularly spent more money on the children than the stipends provided. Foster payments were fixed, with no market incentives for better care, yet she (and others) continually tried to improve the care.

Based on a mothering model, both working-class and middle-class foster mothers reaped rich rewards as they built affectionate bonds and deep emotional attachments with foster children. Caring for foster children became integrally tied with caring about these foster children (Abel and Nelson 1990). Rather than having their feelings for children flattened out due to payment, these foster mothers grew personally attached to the children they cared for daily. Hope foster mothers experienced these loving relationships with foster children as important rewards of their work.

A final source of meaning some women derived from fostering involved the ways that race and ethnicity intersected with gender and class. . . . Latino families explicitly spoke of the ways they understood foster care as a kind of ethnic community care. They believed by taking in Latino children that they were helping Latino families and ultimately the Latino community: *"We want to do this because we want to do something for our people—you know, Mexicans. There are a lot of Mexicans in our old neighborhood [East Los Angeles] . . . that we see that have a lot of problems with their families and with money. We can help them"* (Albert Flores, working-class, Mexican American, married man, 60s).

Connected with this, Latino families often identified with Latino biological families in ways that white foster families seldom did. Latino foster families recognized that they shared with children's biological families similar ethnic, linguistic, and cultural backgrounds, as well as experiences with oppression and discrimination. What is more, they had experienced economic and other hardship in their own lives and believed that a supportive family was essential to overcoming adversity. Sympathizing with the often young, single mothers who had their children removed, they tried to serve as surrogate extended family networks not only for the children but often also for the mothers. In short, many Latino families subscribed to a communal ideal of families that included "fictive kin" (Stack 1974). The nature of

this family vision was evidenced by the way children often referred to their Latino foster parents as *tia* and *tio*—aunt and uncle.

Many Latino foster parents relayed that they wanted to help children maintain cultural and linguistic ties to their biological families and their broader ethnic community with such activities as speaking Spanish to foster children, teaching them Mexican cooking, and taking them to Catholic Mass. In my experience, children felt more at ease in these families with familiar cultural patterns. These relationships facilitated reunification by keeping mothers involved with their kids rather than feeling isolated from them.

All of this was also an important motivation for Latino foster parents in this work and stood in contrast to white foster parents, who did not bring up ethnic and racial motives. I suggest this was due to the invisibility and "taken for grantedness" of whiteness and inattention to race more generally in the white families (Frankenberg 1993). In addition, white respondents more commonly adhered to a private, nuclear family ideal that did not include, or necessitate, fictive kin support systems.

Nakano Glenn argued that caregiving is devalued in the United States due to its relegation to the private sphere and to women (2000:84–85). It is even further devalued, she continued, because caregiving is often performed by people with low status with regard to race, class, or immigration (p. 86). While foster parenting, and carework in general, carries little respect in the larger public culture, Hope foster mothers believed they were doing some of the most important work in society. These findings suggest that even though economic interests are important to foster mothers, they pose little danger of crowding out other deeply embedded intrinsic motivations. However, what did threaten to crowd out or undermine intrinsic motivations were the arrangements of state regulation and professional supervision that I will discuss in the following section.

Part 2: Foster Parents and the Challenges of State-Supervised Carework

Hope foster parents and professionals (echoing U.S. foster care policy as a whole) assumed that children in the system should be placed in private families and care should be based on an intensive mothering model. However, this ideal was never fully realized in actual foster parenting practice because the state and professionals regulated and supervised their mothering. At least four challenges to foster mothers emerged in the context of state oversight. These included the undermining of foster mother competence, their lack of authority, the disruption of their traditional families, and pervasive suspicions about foster mother commitment due to financial interests.

Undermining Foster Mother Competence

To ensure child safety, agency and state regulations required parenting training, weekly social worker home visits, professionally developed and supervised treatment plans, and mandated reporting of all health, psychological,

or behavioral problems. At Hope foster parent orientation, the agency director informed foster parents that "monitoring of your childrearing with the foster child will be done by our agency." In so doing, she conveyed the message that ultimate authority remained with the agency. Thus, although foster mothers were drawn to foster care because it utilized their caregiving expertise, agency and professional childrearing guidance challenged their competence. Because foster mothers valued experiential knowledge over formal knowledge, they often questioned such advice: *"I know more about kids than most social workers. Most social workers that I've met don't even have kids. How are they supposed to tell me what to do if they don't have any children of their own? They might read a lot of books, but if you haven't had a kid in your house 24 hours a day, you really don't know what you're talking about"* (Glenda Frederickson, white, working-class, married woman, 60s). Through foster mothers' eyes, Hope professionals did not really understand children because they had little experience raising children themselves. Working-class foster mothers became especially annoyed with social workers' middle-class expressive communication and discipline styles, which they found unfamiliar and ineffective. Foster mothers experienced the assertion of expert perspectives as discounting their abilities in the domain at which they felt most competent.

On the other hand, social workers viewed their expertise, grounded in science (and validated by their white, middle-class childrearing ideologies and experiences), as more legitimate than foster parents' experiential knowledge. One social worker describes such friction: *"[A challenge] is with foster parents that can be strong willed, well you know the attitude that 'I know what I'm doing, I've raised so many children'"* (Sue, white, middle-class woman, 30s).

It was not just social worker advice that challenged foster mother competence at caregiving. Foster mothers experienced state and agency reporting expectations as unwarranted micromanagement and an indication that their parenting skills were not trusted. State regulations, aimed to protect children, mandated that foster parents report every illness and injury, regardless of the severity. Given the frequency of children's minor ailments, compliant foster mothers were regularly informing agency workers of these problems.

> *It's ridiculous that we have to report every scraped knee or runny nose. Kids . . . are constantly falling down and bumping into things. It doesn't mean that I'm a bad parent. . . . Like when Jimmy was here, he was learning to walk, so he fell down. Nicole [her social worker] said that there were too many incidents and that I had to put him in a playpen. Well, I don't believe in playpens. How is he supposed to learn to walk if he's in a playpen? Well, Nicole wouldn't know; she may be the social worker, but she doesn't know about kids, she doesn't even have any.* (Debbie Watson, white, middle-class, married woman, 30s)

Foster parents worried that too many incidents would be interpreted as poor caregiving and would lead to unfavorable evaluations by social workers who had the institutional authority to remove children and decertify their foster homes. Despite the worthy goal of keeping children safe, foster parents felt that the majority of incidents involved minor childhood problems that should be left to them to handle without the interference of

professionals or excessive judgment. . . . Foster mothers who entered foster care in part because they were skilled caregivers and because they thought the work offered autonomy not permitted in other available jobs found their proficiency challenged by professional and state directives.

Mothers without Power

Although the rewards and meaning derived from this work resembled those received from mothering, fostering lacked the power and permanence of motherhood. Foster mothers became frustrated when they were not able to make decisions about the children in their care or when decisions were made by those far removed from the children (such as courts, professionals, or the birth parents) that went against their judgment. Foster mothers complained that although they were charged with the daily care of children, they sometimes were denied permission to make everyday care decisions such as those about haircuts, ear piercings, or whether children could go to a friend's home after school. While these examples may seem trivial, women experienced such restrictions on their authority as undermining the power earned through motherhood.

The case of two brothers, Juan and Oscar, illustrates how decisions concerning foster children created feelings of disempowerment. Juan and Oscar were seven and eight years old, respectively, and had been in foster care with the Ortega family for two years at the time of this incident. The boys, along with their two younger brothers (placed with a nearby Hope family), were placed in foster care due to severe neglect by their mentally ill mother and her family. The boys were found locked in a room filled with their own waste, and Oscar had to crawl out the window to forage for food from other people's garbage. The youngest child, two years old at placement, came into foster care with burns the shape of an electric stove burner on his bottom from being placed on top of a hot stove. The boys later revealed more stories of burnings, beatings, and their fear of a "bad uncle" who lived with the family.

Given this background, Diana Ortega was stunned when a county worker new to the case recommended to the court that unsupervised weekend visits commence followed by family reunification. Despite the foster mother's concerns and the boys' own declaration that they did not want to return to their birth family, a judge ordered overnight weekend visits and eventual reunification.

Although the boys returned safely from their first weekend visit, and said they wanted to visit their family again, Diana began to suspect that something was not quite right during visits a few weeks later. The boys became uncharacteristically secretive and defiant; they whispered, cried, sometimes sexually touched other children, and oscillated between being aggressive and being withdrawn. From the children's drawings and confused statements, Diana suspected possible abuse of some kind, which she reported to the social workers. However, the bureaucratic layers, institutional hierarchy, and reunification plan muffled the voice of the foster mother, and

no change was made until state-recognized experts became involved. After Juan sexually acted out at school, a police investigation was initiated against the seven-year-old boy that concluded with the child's therapist determining that his uncle had been sexually abusing him during home visits. Only when the credentialed professional advised ceasing visits did the court stop unsupervised home visits.

Throughout the unfolding of this incident, Diana reported her concerns. She was heard but not heeded. Reports to child protection officials recorded what she saw, her interpretations, and her recommendations, but since authority rested with the relatively more distant county workers and court who sought objective proof, the family reunification plan continued as ordered. With the pressures of heavy, crises-laden caseloads, Diana's concerns could be hastily filed and essentially ignored. From the point of view of the system, all she had were suspicions. Although Diana's close familiarity with these children signaled that something was not right, her intimate, particularistic knowledge did not hold weight with authorities who viewed them as the unfounded inferences of a "mother," someone swayed by emotions and intuition. Intimate knowledge and individual responsiveness, so important in the private sphere and the reason the state placed foster children in families in the first place, lacked persuasiveness in the public system. Although Diana was given the responsibility for the daily care of these children, she was not granted authority. This caused great pain for Diana as she watched children whom she loved suffer through this confusing time—especially given her belief that if she had been listened to initially, this would not have happened.

An important irony of this situation was that while Diana had very little power over these decisions, she was left with the responsibility of dealing with the consequences of this situation. She was the one who had to help the boys deal with the abuse, the guilt that they expressed for betraying their family, the termination of the weekend family visits, and the extensive sexual acting out that followed.

This episode reveals both the level of responsibility of foster mothers and their lack of power and influence. Similar situations regularly occurred in serious and not so serious circumstances. Although mothering entailed protecting children from harm, foster mothers experienced powerlessness as state authorities made decisions that discounted foster mothers' intimate knowledge and remained unresponsive to the particular children they cared for deeply.

Disrupting Traditional Families

Paradoxically, the foster family strategy of maintaining a traditional family lifestyle through caring for foster children carried with it unanticipated disruptions and public interventions into their private family lives. This happened in two primary ways.

First, the foster children themselves sometimes changed the lives and routines of foster families. As to be expected, foster families tried to

accommodate the needs and desires of foster children as they would any new addition to the family, but they also had to incorporate treatment and bureaucratic requirements such as therapist appointments, social worker visits, court appearances, and birth family visitation. In addition, foster children's frequent mild to severe emotional and behavioral problems sometimes strained foster families. While a violent tantrum from a preschooler may not constitute a real threat, such behaviors from adolescents understandably alarmed foster families. Several such incidents arose during this ethnographic research. For example, on one occasion, two 12-year-old girls locked their babysitter in a room, claiming they had knives and threatening to burn down the house. Similarly, an 11-year-old girl swung a baseball bat at her foster mother and shattered their curio. At times, foster parents felt these children threatened their families' safety and feared that this behavior would rub off on their own children. Even if most foster children's behavioral issues were minor and could be addressed effectively over time, many children came with problems that tested their care providers and threatened the idyllic family experience they desired.

Second, a great deal of foster family disruption was created by the bureaucratic, regulatory, and supervisory nature of the foster care system. Beyond having to adopt professionally approved childrearing methods, foster families were made to feel that they lived in glass houses as social workers routinely intervened and policies regulated foster homes, collapsing the public-private distinction and undermining family autonomy and authority. The state became a matriarch as differently located professional women intervened in many aspects of foster mothers' family management. Regulations institutionalized middle-class biases that assumed ample resources and space specifying, for example, sleeping arrangements, closet space, and minimum children's wardrobe. State licensing required Hope professionals to conduct quarterly inspections and unannounced foster home visits beyond regular weekly social worker visits. While these rules aimed to protect children and may have prevented the kinds of abuses that have been documented in the county foster care system, it paradoxically also resulted in foster parent dissatisfaction and threatened foster placement stability. Foster mothers felt intruded on when social workers came in with checklists detailing how they needed to reorganize their homes. Foster mothers, who conceived of themselves as caring, child-centered service providers, experienced this regulation and surveillance as excessive and invasive. . . .

Money versus Love

A final tension between foster parent motivations and the institutional context of their labor involved the ways in which compensation sparked suspicions about foster parents' commitment to children. Accompanying the historical and ideological split between the public and the private spheres came the assumption that women engaged in reproductive work within homes should be unconcerned with money. Illustrating this point, although people have not been shy to ask me whether foster parents "do it for the

money," no one has ever asked me whether the social workers, lawyers, or judges involved in the foster care system do it for the money. The fact that carework has been conventionally equated with social value in opposition to market value left foster mothers disempowered in negotiating financial issues and vulnerable to accusations of ulterior, and presumed inappropriate, motives.

Agency and state workers questioned foster parents who called about late stipend checks or requested reimbursement for health care costs that were supposed to be covered by Medicaid. For example, this Hope worker complained about a foster mother's call to the agency when her check was late: *"That Diana Ortega is always calling to make sure that the check will arrive on time, or if it's late just one day, she calls to complain. Makes me wonder why she does this and how much she needs this money"* (Pammy Gover, agency receptionist, white, working-class, married woman, 40s). Similarly, the agency director questioned the foster mother's commitment when, after paying $200 for medical expenses due to a Medicaid bureaucratic error, she requested reimbursement: *"Why couldn't she just pay it and forget it? She should be willing to pay for the children's health. If she's not, we should question whether she is an appropriate foster mother."* When middle-class professionals suspected foster mothers lacked devotion to children because they indicated financial needs, they reinforced white, middle-class assumptions that caring for children could and should be exclusively a selfless labor of love and failed to recognize the material realities of care. Nelson suggested that "the notion that anyone could live somehow above the financial struggles of this world may be a vestige of the image of the white, middle class femininity idealized in the Victorian 'angel of the house'" (1999:49).

One of the most difficult situations I saw working-class foster parents endure was when they were faced with the decision to adopt foster children they dearly loved at the cost of losing stipends they depended on as part of their monthly income. Such parents felt great pains when they were accused of not loving the children and doing it only for the money. This situation faced Rosa Hernandez when she could not afford to adopt the two-year-old boy, David, who had lived with her family his entire life. *"It will break my heart when he is adopted. There is no way you can't get attached if you're supposed to love them and nurture them and give them a good home. But then they turn around and say if you can't adopt them then we'll take them; you must not really care about him after all. But we can't afford it; we would lose his MediCal, and he has asthma. We might lose everything; then we couldn't take care of anybody"* (Latina, working-class, married woman, 40s). Rosa desperately wanted to continue to take care of David and her other foster son. It was not that she lacked emotional commitment; rather, she feared unpredictable financial hardship. The foster parents knew it could prove too difficult to provide for the family of six (including the two foster children) on the father's $1,000 monthly wage, especially as the boys grew. What is more, they feared they would not be able to afford the health care needs of these medically fragile children without the guarantee of health insurance. Nevertheless, the caseworkers and lawyers accused Rosa of fostering only for the money and not truly caring

about the boys if they did not adopt. (Once policies changed a year later and permitted continued health care coverage and minimal stipends for adopted children, the Hernandez family did adopt the boys.)

Similarly, Glenda Frederickson struggled with this dilemma when the caseworker and lawyer asked her to adopt her two foster children:

> *These boys are my life. I would do anything for them. They're my boys. I love them like they were my own, and they love me like I was their own grandma. Of course I want them to stay here until they're grown. But if I lose their foster payment, then I have to go back to work as a sewer [seamstress]. . . . I wouldn't be here to take care of my boys. Me and Steven can take care of ourselves, but we can't take care of the boys, especially as they get bigger and things get more expensive. We need the foster money to buy them food and clothes and everything growing boys need.* (white, working-class, married woman, 60s)

Contrary to the belief that paying for care would diminish the quality of care and preclude authentic affection, foster family feelings of attachment for foster children most often increased over time. Foster mothers anguished when children left their homes, not because they would lose their payments (there were always children in state protection waiting for foster placements) but because they came to love the particular children they cared for. So while some foster parents resisted adopting children without stipends, this pointed to the material realities that coexisted with care but did not indicate lack of affection.

Conclusion

As markets and states take over more responsibility for care, financial compensation, regulation, and oversight are certain to become important and contentious issues in care provision. It is also certain that retaining naturalized and deeply gendered assumptions of care offered selflessly and freely as a labor of love fails to recognize contemporary and future realities. Feminist scholars have begun to attend to the multifaceted complexity of carework by moving beyond a simplistic dichotomous view that people provide caregiving either for love or for money or that financial motives will necessarily diminish care quality.

This fieldwork supports these assertions. Hope foster mothers came to foster care for both self-interested and altruistic reasons and received both pecuniary and nonpecuniary rewards from their carework. In so doing, they delivered high-quality, nurturing care to children under state protection. At the same time, findings in the second half of this article also demonstrate a need for careful consideration about how carework is organized. The conditions of government-contracted foster care with its hierarchical, bureaucratic structure posed serious challenges for foster mothers, making their carework less ideal than they originally had imagined.

Gender stands at the center of all of this. First, the gendered construction of separate private and public spheres shapes these tensions. The assumption of gendered spheres justifies unequal rewards for paid carework in part because it is performed by women with little status in terms of class and race but also because it resembles unpaid work that women have always done in families and is understood to stem from feminine nature. But more than this, the myth of gendered separate spheres suggests that they operate on mutually exclusive and opposing logics. The fear is that injecting individualistic, market motives—traditionally associated with masculinity—into caregiving—traditionally associated with femininity—would undermine the core logic and value of the private sphere rather than adding new dimensions and complexities. To guard against this threat and to preserve the authenticity of caring feelings and the quality of caring acts, the state paradoxically intensifies public surveillance and control of foster mothers' parenting and private lives. Although intended to protect children, this creates an unsupportive context for foster mothers' carework that compromises not only the caregiving experience of foster mothers but the stability and quality of child care itself.

In this study, the numerous regulations and professional interventions diminished foster parent satisfaction and increased foster parent stress and retention problems. In addition, foster parent and social worker attention was diverted away from kids' specific needs and toward compliance and documentation issues. Consequently, children's security and placement stability suffered. While children were certainly safe in Hope homes (there were no substantiated cases of child abuse in Hope foster homes during the time of this research), numerous foster parents resigned, and a few were terminated due to conflict over compliance with agency workers. Foster parent turnover had serious consequences for children, especially when it forced them from families whom they had come to trust and love and required them to move to new homes, new schools, and new communities. . . .

Given the reality that more and more care will be provided for pay, it is important to seek ways to enable and support careworkers who must meet their own material needs at the same time as providing other-centered care. Better pay and adequate benefits would be a good place to start. But as we have seen, the organization of carework is equally important. While safeguards to protect vulnerable populations are imperative, public care programs, policies, and discourse must also recognize and reward careworkers' real skills, knowledge, labor, and devotion as well as integrate and appropriately value an ethic of care in these more public realms.

ENDNOTE

Author's Note: This analysis was supported in part by a National Research Service Award, "Mental Health and Adjustment in the Life Course," from the National Institute of Mental Health (T32 MH19893). I thank Douglas Hartmann, Ann Hironaka, Rebecca Klatch, Barbara Laslett, Richard Madsen, Jeylan Mortimer, Jennifer Pierce, Mary Romero, and three anonymous reviewers and the editors from *Gender & Society* for their insightful and helpful comments.

REFERENCES

Abel, Emily and Margaret Nelson. 1990. *Circles of Care: Work and Identity in Women's Lives.* Albany: State University of New York Press.

The Alliance for Children's Rights. 2004. *Children's Court Project.* Los Angeles: The Alliance for Children's Rights. Available from http://www.kids-alliance.org/programs/childrens_court_project.asp.

Anderson, Troy. 2003. "Foster System among Worst." *Pasadena Star-News,* December 28.

Barbell, Kathy. 1999. "The Impact of Financial Compensation, Benefits, and Supports on Foster Parent Retention and Recruitment." Available from http://casanet.org/library/foster-care/finance.htm.

Cancian, Francesca. 2000. "Paid Emotional Care: Organizational Forms That Encourage Nurturance." In *Care Work,* edited by M. Harrington Meyer. London: Routledge.

Cancian, Francesca and S. Oliker. 2000. *Caring and Gender.* Thousand Oaks, CA: Pine Forge Press.

Christensen, Kathleen. 1987. "Women, Families and Home-Based Employment." In *Families and Work,* edited by N. Gerstel and H. E. Gross. Philadelphia: Temple University Press.

England, Paula, M. Budig, and N. Folbre. 2002. "Wages of Virtue: The Relative Pay of Carework." *Social Problems* 49 (4): 455–73.

Folbre, Nancy. 2001. *Invisible Heart: Economic and Family Values.* New York: New Press.

Folbre, Nancy and Julie Nelson. 2000. "For Love or Money—Or Both?" *Journal of Economic Perspectives* 14 (4): 123–40.

Frankenberg, Ruth. 1993. *White Women, Race Matters: The Social Construction of Whiteness.* Minneapolis: University of Minnesota Press.

Gelles, Richard. 1996. *The Book of David: How Preserving Families Can Cost Children's Lives.* New York: Basic Books.

Harrington Meyer, Madonna. 2000. *Care Work: Gender, Labor and Welfare States.* New York: Routledge.

Hays, Sharon. 1996. *The Cultural Contradictions of Motherhood.* New Haven, CT: Yale University Press.

Hooyman, Nancy and Judith Gonyea. 1995. *Feminist Perspectives on Family Care: Politics for Gender Justice.* Thousand Oaks, CA: Sage.

Kohn, Melvin. 1969. *Class and Conformity: A Study in Values.* Homewood, IL: Dorsey.

Lareau, Annette. 2003. *Unequal Childhoods: Class, Race and Family Life.* Berkeley: University of California Press.

Nakano Glenn, Evelyn. 2000. "Creating a Caring Society." *Contemporary Sociology* 29:84–94.

Nelson, Julie. 1999. "Of Markets and Martyrs: Is It OK to Pay Well for Care?" *Feminist Economics* 5 (3): 43–59.

Newman, Katherine. 1993. *Declining Fortunes: The Withering of the American Dream.* New York: Basic Books.

Romero, Mary. 1992. *Maid in the USA.* New York: Routledge.

Rubin, Lillian. 1994. *Families on the Fault Line.* New York: HarperCollins.

Stack, Carol. 1974. *All Our Kin: Strategies for Survival in a Black Community.* New York: Harper and Row.

Ungerson, Claire. 1990. *Gender and Caring: Work and Welfare in Britain and Scandinavia.* New York: Harvester Wheatsheaf.

Uttal, Lynet. 1996. "Custodial Care, Surrogate Care, and Coordinated Care: Employed Mothers and the Meaning of Child Care." *Gender & Society* 10:291–311.

———. 1999. "Using Kin for Childcare: Embedment in the Socioeconomic Networks of Extended Families." *Journal of Marriage and the Family* 61 (4): 845–57.

24

FATHERING
Paradoxes, Contradictions, and Dilemmas

SCOTT COLTRANE

The beginning of the 21st century offers a paradox for American fathers: Media images, political rhetoric, and psychological studies affirm the importance of fathers to children at the same time that men are becoming less likely to live with their offspring. Although the average married father spends more time interacting with his children than in past decades, marriage rates have fallen, and half of all marriages are predicted to end in divorce. Additionally, the proportion of births to unmarried mothers has increased dramatically for all race and ethnic groups, and single-mother households have become commonplace. These contradictory tendencies— more father–child interaction in two-parent families but fewer two-parent families in the population—have encouraged new research on fathers and spawned debates about how essential fathers are to families and normal child development (Blankenhorn 1995; Silverstein and Auerbach 1999).

Scholars attribute the current paradox in fathering to various economic and social trends. Whereas most men in the 20th century were sole breadwinners, contemporary fathers' wages can rarely support a middle-class standard of living for an entire family. The weakening of the good-provider model, coupled with trends in fertility, marriage, divorce, and custody, has resulted in the average man spending fewer years living with children (Eggebeen 2002). Simultaneously, however, men rank marriage and children among their most precious goals, single-father households have increased, and fathers in two-parent households are spending more time with co-resident children than at any time since data on fathers were collected (Pleck and Masciadrelli 2003). Although married fathers report that they value their families over their jobs, they spend significantly more time in paid work and less time in family work than married mothers, with most men continuing to serve as helpers to their wives, especially for housework and child maintenance activities (Coltrane 2000). Personal, political, religious, and popular discourses about fathers reveal similar ambivalence

about men's family involvements, with ideals ranging from stern patriarchs to nurturing daddies, and public portrayals frequently at odds with the actual behavior of average American fathers (LaRossa 1997). We can understand these contradictions by recognizing that fatherhood has gained symbolic importance just as men's family participation has become more voluntary, tenuous, and conflicted (Griswold 1993; Kimmel 1996).

In this [reading], I summarize how fathering practices have varied across cultures and through history; highlight how different social, economic, and political contexts have produced different types of father involvement; . . . and examine findings about causes and consequences of father involvement. I end with a short analysis of debates over family policy and offer tentative predictions about the future of fathering in America.

Cross-Cultural Variation

Fatherhood defines a biological and social relationship between a male parent and his offspring. *To father* means to impregnate a woman and beget a child, thus describing a kinship connection that facilitates the intergenerational transfer of wealth and authority (at least in patrilineal descent systems such as ours). Fatherhood also reflects ideals about the rights, duties, and activities of men in families and in society and generalizes to other social and symbolic relationships, as when Christians refer to "God the Father," Catholics call priests "Father," and Americans label George Washington "the Father" of the country. Fatherhood thus reflects a normative set of social practices and expectations that are institutionalized within religion, politics, law, and culture. Social theories have employed the concept of *social fatherhood* to explain how the institution of fatherhood links a particular child to a particular man (whether father or uncle) in order to secure a place for that child in the social structure (Coltrane and Collins 2001).

Fathering (in contrast to *fatherhood*) refers more directly to what men do with and for children. Although folk beliefs suggest that fathering entails behaviors fixed by reproductive biology, humans must learn how to parent. In every culture and historical period, men's parenting has been shaped by social and economic forces. Although women have been the primary caretakers of young children in all cultures, fathers' participation in child rearing has varied from virtually no direct involvement to active participation in all aspects of children's routine care. Except for breastfeeding and the earliest care of infants, there are no cross-cultural universals in the tasks that mothers and fathers perform (Johnson 1988). In some societies, the social worlds of fathers and mothers were so separate that they rarely had contact and seldom performed the same tasks; in other societies, men participated in tasks like infant care, and women participated in tasks like hunting (Coltrane 1988; Sanday 1981).

Drawing on worldwide cross-cultural comparisons, scholars have identified two general patterns of fathers' family involvement, one intimate and the other aloof. In the intimate pattern, men eat and sleep with their wives

and children, talk with them during evening meals, attend births, and participate actively in infant care. In the aloof pattern, men often eat and sleep apart from women, spend their leisure time in the company of other men, stay away during births, and seldom help with child care (Whiting and Whiting 1975). Societies with involved fathers are more likely than societies with aloof fathers to be peaceful, to afford women a role in community decision making, to have intimate husband–wife relationships, to feature more gender equality in the society, and to include nurturing deities of both sexes in their religions. Aloof-father societies are more likely to have religious systems with stern male gods, social institutions that exclude women from community decision making, marriage systems in which husbands demand deference from wives, and public rituals that focus on men's competitive displays of masculinity (Coltrane 1988, 1996; Sanday 1981).

Research on fathering among indigenous peoples such as the African Aka suggests why involved fathering and gender egalitarianism are associated (Hewlett 1991). Anthropologists such as Hewlett have drawn on Chodorow's (1974) work to suggest that when fathers are active in infant care, boys develop an intimate knowledge of masculinity, which makes them less likely to devalue the feminine, whereas when fathers are rarely around, boys lack a clear sense of masculinity and construct their identities in opposition to things feminine by devaluing and criticizing women (Hewlett 2000). In reviews of data on father involvement over the past 120,000 years, Hewlett concluded that fathers contribute to their children in many ways, with the relative importance of different contributions varying dramatically; that different ecologies and modes of production have a substantial impact on the contributions of fathers to their children; and that fathers' roles today are relatively unique in human history (Hewlett 1991, 2000).

Historical Variation

Historical studies have focused on practices in Europe, chronicling and emphasizing men's public lives: work, political exploits, literary accomplishments, scientific discoveries, and heroic battles. This emphasis shows how various economic, political, and legal practices have structured privileges and obligations within and beyond families. For example, the historical concept of family in the West is derived from the Latin *famulus*, meaning servant, and the Roman *familia*, meaning the man's domestic property. Linking institutional arrangements with linguistic forms tells us something important about men's relationships to families. Recent historical studies have focused more directly on men's ideal and actual behaviors in families, thereby documenting complexity and diversity in past fathering practices (e.g., Griswold 1993; Kimmel 1996; LaRossa 1997; Mintz 1998; Pleck and Pleck 1997).

Before these studies, many scholars erroneously assumed that changes in fatherhood were linear and progressive (Coltrane and Parke 1998). For example, early family history emphasized that peasant families were extended and governed by stern patriarchs, whereas market societies produced nuclear

families, companionate marriages, and involved fathers. In fact, historical patterns of fathering have responded to a complex array of social and economic forces, varying considerably across regions, time periods, and ethnic or cultural groups. Although it is useful to identify how men's work and production have shaped their public and private statuses, actual family relations have been diverse, and fatherhood ideals have followed different trajectories in different regions of the same country (Griswold 1993; Mintz 1998; Pleck and Pleck 1997).

The economy of the 17th and 18th centuries in Europe and America was based on agriculture and productive family households. For families that owned farms or small artisan shops, their place of work was also their home. Slaves, indentured servants, and others were expected to work on family estates in return for food, a place to live, and sometimes other rewards. In this pattern of household or family-based production, men, women, and children worked together. Regional variations could be large, and fathers and mothers often did different types of work, but many tasks required for subsistence and family survival were interchangeable, and both mothers and fathers took responsibility for child care and training (Coltrane and Galt 2000).

Because most men's work as farmers, artisans, and tradesmen occurred in the family household, fathers were a visible presence in their children's lives. Child rearing was a more collective enterprise than it is today, with family behaviors and attitudes ruled primarily by duty and obligation. Men introduced sons to farming or craft work within the household economy, oversaw the work of others, and were responsible for maintaining harmonious household relations. The preindustrial home was a system of control as well as a center of production, and both functions reinforced the father's authority (Griswold 1993). Though mothers provided most direct care for infants and young children, men tended to be active in the training and tutoring of children. Because they were moral teachers and family heads, fathers were thought to have greater responsibility for and influence on children than mothers and were also generally held responsible for how the children acted outside the home (Pleck and Pleck 1997).

Because the sentimental individualism of the modern era had not yet blossomed, emotional involvement with children in the Western world during the 17th and early 18th centuries was more limited than today. Prevailing images of children also were different from modern ideas about their innocence and purity. Religious teachings stressed the corrupt nature and evil dispositions of children, and fathers were admonished to demand strict obedience and use swift physical punishment to cleanse children of their sinful ways. Puritan fathers justified their extensive involvement in children's lives because women were seen as unfit to be disciplinarians, moral guides, or intellectual teachers. Griswold (1997) pointed out, however, that stern unaffectionate fathering, though not confined to Puritans, was not representative of all of the population. In fact, most American fathers attempted to shape and guide their children's characters, not break them or beat the devil out of them. As more privileged 18th-century fathers gained enough affluence

to have some leisure time, many were affectionate with their children and delighted in playing with them (Griswold 1997).

As market economies replaced home-based production in the 19th and 20th centuries, the middle-class father's position as household head and master and moral instructor of his children was slowly transformed. Men increasingly sought employment outside the home, and their direct contact with family members declined. As the wage labor economy developed, men's occupational achievement outside the household took on stronger moral overtones. Men came to be seen as fulfilling their family and civic duty, not by teaching and interacting with their children as before, but by supporting the family financially. The middle-class home, previously the site of production, consumption, and virtually everything else in life, became a nurturing, child-centered haven set apart from the impersonal world of work, politics, and other public pursuits. The separate-spheres ideal became a defining feature of the late 19th and early 20th centuries (Bernard 1981; Coltrane and Galt 2000; Kimmel 1996).

The ideal that paid work was only for men and that only women were suited to care for family members remained an unattainable myth rather than an everyday reality for most families. Many working-class fathers were not able to earn the family wage assumed by the separate-spheres ideal, and a majority of African American, Latino, Asian American, and other immigrant men could not fulfill the good-provider role that the cultural ideal implied. Women in these families had to either work for wages, participate in production at home, or find other ways to make ends meet. Although the emerging romantic ideal held that women should be sensitive and pure keepers of the home on a full-time basis, the reality was that women in less advantaged households had no choice but to simultaneously be workers and mothers. In fact, many working-class and ethnic minority women had to leave their homes and children to take care of other people's children and houses (Dill 1988). Even during the heyday of separate spheres (in the early 20th century), minority women, young single women, widows, and married women whose husbands could not support them worked for wages.

As noted above, attempts to understand the history of fatherhood have often painted a simple before-and-after picture: *Before* the Industrial Revolution, families were rural and extended, and patriarchal fathers were stern moralists; *after* the Industrial Revolution, families were urban and nuclear, and wage-earning fathers became companionate husbands, distant breadwinners, and occasional playmates to their children. This before-and-after picture captures something important about general shifts in work and family life, but its simple assumption of unidirectional linear change and its binary conceptualization contrasting men's patriarchal roles in the past with egalitarian roles in the present is misleading (Coontz 1992). Stage models of family history have ignored the substantial regional and race/ethnic differences that encouraged different family patterns (Pleck and Pleck 1997). For example, as most of the United States was undergoing industrialization, large pockets remained relatively untouched by it. The experience of white planters in the antebellum South was both like and unlike that of men in the

commercial and industrial North (Griswold 1993). Another major drawback of early historical studies is the tendency to overgeneralize for the entire society on the basis of the experience of the white middle class. Even during the heyday of separate spheres at the turn of the 20th century, minority and immigrant men were unlikely to be able to support a family. Race and class differences also intersect with regional differences: Not only did southern fathering practices differ from northern ones, but slave fathers and freedmen in the South had much different experiences than either group of white men (Griswold 1993; McDaniel 1994).

The Emergence of Modern Fathering

Throughout the 20th century, calls for greater paternal involvement coexisted with the physical presence, but relative emotional and functional absence, of fathers (LaRossa 1997). Nevertheless, some fathers have always reported high levels of involvement with their children. By the 1930s, even though mothers bore most of the responsibility for care of homes and families, three out of four American fathers said they regularly read magazine articles about child care, and nearly as many men as women were members of the PTA (Kimmel 1996). Increases in women's labor force participation during the 1940s briefly challenged the ideal of separate family and work roles, but in the postwar era, high rates of marriage and low rates of employment reinforced the ideology of separate spheres for men and women. The ideal father at midcentury was seen as a good provider who "set a good table, provided a decent home, paid the mortgage, bought the shoes, and kept his children warmly clothed" (Bernard 1981:3–4). As they had during the earlier Victorian era, middle-class women were expected to be consumed and fulfilled by wifely and motherly duties. With Ozzie and Harriet–style families as the 1950s model, women married earlier and had more children than any group of American women before them. Rapid expansion of the U.S. economy fueled a phenomenal growth of suburbs, and the consumer culture from that era idolized domestic life on radio and television. Isolated in suburban houses, many mothers now had almost sole responsibility for raising children, aided by occasional reference to expert guides from pediatricians and child psychologists (Hays 1996). Fathers of the 1950s were also told to get involved with child care—but not *too* involved (Kimmel 1996). The separate spheres of white middle-class men and women were thus maintained, though experts deemed them permeable enough for men to participate regularly as a helper to the mother (Coltrane and Galt 2000; Hays 1996).

During the mid-20th century, separate-spheres ideology and the popularity of Freud's ideas about mother–infant bonding led to widespread acceptance of concepts like *maternal deprivation,* and few researchers asked who besides mothers took care of children, although some researchers began to focus on *father absence* during the baby boom era (roughly 1946–64). Empirical studies and social theories valued the symbolic significance of fathers' breadwinning, discipline, and masculine role modeling, even though few

studies controlled for social class or measured what fathers actually did with children. Studies including fathers found that they were more likely than mothers to engage in rough and tumble play and to give more attention to sons than daughters (Parke 1996; Pleck 1997). In general, research showed that child care was an ongoing and taken-for-granted task for mothers but a novel and fun distraction for fathers (Thompson and Walker 1989).

Compared to the wholesome but distant good-provider fathers pictured on television programs like *Ozzie and Harriet* and *Father Knows Best* in the 1950s, a new father ideal gained prominence in the 1980s (Griswold 1993). According to Furstenberg (1988), "[T]elevision, magazines, and movies herald the coming of the modern father—the nurturant, caring, and emotionally attuned parent. . . . Today's father is at least as adept at changing diapers as changing tires" (p. 193). No longer limited to being protectors and providers, fathers were pictured on television and in magazines as intimately involved in family life. Fatherhood proponents focused on the potential of the new ideals and practices (Biller 1976), but researchers in the 1980s reported that many fathers resisted assuming responsibility for daily housework or child care (Thompson and Walker 1989). Some researchers claimed that popular images far exceeded men's actual behaviors (LaRossa 1988), and others suggested that men, on the whole, were less committed to families than they had been in the past (Ehrenreich 1984). In the 1990s, researchers also began to examine how the modern ideal of the new father carried hidden messages about class and race, with some suggesting that the image of the sensitive and involved father was a new class/ethnic icon because it set middle-class fathers apart from working-class and ethnic minority fathers, who presented a more masculine image (Messner 1993). Others suggested that the sensitive or androgynous parenting styles of new fathers might lead to gender identity confusion in sons (Blankenhorn 1995). . . .

The Potential Influence of Fathers

As scholars pay more attention to fathers, they are beginning to understand what influence their involvement might have on child development. Most researchers find that father–child relationships are influential for children's future life chances (Parke 1996; Pleck and Masciadrelli 2003). The focus of this research tends to be on the positive aspects of fathers' involvement, though it should be noted that because men are more likely than women to abuse children or to use inappropriate parenting techniques, increased male involvement can lead to increased risk and negative outcomes for children, particularly if the father figure does not have a long-term relationship with the mother.

Many researchers continue to focus on fathers' economic contributions to children and report that fathers' resources improve children's life chances. Longitudinal research shows that children from one-parent households (usually mother headed) are at greater risk for negative adult outcomes (e.g., lower educational and occupational achievement, earlier childbirth,

school dropout, health problems, behavioral difficulties) than those from two-parent families (Marsiglio et al. 2000; McLanahan and Sandefur 1994). Although comparisons between children of divorced parents and those from first-marriage families show more problems in the former group, differences between the two are generally small across various outcome measures and do not necessarily isolate the influence of divorce or of father involvement (Crockett, Eggebeen, and Hawkins 1993; Furstenberg and Harris 1993; Seltzer 1994). For children with nonresident fathers, the amount of fathers' earnings (especially the amount that is actually transferred to children) is a significant predictor of children's well-being, including school grades and behavior problems (Amato and Gilbreth 1999; McLanahan et al. 1994; Marsiglio et al. 2000). Because the great majority of children from single-parent homes turn out to be happy, healthy, and productive adults, debates continue about how such large-group comparisons should be made and how we should interpret their results in terms of fathers' economic or social contributions (Amato 2000; Coltrane and Adams 2003).

Earlier reviews suggested that the level of father involvement has a smaller direct effect on infant attachment than the quality or style of father interaction, though time spent parenting is also related to competence (Lamb et al. 1987; Marsiglio et al. 2000). Preschool children with fathers who perform 40% or more of the within-family child care show more cognitive competence, more internal locus of control, more empathy, and less gender stereotyping than preschool children with less involved fathers (Lamb et al. 1987; Pleck 1997). Adolescents with involved fathers are more likely to have positive developmental outcomes such as self-control, self-esteem, life skills, and social competence, provided that the father is not authoritarian or overly controlling (Mosley and Thomson 1995; Pleck and Masciadrelli 2003). Studies examining differences between the presence of biological fathers versus other father figures suggest that it is the quality of the father–child relationship rather than biological relationship that enhances the cognitive and emotional development of children (Dubowitz et al. 2001; Hofferth and Anderson 2003; Silverstein and Auerbach 1999). Reports of greater father involvement when children were growing up have also been associated with positive aspects of adult children's educational attainment, relationship quality, and career success (Amato and Booth 1997; Harris, Furstenberg, and Marmer 1998; Nock 1998; Snarey 1993). Because of methodological inadequacies in previous studies such as not controlling for maternal involvement, most scholars recommend more carefully controlled studies using random samples and multirater longitudinal designs, as well as advocating caution in interpreting associations between fathering and positive child outcomes (Amato and Rivera 1999; Parke 1996; Pleck and Masciadrelli 2003). It will take some time to isolate the specific influence of fathers as against the influence of mothers and other social-contextual factors such as income, education, schools, neighborhoods, communities, kin networks, and cultural ideals.

We do know that when fathers share child care and housework with their wives, employed mothers escape total responsibility for family work, evaluate the division of labor as more fair, are less depressed, and enjoy higher

levels of marital satisfaction (Brennan, Barnett, and Gareis 2001; Coltrane 2000; Deutsch 1999). When men care for young children on a regular basis, they emphasize verbal interaction, notice and use more subtle cues, and treat sons and daughters similarly, rather than focusing on play, giving orders, and sex-typing children (Coltrane 1996, 1998; Parke 1996). These styles of father involvement have been found to encourage less gender stereotyping among young adults and to encourage independence in daughters and emotional sensitivity in sons. Most researchers agree that these are worthy goals that could contribute to reducing sexism, promoting gender equity, and curbing violence against women (but see Blankenhorn 1995).

Demographic Contexts for Father Involvement

As Furstenberg (1988) first noted, conflicting images of fathers are common in popular culture, with nurturing, involved "good dads" contrasted with "bad dads" who do not marry the mother of their children or who move out and fail to pay child support. Recent research suggests that both types of fathers are on the rise and that the demographic contexts for fatherhood have changed significantly over the past few decades. In many industrialized countries, at the same time that some fathers are taking a more active role in their children's lives, growing numbers of men rarely see their children and do not support them financially. In the United States, for example, single-parent households are increasing, with only about half of U.S. children eligible for child support from nonresident parents via court order and only about half of those receiving the full amount (Scoon-Rogers 1999). Both trends in fatherhood—toward more direct involvement and toward less contact and financial support—are responses to the same underlying social developments, including women's rising labor force participation and the increasingly optional nature of marriage.

Marriage rates have fallen in the past few decades, with people waiting longer to get married and increasingly living together without marrying. Women are having fewer children than they did just a few decades ago, waiting longer to have them, and not necessarily marrying before they give birth (Eggebeen 2002; Seltzer 2000). One of three births in the United States is to an unmarried woman, a rate that is three times higher than it was in the 1960s, with rates for African American women highest, followed by Latinas, and then non-Hispanic whites (National Center for Health Statistics 2000). It is often assumed that nonmarital births produce fatherless children, but recent studies show that most of the increase in nonmarital childbearing from the 1980s to the 1990s is accounted for by the increase in the number of cohabiting women getting pregnant and carrying the baby to term without getting married. Historically, if an unmarried woman became pregnant, she would marry to legitimate the birth. Today, only a minority of women do so.

In addition, an increasingly large number of American fathers live apart from their children because of separation or divorce. Because most divorcing men do not seek (or are not awarded) child custody following divorce, the

number of divorced men who are uninvolved fathers has risen (Eggebeen 2002; Furstenberg and Cherlin 1991), although recent research shows that the actual involvement of fathers with children after divorce varies enormously, sometimes without regard to official postdivorce court orders (McLanahan and Sandefur 1994; Seltzer 1998). The number of men with joint physical (residential) custody has grown, though joint legal (decision-making) custody is still a more common postdivorce parenting arrangement (Maccoby and Mnookin 1992; Seltzer 1998). And although single father-households have increased in recent years, single-mother households continue to outpace them five to one. Demographers suggest that because of all these trends, younger cohorts will be less likely to experience sustained involved fathering than the generations that immediately preceded them (Eggebeen 2002).

Marriage and the traditional assumption of fatherhood have become more fragile, in part because an increasing number of men face financial difficulties. Although men continue to earn about 30% higher wages than women, their real wages (adjusted for inflation) have declined since the early 1970s, whereas women's have increased (Bernstein and Mishel 1997). As the U.S. economy has shifted from heavy reliance on domestic manufacturing to global interdependence within an information and service economy, working-class men's prospects of earning a family wage have declined. At the same time, women's labor force participation has risen steadily, with future growth in the economy predicted in the areas where women are traditionally concentrated (e.g., service, information health care, part-time work). The historical significance of this shift cannot be overestimated. For most of the 19th and 20th centuries, American women's life chances were determined by their marriage decisions. Unable to own property, vote, or be legally independent in most states, daughters were dependent on fathers and wives were dependent on their husbands for economic survival. Such dependencies shaped family relations and produced fatherhood ideals and practices predicated on male family headship. As women and mothers have gained independence by entering the labor force in record numbers, it is not surprising that older ideals about marriage to a man legitimating childbearing have been challenged.

Gender and the Politics of Fatherhood

In the 1990s, popular books and articles revived a research and policy focus that had been popular in the 1960s: father absence. For example, Popenoe (1996) suggested that drug and alcohol abuse, juvenile delinquency, teenage pregnancy, violent crime, and child poverty were the result of fatherlessness and that American society was in decline because it had abandoned traditional marriage and child-rearing patterns. Such claims about father absence often rely on evolutionary psychology and sociobiology and define fathers as categorically different from mothers (Blankenhorn 1995; Popenoe 1996). Even some proponents of nurturing fathers warn men against trying

to act too much like mothers (Pruett 1993). Following this reasoning, some argue for gender-differentiated parenting measurement strategies: "[T]he roles of father and mother are different and complementary rather than interchangeable and thus the standards for evaluating the role performance of fathers and mothers should be different" (Day and Mackey 1989:402). Some label the use of measures developed on mothers to study fathers and the practice of comparing fathers' and mothers' parenting as the *deficit model* (Doherty 1991) or the *role inadequacy perspective* (Hawkins and Dollahite 1997).

Because parenting is a learned behavior for both men and women, most social scientists focus on the societal conditions that create gender differences in parenting or find proximate social causes of paternal investment that outweigh assumed biological causes (e.g., Hofferth and Anderson 2003). Nevertheless, questioning taken-for-granted cultural ideals about families can cause controversy. When Silverstein and Auerbach (1999) challenged assertions about essential differences between fathers and mothers in an *American Psychologist* article entitled "Deconstructing the Essential Father," they received widespread public and academic criticism. Their scholarly article (based on a review of research findings) was ridiculed as "silliness" and "junk science" by Wade Horn (1999; formerly of the National Fatherhood Initiative and now Assistant Secretary in the U.S. Department of Health and Human Services), and the U.S. House of Representatives debated whether to pass a resolution condemning the article (Silverstein 2002). Clearly, debates about fathers, marriage, and family values carry symbolic meanings that transcend scientific findings. The contentious political and scholarly debates about fathers that emerged in the 1990s appear to be framed by an older political dichotomy: Conservatives tend to focus on biological parenting differences and stress the importance of male headship and breadwinning, respect for authority, and moral leadership (Blankenhorn 1995; Popenoe 1996), whereas liberals tend to focus on similarities between mothers and fathers and stress the importance of employment, social services, and possibilities for more equal marital relations (Coontz 1992; Silverstein and Auerbach 1999; Stacey 1996).

A full analysis of contemporary family values debates is beyond the scope of this [reading], but elsewhere I analyze marriage and fatherhood movements using data and theories about political opportunities, resource mobilization, and the moral framing of social issues (Coltrane 2001; Coltrane and Adams 2003; see also Gavanas 2002). In general, cultural tensions in the larger society are mirrored in policy proposals and academic debates about the appropriate roles of fathers and the importance of marriage. One cannot adjudicate among various scholarly approaches to fathering without acknowledging gendered interests and understanding the political economy of expert knowledge production. Recent policies and programs promoting marriage and fatherhood using faith-based organizations are designed to advance a particular vision of fatherhood. Whether they will benefit the majority of American mothers and children is a question that cannot be resolved without more sophisticated research with controls for

mothers' parenting and various other economic and social-contextual issues (Marsiglio et al. 2000; Marsiglio and Pleck 2004).

Prospects for the Future

The forces that are driving changes in fathers' involvement in families are likely to continue. In two-parent households (both married and cohabiting), men share more family work if their female partners are employed more hours, earn more money, and have more education. All three of these trends in women's attainment are likely to continue for the foreseeable future. Similarly, fathers share more family work when they are employed fewer hours and their wives earn a greater portion of the family income. Labor market and economic trends for these variables are also expected to continue for several decades. Couples also share more when they believe that family work should be shared and that men and women should have equal rights. According to national opinion polls, although the country has become slightly more conservative about marriage and divorce than it was in the 1970s and 1980s, the belief in gender equality continues to gain acceptance among both men and women. In addition, American women are waiting longer, on average, to marry and give birth, and they are having fewer children—additional factors sometimes associated with more sharing of housework and child care. Thus, I predict that increasing economic parity and more equal gender relations will allow women to buy out of some domestic obligations and/or recruit their partners to do more. Middle- and upper-class wives and mothers will rely on working-class and immigrant women to provide domestic services (nannies, housekeepers, child care workers, fast food employees, etc.), thereby reducing their own hours of family labor but simultaneously perpetuating race, class, and gender hierarchies in the labor market and in the society. Some fathers in dual-earner households will increase their contributions to family work, whereas others will perform a greater proportion of housework and child care by virtue of their wives' doing less. Other men will remain marginal to family life because they do not stay connected to the mothers of their children, do not hold jobs allowing them to support their children, or do not seek custody or make regular child support payments. These two ideal types—of involved and marginalized fathers—are likely to continue to coexist in the popular culture and in actual practice.

The context in which American couples negotiate fathering has definitely changed. The future is likely to bring more demands on fathers to be active parents if they want to stay involved with the mothers of their children. For fathers to assume more responsibility for active parenting, it may be necessary to change cultural assumptions that men are entitled to domestic services and that women are inherently predisposed to provide them. Further changes in fathering are likely to be driven by women's increasing independence and earning power. Ironically, women's enhanced economic position also makes them able to form families and raise children without

the father's being present. In the future, men will be even less able to rely on their superior earning power and the institution of fatherhood to maintain their connection to families and children. Increasingly, they will need to adopt different fathering styles to meet specific family circumstances and to commit to doing things men have not been accustomed to doing. Some men will be able to maintain their economic and emotional commitments to their children, whereas others will not. Some men will participate in all aspects of child rearing, whereas others will hardly see their children. Unless living wages and adequate social supports are developed for all fathers (as well as for mothers and children), we can expect that the paradoxes, contradictions, and dilemmas associated with fathering described in this chapter will continue for the foreseeable future.

ENDNOTE

Author's Note: This chapter incorporates some material from a November 21, 2002, National Council on Family Relations (NCFR) Annual Conference Special Session, "Future Prospects for Increasing Father Involvement in Child Rearing and Household Activities," reprinted as "The Paradox of Fatherhood: Predicting the Future of Men's Family Involvement" in *Vision 2003* (Minneapolis, MN: National Council on Family Relations/Allen). I thank Marilyn Coleman, Lawrence Ganong, Joseph Pleck, Carl Auerbach, and two anonymous reviewers for valuable feedback on an earlier draft of this chapter.

REFERENCES

Amato, P. and F. Rivera. 1999. "Paternal Involvement and Children's Behavior Problems." *Journal of Marriage and the Family* 61:375–384.

Amato, P. 2000. "Diversity within Single-Parent Families." Pp. 149–72 in *Handbook of Family Diversity*, edited by D. H. Demo, K. R. Allen, and M. A. Fine. New York: Oxford University Press.

Amato, P. and A. Booth. 1997. *A Generation at Risk: Growing Up in an Era of Family Upheaval.* Cambridge, MA: Harvard University Press.

Amato, P. and J. Gilbreth 1999. "Nonresident Fathers and Children's Well-Being: A Meta-Analysis." *Journal of Marriage and the Family* 61:557–73.

Bernard, J. 1981. "The Good Provider Role: Its Rise and Fall." *American Psychologist* 36:1–12.

Bernstein, J. and L. Mishel. 1997. "Has Wage Inequality Stopped Growing?" *Monthly Labor Review* 120:3–17.

Biller, H. B. 1976. "The Father and Personality Development." In *The Role of the Father in Child Development*, edited by M. E. Lamb. New York: John Wiley.

Blankenhorn, D. 1995. *Fatherless America.* New York: Basic Books.

Brennan, R. T., R. C. Barnett, and K. C. Gareis. 2001. "When She Earns More than He Does: A Longitudinal Study of Dual-Earner Couples." *Journal of Marriage and the Family* 63:168–82.

Chodorow, N. 1974. "Family Structure and Feminine Personality." Pp. 43–66 in *Woman, Culture and Society*, edited by M. Z. Rosaldo and L. Lampher. Palo Alto, CA: Stanford University Press.

Coltrane, S. 1988. "Father–Child Relationships and the Status of Women." *American Journal of Sociology* 93:1060–95.

———. 1996. *Family Man.* New York: Oxford University Press.

———. 1998. *Gender and Families.* Newbury Park, CA: Pine Forge/Alta Mira.

———. 2000. "Research on Household Labor." *Journal of Marriage and the Family* 62:1209–33.

———. 2001. "Marketing the Marriage 'Solution'." *Sociological Perspectives* 44:387–422.

Coltrane, S. and M. Adams. 2003. "The Social Construction of the Divorce 'Problem': Morality, Child Victims, and the Politics of Gender." *Family Relations* 52:21–30.

Coltrane, S. and R. Collins. 2001. *Sociology of Marriage and the Family.* 5th ed. Belmont, CA: Wadsworth/Thomson Learning.

Coltrane, S. and J. Galt. 2000. "The History of Men's Caring." Pp. 15–36 in *Care Work: Gender, Labor, and Welfare States*, edited by M. H. Meyer. New York: Routledge.

Coltrane, S. and R. D. Parke. 1998. "Reinventing Fatherhood: Toward an Historical Understanding of Continuity and Change in Men's Family Lives." Working Paper No. 98–12A. Philadelphia: National Center on Fathers and Families.

Coontz, S. 1992. *The Way We Never Were.* New York: Basic Books.

Crockett, L. J., D. J. Eggebeen, and A. J. Hawkins. 1993. "Fathers' Presence and Young Children's Behavioral and Cognitive Adjustment." *Journal of Family Issues* 14:355–77.

Day, R. D. and W. C. Mackey. 1989. "An Alternate Standard for Evaluating American Fathers." *Journal of Family Issues* 10:401–08.

Deutsch, F. 1999. *Halving It All.* Cambridge, MA: Harvard University Press.

Dill, B. T. 1988. "Our Mothers' Grief: Racial Ethnic Women and the Maintenance of Families." *Journal of Family History* 13:415–31.

Doherty, W. J. 1991. "Beyond Reactivity and the Deficit Model of Manhood." *Journal of Marital and Family Therapy* 17:29–32.

Dubowitz, H., M. M. Black, C. E. Cox, M. A. Kerr, A. J. Litrownik, A. Radhakrishna, D. J. English, M. W. Schneider, and D. K. Runyan. 2001. "Father Involvement and Children's Functioning at Age 6 Years: A Multisite Study." *Child Maltreatment* 6:300–09.

Eggebeen, D. 2002. "The Changing Course of Fatherhood." *Journal of Family Issues* 23:486–506.

Ehrenreich, B. 1984. *The Hearts of Men.* Garden City, NY: Anchor Press/Doubleday.

Furstenberg, F. F. 1988. "Good Dads—Bad Dads." Pp. 193–218 in *The Changing American Family and Public Policy,* edited by A. Cherlin. Washington, DC: Urban Institute Press.

Furstenberg, F. F. and A. Cherlin. 1991. *Divided Families.* Cambridge, MA: Harvard University Press.

Furstenberg, F. F. and K. Harris. 1993. "When and Why Fathers Matter." Pp. 150–76 in *Young Unwed Fathers,* edited by R. Lerman and T. Ooms. Philadelphia: Temple University Press.

Gavanas, A. 2002. "The Fatherhood Responsibility Movement." Pp. 213–42 in *Making Men into Fathers,* edited by B. Hobson. New York: Cambridge University Press.

Griswold, R. L. 1993. *Fatherhood in America: A History.* New York: Basic Books.

Griswold, R. L. 1997. "Generative Fathering: A Historical Perspective." Pp. 71–86 in *Generative Fathering,* edited by A. J. Hawkins and D. Dollahite. Thousand Oaks, CA: Sage.

Harris, K. H., F. F. Furstenberg, and J. K. Marmer. 1998. "Paternal Involvement with Adolescents in Intact Families." *Demography* 35:201–16.

Hawkins, A. J. and D. C. Dollahite. 1997. "Beyond the Role-Inadequacy Perspective of Fathering." Pp. 3–16 in *Generative Fathering: Beyond Deficit Perspectives,* edited by A. J. Hawkins and D. C. Dollahite. Thousand Oaks, CA: Sage.

Hays, S. 1996. *The Cultural Contradictions of Motherhood.* New Haven, CT: Yale University Press.

Hewlett, B. S. 1991. *The Nature and Context of Aka Pygmy Paternal Infant Care.* Ann Arbor: University of Michigan Press.

———. 2000. "Culture, History, and Sex: Anthropological Contributions to Conceptualizing Father Involvement." *Marriage and Family Review* 29:59–73.

Hofferth, S. L. and K. G. Anderson. 2003. "Are All Dads Equal? Biology versus Marriage as a Basis for Paternal Investment." *Journal of Marriage and the Family* 65:213–32.

Horn, W. 1999. "Lunacy 101: Questioning the Need for Fathers." Retrieved April 29, 2003, from the Smart Marriages Web site (http://listarchives.his.com/smartmarriages/smartmarriages.9907/msg00011.html).

Johnson, M. 1988. *Strong Mothers, Weak Wives.* Berkeley: University of California Press.

Kimmel, M. 1996. *Manhood in America: A Cultural History.* New York: Free Press.

Lamb, M. E., J. Pleck, E. Charnov, and J. Levine. 1987. "A Biosocial Perspective on Parental Behavior and Involvement." Pp. 11–42 in *Parenting across the Lifespan,* edited by J. B. Lancaster, J. Altman, and A. Rossi. New York: Academic Press.

LaRossa, R. 1988. "Fatherhood and Social Change." *Family Relations* 37:451–57.

———. 1997. *The Modernization of Fatherhood: A Social and Political History.* Chicago: University of Chicago Press.

Maccoby, E. and R. Mnookin. 1992. *Dividing the Child.* Cambridge, MA: Harvard University Press.

Marsiglio, W., P. Amato, R. D. Day, and M. E. Lamb. 2000. "Scholarship on Fatherhood in the 1990s and Beyond." *Journal of Marriage and the Family* 62:1173–91.

Marsiglio, W. and J. H. Pleck. 2004. "Fatherhood and Masculinities." Pp. 249–269 in *The Handbook of Studies on Men and Masculinities,* edited by R. W. Connell, J. Hearn, and M. Kimmell. Thousand Oaks, CA: Sage.

McDaniel, A. 1994. "Historical Racial Differences in Living Arrangements of Children." *Journal of Family History* 19:57–77.

McLanahan, S. and G. Sandefur. 1994. *Growing Up with a Single Parent: What Hurts, What Helps.* Cambridge, MA: Harvard University Press.

McLanahan, S., J. Seltzer, T. Hanson, and E. Thomson. 1994. "Child Support Enforcement and Child Well-Being." Pp. 285–316 in *Child Support and Child Well-Being,* edited by I. Garfinkel, S. S. McLanahan, and P. K. Robins. Washington, DC: Urban Institute.

Messner, M. 1993. "'Changing Men' and Feminist Politics in the U.S." *Theory and Society* 22:723–37.

Mintz, S. 1998. "From Patriarchy to Androgyny and Other Myths." Pp. 3–30 in *Men in Families,* edited by A. Booth and A. C. Crouter. Mahwah, NJ: Lawrence Erlbaum.

Mosley, J. and E. Thomson. 1995. "Fathering Behavior and Child Outcomes." Pp. 148–65 in *Fatherhood,* edited by W. Marsiglio. Thousand Oaks, CA: Sage.

National Center for Health Statistics. 2000, January. "Nonmarital Birth Rates, 1940–1999." Retrieved April 29, 2003, from the Centers for Disease Control and Prevention Web site (www.cdc.gov/nchs/data/nvsr/nvsr48).

Nock, S. 1998. *Marriage in Men's Lives.* New York: Oxford University Press.

Parke, R. D. 1996. *Fatherhood.* Cambridge, MA: Harvard University Press.

Pleck, E. H. and J. H. Pleck. 1997. "Fatherhood Ideals in the United States: Historical Dimensions." Pp. 33–48 in *The Role of the Father in Child Development,* 3d ed., edited by M. E. Lamb. New York: John Wiley.

Pleck, J. H. 1997. "Paternal Involvement: Levels, Sources, and Consequences." Pp. 66–103 in *The Role of the Father in Child Development,* 3d ed., edited by M. E. Lamb. New York: John Wiley.

Pleck, J. H. and B. P. Masciadrelli. 2003. "Paternal Involvement: Levels, Sources, and Consequences." In *The Role of the Father in Child Development,* 4th ed., edited by M. E. Lamb. New York: John Wiley.

Popenoe, D. 1996. *Life without Father: Compelling New Evidence That Fatherhood and Marriage Are Indispensable for the Good of Children and Society.* New York: Free Press.

Pruett, K. D. 1993. "The Paternal Presence." *Families in Society* 74:46–50.

Sanday, P. R. 1981. *Female Power and Male Dominance.* New York: Cambridge University Press.

Scoon-Rogers, L. 1999. *Child Support for Custodial Mothers and Fathers.* Current Population Reports, P60–196. Washington, DC: U.S. Bureau of the Census.

Seltzer, J. A. 1994. "Consequences of Marital Dissolution for Children." *Annual Review of Sociology* 20:235–66.

———. 1998. "Father by Law: Effects of Joint Legal Custody on Nonresident Fathers' Involvement with Children." *Demography* 35:135–46.

———. 2000. "Families Formed Outside of Marriage." *Journal of Marriage and the Family* 62:1247–68.

Silverstein, L. B. 2002. "Fathers and Families." Pp. 35–64 in *Retrospect and Prospect in the Psychological Study of Fathers,* edited by J. McHale and W. Grolnick. Mahwah, NJ: Lawrence Erlbaum.

Silverstein, L. B. and C. F. Auerbach. 1999. "Deconstructing the Essential Father." *American Psychologist* 54:397–407.

Snarey, J. 1993. *How Fathers Care for the Next Generation.* Cambridge, MA: Harvard University Press.

Stacey, J. 1996. *In the Name of the Family.* Boston: Beacon.

Thompson, L. and A. J. Walker. 1989. "Gender in Families: Women and Men in Marriage, Work, and Parenthood." *Journal of Marriage and the Family* 51:845–71.

Whiting, J. and B. Whiting. 1975. "Aloofness and Intimacy of Husbands and Wives." *Ethos* 3:183–207.

25

WHAT IT MEANS TO BE DADDY
Fatherhood for Black Men Living Away from Their Children

JENNIFER HAMER

Our story about fatherhood for low-income black American fathers is drawing to a close. It began by asking the reader to look at fatherhood through the eyes of this category of men. Specifically, the audience was asked to place paternal attitudes and activities of these fathers in the context of their surrounding environments and then, given the circumstances of these environments, understand parenting from their perspectives. These tasks are complicated by the barrage of public reports about high school drop-out rates, teenage pregnancy, gang violence, and stark poverty among African American children. Headlines blame fathers for their children's poor life circumstances. They are considered deadbeats, absent, and common villains.

The findings from this study of black live-away fathers move us forward in the public debate about black men and their families. They broaden our analyses and lead us to better understand that low-income black live-away fathers, like all other fathers, continuously negotiate their parenting within particular social, political, cultural, and economic circumstances. These circumstances consist of historical and contemporary social and economic injustices, cultural misrepresentations, unrealistic public expectations, and vague parental agreements with the mothers of their children. In this [reading], the reader is again asked to consider the context of black live-away fatherhood and its meaning in the fathers' world. What follows is a brief explanation of why low-income black fatherhood for them appears to contrast with the dominant paradigm. Finally, this [reading] discusses the implications of these findings for social policy.

Fatherhood on the Margins

"The world is a beautiful place," said one father of two, "if you can ignore the trash on the streets, if you can afford to pay the rent every month and eat . . . and then after all that, if you can still see your kids smile at the end

of the day, the world is a beautiful place." Many black, low-income, live-away fathers experience life on the boundaries. Socially, economically, and culturally they hold a marginal position. The men interviewed worked for low wages and acquired low levels of education. They worked in jobs that required erratic schedules, demanded stringent emotional and physical labor, offered little opportunity for advancement, and afforded them little respect.

Most fathers expressed a desire to one day acquire a single job that would enable them to spend greater leisure time with their families and earn enough money to provide sufficiently for them. Said one father, "I just need to make enough so life is not a struggle . . . so I don't have so many worries." Their occupational aspirations did not seem unreasonable. A few shared their desire to become airplane pilots, corporate CEO's, and self-employed owners of profitable upscale businesses. However, references to these types of positions were generally made in jest and described as "dream" jobs.

Given their backgrounds, these fathers genuinely and realistically aspired for working-class employment. They verbally listed companies such as Coca-Cola, the U.S. Postal Service, United Parcel Service, city sanitation work, and other service or blue-collar occupations. They perceived that these employers would provide them with financial stability, family wages and retirement, paid vacation, health insurance, and other benefits. These were accouterments their low-wage labor, underground employment, and/ or unemployment did not render. Fathers told of a few men that they knew who held or once held these types of occupations. "My uncle, he used to work for the telephone company before they laid him off . . . it was a good job, too," one father reported. "He bought himself a nice house . . . he bought his wife a nice car . . . beautiful." A thirty-six-year-old live-away father recalled his childhood neighbors building a new house "with a finished basement and a pool table" when the father was promoted to a supervisory position in a local glass manufacturing plant. Most surmised that these better-paying positions were today difficult to come by and were virtually nonexistent in the areas surrounding their communities.

They were correct in their assessment. Such manufacturing plants and employers continue to move away from cities and communities that house a disproportionate number of poor African American residents. Many of these fathers lived in East St. Louis, Illinois; Houston, Texas; Chicago, Illinois; St. Louis, Missouri; Detroit, Michigan; and other cities that at one time held economic promise for low-skill workers. Not having access to employment with higher wages and better benefits pained fathers. Said one father, "It's like it makes you feel bad when the snowcone van comes around and you don't have money to give to your child for snowcones . . . and yet and still, he sees all his little friends get to buy a snowcone." Another father recalled the anguish and guilt he felt when he did not visit his daughter on her birthday because he had been fired from his job and could not afford to purchase a birthday gift. "I figured her mother would go off on me for showing up without the present that I had promised," he said sadly. He found out weeks later that the mother of his child was angry not because he did not provide

a gift but because he had chosen to simply not attend the celebration at all. In addition to the poor pay and low benefits of employment, these fathers, like black people in general, were faced with racial prejudices and individual acts of discrimination in their everyday encounters at work, on the bus, in stores, and on the streets.

What Fathers Do

For many black men, their situation has demanded that they develop an "ideal" of fatherhood at variance with dominant cultural and institutional norms. Ironically, their status has provided them with some freedom to set their own code of conduct for proper paternal behavior. This freedom has also enabled low-income, black live-away fathers to develop their own identity outside of mainstream expectations and norms. They are, as Le Roi Jones (1963) explains, "natural nonconformists" because "being Black in a society where such a state is an extreme liability is the most extreme form of nonconformity available."[1]

Regardless of black men's uncertain status, social policies, cultural media, and social institutions direct black people to assimilate and adopt European American mainstream conceptualizations of proper attitudes and behavior. Yet, many researchers have argued that social conditions continuously deny them the means by which to live such a lifestyle. Consequently, black men are expected to assimilate into the dominant society and accept mainstream values and conceptualizations of fatherhood as if these ideals correctly reflect their own reality.[2]

Social researchers and social policy creators tend to view fatherhood in a manner significantly different from that held by the men in my study. Family policies generally reflect a patriarchal perspective that is much in keeping with the historical "ideal" of a father as family head. In this study, black live-away fathers have chosen an alternative to this tradition.

Caregiving and Formation Function

According to the fathers in this study, "ideal" live-away fathers are those who spend as much time as possible with their children. This, they perceived, was their primary paternal function. A review of parenting literature indicates that the amount of time fathers spend with their children is less important than the quality of their interaction. Even without this formal knowledge, most of these fathers attempted to involve themselves as much as possible in the daily aspects of their children's care. Fathers reported managing various responsibilities for their children's care. They picked their children up after school, counseled them, and listened to their concerns. They prepared their meals and helped with homework. When they felt mothers were weak in terms of disciplining their children, they stepped in to fill the void.

Similar to married fathers who reside full-time with their children, these men interacted with children in recreational activities as well. While they took them to various public events, they were more likely to entertain their children with low-cost activities. Such activities would include visiting with relatives, playing cards, eating lunch occasionally at McDonald's, going to the park, or simply taking a leisurely stroll. These findings strengthen research indicating that many live-away fathers may involve themselves extensively in children's caretaking. Moreover, these findings indicate that fathers may continue their involvement throughout their children's development—from infancy through adolescence.

This contrasts with studies indicating that among those experiencing divorce, noncustodial fathers decrease involvement with children over time, particularly those who were "very" involved with children prior to divorce. What this may also suggest is that if the two groups were empirically compared, never-married black live-away fathers may be more "consistently" involved with their children than those experiencing divorce. Research also suggests that married fathers who reside with their children spend about one-third of the time mothers do in direct interaction with their offspring. Additionally, they are less likely than mothers to take on responsibilities for child care, such as changing diapers, giving meals, and making medical appointments. Rather, play time takes up much more of their time with children. Many fathers in this study reported spending time with children. Their involvement was at varying levels. Some never visited their children while others cared for them on an almost daily basis. Moreover, for those who visited or cared for their children one or more times a week, what they provided may not differ markedly from the social and emotional care provided by married fathers who reside full-time with their children.[3]

The implications of this call into question the purpose of marriage as it concerns the care and well-being of children, and the impact of divorce on relationships between fathers and offspring. It may be that having never-married parents and a "very involved father" is better for the emotional stability and well-being of children than having lived with married parents who subsequently divorce. Certainly, the question warrants investigation, given the rate of divorce and rising numbers of single-parenting homes in most demographic groups across the United States.

Ideally, mothers explained, fathers should be sufficient economic providers. However, mothers readily modified this ideal to better fit the financial situations of low-skill, low-income fathers. In so doing, mothers agreed with fathers that the paternal time spent with children was more significant than the receipt of child support, but this did not mean they were completely satisfied with the extent of fathers' activities in this arena. Many expressed disappointment at what was, from their perspective, flaccid male parenting. Some mothers felt men could provide more time for their children than they actually did, particularly since they did not often provide substantial child support. Fathers did not disagree with this, but felt that pressures from work, multiple sets of children, and physical distance from children's homes strained their ability to be accessible and involved at an optimum level.

Mothers acknowledged that black men in general were in a difficult position in today's contemporary social and economic spheres. However, they were often reluctant to accept men's excuses for not spending more time with their children. As one mother stated: "Women always have to make time for their kids, and we always do. . . . Fathers shouldn't be able to get off from that." Mothers too, were stressed economically and would have liked more financial support from fathers. Again, there was general acknowledgment that men also were economically "strapped." Women generally felt that to castigate men and/or pursue them for more money may have a countereffect. From their experiences, it would discourage men from visiting their children, and from contributing what little economic assistance they did provide.

Legal Bonds

Family policies and social institutions expect all fathers to provide their children with a legal bond to their ancestry and formal ties to paternal kin. In this study, none of the men indicated this was a primary element of their roles and functions as fathers. Fathers generally felt it was important for their children to know them as their "daddy." However, knowing paternity was not equated with a legal bond. Whether or not children carried their father's surname seemed of little significance to live-away fathers or custodial mothers. The majority of these men's children did not have their fathers' respective surnames. As in times of slavery, children had access to both maternal and paternal kinship networks despite the absence of sanctioned bonds between father and child.

Traditionally, European American fathers have provided their offspring with paternal surnames so that children are legally recognized as their father's child. In this way, children were able to reap the benefits of significant financial support and inheritance that formal ties to their ancestry might bring. But this particular intent has little meaning for low-income black live-away fathers. In terms of material inheritance, property, wealth, and accompanying accouterments, these men have virtually nothing to pass on to their offspring. "All I can give him," said one father in reference to his three-year-old son, "is my bills."

Provider

In U.S. society, how fathers function in their provider/breadwinner role is the basis for measuring their success or failure. Interviewed black live-away fathers consciously rejected this element as a defining feature of their success or failure as fathers. Furthermore, they considered it to be one of the least important functions of their fatherhood. Those that paid child support on a consistent basis expressed various reasons for doing so. For a few fathers, child support was a legal matter in which their nonpayment could result in

legal action against them. One never-married father lived with his children and their mother for twelve years before separating from them. Without a court order, this father willingly provided consistent monthly economic support to his children. He explained:

> *I have always given them everything . . . my constant love and attention . . . as much of my time as possible . . . and I make a good living so I give that, too. . . . I don't need no judge coming between me and my kids. . . . I told her [the children's mother] as long as it stays between me and you then I'll take care of my own.*

Still other fathers stated that they used child support as a means to make up for the lack of time they spent with their children. Yet, no father viewed the provider role as the most important aspect of his fathering. Nor did they use this as a criterion with which to rate their performance as fathers.

For these fathers, children were primarily cared for by their mothers or another maternal family member. In addition, various maternal and paternal kinfolk provided an array of new and "hand-me-down" goods—clothing, toys, shoes, linens, and furniture that in most cases neither parent could altogether afford to purchase. For most of these fathers at least one set of their children qualified for and received government welfare benefits at some point during their lives, regardless of fathers' economic situation. Welfare benefits addressed children's essential needs—health care, nutrition requirements, and housing; however, no welfare allowances alone were sufficient. Kin networks, social service organizations (food pantries, etc.) contributed to the survival of women and their children. Although such benefits and familial assistance did not guarantee a child the best quality of life, they nonetheless provided fathers and mothers with some sense of comfort.

Although fathers generally looked to others to assume the primary provider role for their children, they looked to themselves to "improve" their children's quality of life. They worked and sought higher education so that in the future they could help their children. In this respect, they expressed attitudes similar to those of custodial black fathers. Like their custodial counterparts, these fathers had great dreams for their offspring, and expected them to attain both academic and professional success (Robinson et al. 1985).

What Mothers Want from Their Children's Daddies

Despite their circumstances, fathers in this study well understood what policy makers and politicians expected of them as fathers. Recent welfare policies demand that states assign paternity to children and secure formal child support from fathers regardless of their economic circumstances. What was unclear to fathers in this study was that the mothers of their children tended to harbor ideals and standards of fatherhood that were similar to those espoused through social policy. They reluctantly relinquish their right to demand child support for fear of what their children may lose in the long run.

For example, custodial mothers of children are compelled to reveal paternity information or face the potential penalties that include the loss of much-needed welfare benefits. However, many of the mothers in this study were reluctant about pursuing fathers for formal payments. Many receive some informal, though inconsistent, support from children's fathers. Consequently, they were concerned that formal pursuit of consistent financial support would not only discourage men from visiting their children but might possibly land fathers in jail if they are unable to meet payment terms. Mothers were also reluctant to pursue child support for another reason: When fathers provide child support through state agencies, the state benefits received for their children are reduced. Moreover, what low-income fathers are able to provide through state agencies does not significantly improve their living conditions.

Nevertheless, mothers often reported feelings of anger toward fathers for not doing more to provide for their children. Fathers, on the other hand, tended to feel they were doing the best they could economically, given the dire straits they often experienced. They felt that relative to their fathers, they were "pretty good" dads. They also felt that mothers had, at least, some support from state and other public and private agencies, which presumably made up for many of the things they could not give. Still, fathers recognized that even these sources did not provide enough, and maintained informal arrangements with the mothers of their children. Upon request, fathers attempted to help mothers and children with purchases of food, clothing, shoes, school supplies, and other needs. They also used various sources to get toys and other extra items for their children. At the time of their interviews, few of these fathers were paying child support through official means. They did, however, feel that there was often more they could do in terms of the social and emotional role they played in their children's lives.

"Bumps in the Road"

Live-away parenting was not always easy. Fathers negotiated their paternal activities in the context of unfriendly attitudes and behaviors from some of the mothers of their children, the lack of support and guidance they received from their own parents, and employment and formal education schedules. Findings from past research on divorced live-away fathers suggest that such circumstances often serve as barriers, inhibiting men's ability to parent their children. Interviewed fathers perceived these elements as making it more difficult to perform fatherhood functions but not necessarily as "barriers" preventing them from doing what they desired to do for their children. One father referred to these "barriers" as "bumps in the road." They were considered small hurdles easily overcome by a determination to be a good father. In fact, these fathers perceived few if any permanent obstacles to their parenting. A "lack of time" and "physical proximity away from children" were the primary hurdles fathers felt that they were constantly leaping. Each was due primarily to fathers having multiple jobs, multiple families, and multiple sets

of children. Mostly, these elements were considered quite simply as negative aspects of live-away fatherhood, of which fathers had little control.

Although fathers' relationships sometimes posed problems for their parenting, they were also a source of strength, providing support to their ability to perform the tasks of fatherhood. Assessing the gate-keeping activities of the mothers of their children was complex. Women generally felt their words and actions encouraged fathers' participation. From their perspective, it was often their encouragement that moved fathers to maintain involvement. From men's view, mothers were simultaneously encouraging and controlling. Women seemed to control when fathers could and could not visit with children, and enlisted the assistance of significant others (boyfriends, mothers, sisters, aunts, brothers, etc.) when fathers did not abide by their rules. Consequently, fathers expressed feelings of powerlessness. They sometimes felt like outsiders in their children's lives.

Nevertheless, most women encouraged fathers to spend time with their children, and fathers perceived that this was the most important expectation of them. Similar to the findings of Stack (1974, 1986), fathers tended to participate in their children's household as a close "friend" to the family. They ran errands, provided child care and transportation, performed yard work, and rendered various other services. In exchange, they sometimes were treated as one of the family. Mothers often provided fathers with meals, allowed them to relax around the house and watch television, and allowed them to spend time with the children in their home.

The mothers of fathers in this study also provided fathers a source of support and encouragement. Fathers' mothers encouraged their sons to spend time with their children, provided sons with comfort, and provided them with advice on childrearing and life in general. In times of disagreements, they also served as mediators between their sons and the mothers of their sons' children. One woman recalled that out of anger and disappointment, she prevented her children's father from visiting with them for three months. She also refused to accept any gifts or money he offered the children. When his prodding to reconsider proved unsuccessful, the father simply took the items to his mother and the woman's mother. These women made certain the items reached their destination. "My children still needed to know I cared about them even though I did their mother wrong," the father explained. The mother agreed and relented. After some time, the two began communicating again.

The Difference between Fathers and Daddies

Fathers distinguished between two types of fathers—those who were "just" fathers and those who acted as "daddies." The former they described as "baby-makers," or those who demonstrated no care for their children. This type was presumed to have multiple children with different women; however, these relationships were rarely sustained for long periods of time. "Daddies," on the other hand, were those who expressed love, provided

social support and companionship, and made their children a central part of their lives. No father in this study fit the "baby-maker" profile. It is important to note that at a glance some may have appeared to, particularly those who had no apparent contact with their children. Upon further exploration of their individual circumstances and decision making, even these relatively few men appeared to fall somewhere in between the definitions of "baby-maker" and "daddy." They expressed great love for their children, but felt overwhelmed and/or constricted by their circumstances. They also seemed to foresee few if any potential opportunities to change their situations. "Daddies" explained that they learned their father role through trial and error and from their own parents.

Mothers of fathers, in particular, provided incentive and inspiration for sons "to do right" by their children—that is, spend time and be a "daddy" to them. Yet, the lack of interaction between men and their own fathers also inspired them to be good daddies. Similar to married fathers mentioned in Blankenhorn's *Fatherless America* (1995), these men were attempting to be better fathers to their children than they felt their fathers had been to them.

Not all fathers were able to negotiate the demands of parenting into their daily lives. Some fathers were quite literally absent from their children's lives. However, none fit the stereotype of the uncaring, selfish, absentee parent circulating in popular media. On the contrary, these fathers expressed deep concern for their children's well-being and shared emotional accounts of how their disengagement from parenting occurred. Many reported their absence was in the best interests of their children. Their ability to parent was overwhelmingly impaired by what seemed to be overlapping experiences in two or more of the following life circumstances: substance abuse, illegal employment, incarceration, and contention between themselves and the mothers of their children. Additionally, some of these fathers appeared to have experienced acute poverty as children themselves and lacked significant sources of social support that may have strengthened their ability to co-parent. While involved fathers tussled with similar obstacles, they seemed to describe having access to various forms of social and economic support throughout their childhood, during pregnancy, and following the birth of their children. Several absent fathers generally felt confounded by their situations and/or felt that their ability to change their situation for their children would be a difficult and complicated task.

Never-Married Co-Parenting Families: An Incomplete Institution

Noncustodial fatherhood was a formal aspect of American slavery. Furthermore, from this period on, the nonresident father–custodial mother family form was sustained through social, economic, and political institutions. Never-married childbearing and co-parenting is historically established and persists in significant proportions in black communities. However, as an institution in U.S. society, it is quite incomplete. Despite its increasing

prevalence among most demographic groups in the United States, it has yet to be accepted and instituted as a legitimate alternative to the nuclear family.[4]

Relative to laws and norms that protect and inform bonds within marital relationships, those that protect relationships and define appropriate behavior for never-married co-parents and partners are still evolving. The never-married live-away father, custodial mother, family has yet to embody a well-established structured pattern of paternal behavior that is a fundamental part of our American culture. What is more, the state's primary emphasis on paternal financial "responsibility" is complicated by the low and inconsistent earnings of many black fathers.

Low-income black fathers and the mothers of their children seem to be developing a definition of fatherhood and a pattern of behavior that best fits these economic circumstances. The mothers of their children, who are also economically deprived, often do their best to maintain paternal ties, even if it means relinquishing their right to child support. Thus, even the development of "child support payments" as a paternal norm for low-income men remains problematic. Custodial mothers and live-away fathers find themselves negotiating and defining their social roles, functions, and interactions with little institutional guidance or support. Consequently, fathers are often unclear about what mothers expect of them as parents. Mothers are constantly assessing and reassessing means to improve fathers' paternal sensibilities and behaviors. This is particularly difficult because there seems to exist so little general public understanding or verbal agreement on what fathers are supposed to do as live-away dads.

Redefining Fatherhood and Adapting Policies to Families

Fathers in this study seemed to discuss fatherhood in a way that best preserved their sense of accomplishment. Their definition of primary paternal roles and functions placed meaning in what they were best able to do for their children. To do otherwise would serve to inhibit their potential as parents and to set themselves up for possible failure as men and as fathers. Their definition of the most important aspects of fatherhood comes from their own interactions with significant others and from their understanding of life's options. It is also within these micro- and meso-systems that live-away fathers look for and find approval for their father functions. Theirs is a "bottom-up" perspective of live-away fatherhood that draws from the daily lives of those most affected by social policy decisions. It is unlike the "top-down" view of the world that characterizes the practices of many social scientists and social policy creators.

These groups tend to view the world and define the functions of black live-away fathers in terms of the values and norms of the dominant culture. Their definition of the most "desirable" father behavior—providing child support and a paternal surname—negates the values and behaviors

of those who hold dissimilar views. At a minimum it places a lesser value on opposing perspectives. Thus, while black live-away fathers express a view of fatherhood that is based on their reality, theirs is a fatherhood that is provided little to no formal support or legitimacy. Social policies addressing child support and support for black fatherless families in general do not factor in the worldview of black live-away fathers. Overall, social policy efforts are far removed from the daily experiences of black men and women. For this reason, Christopher Jencks (1993) argues that many black men and women feel justified in carrying out alternative and adaptive means of survival to provide for themselves and the well-being of their children.

Critics might point out, perhaps correctly, that the evidence presented by fathers in this study is influenced by the tendency people have to present themselves in a favorable light. In fact, measuring the effects of mothers' and fathers' attitudes and behaviors on children's well-being were beyond the scope of this study. Consequently, conclusions drawn are suggestive rather than definitive. Nevertheless, it seems black live-away fathers are developing their own form of fatherhood despite a steady barrage of negative social messages, myths, and negative stereotypes. This attests to the importance black men place on their father/child bonds. Evaluating their fatherhood strictly in terms of the dominant Western paradigm undermines and disregards the subtle strength of what they do provide and can potentially provide for the well-being of their children.

Moving Forward: Improving Circumstances for Parents and Children in Black Noncustodial Father Families

Social policy attempting to address the emotional, social, and economic well-being of black children has—to date—been largely ineffective. Relative to other groups, black children continue to have higher rates of poverty, juvenile delinquency, teenage pregnancies, death from homicide, drug use, school dropouts, and poor health. Social policies have attempted to combat such statistics by attempting to establish children's paternity, subsequently pursuing live-away fathers for formal payment of child support and by implementing various changes in welfare policy. . . .

Supporting Never-Married Co-Parents through Social Policy and Community

American families are increasingly resembling the predominant African American noncustodial father–custodial mother family form. Furthermore, regardless of race and ethnicity, noncustodial fathers frequently do not provide for the financial security of their children, even when they can afford to do so. Addressing the experiences of low-income black fathers and their children may inevitably enable social policy makers and social work practitioners to better understand and assist other groups in similar circumstances.

Low-income live-away fathers must be guaranteed full employment at livable wages if they are expected to fulfill their parental financial obligations. At the macrolevel, local, state, and federal governments must legislate both for all working people if they hope for these parents to have the means to provide enough money to boost themselves and their children out of poverty. Under current conditions and policy emphases, women with children generally gain access to breadwinner's income solely through marriage. Black women are less likely than other demographic groups to marry and/or find mates that earn breadwinner wages. Unless livable wages are instituted, the problem of childhood poverty will remain unbounded in the United States, whether or not parents reside in the same household as their shared offspring (Orloff 1993).

But men's legitimate employment and higher wages alone will not sufficiently improve the well-being of black children. The nurturing and caring aspects of live-away parenting must be further defined and strengthened through institutional and community support. Government attempts to improve the well-being of poor black children and all children will continue to be ill-effective unless researchers and policy creators adapt their perspective of low-income black never-married parents to their reality. Social policy creators must recognize the primary elements of black live-away fatherhood as a "legitimate alternative" to the traditional patriarchal notions of fatherhood, particularly under current economic conditions. Additionally, the definition of fatherhood or the "good father" must be broadened to include the varying characteristics and experiences of low-income black families. Once a more inclusive definition is developed, policy creators can identify and more adequately support family members through legislation and public discourse.

To accomplish this task is complex. Researchers and policy creators must continue to seek to find a balance between the economic provider and nurturing roles. Current policies concerning child support continue to place primary emphasis on the economic support fathers are expected to provide for their children. The everyday nurturance and care for children continues to be gendered labor, and tends to fall most heavily on the shoulders of women. Relatively little importance is placed on the social or emotional relationship between fathers and their children. Yet, the well-being of poor children requires an investment in both time and money, and each element should be a calculated factor in the determination of child support (Klawitter 1994). Some live-away fathers can provide money and time; still others can provide more of one element than the other. Feminists have been arguing for decades that an economic formula should be applied to the caregiving and nurturant roles and functions of childrearing. So too should such a formula be calculated and applied to live-away father/child and mother/child relationships to ensure that children are receiving at least a minimum of what they need for emotional, social, and economic well-being.

Presently, there is no adequate systematic means of accounting for the amount and type of care fathers provide to their children. Nor is there an adequate means of accounting for the informal economic support black

live-away fathers seem to provide. Yet, while popular media, and politicians, and researchers continue to associate the presence of a father with positive well-being and quality of life outcomes for children, they have failed to adequately articulate what it is about fathers that directly links to this phenomenon. Is it, for example, the financial support they provide to the household? Is it their physical presence in the household? Is it the amount and/or type of quality and interactive time they spend with children? Or, is it some or all of the above?

Is it possible to be a good father and not provide significant financial support to one's child? For some directors of father centers in black communities the answer is yes, especially if fathers are doing the most they can for their children. According to one director: "Men want to be fathers to their children and must learn how to do so despite their inconsistent and difficult financial state." He and other program facilitators also argue that men have increased self-esteem and self-confidence, and are more patient and willing to communicate with the mothers of their children, when they are working at legally well-paying jobs. This, they contend, enables them to feel a sense of power in daily parental decision making that affects their children's behavior and well-being. Thus, these programs find themselves attempting to strike a balance between nurturing and economic parenting activities that best fit the lives of their clients.

The goals of father-centered programs would be much easier if they were expressly aided by support from other community entities. In his foreword to Andrew Billingsley's work on the black church and social reform, *Mighty like a River* (1999), C. Eric Lincoln argues that the church is a "vitalizing resource" for all Americans and a "defining reference" in the black community. Faith-based organizations in black communities have historically taken the lead toward social reform. Today they remain the most well-organized and entrenched networks within black America. Moreover, their leadership is often sought by politicians and policy makers for commentary and assessment of conditions for black families.

Yet, under current social and economic conditions, churches must become more ardent and vigilant social activists if they intend to continue as leaders for social change. Their leadership and membership must work as agents to address secular issues confronting black families. Moreover, dwindling resources among the poorest churches and black communities demands that faith-based organizations collaborate with other institutions and activist organizations to identify and address the needs of black mothers, fathers, and children.

Many churches have responded to the sustained secular crises among black families. Over two-thirds of 635 churches surveyed in Billingsley's study operated community outreach programs, a majority of which consisted of adult family support. However, effective support to custodial mothers and noncustodial fathers requires that church leadership and program coordinators think holistically and beyond traditional notions of family. Custodial mothers, live-away fathers, grandparents, aunts, uncles, and fictive kin all play a significant role in raising black children within the noncustodial

father family form. Programs should seek to help family members to define the roles of family members and enhance positive communication and interaction, particularly between mothers and fathers.[5]

Although it exists separately from a church, the Lutheran Child and Family Services Fathers Center of East St. Louis, Illinois, attempts to do just that. Here, the Reverend Phoenix Barnes brings divorced, separated, and never-married fathers and mothers together to discuss their familial circumstances, their parental options and choices, and identify and define their appropriate roles as co-parents. The program also provides opportunities for fathers to seek employment and continued education. It also enables them to spend quality time with their children and arranges familial outings that neither parent could otherwise afford.

Faith-based programs must also be prepared to address many of the problems that may further inhibit familial well-being, such as adult unemployment, substance abuse, incarceration, and low levels of education. Most importantly, as "vitalizing" agents, churches must take the lead in supporting and institutionalizing noncustodial father family forms by articulating their circumstances and needs to social service agencies, educational systems, and cultural media, institutions that can help legitimize this family form. But churches, social service agencies, and the educational system are only part of the solution. They cannot be wholly effective without further attention paid to living wages for poor and working-class people and women's economic ability to develop and maintain autonomous households.

Inevitably, what poor and working-class black live-away fathers actually do for their children rests with society's ability to provide them access to sufficient economic means. It is equally contingent on the legitimacy and support granted to their paternal status. It is also based on their ability to interact and communicate with those who assist in the co-parenting of their children. It is further influenced by black men's ability to define and voice their own vision of fatherhood in the context of their collective economic and social circumstances. For those men who have little else to offer, the provision of nurturance, love, and affection are priceless aspects of fatherhood. Said one father, "No matter what anybody else say, we black men have got to make fatherhood work for *us*. . . . All our babies want is their daddies, and we have got to decide what that means."

ENDNOTES

[1] The quote from Jones is used with caution here. Jones, or Amiri Baraka, is well known for his male chauvinism, and this study's findings and conclusions offer little support for the patriarchal ideals about male and female relationships that he espouses.

[2] See Williams et al. 1995. Also see Jewell 1988; Majors and Billson 1992; Taylor 1994.

[3] See Rivera, Sweeney, and Henderson 1986; Stack 1986; McClanahan 1999. Michael E. Lamb (1995) provides an excellent summary of the literature on what fathers do for their children. He also examines the influence of paternal involvement on child development. It appears that married fathers tend to provide about one-third of what mothers do regardless of whether both parents work 30 hours or more a week. One should note that the studies reviewed consist of primarily white samples. However, there are some indications that black fathers tend to do more in the household than their white counterparts. Yet, there is research that contradicts

this as well. It is important to note that at least one study suggests that relative to middle-class and professional resident fathers, working-class fathers have increased their parental interaction with children more in recent decades. See Ferree (1988), whose work suggests that part of the reason for this is that women in working-class families are more likely to perceive themselves and be perceived by others as sharing the breadwinning role. Thus, she is in a better position than middle-class and professional women to demand and initiate greater participation in household activities and childcare. In middle-class families the need for women's wages is less apparent and more apt to be perceived as a privilege.

[4] The term "noncustodial" is used to describe a live-away father status in slavery only for lack of a better term. There are definite qualitative differences between live-away status during slavery and present-day circumstances. During the former, black men (and women) were bonded labor and had no control over where they lived and sometimes no say in the decision to partner with a particular woman. In contemporary times, blacks have a different relationship to the market. They are no longer bonded. However, their noncustodial status is influenced by (among other factors) their relationship to the free market, their inability to find meaningful employment, and their relationship to the mother of their children.

[5] Billingsley 1999. In the past decade, faith-based initiatives have increased across the nation. Federal grant availability and a general decline in the well-being of poor black communities have spurred the sharp increase in the development of nonprofit programs housed within churches. Grant monies also encourage faith-based organizations to collaborate to provide services to their communities and minimize duplication.

REFERENCES

Billingsley, Andrew. 1999. *Mighty Like a River: The Black Church and Social Reform.* New York: Oxford University Press.

Blankenhorn, David. 1995. *Fatherless America: Confronting Our Most Urgent Social Problem.* New York: Basic Books.

Ferree, Myra Marx. 1988. "Negotiating Household Roles and Responsibilities: Resistance, Conflict, and Change." Paper presented at annual conference of the National Council on Family Relations, Philadelphia, November.

Jencks, Christopher. 1993. *Rethinking Social Policy: Race, Poverty, and the Underclass.* New York: Harper Perennial.

Jewell, K. Sue. 1988. *Survival of the Black Family: The Institutional Impact of U.S. Social Policy.* Westport, CT: Praeger.

Jones, Le Roi. 1963. *Blues People: Negro Music in White America.* New York: William Morrow and Company.

Klawitter, Marieka M. 1994. "Who Gains, Who Loses from Changing U.S. Child Support Policies?" *Policy Sciences* 27 (2–3): 197–219.

Lamb, Michael E. 1995. "The Changing Roles of Fathers." Pp. 18–35 in *Becoming a Father,* edited by Jerrold Shapiro, Michael Diamond, and Martin Greenberg. New York: Springer.

Majors, Richard and Janet Mancini Billson. 1992. *Cool Pose: The Dilemma of Black Manhood in America.* New York: Lexington.

McLanahan, Sara. 1999. "Dispelling Myths about Unwed Parents." National Summit on Supporting Urban Fathers, National Fatherhood Initiative, June 14, Washington, DC.

Orloff, Ann Shola. 1993. "Gender and Social Rights of Citizenship: The Comparative Analysis of Gender Relations and Welfare States." *American Sociological Review* 58 (June): 303–28.

Rivera, F., P. Sweeney, and B. Henderson. 1986. "Black Teenage Fathers: What Happens When the Child Is Born?" *Pediatrics* 78 (1): 151–58.

Robinson, Ira E., Wilfred Bailey, John Smith, and Bernice Bzrnett. 1985. "Self-Perception of the Husband/Father in the Intact Lower-Class Black Family." *Phylon* 46 (2): 136–47.

Stack, Carol. 1974. *All Our Kin: Strategies for Survival in a Black Community.* New York: Harper and Row.

———. 1986. "Sex Roles and Survival Strategies in an Urban Black Community." In *The Black Family: Essays and Studies,* 3d ed., edited by R. Staples. New York: Harper and Row.

Taylor, Ronald. 1994. "Black Males and Social Policy: Breaking the Cycle of Disadvantage." Pp. 147–66 in *The Black Male: His Present and Future Status,* edited by R. G. Majors and J. U. Gordon. Chicago: Nelson-Hall.

Williams, Norma, Kelly Himmel, Andrea Sjoberg, and D. Torrez. 1995. "The Assimilation Model, Family Life, and Race and Ethnicity in the United States: The Case of Minority Welfare Mothers." *Journal of Family Issues* 16:380–405.

26

THE FATHER AS AN IDEA

ROSANNA HERTZ

Abby Pratt-Evans

I sat on my living room floor with all these anonymous donor profiles around me. I had spent hours earlier that day downloading them from the Cryobank Web site. I was trying to look them over before my best friend from college came over to help me. Well, not really help me—she was more there for moral support. I was both excited and nervous, having prepared for this evening for a long time. This evening was about a new beginning, and I went through a lot to get to this point. . . .

I really started seriously considering a donor when I discussed what to do with my therapist. I had heard about a workshop through my HMO for single women considering motherhood. I didn't know anything about support groups or I was clueless to the various options for going about having a child. I remember having a hard time getting there, which is not like me. I was late. I walked in, barely looking at anyone. We went around to do introductions and as soon as I started, I just started blubbering and crying and that was why I was reluctant to go to the meeting 'cause it was real heavy-duty. I was just crying and crying and crying. The anxiety was just all on the surface. It slipped out.

The room felt like it was closing in. I took a deep breath that I learned from my yoga class. I calmed down and tried again to talk. As I talked the women around the table were nodding at me and I heard myself saying, "I thought I would be happily married by this point in my life, not wrestling with the idea that I might not meet someone in time. I really have a very strong desire to have a child. And it doesn't stop. It just keeps growing." Then I looked closely at the women who had just heard years of my life. They shared the feelings I had put to words. I could tell on their faces. I knew that admitting my preoccupation with having a baby was the first step to doing something about it. It seemed like I had entered a secret society. By then I had stopped crying and I felt my body relaxing—I felt relieved. This was a new world and I was applying for membership.

So I went to that workshop and got a lot of information. I scribbled down notes on a yellow legal pad I had taken with me from home about all sorts of things, from opinions on where to get the best sperm to which insurance plan I needed to switch to during my company's open enrollment. And I kept all that information in my head until I needed it. But that workshop turned out to be very useful.

Still, I wasn't sure that I wanted to use an anonymous donor. As I sat on the floor organizing the donor profiles, I recalled why the men I knew were not suitable as known donors. Two years earlier I had written a handful of letters to my best men friends. One was a childhood friend I'd grown up with, another I had met through a youth group and had briefly become my boyfriend, and the third was my sister's husband—this letter I wrote to both my sister and Frank. I recalled each of their responses to my conditions for complete legal rights over the future child. The complexity of those conditions made the profiles spread out in front of me seem somehow less taxing because they lacked strings. Patrick, my childhood friend, responded that his family would want to be involved even though he was "cool" with my wanting nothing from him. I adored his mother and sister and I knew they would be lovingly involved; yet I feared just how involved they would become—I didn't want them hovering around—and Patrick's child would possibly injure my relationship to them. They were local while he had moved away. George, whom I had dated, was skeptical about my motives. He called to say that he did not want to reconnect with me, even if it had been years since we were a couple, and he really thought I would hit him up for child support. Since this was about a hypothetical child, there was no way to assure him to the contrary. And then finally, my sister's husband, Frank, whom I had known for twenty years, had children of his own. He and my sister took my request seriously—as close as we are, I needed to put it all in writing. It felt easier than raising this directly. Frank thought the family relationships would just be too complicated. He said he loved me as his sister-in-law, but why mess with good family relationships? I was disappointed that there were strings attached in ways I hadn't really considered. I knew there could be possible legal entanglements, but I just didn't realize how many people this would involve. For example, I couldn't concede having Patrick's family involved, and he was the one who came the closest to being my known donor. I thought about asking a few more men, but that too seemed futile the more I thought about how a known donor might fit into my life. . . .

Back to the night with the profiles—I was really at a loss as to where to begin. I had almost fifty profiles. It was bizarre because all those profiles around me reminded me of the huge puzzles I always like to do on my floor, except this was about the kid I was about to have. The profiles were actually pretty detailed—they included information like identity release information, family medical histories, physical characteristics, education, occupation, and then there were short-answer questions about hobbies, life goals, why they became donors, and their personality traits.

I didn't know how to weigh the various pieces of information. Suddenly I thought about the internship I had done at a local college's admissions office. Maybe I should come up with a formula for ranking the profiles. I thought to myself, "There must be a method." I struggled with how to equate various medical histories and translate them into phenotypic realities. I highlighted the relevant information on each profile but I couldn't find a common thread. Staring again at the profiles, I found myself rejecting profiles of men who were of different ethnic origins than my own. Short men and men with long, problematic medical histories also didn't appeal to me. But still I was left with a stack of potential donors whom I couldn't differentiate.[1] I liked the idea of an identity release donor. At least the option to meet the donor would be

available. Eighteen years was a long time to wait, but it had the potential to make him less abstract.

I was so totally lost in my own thoughts, trying to figure out a system for finding the one "perfect donor," that I didn't hear the doorbell ring. Nina nearly scared the pants off me—she had let herself in with the emergency key and was standing in the doorway watching me. Nina was shocked by my floor covered in paper and immediately suggested a glass of wine. I thought of Nina as a sister—we were really close in college and now, ten years later, we still share the most intimate details. Nina was the first person I told about my plan to become a single mother. It was such a funny evening when we went through the profiles. I remember Nina picked up the profile lying nearest her, flipped to the questions, and she read out loud, "Why do you want to become a sperm donor?" And in a man's voice—she could always do great voices—she read the answer, something like "I graduated Ivy League with honors in the top 10 percent of my class. My scores on the SAT and GRE correlate to an IQ of 160. My blood relatives are intelligent, athletic, and they tend to live long, healthy lives. I consider donating my sperm to be the greatest act of charity."

I thought he sounded good, like my child would be really smart, but I remember Nina told me to get real. She told me, "Abby, your child would be a narcissistic basket case. What does an IQ score have to do with predicting your future child's intelligence?" Then she flipped over the page and pointed out that on page one, there was information about his twin, who was diagnosed with schizophrenia at age eighteen. So that profile went in the trash. Nina was great to have there; she was catching things I totally had missed.

I remember another profile that cracked us up. There's a question on the profiles asking about artistic abilities and one guy wrote, "Drawing: excellent (stick people)." I remember it made us laugh and we both loved that he had a sense of humor. And his health was perfect; he was a yes identity release, so my kid could meet him. But he was black. While I had dated black men when we were younger, I didn't know if I was prepared to have a mixed-race child alone.

Anyway, we kept going through profiles. Nina was being a goofball, grabbing profiles like she was a magician, all dramatic. There was another one, Dutch-Italian, six foot, medium build, green eyes, fair skin. He was a yes to meet the kid. I remember that one of his grandmothers was an alcoholic, but I didn't really get turned off until I read some of his answers. A couple I remember: to why he became a sperm donor, he said, "The payoff wasn't too bad." And then I was reading to Nina what he said about his math ability, a favorite line of mine, something like "I moderately enjoy math but my skills are above normal if I moderately apply myself." But his writing skill was below normal. Even though he was willing to meet the child and he was a good physical match, I wanted to toss him.

But honestly, none of the profiles really fit. No one grabbed me except the profile of the funny black man. And I couldn't help but think, why couldn't there be a funny white man who is more like me physically? I remember Nina's response to my whining—she reminded me I wasn't picking a boyfriend. She told me, "These aren't guys. This is sperm you're picking. Do you have to like the sperm? Or do we just go with physical information and medical histories 'cause you and I both know that humor isn't genetic, right?"

With Nina's help, I finally was able to decide on an anonymous donor. I called the sperm bank to request donor number 180 and I bought enough vials of frozen sperm for ten tries. After inseminating for six months through my local HMO's clinic, I became pregnant at the age of thirty-three. Occasionally during the pregnancy I thought about the anonymous donor and what he might be like, but those thoughts were fleeting. The profile reassured me that I had at least something to tell my kid about his father.

I'm a diary keeper and I kept one during my pregnancy. When you called me about this interview, I read it over. One of the things that I noticed is that I rarely mention the donor, short of the night that Nina and I chose him. I have a friend who's pregnant right now, and I can't help but wonder what her diary entries must look like as a married woman. It must be different to be drawn closer to a partner who will share the baby. I mean, I talked to friends and family about being excited when I was pregnant, but there was no one special and equally invested in this baby to share my feelings with.

But even without a partner, there were tons of people at the birth, and the first couple of weeks I was never alone in the house, between my mom and Nina and a few other friends. But after the initial rush of new motherhood, I knew I had to establish a routine for myself and the baby. It's worked out okay. . . .

Sometimes I wonder, though. I look at my baby's face and wonder about the sperm donor. Who does my son look like and who will he take after?

Your Father, Your Self

Abby's experience points to the utility of knowing one's biological parents in order to construct an identity. On one hand, the politics of anonymous donor-assisted families do not allow women to answer these fundamental questions of identity for their children (Hood 2002). Humanizing an anonymous sperm donor can only be approached by using the child's own characteristics to sketch the man behind the sperm. On the other hand, women who become pregnant through known donors highlight this man differently, having a tangible man separate from the child to reference.

Women such as Abby and their children grapple not only with the way they see themselves but also with the way they think others see them—something theorist Charles Horton Cooley described as the "looking-glass self." In other words, a child's self-image is composed of many things, but principal among them are how he imagines someone else seeing him, how he imagines that other person judges him (e.g., handsome or clever), and how he feels about that imagined judgment.[2] Mothers who use anonymous or known donors as fathers for their children need to help children imagine how they appear in the eyes of these fathers. In addition, the mother evaluates her route to parenthood positively, including the value of the father as having given her a gift, as we see later on. The mother decides how these traits she has identified from the father should be valued in the child (e.g., intelligence, physical appearance, talent; in the case of an anonymous donor, information she has gleaned from a paper profile). A woman who uses

a known donor also helps the child to imagine the appearance of a positive father through more concrete, personal knowledge. These fathers, the women told me, often appreciate and know the child from a distance. The absence of an actual father makes the mothers' effort to create a looking-glass self (that is, how the child sees the father seeing himself or herself) more central to the child's self. Therefore, in the case of both anonymous and known donors, there is an evaluation and imagination of the self that contrasts sharply with the ideal father-present family.

While "paper fathers" and known donors may periodically enter the scene, offering glimpses of how they influence children's identities, the more enduring and impactful influence on a child's early identity is the active relationship he or she has with his or her mother. Donor gametes are only a token of the child's identity. Mothers, and then mothers and their children, are the ones who create stories about who those men are in order to help children pin down or concretize their self-images. Like all valued objects, the child's sense of self is fragile; it needs to be constantly reaffirmed. This effort at affirmation—to-ing and fro-ing about who the father is and who the child is—also has an effect on the relationship between mother and child. Theorist Anselm Strauss (1959) put it nicely: "involvements become evolvements" that transform the mother–child relationship as together they imagine the father (p. 37).

This [reading] examines fatherhood fantasies as well as various arrangements between fathers and their children. Here, I argue that fathers are more ghostlike than real. I am most interested in the accounts women give to their children about paternal kinship and how those accounts arise. All families tell stories to their children of where they came from as part of the fabric that bonds children to the adults with whom they are close. These early memories are accounts of the self that children love to hear repeated, akin to favorite bedtime stories. An account of the family and each member's story is constantly in progress.

The story woven by the mother combines genetic and social identity. The importance of genetics must be considered apart from the medical perspective, particularly with regard to how much weight to give genetics in shaping lives over nurture. But from a purely social perspective, genetics is both an idea and a road map of identity. These mothers are searching for a means to "locate" their children based on the information they have. Genetics is one of the few building blocks women have to work with as they tell their children about their fathers; for instance, stories become created from anonymous donor profiles. Even though the women are sometimes confused about the meaning and importance of genes, they use them nonetheless as a road map to instill in their children an identity that assumes two parents are essential to create (though not always to raise) a child.

This [reading] focuses on the thirteen women who became pregnant through known donors and the fifteen women who used anonymous donors. They are an interesting subset of this study because they represent women who deliberately sought to give birth to children in a radical way. With one exception, they had no expectations that the men who

fathered their children would become anything other than gamete donors. Even those who became pregnant through known donors wrote contracts before pregnancy specifying that these men would relinquish all rights to their biological children.[3] By looking at these cases we can begin to understand the symbolic ways in which donors' absence forms a presence within families.

In short, the child must rely on the mother's imagination because the child cannot see herself or himself in the glass. Mother and child actively talk about the donor as together they imagine the donor as part of creating a sense of the child's identity. I discuss this in the next sections.

Reconstructing Fathers: Undeniable Imprints of Anonymous Donors

Kerry did not receive unqualified support for her decision to have a child using an anonymous donor:

> *There were people who came to me and said, "Don't do this. My father deserted my mother and it's always been a lifelong thing for me that I never knew him." And I thought, "Well, the mitigating factor is I'm not deserted, I'm not unhappy, I'm not bereft, it's not a tragedy." . . . And in thinking about it, I said, "But I'm not any of those things. And if the choice is between not having a child at all and having a child who's maybe going to have to deal with some of these issues, I choose to have the child." Selfish, but I felt like I would be a good mother, and I think I am.*

Although Kerry's acquaintances' opinions gave her momentary pause about having a child without a dad to raise him, she followed her desire to be a mom by using an anonymous donor. She had the foresight to know that having a child with an anonymous donor, who would most likely be forever unknown, is fraught with complexities. Her future, however, was vague and distant. Becoming pregnant, planning for the child's arrival, and giving birth are more likely to preoccupy these women than existential questions of the meaning of gametes and their relationship to an unknown man. Once children arrive, however, women try to understand what it means to raise a child with only a paper profile of a father.

The women reconstruct the father once their children are born. Birth narratives—the stories parents tell children about their histories from conception on—include the anonymous donor. As the child grows, some of his or her traits—from physical attributes to character, behavior, and interests—become attributed to the anonymous donor. The mother crafts a man out of the limited information she has from the donor profile at the sperm bank and those of her child's traits that she believes are unexplained by the maternal side of the family. That is, the father may be the source of the child's unexplained traits. In this way, the anonymous donor takes on a persona of his own—though it may be more fiction than fact. But through such creation the mother and child take comfort in giving this role of a father meaning in

their lives. Once the donor is acknowledged as being unlike other children's fathers, the mother and child begin to create an imagined man who is a positive yet invisible presence. The "nice man" who helped them to become a family is a worthy human being, if an idealized one.[4]

Birth Narratives: Crafting a Father

In most of these women's narratives, anonymous donors have not rejected their offspring but have instead given the mothers the most awesome gift of their lives. The anonymous donor is not the "bad dad" who walked out (e.g., divorced fathers or birth fathers), but a "good man" who helped the mother and child become a family. These women recast the anonymous donor as doing something positive for them and hence for the child. The mother and child can fantasize together about the genetic father. In addition, the anonymous donor cannot disappoint the child in ways that dads often do. Creating a visual and idealized image has protective power until the child is an adolescent.

All of the children in this study who were conceived from donors knew that they had genetic fathers. Their mothers did not delete the donors from the birth story, instead finding a way to creatively include them. How do children conceived by anonymous donors make sense of a father who is not part of their lives? While mothers attempt to explain to the child his or her origin, they also explain ties to other individuals and the meaning of kinship terminology attached to those individuals. Put differently, family life occurs through naming individuals and interacting with them. In the earliest stories of how they became a family, women use the term *donor* to reinforce this concept as an ordinary way to create a family. The inclusion of a donor is an imaginary leap: the child learns that someone neither she nor her mother knows helped create her. Mothers report that their children's early questions are about kinship boundaries and formation: who's included, who's not, and who's missing. But the questions are not simply an exercise in taxonomy. They are about identity and place, that is, "Who is my dad and where is he?"

Children come to understand the social implications of blood kinship from the language of their births. Melissa, whose twins were born when she was thirty-six years old and were toddlers at the time of the interview, talked of her plans to present the children with an account of their birth:

> *I've read some books and things like that [on children with donor fathers]. I mean, they're really young and I guess I'll just tell them the basics, which is "Your father is in California." I think we're all going to be telling them (because the sperm banks are in California) everybody is going to think their father is in California. Because I guess that's what kids want to know at that young age. And then as they get older, I'll tell them more [from the profile].*

Children will learn from this explanation that a human being exists who is their father. He lives in another place but not in their house or even in their town. Early on, women author narratives of a father and connect the child

to him. They follow professional advice for explaining how children are created, revealing to the child pieces of his or her birth story as requested.

Women contextualize the birth stories of their children by identifying the place and events that transpired. They explain the donor not simply as sperm (a product divorced from a person) but as a man who is located in some place or who was located through someone. A father exists who values their existence.[5] For example, Nadine was under forty when she gave birth to twins. She explained to her preschool children the meaning of the word *donor* as she situated the actors and the action within a medical context. Embedded in her explanation was Nadine's gentle way of connecting the children to their donor through describing the similarities that she guessed they shared.

> *Very recently, one of my sons has begun to ask me about a [father]—I have told them the story at other times about a doctor who helped me find a man. Now it's sort of dovetailed with the facts-of-life discussions. And about eggs and hatching. So that mommies have eggs and fathers have seeds. So I went to a doctor who found a very nice man called a donor who gave me his seed. And that is basically how I've discussed it. And he said, "What's that word, donor?" And then he said, "Will we ever meet him?" And I said, "No, I don't think so. Mommy's never met him." And this was just in the last few weeks. "But he must be very smart and very handsome because look at you," you know? That's been it.*

Although the mother may have received his seed, she transforms the donor into a man and crafts him in her son's image. Yet without a visual image women can only guess at the characteristics of the donor they observe in their children. They piece together the written profiles with the parts of their children they imagine come from the unknown donors. Without a real image to counter the fantasy, the women conjure a wonderful man to tell their children about to buffer the child's feelings of rejection by an unavailable genetic father. The self is fragile and requires affirmation (Strauss 1959). In this case, affirmation of self occurs through the mother's socially shaped imagination about a man she has never met.

Abby, age thirty-six when her child (two years old at the time of the interview) was born, claimed that she preferred an anonymous donor to avoid potential legal hassles. But behind this legal veneer she saw the donor's anonymity as a shield against "letting her child down." By protecting the child from rejection, she also prevented the donor from embracing him. She fantasized with her child about the man they would never know, but the fantasy—like writing letters to Santa Claus—was unattainable.

> *Bryan's father is the best thing that happened to us. He didn't let Bryan down; he didn't let me down, and he never will. And if it were a known donor, he can let Bryan down. I don't have any expectations of anyone, but Bryan might. But at this point, we can both be sad that we don't know who he is, but we both know that he's the best thing that ever happened to us. Or at least I know that, and hopefully Bryan will know that. We can draw pictures of what we think he*

looks like, and we can write letters to him in case we ever know who he is, but he hasn't let us down. Because I chose it this way. And if anything, I let Bryan down, but his father didn't.

These comments reveal a cognitive construction of the genetic father on the part of the mother as a way to protect the child and herself from the "less-than-perfect" way she went about having a child and becoming a mother. Abby, like the majority of women who became pregnant with anonymous donors, could not find a donor in the sperm bank registry that she liked who agreed to have contact with the child at age eighteen if the child wished it. She settled for a donor she thought was a better match even though he would not accept future contact. Few anonymous donors give their consent to later contact with the child. Further, the broader cultural values of privacy and anonymity of donors structure the psychological price the children may pay. The child is denied full knowledge of his or her genealogical heritage and the face of the father.[6]

Half Adopted: The Fantasy Father

From the partial information women have about their donors, we can see how they construct a notion of a whole man—the fantasy father. Instead of denying or remaining silent about him, women make him present in everyday life and conversation. Often these mothers think of their children as "half adopted," a term used by one woman. "Half adopted" is a way to explain the traits that the mother cannot identify in her own extended family. Differences—both physical characteristics and personality—are tentatively assigned to the genetic father. As Nadine commented: "I can see more what comes from me. It's hard for me to know what comes from him [the anonymous donor]. That's the mystery part."

But regardless of whether they believe in environment or nurturance as the primary factors shaping their children, most women would still like to know more about the anonymous donors. Melissa explained why she would like to exchange photographs with the donor:

Their personality, I see their personality as things coming from me, and I think the other things must come from him. Some of their looks come from me, definitely; some of their looks must come from this other person. And I think that those things are important. So I think this person is important, I don't think this person is just nobody. . . . So I would not mind exchanging pictures or things like that. . . . To give them a sense of genetic identity, of who this person is, and who they look like.

Before conception, Melissa believed that environment was more important than genes. But her children's unexplained mannerisms have challenged her former beliefs. That is, the social implications of blood kinship arise as a mother notices parts of the child not recognized in herself.

Melissa's realization is a reminder that the self is not a thing but a process that is developed, sustained, and transformed through social interaction.[7]

Her child's unrecognizable gestures, personality, talents, and physical traits transform Melissa's awareness: she must rethink how to engage characteristics of the child that come from the father's genes. In effect, a profound revelation has occurred. The mother not only perceives the child as containing elements not from her, but also acknowledges that she must socially interact with and embrace those elements in order to affirm the child's sense of unity of self.

Susan, who was thirty-nine when her daughter was born, described how the child's attributes caused her to rethink how to integrate the donor into daily life as an actual person:

> *See, initially I didn't talk about him much and I sort of put it off and I didn't really want to treat him as a person but just a sperm donor. But as time went on, I began to think of him—I changed my attitude about the whole thing and began to see it more as she's half adopted. And that she has, there is this person and he is her biological father and she does have a father . . . and so we talked about him more as a real person. If there are certain traits I don't have in my family, or myself, I might say, "Well maybe you get that from your father." But, like, he was musical and played the piano, and she's musical. And he was athletic, and she's very coordinated. So I just kind of introduced it and then we've talked about him as more of a real person and his different ethnic background . . . and then also, he's someone I can talk positively about. He is a physician. I can say he's smart.*

Susan indicated that conceptualizing her child as "half adopted" is a process of normalization for her and her child that occurred as her thinking shifted from denial to acceptance of the donor. The concept of being "half adopted" may legitimate a procedure that carries great stigma—being created using donor sperm.[8] But "half adopted" may not be sociologically accurate. Susan equated her child's anonymous donor with a birth father. But her child was not adopted. In the case of adoption, the birth father has legal standing until he gives up his legal rights. The anonymous donor never has any legal standing. Fatherhood is given meaning at conception through the social act of intercourse that does not occur when artificial insemination has taken place. The body of a father is missing from the creation of the anonymous donor child. A mother grounds the donor in what she sees in her child, using her child as a reflection of the man she has never met.

The sperm is a detached product that helped to create a baby, what clinical psychologist Diane Ehrensaft refers to in her 2000 article "Alternatives to the Stork" as the part-object father; it does not make the producer of the product, the donor, a dad. Put differently, these mothers may feel the absence of a parenting partner and create a fantasy father for the child, but they are not imagining that man as a parenting partner. Instead, they refuse to leave "the sperm from the vial" in limbo, preferring to construct a man from the gamete. What is the psychological status of the father when the father is only a sperm? It is difficult to imagine that the child is an offspring of a mother and a sperm. Because this situation is psychologically

problematic, Susan borrowed adoption terminology to give meaning to her child's genetic (not birth) father.

The use of adoption terminology allows mother and child to discuss the meaning and implication of genetic heritage and how "pieces" of the child are unexplained and might come from someone else. Children learn to internalize the biological inheritances assigned to them, even if they are fictive. Further, adoption scholars have argued that the search for birth parents by adopted children is a search to establish their genetic heritage and solidify their physical self; that is, the physical traits that they share with other family members are affirmed on meeting genetic kin.[9]

Searching for birth mothers and the relief and realizations that result from such reunions is an important theme in the open adoption literature. Maternal knowledge seems to provide the missing genetic heritage necessary for self-unity. Adopted children find themselves reflected in their biological mothers, and this seems to satisfy the self. In contrast, the children of anonymous donors live with their genetic mothers, whose physical presence echoes in their sense of self. This is not to suggest that birth fathers are not essential. I am only noting that there is an absence of information about birth fathers and how they might contribute to the self of a child created through anonymous donor insemination in ways that might be different from how finding the birth mother operates for adopted children. Certainly these mothers of anonymous donor children sketch fathers based upon profiles that list height, build, eye color, hair color, skin tone, and in some cases other pieces of information about bodily features.

Perhaps more important, the mother and child together consciously help the child see themselves as the offspring of *two* parents, thus recognizing the father as blood kin, if only in their imagination. In this regard, "half adopted" also represents the idea that the sperm is not simply a deconstructed part of a man but is connected to a human being. Therefore, the pieces that the mother regards as unknown become clues to the human being that the mother and child are trying to put together. This process is similar to solving a puzzle without an accompanying picture to guide what the completed puzzle looks like. Putting these clues together provides a way for the child to visualize and identify with the self as an object and the father as an object. By giving an object—in this case, the father—a name, mothers help children figure out how to relate to it and what to expect from it.[10] Of course, a certain mystery remains. In addition, since donors have no place in the nomenclature of the family, their reality is entirely contingent on this talk between mother and child.

Mothers carefully store, as though they are cherished mementos, second-hand information and passing comments given to them by various medical personnel who actually met the anonymous donor. The mementos are eventually passed from mother to child. These clues indicative of a man not only become central pieces but are inflated and conflated as *the* man. Susan continued: "The receptionist in the doctor's office said he was incredibly handsome, drop-dead handsome. So he's handsome, I can describe what he looked like physically, some of his hobbies, things like that."

Even though Susan's child's father was not an anonymous "yes" donor (a man who has agreed to contact with the child when the child is eighteen years old), she and her daughter talked about half siblings and what they would say if they could meet him: "The likelihood [is] that he's a lot younger than I am. And so by the time he went off and got married and had kids, they will probably be a lot younger than she is. But I've talked to her about the possibility that she might someday meet him and that he might have—there might be a whole extended family, half siblings."[11]

These imaginary conversations reinforce the child's bond to a biological family that extends beyond the mother–child dyad. Susan recounted the fantasy conversation she had with her nine-year-old daughter about what each would say if they could meet the anonymous donor.

One time she was saying she thought she would like to meet him sometime, and I said, "Why?" And she said, "I'd like to see what he looks like and if he's nice and if he likes me and things like that." And I said, "Yeah, me too." So we got into this great conversation and I said, "I'd like to meet him too." And she said, "Oh, why? What would you say?" And I said, "I would hug him and kiss him and tell him how much I loved him and how wonderful he was to give me a wonderful daughter and how grateful I was and how I just love this man to pieces even. If I ever met him, I would just thank him and thank him." So she was beaming by the end of the conversation because it made her feel good about him and herself.

Paradoxically, children learn that although men helped to create them, the men remain unavailable to them—even a photograph is lacking. The notion of a father whose presence is felt continuously and may be incorporated into conversations is still more ghostlike than real. They are asked to accept on faith that they have genetic fathers who gave their mothers the most important gift of their lives, but these men do not wish to meet them.

Mother and child cannot help noticing that the genes of an anonymous man have left unanswered questions in their lives. These stories of unknown donors point to the continued importance of blood ties. Mothers believe that their children want the acknowledgment that all children desire: they are loved not only by the people who raise them but also by the men who provided the gametes. Having a social dad might mitigate this importance. Yet grown children whose parents used donor sperm and kept it a secret, as the medical profession once advised, often had haunted childhoods. They felt that they did not belong to the families in which they were raised.[12]

When a child starts to ask questions the mother cannot answer accurately, the mother sometimes returns to the sperm bank to ask that the donor be contacted, despite knowing when she became pregnant that she would never have access to the identity of the genetic father. Since the majority of women in this study had children who were young (under age six) at the time of the interviews, they had not yet actively lobbied the banks for more information. Older children, mothers report, want more information about their genetic fathers than donor profiles give. The women and their children find the present donor system problematic for this reason. However,

bureaucratic control over which pieces of information women can receive in personal and genetic profiles means that they will get, at best, only clues to a genetic father. The profile is static. Updates on medical histories do not exist. Personal information is limited to hobbies, interests, physical traits, and any additional comments the anonymous donor might want to add. Sperm banks are private and self-regulating, and the information a woman receives varies.[13] Susan attempted to relieve the pain of being unable to answer her child's questions by creating a human being for both herself and her daughter. Abby, Susan, Nadine, and Melissa may never know if attributing to the genetic fathers the traits and abilities that they could not find on the maternal side was simply a jointly constructed fiction that they and their children created. . . .

Conclusion

Even as mothers affirm some important ties—most prominently, kinship by blood—they undermine others by separating reproduction from marriage, intercourse, and love. The intimate accounts of these women afford glimpses into how these mothers and their children experience the contested terrain over family life, namely, the power of a two-parent ideology. In part motivated by a cultural ideology that emphasizes the importance of fatherhood and marriage, these women attribute unexplained characteristics of their children to imagined fathers. But ironically, as new reproductive technologies create the possibilities of multiple types of fathers (and mothers), these women work hard to protect the boundaries between social and genetic kinship, in the belief that only one man can be a child's dad. These women protect these boundaries in the hope that another person will come along, marry them, and adopt their children—the ultimate fantasy. Adoption will then give the child a legal second parent. In the uncertain future, middle-class heterosexual women may more readily accept multiple fathers for their children, thus acknowledging genetic ties and social ties as distinct dimensions of family life. However, as children grow up they may make their own set of demands and call for anonymous donors to reveal themselves, not unlike adoptees. Children may also negotiate different relationships with known donors than the ones they currently have.

Although it may be possible to know everything there is to know about our children and ourselves genetically, medical testing cannot produce a man to touch, to hug, or to share the child's deepest hopes and fears. The self emerges in relationship to significant others: the search to know them is deep, and as a culture we deny these children a fundamental right by allowing anonymous donors who never have to reveal themselves to these families. Perhaps the use of anonymous donors needs to be rethought in light of the data I have presented on "imagined fathers."

As medical technology makes possible the ability to uncouple genetic and social parenthood, new forms of families will continue to emerge that

challenge kinship boundaries. One of the most fundamental issues is that of self and other within the family context. In this study I find that biological, social, and sexual sources are distinct but have to be unified in some way that I have called, after Cooley, "the looking-glass self," as mother and child imagine a father. The women's stories show in rich detail the many nuances that anonymous and known donors must cope with in order to sustain the idea of the father for the child and for the mother. There are important distinctions between anonymous donors and known donors. In the former, the crafting of a father is an act of imagination that belies concrete description (characteristics such as smells, sounds, feelings, voice, etc.). A woman must bring to life pieces of information that she feels comfortable loving about this man and, by extension, in their child. The child becomes a looking glass, refracting an image of the man they will probably never meet (which is why contact with other offspring of the same donor becomes an important linkage).

Through deepening love for her child, the mother gradually crafts a man the child believes is a "good" father, and because the mother created this image and mother and child jointly imagine him through this image, the child's self is positively reflected. In the case of known donors, an asymmetry exists between the mother's knowledge and experiences of the known donor and the child's firsthand knowledge of this same person. The mother has intimate knowledge of times shared with the donor that does not usually become the basis for the development of father–child relationships. Children's expectations of known donors are often limited. But innovations that include these men, even in vague and unspecified ways, may have some transformative value and power within individual kinship systems. Although the child is at a distance from the father for the most part, the child sees himself or herself in the man even if he is not a father in the conventional sense.

Donors may become relevant to family life in ways the women themselves do not foresee. Both anonymous donors and known donors are deconstructed, but in different ways. Anonymous donors are fantasy men who provide their sperm without taking on any legal, moral, or social obligation to the child it creates. The deconstructed father is reconstructed by the mother–child dyad as they search to give meaning to the donor in their family. Genealogical lineage remains severed from social kinship on the paternal side, even though the mother and child wish they could meet the man who lives as a vague presence in their lives.

Known donors are also deconstructed because their social role as dad is detached from their genetic relationship to their child. In these cases, the metaphor of the photographic negative is critical: the child knows his or her genetic identity, but the man remains in shadow socially. The asymmetrical knowledge of the mother's relationship to the man versus the child's is striking. Her choice of a known donor derives from a former (and often present) relationship with him, yet she remains a gatekeeper determining how and if a relationship between father and child develops. While multiple

kinds of relationships exist between known donor fathers and their children, in this culture kinship boundaries are tied to particular types of acknowledged paternity that these women and donors prefer to leave legally vague. However, as I have demonstrated, some of these women have expanded the boundaries of kinship, and their children do have relationships with their genetic fathers. Policies that guarantee sperm donor's anonymity may change, and other mothers with biological half siblings may come forward. We have yet to label this possibility or discuss it as part of the broadening of kinship through these new family forms. This transformation of kinship terminology that rests on the relative power of gametes to unravel master narratives is "kin claiming."[14] Attempts by women to label sperm donors "biodads" is an example of kin claiming. However, kinship that continues to be rooted in traditional marriage will preclude the possibility of expanding the ways in which donor father/child relationships develop within the United States.

ENDNOTES

[1] Abby had over fifty profiles from the donor bank. One donor was African American and one donor was Asian (Korean). All the rest were white, but of varying ethnicities. As a white woman, Abby had many choices. Abby, like the other white women, selected a donor who was white. The two black women in this study, one Caribbean American and African American and the other African American, also wished to find an anonymous donor who shared their race. At the time these women searched for available anonymous donors through a major sperm bank, they could find only three and four donors of color, respectively. Nonetheless, both women selected donors who listed their race as mixed but predominately black. The pool of anonymous donors of color is limited.

[2] This is a summary of Cooley's (1983:184) principal elements that comprise the "looking-glass self."

[3] This woman hoped the known donor would want to become a family once the yet-to-be child was born. However, even this woman had a contract saying he had no financial obligation to the child.

[4] This can be likened to the transformation ill individuals experience, which, according to Charmaz's (1995) argument, objectifies their bodies less and allows them to admit cues from their bodies about their illness. Once the illness is acknowledged, they gain control over their lives as they learn how to protect their bodies. When women craft these birth stories about fathers residing in another place, they may master a presentation of conception for the child but mask the acceptance of a man who will never be present in the child's life.

[5] This point is derived from Cooley's (1983) theorizing about the "looking-glass self."

[6] It is ironic that anonymity of gamete donors remains the norm in the United States at the same time that more and more states open up adoption records as a moral obligation to the adopted.

[7] This is a shorthand version of the insights in Mead 1934 on identity formation.

[8] Charlene Miall (1986, 1987, 1989) has done important work on social stigma among childless couples and among adoptive parents. E-mail correspondence with her helped to clarify my thinking concerning the possible roots of "half-adopted" children. In preliminary work with married women who used anonymous donor insemination, the women were encouraged during counseling provided as part of the process they underwent "to think of the donor sperm as part of the adoption spectrum—that is, donor ova or sperm were just adoption one step removed. They were all married and they talked at length about the intimations of adultery that had arisen after conception took place using ADL." Susan most likely borrowed this term and way of conceptualizing a sperm donor from the helping professionals whose workshops she attended.

[9] See especially Weger 1997 and March 2000 on adoption. These scholars analyze the importance of birth families to adoptees. March argues that "this exclusion reaffirms their sense of having no bodily self-reference." Both authors primarily discuss searching (though there are exceptions) for birth mothers and the relief and realizations that result from their reunions.

[10] Strauss put it this way: "The naming of an object provides a directive for action, as if the object were forthrightly to announce, 'You say I am this, then act in the appropriate way toward me.' Conversely, if the actor feels he does not know what the object is, then with regard to it his action is blocked" (1959:22).

[11] Certain sperm banks, though not compelled by anything but the market, have begun to give clients more information about the donor, including a baby photo, an audiotape, and various psychological tests they have administered. Only the women interviewed most recently had these pieces of information. Further, until recently donors checked either yes or no to having contact with the child at the age of eighteen years or older. There is also a new "openness policy" that some banks have instituted. This policy states that at age eighteen the child of a recipient may request additional information about the donor. The bank will maintain records on the donors and recipients. The bank will make a "responsible effort" to supply information from their records or to contact the donor. As one of the major banks writes on its Web site: "We are obligated by mutual agreements to maintain the anonymity and privacy of both the donor and recipient. The only exception to this would be by mutual consent of the involved individuals." This new statement gives women a faint possibility that the donor they used might be amenable to meeting their child. It is far from the guarantee that women I spoke with believe it to be.

[12] Whether children conceived through anonymous donor fathers experience these absent men as missing pieces of their identities similar to adopted children remains a question this study cannot answer. See Ehrensaft 2005 for clinical insights on two-parent families created through donor assistance and surrogacy. See also Orenstein 1995 for an account of adult children conceived through donors. The publication of this story coincided with Father's Day.

[13] States rarely regulate sperm banks, with the exception of California and New York. Sperm banks arose in the 1980s as a way to provide health-screened sperm in order to reduce the rates of reproduction-related HIV transmission and other sexually transmitted diseases. A system that screens donors is safer than either the older practice of private doctors providing fresh sperm from local medical students or a "one-night sexual encounter." Further, the commercialization of sperm banks has created an industry that produces particular knowledge claims about the donor beyond medical information. For instance, the California Cryobank also requires that donors have particular post-high-school educations, a claim that establishes these donors as not "regular Joes." Sperm banks sort semen along a particular set of masculine ideals (Schmidt and Moore 1998), and the same can be claimed about a particular feminine ideal for egg donors. . . .

[14] See Hood 2002:35, where the broadening of kinship systems to include gamete donors and donors' other gamete offspring is dubbed "kin claiming."

REFERENCES

Charmaz, Kathy. 1995. "The Body, Identity, and Self: Adapting to Impairment." *Sociological Quarterly* 36:657–80.

Cooley, Charles Horton. [1902] 1983. *Human Nature and the Social Order.* New Brunswick, NJ: Transaction.

Ehrensaft, Diane. 2005. *Mommies, Daddies, Donors, Surrogates: Answering Tough Questions and Building Strong Families.* New York: Guilford Press.

———. 2000. "Alternatives to the Stork: Fatherhood Fantasies in Sperm Donor Families." *Studies in Gender and Sexuality* 1 (4): 371–97.

Hood, Jane C. 2002. "The Power of Gametes versus the Tyranny of Master Narratives: Commentary." *Symbolic Interaction* 25 (1): 33–39.

March, Karen. 2000. "Who Do I Look Like?: Gaining a Sense of Self-Authenticity through the Physical Reflections of Others." *Symbolic Interaction* 23:359–74.

Mead, George Herbert. 1934. *Mind, Self and Society.* Chicago: University of Chicago Press.

Miall, Charlene. 1986. "The Stigma of Involuntary Childlessness." *Social Problems* 33:268–82.

————. 1987. "The Stigma of Adoptive Parent Status: Perceptions of Community Attitude toward Adoption and the Experience of Informal Sanctioning." *Family Relations* 36:34–39.

————. 1989. "Authenticity and the Disclosure of the Information Preserve: The Case of Adoptive Parenthood." *Qualitative Sociology* 12:279–302.

Orenstein, Peggy. 1995. "Looking for a Donor to Call Dad." *New York Times Magazine,* June 18.

Schmidt, Matthew and Lisa Jean Moore. 1998. "Constructing a 'Good Catch,' Picking a Winner: The Development of Techno-Semen and the Deconstruction of the Monolithic Male." Pp. 21–39 in *Cyborg Babies: From Techno-Sex to Techno-Tots,* edited by Robbie Davis-Floyd and Joseph Dumit. New York: Routledge.

Strauss, Anselm L. 1959. *Mirrors and Masks: The Search for Identity.* Glencoe, IL: Free Press.

Weger, Katrina. 1997. *Adoption, Identity and Kinship: The Debate over Sealed Birth Records.* New Haven, CT: Yale University Press.

PART VI
Parents and Parenting, Children and Childrearing

27

NOT-SO-NUCLEAR FAMILIES
Class, Gender, and Networks of Care

KAREN V. HANSEN

W hen I asked Robert Holcomb, an unmarried father of a six-year-old, "Who helps you care for your son when he visits you?" Robert replied, "Me."[1] Robert views himself as self-reliant, and he leads a full and active life, despite the challenges posed by his paraplegia. Through sheer determination and force of will, he has become independent in most of his daily activities. But I could see that Robert was confined to a wheelchair, and I knew that he did not drive. I also knew that his son lives in a town two hours away. So I probed, "Just you?" He nodded, and nodded again, in response to my questioning. Still, after a pause, a more complicated story unfolded. "I should back up here, when I said that," Robert amended, and then began to describe the dimensions of his support system. He lives with his sister, her husband, and their children. When he needs to pick up his son, his best friend from childhood drives him to the boy's home. This elaboration reveals the interdependent relationships that enable Robert to think of himself as independent. He is not a man who lacks appreciation for others, but from his point of view, he has beaten the odds. Without strength of character, something no one could give him, he would not be alive, let alone be a vigorous, involved father.

Although Robert's physical challenges are unusual, his attitudes about his capabilities are not. The impulse to describe oneself as a can-do, go-it-alone, self-sufficient parent is a typical one. Many, perhaps most, Americans would describe their actions in several realms, including child rearing, in similar terms. Laws in the United States mandate parents' responsibility for and authority over their children. Cultural expectations are no less compelling. American families are assumed to be small, self-reliant units headed by a breadwinning father and cared for by a stay-at-home mother. And yet, over half of all households in the United States with young children have two

---

employed parents (Casper and Bianchi 2002). Do parents go it alone? How do working parents, especially, care for their children? How do they mobilize the help they need? And what enables them to think they are independent when they actually receive a lot of support?

In *Not-So-Nuclear Families*, I probe these questions by investigating the lives of working parents and the networks they construct to help them care for their children. My [research] chronicles the conflicts, hardships, and triumphs of four families and their networks as they navigate the ideology that mandates that parents, mothers in particular, rear children on their own, in the face of a reality that requires that they rely on the help of others.

Employed parents in the United States face a household labor shortage that some have labeled a "crisis of care" (Glenn 2000). Sweeping economic and social changes in the twentieth century altered the landscape for all families, of all races/ethnicities, and classes. The shift from a manufacturing to a service economy has undermined the male wage rate and pushed more and more wives and mothers into paid employment (Casper and Bianchi 2002). Women, historically the chief providers of child care, are increasingly unavailable. The number of mothers in the labor force has risen steadily for decades.[2] What's more, the number of mothers who work full time has increased *fivefold* over the last half century. By 1999, there were 24.6 million school children (63.8 percent of all school-age children) with mothers who were in paid employment (U.S. Census Bureau 2003b).

With so many mothers in the labor force, families must scramble to find child care. Because neighbors, friends, and relatives are as likely as parents to be working, the number of responsible adults with sufficient time available to attend to the needs of school-age children appears to fall far short of the demand. The widespread conception in the culture, and in academic disciplines such as sociology, is that with the depleted ranks of kin and neighbors, the caretakers historically called on to care for children are no longer available. In both popular culture and scholarly research, entrenched assumptions about the "proper" configuration of families with children continue to preserve the power of the ideology of small and independent families.

Caregivers may appear to be disappearing, but children are not. Here is the puzzle: If more mothers are employed, if both men and women are working longer hours (as they are in several economic sectors), and if there have been few significant family-friendly structural transformations in the workplace or state-initiated policies that mandate support for working parents trying to raise children, who then is caring for school-age youngsters in the United States?

Although the national focus is on developing after- and before-school options for school-age children, parents in fact rely much more frequently on informal care. And kin are the mainstay of that informal care. According to U.S. census data for 1999, "other relatives" continue to be the *most common* type of caregivers for grade-school children (U.S. Census Bureau 2003b).

Not-So-Nuclear Families investigates the clash between belief and practice: the ideology of family independence versus the *practice of interdependence*. This research challenges the widespread assumption that nuclear families

raise children without help. And by focusing on white families, assumed to be categorically middle class and nuclear, it challenges the mythology that the United States is a classless society and that middle-class families are disconnected, self-sufficient entities. I find that parents consciously and creatively construct networks of interdependence. They regularly and intentionally tap people beyond their immediate family for aid in the care of their children. I examine the connections among parents, children, and caregivers to illuminate the complex process of creating and sustaining care networks. I show how the networks operate, describing what their members trade and how they conceive of the rights and responsibilities of kinship, children, and reciprocity.

[My research] is focused on the care networks of four families in different class locations (working class, middle class, professional middle class, and upper class) permits me to explore class-based similarities and differences in the arrangements the families make. Although these networks are not offered as typical of their members' class positions, they allow a close examination of how structural transformations unfold on a micro level. Studying them closely results in a detailed understanding of the ways economic and social locations shape what people expect (Kaplan 1997); what they see as possible given their circumstances; and how they make sense of extrahousehold involvements in their efforts to rear children. In several class locations, these parents see their situation as structured by a set of trade-offs: time on the job versus time with family; time with a spouse versus time with the children; reliance on kin versus self-reliance; receiving help versus incurring obligation; exhaustion versus unmet tasks. Consequences follow from each decision about a trade-off, and parents have to determine for themselves the value on each side of the equation.

In this [reading], I explore how the patchwork of parents' caretaking arrangements actually functions (Thorne 2001). When the care occurs outside formal institutions such as schools and day-care centers, to whom do parents turn? And on what grounds? On what principles do the care relationships operate? How do adults and children negotiate needs, and on what terms? Subjects of this research hold a wide range of opinions about child rearing, of philosophies of community and kin involvement, and of attitudes about what children need. Virtually none, however, find it easy to forge and sustain networks of care. In this book, I attempt to see parents' options and decisions from their perspective and to trace empathetically the paths they take to find their way through an ever-changing maze of child-rearing predicaments.

The Power of Ideology in Everyday Life

Why, given the strong empirical evidence to the contrary, are U.S. families assumed to be nuclear in their structure and in their practice? The focus on nuclear household units emphasizes a small insular group that consists of parents and children, a "social nucleus."[3] This emphasis amounts to an ideology of the small and independent family that not only shapes conceptions

held by the general public, but also influences sociologists whose work examines the household and ignores relationships outside it. The ideology of the nuclear family has roots in historical and contemporary evidence of household structure and is augmented by a sociological fascination with families as opposed to kinship (the latter is deemed the provenance of anthropologists). It rests, as well, on certain U.S. beliefs and traditions, including the breadwinner family that Dorothy Smith (1993) calls the "Standard North American Family" (SNAF); the doctrine of privacy in defining families and households; and individualism. In making sense of these sometimes conflicting sets of ideas, people develop expectations about what families and kin should do.

The ideology of the Standard North American Family assumes a heterosexual, two-parent model. Although children are not a necessary component of a Standard North American Family, when they are present, family households constitute the primary site of child rearing. Also implicit in this ideological code is the idea that children continue the legacy of the family materially, culturally, religiously, and, except in cases of adoption, genetically. Therefore, the logic goes, parents have a vested interest in their children's welfare and general well-being.

The male-breadwinner nuclear family has historically been available only to men who could earn a family wage (meaning, primarily, white middle-class men and working-class men in unionized industries). This family structure, moreover, is characterized by an unyielding gender division of labor. Despite its significant problems, this family structure did provide a clear means of caring for children. At the turn of the millennium, however, even that benefit is no longer viable. As families across the economic spectrum search for alternative strategies to make child rearing and family life feasible, white middle-class families are restructuring kin relationships, following the path of African Americans, immigrants, and members of the working class.[4] Historically, families in these groups have relied at least in part on income and resources generated by women. Because of economic need, they have acted independently of the culturally dominant preference for mothers to stay home to rear their children. At the same time, these groups have tended to adopt "attitudes, values, and beliefs that give primacy to the family over the individual," the extended family in particular, a practice known as "familism" (Roschelle 1997:xi–xii). Middle-class and Anglo-American families have tended to present themselves as less familistic in their values. The image of the privileged middle-class family connotes self-reliance, implying that it does not engage in networks. The power of this image has contributed to middle-class white families perceiving themselves as neither asking for nor receiving help from extended kin, even when this image contradicts their lived experience.

The ideology of the small and independent family is also rooted in a belief in the privacy of the family, a notion that arises from the historical role of private property in legally defining the family (Engels 1972; Zaretsky 1986). As with other ideologies, ideas about how private a family should be have changed over time and vary with economic position and cultural

orientation.[5] Equating family life with the private sphere has granted the household a great deal of autonomy in negotiating interpersonal relations and in child-rearing practices. Moreover, since the household is seen as a bounded entity, privacy rights trump outside interference, whether the source be neighborhood gossips or government regulations.[6]

Complementing the doctrine of privacy is the American belief in individualism and self-sufficiency. Sociologist Claude Fischer (2000) defines individualism as "the principle that gives priority to the individual over the group or institution" (p. 4). Indeed, mainstream U.S. culture celebrates the individual and views both success and failure as the result of individual endeavor.[7] This ideology is incorporated into family life in complex, sometimes contradictory, ways because child bearing and rearing require interdependence. But, since children undergo a long period of dependency (how long varies by culture and class), the internal household practice of interdependence counters the hegemonic ideology of individualism. And it is precisely those activities that create the financial dependence of the women who do them. In the United States, people generally believe that families are independent entities but that within any given family, the members are interdependent.[8] Outside the family, however, mainstream U.S. culture stigmatizes dependence as implying weakness, laziness, and incapacity in all but very young children.[9]

Yet parents need help and often seek it. Although the dominant ideology casts the nuclear family as the sole province of child rearing, people other than parents necessarily are involved in children's lives at virtually every developmental stage. For a variety of reasons, the culturally preferred caretaker—the mother—often cannot be the primary caregiver twenty-four hours a day. Nonetheless, "there is a 'moral imperative' that [mothers] continue to provide continuous care for their children" (Daly 1996:133). The ideology of intensive mothering—"emotionally demanding, financially draining, labor consuming child rearing" (Hays 1996:4)—shapes the cultural expectations not only for middle-class parents, but for working-class parents as well. When the mother is unavailable and the father (commonly the next-in-line caregiver) cannot arrange to care for the children, most parents prefer extended family members to substitute for them. In the United States today, this preference for kin is increasingly difficult to satisfy; kin cannot guarantee help. Parents are left to meet the needs of their children in a context of contradictory expectations and assorted impediments and opportunities.

The logic and obligations of kinship do not help a person whose kin are unavailable, dysfunctional, far away, disapproving, or disaffected. Some people reject their family of origin or extended kin, or are rejected by them, long before they have or think about having children (Weston 1991). In the absence of sufficient kin, parents may turn to formal institutions (e.g., schools, child-care centers, after-school programs, religious institutions, recreational activities) and informal networks of interdependence (neighbors and friends).

Still, the ideology and terminology of kinship loom large. Even people who reject or dismiss their biological kin seem to embrace the idea that families are important. Thus the social logic that kin *should* help rear children

surfaces, regardless of how individuals define their kin. Questions remain, however. Which kin help care for children? Whether by biological or social definitions, who constitutes kin? How do people in general and the courts in particular set boundaries around who counts as kin (Minow 1998)? What are the capacities of kin? Not all kin ties are active. Kin may not be geographically close, physically able, or emotionally capable. And although kinship obligations may explain some relatives' motivation to help rear their nieces, nephews, grandchildren, or cousins, they do not explain how that motivation is mobilized.

Perspectives on kinship, networks, and child rearing are profoundly influenced by gender ideology as well. Conceiving of gender as a social construction (as opposed to a biologically assigned identity) helps explain historical fluctuations in men's and women's practices and in culturally bound definitions of appropriate male and female behavior. The construction of gender unfolds in the context of a racial/ethnic- and class-stratified division of labor in society that is shaped by what Gayle Rubin (1990) calls the sex/gender system. For the past two centuries at least, the tasks of child rearing and caregiving have been assigned primarily, although not exclusively, to women. Without trying to specify precisely how individuals come to acquire or enact certain gendered behaviors, I would argue that their behavior is influenced by culturally constructed notions of what is appropriate for good mothers or good fathers or good people to do vis-à-vis children. Most pertinent here is Arlie Hochschild's (1989) concept of gender strategies. A gender strategy is "a plan of action through which a person tries to solve problems at hand, given the cultural notions of gender at play" (p. 15). In *Not-So-Nuclear Families,* women interpret those cultural notions and strategize to mobilize help from the fathers of their children, friends, neighbors, and extended kin to care for their children. Located at the structural nexus of domestic work, child rearing, and paid labor, they nonetheless exercise some discretion about how they act on and interpret their situations. Men strategize to be involved in the lives of their children, nieces, nephews, and grandchildren and, importantly, to support the women who are mothers. They do so from their historical place as family providers, thus needing consciously to break with dominant patterns of behavior. Both men and women rely disproportionately on women as network members, perhaps through a belief that women make better child-care providers and are more readily available to help others.

Most Americans believe the country is composed largely of middle-class people. Unless they are on welfare or fabulously rich and famous, people are assumed to be middle class. This mythology about a middle-class society blurs the very real divisions and inequities that exist. In fact, wealth and income disparities have always existed but have been widening since the 1970s. Demographic data reveal clear evidence of larger concentrations of wealth at the top, creating greater disparities between the top and the bottom quintiles of the population (Mischel, Bernstein, and Boushey 2003:277–307). These "new inequalities" not only have affected those at the bottom but also have placed a greater burden on families in the middle, those who worry

about slipping down the economic ladder (McCall 2001). Katherine Newman (1999) reports that "Americans earning in the middle of the wage scale saw their earnings decline since 1989, after adjustment for inflation" (p. 34). And, according to the Center on Budget and Policy Priorities: "The average income of the middle fifth of families fell by $710 between the late 1970s and the mid-1990s, from $41,430 to $40,720."[10] That drop occurred in the wake of families adding a second wage earner to shore up household earnings. So even with wives and mothers working, family income has declined over the past two decades. Among all groups, these economic inequalities have profound direct and indirect consequences for families, for expectations about what families should do, and for the ways families rear their children. Differences in resources (most particularly in income and wealth, time, and people) often lie obscured in white families who are presumed to be middle class, yet shape the networks parents assemble to help them rear their children.

The Crux of the Family Labor Shortage

As many studies document, two demographic trends in particular have affected, and continue to affect, child-rearing practices: the rising proportion of mothers, particularly mothers of young children, in the paid labor force; and the growth in the proportion of employed mothers who work full time (Casper and Bianchi 2002).

In the immediate aftermath of World War II, following a wartime escalation of women's entry into paid employment, women were ideologically and structurally encouraged to head back to the home (Coontz 1992). However, after a brief postwar drop, the number of women in the labor force steadily increased through the 1990s (Goldin 1990:10–57). By 2000, married and formerly married women with children were more likely to work than those without children. In 1958, 3,033,654 children ages six to eleven had mothers who were employed full time (Lajewski 1959:10). In 1999, there were 17,307,000 children ages five to fourteen with full-time working mothers (U.S. Census Bureau 2003b). The magnitude of the increase in the number of children with working mothers is staggering in its social consequences.

The increase of women in the paid labor force has not been accompanied by structural transformations in the workplace or by policies instituted by the state that would create family-supportive conditions for rearing children. The paid employment of women decreases the amount of time they are available to be involved in child rearing, helping others care for their children, kin keeping, and doing other kinds of community work. Especially hard hit have been poor and working-class communities that rely on the activism and presence of women, many of whom have been pressed into paid employment as a result of the 1990s welfare "reform" (Oliker 2000).

Work, which determines the contours of much of an employed parent's day, and schooling, which centrally organizes children's time, shape and mediate the legal and moral responsibilities of parents to provide food, clothing, and shelter for their children. The workplace assumes workers are

independent wage earners who can entirely devote themselves to the job at hand, and who have families at home to take care of them (Williams 2000). Neither assumption is valid for most employed women. While women have increased their numbers in professional and managerial occupations, they continue to be concentrated in the female-dominated occupational categories of clerical and service work (Goldin 1990). Not coincidentally, women in the workplace generally have fewer benefits and less flexibility in their jobs than men have. Moreover, as Jody Heymann (2000) points out, "while working women are disproportionately responsible for caring for children, the elderly and disabled adults, they face significantly greater work-related barriers to providing that care than men do" (p. 13). Families' efforts to adapt to inflexible structures result in mothers getting less sleep; fathers doing more child care; children taking care of themselves; and relatives, neighbors, or friends helping out.

The structure schools impose is, like that of the workplace, large and inflexible. The school day averages about six hours, ending at various times in the early to midafternoon. Trying to close the care gap using day care is expensive and often not comprehensive (Hofferth et al. 1991). For children in elementary school, there are a growing number of "out of school time" care options provided at school sites, but the quality, staffing, cost, and availability of such programs vary widely (Bundy 1998).

Overall, the structures of work and school combine to make providing care for school-age children an ongoing challenge for employed parents. No matter how well organized, no matter how reliable, no matter how hardworking, these parents have difficulty making sure their children are supervised during the care gap. As one of the uncles in my study points out, "There're times when you have little kids and you're just totally frazzled. And, you know, there's just a zillion things to do, and you can't be a zillion places at once or doing a thousand things, so you gotta ask for help." This is one reason networks become so important.

The acute need for a network of care among all classes of families seems particular to the gendered organization of labor in a specific historical moment.[11] When mothers are expected to take the primary responsibility for rearing children, and those mothers work for wages, they need help. One woman reports that working has pressed her to engage in give-and-take relationships: "Because I work, I've had to rely on others." Women of color, immigrant women, and working-class women have always had such a need. Now women of the middle classes share that need. They are experiencing a keen family labor shortage that networks help alleviate.

Care for School-Age Children

Nostalgic for an idealized family life, some scholars and a sector of the public imagine a time, often focusing on the fifties, when more relatives supported parents in rearing their children (Coontz 1992). Census data confirm that, indeed, "other relatives" were the most common category of caretaker for

schoolchildren of full-time working mothers in the fifties. In 1958, individuals in this category—including older siblings aged thirteen to eighteen, grandparents, and extended kin (but not fathers)—accounted for 39.8 percent of the caretakers of children with full-time working mothers (Lajewski 1959:11). Interestingly, however, in 1999, "other relatives" cared for 40.6 percent of the school-age children whose mothers worked full time (U.S. Census Bureau 2003b). The widespread perception that fewer people help their extended kin in child rearing is simply not supported by the data. To the contrary, kin continue to step forward as important players in the lives of children.[12]

What *is* very different between 1958 and 1999 is that, with the huge increase in the number of children whose mothers work part-time and full time, the absolute demand for care has skyrocketed. While the proportion of families that enlists relatives has remained relatively constant, the need for caretakers of children has ballooned, and it has done so across the economic spectrum. At the turn of the twenty-first century, more day-care centers and after-school programs exist than ever before, and they are commonly used if available (Casper and Bianchi 2002). But nowhere does the supply meet the demand. This gap in care has put pressure on kinship systems that were already overextended.

Employed mothers historically have relied on a patchwork of caregivers, whereby multiple people fill in various time slots. Reliance on multiple caregivers enables parents to ensure their children have adult supervision even in those small gaps between formal arrangements. This interstitial coverage can make a critical difference, regardless of the number of hours a caregiver provides. A mere five to ten hours per week can be indispensable to the economic arrangements of a family and the well-being of a child. Child-care providers can supplement institutional care and yet make the crucial difference in whether a parent can work, or whether a child is safe.

Family Reliance on Networks

Networks make a difference, usually positive, sometimes negative, in people's lives. Researchers have reached different conclusions, however, about who relies on kin networks more—Euro-Americans or people of color, members of the working class or those of the middle class—and why.[13] The debate on this question has persisted, in part, because of research design. Many network studies either "examine poverty populations in isolation" or have not been designed with sufficient comparability to enable scholars to disentangle race and class effects (Roschelle 1997:81). Studies that compare a working-class Latino neighborhood to a middle-class Anglo one, for instance, cannot shed much light on the relative importance of either race/ethnicity or class. After conducting an extensive study of kin networks herself, Anne Roschelle (1997) recommends that "scholars must begin to examine the different types of network participation engaged in by different groups under different circumstances" (p. 81). Accordingly, some scholars are beginning to devise successful strategies for parsing the race-ethnic variation and class

dimensions in domestic networks. Ironically, because native-born Euro-Americans have been assumed not to have kin networks, they have not been studied as a parallel subpopulation.[14] This oversight, along with my desire to compare networks across class, motivated me to begin my research with white parents.

Recent research based on national surveys has investigated the impact of differential resources on network formation. Large-scale quantitative studies show that those in the middle class are more likely to have networks than the poor or those in the working class (Hogan, Hao, and Parish 1990). This research finds that the more economic and educational resources a family has to draw upon, the more it helps others and receives help in turn (Roschelle 1997). These findings contradict those of earlier, qualitative, ethnographic studies that found domestic networks to be the province of poor, working-class, and immigrant communities. While most of the earlier studies were not comparative, subsequent theory and research built on the assumption that networks were a product of necessity in the U.S. context, and social scientists continued to interpret their findings in that vein. As a result, families were assumed to participate in networks of support only if they could not purchase what they needed, making them deviant according to the Standard North American Family ideal.

Notably, interpretations of the value of and motivation for building networks have flip-flopped with the more recent quantitative results. The emergent interpretation is that families with more resources are better equipped to participate in a network; in effect, they have more to contribute, especially when compared to poorer families who risk their own well-being by sharing and participating in a network. Having been discovered, the connectedness of middle-class families is now taken to be a marker of health and vibrancy and a measure of these families' success. No longer are extended domestic networks treated as pathological, aberrant phenomena that need to be explained. Rather, such networks are deemed a normative asset for the middle class and are associated with relative privilege. The end result, however, is that poor, working-class, and racial-ethnic communities continue to be seen as aberrant, but now by a new norm, one for which previously they had been the standard-bearers.

Sociologists have searched for both structural and cultural reasons to explain the dramatic shift in the kinds of families now identified as building and relying upon networks (Roschelle 1997). Some argue that the shift in findings could reflect a genuine inversion of the resources available to families (Brewster and Padavic 2002; Roschelle 1997). That is, the change may be the result of social and economic processes that have impoverished the basic landscape of poor, working-class, and/or African American communities (Brewster and Padavic 2002). This includes the transformation to a postindustrial economy, which has reduced the number of manufacturing jobs in general, but especially in inner cities (Newman 1999; Wilson 1987). It also has pulled more women into the paid labor force. And, as Roschelle (1997) aptly points out, the eighties hit poor and working-class families particularly hard. Crack cocaine invaded poor neighborhoods, and the federal government

implemented policies that widened wealth and income gaps by reforming tax legislation, dismantling affirmative action, and busting unions. In sum, the profound structural changes over the past three decades offer a compelling, although partial, explanation of shifts over time in various groups' use of networks.

Another explanation for the reversal in findings about network involvement looks to differences in methodological approach. The earlier studies tended to be largely ethnographic, while some of the more recent studies use large quantitative data sets that are representative of the U.S. population as a whole (Brewster and Padavic 2002; Roschelle 1997; Stack 1974). Large multivariate studies are good at counting things that can be measured. Ethnographic studies examine interstices among people that surveys cannot capture.

Another way to think about the increase in middle-class families' reliance on networks is that they have greater labor-power needs than they had thirty years ago and therefore create networks to help them rear children and do kin work. I would argue that structural shifts have created harsher conditions in middle-class communities, as well as in working-class ones, and that middle-class families are clambering to assemble networks out of necessity. The greater contemporary precariousness of middle-class families stems both from employment insecurity and longer work hours, and from a shortage of kin workers. Family households have been able to hold their ground financially only because the wages women earn by going into the labor force are added to the household coffer (Faludi 1991). But some families then have fewer people resources and less time to engage in family activities (Daly 1996; Jacobs and Gerson 1998). The parallel decline in resources within poor communities may push people below a threshold level of comfort, making it impossible for them to share child care and other commodities as readily as they did before the economic restructuring.

Studying Interdependent Networks that Care for Children

I focus my attention on networks of differing social and economic resources. How do those in the structural middle find help? How do their strategies differ from those at the bottom? From those at the top? What similarities do they share?

I examine a specific kind of interdependent network—a network of care, that is, one organized to help parents care for their children while they are on the job and the children are not in school. How do parents cover that weekly gap between work and school that the Annie E. Casey Foundation (1998) estimates to be as high as twenty-to-twenty-five hours? The help provided ranges from practical hands-on care, those activities that some researchers frame as *care for*, to advice and emotional support, which they label *care about* (Tronto 1993; Ungerson 1983). I illustrate how parents in several economic locations construct informal networks of interdependence to substitute for and supplement institutions that cover the gap in after-school and before-school care.

I begin by identifying white parents in different class positions. The homogeneity of race-ethnicity across the cases enables me to explore similarities and differences across class location. That comparability also allows me to focus attention on the ways white families define their care assets and deficits and how they mobilize their differential resources to address these issues.

My goal of understanding the *internal processes* of networks seems best accomplished through qualitative, open-ended interviews. I seek to understand why parents rely on particular people, how they feel about this interdependence, what they trade, and what they think they have gained and lost in the process. Rather than interview independent individuals, I chose to study connected individuals who are part of a parent's network of care. My method—to approach each network as a case study—is motivated by my desire to analyze particular networks in their entirety and to get a fuller picture, from multiple vantage points, of approaches to caring for children and to supporting parents. Each of the four case studies thus focuses on a network, a web of people, rather than on a collection of separate individuals. While the particulars of the cases are idiosyncratic rather than representative in some kind of statistical sense, by delving into the network dynamics, I am able to probe the interpretations and meanings people assign to their involvements and interactions with other people. The cases include people who struggle with the contradictions of their circumstances—trying to raise their children responsibly while trying to earn a living, engaging others to help them in those inevitable yet impossible moments when the care puzzle pieces fail to come together. It is less their particular decisions that interest me, and more their deliberations, the patterns of their interactions, and the ways that others respond to them.

Large-scale surveys of patterns of exchange analyze the *structures* of networks, rather than the *processes* of mobilizing them (Osnowitz 2002; Wellman 1990). They focus on the size, composition, and density of networks, on those things that can be measured or counted—money, material goods, and concrete favors. Other aspects of network relationships, such as support or advice, are difficult to assign value to and, other researchers have found, harder to assess and track (Nelson 1999; Weinberg 1994). While useful, the survey approach fails to provide sufficient insight into the internal dynamics of a network. A random, nationally representative sample that produces statistically generalizable findings may miss the very essence of networks—that is, their overlapping circles of interdependency—and may methodologically tilt findings toward a more disconnected portrait of the world. However, looking at a network from multiple participants' points of view can be done only through intensive study. Because perception and subjectivity are part of an ongoing construction and negotiation of network relations, they are best studied using an interpretive, qualitative analysis. . . .

In the comparative tradition of network studies, this investigation includes one network each from four economic locations: working class, middle class, professional middle class, and upper class (Bott 1957; Young and Willmott 1992). By including an upper-class case, my research design extends the class

categories beyond the construct of working class versus middle class commonly found in comparative research. In stratifying my sample by class, I am trying to understand the ways that economic conditions shape people's lives, the needs of their children, people's perceptions of the needs of their children, and hence the contours of their networks. I define class location as a product of several economic and social forces, including a person's current occupation and job history, education, and wealth, with particular attention to home ownership, in addition to income (Keister 2000; Townsend 2002). In conceiving of class as a complex relationship of economic and social dimensions, I posit that experiences and ideologies are shaped by class location. I am interested in the contingencies of class, that is, occurrences or dynamics connected to class but not determined by it. Class contingencies shape and reflect a particular "constellation of resources," as Anita Ilta Garey puts it. Garey's notion of resource constellations broadens the concept of assets beyond the narrowly conceived categories of income or education. She identifies racial-ethnic privilege, neighborhood context, relationship status, transportation options, family size and ages of children, and physical health as different aspects of one's constellation of resources, and therefore one's social capital (Garey 1999). I recognize all these dimensions as shaping ideas and practice, although in this research, I focus most particularly on the time, money, and people to which networks have access in varying degrees.

At the end of my first interview with each anchor, I asked her or him to enumerate those who helped rear her or his children. I respected the list constructed by the anchor and the boundaries placed by the anchor around whom to include and exclude. By openly asking who made up the network, I was able to explore the anchor's on-the-ground definition of a network of care. The lists the anchors generated included both primary and secondary caregivers: neighbors, grandmothers, friends, uncles, aunts, babysitters, and nannies. The network participants ranged from those involved in daily interactions with the children (including providing transportation or direct supervision) to those who live outside the geographic orbit of daily life, but who contribute invaluable advice and emotional support (Holloway and Valentine 2000). Over a nine-month period, I interviewed *all* the participants named by the anchors, asking each about his or her role as a giver of care and a recipient of care, advice, or favors. I also asked the network members about the tending of their own children, if they had them, and about their childhood experiences as recipients and providers of care. The network participants' lives are ever changing and my portraits are necessarily provisional. After interviewing the adults, I interviewed all the anchors' school-age children. Speaking with the children gave me an opportunity for a final visit to the anchors' households and provided insight into the children's specific needs and capacities. In addition, I interviewed three people whose lives touched the anchors in tangential ways, but who were not identified as network members. In total, across all four networks, I interviewed forty individuals.

There are several advantages to profiling an entire network rather than disparate individuals. First, my approach allowed repeated contacts with

each network and provided glimpses of its issues at different moments in time. So, for example, as the health crisis of the mother of the working-class anchor evolved, the network needs and activities shifted. I interviewed the anchor three times. In addition, since she acted as the interview broker and family scheduler, I saw and spoke to her when I made arrangements to interview her mother, her grandmother, her close friend, and her son. And each time I interviewed a participant in this network, I also talked briefly to the anchor. Each of these contacts gave me the opportunity to get a snapshot of the network as the health crisis unfolded.

A second advantage of approaching the network as a case study is that I was able to observe one system of caregiving from several different vantage points. By building in triangulation, the research design transcends self-reports, which in network studies are especially limiting. For example, the working-class father told me he was deeply involved with his six-year-old son, yet he had never married his son's mother and lived one hundred miles away. The respect for him expressed by the boy's grandmother gave this father's account more gravity. His self-description was also strengthened by the boy's mother, who said that she turned to him for advice and support in child rearing. And, finally, the boy himself made it clear that he idolized his father. These separate accounts combined to give me greater confidence in the validity of the father's self-report.

Last, the network approach enhanced my ability to solicit disclosure. The personal-contact structure of recruitment made it easier to establish rapport and build trust during my initial interview with each anchor. The anchor's introduction to the other network members in turn helped establish my credibility and created opportunities for open communication. When I arrived for interviews, people generally already knew something about me and the study.

ENDNOTES

[1] All names and place names in the book are pseudonyms.

[2] In 1958, for example, 7.5 million of the married or formerly married women (the census defines the second group as "separated, divorced, and widowed") in the labor force had children under eighteen (Lajewski, "Working Mothers," 8). In 2000, 22.7 million had children under eighteen (U.S. Census Bureau, *Statistical Abstract*, Table 577).

[3] In sociology, the enduring pervasiveness of the functionalist theoretical approach shapes the ideology of families. Functionalists argue that the nuclear family form is an adaptive response to economic circumstances (Goode, *World Revolution and Family Patterns;* Parsons and Bales, *Family, Socialization, and Interaction Process*). That is, they maintain that families dropped the extended ties that had helped sustain agricultural life to enhance their ability to respond effectively to the new conditions imposed by industrialization. Despite historical evidence that nuclear households pre-dated industrialization and that the industrial revolution did not alter household structure, the functionalist perspective has continued to influence U.S. sociology (Laslett, *Household and Family*). As early as 1961, social scientists challenged that portrait. Elaine Cumming and David Schneider wrote: "The ideal American family is a nuclear family, but the real American family is often an extended one" ("Sibling Solidarity in American Kinship," 499). Feminists have criticized the gendered and ahistorical assumptions of functionalism and pointed to its mythic qualities but have not succeeded in supplanting the functionalist paradigm in the practice of family sociology.

[4] Stacey, *Brave New Families*, 251–71. Given the ubiquity of the SNAF ideal, it is interesting to note that historians find extensive evidence of nuclear families embedded in extended kin

networks, evidence largely ignored by sociologists in conducting contemporary research (Hareven, *Family Time and Industrial Time*). In keeping with the Standard North American Family ideal, this nuclear structure and ideology have been interpreted as a sign of greater self-sufficiency and a measure of success.

[5] Historically, family members were considered the private property of the male head of household. That ownership gave men dominion over their wives, children, and servants. In other words, male heads of households had ultimate say in decisions, financial or social, and discretion in how they spent their own time and money and in how they directed others to spend theirs. Even with women's increased economic independence that accompanied wage earning and the passage of the married women's property acts of the mid-nineteenth century, the structure of labor markets and the differential legal status of women and men in marriage have continued to undercut women's equality within families as well as outside them (Basch, *Eyes of the Law*). Although women in the twenty-first century are no longer men's private property, the legal situation of children is more contested. Children remain under the legal jurisdiction of their fathers and mothers; how much "voice" they have in their treatment and futures is debated (Beck, "Democratization of the Family").

[6] In the nineteenth century, the male head of household's discretionary power was circumscribed by his neighbors and extended kin; the community monitored heads of households to curb their excessive use of force in dealing with family members. Over the course of the twentieth century, the increase in single-family dwellings, the geographic dispersion of kin, and the growth of urban/metropolitan areas have rendered the community irrelevant as a control for internal household behaviors. Scholars debate the degree to which state control over family activities has increased apace through laws designed to prevent the exploitation and abuse of children, and laws regarding public education, the welfare state, "child saving" agencies, and so on. In spite of the shift from social to legal control, the importance of the privacy of the household has not diminished ideologically; indeed, it has grown (D'Emilio and Freedman, *Intimate Matters*; Gordon, *Heroes of Their Own Lives*).

[7] Fischer notes that there are different types of individualism—political, economic, and familial. His review of debates about individualism points to contradictory cultural impulses that coexist with a focus on the self. It is precisely those contradictions that can produce a belief that families are self-contained units that can go it alone ("Was There a Moment?" 10).

[8] Fischer points out that beliefs in individualism vary by sphere, so although Americans, in comparison to people in other countries, may express a more individualist set of beliefs about government and the economy, they tend to articulate more collectivist values in regard to families ("Was There a Moment?"). Thorne notes, for example, that families have been associated with the values of nurturance and community ("Feminism and the Family").

[9] This portrait of dependence is challenged by the new debates about care among feminists (see Fraser and Gordon, "A Genealogy of Dependency"; Garey et al., "Care and Kinship"; Kittay, *Love's Labor*). See also Kittay and Feder, *The Subject of Care*.

[10] These figures are adjusted for inflation to 1997 dollars (Center on Budget and Policy Priorities, "Pulling Apart," www.cbpp.org/pa-statelist.htm).

[11] By this, I do not mean to suggest that families have not experienced labor shortages in other time periods under different economic systems, but rather that the one this country is facing now is uniquely shaped by historical circumstance and particular expectations about gendered behavior.

[12] Interestingly, the proportion of nonrelatives (babysitters, friends, and neighbors) caring for children in the child's home has declined from the fifties. *Nonrelative care in the child's home* was provided to 10 percent of the children whose mothers worked full time in 1958 (Lajewski, "Working Mothers," 11) compared to 3.6 percent in 1999 (U.S. Census Bureau, "Who's Minding the Kids?" PPL Table 3B).

One of the biggest changes in the forty-year period is in the area of group-care and day-care centers. Very few day-care centers and after-school programs existed in 1958; therefore, *group care* accounted for a miniscule 1.0 percent of school-age children whose mothers worked full time (Lajewski, "Working Mothers," 11). In 1999, 17.6 percent of grade-school children were involved in organized care or at a day-care center before and after school (U.S. Census Bureau, "Who's Minding the Kids?" PPL Table 3B).

In 1958, the remaining children were either in "self-care" or in some combination of caregiving situations that were not easily placed in the census categories. The issue of "self-care" sparked controversies in the fifties. Legislators, psychologists, and PTA members debated the wisdom of allowing "latch-key children" to be at home without on-site adult supervision.

The controversies surrounding this issue are many, and the challenge of counting is huge. No less controversial today, this category of care appears to have increased dramatically. In 1958, 12.8 percent of children five to eleven were identified as being in self-care. The comparable figure for 1999 is 20.6 percent (U.S. Census Bureau, "Who's Minding the Kids?" PPL Table 3B). This may be due simply to the inclusion of older children (twelve- to fourteen-year-olds) not included in 1958.

[13] Bott, *Family and Social Network;* Hofferth, "Kin Networks"; Hogan, Hao, and Parish, "Race, Kin Networks, and Assistance"; L. Rubin, *Worlds of Pain;* Young and Willmott, *Family and Kinship.*

[14] For an exception, see Stacey, *Brave New Families.* In one sense, this is not at all ironic. In general, "whiteness" is associated with middle-class status. Until researchers released the findings of studies conducted in the early 1990s, the middle classes were assumed *not* to have extensive kin networks.

REFERENCES

Annie E. Casey Foundation. 1998. "Care for School-Age Children" ("Kids Count" brochure). Baltimore, MD: Annie E. Casey Foundation.

Basch, Norma. 1982. *In the Eyes of the Law: Women, Marriage, and Property in Nineteenth-Century New York.* Ithaca, NY: Cornell University Press.

Beck, Ulrich. 1997. "Democratization of the Family." *Childhood: A Global Journal of Child Research* 4 (2): 151–68.

Bott, Elizabeth. 1957. *Family and Social Network: Roles, Norms, and External Relationships in Ordinary Urban Families.* New York: Free Press.

Brewster, Karin L. and Irene Padavic. 2002. "No More Kin Care? Changes in Black Mothers' Reliance on Relatives for Child Care, 1977–1994." *Gender and Society* 16 (4): 564–63.

Bundy, Andrew. 1998. "National School-Based Out of School Time Survey." Boston: Parents United for Childcare.

Casper, Lynne M. and Suzanne M. Bianchi. 2002. *Continuity and Change in the American Family.* Thousand Oaks, CA: Sage.

Center on Budget and Policy Priorities. 2000. *Pulling Apart: A State-by-State Analysis of Income Trends.* Center on Budget and Policy Priorities. Cited March 18, 2003. Available from www.cbpp.org/pa-statelist.htm.

Coontz, Stephanie. 1992. *The Way We Never Were: American Families and the Nostalgia Trap.* New York: Basic Books.

Cumming, Elaine and David M. Schneider. 1961. "Sibling Solidarity: A Property of American Kinship." *American Anthropologist* 63:298–507.

Daly, Kerry J. 1996. *Families and Time: Keeping Place in a Hurried Culture.* Thousand Oaks, CA: Sage.

D'Emilio, John and Estelle Freedman. 1988. *Intimate Matters.* New York: Harper and Row.

Engels, Fredrich. 1972. *The Origin of the Family, Private Property, and the State.* New York: International.

Faludi, Susan. 1991. *Backlash: The Undeclared War Against American Women.* New York: Crown.

Fischer, Claude. 2000. "Just How Is It That Americans Are Individualistic?" Presented at the annual meeting of American Sociological Association, Washington, DC.

———. 2001. "Was There a Moment (When Americans Became Individualists?)" Paper presented at the annual meeting of the American Sociological Association, Anaheim, CA.

Fraser, Nancy and Linda Gordon. 1994. "A Genealogy of Dependency: Tracing a Keyword of the U.S. Welfare State." *Signs* 19 (21): 309–36.

Garey, Anita Ilta. 1999. *Weaving Work and Motherhood.* Philadelphia: Temple University Press.

Garey, Anita Ilta, Karen V. Hansen, Rosanna Hertz, and Cameron Macdonald. 2002. "Care and Kinship: An Introduction." *Journal of Family Issues* 23 (6): 703–15.

Glenn, Evelyn Nakano. 2000. "Creating a Caring Society." *Contemporary Sociology* 29 (1): 84–94.

Goldin, Claudia. 1990. *Understanding the Gender Gap: An Economic History of American Women.* New York: Oxford University Press.

Goode, William J. 1963. *World Revolution and Family Patterns.* New York: Free Press.

Gordon, Linda. 1988. *Heroes of Their Own Lives: The Politics and History of Family Violence, Boston 1880–1960.* New York: Penguin.

Hareven, Tamara. 1982. *Family Time and Industrial Time: The Relationship between the Family and Work in a New England Industrial Community.* New York: Cambridge University Press.

Hays, Sharon. 1996. *The Cultural Contradictions of Motherhood.* New Haven, CT: Yale University Press.

Heymann, Jody. 2000. *The Widening Gap: Why America's Working Families Are in Jeopardy and What Can Be Done about It.* New York: Basic Books.

Hochschild, Arlie Russell, with Anne Machung. 1989. *The Second Shift: Working Parents and the Revolution at Home.* New York: Viking.

Hofferth, Sandra L. 1984. "Kin Networks, Race, and Family Structure." *Journal of Marriage and the Family* 46 (4): 791–806.

Hofferth, Sandra L., April Brayfield, Sharon Deich, and Pamela Holcomb. 1991. "National Child Care Survey, 1990." Washington, DC: Urban Institute Press.

Hogan, Dennis P., David J. Eggebeen, and Clifford C. Clogg. 1993. "The Structure of Intergenerational Exchanges in American Families." *American Journal of Sociology* 98 (6): 1428–58.

Hogan, Dennis P., Ling-Xin Hao, and William L. Parish. 1990. "Race, Kin Networks, and Assistance to Mother-Headed Families." *Social Forces* 68 (3): 797–812.

Holloway, Sarah L. and Gill Valentine, eds. 2000. *Children's Geographies: Playing, Living, Learning.* New York: Routledge.

Jacobs, Jerry and Kathleen Gerson. 1998. "Who Are the Overworked Americans?" *Review of Social Economy* 56 (4): 443–60.

Kaplan, Elaine Bell. 1997. *Not Our Kind of Girl: Unraveling the Myths of Black Teenage Motherhood.* Berkeley and Los Angeles: University of California Press.

Keister, Lisa A. 2000. *Wealth in America: Trends in Wealth Inequality.* New York: Cambridge University Press.

Kittay, Eva Feder. 1999. *Love's Labor: Essays on Women, Equality, and Dependency.* New York: Routledge.

Kittay, Eva Feder and Ellen K. Feder, eds. 2002. *The Subject of Care: Feminist Perspectives on Dependency.* Lanham, MD: Rowman and Littlefield.

Lajewski, Henry C. 1959. "Working Mothers and Their Arrangements for Care of Their Children." *Social Security Bulletin,* pp. 8–13.

Laslett, Peter. 1972. *Household and Family in Past Time.* Cambridge: Cambridge University Press.

McCall, Leslie. 2001. *Complex Inequality: Gender, Race, and Class in the New Economy.* New York: Routledge.

Minow, Martha. 1998. "Who's In and Who's Out." Pp. 7–19 in *Families in the U.S.: Kinship and Domestic Politics,* edited by Karen V. Hansen and Anita Ilta Garey. Philadelphia: Temple University Press.

Mishel, Lawrence, Jared Bernstein, and Heather Boushey. 2003. *The State of Working America 2002/2003.* Ithaca, NY: ILR Press.

Nelson, Margaret and Joan Smith. 1999. *Working Hard and Making Do.* Berkeley and Los Angeles: University of California Press.

Newman, Katherine S. 1999. *Falling from Grace: Downward Mobility in the Age of Affluence.* Berkeley and Los Angeles: University of California Press.

Oliker, Stacey J. 2000. "Examining Care at Welfare's End." Pp. 167–85 in *Care Work: Gender, Labor, and the Welfare State,* edited by Madonna Harrington Meyer. New York: Routledge.

Osnowitz, Debra. 2002. "Constructing Opportunity and Choice: Contract Professionals in Comparative Context." Presented at the annual meeting of Society for the Study of Social Problems, Chicago.

Parsons, Talcott and Robert F. Bales. 1955. *Family, Socialization and Interaction Process.* New York: Free Press.

Roschelle, Anne R. 1997. *No More Kin: Exploring Race, Class, and Gender in Family Networks.* Thousand Oaks, CA: Sage.

Rubin, Gayle. 1990. "The Traffic in Women: Notes on the 'Political Economy' of Sex." Pp. 74–113 in *Women, Class, and the Feminist Imagination,* edited by Karen V. Hansen and Ilene J. Philipson. Philadelphia: Temple University Press.

Rubin, Lillian. 1992. *Worlds of Pain: Life in the Working-Class Family.* New York: Basic Books.

Smith, Dorothy. 1993. "The Standard North American Family: SNAF as an Ideological Code." *Journal of Family Issues* 4:50–65.

Stacey, Judith. 1998. *Brave New Families: Stories of Domestic Upheaval in Late-Twentieth-Century America.* New York: Basic Books.

Stack, Carol. 1974. *All Our Kin: Strategies for Survival in a Black Community.* New York: Harper and Row.

Thorne, Barrie. 1992. "Feminism in the Family." Pp. 3–30 in *Rethinking the Family,* edited by Barrie Thorne with Marilyn Yalom. Boston: Northeastern University Press.

———. 2001. "Pick-up Time at Oakdale Elementary School: Work and Family from the Vantage Points of Children." Pp. 354–76 in *Working Families: The Transformation of the American Home,* edited by Rosanna Hertz and Nancy L. Marshall. Berkeley: University of California Press.

Townsend, Nicholas. 2002. *The Package Deal: Marriage, Work, and Fatherhood in Men's Lives.* Philadelphia: Temple University Press.

Tronto, Joan C. 1993. *Moral Boundaries: A Political Argument for an Ethic of Care.* New York: Routledge.

Ungerson, Clare. 1983. "Why Do Women Care?" Pp. 31–49 in *A Labor of Love: Women, Work, and Caring,* edited by Janet Finch and Dulcie Groves. Boston: Routledge and Kegan Paul.

U.S. Census Bureau. 2003a. *Statistical Abstract of the United States.* Washington, DC: U.S. Bureau of Labor Statistics, Bulletin 2307.

———. 2003b. "Who's Minding the Kids? Child Care Arrangements: Spring 1999." Detailed Tables (PPL-168). Washington, DC: U.S. Census Bureau.

Weinberg, Davida Jean. 1994. "Reciprocity Reconsidered: Motivations to Give and Return in the Everyday Exchange of Favors." Ph.D. dissertation, University of California.

Wellman, Barry. 1990. "The Place of Kinfolk in Personal Community Networks." *Marriage and Family Review* 15:195–228.

Weston, Kath. 1991. *Families We Choose: Lesbians, Gays, Kinship.* New York: Columbia University Press.

Williams, Joan. 2000. *Unbending Gender: Why Family and Work Conflict and What to Do about It.* New York: Oxford University Press.

Wilson, William Julius. 1987. *The Truly Disadvantaged.* Chicago: University of Chicago Press.

Young, Michael and Peter Willmott. 1992. *Family and Kinship in East London.* 2d ed. Berkeley and Los Angeles: University of California Press.

Zaretsky, Eli. 1986. *Capitalism, the Family and Personal Life.* New York: Perennial Library.

28

BEYOND THE BIRTH FAMILY
African American Children
Reared by Alternative Caregivers

ELLEN E. PINDERHUGHES • BRENDA JONES HARDEN

African American children grow up in diverse family settings, ranging from "nuclear" families to households headed by single parents to a variety of extended family situations. A small but significant group of African American children do not reside with their birth parents, but are reared by kin (blood relatives), foster and adoptive families, as well as families united through legal guardianship. Across these diverse family arrangements there are common challenges or issues confronting parents and caregivers of African American children. As in all families, one set of challenges includes using a parenting style and engaging in parenting processes that will facilitate effective childrearing. Unique to families of color,

Ellen E. Pinderhughes and Brenda Jones Harden, "Beyond the Birth Family: African American Children Reared by Alternative Caregivers" from *African American Family Life: Ecological and Cultural Diversity,* edited by Vonnie C. McLoyd, Nancy E. Hill, and Kenneth A. Dodge. Copyright © 2005 by The Guilford Press. Reprinted with permission.

another challenge is helping children develop with an appreciation of their cultural legacy and an understanding of the potential discrimination they will face. . . . This [reading] . . . examines issues unique to African American children in the most common alternative caregiving arrangements—specifically, kinship care, foster care, and adoption.

Because these families are created by the removal of children from their biological parents, there are unique challenges with which caregiver, child, and biological parent must contend. Whether the removal is voluntary or involuntary, it signals the perspective that the child's needs are better met in another family setting. Whereas in some cases caregivers and birth parents privately or informally negotiate the kinship arrangement, many kinship, foster, and adoptive families are formed through the intervention of the child welfare system. Too often the intervention is prompted by a reported failure of the biological parents to ensure the safety and well-being of their children (Berrick 1998). When this occurs, a judgment is made by child welfare and legal professionals that a child's needs for safety and protection cannot be met by his or her biological parents and the child must be placed with a family competent to meet these needs.

The Overrepresentation of African American Children in Alternative Caregiving Arrangements

As compared with children in other racial-ethnic groups, African American children are more likely to live apart from their birth parents. Census data (U.S. Bureau of the Census 2002) indicate that approximately 8 percent of African American children reside in households that do not include either of their birth parents. In contrast, approximately 3 percent of European American children live in such households. The proportion of American children living with their grandparents varies by race-ethnicity as well. Nine percent of African American children reside with their grandparents, as opposed to 4 percent of European American children, 6 percent of Hispanic children, and 3 percent of Asian American children (Fields 2003). Evidence from empirical studies across the nation has confirmed the findings yielded by census data. Multiple studies of families in which children are being reared by relatives have suggested that these arrangements are more commonly found among the African American population.

In addition, African American families are more likely to be involved in the child welfare system than would be expected, given their general numbers in the population. Although the evidence suggests that African American children are no more vulnerable to maltreatment than other children (particularly when socioeconomic factors are controlled for; e.g., Sedlak and Broadhurst 1996), the proportion of African American children in the foster care system far exceeds their proportion in the general population (Courtney et al. 1996; Lau et al. 2003). Specifically, Adoption and Foster Care Analysis and Reporting System (AFCARS) data reveal that 38 percent of children in foster care are of African American descent, despite the fact that

they represent only 15 percent of the U.S. child population (U.S. Department of Health and Human Services [USDHHS] 2003a).

Once in the foster care system, African American children are less likely to be returned to their biological families (Courtney 1994; Wells and Guo 1999; Wulczyn et al. 2001). They also tend to remain in the foster care system longer than children of other racial groups (Barth 1997; Courtney 1994; Wulczyn, Hislop, and Goerge 2001). There are also racial disparities in the number and quality of services foster children receive, with African American children faring the worst. African American children have fewer contacts with their caseworkers and have fewer written case plans (Courtney et al. 1996). They also are less likely to receive developmental and psychological assessments and mental health treatment while in care (Garland, Landsverk, and Lau 2003). They have fewer parental visits, and their biological parents are less likely to receive family preservation and reunification services (Brown and Bailey-Etta 1997; Lawrence-Webb 1997).

In regard to the settings in which foster children are reared, African American children tend to be cared for by unrelated persons in traditional foster family homes. However, they are more likely to be placed temporarily or permanently with relatives than their European American counterparts (Ehrle and Geen 2002). Thus, they are slightly less likely than European American children to be placed in traditional foster home settings. In specific urban areas, relative placements have exceeded foster home placements for African American children (e.g., Chicago; Testa 2001). Although African American children are less likely to be placed in adoptive homes than their European American counterparts (Barth 1997; USDHHS 2003b), increasingly they are being adopted, sometimes by their own relatives (Testa 2004). In fact, data from the Multistate Data Archive suggest that the adoption of African American infants may be closing the gap between the rates of foster care exits experienced by African American and European American children (Wulczyn 2003).

In sum, African American children have a higher likelihood than European American children of residing in homes without the presence of their birth parents. This holds true across a variety of settings, including "informal" arrangements between their parents and relatives and placements that are facilitated by the child welfare system. These alternative arrangements have multiple implications for the experiences of African American children and their developmental outcomes. These issues are discussed in turn in the sections on the various family arrangements—non-kinship foster care, kinship care, and adoption.

Non-Kinship Foster Care

Originating in the 1800s, and organized on a state-by-state basis, the foster care system is charged with ensuring the safety of, permanency for, and well-being of all children in the system (Berrick 1998; Waldfogel 2000). Traditional foster care has a long, complex history in the United States with respect to

African American children and families. According to some scholars, this service sector basically ignored African American children prior to the 1960s. For example, most public and private child welfare agencies did not provide foster and adoptive placement services for African American children (Billingsley and Giovannoni 1972; Everett, Chipungu, and Leashore 1991; Smith and Devore 2004). During this era, some agencies were created specifically to serve African American children in vulnerable family situations, such as New York's Harlem-Dowling agency. With increased national attention in the ensuing decades given to the civil rights of African Americans across social institutions, African American children and families increasingly became consumers of child welfare services (Everett et al. 1991; Smith and Devore 2004).

The child welfare system includes a complex array of services, including child protection, foster care, and adoption. Foster care is defined as the temporary placement of a child in a stable family setting, during which time a permanent home is sought for the child: a return to a "rehabilitated" biological parent, placement with a relative, or adoption (Berrick 1998). Foster parents are licensed to care for children on a 24-hour basis. To be licensed, they must attend extensive preservice training and undergo a "home study," a process in which their individual, family, and home characteristics are examined to determine whether they meet the criteria for the license. African American families may be less likely to meet the licensing requirements than European American families (Chipungu and Bent-Goodley 2004; Denby and Rindfleisch 1996). For example, they may be less likely to complete the training and paperwork required for licensure or to have homes that meet the stringent safety and space mandates.

While caring for children, foster parents receive a monthly stipend to pay for the children's board and maintenance expenses. The limited data on foster care payments suggest that this financial assistance is critical for African American families (Fees et al. 1998). Foster parents must attend regular "booster" trainings and receive regular home visits while actively caring for children. The cultural competence of both the preservice and in-service trainings that African American foster parents receive has been called into question (Chipungu and Bent-Goodley 2004; Smith and Devore 2004). Similarly, the cultural competence of the foster care social workers has been noted as crucial to maintaining a positive relationship between African American foster families and the child welfare agencies (McPhatter 1997; Pinderhughes 1991).

Non-Kin Foster Caregivers

Over the last few decades, the needs of the foster care system and the characteristics of foster families have changed appreciably. Regardless of race, child welfare systems are losing record numbers of foster parents as a result of foster parent adoptions, the demands of being a foster parent, and economic demands requiring more women in the workforce (Barbell and Freundlich 2001; Chipungu and Bent-Goodley 2004). Because of the dwindling supply of traditional foster parents and efforts at recruiting a new cadre of potential

foster families, the population of foster parents has become considerably more diverse (Orme et al. 2004). Specifically, although caregivers are still predominately female, there is now a small but growing number of male foster care providers. In addition, many foster parents are single parents and are members of multigenerational households. There is greater age variability as well, with many traditional foster parents reaching their older years and many young persons being licensed as foster parents. Although most foster parents are of European American ancestry, expansion of the requirements for foster parent licensure has increased the proportion of African American foster parents over the last few decades. Some of this increase is attributable to the rising number of relatives who are approved as foster parents (Testa and Slack 2002; USDHHS 2000).

Perhaps related to the increasing racial and economic diversity of the foster parent population, current foster parents are a fairly vulnerable group of families. Findings from various studies indicate that foster parents have poorer physical health, higher rates of mental health difficulties, more compromised parenting, greater family dysfunction, and lower socioeconomic levels than their counterparts in the general population (Orme et al. 2004). These risk factors must be addressed in the context of the unique cultural characteristics of the African American foster family population. African American foster caregivers tend to be older and in poorer health than their European American counterparts (USDHHS 2000), thus experiencing more personal constraints on their ability to provide effective care and supervision. Despite these higher individual stressors, as well as the stress associated with minority status in the United States, one study of the quality of family functioning found more similarities than differences between African American and European American foster families (Seaberg and Harrigan 1999). African American foster caregivers receive fewer supports than do their European American counterparts (e.g., Courtney et al. 1996).

African American Children in Non-Kinship Care

There are limited data on the functioning of children in foster care, and even less on African American children in such care. The National Survey of Child and Adolescent Well-Being (NSCAW Research Group 2002) has brought the field closer to a solid knowledge base about the developmental functioning of foster children. This study examines the needs of foster children being reared in a variety of contexts, including foster family and kinship settings. Findings from this and other studies present a profile of foster children that suggests that they are more compromised than are children in the general population across developmental domains. Although most of the extant studies generally control for race and ethnicity, the available evidence is particularly germane to African American children, given their overrepresentation in the foster care system.

Before considering developmental outcomes in foster children, one must note an important caveat to the evidence. It is difficult to disentangle the

multiple preplacement influences on foster child outcomes from the impact of foster care experience per se. Children in foster care are biologically vulnerable to many poor developmental outcomes because of genetic factors, prenatal drug exposure, and other physical health issues. The majority of these children have experienced maltreatment prior to foster care entry as well, which has been documented to have a major impact on children's outcomes across domains (Hildeyard and Wolfe 2001). Moreover, the child's experiences while in foster care have an impact on developmental outcome. For example, the placement instability while in care (number of foster homes) influences how the child adjusts (James, Landsverk, and Slymen 2004; Newton, Litrownik, and Landsverk 2000). Facilitating the integration of a foster child into the family is very risky; foster families may function with different boundaries, rules, and patterns of interactions than those with which foster children have experience. The quality of the parenting in foster families also contributes to the child's development. Such issues as subsequent experiences of maltreatment and the emotional commitment of the foster parent also have great effects on the child (Zuravin, Benedict, and Somerfield 1993).

Despite the preceding caveat, many studies have pointed to the deleterious impact of foster care on children's physical health, cognitive and academic functioning, and social-emotional well-being. In regard to physical health, pediatric and public health scholars have documented that foster children have a higher level of morbidity throughout childhood, higher rates of growth abnormalities, and more untreated health problems than children not involved in the foster care system (Halfon, Berkowitz, and Klee 1992; Risley-Curtiss et al. 1996). Data from the NSCAW study and smaller studies point to cognitive developmental delays in this population of children as well (NSCAW Research Group 2002). In addressing academic achievement, some studies have found that foster children perform more poorly on academic achievement tests, have poorer grades, and have higher rates of grade retention and special education placement (Konenkamp and Ehrle 2002; Yu, Day, and Williams 2002).

The social-emotional development of foster children is the domain that has received the most empirical attention. Research has suggested that foster children are more likely to have insecure or disordered attachments and the adverse long-term outcomes associated with such attachments (Dozier et al. 2001). Most studies have estimated that at least 50 percent of foster children also have mental health difficulties, including higher rates of depression, poorer social skills, lower adaptive functioning, and more externalizing behavior problems such as aggression and impulsivity (USDHHS 2003a). Research has also documented high levels of mental health service utilization among foster children (Garland et al. 2003; Halfon et al. 1992).

Race-ethnicity is a salient factor in understanding the well-being of children in the foster care system. The relation between race-ethnicity and outcomes is fairly complex. Diverse studies point to the variability in findings. In one investigation, few differences were found between European American, Latino, and African American youth in their levels of psychosocial

functioning and engagement in risk behaviors (Taussig and Talmi 2001). Another study found that African American foster children had death rates comparable to their peers in the general population, whereas the death rates for European American and Latino foster youth were considerably higher than those of their counterparts in the general population (Barth and Blackwell 1998). In a study of preschool foster children, African American children had significantly lower scores on tests of cognitive and language functioning than a group of children from a combination of other racial and ethnic groups (Jones Harden and Clyman 2004). As with African American foster parents, the psychosocial needs of African American foster children do not translate into the receipt of higher levels of service. For example, Garland and colleagues (2000, 2003) have found that African American foster children consistently receive fewer mental health services than European American foster children.

Transracial Foster Placements

Some African American children experience transracial placements (i.e., are cared for by non–African American foster parents). With the insufficient availability of African American foster parents, children sometimes are placed with European American parents who have different cultural backgrounds and experiences. For all children who have been removed from their birth families and placed in foster care, the maintenance of links to their culture of origin is critical (Jones Harden 2004). When children are placed transracially, the maintenance of these links becomes more challenging. Transracial foster caregivers are engaged in learning about African American culture and normative practices simultaneously as they face incorporating the child into their family and their community and negotiating visits with birth parents. Birth parents may display resentment and hostility about the transracial placement, further constraining foster caregiver–birth parent relations. Racial socialization, parental messages designed to help children develop a healthy racial identity, and found to be linked to youth adjustment (Bowman and Howard 1985; Stevenson 1995), may also be challenging. The only known study on transracial foster placements suggests that foster caregivers receive insufficient support to racially socialize their children (Campbell 2002).

Kinship Arrangements

Kinship care has a rich history in the African American community, being viewed by some scholars as a vestige of African-based practices that survived the devastating effects of the middle passage and slavery (e.g., Hill 1997), or by other scholars as an adaptive response to the destruction of families in slavery and the repressive welfare practices of the early to mid-20th century (Roberts 2002). Irrespective of its actual origin, kinship care provides a family resource for birth parents who, for various reasons, are

unable to care for and protect their children. There are three types of kinship care: (1) private kinship care, whereby the birth parent and kin caregiver informally agree that the caregiver will assume caregiving responsibility; (2) voluntary kinship care, in which a child is placed with a state-approved relative, but the relative is not licensed as a foster parent; and (3) kinship foster care, in which the state has placed the child with relatives who become licensed foster parents (Ehrle, Geen, and Clark 2001).

Kinship foster care has emerged in the past 20 years as a critical strategy for the care and protection of African American children (Geen 2004; Testa and Slack 2002). Due in part to a dwindling foster family base and an increase in the number of children cared for by kin, the increase in state-recognized kinship placements has also reduced the racial disparity in numbers of children in foster care in some jurisdictions (Testa 2004). Although the involvement of the child welfare system distinguishes kinship foster care from private or voluntary kinship care, there are many similar challenges for kin arrangements. There is some evidence that private kinship and voluntary kinship care providers, as well as the children for whom they care, are similarly vulnerable groups (Ehrle and Geen 2002; Goodman et al. 2004). In this section, we address common issues for kinship arrangements and note unique issues specific to each kinship arrangement.

Kinship Caregivers

Kinship caregivers tend to be older (Chipungu et al. 1998) and to have more physical health complications than do licensed foster caregivers (USDHHS 2000), thus facing more challenges to their ability to be effective caregivers. The literature on grandparents raising grandchildren points to the poor mental health of these caregivers and suggests that their health and mental health may worsen under the burden of caring for children (Minkler and Fuller-Thompson 2000). Many studies have pointed to their socioeconomic vulnerability, including being more likely than non-kin foster parents to lack a high school diploma, to be single parents, and to live in poverty (Cuddeback 2004; Geen 2004). Research has also suggested that their parenting and home environments may be more compromised than those of non-kin foster parents (Brooks and Barth 1998; Jones Harden et al. 2004).

Kinship caregivers not only face the numerous challenges that characterize foster caregiving, but also face these challenges with less support from the child welfare system. Although foster kin caregivers are licensed and eligible to receive services, they typically receive fewer services than do non-kin foster caregivers (Chipungu et al. 1998; Cuddeback 2004). Some states do not provide subsidies to non-licensed private kin caregivers (Ehrle et al. 2001). Lacking state recognition for foster care status also excludes private kin caregivers from eligibility for social casework and other supports available to foster caregivers. In the context of very limited systemic support, as well as the external neighborhood and societal stressors that confront African American caregivers (McLoyd 1990), private kin caregivers must

provide concrete and psychological caregiving and obtain needed services for the children in their homes.

African American Children in Kinship Care

Because African American children are more likely to be in kinship care arrangements than are European American children, it is important to consider the effects of kinship placement on children in any discussion of African American children. Most African American children in kinship settings live in private kinship arrangements (Geen 2004). There is limited research on the developmental outcomes for children who are reared by relatives, whether through informal arrangements or formal placement through the child welfare system. Available evidence from several strands of the literature, including foster care, custodial grandparents, and multigenerational families, indicates considerable variability in developmental outcomes. As with the research on foster children, there is limited research that specifically addresses outcomes for African American children in kinship care. Again, the significant overrepresentation of African American children in this population renders the available evidence particularly relevant.

The data on the effects of kinship care on child outcomes yield a complicated picture. Early research suggested that children in kinship care were faring at least as well as other foster children (Benedict, Zuravin, and Stallings 1996), whereas other studies found that children in kinship care had more behavior problems (Berrick et al. 1994; Keller et al. 2001). Research on academic functioning suggests that these children are less likely to repeat a grade or to be enrolled in special education (Brooks and Barth 1998). Retrospective research of adults who were in foster care also yields contrasting findings: One study found that women formerly in kinship care had more psychological vulnerabilities (Carpenter and Clyman 2004), whereas another study reported comparable functioning among those formerly in kinship care and nonrelative care (Benedict et al. 1996). This complicated picture suggests that the critical question is not whether kinship care is better than nonrelative care, but rather is for whom and under what circumstances kinship care is effective. In short, research should next cast its focus on moderators of kinship experiences.

In the NSCAW study, children in kinship care had fewer scores in the clinical range on a variety of developmental measures than children in non-kin foster care (Administration on Children and Families 2003). However, the data in this study suggest that kinship caregivers may choose to care only for children who are functioning well, or that child welfare workers may elect to place less problematic children with kinship care providers. It has also been documented that kinship care providers tend to take younger children (Geen 2004), who may have fewer problems. Thus, decisions by child welfare workers and kinship care providers may explain the better outcomes found among children in kinship homes.

The data on the children's experience of kinship placements are far less equivocal than those regarding their outcomes. Multiple studies have documented that kinship homes are more stable and permanent for children

than non-kin foster homes (Cuddeback 2004; Geen 2004; USDHHS 2000), although kinship placements "disrupt" as well (Testa 2001). Children in these placements live in closer proximity to their neighborhoods of origin and are more able to maintain cultural linkages (Chipungu et al. 1998). Moreover, children in kinship placements do not experience the trauma of being separated from familiar social networks. Specifically, they are more likely to have contact with their birth parents and siblings, and to be placed with their siblings (Chipungu et al. 1998; Geen 2004). In contrast, they are less likely to be reunified with their birth parents and less likely to be adopted (Geen 2004).

This evidence underscores the complex relationship dynamics created for children and their caregivers in kinship arrangements. The implications of these experiences for children remain unclear. For example, the impact of more frequent access to birth parents is not empirically known (USDHHS 2000) and must be disentangled from the reason for the kin placement. In addition, the fewer financial and psychological resources of kinship caregivers certainly influences the caregiving environment their children experience, including how parents under such stress are able to relate to the children in their care. In fact, some studies have documented that the home environments of kinship caregivers are more compromised than those of foster care providers (Barth 2001). Other evidence suggests that the kinship caregiving environment, although not optimal, is generally positive for children (USDHHS 2000). For example, kinship caregivers demonstrate a higher level of commitment to and acceptance of the children in their care and are less likely to maltreat them.

Adoptive Family Arrangements

When parental rights are voluntarily or involuntarily terminated, children become eligible for adoption. In recent years, averages of 120,000 children have been adopted each year in the United States (National Information Adoption Clearinghouse 2003). Although African American children in the child welfare system have lower rates of adoption than European American children (Brooks and James 2003), adoptions of African American children have increased over the last decade largely as a result of the provisions of the Adoption and Safe Families Act and the federal Adoption 2002 initiative (Testa 2004). In fact, African American children represented the largest share of children who were adopted from the foster care system in 2000 (Testa 2004). Based on data from the Multistate Data Archive, African American infants appear to be moving much more quickly through the foster care system toward adoption, a trend that is reducing racial disparities in foster care length of stay in these states (Wulczyn 2003). In addition, foster parents and relatives are increasingly becoming adoption resources for foster children (Testa 2004). Although more long-term research is needed, it does not seem that the passage of the Multiethnic Placement Act of 1994 and the Interethnic Placement Act of 1996 (MEPA/IEPA) is the factor that is increasing the adoption of African American children (Testa 2004).

Most placements involve adoptions of infants through licensed private adoption agencies, whereas about 15–18 percent involve placements of children over age 3, usually from foster care. Whereas international adoptions, involving placement of children from outside the United States are common for children from Asian, Eastern European, and Latin American countries, they are rare for children of African descent. Special needs adoptions involve placement of children who have a developmental, physical, or emotional disability, are members of a sibling group or a minority group, or meet a given state's criteria for being an older child. Transracial adoptions involve placement of an adoptee with a family of a different race.

There are several common issues facing all adoptive families: acknowledgment of similarities and differences in the adoptive and birth families' life cycles (Kirk 1964), parenting adopted children (Brodzinsky and Pinderhughes 2003), the adoptee's adjustment and identity development (Brodzinsky 1990), and the degree of contact or openness (Grotevant and McRoy 1998) between adoptive and birth families. Among the issues facing families adopting African American children, two stand out as particularly salient: openness and transracial adoption.

Openness in Adoption

Over the past few decades, adoptions have become increasingly more open, in large part due to the expectations of birth parents relinquishing their infants to know about, in some cases to choose, and in other cases to meet the adoptive parents (National Adoption Information Clearinghouse 2003). Nowadays, adoptions vary in how much contact or information is shared, ranging from no contact at all (confidential adoption), to exchange of nonidentifying information through a third party (mediated adoption), to exchange of identifying information and, perhaps, face-to-face meeting (fully disclosed adoption) (Grotevant and McRoy 1998). Estimates of placement characterized by these different levels of contact are extremely sketchy; one study found that 69 percent of adoptions involved some contact (Berry 1991).

A highly controversial aspect of adoption, openness, became a research topic relatively recently. Findings from a respected longitudinal research program on infant adoptions (Grotevant and McRoy 1998; Grotevant et al. 1999; Wrobel et al. 1996) found that contrary to the concerns of those opposed to open adoption, birth parents are no more likely to seek to reclaim custody, adoptive parents' sense of entitlement to be parents is not jeopardized, and adoptees can experience a healthy adjustment. However, contrary to those extolling the benefits of open adoption, the resolution of grief for birth parents was not guaranteed. In sum, mutual agreement about the level of contact between adoptive and birth parents is the critical element. Another important element is flexibility for changing the arrangements over time—in either direction on the continuum.

This small and growing body of literature lacks the participation of African American families, so we know little about the numbers or

experiences of African American families involved in mediated or fully disclosed adoptions. It is not easy to forecast the patterns of participation or outcomes for African American families, because of two competing historical patterns. Although African Americans have a rich and long tradition of private kinship placements (Hill 1997), suggesting an inclination toward more openness in adoptions, these families also have a history of neglect by social service and child welfare agencies (Billingsley and Giovannoni 1972; Roberts 2002), pointing to a wariness of agency mediation in or facilitation of adoption contact. However, socioeconomic differences in adoptions involving different levels of openness may emerge. A common pattern in adoption is that lower-income African American families tend to have more success adopting older children from foster care than do middle-income families (Rosenthal 1993). Middle- to upper-income African Americans are more likely to have the resources to adopt infants through private agency placements. Older child foster placements present a mixed picture of openness: whereas parental rights have been permanently terminated, the adoptee intimately knows who his or her birth parents and family are. The adoptee also may have occasional contact with the extended birth family. Thus, lower-income families may experience more contact with birth families than do middle-income families. Clarification of these issues awaits the focus on African American families in research on openness.

Transracial Adoption

From the era of the civil rights movement through the nascence of the Black Power era, transracial adoption emerged as an option of choice for European American parents. In 1971, during the height of this period, 2,500 children were placed in transracial adoptions. Abruptly reduced by reactions to the National Association of Black Social Workers' dictum that transracial adoption was tantamount to cultural genocide, transracial adoption became rarer over the next 20–25 years. Recent federal policies supportive of transracial placements (i.e., MEPA, IEPA) have again placed transracial adoption on the adoption map. In this country, where the salience of race still occupies local, state, and national discourse, parents raising African American children face the challenge of preparing their children to succeed as adults of color. This may mean providing support and advocacy for a child's success in school and in the community, as well as active support for the child's development of his or her ethnic identity. However, parents in transracial adoptions must also anticipate the placement's impact on the family, for the perception of the family by the community and society may change.

Although African American parents vary as to the amount and content of race-related information they share with children, two important findings have emerged in the developing literature on racial socialization. First, African American children whose parents highlight their group's cultural history have higher self-esteem and more positive attitudes toward their cultural group (Stevenson 1995). Second, messages about racial barriers are linked to higher grades and feelings of efficacy among children, as well as

less depression (Bowman and Howard 1985; Stevenson 1995). Thus, this literature suggests the importance of racial socialization messages for youth adjustment.

The literature on the impact of transracial placements on adoptee development yields some inconsistencies (Lee 2003). On one hand, several studies suggest that individual and group identity do not suffer, despite great variation in adoptive parents' attention to racial socialization (Brooks and Barth 1999; Simon, Alstein, and Melli 1994). On the other hand, some studies report that group identity is negatively affected. Deberry and colleagues (1996) noted a concerning pattern among a small sample of families in which parents' racial socialization practices decreased as the children moved into adolescence, with corresponding shifts in adoptees' Eurocentric and Afrocentric values. Case study accounts from adults raised in transracial placements highlight not only the love and appreciation of the adoptees for their families, but also the struggles they have encountered with their sense of self as African Americans (Pinderhughes 1997; Simon and Rhoorda 2000).

In sum, the complexities of transracial adoption highlight multiple levels of parenting challenges faced in these families: common childrearing challenges faced by all parents, adoption-related challenges faced by all parents raising adopted children, challenges faced by parents raising children of color, and challenges faced by parents whose children are from a different cultural group. Despite these multiple layers of challenge in transracial placements, there is no systematic emphasis set forth in the MEPA, IEPA, or related regulations on assessing or training prospective transracial adoptive parents. This hole in adoption policy and practice must be addressed.

Policy Issues

Family policy in the United States emanates from a complex set of laws, regulations, and procedures that lacks a cohesive philosophy and an interconnected funding stream (Kamerman 1996). There are multiple national policies that may affect children in these alternative caregiving environments, including those addressing child maltreatment and income supports for low-income families. . . . The ensuing discussion addresses the policy landscape specific to African American children and families in these diverse caregiving situations.

The leading legislation affecting the families discussed in this chapter is the Adoption and Safe Families Act (ASFA). Proponents of ASFA assert that this legislation moves the field forward in meeting the developmental needs of children by mandating expeditious permanency decisions for them. However, other scholars (e.g., Roberts 2001) suggest that the practices emanating from such legislation may sever the ties that African American families may have. These scholars argue that the supports to help families care for their children and rehabilitate themselves are not available, so the ultimate effect of such policies as ASFA is to achieve permanency for children outside their birth families.

There are other specific policies that support families, such as the Safe and Stable Families Act. In addition, currently there are funds available through child welfare "waivers," by which localities can divert funds saved through reductions of their numbers of children in foster care to other purposes, such as family support, preservation, and reunification. Despite these policies, the resources for such family-centered services are severely lacking (Wulczyn 2004). The financial incentives states and counties may receive for adoption and the financial reimbursements they receive for foster care clearly outstrip the meager resources available for services to promote the stability and well-being of maltreating families. The insufficiency of these latter resources compound the inequities in resources available for African American families involved with the child welfare system.

Policies for kinship care suffer from a lack of cohesion and direction from the national level. Thus, kinship care policies are quite variable across states (Ehrle et al. 2001; Geen 2004). Some states routinely provide relative caregivers with foster care board rates and services, whereas others provide them only with public assistance allotments (i.e., Temporary Assistance for Needy Families [TANF] payments). Some states have created comprehensive service networks targeted specifically to relative caregivers who provide legal, family support, mental health, and other ancillary services. Relatedly, in some jurisdictions, relatives are encouraged to make informal arrangements to care for the vulnerable children in their midst, and therefore the children never become "cases" in the child welfare system. Other jurisdictions may require formal involvement with the child welfare system whenever a child is removed from a biological parent. Thus, what occurs in practice in regard to families in which a relative is caring for a minor child differs from jurisdiction to jurisdiction, from family to family.

Two race-specific policies, MEPA and its successor IEPA, grew out of the concern of some practitioners and policymakers that African American and other minority children were not being placed in permanent homes as expeditiously as possible. Adoption practices favoring in-race placements provided few options for majority families seeking to adopt. Indeed, national trends indicated that many European American families were waiting for children to adopt and many African American children were waiting for adoptive placement (Brooks and James 2003). Although the data on the long-term impact of these policies are not yet available, preliminary evidence suggests that MEPA and IEPA have not had an appreciable impact on the adoption of African American children by European American families (Testa 2004). However, the press of legislation such as this to secure permanency for African American children has led to more permanent relative placements and an increased emphasis and effort relative to the adoption of minority children.

Conclusion

Five critical surrogate arrangements for African American children include non-kinship foster care, three variations of kinship care—private kinship

care, voluntary kinship care, and kinship foster care—and adoption. As this [reading] has examined the issues facing caregivers, children, and birth parents in each of these placements, several themes have emerged. First, the knowledge base of the impact of these arrangements on the functioning of African American caregivers and children is woefully insufficient. Emerging research in this area, particularly regarding kinship arrangements, suggests that these placements warrant greater understanding. Although the new NSCAW study on children in foster care may contribute to rectifying the literature gap, other studies are needed as well. Second, consideration of issues associated with these placements, beyond the typical challenges confronting parents described elsewhere . . . , illustrates that surrogate arrangements complicate childrearing in ways that suggest the importance of additional services for families united through foster care, kinship care, or adoption. Although the developmental implications of these caregiving experiences are yet to be fully understood, it is certain that these alternative family arrangements provide a critical resource for African American children whose birth parents are unable to care for them.

REFERENCES

Administration on Children and Families. 2003. *National Survey of Child and Adolescent Well-Being, One Year in Foster Care, Wave 1 Data Analysis Report.* Washington, DC: U.S. Department of Health and Human Services.

Barbell, K. and M. Freundlich. 2001. *Foster Care Today.* Washington, DC: Casey Family Programs.

Barth, R. 2001. "Policy Implications of Foster Family Characteristics." *Family Relations* 50 (1): 16–19.

Barth, R. and D. Blackwell. 1998. "Death Rates among California's Foster Care and Former Care Populations." *Children and Youth Services Review* 20 (7): 577–604.

Benedict, M., S. Zuravin, and R. Stallings. 1996. "Adult Functioning of Children Who Lived in Kin vs. Non-Relative Foster Homes." *Child Welfare* 75:529–49.

Berrick, J. D. 1998. "When Children Cannot Remain Home: Foster Family Care and Kinship Care." *The Future of Children* 8:72–87.

Berry, M. 1991. "The Practice of Open Adoption: Findings from a Study of 1,396 Families." *Children and Youth Services Review* 13:379–95.

Billingsley, A. and J. Giovannoni. 1972. *Children of the Storm: Black Children and American Child Welfare.* New York: Harcourt Brace Jovanovich.

Bowman, P. J. and C. Howard. 1985. "Race-Related Socialization, Motivation, and Academic Achievement: A Study of Black Youth in Three-Generation Families." *Journal of the American Academy of Child Psychiatry* 24:134–41.

Brodzinsky, D. M. 1990. "A Stress and Coping Model of Adoption Adjustment." Pp. 212–43 in *The Psychology of Adoption,* edited by D. Brodzinsky and M. Schechter. New York: Oxford University Press.

Brodzinsky, D. M. and E. E. Pinderhughes. 2003. "Parenting and Child Development in Adoptive Families." Pp. 279–312 in *Handbook of Parenting.* Mahwah, NJ: Erlbaum.

Brooks, D. and R. P. Barth. 1999. "Adult Transracial and Inracial Adoptees: Effects of Race, Gender, Adoptive Family Structure, and Placement History on Adjustment Outcomes." *American Journal of Orthopsychiatry* 69:87–99.

Brooks, D. and S. James. 2003. "Willingness to Adopt Black Foster Children: Implications for Child Welfare Policy and Recruitment of Adoptive Families." *Children and Youth Services Review* 25:463–87.

Campbell, H. M. 2002. "Psychological Adjustment of Same Race and Transracially Placed African American Foster Children and Racial Socialization Practices of Foster Parents: An Exploratory Study." *Dissertation Abstracts International* 63 (1-B): 563.

Chipungu, S. and T. Bent-Goodley. 2004. "Challenges of Contemporary Foster Care." *The Future of Children* 14 (1): 75–93.

Chipungu, S., J. Everett, M. Verduik, and J. Jones. 1998. *Children Placed in Foster Care with Relatives: A Multi-State Study.* Washington, DC: U.S. Department of Health and Human Services.

Courtney, M. E., R. P. Barth, J. Duerr Berrick, J. Berrick, D. Brooks, B. Needell, and L. Park. 1996. "Race and Child Welfare Services: Past Research and Future Directions." *Child Welfare* 75:99–137.

Cuddeback, G. 2004. "Kinship Family Foster Care: A Methodological and Substantive Synthesis of Research." *Children and Youth Services Review* 26 (7): 623–39.

Deberry, K., S. Scarr, and R. Weinberg. 1996. "Family Racial Socialization and Ecological Competence: Longitudinal Assessments of African-American Transracial Adoptees." *Child Development* 67:2375–99.

Denby, R. and N. Rindfleisch. 1996. "African American Foster Parenting Experiences: Research Findings and Implications for Policy Practice." *Children and Youth Services Review* 18 (6): 523–52.

Dozier, M., K. C. Stovall, K. E. Albus, and B. Bates. 2001. "Attachment for Infants in Foster Care: The Role of Caregiver State of Mind." *Child Development* 72:1467–77.

Ehrle, J., R. Geen, and R. Clark. 2001. "Children Cared for by Relatives: Who Are They and How Are They Faring?" *New Federalism: National Survey of America's Families*. Washington, DC: Urban Institute.

Everett, J., S. Chipungu, and B. Leashore, eds. 1991. *Child Welfare: An Africentric Perspective*. New Brunswick, NJ: Rutgers University Press.

Fees, B., B. Stockdale, S. Crase, K. Riggins-Caspers, A. Yates, K. Lekies, and R. Gillis-Arnold. 1998. "Satisfaction with Foster Parenting: Assessment One Year after Training." *Children and Youth Services Review* 20:347–63.

Fields, J. 2003. "Children's Living Arrangements and Characteristics: March 2002." *Current Population Reports*, series P20–547. Washington, DC: U.S. Bureau of the Census.

Garland, A., R. Hough, J. Landsverk, K. McCabe, M. Yeh, W. Ganger, and B. Reynolds. 2000. "Racial and Ethnic Variations in Mental Health Service Utilization among Children in Foster Care." *Children's Services: Social Policy, Research and Practice* 3 (3): 133–46.

Garland, A., J. Landsverk, R. Hough, and E. Ellis-MacLeod. 1996. "Type of Maltreatment as a Predictor of Mental Health Service Use in Foster Care." *Child Abuse and Neglect* 20:675–88.

Garland, A., J. Landsverk, and A. Lau. 2003. "Racial-Ethnic Disparities in Mental Health Service Use among Children in Foster Care." *Children and Youth Services Review* 25:489–505.

Geen, R. 2004. "The Evolution of Kinship Care Policy and Practice." *The Future of Children* 14 (1): 131–50.

Grotevant, H. D. and R. G. McRoy. 1998. *Openness in Adoption: Connecting Families of Birth and Adoption*. Thousand Oaks, CA: Sage.

Grotevant, H. D., H. M. Ross, M. A. Marchel, and R. G. McRoy. 1999. "Adaptive Behavior in Adopted Children: Predictors from Early Risk, Collaboration in Relationships within the Adoptive Kinship Network, and Openness Arrangements." *Journal of Adolescent Research* 14:231–47.

Halfon, N., G. Berkowitz, and L. Klee. 1992. "Mental Health Service Utilization by Children in Foster Care in California." *Pediatrics* 89:1238–44.

Hildeyard, K. and D. Wolfe. 2001. "Child Neglect: Developmental Issues and Outcomes." *Child Abuse and Neglect* 26 (6–7): 679–95.

Hill, R. 1997. *The Strengths of African American Families: Twenty-Five Years Later*. Washington, DC: R & B.

James, S., J. Landsverk, and D. Slymen. 2004. "Placement Movement in Out-of-Home Care: Patterns and Predictors." *Children and Youth Services Review* 26 (2): 185–206.

Jones Harden, B. 2004. "Safety and Stability for Foster Children: A Developmental Perspective." *Future of Children* 14 (1): 31–48.

Jones Harden, B., R. Clyman, D. Kriebel, and M. Lyons. 2004. "Kith and Kin Care: Parental Characteristics and Attitudes of Foster and Kinship Caregivers." *Children and Youth Services Review* 26 (7): 657–71.

Kamerman, S. 1996. "Child and Family Policies: An International Review." Pp. 31–50 in *Children, Families and Government*, edited by E. Zigler, S. L. Kagan, and N. Hall. New York: Cambridge University Press.

Kirk, H. D. 1964. *Shared Fate*. New York: Free Press.

Konenkamp, K. and J. Ehrle. 2002. *Well-Being of Children Involved in the Child Welfare System: A National Overview*. Washington, DC: Urban Institute.

Lau, A., K. McCabe, M. Yeh, A. Garland, R. Hough, and J. Landsverk. 2003. "Race/Ethnicity and Rates of Self-Reported Maltreatment among High-Risk Youth in Public Sectors of Care." *Child Maltreatment* 8 (3): 183–94.

Lee, R. 2003. "The Transracial Adoption Paradox: History, Research, and Counseling Implications of Cultural Socialization." *Counseling Psychologist* 31 (6): 711–44.

Minkler, M. and E. Fuller-Thomson. 1999. "The Health of Grandparents Raising Grandchildren: Results of a National Study." *American Journal of Public Health* 89 (9): 1384–89.

National Information Adoption Clearinghouse. 2003. *Adoption: Numbers and Trends.* Retrieved July 1, 2004, from http://naic.afc.hhs.gov.

Newton, R. R., A. J. Litrownik, and J. A. Landsverk. 2000. "Children and Youth in Foster Care: Disentangling the Relationship between Problem Behaviors and Number of Placements." *Child Abuse and Neglect* 24:1363–74.

NSCAW Research Group. 2002. "Methodological Lessons from the National Survey of Child and Adolescent Well-Being: The First Three Years of the USA's First National Probability Study of Children and Families Investigated for Abuse and Neglect." *Children and Youth Services Review* 24:513–41.

Orme, J., C. Buehler, M. McSurdy, K. Rhodes, M. Cox, and D. Patterson. 2004. "Parental and Familial Characteristics of Family Foster Care Applicants." *Children and Youth Services Review* 26 (3): 307–29.

Pinderhughes, R. B. 1997. "The Experience of Racial Identity Development for Transracial Adoptees." Unpublished doctoral dissertation, Massachusetts School of Professional Psychology, Boston.

Risley-Curtiss, C., T. Combs-Orme, R. Chernoff, and A. Heisler. 1996. "Health Care Utilization by Children Entering Foster Care." *Research on Social Work Practice* 6 (4): 442–61.

Roberts, D. 2002. *Shattered Bonds: The Color of Child Welfare.* New York: Basic Civitas Books.

Seaberg, J. and M. Harrigan. 1999. "Foster Families' Functioning Experiences and Views: Variations by Race." *Children and Youth Services Review* 21 (1): 31–55.

Sedlak, A. and D. Broadhurst. 1996. *Third National Incidence Study of Child Abuse and Neglect.* Washington, DC: U.S. Department of Health and Human Services.

Simon, R. J., H. Alstein, and M. S. Melli. 1994. *The Case for Transracial Adoption.* Washington, DC: American University Press.

Simon, R. J. and R. M. Rhoorda. 2000. *In Their Own Voices: Transracial Adoptees Tell Their Stories.* New York: Columbia University Press.

Smith, C. and W. Devore. 2004. "African American Children in the Child Welfare and Kinship System: From Exclusion to Over Inclusion." *Children and Youth Services Review* 26 (5): 427–46.

Stevenson, H. C. 1995. "Relationships of Adolescent Perceptions of Racial Socialization to Racial Identity." *Journal of Black Psychology* 21 (1): 49–70.

Taussig, H. and A. Talmi. 2001. "Ethnic Differences in Risk Behaviors and Related Psychosocial Variables among a Cohort of Maltreated Adolescents in Foster Care." *Child Maltreatment* 6 (2): 180–92.

Testa, M. 2001. "The Changing Significance of Race and Kinship for Achieving Permanency for Foster Children." Presented at Race Matters: A Research Forum. Washington, DC: Children and Family Research Center.

———. 2004. "When Children Cannot Return Home: Adoption and Guardianship." *The Future of Children* 14 (1): 115–30.

Testa, M. and K. Slack. 2002. "The Gift of Kinship Foster Care." *Children and Youth Services Review* 24 (1–2): 79–108.

U.S. Bureau of the Census. 2002. *Current Population Survey Report.* Washington, DC: U.S. Bureau of the Census.

U.S. Department of Health and Human Services. 2000. *Report to the Congress on Kinship Foster Care.* Washington, DC: U.S. Government Printing Office.

U.S. Department of Health and Human Services. 2003a. *The Adoption and Foster Care Analysis and Reporting System (AFCARS) Report: Preliminary FY 2001 Estimates as of March 2003.* Washington, DC: U.S. Government Printing Office.

Waldfogel, J. 2000. "Child Welfare for the 21st Century." *Children and Youth Services Review* 22:681–83.

Wrobel, G., S. Ayers-Lopez, H. D. Grotevant, R. G. McRoy, and M. Friedrick. 1996. "Openness in Adoption and the Level of Child Participation." *Child Development* 67:2358–74.

Wulczyn, F. 2003. "Closing the Gap: Are Changing Exit Patterns Reducing the Time African American Children Spend in Foster Care Relative to Caucasian Children?" *Children and Youth Services Review* 25:393–408.

———. 2004. "Family Reunification." *Children, Families and Foster Care* 14 (1): 95–113.

Yu, E., P. Day, and M. Williams. 2002. *Improving Educational Outcomes for Youth in Care: A National Collaboration.* Washington, DC: Child Welfare League of America.

29

OUT OF SORTS
Adoption and (Un)Desirable Children

KATHERIN M. FLOWER KIM

Adoption has become an increasingly important and common path for forming a family with children, and it illustrates the importance adopters place on having a family that includes children. Yet adoption is not simply a case of adopting any child. Differential rates of adoption for different groups of children as well as categories of "waiting children" reflect the ways some children are considered more desirable than other children and helps explain why some children are more likely to be adopted, and adopted more quickly, than are other children. I draw on interview data collected during 1997–1999 from 43 mothers and 30 of their husbands in Central City, a pseudonym for a city in central New York, who adopted children from Korea in the 1980s and 1990s, to investigate the sorting, and in many instances ranking, of children throughout the adoption process. All but one of the participants identified themselves as white.[1] While their comments indicated that a range of factors contributed to parental perceptions and talk about (un)desirable children, this reading is principally concerned with exploring and analyzing the ways race shaped American parents' thinking and discourse about who was more or less desirable as a potential family member. More specifically, I use parents' descriptions of assembling their families to explore and highlight how they came to explain the desirability of children from Korea and the undesirability of African American children.

A key aspect of understanding constructions of desirable children and parental preferences for certain children is clarifying who the adopters are, particularly in terms of race. More specifically, the majority of parents who adopt through formal, legal channels[2] were, and continue to be, whites who experience fertility problems (May 1995; Roberts 1997). As Elaine Tyler May (1995) noted,

> "Barren" is a term laden with historical weight. It carries negative meanings: unproductive, sterile, bare, empty, stark, deficient, lacking, wanting, destitute, devoid. It is the opposite of fertile, lavish, abounding, productive. . . . Until the mid-nineteenth century, men were believed to be fertile if they were not impotent, so "barren" women carried the

blame if a married couple did not have children. The term, like the condition, suggested moral and spiritual failure, and the words like "blame," "fault" and "guilt" have been attached to childlessness ever since. (P. 11)

From this perspective, the desire for white children was connected to the potential for parents, especially women, to avoid the social stigma of infertility.[3] Racial matching policies were, however, not only about avoiding the social stigma of infertility. Rather, preferences and policies regarding racial matching were also about supporting social norms related to race relations. More to the point, given the tension and polarization between U.S. whites and racial-ethnic minorities (especially those between whites and blacks), adopting white children and avoiding other children was not just about masking infertility; it was also a way of managing race relations and racism. Thus, the social location and characteristics of the majority of formal–legal adopters (i.e., whites), in conjunction with the sociohistorical context, offers a more complete explanation of why white infants were more desirable (and therefore adopted) and other infants and children were considered undesirable and subsequently not adopted.

Following World War II, a number of social changes occurred in the United States, which had important ramifications for adoption policies and practices, especially in relation to the availability of healthy, white infants. Factors, such as postwar affluence as well as changes in the age, education, and occupation of "birth" parents and adoption applicants, impacted adoption trends (Carp 2002). In addition, two of the most commonly cited shifts in sociocultural norms influencing adoption in the United States are the availability of contraception and abortion as well as an increased acceptance of out-of-wedlock births (Luker 1996; May 1995; Solinger 1992). These changes drastically decreased the number of healthy, white infants available for adoption, creating an atmosphere of scarcity for "desirable" children. The imbalance in formal legal adoption between the adopters (white middle/upper class) and the desirable child (a healthy, white infant) was such that by the 1970s a "healthy white baby" was a request deemed unrealistic by social workers (Melosh 2002:162). In light of the "context of scarcity," some parents looked for alternatives to a healthy, white infant. One alternative was to reconstruct the desirable child to include non-white children as acceptable and pursue transracial adoption. Two options for transracial adoption were racial-ethnic minority children in the United States or children born outside the United States.

Healthy, but . . .

In my interviews, most parents pointed out that a notable and unique aspect of the adoption process was the opportunity to make specific choices about the children they would adopt. In various ways, they could sort potential family members as more or less desirable by indicating what types of children they were willing to adopt.[4] As such, notions of "choices" and

"choosing" were central to parents' adoption narratives and practices,[5] and parents and adoption agencies expressed a range of feelings and practices regulating the choices parents could or could not make. Most adoptive parents initially indicated resistance, or at least ambivalence, to indicating preferences for certain characteristics of children. As if given a script, the majority of parents in my sample responded to the question "When thinking about adopting a child, what was important to you?" by noting they wanted only *a healthy* child. The consistency of the response was not entirely surprising given available cultural discourses and norms that emphasize the idea of wanting a healthy child.

Parents' responses indicated that when they expressed a desire for a healthy child, part of their wish did, in fact, translate into the literal physical health of the child. For instance, Paula, a mother of two adopted children, described taking the information provided by the adoption agency to the pediatrician to interpret the child's health. She noted,

> *Part of the issue was we certainly wanted and wished [for] a child who was in good health, and what do we know, we were sent these things that were both vague or unfamiliar to us, birth weights and heights and we had no sense of how to see if that meant anything, so I think one thing we did do was go to our pediatrician with the information we had. . . .*

Her response was typical of other adoptive parents' remarks as others noted seeking advice from a physician to evaluate the health status of the child.

Thus, parents' descriptions of their search for healthy children were remarkably similar. In general, they began their search for healthy children by exploring domestic adoptions. One mother, Erin, offered,

> *We looked at domestic . . . and we thought we'd talked with just about everybody in town and we were really discouraged because [my husband] was already thirty-nine and I was thirty-six and we thought [pause] you know if we have to wait ten years, that's too, we're too old. So we were really discouraged about it.*

Notably, although parents talked about pursuing "domestic adoption," they generally pursued only one specific type of domestic adoption. For most parents, "domestic" adoptions were understood and coded almost exclusively as the search for healthy, *white* infants. One clue to decoding parents' particular understanding of domestic adoption was the time frames they cited. More specifically, the waiting time this mother and others in my sample cited was, in fact, only reflective of the waiting time for healthy, white infants in the United States. Other children in the United States were more readily available and did not have an extensive waiting time. For instance, in my interview with Amy, she described her experience with domestic adoption, and at one point in the interview, I attempted to clarify who was included in her domestic adoption search by asking her if she and her husband had investigated children other than healthy, white infants. She responded, ". . . but as far as other nationalities here [in the United States], I don't think that even occurred to us, come to think of it." Amy's comments reinforced the idea that adoption was not about adopting any child and illustrated how some

children were not included in domestic adoption searches. Importantly, rather than address the issue in terms of race, Amy took up the question of nonwhite children in terms of nationalities. While it is possible that she might not have understood my question, my strong sense is that answering it using the term "nationalities" may have allowed her to verbally maneuver through contested terrain. Furthermore, Amy does not make a distinction between the health status of children from other "nationalities" (likely coded as racial-ethnic minorities) here in the United States. Instead, the undesirability of children from "other nationalities here" was not necessarily linked to their health status. Rather, their "nationality" appeared to trump their health status, as well as their age. "Nationality" was used by parents as a primary factor for sorting children as undesirable.

Amy's report of not having children from "other nationalities" in the United States on her list of potentially adoptable children was not an isolated response. Although Amy was unique in invoking a language of "nationality," the claim that it did not occur to her to consider nonwhite children was shared by half of the participants. That it did not even occur to 50 percent of the participants to consider adopting children of color was a powerful statement about how race privilege operated, since one way privilege works is to socially buffer those in privileged positions from having to be aware of or consider minorities. In addition, it illustrated strong support for the contention that even when faced with the desire to have "healthy" children (and with the knowledge that there are children more readily available for adoption in the United States), some children were not considered desirable as potential family members because of their race-ethnicity or their nationality.[6]

On many occasions, getting informants to be specific and direct about their view on racial preference was difficult because rather than specifically articulating or addressing race, parents used language that was racially coded. As Amy's comments demonstrated, for example, one way to talk about race without specifying it was to substitute "nationalities," or as discussed earlier, parents frequently used "healthy child" and "domestic adoptions" to signal the search for healthy, white infants. The language choices were likely due to convention as well as more conscious efforts to avoid the appearance of racism. Regardless, parents traded on common assumptions about who were perceived as desirable children for adoption and with what characteristics.

In fact, all but two parents—of the 73 parents in my sample—talked about domestic adoptions almost exclusively in terms of white children, as evidenced by the extensive wait times they cited. Thus, by not specifying and articulating whiteness and still finding an interpretive community that understood what was meant without being explicit about the racialized dimensions, whiteness was, in a very real sense, so normative as to be taken for granted. While some may discount this point, I think it was precisely the subtlety of the racial codes and the ability of whiteness to remain hidden and taken for granted that was so powerful. For example, in the following excerpt, Donna talked about the advice she received from an adoption

agency. Consider the way Donna and the adoption agency used the term "American." She said,

> *We had gone to [the adoption agency] for an American adoption. . . . But I hate to say this, but it was true, [the agency], they said, don't even try for them because they're hard to get. . . . The waiting list [was] as long as it would take for an American child.*

In this case, both the agency and parents had a common understanding of "American child." Her description regarding difficulties of getting an "American child" and her focus on the waiting list indicated that the agency and the parents understood the search for an "American child" as the search for a healthy, white infant.

In another example that illustrated the narrow way "American" was used, Linda stated,

> *Well, we were married for several years and um, unable to have children, and we finally decided that we would adopt. [Pause] So we started with um, like every other person, I guess, thinking about adopting an American baby. You know, so we started off with [the adoption agency], and um, . . . so we knew [this adoption agency] did adoption, so we went to a meeting, [pause] and um, to adopt an American baby, at that point it was like a 7-year wait, they just, I think, [were] not readily available. So we thought well, this is not going to do, because we were not terribly young at that point, um, [pause]. So we decided that we could go with a foreign adoption.*

This mother considered it normative to start with an American baby. Yet, similar to other parents, as revealed by the extensive waiting period (7 years), it was normative for this mother to investigate only certain American children (i.e., whites), since other American children (i.e., racial-ethnic minorities) were, in fact, more readily available and did not necessarily have the extensive waiting period.

In contrast to those who were vague or used coded racial language, some parents were quite clear in verbalizing their unwillingness to consider adopting a child who was African American. In sharing her recollection of the adoption process, Marlene brought up her distress about the possibility of not being able to adopt a child.

> K: *And so, . . . in pursuing avenues for adoption, how did you make that transition?*
>
> M: *Um, oh boy, all I remember is for me it was very traumatic because I was afraid that we wouldn't be able to [adopt]. Um. . . . If we wanted a Black or Hispanic, if we wanted a Black or Hispanic child, [we could adopt] which we did not, so we ruled that out.*

Marlene was fairly definitive about not wanting a Black or Hispanic child. She did not expand her explanation and specify that she would not accept a Black or Hispanic child who was not healthy. Instead, race (for Hispanics and Blacks) became a master status of children waiting to be adopted,

and they were, quite literally, sorted out of the adoption process by white parents.

In the following selection, Molly, a mother of one adopted boy and one genetically related daughter, clearly illustrated the desire for a healthy baby, but not a healthy African American baby. Her account highlighted the way some children were not able to shed the stigma associated with their racial status. She stated,

> *We wanted a healthy baby, we just wanted a healthy baby and um, . . . we had thought briefly about an African American baby . . . and I had some reservations about that also because I thought we would grow up right next to a culture that I don't always like very well. You know, and so that would be real strange if he felt like he had to act like, you know, one of the boys from the hood. That would be hard for us.*

Molly's statement was important because it offered clues about why race was a salient factor influencing the desirability of a child for some white parents. I read Molly's explanation for not wanting an African American baby as a comment on the way race (understood as socially created) was frequently used as a proxy for cultural practices. In this case, race had a specific meaning for Molly. "African American" was understood as a set of distinct (gendered) cultural practices, i.e., acting like a "boy from the hood." Thus, it was not simply resistance to adopting an "African American" child as such, but resistance to adopting what "African American" was presumed to mean and signify culturally. From Molly's perspective, African American cultural practices were oppositional to and incompatible with white cultural practices as indicated by her statement "That would be hard for us." Some parents, like Molly, seemed to believe that racial culture was so powerful that their child would participate in it, regardless of how the family might socialize the child. Thus, the connection between race and presumed cultural practices was so strong that for some parents, it did not appear to make a difference whether the African American child was adopted as an *"infant."* Parents' comments indicated that socialization could not erase the propensity for oppositional racial and cultural practices.

There are different ways to think about and situate her comments. On the one hand, it is possible that the resistance to adopting African American children (including healthy infants) was because Molly and other parents who shared similar perspectives, were aware of and sensitive to larger structures of racism. For instance, although she did not cite the NABSW's (National Association of Black Social Workers') position on transracial adoption (read: as whites adopting Black children), she might have been aware of their statement. It is also possible that she (and others) anticipated ways that race would influence her child's behavior. That is, in the face of oppression and a society structured by and through racism, the family is only one agent of socialization and perhaps they felt truly unprepared and unequipped to deal with it.

Yet her statements also revealed a personal ambivalence—for Molly, adopting an African American meant engaging and confronting a culture

that she "didn't always like very well." Her feelings concerning African Americans were focused on particular aspects of African American culture and reflected common stereotypes of "hood culture." Molly and other prospective parents relied on negative racial stereotypes (and therefore, incomplete and inaccurate information) throughout the decision-making process. From this framework, her sentiments were likely magnified when she considered that this child (read: bad boy from the hood) would be in the intimate and daily setting of her family.

In contrast to Molly and Marlene, who illustrated how race activated a wholesale rejection of some African American children, another respondent, Rachel, noted that an African American baby was not desirable unless the option was no baby. The following is an excerpt from the beginning of our conversation.

> K: *Did you know where you wanted to adopt from?*
>
> R: *Well, we probably didn't, you know, think that far ahead, you know, we were, um* [pause] *the way you mean it started for Korean?*
>
> K: *Yes.*
>
> R: *Well, okay, plain and simple in my mind, um* [pause] *if you waited for, . . . so, hey, you know, so I think anything, we probably didn't want to go* [pause] *I,* [pause] *I don't, I shouldn't say didn't, we wanted a baby, I was going to say didn't want an African American, but you know, we didn't really, we didn't really have to, ah, I mean versus no baby, I mean, I know we would have, but I'm just saying, because my son's godfather is African American, so we don't have anything against it, but, we're just saying, I'm white. . . .*

Both the format and content of Rachel's comments are instructive for a number of reasons. First, her explanation of how she came to adopt from Korea focused on her standpoint on adopting African American children. Rachel's feelings about adopting African American children were strong enough that, even without direct probing (and even though we had just met and started the interview), she still shared information that is commonly considered taboo. In addition, her comments illustrated the ways hierarchies of racial desirability were constructed as well as how unstable these notions of desirability were. More specifically, the possibility of *not* having a child was able to transform Rachel's opinion about race. Although Rachel initially had reservations about adopting an African American child, an African American child would be desirable if it was the only way to have a family with children. As she described her feelings, Rachel indicated that they may not be popular or acceptable to say. I read her pauses and self interruptions (i.e., "um") as underscoring the difficulties of being honest about and articulating such sentiments, and thus raised larger issues about what the available and acceptable ways to talk about these feelings were. For instance, offering statements like "we don't have anything against it" is a common rhetorical strategy used in deflecting perceptions of racist attitudes. Noting that the godfather of one of their children is African American also may be perceived as a way to socially buffer against accusations of being a racist.

These strategies perhaps serve as a method of contemporary racial etiquette (Collins 1998; Park 1950) thus making it seem more acceptable to have these feelings, or at least make it feel safer to express these feelings.

One of the two families who talked about being open to the possibility of adopting an African American child reported that it would present problems with their extended family. One mother, Becca, recalled phoning her mother after they received news that she and her husband were matched with a child and shared her experience of telling her mother. She stated,

> So [my husband and I] decided to tell our parents, so we called up all excited that we were gonna be adopting, and [my mother] said after a dead silence, "Is the baby Black?" Interesting reaction. [Pause] And we said, "No," and [my mother] said, "That's fine."

In this mother's adoption experience, the issue of race dominated the interaction with her biological family. For the soon-to-be grandmother, race was framed as a binary: Black and not Black. Knowing the child was not Black appeared to be sufficient for accepting the child.

International: Why Korea?

> It was quick, it was easy, and they were Oriental, I mean that seemed like a nice thing. . . .

In deciding that "domestic" adoptions were not a viable option (because of the lengthy waiting period for healthy, white infants coupled with resistance to adopting African American children (whether or not they were healthy infants) or other special needs children, parents shifted their attention to intercountry adoptions. Historically, Korea has been an important sending country of children for adoption, and during the 1980s, it was by far the largest sending country. Yet, Korea has never been the sole country available to parents. Given the choices for intercountry adoption, why were children from Korea perceived and sorted as desirable?

A range of pragmatic factors influenced parental decisions to adopt from Korea. Since each sending country, as well as each adoption agency, constructed (un)desirable parents differently, participants said that Korea was an attractive country to adopt from because they met the eligibility requirements and were considered desirable parents. In addition, Korea met many of the other factors parents felt were important. Adopting a healthy infant was possible in a short period of time, it was generally convenient (e.g., parents were not required to travel to Korea), and parents felt that when adopting from Korea they were working with a well-established program.

Moreover, while all of these aspects were relevant to parents, as the quotation that opens this section states, unlike sentiments parents expressed about Black children, the racial status of a child from Korea was seen as a "nice thing." While some parents initially indicated ambivalence or trepidation about adopting a child from Korea, each of the parents came to view

children from Korea as desirable. One way of explaining this change is that some contemporary stereotypes of Asians make Asian children seem more compatible with white, middle-class culture. For example, stereotypes of Asians as the model minority (Kibria 2002; Min 1995) or as "Honorary Whites" (Bonilla-Silva 2004; Tuan 1998) likely promote Asians, especially Asian females, as less oppositional and more compatible to whites than other racial-ethnic minorities.

In fact, most parents expressed fairly positive attitudes about the racial status and characteristics of children adopted from Korea. Kara, for example, did not recall investigating countries other than Korea. She shared,

> . . . *we never really looked at others, no, um, there, you know, there was something about the Asian culture, I don't know what it is, you know. I hate to sound hoaky but um, there's something that, I don't know.* [Pause] *I remember one time* [my husband] *and I went out to dinner and we saw this family, mother, father and ah, a little Korean girl, she was only about 10 and we were just watching, and we just like couldn't take our eyes off her, you know? And we didn't want to stare but, you know, it's just, it just gave us a good feeling.*

Thus, Kara felt positively about Asian culture, and seeing another Korean child before she adopted gave her a good feeling about Korean features.

Molly also expressed enthusiasm regarding the physical characteristics of children adopted from Korea. After describing a meeting with a social worker who worked with Korean adoptions, Molly emphatically stated,

> *So you know,* [my husband and I said], *"Oh, the babies are beautiful!" We saw the babies and they had pictures of all these little toddlers, and they were so pretty.*

Amy echoed Molly's positive sentiments. At one point in our conversation, I asked her to expand on the process of adopting from Korea.

> K: *So how did you come up with Korea?*
>
> A: *Well, you know, that's a good question. My husband, I think* [pause] *thought of that idea because he thinks Asian people are beautiful, and they are beautiful . . . so he, I think he came up with that. He was kind of drawn to that.*

In Amy's and Molly's opinions, Asian babies were physically attractive, and thus, one nice thing about adopting children from Korea was the appeal of their physical characteristics.

In contrast to the examples above, Lois, a mother of an adopted son and daughter (both from Korea) noted that it was not necessarily anything about the racial status of Asians in particular that she was attracted to. Unlike Amy and Molly, Lois did not focus on the beauty of Asian babies. Rather, for her, there came a point where having a baby that physically resembled them in terms of race became secondary. She stated,

> [We] *had contacted our attorney, actually, um,* [pause] *who had done a lot of adoptions and asked him, you know, what avenue, which avenues he thought would be best. And he sort of* [pause] *told us about a few different things, because at this point we also were looking at a time frame where we didn't want*

to wait another 7 years, [pause] it wasn't important to us, to, to have [pause] um, [pause] a, you know, [pause] Caucasian baby that looks similar to us, or, or whatever, so [pause] so I contacted all these different agencies and asked them to send some information.

Lois' comments were instructive because they suggested that whiteness was pivotal to her decision-making process. Similar to other respondents, it was only in the face of a substantial wait time for healthy, white infants that the idea of having a baby that looks similar (i.e., racial matching) became less important for her.

While Lois' description indicated that it was "not important" to have a Caucasian baby, her description of the adoption process still points to an important tension. As previously discussed, there were children available in the United States who did not have an extended waiting period (i.e., Black and Latino infants). Yet, Black children and infants of color who were more readily available would not look like them, especially in terms of racial matching. Although I do not have specific evidence from this mother, one interpretation might be that even though it was not important to have a baby that looked similar, it was important that the child not look *too different*. More specifically, while Asian children might not provide an exact match, Asians might signal an acceptable amount of racial-ethnic difference. Additionally, the racial-ethnic differences may be perceived as compatible (and perhaps complementary to) whiteness, especially within a framework of viewing Asians as "Honorary Whites." For instance, in an ironic twist, at different moments, some parents noted that they thought their adoptive kids looked like them. For example, Shelby described telling others about the physical features she felt were similar between her and her son. She stated, *"What we used to say to people when [my son came], and we still do, 'I think he has my straight hair and his father's brown eyes.' So we tell him he looks like us too."* These cases may suggest that it is not just the racial status of Asians that is considered a "nice thing," but that parents needed to feel like they could make connections with their children about how similar they look. For instance, Holly pointed out that her daughters initiated comments about the physical similarities. She recalled her daughters saying, *"Mommy, aren't we starting to look more like you?"* Another mother, Ellen, commenting on her age and the fact that she was starting to color her hair and consequently every month it was a different color, noted how much she liked her daughter's hair. She stated, *"I have always strived to have the same color as [my daughter]. I want to have the same color hair as her."* While talking about physical similarities between parents and children is not exclusive to families who adopt, such conversations do take on particular significance in adoption, especially in the context of race and racial dynamics. In light of racism, white parents adopting children from Korea might be understood as a way of avoiding direct engagement with racial dynamics that feel oppositional and, instead, engaging with parts that feel more comfortable. As illustrated by this mother's comments, in some cases, it may be more than merely comfort—it could be envy and admiration for certain characteristics like her daughter's hair.[7]

Discussion

This reading explored the ways adoptive parents used various characteristics to sort children as desirable or undesirable. While parents generally began their explanations by framing their responses such that having a healthy child was paramount, health was not necessarily the most important characteristic that shaped decisions about who parents would adopt. Instead, other factors, most notably, race, appeared to be significant, although at times it remained "unmarked" or racially coded. For Asians, specifically those from Korea, racial stereotypes appeared to act as a resource, which allowed them to be sorted as desirable potential family members in transracial adoptions. Conversely, for African Americans, race became their master status and, as signaled by the title of this piece, they were quite literally sorted out of the adoption process. As such, my data on adoption indicate support for Bonilla-Silva's (2004) contention that a system of tri-racialization is at work in the United States.

Studying adoption in general, and transracial, intercountry adoptions in particular, is sociologically relevant for a number of reasons. For one, written within constructions of racial desirability are constructions of undesirability. As such, racial-ethnic hierarchies (and at times binaries) are produced in which the desirable and the preferable child is understood and constructed in direct relation to the undesirable child (i.e., knowing who and what is desirable offers clues about what is undesirable and vice versa).

Additionally, interpretations and constructions of racial and gender desirability are, in large part, contingent upon and reflective of the preferences of the adopters. While parents' preferences for certain children might be framed as matters of individual choice and personal taste, focusing on their choices as merely individual preferences or private decisions, leaves issues of larger social structures, such as racism and white privilege, unchallenged.[8] It is critical to realize that individual choices and preferences are inextricably linked and indeed embedded in broader social, cultural, and historical contexts—families and adoption do not occur outside of or independent from other sociohistorical forces. Thus, in terms of racial-ethnic preferences, parental decisions and inclinations for whites and Asians, and an avoidance of adopting Blacks and Latinos, can (and should) be understood within larger sociohistorical contexts and processes. In short, the issues, questions, and struggles adoptive parents described are significant not only because of the constructions of desirability themselves (i.e., which children are perceived as adoptable and which children are actually (not) adopted) but given historical and current social inequalities, these issues also contribute to our understanding of the ways privilege, especially parents' racial privilege, operates and, at certain moments, perpetuates social inequalities.

Finally, while one way of interpreting parents' accounts and standpoints is to view parents who would not adopt (or who showed hesitancy toward adopting) Black and Latino children as racist, those who were willing to adopt children of color as not racist, such a binary is weak and much too simplistic. Indeed, it is more complicated and complex than this statement.

Certainly, those who (more openly) expressed hostility and ambivalence toward adopting Black children reflected and perpetuated racist ideologies. But those who were willing to adopt nonwhites also operated and were embedded in sociohistorical forces that were deeply implicated in racist ideologies and practices. Thus, openness to adopting a racial-ethnic minority, and a Black child in particular, does not mean adoptive parents have not absorbed and subscribed to other pieces of racism in the culture.

ENDNOTES

[1] The one exception to this was a father who identified himself as second-generation Chinese.

[2] I highlight the "formal legal" aspect of this process in an effort to address common assumptions and misperceptions that African Americans do not adopt or do not want to adopt. It is important to note that alternatives to the formal legal channels have been established and utilized by African Americans but have not been recognized as legitimate adoptions by the legal system. Often labeled "kinship adoptions" (Hill 1977; Stack 1974), these have been an important and integral part of African American family life, especially in light of persistent structural challenges (such as poverty) and oppression. In addition, current scholarship indicates that African Americans are just as likely to adopt as whites. One way to interpret the lack of parity in adoptions, then, is to revisit Joyce Ladner's (1977) assertion: "The fact that adoption agencies do not carry out a brisk business in placing children in black homes should not be used as documentation for the myth that blacks do not adopt. It is probably more reasonable to examine the effectiveness of agencies in locating and recruiting black adoptive parents" (p. 68). Part of a larger research project could indeed expand on this idea.

[3] Racial matching also allowed parents a degree of freedom in "hiding" the adoption from their child. In fact, until recently, concealing adoptions from children was not uncommon and was even advocated by some parents and professionals. For further discussion of secrecy and disclosure issues, see Baran, Reuben, and Sorosky 1997; Carp 1998; and Grotevant and McRoy 1997.

[4] In some cases, adoptive parents were required to choose or reject the actual children.

[5] The attention to the ways parents who adopt make "choices" often obscures and/or ignores the range of choices that parents who have genetically-related children make as well, e.g., who their partners or spouses are (their race-ethnicity, body type, etc.).

[6] Moreover, this highlights an important tension, since Amy's family, as well as that of others in this study, included children adopted from Korea. Her description revealed a common pattern—attention to other nationalities was directed toward Korea, not "other nationalities here," in the United States.

[7] Significantly, given cultural scripts, it is difficult to imagine substituting African American in this situation.

[8] As I write this conclusion, there is a small movement trying to bring awareness to the disparity in adoption fees for babies of different races. One U.S. ad campaign has a picture of three infants, one white, one Black, and one who is a racial-ethnic minority with skin coloring in between the white and Black infants. Across each of the infants is their "value"—the white child has $35,000, the Black child has $4,000, and the child with the skin coloring in between the white and Black infants says $10,000.

WORKS CITED

Baran, Annette, P. Reuben, and A. Sorosky. 1997. "Open Adoption." *Social Work* 21 (2): 97–100.

Bonilla-Silva, Eduardo. 2004. "From Bi-Racial to Tri-Racial: Towards a New System of Racial Stratification in the USA." *Ethnic and Racial Studies* 27 (6): 931–50.

Carp, Wayne E., ed. 1998. *Family Matters: Secrecy and Disclosure in the History of Adoption.* Cambridge: Harvard University Press.

———, ed. 2002. *Adoption in America: Historical Perspectives.* Ann Arbor: University of Michigan Press.

Collins, Patricia Hill. 1998. *Fighting Words: Black Women and the Search for Justice.* Minneapolis: University of Minnesota Press.

Grotevant, Harold and R. McRoy. 1997. "The Minnesota/Texas Adoption Research Project: Implications of Openness in Adoption for Development and Relationship." *Applied Developmental Science* 1 (4): 168–87.

Hill, Robert. 1977. *Informal Adoption among Black Families*. Washington, DC: National Urban League Research Department.

Kibria, Nazli. 2002. *Becoming Asian American: Second-Generation Chinese and Korean American Identities*. Baltimore: Johns Hopkins University Press.

Ladner, Joyce. 1977. *Mixed Families: Adopting across Racial Boundaries*. New York: Anchor Press/Doubleday.

Luker, Kristin. 1996. *Dubious Conceptions: The Politics of Teenage Pregnancy*. Cambridge, MA: Harvard University Press.

May, Elaine Tyler. 1995. *Barren in the Promised Land: Childless Americans and the Pursuit of Happiness*. Boston: Harvard University Press.

Melosh, Barbara. 2002. *Strangers and Kin: The American Way of Adoption*. Cambridge, MA: Harvard University Press.

Min, Pyong Gap. 1995. "Major Issues Relating to Asian American Experiences." In *Asian Americans: Contemporary Trends and Issues*, 1st ed., edited by Pyong Gap Min. Thousand Oaks: Sage.

Park, Robert. 1950. *Race and Culture*. Glencoe: Free Press.

Roberts, Dorothy. 1997. *Killing the Black Body: Race, Reproduction and the Meaning of Liberty*. New York: Pantheon.

Solinger, Rickie. 1992. "Race and 'Value': Black and White Illegitimate Babies, in the U.S., 1945–1965." In *Unequal Sisters: A Multicultural Reader in U.S. Women's History*, edited by Vicki L. Ruiz and Ellen Carol Dubois. New York: Routledge.

———. 1992. *Wake Up Little Susie: Single Pregnancy and Race before Roe v. Wade*. New York: Routledge.

Stack, Carol. 1974. *All Our Kin*. New York: Basic Books.

Tuan, Mia. 1998. *Forever Foreigners or Honorary Whites? The Asian Ethnic Experience Today*. New Brunswick, NJ: Rutgers University Press.

30

(HOW) DOES THE SEXUAL ORIENTATION OF PARENTS MATTER?

JUDITH STACEY • TIMOTHY J. BIBLARZ

"Today, gay marriage is taking on an air of inevitability" (*Detroit News*, "Middle Ground Emerges for Gay Couples," October 4, 1999, p. A9). So observed a U.S. newspaper from the heartland in September 1999, reporting that one-third of those surveyed in an *NBC News/Wall Street Journal* poll endorsed the legalization of same-sex marriage, while 65 percent predicted such legislation would take place in the new century

Judith Stacey and Timothy J. Biblarz, "(How) Does the Sexual Orientation of Parents Matter?" from *American Sociological Review* 66 (April 2001): 159–183. Copyright © 2001 by the American Sociological Association. Reprinted with the permission of the authors and the American Sociological Association.

(Price 1999). During the waning months of the last millennium, France enacted national registered partnerships, Denmark extended child custody rights to same-sex couples, and the state supreme courts in Vermont and in Ontario, Canada, ruled that same-sex couples were entitled to full and equal family rights. Most dramatically, in September 2000 the Netherlands became the first nation to realize the inevitable when the Dutch parliament voted overwhelmingly to grant same-sex couples full and equal rights to marriage. As the new millennium begins, struggles by nonheterosexuals to secure equal recognition and rights for the new family relationships they are now creating represent some of the most dramatic and fiercely contested developments in Western family patterns.

It is not surprising, therefore, that social science research on lesbigay family issues has become a rapid growth industry that incites passionate divisions. For the consequences of such research are by no means "academic," but bear on marriage and family policies that encode Western culture's most profoundly held convictions about gender, sexuality, and parenthood. As advocates and opponents square off in state and federal courts and legislatures, in the electoral arena, and in culture wars over efforts to extend to nonheterosexuals equal rights to marriage, child custody, adoption, foster care, and fertility services, they heatedly debate the implications of a youthful body of research, conducted primarily by psychologists, that investigates if and how the sexual orientation of parents affects children.

This body of research, almost uniformly, reports findings of no notable differences between children reared by heterosexual parents and those reared by lesbian and gay parents, and that it finds lesbigay parents to be as competent and effective as heterosexual parents. Lawyers and activists struggling to defend child custody and adoption petitions by lesbians and gay men, or to attain same-gender marriage rights and to defeat preemptive referenda against such rights (e.g., the victorious Knight Initiative on the 2000 ballot in California), have drawn on this research with considerable success (cf. Wald 1999). Although progress is uneven, this strategy has promoted a gradual liberalizing trend in judicial and policy decisions. However, backlash campaigns against gay family rights have begun to challenge the validity of the research.

In 1997, the *University of Illinois Law Review Journal* published an article by Wardle (1997), a Brigham Young University law professor, that impugned the motives, methods, and merits of social science research on lesbian and gay parenting. Wardle charged the legal profession and social scientists with an ideological bias favoring gay rights that has compromised most research in this field and the liberal judicial and policy decisions it has informed. He presented a harshly critical assessment of the research and argued for a presumptive judicial standard in favor of awarding child custody to heterosexual married couples. The following year, Wardle drafted new state regulations in Utah that restrict adoption and foster care placements to households in which all adults are related by blood or marriage. Florida, Arkansas, and Mississippi also have imposed restrictions on adoption and/or foster care, and such bills have been introduced in the legislatures of 10 additional states

(Leslie Cooper, ACLU gay family rights staff attorney, personal communication, September 27, 2000). In March 2000, a paper presented at a "Revitalizing Marriage" conference at Brigham Young University assailed the quality of studies that had been cited to support the efficacy of lesbigay parenting (Lerner and Nagai 2000). Characterizing the research methods as "dismal," Lerner and Nagai claimed that "the methods used in these studies were sufficiently flawed so that these studies could not and should not be used in legislative forums or legal cases to buttress any arguments on the nature of homosexual vs. heterosexual parenting" (p. 3). Shortly afterward, Gallagher (2000), of the Institute for American Values, broadcast Lerner and Nagai's argument in her nationally syndicated *New York Post* column in order to undermine the use of "the science card" by advocates of gay marriage and gay "normalization."

We depart sharply from the views of Wardle and Gallagher on the merits and morals of lesbigay parenthood as well as on their analysis of the child development research. We agree, however, that ideological pressures constrain intellectual development in this field. In our view, it is the pervasiveness of social prejudice and institutionalized discrimination against lesbians and gay men that exerts a powerful policing effect on the basic terms of psychological research and public discourse on the significance of parental sexual orientation. The field suffers less from the overt ideological convictions of scholars than from the unfortunate intellectual consequences that follow from the implicit hetero-normative presumption governing the terms of the discourse—that healthy child development depends upon parenting by a married heterosexual couple. While few contributors to this literature personally subscribe to this view, most of the research asks whether lesbigay parents subject their children to greater risks or harm than are confronted by children reared by heterosexual parents. Because anti-gay scholars seek evidence of harm, sympathetic researchers defensively stress its absence.

We take stock of this body of psychological research from a sociological perspective. We analyze the impact that this hetero-normative presumption exacts on predominant research strategies, analyses, and representations of findings. After assessing the basic premises and arguments in the debate, we discuss how the social fact of heterosexism has operated to constrain the research populations, concepts, and designs employed in the studies to date.

We wish to acknowledge that the political stakes of this body of research are so high that the ideological "family values" of scholars play a greater part than usual in how they design, conduct, and interpret their studies. Of course, we recognize that this is equally true for those who criticize such studies (including Wardle [1997], Lerner and Nagai [2000], and ourselves). The inescapably ideological and emotional nature of this subject makes it incumbent on scholars to acknowledge the personal convictions they bring to the discussion. Because we personally oppose discrimination on the basis of sexual orientation or gender, we subject research claims by those sympathetic to our stance to a heightened degree of critical scrutiny and afford the fullest possible consideration to work by scholars opposed to parenting by lesbians and gay men.

The Case against Lesbian and Gay Parenthood

Wardle (1997) is correct that contemporary scholarship on the effects of parental sexual orientation on children's development is rarely critical of lesbigay parenthood. Few respectable scholars today oppose such parenting. However, a few psychologists subscribe to the view that homosexuality represents either a sin or a mental illness and continue to publish alarmist works on the putative ill effects of gay parenting (e.g., Cameron and Cameron 1996; Cameron, Cameron, and Landess 1996). Even though the American Psychological Association expelled Paul Cameron, and the American Sociological Association denounced him for willfully misrepresenting research (Cantor 1994; Herek 1998, 2000), his publications continue to be cited in amicus briefs, court decisions, and policy hearings. For example, the chair of the Arkansas Child Welfare Agency Review Board repeatedly cited publications by Cameron's group in her testimony at policy hearings, which, incidentally, led to restricting foster child placements to heterosexual parents (Woodruff 1998).

Likewise, Wardle (1997) draws explicitly on Cameron's work to build his case against gay parent rights. Research demonstrates, Wardle maintains, that gay parents subject children to disproportionate risks; that children of gay parents are more apt to suffer confusion over their gender and sexual identities and are more likely to become homosexuals themselves; that homosexual parents are more sexually promiscuous than are heterosexual parents and are more likely to molest their own children; that children are at greater risk of losing a homosexual parent to AIDS, substance abuse, or suicide, and to suffer greater risks of depression and other emotional difficulties; that homosexual couples are more unstable and likely to separate; and that the social stigma and embarrassment of having a homosexual parent unfairly ostracizes children and hinders their relationships with peers. Judges have cited Wardle's article to justify transferring child custody from lesbian to heterosexual parents.[1]

Wardle (1997), like other opponents of homosexual parenthood, also relies on a controversial literature that decries the putative risks of "fatherlessness" in general. Thus, Wardle cites books by Popenoe (1993, 1996), Blankenhorn (1995), and Whitehead (1993) when he argues:

> [C]hildren generally develop best, and develop most completely, when raised by both a mother and a father and experience regular family interaction with both genders' parenting skills during their years of childhood. It is now undeniable that, just as a mother's influence is crucial to the secure, healthy, and full development of a child, [a] paternal presence in the life of a child is essential to the child emotionally and physically. (P. 860)

Wardle, like Blankenhorn, extrapolates (inappropriately) from research on single-mother families to portray children of lesbians as more vulnerable to everything from delinquency, substance abuse, violence, and crime, to teen pregnancy, school dropout, suicide, and even poverty.[2] In short, the few

scholars who are opposed to parenting by lesbians and gay men provide academic support for the convictions of many judges, journalists, politicians, and citizens that the sexual orientation of parents matters greatly to children, and that lesbigay parents represent a danger to their children and to society. Generally, these scholars offer only limited, and often implicit, theoretical explanations for the disadvantages of same-sex parenting—typically combining elements of bio-evolutionary theory with social and cognitive learning theories (e.g., Blankenhorn 1995). Cameron et al. (1996) crudely propose that homosexuality is a "learned pathology" that parents pass on to children through processes of modeling, seduction, and "contagion." The deeply rooted hetero-normative convictions about what constitutes healthy and moral gender identity, sexual orientation, and family composition held by contributors to this literature hinders their ability to conduct or interpret research with reason, nuance, or care.

The Case for Lesbian and Gay Parenthood

Perhaps the most consequential impact that heterosexism exerts on the research on lesbigay parenting lies where it is least apparent—in the far more responsible literature that is largely sympathetic to its subject. It is easy to expose the ways in which the prejudicial views of those directly hostile to lesbigay parenting distort their research (Herek 1998). Moreover, because anti-gay scholars regard homosexuality itself as a form of pathology, they tautologically interpret any evidence that children may be more likely to engage in homoerotic behavior as evidence of harm. Less obvious, however, are the ways in which heterosexism also hampers research and analysis among those who explicitly support lesbigay parenthood. With rare exceptions, even the most sympathetic proceed from a highly defensive posture that accepts heterosexual parenting as the gold standard and investigates whether lesbigay parents and their children are inferior.

This sort of hierarchical model implies that *differences* indicate *deficits* (Baumrind 1995). Instead of investigating whether (and how) differences in adult sexual orientation might lead to meaningful differences in how individuals parent and how their children develop, the predominant research designs place the burden of proof on lesbigay parents to demonstrate that they are not less successful or less worthy than heterosexual parents. Too often scholars seem to presume that this approach precludes acknowledging almost any differences in parenting or in child outcomes. A characteristic review of research on lesbian-mother families concludes:

> [A] rapidly growing and highly consistent body of empirical work has failed to identify significant differences between lesbian mothers and their heterosexual counterparts or the children raised by these groups. Researchers have been unable to establish empirically that detriment results to children from being raised by lesbian mothers. (Falk 1994:151)

Given the weighty political implications of this body of research, it is easy to understand the social sources of such a defensive stance. As long as sexual orientation can deprive a gay parent of child custody, fertility services, and adoption rights, sensitive scholars are apt to tread gingerly around the terrain of differences. Unfortunately, however, this reticence compromises the development of knowledge not only in child development and psychology, but also within the sociology of sexuality, gender, and family more broadly. For if homophobic theories seem crude, too many psychologists who are sympathetic to lesbigay parenting seem hesitant to theorize at all. When researchers downplay the significance of any findings of differences, they forfeit a unique opportunity to take full advantage of the "natural laboratory" that the advent of lesbigay-parent families provides for exploring the effects and acquisition of gender and sexual identity, ideology, and behavior.

This reticence is most evident in analyses of sexual behavior and identity—the most politically sensitive issue in the debate. Virtually all of the published research claims to find no differences in the sexuality of children reared by lesbigay parents and those raised by nongay parents—but none of the studies that report this finding attempts to theorize about such an implausible outcome. Yet it is difficult to conceive of a credible theory of sexual development that would not expect the adult children of lesbigay parents to display a somewhat higher incidence of homoerotic desire, behavior, and identity than children of heterosexual parents. For example, biological determinist theory should predict at least some difference in an inherited predisposition to same-sex desire; a social constructionist theory would expect lesbigay parents to provide an environment in which children would feel freer to explore and affirm such desires; psychoanalytic theory might hypothesize that the absence of a male parent would weaken a daughter's need to relinquish her pre-oedipal desire for her mother or that the absence of a female parent would foster a son's pre-oedipal love for his father that no fear of castration or oedipal crisis would interrupt. Moreover, because parents determine where their children reside, even one who subscribed to J. Harris' (1998) maverick theory—that parents are virtually powerless when compared with peers to influence their children's development—should anticipate that lesbigay parents would probably rear their children among less homophobic peers.

Bem's (1996) "exotic becomes erotic" theory of sexual orientation argues that in a gender-polarized society, children eroticize the gender of peers whose interests and temperaments differ most from their own. Most children thereby become heterosexual, but boys attracted to "feminine" activities and girls who are "tomboys" are apt to develop homoerotic desires. The impact of parental genes and child-rearing practices remains implicit because parents contribute genetically to the temperamental factors Bem identifies as precursors to a child's native activity preferences, and parental attitudes toward gender polarization should affect the way those innate preferences translate into children's cognition and play. In fact, the only "theory" of child

development we can imagine in which a child's sexual development would bear no relationship to parental genes, practices, environment, or beliefs would be an arbitrary one.[3] Yet this is precisely the outcome that most scholars report, although the limited empirical record does not justify it.

Over the past decade, prominent psychologists in the field began to call for less defensive research on lesbian and gay family issues (G. Green and Bozett 1991; Kitzinger and Coyle 1995; Patterson 1992). Rethinking the "no differences" doctrine, some scholars urge social scientists to look for potentially beneficial effects children might derive from such distinctive aspects of lesbigay parenting as the more egalitarian relationships these parents appear to practice (Patterson 1995; also see Dunne 2000). More radically, a few scholars (Kitzinger 1987, 1989; Kitzinger and Coyle 1995) propose abandoning comparative research on lesbian and heterosexual parenting altogether and supplanting it with research that asks "why and how are lesbian parents oppressed and how can we change that?" (Clarke 2000:28, paraphrasing Kitzinger 1994:501). While we perceive potential advantages from these agendas, we advocate an alternative strategy that moves beyond heteronormativity without forfeiting the fruitful potential of comparative research. Although we agree with Kitzinger and Coyle (1995) and Clarke (2000) that the social obstacles to lesbian (and gay) parenthood deserve rigorous attention, we believe that this should supplement, not supplant, the rich opportunity planned lesbigay parenthood provides for the exploration of the interactions of gender, sexual orientation, and biosocial family structures on parenting and child development. Moreover, while we welcome research attuned to potential strengths as well as vulnerabilities of lesbigay parenting, we believe that knowledge and policy will be best served when scholars feel free to replace a hierarchical model, which assigns "grades" to parents and children according to their sexual identities, with a more genuinely pluralist approach to family diversity. Sometimes, to bowdlerize Freud's famous dictum, a difference *really is* just a difference!

Problems with Concepts, Categories, and Samples

The social effects of heterosexism constrain the character of research conducted on lesbigay parenting in ways more profound than those deriving from the ideological stakes of researchers. First, as most researchers recognize, because so many individuals legitimately fear the social consequences of adopting a gay identity, and because few national surveys have included questions about sexual orientation, it is impossible to gather reliable data on such basic demographic questions as how many lesbians and gay men there are in the general population, how many have children, or how many children reside (or have substantial contact) with lesbian or gay parents. Curiously, those who are hostile to gay parenting tend to minimize the incidence of same-sex orientation, while sympathetic scholars typically report improbably high numerical estimates. Both camps thus implicitly presume that the rarer the incidence, the less legitimate would be lesbigay claims to

rights. One could imagine an alternative political logic, however, in which a low figure might undermine grounds for viewing lesbigay parenting as a meaningful social threat. Nonetheless, political anxieties have complicated the difficulty of answering basic demographic questions.

Since 1984, most researchers have statically reproduced numbers, of uncertain origin, depicting a range of from 1 to 5 million lesbian mothers, from 1 to 3 million gay fathers, and from 6 to 14 million children of gay or lesbian parents in the United States (e.g., Patterson 1992, 1996).[4] More recent estimates by Patterson and Freil (2000) extrapolate from distributions observed in the National Health and Social Life Survey (Laumann et al. 1995). Depending upon the definition of parental sexual orientation employed, Patterson and Freil suggest a current lower limit of 800,000 lesbigay parents ages 18 to 59 with 1.6 million children and an upper limit of 7 million lesbigay parents with 14 million children. However, these estimates include many "children" who are actually adults. To estimate the number who are dependent children (age 18 or younger), we multiplied the child-counts by .66, which is the proportion of dependent children among all offspring of 18- to 59-year-old parents in the representative National Survey of Families and Households (Sweet and Bumpass 1996).[5] This adjustment reduces the estimates of current dependent children with lesbigay parents to a range of 1 to 9 million, which implies that somewhere between 1 percent and 12 percent of all (78 million) children ages 19 and under in the United States (U.S. Census Bureau 1999) have a lesbigay parent. The 12 percent figure depends upon classifying as a lesbigay parent anyone who reports that even the idea of homoerotic sex is appealing, while the low (1 percent) figure derives from the narrower and, in our view, more politically salient, definition of a lesbigay parent as one who self-identifies as such (also see Badgett 1998; Black, Maker, et al. 1998).

Across the ideological spectrum, scholars, journalists, and activists appear to presume that the normalization of lesbigay sexuality should steadily increase the ranks of children with lesbian and gay parents. In contrast, we believe that normalization is more likely to reduce the proportion of such children. Most contemporary lesbian and gay parents procreated within heterosexual marriages that many had entered hoping to escape the social and emotional consequences of homophobia. As homosexuality becomes more legitimate, far fewer people with homoerotic desires should feel compelled to enter heterosexual marriages, and thus fewer should become parents in this manner.

On the other hand, with normalization, intentional parenting by self-identified lesbians and gay men should continue to increase, but it is unlikely to do so sufficiently to compensate for the decline in the current ranks of formerly married lesbian and gay parents. Thus, the proportion of lesbian parents may not change much. Many women with homoerotic desires who once might have married men and succumbed to social pressures to parent will no longer do so; others who remained single and childless because of their homoerotic desires will feel freer to choose lesbian maternity. It is difficult to predict the net effect of these contradictory trends. However, as fewer

closeted gay men participate in heterosexual marriages, the ranks of gay fathers should thin. Even if gay men were as eager as lesbians are to become parents, biology alone sharply constrains their ability to do so. Moreover, there is evidence that fewer men of any sexual orientation actually desire children as strongly as do comparable women (cf. Groze 1991; Shireman 1996), and most demographic studies of sexual orientation find a higher incidence of homosexuality among men than women (Kinsey, Pomeroy, and Martin 1948; Kinsey et al. 1953; Laumann et al. 1994; Michael et al. 1994). Thus, although the ranks of intentional paternity among gay men should increase, we do not believe this will compensate for the declining numbers of closeted gay men who will become fathers through heterosexual marriages. Hence the estimate of 1 to 12 percent of children with a lesbigay parent may represent a peak interval that may decline somewhat with normalization.

A second fundamental problem in sampling involves the ambiguity, fluidity, and complexity of definitions of sexual orientation. "The traditional type of surveys on the prevalence of 'homosexuality,'" remarks a prominent Danish sociologist, "are already in danger of becoming antiquated even before they are carried out; the questions asked are partially irrelevant; sexuality is not what it used to be" (Bech 1997:211). What defines a parent (or adult child) as lesbian, gay, bisexual, or heterosexual? Are these behavioral, social, emotional, or political categories? Historical scholarship has established that sexual identities are modern categories whose definitions vary greatly not only across cultures, spaces, and time, but even among and within individuals (Katz 1995; Seidman 1997). Some gay men, for example, practice celibacy; some heterosexual men engage in "situational" homosexual activity. Some lesbians relinquish lesbian identities to marry; some relinquish marriage for a lesbian identity. What about bisexual, transsexual, or transgendered parents, not to mention those who re-partner with individuals of the same or different genders? Sexual desires, acts, meanings, and identities are not expressed in fixed or predictable packages.

Third, visible lesbigay parenthood is such a recent phenomenon that most studies are necessarily of the children of a transitional generation of self-identified lesbians and gay men who became parents in the context of heterosexual marriages or relationships that dissolved before or after they assumed a gay identity. These unique historical conditions make it impossible to fully distinguish the impact of a parent's sexual orientation on a child from the impact of such factors as divorce, re-mating, the secrecy of the closet, the process of coming out, or the social consequences of stigma. Only a few studies have attempted to control for the number and gender of a child's parents before and after a parent decided to identify as lesbian or gay. Because many more formerly married lesbian mothers than gay fathers retain custody of their children, most research is actually on post-divorce lesbian motherhood. A few studies compare heterosexual and gay fathers after divorce (Bigner and Jacobsen 1989, 1992). If fewer self-identified lesbians and gay men will become parents through heterosexual marriages, the published research on this form of gay parenthood will become less relevant to issues in scholarly and public debates.

Fourth, because researchers lack reliable data on the number and location of lesbigay parents with children in the general population, there are no studies of child development based on random, representative samples of such families. Most studies rely on small-scale, snowball and convenience samples drawn primarily from personal and community networks or agencies. Most research to date has been conducted on white lesbian mothers who are comparatively educated, mature, and reside in relatively progressive urban centers, most often in California or the Northeastern states.[6]

Although scholars often acknowledge some of these difficulties (Bozett 1989; Patterson and Freil 2000; Rothblum 1994), few studies explicitly grapple with these definitional questions. Most studies simply rely on a parent's sexual self-identity at the time of the study, which contributes unwittingly to the racial, ethnic, and class imbalance of the populations studied. Ethnographic studies suggest that "lesbian," "gay," and "bisexual" identity among socially subordinate and nonurban populations is generally less visible or less affirmed than it is among more privileged white, educated, and urban populations (Boykin 1996; Cantu 2000; Carrier 1992; Greene and Boyd-Franklin 1996; Hawkeswood 1997; Lynch 1992; Peterson 1992).

Increasingly, uncloseted lesbians and gay men actively choose to become parents through diverse and innovative means (Benkov 1994). In addition to adoption and foster care, lesbians are choosing motherhood using known and unknown sperm donors (as single mothers, in intentional co-mother couples, and in complex variations of biosocial parenting). Both members of a lesbian couple may choose to become pregnant sequentially or simultaneously. Pioneering lesbian couples have exchanged ova to enable both women to claim biological, and thereby legal, maternal status to the same infant (Bourne 1999). It is much more difficult (and costly) for gay men to choose to become fathers, particularly fathers of infants. Some (who reside in states that permit this) become adoptive or foster parents; others serve as sperm donors in joint parenting arrangements with lesbian or other mothers. An affluent minority hire women as "surrogates" to bear children for them.

The means and contexts for planned parenthood are so diverse and complex that they compound the difficulties of isolating the significance of parental sexual orientation. To even approximate this goal, researchers would need to control not only for the gender, number, and sexual orientation of parents, but for their diverse biosocial and legal statuses. The handful of studies that have attempted to do this focus on lesbian motherhood. The most rigorous research designs compare donor-insemination (DI) parenthood among lesbian and heterosexual couples or single mothers (e.g., Chan, Brooks, et al. 1998; Flaks et al. 1995). To our knowledge, no studies have been conducted exclusively on lesbian or gay adoptive parents or compare the children of intentional gay fathers with children in other family forms. Researchers do not know the extent to which the comparatively high socioeconomic status of the DI parents studied accurately reflects the demographics of lesbian and gay parenthood generally, but given the degree of effort,

cultural and legal support, and, frequently, the expense involved, members of relatively privileged social groups would be the ones most able to make use of reproductive technology and/or independent adoption.

In short, the indirect effects of heterosexism have placed inordinate constraints on most research on the effects of gay parenthood. We believe, however, that the time may now be propitious to begin to reformulate the basic terms of the enterprise.

Reconsidering the Psychological Findings

Toward this end, we examined the findings of 21 psychological studies published between 1981 and 1998 that we considered best equipped to address sociological questions about how parental sexual orientation matters to children. One meta-analysis of 18 such studies (11 of which are included among our 21) characteristically concludes that "the results demonstrate no differences on any measures between the heterosexual and homosexual parents regarding parenting styles, emotional adjustment, and sexual orientation of the child(ren)" (Allen and Burrell 1996:19). To evaluate this claim, we selected for examination only studies that: (1) include a sample of gay or lesbian parents and children and a comparison group of heterosexual parents and children; (2) assess differences between groups in terms of statistical significance; and (3) include findings directly relevant to children's development. The studies we discuss compare relatively advantaged lesbian parents (18 studies) and gay male parents (3 studies) with a roughly matched sample of heterosexual parents. Echoing the conclusion of meta-analysts Allen and Burrell (1996), the authors of all 21 studies almost uniformly claim to find no differences in measures of parenting or child outcomes. In contrast, our careful scrutiny of the findings they report suggests that on some dimensions—particularly those related to gender and sexuality—the sexual orientations of these parents matter somewhat more for their children than the researchers claimed. . . .

Our discussion here emphasizes findings from six studies we consider to be best designed to isolate whatever unique effects parents' sexual orientations might have on children. Four of these—Flaks et al. (1995); Brewaeys et al. (1997); Chan, Raboy, and Patterson (1998); and Chan, Brooks, et al. (1998)—focus on planned parenting and compare children of lesbian mothers and heterosexual mothers who conceived through DI. This focus reduces the potential for variables like parental divorce, re-partnering, coming out, and so on to confound whatever effects of maternal sexual orientation may be observed. The other two studies—R. Green et al. (1986) and Tasker and Golombok (1997)—focus on children born within heterosexual marriages who experienced the divorce of their biological parents before being raised by a lesbian mother with or without a new partner or spouse. Although this research design heightens the risk that in statistical analyses the effect of maternal sexual orientation may include the effects of other factors, distinctive strengths of each study counterbalance this limitation.

R. Green et al. (1986) rigorously attempt to match lesbian mothers and heterosexual mothers on a variety of characteristics, and they compare the two groups of mothers as well as both groups of children on a wide variety of dimensions. Tasker and Golombok (1997) offer a unique long-term, longitudinal design. Their data collection began in 1976 on 27 heterosexual single mothers and 39 of their children (average age 10) and 27 lesbian mothers and 39 of their children (also average age 10) in England. Follow-up interviews with 46 of the original children were conducted 14 years later, allowing for a rare glimpse at how children with lesbian mothers and those with heterosexual mothers fared over their early life courses into young adulthood. . . .

No Differences of Social Concern

The findings summarized in our meta-analysis show that the "no differences" claim does receive strong empirical support in crucial domains. Lesbigay parents and their children in these studies display no differences from heterosexual counterparts in psychological well-being or cognitive functioning. Scores for lesbigay parenting styles and levels of investment in children are at least as "high" as those for heterosexual parents. Levels of closeness and quality of parent–child relationships do not seem to differentiate directly by parental sexual orientation, but indirectly, by way of parental gender. Because every relevant study to date shows that parental sexual orientation per se has no measurable effect on the quality of parent–child relationships or on children's mental health or social adjustment, there is no evidentiary basis for considering parental sexual orientation in decisions about children's "best interest." In fact, given that children with lesbigay parents probably contend with a degree of social stigma, these similarities in child outcomes suggest the presence of compensatory processes in lesbigay-parent families. Exploring how these families help children cope with stigma might prove helpful to all kinds of families.

Most of the research to date focuses on social-psychological dimensions of well-being and adjustment and on the quality of parent–child relationships. Perhaps these variables reflect the disciplinary preferences of psychologists who have conducted most of the studies, as well as a desire to produce evidence directly relevant to the questions of "harm" that dominate judicial and legislative deliberations over child custody. Less research has explored questions for which there are stronger theoretical grounds for expecting differences—children's gender and sexual behavior and preferences. In fact, only two studies (R. Green et al. 1986; Tasker and Golombok 1997) generate much of the baseline evidence on potential connections between parents' and child's sexual and gender identities. Evidence in these and the few other studies that focus on these variables does not support the "no differences" claim. Children with lesbigay parents appear less traditionally gender-typed and more likely to be open to homoerotic relationships. In addition, evidence suggests that parental gender and sexual identities interact to create distinctive family processes whose consequences for children have yet to be studied.

How the Sexual Orientation of Parents Matters

We have identified conceptual, methodological, and theoretical limitations in the psychological research on the effects of parental sexual orientation and have challenged the predominant claim that the sexual orientation of parents does not matter at all. We argued instead that despite the limitations, there is suggestive evidence and good reason to believe that contemporary children and young adults with lesbian or gay parents do differ in modest and interesting ways from children with heterosexual parents. Most of these differences, however, are not causal, but are indirect effects of parental gender or selection effects associated with heterosexist social conditions under which lesbigay-parent families currently live.

First, our analysis of the psychological research indicates that the effects of parental gender trump those of sexual orientation (Brewaeys et al. 1997; Chan, Brooks, et al. 1998; Chan, Raboy, and Patterson 1998; Flaks et al. 1995). A diverse array of gender theories (social learning theory, psychoanalytic theory, materialist, symbolic interactionist) would predict that children with two same-gender parents, and particularly with co-mother parents, should develop in less gender-stereotypical ways than would children with two heterosexual parents. There is reason to credit the perception of lesbian co-mothers in a qualitative study (Dunne 2000) that they "were redefining the meaning and content of motherhood, extending its boundaries to incorporate the activities that are usually dichotomized as mother and father" (p. 25). Children who derive their principal source of love, discipline, protection, and identification from women living independent of male domestic authority or influence should develop less stereotypical symbolic, emotional, practical, and behavioral gender repertoires. Indeed, it is the claim that the gender mix of parents has no effect on their children's gender behavior, interests, or development that cries out for sociological explanation. Only a crude theory of cultural indoctrination that posited the absolute impotence of parents might predict such an outcome, and the remarkable variability of gender configurations documented in the anthropological record readily undermines such a theory (Bonvillain 1998; Brettell and Sargent 1997; Ortner and Whitehead 1981). The burden of proof in the domain of gender and sexuality should rest with those who embrace the null hypothesis.

Second, because homosexuality is stigmatized, selection effects may yield correlations between parental sexual orientation and child development that do not derive from sexual orientation itself. For example, social constraints on access to marriage and parenting make lesbian parents likely to be older, urban, educated, and self-aware—factors that foster several positive developmental consequences for their children. On the other hand, denied access to marriage, lesbian co-parent relationships are likely to experience dissolution rates somewhat higher than those among heterosexual co-parents (Bell and Weinberg 1978; Weeks, Heaphy, and Donovan forthcoming, chap. 5). Not only do same-sex couples lack the institutional pressures and support for commitment that marriage provides, but qualitative studies suggest that they tend to embrace comparatively high standards of emotional intimacy

and satisfaction (Dunne 2000; Sullivan 1996; Weeks et al. 2001). The decision to pursue a socially ostracized domain of intimacy implies an investment in the emotional regime that Giddens (1992) terms "the pure relationship" and "confluent love." Such relationships confront the inherent instabilities of modern or postmodern intimacy, what Beck and Beck-Gersheim (1995) term "the normal chaos of love." Thus, a higher dissolution rate would be correlated with but not causally related to sexual orientation, a difference that should erode were homophobia to disappear and legal marriage be made available to lesbians and gay men.

Most of the differences in the findings discussed above cannot be considered deficits from any legitimate public policy perspective. They either favor the children with lesbigay parents, are secondary effects of social prejudice, or represent "just a difference" of the sort democratic societies should respect and protect. Apart from differences associated with parental gender, most of the presently observable differences in child "outcomes" should wither away under conditions of full equality and respect for sexual diversity. Indeed, it is time to recognize that the categories "lesbian mother" and "gay father" are historically transitional and conceptually flawed, because they erroneously imply that a parent's sexual orientation is the decisive characteristic of her or his parenting. On the contrary, we propose that homophobia and discrimination are the chief reasons why parental sexual orientation matters at all. Because lesbigay parents do not enjoy the same rights, respect, and recognition as heterosexual parents, their children contend with the burdens of vicarious social stigma. Likewise, some of the particular strengths and sensitivities such children appear to display, such as a greater capacity to express feelings or more empathy for social diversity (Mitchell 1998; O'Connell 1994), are probably artifacts of marginality and may be destined for the historical dustbin of a democratic, sexually pluralist society.

Even in a utopian society, however, one difference seems less likely to disappear: The sexual orientation of parents appears to have a unique (although not large) effect on children in the politically sensitive domain of sexuality. The evidence, while scanty and underanalyzed, hints that parental sexual orientation is positively associated with the possibility that children will be more likely to attain a similar orientation—and theory and common sense also support such a view. Children raised by lesbian co-parents should and do seem to grow up more open to homoerotic relationships. This may be partly due to genetic and family socialization processes, but what sociologists refer to as "contextual effects" not yet investigated by psychologists may also be important. Because lesbigay parents are disproportionately more likely to inhabit diverse, cosmopolitan cities—Los Angeles, New York and San Francisco—and progressive university communities—such as Santa Cruz, Santa Rosa, Madison, and Ann Arbor (Black, Gates, et al. 2000)—their children grow up in comparatively tolerant school, neighborhood, and social contexts, which foster less hostility to homoeroticism. Sociology could make a valuable contribution to this field by researching processes that interact at the individual, family, and community level to undergird parent–child links between gender and sexuality.

Under homophobic conditions, lesbigay parents are apt to be more sensitive to issues surrounding their children's sexual development and to injuries that children with nonconforming desires may experience, more open to discussing sexuality with their children, and more affirming of their questions about sexuality (Mitchell 1998; Tasker and Golombok 1997). It therefore seems likely, although this has yet to be studied, that their children will grow up better informed about and more comfortable with sexual desires and practices. However, the tantalizing gender contrast in the level of sexual activity reported for sons versus daughters of lesbians raises more complicated questions about the relationship between gender and sexuality.

Even were heterosexism to disappear, however, parental sexual orientation would probably continue to have some impact on the eventual sexuality of children. Research and theory on sexual development remain so rudimentary that it is impossible to predict how much difference might remain were homosexuality not subject to social stigma. Indeed, we believe that if one suspends the hetero-normative presumption, one fascinating riddle to explain in this field is why, even though children of lesbigay parents appear to express a significant increase in homoeroticism, the majority of all children nonetheless identify as heterosexual, as most theories across the "essentialist" to "social constructionist" spectrum seem (perhaps too hastily) to expect. A nondefensive look at the anomalous data on this question could pose fruitful challenges to social constructionist, genetic, and bioevolutionary theories.

We recognize the political dangers of pointing out that recent studies indicate that a higher proportion of children with lesbigay parents are themselves apt to engage in homosexual activity. In a homophobic world, anti-gay forces deploy such results to deny parents custody of their own children and to fuel backlash movements opposed to gay rights. Nonetheless, we believe that denying this probability capitulates to heterosexist ideology and is apt to prove counterproductive in the long run. It is neither intellectually honest nor politically wise to base a claim for justice on grounds that may prove falsifiable empirically. Moreover, the case for granting equal rights to non-heterosexual parents should not require finding their children to be identical to those reared by heterosexuals. Nor should it require finding that such children do not encounter distinctive challenges or risks, especially when these derive from social prejudice. The U.S. Supreme Court rejected this rationale for denying custody when it repudiated discrimination against interracially married parents in *Palmore v. Sidoti* in 1984: "[P]rivate biases may be outside the reach of the law, but the law cannot, directly or indirectly, give them effect" (quoted in Polikoff 1990:569–70). Inevitably, children share most of the social privileges and injuries associated with their parents' social status. If social prejudice were grounds for restricting rights to parent, a limited pool of adults would qualify.

One can readily turn the tables on a logic that seeks to protect children from the harmful effects of heterosexist stigma directed against their parents. Granting legal rights and respect to gay parents and their children should lessen the stigma that they now suffer and might reduce the high rates of

depression and suicide reported among closeted gay youth living with heterosexual parents. Thus, while we disagree with those who claim that there are no differences between the children of heterosexual parents and children of lesbigay parents, we unequivocally endorse their conclusion that social science research provides no grounds for taking sexual orientation into account in the political distribution of family rights and responsibilities.

It is quite a different thing, however, to consider this issue a legitimate matter for social science research. Planned lesbigay parenthood offers a veritable "social laboratory" of family diversity in which scholars could fruitfully examine not only the acquisition of sexual and gender identity, but the relative effects on children of the gender and number of their parents as well as of the implications of diverse biosocial routes to parenthood. Such studies could give us purchase on some of the most vexing and intriguing topics in our field, including divorce, adoption, step-parenthood, and domestic violence, to name a few. To exploit this opportunity, however, researchers must overcome the hetero-normative presumption that interprets sexual differences as deficits, thereby inflicting some of the very disadvantages it claims to discover. Paradoxically, if the sexual orientation of parents were to matter less for political rights, it could matter more for social theory.

ENDNOTES

Authors' Note: We are grateful for the constructive criticisms on early versions of this article from: Celeste Atkins, Amy Binder, Phil Cowan, Gary Gates, Adam Green, David Greenberg, Oystein Holter, Celia Kitzinger, Joan Laird, Jane Mauldon, Dan McPherson, Shannon Minter, Valory Mitchell, Charlotte Patterson, Anne Peplau, Vernon Rosario, Seth Sanders, Alisa Steckel, Michael Wald, and the reviewers and editors of *ASR*. We presented portions of this work at UCLA Neuropsychiatric Institute Symposium on Sexuality; the Feminist Interdisciplinary Seminar of the University of California, Davis; and the Taft Lecture Program at the University of Cincinnati.

[1] In *J.B.F. v. J.M.F.* (Ex parte J.M.F. 1970224, So. 2d 1190, 1988 Ala. LEXIS 161 [1998]), for example, Alabama's Supreme Court quoted Wardle's (1997) essay to justify transferring custody of a child from her lesbian mother to her heterosexual father.

[2] The extrapolation is "inappropriate" because lesbigay-parent families have never been a comparison group in the family structure literature on which these authors rely (cf. Downey and Powell 1993; McLanahan 1985).

[3] In March 2000, Norwegian sociologist Oystein Holter (personal communication) described Helmut Stierlin's "delegation" theory (published in German)—that children take over their parents' unconscious wishes. Holter suggests this theory could predict that a child who grows up with gay parents under homophobic conditions might develop "contrary responses." We are unfamiliar with this theory but find it likely that under such conditions unconscious wishes of heterosexual and nonheterosexual parents could foster some different "contrary responses."

[4] These estimates derive from an extrapolation of Kinsey data claiming a roughly 10 percent prevalence of homosexuality in the adult male population. Interestingly, Michael et al.'s (1994) revisiting of Kinsey (Kinsey, Pomeroy, and Martin 1948; Kinsey, Pomeroy, Martin, and Gebhard 1953) suggests that Kinsey himself emphasized that different measures of sexual orientation yield different estimates of individuals with same-sex sexual orientations in the population. Had scholars read Kinsey differently, they might have selected his figure of 4 percent of the men in his sample who practiced exclusive homosexual behavior from adolescence onward, rather than the widely embraced 10 percent figure. In fact, the 10 percent number is fundamentally flawed: Kinsey found that of the 37 percent of the white men in his sample who had at least one sexual experience with another man in their lifetime, only 10 percent of them (i.e., 3.7 percent of the entire white male sample) had exclusively same-sex sexual experiences for any three-year period between ages 16 and 55.

[5] This assumes that the ratio of number of dependent children to total offspring among current lesbigay parents will be roughly the same as that for all parents and children.

[6] The field is now in a position to take advantage of new data sources. For example, the 1990 U.S. census allows (albeit imperfectly) for the first time the identification of gay and lesbian couples, as will the 2000 census (Black, Gates, et al. 2000). From 1989 to the present, the U.S. General Social Surveys (http://www.icpsr.umich.edu/GSS/index.html) have also allowed for the identification of the sexual orientation of respondents, as does the National Health and Social Life Survey (Laumann et al. 1995).

REFERENCES

Allen, Mike and Nancy Burrell. 1996. "Comparing the Impact of Homosexual and Heterosexual Parents on Children: Meta-Analysis of Existing Research." *Journal of Homosexuality* 32:19–35.

Badgett, M. V. Lee. 1998. "The Economic Well-Being of Lesbian, Gay, and Bisexual Adults' Families." Pp. 231–48 in *Lesbian, Gay and Bisexual Identities in Families: Psychological Perspectives*, edited by C. J. Patterson and A. R. D'Augelli. New York: Oxford University Press.

Baumrind, Diana. 1980. "New Directions in Socialization Research." *American Psychologist* 35:639–52.

———. 1995. "Commentary on Sexual Orientation: Research and Social Policy Implications." *Developmental Psychology* 31:130–36.

Bech, Henning. 1997. *When Men Meet: Homosexuality and Modernity.* Chicago: University of Chicago Press.

Beck, Ulrich and Elisabeth Beck-Gersheim. 1995. *The Normal Chaos of Love.* London: Polity.

Bell, Alan P. and Martin S. Weinberg. 1978. *Homosexualities: A Study of Diversity among Men and Women.* New York: Simon and Schuster.

Bem, Daryl J. 1996. "Exotic Becomes Erotic: A Developmental Theory of Sexual Orientation." *Psychological Review* 103:320–35.

Benkov, Laura. 1994. *Reinventing the Family: Lesbian and Gay Parents.* New York: Crown.

Bigner, Jerry J. and R. Brooke Jacobsen. 1989. "Parenting Behaviors of Homosexual and Heterosexual Fathers." *Journal of Homosexuality* 18:73–86.

———. 1992. "Adult Responses to Child Behavior and Attitudes toward Fathering: Gay and Nongay Fathers." *Journal of Homosexuality* 23:99–112.

Black, Dan A., Gary Gates, Seth Sanders, and Lowell Taylor. 2000. "Demographics of the Gay and Lesbian Population in the United States: Evidence from Available Systematic Data Sources." *Demography* 37:139–54.

Black, Dan A., Hoda R. Maker, Seth G. Sanders, and Lowell Taylor. 1998. "The Effects of Sexual Orientation on Earnings." Working paper, Department of Economics, Gatton College of Business and Economics, University of Kentucky, Lexington, KY.

Blankenhorn, David. 1995. *Fatherless America: Confronting Our Most Urgent Social Problem.* New York: Basic.

Bonvillain, Nancy. 1998. *Women and Men: Cultural Constructs of Gender.* 2d ed. Upper Saddle River, NJ: Prentice Hall.

Bourne, Amy E. 1999. "Mothers of Invention." *San Francisco Daily Journal*, May 21, pp. 1, 9.

Boykin, Keith. 1996. *One More River to Cross: Black and Gay in America.* New York: Anchor.

Bozett, Frederick W. 1989. "Gay Fathers: A Review of the Literature." Pp. 137–62 in *Homosexuality and the Family*, edited by F. W. Bozett. New York: Haworth Press.

Brettell, Caroline B. and Carolyn F. Sargent, eds. 1997. *Gender in Cross-Cultural Perspective.* 2d ed. Upper Saddle River, NJ: Prentice Hall.

Brewaeys, A., I. Ponjaert, E. V. Van Hall, and S. Golombok. 1997. "Donor Insemination: Child Development and Family Functioning in Lesbian Mother Families." *Human Reproduction* 12:1349–59.

Cameron, Paul and Kirk Cameron. 1996. "Homosexual Parents." *Adolescence* 31:757–76.

Cameron, Paul, Kirk Cameron, and Thomas Landess. 1996. "Errors by the American Psychiatric Association, the American Psychological Association, and the National Educational Association in Representing Homosexuality in Amicus Briefs about Amendment 2 to the U.S. Supreme Court." *Psychological Reports* 79:383–404.

Cantor, David. 1994. *The Religious Right: The Assault on Tolerance and Pluralism in America.* New York: Anti-Defamation League.

Cantu, Lionel. 2000. "Entre Hombres/Between Men: Latino Masculinities and Homosexualities." Pp. 224–46 in *Gay Masculinities*, edited by P. Nardi. Thousand Oaks, CA: Sage.

Carrier, Joseph. 1992. "Miguel: Sexual Life History of a Gay Mexican American." Pp. 202–24 in *Gay Culture in America: Essays from the Field*, edited by G. Herdt. Boston: Beacon.

Chan, Raymond W., Risa C. Brooks, Barbara Raboy, and Charlotte J. Patterson. 1998. "Division of Labor among Lesbian and Heterosexual Parents: Associations with Children's Adjustment." *Journal of Family Psychology* 12:402–19.

Chan, Raymond W., Barbara Raboy, and Charlotte J. Patterson. 1998. "Psychosocial Adjustment among Children Conceived Via Donor Insemination by Lesbian and Heterosexual Mothers." *Child Development* 69:443–57.

Clarke, Victoria. 2000. "Sameness and Difference in Research on Lesbian Parenting." Working paper, Women's Studies Research Group, Department of Social Sciences, Loughborough University, Leicestershire, UK.

Downey, Douglas B. and Brian Powell. 1993. "Do Children in Single-Parent Households Fare Better Living with Same-Sex Parents?" *Journal of Marriage and the Family* 55:55–72.

Dunne, Gillian A. 2000. "Opting into Motherhood: Lesbians Blurring the Boundaries and Transforming the Meaning of Parenthood and Kinship." *Gender and Society* 14:11–35.

Falk, Patrick J. 1994. "The Gap between Psychosocial Assumptions and Empirical Research in Lesbian-Mother Child Custody Cases." Pp. 131–56 in *Redefining Families: Implications for Children's Development*, edited by A. E. Gottfried and A. W. Gottfried. New York: Plenum.

Flaks, David K., Ilda Ficher, Frank Masterpasqua, and Gregory Joseph. 1995. "Lesbians Choosing Motherhood: A Comparative Study of Lesbian and Heterosexual Parents and Their Children." *Developmental Psychology* 31:105–14.

Gallagher, Maggie. 2000. "The Gay-Parenting Science." *New York Post*, March 30, p. 3.

Giddens, Anthony. 1992. *The Transformation of Intimacy: Sexuality, Love and Eroticism in Modern Societies*. Stanford, CA: Stanford University Press.

Green, G. Dorsey and Frederick W. Bozett. 1991. "Lesbian Mothers and Gay Fathers." Pp. 197–214 in *Homosexuality: Research Implications for Public Policy*, edited by J. C. Gonsiorek and J. D. Weinrich. Newbury Park, CA: Sage.

Green, Richard, Jane Barclay Mandel, Mary E. Hotvedt, James Gray, and Laurel Smith. 1986. "Lesbian Mothers and Their Children: A Comparison with Solo Parent Heterosexual Mothers and Their Children." *Archives of Sexual Behavior* 15:167–84.

Greene, Beverly and Nancy Boyd-Franklin. 1996. "African-American Lesbians: Issues in Couple Therapy." Pp. 251–71 in *Lesbians and Gays in Couples and Families: A Handbook for Therapists*, edited by J. Laird and R. J. Green. San Francisco, CA: Jossey-Bass.

Groze, Vic. 1991. "Adoption and Single Parents: A Review." *Child Welfare* 70:321–32.

Harris, Judith Rich. 1998. *The Nurture Assumption: Why Children Turn Out the Way They Do*. New York: Free Press.

Hawkeswood, William. 1997. *One of the Children: Gay Black Men in Harlem*. Berkeley: University of California Press.

Herek, Gregory M. 1998. "Bad Science in the Service of Stigma: A Critique of the Cameron Group's Survey Studies," Pp. 223–55 in *Stigma and Sexual Orientation: Understanding Prejudice against Lesbians, Gay Men, and Bisexuals*, edited by G. M. Herek. Thousand Oaks, CA: Sage.

———. 2000. "Paul Cameron Fact Sheet" (Copyright 1997–2000 by G. M. Herek). Retrieved (http://psychology.ucdavis.edu/rainbow/html/facts_cameron_sheet.html).

Katz, Jonathan Ned. 1995. *The Invention of Heterosexuality*. New York: Dutton.

Kinsey, Alfred C., Wardell B. Pomeroy, and Clyde E. Martin. 1948. *Sexual Behavior in the Human Male*. Philadelphia: W. B. Saunders.

Kinsey, Alfred C., Wardell B. Pomeroy, Clyde E. Martin, and Paul H. Gebhard. 1953. *Sexual Behavior in the Human Female*. Philadelphia: W. B. Saunders.

Kitzinger, Celia. 1987. *The Social Construction of Lesbianism*. London, England: Sage.

———. 1989. "Liberal Humanism as an Ideology of Social Control: The Regulation of Lesbian Identities." Pp. 82–98 in *Texts of Identity*, edited by J. Shotter and K. Gergen. London: Sage.

———. 1994. "Should Psychologists Study Sex Differences? Editor's Introduction: Sex Differences Research: Feminist Perspectives." *Feminism and Psychology* 4:501–506.

Kitzinger, Celia and Adrian Coyle. 1995. "Lesbian and Gay Couples: Speaking of Difference." *The Psychologist* 8:64–69.

Laumann, Edward O., John H. Gagnon, Robert T. Michael, and Stuart Michaels. 1994. *The Social Organization of Sexuality: Sexual Practices in the United States*. Chicago: University of Chicago Press.

———. 1995. *National Health and Social Life Survey, 1992* [MRDF]. Chicago: University of Chicago and National Opinion Research Center [producer]. Ann Arbor, MI: Inter-university Consortium for Political and Social Research [distributor].

Lerner, Robert and Althea K. Nagai. 2000. "Out of Nothing Comes Nothing: Homosexual and Heterosexual Marriage Not Shown to Be Equivalent for Raising Children." Presented at the Revitalizing the Institution of Marriage for the 21st Century conference, Brigham Young University, March, Provo, UT.

Lynch, F. R. 1992. "Nonghetto Gays: An Ethnography of Suburban Homosexuals." Pp. 165–201 in *Gay Culture in America: Essays from the Field*, edited by G. Herdt. Boston, MA: Beacon.

McLanahan, Sara S. 1985. "Family Structure and the Reproduction of Poverty." *American Journal of Sociology* 90:873–901.

Michael, Robert T., John H. Gagnon, Edward O. Laumann, and Gina Bari Kolata. 1994. *Sex in America: A Definitive Survey*. Boston, MA: Little, Brown.

Mitchell, Valory. 1998. "The Birds, the Bees . . . and the Sperm Banks: How Lesbian Mothers Talk with Their Children about Sex and Reproduction." *American Journal of Orthopsychiatry* 68:400–409.

O'Connell, Ann. 1994. "Voices from the Heart: The Developmental Impact of a Mother's Lesbianism on Her Adolescent Children." *Smith College Studies in Social Work* 63:281–99.

Ortner, Sherry and Harriet Whitehead. 1981. *Sexual Meanings: The Cultural Construction of Gender and Sexuality*. Cambridge, England: Cambridge University Press.

Patterson, Charlotte J. 1992. "Children of Lesbian and Gay Parents." *Child Development* 63:1025–42.

———. 1995. "Families of the Lesbian Baby Boom: Parents' Division of Labor and Children's Adjustment." *Developmental Psychology* 31:115–23.

——— 1996. "Lesbian and Gay Parents and Their Children." Pp. 274–304 in *The Lives of Lesbians, Gays, and Bisexuals: Children to Adults*, edited by R. C. Savin-Williams and K. M. Cohen. Fort Worth, TX: Harcourt Brace College Publishers.

Patterson, Charlotte J. and Lisa V. Freil. 2000. "Sexual Orientation and Fertility." In *Infertility in the Modern World: Biosocial Perspectives*, edited by G. Bentley and N. Mascie-Taylor. Cambridge, England: Cambridge University Press.

Peterson, John. 1992. "Black Men and Their Same-Sex Desires and Behaviors." Pp. 147–64 in *Gay Culture in America: Essays from the Field*, edited by G. Herdt. Boston: Beacon.

Polikoff, Nancy D. 1990. "This Child Does Have Two Mothers: Redefining Parenthood to Meet the Needs of Children in Lesbian-Mother and Other Nontraditional Families." *Georgetown Law Journal* 78:459–575.

Popenoe, David. 1993. "American Family Decline, 1960–1990: A Review and Appraisal." *Journal of Marriage and the Family* 55:527–41.

———. 1996. *Life without Father*. New York: Free Press.

Price, Deb. 1999. "Middle Ground Emerges for Gay Couples." *Detroit News*, October 4.

Rothblum, Ester D. 1994. "'I Only Read About Myself on Bathroom Walls': The Need for Research on the Mental Health of Lesbians and Gay Men." *Journal of Consulting and Clinical Psychology* 62:213–20.

Seidman, Steven. 1997. *Difference Troubles: Queering Social Theory and Sexual Politics*. New York: Cambridge University Press.

Shireman, Joan F. 1996. "Single-Parent Adoptive Homes." *Children and Youth Services Review* 18:23–36.

Sullivan, Maureen. 1996. "Rozzie and Harriet?: Gender and Family Patterns of Lesbian Coparents." *Gender and Society* 10:747–67.

Sweet, James and Larry Bumpass. 1996. *The National Survey of Families and Households—Waves 1 and 2: Data Description and Documentation*. Center for Demography and Ecology, University of Wisconsin–Madison, Madison, WI (http://www/ssc.wisc.edu/nsfh/home.htm).

Tasker, Fiona L. and Susan Golombok. 1997. *Growing Up in a Lesbian Family*. New York: Guilford.

U.S. Census Bureau. 1999. "Population Estimates Program." Population Division, Washington, DC. Retrieved January 5, 2000 (http://www.census.gov/population/estimates/nation/intfile2–1.txt, and natdoc.txt).

Wald, Michael S. 1999. "Same-Sex Couples: Marriage, Families, and Children, An Analysis of Proposition 22, The Knight Initiative." Stanford Institute for Research on Women and Gender, Stanford University, Stanford, CA.

Wardle, Lynn D. 1997. "The Potential Impact of Homosexual Parenting on Children." *University of Illinois Law Review* 1997:833–919.

Weeks, Jeffrey, Brian Heaphy, and Catherine Donovan. 2001. *Families of Choice and Other Life Experiments: The Intimate Lives of Non-Heterosexuals*. Cambridge, England: Cambridge University Press.

Whitehead, Barbara Dafoe. 1993. "Dan Quayle Was Right." *Atlantic Monthly*, April, vol. 271, pp. 47–50.

Woodruff, Robin. 1998. Testimony re: "Subcommittee Meeting to Accept Empirical Data and Expert Testimony Concerning Homosexual Foster Parents." Hearing at the Office of the Attorney General, September 9, 1998. Little Rock, AR. Available from the authors on request.

31

INVISIBLE INEQUALITY
Social Class and Childrearing in Black Families and White Families

ANNETTE LAREAU

In recent decades, sociological knowledge about inequality in family life has increased dramatically. Yet, debate persists, especially about the transmission of class advantages to children. Kingston (2000) and others question whether disparate aspects of family life cohere in meaningful patterns. Pointing to a "thin evidentiary base" for claims of social class differences in the interior of family life, Kingston also asserts that "class distinguishes neither distinctive parenting styles or distinctive involvement of kids" in specific behaviors (p. 134).

One problem with many studies is that they are narrowly focused. Researchers look at the influence of parents' education on parent involvement in schooling *or* at children's time spent watching television *or* at time spent visiting relatives. Only a few studies examine more than one dynamic inside the home. Second, much of the empirical work is descriptive. For example, extensive research has been done on time use, including patterns of women's labor force participation, hours parents spend at work, and mothers' and fathers' contributions to childcare. . . .

Third, researchers have not satisfactorily explained how these observed patterns are produced. Put differently, *conceptualizations* of the *social processes* through which families differ are underdeveloped and little is known about how family life transmits advantages to children. Few researchers have attempted to integrate what is known about behaviors and attitudes taught inside the home with the ways in which these practices may provide unequal resources for family members outside the home. . . .

Fourth, little is known about the degree to which children adopt and enact their parents' beliefs. Sociologists of the family have long stressed the importance of a more dynamic model of parent–child interaction, but empirical research has been slow to emerge. . . .

I draw on findings from a small, intensive data set collected using ethnographic methods. I map the connections between parents' resources and their children's daily lives. My first goal, then, is to challenge Kingston's

Annette Lareau, excerpts from "Invisible Inequality: Social Class and Childrearing in Black Families and White Families" from *American Sociological Review* 67 (October 2002): 747–776. Copyright © 2002 by American Sociological Association. Reprinted with the permission of the author and the American Sociological Association.

(2000) argument that social class does not distinguish parents' behavior or children's daily lives. I seek to show empirically that social class does indeed create distinctive parenting styles. I demonstrate that parents differ by class in the ways they define their own roles in their children's lives as well as in how they perceive the nature of childhood. The middle-class parents, both white *and* black, tend to conform to a cultural logic of childrearing I call "concerted cultivation." They enroll their children in numerous age-specific organized activities that dominate family life and create enormous labor, particularly for mothers. The parents view these activities as transmitting important life skills to children. Middle-class parents also stress language use and the development of reasoning and employ talking as their preferred form of discipline. This "cultivation" approach results in a wider range of experiences for children but also creates a frenetic pace for parents, a cult of individualism within the family, and an emphasis on children's performance.

The childrearing strategies of white and black working-class and poor parents emphasize the "accomplishment of natural growth." These parents believe that as long as they provide love, food, and safety, their children will grow and thrive. They do not focus on developing their children's special talents. Compared to the middle-class children, working-class and poor children participate in few organized activities and have more free time and deeper, richer ties within their extended families. Working-class and poor parents issue many more directives to their children and, in some households, place more emphasis on physical discipline than do the middle-class parents. These findings extend Kohn and Schooler's (1983) observation of class differences in parents' values, showing that differences also exist in the *behavior* of parents *and* children.

Quantitative studies of children's activities offer valuable empirical evidence but only limited ideas about how to conceptualize the mechanisms through which social advantage is transmitted. Thus, my second goal is to offer "conceptual umbrellas" useful for making comparisons across race and class and for assessing the role of social structural location in shaping daily life.

Last, I trace the connections between the class position of family members—including children—and the uneven outcomes of their experiences outside the home as they interact with professionals in dominant institutions. The pattern of concerted cultivation encourages an *emerging sense of entitlement* in children. All parents and children are not equally assertive, but the pattern of questioning and intervening among the white and black middle-class parents contrasts sharply with the definitions of how to be helpful and effective observed among the white and black working-class and poor adults. The pattern of the accomplishment of natural growth encourages an *emerging sense of constraint*. Adults as well as children in these social classes tend to be deferential and outwardly accepting in their interactions with professionals such as doctors and educators. At the same time, however, compared to their middle-class counterparts, white and black working-class and poor family members are more distrustful of professionals. These are differences with potential long-term consequences. In an historical moment when the dominant society privileges active, informed, assertive clients of

health and educational services, the strategies employed by children and parents are not equally effective across classes. In sum, differences in family life lie not only in the advantages parents obtain for their children, but also in the skills they transmit to children for negotiating their own life paths.

Methodology

Study Participants

This study is based on interviews and observations of children, aged 8 to 10, and their families. The data were collected over time in three research phases. Phase one involved observations in two third-grade classrooms in a public school in the midwestern community of "Lawrenceville."[1] After conducting observations for two months, I grouped the families into social class (and race) categories based on information provided by educators. I then chose every third name, and sent a letter to the child's home asking the mother and father to participate in separate interviews. Over 90 percent of parents agreed, for a total of 32 children (16 white and 16 African American). A black graduate student and I interviewed all mothers and most fathers (or guardians) of the children. Each interview lasted 90 to 120 minutes, and all took place in 1989–1990.

Phase two took place at two sites in a northeastern metropolitan area. One school, "Lower Richmond," although located in a predominantly white, working-class urban neighborhood, drew about half of its students from a nearby all-black housing project. I observed one third-grade class at Lower Richmond about twice a week for almost six months. The second site, "Swan," was located in a suburban neighborhood about 45 minutes from the city center. It was 90 percent white; most of the remaining 10 percent were middle-class black children.[2] There, I observed twice a week for two months at the end of the third grade; a research assistant then observed weekly for four more months in the fourth grade. At each site, teachers and parents described their school in positive terms. The observations took place between September 1992 and January 1994. In the fall of 1993, I drew an interview sample from Lower Richmond and Swan, following the same method of selection used for Lawrenceville. A team of research assistants and I interviewed the parents and guardians of 39 children. Again, the response rate was over 90 percent but because the classrooms did not generate enough black middle-class children and white poor children to fill the analytical categories, interviews were also conducted with 17 families with children aged 8 to 10. . . . Thus, the total number of children who participated in the study was 88 (32 from the Midwest and 56 from the Northeast).

Family Observations

Phase three, the most intensive research phase of the study, involved home observations of 12 children and their families in the Northeast who had been previously interviewed. Some themes, such as language use and families' social connections, surfaced mainly during this phase. . . .

TABLE 1 Summary of Differences in Childrearing Approaches

Dimension Observed	Childrearing Approach	
	Concerted Cultivation	Accomplishment of Natural Growth
Key elements of each approach	Parent actively fosters and assesses child's talents, opinions, and skills	Parent cares for child and allows child to grow
Organization of daily life	Multiple child leisure activities are orchestrated by adults	Child "hangs out" particularly with kin
Language use	Reasoning/directives Child contestation of adult statements Extended negotiations between parents and child	Directives Rare for child to question or challenge adults General acceptance by child of directives
Social connections	Weak extended family ties Child often in homogeneous age groupings	Strong extended family ties Child often in heterogeneous age groupings
Interventions in institutions	Criticisms and interventions on behalf of child Training of child to intervene on his or her own behalf	Dependence on institutions Sense of powerlessness and frustration Conflict between childrearing practices at home and at school
Consequences	Emerging sense of entitlement on the part of the child	Emerging sense of constraint on the part of the child

Concerted Cultivation and Natural Growth

The interviews and observations suggested that crucial aspects of family life *cohered*. Within the concerted cultivation and accomplishment of natural growth approaches, three key dimensions may be distinguished: the organization of daily life, the use of language, and social connections. . . . These dimensions do not capture all important parts of family life, but they do incorporate core aspects of childrearing (table 1). Moreover, our field observations revealed that behaviors and activities related to these dimensions dominated the rhythms of family life. Conceptually, the organization of daily life and the use of language are crucial dimensions. Both must be present for the family to be described as engaging in one childrearing approach rather than the other. Social connections are significant but less conceptually essential.

All three aspects of childrearing were intricately woven into the families' daily routines, but rarely remarked upon. As part of everyday practice, they were invisible to parents and children. Analytically, however, they are useful means for comparing and contrasting ways in which social class differences shape the character of family life. I now examine two families in terms of these three key dimensions. I "control" for race and gender and contrast the lives of two black boys—one from an (upper) middle-class family and one from a family on public assistance. I could have focused on almost any of the other 12 children, but this pair seemed optimal, given the limited number of studies reporting on black middle-class families, as well as the aspect of my argument that suggests that race is less important than class in shaping childrearing patterns.

Developing Alexander Williams

Alexander Williams and his parents live in a predominantly black middle-class neighborhood. Their six-bedroom house is worth about $150,000. Alexander is an only child. Both parents grew up in small towns in the South, and both are from large families. His father, a tall, handsome man, is a very successful trial lawyer who earns about $125,000 annually in a small firm specializing in medical malpractice cases. Two weeks each month, he works very long hours (from about 5:30 A.M. until midnight) preparing for trials. The other two weeks, his workday ends around 6:00 P.M. He rarely travels out of town. Alexander's mother, Christina, is a positive, bubbly woman with freckles and long, black, wavy hair. A high-level manager in a major corporation, she has a corner office, a personal secretary, and responsibilities for other offices across the nation. She tries to limit her travel, but at least once a month she takes an overnight trip.

Alexander is a charming, inquisitive boy with a winsome smile. Ms. Williams is pleased that Alexander seems interested in so many things:

> *Alexander is a joy. He's a gift to me. He's very energetic, very curious, loving, caring person, that, um . . . is outgoing and who, uh, really loves to be with people. And who loves to explore, and loves to read and . . . just do a lot of fun things.*

The private school Alexander attends has an on-site after-school program. There, he participates in several activities and receives guitar lessons and photography instruction.

Organization of Daily Life Alexander is busy with activities during the week and on weekends (table 2). His mother describes their Saturday morning routine. The day starts early with a private piano lesson for Alexander downtown, a 20-minute drive from the house:

> *It's an 8:15 class. But for me, it was a tradeoff. I am very adamant about Saturday morning TV. I don't know what it contributes. So . . . it was . . . um . . . either stay at home and fight on a Saturday morning [laughs] or go do something constructive. . . . Now Saturday mornings are pretty booked up. You know, the piano lesson, and then straight to choir for a couple of hours. So, he has a very full schedule.*

TABLE 2   Participation in Activities Outside of School: Boys

Boy's Name/Race/ Class	Activities Organized by Adults	Informal Activities
Middle Class		
Alexander Williams (black)	Soccer team	Restricted television
	Baseball team	Plays outside occasionally with two other boys
	Community choir	Visits friends from school
	Church choir	
	Sunday school	
	Piano (Suzuki)	
	School plays	
	Guitar (through school)	
Poor		
Harold McAllister (black)	Bible study in neighbor's house (occasionally)	Visits relatives
	Bible camp (1 week)	Plays ball with neighborhood kids
		Watches television
		Watches videos

Ms. Williams' vehement opposition to television is based on her view of what Alexander needs to grow and thrive. She objects to TV's passivity and feels it is her obligation to help her son cultivate his talents.

Sometimes Alexander complains that "my mother signs me up for everything!" Generally, however, he likes his activities. He says they make him feel "special," and without them life would be "boring." His sense of time is thoroughly entwined with his activities: He feels disoriented when his schedule is not full. This unease is clear in the following field-note excerpt. The family is driving home from a Back-to-School night. The next morning, Ms. Williams will leave for a work-related day trip and will not return until late at night. Alexander is grumpy because he has nothing planned for the next day. He wants to have a friend over, but his mother rebuffs him. Whining, he wonders what he will do. His mother, speaking tersely, says:

> You have piano and guitar. You'll have some free time. [Pause] I think you'll survive for one night. [Alexander does not respond but seems mad. It is quiet for the rest of the trip home.]

Alexander's parents believe his activities provide a wide range of benefits important for his development. In discussing Alexander's piano lessons, Mr. Williams notes that as a Suzuki student,[3] Alexander is already able to read music. Speculating about more diffuse benefits of Alexander's involvement with piano, she says:

> I don't see how any kid's adolescence and adulthood could not but be enhanced by an awareness of who Beethoven was. And is that Bach or Mozart? I don't

know the difference between the two! I don't know Baroque from Classical—but he does. How can that not be a benefit in later life? I'm convinced that this rich experience will make him a better person, a better citizen, a better husband, a better father—certainly a better student.

Ms. Williams sees music as building her son's "confidence" and his "poise." In interviews and casual conversation, she stresses "exposure." She believes it is her responsibility to broaden Alexander's worldview. Childhood activities provide a learning ground for important life skills:

Sports provide great opportunities to learn how to be competitive. Learn how to accept defeat, you know. Learn how to accept winning, you know, in a gracious way. Also it gives him the opportunity to learn leadership skills and how to be a team player. . . . Sports really provides a lot of really great opportunities.

Alexander's schedule is constantly shifting; some activities wind down and others start up. Because the schedules of sports practices and games are issued no sooner than the start of the new season, advance planning is rarely possible. Given the sheer number of Alexander's activities, events inevitably overlap. Some activities, though short-lived, are extremely time consuming. Alexander's school play, for example, requires rehearsals three nights the week before the opening. In addition, in choosing activities, the Williamses have an added concern—the group's racial balance. Ms. Williams prefers that Alexander not be the only black child at events. Typically, one or two other black boys are involved, but the groups are predominantly white and the activities take place in predominantly white residential neighborhoods. Alexander is, however, part of his church's youth choir and Sunday School, activities in which all participants are black. . . .

Language Use   Like other middle-class families, the Williamses often engage in conversation that promotes reasoning and negotiation. An excerpt from a field note (describing an exchange between Alexander and his mother during a car ride home after summer camp) shows the kind of pointed questions middle-class parents ask children. Ms. Williams is not just eliciting information. She is also giving Alexander the opportunity to develop and practice verbal skills, including how to summarize, clarify, and amplify information:

As she drives, [Ms. Williams] asks Alex, "So, how was your day?"

Alex: *"Okay. I had hot dogs today, but they were burned! They were all black!"*

Mom: *"Oh, great. You shouldn't have eaten any."*

Alex: *"They weren't all black, only half were. The rest were regular."*

Mom: *"Oh, okay. What was that game you were playing this morning? . . .*

Alex: *"It was [called] 'Whatcha doin?'"*

Mom: *"How do you play?"*

Alexander explains the game elaborately—fieldworker doesn't quite follow. Mom asks Alex questions throughout his explanation, saying, "Oh, I see,"

when he answers. She asks him about another game she saw them play; he again explains. . . . She continues to prompt and encourage him with small giggles in the back of her throat as he elaborates. . . .

Not all middle-class parents are as attentive to their children's needs as this mother, and none are *always* interested in negotiating. But a general pattern of reasoning and accommodating is common.

Social Connections   Mr. and Ms. Williams consider themselves very close to their extended families. Because the Williamses' aging parents live in the South, visiting requires a plane trip. Ms. Williams takes Alexander with her to see his grandparents twice a year. She speaks on the phone with her parents at least once a week and also calls her siblings several times a week. Mr. Williams talks with his mother regularly by phone (he has less contact with his stepfather). With pride, he also mentions his niece, whose Ivy League education he is helping to finance.

Interactions with cousins are not normally a part of Alexander's leisure time. . . . Nor does he often play with neighborhood children. The huge homes on the Williamses' street are occupied mainly by couples without children. Most of Alexander's playmates come from his classroom or his organized activities. Because most of his school events, church life, and assorted activities are organized by the age (and sometimes gender) of the participants, Alexander interacts almost exclusively with children his own age, usually boys. Adult-organized activities thus define the context of his social life.

Mr. and Ms. Williams are aware that they allocate a sizable portion of time to Alexander's activities. What they stress, however, is the time they *hold back*. They mention activities the family has chosen *not* to take on (such as traveling soccer).

Summary   Overall, Alexander's parents engaged in concerted cultivation. They fostered their son's growth through involvement in music, church, athletics, and academics. They talked with him at length, seeking his opinions and encouraging his ideas. Their approach involved considerable direct expenses (e.g., the cost of lessons and equipment) and large indirect expenses (e.g., the cost of taking time off from work, driving to practices, and forgoing adult leisure activities). Although Mr. and Ms. Williams acknowledged the importance of extended family, Alexander spent relatively little time with relatives. His social interactions occurred almost exclusively with children his own age and with adults. Alexander's many activities significantly shaped the organization of daily life in the family. Both parents' leisure time was tailored to their son's commitments. Mr. and Ms. Williams felt that the strategies they cultivated with Alexander would result in his having the best possible chance at a happy and productive life. They couldn't imagine themselves not investing large amounts of time and energy in their son's life. But, as I explain in the next section, which focuses on a black boy from a poor family, other parents held a different view.

Supporting the Natural Growth of Harold McAllister

Harold McAllister, a large, stocky boy with a big smile, is from a poor black family. He lives with his mother and his 8-year-old sister, Alexis, in a large apartment. Two cousins often stay overnight. Harold's 16-year-old sister and 18-year-old brother usually live with their grandmother, but sometimes they stay at the McAllister's home. Ms. McAllister, a high school graduate, relies on public assistance (AFDC). Hank, Harold and Alexis' father, is a mechanic. He and Ms. McAllister have never married. He visits regularly, sometimes weekly, stopping by after work to watch television or nap. Harold (but not Alexis) sometimes travels across town by bus to spend the weekend with Hank.

The McAllisters' apartment is in a public housing project near a busy street. The complex consists of rows of two- and three-story brick units. The buildings, blocky and brown, have small yards enclosed by concrete and wood fences. Large floodlights are mounted on the corners of the buildings, and wide concrete sidewalks cut through the spaces between units. The ground is bare in many places; paper wrappers and glass litter the area.

Inside the apartment, life is humorous and lively, with family members and kin sharing in the daily routines. Ms. McAllister discussed, disdainfully, mothers who are on drugs or who abuse alcohol and do not "look after" their children. Indeed, the previous year Ms. McAllister called Child Protective Services to report her twin sister, a cocaine addict, because she was neglecting her children. Ms. McAllister is actively involved in her twin's daughters' lives. Her two nephews also frequently stay with her. Overall, she sees herself as a capable mother who takes care of her children and her extended family.

Organization of Daily Life   Much of Harold's life and the lives of his family members revolve around home. Project residents often sit outside in lawn chairs or on front stoops, drinking beer, talking, and watching children play. During summer, windows are frequently left open, allowing breezes to waft through the units and providing vantage points from which residents can survey the neighborhood. A large deciduous tree in front of the McAllisters' apartment unit provides welcome shade in the summer's heat.

Harold loves sports. He is particularly fond of basketball, but he also enjoys football, and he follows televised professional sports closely. Most afternoons, he is either inside watching television or outside playing ball. He tosses a football with cousins and boys from the neighboring units and organizes pick-up basketball games. Sometimes he and his friends use a rusty, bare hoop hanging from a telephone pole in the housing project; other times, they string up an old, blue plastic crate as a makeshift hoop. One obstacle to playing sports, however, is a shortage of equipment. Balls are costly to replace, especially given the rate at which they disappear—theft of children's play equipment, including balls and bicycles, is an ongoing problem. During a field observation, Harold asks his mother if she knows where the ball is. She replies with some vehemence, "They stole the blue and yellow ball, and they stole the green ball, and they stole the other ball."

Hunting for balls is a routine part of Harold's leisure time. One June day, with the temperature and humidity in the high 80's, Harold and his cousin Tyrice (and a fieldworker) wander around the housing project for about an hour, trying to find a basketball:

We head to the other side of the complex. On the way . . . we passed four guys sitting on the step. Their ages were 9 to 13 years. They had a radio blaring. Two were working intently on fixing a flat bike tire. The other two were dribbling a basketball.

Harold: *"Yo! What's up, ya'll."*

Group: *"What's up, Har." "What's up? "Yo."*

They continued to work on the tire and dribble the ball. As we walked down the hill, Harold asked, "Yo, could I use your ball?"

The guy responded, looking up from the tire, "Naw, man. Ya'll might lose it."

Harold, Tyrice, and the fieldworker walk to another part of the complex, heading for a makeshift basketball court where they hope to find a game in progress:

No such luck. Harold enters an apartment directly in front of the makeshift court. The door was open. . . . Harold came back. "No ball. I guess I gotta go back."

The pace of life for Harold and his friends ebbs and flows with the children's interests and family obligations. The day of the basketball search, for example, after spending time listening to music and looking at baseball cards, the children join a water fight Tyrice instigates. It is a lively game, filled with laughter and with efforts to get the adults next door wet (against their wishes). When the game winds down, the kids ask their mother for money, receive it, and then walk to a store to buy chips and soda. They chat with another young boy and then amble back to the apartment, eating as they walk. Another afternoon, almost two weeks later, the children— Harold, two of his cousins, and two children from the neighborhood—and the fieldworker play basketball on a makeshift court in the street (using the fieldworker's ball). As Harold bounces the ball, neighborhood children of all ages wander through the space.

Thus, Harold's life is more free-flowing and more child-directed than is Alexander Williams'. The pace of any given day is not so much planned as emergent, reflecting child-based interests and activities. Parents intervene in specific areas, such as personal grooming, meals, and occasional chores, but they do not continuously direct and monitor their children's leisure activities. Moreover, the leisure activities Harold and other working-class and poor children pursue require them to develop a repertoire of skills for dealing with much older and much younger children as well as with neighbors and relatives.

Language Use   Life in the working-class and poor families in the study flows smoothly without extended verbal discussions. The amount of talking

varies, but overall, it is considerably less than occurs in the middle-class homes.[4] Ms. McAllister jokes with the children and discusses what is on television. But she does not appear to cultivate conversation by asking the children questions or by drawing them out. Often she is brief and direct in her remarks. For instance, she coordinates the use of the apartment's only bathroom by using one-word directives. She sends the children (there are almost always at least four children home at once) to wash up by pointing to a child, saying one word, "bathroom," and handing him or her a washcloth. Wordlessly, the designated child gets up and goes to the bathroom to take a shower.

Similarly, although Ms. McAllister will listen to the children's complaints about school, she does not draw them out on these issues or seek to determine details, as Ms. Williams would. . . .

Social Connections   Children, especially boys, frequently play outside. The number of potential playmates in Harold's world is vastly higher than the number in Alexander's neighborhood. When a fieldworker stops to count heads, she finds 40 children of elementary school age residing in the nearby rows of apartments. With so many children nearby, Harold could choose to play only with others his own age. In fact, though, he often hangs out with older and younger children and with his cousins (who are close to his age).

The McAllister family, like other poor and working-class families, is involved in a web of extended kin. As noted earlier, Harold's older siblings and his two male cousins often spend the night at the McAllister home. Celebrations such as birthdays involve relatives almost exclusively. Party guests are not, as in middle-class families, friends from school or from extra-curricular activities. Birthdays are celebrated enthusiastically, with cake and special food to mark the occasion; presents, however, are not offered. Similarly, Christmas at Harold's house featured a tree and special food but no presents. At these and other family events, the older children voluntarily look after the younger ones: Harold plays with his 16-month-old niece, and his cousins carry around the younger babies.

The importance of family ties—and the contingent nature of life in the McAllisters' world—is clear in the response Alexis offers when asked what she would do if she were given a million dollars:

> *Oh, boy! I'd buy my brother, my sister, my uncle, my aunt, my nieces and my nephews, and my grandpop, and my grandmom, and my mom, and my dad, and my friends, not my friends, but mostly my best friend—I'd buy them all clothes . . . and sneakers. And I'd buy some food, and I'd buy my mom some food, and I'd get my brothers and my sisters gifts for their birthdays.*

Summary   In a setting where everyone, including the children, was acutely aware of the lack of money, the McAllister family made do. Ms. McAllister rightfully saw herself as a very capable mother. She was a strong, positive influence in the lives of the children she looked after. Still, the contrast with Ms. Williams is striking. Ms. McAllister did not seem to think that Harold's

opinions needed to be cultivated and developed. She, like most parents in the working-class and poor families, drew strong and clear boundaries between adults and children. Adults gave directions to children. Children were given freedom to play informally unless they were needed for chores. Extended family networks were deemed important and trustworthy. . . .

Impact of Childrearing Strategies on Interactions with Institutions

. . . I now follow the families out of their homes and into encounters with representatives of dominant institutions—institutions that are directed by middle-class professionals. Again, I focus on Alexander Williams and Harold McAllister. Across all social classes, parents and children interacted with teachers and school officials, healthcare professionals, and assorted government officials. Although they often addressed similar problems (e.g., learning disabilities, asthma, traffic violations), they typically did not achieve similar resolutions. The pattern of concerted cultivation fostered an *emerging sense of entitlement* in the life of Alexander Williams and other middle-class children. By contrast, the commitment to nurturing children's natural growth fostered an *emerging sense of constraint* in the life of Harold McAllister and other working-class or poor children.

Both parents and children drew on the resources associated with these two childrearing approaches during their interactions with officials. Middle-class parents and children often customized these interactions; working-class and poor parents were more likely to have a "generic" relationship. When faced with problems, middle-class parents also appeared better equipped to exert influence over other adults compared with working-class and poor parents. Nor did middle-class parents or children display the intimidation or confusion we witnessed among many working-class and poor families when they faced a problem in their children's school experience.

Emerging Signs of Entitlement

Alexander Williams' mother, like many middle-class mothers, explicitly teaches her son to be an informed, assertive client in interactions with professionals. For example, as she drives Alexander to a routine doctor's appointment, she coaches him in the art of communicating effectively in healthcare settings:

> *Alexander asks if he needs to get any shots today at the doctor's. Ms. Williams says he'll need to ask the doctor. . . . As we enter Park Lane, Mom says quietly to Alex: "Alexander, you should be thinking of questions you might want to ask the doctor. You can ask him anything you want. Don't be shy. You can ask anything."*

> *Alex thinks for a minute, then: "I have some bumps under my arms from my deodorant."*

Mom: *"Really? You mean from your new deodorant?"*

Alex: *"Yes."*

Mom: *"Well, you should ask the doctor."*

Alexander learns that he has the right to speak up (e.g., "don't be shy") and that he should prepare for an encounter with a person in a position of authority by gathering his thoughts in advance. . . .

Middle-class parents and children were also very assertive in situations at the public elementary school most of the middle-class children in the study attended. There were numerous conflicts during the year over matters small and large. For example, parents complained to one another and to the teachers about the amount of homework the children were assigned. A black middle-class mother whose daughters had not tested into the school's gifted program negotiated with officials to have the girls' (higher) results from a private testing company accepted instead. The parents of a fourth-grade boy drew the school superintendent into a battle over religious lyrics in a song scheduled to be sung as part of the holiday program. The superintendent consulted the district lawyer and ultimately "counseled" the principal to be more sensitive, and the song was dropped.

Children, too, asserted themselves at school. Examples include requesting that the classroom's blinds be lowered so the sun wasn't in their eyes, badgering the teacher for permission to retake a math test for a higher grade, and demanding to know why no cupcake had been saved when an absence prevented attendance at a classroom party. In these encounters, children were not simply complying with adults' requests or asking for a repeat of an earlier experience. They were displaying an emerging sense of entitlement by urging adults to permit a customized accommodation of institutional processes to suit their preferences. . . .

Emerging Signs of Constraint

The interactions the research assistants and I observed between professionals and working-class and poor parents frequently seemed cautious and constrained. This unease is evident, for example, during a physical Harold McAllister has before going to Bible camp. Harold's mother, normally boisterous and talkative at home, is quiet. Unlike Ms. Williams, she seems wary of supplying the doctor with accurate information:

Doctor: *"Does he eat something each day—either fish, meat, or egg?"*

Mom, response is low and muffled: *"Yes."*

Doctor, attempting to make eye contact but mom stares intently at paper: *"A yellow vegetable?"*

Mom, still no eye contact, looking at the floor: *"Yeah."*

Doctor: *"A green vegetable?"*

Mom, looking at the doctor: *"Not all the time."* [Fieldworker has not seen any of the children eat a green or yellow vegetable since visits began.]

Doctor: *"No. Fruit or juice?"*

Mom, low voice, little or no eye contact, looks at the doctor's scribbles on the paper he is filling out: *"Ummh humn."*

Doctor: *"Does he drink milk every day?"*

Mom, abruptly, in considerably louder voice: *"Yeah."*

Doctor: *"Cereal, bread, rice, potato, anything like that?"*

Mom, shakes her head: *"Yes, definitely."* [Looks at doctor.]

Ms. McAllister's knowledge of developmental events in Harold's life is uneven. She is not sure when he learned to walk and cannot recall the name of his previous doctor. And when the doctor asks, "When was the last time he had a tetanus shot?" she counters, gruffly, "What's a tetanus shot?" . . .

[N]either Harold nor his mother seemed as comfortable as Alexander had been. Alexander was used to extensive conversation at home; with the doctor, he was at ease initiating questions. Harold, who was used to responding to directives at home, primarily answered questions from the doctor, rather than posing his own. Alexander, encouraged by his mother, was assertive and confident with the doctor. Harold was reserved. Absorbing his mother's apparent need to conceal the truth about the range of foods he ate, he appeared cautious, displaying an emerging sense of constraint.

We observed a similar pattern in school interactions. Overall, the working-class and poor adults had much more distance or separation from the school than their middle-class counterparts. Ms. McAllister, for example, could be quite assertive in some settings (e.g., at the start of family observations, she visited the local drug dealer, warning him not to "mess with" the black male fieldworker). But throughout the fourth-grade parent-teacher conference, she kept her winter jacket zipped up, sat hunched over in her chair, and spoke in barely audible tones. She was stunned when the teacher said that Harold did not do homework. Sounding dumbfounded, she said, "He does it at home." The teacher denied it and continued talking. Ms. McAllister made no further comments and did not probe for more information, except about a letter the teacher said he had mailed home and that she had not received. The conference ended, having yielded Ms. McAllister few insights into Harold's educational experience.[5]

Other working-class and poor parents also appeared baffled, intimidated, and subdued in parent-teacher conferences. . . . Working-class and poor children seemed aware of their parents' frustration and witnessed their powerlessness. Billy Yanelli, for example, asserted in an interview that his mother "hate[d]" school officials.

At times, these parents encouraged their children to resist school officials' authority. The Yanellis told Billy to "beat up" a boy who was bothering him. Wendy Driver's mother advised her to punch a male classmate who pestered her and pulled her ponytail. Ms. Driver's boyfriend added, "Hit him when the teacher isn't looking."

In classroom observations, working-class and poor children could be quite lively and energetic, but we did not observe them try to customize their environments. They tended to react to adults' offers or, at times, to

plead with educators to repeat previous experiences, such as reading a particular story, watching a movie, or going to the computer room. Compared to middle-class classroom interactions, the boundaries between adults and children seemed firmer and clearer. Although the children often resisted and tested school rules, they did not seem to be seeking to get educators to accommodate their own *individual* preferences.

Overall, then, the behavior of working-class and poor parents cannot be explained as a manifestation of their temperaments or of overall passivity; parents were quite energetic in intervening in their children's lives in other spheres. Rather, working-class and poor parents generally appeared to depend on the school (Lareau 2000), even as they were dubious of the trustworthiness of the professionals. This suspicion of professionals in dominant institutions is, at least in some instances, a reasonable response.[6] The unequal level of trust, as well as differences in the amount and quality of information divulged, can yield unequal *profits* during an historical moment when professionals applaud assertiveness and reject passivity as an inappropriate parenting strategy (Epstein 2001). Middle-class children and parents often (but not always) accrued advantages or profits from their efforts. Alexander Williams succeeded in having the doctor take his medical concerns seriously. Ms. Marshall's children ended up in the gifted program, even though they did not technically qualify. Middle-class children expect institutions to be responsive to *them* and to accommodate their individual needs. By contrast, when Wendy Driver is told to hit the boy who is pestering her (when the teacher isn't looking) or Billy Yanelli is told to physically defend himself, despite school rules, they are not learning how to make bureaucratic institutions work to their advantage. Instead, they are being given lessons in frustration and powerlessness.

Why Does Social Class Matter?

Parents' economic resources helped create the observed class differences in childrearing practices. Enrollment fees that middle-class parents dismissed as "negligible" were formidable expenses for less affluent families. Parents also paid for clothing, equipment, hotel stays, fast-food meals, summer camps, and fundraisers. In 1994, the Tallingers estimated the cost of Garrett's activities at $4,000 annually, and that figure was not unusually high.[7] Moreover, families needed reliable private transportation and flexible work schedules to get children to and from events. These resources were disproportionately concentrated in middle-class families.

Differences in educational resources also are important. Middle-class parents' superior levels of education gave them larger vocabularies that facilitated concerted cultivation, particularly in institutional interventions. Poor and working-class parents were not familiar with key terms professionals used, such as "tetanus shot." Furthermore, middle-class parents' educational backgrounds gave them confidence when criticizing educational professionals and intervening in school matters. Working-class and poor parents viewed educators as their social superiors.

Kohn and Schooler (1983) showed that parents' occupations, especially the complexity of their work, influence their childrearing beliefs. We found that parents' work mattered, but also saw signs that the experience of adulthood itself influenced conceptions of childhood. Middle-class parents often were preoccupied with the pleasures and challenges of their work lives.[8] They tended to view childhood as a dual opportunity: a chance for play and for developing talents and skills of value later in life. Mr. Tallinger noted that playing soccer taught Garrett to be "hard nosed" and "competitive," valuable workplace skills. Ms. Williams mentioned the value of Alexander learning to work with others by playing on a sports team. Middle-class parents, aware of the "declining fortunes" of the middle class, worried about their own economic futures and those of their children (Newman 1993). This uncertainty increased their commitment to helping their children develop broad skills to enhance their future possibilities.

Working-class and poor parents' conceptions of adulthood and childhood also appeared to be closely connected to their lived experiences. For the working class, it was the deadening quality of work and the press of economic shortages that defined their experience of adulthood and influenced their vision of childhood. It was dependence on public assistance and severe economic shortages that most shaped poor parents' views. Families in both classes had many worries about basic issues: food shortages, limited access to healthcare, physical safety, unreliable transportation, insufficient clothing. Thinking back over their childhoods, these parents remembered hardship but also recalled times without the anxieties they now faced. Many appeared to want their own youngsters to concentrate on being happy and relaxed, keeping the burdens of life at bay until they were older.

Thus, childrearing strategies are influenced by more than parents' education. It is the interweaving of life experiences and resources, including parents' economic resources, occupational conditions, and educational backgrounds, that appears to be most important in leading middle-class parents to engage in concerted cultivation and working-class and poor parents to engage in the accomplishment of natural growth. Still, the structural location of families did not fully determine their childrearing practices. The agency of actors and the indeterminacy of social life are inevitable.

ENDNOTES

[1] All names of people and places are pseudonyms. The Lawrenceville school was in a white suburban neighborhood in a university community a few hours from a metropolitan area. The student population was about half white and half black; the (disproportionately poor) black children were bused from other neighborhoods.

[2] Over three-quarters of the students at Lower Richmond qualified for free lunch; by contrast, Swan did not have a free lunch program.

[3] The Suzuki method is labor intensive. Students are required to listen to music about one hour per day. Also, both child and parent(s) are expected to practice daily and to attend every lesson together.

[4] Hart and Risley (1995) reported a similar difference in speech patterns. In their sample, by about age three, children of professionals had larger vocabularies and spoke more utterances per hour than the *parents* of similarly aged children on welfare.

[5] Middle-class parents sometimes appeared slightly anxious during parent–teacher conferences, but overall, they spoke more and asked educators more questions than did working-class and poor parents.

[6] The higher levels of institutional reports of child neglect, child abuse, and other family difficulties among poor families may reflect this group's greater vulnerability to institutional intervention (e.g., see L. Gordon 1989).

[7] In 2002, a single sport could cost as much as $5,000 annually. Yearly league fees for ice hockey run to $2,700; equipment costs are high as well (Halbfinger 2002).

[8] Middle-class adults do not live problem-free lives, but compared with the working class and poor, they have more varied occupational experiences and greater access to jobs with higher economic returns.

REFERENCES

Epstein, Joyce. 2001. *Schools, Family, and Community Partnerships.* Boulder, CO: Westview.

Gordon, Linda. 1989. *Heroes of Their Own Lives: The Politics and History of Family Violence.* New York: Penguin.

Halbfinger, David M. 2002. "A Hockey Parent's Life: Time, Money, and Yes, Frustration." *New York Times,* January 12, p. 29.

Hart, Betty and Todd Risley. 1995. *Meaningful Differences in the Everyday Experience of Young American Children.* Baltimore, MD: Paul Brooks.

Kingston, Paul. 2000. *The Classless Society.* Stanford, CA: Stanford University Press.

Kohn, Melvin and Carmi Schooler, eds. 1983. *Work and Personality: An Inquiry into the Impact of Social Stratification.* Norwood, NJ: Ablex.

Lareau, Annette. 2000. *Home Advantage: Social Class and Parental Intervention in Elementary Education.* 2d ed. Lanham, MD: Rowman and Littlefield.

———. 2002. "Doing Multi-Person, Multi-Site 'Ethnographic' Work: A Reflective, Critical Essay." Department of Sociology, Temple University, Philadelphia, PA. Unpublished manuscript.

Newman, Kathleen. 1993. *Declining Fortunes: The Withering of the American Dream.* New York: Basic Books.

32

CONSUMPTION AS CARE AND BELONGING
Economies of Dignity in Children's Daily Lives

ALLISON J. PUGH

Introduction

When I asked Judy Berger, a quiet, reflective, white middle-class mother, if she regretted buying anything for her 8-year-old son Max, it would not have been surprising had she named the GameBoy. She had just finished telling me in great detail about the extent of her son's obsession with the

electronic handheld toy, and the deep misgivings she had about it. After all that, I almost felt silly asking the question—but her answer startled me. It is not that she rued buying the GameBoy for Max, she insisted. "I guess I felt almost like it wasn't really, like I couldn't have not bought it, because now we are there in our life," she said, her words tripping over each other uncharacteristically. While she wanted Max to be happy, for two years that desire had not been enough to overcome her intense dislike of the gaming systems, which she regarded as addictive, violent, and sedentary. The turning point was when she came to realize that GameBoys had so saturated the social lives of 8-year-old boys they knew, that she did not think she could relegate Max to the kind of social pathos of the outsider. It was not the thought of Max's happiness that led her to buy the gaming system but, rather, the prospect of his social exclusion that made her re-evaluate her opposition. But her distaste for the GameBoy remained. "It is kind of sad that it feels like it is a given that you will have one," she finally conceded. "It is too bad that that is where we are."[1]

The commodification of childhood is advancing, with children spending some $30 billion themselves, and influencing another $670 billion spent on their behalf in the United States (Schor 2004). The daily lives of children are permeated now with moments of buying, from symbolic rituals to transportation to lunches. As Arlie Hochschild (2003) observed, increasingly, "companies . . . expand the number of market niches for goods and services covering activities that, in yesteryear, formed part of unpaid 'family life'" (p. 36).

As the market seeps into childhood, scholars debate whether or not we should be worried. Are children the victims of an ever more sophisticated onslaught by powerful corporate interests (Schor 2004)? Or are they "wise consumers," savvy social actors who can innovate, using advertising content for their own strategic ends (Buckingham 2000)? Is the commercialization of childhood a new and alarming trend (Kline 1993; Linn 2004), or is it the outgrowth of long-standing historical practices of intermingling economic exchange and personal lives (Zelizer 2004)? Should we shield children from the more sexual, violent, exploitative or materialistic corners of adult culture, or is it impossible to separate childhood from the features of the wider culture in which it is embedded (Cook 2004; Williams 2005)?

The reader might be forgiven for thinking that the answer to all of these questions, however contradictory, is "yes." I argue that these debates, while important, miss a central point about spending on children: the impact of commercialization on the emotional experience of childhood, specifically, on children's relationships with parents and with friends. Just like the rise of a "divorce culture" generated by the prevalence of divorced couples changed widespread cultural assumptions about the expectations of trust and obligation in marriage (Hackstaff 1999), the rise of children's consumer culture has so permeated children's daily lives as to establish a new cultural environment in which to grow up. By its sheer domination of childhood today, commodification has reframed expectations about what parents should provide, what children should have, and what having, or not having, signifies.

In this [reading], I consider these developments from the perspective of three years of ethnographic research on children's consumer culture and families in California. I found that Judy Berger's dilemma exemplifies that of many parents: she did not regret her decision to buy the GameBoy, but she regretted the cultural imperative that necessitated its buying—an imperative stemming from Max's relationships with others.

Consumption, Care, and Belonging

For thousands of years, we have understood consumption as a means of distinguishing those like ourselves from others who are not, most often from others below. In a particularly influential argument, Pierre Bourdieu (1984) contended that parents and schools socialize children into having tastes that ultimately stratify them, through at times unconscious cultural practices inculcating a certain approach to particular cultural goods, such as classical music. While his focus was on inequality, Bourdieu's argument presaged a dual sense of consumption as a means of forging group bonds, or a sense of belonging, and as a component of childrearing, or care.

Some scholars have focused on the latter sense, arguing that consumption can be a form of care located at the intersections of the market and intimacy, forging "connected lives," as Viviana Zelizer (2004) observed. These researchers suggest that consumption acts as a symbolic language through which buyers make connections to others, a devotional rite involving what British anthropologist Daniel Miller (1998) called "the material culture of love." In this vein, parents buy for children to strengthen emotional bonds, bonds under some strain from such stressors as increasing work hours (Hochschild 1997; Thompson 1996), divorce (Pugh 2002), or poverty (Edin and Lein 1997; Power 2003). As Sharon Zukin (2004) observed, "the things we need to buy are framed by our love for the significant others we buy for" (p. 30). These studies portray consumption as a form of care.

Other researchers look not at buying as caring, but on having (as in having a particular good or experience) as belonging. A British study of youth and advertising found that many teenagers agonized over moments of being unable to participate when their friends recalled commercials or sang jingles, which the authors considered the rites of group membership (Ritson and Elliott 1999; see also Chee 2000). Teenagers told the researchers about their experience of being "left out," "talked around," or "blanked" when they could not take part in the conversation. At stake was a form of social invisibility, an exclusion from social participation or citizenship.

Corporate advertisers work with all of these hypotheses—attaching to commodities meanings of distinction, care, and belonging. With more than $17 billion spent per year targeting children, corporate marketing is increasingly sophisticated and unfettered, and children are particularly vulnerable to their tactics, as consumer researchers have found they are unaware even of the advertisers' persuasive intent until about the age of seven (Horovitz 2006; for a review, see John 1999). Some important recent scholarship has documented the onslaught of campaigns to tap into children's desires, brought

on in part by the deregulation of children's television in the 1980s and the development of powerful market tactics to lure buyers (Cook 2004; Cross 1997, 2000; Schor 2004). While it is clear, then, that childhood is a media-rich environment, we know less about what this environment means for the children and parents who live in it. Eva Illouz (2007) counsels against knee-jerk assumptions about the pernicious effects of commodification, but none-theless points us in the direction of relationships: "We need not "presume that the realm of commodities debases the realm of sentiment," she wrote, but "the vocabulary of emotions is now more exclusively dictated by the market" (p. 91).

From this scholarship, we can understand that consumption for children permeates their relationships, sometimes as an arbiter of belonging, some-times as a conduit for care. How do parents and children view these dual roles for commodified goods and experiences? How do these twin tasks reveal themselves in children's daily lives? How does commercial culture thread its way through children's emotional connections, with peers and with parents?

Methods

I investigated these questions by conducting an ethnography of childhood consumer culture in Oakland, California. For three years, I observed children aged five to nine at a low-income after-school setting, and for six months each at two other, more affluent, school sites, one private school and one public. I helped children while they did their homework, pushed them on the swings, sat on the sidelines while they climbed in play structures, held their hands while we went on field trips. I listened to their jokes and stories, went to birth-day parties, took them to the library or to free concerts, ate with them, and watched them receive awards or go on parades. I also listened to parents from 54 families, in interviews generally lasting for two to four hours, sometimes over several visits. Through these efforts, I immersed myself in everyday child-hoods of divergent class and racial backgrounds and in the worlds of parents struggling with the practices and meanings of consuming for children. In my book, *Longing and Belonging: Parents, Children and Consumer Culture* (2009), I trace how children navigate the world of commodified goods and experiences, particularly when they lack specific items that seem to matter socially. I also explore parents' motivations and fears, including the prospect and meaning of their children's experiences of being different at school. In this [reading], I delve into how consumer culture permeates children's emotional connections to others, through the twin prongs of belonging and care, and the implications this development has for contemporary childhood and parenthood.

The Economy of Dignity

One day, on a cold afternoon at the private school Arrowhead Academy, some children sought refuge from the damp chill in a one-room portable building

they called the Addition, where the school's after-school program hosted the knitting club and other activities. Some children sat or lay down on the carpet turning yarn into "puffballs," small round balls of yarn sold around the school for a penny each. Two first-grade boys built with Legos in the corner, and another group of four played a board game, while two staff members helped knitters begin or end projects. One child made a purple scarf for her mother, proudly announcing that "knitting is better than buying."

There were several low conversations taking place among the children, and one group of second-grade girls began to talk about birthday parties. Tamsin was excited about her upcoming party, in which her mother planned to repeat a favorite ritual. Every year, Tamsin explained, her mother would devise a treasure hunt, in which all the guests would search throughout her house, spurred on by little rhyming clues and small presents. The girls in the small group around Tamsin are curious, interested. It is clear that they will be invited, although others nearby—including some boys and other children in other grades—will not. Tamsin describes the trinkets her mother has given in preceding years while the surrounding girls exclaim or ask questions.

While the rest of us listen, Claire, a first grader sitting near the couch and some distance away from Tamsin, chimes in. Claire bends over her puffballs and remarks that she herself had a birthday party a few weeks ago, at the "Bladium," an indoor sports palace where birthday parties start at $300. Claire, who had turned seven at this party, was younger than some of the other children in the Addition, but she nonetheless cheerily described her party—how many guests there were, the soccer they played—while the knitters listened. "I was the worst goalie," she said, smiling ruefully. Tamsin and the other girls listen, as do the rest of the knitters, and no one scoffs, rolls her eyes, or patently ignores Claire; indeed, she secures the momentary dignity of their attention, and the fleeting connection to others, made slightly unusual by the fact that she is younger.

In some ways, this vignette—mundane and without undue drama—captures important features about contemporary childhood. The ambiance is not wholly permeated with rank materialism—witness the pronouncement "knitting is better than buying"—and neither is every object branded. It is not that a child's every moment is spent acquiring, selling, or thinking about consumer goods. Yet market culture is often present in the children's conversations, an important arbiter of who gets to pipe up and who stays silent, a passport for their participation in their social world. As Randall Collins (2004) suggests, talk is a kind of ritual, serving to "mark boundaries of inclusion and exclusion" (p. 297). In order to join in the birthday party conversation, the norms of children's talk rituals meant that only children with celebrations somehow equal in stature—in elaborate preparations, in rarity, in superior fun, in commodified "enchantment" (Ritzer 1999)—could leap in to share, while children who celebrated their birthday in the park with pizza and a cake could not speak up, silenced by their lack of relevant possession or experience.

Such conversations form the crux of what I have termed the "economy of dignity," the system by which children make themselves audible and therefore relevant to their peers. Similar to Hochschild's (1989) "economy of

gratitude," in which married couples exchange recognition of gifts of time, work or feeling, the economy of dignity refers to an emotional market of recognition, in this case of children's claims to belong in their social world. In their daily, ordinary talk, children negotiate what sort of commodities or experiences count for belonging, enabling them to participate. I call this an emotional market because children's participation creates both their visibility and their connection to others, and the processes that engender children's talk evoke intense feelings among the children, which then create their own ramifications in school and in their homes.

I use dignity to capture the sense of this participation as a fundamental psychological and social need, what Amartya Sen (1999) called an "absolute capability . . . to take part in the life of the community" (pp. 361–62). With dignity, children are visible to their peers, and granted the aural space, the very right to speak in their own community's conversation. While dignity specifically does not refer to the competitive status-seeking behavior widely assumed to underlie consumer desire, I do not mean to suggest that I never saw children seeking to induce the jealousy of others. Rather, in view of Veblen's ([1899] 1994) observation that buyers buy to "gain the esteem and envy of one's fellow-men" (p. 21), children seemed to spend as much or more time and energy searching for esteem than for envy, seeking to join the circle rather than better it.

Sometimes children argued about what was valuable, as in one note-worthy exchange at the low-income after-school center I call Sojourner Truth, in which the children who attended were supposed to make posters listing what they were thankful for. One African American girl, Loretta, urged her classmate to write "thankful for what you have," to which Marco, a recent Mexican immigrant, retorted, "I am thankful for my ancestors." But it was rare for children's interactions to feature such a direct conversation about what might count as tokens worthy of dignity. More commonly, children seemed to avoid comparison and, instead, would mention their own experiences or possessions without weighing the advantages or disadvantages of theirs versus those of another. Would they not have made observations of this sort more directly if they sought a triumphant domination over others based on superiority, instead of a connection to others based on similarity? Claire might have argued that the Bladium was an improvement over any home birthday, no matter how many trinkets were involved, while Tamsin might have disparaged the Bladium for its impersonality. By adding their own experience alongside that of their peers, rather than forcing a win-or-lose challenge, these young children seem to be less striving to conquer than forging connections based on the scrip of the moment, which, for Claire, was "those of us with fun birthday parties."

What Scrip Signifies: The Claim to Care

Children in all three sites experienced economies of dignity that they then had to navigate with the resources at their disposal. While the schools in this study differed vastly by income and by "school climate," meaning their

explicit attention to how children treat each other, what counted as scrip in these economies varied more in degree than kind and, at each fieldsite, was a fluid and dynamic set. Children found they could achieve visibility through claims to particular skills or knowledge, or other prized characteristics, but they often made the most symbolic value out of claiming access to popular culture—from actually owning or using to merely knowing about many objects or experiences that were advertised in their worlds, such as sneakers, movies or collectible cards and toys. The prominence of popular culture both reflected and shaped the power of corporate marketers to at least establish the menu from which children would select what mattered at the moment.

Children used these forms of scrip to enter their conversations and, along the way, to symbolize sought-after qualities, such as relative autonomy, talent, wealth, skill or long family pedigrees. But children's tokens of value also established the bona fides of another claim: that of the child as "cared for." Care scholars have documented the ways in which care is both "labor and relationship," involving at once the interactive tasks and feelings of caring for another (Ruddick 1998). In my research, I saw children add another dimension to care, in the social uses to which they put the caring consumption they received from parents, as a form of scrip in their economies of dignity. This action, which we might call "care-displaying," is one that struck at the core of children's identity as worthwhile, that traversed income inequality, and that linked the dual uses of consumption as both belonging and care.

Under this logic, then, for children, possessions signaled that they were cared for. Poignant examples abounded at Sojourner Truth. On numerous occasions, the children seemed to equate care with provisioning, as was visible in the Mother's Day cards they created one day. "My mom is special to me because she keeps me warm, she buys me clothes, she buys me toys and food, walks with me, reads to me, pays for the house. That's why I think my mother is special," read one card. Another day, a diminutive Chinese American boy declared that his mother refused to let him accept candy from other students and, in the same breath, that she was taking him to McDonald's that weekend. Rather than contradictory statements, we might surmise both served as evidence of care: his mother cares about him enough to shield him from the implied danger in others' candy *and* to indulge him in commercialized pleasure.

Ultimately, part of the deeper appeal of possessions, destinations, and other mediated claims—in which the child used particular objects or events to represent good qualities about themselves—was in their ability to symbolize the child's membership in a larger community of care. We can read these symbolic efforts like the "negative space" of a painting, to gather a sense of children's anxieties about what they actually lacked—such as autonomy, age, wealth, or the claim to someone's loving attention. These pointed demonstrations (and its underlying anxiety) were not limited to low-income children, as children in more affluent locales seemed also to work hard to convey that they were cared for, and often seemed to be intentionally portraying themselves as somebody's focal point. The difference was that affluent children used a wider variety of tactics to do so: Tamsin used the

elaborate preparation her mother undertook to represent her own centrality as the object of somebody's extensive caring, and other children talked about their extracurricular lessons in the same way, as if the "concerted cultivation" (Lareau 2003) of their individual talents and skills was, similarly, evidence of care. Annette Lareau (2003) observed that through such middle-class cultivation, "children learn they are special" (p. 39). Data from my fieldwork suggest they also learned to equate parental scrutiny, especially that accompanied by parental spending, with what it meant to be cared for.

The Equation of Belonging and Care

There is evidence that parents made the same equation of care with the consuming they did to ensure children's belonging. Like Judy Berger, children's belonging needs could vanquish the affluent parent's abiding distaste for particular commodities. Katerina, from the affluent public school Oceanview, was second-guessing her television restrictions, because "sometimes I worry. I don't know if that's the thing to do, because in the school they talk, and other children have seen so many shows." Birthdays were an important moment, Deborah Lamont observed. "Birthday parties are a lot of pressure," she said. "You have to come up with these ideas that are fun and the children want to go to. And that are novel, . . . in addition to being expensive. It's really common to spend $500 on a birthday party." Yet she didn't question the necessity of the practice nor the influence it wielded in the children's economy of dignity at Oceanview. "Party bags are an important thing," she noted. "You have to have cool things for the guests."

For low-income parents, the pressure was acute and could trump other budgetary priorities. Askia Jenkins, who lived in subsidized housing with her three kids, lamented the stress she felt because of the things her children wanted. "The thing that I hate about society is that they put so much emphasis that things have to have a certain name brand," Askia said. "You know, it has to be . . . with our kids—Sean John, Rocawear, Air Force One, Jordans. You know, these are the styles that my kids like to wear and that they see other kids wearing." While Askia complained that those styles were name brands, however, she did not question the fact that her children cared about what other people wore. She understood the source of her children's consumer desire as the social meaning generated by their economy of dignity.

Sandra Perkins, a nursing aide with three children, railed against buying Michael Jordan-branded sneakers for her son, who thought he was going to be "some big record producer." Yet other purchases were unavoidable, despite her disinclination:

> Well, I do Halloween. I buy Rasheed and Lexine costumes. I really don't like to because I really think it's a waste of money, really. To spend all that money on a costume and they're only going to wear it one time. But I do it because they have the parades and stuff at school.

Sandra knew that the "parades and stuff at school" meant that having a costume would be an essential component of dignity, and that the children's

peers would notice if they did not participate. For Sandra, as for other low-income mothers, the symbolic import of Halloween costumes meant that the children had to have them, and elevated their desires to the level of needs, even as others might discount these needs as "only" psychological.

Angela Lincoln, a janitor, reported struggling to make the food last for herself and her three children before the end of her monthly paycheck. Yet when she talked about getting her son a Playstation, she was matter-of-fact. "You have to manage your money," she said, dolefully. "You can't neglect the kids, though." Shirley, an African American mother of three, described how she managed to buy her son the electronic games he wants. "What I do is I just sacrifice something. I'll work extra hours somewhere just so this can be the Christmas." Thus children's consumption desires, transformed into needs by the economy of dignity, were a top priority for low-income parents, sometimes even pegged ahead of other basics like clothes, food or even rent, and worth extraordinary efforts to procure.

Discussion and Conclusion

The emotional impact of the commercialization of childhood reverberates in two directions, in the ratcheting up of what it takes to belong, and in the equation of parent spending with care. These effects are relational, they transform the webs of connection which children inhabit, and they are felt in affluent and low-income communities alike. In other work (Pugh 2009), I explore how children's lives, and that of American families generally, have changed to help produce the conditions in which these reverberations are so powerfully felt. For our purposes here, however, my research demonstrates that the economy of dignity reaches across class lines to shape children's relationships everywhere.

The implications are vast, but three are particularly important. First, because children hitch so many of their bids for connection to others to their demonstrated knowledge of popular culture, corporate marketing has a direct conduit to their hearts. Children are thus subject to the planned obsolescence, the fleeting nature of popular fads generated by the market cycle. This is not to say that all intimacy should be devoid of "pollution" by market exchange, in some variation of the "hostile worlds" argument Zelizer (2004) rejected. But the harnessing of children's social bonds to profit-seeking forces is more than just the neutral commingling of cultural symbols; any reckoning of the economy of dignity must incorporate the powerful targeted marketing efforts as that which largely establishes the framework of options from which children draw their meaningful tokens of belonging.

Second, like "divorce culture," the commodification of childhood changes the environment for all children, affecting even those children whose parents have attempted to curtail their exposure to corporate marketing. Thus the economy of dignity demonstrates that individual parents—however much they say "no" in their own homes, however much they restrict or prohibit "screen time," or otherwise follow expert counsel—are

limited in their ability to protect their children from consumer culture. Children are immersed in this environment, in part defined by the media exposure of some sort of critical mass, and thus any successful attempt to control or change childhood culture can be only a collective one, at the school, neighborhood or media level.

This inescapability has its most pernicious effects on low-income parents, who struggle to meet the basic needs of children, and whose struggles are increased when those basic needs expand. While parents and children can engage in protracted negotiations in which they contest just how necessary a given item is, ultimately, low-income parents viscerally recognize the importance of their children's tokens of dignity. As the standards of a good-enough childhood increase, however, parents face new tokens again and again, posing particular challenges for low-income families, who stand between the rock of their children's psychological needs and the wall of their limited means to meet them.

But perhaps the most poignant of implications of the economies of dignity is the contrast between what children reach for, in yearning, and what they manage to obtain. The commodified object or experience through which children seek to link to others mediates human connection through the market, often serving as much to distance people as to bring them together. If what children want is to belong to their communities, or to experience care from loving adults, then surely buying the GameBoy is like treating not the cause of their longing but the "referred pain" of their consumer desires (Hochschild 2003). The shifting sands of children's consumer culture are unstable grounds on which children find themselves daily having to build their relationships.

ENDNOTES

Author's Note: I would like to thank Anita Garey and Karen Hansen for their comments on earlier drafts. This essay is based on research I conducted for my book, *Longing and Belonging: Parents, Children and Consumer Culture* (2009), which was written with the help of a grant from the Alfred P. Sloan Foundation's Workplace, Work Force and Working Families program. In addition, the research was supported by the National Science Foundation under Grant No. 0221499, as well as by the Center for Working Families and the Institute for the Study of Social Change, both at the University of California, Berkeley.

[1] All names of people and institutions, and some of their identifying characteristics, have been changed to preserve their confidentiality.

REFERENCES

Bourdieu, Pierre. 1984. *Distinction: A Social Critique of the Judgement of Taste.* Translated by Richard Nice. Cambridge, MA: Harvard University Press.

Buckingham, David. 2000. *After the Death of Childhood.* Cambridge and Malden, MA: Polity Press.

Chee, Bernadine. 2000. "Eating Snacks, Biting Pressure: Only Children in Beijing." Pp. 48–70 in *Feeding China's Little Emperors: Food, Children and Social Change,* edited by Jun Jing. Stanford, CA: Stanford University Press.

Collins, Randall. 2004. *Interaction Ritual Chains.* Princeton, NJ: Princeton University Press.

Cook, Dan. 2004. *The Commodification of Childhood: The Children's Clothing Industry and the Rise of the Child Consumer.* Durham, NC: Duke University Press.

Cross, Gary. 1997. *Kids' Stuff: Toys and the Changing World of American Childhood.* Cambridge, MA: Harvard University Press.

———. 2000. *An All-Consuming Century: Why Commercialism Won in Modern America.* New York: Columbia University Press.

Edin, Kathryn and Laura Lein. 1997. *Making Ends Meet.* New York: Russell Sage Foundation.

Hackstaff, Karla. 1999. *Marriage in a Divorce Culture.* Philadelphia: Temple University Press.

Hochschild, Arlie, with Anne Machung. 1989. *The Second Shift.* New York: Avon Books.

———. 1997. *The Time Bind.* New York: Metropolitan Books.

———. 2003. *The Commercialization of Intimate Life.* Berkeley: University of California Press.

Horovitz, Bruce. 2006. "Six Strategies Marketers Use to Make Kids Want Things Bad." *USA Today,* November 22, p. 1B, as cited by The Campaign for a Commercial Free Childhood, "Marketing to Children Overview." Accessed May 26, 2009, at http://www.commercialexploitation.org/factsheets/overview.pdf.

Illouz, Eva. 2007. *Cold Intimacies: The Making of Emotional Capitalism.* Malden, MA: Polity Press.

John, Deborah Roedder. 1999. "Consumer Socialization of Children: A Retrospective Look at Twenty-Five Years of Research." *Journal of Consumer Research* 26 (December 1999): 183–213.

Kline, Stephen. 1993. *Out of the Garden: Toys, TV and Children's Culture in the Age of Marketing.* New York: Verso.

Lareau, Annette. 2003. *Unequal Childhoods.* Berkeley: University of California Press.

Linn, Susan. 2004. *Consuming Kids: The Hostile Takeover of Childhood.* New York and London: The New Press.

Miller, Daniel. 1998. *A Theory of Shopping.* Ithaca, NY: Cornell University Press.

Power, Elaine. 2003. "Freedom and Belonging through Consumption: The Disciplining of Desire in Single Mothers on Welfare." Presented at the annual meeting of the British Sociological Association, University of York, UK.

Pugh, Allison. 2002. "From Compensation to Childhood Wonder: Why Parents Buy." Working Paper No. 39, Center for Working Families, University of California, Berkeley.

———. 2009. *Longing and Belonging: Parents, Children and Consumer Culture.* Berkeley: University of California Press.

Ritson, Mark and Richard Elliott. 1999. "The Social Uses of Advertising: An Ethnographic Study of Adolescent Advertising Audiences." *Journal of Consumer Research* 26:260–77.

Ritzer, George. 1999. *Enchanting a Disenchanted World: Revolutionizing the Means of Consumption.* Thousand Oaks, CA: Pine Forge Press.

Ruddick, Sara. 1998. "Care as Labor and Relationship." Pp. 3–25 in *Norms and Values: Essays on the Work of Virginia Held,* edited by J. G. Haber and M. S. Halfon. Lanham, MD: Rowman and Littlefield.

Schor, Juliet. 2004. *Born to Buy.* New York: Scribner.

Sen, Amartya. 1999. "The Possibility of Social Choice." *The American Economic Review* 89 (3): 349–78.

Thompson, Craig. 1996. "Caring Consumers: Gendered Consumption Meanings and the Juggling Lifestyle." *Journal of Consumer Research* 22 (4): 388–407.

Veblen, Thorstein. [1899] 1994. *The Theory of the Leisure Class.* New York: Dover.

Williams, Christine. 2005. *Inside Toyland: Working, Shopping and Social Inequality.* Berkeley: University of California Press.

Zelizer, Viviana. 2004. *The Purchase of Intimacy.* Princeton, NJ: Princeton University Press.

Zukin, Sharon. 2004. *Point of Purchase: How Shopping Changed American Culture.* New York: Routledge.

PART VII

Grandparents and Multigenerational Relationships

33

GRANDPARENTING

LYNNE M. CASPER • SUZANNE M. BIANCHI

The most recent estimates indicate that there are 53 million grandparents in the United States and that about 70 percent of adults over age 50 are grandparents (Watson and Koblinsky 1997). Although the majority of Americans will experience the role of grandparent as they age, just how they carry out this role is likely to vary greatly. Grandparent–grandchild relations are embedded in societal, environmental, cultural, familial, and individual contexts that are interdependent and change over time (King, Russell, and Elder 1998). Because of differences in these contexts, grandparenting styles are diverse; they can range from extremely involved, as in the case of a grandparent raising a grandchild without the help of the child's parents, to very remote, as in the case of grandparents who live on the opposite coast from their grandchildren.

Since the 1940s, grandparents have often been portrayed as "rescuers" in family crises, stepping in to help out after wartime marriages dissolved due to death or divorce, or in times of economic crisis (Szinovacz 1998). More recently, increases in drug abuse, child abuse, teen and nonmarital births, divorce, the incidence of AIDS, and changes in welfare laws have presented families with new crises. The increased severity and prevalence of these crises has meant that more and more grandparents are raising their grandchildren on their own (Bryson and Casper 1999; Casper and Bryson 1998). At the same time, increased longevity and continued preferences for noninstitutional living have meant that other grandparents are in need of care and assistance and may reside with their children and grandchildren for the help they can provide (Bryson and Casper 1999). These grandparents may be in need of assistance, but they may also be able to help out with child care, light household chores, and financial contributions, although they have much less responsibility in the rearing of their grandchildren than do grandparents who are raising their grandchildren alone.

A front-page feature in *USA Today* highlighted three families that included grandparents and described the circumstances through which each family came to be formed. Grandparents Tom and Pat Torkelson went to live with Tom's daughter and her husband after Pat was hospitalized for cardiac problems (Kasindorf 1999). The family is doing well financially and Mr. Torkelson works almost full-time to contribute. He enjoys a close relationship with his grandchildren, talking to them frequently and giving them advice. He also drives the youngest children to piano, dance, singing, and soccer practices. Mrs. Torkelson is home when the children get home from school and keeps an eye on them.

In contrast, Cora Stewart, a 63-year-old single grandmother in ill health, is raising her four grandchildren whose mothers could not raise them because of drug problems (Sharp 1999). The Stewart family survives on $250 a month in food stamps and $364 a month in welfare payments. For all intents and purposes, Mrs. Stewart acts as both mother and father to her grandchildren and is fully responsible for their upbringing.

The third family highlighted in the *USA Today* feature includes Mr. and Mrs. Gibson, their daughter, Amy, and their granddaughter, Nicole (El Nasser 1999). Amy Gibson got pregnant when she was 13 years old. Rather than give the baby up for adoption, the Gibsons raised their daughter and granddaughter together and say the two girls grew up more like sisters. The Gibsons are fairly well-off, and Mrs. Gibson quit her job to be home full-time with Nicole.

These stories not only illustrate the diversity of grandparent–grandchildren families and the different types of interactions grandparents and grandchildren can have, they highlight the unique processes through which each family was formed. These families were joined together by circumstances brought about by illness, drug abuse, and nonmarital childbearing, and they bear testimony to the resilience of the American family and its ability to cope with even the most severe crises. The diversity of these families also illustrates the blurring of the definition of family and of the traditional roles each member performs. In some of these families the parents are fulfilling their legal, moral, and social obligations to their children; in others, parents are sharing these responsibilities with the grandparents; and in still others, the grandparents have full responsibility.

Other demographic shifts, including improvements in life expectancy and declines in fertility and immigration, have altered opportunities for interaction between grandparents and grandchildren (Uhlenberg and Kirby 1998). Because more people are surviving to older ages, more children today will have the opportunity to establish relationships with several grandparents than was true in the past. And more grandparents will live long enough to have adult grandchildren. . . .

How Has Grandparenthood Changed over the Years?

Social and demographic shifts have altered the face of grandparenthood over the past century. Changes in mortality, fertility, and immigration can greatly

affect how people experience the roles of grandparent and grandchild. In the past, when mortality was higher among adults, children and young adults were less likely than they are today to have living grandparents. Uhlenberg (1996) used life table techniques to estimate the proportion of people who, at various ages, would have had a living grandparent at the beginning and end of the twentieth century. Less than one-fourth of infants born in 1900 would have had four living grandparents. By 2000, life expectancy among adults had improved to such an extent that more than two-thirds of newborns had all four grandparents alive. Only one-fifth of adults age 30 would have had any living grandparents in 1900, compared with more than three-fourths of those turning 30 in 2000. Many scholars have maintained that at the beginning of the twentieth century very few grandparents were alive. Although it is true that children today are more likely to have living grandparents than were children in the past, even a century ago more than 90 percent of 10-year-old children had at least one living grandparent.

Throughout most of the century, the gender gap in mortality grew and the likelihood of having a living grandmother increased more rapidly than the probability of having a surviving grandfather, especially for young adults (Uhlenberg and Kirby 1998). These differences in mortality also mean that a larger proportion of living grandparents are grandmothers and that the vast majority of great-grandparents are female.

The number of grandchildren a grandparent can expect to have is affected by the level of fertility—higher fertility rates imply more grandchildren and lower fertility rates imply fewer grandchildren. The likelihood of being a grandparent is also affected by changes in childlessness and the timing of births within the population. Changing fertility patterns over the twentieth century affected grandparenthood in three major ways (Uhlenberg and Kirby 1998). First, because of declining fertility, grandparents have fewer grandchildren today than they did in 1900. For example, it is estimated that a woman aged 60 to 64 in 1900 would have had 12.1 grandchildren; a woman in the same age group in the 1990s would have had fewer than 6 grandchildren. Second, due to a decline in childlessness, a higher proportion of older Americans are grandparents than was true a century ago. Third, because of changes in the age at which women complete their childbearing, people today are less likely than they were in 1900 still to be raising their own children when they become grandparents. This is not to say that early childbearing today does not produce overlap in these roles for some people. For example, because childbearing occurs at younger ages for blacks and Hispanics, they are more likely than whites (or Asian Americans) to become grandparents while still raising their own children (Morgan 1996). Yet overall, as fertility declines for all groups, fewer people are likely to experience this overlap than in the past.

Record numbers of immigrants poured into the United States at the beginning of the twentieth century before restrictive laws that limited immigration were passed in the 1920s. This meant that the children of immigrants typically lived in a different country than did their grandparents, and interaction between grandparents and grandchildren was infrequent. One-third

of children under age 15 in 1900 had a parent who was born in another country, compared with one-fourth of children in that age group in the late 1990s (Uhlenberg and Kirby 1998).

Other social changes occurring throughout the twentieth century were also important in transforming grandparenthood. The changing economic fortunes of the older population and improvements in health have meant that grandparents today have greater opportunities for more meaningful interaction with their grandchildren. Today's grandparents are also likely to have more free time to spend with their grandchildren; they have more post-retirement years and more years after they raise their own children to pursue relationships with their grandchildren. Prior to the 1960s, many documents portrayed grandparents' interactions with grandchildren in a negative light (Szinovacz 1998). Judging from the articles in *USA Today* described above, these views have diminished substantially.

Grandparenting

Styles of grandparenting are defined in part by the extent of the connectedness between grandparents and their grandchildren. The degree of this connectedness is influenced by norms, roles, interactions, sentiments, and exchanges of support (Silverstein, Giarrusso, and Bengtson 1998). Bengtson and his colleagues suggest that intergenerational connectedness between grandparents and grandchildren must be measured along a number of dimensions (Bengtson 2001; Bengtson and Schrader 1982; Mangen, Bengtson, and Landry 1988; Silverstein and Bengtson 1997). The degree of emotional closeness felt between grandparents and grandchildren and the degree to which they share beliefs and values affect connectedness. Closeness between the generations depends on structural factors that facilitate interaction between the grandparents and grandchildren, such as geographic distance and family structure. Grandparenting styles are affected by the number of activities grandparents and grandchildren share and how often they see each other. The extent to which grandparents and grandchildren receive assistance from each other is another important factor. And finally, the degree to which grandparents and grandchildren have a sense of familial duty to each other and share family values affects grandparenting styles.

In general, very few normatively explicit expectations are placed on the role behavior of grandparents. However, American grandparents generally adhere to the norm of noninterference; that is, they believe that parents should be free to raise their children as they see fit (Cherlin and Furstenberg 1985, 1986). Yet most Americans also feel obligated to provide assistance when close relatives are in need (Rossi and Rossi 1990). These two contrasting norms, along with variations in the six dimensions of grandparent–grandchild connectedness, help to explain why there is such broad diversity in grandparenting styles.

In one of the earliest studies on grandparenting, Neugarten and Weinstein (1964) used factors such as biologic continuity, emotional self-fulfillment,

teaching, vicarious accomplishment, degree of formality, authority, contact, the transmission of family wisdom, and having fun to categorize the meaning of grandparenthood and the style of grandparenting. They identified the following types of grandparents: "formal," "funseeker," "surrogate parent," "reservoir of family wisdom," and "distant."

Cherlin and Furstenberg (1985, 1986), in one of the benchmark studies on grandparenthood, used nationally representative data to develop a typology of grandparenting styles based on the extent of exchange of services, the degree of parentlike behavior (authority), and frequency of contact. They labeled those who scored low on exchange of services, demonstrated little parentlike behavior, and had little contact with their grandchildren "detached" grandparents. "Passive" grandparents reported minimal exchange of services and little parentlike behavior, but had more frequent contact with their grandchildren. "Active" grandparents were those who exchanged services and/or had some parentlike influence in their grandchildren's lives. Cherlin and Furstenberg (1985) further categorized active grandparents as "supportive" (those scoring high only on exchange), "authoritative" (those scoring high only on authority), or "influential" (those scoring high in both areas). Using this typology, they found that 26 percent of the grandparents in their sample were detached, 29 percent were passive, 17 percent were supportive, 9 percent were authoritative, and 19 percent were influential. According to this typology, more than 70 percent of grandparents do not assume parentlike roles with their grandchildren. Thus, even though most grandparents have involvement with their grandchildren, the majority seem to adhere to the norm of noninterference.

In their study, Cherlin and Furstenberg (1985) also examined other differences across grandparenting styles. They found that detached and passive grandparents were much older than supportive and authoritative grandparents and that influential grandparents tended to be the youngest. They interpret this finding as evidence that grandparental activity levels are determined in part by the aging process. They also found that detached grandparents had less contact with and lived farther away from their grandchildren than other grandparents. They suggest that because 63 percent of detached grandparents lived more than 100 miles from their grandchildren, geographic limitations may impede such grandparents from adopting more active roles. Cherlin and Furstenberg also found that about half of the passive, supportive, and authoritative grandparents saw their grandchildren at least once a week. Therefore, the degree of contact between grandparents and grandchildren was not necessarily indicative of whether grandparents had a passive or moderately active style of grandparenting. In contrast, influential grandparents lived very close to their grandchildren and had a very high degree of contact. In regard to this finding, Cherlin and Furstenberg note that near daily contact seems to be essential to a grandparent's maintaining an influential grandparenting style.

Although family rituals, such as special family recipes and dishes, jokes, common expressions, songs, and sharing special events, were common among all grandparents, detached grandparents were the least likely to acknowledge such rituals (Bengtson 2001; Cherlin and Furstenberg 1985). They were also

the least likely to report that they had close or extremely close relationships with their grandchildren.

Styles of grandparenting are related to other factors as well, including gender, lineage (paternal or maternal relation), ages of grandparents and grandchildren and their relative ages, family structure, and race. (For a recent review of this literature, see Aldous 1995.) Studies have shown that grandmothers generally have closer relationships with their grandchildren than do grandfathers (Cherlin and Furstenberg 1986). Grandmothers also interact differently with grandchildren than do grandfathers; they are more likely to interact as caregivers, whereas grandfathers are more likely to interact as mentors (Eisenberg 1988).

Divorce and premarital fertility in the parental generation also affect grandparenting styles. Grandparents are more likely to assist the middle generation when daughters are single mothers (Aldous 1985; Eggebeen and Hogan 1990). In addition, when parents divorce, the mother usually retains custody and her parents tend to have greater access to the grandchild. Aldous (1995) suggests that one of the consequences of these customary custody arrangements is that grandparents are generally less important in the lives of their descendants in the male line. This may be particularly salient for black families, because single-mother families are more prevalent among blacks.

Yet even apart from single parenting, the intergenerational linkages between mothers and adult daughters tend to be somewhat stronger than those between mothers and sons (Silverstein and Bengtson 1997). This predisposes grandchildren to have more contact with maternal grandparents. Feelings of closeness are also stronger between adult children and mothers (Bengtson 2001; Silverstein and Bengtson 1997), further increasing the likelihood that grandmothers more than grandfathers will be influential in the lives of their grandchildren.

The ages of the grandparents and grandchildren also affect grandparenting styles. Younger grandparents are more likely to be involved with their grandchildren (Troll 1983), yet grandparents who are too young may not be prepared for the role of grandparent and may feel overburdened by the prospect of having to raise both their own children and their children's children (Burton and Bengtson 1985; Troll 1985). Older grandparents are more often detached or passive in their grandparenting styles. Research suggests that older grandparents often lack the energy to interact with their grandchildren (Burton and Dilworth-Anderson 1991). Grandchildren's ages also matter; grandparents tend to be more highly involved with young grandchildren and less involved with adolescent grandchildren (Troll 1983). In addition, whereas grandparents feel responsible for disciplining and advising younger grandchildren, they feel responsible for sharing wisdom with older grandchildren (Thomas 1989).

Research in the area of grandparent roles and grandparent–grandchild relationships has also focused on how historical and experimental events shape the way the grandparent role is enacted (Cherlin and Furstenberg 1986; Hagestad 1985). Children who grew up in cohesive families with affectionate parents exhibit stronger feelings of obligation as mature adults when they are

enacting the grandparent role (Rossi and Rossi 1990). Childhood experiences with grandparents also influence how grandparents interact with their own grandchildren (King and Elder 1997). Also, relations between grandchildren and grandparents depend on current relations between grandchildren and their parents and, more important, on relations between their parents and grandparents (King and Elder 1995).

A few researchers have also investigated cultural differences in grandparenting styles. Young black adults tend to believe that grandparents should have a parental role in rearing grandchildren and that the boundary between parent and grandparent roles is malleable. In contrast, young white adults hold attitudes consistent with the norm of noninterference—grandparents should maintain contact, but leave the role of parenting to the parent (Kennedy 1990). Cherlin and Furstenberg (1985) report similar black–white differences with regard to the norm of noninterference. Sotomayor (1989) found that Mexican American grandparents believe they have an important function in helping to rear their grandchildren. Asian American families are more likely to reject the norm of noninterference; Kamo (1998) suggests that this may be explained in part by Confucian ethics, under which children belong to the entire extended family.

Grandparents and Single Parenting

The involvement of grandparents in the lives of their daughters (and sons) who become single parents is receiving increased attention with court cases over grandparents' visitation rights and welfare reform measures that highlight the responsibilities of (grand)parents whose teenage daughters become mothers. The 2000 Census even included a new set of questions, mandated as part of welfare reform, on grandparents' support of grandchildren to address this important issue.

Research suggests that grandparents increase the assistance they provide to their adult children after their children experience divorce (Hirshorn 1998). As in the case of the Gibsons in the *USA Today* article cited earlier, grandparents also frequently coparent or raise their grandchildren who are born into single-parent families. In these cases grandparents may provide child care, act as coparents or as surrogate parents, and help out with expenses.

Table 1 illustrates the importance of grandparents in mother–child families. In 1998, about 17 percent of unmarried mothers with children lived in the homes of their parents. These single mothers are likely to benefit from sharing residences with their parents; grandparents can help out by providing food and shelter, caring for their grandchildren, and providing parenting advice. The table also shows that the proportion of single mothers living with their parents is the highest for Hispanics (22 percent), followed by blacks (18 percent) and whites (15 percent). These findings provide further evidence that "distant grandparenting" and the norm of noninterference may be more prevalent among whites, perhaps in part because the higher economic status of white single-parent families, on average, means they less often require

TABLE 1   Coresidence with Parents and Receipt of Child Care in Single-Mother Families by Race (in percentages)

	Total	White	Black	Hispanic
Single mothers living with their parents	16.7	14.5	17.5	21.7
Preschoolers with grandparents as primary child-care providers[a]				
All preschoolers of employed mothers	16.3	14.1	22.1	22.4
With married mothers	13.5	12.1	18.0	19.5
With unmarried mothers	25.4	24.8	25.1	29.2

Source: Data on single mothers living with parents are from the Current Population Survey, March supplement, 1998; data on preschoolers are from the Survey of Income and Program Participation, 1994.

Note: Race-ethnicity categories are white, non-Hispanic; black, non-Hispanic, and Hispanic.

[a]Care provided while the mother was at work.

direct (grand)parental assistance. Grandparents also coreside with and provide support to sons who are single fathers. Data . . . indicate that about 1 out of 10 single fathers lived with his children's grandparent(s) in 1998. Hagestad (1996) has used the expression "Family National Guard" to describe the ways in which elders, especially grandparents, provide assistance when necessary, and the living arrangement data are consistent with this notion of grandparents as a reserve to be called upon during times of need.

Living arrangements data such as those shown in Table 1 provide only a snapshot of grandparental assistance to single mothers and underestimate the proportion of single mothers who ever receive assistance from their parents during their years of single parenting. A much higher 36 percent of single mothers live at some point in their parents' homes (Bumpass and Raley 1995, table 3). Coresidence with a parent is especially prevalent among black single mothers, 57 percent of whom have lived in their mothers' (and/or fathers') homes while raising children without their children's father present. Grandparent coresidence is especially likely in cases where there is a birth before marriage: 60 percent of white and 72 percent of black single mothers who had a child before marrying resided at some point with their parent(s).

Data from the Survey of Income and Program Participation give us an idea of another type of help grandparents provide to single parents: child care. In 1994, one-fourth of preschoolers with unmarried mothers had grandparents as primary child-care providers while their mothers worked, compared with only 14 percent of children with married mothers (see Table 1). Slightly more Hispanic preschoolers with unmarried mothers had grandparents as their primary care providers than did their black and white counterparts (29 percent, 25 percent, and 25 percent, respectively). Data also suggest that grandparents are more likely to provide primary care for their grandchildren when their children are never married than when they are divorced or separated (Casper 1997, table 2). Thus, as single parenthood shifts toward

women who have never married, grandparents may be providing financial and child-care assistance for increasing numbers of single mothers and their children (Ghosh, Easterlin, and Macunovich 1993).

Grandparent interaction with grandchildren in single-parent families blurs the boundaries of the traditional roles of parenthood and grandparenthood. To the extent that grandparent involvement substitutes for the nonresident parent's involvement or compensates for time and resources the single parent cannot give to children, single parents may experience different "degrees" of raising children alone and grandparents may experience different degrees of parenting and grandparenting.

Multigenerational Families with Grandparents

In the 1990s, amid the passage of the new welfare legislation and continued discussion of the decline of the family, grandparenting research shifted toward the examination of different kinds of households containing grandparents and grandchildren (Szinovacz 1998). The three types of grandparent–grandchild families depicted in the *USA Today* articles noted earlier provide a real-life example of the diversity of these families. The main structural difference among these families is that Mrs. Stewart and the Gibsons took their grandchildren into their homes and had primary responsibility for parenting them, whereas the Torkelsons moved in with their adult children and were supplemental caregivers for their grandchildren. These two household structures, with homes maintained by either the grandparents or the parents, imply different caregiving scenarios in which the roles of the grandparents vary enormously.

Researchers, public policy makers, and the media first began to notice the increases in grandparent-maintained households around 1990, prompting them to question why this was happening. An explosion of analytic research occurred in the early to mid-1990s that sought to answer this question and to examine further the area of grandparent caregiving in general. These studies identified several explanations for the increase in the numbers of grandparents raising and helping to raise their grandchildren. Increasing drug abuse among parents, teen pregnancy, divorce, the rapid rise of single-parent households, mental and physical illnesses of parents, AIDS, crime, child abuse and neglect, and incarceration are a few of the most common explanations offered (for a review of these causes, see Minkler 1998).

CPS data for the 1990s confirm the researchers' impressions, showing that more grandparents were taking their children and grandchildren into their homes. In 1990, there were 2.1 million grandparent-maintained households in the United States, constituting 6.3 percent of all family households. By 1998, this number had increased to 2.6 million, representing 7.4 percent of all family households. The number of children residing with grandparents increased as well. Figure 1 shows that in 1970, 2.2 million or 3.2 percent of American children lived in households maintained by grandparents. By 1998, this number had risen to 4 million, or 5.6 percent. Thus the number of children living in their grandparents' homes increased by more than

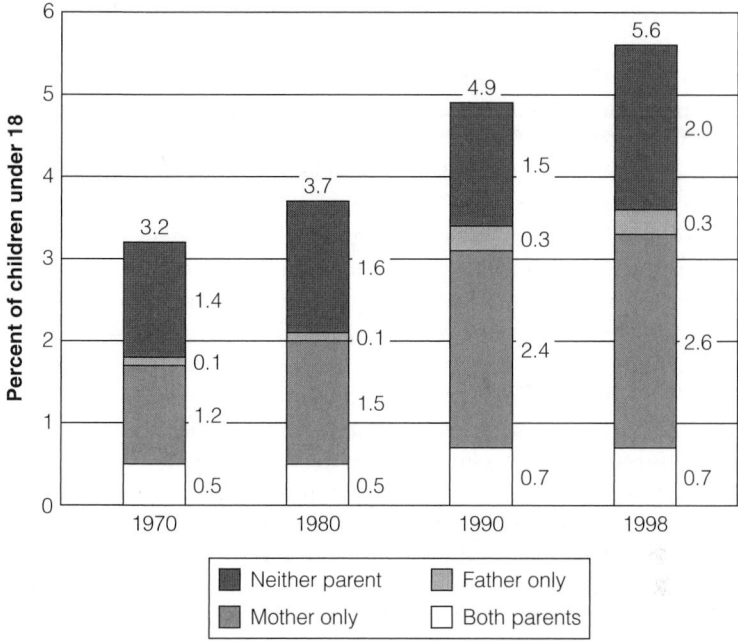

FIGURE 1   Grandchildren in Grandparents' Homes by Presence of Parents
Source: U.S. Census, 1970, 1980; Current Population Survey, March Supplements, 1990, 1998.

80 percent over the 28-year period. Substantial increases occurred among all types of households maintained by grandparents, regardless of the presence or absence of the grandchildren's parents, but increases were greatest among children with only one parent in the household. The majority of change for most household types occurred in the decade of the 1980s. Although the proportion of children living *only* with their grandparents (i.e., no parent present) did not increase in the 1970s and 1980s, the greatest growth in the 1990s was registered in these skipped-generation living arrangements. This means that the 1990s was a decade marked by increasing numbers of grandparents with sole responsibility for raising their grandchildren.

Given the increase in this type of family, it is not surprising that the popular media began to focus attention on the growing number of children being raised by their grandparents (e.g., Culter 1991; Norris 1991). It wasn't long before federal lawmakers followed suit—both the Senate and the House of Representatives recognized that this trend constituted a pressing issue for public policy and held congressional hearings on the matter in 1992. The Senate hearings of the Special Committee on Aging focused on the causes of the trend (U.S. Senate 1992), whereas the House hearings, held by the Select Committee on Aging, examined the new roles and responsibilities of grandparents (U.S. House of Representatives 1992). Both sets of hearings also highlighted policy deficiencies in the areas of grandparents' rights and grandparents' access to public assistance. In January 1995, then-President Clinton signed a formal proclamation declaring 1995 the "Year of

the Grandparent," recognizing the "extraordinary place that grandparents hold in our families and communities."

The recent increase in numbers of grandparents raising their grandchildren is particularly troubling because both these grandparents and their grandchildren often suffer significant health problems. Researchers have documented high rates of asthma, weakened immune systems, poor eating and sleeping patterns, physical disabilities, and hyperactivity among grandchildren being raised by their grandparents (Dowdell 1995; Minkler and Roe 1996; Shore and Hayslip 1994). Grandparents raising grandchildren also appear to be in poorer health than their counterparts; studies have noted high rates of depression, poor self-rated health, and multiple chronic health problems among grandparents raising their grandchildren (Dowdell 1995; Minkler and Roe 1993). For example, Minkler et al. (1997) found that grandparents raising grandchildren were twice as likely to be clinically depressed as were grandparents who play more traditional roles.

These families are also more likely than other kinds of families to experience economic hardship. A number of studies have focused on the economic well-being of grandparents and their grandchildren, documenting their disproportionately high poverty rates (Bryson and Casper 1999; Casper and Bryson 1998; Chalfie 1994; Fuller-Thomson, Minkler, and Driver 1997; Rutrough and Ofstedal 1997).

At the other end of the spectrum are growing concerns for the well-being of adults who are taking their aging mothers and fathers into their homes and providing care for them, often at the same time they are raising children of their own. Demographic shifts—the extension of the life span, aging of the population, fewer children per family, increasing divorce and remarriage, and the delay in childbearing—have contributed to the sense of urgency in this matter. In this type of household, the flow of resources is usually from the parent to the grandparent. Grandparents in this situation may be more limited in the roles they can play in their grandchildren's lives. They are likely to be older and to have older grandchildren than grandparents who provide homes for their grandchildren. They are also more likely to have health problems (Bryson and Casper 1999).

Despite the trend toward independent living among older Americans, research has shown that many families who have older kin in frail health provide extraordinary care (Horowitz 1985; Stone, Cafferata, and Sangl 1987). Providing intensive care can have many negative consequences for caregivers, including increased stress and strained relationships (Semple 1992; Stommel et al. 1995). The level of stress in these households is also likely to affect how grandparents and grandchildren experience their relationships.

REFERENCES

Aldous, Joan. 1985. "Parent–Adult Child Relations as Affected by the Grandparents' Status." Pp. 117–32 in *Grandparenthood*, edited by Vern L. Bengtson and Joan F. Robertson. Beverly Hills, CA: Sage.

———. 1995. "New Views of Grandparents in Intergenerational Context." *Journal of Family Issues* 16:104–22.

Bengtson, Vern L. 2001. "Beyond the Nuclear Family: The Increasing Importance of Multigenerational Bonds." *Journal of Marriage and the Family* 63:1–16.

Bengtson, Vern L. and Sandi S. Schrader. 1982. "Parent–Child Relations." Pp. 115–86 in *Research Instruments in Social Gerontology*, vol. 2, *Social Roles and Social Participation*, edited by David J. Mangen and Warren A. Peterson. Minneapolis: University of Minnesota Press.

Bryson, Ken and Lynne M. Casper. 1999. *Co-resident Grandparents and Their Grandchildren.* Current Population Reports, Series P-23, No. 198. Washington, DC: Government Printing Office.

Bumpass, Larry L. and R. Kelly Raley. 1995. "Redefining Single-Parent Families: Cohabitation and Changing Family Reality." *Demography* 32:97–109.

Burton, Linda M. and Peggy Dilworth-Anderson. 1991. "The Intergenerational Family Roles of Aged Black Americans." *Marriage and Family Review* 16:311–30.

Casper, Lynne. 1997. *Who's Minding Our Preschoolers? Fall 1994 (Update).* Current Population Reports, Series P-70, No. 62. Washington, DC: Government Printing Office.

Casper, Lynne M. and Ken Bryson. 1998. "Co-resident Grandparents and Their Grandchildren: Grandparent-Maintained Families." Working Paper No. 26, Population Division, U.S. Bureau of the Census, Washington, DC.

Chalfie, Deborah. 1994. *Going It Alone: A Closer Look at Grandparents Rearing Grandchildren.* Washington, DC: American Association of Retired Persons.

Cherlin, Andrew J. and Frank F. Furstenberg, Jr. 1985. "Styles and Strategies of Grandparenting." Pp. 97–116 in *Grandparenthood,* edited by Vern L. Bengtson and Joan F. Robertson. Beverly Hills, CA: Sage.

———. 1986. *The New American Grandparent: A Place in the Family, a Life Apart.* New York: Basic Books.

Culter, Lawrence. 1991. "More and More, Grandparents Raise Grandchildren." *New York Times,* April 7, p. C12.

Dowdell, Elizabeth B. 1995. "Caregiver Burden: Grandparents Raising Their High-Risk Children." *Journal of Psychosocial Nursing* 33 (3): 27–30.

Eggebeen, David J. and Dennis P. Hogan. 1990. "Giving between Generations in American Families." *Human Nature* 1:211–32.

Eisenberg, Anne R. 1988. "Grandchildren's Perspectives on Relationships with Grandparents: The Influence of Gender across Generations." *Sex Roles* 19:205–17.

El Nasser, Haya. 1999. "Raising Grandkids: No Day at the Beach." *USA Today,* July 1, p. A1.

Fuller-Thomson, Esme, Meredith Minkler, and Diane Driver. 1997. "A Profile of Grandparents Raising Grandchildren in the United States." *Gerontologist* 37:406–11.

Ghosh, Susmita, Richard A. Easterlin, and Diane J. Macunovich. 1993. "How Badly Have Single Parents Done? Trends in the Economic Status of Single Parents since 1964." Presented at the annual meeting of the Population Association of America, March, Cincinnati.

Hagestad, Gunhild O. 1985. "Continuity and Connectedness." Pp. 31–48 in *Grandparenthood,* edited by Vern L. Bengtson and Joan F. Robertson. Beverly Hills, CA: Sage.

———. 1996. "On-Time, Off-Time, Out of Time? Reflections of Continuity and Discontinuity from an Illness Process." Pp. 204–22 in *Adulthood and Aging: Research on Continuities and Discontinuities,* edited by Vern L. Bengtson. New York: Springer.

Hirshorn, Barbara A. 1998. "Grandparents as Caregivers." Pp. 200–14 in *Handbook on Grandparenthood,* edited by Maximiliane E. Szinovacz. Westport, CT: Greenwood.

Horowitz, Amy. 1985. "Family Caregiving to the Frail Elderly." Pp. 194–246 in *Annual Review of Gerontology and Geriatrics,* vol. 5, edited by Carl Eisdorfer. New York: Springer.

Kamo, Yoshinori. 1998. "Asian Grandparents." Pp. 97–112 in *Handbook on Grandparenthood,* edited by Maximiliane E. Szinovacz. Westport, CT: Greenwood.

Kasindorf, Martin. 1999. "Three Generations, One Happy Family." *USA Today,* July 1, p. D8.

Kennedy, Gregory E. 1990. "College Students' Expectations of Grandparent and Grandchild Role Behaviors." *Gerontologist* 30:43–48.

King, Valerie and Glen H. Elder, Jr. 1995. "American Children View Their Grandparents: Linked Lives across Three Rural Generations." *Journal of Marriage and the Family* 57:165–78.

———. 1997. "The Legacy of Grandparenting: Childhood Experiences with Grandparents and Current Involvement with Grandchildren." *Journal of Marriage and the Family* 59:848–59.

King, Valerie, Steven T. Russell, and Glen H. Elder, Jr. 1998. "Grandparenting in Family Systems: An Ecological Perspective." Pp. 53–69 in *Handbook on Grandparenthood,* edited by Maximiliane E. Szinovacz. Westport, CT: Greenwood.

Mangen, David J., Vern L. Bengtson, and Pierre H. Landry. 1988. *Measurement of Intergenerational Relations.* Newbury Park, CA: Sage.

Minkler, Meredith. 1998. "Intergenerational Households Headed by Grandparents: Demographic and Sociological Contexts." Pp. 3–18 in *Grandparents and Other Relatives Raising Children: Background Papers from Generations United's Expert Symposium,* edited by Generations United. Washington, DC: Generations United.

Minkler, Meredith, and Esme Fuller-Thomson, Doriane Miller, and Diane Driver. 1997. "Depression in Grandparents Raising Grandchildren: Results of a National Longitudinal Study." *Archives of Family Medicine* 6:445–52.

Minkler, Meredith and Kathleen M. Roe. 1993. *Grandmothers as Caregivers: Raising Children of the Crack Cocaine Epidemic.* Newbury Park, CA: Sage.

———. 1996. "Grandparents as Surrogate Parents." *Generations* 20:34–38.

Morgan, S. Philip. 1996. "Characteristic Features of Modern American Fertility." Pp. 19–66 in *Fertility in the United States: New Patterns, New Theories,* edited by J. B. Casterline, Ronald D. Lee, and Karen A. Foote. New York: Population Council.

Neugarten, Bernice L. and Karol K. Weinstein. 1964. "The Changing American Grandparent." *Journal of Marriage and the Family* 26:199–204.

Norris, Michele. 1991. "Grandmothers Who Fill Void Carved by Drugs." *Washington Post,* August 30, p. C12.

Rossi, Alice S. and Peter H. Rossi. 1990. *Of Human Bonding: Parent–Child Relations across the Life Course.* New York: Aldine de Gruyter.

Rutrough, Thyne S. and Mary Beth Ofstedal. 1997. "Grandparents Living with Grandchildren: A Metropolitan–Nonmetropolitan Comparison." Presented at the annual meeting of the Population Associate of America, March.

Semple, Shirley J. 1992. "Conflict in Alzheimer's Caregiving Families: Its Dimensions and Consequences." *Gerontologist* 32:648–55.

Sharp, Deborah. 1999. "After a Lifetime of Work, a Second Family to Raise." *USA Today,* July 1, p. D8.

Shore, Ron J. and Bert Hayslip, Jr. 1994. "Custodial Grandparenting: Implications for Children's Development." Pp. 171–218 in *Redefining Families: Implications for Children's Development,* edited by Adele Eskeles Gottfried and Allen W. Gottfried. New York: Plenum.

Silverstein, Merril and Vern L. Bengtson. 1997. "Intergenerational Solidarity and the Structure of Adult Child–Parent Relationships in American Families." *American Journal of Sociology* 103:429–60.

Silverstein, Merril, Roseann Giarrusso, and Vern L. Bengston. 1998. "Intergenerational Solidarity and the Grandparent Role." Pp. 144–58 in *Handbook on Grandparenthood,* edited by Maximiliane E. Szinovacz. Westport, CT: Greenwood.

Sotomayor, M. 1989. "The Hispanic Elderly and the Intergenerational Family." *Journal of Children in Contemporary Society* 20:55–65.

Stommel, Manfred, Barbara A. Given, Charles W. Given, and Clare Collins. 1995. "The Impact of the Frequency of Care Activities on the Division of Labor between Primary Caregivers and Other Care Providers." *Research on Aging* 17:412–33.

Stone, Robyn, Gail Lee Cafferata, and Judith Sangl. 1987. "Caregivers of the Frail Elderly: A National Profile." *Gerontologist* 27:616–26.

Szinovacz, Maximiliane E. 1998. "Grandparent Research: Past, Present, and Future." Pp. 1–22 in *Handbook on Grandparenthood,* edited by Maximiliane E. Szinovacz. Westport, CT: Greenwood.

Thomas, Jeanne L. 1989. "Gender and Perceptions of Grandparenthood." *International Journal of Aging and Human Development* 29:269–82.

Troll, Lillian E. 1983. "Grandparents: The Family Watchdogs." Pp. 63–74 in *Family Relationships in Later Life,* edited by Timothy H. Brubaker. New York: Free Press.

———. 1985. "The Contingencies of Grandparenting." Pp. 135–49 in *Grandparenthood,* edited by Vern L. Bengtson and Joan F. Robertson. Beverly Hills, CA: Sage.

Uhlenberg, Peter. 1996. "Mortality Decline in the Twentieth Century and Supply of Kin over the Lifecourse." *Gerontologist* 36:681–85.

Uhlenberg, Peter and James B. Kirby. 1998. "Grandparenthood over Time: Historical and Demographic Trends." Pp. 23–39 in *Handbook on Grandparenthood,* edited by Maximiliane E. Szinovacz. Westport, CT: Greenwood.

U.S. House of Representatives. 1992. *Grandparents: New Roles and Responsibilities.* Select Committee on Aging Publication No. 102-876. Washington, DC: Government Printing Office.

U.S. Senate. 1992. *Grandparents as Parents: Raising a Second Generation.* Special Committee on Aging Serial No. 102-24. Washington, DC: Government Printing Office.

Watson, Jeffrey A. and Sally A. Koblinsky. 1997. "Strengths and Needs of Working-Class African-American and Anglo-American Grandparents." *International Journal of Aging and Human Development* 44:149–65.

34
_____

THE STRENGTHS OF APACHE GRANDMOTHERS
Observations on Commitment, Culture, and Caretaking

KATHLEEN S. BAHR

"**M**y great grandmother is a special person to me because she did a good job of raising my mother. I am happy for what she has done and for what she is still doing for us." So begins a tribute written by Garrett Dazen, a fifth grader, published in the *Fort Apache Scout,* June 1, 1990. To persons unacquainted with Apachean families (including several Apache populations as well as the Navajo), this tribute may hint of possible failure in the family system: What happened that made it necessary for the great grandmother to raise the mother? In fact, rather than signaling family failure, the statement is testimony to one of the great strengths of Apache families, a traditional pattern of responsibility and care that continues to serve families and protect children.

This [reading] compares two normative models of grandparenting, one common in Anglo American culture and the other an Apache pattern. The introduction of these contrasting models is followed by a description of contemporary Apache grandmothering and its social context, as enacted by White Mountain Apache grandmothers living on the Fort Apache Indian Reservation. Finally, there is a systematic comparison of selected themes and issues in both ethnic contexts, and of the meanings and consequences of grandparenting for community and family life.

Ethnicity and "Normal" Family Development

Wilson (1984a), commenting on social scientific studies of black families, observed that there had been much more attention paid to their pathologies and disorganization than to their remarkable strength and resilience. So it also is with studies of Indian families. People who know very little else about Indian Americans share stereotypes about the poverty, violence, and alcoholism that characterize their families. Yet Anglo Americans are generally unaware of the tenacity of Indian family values and the maintenance

Kathleen S. Bahr, "The Strengths of Apache Grandmothers: Observations on Commitment, Culture and Caretaking" from *Journal of Comparative Female Studies* 25, No. 2 (Summer 1994). Copyright © 1994 by Kathleen S. Bahr. Reprinted with permission.

of strong kinship ties and family identity among them in the face of almost insurmountable odds.

In family matters, as in other patterns of behavior, it has been assumed by white Americans that their own cultural norms for acceptable behavior are the "right" ones, normal and morally superior to other patterns. Thus, in scholarship as well as popular stereotypes, Anglo American family patterns have been held up as optimal standards. To the degree that the families of ethnic minorities have differed, they have been defined as deficient, disorganized, or immoral (Wilson 1984b:1333). "Help" in better adjusting and conforming to majority standards, often unsought, has been offered or imposed on Indian peoples by teachers, counselors, missionaries, social workers, politicians, and other professionals.

One of the purposes of this [reading] is to call into question the superiority of the standard "white" family pattern as it applies to grandparenting. Another is to document the continuing commitment of many Apachean grandmothers as bearers of the cultural heritage and of ultimate responsibility for the physical well-being of their families. Defined by her culture and often by circumstance as "caretaker of last resort," she devotes extraordinary effort and personal sacrifice to performing the grandmother role.

Models of Grandparenting: Anglos and Apacheans

Family scientists sometimes talk of "the" family life cycle, or "developmental stages," as if such cycles and stages were part of humanity's genetic heritage rather than social constructions. In practice, there are many ethnic and individual variations in such stages and cycles. With respect to grandparenting, many of the standard models of family life in America assume a configuration where grandparents are acknowledged as kin, but play a peripheral role in the lives of the families of their children and grandchildren. In the usual "family life cycle" model, with "stages" often presented as universals without significant ethnic qualification, American older couples "launch" their children and move into an "empty nest" stage. This is described as a stage when parents should be able to consider their parenting tasks "done," and now are free to pursue their own interests in ways heretofore impossible because of child-rearing responsibilities.

In reality, many parents do not "launch" their adult children and many are directly involved in the care of grandchildren (according to the U.S. Census Bureau, 24 percent of unmarried adults aged 25 to 39 were living in the parental household, and about 5 percent of American grandchildren live in a grandparent-headed household [1991b:9, 11]). However, these variations do little to weaken the strength of the norm. In fact, to vary from this norm is sometimes labeled as being "out of phase," that is, not finished with parenting at ages when most people are said to be enjoying the "freedom" associated with an "empty nest."

Being thus out of phase is reported to be associated with perceptions of high personal stress and unhappiness. The stresses are assumed to be severe

if adult children and grandchildren return to live in the grandparental home. Such grandparents are said to be "developmentally disadvantaged":

> In the home with adult children, the parents' development may also suffer. As individuals, these parents are often prevented from experiencing the freedom necessary to develop further interests without the burdens of children at home. (Clemens and Axelson 1985:262)

The family structure of this three-generation household is described as "inappropriate or off-balance." It is said that "most parents do not welcome the return of these children and view their stay as a short-term arrangement," and that "older adult children and those whose sojourn [in the parental household] becomes long-term appear to both cause and experience more stress" (p. 263). In the same vein, Hagestad and Burton (1986) argue that

> the entry into grandparenthood has become a normal, expectable part of middle age, *a time when daily involvement in the demands of parenthood have ceased.* When the transition does not come in the expected life context, it may disrupt resolution of developmental tasks and hamper involvement in other roles. [Emphasis added] (P. 471)

Beyond the expectation that they will be "freed from the commitments of the child-rearing years," "the normal expectable life" of the modern Anglo grandparent also includes the assumption that they "have attained a certain level of economic security, and at a time when they are still healthy and vigorous" (Hagestad and Burton 1986:473). The combination of health and a degree of economic security means that many continue to maintain a social and economic life independent of children and grandchildren. Consider Cowgill's (1986) depiction of "Western" grandparenting:

> In Western society, despite the fact that grandparents have generally been relieved of any authoritative responsibility for the discipline and upbringing of grandchildren, the relationship is usually rather formal and distant. Grandparents are interested in and take pride in the accomplishments of grandchildren, but they are not usually intimate with them, and there is relatively little affect in the relationship. But in this case, the distance results not from any interference based on authority but from physical separation and conflicting social involvement. . . . Thus both grandparents and grandchildren tend to be preoccupied with interests and activities with their age peers, and all of this tends to minimize contacts, reduce interaction, and attenuate the relationship. (P. 92)

In contrast to this normative Anglo American pattern[1] is an American Indian standard that defines the grandparent as very important in the socialization and care of children. Rather than being without responsibility or right to intervene in the rearing of the new generation, grandparents are both authorized and expected to play a major role. Among the Sioux, a new child is called "little grandmother" or "little grandfather" to help impress on her the important role of the grandparent. This custom also encourages respect for the very young and is a reminder that the grandparent generation

is the model, "that you are going to grow up to be a grandparent some day and, as such, you must remember to keep these things in mind. And mutual respect and affection develop because this is a known role for the future as well as the kind one can play at when one is a child. It is a very important thing" (Attneave 1981:47).

The expectation that grandparents will play a major role in the physical care and training of their grandchildren is common among most Indian peoples. In fact, it is one of the notable similarities among the wide diversity of tribes (Ryan 1981).

Many ethnographic reports emphasize the key role Apachean grandparents have played in the rearing of their grandchildren. Shomaker (1989) notes that among the Navajo the grandparent often adopted the grandchild, and the alliance between the grandparent and grandchild was considered

> the strongest bond in Navajo culture; this was a warm association in which perpetuation of traditional teaching could be effected. The fostered child became known to others as *child of the grandparent,* changing in status from that of the biological grandchild. The biological mother withdrew from her role as parent to a more distant relationship, similar to that of an older sister. The grandchild lived with the grandparents until adulthood. [Emphasis added] (P. 3)

Historically, the Apaches were hunters, gatherers, and farmers, and Apache women played a major role in providing for their families (Stockel 1991). Their involvement as providers began when they were young girls and continued into old age for as long as they were physically able. Young Apache mothers, perhaps accompanied by an older daughter, roamed long distances to gather food and fuel. Grandmothers, less physically able, stayed close to home and cared for the children. "Older women supervised, answered questions, trained the girls, and taught them to identify various plants and how to shell, husk, and strip wild foods to obtain the edible parts" (Stockel 1991:14).

Goodwin (1942), a close observer of the Western Apache in the 1930s, described the relationship between grandmothers and grandchildren this way:

> Grandparents love to watch their grandchildren at play. It is common for a grandmother to give a small child the run of her wickiup, the child passing and repassing in front of her with a most annoying frequency, stepping over her, lolling against her, pulling at her dress, all of which she accepts with a calm inattention truly remarkable. If the child is too much in the way, the grandparent may turn about in feigned anger and dismiss it with a sharp word. The child usually obeys. Occasionally, a child will defy a grandparent. *The parents do not interfere but leave the matter to the grandparent entirely.* If the encounter ends in the child's crying, it cannot run to the parents for sympathy. *The child's attitude toward its grandparents is not duplicated with* any other relative. The grandparent's good-naturedness and willingness to do things are taken for granted, and I have never heard a maternal grandparent mentioned with any

dislike or fear. They are usually spoken of with a feeling of affection, intimacy, and respect. [Emphasis added] (P. 218)

Goodwin (1942) also writes of "a decided lack of restraint" among grown grandchildren in asking for help from grandparents. "Where a young man hesitates to use another relative's dwelling, he makes himself entirely at home with his maternal grandparents, using their belongings, lying on their beds, asking for food and money" (p. 219). To some degree, the generosity of grandparents was reciprocated by the grandchildren. At the very least, they were expected to respect the grandparents. Among the Navajo at the turn of the century, "Grandchildren served as eyes, ears, hands, and feet for their frail elderly grandparents" (Shomaker 1989:2). Adult daughters assumed the primary responsibility for the care of their elderly parents, but they were often assisted in this effort by young grandsons and granddaughters.

In a 1989 interview, an Apache medicine man told me about his relationship with his grandmother in these words:

Grandmother and I took care of each other, in her wickiup. When I was little, grandmother and I went on a donkey to get wood. My mother was with my dad, but I was with grandmother. My mother sent my sister and I to sleep with my grandmother. They [your parents] always want you to respect the older people. You never walk over them and you never talk back to them. You always listen and then they cook for you and you learn a lot of things from them.

When the Apaches lived off the land, this system of cross-generational reciprocity ensured that family members shared the necessities of life and also knowledge about life. A changing tribal economy in a changing regional and national economic system, including the modern trend toward a cash economy, has complicated but not eliminated the traditional system of reciprocal amity and responsibility.

Apache Grandmothering Today:Patterns and Contexts

As part of an exploratory study of grandparenting and family change among Navajo and Apache grandmothers, beginning in 1989 and continuing through 1991, I conducted loosely structured, in-depth interviews with 13 grandmothers, four adult daughters, a medicine man, and an Anglo elementary school teacher, all residents of the Fort Apache reservation in Arizona.[2] Potential respondents were chosen by a "snowball sampling" technique. They were members of a network that included a long-term friend and former student of mine who had been raised on the reservation.

Early in each interview, I questioned the grandmother about her children and grandchildren and sketched a genogram (Bahr 1990) of her extended family. The genogram then served as a systematic guide or "map" to her family, helping me to keep relationships straight and ask appropriate questions as the interview proceeded.

The interview data have been supplemented by published research on Apachean peoples and occasional references in the tribal newspaper to

problems of parenting and grandparenting in the White Mountain Apache community. The following descriptions of contemporary Apache summarize and illustrate behaviors that I observed or that were reported by my informants or other cited sources. It is not maintained that they are statistically representative of all Apache grandmothers.

The project's initial focus was on the place of grandmothers in transmitting traditional values and teaching family work skills, that is, on grandmothers as the custodians of culture. However, I was quickly impressed by the creativity and strength shown by these grandmothers in provisioning their households. They are custodians of the culture, but many of them are also responsible for the sheer physical support of their children and grandchildren. The present discussion emphasizes their responsibilities as providers and nurturers more than their role as custodians of culture.

Role Expectations and Performance

Apache culture values the extended family and exemplifies it in many forms. In these multigenerational settings family members feel, as one respondent put it, that "there is always someone to care for the children." In many instances, the household member who seems to feel the greatest obligation to the children is the grandmother. Therefore, she tends to be the "someone" of last resort.

I was particularly interested by the acceptance of heavy obligations of child care and support by women whose counterparts in Anglo society tend to celebrate their freedom from such responsibilities. Although it is not clear precisely what percentage of Apache grandmothers assume such obligations, the pattern is well-known and quite visible in the community. Rough estimates of its frequency may be made from results of the 1990 U.S. Census. Because the Census reports list heads of household by age but not grandparent status, we cannot tell how many grandparents are caring for grandchildren. However, there are published figures for total numbers of grandchildren living in grandparent-headed households. In 1990 an Apache child was at least 3.5 times more likely to be living in the home of a grandparent than was her Anglo American counterpart.[3] Judging from what I saw and was told, the number of grandchildren living with grandparents varies considerably from day to day and week to week. Nevertheless, it is clear this is a fairly common arrangement, affecting at least one-fifth of the children on a continuing basis.[4]

The recognition of the grandmothers' ultimate responsibility is a well-established part of the Apachean culture. There is general recognition and respect in the community for these women who carry on the nurturing and caretaking functions of the "grandmother role" with energy and deep commitment until incapacitated by illness or taken by death. There are many reasons for this pattern. As indicated earlier, it is "traditional" in the sense that historically the grandmother's role was a well-defined, essential part of normal family life. For many Apache families, the need for traditional grandmothering continues and is perhaps heightened by the modern pattern of

women's employment outside the home, which means that many children need supplemental care. High rates of single parenthood and of alcohol abuse put additional children at risk. There are also many grown children, marginally employed or unemployed, who continue to be supported, at least in part, by their parents or grandparents.

Many of the more economically stable members of Apache families live off the reservation, often in another state, insulated from much of the day-to-day pressure to make ends meet. When things get hard for the unemployed on the reservation, it is culturally appropriate to call upon grandparents for aid. Under such circumstances it is fairly common for adult children, with or without partners, to live with their parents, and in many cases the task of caring for and teaching their children falls almost entirely to the grandmothers.

There is also the powerful force of cultural tradition and family example. For some of these women, the memory of having been raised by a grandmother translates into the expectation that they themselves need not be a truly responsible "parent" until they reach the grandmother stage. At that point, however, they recognize that the responsibility to be "parent of last resort" is now theirs.

A related explanation for the willingness to continue nurturing behavior at an age when many women in the wider society have "graduated" to leisure and, at most, sporadic child care is that the grandmothers feel fulfilled by doing it. Caring for children and grandchildren is a source of deep satisfaction for them. In fact, the chief regret expressed by the grandmothers I interviewed was that they couldn't do more for their children and grandchildren. That sense of needing to do more was cited as the most difficult thing about being a grandmother:

> *It's finding the time . . . having the chance to really talk with my teenage grandson and granddaughter. She needs to be advised about different ways of dressing and caring for herself and all these things. It seems that the time is too limited, that you can't sit down and talk without having [all of my grandchildren] pulling at me. . . . There are ways that we can deal with it, like go by yourself and get [that one] individual, but then I always feel guilty [when] the other one says, "Can I go? I want to go with you." Before I know it, I have two or three with me, without getting the chance with that one. . . . You know you are swamped by them, and then my daughter, too, still needs advice, and I need the time to spend with [her], and it is getting so that she is pushed out by these [grand]kids.*

In the past few years of economic recession, Apache grandmothers enacting their traditional roles, serving as caretakers of last resort for adult children and grandchildren, have been especially hard hit. What is remarkable is that their definitions of their problems do not question the role definition that assigns them ultimate responsibility but, rather, focus on changes and other obstacles that make it harder for them to live up to the cultural expectations. A mother of five with 11 grandchildren acknowledged that the challenge of trying to feed her household kept her in a state of continual stress. Like many Apache grandmothers, the size of her household varies. At the time of the interview, two preschool-aged grandchildren, two adult

daughters, and an ex-son-in-law were living with her. Other adult children and grandchildren lived nearby and were frequent visitors. She was proud to have "a real close family." Her only problem was

> *the feeding part of it. It is hard to feed a big family, and it is hard when just one family is not up to feeding the children, and they have to come over here and we feed them. But my grandmother, she only had a bag of beans, flour, salt and baking soda, and a bag of potatoes. But we ate good; it didn't hardly cost her anything. She fed us three times a day. But with these children [who belonged to a daughter who had recently quit work following the birth of another baby] . . . seems like we don't have anything to eat half the time. But in those days, I don't know how my grandmother managed, [but we seemed] to have plenty all of the time.*

Many community members continue to recognize the grandmothers as the last line of responsibility for families in trouble. An elementary school teacher and long-term observer of the community commented,

> *When you hear of a death in the family . . . you pray it's not the grandmother, because they are the only ones there for the children in many families. I would say, in at least 15, maybe 20, percent of the students I have had, they live with their grandmother. Their mother may be around part of the time, but it is the grandmother they go home to, who comes to school to see how they are doing. . . . And they really are the only ones many times that aren't drinking. . . . And they many times are the ones who worry about getting kids their clothes and get-ting them into school and trying to make sure that the kids are there [attending school].*

Children who do not have an able grandmother to supplement and back up the efforts of their other caretakers are disadvantaged.

What happens if the grandmother has passed away? One of the grand-mothers I talked to said that sometimes other relatives don't want to take the responsibility for the children the deceased grandmother was caring for, and then they are taken to a group home sponsored by the tribe. Usu-ally, however, some close relative will assume responsibility. In her own case, this informant recalled, she was fortunate because she had a third "grandmother," a caring older relative in addition to her two grandmothers. "I guess [she] was my mom's aunt," she said:

> *my grandmother's sister, and after my grandmother passed away she kind of took over. . . . She taught us a lot of things. By this time my other sisters were too small to remember my real grandmother. . . . They more or less thought of her as our real grandmother.*

The grandmothers I interviewed were committed to their families and devoted their lives to them. They were models of energy and indus-try. Such characteristics are expected of Apache grandmothers, and it was apparent that there was an accepted standard of grandmother behavior. Everyone seemed to know a grandmother or two who didn't fare too well, and some of the grandmothers I interviewed had things to say about other

grandmothers—and grandchildren—who didn't measure up. For example, grandmothers whose caring behavior consisted merely of "baby-sitting" were seen as deficient, and so were some whose drinking habits made them incapable of caring for their households. Others manifested less commitment than my informants thought appropriate. I did not interview any of these "below-par" grandmothers—they were not identified to me by name—but plainly they were defined as a small and deviant minority.

Many grandmothers that outsiders might define as exploited or dominated by children and grandchildren do not see themselves as "giving in" but, rather, define their actions as the most loving, altruistic responses they know how to give, under the circumstances. They may not define being "used" by their children as exploitation. The caring grandmother is unlikely to assert herself. Rather, she gives in because "she loves her children and grandchildren," and she feels "like they are part of her." Take the grandmother who, when asked what was the most difficult thing about being a grandmother, was interrupted by her grown daughter who insisted, "Let me answer for her: Saying 'No.'" The daughter elaborated,

> Like if one of my sisters comes and says, "I want to go here and I want you to take care of my children," when my Mom would want to do something else, she doesn't know how to say no. So she ends up with the kids. That's the problem.

The grandmother's reply revealed a different ethic: "I don't mind them being there. I raised a lot of my own, so having my grandkids there doesn't make too much difference." She further showed her priorities in answering a question about what was most difficult about being a grandmother: "the worry." She said she worried especially about the grandchildren who did *not* live with her and who, she felt, were not well supervised at home.

Most of these grandmothers impressed me as pragmatic and worldwise. They knew that generosity required wisdom, that gifts should not be given indiscriminately. Also, they recognized that they were personally vulnerable and were sometimes exploited. Some were openly critical of the grown children—generally not their own—who they thought took unfair advantage of parental generosity. One told of seeing a grandmother in a grocery store spending her meager Social Security checks on disposable diapers, and offered her opinion that "Grandmother shouldn't be buying those. Grandmother should buy herself good food that she likes to eat."

It was also suggested that some grandmothers might appear to be overly tolerant or generous because they were trying to make up for past mistakes. In the words of one Apache mother,

> This one grandmother, she's trying to win their love. Try to win their love back. Somewhere she made a mistake, maybe through her drinking in her younger days, maybe the days when she was having a good time.

There was some evidence to support her judgment. While I did not specifically ask, two grandmothers volunteered that they had been fairly heavy drinkers when their children were young, and often had left their children either to care for themselves or in the care of a grandmother. Their

recollections were often poignant: "And the kids would be wondering, 'what happened to my mom?'"

Coping Strategies

Apache grandmothers, despite their limited resources, rarely turn away their own. Grandmothers too old or unskilled to participate in the conventional labor market somehow manage, as "caretakers of last resort," to support themselves and their households. Often they survive by the creative application of traditional skills.

Many are still "gatherers," combing nearby lands for anything that can be sold for cash. "Anything" includes digging for worms to sell to fishermen, retrieving quills from roadkill porcupines to use in making earrings, scavenging the countryside for aluminum cans to sell to recycling centers, and harvesting native plants to sell and to supplement the family diet. They make lunches to sell in town, sew traditional dresses, or do craftwork, making dolls, cradle boards, beadwork, and jewelry. The usual market for these products is local residents more than tourists. Often such products are sold at places of employment on paydays.

A key to the grandmother's very survival is the operation of the informal economy, whereby goods, services, and money are exchanged and transferred. The system does not always work smoothly and predictably, particularly where alcohol is involved. There also seems to be a pattern where men—sons, brothers, husbands—are more willing than daughters or sisters to take advantage of the generosity of the grandmothers. On the other hand, a daughter with an alcohol or drug problem can be as exploitive as any man.

Creative coping strategies and the workings of the informal economy are illustrated in the following brief profiles of two of the grandmothers. Grandmother A has 10 children and 17 grandchildren. When I interviewed her, two grown daughters and a preschool grandson were living with her. Three teenaged grandsons and their mother live nearby and spend a lot of time with her. When I first arrived at her home, she was mixing dough to make tortillas for another of her daughters who lives in the area.

Grandmother A receives a small income from the Veterans Administration and from Social Security, "not much, but it helps out a little." The daughter who lives nearby receives AFDC and food stamps and contributes about $10 a month to the family income, "to buy meat sometimes, or whatever." One of her sons also helps out, "off and on, not that much."

How does Grandmother A supplement this meager income? I asked if she made crafts or helped the resident grandson's other grandmother "pick worms" for sale to fishermen. "No," she said, "I have a bad heart and I have rheumatoid arthritis. What I usually do is chop wood and wash and that is about it." She is resourceful and lives simply, cooking with wood, making her own tortillas. Because of her health problems, she has not grown a garden for several years. She does, however, gather the yellow pollen from cattails and sells that to get a little extra cash.

She takes her grandchildren with her to gather the cattails, because she can't get into the water where they grow but the children can. Then she lays the cattails in the sun to dry. As they dry, she shakes out the pollen. It is a time-consuming process. It takes many cattails to get enough pollen to fill one baby-food jar. This year, she said, a jar of pollen sells for about $20, or about $5 for one tablespoon. The pollen is used in Sunrise Dance ceremonies throughout the year.

I had difficulty discovering just how much money the pollen harvest yields. When I expressed surprise that all that work would net her only about a hundred dollars, she explained, in the essential spirit of the nurturing grandmother, that

> *sometimes I just give it out free, 'cause a lot of our people are on welfare and food stamps, and it is really hard for them. . . . If they have money, they can go ahead and buy yellow powder but they can't do that with their food stamps.*

Her grandsons contribute to the welfare of the household by gathering and chopping wood and cleaning house. They sweep and mop the floors and wash the dishes. She told me with satisfaction that her 3½-year-old grandson

> *picks up the broom and says, "Grandma, let me sweep." He brings the wood in. And sometimes he wants to help me with the dishes, and he pulls up a chair and is standing there.*

How does she see her role as grandmother? She insisted that what she does is assuredly "not baby-sitting." Instead, "They need me, and I need to be there with them to talk with them or do something with them."

Grandmother B bore 11 children, four of whom grew to adulthood. Three are still living. At present her brother lives with her. Much of the time, so do three grandsons, children of her oldest son. Her aged mother lived with her until her death a few months ago. Her mother's passing has taken away the Social Security checks that for several years were the household's only regular income. A sister who provided moral support and occasional transportation also died recently. Now the challenges of paying the rent, buying food, and making the lengthy trip to the tribal offices to apply for her monthly allotment of food stamps are much harder than before.

After her mother's death, Grandmother B went to a daughter's home in another state. On her return she discovered that her alcoholic son, father of the three grandsons who often live in her home, had claimed her food stamps. There was nothing left to enable her to buy food for the month. I asked what she thought she would do about this crisis. She looked around her home and said, "I've been thinking I could have a yard sale. I could sell a lot of this stuff."

She has only limited reading skills, and in the wake of her mother's recent death her life has been further complicated by the arrival of various official forms that must somehow be interpreted and dealt with. Even taking advantage of the transfer payments available to her ends up being a hardship. To obtain food stamps, she must apply in person each month at an office many miles away, and then, two weeks later, she must again make the

trip to personally pick up the stamps. If she is unable to get a ride, she hitch-hikes, and the round trip plus the waiting in line and application process may take an entire day. It can be even worse for mothers with small children in tow who have to wait in the food-stamp line in wet or freezing weather.

After the food stamps, her main source of income is "picking worms" for fishermen. Her grandsons help in this enterprise, and sometimes so do other kinfolk or temporary household members. One morning when I picked Grandmother B up to accompany me to some interviews, she told how the night before her grandsons had come to report that they had watered the grass "real good" at their maternal grandmother's house and now there were lots of worms coming up. So they had all gone over there and within about 30 minutes had picked up enough worms to make a two-inch layer in the bottom of a large can. As we drove away, we saw the boys out on the road selling worms. On a good day in summer—a weekend or holiday—Grandmother B may gross as much as $50 selling worms. Week-days are slower: A good day's receipts may total only $10 to $15. Winters are hard. When the ground freezes worm-picking is over, and along with that loss of income comes the additional expense of having to buy wood to heat her modest home. Sometimes members of her church help out and give her wood.

As summer wanes, Grandmother B becomes a crafts worker. When she can get the materials, she makes dolls and beautiful doll clothes. When she can get silver, she makes jewelry. Her out-of-state daughter often sends fabrics and trims for the dolls. Finding an effective way to market her products is always a challenge. Grandmother B has no car and must depend on others for transportation. The small community where she lives has no stores, and the nearest commercial center is about 15 miles away. Relatives and friends passing through sometimes deliver items to distant customers or even market them for her.

There is also some direct sustenance from the land. The grandsons fish at a nearby lake. When they are successful, their catch is a significant addition to family meals. When someone kills an elk, it is butchered, cut up, and distributed to friends and relatives. Of course, Grandmother B and many others like her, grandmothers whose lives exemplify the tribal ethic of sharing and who are known to be primary economic supports for children and grandchildren, are included in the community distribution network.

And so the stories go. One grandmother makes and sells cradle boards, real ones for the Apache mothers who use them and miniature decorative models for the tourist trade. Another makes and sells the traditional Apache "camp dresses." Another walks along the riverbanks gathering aluminum cans to sell and occasionally is paid to teach special classes at local schools. Yet another works two jobs, as support staff in the local public schools during the school year and in a forestry camp during the summer.

Finally, as indicated above, some grandmothers also receive financial support from children and other relatives who live off-reservation. The Apache values of sharing, family commitment, and community support extend beyond the reservation boundary lines.

Summary and Discussion

In the modern Anglo milieu of "expressive individualism" (Bellah et al. 1985), older adults, and especially retired adults, are often portrayed as having reached an age of entitlement, when they deserve to be rewarded for years of work and can expect to "enjoy the good life." To those so entitled, high levels of family demand, conflict, and stress signal pathology, not maturity.

In contrast, the Apache grandmothers I talked to seemed reconciled to a "conflict" orientation to life: They accepted the reality that conflict and stress were embedded in the processes of family living. Whether they saw such experiences as growth-producing, at least they seemed to recognize that now, in the full strength of their maturity, such experiences and the responsibility to make the best of them were their lot as *grandmothers*. Resourceful, patient, even resigned, most were willing to lose themselves in the service of their families. At a life stage when many in Anglo society defined themselves as "retired" and perhaps redundant, the Apache grandmothers had arrived at the pinnacle of maturity and responsibility.

The other side of the coin is that many young Apache mothers seem to feel that now is their time to serve individualistic interests, to seek personal goals, or simply to "have a good time." Their attitudes and activities, while not always approved by the grandmothers, are defined as a normal stage of life. But if the mothers can sometimes avoid the challenging responsibilities of child care and child rearing, the grandmothers cannot. The developmental sequence has run its course, and their time has come.

It is instructive to compare some specific aspects of Apache (A) and Anglo American grandparenting (AA). In making these comparisons, I have cited some relevant descriptions of grandparenting in other tribes where they parallel my own observations of Apache grandparenting. Also, I generalize about Anglo American grandparenting according to what I perceive are central tendencies or dominant patterns reported in the literature. It is recognized that there are many other Anglo American patterns, including some that involve high commitment, frequent interaction, active economic support of grown children and grandchildren, and even formal educational efforts to improve grandparenting performance.[5]

1. Obligation and Responsibility

AA: A grandparent is a "spoiler" of grandchildren, one who may interact or give gifts but who "can have meaningful relationships with their grandchildren with minimal obligation and responsibility" (Link 1987:29).

A: For grandmothers in particular, grandparenting means heavy obligation and responsibility: "The older woman's role was that of a parent substitute within the family system" (Ryan 1981:35).

2. Gender Differences in Grandparental Role Behavior

AA: Grandmothers are more important than grandfathers in both role definition and role enactment. "Grandmothers tend to have warmer and closer

relationships and serve more often as surrogate parents than grandfathers. Their close involvement in the mother role in relationships with their own children is a determining factor" (Link 1987:31).

A: Grandmothers are much more important than grandfathers. In this characteristic the Apache and Anglo patterns are similar in direction, but the role of the grandmother as provider is much enhanced among the Apache, and so is her position in the memory of Apache children (and among Indian children of other tribes as revealed in their writings as adults). In both Anglo and Apache society, the grandmothers' priority over grandfathers is partly a function of their greater longevity and partly a culturally prescribed greater affinity and responsibility for children generally.

3. Grandparents as Part of a Viable, Functioning Family Network

AA: Kinship ties are valued and maintained between parents, adult children, and grandchildren, but economic and residential units families tend to be nuclear and two-generational (parents and children). Family households have well-defined, fairly stable boundaries. Individual households tend to be independent.

A: Kinship ties are valued and maintained, and individual households are likely to involve cross-generational and multinuclear (e.g., cousins, aunts, and uncles) members. Family households have loosely defined, rather permeable, boundaries. Individual households tend to be interdependent. Ryan (1981:28) identifies the traditional interdependent family as the key to overcoming the problems faced by many American Indians today. "The individuals I knew who were not successful were not successful because their family was not complete," he says, and the missing elements he points to are grandmothers, grandfathers, aunts and uncles.

4. Economic Security and Economic Responsibilities

AA: Elder status, retirement, and grandparenthood are typically times of fairly secure economic status. Grandparents are more likely than others to own their homes and have accumulated savings. Financial costs of rearing and educating their grandchildren are expected to be borne by the children's parents.

A: Elder status and grandparenthood are times of heavy economic demand. Adult children and grandchildren may become the economic responsibility of the grandparents, adding to the financial burdens of the older years because in the low-income reservation milieu it has been difficult to accumulate savings. Pensions, Social Security, food stamps, and other transfer payment programs do not begin to cover the Apache grandmother's expenses, and, as a consequence, she often works as hard as ever in her life, for as long as she is able.

Apache grandmothers are busy in good causes. Some of them are elderly, many have health problems, but they exhibit a rich variety of economic

activities, in both the informal and the formal economy. Generally they not only make enough to support themselves, but also provide much and sometimes all of the support for their large, often-multigenerational households. Whether married or single, they take financial responsibility for themselves and many others.

These are strong, industrious women. Only one of more than a score of Apache and Navajo grandmothers I got to know in the course of this research was not actively working at cottage enterprises or formal employment, or both, in an effort to improve the economic status of her family. That lone exception was also the oldest grandmother I encountered. Many of these women were suffering considerable physical hardship, from handicaps, accidents, aging, and illness; several showed signs of sheer physical exhaustion; some were psychologically stretched by the responsibilities of child care along with serving as economic providers and cultural models. Most had relatively low-level job skills, in the accepted sense of formal education, human capital, and preparation for successful competition in the labor force.

Despite multiple disadvantages, these Apache grandmothers were among the most influential and active participants in community life. Occupying the respected role of grandmother, enacting a tribal role definition that includes wisdom, energy, and resourcefulness, they stand out as the effective "managers" of much of the local economy and models of independence, courage, and strength in contexts where dependence, frustration, and resignation might be seen as more realistic adjustments.

It is not merely that they are individually strong and committed. To the degree that anyone is truly responsible for the future of the Apache society and culture, I believe it is the grandmothers. More than the tribal politicians, the medicine men, the teachers, the local celebrities, or the upwardly mobile migrants to urban America, it is the local grandmothers who anchor the heritage and, very often, the physical well-being of the Apache people.

Like families in the rest of America, the Apache family is experiencing strain and undergoing change. Like families elsewhere, many Apache mothers and fathers have occupations and lifestyles that take them away from home and severely limit their time with their children. It might even be argued that the poverty and accompanying social problems that afflict the Apache people make their families particularly vulnerable to a host of problems that would have destroyed a lesser people. In the face of the problems they confront, it is fortunate that, unlike much of the rest of America, they do not set aside their older women as "retired" or irrelevant. Rather, they place them in demanding, high-status, high-intensity roles that direct their insights and energies to the benefit of the community's youngest and most helpless members. The combination of high role expectations and the sheer scale of physical and emotional need they confront seem to inspire almost superhuman efforts from them. Looking at their lives and challenges, one may conclude that Apache grandmothering is very hard on the grandmothers. On the other hand, it plainly is very good for the Apache community as a whole and for Apache posterity.

ENDNOTES

[1] In highlighting this general or "normative" pattern, I do not mean to downplay the diversity of grandparenting behavior among both Anglo and Indian populations. There is exceptional and deficient grandparenting in all societies, and millions of American grandparents are currently raising their grandchildren. Even so, I believe the literature in general, and the illustrative works cited, support a clear Anglo–Apache difference in cultural expectations about what constitutes good grandparenting and the social status accorded grandparents.

[2] The Fort Apache Reservation occupies portions of Navajo, Gila, and Apache counties in east central Arizona. In 1990 the population of the Fort Apache Reservation was 10,394, of whom 9,825 were Indian Americans. There were 2,232 households (1,974 family households), with an average household size of 4.35. The Apache population is young: 45 percent are under age 18, and the median age is 20.9. Of the family households, 31 percent were headed by women ("female householder, no husband present") (U.S. Bureau of the Census 1991a:58, 1992:285).

[3] According to the 1990 U.S. Census, of the 4,453 children under age 18 on the Fort Apache Reservation, 759 (17.0 percent) lived in households headed by one or both grandparents. In the entire United States, the corresponding rate was 4.9 percent (U.S. Bureau of the Census 1991b:9, 1992:285).

[4] Of course this pattern is not the only pattern among the White Mountain Apache, nor the typical one. In addition to the 17 percent of all children living in households headed by a grandparent, 55 percent lived in married-couple families including at least one of their parents, 17 percent in single-parent families headed by their mothers, 4 percent in single-parent families headed by their fathers, and the remainder with other relatives or nonrelatives or in institutions (U.S. Bureau of the Census 1992:285). Plainly, the parent or parents are still the primary caretakers for the majority of children. However, even where parents are in place and functioning, Apache culture strongly encourages grandparents to participate in the socialization and nurturing of their grandchildren. Both patterns—grandparent dominant and grandparent supportive and supplemental—seem to be within the "norm."

[5] As with Cowgills' statement, quoted earlier, that in the "Western" model of grandparenting, grandchild–grandparent relationships usually are "rather formal and distant," so also the following generalizations on "minimal obligation and responsibility" need to be qualified. Not only are millions of American grandparents standing in for parents and raising their grandchildren, but substantial numbers are making a conscious effort to improve their grandparenting skills, as indicated in the emergence of formal curricula and a published literature on grandparent education (cf. Strom and Strom 1991a, 1991b, 1992).

REFERENCES

Attneave, Carolyn. 1981. "Discussion." Pp. 46–51 in *The American Indian Family: Strength and Stresses*, edited by John Red Horse, August Shattuck, and Fred Hoffman. Isleta, NM: American Indian Social Research and Development Associates.

Bahr, Kathleen. 1990. "Student Responses to Genogram and Family Chronology." *Family Relations* 39:243–49.

Bellah, Robert N., Richard Madsen, William M. Sullivan, Ann Swidler, and Steven M. Tipton. 1985. *Habits of the Heart: Individualism and Commitment in American Life*. Berkeley: University of California Press.

Clemens, Audra W. and Leland J. Axelson. 1985. "The Not-So-Empty-Nest: The Return of the Fledgling Adult." *Family Relations* 34:259–64.

Cowgill, Donald O. 1986. *Aging Around the World*. Belmont, CA: Wadsworth.

Goodwin, Grenville. 1942. *The Social Organization of the Western Apache*. Chicago: University of Chicago Press.

Hagestad, Gunhild O. and Linda M. Burton. 1986. "Grandparenthood, Life Context, and Family Development." *American Behavioral Scientist* 29 (4, March/April): 471–84.

Link, Mary S. 1987. "The Grandparenting Role." *Lifestyles: A Journal of Changing Patterns* 8 (3 & 4, Spring/Summer): 27–45.

Ryan, Robert A. 1981. "Strengths of the American Indian Family: State of the Art." Pp. 25–43 in *The American Indian Family: Strength and Stresses*, edited by John Red Horse, August Shattuck, and Fred Hoffman. Isleta, NM: American Indian Social Research and Development Associates.

Shomaker, Dianna J. 1989. "Transfer of Children and the Importance of Grandmothers among the Navajo Indians." *Journal of Cross-Cultural Gerontology* 4:1–18.

Stockel, H. Henrietta. 1991. *Women of the Apache Nation.* Reno: University of Nevada Press.
Strom, Robert D. and Shirley K. Strom. 1991a. *Becoming a Better Grandparent: Viewpoints on Strengthening the Family.* Newbury Park, CA: Sage.
————. 1991b. *Grandparent Education: A Guide for Leaders.* Newbury Park, CA: Sage.
————. 1992. *Achieving Grandparent Potential: Viewpoints on Building Intergenerational Relationships.* Newbury Park, CA: Sage.
U.S. Bureau of the Census. 1991a. *1990 Census of Population and Housing, Summary Population and Housing Characteristics: Arizona.* Washington, DC: U.S. Government Printing Office.
————. 1991b. *Marital Status and Living Arrangements, March 1990.* Current Population Reports, Series P-20, No. 450. Washington, DC: U.S. Government Printing Office.
————. 1992. *1990 Census of Population, General Population Characteristics: Arizona.* Washington, DC: U.S. Government Printing Office.
Wilson, Melvin N. 1984a. "The Black Extended Family: An Analytical Consideration." *Developmental Psychology* 22:246–58.
————. 1984b. "Mothers' and Grandmothers' Perceptions of Parental Behavior in Three-Generational Black Families." *Child Development* 55:1333–39.

35

MY MOTHER'S HIP
Lessons from the World of Eldercare

LUISA MARGOLIES

The question of who will care for the elderly is not as simple as it used to be. Fifty years ago, few middle-aged people had frail, elderly parents. Now, nearly 90 percent of baby boomers have parents who survive to advanced ages. Families composed of several generations are not unusual; nor is it uncommon for an elderly child to care for an aged parent. Parents may require different types and degrees of care, depending on their age and health status. Many people older than eighty-five can manage on their own, particularly if they have a spouse to share the tasks, but nearly half need limited to substantial assistance in carrying out their daily activities and can remain at home only with the help of family caregivers or hired aides.

Transformations in family structure have wrought fundamental changes in the nature of caregiving. Thanks to geographical mobility and the decline in fertility, the extended family is almost extinct, and fewer children are around to care for aging parents. Divorce, remarriage, and multiple career paths for men and women have made rendering consistent care increasingly difficult.

The issue of who should care for the elderly has become muddled with moralistic arguments. Some historians contend that economic imperatives

were the moral underpinning of the large extended families of the past. In the countryside, adult children toed the line because their parents controlled the means of production and allocated the family's economic resources. One honored one's parents and took care of them in their old age. Ireland's system of impartible inheritance, for instance, obligated children to seek their fortunes elsewhere. The youngest son, however, continued to live with his parents and was committed to caring for them throughout their lives. This child was amply compensated on his parents' death by being made the sole recipient of the family estate.

Even among urban families, where no such economic imperative reigned, adult children felt a heavy obligation to care for their surviving parents. Numerous children worked out the logistics of caregiving without the aid of Social Security and national medical entitlements. Surviving parents normally lived with a primary caregiver but also rotated among their other children. The children had an unquestioned duty to their parents, and the lines of caregiving were clearly delineated.

When I think about my grandparents and great-grandparents, the idea of removing them from home was inconceivable. Both sets of paternal great-grandparents lived to advanced ages and were cared for by my paternal grandparents. My father had fond memories of talking to his grandparents daily: All he had to do was walk down the long hallway of the large apartment to their separate quarters. Both sets of his grandparents died naturally at home of "old age." My paternal grandfather "dropped dead" at the relatively young age of fifty-seven, but my paternal grandmother lived into her eighties in her only daughter's home. When she grew senile and frail, her three sons contributed a monthly stipend for her medical care. My maternal grandmother also died young, but my maternal grandfather was lucky to have had four adoring daughters who spoiled him after he was widowed. He continued to live with his youngest daughter after she married, but he liked to circulate among his other daughters for weeks at a time. He helped raise his youngest daughter's children, and he was an integral member of her household until his sudden death at age seventy-four from a ruptured hernia.

It was not until the Medicare and Medicaid Acts of 1965 were passed that the idea of living with and being cared for by one's family changed. In one swift moment, the extended family was rendered superfluous as commercial nursing homes, financed by government contributions, took over the role of caring for the frail elderly. The cultural ties that bound multiple generations together in a single household rapidly attenuated, and the first Medicare generation to reach old age gained the dubious distinction of caring for itself.

Today, filial piety is nearly an anachronism, and ethicists argue about the moral obligations children should have toward their aging parents. The argument goes something like this: Children did not ask to be born and therefore do not have the same degree of commitment toward their parents that parents have toward them. Parents must raise their children and see them safely into young adulthood, but this does not necessarily obligate children to bear the burden of caring for a failing parent later. Because parents

are simply discharging their normal responsibilities, the "parental sacrifice account" of filial obligation in which grown children "owe" their old parents care is nonsense (even though many grown children still subscribe to it). In *Am I My Parents' Keeper?* (1988), Norman Daniels argues that we cannot view children's obligations as equivalent to parental duties. We should not fall into the trap of appealing to the "traditionalist" view of a golden age of moral and emotional bonds as a signal for returning to outmoded values. Caregiving obligations were different in the "good old days," when parents died relatively young after brief illnesses. Long-term care duties can now be so burdensome, he adds, that it would be imprudent to depend exclusively on individuals to care for their elderly.

What ethicists are trying to tell us is that we should not rely indiscriminately on implicit contracts to ensure that growing numbers of frail elders are properly cared for. Daniel Callahan, founding director of the bioethics research institute The Hastings Center, observes that some moral obligations *do* exist for family members to care for one another. But he also warns that "unlimited self-sacrifice on the part of the caregiver, in a time of rapidly increasing life expectancy and chronic illness, encounters heavy, and perhaps mounting resistance" (1987:101). . . .

Today, seven in ten care recipients suffer from medical conditions that are long term or chronic in nature (AARP 1997:14). Chronic conditions can turn caregiving into an endless nightmare, because the elderly are older, sicker, and frailer than ever before. Living with a chronic condition is like living with an uninvited guest who refuses to leave, no matter how many hints are given. Chronic diseases are incurable and relentlessly progressive. They sap one's strength even as one tries to manage them. These are just the physical effects. The illness is also the main element that segregates the sufferer from normal interactions with the outer world, taking on a dynamic of its own and tightening its tedious grip over every aspect of his or her daily life.

The chronically ill exist in a state of limbo. My colleague Robert Murphy, who suffered from the disabling effects of an inoperable tumor on the spine, described his feelings of alienation and sense of stigmatization in *The Body Silent* (1987):

> *My identity has lost its stable moorings and has become contingent on a physical flaw. . . . The long-term physically impaired are neither sick nor well, neither dead nor fully alive, neither out of society nor wholly in it. They are human beings but their bodies are warped or malfunctioning, leaving their full humanity in doubt. . . . The sick person lives in a state of social suspension until he or she gets better. The disabled spend a lifetime in a similar state. They are neither fish nor fowl; they exist in partial isolation from society as undefined, ambiguous people.* (Pp. 104, 131)

Chronic diseases have to be nurtured because they form a permanent part of one's life. One has to both monitor the illness and learn how to cope. All this takes up a lot of time and energy. In *Good Days, Bad Days* (1991), Kathy Charmaz notes that chronic illness is "intrusive" because it forces its sufferer to make constant adjustments. The illness is like being

on a roller-coaster—there are good days and bad days, depending on the "intrusiveness" of the symptoms (pp. 42–49). When chronically ill people feel "well," they push themselves in the foolish attempt to persuade themselves that they are not actually ill. Then they become overtaxed and relapse quickly, only to be bitterly reminded of their illness by experiencing renewed episodes of pain and fatigue. . . .

How many times have chronically ill people been asked by well-meaning observers, "What do you do with yourself all day?" Just going to the supermarket may constitute the day's major outing and consume all of one's meager resources. How many adult children wonder why a parent takes "all day" to accomplish a "minor" task because they are insensitive to the illness's dominant role in limiting a person's capacity to perform routine chores? The interrogators cannot understand how pervasive the consequences of chronic disease are.

Each modification of one's surroundings to eliminate physical obstacles, and each limitation of activities, is a reminder of one's condition. One is forced to simplify as the illness progresses. People give up cherished activities like driving and entertaining and differentiate themselves from the people around them by parking in special handicapped spots or sitting down in the supermarket. They may have to purchase adaptive devices to compensate for physical limitations. They may stop picking up relatives at the airport, stop going to the mall, and "forget" to walk or exercise. Sick people often cannot be bothered with such niceties as setting a pretty table or filling the house with plants, and they may dispense with common courtesies because they feel "entitled." Chronic sufferers may end up reducing their living space to a well-traveled path between one room and another or confining themselves to a favorite chair. Nothing is more painful than the day the chronically ill person realizes he or she cannot manage alone. Caregiving then becomes a question of not only helping the elderly run their households, but also of providing them with hands-on continuing care. The caregiver must come to accept that she or he may not be able to alleviate the suffering of an ailing parent who is on a downhill course. "Sometimes, it means sharing their suffering, helping them to shoulder the burden," notes Richard Gunderman (2002:42).

Paradoxically, technological advances, which seemed to offer so much promise for the elderly, have scarcely affected our ability to care equitably for those who have most benefited from them. We have yet to come up with morally comfortable solutions that will ensure the continuing well-being of our aging society and keep pace with the remarkable achievements of modern medicine. Although the biomedical approach to medicine has dealt admirably with acute diseases, it has shortchanged the care of our senior population. According to a report on eldercare, "The gap is plugged by programs of long-term institutional care and informal home care that are at worst inhumane and niggardly, and at best starved for adequate funds and well-trained health care workers and social workers" (JIRGIB 1994:S11). Callahan posed the right question when he asked what the appropriate balance should be between the provision of acute health care and the provision

of long-term care for the chronically ill elderly. He calls for a different type of medicine today—one that knows its limitations and focuses on the care of the chronically ill (1993:209).

Family members currently provide the bulk of long-term care services to the elderly and underwrite some $38 billion of the $70 billion expended on long-term care. Recent projections suggest that these expenditures will more than double in the next twenty-five years to keep pace with the galloping growth of the senior population. Meanwhile, Medicare entitlements continue to rest on theories about aging that prevailed more than forty years ago. Families who care for ailing relatives at home rarely receive the benefit of community-based programs or services because of Medicare's skewed emphasis on acute-care reimbursements for inpatients. Compare our glaringly deficient programs with those in many European countries, where both home-nursing and institutional care are incorporated into comprehensive social-security systems that are financed by a percentage of the wage base assessed exclusively for eldercare. Germany, for example, has a universal, compulsory long-term care program that is administered by a sickness fund whose contributions come from monthly deductions shared equally between employees and employers. The elderly are provided with nursing-home and home-health care benefits, and family caregivers receive formal training and earn pension credits (Wiener and Cuellar 1999). Those who choose to stay at home (the majority) receive a monthly stipend; their caregivers are covered by social-security insurance and receive various supports, such as respite care. In contrast, the American system puts the onus of caregiving squarely on the patient's family. It fails both the recipient and the giver of care.

Who are the care recipients, and how are they cared for? A national survey of family caregiving shows that the mean age of care recipients is seventy-seven years and seven months, but nearly 25 percent are older than eighty-five. Sixty percent are female, and a little more than 40 percent are widowed. Some 22.4 million families provide assistance to an aging relative. Adult children constitute 37 percent of all caregivers, and nearly one-fifth of care recipients live with their caregivers. The majority of family caregivers devote an average of three hours each day to rendering care, despite such competing demands as paid employment. Forty percent of caregivers perform the equivalent of a full-time job and have borne the responsibility for an average of four-and-a-half years. Twenty percent of caregivers have been fulfilling this role for more than five years (AARP 1997).

Family caregivers provide an eclectic variety of services for the elderly, including assistance with marketing, shopping, banking, car repairs, housekeeping, cooking, assorted chores, doctors' appointments, and financial management. The next level of attention involves hands-on personal care, such as bathing, dressing, toileting, and administering medication. Another type of assistance falls within the rubric of nursing and may involve the performance of complicated medical procedures.

One usually takes on the role of caregiver spontaneously, without anticipating the enormous complications to come. Caregiving functions tend to expand almost insidiously as the care recipients grow increasingly infirm or

have unexpected crises. Caregivers will go to considerable lengths to provide the necessary care at home, even if they have to hire full-time aides or
appeal to the services of a case manager to coordinate the different types
of care. Nursing homes, for the most part, are still considered places of last
resort. Brakman (1994) concludes that, "when elder parents do take up residence in a nursing home, this is often experienced by the child and the elder
as a moral, emotional, and physical failure" (p. 27).

Caregiving is overwhelmingly women's work. Women make up 77 percent of the adult children providing hands-on care and are likely to rearrange
their professional and personal lives to manage the unpredictable needs of
their parents. Caregiving takes an important place alongside women's other
roles as workers, wives, mothers, and homemakers. The typical caregiving daughter is middle-aged and squarely "in the middle" in terms of the
demands competing for her time and energy. Some 41 percent of caregivers
are still raising children younger than eighteen when they first undertake
the caregiving role. Women generally serve as primary caregivers to an older
female relative; today, that relative is likely to be one's mother. In the past
forty years, the proportion of fifty-year-old women with living mothers has
risen from 37 percent to nearly 70 percent. It is common for a fifty-year-old
woman to have a mother who is living but perhaps not well—that is, with a
chronic illness or some frailty. This daughter may have put off childbearing
in favor of career development during her thirties; now she finds herself the
mother of children approaching adulthood while confronting menopause
and her own eventual mortality. She may end up spending more years caring for an elderly parent than raising her children. For these women, the
issues surrounding caregiving pose an enormous challenge.

Various researchers have commented that daughters look on caregiving
not as a set of discrete tasks but as a diffuse responsibility that never ends
(Brody 1981; Rutman 1996). Daughters feel intimately responsible for their
parents' well-being and will go to great lengths to preserve the recipient's
sense of dignity. They try to uphold an image of the parent as he or she was
by presenting that fictional vision, as far as possible, to the public sphere. In
Who Cares for the Elderly? Public Policy and the Experiences of Adult Daughters
(1991), Emily Abel views this act of protecting a parent's sense of person-
hood as a kind of moral guardianship. Daughters seem to have an intuitive,
nonverbal engagement with their parents that allows them to translate their
parents' feelings.

Why do middle-aged women have such a difficult time setting limits
on their role as caregivers to their parents? First, these women traditionally
have been raised to be nurturers and expect to make sacrifices. They learned
this from their stay-at-home mothers, and even though women are now in
the working world, shrugging off old values is hard. Daughters are still the
ones who hold families together and embody the moral underpinnings of the
family unit, even though the nature of family dynamics has clearly changed.

Caregiving is not something most daughters have to think about very
hard. They just do it because they have to. Caregiving is often a natural,
spontaneous act for one's parents. Daughters have an overwhelming desire

to provide care when a parent needs it and do not expect anything in return. I have yet to come across a daughter who can proceed comfortably with her own life while ignoring the obvious needs of a parent. Take the case of Elaine Simmons, the visiting nurse who came to my parents' home for eighteen months to give Mother her Calcimar injections. Elaine held a full-time job while caring for a daughter with developmental difficulties and a husband brain-disabled in a freak accident. She also found time to be a caring daughter to an ailing father who traveled between his home up North and hers in South Florida. She coordinated every detail of her father's care for several years while respecting his wishes to retain a separate and distant household. Elaine was so good-natured and concerned about her patients that one would never know she carried such weighty responsibilities at home. She juggled her affairs so that each family member received attention without feeling slighted. Such intense caregiving seems to emanate from a sense of connectedness, according to Abel (1991:91), rather than from any notion of repaying a parent or canceling a moral debt.

Two of my closest friends cared for their fathers with such abnegation that they had to rework their professional lives. George Ann worked for a global nonprofit organization, a job that kept her traveling much of the year. When her widowed father broke his hip, she bought a house in Vermont, moved him in with her, and took a more sedentary job. Her father had emphysema and had been seriously depressed since his wife's death. George Ann saw him through congestive heart failure, several minor strokes, and many bouts of pneumonia, but she never considered putting him in a nursing home, even though her absent brother kept urging her to take the step. During the nearly four years George Ann lived in Vermont, her brother visited their father once. Two years after her father's death, George Ann still could not forgive her brother for his failure to participate in their father's care. By contrast, Carmen Nieves, a colleague in the Canary Islands, was fortunate to have both a brother and a husband to share in caregiving tasks. Nevertheless, she refused to leave her father for more than a few days at a time, despite numerous professional invitations abroad. Her father suffered from advanced Parkinson's disease and was eventually confined to a wheelchair. Not only did Carmen Nieves cater to his bodily needs; she also made sure he took part in the family's activities by seating him in the front parlor, where he could greet and chat with everyone who entered the house. He was a retired schoolmaster and enjoyed the comings and goings of his granddaughter and her friends. Carmen Nieves' brother occasionally covered for her when she went out in the evening; it was understood that they would share the responsibility for their ailing father. The care was accomplished in a low-key, unobtrusive manner, and her father's death was a blow to the entire family.

Aspects of caregiving can be gratifying, but as the parent's needs increase, caregiving takes over more and more of a daughter's life. Women may assume the tasks willingly when a parent is relatively independent or step in for an emergency without knowing what to expect in the future (Guberman, Maheu, and Maille 1992). Daughters are likely to take unpaid

leaves of absence, reduce their working hours, relinquish their jobs, eliminate their vacations, and abandon their social activities to keep pace with the pressing demands of caregiving. But the progressive deterioration of the parent cannot be stemmed, and in the end daughters often feel frustrated and angry about their own powerlessness.

Caregiving is hard work. It is not something to undertake lightly or to walk away from in the middle. It is not only physically taxing; it is emotionally wearing. Eldercare is also more complicated than it was in the past and can involve multiple tasks over many years. "It is hypocritical to envision it as anything but a hard, bankrupting job," says Theodore Roszak (2001). "The extensive care that the frail and infirm require is uniquely the result of modern medicine. Nobody in any previous culture was expected to handle demands of this magnitude and live a life of their own" (p. 121). The caregiver must give unconditional support and function as the parent's advocate without being patronizing. Many daughters have likened the experience of caring for a frail parent to that of caring for a growing child, because the daughter assumes the role of parent. Yet the experience is inherently different because the daughter is a witness to her parent's decline, and the result is not hard to envision. What the daughter does to make an ailing parent more comfortable may ensure the status quo for a while, but it is never enough in the long run. Women tend to see the deterioration of a parent under their care as a personal affront and are burdened with guilt. It is hard for a daughter to act objectively amid such intense involvement.

Daughters who care for their mothers are particularly stressed because they identify so closely with their mothers' decline. Although their roles are now reversed, daughters continue to look upon mothers as the original nurturers. Daughters are not only constantly reminded of how their mothers used to be; they are also terrified of their mothers' infirmities, which "foreshadow" their coming old age. The anthropologist Robert Rubinstein, who studied the social context of caregiving by collecting daughters' narratives, concludes that, no matter how dependent mothers are on daughters, the relationship continues to remain one between a mother who has raised a child and her middle-aged daughter. This is the last chance for mothers and daughters to examine and work out crucial aspects of their relationship (1995:258).

When elderly people have both sons and daughters, the daughters inevitably end up as the primary caregivers. Sometimes, adult daughters share equally in the tasks of caregiving, but that is the exception rather than the rule. "Contingencies such as geographical proximity, gender roles, or interpersonal relationships conspire to make the burdens unequal, and often unfair, in practice," notes Harry Moody (1992:92). Sons who share in caregiving tasks usually expect their sisters to provide the personal care while they carry out the more "masculine" tasks related to managing the household.

Considering the broad range of caregiving duties performed by family members, the need to share the responsibility becomes obvious. Barbara Tarlow (1996) believes that the caregiving role should be negotiated among adult children because not everyone is cut out to be a good caregiver or is willing to make the necessary sacrifices. Good caregiving encompasses a

number of indispensable qualities without which the experience can be transformed into a traumatic burden for all concerned. Some children may feel that a paid surrogate is an adequate substitute for personal caregiving. The neglected parent's emotional hurt is not easily forgotten. It is not uncommon for the elderly care recipient to feel abandoned when adult children are distant and uninvolved.

Men rise admirably to the occasion when daughters are lacking. Some of the finest stories in the caregiving literature are about men caring tenderly for their parents and feeling as much of a moral responsibility as women do. In *The Time of Their Dying* (1977), Stephen Rosenfeld talks about the importance of investing time, unstintingly, in the care of a parent: "One must be there. Time and again I realized how futile it was to extract information or convey emotion at a distance" (p. 180). The journalist and writer Nick Taylor, who was sucked into the caregiving vortex as an only child, also experienced such sentiments. His memoir, *A Necessary End,* should be read by every potential caregiver because it depicts so nakedly his intense involvement with both parents as they declined. His caretaking career encompassed the period from 1983 to 1991. At first he felt he had to decide how much of his life he should sacrifice to care for his ailing parents. But then he plunged fully into the caregiving fray as he tried to deal with one crisis after another. . . . No matter what he did, he never felt he had a handle on the situation, and he had no siblings to share his pain. . . .

Tom Koch, the author of *Mirrored Lives: Aging Children and Elderly Parents* (1990), cared for his father with total dedication. He became a frequent flyer between Vancouver and Buffalo, New York,

> *unable to stay in Buffalo and unwilling to stay away. Each new medical crisis returned me to Norm's house, and as he grew weaker, each new responsibility tied me closer to the world that Norm progressively relinquished. . . . I could not leave; it was impossible for me to fly that far knowing how tenuous was the balance in our Buffalo world. . . . This was the pattern, a gradual diminishment and a series of small incidents, as we waited for calamity to strike.* (Pp. 173, 175)

Koch's book illustrates how the strands of connectedness bind failing parents and caring children even closer together as their private world crumbles. . . .

In *Looking After* (1996), John Daniel depicts the nitty-gritty of caregiving in frank, unapologetic terms. He was a reluctant caregiver for a mother who had moved into his home after she became increasingly forgetful. Daniel had conflicting feelings because she had never been a "mothering" type. He was annoyed and acted churlishly at times: "My mother had been a strong and vibrant woman. It grieved me to see her reduced to a stooped crone who dithered over vegetables at the store, who couldn't remember what she'd read half an hour before, who forgot to take the pills I placed directly in front of her at breakfast. It more than grieved me—it enraged me . . . because I was stuck with caring for a feeble old mother and didn't want to be" (p. 92). Yet he mourned his mother after she died and chastised himself. "In the time since her death, I've found myself saying, 'I'm sorry, Mama, I'm so sorry.' . . . I berated myself for not being strong enough to bear the modest office of

caregiving. I blamed myself for my mother's irrevocable absence from the world" (pp. 204, 214).

Researchers have consistently shown that family caregiving engenders family conflicts. Rare is the family that manages to stay together and act harmoniously under the multiple stresses of caring for failing parents. The national survey on family caregiving found that some 25 percent of caregivers report family conflict (AARP 1997:22). The conflict generally arises between the primary caregiver and the other siblings (Brody et al. 1989). Because most primary caregivers are women, sisters frequently find themselves on the outs with their brothers. "When caregivers are asked directly about relations with siblings," writes Amy Horowitz (1985), "significant numbers do report deteriorated relations" (p. 210). Many siblings care deeply about their parents but do not engage in the actual care. Brothers may feel that hands-on care can be provided adequately by hiring outsiders, but daughters often believe that no outsider can care for their parents the way they do and are more sensitive to the fact that vulnerable parents may prefer their children's help. Brothers may act as though their sisters' careers are expendable or less relevant because they cling to the outmoded, sexist notion that men are the principal wage earners. Caregiving itself is devalued because it is an unremunerated personal activity—women's work—that receives little recognition beyond the family sphere.

Many wonder how much longer women can bear the emotional burden of caregiving. The responsibility is often imposed on the daughter with little discussion or planning, because girls have been socialized to "care" while boys are directed to "act." Despite the revolution in gender roles, people still assume that women will continue to provide the bulk of the hands-on care. Richard Martin and Stephen Post note that some women may have the inner resources to "shoulder this monumental responsibility" and may "live lives of significant self-abnegation," yet they question the ability of women to hold up under the increasing pressure (1992:62).

Explosions are likely to occur when the primary caregiver feels the effects of burnout and verbalizes her resentment to less involved siblings. A little more than half of all caregivers feel that other relatives are not doing their share. Caregivers are distressed not only by their siblings' lesser participation but also by their siblings' lack of emotional and instrumental support for their role as principal caregiver. The other siblings often take the caregiving sister for granted. Caregivers rightly feel that absent siblings are the least fit to criticize their efforts or offer unsolicited advice, especially when they are not there to witness the daily happenings. Absent children, however, may feel slighted by the primary caregiver because they are not consulted or kept abreast of changes. . . .

Numerous factors affect the quality of sibling relationships. First and foremost, siblings cannot afford to be angry with their parents, so they must take out their fear and frustration on one another. A failing parent is too often caught up in his or her own problems to focus on the undercurrents of care. Some siblings revive childhood rivalries and other old conflicts in the context of caregiving. Yet caregiving is sufficiently stressful to produce

conflicts among siblings who previously enjoyed harmonious relationships. Adult children bicker about the type of care that is appropriate—should it be a nursing home or some sort of home arrangement? They squabble over the disbursement of the parents' funds—one sibling may feel that the parents' savings should be used to fund their care, another that those life savings are sacred and should be held for eventual inheritance. Parents who lived through the Depression may be loath to deplete the savings that took a life-time to amass and worry that their medical expenses will leave nothing for the children. Siblings may have questions about inheritance and wills but feel that discussing such matters in the context of caregiving is tasteless. So they remain silent, and their silence breeds tension and taints their relation-ship. The possibilities for friction among siblings are endless. Primary care-givers may be so depressed and exhausted from sleeplessness, poor diet, lack of respite, and the endless routine that they cannot cope graciously with a difficult sibling. "Coming together to face a parent's illness requires an altogether different degree of cooperation and communication among sib-lings than organizing holiday dinners and family reunions," warn Nancy Hooyman and Wendy Lustbader in *Taking Care of Your Aging Family Members* (1986:45).

If filial obligations were shared more evenly and not simply left to duti-ful daughters, families would be able to function as more effective caregivers to their parents. The burdens of contemporary caregiving can be extremely unfair, creating a new class of human casualties who will be unable to age successfully because of the disproportionate demands on their time and resources. "Increasing pressures on adult children to personally take care of their frail relative's every need is socially irresponsible," says Laura Olson in a detailed study of the political economy of long-term care (1993:179). The solution, she says, is to implement social policies that will address not only the needs of the care recipients but also those of the caregivers.

In a cogent summing up of the problem, Carol Levine (2000) notes that she eventually realized she had done nothing wrong in her caregiving. It was the system that was out of whack. "I feel abandoned by a health care system that commits resources and rewards to rescuing the injured and ill, but then consigns such patients and their families to the black hole of chronic 'custo-dial' care" (p. 74). Only in the United States are family members inducted into a volunteer labor force because the health-care system, predicated on outmoded social policies, has not yet grappled with the issue of caring for our nation's oldest citizens. The void in long-term care programs will only expand unless Medicare abandons its antiquated premises and comes to terms with the pressing needs of our rapidly aging society.

An equitable health-care system would empower potential caregivers by allowing them to choose to take on the caregiving role rather than forcing the role on them. In a timely essay on the institutional care of the elderly, Bela Blasszauer (1994) puts it aptly: "A society can, indeed, very well be judged on the basis of how it takes care of its elderly" (p. 14). Good care must be an ethical concern for everyone, and caring for the frail elderly must be the social responsibility of an entire nation.

REFERENCES

AARP. 1997. *Family Caregiving in the U.S.: Findings from a National Survey.* Final Report. Washington, DC: National Alliance for Caregiving and American Association of Retired Persons (AARP).

Abel, Emily K. 1991. *Who Cares for the Elderly? Public Policy and the Experiences of Adult Daughters.* Philadelphia: Temple University Press.

Blasszauer, Bela. 1994. "Institutional Care of the Elderly." *Hastings Center Report* 24 (5): 14–17.

Brakman, Sarah-Vaughan. 1994. "Adult Daughter Caregivers." Symposium. Caring for an Aging World: Allocating Scarce Resources. *Hastings Center Report* 24 (5): 26–28.

Brody, Elaine M. 1981. "Women in the Middle and Family Help to Older People." *Gerontologist* 21 (5): 471–80.

Brody, Elaine M., Christine Hoffman, Morton H. Kleban, and Claire B. Schoonover. 1989. "Caregiving Daughters and Their Local Siblings: Perceptions, Strains, and Interactions." *Gerontologist* 29 (4): 529–38.

Callahan, Daniel. 1987. *Setting Limits: Medical Goals in an Aging Society.* Washington, DC: Georgetown University Press.

———. 1993. *The Troubled Dream of Life: Living with Mortality.* New York: Simon and Schuster.

Charmaz, Kathy. 1991. *Good Days, Bad Days: The Self in Chronic Illness and Time.* New Brunswick, NJ: Rutgers University Press.

Daniel, John. 1996. *Looking After: A Son's Memoir.* Washington, DC: Counterpoint.

Daniels, Norman. 1988. *Am I My Parents' Keeper? An Essay on Justice between the Young and the Old.* New York: Oxford University Press.

Guberman, N., P. Maheu, and C. Maille. 1992. "Women as Family Caregivers: Why Do They Care?" *Gerontologist* 32 (5): 607–17.

Gunderman, Richard B. 2002. "Is Suffering the Enemy?" *Hastings Center Report* 32 (2): 40–44.

Hooyman, Nancy R. and Wendy Lustbader. 1986. *Taking Care of Your Aging Family Members: A Practical Guide.* New York: Free Press.

Horowitz, Amy. 1985. "Family Caregiving to the Frail Elderly." Pp. 194–246 in *Annual Review of Gerontology and Geriatrics.* New York: Springer.

JIRGIB (Joint International Research Group of the Institute of Bioethics). 1994. "What Do We Owe the Elderly? Allocating Social and Health Care Resources." *Hastings Center Report, Special Supplement* 24 (2).

Koch, Tom. 1990. *Mirrored Lives: Aging Children and Elderly Parents.* Westport, CT: Praeger.

Levine, Carol. 2000. "The Loneliness of the Long-Term Care Giver." Pp. 71–80 in *Always on Call: When Illness Turns Families into Caregivers,* edited by Carol Levine. New York: United Hospital Fund of New York.

Martin, Richard J. and Stephen G. Post. 1992. "Human Dignity, Dementia and the Moral Basis of Caregiving." Pp. 55–68 in *Dementia and Aging: Ethics, Values and Policy Choices,* edited by Robert H. Binstock, Stephen G. Post, and Peter J. Whitehouse. Baltimore: Johns Hopkins University Press.

Moody, Harry R. 1992. "A Critical View of Ethical Dilemmas in Dementia." Pp. 86–106 in *Dementia and Aging: Ethics, Values and Policy Choices,* edited by Robert H. Binstock, Stephen G. Post, and Peter J. Whitehouse. Baltimore: Johns Hopkins University Press.

Murphy, Robert F. 1987. *The Body Silent.* New York: Henry Holt.

Olson, Laura Katz. 1993. "The Political Economy of Productive Aging: Long-Term Care." Pp. 167–85 in *Achieving a Productive Aging Society,* edited by Scott A. Bass, Francis G. Caro, and Yung Ping Chen. Westport, CT: Auburn House.

Rosenfeld, Stephen S. 1977. *The Time of Their Dying.* New York: W. W. Norton.

Roszak, Theodore. 2001. *Longevity Revolution: As Boomers Become Elders.* Berkeley, CA: Berkeley Hills Books.

Rubinstein, Robert L. 1995. "Narratives of Elder Parental Death: A Structural and Cultural Analysis." *Medical Anthropological Quarterly* 9 (2): 257–76.

Rutman, Deborah. 1996. "Caregiving as Women's Work: Women's Experiences of Powerfulness and Powerlessness as Caregivers." *Qualitative Health Research* 6 (1): 90–111.

Tarlow, Barbara. 1996. "Caring: A Negotiated Process That Varies." Pp. 56–82 in *Caregiving: Readings in Knowledge, Practice, Ethics and Politics,* edited by Suzanne Gordon, Patricia Benner, and Nel Noddings. Philadelphia: University of Pennsylvania Press.

Taylor, Nick. 1994. *A Necessary End.* New York: Doubleday/Nan A. Talese.

Wiener, Joshua M. and Alison Evans Cuellar. 1999. "Public and Private Responsibilities: Home- and Community-Based Services in the United Kingdom and Germany." *Journal of Aging and Health* 11 (2): 417–44.

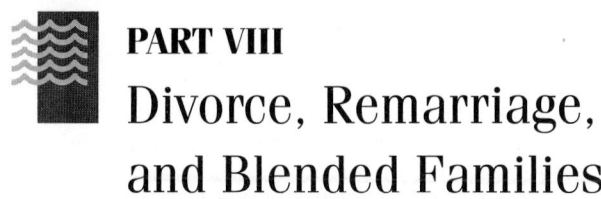

PART VIII

Divorce, Remarriage, and Blended Families

36

FRAMING DIVORCE REFORM
Media, Morality, and the Politics of Family

MICHELE ADAMS • SCOTT COLTRANE

Public rhetoric suggests that we have entered a new era of divorce and marriage reform, but current public discourse bears a striking resemblance to earlier eras. Post-no-fault divorce reform efforts were intended to make it easier, more fair, or just plain nicer when marriage was no longer a viable option for spouses. Recent events, however, have conspired to change divorce reform discourse into marriage promotion discourse. As marriage reform has come to represent the contemporary approach to reforming divorce, creating "better" divorces has essentially dropped off the policy radar screen, and divorcing couples are increasingly at risk for being labeled as deviant and morally deficient.

As the organized Marriage Movement and the Bush administration enthusiastically promoted marriage, divorce was relegated to the margins of public consciousness. The movement's assumption that "healthy" marriage would make divorce go away set up the two as polar opposites, associating the former with moral good and the latter with evil. In the process, making divorce "better" for present and future unhappily marrieds and their children took a distant back seat to marriage education, premarital counseling, reducing marriage license fees, and proposing waiting periods for those who wanted to divorce (Brotherson and Duncan 2004). Although denying their intent to stigmatize single mothers and their offspring, marriage promoters who insisted that "clearly, we are losing many marriages that could and should be saved" (Waite and Gallagher 2000:149) may be inadvertently stigmatizing those who feel that their marriages cannot (and should not) last.

In this context, there are indications that divorce is once again becoming a venue for moral evaluation, and those desirous of ending their marriages, for whatever reason, including conflict and hostility, may find

---

Michele Adams and Scott Coltrane, "Framing Divorce Reform: Media, Morality, and the Politics of Family" from *Family Process* 46, no. 1 (March 2007): 17–34. Copyright © 2006 by Family Process, Inc. Reprinted with the permission of Wiley-Blackwell.

themselves subject to public and professional disapproval. To what extent are dysfunctional and unhealthy marriages "saved" when, for instance, a conflicted couple arrives on the doorstep of a counselor belonging to the National Registry of Marriage-Friendly Therapists, a group whose participating therapists must sign a value statement that says, "Because as a marriage therapist *I believe that many and maybe even most marriages can be restored to health even when the spouses are unhappy, conflicted, or demoralized,* my first stance is to explore how the couple might preserve their marriage" (Doherty 2005; italics added)? Although this national registry and most marriage promoters explicitly deny trying to preserve violent or dangerous marriages, their implicit message is that *all* marriages are good and *all* divorces are bad, and the burden of proof falls on the unhappily married couple to show otherwise.

In 1994, psychologist and family therapist Constance Ahrons introduced the phrase *the good divorce* as one in which families can stay together and interact harmoniously even after the parents dissolve their marriage (Ahrons 1994). Her admonition that we lack a language to accommodate the concept of a positive divorce experience is instructive; linguists have for some time noted that without naming a concept, we have no recourse to thinking about or enacting it. As Ahrons observed, the negative language used to frame divorce has marginalized and stigmatized families for whom divorce is a fact. Today, the obliteration of the process of divorce (and its frequently positive aspects) from the discourse of family reform is once again threatening to restigmatize divorced individuals and their families. The concept of the "good divorce" has, that is, been replaced by the concept of the "healthy marriage." Although coexistence of the two, side by side, in the marital relationship marketplace is, undoubtedly, something to be desired, we suggest that substitution of the former by the latter is problematic to the extent that it demonizes divorced individuals and precludes policy reforms to make divorce better for all involved, including children. Moreover, the push to "reinstate" a "marriage culture" over a "culture of divorce" implicitly overlooks the problems of the former, foremost among which is the assumption of gendered family arrangements that underlies the institution of marriage in the United States.

In this [reading], we examine divorce reform over time, demonstrating how it is socially constructed within particular historical and moral contexts. We use archival materials to discuss the broad historical outlines of divorce reform, and more focused content analysis to describe more recent media framing. We begin with a brief history of divorce in the United States, moving on to a closer examination of the social and political contexts of the no-fault divorce revolution and the "healthy marriage" counterrevolution. Following a discussion of media participation in framing social concerns, we examine divorce reform media frames in 89 newspaper articles extending from 1968 through April 2005. We discuss the implications of findings that illustrate the evolution of divorce reform discourse to "healthy marriage" discourse over the course of the study

period, and we conclude by recommending that [family scholars] take into account the socially and politically constructed nature of marriage reform as a substitute for divorce reform. . . .

Divorce in the United States

Historical Background

In the early days of the American republic, divorce, tied metaphorically to the new nation's "divorce" from England, was essentially a symbol of social order, representing the ability of the community to enforce standards for marital (and other governing) contracts (Basch 1999; Cott 2000). The 18th- and 19th-century privileging of contract relations allowed lifelong marriage to coexist with the acceptance of divorce if one of the spouses failed to live up to the marital contract. Such thinking affirmed the nature of marriage as not only between marrying partners but also as an agreement with the state that marriage was to be conducted along certain socially understood lines and in accordance with agreed-upon family roles. Divorce, then, was the community's way of showing its disapproval when one spouse broke the marital contract. The evolution of fault bases for divorce corresponded to a showing that one spouse was no longer keeping up his or her end of the marital bargain, not only with the other spouse but also with the state in general. Early bases of fault were largely limited to adultery, sexual incapacity, and desertion (Cott 2000), but by the 19th century, provisions for divorce were expanded and grounds were added. Although 19th-century family moralists decried the "laxity" in divorce legislation (see, for instance, Woolsey 1869), in fact, the expansion of grounds was more indicative of the state's increased control over the marriage contract than it was of the absence of state involvement or concern (Cott). Although divorcing created significant social stigma and hardship, particularly for women (see Riley 1991), it was not seen as antithetical to marriage and coexisted, therefore, with the ideal of lifelong marriage.

Nevertheless, as massive 19th-century economic, social, and demographic changes swept the United States, divorce was increasingly blamed for the resulting social disorder. The number of divorces did in fact increase over the course of the century, as did the perception that the family was in a state of crisis. Adding to the angst, women's rights advocates such as Elizabeth Cady Stanton began to promote divorce as a tool for women's emancipation from bad marriages (DuBois 1998). An organized antidivorce movement arose by about 1870 (Grossberg 1985), reacting both to the rise in divorce and to the campaign for women's rights (see Coltrane and Adams 2003; Faludi 1991). The leaders of the movement, organized as the National League for the Protection of the Family,[1] consisted largely of White male clergy, lawyers, judges, academics, and politicians. One of their primary tasks involved motivating an "educational" campaign to associate divorce with family breakdown and social disorder (Dike 1888), a project that we might today view as akin to an antidivorce public relations campaign.

As a result, divorce and marriage came to be seen as oppositional processes, and divorce was equated generally with social disorder. Envisioning divorce as a moral evil to be fought in America's homes and on the legislative front, the antidivorce crusaders focused on tightening state restrictions on divorce and promoting national uniformity in grounds and regulation.

Generally speaking, the 19th-century divorce reform movement is considered a failure by historians, who cite the movement's long-term inability to reduce divorce (O'Neill 1967). Nevertheless, a number of states did move to limit access to divorce by reducing the number of available grounds, and states with omnibus clauses repealed them and reinstated definitive grounds for divorce (Grossberg 1985). Although the 19th-century antidivorce movement was somewhat successful at encouraging uniformity across states, it was less successful in promoting uniformity in divorce regulation at a national level, although uniform divorce laws were introduced in Congress on several occasions (Grossberg; Riley 1991). The present analysis suggests that, although that fight was "lost" in the early part of the 20th century, an analogous fight has resurfaced recently at the national level as the federal government, in alliance with marriage promotion advocates, has moved to make "healthy marriage" the standard for reform activity across the nation.

From Fault to No-Fault to "Healthy Marriage"

Over the next half-century, divorce laws remained relatively unchanged. The requirement that grounds be proved in court before a divorce could be granted necessitated an overtly adversarial judicial proceeding that pitted a "blameless" victim against a "blameworthy" victimizer (see Coltrane and Adams 2003). Although divorces were often mutually desired, the legal requirement for blame mandated divorce actions filled with collusion between the spouses, their lawyers, and judges themselves (see Ellman and Lohr 1997; Hill Kay 2000). Revelation of (staged) trysts, replete with private investigators hired to "uncover" the adultery, consumed an undue amount of court activity and energy, increasing an atmosphere of legal hypocrisy that many felt demeaned the courts, the law, and the involved couple (Ellman and Lohr). Moreover, the mandated finding of blame was, in many cases, undeserved but required, and the animosity that resulted as couples debated who was to "take the hit" exacerbated acrimonious outcomes (see, for instance, Ahrons 1994). In response to this divorce miasma, the legal community undertook divorce reform that moved divorce from a fault-based to a no-fault regime (Hill Kay 1987, 2000).

No-fault divorce statutes, the first of which was enacted in California in 1969–1970, made divorce proceedings officially nonadversarial as the requirement to prove one party's guilt was eliminated (Hill Kay 2000). Irreconcilable differences or incompatibility replaced, or was added to, the laundry list of grounds for which a divorce could be granted. This reform also did away with much of the hypocrisy embedded in a system that

required collusion between the participants and the court (Bradford 1997; Friedman 2000). Other states followed California in quick succession and, by about 1985, all had some provision for no-fault divorce on their books (Singer 1992). The decision for divorce moved from the state to the divorcing couple as the former moved from a regulatory to a procedural role. Most states, however, did not completely break from grounding divorce in fault, at the very least continuing to require a mandated waiting period before divorce could be granted (Butler 2000).

A number of symbolic and conceptual shifts occurred with the implementation of no-fault statutes. Divorces were essentially privatized; couples could make their own divorce decisions without being subject to the public moralizing implicit in fault-based regimes. The state had "abandoned its role as the moral arbiter of marital behavior" (Singer 1992:1472). Severing the conceptual divorce relationship between victim and victimizer (generally conceived as wife and husband, respectively) also broke the implicit symbolic connection of divorce with social disintegration, which was embedded in the symbolism of divorce law since the late 1800s. Divorce became a process between ostensible legal equals rather than one that allowed the state to reinforce one spouse's legal dependency by conjuring up images of an injured and an injuring party (see Biondi 1999). In this way, divorce could be seen, as early feminists had envisioned, as a mechanism for release from a bad marriage. Moreover, as sociologist Karla Hackstaff (1999) observed, a "culture of divorce" could serve as a negotiating tool for empowering women within the context of marriage.

Implementation of no-fault divorce initially created a number of financial problems for ex-wives because their property and support settlements were now premised on their legal status as equal marital partners. Some states continued to regard property as belonging to the person in whom title vested (generally the man); moreover, exactly what belonged in the realm of marital property was unclear. Alimony, previously considered a divorced wife's "right" based on her husband's abrogation of the marital contract, had been discontinued and replaced by a new ideal of spousal support premised on the notion that men and women were equally capable of supporting themselves (Brobeil 2004). That women were disadvantaged by the gender pay gap was overlooked, and divorced women suffered financially as a result (Weitzman 1985). Moreover, women continued to be the primary postdivorce custodians of children, a fact that further exacerbated their financial hardship (see, for instance, Arendell 1986). For these reasons, early post-no-fault reform efforts, promoted largely by feminists, focused on such topics as financial awards (both spousal and child), the legal parameters of "equity" versus "equality," and the types and extent of property to be distributed at divorce (Hill Kay 1987). Although they had limited success in increasing divorced mothers' standard of living (see Arendell), feminists were able to increase the visibility of the problems in the system and slowly make the new divorce regime fairer for women (Hill Kay). A number of states passed equitable distribution laws, and many broadened the scope of marital property distributed at divorce (Burke 1987; Hill Kay).

One area of increased concern for women was child support. Even before implementation of no-fault, noncustodial fathers rarely made court-mandated child support payments, and states found it difficult to force them to pay (Walters and Elam 1985). Because of early problems with the no-fault system, custodial mothers found themselves shortchanged both by the presumption of equal partnership in distribution of assets and by fathers' continued nonpayment of child support. Although the post-no-fault divorce standard of equality evaluated both mothers and fathers for their potential to pay, generally fathers were found to have the greater ability and were therefore most often obligated for the financial support of their children (Carbone 2000). Although states had a difficult time persuading non-custodial fathers to pay, by the 1980s, the federal government had involved itself in ensuring and enforcing child support awards (Walters and Elam; see Coltrane and Hickman 1992).

By the late 1970s, reacting at least in part to their responsibility for increased child support payments, noncustodial fathers organized around their perceived disadvantage in the no-fault divorce regime. Observing continued judicial preference for maternal custody (Carbone 2000), a fathers' rights movement emerged to promote joint child custody, a new ideal that was institutionalized in some states' statutes (Coltrane and Hickman 1992). Drawing on social science literature that portrayed fathers as necessary for a child's healthy development (Lamb 1981), the fathers' rights movement constructed a cultural ideology that typified the "new" father as child centered and nurturing, and their children as deprived by divorce of their father's love and care (Coltrane and Hickman; Drakich 1989). The fathers' rights movement was part of a larger men's rights movement that emerged during the 1970s, partly in reaction to the women's movement and to the privatization of family law that was reflected in no-fault divorce statutes. Both adopted a discourse of men's victimization that blamed women (and particularly feminists) for men's (and fathers') perceived loss of privilege (Messner 1997). . . .

As divorce repeal rhetoric and policies multiplied, covenant marriage emerged as the beginning of a third phase of divorce reform. Although we date the third phase to the 2001 inauguration of President George W. Bush, covenant marriage got a somewhat earlier start, creating some overlap between the discourse of divorce repeal and that of marriage reform. This overlap reflects, we suggest, the ambivalence that Americans feel about repealing divorce or even making it more difficult. For instance, responding to a question on a Time/CNN poll (May 7–8, 1999), 59 percent said that government should not make it harder for people to get divorced; nevertheless, 64 percent agreed that people should be required to take a marriage education course before they could get a marriage license (Time/CNN 1999).[2] The third phase of divorce reform discourse suggests that policy makers interpret such polls to mean that "frontloading" marriage is a more publicly palatable approach to divorce reduction than is making divorce less accessible.

Covenant marriage was perhaps the first attempt to make divorce harder to get by tapping into a couple's commitment level as they first approach the altar. Passed originally in Louisiana in 1997, covenant marriage

is also currently available in Arizona and Arkansas. These statutes provide a voluntary alternative to "regular" marriage whereby partners commit to three primary practices: (1) mandatory premarital counseling; (2) a "legally binding agreement" that they will privilege preservation of the marriage; and (3) return to fault-based divorce provisions or an extended period of separation (up to 2 years) if divorce ultimately becomes necessary (Spaht 2004). Although covenant marriage has been promoted extensively by conservative political and religious groups and has been introduced in a number of additional state legislatures, it has not taken hold of the public imagination and, to date, has been chosen by relatively few marrying couples (Feld, Rosier, and Manning 2002; Zurcher 2004).

Although covenant marriage has failed to mobilize a substantial following, it does illustrate a conceptual shift in the rhetoric of divorce reform, whereby reforming marriage (making marriage "better") has become the latest method for attempting to reduce what is considered to be an unreasonably high divorce rate. The conceptual and ideological shift represented by the "strengthening marriage as divorce reform" approach has occurred in the context of a conservative reaction to no-fault reforms and an increased political opportunity that has energized conservative evangelical groups to elect politicians holding traditional family worldviews (see Coltrane 2001). Elements of the shift include focus on better marriage, often to the near total exclusion of fostering better divorces. This latest phase in divorce reform strategizing has been adopted by an amorphous grouping of academics, therapists, clergy, and others who call themselves the "Marriage Movement."

The Marriage Movement was built on aversion to high divorce rates and fueled by a particular body of social science research connecting divorce to lifelong damage to children (see Wallerstein, Lewis, and Blakeslee 2000) and marriage to unrealistic expectations for health, wealth, and social prosperity (see Nock 1998; Waite and Gallagher 2000). Originally organized in 2000 through the Institute for American Values, the Marriage Movement claims to represent a nonpartisan "grassroots" effort to "strengthen marriage" (Marriage Movement 2004). Its Statement of Principles, created in 2000, and 2004 update set forth its determination to lead a "marriage renaissance" and create a "marriage culture" in the United States (Marriage Movement).

Although the organization is of relatively recent vintage, momentum has been building for some time, drawing strength from groups who have become disenchanted with the loss of male privilege associated with symbolic and material changes to family life (see Coltrane 2001). For instance, Promise Keepers, an evangelical men's movement organized in the 1990s by former professional football coach Bill McCartney, filled football stadiums as it combined sports and religious metaphors to demand men's "reinstatement" as spiritual, physical, and moral family leaders (Janssen 1994). A somewhat less spectacular, but more overtly political, organization, the National Fatherhood Initiative, was organized in 1994 as an advocacy group to "counter what . . . activists saw as 'the growing problem of fatherlessness'" and promote "responsible fatherhood as a national priority" (Coltrane, p. 398). Ostensibly, this organization could be seen as a distant

cousin to the (distinctly antifeminist) fathers' rights groups organized in the 1970s and 1980s. In a sort of cross-pollination between groups, David Blankenhorn, a leader of the organized Marriage Movement, and presidential appointee Wade Horn, who headed the Bush administration's Healthy Marriage Initiative, both presided over the National Fatherhood Initiative (see Coltrane). As president of the National Fatherhood Initiative, Horn pitted feminists against fatherhood in stating, "Radical feminists trumpet the demise of in-the-home fatherhood as a victory for the independence of the modern woman, but fathers make unique and irreplaceable contributions to the well-being of children" (quoted in Pear 2001:24).

The Bush administration's Healthy Marriage Initiative proposed to expend $1.5 billion over a period of 5 years on programs to "strengthen marriage." Tied to reauthorization of the 1996 welfare reform bill, the initiative attempted to earmark those funds for marriage strengthening among the poor and encouraged "faith-based" organizations to develop programs for its implementation (see, for instance, Brotherson and Duncan 2004). Although enabling legislation is still pending, administration officials have used loopholes in the budgetary process to distribute funds for the initiative's enactment, funding programs that promote marriage through marriage preparation, premarital counseling, reductions in marriage license fees, and other programs that "jump-start" marriage. Because the "official" motivation for the initiative is the high divorce rate, the Healthy Marriage Initiative can be viewed as one form of divorce reform. In this sense, the Healthy Marriage Initiative organizes the marriage, fatherhood, and fathers' rights movement concerns about (no-fault) divorce into a broader concern about divorce's alleged connection with children and men as victims of (easy) divorce, and reinforces the symbolic image of divorce as social disorder.

The above discussion addresses divorce reform at the larger policy level and the discourse deployed by politicians, social scientists, and activists to influence policy decisions. Below, we address how that discourse becomes part of the larger public conversation on divorce reform. For this discussion, we turn to an analysis of media framing of divorce reform that can help us better understand how politicized worldviews such as these become part of the public's taken-for-granted stock of knowledge.

Media and Framing

According to sociologists and media scholars, newspapers both reflect public opinion and contribute to its creation. A media frame, according to Gamson and Modigliani (1989), is a "central organizing idea . . . for making sense of relevant events, suggesting what is at issue" (p. 3). Media frames are not policy positions; media frames are interpretive structures broad enough to encompass "disagreement within the overall frame" (p. 4). In this respect, frames essentially provide the boundaries of reasonable discourse and the limits of rational argument. Accordingly, frames encourage particular ways of thinking by selecting out and highlighting certain

"aspects of a perceived reality . . . in such a way as to promote particular problem definition, causal interpretation, moral evaluation" and problem solution (Entman 1993:52).

Social scientists suggest that media framing is a "central political activity" (Baysha and Hallahan 2004:235) because the "entrenchment of some terms, and the disappearance of others, is often a signal of political triumph and defeat" (Callaghan and Schnell 2001:184). Thus, to the extent that certain frames appear or disappear from the mediated public discourse, intentional media framing can be seen as political practice, particularly because studies have found that decision makers frequently use the media as their primary information source (see, for instance, Featherman and Vinovskis 2001). Moreover, selective (and decontextualized) use of social scientific statistics and findings can be seen as legitimating media frames that might otherwise be perceived as "too opinionated" to be objective fact.

Contemporary Media Framing

This portion of our study examines popular news media framing of divorce reform between the time of implementation of the first no-fault divorce statute in California in 1968 and April 2005. Drawing on the literature on media frames and their political nature, we address two main questions: (1) What are the defining media frames that are used by news media in reporting divorce reform? and (2) How has deployment of those frames changed over time?

We use a content analytic approach to address these questions, focusing on articles from three popular newspapers available from two online news databases, *Lexis/Nexis* online and *Proquest Historical Newspapers*. Our general time period of interest is 1968 through April 2005, which encompasses the inception of no-fault statutes around the nation. Specifically, the data are taken from the *Christian Science Monitor*, the *New York Times*, and the *Washington Post*. The bulk of the analysis was drawn from the *Lexis/Nexis* database, which provided extensive coverage after 1980, but minimal coverage before. To include earlier media discourse relative to the burgeoning of no-fault divorce laws, we used the *Proquest Historical Newspapers* database to find articles from the *New York Times* prior to 1980. Using the search terms "(divorce reform or marriage reform) or (healthy marriage and divorce)," we uncovered a total of 127 articles in *Lexis/Nexis* and 65 articles in *Proquest Historical Newspapers*. We excluded all articles on same-sex marriage and those primarily concerned with divorce policy outside the United States. We also excluded articles with no clear divorce media frame. Our sample after applying these criteria incorporated 60 articles from *Lexis/Nexis* and 29 articles from *Proquest* (total $n = 89$ articles; 11 from the *Christian Science Monitor*, 63 from the *New York Times*, and 15 from the *Washington Post*). We chose these three news publications for both substantive and pragmatic reasons. Both the *New York Times* and the *Washington Post* are major national newspapers whose influence and circulation statistics—exceeding a total of 2.5 million subscribers (Audit Bureau of Circulations 2005)—reach well beyond their regional

boundaries. The *Christian Science Monitor,* distributed both nationally and internationally, is described by *Lexis/Nexis* online as "one of the world's great newspapers." We believe that the quality, extent of readership, and level of influence of these three media sources combine to provide a good basis for analyzing the public presentation of the divorce reform debate. Moreover, our ability to access the full texts of articles from 1968 to 1980 (*New York Times*) and from 1980 to April 2005 for all three media outlets through *Lexis/Nexis* and *Proquest Historical Newspapers* provided us with enough contextual detail to enable categorization of each article by media frame. . . .

Analytic Approach

Drawing on Gamson and Modigliani's (1989) definition of media frames, we examined each of the articles for presence of a divorce media frame. Preliminary reading of the articles suggested the involvement of three such frames, each engaging a different "storyline" about divorce policy. The *divorce reform frame* provides an organizing framework for answering the question of how divorce can be made easier or better for the participants (divorcing couple and/or their children). This frame engages a discussion of divorce, usually with the implicit assumption that access to divorce itself is good or at least preferable to not having such access. The *divorce repeal frame,* on the other hand, organizes the storyline of divorce itself as a bad (or morally evil) institution, for the participants and/or society. This frame is also about divorce but implies that divorce should be abolished entirely or should be made more difficult to obtain. The *marriage reform frame* co-opts and incorporates the divorce repeal frame and provides an interpretive structure whereby "strengthening" marriage is viewed as the ultimate way to eliminate divorce. This frame implies that frontloading marriage— through such programs as marriage education, premarital counseling, or "healthy" marriage incentives—will prevent divorce at some future time. We coded each of the 89 selected articles using the above frame definitions, keeping in mind the admonition that arguments both pro and con could fit into the context of each of these overall frames. We also coded for the date of the article and for the presence of reference to social science research regarding divorce or marriage.

Findings and Discussion

The results of our analyses are shown in Figure 1. Results are divided into three time periods, as shown, each of which depicts the proportional composition of divorce policy media frames discussed above. Most articles were structured by one main divorce policy frame, although in four cases, two frames were given roughly equal play, so we coded for the presence of both frames used. Time periods chosen are subjective, reflecting our understanding of changing perceptions of divorce relating to larger cultural and political shifts.

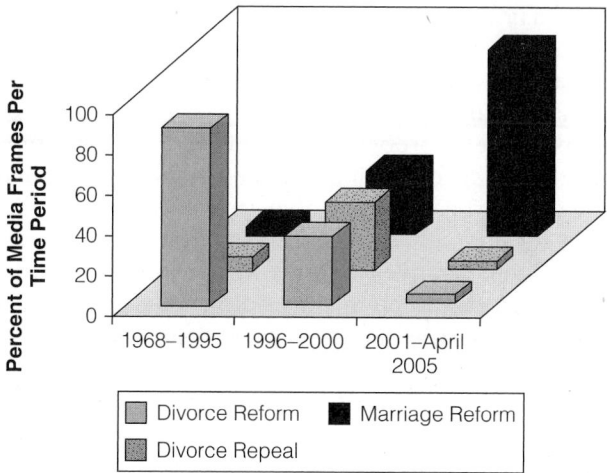

FIGURE 1   Divorce Policy Media Frames, 1968 through April 2005

The first time period includes articles dated from 1968 through 1995. At a policy level, during this period, no-fault divorce was developed and implemented throughout the country and, after implementation, statutes were reworked to "iron out" difficulties. At a social level, this period saw the rise of, and subsequent backlash to, second-wave feminism, the rise of pro- and antifeminist men's movements (Messner 1997), and the rise of the conservative religious right (see Himmelstein 1990). The large majority of divorce reform media frames were identified during this period ($n = 53$), with divorce repeal ($n = 4$) and marriage reform ($n = 3$) frames lagging well behind in use. . . . The beginning of the second time period, 1996, marked legislative adoption of changes in welfare law that included language on strengthening marriage and family. The second time period extends through 2000, the year of G. W. Bush's election as president. During this second period, there was a marked reduction in media attention to divorce, and the coded frames reflect this reduction. Notably, although the divorce repeal and marriage reform frames remained relatively stable, use of the divorce reform frame dropped substantially, from 53 identified frames to only 3 during the second time period. Although this is undoubtedly an artifact of the uneven time periods, at least part of the reduced deployment of the divorce reform frame likely reflects the increased political organization of the religious right and the rise of the National Fatherhood Initiative, both of which tend to disparage divorce and call for policies that make it less accessible. Increasingly prevalent was discourse discouraging divorce but not yet explicitly promoting marriage reform.

The third time period, 2001 through April 2005, begins with the inauguration of G. W. Bush and parallels his administration's efforts to promote two-parent, married, heterosexual families. The political entrenchment of the religious right has, by this time, coalesced with the increased organization of the Marriage Movement to provide a united front in the war on divorce, and

both have found a home with the administration and its promotion of "faith-based" programs. In the process, the divorce reform frame is essentially redefined as marriage reform, and the marriage reform frame assumes that the programmatic result will be elimination of future divorces. Thus, the marriage reform frame incorporates elements of the divorce repeal frame as well; that is, premarital counseling may be combined with longer waiting periods before divorce becomes effective. Use of the marriage reform media frame increases substantially over this time period ($n = 22$) even though the time frame analyzed is relatively short. Thus, the number of articles deploying the marriage reform frame in the approximately 4 1/2 years between 2001 and April 2005 is nearly half the number of articles deploying a divorce reform frame in the 27 years between the inception of no-fault and 1995. This analysis is, moreover, conservative, because our search frame precluded use of a strictly healthy marriage frame by requiring that articles refer to both "healthy marriage and divorce."

As suggested previously, the news media both reflect and inform public opinion. In this regard, Entman and Herbst (2001) suggested that public opinion is largely a myth constructed through media framing processes. Our analysis has illuminated the media framing that evolved over the course of the last several decades in terms of divorce reform discourse. Nevertheless, this framing has not been solely the product of the media; various claimsmakers, such as fathers' rights advocates and marriage promoters, have been involved in the construction and promotion of divorce as a social problem (Coltrane and Adams 2003). Moreover, these claimsmakers, particularly those involved in the promarriage movement, have benefited from the pseudo-scholarly contributions of well-funded, often conservative, think tanks that sponsor public dissemination of the movement's political agenda. These think tanks (e.g., the Heritage Foundation, the Institute for American Values, and the American Enterprise Institute) help to establish and promote media "experts," largely outside the peer review process, whose research and opinions may then appear as legitimating forces in the context of media frames (see Coltrane and Adams). Our analysis of divorce reform frames by time period supports the notion that a political opportunity for the promarriage/antidivorce movement agenda was created with the election and reelection of G. W. Bush in 2000 and 2004. An often symbiotic relationship developed between the Bush administration and this movement, such that the policies of one support and legitimate the political agenda of the other (see Coltrane 2001). . . .

Of additional note is the increased use over time of social science research to legitimate journalistic accounts of divorce policy. Although only 10% of articles drew on social science in the first time period (6/60), the proportion climbed to 44 percent in the second time period (4/9). In the most recent period, two-thirds (16/22) of the articles relied on social science to bolster their claims. We thus observed the blending of social science and moral claims about divorce and its repercussions. This finding resonates, moreover, with the increasing use of "experts," discussed above, by conservative think tanks to legitimate claims of the promarriage movement.

Our analysis suggests that divorce reform policy is no longer about divorce reform, at least as presented through the context of the news media, but is instead about marriage promotion. In this regard, the news stories analyzed reflect the general trend over time for divorce reform to become less "divorce centered" and more concerned with frontloading marriage to forestall later divorce. Although we have identified three different media frames, the divorce reform and marriage reform frames are the dominant frames deployed. . . .

Conclusion

As the fault-based divorce regime demonstrated, laws go only so far in restricting marital behavior; if one spouse wants out of a marriage bad enough, he or she is likely to find a way to "escape" regardless of whether such escape accords with extant divorce laws. No one can argue with the benefits of a healthy, stable family life, and few people try. But because the issue of family has become an increasingly political one, it behooves us, as researchers and therapists, to understand that the way the issue is framed can incorporate a particular politicized worldview. Moreover, it is important to be cognizant of the ways that the media, as a representative of the culture at large, transmits that worldview and makes it seem natural. . . .

Like it or not, divorce is here to stay. Most estimates are that almost one half of all marriages will continue to end in divorce. What purpose is then served by routinely discouraging divorce and ignoring legal reforms that might make it less onerous and contentious? To the extent that we eliminate a discussion of "good" divorce, or a search for ways to have good divorces, we will be reducing the opportunities and life chances for those availing themselves of divorce and for their children. Because increasing the well-being of children is the alleged goal of the marriage reformers, we would hope that they would see the logic in keeping good divorce on the table as an option. Moreover, idealization of marriage implicitly stigmatizes those who do not, or cannot, marry. For instance, as Edin and Reed (2005) observed, the poor, a group specifically targeted for marriage by the profamily movement, are often desirous of marrying. Nevertheless, social and economic barriers tend to prevent them from doing so in spite of the high value that they place on marriage. Stigma and increased pressure to marry, in the form of reduced access to welfare benefits, often follow. Same-sex couples form another group stigmatized by the push for heterosexual marriage. To the extent that same-sex couples, many of whom are parents, are denied access to marriage, its idealization and promotion relegates them and their children to the status of second-class citizens. Finally, as suggested by Elizabeth Cady Stanton nearly 150 years ago and as our analysis of the gendered implications of divorce reform has reiterated, divorce is an option that empowers women in the context of marriage. Although marriage promoters suggest that abandoning the search for the good divorce benefits fathers (Blankenhorn 1995) and, possibly, children (Wallerstein et al. 2000), we believe it would do little to increase women's marital well-being.

ENDNOTES

[1] Organized in 1881 as the New England Divorce Reform League, the group went through two additional name changes, first to the National Divorce Reform League and, in 1897, to the National League for the Protection of the Family.

[2] Interestingly, responses to the divorce question depended on the wording. When asked, "Do you believe it should be harder than it is now for married couples to get a divorce?" 50 percent of respondents answered Yes. When asked, "Should it be harder than it is now for married couples with young children to get a divorce?" 61 percent said Yes.

REFERENCES

Ahrons, C. 1994. *The Good Divorce.* New York: HarperCollins.

Arendell, T. 1986. *Mothers and Divorce: Legal, Economic, and Social Dilemmas.* Berkeley: University of California Press.

Audit Bureau of Circulations. 2005. *Top 200 Newspapers by Largest Reported Circulation.* Retrieved January 27, 2006, from http://www.accessabc.com/reader/top150.htm.

Basch, N. 1999. *Framing American Divorce: From the Revolutionary Generation to the Victorians.* Berkeley: University of California Press.

Baysha, O. and K. Hallahan. 2004. "Media Framing of the Ukrainian Political Crisis, 2000–2001." *Journalism Studies* 5:233–46.

Biondi, J. 1999. "Who Pays for Guilt? Recent Fault-Based Divorce Reform Proposals, Cultural Stereotypes, and Economic Consequences." *Boston College Law Review* 40:611–32.

Blankenhorn, D. 1995. *Fatherless America: Confronting Our Most Urgent Social Problem.* New York: Basic Books.

Bradford, L. 1997. "The Counterrevolution: A Critique of Recent Proposals to Reform No-Fault Divorce Laws." *Stanford Law Review* 49:607–36.

Brobeil, A. 2004. "Family Law Chapter: Marriage and Divorce." *Georgetown Journal of Gender and the Law* 5:529–44.

Brotherson, S. E. and W. C. Duncan. 2004. "Rebinding the Ties That Bind: Government Efforts to Promote and Preserve Marriage." *Family Relations* 53:459–68.

Burke, D. E. 1987. "Til Graduation Do We Part—the Professional Degree Acquired during Marriage as Marital Property upon Dissolution. An Evaluation and Recommendation for Ohio." *University of Cincinnati Law Review* 56:227.

Butler, M. 2000. "Getting Divorced: Grounds for Divorce, a Survey." *Journal of Contemporary Legal Issues* 11:164–73.

Callaghan, K. and F. Schnell. 2001. "Assessing the Democratic Debate: How the News Media Frame Elite Policy Discourse." *Political Communication* 18:183–212.

Carbone, J. 2000. *From Partners to Parents: The Second Revolution in Family Law.* New York: Columbia University Press.

Coltrane, S. 2001. "Marketing the Marriage 'Solution': Misplaced Simplicity in the Politics of Fatherhood." *Sociological Perspectives* 44:387–418.

Coltrane, S. and M. Adams. 2003. "The Social Construction of the Divorce 'Problem': Morality, Child Victims, and the Politics of Gender." *Family Relations* 52:363–72.

Coltrane, S. and N. Hickman. 1992. "The Rhetoric of Rights and Needs: Moral Discourse in the Reform of Child Custody and Child Support Laws." *Social Problems* 39:400–20.

Cott, N. 2000. *Public Vows: A History of Marriage and the Nation.* Cambridge, MA: Harvard University Press.

Dike, S. W. 1888. *Annual Report of the National Divorce Reform League, Year Ending 1888.* Boston: C. H. Simonds and Co.

Doherty, W. J. 2005. *Values Statement* [National Registry of Marriage-Friendly Therapists]. Retrieved August 23, 2005, from http://marriagefriendlytherapists.com/values.php.

Drakich, J. 1989. "In Search of the Better Parent: The Social Construction of Ideologies of Fatherhood." *Canadian Journal of Women and the Law* 3:69–87.

DuBois, E. C. 1998. *Woman Suffrage and Women's Rights.* New York: New York University Press.

Edin, K. and J. M. Reed. 2005. "Why Don't They Just Get Married? Barriers to Marriage among the Disadvantaged." *The Future of Children* 15 (2): 117–37.

Ellman, I. M. and S. Lohr. 1997. "Marriage as Contract, Opportunistic Violence, and Other Bad Arguments for Fault Divorce." *University of Illinois Law Review* 1997 719–72.

Entman, R. M. 1993. "Framing: Toward Clarification of a Fractured Paradigm." *Journal of Communication* 43:51–58.

Entman, R. M. and S. Herbst. 2001. "Reframing Public Opinion as We Have Known It." Pp. 203–25 in *Mediated Politics: Communication in the Future of Democracy*, edited by W. L. Bennett and R. M. Entman. Cambridge, England: Cambridge University Press.

Faludi, S. 1991. *Backlash: The Undeclared War Against American Women*. New York: Crown.

Featherman, D. L. and M. A. E. Vinovskis. 2001. *Social Science and Policy-Making: A Search for Relevance in the Twentieth Century*. Ann Arbor: University of Michigan Press.

Feld, S. L., K. B. Rosier, and A. Manning. 2002. "Christian Right as Civil Right: Covenant Marriage and a Kinder, Gentler, Moral Conservatism." *Review of Religious Research* 44:173–83.

Friedman, L. M. 2000. "A Dead Language: Divorce Law and Practice before No-Fault." *Virginia Law Review* 86:1497–1536.

Gamson, W. A. and A. Modigliani. 1989. "Media Discourse and Public Opinion on Nuclear Power: A Constructionist Approach." *American Journal of Sociology* 95:1–37.

Grossberg, M. 1985. *Governing the Hearth: Law and the Family in Nineteenth-Century America*. Chapel Hill: University of North Carolina Press.

Hackstaff, K. B. 1999. *Marriage in a Culture of Divorce*. Philadelphia: Temple University Press.

Hill Kay, H. 1987. "Equality and Difference: A Perspective on No-Fault Divorce and Its Aftermath." *University of Cincinnati Law Review* 56:1–90.

———. 2000. "From the Second Sex to the Joint Venture: An Overview of Women's Rights and Family Law in the United States during the Twentieth Century." *California Law Review* 88:2017–93.

Himmelstein, J. 1990. *To the Right: The Transformation of American Conservatism*. Berkeley: University of California Press.

Janssen, A. 1994. *The Seven Promises of a Promise Keeper*. Colorado Springs, CO: Focus on the Family Publishers.

Lamb, M. E., ed. 1981. *The Role of the Father in Child Development*. New York: Wiley.

Marquardt, E. 2005. "The bad divorce." *First Things* 150:24–28.

Marriage Movement. 2004. *Resources for the Marriage Movement*. Retrieved August 23, 2005, from http://www.marriagemovement.org.

Messner, M. A. 1997. *Politics of Masculinities: Men in Movements*. Thousand Oaks, CA: Sage.

Nock, S. L. 1998. *Marriage in Men's Lives*. New York: Oxford University Press.

O'Neill, W. L. 1967. "Samuel W. Dike and the Hazards of Moral Reform." *Vermont History: The Proceedings of the Vermont Historical Society* 35 (3): 160–68.

Pear, R. 2001. "Human Services Nominee's Focus on Married Fatherhood Draws Both Praise and Fire." *The New York Times*, June 7, p. 24.

Riley, G. 1991. *Divorce: An American Tradition*. New York: Oxford University Press.

Schoenfeld, E. 1996. "Drumbeats for Divorce Reform." *Policy Review* 7. Retrieved August 25, 2005, from http://www.policyreview.org/may96/homef.html.

Singer, J. B. 1992. "The Privatization of Family Law." *Wisconsin Law Review* 1992 1443–1567.

Spaht, K. S. 2004. "A Proposal: Legal Re-regulation of the Content of Marriage." *Notre Dame Journal of Law, Ethics and Public Policy* 18:243–62.

Time/CNN. 1999. *Time/CNN Poll: Divorce*. Retrieved August 23, 2005, from http://patriot.net/~crouch/wash/timetable.html.

Waite, L. J. and Gallagher, M. 2000. *The Case for Marriage: Why Married People Are Happier, Healthier, and Better Off Financially*. New York: Doubleday.

Wallerstein, J., J. Lewis, and S. Blakeslee. 2000. *The Unexpected Legacy of Divorce: A 25-Year Landmark Study*. New York: Hyperion.

Walters, L. H. and A. W. Elam. 1985. "The Father and the Law." *American Behavioral Scientist* 29:78–111.

Weitzman, L. J. 1985. *The Divorce Revolution*. New York: Free Press.

Woolsey, T. 1869. *Essay on Marriage and Divorce Legislation*. New York: Scribner.

Zurcher, K. E. 2004. "'I Do' or 'I Don't'? Covenant Marriage after Six Years." *Notre Dame Journal of Law, Ethics & Public Policy* 18:273–301.

37

DIVORCE CULTURE AND MARITAL GENDER EQUALITY
A Cross-National Study

CARRIE YODANIS

One in two marriages ends in divorce. This statistic is a source of much attention in the United States. The focus, however, has largely been on the marriage that ends. Research examining why divorces occur and the impact of divorce on the members of divorcing families is abundant. This [reading] takes a different focus and looks at the one marriage out of two that does not end. Previous research and theory propose that intact marriages and the level of marital gender equality are affected by a growing divorce culture, including both increasing divorce rates and acceptance of divorce. In this article, I explore these ideas cross-nationally and look to see if a national divorce culture is associated with more or less gender equality in marriage.

Marital Gender Inequality in a Divorce Culture

Most studies on divorce examine the consequences of personally experiencing divorce for individual women, men, and children. However, divorce can also be viewed as part of a macro, cultural-level phenomenon affecting people throughout a society regardless of whether they individually experience divorce. In her book *Marriage in a Culture of Divorce*, Karla Hackstaff (1999) contrasts marriage culture and divorce culture. A marriage culture includes the belief, assumption, and practice that marriage is a given and forever. A divorce culture, in comparison, is a set of beliefs and practices that define marriage as optional and conditional, with divorce being an option if the marriage does not work.

Research on the consequences of rising divorce rates and especially changing attitudes toward divorce on a national level is limited. There is some evidence that high national divorce rates are related to lower fertility rates, later age at marriage, and lower rates of spousal violence (Gibson 1976; Lester 1996; Sleebos 2003; Stevenson and Wolfers 2003; Wolfinger 2003). In addition, some research suggests that women's increasing labor force participation is an outcome of high divorce rates. In societies characterized by

high divorce rates, women may be less willing to be financially dependent on men in marriage and therefore more likely to participate in the labor force throughout the life course (Diekmann 1994; Hou and Omwanda 1997). Most notably, a debate continues regarding how a growing divorce culture affects gender equality in intact marriages. This [reading] contributes to this debate.

Bargaining theory focuses on how couples negotiate agreements in the relationship, including how to divide the work. According to bargaining theory, partners have options both within and outside of marriage, and each partner's ability to negotiate in the bargaining process is based on the options that are available to him or her. Particularly relevant is the concept of a "divorce threat point." When bargaining occurs within the context of the possibility of divorce, partners consider their alternatives if their relationship should end, and the attractiveness of their anticipated alternatives affect their negotiations (Lundberg and Pollak 1996; Manser and Brown 1980; Muthoo 2000).

The divorce threat point operates on an individual level and is dependent on environmental factors, such as the level of public assistance to divorced single mothers and divorce laws regarding the division of property (Lundberg and Pollak 1996). Stevenson and Wolfers (2003) find support for the importance of the contextual dimension of the threat point when they find that the introduction of no-fault divorce laws across U.S. states is related to significant decreases in rates of spousal violence in the states. In other words, when it became easier to leave a relationship, gender dynamics within the relationship improved. As they conclude, "unilateral divorce changed the bargaining power in marriage and therefore impacted many marriages—not simply the extra few divorces enabled by unilateral divorce" (p. 19).

This [reading] adds a cross-national component to this argument. Nations, more so than the 50 states in the United States, have varying laws and dominant ideologies that make it easier or harder for individuals to divorce whether or not they want to. In the context of strict laws and attitudes against divorce, individual divorce threat points will be high or nonexistent.

Building on bargaining theory, the literature outlines two possible ways that a divorce culture on a national level can affect the level of gender equality in marriages. An enhanced equality hypothesis suggests that divorce culture may increase equality between partners. Unlike in a marriage culture where women stay in the relationship no matter how unsatisfied or unequal they are, men risk losing women in a divorce culture if the relationship does not move toward equality. Thus, divorce becomes a tool that women use to secure change and greater equality in marital relationships. . . .

In a counter diminished equality hypothesis, a divorce culture may increase inequality between marriage partners. The divorce alternative increases men's power relative to women's. In a marriage culture, men stay in the marriage no matter what. In a divorce culture, in comparison, women risk losing men if they push for change in the relationship. Divorce can be a threat that men use against women in an effort to thwart their attempts at

marital equality and thereby can reduce women's power in marriage. Given that women often experience declines in economic well-being with divorce, this threat can be powerful in controlling women's attempts to strive for equality. In her classic study of dual-career couples, Hochschild (1989) finds support for the diminished equality hypothesis that women are not able to push for change in the unequal distribution of work in relationships because of the threat of divorce. . . .

In this [reading], I address the question, How is a divorce culture, measured as both national practices and attitudes toward divorce, related to gender equality in marriage on an individual level? In addressing this question, this [reading] provides a cross-national examination of the enhanced and diminished marital equality hypotheses of divorce culture. Most of the research about these hypotheses is based on data from the United States, a country with a very high divorce culture. Looking across nations makes it possible to see if the theories hold up in different cultural contexts and if variation between countries in divorce culture is related to variation in marital relationships (Kohn 1987). This is what I set out to do in this [reading]. . . .

Method

The data used in this [reading] come primarily from the International Social Survey Programme (ISSP). The ISSP, analogous to a cross-nationally comparative General Social Survey, is an annual social survey conducted in countries throughout the world. Since 1986, a different topic is selected each year as a module of focus in addition to the repeated items. For this analysis, data from the 1994 Family and Changing Gender Roles module are used.

The data are gathered through a 15-minute questionnaire, conducted as a supplement to regular national surveys or as a separate survey. The samples for each country are national household probability samples. The questionnaire is originally written in English and translated into the national language(s) for conducting the survey. The data are then compiled into English-language data sets.

Twenty-two countries are included in the analysis. In the 1994 ISSP data set, Spain and the Netherlands were dropped due to insufficient data. For this analysis, I use two levels of data: country and individual level. At the individual level, the total sample is 9,529 married women. To be included in the sample, participants had to be currently married. People who were currently cohabiting were dropped from the sample. Only women were included in the analysis. This decision was made based on the nature of the research questions as well as the fact that key variables about wives, such as education, age, gender ideology, and opinions about women's employment, were available only for the respondent.

At the country level, data are based on the entire sample, including married and not married women and men. This decision is based on the need to measure the overall dominant ideology and practices of the country.

Outcome Variable: Marital Gender Inequality

The level of marital gender inequality is measured using the division of household labor. The distribution of housework between husband and wife is measured using reports of who does the following four household tasks: shopping for groceries, deciding what to have for dinner, doing the laundry, and caring for the sick. Responses include "always or usually the woman," "equally," "usually or always the man," and "a third person." Those who responded that a third person did the task were dropped. A mean score was computed by summing the responses and dividing by the number of completed answers for each case. The scale has a Cronbach's alpha of .68. A high score indicates a traditional division of labor with women doing more housework than do men. . . .

Individual-Level Independent Variables

Gender role ideology is conceptualized as beliefs about gender roles in marriage. The variable is a composite measure of the following three questions from the ISSP: "Do you agree or disagree . . . (1) A job is all right, but what most women really want is a home and children, (2) Being a housewife is just as fulfilling as working for pay, (3) A man's job is to earn money; a woman's job is to look after the home and family." For each statement, respondents indicated whether they *strongly agree, agree, neither agree nor disagree, disagree,* or *strongly disagree.* These three indicators were confirmed for selection based on factor analysis and theory. The composite measure was created by summing the scores on the items and dividing by the number of the responses given. A high score indicates a nontraditional gender ideology. The scale has a Cronbach's alpha of .68. The range in average scores across countries is not large. The most traditional ideology is found in Russia, with a mean score of 2.16, and the most nontraditional ideology is in East Germany, with a mean score of 3.80.

Relative earnings is included to account for the relative resource theory of marital gender equality, which explains that valued resources, including income, can be exchanged within the relationship to opt out of doing housework (Brines 1993). This variable measures who earns more, the husband or wife. The five responses include "the man earns much more," "the man earns a bit more," "we earn about the same amount," "the woman earns a bit more," and "the woman earns much more." A high score indicates the woman earns more. The variable was recoded to include respondents who were not employed. Using questions regarding the employment status of each partner, the variable is coded as "man earns much more" if the husband is employed and the wife is not. Likewise, the variable is coded "woman earns much more" if the wife is employed and the husband is not. Slightly more than 68 percent of the women are employed either full- or part-time or retired. In nearly 77 percent of the couples, the man earns much or a bit more, while in 10 percent of the couples, women do. . . .

Age is included in the equation to control for cohort effects in marital relations. The respondent's age is measured in years. For the sample, the mean age is 45 years.

Education is constructed as a dummy variable, indicating whether the respondent has a university degree (1 = university degree). Nearly 11 percent of the sample has a university degree.

Cohabitation is also associated with greater marital equality (Batalova and Cohen 2002). Thus, a dummy variable is included in the equation, indicating whether the couple lived together before marrying (1 = cohabited). Nearly 29 percent of the sample cohabited before marriage.

Additional people in the household is a variable included to serve as a proxy for presence of children in the household. The presence of children affects gender roles in marriage, often resulting in more traditional gender arrangements (Nomaguchi and Milkie 2003). In the ISSP, the best variable available to control for the presence of children is the measure of number of people in the household. The variable is dichotomized, with three or more people in the household coded as 1. While this variable indicates the possibility that children live with the married couple, it cannot distinguish between children and others, such as an elderly parent or other adults. The average number of people in a household is 3.5, and 71.4 percent of the sample are households with three or more people.

Divorce attitudes are based on the following three questions from the ISSP: "Do you agree or disagree . . . (1) Divorce is usually the best solution when a couple can't seem to work out their marriage problems, (2) When there are children in the family, parents should stay together even if they don't get along, (3) Even when there are no children, a married couple should stay together even if they don't get along." Responses are given on a 5-point Likert-type scale ranging from *strongly agree* to *strongly disagree.* Items were coded so that a high score indicates an acceptance of divorce or high divorce culture. Items were combined by summing the scores and dividing by the number of responses given. The scale has a Cronbach's alpha of .57.

Divorce experiences can also be related to gender equality in marriage. In particular, there is evidence that women who have been previously divorced may be more reluctant to remarry and thereby have more power when they do (Pyke 1994). Therefore, two variables measuring if the husband and wife had been previously divorced are included in the models (1 = has been divorced). More than 13 percent of women and men report a previous divorce. In 4 percent of couples, both the husband and wife were previously divorced. Divorce experience of respondent and partner explains 1 percent of the variance in divorce attitudes.

Country-Level Independent Variables

Divorce culture is a composite measure of attitudes toward divorce and divorce rates. The measure is a factor score combining these two items using principal components analysis. National aggregates of divorce attitudes, based on the mean score on the divorce attitudes measure for each country, are used. Divorce rates are based on data from the 1997 and 1998 *United Nations Demographic Yearbooks.* For each country, the rates are based on the number of divorces per 1,000 midyear population, and the running average

of divorce rates from 1993, 1994, and 1995 are used to correspond with the 1994 ISSP data. . . .

Gender Role Ideology   A second country-level variable, dominant gender ideology, is included to account for the fact that part of the country-level effect of a divorce culture on marital equality may be spurious since nontraditional values are related both to greater marital equality (Komter 1989) and to a higher divorce culture. Gender ideology on the country level is measured using the mean score for each country on the individual-level gender role ideology index. The correlation between the national measures of divorce culture and gender role ideology is rather weak ($r = .386$, $p = .076$).

Analysis

. . . The analysis presented in this [reading] incorporates two levels of data—individual- and country-level variables on the outcome variable, marital equality.

On the individual level, relative income, individual gender ideology, age, education, and divorce attitudes are centered at the grand mean. To explore the country-level impact, I test if the intercept of the individual-level equation varies by levels of divorce culture and gender ideology. Both country-level variables are centered at the grand mean. Age, education, relative income, cohabitation, presence of children, and individual divorce attitudes have fixed effects across countries.

Results

Country-Level Description of Divorce Culture and Marital Equality

Country-level descriptive statistics are presented in table 1. Countries are ranked according to the level of divorce culture. Surprisingly, given the vast variation between countries in their history, religion, family laws, and the status of women, there is not a large amount of variation in attitudes toward divorce. Austria has the strongest acceptance of divorce (with a mean score of 4 on a 5-point scale), and Japan has the lowest acceptance (with a mean score of 2.87). Divorce rates range from a high of 4.29 in the United States to lows of .46 in Italy and 0 in Ireland and the Philippines, where divorce is not legal. The United States has the strongest divorce culture. Catholic, familialistic, and collectivist countries, including Italy, Ireland, Poland, and the Philippines, have the lowest culture of divorce.

Turning to average measure of marital equality across countries, again it is interesting to see that despite large variation between the countries, the housework on average remains unequally distributed, with women being responsible for most of the work. In no country was the housework on average distributed equally or primarily done by men (as would be indicated by a score of 1 to 3).

TABLE 1　Descriptive Statistics for Measures of Divorce Culture and Marital Gender Inequality

Country [a]	Divorce Culture			Marital Inequality [d]
	Attitude	Rate [b]	Index Score [c]	Housework [e]
United States	3.60	4.54	1.23	3.85
Russia	3.55	4.53	1.13	4.01
Austria	4.00	2.14	0.90	4.18
East Germany	3.96	2.01 [f]	0.76	3.80
Canada	3.79	2.67	0.71	3.82
Czech Republic	3.70	2.97	0.67	4.14
Great Britain	3.64	2.98 [g]	0.54	4.04
West Germany	3.85	2.01 [f]	0.51	3.99
New Zealand	3.71	2.61	0.51	3.95
Australia	3.68	2.73	0.50	4.13
Sweden	3.72	2.52	0.48	3.84
Hungary	3.69	2.29	0.31	4.01
Northern Ireland	3.49	2.98 [g]	0.23	4.12
Norway	3.57	2.49	0.15	3.82
Israel	3.73	1.47	−0.01	3.92
Bulgaria	3.71	1.02	−0.29	4.06
Slovenia	3.71	0.92	−0.33	4.02
Italy	3.63	0.46	−0.75	4.33
Ireland	3.51	0.00 [h]	−1.24	4.22
Japan	2.87	1.55	−1.84	4.62
Poland	3.01	0.84	−1.88	4.16
Philippines	3.03	0.00 [h]	−2.28	4.16

[a]Countries are ranked according to divorce culture.
[b]Divorce rate (divorces per 1,000 population), average of 1993, 1994, and 1995.
[c]Factor score from factor analysis with divorce attitudes and divorce rates.
[d]Based on the sample of married women.
[e]Score on division of housework index, ranges from 1 to 5, with a high score indicating women's doing more of the work.
[f]Given the rates for Germany.
[g]Given the rates for the United Kingdom.
[h]Divorce was illegal in the Philippines and Ireland (until 1997).

Multilevel Analysis

Individual-Level Effects　Looking first at the relationship between individual-level variables and the division of housework, findings from previous research are supported. Results are shown in table 2. Model 1 shows the effects of individual-level variables commonly used to explain the division of household labor. Supporting resource theory, the more women earn relative to men, the more equal the division of housework. In addition, women with university degrees report a more egalitarian division of labor than women with less

TABLE 2 **Hierarchical Linear Model of Individual- and Country-Level Effects on Division of Housework** [a]

	Model 1	Model 2	Model 3	Model 4
Intercept	3.9814***	3.9828***	3.9833***	3.9834***
Individual level				
Relative income	−0.0620***	−0.0616***	−0.0617***	−0.0618***
Gender ideology (individual)	−0.0663***	−0.0676***	−0.0673***	−0.0667***
Age	0.0049***	0.0049***	0.0050***	0.0050***
Education	−0.0794***	−0.0803***	−0.0806***	−0.0807***
Cohabitation	−0.0706***	−0.0665***	−0.0656***	−0.0655***
People in household	0.1483***	0.1485***	0.1474***	0.1471***
Missing value: income	−0.0359	−0.0368	−0.0388*	−0.0389*
Divorce attitudes (individual)		0.0077	0.0087	0.0087
Wife previously divorced		−0.0356	−0.0353	−0.0356
Husband previously divorced		0.0060	0.0066	0.0065
Country level				
Divorce culture			−0.0924**	−0.0835*
Gender ideology (country)				−0.0500
Variance components				
Intercept	0.0234***	0.0236***	0.0159***	0.0163***
Level 1	0.3514	0.3514	0.3514	0.3514

[a]Measured on a 5-point scale with a high score indicating that women do more of the housework than do men.
*$p < .05$ **$p < .01$ ***$p < .001$

education. In models 1 and 2, the nonresponses for the income variable do not differ significantly on the division of household labor. In the later models, there is a small yet significant difference.

Previous findings regarding the effect of gender ideology on the distribution of housework are also supported. When women have a nontraditional gender role ideology, the division of labor is less unequal. In addition, as a cohort effect would expect, older women do significantly more housework compared to younger women. Women who cohabited before marriage are significantly more likely to report greater equality in the distribution of housework, and the number of people in the household is related to women's doing more housework relative to men.

Model 2 adds individual-level variables regarding divorce experience and attitudes. Neither husbands' nor wives' previous experiences with divorce nor women's individual divorce attitudes are significantly related to the distribution of housework.

Country-Level Effects   Model 3 adds the country-level measure of divorce culture, the focus of this [reading]. In this multilevel model, the intercept of housework, or the mean distribution of housework across countries of

average divorce culture for women of average age, gender ideology, and relative income; with no university education; and who did not cohabit before marriage, is 3.98, indicating a general tendency toward women's doing most of the work. The divorce culture of a country is related to the distribution of housework within marriage. The stronger the divorce culture, the more equal the division of housework. Specifically, controlling for women's resource contribution, gender role ideology, and other characteristics found to be related to marital equality, with each increase of 1 on the divorce culture index, the average score on the housework index decreases by .09, moving toward a more equal division of labor. The size of the effect is not very large but is not inconsequential given the rigidity of the gendered division of labor across cultures. This is addressed in more detail in the Discussion. Model 4 adds the country-level variable, dominant gender ideology, to the model. The gender ideology of a country is not directly related to the distribution of housework.

Comparing the variance components between models 1 and 2, individual-level divorce variables do not explain additional variation in the division of household labor. Looking at model 3, it is apparent that national divorce culture explains a substantial portion of the variation in the intercept across countries. Divorce culture reduces the amount of unexplained variance in the intercept by a third.

Discussion

The main objective of this [reading] is to examine the cross-national relationship between a divorce culture on a national level and gender equality in intact marriages. In particular, I look across countries to see if there is more support for the argument that a divorce culture is associated with enhanced or diminished equality for women in marriage.

Overall, the results provide support for the enhanced equality theory over the diminished equality hypothesis. A strong divorce culture on the national level is associated with a more, not less, equal distribution of work in marriages. Thus, it appears that the concern that divorce would limit women's ability to push for equality in marriage does not appear to be the overall pattern. In countries where divorce is more accepted and widely practiced, women's position within marriages is better.

In addition, the national divorce culture of a country, rather than individual divorce attitudes or experiences, appears to be particularly important. This adds confirmation to the argument that divorce threat points and, correspondingly, women's and men's options and perceived alternatives within relationships are influenced by social and cultural context. If divorce is not an accepted or available option within a society, the divorce threat point is remote, limiting the extent to which alternatives to the relationship can be used to bargain for equality within the relationship.

This study also adds new perspectives on the study of divorce. First, the findings raise the often underresearched issue that divorce is not merely

behavior on the micro level but is associated with shifting cultures on the macro level. By conceptualizing and operationalizing divorce culture as a composite measure of both the attitudes toward and the practices of divorce on a national level, divorce can be viewed as not merely a personal experience but a part of a dramatic cultural and social change. As such, the influence of these changes may not be limited to those individuals and families who directly experience divorce. Rather, these changes affect everyone within a society, including married couples. This follows the longtime call by feminist researchers to move away from thinking about the family as an autonomous unit and toward realizing the complex ways in which the social contextual shapes family relationships (Little Fox and McBride Murry 2000; Thorne and Yalom 1982).

Second, the research reaffirms that like many social and cultural changes, the correlates of a growing divorce culture are complex, including simultaneous advantages and disadvantages. While much research shows the potential negative consequences of divorce, this study provides support for the often overlooked positive correlates of a divorce culture. Researchers have long argued that divorce can provide physical and psychological safety for women and children by providing opportunities to leave abusive or unhealthy relationships (Katz et al. 1995). This study adds to the evidence that there may be benefits to the availability of divorce that extend beyond extreme, life-threatening situations and ironically may contribute to the strengthening of marriages. At a time when efforts such as the implementation of covenant marriages are trying to reverse the divorce culture and make it more difficult to leave marriages, understanding the positive outcomes of a divorce culture is more important than ever (Rosier and Feld 2000).

When considering the results, there are some methodological limitations to keep in mind. First, the relationship between the divorce culture and the division of housework is present and significant but not very strong. This is not surprising given previous research that shows a strong persistence of an unequal division of household labor regardless of women's resource contribution or couples' gender ideology (Bittman et al. 2003; Brines 1994; Greenstein 2000). The striking consistency in women's responsibility for household labor across countries that vary greatly in culture, social structures, and social institutions is itself a testament to the rigidity of the gender imbalance in the division of labor. Under these conditions, a weak relationship is to be expected. Indeed, it is not unreasonable to argue that the relationship is substantial given the phenomenon under study.

As is often the case with cross-sectional data, it is important to caution against making claims of causal order. It is possible that divorce is more likely to be accepted and possible in countries characterized by greater marital equality. Nonetheless, this does not negate the finding that marriages are less, not more, unequal in strong divorce cultures.

Furthermore, the possibility of a selectivity bias should also be considered. According to the enhanced equality hypothesis, women in unequal couples will use divorce as a threat to create change. Following from this reasoning, unequal couples may be selected out of the sample in divorce

cultures because they have already divorced. Again, however, the dissolution of unequal marriages and the persistence of egalitarian marriages in a divorce culture do not contradict the support for the enhanced equality hypothesis.

Gender role ideology is included in the analysis to try to rule out some possible spurious national-level factors that might explain the relationship between divorce culture and marital gender equality. There are likely to be other variables that affect this relationship. For example, religious history and culture unquestionably explain variation in the divorce culture across countries. Some of these variables, such as religion, may be less likely to have direct relationships to marital equality than indirect relationships through such variables as gender ideology. Other variables such as women's political and occupational status relative to men's may also explain part of the relationship. . . .

. . . In research focusing on a few countries, it is possible to consider the detailed specifics of each case and variable, such as marital gender equality, and to consider the complex factors that led to variation in divorce cultures across countries. This unquestionably is an interesting future direction for cross-national research on divorce culture. Such questions, however, involve a different type of cross-national research than the one presented in this [reading]. This study seeks to examine patterns across a larger sample of countries—an approach that Kohn (1987) calls "country as the unit of analysis." While this approach necessitates a loss in the depth of detail for each specific variable and case, it provides the advantage of a breadth of information across more cases. Using this approach, Kohn argues that it is not imperative to explain how the countries got to their current status. Such questions are better left to other cross-national research designs. Rather, the focus is on studying the correlates of the current social circumstances of nations, regardless of the various historical or cultural processes that lead to them.

REFERENCES

Batalova, Jeanne A. and Philip N. Cohen. 2002. "Premarital Cohabitation and Housework: Couples in Cross-National Perspective." *Journal of Marriage and the Family* 64:743–55.

Bittman, Michael, Paula England, Liana Sater, Nancy Folbre, and George Matheson. 2003. "When Does Gender Trump Money? Bargaining and Time in Household Work." *American Journal of Sociology* 100:652–88.

Brines, Julie. 1993. "The Exchange Value of Household Work." *American Journal of Sociology* 109:186–214.

———. 1994. "Economic Dependency, Gender, and the Division of Labor at Home." *American Journal of Sociology* 100:652–88.

Diekmann, Andrea. 1994. "Is Women's Labor Force Participation Caused by Increasing Divorce Risks?" *Soziale Welt* 45:83–97.

Gibson, Campbell. 1976. "The U.S. Fertility Decline, 1961–1975: The Contribution of Changes in Marital Status and Marital Fertility." *Family Planning Perspectives* 8:249–52.

Greenstein, Theodore N. 2000. "Economic Dependence, Gender, and the Division of Household Labor in the Home: A Replication and Extension." *Journal of Marriage and the Family* 62:322–35.

Hackstaff, Karla B. 1999. *Marriage in a Culture of Divorce.* Philadelphia: Temple University Press.

Hochschild, Arlie. 1989. *The Second Shift.* New York: Avon.

Hou, Feng and Lewis O. Omwanda. 1997. "A Multilevel Analysis of the Connection between Female Labour Force Participation and Divorce in Canada, 1931–1991." *International Journal of Comparative Sociology* 38:271–88.

Katz, Jennifer, Ilena Arias, Steven Beach, Gene Brody, and Paul Roman. 1995. "Excuses, Excuses: Accounting for the Effects of Partner Violence on Marital Satisfaction and Stability." *Violence and Victims* 10:315–26.

Kohn, Melvin. 1987. "Cross-National Research as an Analytic Strategy." *American Sociological Review* 52:713–31.

Komter, A. 1989. "Hidden Power in Marriage." *Gender & Society* 3:187–216.

Lester, David. 1996. "Trends in Divorce and Marriage around the World." *Journal of Divorce and Remarriage* 25:169–71.

Little Fox, Greer and Velma McBride Murry. 2000. "Gender and Families: Feminist Perspectives and Family Research." *Journal of Marriage and the Family* 62:1160–72.

Lundberg, Shelly and Robert Pollak. 1996. "Bargaining and Distribution in Marriage." *Journal of Economic Perspectives* 10:139–58.

Manser, Marilyn and Murray Brown. 1980. "Marriage and Household Decision Making: A Bargaining Analysis." *International Economic Review* 21:31–44.

Muthoo, Abhinay. 2000. "A Non-Technical Introduction to Bargaining Theory." *World Economics* 1:145–66.

Nomaguchi, Kei and Melissa Milkie. 2003. "Costs and Rewards of Children: The Effects of Becoming a Parent on Adults' Lives." *Journal of Marriage and the Family* 65:356–74.

Pyke, Karen. 1994. "Women's Employment as Gift or Burden? Marital Power across Marriage, Divorce and Remarriage." *Gender & Society* 8:73–91.

Rosier, Katherine and Scott Feld. 2000. "Covenant Marriage: A New Alternative for Traditional Families." *Journal of Comparative Family Studies* 31:385–94.

Sleebos, J. E. 2003. "Low Fertility Rates in OECD Countries: Facts and Policy Responses." Working Paper No. 15, OECD Social, Employment, and Migration Working Papers. Paris: OECD.

Stevenson, Betsey and Justin Wolfers. 2003. "Bargaining in the Shadow of the Law: Divorce Laws and Family Distress." Paper No. 1828, Stanford Graduate School of Business Research Paper Series.

Thorne, Barrie and Marilyn Yalom. 1982. *Rethinking the Family: Some Feminist Questions.* New York: Longman.

Wolfinger, Nicholas H. 2003. "Parental Divorce and Offspring Marriage: Early or Late?" *Social Forces* 82:337–54.

38

ACCOUNTING FOR DIVORCE
Gender and Uncoupling Narratives

SUSAN WALZER • THOMAS P. OLES

A divorced man explained in an interview that he and his wife should never have married in the first place. Early in their relationship, they had gone on a vacation together—he figured that he could "get laid five or six times"—but she had become pregnant and they had married. Although he didn't "enjoy" being married, he "wouldn't have broken up the family." When he was delivered some paperwork from family court,

Susan Walzer and Thomas P. Oles, "Accounting for Divorce: Gender and Uncoupling Narratives" from *Qualitative Sociology* 26, no. 3 (2003). Copyright © 2003 by Human Sciences Press, Inc. Reprinted with permission.

however, he waited a year and then filed for divorce because he realized that his wife was going to do it. He described her "bitterness" toward him as "ruining" their children's lives; they were currently engaged in a custody battle. From his point of view, his ex-wife was attempting to "control" and "alienate" the children from him. She had "allowed the heat of battle to consume her" and he had to fight back. "Like countries," he commented, "if one wants to remain at war, peace cannot be achieved."

In another interview, a former wife described coming upon her husband and another woman in a restaurant. She described it as "a terrible shock"— not just the girlfriend, but also "the realization this was no kind of partnership." When they talked, her husband admitted that he had met the other woman four months before they married, which "kind of invalidated our whole marriage . . . I was totally demoralized," she said, and "there just didn't seem to me to be any way out of it." On the way home from the restaurant, she declared that they were going to have to get a divorce, hoping that he would disagree. But he didn't: "Just: 'Guess you're right. The jig is up. I'm caught.' If he couldn't go on with this triangle thing, I don't think he wanted the marriage."

Scott and Lyman (1968) identify the kind of talk that is meant to bridge a gap between actions and expectations as an "account or a 'statement' made by a social actor to explain unanticipated or untoward behavior" (p. 46). Our concern in this [reading] is with the kinds of accounts that people provide when they experience the ending of a relationship that is institutionalized as one that is not supposed to end: a marriage. As Hopper (2001a) writes, "Marriage is valued both as an institution and as a personal accomplishment, and it is a relationship that is supposed to last forever. Divorce violates the profound value we attach to marriage, and it represents a personal failure for both spouses" (p. 129). Because divorce violates deeply entrenched individual and social expectations, it generates explanations both from people who experience it and from people who study it.

To the extent that narratives of uncoupling have been studied, previous analyses have focused on rhetorical differences between the accounts of initiating and non-initiating partners (Hopper 1993, 2001a, 2001b; Vaughan 1986). Hopper (2001a:129) notes that the identification of oneself as either an initiator or a non-initiator helps divorcing people to address the morality of their position, to form accounts that "neutralize their own culpability" and "emphasize compelling cultural values" (see also Riessman 1990). Our purpose in this [reading] is to extend previous work on divorce narratives by making the argument, grounded in qualitative interview data, that gender norms are among the cultural values that mediate how divorcing people explain their experiences (see also Arendell 1995).

We suggest that bringing gender into an analysis of divorce complicates the distinction between initiator and non-initiator identities because of potential tensions between narrating one's life as a woman or man and narrating one's part as an initiator or non-initiator of divorce. As people go through the process of divorce, they also "do gender": create, sustain and/or answer for an expected differentiation between women and men, the content of which

includes female deference and male control (West and Fenstermaker 1993; West and Zimmerman 1987). When women initiate divorces, and men have them initiated, they may offer narratives that are accountable to gender— a process that lends ambiguity to the categories of initiator and partner and unmasks motives for divorce that do not necessarily surface in survey data or reflect the emphasis on individualism in current understandings of divorce (Hackstaff 1999).

The Social Significance of Divorce Narratives

As C. Wright Mills notes (1940:904, 908), the differing reasons that people give for their actions "are not themselves without reasons." Motives must be situated, Mills argues; they "line up conduct with norms." This process of "aligning" behavior with cultural expectations happens largely through a variety of verbal efforts—through actions directed at addressing "discrepancies between what is actually taking place in a given situation and what is thought to be typical, normatively expected, probable, desirable or, in other respects, more in accord with what is culturally normal" (Stokes and Hewitt 1976:843). In this sense, then, not only do we tell stories about our lives; our lives are shaped by the stories we tell and how others hear our narratives (Chase 1995).

Goffman (1967:10) argues that we do not have "face"—a sense of having positive social value—without confirmation from other people. A person's social face can be his or her "most personal possession," but "it is only on loan . . . from society"; it can be withdrawn if a person's conduct is not worthy of it. This, Goffman writes, is a "fundamental social constraint." Indeed, he argues, it is the basis of morality and social order. Narration, therefore, is a form of social action aimed at constructing and communicating meaning—and one that both "draws on and is constrained by the culture in which it is embedded" (Chase 1995:7). Our explanations may reflect attempts to maintain face—to convince our audience that we are okay—by framing our actions in terms we perceive to be acceptable. When we behave in ways that appear to deviate from social norms, we have more explaining to do.

Scott and Lyman (1968) identify two types of accounts: justifications, in which responsibility is taken, but the pejorative quality of an act is denied; and excuses, in which the act is acknowledged as wrong in some way, but full responsibility is denied. Both kinds of accounts tell us about social norms—justifications serving as attempts to reconstruct social perceptions of what is right and wrong, and excuses reproducing social views of unacceptable behavior. Both kinds of accounts surface from divorcing people. Some try to offer justification for an act they want to convince their audience is right; others offer excuses for an act they perceive as wrong. Accounting for divorce may be an adaptive strategy for people who experience themselves as having "failed" and are attempting to organize trying events into a coherent story (Riessman 1990; Weber 1992; Weiss 1975). Social psychological research

supports the notion that feeling a sense of control enhances adjustment to change, and post-marital accounting helps people attain a sense of control (Grych and Fincham 1992), perhaps especially when they can tell their story "in a biased and ego-enhancing fashion" (Gray and Silver 1990:1180).

Gender and Meanings of Initiation

Although research about uncoupling processes has tended to focus on differences between initiator and non-initiator experiences, there is more than one way to identify who initiates the end of a marriage. Braver, Whitley, and Ng (1993) point out that initiation can be operationalized in a number of ways: who was the most unhappy, who was to blame, who suggested the divorce first, whose decision it was to divorce, who filed the legal documents. They find that the "dumper" is not necessarily the one who files the divorce papers, for example. As we began to analyze accounts from our own interview data, there were even more areas of ambiguity, such as who asked whom to leave. The answers to questions that seemed empirical were inconsistent at times.

Sociological conceptualizations of the roles of initiator and non-initiator capture some of this ambiguity. In Diane Vaughan's (1986) analysis, initiators want distance from their partners and move, not always consciously, toward ending relationships; the non-initiators are people who (eventually) recognize that their partners want their relationships to end and resist the break-ups, although their partners' behavior may ultimately lead them to end the relationship. These experiences result in two transitions: one that begins earlier for initiators, who are secretly aware of their own dissatisfaction; and a later, more involuntary one for the non-initiator. The post-separation experience is determined, in Vaughan's view, by whether one is the initiating or the non-initiating partner during the process of the relationship turning point.

In contrast to the idea that initiator/non-initiator identities are embedded in actual relationship processes, Joseph Hopper (1993:804–5) argues that identification of each is rather arbitrary—that divorces are complex and chaotic experiences in which the initiator and non-initiator roles surface only after a decision to divorce has been made. Unlike Vaughan, he does not root post-separation identities in the experience of the relationship itself; most relationships prior to divorce, he argues, are characterized by "a long period of discontent, multiple complaints, and ambivalence" on the part of both people that could result in any number of outcomes. People make distinctions only after the divorce, Hopper suggests, as they interpret their behavior with "an emergent symbolic order structured around initiator and non-initiator identities."

While Hopper sees the initiator and partner identities as rhetorical devices through which divorcing people construct motives retrospectively, Vaughan suggests that these roles emerge from some real process in the ending of the relationship—that initiators and partners actually feel and

act differently from each other. We think that both positions are useful for making sense of uncoupling processes. We agree, as Vaughan suggests, that the identities are linked to real experiences in the relationship. We also agree with Hopper's assertion that the retrospective accounts of "exes" tend to consolidate a particular status as partner or initiator. What we wish to add to the analysis of divorce accounts is attention to how gendered meanings associated with initiation may complicate the narrative processes of divorcing women and men.

When we talk about gender, we are not referring simply to the sexes of the divorcing partners, but to the gendered content of their narratives. Gender beliefs in North American society are frequently organized around the assumptions that men are more agentic, instrumental, and competent at most things while women are more communal and competent at nurturing (Ridgeway and Correll 2000). These socialized gender expectations make their way into the verbal presentations men and women make about their lives. Research comparing communication approaches suggests that men's style of talk tends to reflect a greater emphasis on establishing social position while women tend to be more oriented toward connection and collaboration (Pierce 1995; Tannen 1990; Wood 1999). . . .

Given that more women than men are apparently initiating divorces (Braver, Whitley, and Ng 1993), certain narrative dilemmas are posed for individuals who are accountable to dominant notions that men are in control and decide their own fates while women hold families together and put others' needs before their own. These dilemmas surface in incongruities in the narratives of divorced individuals that have not previously been identified in analyses of uncoupling narratives and are not represented in aggregated data about divorce initiation.

The man we quoted above, for example, sounds rhetorically like both an initiator and a non-initiator. On one hand, he believes in keeping "the family" together; on the other hand, he suggests that his marriage should never have happened—that he hadn't particularly cared for his wife or enjoyed their marriage. Although his narrative reflects that he did not initiate his divorce, he presents himself as the one in control while suggesting that his ex-wife is consumed by their battle. The woman we quoted also sounds like both an initiator and a non-initiator. She responds to her husband's affair with the idea that they should divorce (since he had not perceived it as a reason not to marry in the first place, he apparently did not perceive it as a reason to initiate a divorce). Yet she presents herself as out of control of the decision—hopeful that he would think it was the wrong course of action. She perceived him as the one who had not wanted the marriage and whose behavior gave her no other way. The categories of initiator and non-initiator are embedded with imageries of power and victimization that have implications for how men and women construct themselves within them. If every account "is a manifestation of the underlying negotiation of identities," as Scott and Lyman (1968:59) write, accounting for oneself as a socially defined man or woman is one of the identities that divorcing people negotiate.

Method

Our argument is grounded in excerpts from qualitative, semi-structured interviews that we conducted as part of an inductive study of post-marital relationships. Motivated by an interest in understanding more about how formerly married people interpret and renegotiate their relationships, we spoke with twenty-five individuals (including five former couples, interviewed separately) who had been divorced or separated from their partners for at least one year. This parameter was established so that couples would be over the distress that often accompanies the first year of divorce or separation (see studies cited in Cherlin 1981), enabling us to focus on people's retrospective accounts of what had happened in their marriages. . . .

Of the twenty-five individuals we interviewed, thirteen were men and twelve were women. Ten of these participants were formerly married to each other. Four were cohabiting with each other, having ended previous marriages. The age range of the participants interviewed was 29 to 68. Most of them were white; one person identified as Latina and another as Native American. The sample was mixed in class, ranging from very low income to middle- and upper middle-class household incomes. Most of the sample interviewed discussed a first marriage; two people were ending a second marriage; and one person had been married four times. The length of former marriages described ranged from less than two years to thirty-nine years.

The focus of this particular article is an outgrowth of our serendipitous difficulty in categorizing some of the people in our sample as initiators or non-initiators of their divorces. Although initiation can be operationalized in a number of ways (Braver, Whitley, and Ng 1993), we had learned that most divorcing people do not perceive their marriages to have ended by mutual consent and are able to identify who decided on a divorce and who did not (Hopper 1993). Our intention was to use a constant comparative approach (Glaser and Strauss 1967) to understand more about the roles that initiator/non-initiator identities play in conflict after marriages end. . . .

. . . [O]f the twenty-five people we interviewed, only one man presented himself as an initiator driven by his own needs (the individualistic rhetoric expected of an initiator). Nine other people who, we could agree, identified as initiators focused on how their behavior had been driven by behaviors of their spouses in ways that made them concerned for their children as well as for themselves. When we examined those who used this different kind of initiator discourse in which the decision to divorce was not presented as an act of self-fulfillment, and the needs of others were placed in the foreground (what we call "collectivist" rhetoric), we found that they all were women, with the exception of one man who described himself as having been a battered husband. As for accounts in which the claimed identity did not seem to fit the narrative, we found that those who claimed to be initiators, while they hadn't seemed to be, were primarily men, and at least two women denied being initiators while it seemed to us they had been.

The next section describes how bringing gender into our reading of these narratives illuminated these ambiguities. In some ways it should not

be a surprise that gender is relevant to divorce narratives at this particular historical moment. As Hackstaff's (1999) analysis reveals, couples who married in the 1970s, compared with those who married in the 1950s, brought to marriage an alternative set of meanings, including a shift from an assumption of male dominance to a quest for gender equality. The people that we interviewed—most of them having married in the 1970s or later—were well into what Hackstaff (1999) identifies as a social shift from an assumption of marital permanence to a culture of divorce in which gender issues figure prominently. This makes it all the more interesting to examine how gender accountability that is not necessarily recognized as such complicates some of their uncoupling narratives.

Intersections of Divorce Accounting and Gender

We first present two voices in which the narratives are congruent with normative expectations of men and women. We then discuss some of the incongruent accounts that generated our identification of gender accountability as a mediating factor in initiator and non-initiator identities. Finally, we look at an example of gender accountability itself becoming an explicit part of an uncoupling narrative, and how its presence in the narrative subverts the initiator/non-initiator dichotomy.

Conventional Scripts

Our first example is a man we interviewed who actively decided to end his marriage and spoke about his decision in utilitarian individualistic rhetoric—the only one in our sample who did so. This man's account is a justification for his divorce. He does not suggest that he has done something wrong that should be excused; rather, he acknowledges responsibility for ending his marriage, and justifies it through the individualistic value of putting the self first:

> Respondent: *I was on an overseas mission for six months and when I came home I think that's when I realized something had to give in my marriage . . . it had to meet more things that I thought I was looking for in one way, shape or another. . . . We went to one session of counseling. She openly expressed her positive feelings towards me and I was neutral and ambivalent. So that was devastating [for her]. Probably two months later is when I finally just said, you know, it wasn't working and two or three months later. . . . I just said I didn't think I wanted to keep the marriage alive. Shortly after that was when I got involved with the other lady.*
>
> Interviewer: *So that didn't precede this?*
>
> Respondent: *No. Probably pretty close, but the thing is I had definitely resolved that I wasn't having a healthy relationship at home and I just wasn't having needs met.*

This man was resolved that his needs weren't being met and "something had to give." He was able to provide a justifying account because there was

congruence for him between his act of ending his marriage and the social norm of individualism.

Our next example is the narrative of a non-initiating woman who expressed contempt for her ex-husband's self-focus. Married for over thirty-five years to a prominent man in the community, she reported that "the bottom line" was that he had left her for another woman, although he had not mentioned the other woman during their uncoupling. She related great humiliation and a sense of victimization, describing her ex-husband as someone who had "stepped on" her. She talked about her desire to have had a cordial relationship on her children's behalf, but said that she was unable to make this happen because her ex-husband was "still very wrapped up in himself." This woman's account was not a justification for divorce, nor did she place the same value on taking care of the self as the man cited earlier did. What this woman offered, rather, was an excuse for why she was unable to maintain her marriage or to construct a congenial post-marital relationship for her children.

Variations on Uncoupling Scripts

The accounts that we heard from these two people describe routes to marital dissolution that correspond to stereotypical gender expectations. The man was in control; the woman was not. His rhetoric contained the self-focus of initiator narratives, while she sounded like a non-initiator, victimized by a selfish partner. But what happens when women end marriages and men have them ended, which is the more typical national pattern reported in survey data?

While women appear in aggregated data to be initiating divorces much more than men, we want to suggest that the individualism previously identified as underlying initiator accounts does not fully capture the ways that marital and divorce experiences and accounts are mediated by gender. As Hackstaff (1999:214) points out, individualism may have different meanings for men and women. She notes that refusing to be subordinated or removing children from violent households is a way of using individualism for relational ends. We did not hear accounts from women whose primary justification for divorce was putting themselves first. Even in cases of abuse, our informants tended to justify initiating their divorces based on the effects of their ex-husbands' behavior on their children as well as on themselves (see also Kurz 1995). Their narratives, rather than being grounded in individualistic rhetoric, tended to be what we call more collectivist.

One woman, who presented herself as having reluctantly initiated her divorce, said, "It was a tragedy for us. For our family. It really was. But here we are. And like I say, I don't think he's changed." Another woman said of her ex-husband:

> He was staying out late all the time, verbally abusive, not doing anything in the house, never spending time with us as a family, and as the marriage progressed, it was less and less. Then it got to the point where he was barely sitting down to dinner. I mean, he was out gambling and going out and I was home with the kids. . . . I asked him to go to counseling; he didn't want to go.

Although this couple went on to become legally separated, this woman reported that her husband still hadn't wanted to leave; he had wanted to remain married. Her decision was made in the context of what was happening to them "as a family."

Did this woman present herself as an initiator? Yes and no. We suggest that the ambiguity in her account may be explained by gender accountability. Her first choice was for her husband to shape up; and she spoke in the rhetoric of non-initiators, as described by Hopper (1993), concerned about family and commitment: "I felt bad for the children. And I don't believe in divorce, personally, and I don't like it, especially when there's kids involved." Her account was an excuse rather than a justification; she presented her act as something that she was driven to rather than in control of, and as something that was in some way wrong. This woman perceived herself as a non-initiating partner, as Vaughan (1986) describes it—ending the marriage only when she was pushed to by her husband. On the other hand, she did make the call; she ended a marriage that her husband, according to her, had not wanted to end. Our point is that there may be women who do not necessarily experience or want to claim the sense of control implied in the initiator identity. There are also men who have not, by definition, initiated, but would like to present themselves as having been in control.

Among our informants, there were several men who claimed initiator status despite their wives having been the ones to commit the kind of rule violations that Vaughan attributes to initiators—in two of these cases, infidelity. One husband described his wife as having wanted to "find herself." His reaction to his wife's initiation was a face-saving account in which he asserted control of the ending of his marriage:

I: *So it sounds like she initiated the separation?*

R: *I did.*

I: *You did?*

R: *Yep. The boyfriend in the picture kind of put a stumbling block in the marriage.*

Another man in our sample claimed to be the initiator after having described a number of initiating moves on his wife's part, which generated the following interchange (with a confused interviewer) about whose decision it was to break up:

I: *It wasn't your choice to split up?*

R: *It was.*

I: *It was your choice?*

R: *It was.*

I: *Was it like a mutual thing or you made the call?*

R: *No, it wasn't mutual. . . . There was somebody else involved in the relationship and I couldn't deal with that.*

Accounts do not reveal a clear "truth"; they reveal interpretations that are generated in interaction with some kind of social audience (Riessman 1990). This man's ex-wife told us that she had not been having an affair and that her ex-husband's alcoholism had precipitated their separation. She also said that he had asked for a reconciliation that she turned down. In his narrative he asserted control, however, telling us that he had refused a request from his ex-wife to get back together. . . .

Ahrons (1994) interprets women leaving men as an assumption of power, and she suggests that the loss of power men experience in being left has special meaning for them because they are men. A woman whose husband wanted to have her killed agreed: "It was something he just didn't want to accept. . . . The divorce was just sort of a blow in the head to his ego, being a man." Joseph Hopper (1999) provided us with interview data from an attorney who described some male clients "who by and large are pretty controlling people . . . frequently get very, very obsessive about maintaining the relationship that the other person doesn't want. And you get a real strong sense from that, that they're not missing the person so much as they're missing the control over the person."

Some of the men we interviewed who did not actively decide to end their marriages, like the men quoted here, nevertheless claimed initiator status. Other men's behavior is captured in Vaughan's initiator category; i.e., their actions pushed their wives to divorce. These men spoke in individualistic initiator rhetoric, but it's not clear that they would have ever ended their marriages had they not been "caught" in behavior that their wives deemed marriage-ending. One example of this is the man whose ex-wife we quoted earlier, whose marriage ended after she learned of his affair that had begun at the time they married. He said of his marriage:

> The problem with the relationship was that . . . I didn't really feel the kind of a yen you need to feel where you say that you'd fallen in love with her. . . . I met someone who was particularly younger—half my age. At the time she was very forward, and I guess she was intriguing, really passionate.

While this man offered a justifying account, he had not embarked on this affair to initiate an end to his marriage; in fact, he was making secret calls to his girlfriend during his honeymoon. Yet in his retrospective account, he attempted to position himself differently, as having been more in control of choosing between his marriage and this other relationship, despite the stigma associated with leaving his wife for another woman (Gerstel 1987).

In contrast to the men quoted above, the accounts of women in our sample who decided to get divorced in the context of their husbands having had affairs were different in tone. These women did not necessarily want to claim the status of having initiated a divorce. As we saw, one wife hoped that her husband wouldn't take her up on the divorce:

> We drove home together and I said, "We are going to have to get a divorce," and he said, "I guess so"; and I guess in the back of my mind I was hoping he'd say, "Well, let's think it over, it's not that important to me." But he never said that. . . .

Another woman described being in an auto accident with her child and being unable to reach her husband. "Now where was my husband at midnight?" she asked. But she did not necessarily want to claim to have initiated a divorce in response to his affair:

I: *So it was your call?*

R: *I think he would have left eventually because I think he was probably seeing someone anyway.*

This woman was reluctant to identify as an initiator—at least in terms of her response to her husband's affair—yet later in the interview she invoked the accident as crystallizing her decision:

R: *I said, "You couldn't be reached." He was like, "Well, what could I have done?" That was it. That showed me that, you know, he was like so into himself and his own things, he wasn't even available to, you know, your wife, and you almost lost your daughter. If she hadn't been in a seat belt in the booster seat, she would have been out in the street.*

I: *So that was the moment where you thought . . .*

R: *That was it. That was it. There was no turning back after that.*

In this woman's account, her decision was made especially after she perceived her husband's indifference to their daughter's well-being.

Although this woman was ambivalent about identifying herself as the initiator of her divorce, her ex-husband found it distasteful not to have initiated. When asked whose decision it was to end the marriage, he responded, "I'd rather not go there." Later in the interview he said, "Let me put it this way, I was happier than she was about the divorce." Finally, he said that he suspected that his ex-wife "could be gay."

Of the twenty-five people we interviewed, there was one non-initiating woman who offered an initiator account. She responded to our question about her current relationship with her ex-husband by saying, "He had an affair. I threw his ass out. Okay? Point blank. People don't do that to me." As her narrative continued, we found that she had discovered the affair only after her husband had left and she'd hired a detective, because her lawyer and others suspected a third party involvement.

We will speculate that one reason this woman presented a forthright justifying account in which she was in control and taking care of herself is that she and her ex-husband were childless. She was not accountable as a mother, as the other women in the sample were, and did not have to answer to the same expectation that she would try to hold the family together. In other words, if there are gendered experiences of uncoupling, they are likely to be linked to the gendered experiences of marriage and parenthood, in which women are held ultimately responsible for maintaining relationships and children's well-being (e.g., Walzer 1998). Gerstel (1987) notes, for example, that mothers who get divorced perceive more disapproval than do childless women, and in a way that men do not. In the next section we look

at one former couple who illustrate the possible ways that making gender dynamics explicit can transform uncoupling rhetoric.

The Invisible Initiator: Gender in Marriage

Accounting for divorce generally leads to finger-pointing at a specific person or marriage, but not at the institution of marriage itself (Hopper 2001b; Stewart et al. 1997). One of the former couples we interviewed, however, spoke to the tensions that marital roles generated in their marriage. Their post-marital accounts were more "androgynous" in the sense that they both identified as initiators and non-initiators, and their accounts reflected some analysis of the role that gender and marital expectations had played in their relationship.

In terms of the initiator/partner dichotomy, this man and woman (we will call them Lyle and Melanie) had each been both. Lyle told us that Melanie had left, but their history was more complicated than that, as his narrative reflects:

> We both understand that we both made mistakes. I had an affair way back in '76. That was probably one of the keys because she didn't trust me after that and all that. I would never do that again. . . . She basically forgave me but the trust takes a long time to get back. But that was like so . . . I mean, we did not split because of that reason, another woman or any of that kind of stuff. So maybe that made it also better in the sense that it wasn't anger-at-each-other type thing. We both kind of realized at this point in time that neither one of us were happy and I remember her saying to me one time, she says, "Look, we're both good people. Why don't we just split and move on?" And we eventually did. It took a long time. . . . I had left one time. . . . I didn't leave, no, I went out and I put a deposit on an apartment for myself. I had just had enough. . . . I came home and I told her, cause we hadn't really discussed it. She had talked earlier that she wanted to leave and she hadn't done anything, so I did. And boy, did I catch hell for that. She was angry with me because she felt that I didn't discuss it with her first. She's right . . . I lost my hundred bucks. I didn't leave. She said, "No, I want you to stay," and . . . she left [about a year later]. So it did go on another year . . . we tolerated each other kind of. It was like two ships moving apart.

Although Lyle said that he "had just had enough," taking care of himself by leaving was not a good enough justification; rather, he waited for Melanie to be ready to separate, or for their split to be perceived as more mutual.

Consideration of their children was embedded in Melanie's account, but she was straightforward about her need to act on her own unhappiness:

> For a long time we had talked about splitting up. At one point he had gotten an apartment. He was gonna leave and it's difficult. It's very, very difficult. . . . I was just completely lost. Even though I was alive I was not living. I was lonely all the time. I was angry all the time. So I got an apartment with the help of friends and a little support. I asked my daughter to leave—she wouldn't go. She wanted to stay in the house, which made it even harder. She was thirteen at the time but I moved like two miles down the road so I saw her all the time. I think

*both of us wanted it, but it just took somebody to actually make the move. . . .
I think I was maybe more unhappy than he was, at least for a longer time. And
our son was in college, he was away, and we just had to do something.*

While Lyle was an initiator in a couple of different ways, in the end he conceded this status to Melanie; she, in turn, allowed him primary ownership
of the care of their daughter. Both, in other words, subverted the gendered
expectations in the uncoupling process and in their accounts of the process.

When Lyle and Melanie reflected on the sources of their stress, they
invoked observations about the institution of marriage and gender. As Lyle
said:

*We had our problems in the marriage just like everybody else does. And a lot of
our problems were . . . "the ones everybody has" type thing. . . . I would say I
was not ready for marriage. I was ready for the marriage to the extent of a wife,
but not kids. . . . A child comes into it, the woman really kind of takes on the burden of the child, it came from her, you are kind of put on the back burner. . . . All
of sudden she's tired at night when you wanted something else. . . . It's funny
how at that point in time I didn't understand it real well, where now I think one
of the biggest changes is when you . . . do what the other person did. . . . When
you walk in the other person's shoes, you find out real fast that that person had
an awful lot to do. You know, maintain the house, clean the house, do the dishes,
take care of the kids. . . . And I realized that after. It took me a long time before
I realized. Holy smokes, when you walk in their shoes you find out this person
needs help. But as a 20-some-year-old, I was just probably too immature to be
married and I realize it now what it amounted to—it's a lot. I'm not alone when
it comes to that. . . .*

Melanie and Lyle concurred on the impact that traditional gender
arrangements had had on their marriage and found in their uncoupling what
they had not been able to find while they were together: a sense that rigid differentiation in roles did not work for them. Unlike divorced people who do
not conceptualize gender roles as problematic and attribute difficulties to the
personality or values of their partner (Stewart et al. 1997), Lyle and Melanie's
recognition of their accountability to gender within their marriage allowed
them to account for their divorce in ways that did not implicate each other as
individuals. Their narratives also combined individualistic and collectivist
orientations: attention to their children's and to each other's needs as well as
their own, and a sense of joint responsibility for ending their marriage.

Discussion

The accomplishment of gender does not necessarily occur behaviorally,
but in accounting for behavior in terms of femininity and masculinity
(West and Zimmerman 1987). Our argument has been that incongruities in
some divorce narratives may be explained by an accountability to gender
that has not previously been identified in analyses of uncoupling identities and do not surface in aggregated data about divorce initiation. This

negotiation is especially apparent when the uncoupling experiences of men and women violate dominant cultural associations surrounding masculinity and femininity. For some initiating women, there may be a tension between claiming control and accounting to a socially constructed definition of themselves as women. And for non-initiating men—a population that has been referred to in clinical literature as "angry, abandoned husbands" (Myers 1986)—there may be a tension in not having had the control that men are supposed to have.

Just as gender rigidity in marital and parenting roles may jeopardize marriage, gender accountability in post-marital roles is also risky. There is evidence, for example, that non-initiating partners may try to regain power through post-marital struggles, most unfortunately, around children (Hopper 2001a). The man whom we first cited in this [reading] telephoned a couple of years after his initial interview to report that he had "nuked" his wife in their custody battle; she was "toast." This informant was among the people we interviewed who called on initiator rhetoric in the context of a narrative that suggested he had not chosen to end his marriage. His status as a man, jeopardized by his ex-wife's dissatisfaction with their relationship, was perhaps re-established (from his perspective) through his use of aggression and intimidation in court (see Pierce 1995).

Conversely, women who finally end a marriage may not always narrate their actions as the assertive acts of self-fulfillment previously identified in initiator accounts. Rather, several of the women that we interviewed tended to frame divorce as a last-resort response to men's behavior (see also Ahrons 1994 and Kurz 1995), with the consequences of men's behavior for children figuring especially prominently in some of their accounts. In this sense, "doing" divorce, like "doing gender" through housework (see South and Spitze 1994), may for some women initiators be another way in which they take disproportionate responsibility for cleaning up family messes.

Our analysis is supported by other research that identifies the role of gendered experiences and expectations in divorce. In a quantitative analysis, Pettit and Bloom (1984) find an interaction between sex and initiation in whether a spouse's problems with children were identified as a determinant of divorce. In other words, women initiators in their sample cited their partners' relationships with children as a factor in their divorces while men did not. Men may save face on the other side of divorce with the masculinist discourse that Arendell (1995) identifies, in which they blame ex-wives for alienation in their own relationships with their children. Kurz (1995) argues that women leave marriages, in large part, because of conditions and behavior associated with the conventional male role (see also Riessman 1990). A majority of Kurz's representative sample of divorced women cited husbands' violence, infidelities, and "hard living" (alcoholism, absenteeism, and other negative behaviors) as reasons for their divorces as opposed to personal dissatisfaction per se. Ahrons (1994:93) also points out that women frequently describe their divorce as an action to which they are finally led by husbands' behavior: "Stories of years of abuse, betrayal, or absenteeism by their ex-husband are rife" (p. 93). Many women say that they left "because they had no choice.". . .

We also suggest that identifying differences by gender in divorce accounts provides further perspective on the tendency, in the aggregate, for women to be reported as initiators of divorce. While analyses of uncoupling discourse suggest an equation of initiation with self-focus, we suggest that a missing piece of the story is the gender imbalances in marriage that result in interactions and behavior that become unacceptable for families as collectives and that push women to end marriages they are not easily inclined to end.

ENDNOTE

Authors' Note: This article is a revised version of a paper presented at the 94th Annual Meeting of the American Sociological Association. Our research was funded by a Faculty Development Grant from Skidmore College. We thank John Brueggemann, Michael Ennis-McMillan, Frances Hoffmann, David Karp, Jennifer Pierce, Glenna Spitze, Christopher Wellin, Robert Zussman and one anonymous reviewer for their helpful comments and Jessica Dorrance, Cynthia Ferguson Wheeler, Sarah Winslow, and Elizabeth Umbro for research assistance. A special thanks to Joseph Hopper for providing us with useful consultation and data.

REFERENCES

Ahrons, C. 1994. *The Good Divorce.* New York: HarperCollins.

Arendell, T. 1995. *Fathers and Divorce.* Thousand Oaks, CA: Sage.

Braver, S. L., M. Whitley, and C. Ng. 1993. "Who Divorced Whom? Methodological and Theoretical Issues." *Journal of Divorce and Remarriage* 20:1–19.

Chase, S. E. 1995. *Ambiguous Empowerment: The Work Narrative of Women School Superintendents.* Amherst: University of Massachusetts Press.

Cherlin, A. 1981. *Marriage, Divorce, Remarriage.* Cambridge, MA: Harvard University Press.

Gerstel, N. 1987. "Divorce and Stigma." *Social Problems* 34:172–86.

Glaser, B. G. and A. L. Strauss. 1967. *The Discovery of Grounded Theory.* New York: Aldine de Gruyter.

Goffman, E. 1967. *Interaction Ritual: Essays on Face-to-Face Behavior.* New York: Pantheon Books.

Gray, J. D. and R. C. Silver. 1990. "Opposite Sides of the Same Coin: Former Spouses' Divergent Perspectives in Coping with Their Divorce." *Journal of Personality and Social Psychology* 90:1180–91.

Grych, J. H. and F. D. Fincham. 1992. "Marital Dissolution and Family Adjustment: An Attributional Analysis." *Close Relationship Loss: Theoretical Approaches,* edited by T. L. Orbuch. New York: Springer-Verlag New York.

Hackstaff, K. B. 1999. *Marriage in a Culture of Divorce.* Philadelphia: Temple University Press.

Hopper, J. 1993. "The Rhetoric of Motives in Divorce." *Journal of Marriage and the Family* 55:801–13.

———. 1999. Personal communication.

———. 2001a. "Contested Selves in Divorce Proceedings." Pp. 127–41 in *Institutional Selves: Troubled Identities in a Postmodern World,* edited by J. F. Gubrium and J. A. Holstein. New York: Oxford University Press.

———. 2001b. "The Symbolic Origins of Conflict in Divorce." *Journal of Marriage and the Family* 63:430–45.

Kurz, D. 1995. *For Richer, for Poorer: Mothers Confront Divorce.* New York: Routledge.

Mills, C. W. 1940. "Situated Actions and Vocabularies of Motive." *American Sociological Review* 5:904–13.

Myers, M. F. 1986. "Angry, Abandoned Husbands: Assessment and Treatment." *Marriage and Family Review* 9:31–42.

Pettit, E. J. and B. L. Bloom. 1984. "Whose Decision Was It? The Effects of Initiator Status on Adjustment to Marital Disruption." *Journal of Marriage and the Family* 46:587–95.

Pierce, J. L. 1995. *Gender Trials: Emotional Lives in Contemporary Law Firms.* Berkeley: University of California Press.

Ridgeway, C. and S. Correll. 2000. "Limiting Gender Inequality through Interaction: The End(s) of Gender." *Contemporary Sociology* 29:110–20.

Riessman, C. K. 1990. *Divorce Talk.* New Brunswick: Rutgers University Press.

Scott, M. B. and S. M. Lyman. 1968. "Accounts." *American Sociological Review* 33:46–62.

South, S. and G. Spitze. 1994. "Housework in Marital and Nonmarital Households." *American Sociological Review* 59:595–618.

Stewart, A. J., A. P. Copeland, N. L. Chester, J. E. Malley, and N. B. Barenbaum. 1997. *Separating Together: How Divorce Transforms Families.* New York: Guilford Press.

Stokes, R. and J. P. Hewitt. 1976. "Aligning Actions." *American Sociological Review* 41:838–49.

Tannen, D. 1990. *You Just Don't Understand: Women and Men in Conversation.* New York: William Morrow.

Vaughan, D. 1986. *Uncoupling.* New York: Vintage Books.

Walzer, S. 1998. *Thinking about the Baby: Gender and Transitions into Parenthood.* Philadelphia: Temple University Press.

Weber, A. L. 1992. "The Account-Making Process: A Phenomenological Approach." Pp. 174–91 in *Close Relationship Loss: Theoretical Approaches,* edited by T. L. Orbuch. New York: Springer-Verlag New York.

Weiss, R. S. 1975. *Marital Separation.* New York: Basic Books.

West, C. and S. Fenstermaker. 1993. "Power, Inequality, and the Accomplishment of Gender: An Ethnomethodological View." Pp. 151–174 in *Theory on Gender/Feminism on Theory,* edited by P. England. New York: Aldine de Gruyter.

West, C. and D. Zimmerman. 1987. "Doing Gender." *Gender and Society* 1:125–51.

Wood, J. T. 1999. *Gendered Lives.* Belmont, CA: Wadsworth.

39

THE MODERN AMERICAN STEPFAMILY
Problems and Possibilities

MARY ANN MASON

Cinderella had one, so did Snow White and Hansel and Gretel. Our traditional cultural myths are filled with the presence of evil stepmothers. We learn from the stories read to us as children that stepparents, particularly stepmothers, are not to be trusted. They may pretend to love us in front of our biological parent, but the moment our real parent is out of sight they will treat us cruelly and shower their own children with kindnesses. Few modern children's tales paint stepparents so harshly, still the negative image of stepparents lingers in public policy. While the rights and obligations of biological parents, wed or unwed, have been greatly strengthened in recent times, stepparents have been virtually ignored. At best it is fair to say that as a society we have a poorly formed concept of the role of stepparents and a reluctance to clarify that role.

Indeed, the contrast between the legal status of stepparents and the presumptive rights and obligations of natural parents is remarkable. Child support obligations, custody rights, and inheritance rights exist between

children and their natural parents by virtue of a biological tie alone, regardless of the quality of social or emotional bonds between parent and child, and regardless of whether the parents are married. In recent years, policy changes have extended the rights and obligations of natural parents, particularly in regard to unwed and divorced parents, but have not advanced with regard to stepparents. Stepparents in most states have no obligation during the marriage to support their stepchildren, nor do they enjoy any right of custody or control. Consistent with this pattern, if the marriage terminates through divorce or death, they usually have no rights to custody or even visitation, however long-standing their relationship with their stepchildren. Conversely, stepparents have no obligation to pay child support following divorce, even if their stepchildren have depended on their income for many years. In turn, stepchildren have no right of inheritance in the event of the stepparent's death (they are, however, eligible for Social Security benefits in most cases).[1]

Policymakers who spend a great deal of time worrying about the economic and psychological effects of divorce on children rarely consider the fact that about 70 percent of mothers are remarried within six years. Moreover, about 28 percent of children are born to unwed mothers, many of whom eventually marry someone who is not the father of their child. In a study including all children, not just children of divorce, it was estimated that one-fourth of the children born in the United States in the early 1980s will live with a stepparent before they reach adulthood.[2] These numbers are likely to increase in the future, at least as long as the number of single-parent families continues to grow. In light of these demographic trends, federal and state policies affecting families and children, as well as policies governing private-sector employee benefits, insurance, and other critical areas of everyday life, may need to be adapted to address the concerns of modern stepfamilies.

In recent years, stepfamilies have received fresh attention from the psychological and social sciences but little from legal and policy scholars. We now know a good deal about who modern stepfamilies are and how they function, but there have been few attempts to apply this knowledge to policy. This [reading] first of all reviews the recent findings on the everyday social and economic functioning of today's stepfamilies, and then examines current state and federal policies, or lack of them in this arena. Finally, the sparse set of current policy recommendations, including my own, are presented. . . .

The Modern Stepfamily

The modern stepfamily is different and more complex than Cinderella's or Snow White's in several important ways. First, the stepparent who lives with the children is far more likely to be a stepfather than a stepmother, and in most cases the children's biological father is still alive and a presence, in varying degrees, in their lives. Today it is divorce, rather than death, which usually serves as the background event for the formation of the stepfamily,

and it is the custodial mother who remarries (86 percent of stepchildren live primarily with a custodial mother and stepfather),[3] initiating a new legal arrangement with a stepfather.[4] . . .

In most stepfamilies the noncustodial parent, usually the father, is still alive (only in 25 percent of cases is the noncustodial parent dead or his whereabouts unknown). This creates the phenomenon of more than two parents, a situation that conventional policymakers are not well equipped to address. However, according to the National Survey of Families and Households (NSFH), a nationally representative sample of families, contact between stepchildren and their absent natural fathers is not that frequent. Contact falls into four broad patterns: Roughly one-quarter of all stepchildren have no association at all with their fathers and receive no child support; one-quarter see their fathers only once a year or less often and receive no child support; one-quarter have intermittent contact or receive some child support; and one-quarter may or may not receive child support but have fairly regular contact, seeing their fathers once a month or more. Using these data as guides to the quality and intensity of the father–child relationship, it appears that relatively few stepchildren are close to their natural fathers or have enough contact with them to permit the fathers to play a prominent role in the children's upbringing. Still, at least half of natural fathers do figure in their children's lives to some degree.[5] The presence of the noncustodial parent usually precludes the option of stepparent adoption, a solution that would solve the legal ambiguities, at least, of the stepparent's role. . . .

Some children may spend time a good deal of time with nonresidential stepparents, and they may become significant figures in the children's lives. But for our purpose of reassessing the parental rights and obligations of stepparents, we will focus only on residental stepparents, since they are more likely to be involved in the everyday support and care of their stepchildren. Moreover, the wide variety of benefits available to dependent children, like Social Security and health insurance, are usually attached only to a residential stepparent. . . .

The classic longitudinal studies by Hetherington and colleagues,[6] spanning the past two decades, provide a rich source of information on how stepfamilies function. Hetherington emphasizes that stepchildren are children who have experienced several marital transitions. They have usually already experienced the divorce of their parents (although the number whose mothers have never before wed is increasing) and a period of life in a single-parent family before the formation of the stepfamily. In the early stages of all marital transitions, including divorce and remarriage, child–parent relations are often disrupted and parenting is less authoritative than in nondivorced families. These early periods, however, usually give way to a parenting situation more similar to nuclear families.[7]

The Heatherington studies found that stepfathers vary in how enthusiastically and effectively they parent their stepchildren, and stepchildren also vary in how willingly they permit a parental relationship to develop. Indeed, many stepfather–stepchild relationships are not emotionally close. Overall, stepfathers in these studies are most often disengaged and less authoritative

as compared with nondivorced fathers. The small class of residential step-mothers exhibits a similar style.[8] . . .

The age and gender of the child at the time of stepfamily formation are critical in his or her adjustment. Early adolescence is a difficult time in which to have remarriage occur, with more sustained difficulties in stepfather–stepchild relations than in remarriages where the children are younger. Young (preadolescent) stepsons, but not necessarily stepdaughters, develop a closer relationship to their stepfathers after a period of time; this is not as likely with older children.[9]

Other researchers have found that in their lives outside the family, step-children do not perform as well as children from nondivorced families, and look more like the children from single-parent families. It seems that divorce and remarriage (or some factors associated with divorce and remarriage) increase the risk of poor academic, behavioral, and psychological outcomes.[10]

The difficulties of the stepfamily relationship are evident in the high divorce rate of such families. About one-quarter of all remarrying women separate from their new spouses within five years of the second marriage, and the figure is higher for women with children from prior relationships. A conservative estimate is that between 20 percent and 30 percent of step-children will, before they turn eighteen, see their custodial parent and stepparent divorce.[11] This is yet another disruptive marital transition for children, most of whom have already undergone at least one divorce.

Other researchers look at the stepfamily more positively. Amato and Keith analyzed data comparing intact, two-parent families with stepfami-lies and found that while children from two-parent families performed sig-nificantly better on a multifactored measure of well-being and development, there was a significant overlap. A substantial number of children in stepfam-ilies actually perform as well as or better than children in intact two-parent families. As Amato comments, "Some children grow up in well-functioning intact families in which they encounter abuse, neglect, poverty, parental mental illness, and parental substance abuse. Other children grow up in well-functioning stepfamilies and have caring stepparents who provide affection, effective control and economic support."[12] Still other researchers suggest that it may be the painful transitions of divorce and economically deprived single-parenthood which usually precede the formation of the stepfamily that explain the poor performance of stepchildren.[13]

Perhaps a fairer comparison of stepchildren's well-being is against single-parent families. Indeed, if there were no remarriage (or first marriage, in the case of unmarried birth mothers), these children would remain a part of a single-parent household. On most psychological measures of behavior and achievement, stepchildren look more like children from single-parent fami-lies than children from never-divorced families, but on economic measures it is a different story. The National Survey of Families and Households (NSFH) data show that stepparents have slightly lower incomes and slightly less edu-cation than parents in nuclear families, but that incomes of all types of mar-ried families with children are three to four times greater than the incomes of single mothers. Custodial mothers in stepfamilies have similar incomes to

single mothers (about $12,000 in 1987). If, as seems plausible, their personal incomes are about the same before they married as after, then marriage has increased their household incomes more than threefold. Stepfathers' incomes are, on average, more than twice as great as their wives' and account for nearly three-fourths of the family's income.[14]

In contrast to residential stepparents, absent biological parents only rarely provide much financial or other help to their children. Some do not because they are dead or cannot be found; about 26 percent of custodial, remarried mothers and 28 percent of single mothers report that their child's father is deceased or of unknown whereabouts. Yet even in the three-quarters of families where the noncustodial parent's whereabouts are known, only about one-third of all custodial mothers (single and remarried) receive child support or alimony from former spouses, and the amounts involved are small compared to the cost of raising children. According to NSFH data, remarried women with awards receive on average $1780 per year, while single mothers receive $1383. Clearly, former spouses cannot be relied on to lift custodial mothers and their children out of poverty.[15]

The picture is still more complex, as is true with all issues relating to stepfamilies. Some noncustodial fathers have remarried and have stepchildren themselves. These relationships, too, are evident in the NSFH data. Nearly one-quarter (23 percent) of residential stepfathers have minor children from former relationships living elsewhere. Two-thirds of those report paying child support for their children.[16] [There] is a growing class of fathers who frequently feel resentful about the heavy burden of supporting two households, particularly when their first wife has remarried.

In sum, although we have no data which precisely examine the distribution of resources within a stepfamily, it is fair to assume that stepfathers' substantial contributions to family income improve their stepchildren's material well-being by helping to cover basic living costs. For many formerly single-parent families, stepfathers' incomes provided by remarriage are essential in preventing or ending poverty among custodial mothers and their children. (The data are less clear for the much smaller class of residential stepmothers.)

While legal dependency usually ends at eighteen, the economic resources available to a stepchild through remarriage could continue to be an important factor past childhood. College education and young adulthood are especially demanding economic events. The life-course studies undertaken by some researchers substantiate the interpersonal trends seen in stepfamilies before the stepchildren leave home. White reports that viewed from either the parent's or the child's perspective, relationships over the life-course between stepchildren and stepparents are substantially weaker than those between biological parents and children. These relationships are not monolithic, however; the best occur when the stepparent is a male, there are no stepsiblings, the stepparent has no children of his own, and the marriage between the biological parent and the stepparent is intact.[17] On the other end, support relationships are nearly always cut off if the stepparent relationship is terminated because of divorce or the death of the natural parent. . . .

. . . One study of perceived normative obligation to stepparents and step-children suggests that people in stepfamilies have weaker, but still important, family ties than do biological kin.[18] In terms of economic and other forms of adult support, even weak ties cannot be discounted. They might, instead, become the focus of public policy initiatives.

Stepfamilies in Law and Public Policy

Both state and federal law set policies that affect stepfamilies. Overall, these policies do not reflect a coherent policy toward stepparents and stepchildren. Two competing models are roughly evident. One, a "stranger" model, followed by most states, treats the residential stepparent as if he or she were a legal stranger to the children, with no rights and no responsibilities. The other, a "dependency" model, most often followed by federal policymakers, assumes the residential stepfather is, in fact, supporting the stepchildren and provides benefits accordingly. But there is inconsistency in both state and federal policy. Some states lean at times toward a dependency model and require support in some instances, and the federal government sometimes treats the stepparent as if he or she were a stranger to the stepchildren, and ignores them in calculating benefits.

State law governs the traditional family matters of marriage, divorce, adoption, and inheritance, while federal law covers a wide range of programs and policies which touch on the lives of most Americans, including stepfamilies. As the provider of benefits through such programs as [TANF] and Social Security, the federal government sets eligibility standards that affect the economic well-being of many stepfamilies. In addition, as the employer of the armed forces and civil servants, the federal government establishes employee benefits guidelines for vast numbers of American families. And in its regulatory role, the federal government defines the status of stepfamilies for many purposes ranging from immigration eligibility to tax liability. . . .

State Policies

State laws generally give little recognition to the dependency needs of children who reside with their stepparent; they are most likely to treat the step-parent as a stranger to the children, with no rights or obligations. In contrast to the numerous state laws obligating parents to support natural children born out of wedlock or within a previous marriage, only a few states have enacted statutes which specifically impose an affirmative duty on steppar-ents. The Utah stepparent support statute, for example, provides simply that "[a] stepparent shall support a stepchild to the same extent that a natural or adoptive parent is required to support a child."[19] This duty of support ends upon the termination of the marriage. Most states are silent on the obligation to support stepchildren.[20]

A few states rely on common law, the legal tradition stemming from our English roots. The common law tradition leans more toward a dependency model. It dictates that a stepparent can acquire the rights and duties of a

parent if he or she acts *in loco parentis* (in the place of a parent). Acquisition of this status is not automatic; it is determined by the stepparent's intent. A stepparent need not explicitly state the intention to act as a parent; he or she can "manifest the requisite intent to assume responsibility by actually providing financial support or by taking over the custodial duties."[21] Courts, however, have been reluctant to grant *in loco* parental rights or to attach obligations to unwilling stepparents. In the words of one Wisconsin court, "A good Samaritan should not be saddled with the legal obligations of another, and we think the law should not with alacrity conclude that a stepparent assumes parental relationships to a child."[22]

At the extreme, once the status of *in loco parentis* is achieved, the stepparent "stands in the place of the natural parent, and the reciprocal rights, duties, and obligations of parent and child subsist." These rights, duties, and obligations include the duty to provide financial support, the right to custody and control of the child, immunity from suit by the stepchild, and, in some cases, visitation rights after the dissolution of the marriage by death or divorce.

Yet stepparents who qualify as *in loco parentis* are not always required to provide support in all circumstances. A subset of states imposes obligation only if the stepchild is in danger of becoming dependent on public assistance. For example, Hawaii provides that

> [a] stepparent who acts in loco parentis is bound to provide, maintain, and support the stepparent's stepchild during the residence of the child with the stepparent if the legal parents desert the child or are unable to support the child, thereby reducing the child to destitute and necessitous circumstances.[23]

Just as states do not regularly require stepparents to support their stepchildren, they do not offer stepparents the parental authority of custody and control within the marriage. A residential stepparent generally has fewer rights than a legal guardian or a foster parent. According to one commentator, a stepparent "has no authority to make decisions about the child—no authority to approve emergency medical treatment or even to sign a permission slip for a field trip to the fire station."[24]

Both common law and state statutes almost uniformly terminate the stepparent relationship upon divorce or the death of the custodial parent. This means that the support obligations, if there were any, cease and that the stepparent has no rights to visitation or custody. State courts have sometimes found individual exceptions to this rule, but they have not created any clear precedents. Currently only a few states authorize stepparents to seek visitation rights, and custody is almost always granted to a biological parent upon divorce. In the event of the death of the stepparent's spouse, the noncustodial, biological parent is usually granted custody even when the stepparent has, in fact, raised the child. In the 1987 Michigan case, *Henrikson* v. *Gable*,[25] the children, aged nine and ten when their mother died, had lived with their stepfather since infancy and had rarely seen their biological father. In the ensuing custody dispute, the trial court left the children with their stepfather, but an appellate court, relying upon a state law that created a

strong preference for biological parents, reversed this decision and turned the children over to their biological father.

Following the stranger model, state inheritance laws, with a few complex exceptions, do not recognize the existence of stepchildren. Under existing state laws, even a dependent stepchild whose stepparent has supported and raised the child for many years is not eligible to inherit from the stepparent if there is no will. California provides the most liberal rule for stepchild recovery when there is no will, but only if the stepchild meets relatively onerous qualifications. Stepchildren may inherit as the children of a deceased stepparent only if "it is established by clear and convincing evidence that the stepparent would have adopted the person but for a legal barrier."[26] Very few stepchildren have been able to pass this test. Similarly, a stepchild cannot bring a negligence suit for the accidental death of a stepparent. In most instances, then, only a biological child will inherit or receive legal compensation when a stepparent dies.

Federal Policies

The federal policies that concern us here are of two types: federal benefit programs given to families in need, including AFDC (until 1997) and Supplemental Security Income (SSI), and general programs not based on need, including Social Security as well as civil service and military personnel employee benefits. Most of these programs follow the dependency model. They go further than do most states in recognizing or promoting the actual family relationship of residential stepfamilies. Many of them (although not all) assume that residential stepparents support their stepchildren and accordingly make these children eligible for benefits equivalent to those afforded to other children of the family.

Despite the fact that federal law generally recognizes the dependency of residential stepchildren, it remains wanting in many respects. There is a great deal of inconsistency in how the numerous federal programs and policies treat the stepparent–stepchild relationship, and the very definitions of what constitutes a stepchild are often quite different across programs. Most of the programs strive for a dependency-based definition, such as living with or receiving 50 percent of support from a stepparent. However, some invoke the vague definition "actual family relationship," and some do not attempt any definition at all, thus potentially including nonresidential stepchildren among the beneficiaries. In some programs the category of stepchild is entirely absent or specifically excluded from the list of beneficiaries for some programs. . . .

Stepchildren are even more vulnerable in the event of divorce. Here the stranger model is turned to. As with state law, any legally recognized relationship is immediately severed upon divorce in nearly all federal programs. The children and their stepparents become as strangers. Social Security does not provide any cushion for stepchildren if the deceased stepparent is divorced from the custodial parent. Under Social Security law, the stepparent–stepchild relationship is terminated immediately upon divorce

and the stepchild is no longer eligible for benefits even if the child has in fact been dependent on the insured stepparent for the duration of a very long marriage.[27] If the divorce were finalized the day before the stepparent's death, the child would receive no benefits. . . .

New Policy Proposals

. . . All of the proposals I review base their arguments to a greater or lesser degree on social science data, although not always the same data. The proposers may roughly be divided into three camps. The first, and perhaps smallest camp, I call *negativists*. These are scholars who view stepfamilies from a sociobiological perspective and find them a troublesome aberration to be actively discouraged. The second, and by far largest group of scholars, I term *voluntarists*. This group acknowledges both the complexity and the often distant nature of stepparent relationships, and largely believes that law and policy should leave stepfamilies alone, as it does now. If stepparents wish to take a greater role in their stepchildren's lives, they should be encouraged to do so, by adoption or some other means. The third camp recognizes the growing presence of stepfamilies as an alternate family form and believes they should be recognized and strengthened in some important ways. This group, I call them *reformists*, believes the law should take the lead in providing more rights or obligations to stepparents. The few policy initiatives from this group range from small specific reforms regarding such issues as inheritance and visitation to my own proposal for a full-scale redefinition of stepparents' rights and obligations.

The negativist viewpoint on stepparenting, most prominently represented by sociologist David Popenoe, relies on a sociobiological theory of reproduction. According to this theory, human beings will give unstintingly to their own biological children, in order to promote their own genes, but will be far less generous to others. The recent rise in divorce and out-of-wedlock births, according to Popenoe, has created a pattern of essentially fatherless households that cannot compete with the two-biological-parent families.

Popenoe believes the pattern of stepparent disengagement revealed by many researchers is largely based on this biological stinginess.

> If the argument . . . is correct, and the family is fundamentally rooted in biology and at least partly activated by the "genetically selfish" activities of human beings, childbearing by non-relatives is inherently problematic. It is not that unrelated individuals are unable to do the job of parenting, it is just that they are not as likely to do the job well. Stepfamily problems, in short, may be so intractable that the best strategy for dealing with them is to do everything possible to minimize their occurrence.[28] . . .

Popenoe goes beyond the stranger model, which is neutral as to state activity, and suggests an active discouragement of stepparent families. He believes the best way to obstruct stepfamilies is to encourage married

biological two-parent families. Premarital and marital counseling, a longer waiting period for divorce, and a redesign of the current welfare system so that marriage and family are empowered rather than denigrated are among his policy recommendations. . . .

The second group of scholars, whom I call voluntarists, generally believe that the stepparent relationship is essentially voluntary and private and the stranger model most clearly reflects this. The legal bond formed by remarriage is between man and wife—stepchildren are incidental; they are legal strangers. Stepparents may choose, or not choose, to become more involved with everyday economic and emotional support of their stepchildren; but the law should not mandate this relationship, it should simply reflect it. These scholars recognize the growth of stepfamilies as a factor of modern life and neither condone nor condemn this configuration. Family law scholar David Chambers probably speaks for most scholars in this large camp when he says,

> In most regards, this state of the law nicely complements the state of stepparent relationships in the United States. Recall the inescapable diversity of such relationships—residential and non-residential, beginning when the children are infants and when they are teenagers, leading to comfortable relationships in some cases and awkward relationships in others, lasting a few years and lasting many. In this context it seems sensible to permit those relationships to rest largely on the voluntary arrangements among stepparents and biological parents. The current state of the law also amply recognizes our nation's continuing absorption with the biological relationship, especially as it informs our sensibilities about enduring financial obligations.[29]

Chambers is not enthusiastic about imposing support obligations on stepparents, either during or following the termination of a marriage, but is interested in promoting voluntary adoption. He would, however, approve some middle ground where biological parents are not completely cut off in the adoption process.

Other voluntarists are attracted by the new English model of parenting, as enacted in the Children Act of 1989. Of great attraction to American voluntarists is the fact that under this model a stepparent who has been married at least two years to the biological parent may voluntarily petition for a residence order for his or her spouse's child. With a residence order the stepparent has parental responsibility toward the child until the age of sixteen. But this order does not extinguish the parental responsibility of the noncustodial parent.[30] In accordance with the Children Act of 1989, parents, biological or otherwise, no longer have parental rights; they have only parental responsibilities, and these cannot be extinguished upon the divorce of the biological parents. In England, therefore, it is possible for three adults to claim parental responsibility. Unlike biological parental responsibility, however, stepparent responsibility does not usually extend following divorce. The stepparent is not normally financially responsible following divorce, but he or she may apply for a visitation order.

The third group, whom I call reformists, believe that voluntary acts on the part of stepparents are not always adequate, and that it is necessary to reform the law in some way to more clearly define the rights and responsibilities of stepparents. The American Bar Association Family Law Section has been working for some years on a proposed Model Act to suggest legislative reforms regarding stepparents' obligations to provide child support and rights to discipline, visitation, and custody. A Model Act is not binding anywhere; it is simply a model for all states to consider. Traditionally, however, Model Acts have been very influential in guiding state legislative reform. In its current form, the ABA Model Act would require stepparents to assume a duty of support during the duration of the remarriage only if the child is not adequately supported by the custodial and noncustodial parent. The issue is ultimately left to the discretion of the family court, but the Model Act does not require that the stepparent would need to have a close relationship with a stepchild before a support duty is imposed. The Model Act, however, does not describe what the rule should be if the stepparent and the custodial parent divorce.

The proposed statute is rather more complete in its discussion of stepparent visitation or custody rights following divorce. It takes a two-tiered approach, first asking if the stepparent has standing (a legal basis) to seek visitation and then asking if the visitation would be in the best interests of the child. The standing question is to be resolved with reference to five factors, which essentially examine the role of the stepparent in the child's life (almost an *in loco parentis* question), the financial support offered by the stepparent, and the detriment to the child from denying visitation. The court, if it finds standing, then completes the analysis with the best interests standard of the jurisdiction. The Model Act's section on physical custody also requires a two-tiered test, requiring standing and increasing the burden on the stepparent to present clear and convincing proof that he or she is the better custodial parent.

The ABA Model Act is a worthwhile start, in my opinion, but it is little more than that. At most it moves away from a stranger model and provides a limited concept of mandatory stepparent support during a marriage, acknowledging that stepchildren are at least sometimes dependent. It also gives a stepparent a fighting chance for visitation or custody following a divorce. It fails to clarify stepparents' rights during the marriage, however, and does not deal with the issue of economic support at the period of maximum vulnerability, the termination of the marriage through death and divorce. Moreover, the Model Act, and, indeed, all the existing reform proposals, deal only with traditional legal concepts of parenthood defined by each state and do not consider the vast range of federal programs, or other public and private programs, that define the stepparent–stepchild relationship for purposes of benefits, insurance, or other purposes.

I propose, instead, a new conceptualization of stepparent rights and responsibilities, a de facto parent model, that will cover all aspects of the stepparent–stepchild relationship and will extend to federal and private policy as well. My first concern in proposing a new framework is the welfare of

the stepchildren, which is not adequately dealt with in either the stranger or the dependency model. The failure of state and, to a lesser extent, federal policy to address coherently the financial interdependencies of step relationships, described earlier, means that children dependent upon a residential stepparent may not receive adequate support or benefits from that parent during the marriage, and they may not be protected economically in the event of divorce or parental death. . . .

A second reason for proposing a new framework is to strengthen the relationship of the stepparent and stepchildren. While research generally finds that stepparents are less engaged in parenting than natural parents, research studies do not explain the causes; others must do so. In addition to the sociobiologists' claim for stingy, genetically driven behavior, sociologists have posited the explanation of "incomplete institutionalization."[31] This theory is based on the belief that, by and large, people act as they are expected to act by society. In the case of stepfamilies, there are unclear or absent societal norms and standards for how to define the remarried family, especially the role of the stepparent in relation to the stepchild.

Briefly, my new model requires, first of all, dividing stepparents into two subclasses: those who are de facto parents and those who are not. De facto parents would be defined as "those stepparents legally married to a natural parent who primarily reside with their stepchildren, or who provide at least 50 percent of the stepchild's financial support." Stepparents who do not meet the de facto parent requirements would, in all important respects, disappear from policy.

For the purposes of federal and state policy, under this scheme, a de facto parent would be treated virtually the same as a natural parent during the marriage. The same rights, obligations, and presumptions would attach vis-à-vis their stepchildren, including the obligation of support. These rights and duties would continue in some form, based on the length of the marriage, following the custodial parent's death or divorce from the stepparent, or the death of the stepparent. In the event of divorce the stepparent would have standing to seek custody or visitation, but the stepparent could also be obligated for child support of a limited duration. Upon the death of a stepparent, a minor stepchild would be treated for purposes of inheritance and benefits as would a natural child.

So far this proposal resembles the common law doctrine of *in loco parentis*, described earlier, where the stepparent is treated for most purposes (except inheritance) as a parent on the condition that he or she voluntarily agrees to support the child. In the de facto model, however, support is mandatory, not voluntary, on the grounds both that it is not fair to stepchildren to be treated by the law in an unequal or arbitrary manner and that child welfare considerations are best met by uniform support of stepchildren. Furthermore, in the traditional common law *in loco parentis* scenario, the noncustodial parent had died and was not a factor to be reckoned with. Under this scheme, creating a de facto parent category for stepparents would not invalidate the existing rights and obligations of a noncustodial biological parent. Rather, this proposal would empower a stepparent as an additional parent.

Multiple parenting and the rights and obligations of the stepparent and children following divorce or death are controversial and difficult policy matters that require more detailed attention than the brief exposition that can be offered here. Multiple parenting is the barrier upon which many family law reform schemes, especially in custody and adoption, have foundered. It is also one of the reasons that there has been no consistent effort to reformulate the role of stepparents. Working out the details is critical. For instance, mandating stepparent support raises a central issue of fairness. If the stepparent is indeed required to support the child, there is a question about the support obligations of the noncustodial parent. Traditionally, most states have not recognized the stepparent contribution as an offset to child support.[32] While this policy promotes administrative efficiency, and may benefit some children, it may not be fair to the noncustodial parent. An important advance in recognizing the existence of multiple parents in the nonlinear family is to recognize multiple support obligations. The few states that require stepparent obligation have given limited attention to apportionment of child support obligations, offering no clear guidelines. I propose that state statutory requirements for stepparent obligation as de facto parents also include clear guidelines for apportionment of child support between the noncustodial natural parent and the stepparent. . . .

Another facet of multiple parenting is legal authority. If stepparents are required to accept parental support obligations, equal protection and fairness concerns dictate that they must also be given parental rights. Currently, state laws, as noted earlier, recognize only natural or adoptive parents; a stepparent currently has no legal authority over a stepchild, even to authorize a field trip. If stepparents had full parental rights, in some cases, as when the parents have shared legal custody, the law would be recognizing the parental rights of three parents, rather than two. While this sounds unusual, it is an accurate reflection of how many families now raise their children. Most often, however, it would be only the custodial parent and his or her spouse, the de facto parent, who would have authority to make decisions for the children in their home.

Critics of this scheme may argue that adoption, not the creation of the legal status of de facto parent, is the appropriate vehicle for granting a stepparent full parental rights and responsibilities.[33] If, as discussed earlier, nearly three-quarters of stepchildren are not being supported by their noncustodial parents, policy initiatives could be directed to terminating the nonpaying parents' rights and promoting stepparent adoption. Adoption is not possible, however, unless the parental rights of the absent natural parent have been terminated—a difficult procedure against a reluctant parent. Normally, the rights of a parent who maintains contact with his or her child cannot be terminated even if that parent is not contributing child support. And when parental rights are terminated, visitation rights are terminated as well in most states. It is by no means clear that it is in the best interests of children to terminate contact with a natural parent, even if the parent is not meeting his or her obligation to support.[34] As discussed earlier, a large percentage (another 25 percent or so), of noncustodial parents continue some

contact with their children, even when not paying support.[35] And while stepparent adoption should be strongly encouraged when it is possible, this solution will not resolve the problem of defining the role of stepparents who have not adopted.

Extending, in some form, the rights and obligations following the termination of the marriage by divorce or death is equally problematical. Currently, only a few courts have ruled in favor of support payments following divorce, and these have been decided on an individual basis. Only one state, Missouri, statutorily continues stepparent support obligations following divorce.[36] It would clearly be in the best interests of the child to experience continued support, since a significant number of children may sink below the poverty line upon the dissolution of their stepfamily.[37]

Since the de facto model is based on dependency, not blood, a fair basis for support following divorce or the death of the custodial parent might be to require that a stepparent who qualified as a de facto parent for at least one year must contribute child support for half the number of years of dependency until the child reached maturity. If a child resided with the stepparent for four years, the stepparent would be liable for support for two years. If the biological noncustodial parent were still paying support payments, the amount could be apportioned. While it may be said that this policy would discourage people from becoming stepparents by marrying, it could also be said to discourage divorce once one has become a stepparent. Stepparents might consider working harder at maintaining a marriage if divorce had some real costs.

Conversely, stepparents should have rights as well as responsibilities following divorce or the death of the custodial parent. Divorced or widowed stepparents should be able to pursue visitation or custody if they have lived with and supported the child for at least one year. Once again, multiple parent claims might sometimes be an issue, but these could be resolved, as they are now, under a primary caretaker, or a best interest standard.

The death of a stepparent is a particular period of vulnerability for stepchildren for which they are unprotected by inheritance law. While Social Security and other federal survivor benefits are based on the premise that a stepchild relies on the support of the residential stepparent and will suffer the same hardship as natural children if the stepparent dies, state inheritance laws, notoriously archaic, decree that only biology, not dependency, counts. State laws should assume that a de facto parent would wish to have all his dependents receive a share of his estate if he died without a will. If the stepchildren are no longer dependent, that assumption would not necessarily prevail. The same assumption should prevail for insurance policies and compensation claims following an accidental death. A dependent stepchild, just as a natural child, should have the right to sue for loss of support.

On the federal front, a clear definition of stepparents as de facto parents would eliminate the inconsistencies regarding stepparents which plague current federal policies and would clarify the role of the residential stepparent. For the duration of the marriage, a stepchild would be treated as a natural child for purposes of support and the receipt of federal benefits.

This treatment would persist in the event of the death of the stepparent. The stepchild would receive all the survivor and death benefits that would accrue to a natural child.[38]

In the case of divorce, the issue of federal benefits is more complicated. Stepchildren and natural children should not have identical coverage for federal benefits following divorce, again, but neither is it good policy to summarily cut off children who have been dependent, sometimes for many years, on the de facto parent. A better policy is to extend federal benefits for a period following divorce, based on a formula which matches half the number of years of dependency, as earlier suggested for child support. For instance, if the stepparent resided with the stepchild for four years, the child would be covered by Social Security survivor benefits and other federal benefits, including federal employee benefits, for a period of two years following the divorce. This solution would serve children by at least providing a transitional cushion. It would also be relatively easy to administer. In the case of the death of the biological custodial parent, benefits could be similarly extended, or continued indefinitely if the child remains in the custody of the stepparent. . . .

Ultimately, state law defines most of these stepfamily relationships, and it is difficult, if not impossible to achieve uniform reform on a state-by-state basis. In England it is possible to pass a single piece of national legislation, such as the Children Act of 1989, which completely redefines parental roles. In America, the process of reform is slower and less sure. Probably the first step in promoting a new policy would be for the federal government to insist all states pass stepparent general support obligation laws requiring stepparents acting as de facto parents (by my definition) to support their stepchildren as they do their natural children. This goal could be accomplished by making stepparent general support obligation laws a prerequisite for receiving federal welfare grants. Federal policy already assumes this support in figuring eligibility in many programs, but it has not insisted that states change their laws. Precedent for this strategy has been set by the Family Support Acts of 1988 in which the federal government mandated that states set up strict child support enforcement laws for divorced parents and unwed fathers at AFDC levels in order to secure AFDC funding.[39] The second, larger step would be to require limited stepparent support following divorce, as described previously. Once the basic obligations were asserted, an articulation of basic rights would presumably follow.

Conclusion

Stepfamilies compose a large and growing sector of American families that is largely ignored by public policy. Social scientists tell us that these families have problems. Stepparent–stepchildren relationships, poorly defined by law and social norms, are not as strong or nurturing as those in nondivorced families, and stepchildren do not do as well in school and in other outside settings. Still, stepfamily relationships are important in lifting single-parent

families out of poverty. When single or divorced mothers marry, the household income increases by more than threefold, rising to roughly the same level as nuclear families. A substantial portion of these families experiences divorce, however, placing the stepchildren at risk of falling back into poverty. It makes good public policy sense then, both to strengthen these stepfamily relationships and to cushion the transition for stepchildren should the relationship end.

ENDNOTES

[1] Mary Ann Mason and David Simon, "The Ambiguous Stepparent: Federal Legislation in Search of a Model," *Family Law Quarterly* 29:446–48, 1995.

[2] E. Mavis Hetherington and Kathleen M. Jodl, "Stepfamilies as Settings for Child Development," in Alan Booth and Judy Dunn (eds.), *Stepfamilies: Who Benefits? Who Does Not?* New Jersey: Erlbaum, 1994, 55; and E. Mavis Hetherington, "An Overview of the Virginia Longitudinal Study of Divorce and Remarriage: A Focus on Early Adolescence," *Journal of Family Psychology* 7:39–56, 1993.

[3] U.S. Bureau of Census, 1989.

[4] Divorce is not always the background event. An increasing, but still relatively small number of custodial mothers have not previously wed.

[5] Mary Ann Mason and Jane Mauldon, "The New Stepfamily Needs a New Public Policy," *Journal of Social Issues* 52(3):5, Fall 1996.

[6] Hetherington and Jodl, "Stepfamilies as Settings for Child Development," 55–81.

[7] Ibid., 76.

[8] E. Mavis Hetherington and William Clingempeel, "Coping with Marital Transitions: A Family Systems Perspective," *Monographs of the Society for Research in Child Development* 57:2–3, Serial No. 227, 1992; E. Thomson, Sara McLanahan, and R. B. Curtin, "Family Structure, Gender, and Parental Socialization," *Journal of Marriage and the Family* 54:368–78, 1992.

[9] Hetherington and Jodl, "Stepfamilies as Settings for Child Development," 64–65.

[10] Thomson, McLanahan, and Curtin, "Family Structure, Gender, and Parental Socialization," 368–78.

[11] L. Bumpass and J. Sweet, *American Families and Households*, New York: Russell Sage Foundation, 1987, 23.

[12] Paul Amato, "The Implications of Research Findings on Children in Stepfamilies," in Alan Booth and Judy Dunn (eds.), *Stepfamilies: Who Benefits? Who Does Not?* New Jersey: Erlbaum, 1994, 84.

[13] Nicholas Zill, "Understanding Why Children in Stepfamilies Have More Learning and Behavior Problems than Children in Nuclear Families," in Alan Booth and Judy Dunn (eds.), *Stepfamilies: Who Benefits? Who Does Not?* New Jersey: Erlbaum, 1994, 89–97.

[14] Mason and Mauldon, "The New Stepfamily Needs a New Public Policy," 7.

[15] Ibid., 8.

[16] Ibid.

[17] Lynn White, "Stepfamilies over the Lifecourse: Social Support," in Alan Booth and Judy Dunn (eds.), *Stepfamilies: Who Benefits? Who Does Not?* New Jersey: Erlbaum, 1994, 109–139.

[18] A. S. Rossi and P. H. Rossi, *Of Human Bonding: Parent–Child Relations across the Life Course*, New York: A. de Gruyter, 1990.

[19] Utah Code Ann. 78-45-4.1.

[20] Margaret Mahoney, *Stepfamilies and the Law*, Ann Arbor: University of Michigan Press, 1994, 13–47.

[21] *Miller v. United States*, 123 F.2d 715, 717 (8th Cir, 1941).

[22] *Niesen v. Niesen*, 157 N. W.2d 660 664 (Wis. 1968).

[23] Hawaii Revised Stat. Ann., Title 31, Sec. 577-4.

[24] David Chambers, "Stepparents, Biologic Parents, and the Law's Perceptions of 'Family' after Divorce," in S. Sugarman and H. H. Kay (eds.), *Divorce Reform at the Crossroads*, New Haven: Yale University Press, 1990, 102–29.

[25] *Henrikson v. Gable,* 162 Mich. App 248 (1987).

[26] Cal. Prob. Code, Sec. 6408.

[27] 42 U.S.C. sec. 416(e), 1994.

[28] David Popenoe, "Evolution of Marriage and Stepfamily Problems," in Alan Booth and Judy Dunn (eds.), *Stepfamilies: Who Benefits? Who Does Not?* New Jersey: Erlbaum, 1994, 3–28.

[29] Chambers, "Stepparents, Biologic Parents, and the Law's Perceptions of 'Family' after Divorce," 26.

[30] Mark A. Fine, "Social Policy Pertaining to Stepfamilies: Should Stepparents and Stepchildren Have the Option of Establishing a Legal Relationship?" in Alan Booth and Judy Dunn (eds.), *Stepfamilies: Who Benefits? Who Does Not?* New Jersey: Erlbaum, 1994, 199.

[31] Andrew Cherlin, "Remarriage as an Incomplete Institution," *American Journal of Sociology* 84:634–49, 1978.

[32] S. Ramsey and J. Masson, "Stepparent Support of Stepchildren: A Comparative Analysis of Policies and Problems in the American and British Experience," *Syracuse Law Review* 36:649–66, 1985.

[33] Joan Hollinger (ed.-in-chief), et al., *Adoption Law and Practice,* New York: Matthew Bender, 1988.

[34] Katherine Bartlett, "Re-thinking Parenthood as an Exclusive Status: The Need for Alternatives When the Premise of the Nuclear Family Has Failed," *Virginia Law Review* 70:879–903, 1984.

[35] Mason and Mauldon, "The New Stepfamily Needs a New Public Policy," 5.

[36] Vernon's Ann. Missouri Stats. 453.400, 1994.

[37] Mason and Mauldon, "The New Stepfamily Needs a New Public Policy," 5.

[38] Mason and Simon, "The Ambiguous Stepparent: Federal Legislation in Search of a Model," 471.

[39] 100 P.L. 485; 102 Stat. 2343 (1988).

40

OVERLOOKED ASPECTS OF STEPFATHERING

WILLIAM MARSIGLIO

When we think about the everyday issues and implications associated with stepfathering, our attention likely drifts to obvious activities like discipline, supervision, financial support, and playing.[1] How assertive is the stepfather in defining the house rules or looking after his partner's child? Does he help pay for the child's food, clothes, and activities? If the mother works, does the stepdad take on the role of babysitter when she's away from home? Does he spend time doing fun things with the child?

We seldom reflect on the indirect ways a stepfather can influence a stepchild's life. Without this broader view, though, much goes unnoticed about how the complex and often ambiguous nature of stepfamily dynamics

provides the stepfather with unique opportunities to make a difference in a child's life. A stepfather, just like a biological father, can influence a child's well-being in many ways, some direct, others indirect. The stepfathers' stories in my study shed light on two key indirect avenues for making a difference: contributions to building social capital and efforts to support the biological father, or, as I put it, to be the father's ally.

Another dimension of stepfathering that often flies beneath the radar is that the experience of stepfathering, like fathering, is not a one-way street. A man's willingness to get involved with his partner's child in a fatherly way means that he too may be changed by the experience. The stepfather who is mindful of how he makes a difference in a stepchild's life, as well as how he develops because of his involvement, is likely to have a much deeper understanding of what stepfamily life means to him.

Social Capital

Under the right circumstances, a father, either biological or step, can contribute to his child's well-being indirectly by providing the child with what sociologists call social capital.[2] This type of contribution goes beyond the typical cognitive and financial resources a parent can provide a child. In this study, it refers to the stepfather's contributions to either family-based or community-based relations that can affect a child's cognitive, emotional, and physical well-being. In terms of family relations, it captures a stepfather's relations with his child, the extent of his positive involvement and support. It also focuses on the extent to which a stepfather maintains a relationship with the mother based on trust, mutual respect, and a sense of loyalty. Does the stepfather share similar parenting values and conflict resolution strategies with the child's birth mother? To what extent and in what ways is the stepfather supportive of the birth mother, especially in ways that the child can notice? Is the stepfather an integral part of a coparenting team with the birth mother in which they routinely share with each other information about the child, a practice that allows each to know what is taking place in the child's life from day to day?

The other domain in which social capital comes into play involves the stepfather's set of relations with individuals and organizations directly involved with the stepchild. The individuals either interact with the child or are in a position to provide resources and opportunities if needed. Included among them are teachers, coaches, ministers, camp counselors, medical personnel, neighbors, and the child's friends, as well as the friends' parents. Individuals who presently are not involved with the child can also be viewed as part of this potential network if the stepfather has the option of bringing them into the picture to benefit the child (an acquaintance of the stepfather who hires the child for a summer job).

Taken together, these two general forms of social capital are meaningful because they enable a stepfather to expose a child to a healthy model of adult interaction, bring about closure in the child's social networks so that

people important to the child can share vital information about him or her, and act as a liaison to valuable community resources for the child. If persons in the community share the stepfather's interests in helping the child, they can provide an important source of supervision while reinforcing or sanctioning the child's behavior. Similarly, if the stepfather is integrated into a larger network or community where mutual obligations, expectations, and trustworthiness prevail, the child will be exposed to social capital. Focusing on these types of connections and fatherly contributions reminds us that the stepfamily (or family) is a social system embedded in a larger social ecology replete with neighborhood, school, and peer contexts.[3] How then can a stepfather, given the ambiguous norms often associated with stepfamily life, contribute to a child's social capital and thereby affect the child's quality of life? Because the norms and arrangements associated with stepfamily life are sometimes unclear to family members[4] and are often muddled in the public eye,[5] a stepfather may be forced to work harder than a biological father if he wishes to develop social capital on behalf of a child.

When stepfathers describe their parenting circumstances, they often emphasize their desire to be part of a team. As already noted, some are more successful in achieving this arrangement than others. The "team" mentality that some of the stepfathers experience can be thought of as part of the family-based social capital they contribute to their stepchildren. This is one form of social capital that requires the birth mother's cooperation. The men's efforts to promote a team approach can sometimes be viewed as part of their general attempt to provide social support for the birth mother. When men take an active role in the hands-on parenting of stepchildren with the mother's blessing, her life becomes easier. . . .

From a practical standpoint, opportunities to create community-based social capital are more readily available for men with school-age children who are involved in school and other activities outside the home. Because a number of the men I interviewed were involved with stepchildren who were still quite young and had little exposure to the world beyond their home, my sample is a bit limited in the breadth and depth of insights it can generate on this topic. Nevertheless, a third of the stepfathers in my sample met the target stepchild when he or she was at least seven years old, and two-thirds were currently involved with a stepchild who had reached school age. The stepfather's experiences with school-age children highlight several points germane to the development of social capital.

Several of the stepfathers spoke about how they took it upon themselves to have discussions with teachers and other child care professionals in order to understand their stepchild better and to intervene on his or her behalf. Some of these kids had been diagnosed with a learning disability or behavioral problem (for example, ADHD—attention deficit hyperactive disorder) and/or were having problems at school. Although they varied in how they went about getting involved, a number of the stepdads took their roles quite seriously. Randy, for example, describes his experience with his wife, Molly, and her son Jamie. Talking about how he and his

wife responded to a teacher's suggestion that Jamie probably had ADHD, Randy says, "We were able to get him tested early and have a firm handle on all the problems, before he got into public schools. So we have in some ways been really tight with all his teachers." Continuing, "We interact with the teachers. And basically we have to because if anything happens to Jamie, Molly's going to be in somebody's face about it. So I've got to be right there to make sure she doesn't overdo the 'in the face' stuff, . . . we're kind of a good cop, bad cop team, when it comes to Jamie." By using "we" and "team" to characterize his involvement, Randy apparently sees his role in Jamie's life from a coparenting perspective. His consistent use of these words illustrates that he perceives himself as playing a critical role alongside his wife in looking out for Jamie and developing social capital to serve the child's best interests.

Brad similarly describes his initial contribution to a coparenting approach to developing social capital and being involved with his stepson Bobby, diagnosed with ADHD. He entered the picture at a time when Bobby was struggling at school and his mother was distraught over what she could do to help him improve. She had been particularly upset over one teacher's treatment of her son, while being generally dissatisfied with the response she was receiving from school personnel. Given this awkward context, Brad's initial involvement in confronting school representatives meant that he was jumping into an already volatile situation. Referring to this first meeting, Brad says, "I went basically to try and help her keep her temper, help keep the discussion at a level that was rational and not just angry at the school, expressing anger to the teachers. I failed miserably." Although Brad does not view his initial experience as a success, he recognizes that he has made a difference since then.

Like Randy, Brad felt that he was part of a parental team, with his specific role being to bring a calm and sober perspective to the meetings with school personnel. Presumably, both these men, as well as their partners, assumed that they could provide this perspective because, compared to the birth mother, they did not have the same history with and investments in the child. However, these men still saw themselves as having a vested interest in looking out for their respective stepchildren, but they implicitly recognized that their best shot at building social capital and helping the child was to monitor the birth mother. . . .

The same sort of paternal commitment is expressed by Doug as he talks about how he became very active in his nonbiological son Sammy's academic life a few years ago, when the boy was in his senior year of high school. Doug differs from Randy and Brad in that he assumes a more proactive and independent role. He describes at length a situation in which Sammy (who had on his own stopped taking the drug Ritalin earlier in the year) announced near the end of the academic year that he was probably not going to graduate with his class. On hearing the news, Doug immediately called the school principal and arranged a joint meeting the next day with a few of Sammy's teachers, the principal, Sammy, and himself. As Doug describes it, it was an intense meeting where he confronted both the teachers and Sammy about

Sammy's predicament. He recalls telling the school officials: "I am here on behalf of my son. . . . He's what matters to me. . . . He's going to graduate." During that meeting, Doug negotiated an arrangement whereby the teachers agreed to tutor Sammy and Sammy agreed to resume taking Ritalin. Doug proudly finishes the story by noting that Sammy graduated on time that spring, adding "had it been let go the way it was, Sammy would not have graduated." Although Doug's wife supported his intervention on Sammy's behalf, she did so from a distance. . . .

Although situations like those described above are noteworthy in their own right, a stepfather can experience plenty of less dramatic, more pleasant opportunities to build social capital for a child. Under the right circumstances, a stepfather, like a biological father, can volunteer to participate in various school activities, affording him a chance to build relations with persons who may have contact with or be in a position to monitor his stepchild. This rings true for Calvin. While talking about his experiences at the charter school his stepdaughter Rebecca attends, he mentions that parents are required to volunteer for a certain amount of time. For his part, Calvin has stuffed packets, participated in an area cleanup, taken charge of selling candy for the safety patrol, and managed a listserv—a newsgroup for the parents. He also describes himself as having "positive interactions with the teachers." Many of these interactions occur spontaneously while he's waiting to pick Rebecca up from school. "I'll see them and talk to them at that time. There are three or four of them that were there last year and I've kind of gotten to know. . . . I'll talk to them about whatever's going on and if there's a problem. And Rebecca is usually good in school, but if there's a problem, I'll talk to them about that." Calvin's last comment highlights the opportunities parents have to develop social capital stemming from their children's needs and experiences. Both minor and more serious kinds of needs can provide an impetus for parental action. When children struggle in some way, parents are often compelled to contact members of the child's network outside the family. Building social capital for a child who has not experienced significant problems may help some parents prevent specific problems from ever occurring.

Let's stay with Calvin's story to illustrate another example of how social capital can be developed, while interpreting social capital broadly. Calvin stresses how he and his wife, Kristin, need to talk more about helping Rebecca in school because in his opinion, he and Kristin "haven't really gotten on the same page" yet. Prompted by his concerns for Rebecca's behavior, he went to a community-sponsored "parenting fair" a few days prior to the interview with Rebecca in tow. The listserv he manages came in handy because he learned about the program from one of the parents who posted information on the listserv about it. One of the workshops he attended dealt with children's problem behaviors and how to help children build self-esteem. Calvin plans to talk to Kristin about what he learned when they have some free time. This example is useful because it depicts how a stepfather, under the right set of circumstances, can serve as a liaison between the community and his family. . . .

Father Ally

One of the indirect ways stepdads can leave their mark on their stepchildren that goes largely unnoticed in the literature about stepfamilies is how step-dads relate to biological fathers.[6] Do stepfathers make it easier or more difficult for biological fathers to maintain contact and a close relationship with children with whom they do not live?

Some stepdads have little or nothing to do with biological fathers because these fathers have either walked away or been pushed away from their children, sometimes completely. A significant minority of the men who participated in my study describes the biological fathers as being out of the picture. In a small number of cases, the biological fathers may not even be aware that they have fathered a child. But most of the stepdads are directly or indirectly aware of the biological father's presence in the children's lives as well as his interaction with the children's mother. Not surprisingly, a number of the stepdads are accustomed to dealing with the biological father's continued involvement with his children. In some cases, the biologi-cal fathers are even involved on a limited basis with the children and mother together. Some of the stepdads find it eye opening, being nonresident fathers themselves, because they sometimes develop a more well-rounded view of stepfamily arrangements when they have contact with men serving as step-fathers to their own children. This allows certain stepdads to relate more easily to issues involving the intersection between their roles and those of the biological father.

As my participants clearly illustrate, stepdads face a range of possible stepfamily scenarios. These scenarios differ in the frequency, type, and qual-ity of the biological father's involvement with the children.[7] Though many of the patterns are stable over an extended period of time, they are not etched in stone. A scenario familiar today may be gone tomorrow as biological fathers get more involved or distance themselves from their children. Biological fathers may also change how they're involved. A sudden job loss may result in a father not being able to pay child support, but he may have more free time to spend with his child. Or a father may get involved, perhaps marry a woman who has her own child and begin to invest time, energy, and money in this new family. Given this type of uncertainty within stepfamilies, step-dads may, over time, face differing stepfamily scenarios where the biological father's role varies considerably.

When dealing with a biological father who is at least moderately involved in a hands-on way, a stepdad is likely to be concerned with how his own involvement will be supported or challenged. Will a biological father try to undermine the stepdad's household authority or will he encourage his child to respect the stepfather? By paying child support, being consis-tent with scheduled visits, speaking respectfully to the child and mother about the stepdad, and treating the stepfather cordially, a father has plenty of opportunities to ease the stepfather's transition into his various familial roles. The father can also help the stepfather thrive in the new roles. Addi-tionally, the biological father who interacts with a stepdad in supportive

ways can often improve his chances of having the stepdad act on his behalf in return. Along these lines, William, a twenty-seven-year-old man who was acting as a stepfather for his fiancée's two young boys, knew the boys' father before he became involved with the kids. William recalls having a conversation with the father during the early phases of becoming involved with the boys. He said the father "was just telling me that he was sorry that he wasn't there, but since I was there and he knows what kind of person I am, he said he felt that his kids were in competent hands. He told me that to my face." Hearing the father's sentiments made William "feel pretty good" about himself. It also helped reinforce his willingness not to say anything negative about the father in front of the kids.

The biological father who wants to remain involved in his child's life, even though he is no longer romantically involved with the child's mother, is likely to be concerned with how the stepdad affects his ability to retain his fatherly roles. A father may feel this way irrespective of the custody or residency arrangement. In many situations, the father's and stepfather's perceptions and actions can influence each other, even though they may not be conscious of their effect or acknowledge it directly. The old adage "scratch my back and I'll scratch yours" captures the experiences of many men with children as they try to settle on new ways of organizing their family roles, rights, and responsibilities in a wide range of different family settings. Although this agreement is often left unspoken, it exists nonetheless. This kind of arrangement eventually unfolded between Barry and his stepchildren's father, Sam, who had known and disliked Barry for some time before Barry got involved with his ex-wife (Lucy) and children. In Barry's words:

> I would hear back from the kids and from other people that he overcame his dislike of me, so to speak, because he felt I was being so nice to the kids and I wasn't trying to replace him, that I was in fact saying positive things about him and trying to encourage Lucy not to be bitter. He really encouraged that. In fact, I was getting Christmas presents from them [biological father and his current wife] and a birthday present, things like that. He'd call me up. But we never sat down and said oh, you're a great guy, I love what you're doing.

One distinct pattern that emerged from my interviews with the stepdads was that many acted in ways that had the effect of helping the father remain active in a positive way in his child's life. From the stepfather's perspective, this activity sometimes enabled the biological father to strengthen his emotional ties with his child. Some stepfathers' efforts were intended and obvious, while others were much more subtle. If the term "ally" is used loosely, some stepdads acted like an ally to the father because they helped prevent problems or smooth over ones that probably would have tainted the father's relationship with his child had they gone unattended. For instance, a number of the stepfathers said they encouraged mothers not to say anything negative about the father in front of the children. Those who took this position thought it was counterproductive to "bad-mouth" a father in a child's presence, even though some mothers might have found this to be an effective short-term strategy to release stress. . . .

Stepdads who had kids of their own living elsewhere appeared to be the most sensitive to giving the biological father a fair shake in the stepfamily household. From their own experience, they knew how they would like to be represented to their children when they were absent. However, even stepdads who don't have their own children living elsewhere can develop empathy for a nonresident father. . . .

A stepdad has various opportunities to be an ally to a father by how he speaks to or interacts with the child directly. He might, for instance, make a point of saying nice things about the father, jump in to defend the father if circumstances call for it, or give advice on how to communicate with the father. Without being in the home himself, the nonresident father has a more difficult time speaking on his own behalf and explaining his behavior in a convenient and timely manner. One stepfather, Eddie, recalls several times when he consoled his stepdaughter Melissa on being disappointed by her father's irresponsible behavior. Asked if his efforts minimized Melissa's pain, and in the process helped the father's relationship with her, Eddie replies:

> *Well, the damage is when he does it—the damage is already done. I'm just trying to make her feel a little bit better. I guess you can say, because if he does something—if he don't call or he don't pick her up when he says he's going to pick her up, then I guess I kind of smooth things over for him. I guess you can say that. I mean—I try to make him—he's not bad. I try to make him, when he do bad things, whether he do it intentionally or not—I try to make him look like he—it's a mistake, nobody's perfect. Dad is going to make mistakes. It's okay for dad to make mistakes. He's human. It's going to be all right. He'll call you the next time. . . .*

As his comments indicate, Eddie acknowledges that he probably helps minimize his stepdaughter's disappointment and anger with her father. But when I asked Eddie specifically if he feels comfortable with the language of being called the father's "ally," he said he felt a bit uneasy with the label. Apparently Eddie has difficulty thinking of himself as the father's ally because "he [father] doesn't know half the times I cleaned up his mess." For Eddie, thinking of himself as an ally seems to necessitate an explicit agreement between the two men. It seems reasonable to conclude that Eddie acts like an ally in a functional sense, even if he does not clearly see himself as doing so and if the father is unaware of his efforts. The bottom line is that he does things as a stepdad that help the father maintain the quality of his relationship with his daughter.

Eddie's experience highlights two distinctions relevant to situations in which a stepdad acts like an ally to the father. First, does the stepfather do his work behind the scenes away from the father's view or does he actively work with the father, telling him what he is trying to accomplish? Eddie is essentially a "secret" ally because the father remains in the dark about much of what he does. A selective few, however, are more direct in making their approach and intentions known. The second distinction involves the stepfather's motivation for doing the things that are intended to enhance the father's relationship with his child. Is the stepfather making this effort because of his concern for the child, the father, or both? The driving force

behind Eddie's efforts is his desire to look out for his stepdaughter's feelings. He is not particularly concerned about the father's dilemmas or feelings. In some instances, though, the stepdad empathizes with a father and goes out of his way to help him. Sometimes the stepfather may choose to play this role because he wants to be treated similarly.

Herman, a gregarious forty-two-year-old man, provides a detailed account of what it means to be an active and open father ally. In addition, he expresses his interest in helping both his stepdaughter and her father. He goes to considerable lengths to describe how he tries to keep the biological father of his three stepchildren involved in their lives. A self-described "initiator" when it comes to conversations, Herman explains that he once talked to the father on the phone and candidly told him that "you need to spend time with your kids." Compared to many stepfathers, Herman has gone the extra mile to reach out to the father and develop his own line of communication with him. Seeing the father in the stands at a high school football game, for example, Herman made a point of introducing himself to him and his current wife. Herman clarifies his assertiveness by explaining his line of thinking. "We don't have a reason not to be civil because—it's four different lives now [Herman and his wife, the father and his wife]. . . . There's no reason for us not to be civil together. Plus, we need to be civil for the kids anyhow." According to Herman, the father eventually embraced this view and they had subsequent conversations.

In addition to talking to the father directly, Herman talks frankly and forcefully to his stepchildren. He is particularly eager to have his fourteen-year-old stepdaughter, Annette, maintain contact with her father. In one instance, after Herman convinced Annette to rejoin the band, he asked her if she had told her father that she was involved in a jamfest at one of the universities in the region. As he explains,

> *See, what I'm doing is, I'm pushing her up to do it, because I don't want it to seem—granted, like I told him on the phone—look man, I don't have a problem with you calling my house. I don't have a problem with you coming to my house. She's my wife now. I'm not insecure about that. I'm not insecure about anything. I want you to spend time with your children, because they're your children.*

Herman also makes a point of asking Annette if her father knows about her other school and recreational functions as they approach. In his words, "I make sure that she initiates with her father, let him know what's happening. . . . One day he's going to need you [Annette]."

Herman offers other astute comments that reveal how he believes Annette is growing closer to him over time because they live together. He worries about this and reflects on how his own fathering experiences with his son, who lives elsewhere with his mother, enable him to empathize with Annette's father.

> *She's coming more to my side because I'm with her all the time. . . . he's going to be distanced but—and that's the thing that concerns me, that after awhile I'll take on the persona of being her father and her father will be just a memory. I don't*

want that to be. I want him to actually be in her life. Because I'm going to be there. . . . But he'll be missing the growing-up stages in her life. She'll end up getting married and he'll miss that. Like with my son, I miss stuff. He's eleven years old now. Out of his entire life I think I've—if you put all the time that we've spent together, I've had two years, maybe three years of his life. . . . My son's got his own life now. It hurts because I've missed . . . ten years of his life that I don't even know what happened to him. I don't even know when he was sick. Did he cry? I taught him how to ride a bike. I bought him stuff. But then I miss days in the wintertime coming home, sitting out in the yard and he coming out there and sitting in the yard or helping me mow the yard. Well, I got a few days of that. So, I don't want this guy to miss that. He's got a girl. She's going to give him grandchildren. . . . She's going to go to the prom. I'm going to be there. Okay, I'm going to enjoy that because she's in the house with me, but that's one of his privileges. . . . Who's going to be there on her first date? I'm going to be the one scrutinizing this rookie coming up. Where you from, son? Okay. Tell me about yourself. He's going to miss that. You see? It's just not a good thing. I mean, it's a good thing for me, but I'm sure he should be in on that. She's his daughter. But now she's my daughter. I'm going to take responsibility for her. I have taken responsibility . . . everything I would do with my child, she gets the same.

Listening to Herman's thought-provoking, emotional description of his efforts, it is clear that he takes pride as a proactive, nurturing, and protective father in overseeing Annette's life. In a separate interview, Herman's wife attests to his commitment to Annette. Unlike some stepfathers, Herman has a sense of security in his relationships with both his wife and Annette that provide him with the confidence necessary to incorporate the father more fully into the network of adults who have an interest in supporting Annette's transition through her teen years. In addition, the intense frustration and pain he has experienced as a nonresident father provide him a reservoir of feelings enabling him to relate to and empathize with Annette's father. As suggested previously, Herman's compassionate approach seems motivated by a genuine concern for both Annette's and her father's emotional and psychological well-being. . . .

Kids Making a Difference

Sometimes a stepfather's active involvement with a child leads him to make fundamental changes in the way he lives and sets his priorities. He may gain insights about himself, others, and life in general. When a stepfather seizes these opportunities, he often feels differently about himself.[8]

The stories the men tell about how they have been affected by being involved with stepchildren are similar in many ways to those typically shared by biological fathers. Unlike many biological fathers who make a conscious decision to have a child with their partner, most stepfathers become active with children because they get romantically involved with a woman who happens to be a mother. Concerns about how being

involved with stepchildren may affect their lives may not fully register with stepfathers. They may not plan for or anticipate these consequences prior to getting seriously involved with the mother. But whether the consequences of their involvement with the kids are expected or not, some men are aware after the fact that their experiences as stepfathers have affected them.

Not surprisingly, some of the men comment on how involvement with stepchildren helped them develop a sense of purpose, become more responsible, and feel grounded. Among these men, Keith, Carl, Eddie, and Ray provide excellent examples of how being an active stepfather can affect men's lives. Keith, a stepfather of two young adolescent girls, says with conviction, "I have purpose now. That's something to do besides work and take care of Keith. That seems to be very important to me. I don't know why though. I need to have something to turn around and look back on, that's more than me, I guess." Keith's reference to being able to "look back on" his stepdaughters captures his feelings about helping others grow. These feelings are not new to Keith because he spent a number of years in a previous marriage helping raise a stepson who is now thirty years old. His long-standing and strong relationship with his stepson enabled him to feel comfortable about the prospects of devoting himself to raising children who are not biologically related to him. He anticipates that they will remain a part of his life forever. . . .

Eddie identifies only one way in which being a stepfather for eight-year-old Rhendy has changed him, but he feels it is significant.

> *My sense is I know I have to work harder. . . . it's the extra stuff that she wants, so I figure I'll go out, I'll sacrifice my time for a little extra. Why not? You only live once. If I didn't get it when I was little, and my kids want it, by golly I'm going to go out and work and make sure they have it. . . . I've had to work harder just to make her happy, her life comfortable.*

Eddie's willingness to work longer hours relates partly to his interest in providing financially for his three biological children, but he focuses his remarks primarily on his current responsibilities for Rhendy. Consistent with his traditional view of men's fatherly responsibilities, Eddie takes his financial provider role quite seriously. Thus Eddie's desire to make Rhendy happy has led him to deepen his commitment to being a family man who expresses himself through his financial contribution to the family.

For Ray, being a stepfather and biological father helps him feel "grounded." Being involved in a fatherly way with his two stepchildren and one biological child gives him a "good feeling" about the "responsibility angle" of raising kids. "I like responsibility. To see that well, hey, I'm not a scared little child. I'm actually doing this. I'm actually taking care of this. This feels good. I feel strong. I feel powerful. I feel confident. That's a good deal." Ray conveys the idea that the kids in his life provide him with opportunities to perform certain adult, fatherly roles that in turn give him a sense of empowerment. Although most might find it a little odd that Ray, at age forty-two, refers to his contentment with being able to avoid the "scared little child" role, Ray's comments apparently reflect his sincere feelings about his contribution to his kids.

In some respects, Keith, Carl, and Eddie represent men who have become more future oriented because of their involvement with stepchildren. The men have a heightened sense that they need to provide for their stepkids now, as well as plan for the future. But for some of the stepfathers, their experiences with children actually encourage them to slow down and pay more attention to the present. This is what happened with Jackson, an introspective thirty-nine-year-old man who decided that he wanted to have a child with his former wife several years ago and was disappointed when he realized that she was unwilling to do so. His desire for a child was so strong that he divorced his first wife and pursued a new relationship with a long-time friend who has a small son. Jackson, who is now living his dream of being involved with a child, has found new inspiration by being around his five-year-old stepson, Mason.

> *He really got me to slow down from the—I guess I lived for quite a long time in future-oriented goals and trying to achieve something that's tomorrow, tomorrow, tomorrow. It's really pulled me into the present more, because just answering the questions of someone who's trying to define the world and is working very hard to define the world is—it takes a lot of energy so I can't be as future-oriented or worry about tomorrow and the next day, so that's one way, I've slowed down. And he's given me remarkable opportunities to be introspective, to think about what's important to me. . . . He says something like well, light reflects—we've got colors because light reflects off of the surface and—as he's learning these things and repeating different, very basic concepts that I have just taken for granted for most of my life, it's kind of wondrous. It makes me realize that, well, as corny as it sounds, this is really a precious thing we have. And it's very easy to get lost chasing the goals that we think are important when we're twenty or twenty-five that don't really mean that much later in life.*

Here, and in other portions of his interview, Jackson emphasizes that Mason has affected his outlook on life. Jackson thinks less about promoting his business and acquiring the material symbols of success. He is more inspired by the beauty of life, nature, and being a family man. Mason has brought Jackson back to the present and into a world where he values his personal connections to others much more. . . .

Just as Jackson spoke about the ways Mason gets him to think about things that he hasn't thought about since he was a kid, other men comment on how being with their stepchildren helped them remain young. Carl, for instance, mentions that Vicky has "just done wonders for me as far as making sure that I stay with my kid-self, staying with being able to read children's books and seeing it from a kid's point of view and seeing all the wonderful things that I remember as a kid, that you forget when you get into the workplace and you, the day-in-day-out drudgery of paperwork." Similarly, Rodney offers that his two teenage stepchildren are responsible for making "me stay on my toes and I think they're helping me think younger than I would if I didn't have kids their age." A stepfather may not initially seek experiences such as these when he gets involved with a woman who is a mother, but they can nonetheless become powerful experiences over time.

For stepfathers who assume their place in a stepfamily without ever having kids of their own, being involved with stepchildren can offer them a unique opportunity to become less ego-centered. Gerald, even though he lived with a woman who had kids for several years, had for the most part lived the bachelor life, growing accustomed to having his living space to himself. Becoming a stepfather and living with his thirteen-year-old step-daughter Sabrina has given Gerald a chance to expand his perspective. In his words, Sabrina

> *caused me, forced me, allowed me to just open my heart a little bit more than maybe I normally would. Just learning to live with somebody makes changes in an individual. I'm probably less spoiled than I was. You live with a kid you can't be—even if you want to be, you've gotta set a good example. . . . when you have kids, you have to give and take. . . . You can't necessarily show your true self.*

Throughout the interview Gerald describes himself as "pissy," so his involvement with Sabrina has allowed him to change his personality while learning how to "chill a bit." Presumably, when Gerald talks about not showing his "true self," he means that he wants to shelter Sabrina from the less congenial aspects of his personality. Although he still enjoys his alone time, I got the sense that Sabrina has been drawing him out a bit from his self-centered ways, encouraging him to think of others more. Sabrina is basically helping Gerald mature.

Along similar lines, Randy, a stepfather who is unemployed because of serious physical disabilities that confine him to a wheelchair, feels that his nine-year-old stepson has made him a "better person" and forced him to think of others more. Since becoming a stepfather, Randy has become more concerned with presenting his genuine self. "He's made me realize that I got to be more truthful with myself and I can't like tell him to do something and then not really do it myself." . . . Randy's appreciation for his stepson is perhaps best captured in a simple statement he made: "He has given me tons more than I think I've given him."

For men who were fathers prior to getting involved with their current partner who was a single mother, becoming a stepfather meant that they were in most cases spending more time with children than they had in the recent past or, in some cases, ever. Because some of the men miss living with their children and seeing them as much as they once did, getting involved in their stepchildren's lives gives some a chance to fulfill their desires to be around children. . . .

The stories I use to capture the nature and significance of the impact stepfathers and children have on each other come from the minds, hearts, and mouths of stepfathers, and to a lesser extent the birth mothers. A more complete portrait of this impact awaits future research incorporating children's voices directly. For now, we glimpse the power a child's perspective can bring to the story of stepfatherhood by turning to Danny, one of the two fourteen-year-olds I interviewed and discussed earlier in connection with his stepfather, Thomas. After I asked him what letter grade he would assign to his stepfather, Danny was quick to reply, "I would give him an A plus.

Because he's just the best thing that has happened to me. So, it's like I really appreciate what he's done and how he's affected my life and helped me get through my father leaving me and stuff." Later, while discussing different aspects of his relationship with his stepfather, Danny talks about the pride his stepfather takes in him. At one point he says, "He's like very quick to tell people how smart I am and what good grades I get and stuff. It's like, he really likes to tell people how good I am and stuff." [I: "And what does that do for you or how does that make you . . . ?"] "It just makes me feel proud, it's like . . . makes me feel proud of what I'm doing and it kind of encourages me to do more." Danny's heartfelt, thoughtful analysis pinpoints the value of parental support, whether it's from a biological father or stepfather. In this case, it is Danny's stepfather who lets him know that he is appreciated for who he is and what he does. In a number of cases, this sense of pride can be heard in the stepfathers' voices as they glowingly talk about their stepchildren. A sampling of these comments:

> *They're both great kids. They're fabulous kids.* [Barry, 52]

> *She has an incredible voice, a beautiful singing voice. She's really very naturally talented.* [Brad, 38]

> *She's a great kid. She's smart and she's added a whole new dimension to my life.* [Calvin, 38]

> *When you see her contemporaries acting certain ways. It made me appreciate even more what a good kid she is. I mean, she's not a typical thirteen-year-old. I think she's more sensitive. . . . She does not get into any trouble. . . . She really does occupy her time quite productively.* [Gerald, 44]

Not all the stepfathers, of course, praise their stepchildren. However, most feel at least reasonably content with their stepchildren's character. Most of the stepfathers also tend to think that they have lent a helping hand in shaping these kids. Once again, we must keep in mind that the sample of stepfathers who volunteered to be in my study probably does not fully tap the men who are struggling in their stepfathering roles or those who walked away from them. That said, the overriding impression I formed from my interviews is that most of the stepfathers are proud to be around their stepchildren and delighted to have others see them together.

ENDNOTES

[1] For national survey studies of what stepfathers do with children, see Hofferth and Anderson 2003; Hofferth et al. 2002.

[2] Amato 1998; Coleman 1988, 1990; Furstenberg 1998; Furstenberg and Hughes 1995; Marsiglio and Cohan 2000; Seltzer 1998a; Teachman, Paasch, and Carver 1996.

[3] Conceptual discussions about fathering using a systems or ecological approach (Doherty, Kouneski, and Erickson 1998) or a scripting perspective (Marsiglio 1995, 1998) are also relevant to stepfathers.

[4] Although there is some disagreement between the way parents and stepparents perceive the stepparent's role in a stepfamily, the greatest discrepancy is found when comparing stepchildren's perceptions (Fine, Coleman, and Ganong 1998, 1999).

[5] Cherlin 1978; Ganong and Coleman 1997.

[6] Ahrons and Wallisch (1987) provide one of the few empirically based discussions of the relations between biological father and stepfathers, biological mothers and stepmothers, and stepfathers and stepmothers. . . .

[7] A considerable amount of research has focused on different aspects of nonresident fathers' involvement with their children, especially visitation and child support (Arendell 1995; Braver and O'Connell 1998; Cooksey and Craig 1998; Leite and McKenry 2002; Manning and Smock 1999; Seltzer 1991, 1998b; Seltzer and Brandeth 1995). A number of studies have also focused on how nonresident fathers' actions are related to child outcomes (for a review, see Amato and Gilbreth 1999). The main conclusion from these latter studies is that it is not how much time nonresident fathers spend with their kids that matters, but how they interact with them. . . .

[8] Although researchers have done little to explore systematically how becoming a stepfather influences men's personal lives—beyond marital adjustment, several researchers have explored the implications of biological fathers getting involved actively with their children, especially in a marital context. Hawkins and Belsky (1989) argue that by being involved in their young children's lives, fathers develop more nurturing traits. . . .

REFERENCES

Ahrons, C. A. and L. Wallish. 1987. "Parenting in the Binuclear Family: Relationships between Biological and Stepparents," Pp. 225–56 in *Remarriage and Stepparenting: Current Research and Theory*, edited by K. Pasley and M. Ihinger-Tallman. New York: Guilford.

Amato, P. 1998. "More than Money? Men's Contributions to Their Children's Lives." Pp. 241–78 in *Men in Families: When Do They Get Involved? What Difference Does It Make?*, edited by A. Booth and N. Crouter. Mahwah, NJ: Erlbaum.

Amato, P. R. and J. G. Gilbreth. 1999. "Nonresident Fathers and Children's Well-Being: A Meta-Analysis." *Journal of Marriage and the Family* 61:557–73.

Arendell, T. 1995. *Fathers and Divorce*. Thousand Oaks, CA: Sage.

Braver, S. L. and D. O'Connell. 1998. *Divorced Dads: Shattering the Myths*. New York: Tarcher/Putnam.

Cherlin, A. J. 1978. "Remarriage as an Incomplete Institution." *American Journal of Sociology* 84:634–50.

Coleman, J. 1988. "Social Capital in the Creation of Human Capital." *American Journal of Sociology* 94:S95–S120.

———. 1990. *Foundations of Social Theory*. Cambridge, MA: Harvard University Press.

Cooksey, E. C. and P. H. Craig. 1998. "Parenting from a Distance: The Effects of Paternal Characteristics on Contact between Nonresidential Fathers and Their Children." *Demography* 35:187–200.

Doherty, W. J., E. F. Kouneski, and M. F. Erickson. 1998. "Responsible Fathering: An Overview and Conceptual Framework." *Journal of Marriage and the Family* 60:277–92.

Fine, M. A., M. Coleman, and L. H. Ganong. 1998. "Consistency in Perceptions of the Stepparent Role among Stepparents, Parents and Stepchildren." *Journal of Social and Personal Relationships* 15:810–28.

———. 1999. "A Social Constructionist Multi-Method Approach to Understanding the Stepparent Role." In *Coping with Divorce, Single Parenting, and Remarriage: A Risk and Resiliency Perspective*, edited by E. M. Hetherington. Mahwah, NJ: Erlbaum.

Furstenberg, F. F., Jr. 1998. "Social Capital and the Role of Fathers in the Family." Pp. 295–301 in *Men in Families: When Do They Get Involved? What Difference Does It Make?*, edited by A. Booth and N. Crouter. Mahwah, NJ: Erlbaum.

Furstenberg, F. F., Jr. and M. E. Hughes. 1995. "Social Capital and Successful Development among At-Risk Youth." *Journal of Marriage and the Family* 57:580–93.

Ganong, L. H. and M. M. Coleman. 1997. "How Society Views Stepfamilies." *Marriage and Family Review* 26:85–106.

Hawkins, A. J. and J. Belsky. 1989. "The Role of Father Involvement in Personality Change in Men across the Transition to Parenthood." *Family Relations* 38:378–84.

Hofferth, S. L. and K. G. Anderson. 2003. "Are All Dads Equal? Biology versus Marriage as a Basis for Parental Investment." *Journal of Marriage and the Family* 65:213–32.

Hofferth, S. L., J. Pleck, J. L. Stueve, S. Bianchi, and L. Sayer. 2002. "The Demography of Fathers: What Fathers Do." Pp. 63–90 in *Handbook of Father Involvement: Multidisciplinary Perspective*, edited by C. S. Tamis-LeMonda and N. Cabrera. Mahwah, NJ: Erlbaum.

Leite, R. W. and P. C. McKenry. 2002. "Aspects of Father Status and Postdivorce Father Involvement with Children." *Journal of Family Issues* 23:601–23.

Manning, W. D. and P. J. Smock. 1999. "New Families and Nonresident Father–Child Visitation." *Social Forces* 78:87–116.

Marsiglio, W. 1995. "Fathers' Diverse Life Course Patterns and Roles: Theory and Social Interventions." Pp. 78–101 in *Fatherhood: Contemporary Theories, Research, and Social Policy*, edited by W. Marsiglio. Thousand Oaks, CA: Sage.

———. 1998. *Procreative Man.* New York: New York University Press.

Marsiglio, W. and M. Cohan. 2000. "Contextualizing Father Involvement and Paternal Influence: Sociological and Qualitative Themes." *Marriage and Family Review* 29:75–95.

Seltzer, J. 1991. "Relationships between Fathers and Children Living Apart: The Father's Role after Separation." *Journal of Marriage and the Family* 53:79–101.

———. 1998a. "Men's Contributions to Children and Social Policy." Pp. 303–14 in *Men in Families: When Do They Get Involved? What Difference Does It Make?*, edited by A. Booth and N. Crouter. Mahwah, NJ: Erlbaum.

———. 1998b. "Father by Law: Effects of Joint Legal Custody on Nonresident Fathers' Involvement with Children." *Demography* 35:135–46.

Seltzer, J. and Y. Brandeth. 1995. "What Fathers Say about Involvement with Children after Separation." Pp. 166–92 in *Fatherhood: Contemporary Theory, Research, and Social Policy*, edited by W. Marsiglio. Thousand Oaks, CA: Sage.

Teachman, J. D., K. Paasch, and K. Carver. 1996. "Social Capital and Dropping Out of School Early." *Journal of Marriage and the Family* 58:773–83.

41

GENDER, DIVERSITY, AND VIOLENCE
Extending the Feminist Framework

KERSTI A. YLLÖ

Violence within the family is as complex as it is disturbing. Compressed into one assault are our deepest human emotions, our sense of self, our power, and our hopes and fears about love and intimacy, as well as the social construction of marriage and its place within the larger society. Despite the issue's complexity, the most fundamental feminist insight into all of this is quite simple: Domestic violence cannot be adequately understood unless gender and power are taken into account.

Looking at domestic violence through a feminist lens is not a simple matter, however. Developing a theoretical, empirical, political, and personal understanding of violence requires us to analyze its complex gendered nature. This involves the psychologies of perpetrator and victim and their interactions, gendered expectations about family relationships and dynamics, and the patriarchal ideology and structure of society within which individuals and relationships are embedded. Increasingly, feminists of color are pointing to the important impact of race-ethnicity and class in shaping all of these dimensions. Although there is a range of feminist perspectives, there is a broad consensus that family violence is profoundly shaped by gender and power.

Feminist understanding of domestic violence has its roots in social action. Feminist academic work, theoretical analyses, and methodological debates flow out of feminist practice. The feminist perspective, with its origins in social movements, is strong on practical programs and critiques of prevailing perspectives. But it is not yet a fully developed, distinctive framework for the explanation of domestic violence, and in this limitation we are in good company, for no single view is complete. Although a feminist lens may not be sufficient for seeing the full picture of domestic violence, I believe that it is a necessary lens without which any other analytic perspective is flawed. Gender and power are key elements of domestic violence, whether one takes a sociological or a psychological perspective.

After briefly reviewing the gender and power analysis so central to the feminist perspective, I turn to one of the pressing issues feminists are now addressing: a fuller, more nuanced incorporation of race-ethnicity and class into our analysis. The feminist focus on women as a victimized class has obscured the diversity among women (as well as among the men who perpetrate the violence). I point to new directions in feminist theory that, I believe, hold the potential to move us to a more inclusive and more powerful analysis.

Domestic Violence, Gender, and Control

As social constructionists point out, the phenomena we study (including physical violence) are not simply "out there" to be discovered through direct observation. Rather, definitions of problems are socially created through ongoing controversy as well as collaboration. Observation is always theory laden, and this is especially true when the phenomenon under scrutiny is as politically and emotionally fraught as violence (see Yllö 1988).

The focus we choose for our work (including our theoretical formulations, our empirical research, our policy recommendations, and our social activism) is crucially important. . . . The family [is] the overarching rubric for defining the problem. It then falls to feminists, who tend to focus on *domestic violence* (a term that has become synonymous with battering), to explain why our analysis is largely limited to woman abuse. In the *Handbook of Marriage and the Family,* for example, Suzanne Steinmetz (1987) dismisses feminist theory as "constricted" and of "limited utility as a theory of family violence" (p. 749).

An important question that has been largely overlooked during the 30-year explosion of the family violence field is whether "family violence" is a unitary phenomenon that requires an overarching theory. I argue that feminist analysis has made an enormous contribution to our understanding of wife abuse, yet it has produced relatively less insight into child abuse or elder abuse. However, I do not regard this as evidence that feminist theory is constricted, since it has also made significant contributions to our understanding of stranger rape, acquaintance rape, sexual harassment in the workplace, and murder. Further, this analysis of violence against women (whether in the family or outside it) rests within even broader feminist analysis of all aspects of women's lives in patriarchal society. A feminist analysis of violence connects it to the pervasive sexism in our norms, values, and institutions.

When a man rapes his wife because he feels that it is her "wifely duty" to submit, this is not just a conflict of individual interests, as a sociological analysis might contend. This conflict is deeply gendered, and the husband's perceived entitlement has strong institutional support. When a man with a personality disorder batters his wife when she burns his dinner or tries to get a job, our understanding of the violence is incomplete if we deny the gendered aspects of his controlling behavior. To say simply that domestic violence is about gender and power may seem like nothing more than a sound

bite. But it is far more than that—it is a concise expression of a complex body of feminist theory and research. A full discussion of this work would fill volumes; in this [reading] I can only outline the coercive control view of domestic violence.

In her review essay on feminism and family research, Myra Marx Ferree (1990) states that "feminists agree that male dominance within families is part of a wider system of male power, is neither natural nor inevitable, and occurs at women's cost" (p. 866). Feminist work in family violence explores and articulates the ways in which violence against women in the home is a critical component of the system of male power. Violence grows out of inequality within marriage (and other intimate relations that are modeled on marriage) and reinforces male dominance and female subordination within the home and outside it. In other words, violence against women (whether in the form of sexual harassment at work, rape by a date, or a beating at home) is a part of male control (Dobash and Dobash 1998; Hanmer and Maynard 1987). It is not gender neutral any more than the economic division of labor or the institution of marriage is gender neutral.

The conceptualization of violence as coercive control was not deduced from an abstract theoretical model. Rather, it grew inductively out of the day-to-day work of battered women and activists who struggled to make sense of the victimization they saw. As the shelter movement grew and survivors and activists joined together to discuss their experiences, a clearer vision of what domestic violence is and how to challenge it emerged.

A control model of domestic violence, known as the "Power and Control Wheel," developed by the Domestic Abuse Intervention Project in Duluth, Minnesota, is shown in Figure 1. This model has been used across the country in batterers' groups, support groups, and training sessions, as well as in empirical studies (see Shepard and Pence 1999). It provides a valuable, concise framework for seeing the interconnections between violence and other forms of coercive control or *control tactics*. The wheel connects physical and sexual violence to the hub of power and control with a number of "spokes": minimization and denial, intimidation, isolation, emotional abuse, economic abuse, use of children, threats, and assertion of male privilege.

When one looks at these control tactics in a bit more detail, through research based on extensive interviews with battered women and batterers (Jones and Schechter 1992; Ptacek 1988), the close-up picture of domestic violence that develops is one of domination. The following is an interview excerpt from my study of women who were physically abused during their pregnancies.

S., a 31-year-old white woman, describes the control and violence in her marriage that eventually resulted in a miscarriage:

> *I didn't even realize he was gaining control and I was too dumb to know any better. . . . He was gaining control bit by bit until he was checking my pantyhose when I'd come home from the supermarket to see if they were inside out. . . . He'd time me. He'd check the mileage on the car. . . . I was living like a prisoner. . . . One day I was at Zayers with him . . . and I was looking at a sweater. He insisted*

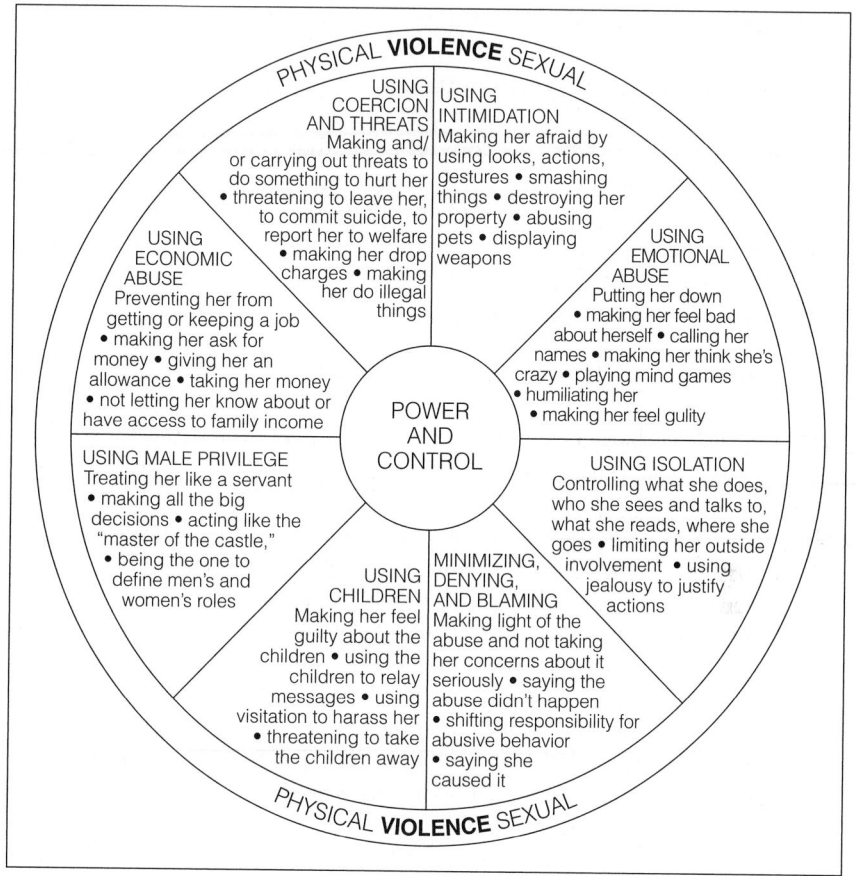

FIGURE 1 Power and Control Wheel

Source: Reprinted with permission from Minnesota Program Development, Inc., Domestic Abuse Intervention Project, 206 W. 4th Street, Duluth, MN 55806.

> *I was looking at a guy. I didn't even know there was a guy in the area, because it got to the point that I, I had to walk like I had horse-blinders on. . . . You don't look anybody in the eye. You don't look up because you are afraid.*

At one point, S. was insulted by a friend of her husband's, and she was furious. She recalls:

> *I told him, who the hell was he? And I threw a glass of root beer in his face. My husband gave me a back hand, so I just went upstairs to the bedroom and got into a nightgown. And he kept telling me to come downstairs and I said "No—just leave me alone." . . . He come up and went right through the door. Knocked the whole top panel off the door and got into the room. Ripped the nightgown right off my back, just bounced me off every wall in that bedroom. Then he threw me down the stairs and . . . outside in the snow and just kept kicking me and saying it was too soon for me to be pregnant. . . . His friend was almost rooting him on.*

The coercive control model of domestic violence is an important theoretical alternative to psychological explanations focused only on personality disorders and the sociology of interpersonal conflict. It identifies violence as a tactic of entitlement and power that is deeply gendered, rather than as a symptom of a disorder or as a conflict tactic that is individual and gender neutral. It has deepened our understanding of family violence in substantial and significant ways. However, it is not the final analysis. Although it provides a potent description of violence and its context, it should be seen as the beginning, not the completion of our work.

Commonality and Diversity

One area where feminist theory has fallen short concerns the racial-ethnic and class diversity among women. Drawing on radical feminist analysis, we have conceptualized women as a class, oppressed in a dichotomous sex-gender system. During the last decade, important work by feminists of color have challenged this view as simplistic and limiting (Crenshaw 1994; Richie 1996). This conceptualization is constricted by what Adrienne Rich (1979) called "white solipsism"—a type of tunnel vision in which white experience is assumed to describe human experience.

We are currently undergoing a period of rich intellectual and political debate about the interconnections among gender, race, and class and their implications for understanding violence. I suggest that feminist theory stands out among the different family violence frameworks in addressing these issues. Race is far more than a variable affecting rates of violence or a factor to be controlled. Like gender, race-ethnicity infuses all aspects of family life and its social context. I next touch upon promising theoretical work, mostly by women of color, that needs more attention and integration into our analyses and practices.

An important concept for analyzing diversity and violence is the idea of intersectionality, developed by legal scholar Kimberlé Crenshaw (1993, 1994). She makes the point that

> although violence is a common issue among women, such violence usually occurs within a specific context—that often varies considerably depending on the race, class, and other social characteristics of the woman.... These characteristics can be better understood and addressed through a framework that links them to broader structures of subordination which intersect sometimes in fairly predictable ways. (1993:15)

Further, she suggests that we consider both structural and political intersectionality. Structurally, the intersection of race, class, and gender creates particular circumstances for different battered women. Deciding how to respond to abuse is very different for a Latina who is trying to establish legal residence through her husband than it is for an employed white woman who is a U.S. citizen. Politically, intersectionality has implications for activism and intervention. Crenshaw urges us to supersede identity politics and

the notion of unitary groups in conflict (blacks versus whites, males versus females, gays versus straights, and so on) and to recognize each of these groups as multidimensional within themselves and, at their best, effective coalitions. So, women can be a coalition of gay, straight, Latina, middle class, poor, African American, white, and so on with structural and political commonalities and differences. A feminist theory that emphasizes only the commonality of gender erases the texture of women's lives and is less useful than it might be. Feminist scholars and activists who are mindful of these intersections can develop theory, research, and interventions to move us forward.

In *The Color of Privilege: Three Blasphemies on Race and Feminism* (1996), Aida Hurtado offers a useful and challenging framework for considering intersectionality, although she does not address domestic violence directly. She develops a theory of gender subordination as relational, explaining why subordination is experienced differently by white women and women of color. It is often tempting to see these as differences in attitude—as simple reflections of culture (for example, different values regarding family)—or social location (the greater likelihood that women of color live in poverty). Hurtado argues that the theoretically important factor is women's *relationship* to white male power. She points out that women of color have been exploited for their labor and sexuality, yet they have been rejected as legitimate reproducers of white men's offspring. White women, in contrast, have been seduced into compliance because they are needed to biologically reproduce the next generation of the power structure (p. vii). White women, especially of the upper and middle classes, live *within* circles of power and are intimately connected to those who subordinate them.

Hurtado's theory is particularly useful in an analysis of violence in the home, because she helps us see how feminist theory to date has been myopic. The political consciousness that has informed the women's movement grew out of an examination of the public-private distinction and the realization by white, educated women that gender oppression occurred in the intimacy of their own homes. The radical slogan "The personal is political," according to Hurtado, "identifies and rejects the public-private distinction as a tool by which women are excluded from public participation while the daily tyrannies of men are protected from public scrutiny" (p. 18). From this viewpoint, battering is a prime example of this intimate oppression, and much of feminist activism has attempted to bring it to public attention, to sanction it through the criminal justice system, and to offer women refuge from their homes.

This work has undoubtedly been important and has saved lives. It has, however, assumed that the private-public split applies similarly to all women. Hurtado contends that "the political consciousness of women of color stems from an awareness that the public is personally political" (p. 18). People of color have not had the luxury of a private realm. Through welfare programs, public housing, sterilization programs, police presence, and disproportionate arrest and incarceration rates, public systems of social control invade their private realm. Poor women of color are acutely aware of their distance from the white male power structure that may evict or deport them or imprison their sons. Their activism, then, more often focuses on these

public issues rather than the subordination or abuse they may experience from their intimate partners who are, otherwise, relatively powerless. Their experiences with the racism of the criminal justice system and other service providers make them reluctant to use the same avenues of redress that white battered women turn to.

In contrast, women who are physically integrated into the centers of power have a very different experience of gender subordination. Thus white feminists have been more concerned with expectations of docility, gender socialization, housework, body image, and intimate violence. These observations have been made before; however, the implication usually has been that some essential difference exists between the submissive, white women victimized within their homes and the strong, black women heading families. A relational theory of gender subordination offers a clear structural explanation for the differences: They reflect women's connection to or distance from white male power.

As Hurtado points out, the women's movement is the only political movement in history to develop its own clinical approach—feminist therapy (p. 18). There is a real question about the extent to which therapy, which deals with oppression at the individual and interpersonal level, can address the needs of all women. So far, feminist therapy has focused heavily on issues of intimacy with white men and has been utilized largely by those women who are struggling with the seduction of men in power. Yet, feminist therapy, like feminist theory, is addressing the challenges posed by feminists of color who question its assumptions (Bograd 1999). This is not to argue that feminist therapy has not made important contributions, but rather that we should not assume that approaches of value for some women will be of value for all women. Further, a truly radical feminist therapy will help to transcend the divisions between those women privileged by their association with white male power and those distanced and oppressed by it.

The discussion in this [reading] has been largely about gender subordination and rather little about family violence. Nevertheless, I hope that the implications for our work, both scholarly and applied, are becoming clear. The feminist approach to violence will become more analytically powerful and more practically useful if we add to its depth and complexity by addressing the intersection of race-ethnicity, class, and gender. It is not enough to include these factors as variables in models that ignore the structural conditions of oppression. Nor is it enough to invoke "race-class-gender" as a political mantra in superficial analyses. There is an enormous amount of intellectual, political, and practical work to be done to reach more synthetic understandings and solutions.

Research and Intervention at the Intersection

The feminist analysis of intimate violence to date has emphasized women's commonality. The point feminists have made over and over again has been that *all* women are vulnerable to such violence, which cuts across racial,

ethnic, and class lines. This position has proven to be very effective politically precisely because of the relational character of gender subordination that Hurtado identifies. Whether we're training judges, police, or medical doctors, or lobbying for stronger criminal justice sanctions or the Violence against Women Act, we have made the point that the victims can be *"your* sisters, daughters, and friends." We have seen that Social Security is sacred, while welfare is vilified. Therefore, we have emphasized the connections to the white men in power and downplayed violence in poor communities of color because we knew that funding would not be forthcoming if victims were seen as "other." Political favor flows more easily to "worthy" (read white, middle-class) victims. Using the strategy, feminists have successfully changed laws, policies, and procedures and gained funding for services that have helped large numbers of women.

However, Crenshaw (1994:105) points out that there is a thin line between debunking the stereotypical beliefs that only poor and minority women are battered and pushing them aside to focus on victims for whom mainstream politicians and media are more likely to express concern.

Unfortunately, one of the unintended consequences of this approach is that the differences among women have been "white-washed" and that those who are most victimized have been pushed aside. The reality that poor women (who are disproportionately women of color) experience more extensive and severe violence coupled with fewer options tends to become lost.

Angela Browne and her colleagues (Browne and Bassuk 1997) have done important work on the relationship between poverty and intimate violence. Their well-designed study of housed and homeless poor women revealed horrific rates of physical and sexual abuse. The researchers found that an astounding 83 percent of very low-income mothers had been victims of severe physical violence and/or sexual abuse during their lifetimes. Homelessness and substance abuse were closely connected problems. The enormity of these women's troubles can be more fully understood through such examinations of class, poverty, and the welfare system; a gender analysis alone is inadequate.

The gender-race-class intersection was an unexpected finding in a study by Eileen Abel (1999) that compared female "victims" with women who had been adjudicated as "batterers." The study was based on a sample of women drawn from three domestic violence victim service programs ($N = 51$) and three batterer intervention programs ($N = 67$) in the state of Florida. There were few statistical differences between the "victims" and "batterers" in exposure to violence *by their partners,* except that the women identified as batterers were *more* likely to have been threatened and forced to have sex than their victim counterparts. The women who had been labeled as batterers were also more likely to have previously sought medical treatment (62 percent versus 38 percent), whereas victims were more likely to have previously used domestic violence victim services (67 percent versus 33 percent). Abel discovered another important difference between the two groups: Women of color were overrepresented in the batterers group (42 percent nonwhite) compared to the victims group (26 percent). The mean income of women

in the batterers group was $26,000; in the victims group it was more than $46,000. So, despite higher levels of victimization and injury, poorer and minority women are more likely to be mandated into batterer treatment through the criminal justice system, while victim services are more likely to offer support to white, financially more stable women. While the Abel study offered no details of the women's use of violence or the process by which they came to be in the two groups, her research does raise questions about the impact of class and race on battered women's experiences with state intervention and social services.

The race-gender intersection also proved critical in a study of 1,870 partner violence reports to police by Bourg and Stock (in Marin and Russo 1999). They found that, overall, men were more likely to be identified as batterers; however women who were so identified were more likely to be charged with a serious crime. In particular, "black women were more likely to be arrested on felony charges (84 percent) than white men were (19 percent) *for similar behavior*" (p. 23, emphasis mine). Given the overall high arrest rates in communities of color, it is not surprising that black women are arrested and charged disproportionately.

These studies provide support for the proposition that individuals' distance from the white male power structure shapes their chances of abuse as well as the response of social services and the criminal justice system. However, these studies offer just a glimpse of how race intersects with gender in the institutional response to violence, since race was not their main focus. One study that does take this intersection as its central concern is Beth Richie's *Compelled to Crime: The Gender Entrapment of Battered Black Women* (1995). Her research on battered women jailed on Rikers Island, New York, reveals just how complex the race-class-gender intersection is. The battered African American women she interviewed were entrapped in a series of paradoxes. For example, Richie found that the battered women in her sample were more likely to come from stable families in which their parents had high expectations of them. These women struggled to maintain relationships despite ongoing abuse because they were so committed to traditional gender norms and family values. Unfortunately for these women, these efforts led to illegal activities in response to violence and coercion by their male partners (p. 4). Women from more disadvantaged and unstable families were more likely to walk away from violent partners because they had few expectations of an enduring family.

Compounding what Richie refers to as the battered women's "gender entrapment" in their abusive relationships are their experiences with social services and the criminal justice system. Compared to the white battered women in the study, the African American women were less likely to turn to social services for help. Further, none wanted their partners arrested or jailed, whereas the white women had often turned to the police for help. Here, Hurtado's (1996) emphasis on distance from the white male power structure is illuminating. The institutions that feminists have worked hard to make responsive to battered women have certainly changed, but those changes seem to better serve white women rather than all women.

Richie's (1996) study serves as a warning to those who ignore race or who might too easily assume that the effects of race, class, and gender are simply additive. Although Richie focused on the most extreme cases, her nuanced analysis of the intersection of race, class, and gender serves as a model of feminist research that can guide us in further work on the full spectrum of family violence.

Looking Forward

Feminists have made enormous contributions to our understanding of and interventions in intimate violence. Gender and coercive control remain critical conceptual tools in this work. The challenge before us is to deepen and extend our analysis. The centrality of gender is the subject of as much controversy as ever. From researchers using the Conflict Tactics Scales comes the assertion that women are as violent as men in the home. Antifeminist activists use these data to champion an artificial "equality" of abuse that erases the terror and injury of battering and undermines programs designed to intervene with violent men and support battered women. In response, feminists must work hard to elucidate women's shared subjection. We must not relent in asserting women's commonality of experience with coercive control. The Power and Control Wheel (which has been translated into dozens of languages and dialects) speaks to battered women of every color in disparate communities around the globe.

Yet, as surely as we must assert women's commonality in response to the antifeminist backlash, we must recognize, understand, and draw on the power of the diversity among us. A feminist analysis that assumes gender oppression is a unitary phenomenon will fall far short of its transformative potential. The social location of a black battered woman or an abused illegal immigrant is profoundly different from that of a beaten middle-class white woman—despite the subjection of all three to the coercive control of their partners. These differences are not essential to racial or ethnic groups. Rather, they reflect cultural differences, structural inequalities, and our differing relationships to white male power.

Doing feminist work in this field is, in many ways, more challenging than ever. It is certainly true that we have been heard and have more funding and more influence than in the early years of the movement. We have succeeded in making what was once a private trouble into a public issue. Feminist research and activism have influenced institutional realms from the police and courts to medical, mental health, and social services. After more than 25 years of work, we are at a point where the once glaring indifference to violence against women has been confronted and, in many places, transformed. There have been dramatic changes in law, policy, protocols, and practice. In an address titled "The Color of Violence against Women," Angela Davis (2000) pays tribute to the anti-violence movement that has criminalized the once-private act of battering. Yet she challenges us by arguing that "given the racist and patriarchal patterns of the state, it is difficult

to envision the state as the holder of solutions to the problem of violence against women of color." A critical task now is to develop more of what some have called "culturally sensitive" or "culturally competent" analysis and interventions. We must remember that this cultural sensitivity must be linked to challenges of structural inequalities and power relations. The work before us is, in many ways, more complex and difficult than what we have accomplished thus far.

The final point I make is not about feminism or violence per se, but about the nature of the debate and controversy around these issues. I am disturbed by the deep cleavages that have resulted from attacks, counterattacks, and highbrow name calling. Feminist scholars and activists with strong convictions are labeled ideologues, "feminist fundamentalists" (Erickson 1992), and "dogmatic." At the same time, feminists deepen the chasm by dismissing nonfeminist insights too quickly and hastily deciding who "gets it" and who doesn't. In the early years of family violence research and the battered women's movement, these divisions were largely focused on gender politics. More recently, challenges from scholars and activists of color (some feminists, some not) are pushing us forward toward more inclusive and transformative work. Our contentious history should give us pause. White feminists taking up the challenge to address race must recognize the potential dangers of this work. As Jim Ptacek (1999) notes, "In a fiercely divided society, public discussions of class, race, and violence entail risks. Wittingly or unwittingly, those who name these interconnections arouse powerful racist images, even when their goals are to displace them" (p. 19).

One way that white feminists can further the work on the race-class-gender intersection is to interrogate our own racial privilege (Lewis 1997). "Culturally sensitive" theories and interventions focused on people of color should not be seen as alternatives to the prevailing work, which is somehow assumed to be culturally neutral. Race is not a black issue any more than gender is a women's issue.

I believe that our future work cannot evade these difficult matters. Openness and respectful listening to different viewpoints will be essential. Careful consideration of potential unintended consequences of our work will be more important than ever. Recognition of the power of the coalitions (rather than the divisions) among us will be crucial. It will not be easy to answer Angela Davis's (2000) question, "How do we develop analyses and organizing strategies against violence against women that acknowledge the race of gender and the gender of race?" It will be difficult. But in addressing this question, I believe, lies the radical potential of feminism.

ENDNOTE

Author's Note: Thanks are given to Michelle Harris for her comments and suggestions.

REFERENCES

Abel, E. 1999. "Comparing the Social Service Utilization, Exposure to Violence, and Trauma Symptomology of Domestic Violence 'Victims' and Female 'Batterers.'" Presented at the Seventh International Family Violence Research Conference, University of New Hampshire.

Bograd, M. 1999. "Strengthening Domestic Violence Theories: Intersections of Race, Class, Sexual Orientation, and Gender." *Journal of Marital and Family Therapy* 25:275–89.

Browne, A. and S. Bassuk. 1997. "Intimate Violence in the Lives of Homeless and Poor Housed Women." *American Journal of Orthopsychiatry* 67 (2): 261–78.

Crenshaw, K. 1993. "Race, Gender, and Violence against Women." Pp. 230–32 in *Family Matters: Readings on Family Lives and the Law,* edited by M. Minow. New York: New Press.

———. 1994. "Mapping the Margins: Intersectionality, Identity Politics, and Violence against Women of Color." Pp. 93–118 in *The Public Nature of Private Violence,* edited by M. Fineman and R. Mykitiuk. New York: Routledge.

Davis, A. 2000. "The Color of Violence against Women." Keynote address of the Color of Violence Conference at the University of California at Santa Cruz. Retrieved April 29, 2004 (www.arc.org/C_Lines/CL Archive/story3_3_02.html).

Dobash, R. E. and R. P. Dobash. 1998. *Rethinking Violence against Women.* Thousand Oaks, CA: Sage.

Erickson, B. 1992. "Feminist Fundamentalism: Reactions to Avis, Kaufman, and Bograd." *Journal of Marital and Family Therapy* 18:263–67.

Ferree, M. M. 1990. "Beyond Separate Spheres: Feminism and Family Research." *Journal of Marriage and the Family* 52:866–84.

Hanmer, J. and M. Maynard. 1987. *Women, Violence, and Social Control.* Atlantic Highlands, NJ: Humanities.

Hurtado, A. 1996. *The Color of Privilege: Three Blasphemies on Race and Feminism.* Ann Arbor: University of Michigan Press.

Jones, A. and S. Schechter. 1992. *When Love Goes Wrong.* New York: HarperCollins.

Lewis, A. 1997. "Theorizing Whiteness: Interrogating Racial Privilege." Working Paper No. 568, Center for Research on Social Organization, University of Michigan.

Marin, A. and N. Russo. 1999. "Feminist Perspectives on Male Violence against Women." Pp. 18–35 in *What Causes Men's Violence against Women?,* edited by M. Harway and J. O'Neil. Thousand Oaks, CA: Sage.

Ptacek, J. 1988. "Why Do Men Batter Their Wives?" Pp. 133–57 in *Feminist Perspectives on Wife Abuse,* edited by K.Yllö and M. Bograd. Newbury Park, CA: Sage.

———. 1999. *Battered Women in the Courtroom.* Boston: Northeastern University Press.

Rich, A. 1979. *On Lies, Secrets, and Silence: Selected Prose, 1966–1978.* New York: Norton.

Richie, B. E. 1995. *Compelled to Crime: The Gender Entrapment of Battered Black Women.* New York: Routledge.

———. 1996. "Battered Black Women: A Challenge for the Black Community." *Black Scholar* 16 (2): 40–44.

Shepard, M. and E. Pence, eds. 1999. *Coordinating Community Response: Lessons from Duluth and Beyond.* Thousand Oaks, CA: Sage.

Steinmetz, S. K. 1987. "Family Violence: Past, Present, and Future." Pp. 725–65 in *Handbook of Marriage and the Family,* edited by M. B. Sussman and S. K. Steinmetz. New York: Plenum.

Yllö, K. 1988. "Political and Methodological Debates in Wife Abuse Research." Pp. 28–50 in *Feminist Perspectives on Wife Abuse,* edited by K. Yllö and M. Bograd. Newbury Park, CA: Sage.

42

LIFTING THE VEIL OF SECRECY
Domestic Violence against South Asian Women in the United States

SATYA P. KRISHNAN   •   MALAHAT BAIG-AMIN
•   LOUISA GILBERT   •   NABILA EL-BASSEL   •   ANNE WATERS

I would always be in fear. Even though I worked, I had to be home at a certain time. Even if I was five minutes late or if there was a traffic jam or something, I could not tell him that. I was in fear all the time. I was in fear that I would lose my mind if I go home late. I constantly made plans to be home on time.

—AN INTERVIEWEE'S COMMENTS

The image of a woman being abused by those who claim to love and honor her is horrifying. However, such abuse is one that many of us have heard of or, perhaps, experienced in our own lives. Domestic violence has been a part of our living landscape since the beginning of time and is still a significant component of many women's lives. Despite their abusive domestic circumstances, many women strive to work quietly, raise children, care for their families, and try to establish a "normal" existence in society.

Owing to the efforts of many dedicated community activists, the prevalence of domestic violence among South Asian women in the United States is no longer a secret. The efforts of these advocates have been crucial in bringing acknowledgment, recognition, and understanding to the issues surrounding domestic violence in South Asian immigrant communities. As the number of immigrants to the United States increases, the endeavors of these activists have begun to shed light on a neglected public health issue in a singularly underserved group, the South Asian American community.[1] Our interests in the issues of domestic violence among South Asian women stem from our research interests in immigrant women's health issues in general and our commitment to [ending] violence against women. . . .

Violence in Intimate Relationships: Issues in the Larger Society

Women often experience their greatest risk of violence not from acquaintances and strangers but from their intimate male partners.[2] Domestic violence is one of the most significant causes of injury to women, affecting about two million women in the United States every year. Today, domestic violence is being referred to as a "national epidemic" by physicians, public health experts, and politicians and is slowly becoming a part of the public consciousness in the United States.[3] Domestic violence, specifically intentional physical or nonphysical harm, or both, perpetrated by an intimate partner against a woman is pervasive and often an unrecognized cause of chronic physical and mental health problems.[4] These chronic health problems include such physical traumas as multiple contusions, fractures, bruises, bites, as well as burns on the face, head, abdomen, or genitals. In addition to direct injuries, victims may also suffer from chronic stress-related disorders such as gastric distress, lower back and pelvic pain, headaches, insomnia, and hyperventilation.[5] A variety of psychological and mental health symptoms such as anxiety disorders and panic attacks, depression, sense of helplessness and declining coping skills, self-blame, as well as lowered self-esteem may further accompany these physical impairments.[6]

Domestic Violence in South Asian Communities

The recent recognition of domestic violence in the United States and around the world as an extensive and long-existing phenomenon is largely due to the global efforts of battered women themselves. It is undeniable that the activities of community-based agencies and women's organizations have brought increasing policy, media, and research attention to intimate violence.[7] As the issues of domestic violence move from the private to the public arena in the larger community, a similar trend is reflected among South Asians in the United States.[8] Two factors appear to influence this shift: (1) the emergence and investment of South Asian women's groups and community-based organizations such as Manavi, Apna Ghar, and Sakhi for South Asian women and (2) the increased willingness of South Asian battered women to tell their stories to formal support systems.

In fact, South Asian community organizations and women's groups have played a pivotal role in bringing recognition to domestic violence within their communities. While they serve as safe havens for individual battered women, these agencies simultaneously aim to bring about social change by focusing attention on domestic violence itself. Generally, individual care comes in the form of counseling and emotional support, as well as intervention during emergencies. Social change, on the other hand, is attempted through publicizing particular issues of South Asian women in abusive relationships, training social and health-care workers, and influencing as well as

improving legislation regarding domestic violence. Consequently, the visibility of women's groups and community-based organizations, and the willingness of South Asian women to talk about their experiences of violence, have begun to construct a clearer and more realistic picture of women's lives in South Asian immigrant communities.

Of the immigrants living in the United States, 2.8 percent are Asian, and the 1990 census indicates that a million are South Asians—Bangladeshi, Indian, Pakistani, Nepali, and Sri Lankan.[9] One estimate suggests that the incidence of domestic violence in these communities is about 20 to 25 percent.[10] However, this may be an underestimation because domestic violence cases in these communities often are underreported owing to underutilization of existing social and health services.[11] Issues such as immigration status, language barriers, lack of knowledge about helping services and organizations, social and cultural barriers, fear and isolation, as well as concerns of safety for themselves and their children, are often responsible for this underutilization. This constellation of issues can have a profound effect on how South Asian women respond to violence in intimate relationships. These issues, real and perceived, add to the vulnerability of battered South Asian women and influence the way they address violence in their personal lives.

Despite the prevalence of domestic violence among South Asian women living in the United States, little systematic understanding and documentation of the problem exists.[12] A lack of comprehension of the cultural and social factors that define domestic violence, difficulties in reaching out to victims, and the continued reluctance of many women to seek help all contribute to perpetuating intimate violence in our communities. However, current changing conditions within South Asian communities suggest the need for research approaches that can systematically record the scope and particularities of that violence. Such research will also provide better understanding of the factors and correlates of intimate violence, so that culturally appropriate and effective prevention and intervention strategies can be designed.

In this [reading], we hope to lift the veil of secrecy shrouding domestic violence by offering realistic views of South Asian women's experiences, concerns, needs, solutions, and hopes through the words, thoughts, ideas, and courage of the women themselves.

Domestic Violence Research and Focus Groups

In our work, we have used focus groups extensively to explore, discuss, and elaborate on a variety of issues concerning domestic violence among South Asian women living in the United States. A focus group discussion, very simply, is a qualitative method of gathering information from a group of eight to fifteen people who have at least one interest in common.[13] We chose to use focus groups over other methods because of their comfortable, safe, and sharing format. We observed that while participants told their own

stories in these groups, they also heard from other women in similar circumstances and developed a sense of kinship and support for one another.

We conducted several focus groups in Chicago and in New York City, where the local South Asian women's organizations assisted us in contacting and recruiting participants for groups. Between five and ten South Asian (Indian, Pakistani, and Bangladeshi) women participated in each of the discussion groups. Some of the issues explored during the group sessions included

- ▾ Personal, family, and community definitions and perceptions of domestic violence and its consequences;
- ▾ The type, context, and circumstances in which violence occurred;
- ▾ Effects and consequences of this violence on the women themselves and their children, and on other aspects of women's lives;
- ▾ Personal, family, and community norms, attitudes, perceptions, and acceptance of domestic violence;
- ▾ The issues of social support, both formal and informal, and the types of coping strategies used;
- ▾ Factors that perpetuate domestic violence in women's lives and those that alleviate the problem;
- ▾ Barriers to care- and help-seeking behaviors and the women's suggestions for change; and
- ▾ Whether migration has affected women's domestic violence experiences.

The focus group discussions were led by two facilitators who helped to moderate the discussions among participants. For South Asian women who were still in abusive situations, these discussion sessions proved to be "safe havens" where they felt comfortable about articulating their experiences of domestic violence and discussing a variety of other related issues. Furthermore, these discussions also appeared to be "therapeutic" and "empowering," as the participants themselves indicated that they welcomed the opportunity to talk about their lives and the violence and meet others in situations similar to theirs.

South Asian Women Define Domestic Violence

The recent interest in domestic violence has fueled a debate about what constitutes the phenomenon. Experts, politicians, activists, advocates, and academics have suggested varying definitions, including those rooted in feminist perspectives, those from the family preservation point of view, and others from the ecological standpoint. An important missing ingredient in this ongoing argument is the viewpoint of battered women, in this case, South Asian women in abusive relationships. Although their definitions may differ from those of the professionals, the South Asian women participating in our focus groups knew intuitively what was "not right" or what was "wrong" in their domestic lives. Meena, a young Indian woman who

recently moved to the United States, had a very simple definition of violence and declared, "Beating is domestic violence."[14]

While Meena focused on the physical aspects of domestic violence, Kismat, a Pakistani mother of four, emphasized the psychological aspects of such abuse. She focused on the constant lack of respect from her spouse, which constituted domestic violence to her. This lack of respect often translated into jealousy and suspicion and led to various types of abuse and violence, including physical beatings. She said, "[Domestic violence] is when husbands do not give respect to their wives and are always suspicious. The persons who live with each other must have respect for each other."

Definitions of spousal violence offered by the women participating in the focus groups were not limited to physical or overt forms of abuse only. Their notion of ill treatment included emotional and verbal abuse, as well as subtle mistreatments such as standing around to overhear conversations with friends and family members. Munni, an Indian woman living in the Chicago area for a number of years, provided quite a comprehensive definition of domestic violence: "Emotional abuse is domestic violence. And verbal abuse, being suspicious, beating, and not supporting financially is domestic violence. Sometimes men think that they should treat women like a pair of shoes."

These interpretations of domestic violence indicate that the South Asian women in the focus groups understood intuitively that their experiences of physical, emotional, and psychological abuse were not normative. They were also able to distinguish among various types of domestic violence such as physical, psychological, emotional, verbal, and sexual. This distinction affected the consequences of abuse, as well as the demands on the women's coping skills. Clearly, these women recognized abuse in their relationships, even when it was perpetrated in subtle and quiet ways.

Although the women were quite willing to discuss their overall situations, cultural as well as community influences were obvious in the emphasis they placed on certain types of abuse and their reluctance to discuss others. For example, many of the focus group participants felt that verbal, psychological, and emotional abuse were more pervasive and therefore critical in their lives but felt that, unlike physical abuse, these were harder to document and explain. Furthermore, all women were significantly more reticent about broaching the subject of sexual abuse.

Another culture-specific aspect was that the women did not necessarily blame themselves for the violence in their domestic relationships but considered it more a consequence of "bad fate." This ability to contextualize domestic violence in terms of bad fate gave the participants the patience, tolerance, and dignity they needed to cope with it. Sheba, an Indian mother of two grown-up children, explained: "I don't think it was my fault at all. This was my fate. I just thought that this was part of my life. You know, no one's life is perfect. There's one thing or another in everyone's life. And I just look at this [domestic violence] as something that I had to tolerate."

Obedient Daughters, Faithful Wives, and Caring Mothers: Sexual Abuse in Conjugal Relationships

All of the participating women were very reluctant to acknowledge, include, and discuss sexual abuse as an integral part of domestic violence. Sexual abuse was by far the hardest topic to introduce in the discussions, and the women even refused to elaborate on the reasons for this discomfort. One can only speculate about their rationale in terms of the women's lack of ease with issues of sex, sexuality, and self-disclosure. Although they perceived the focus groups to be "safe" and "nonjudgmental," the majority of women were conscious of the constraints of their social norms. They were socialized to be "obedient daughters," "faithful wives," and "caring mothers," and these social norms required conformity to certain behavioral standards: subservience, propriety, and putting others' needs ahead of their own. These expectations ruled out any discussion regarding sex, pleasure, and personal enjoyment. The fact that they had moved into the public arena with their stories of domestic violence was already a great departure from tradition, and to discuss sexual abuse, another taboo issue, would have further taxed their coping skills.

Decision to Stay: Insights into a Process

Recent research indicates that women's length of stay in violent relationships varies with ethnicity, assimilation to the dominant culture and acculturation levels, attitudes, and norms about family, marriage, sex roles, and domestic violence, as well as other sociodemographic characteristics. In light of these studies, we tried to examine the factors that affect South Asian women's motivations to remain in violent relationships. Thus, the women participating in the focus groups spent a substantial amount of time exploring why each stayed in their abusive situations. Their discussions indicated a decision-making process that was personal, yet complex. The following were some considerations extracted from the women's testimonies regarding the process itself:

1. Evaluation of the pros and cons of their domestic circumstances;
2. Perceived choices and options available to them;
3. Concern for their children's safety and future;
4. Immigration status and financial stability;
5. Value placed on opinions and concerns of family members and community;
6. A sense of self-blame, guilt, and personal responsibility; and
7. Perceptions of societal norms and expectations of them.

Contrary to popular belief, the decisions these women made were neither irrational nor arbitrary. Most women based their decisions on a clear rationale. For example, Hala, a young Muslim woman, assessed her situation and found no relevant and viable solutions to her problem. In addition,

she believed that she was expected to "tolerate" the violence she was experiencing. Thus, she based her decision to stay with her abusive spouse on these perceptions: I guess that's the way its supposed to be. Women, they take it. They don't fight back, you know, like women here [American women in the United States] do. Asian women, however much educated they are, they don't fight back. That's the way I was—just be quiet, or walk out, or get out of the house, or go to the other room. Roja, another focus group participant, declared unceremoniously, "In my case, it was financial dependence."

The issue of economic dependency as a salient reason for continuing in a violent relationship was a theme that emerged often. Many of the participants were partially or totally dependent on their spouses for their finances, as well as other resources. Some perceived this dependency to be stronger than it may have been in actuality. Social isolation and lack of information about formal service provisions also contributed to exaggerating this problem of dependency. For some women in the focus groups, marriage had provided them with financial resources, a decent home, class privileges, respectability, and legitimacy in their community and families that they did not have before. In essence, the women had received respectability, a higher social class, and material comforts in exchange for private mistreatments. This exchange was a strategic choice that some participants indicated they made consciously, for themselves and for their children, for a limited length of time or for a lifetime.

For some participants, social norms, family traditions and marriage, and acceptance of men as authorities in the family were adequate reasons for maintaining their abusive relationships. Jila, a focus group participant, succinctly stated her reason for not leaving her violent husband: "Because we feel respect for our parents [and] we should try to keep good relations with our husbands—no matter what." Kamini, another woman in the groups, expressed similar sentiments: "For me, it's like everyone should be together, sit together, and there should be love amongst everyone. And it is a good impression for the children. This is what is in my faith and in my culture. Divorce in our family is very difficult. If you have children, you have to stay together for their sake. Children need to have both mother and father."

Barriers to Leaving: A Glimpse into South Asian Women's Worlds

For most people, it is extremely difficult to comprehend why a woman continues to endure and cope with violence in her home. In our group discussions, South Asian women provided glimpses into a process of decision making that is often poorly understood and judged harshly. Despite the fear and uncertainty that most of these women face daily they seem to find a way to examine their own lives, available options, and their own capabilities in terms of complexities engendered by living in a "foreign" country. This rather calm and rational scrutiny in the midst of an otherwise chaotic life

seemingly helped the group participants find reasons for continuing in their violent relationships and coming to terms with it.

Values and Norms-Related Factors

Many of the barriers to leaving that these women experienced were not individual at all. Rather, women based their decisions to stay on factors such as family and cultural values. [The values and norms that created barriers for these women include:]

1. Societal, community, and family norms;
2. Community and family expectations; and
3. Patriarchy and prescribed gender roles.

The effects of these factors are illustrated in Munni's account of the circumstances of her marriage and conjugal life: "When I got married, my father said to my husband, 'My respect and honor is in your hands. Please take care of my daughter.' From then on he was my husband. It was my job to take care of him. For my family honor, family respect, and to maintain [this] respect, we have to just put up with it [violence]. Because of the family!" This is even more clear in Nilufer's statement "My husband forced me to have more children for citizenship purposes. I am sure that what he really wanted was to have sons. He hates daughters. I couldn't even tell you how much. Back in Pakistan, it is understood that girls are no good, and you shouldn't have them." Along with the perceived relevance of patriarchy in families, Nilufer's understanding and acceptance of gender positions is evident in this statement.

Support Factors

[The focus group discussions also centered on three support factors:]

1. Lack of social support;
2. Lack of structural support and material resources; and
3. Lack of knowledge of available formal support networks and systems.

Suman, an Indian single mother living in New York with a young daughter, discussed the lack of social support she experienced: "I have no relatives. I have nobody, just me and my daughter now. It is hard, very hard." Savitri, a mother of three children, discussed the lack of structural support and material resources in terms of the availability of affordable baby-sitting and public transportation. She felt that a scarcity of both had prevented her from developing necessary skills to become self-sufficient and independent. "I have a baby-sitting problem. The day care that is on our side is very expensive. Taking the public transport to another place itself costs five dollars," she lamented.

The lack of knowledge about available formal assistance programs can often prove to be an important reason why some South Asian women choose to continue in their violent domestic relationships. Roja, who had recently moved to Chicago from India, expressed her dilemma and her

reasons for staying in her violent relationship: "And this is a new culture [the United States], language problem, no money, and with children. Where to go? And moreover, no relatives. There is nowhere to go. And there is no way to get out."

During discussions about support factors, focus group participants indicated the magnitude of their sense of isolation when they were attempting to address problems surrounding abuse in their lives. Suman declared, "It's quite difficult to make the adjustment and adapt to the new culture, and it takes quite a bit of time. There are difficulties and problems. Especially when there is no one to turn to."

Individual Factors

These individual factors emerged from the focus group discussions:

1. Fear for safety for themselves and their children;
2. Fear for their future and possible deportation;
3. Inability to handle and cope with the stress of living alone in the United States;
4. Lack of job skills, language skills, and other life skills;
5. Desire to stay in the relationship or inability to accept and address the violence in their lives; and
6. Fear for the children's future.

Leela, a woman living in Chicago, focused on some of the personal factors that formed barriers for her: "My English speaking isn't very good. So getting a job and working is not a possibility yet. So I cannot get the things I need without the English. In addition I do not have a green card." Roja, another woman in Chicago, indicated racism as a factor contributing to her abusive situation: "My life now is for my children. That's why I need to work and support them. I had to swallow my hopes. I have to put all my hopes in my children. There are many tensions from the outside. He [the husband] wants what he had back home [in terms of a job]. A woman accepts whatever she can get, because we want to survive and support the family. Although the men have the education, they cannot find a suitable job or sometimes they do not want to work. So there is frustration outside and inside the home for all of us."

Why Leave Now? Why South Asian Women Walk Out of Their Marriages

Despite the hopelessness and lack of support they experienced, some of the South Asian women took the "uncharacteristic" and "unlikely" step of leaving their abusive relationships for good. Many indicated that they were seriously considering this option. Others stated that they were trying hard to cope with their present, violence-filled circumstances and hoping to "make them [their marriages] work."

Those who walked away from their abusive relationships indicated that they did so not because of one defining moment, or a single violent episode, but because of the sum total of their experiences. They had reached the end of their tolerance and recognized that they could seek and receive support and assistance from formal systems. Those who had walked away from their violent relationships, however, also acknowledged that it had been excruciatingly difficult and painful to start living on their own. They indicated that the support they received from local South Asian women's organizations and culturally sensitive domestic violence shelters was crucial in their decision making and follow-through processes. Also significant in their decision making was the support they received from informal kin and friendship networks such as friends, family members, neighbors, and co-workers. For those who were continuing in their present abusive circumstances, having a job and interacting with their colleagues at work, talking to supportive siblings, family members, and friends, the support and understanding of their children, and their own unwavering religious faith had all helped them to continue to cope. These factors gave them hope for a better future and life.

Hopes for the Future: Living in Peace and Tranquillity

Despite difficult circumstances and lives filled with violence and fear, the participating South Asian women expressed hopes and expectations for a better future. Those who had left their violent lives encouraged others to consider this option and offered to help in any way possible. Madhu, an Indian woman who participated in one of the focus groups in Chicago, voiced this optimism: "My hopes are that I want to study [and] I am doing a job in the library now. It's a good position, but I want to move ahead. So that's why I want to study more. I don't want a restaurant or a store job." Kismat, a Pakistani woman and a mother of four, expressed her desires in terms of her children. She remarked, "My life is with my children. I want to see my children have a good life with a good education, have good jobs. This is my biggest wish and hope." Sheba, who had started a life on her own, had this advice for other participants: "You need to make yourself good and show that you don't have less of anything. You can raise your children without him. And better than him. And you can be happy. You need to begin to say this to yourself and foster these kinds of thoughts."

During these discussions, the participants indicated that it was important to address domestic violence through simple and tangible strategies that were empowering and meaningful to women. They suggested that these strategies need to focus first and foremost on providing life skills, job skills, and language skills so that women could slowly find the peace and tranquillity that had eluded them for so long. Their suggestions included providing the following services: English classes, transportation, baby-sitting services, advice about legal issues and immigration laws, job training such as computer classes, some seed money to start their lives again, and support groups where they can talk with others and help others.

Their focus was simple, narrow, and targeted toward themselves. They felt that with these kinds of tangible assistance and services, they could emerge from behind the veil of secrecy, talk about their lives in public, not feel responsible for the violence in their lives, and, like other people, live a life of dignity and peace. . . .

Learning from Women

Although there has been a long history of domestic violence in South Asian communities, only recently have attempts been made to document these issues systematically in these communities in the United States. Our experience is that focus group discussions are extremely effective in exploring a variety of issues regarding domestic violence in these communities. Our work with South Asian women revealed that violence experienced by South Asian women was defined by a variety of unique cultural, familial, and community factors and norms. Socioeconomic factors, immigration status, and a host of perceived barriers, including linguistic ones, further defined their experiences. Our focus group discussions revealed a complex picture of domestic violence among the participating South Asian women. Issues of patriarchy, gender roles and expectations, constricting family and community norms, attitudes and traditions about spousal violence, lack of decision-making power, and economic independence are still important in South Asian communities and have aggravated the problem of domestic violence further. Despite this bleak picture, the South Asian women who participated in our groups exhibited enviable resiliency and coping abilities. Their hopes for a peaceful and violence-free life for themselves and their children spoke volumes about their courage. With the help of South Asian women's organizations and other community-based organizations, and through their own willingness to speak out, South Asian women have begun to challenge their communities to confront domestic violence with sensitivity and urgency. Although the process has been initiated, there is much work to be done. Part of the task is to document the nature and incidence of this atrocity systematically and implement culturally sensitive, as well as effective, interventions that address issues in South Asian contexts.

ENDNOTES

[1] K. A. Huisman, "Wife Battering in Asian American Communities," *Violence against Women* 2 (1996): 260–83.

[2] M. P. Koss, L. A. Goodman, A. Browne, L. F. Fitzgerald, G. P. Keita, and N. F. Russo, *No Safe Haven: Male Violence against Women at Home, at Work, and in the Community* (Washington, DC: American Psychological Association, 1994).

[3] J. Abbott, J. McLain-Koziol, and S. Lowenstein, "Domestic Violence against Women: Incidence and Prevalence in an Emergency Department Population," *Journal of the American Medical Association* 273 (1995): 1763–77.

[4] D. Berrios and D. Grady, "Domestic Violence. Risk Factors and Outcomes," *Western Journal of Medicine* 155, no. 2 (1991): 133–35.

[5] V. F. Parker, "Battered," *RN (TWP)* 58, no. 1 (1995): 26–29.

[6] A. L. Kornblit, "Domestic Violence: An Emerging Health Issue," *Social Science and Medicine* 39 (1994): 1181–88.

[7] S. D. Dasgupta and S. Warrier, "In the Footsteps of 'Arundhati': Asian Indian Women's Experience of Domestic Violence in the United States," *Violence against Women* 2, no. 3 (1996): 238–59.

[8] M. Abraham, "Addressing the Problem of Marital Violence among South Asians in the United States: A Sociological Study of the Role of Organizations," paper presented at the meetings of the International Sociological Association (1994); and "Transforming Marital Violence from a 'Private Problem' to a 'Public Issue': South Asian Women's Organizations and Community Empowerment," paper presented at the meetings of the American Sociological Association (1995). These papers have since been published as "Ethnicity, Gender, and Marital Violence: South Asian Women's Organizations in the United States," *Gender and Society* 9 (1995): 450–68; and "Speaking the Unspeakable: Marital Violence against South Asian Immigrant Women in the United States," *Indian Journal of Gender Studies* 5, no. 2 (June–December 1998).

[9] U.S. Bureau of the Census, *1990 Census of the Population: Social and Economic Characteristics, United States* (Washington, DC: U.S. Government Printing Office, 1993).

[10] Koss et al., *No Safe Haven.*

[11] C. K. Ho, "An Analysis of Domestic Violence in Asian American Communities: A Multicultural Approach to Counseling," *Women and Therapy* 9 (1990): 129–50.

[12] Abraham, "Addressing the Problem" and "Transforming Marital Violence."

[13] T. L. Greenbaum, *The Practical Handbook and Guide to Focus Groups Research* (Lexington, MA: Lexington, 1988).

[14] Names of all participants have been changed to protect their identity.

43

TOWARD A BETTER UNDERSTANDING OF LESBIAN BATTERING

CLAIRE M. RENZETTI

What do we now know about violence in lesbian relationships, and where do we go from here? . . .

It appears that violence in lesbian relationships occurs at about the same frequency as violence in heterosexual relationships. The abuse may be physical and/or psychological, ranging from verbal threats and insults to stabbings and shootings. Indeed, batterers display a terrifying ingenuity in their selection of abusive tactics, frequently tailoring the abuse to the specific vulnerabilities of their partners. We have seen that there is no "typical" form of abuse, even though some types of abuse are more common than others. What emerged as significant in my research was not the forms of abuse

inflicted, but, rather, the factors that appear to give rise to the abuse, and the consequences of the abuse for batterers and especially for victims.

The factor that in this study was most strongly associated with abuse was partners' relative dependency on one another. More specifically, batterers appeared to be intensely dependent on the partners whom they victimized. The abusive partner's dependency was a central element in an ongoing, dialectic struggle in these relationships. As batterers grew more dependent, their partners attempted to exercise greater independence. This, in turn, posed a threat to the batterer, who would subsequently try to tighten her hold on her partner, often by violent means. The greater the batterer's dependency, the more frequent and severe the abuse she inflicted on her partner. In most cases, the batterer eventually succeeded in cutting her partner off from friends, relatives, colleagues, and all outside interests and activities that did not include the batterer herself. Still, though she apparently had her partner all to herself in a sense, her success in controlling her partner seemed only to fuel her dependency rather than salve it.

The intense dependency of the batterer typically manifests itself as jealousy. It is not enough for the batterer to possess her partner; she must also guard her from all others who could potentially lure her away. The battering victim is subjected to lengthy interrogations about her routine activities and associations. She is repeatedly accused of infidelity, and although the accusations are almost always groundless, her denials rarely satisfy the batterer. Violence is a frequent end product of the batterer's jealous tirades. The overdependency of the batterer may also manifest itself through substance abuse, especially alcohol abuse. When under the influence of alcohol or drugs, she may feel strong, more independent, more aggressive. She may act on these perceptions by becoming violent and abusive, especially toward her partner. This is particularly likely if, along with the belief that alcohol or drugs make her powerful, she or her partner or both of them also believe that an individual under the influence of alcohol or drugs is not responsible for her actions. Thus substance abuse appears to be a facilitator rather than a cause of lesbian battering.

Another factor that emerged as a potential facilitator of lesbian partner abuse was a personal history of family violence. Although a number of researchers have found that childhood exposure to domestic violence may increase one's likelihood of being victimized in an intimate relationship as an adult, the participants in my study did not report a high incidence of exposure to domestic violence in their families of origin. Their batterers were more likely than they were to have been victimized, but there were almost as many abusive partners who grew up in nonviolent households as there were those who grew up in violent ones.

Exposure to domestic violence as a child may put one at risk of becoming abusive toward one's own partner as an adult, but the data from my study also suggest that a personal history of abuse can become, for both batterer and victim, a means to legitimate the battering. In other words, the belief that childhood exposure to domestic violence predisposes one toward violent behavior or victimization as an adult may facilitate lesbian battering

much the same way substance abuse does—that is, by forming the basis of an excuse for the batterer's behavior.

One issue that remains unclear is how an imbalance of power in the relationship may contribute to partner abuse. Like other researchers who have examined the relationship between power imbalance and battering among homosexual couples, few strong associations emerged from my study. This is probably due in large part to the complexity of the concept of power. Power is multifaceted. With respect to some dimensions of power (e.g., decision making, the division of household labor), batterers could be considered the more powerful partners. However, in terms of other indicators of power (e.g., economic resources brought to the relationship), victims tended to be more powerful. It is also unclear when an imbalance of power in these terms emerges in abusive relationships; the data from my study indicate that, at least with regard to decision making, victims often ceded power to batterers in an attempt to appease them and perhaps avoid further abuse. This evidence lends support to the hypothesis that batterers are individuals who feel powerless and use violence as a means to achieve power and dominance in their intimate relationships.

The power imbalance–domestic violence link is one that obviously deserves further attention in future research. If batterers use violence as a means to overcome feelings of powerlessness, what are the sources of these feelings? Are they a further outgrowth of dependency needs? In addition, researchers need to clarify what elements compose the power construct so that the dimensions of power relevant to the etiology of lesbian partner abuse can be distinguished and addressed.[1]

It is doubtful that we will ever be able to predict with precision which relationships, be they homosexual or heterosexual, will become violent. However, findings from my research and that of others we have reviewed point to several factors that may serve as markers for identifying lesbian relationships that are particularly at risk for violence. Figure 1 presents a decision tree designed to assist lesbian partners, counselors, battered women's advocates, and others in assessing this risk. I also urge readers who feel they are at risk, or who think they may be involved in a battering relationship, to apply Figure 1 as a checklist to their own relationships.

What if one is involved in an abusive relationship? Where may one go for help? . . . As the findings of my research make clear, battered lesbians experience tremendous difficulty obtaining the help they want and need. Help sources available to battered heterosexual women (e.g., the police and the legal system, shelters, relatives) generally are not perceived by lesbian victims as viable sources of help. Or, if help is sought from these sources, lesbian victims do not typically rate it as highly effective. Even those whom lesbian victims consider to be good sources of help (i.e., counselors and friends) frequently deny the abuse or refuse to name it battering.

Based on the data gathered in my study, it is not overstating the point to say that battered lesbians are victimized not only by their partners, but also by many of those from whom they seek help. Consequently, additional research is urgently needed on ways to improve help providers' responses to battered lesbians. We will take up this issue in the sections that follow.

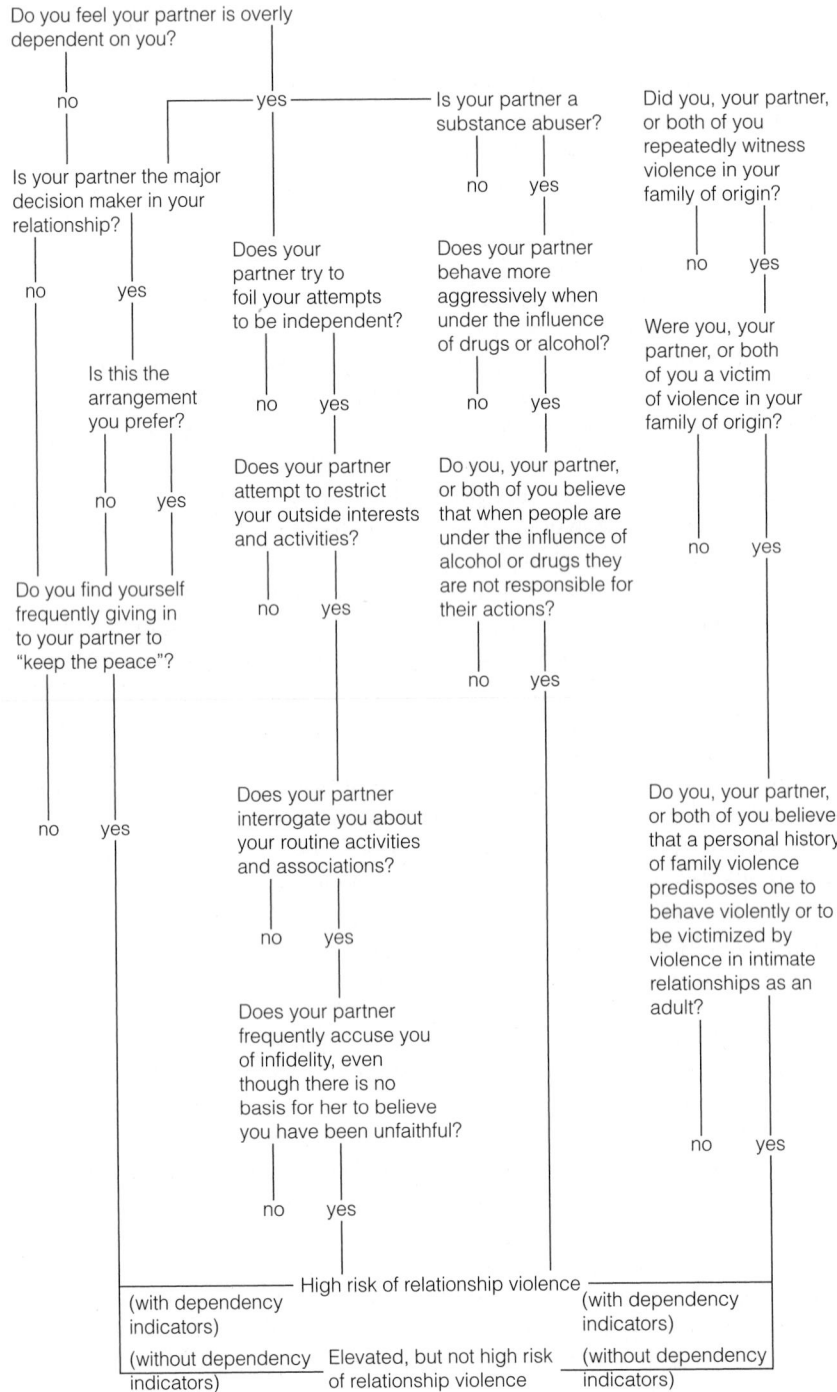

FIGURE 1 Decision Tree for Assessing Risk for Violence in Lesbian Relationships

Providing Help to Battered Lesbians

Research has consistently documented the difficulties battered heterosexual women encounter when they seek help to address the battering. Nevertheless, battered heterosexual women appear to have considerably more success in getting effective help—or at least in eliciting positive responses from help providers—than battered lesbians do. As Pharr (1986) has pointed out:

> There is an important difference between the battered lesbian and the battered non-lesbian: the battered non-lesbian experiences violence within the context of a misogynist world; the lesbian experiences violence within the context of a world that is not only woman-hating, but is also homophobic. And that is a great difference. Therefore, an initial step in improving responses to battered lesbians is for help providers to confront and overcome their homophobia. (P. 204)

As Elliott (1990) says, "Before you . . . can acknowledge lesbian battering, you must first acknowledge lesbian relationships" (n.p.).

While informal help providers (e.g., heterosexual friends, family members) cannot be forced to attend homophobia workshops, all official or formal help providers—that is, police personnel, shelter volunteers and paid staff, crisis hotline staffers, counselors, physicians, and emergency room personnel—should be required to participate in such workshops as part of their routine training. There are a number of excellent resources available that can be utilized for such sessions. Perhaps the best is *Confronting Homophobia*, edited by Julie Guth and Pamela Elliott of the Lesbian Advocacy Committee of the Minnesota Coalition for Battered Women. The manual includes not only training materials, but also suggestions for trainers and workshop leaders, sample training formats, and evaluation forms.

Confronting Homophobia is part of a two-volume set; the second volume, *Confronting Lesbian Battering,* is specifically designed for battered women's advocates as a resource for developing effective responses to lesbian victims. The value of *Confronting Lesbian Battering* is that it addresses the many myths that surround lesbian partner abuse and sensitively guides readers through a rethinking of our operating models of intimate violence.

In a survey of 1,505 service providers that I conducted in 1991, two-thirds (66.6 percent) of the 557 service providers who responded indicated that their staff receive antihomophobia training; 56.4 percent indicated that volunteers also receive this training. However, only 47.9 percent reported that their staff received any training specifically about lesbian battering and 40.6 percent reported that volunteers receive such training. Thus, in addition to homophobia workshops, help providers also must be educated about lesbian battering, and this education must include an analysis of the many myths about partner abuse: that it is a male/female problem; that it typically involves "mutual battering"; that it is always the physically larger or "masculine" partner who batters. Education in this regard, however, should extend beyond official help providers to the communities, both lesbian and non-lesbian. This may be undertaken in the context of community

speak-outs in which participants are assured safe space. It may also be done through the distribution of pamphlets or flyers and through public service advertisements. In particular, battered women's agencies should determine if their ads and literature imply (or explicitly state) that all batterers are heterosexual men and all victims of battering are heterosexual women. Often, the sex-specific pronoun "he" is used in reference to batterers, and "she" is used in reference to victims. In my survey of service providers, 96.4 percent of those who responded said they welcome battered lesbians as clients, yet just 37 percent reported that they do outreach to lesbians. Similarly, 77.7 percent said that at least some of the written materials they make available use inclusive language, but only 25.9 percent indicated that their written materials explicitly address the problem of lesbian battering and just 29.8 percent reported that they have written material specifically about lesbian battering available. Just as efforts have been made to make agency materials racially-inclusive, so too should they be inclusive of lesbians and gay men.

Strategies such as these not only educate help providers, the lesbian and gay community in general, and the heterosexual public, but may also assist lesbians involved in abusive relationships in recognizing themselves as battered, which is their first step in getting free. Still, education without action is of little use. What responses from others would lesbian victims find most helpful? This question was posed to the participants in my study of lesbian battering. Their answers have been incorporated into the following discussions.[2]

The Legal System and Alternatives

A current debate among advocates for battered lesbians is whether or not the legal system should be utilized to resolve the problem of violence in lesbian relationships. Those who support the use of the legal system maintain that bringing the force of legal authority to bear on the batterer can effectively put an end to her abuse and, at the same time, hold her accountable for her actions. From this perspective, lesbians are entitled to equal protection by the law. The difficulties are that in most states, the domestic violence statutes do not explicitly apply to homosexual couples, and in those states where they do apply, the police and the courts do not consistently or fairly enforce them in cases involving homosexual couples. Those who hold this position maintain that advocates should lobby for the revision of domestic violence statutes to include homosexual couples, and serve as watchdogs to ensure that the statutes are consistently and fairly enforced when lesbians and gay men turn to the police and courts for help.[3]

Opponents of utilizing the legal system in cases of lesbian battering point first to its well-documented mistreatment of cases involving heterosexual couples. According to Irvine (1990), "The courts deal so poorly with heterosexual abuse cases that in a case involving two lesbians they would have a 'field day'" (p. 29). Second, many see the legal system as inappropriate for resolving problems between lesbian partners. As one advocate put it: "I have a personal hatred and bias against women using the

legal system and the police system in their fights with each other. I find it offensive as a feminist. Resolution of disputes between lesbians should not take place in a white male judicial court" (quoted in Irvine 1990:29).

Only two of the participants in my study indicated that they would find intervention by the police and the courts helpful. One said she would like to have legal sanctions available that are tougher than restraining orders. The second participant said that the homophobia of the police needs to be addressed. She found the police to be helpful in stopping the battering in the short-run, but reported that they were blatantly homophobic in their response to her.

If the police and the legal system should not be utilized by battered lesbians, what are their alternatives? One is mediation. The role of the mediator is to facilitate communication between partners so that they themselves can develop a mutually beneficial and impartial resolution to their conflicts (e.g., separation, a signed agreement in which the abusive partner promises to end the violence) without resorting to formal legal action (Felstiner and Williams 1978; Folberg and Taylor 1984).

The informal and private nature of mediation may make it especially appealing to lesbian victims, particularly if they prefer that most people (e.g., their families, colleagues at work, etc.) not know about their sexual orientation. However, Ellis (1988) and others (e.g., Bahr, Chappell, and Marcos 1987) warn that mediation may have limited success in ending partner abuse. Their research indicates that the more hostile the relations between partners, the less likely they are to successfully complete mediation. In addition, mediators, in their effort to be impartial, may overlook inequalities of power between partners, not only with regard to economic resources, but also in terms of fear or psychological domination. Mediation also implies co-responsibility on the part of the partners and fails to hold batterers accountable for their behavior. Weighing these findings against the potential value of mediation for lesbian victims, research should be undertaken to evaluate the effectiveness of existing mediation programs in assisting both lesbian and heterosexual clients.

Apart from the police, the courts, and mediators, battered lesbians may also turn to other formal help providers, especially shelters and counselors, for assistance. How might the responses of these professionals be improved?

Shelters and Counselors

Nineteen participants in my study stated that having a safe place to which they could go for refuge from their batterers would have been most helpful to them.[4] We have already noted that shelters can only become viable sources of help to battered lesbians when shelter staff confront and overcome their homophobia, and when lesbian partner abuse is explicitly recognized as a serious problem in public service advertisements and literature for battered women. Lesbian victims of partner abuse need to know that local battered women's shelters are open to them and that they are welcome there.

Once the battered lesbian arrives at the shelter, staff there must, of course, make good on their promise of providing her with safe space, emotional support, and other assistance that they routinely provide to battered heterosexual women. Shelter staff must not minimize the abuse experienced by the battered lesbian simply because her batterer is a woman. Lesbian battering is "real" battering, and many of the needs of battered lesbians are the same as those of battered heterosexual women.

At the same time, however, battered lesbians have several unique concerns. One of the most important is deciding to whom among shelter staff and residents one will make one's sexual orientation known. As Geraci (1986) explains:

> If a lesbian does not choose to come out this right must be respected. It is important to keep in mind that in the lesbian community at large, battering between women is a non-issue—it violates the idea of a safe, peaceful world of women. . . . A battered lesbian who seeks shelter is making a very courageous step which could cause her to lose the support of many of her lesbian sisters. (P. 78)

She also runs the risk of incurring hostility and ostracism from other shelter residents.[5] Among the service providers I surveyed, 92.3 percent said that their clients' sexual orientation was treated confidentially, although the majority also indicated their confidentiality policies regarding sexual orientation were not explicit.

Another serious concern of battered lesbians in shelters is the extent to which they are actually safe from their batterers. While shelter locations are well-guarded secrets from men, and both staff and residents are severely sanctioned if they disclose this information, we have already noted that the location of shelters is often well-known in the lesbian community, primarily because lesbians have been very active in the battered women's movement and because of the widely held belief that all batterers are men. Consequently it has been suggested that as an alternative to traditional residential shelters, a network of safe houses be established for battered lesbians (Irvine 1990). In Minneapolis–St. Paul, for example, a network of lesbians takes victims into their individual homes (Ojeda-Zapata 1990). Irvine (1990) points out that a drawback of this approach is that lesbian victims are not afforded the peer support that may be available at the shelters. However, a support group for battered lesbians may fill this gap (Porat 1986).

The Lesbian Battering Intervention Project of the Minnesota Coalition for Battered Women has compiled a checklist to assist shelter staff in determining if they are adequately prepared to serve battered lesbians. They have kindly permitted me to reprint it here (see Table 1). Many of the issues raised in this checklist also apply to counselors from whom lesbian victims seek help. Seventeen of the lesbian victims in my study identified specific responses from counselors that they would have found helpful. Three were cited repeatedly.

First, participants indicated that they needed professional help in regaining their self-esteem and building a strong sense of self-worth. They

TABLE 1   Checklist for Shelter Programs

1. Do all written materials use inclusive language (no pronouns) and address the issue of lesbian battering?
   Mission
   Philosophy statement
   Brochures
   Arrival and departure forms
   Welcome letters, house rules, etc.

2. Is homophobia identified as an oppression and a form of violence?
   In the philosophy statement
   In the house rules

3. Are policies inclusive of lesbians?
   Does the definition of family in personal policies include lesbian families?
   Does the affirmative action statement include sexual/affectional orientation?
   Does the policy on confidentiality include confidentiality for lesbians and consequences for violating the policy?

4. Is the recruitment of staff, volunteers, and board members addressing homophobia?
   Are candidates questioned about homophobia and providing services to lesbians?
   Are position announcements distributed to reach lesbians?
   Do job qualifications include commitment to confront homophobia?
   Is homophobia training included for all new staff, volunteers, and board members?
   Does the program have a commitment to lesbian involvement at all levels?

5. Is the program prepared to respond to the needs of battered lesbians?
   Is information available on resources for battered lesbians?
   Does the library, video library, and/or magazine rack contain lesbian books, videos, periodicals, or articles?
   Is the Children's Program staff familiar with issues confronting lesbian mothers? (custody, coming out to children, etc.)
   Is the Women's Program familiar with issues confronting battered lesbians? (dangers of using the "system," closeting, etc.)
   Are all services prepared to include battered lesbians? (support group, intervention program, legal advocates, etc.)

6. Has the issue of lesbian battering been integrated into the program on an ongoing basis? (One or two trainings will not remove barriers or fix the problem.)

Source: Written by Lisa Vecoli for the Minnesota Coalition for Battered Women, Lesbian Battering Intervention Project; printed in Elliott 1990, pp. 73–74.

expressed the desire for counselors to focus therapy sessions on these goals. Importantly, however, respondents emphasized that counselors should not treat their low self-esteem as a cause of their battering but, rather, as a result of it. Lenore Walker's (1979:239) suggestions with respect to counseling battered heterosexual women are applicable here. Walker maintains that individual therapy with battered women should be more action-oriented than analytic. "The realities of present alternatives and future goal planning are

explored in individual therapy. The battered woman needs to recognize concrete steps she can take to improve her situation. . . . Intervention and collaboration with other helpers are important corollaries of individual psychotherapy." These methods will help the battered woman rebuild her self-esteem and recognize and constructively experience her feelings of anger.

Closely related to this were the two other responses participants most would have appreciated from counselors—specifically, for counselors to identify their experiences as battering and for them not to lay blame for the abuse on those who were victimized. Like shelter staff, counselors must not minimize the abuse because it was inflicted by a woman, nor deflect attention away from the abuse and onto the abused's "other problems." Battered lesbians, like battered heterosexual women, may also benefit from group therapy and support groups, but counselors should not assume that couples counseling is more appropriate for lesbian partners involved in abusive relationships than for heterosexual couples. As Lydia Walker (1986) has pointed out, why should counselors assume that lesbian batterers are less manipulative and more likely than men to control their violence? These are false assumptions.

This is not to say that treatment for batterers should be ignored. To the contrary, a focus of future research should be on identifying the unique treatment needs of lesbian batterers and developing treatment programs specifically for them. (The vast majority of treatment programs for batterers are male-centered, and men who batter women also tend to be overtly homophobic. Thus such programs would be inappropriate and probably ineffective for lesbian batterers.) If a lesbian victim presents herself for treatment, however, the counselor must keep in mind that she alone—not her partner, nor she and her partner as a couple—is the client. Couples counseling should only be attempted at the request of the victim. The model offered by Walker (1979:245–48) may be applicable to lesbian couples, if both therapists involved are lesbians. However, even if a battered lesbian requests couples counseling, it should be attempted only if her safety can be ensured, and she should be apprised of its low probability of success in abusive relationships.

As noted [by other researchers], the couples counseling approach is based on a family systems or codependency model that sees both partners sharing responsibility for the abusive nature of their relationship. Although it has, perhaps, intuitive appeal, the codependency model is inherently victim-blaming. It may be especially damaging when the woman who has been abused fought back or defended herself against the battering. Victims who have fought back or defended themselves, we have seen, typically experience guilt or shame over their use of violence. They often question whether they are truly victims or are batterers themselves. Counselors, like others, appear to apply the label "mutually abusive" too readily and uncritically to lesbian victims who come to them for help. Thus they reinforce rather than reverse the women's low self-esteem and perpetuate the myth that the abuse is at least partially their fault.

Counselors must learn to evaluate the dialectic nature of the abusive relationship and to distinguish between battering and self-defense (or fighting back). To do this, they, along with shelter staff and other advocates, must

first ask themselves some hard questions about their own acceptance of the myth of mutual battering (Walker 1986:76):

> Why are female batterers more "believable" when they blame their partner, why do workers see self-defense as "mutual battering" if the batterer is a woman, and why is it easier to believe that somehow a battered lesbian is part of the "violence problem" than to believe that a heterosexual woman is part of the "violence problem"? I challenge workers in the movement to think about how they would respond to a battered woman who says she provokes him or that she is as much to blame as him because she hits him first sometimes.

Relatives, Friends, and Community

The major barrier to relatives becoming viable sources of help for battered lesbians, as they are for battered heterosexual women, is their homophobia. However, it is probably more difficult to convince relatives to attend homophobia workshops than it is for any other group of help providers we have discussed here. Perhaps family members will be motivated by the fact that if they do confront and overcome their homophobia, they can effectively help their loved ones free themselves from abusive relationships: Recall our finding that the more helpful lesbian victims found their relatives to be, the sooner they ended the abusive relationship.

It is friends, though, especially friends in the lesbian community, from whom battered lesbians most often seek help. And it was to friends and the community that the majority of the study participants directed their suggestions for improving responses to lesbian victims.

The primary need expressed by lesbian victims is for their friends to allow them to confide in them. Thirty-two of the study participants wrote that they wanted their friends to lend emotional support, listen to them when they tried to make them aware of the problem, and reassure them that the abuse was not their fault. Twenty women said they wished their friends had named the violence "battering" instead of excusing or denying it. Fifteen women would have liked their friends to help them leave the relationship, either by offering physical assistance in moving or by verbally affirming their decision to end the relationship.

In short, friends and the community itself must recognize that battering is a problem among lesbian couples, and that its consequences are as serious as those of heterosexual battering—perhaps more serious, in fact, given that lesbians who are victimized are doubly stigmatized and have fewer sources of help available to them. Belief is essential, and like other help providers, friends and the community must not reflexively apply the label "mutual battering" simply because the partners involved are both women or because they know that the victim sometimes fought back. The words of the study participants, of course, convey these sentiments best:

> *Most helpful would have been the respect shown by believing that there actually was a problem—my friends brushed it off, didn't believe [she] was abusive, said it was a two-way street.*

To listen, believe, ask questions to gain understanding, but no "Why didn't you just do . . . ?" Offer practical help to get away. Encouragement to talk about it. No victim blaming. No judgmental crap about how my batterer is really my sister. Treat me as you would treat any woman who has been the victim of a violent crime.

Support, genuine understanding. My friends knew but tried to ignore it and suggested that I overlook her "moods" because "she's just that way."

Acknowledging that lesbian battering is a serious problem may indeed be unpleasant, even painful, for the lesbian community. But until such acknowledgment is made, until victims' needs are effectively and sensitively met, and until batterers are challenged and held accountable for their behavior, all lesbians are unsafe and the struggle for the creation of a peaceful, egalitarian community of women is violently betrayed.

ENDNOTES

[1] Others (see, e.g., Island and Letellier 1991 and Coleman 1990) have hypothesized that internalized homophobia may be an underlying factor in homosexual partner abuse either by motivating a partner to be violent or by increasing one's risk of victimization. Although I did not examine internalized homophobia in my study, the issue was the focus of much discussion at my meetings with the Working Group on Lesbian Battering. Certainly the phenomenon of internalized homophobia deserves attention in future studies of homosexual partner abuse. However, the problem of developing a reliable and valid measure of internalized homophobia—a problem perhaps more difficult to resolve than that of measuring partners' relative power in a relationship—confronts researchers who wish to explore this issue further.

[2] Eighty-nine participants responded to the questionnaire item, "Whether or not you sought help, please describe what response from others would have been most helpful to you." One woman wrote simply that she had gotten the help she needed. One felt that money/financial assistance would have been most helpful. And a third participant wrote, "Take my alcohol away." The majority of the women, however, responded with more than one answer.

[3] According to Fagan (1989), research on heterosexual domestic violence indicates that legal sanctions appear to be most effective in deterring batterers with brief and relatively nonsevere histories of abusive behavior. At the same time, however, Fagan notes that, for any legal sanctions to be effective, they cannot be weak. Weak legal interventions may reinforce violence simply by not adequately penalizing it.

[4] Two participants indicated that in addition to safe shelter space, they needed transportation. One suggested establishing an escort service that could be called upon at any time to transport victims to a safe space. Four women also requested hotline services, and four felt that a support group for battered lesbians would be helpful.

[5] Grover (1990:43) points out that children of battered lesbians who accompany their mothers to shelters must also have their privacy rights respected. "Children may be used as closeting for their mothers and themselves. They may not know who is safe to come out to and who is not. A conversation with mom about how her family typically handles this is essential."

REFERENCES

Bahr, S., C. B. Chappell, and A. Marcos. 1987. "An Evaluation of a Trial Mediation Programme." *Mediation Quarterly* (Winter):37–52.

Coleman, V. E. 1990. "Violence between Lesbian Couples: A Between Groups Comparison." Ph.D. dissertation. University Microfilms International (9109022).

Elliott, P. 1990. "Introduction." In *Confronting Lesbian Battering*, edited by P. Elliott. St. Paul: Minnesota Coalition for Battered Women.

Ellis, D. 1988. "Marital Conflict Mediation and Post-Separation Wife-Abuse." Presented at the annual meeting of the American Society of Criminology, Chicago, November.

Fagan, J. 1989. "Cessation of Family Violence: Deterrence and Discussion." Pp. 377–425 in *Family Violence,* edited by L. Ohlin and M. Tonry. Chicago: University of Chicago Press.

Felstiner, W. and L. Williams. 1978. "Mediation as an Alternative to Criminal Prosecution: Ideology and Limitations." *Law and Human Behavior* 2:221–39.

Folberg, J. and A. Taylor. 1984. *Mediation.* San Francisco: Jossey-Bass.

Geraci, L. 1986. "Making Shelters Safe for Lesbians." Pp. 77–79 in *Naming the Violence,* edited by K. Lobel. Seattle, WA: Seal.

Grover, J. 1990. "Children from Violent Lesbian Homes." Pp. 42–43 in *Confronting Lesbian Battering,* edited by P. Elliott. St. Paul: Minnesota Coalition for Battered Women.

Guth, J. and P. Elliott, eds. 1991. *Confronting Homophobia.* St. Paul: Minnesota Coalition for Battered Women.

Irvine, J. 1990. "Lesbian Battering: The Search for Shelter." Pp. 25–30 in *Confronting Lesbian Battering,* edited by P. Elliott. St. Paul: Minnesota Coalition for Battered Women.

Island, D. and P. Letellier. 1991. *Men Who Beat the Men Who Love Them.* New York: Harrington Park.

Ojeda-Zapata, J. 1990. "Battering No. 1 Lesbian Problem." *St. Paul Pioneer Press-Dispatch,* October 21. (Located in *Newsbank* [microform], Social Relations, 1990, 72:D3-5, fiche.)

Pharr, S. 1986. "Two Workshops on Homophobia." Pp. 202–22 in *Naming the Violence,* edited by K. Lobel. Seattle, WA: Seal.

Porat, N. 1986. "Support Groups for Battered Lesbians." Pp. 80–87 in *Naming the Violence,* edited by K. Lobel. Seattle, WA: Seal.

Walker, L. 1986. "Battered Women's Shelters and Work with Battered Lesbians." Pp. 73–76 in *Naming the Violence,* edited by K. Lobel. Seattle, WA: Seal.

Walker, L. E. 1979. *The Battered Woman.* New York: Harper & Row.

44

ABUSE OF ELDERS

OLA BARNETT • CINDY L. MILLER-PERRIN
• ROBIN D. PERRIN

Case History: Jenny and Jeff Jr.—Dwindling Assets, Dwindling Devotion

Several years after my husband's death, my mother-in-law, Jenny, who was 91, became unable to care for herself. She went to live with my brother-in-law, Jeff Jr., and his wife, Marianne. Although my own aging mother was dying, I took time to visit Jenny, who had always been a loving mother-in-law.

Over the next year, Jeff Jr. became Jenny's guardian, and she made out a new will giving one-third of her estate to each of us—myself, Jeff Jr., and Marianne. I didn't understand this sudden change from the previous division of half for each son, but I said nothing; after all, I was a widowed daughter-in-law. As Jenny continued to deteriorate, I asked Jeff Jr. if he was planning to put Jenny in a retirement home where she would receive

around-the-clock care. He said he couldn't afford to place her in a home and that he and Marianne would care for her at home. I was amazed. Jeff Jr. had sold Jenny's home for a probable yield of $150,000 in cash. Jeff Jr. and Marianne owned a mini-estate as well as stocks and bonds; they were probably worth $2 million.

I was puzzled by what was going on with Jenny and Jeff Jr., but then I became seriously concerned when I heard a number of rumors from Jenny's other relatives and friends. They said that Jeff Jr. and Marianne had offered financial advice to several aging relatives. Each had changed his or her will to name Jeff Jr. and Marianne the beneficiaries, and each had died shortly thereafter of neglect and malnutrition.

Over the next few months, I became alarmed when Jenny "refused to come to the phone" to speak to me. Marianne told me that "Jenny couldn't walk far enough to get to the phone." After 2 weeks, I drove several hours to visit her. I was appalled when I arrived. There was Jenny, sitting alone in a hot room that smelled like urine. She would not speak to me. She was in the maid's quarters, with no television and no phone. She was dirty and unkempt. There were no diapers in the room, the small refrigerator held only a piece of moldy bologna, and Jenny had not taken her medications. Later, when I expressed my concern to Jeff Jr., he said that he was going to hire a couple to come in and take care of her. I left feeling some sense of relief that Jenny's ordeal would soon be over.

A week later, I received a call from the caretaker couple. Frightened by Jenny's condition when they arrived to care for her, they had called the paramedics, who took Jenny to the hospital, and then they called me. Doctors diagnosed Jenny's condition as malnutrition, dehydration, and "neglect." The caretakers said that Jeff Jr. and Marianne had gone on a vacation, leaving no money for food or diapers, no instructions, no telephone numbers or itinerary—not even any information about when they would return. Finally, I felt compelled to call the county adult protective services (APS) agency. Someone there promised to visit the premises and soon did so. I also called some other relatives, who started making unscheduled visits to see Jenny.

Jeff Jr. and Marianne continue to take unexpected vacations to visit other aging relatives who may "need financial management services in the near future." I fear that Jeff Jr. and Marianne hope to come home someday to find that Jenny has simply "passed away in her sleep." I am constantly uneasy about Jenny's situation. I frequently call APS to see if they can do something more, and I keep "popping in" to check up on Jenny when Jeff Jr. and Marianne are away from home.

Jenny, by all accounts, is doing better now. She is clean and has food in the refrigerator. The caretakers drop in every day briefly and bring in food and diapers on their own. Jenny is still alone most of the time, and she seems too frightened to say much. As Jenny's life is slowly ending, I feel that my life is "on hold." I wish I knew for sure that everything that can be done to protect Jenny is being done. It's in God's hands now.

Violence against elders has been a perpetual feature of American social history. As with other forms of family violence, however, there has been an ebb and flow in the visibility and invisibility of elder abuse. During the 1980s, violence against elders received heightened consideration, especially violence perpetrated by informal caretakers, such as relatives (Social Services Inspectorate 1992). The year 2002 brought international attention to elder abuse through the work of the World Health Organization (cited in Cook-Daniels 2003; Nelson 2002). Only recently, however, has elder abuse attracted scholarly examination at all consonant with other subfields of family violence. As a result, there is a surprising dearth of methodologically sound research on violence against elders.

Any type of problem afflicting the elderly, of course, is likely to multiply with the rapid increase of elderly in the population. According to the U.S. Bureau of the Census (2000), in 2000 there were almost 35 million elderly (65+ years of age) in the United States, 12.4% of the total population. This figure is apt to rise through at least the first few decades of the twenty-first century, as the post–World War II baby boom generation ages.

Changes in economic conditions, families and family mobility, women's roles, and traditional methods of elder care appear to have contributed to increasing rates of elder abuse (see Kosberg and Garcia 1995; Kwan 1995). One dilemma is that in American society there are no clear norms or moral rules about who is responsible for elder care (Phillipson 1993). Adult children are not legally required to help elderly parents in need. Moreover, many elders are childless, homosexual elders in particular (Cahill and Smith 2002). Because of this lack of moral and legal standards concerning responsibility for the elderly, it is difficult to know who society should hold accountable for their care or neglect. This ambiguity places the elderly in an especially vulnerable position.

Further complicating matters is the fact that even in cases of interpersonal violence involving elderly persons, it is often not clear who is the victim and who is the perpetrator. Indeed, some violence in which elders are involved can be categorized as mutual violence (e.g., Phillipson 1992). Elders may strike out at their caregivers, for instance, in reaction to the loss of personal freedom they feel when the caregivers find it necessary to curtail the elders' behavior (e.g., when the caregiver will not let the elder leave the house alone) (Meddaugh 1990). Taken together, these problems have generated a literature on elder abuse that lacks coherence and precision. In sum, the nascency of research on elder abuse leaves numerous gaps in current knowledge, thus creating a large number of uncertainties. . . .

Scope of the Problem

If an elderly father wishes to wear a food-stained jacket, are his offspring-caregivers supposed to enforce some sort of cleanliness standard to avoid being neglectful? What can a caregiver do if an elder decides to drink too

much alcohol or otherwise act foolishly? What if an adult son decides to let his increasingly dependent father fend for himself? Is the son an abuser?

What Is Elder Abuse?

Arguably, the debate about what constitutes family violence is more pronounced in the area of elder abuse than in other subfields. State legislatures and various professional groups (e.g., in the fields of medicine and social work) all define elder abuse dissimilarly. In addition to definitional questions, additional challenges have arisen. To define elder abuse, one must, for example, specify the meanings of *elder* (i.e., age requirements), *dependency*, and *self-neglect*. The Joint Commission on Accreditation of Healthcare Organizations (JCAHO 2002) suggests defining an elder as someone 60 years of age or older. Congress also favors age 60 (Stiegel 2003).

Sexual Abuse   Direct forms of sexual abuse of elders encompass intercourse, molestation, sexualized kissing, oral/genital contact, and digital penetration. Indirect forms of sexual abuse include unwanted sexual discussions, exhibitionism, forced viewing of pornography, and exposed masturbation (see Ramsey-Klawsnik 1991). A surprising newer type of sex abuse has come to light in the form of pornographic Web sites that display older victims who were too mentally incapacitated to give consent. These sites offer still photographs of elderly women posed in every conceivable sexual activity. Viewers can also play short video clips of elderly women engaged in sexual activities. These media materials are classified as pornography, but laws regarding the use of older women hinge on the adults' ability to consent. Police officers who are specially trained in child and elder sexual abuse investigate these cases (Calkins 2003).

Financial Abuse   Financial abuse of elders consists of a number of behaviors: (a) misusing a durable power of attorney, bank account, or guardianship; (b) failing to compensate transfers of real estate; (c) charging excessive amounts for goods and services delivered to an elder; (d) using undue influence to gain control of an elder's money or property; and (e) predatory lending, Internet, telemarketing, or other frauds (Sweeney 2003).

Taxonomies of Elder Abuse   Boudreau (1993) distinguishes five broad categories of abuse most frequently cited in the literature: physical, psychological, financial/material, unsatisfactory living arrangement (e.g., unclean home), and violation of individual or constitutional rights. Although experts concur that physical violence constitutes abuse, they disagree over whether some behaviors, such as "violation of constitutional rights," are abuse. At what point, for example, do a caregiver's actions become a violation of an elder's constitutional rights? Does a daughter who makes her elderly mother wear a bib at dinner violate the mother's constitutional rights?

In creating a more widely acknowledged classification system, Hudson (1991) solicited opinions from 63 professionals in diverse specialties such as law, medicine, psychology, public health, and social work. Over three successive rounds of decision making, these experts attempted to reach consensus about

the appropriateness of certain theoretical definitions of elder abuse. Representative of one series of judgments, participants categorized mistreatment into two major classes (elder abuse and elder neglect) with two modes of intent (unintentional and intentional). Each round resulted in greater and greater specificity with more and more subdefinitions. The final taxonomy consists of four forms of elder abuse: physical, social, psychological, and financial. With one exception, senior adults in a follow-up study agreed with the experts' definitions. Leaders in the field believe that some forms of abuse (e.g., yelling) must occur several times to reach the level of abuse, whereas the interviewed elders believed even one such occurrence is abusive (Hudson et al. 2000). It is important to acknowledge that elders find disrespect a very painful type of abuse, although it is not included in these taxonomies (Cook-Daniels 2003). Note that the taxonomy excludes self-neglect and does not list sexual abuse separately. Insertion of sexual abuse into the physical abuse category may be unfortunate, because sexual abuse represents a distinctive form of elder abuse. Table 1 presents the taxonomy of elder abuse developed by Hudson et al. (2000).

Gay, Lesbian, Bisexual, and Transgendered Elders Although dating violence and intimate partner violence (IPV) among younger gay, lesbian, bisexual, and transgendered (GLBT) persons have gained some recognition, older GLBT individuals often go unidentified and unassisted by medical and mental health personnel. Both **heterosexism** (denigration of non-heterosexual behavior) and **homophobia** (fear or hatred of homosexual orientation) plague GLBT elders. An abusive caregiver, as one example, can threaten to "out" a gay elder if the gay elder will not comply with the caregiver's demands (see Cahill and Smith 2002).

Elder Abuse among Minorities Some racial-ethnic groups have distinctive views about elder abuse (Hudson et al. 2000). Korean Americans, for example, traditionally participate in a type of co-ownership of elder parents' financial assets, an arrangement that many African Americans and Whites consider a form of financial exploitation. Another cultural difference is that Korean Americans judge it inappropriate to tell outsiders "family business"; thus they do not report elder abuse at a rate comparable to either African Americans or Whites (Moon and Benton 2000). Korean Americans are also especially likely to blame elder victims for their own abuse (Moon and Benton 2000). Interestingly, as Asian immigrants' children become Americanized, they are beginning to change the habit of keeping aging parents at home and are putting them in assisted living centers (Kershaw 2003). A survey of 2,702 White, African American, and Hispanic female victims in Illinois found some differences among types of abuse experienced. In particular, about four times as many Hispanic women and three times as many White women reported sexual abuse as did African American women (Grossman and Lundy 2003). . . .

Prevalence of Abuse

The rates of elder abuse in Australia, Canada, Great Britain, and Norway appear to be roughly similar to estimated rates in the United States (Kurrle and Sadler 1993; Ogg and Bennett 1992; Podnieks 1992). The estimated

TABLE 1   Theoretical Definitions of Elder Mistreatment and Abuse by Delphi Panel of Elder Mistreatment Experts

Level I	
Elder mistreatment	Destructive behavior that is directed toward an older adult; occurs within the context of a relationship connoting trust; and is of sufficient intensity and/or frequency to produce harmful physical, psychological, social, and/or financial effects of unnecessary suffering, injury, pain, loss, and/or violation of human rights and poorer quality of life for the older adult
Personal/social relationship	Persons in close personal relationships with an older adult connoting trust and some socially established behavioral norms, for example, relatives by blood or marriage, friends, neighbors, any "significant other"
Professional/business relationship	Persons in a formal relationship with an older adult that denotes trust and expected services, for example, physicians, nurses, social workers, nursing aides, bankers, lawyers, nursing home staff, home health personnel, and landlords
Level II	
Elder abuse	Aggressive or invasive behavior/action(s), or threats of same, inflicted on an older adult and resulting in harmful effects for the older adult
Elder neglect	The failure of a responsible party(ies) to act so as to provide, or to provide what is prudently deemed adequate and reasonable assistance that is available and warranted to ensure that the older adult's basic physical, psychological, social, and financial needs are met, resulting in harmful effects for the older adult
Level III	
Intentional	Abusive or neglectful behavior or acts that are carried out for the purpose of harming, deceiving, coercing, or controlling the older adult so as to produce gain for the perpetrator (often labeled *active* abuse/neglect in the literature)
Unintentional	Abusive or neglectful behavior or acts that are carried out, but *not* for the purpose of harming, deceiving, coercing, or controlling the older adult, so as to produce gain for the perpetrator (often labeled *passive* abuse/ neglect in the literature)
Level IV	
Physical	Behavior(s)/actions in which physical force(s) is used to inflict the abuse; or available and warranted physical assistance is not provided, resulting in neglect

Psychological	Behavior(s)/action(s) in which verbal force is used to inflict the abuse; or available and warranted psychological/emotional assistance/support is not provided, resulting in neglect
Social	Behavior(s)/action(s) that prevents the basic social needs of an older adult from being met; or failure to provide available and warranted means by which an older adult's basic social needs can be met
Financial	Theft or misuse of an older adult's funds or property; or failure to provide available and warranted means by which an older adult's basic material needs can be met

Source: "Elder Mistreatment: A Taxonomy with Definitions by Delphi," by M. F. Hudson, 1991, *Journal of Elder Abuse and Neglect,* 3 (2): 14. Copyright 1991 by Margaret F. Hudson. Reprinted with permission.

proportion of Finnish elders seeking shelter from abuse is 3% to 6% (cited in Kivela 1995). In Greece, the estimate for physical abuse is quite high, 15% (Pitsiou-Darrough and Spinellis 1995). A recent survey of 355 elderly Chinese in Hong Kong revealed a 2% rate for physical abuse and a 20.8% rate for verbal abuse (Yan and Tang 2001). In another study, 18% of 4,000 elderly Japanese reported knowing of an elder victim (Tsukada, Saito, and Tatara 2001). A survey of older women ($M = 75$ years) in Ireland, Italy, and the United Kingdom suggested the elder abuse rate was approximately 20% (Ockleford et al. 2003).

In most foreign countries, elders receive support and care through informal care systems (i.e., family) rather than through formal institutions (e.g., nursing homes). In Finland there are no government programs of any sort for elder care (cited in Kivela 1995), and in Australia there are no adult protective services (Dunn 1995). In Israel, only 15% of dependent elderly receive help from public authorities; the rest rely on informal sources (Lowenstein 1995). In Greece, elder abuse is "just one more problem," and victims must wait their turn for help from social agencies (Johns and Hydle 1995). European support services are only marginally involved in assisting elder abuse victims. Less than a third of victims report receiving any assistance, and agencies fail to collect data on elder victims who seek assistance (Ockleford et al. 2003).

Laws regarding elder abuse vary throughout the world. In contrast to the United States, many countries assign responsibility for elder care to adult children. In India, all financially able children are legally responsible for parental care (Shah, Veedon, and Vasi 1995). In Finland, however, as many as 20% of elders have no children or family of any sort to offer support (or abuse) (cited in Kivela 1995). In Ireland, refusing to provide necessities of life to any child or any aged or sick person is a misdemeanor (Horkan 1995). Israel has no special legal provisions for elders, but they are protected under a general Protection of Helpless Persons law (Lowenstein 1995). As of 1994, South Africa had no laws dealing with elder abuse (Eckely and Vilakazi 1995). . . .

Because elder abuse is particularly underrecognized and underreported, prevalence estimates are complicated. Unlike children, who usually go out of the house at least to attend school, elders who live alone and seldom leave their homes are practically invisible. Although similar to other intimate violence victims in not reporting all of their mistreatment, elders are more likely than younger victims to report crimes (Klaus 2000). The National Elder Abuse Incidence Study (NEAIS), based on APS data, showed that reports of elder abuse rose significantly over the period from 1986 to 1996. Apparently, elder abuse is not as hidden as it once was (National Center on Elder Abuse [NCEA] 1998).

Nonetheless, the NEAIS found more than five times as many unreported cases as reported cases. Some elements of reluctance to report are mental incapability, nonrecognition of abuse, fear of others' disbelief, stigma, and fear of loss of independence (Stiegel 2001). By contrast, increased reporting rates are associated with lower SES [socioeconomic status] of elders, more community training of area professionals, and higher agency service rating scores (Wolf and Donglin 1999). . . .

Official Estimates   The U.S. Bureau of Justice Statistics recently disseminated analyses of criminal victimization of persons age 65 and older averaged over the years 1992–1997. Although the research was somewhat limited by government-specified samples and methodology, statistician Patsy A. Klaus (2000) provided a large number of core findings about elder abuse. She established that, compared with younger persons, elders suffer a much smaller proportion of violent crimes, including murders—about one-tenth as many as younger people.

Klaus used the FBI's *Supplementary Homicide Reports (SHR)* to estimate murder rates. One unexpected factor related to eldercide is that a number of "gray murders," unrecognized murders of elderly people, have occurred. An obstacle in grappling with this issue is the low autopsy rate for elder deaths, less than 1% in recent years. Attending physicians, not pathologists, determine cause of death for most seniors, and research has found a discordance rate of 44% between physicians' and pathologists' determinations of cause of death (Burton, as cited in Soos 2000).

Annual homicide rates averaged over the years 1992–1997 from *SHR* analyses revealed gender and racial differences. Elder males were perpetrators of homicide at a rate twice as great as females. Blacks were overrepresented as murder victims and perpetrators. Males also committed the majority of homicide-suicides occurring at age 55+ years (Cohen, Llorente, and Eisendorfer 1998). Dawson and Langan (1994) found in a study for the U.S. Bureau of Justice Statistics that sons and daughters commit only 11% of all homicides of victims age 60+ years. Of these patricides and matricides, sons kill fathers (53%) about as often as they kill mothers (47%), but daughters kill fathers (81%) much more often than they kill mothers (19%). . . .

In a survey conducted in 2000 under the auspices of the National Association of Adult Protective Services Administrators, Teaster (2003) amassed reports on elder/adult abuse from state APS agencies. The number of

elder/adult abuse reports received by APS associations reached 472,813. In states that responded, APS investigated 396,398 reports, and APS workers confirmed 166,019 cases. Data from 40 states indicated that 41.9% of the unsubstantiated reports were for self-neglect, 20.1% were for physical abuse, and 13.2% were for caregiver neglect/abandonment. The amount of financial abuse of the elderly is unknown, but may affect 10.5% to 49.3% of abused elders (NCEA 1998; Teaster 2003).

Self-Report Estimates   Recognizing the need for more generalizable and inclusive data, Pillemer and Finkelhor (1988) conducted telephone interviews with 2,020 Boston area residents age 65 and older. They estimated prevalence rates of three different kinds of elder abuse: physical, psychological, and neglect. They did not, however, assess financial abuse. Using a modified version of the Conflict Tactics Scale (CTS1; Straus 1979), they defined physical abuse as any violent act (e.g., pushed, grabbed, shoved, beat up) committed by a caregiver (spouse, child, or other coresident) since the respondent had turned 65. They defined neglect as withholding assistance with daily living (e.g., meal preparation, housework) 10 or more times in the preceding year. Finally, they designated psychological abuse as "chronic verbal aggression" (e.g., insulted, swore at, threatened) occurring more than 10 times a year.

Of 2,020 elders interviewed, 63 (3.2%) reported being abused. Specifically, 2% reported being physically abused, 1.1% reported being psychologically abused, and 0.4% reported being neglected (in the past year) (Pillemer and Finkelhor 1988). From these figures, the researchers estimated that 701,000–1,093,560 elders were abuse victims each year in the United States. Findings of the NEAIS indicated that the number of older people abused annually was much smaller, 450,000 (NCEA 1998). The sampling procedure for the NEAIS, however, garnered extensive criticism (e.g., Cook-Daniels 1999; Otto and Quinn 1999). A group of studies pinpointed the level of any elder abuse as falling between 19.1% and 59.4% (cited in Brandl and Cook-Daniels 2002). . . .

As expected, nearly all elderly sexual assault victims are women and nearly all perpetrators are men. In a small study, Mouton, Rovi, Furniss, and Lasser (1999) found that husbands were guilty of forcing sex among 7% of older women. These older women had been battered throughout their lifetimes. A large percentage (80%) of sexual assault victims in a nursing home study were impaired. These women were in wheelchairs, were bedridden, or had dementia.

Injury Estimates   Injury estimates arise from both official and self-report data. The latest official numerical summary from the National Electronic Injury Surveillance System–All Injury Program provides the most comprehensive and reliable data concerning injuries of elders seeking treatment at hospital emergency departments ("Public Health" 2003). This program furnishes national, annualized, weighted estimates of nonfatal, nonsexual, physical assaults categorized by intent. During 2001, roughly 33,026 elders received treatment in emergency departments (rate = 72/100,000). The majority of elders treated were men (55.4%). Primary injuries were as

follows: (a) contusion/abrasion, 31.9%; (b) laceration, 21.1%; and (c) fracture, 12.7%. The primary sources of injury were assaults as follows: (a) by body part, 20.3%; (b) blunt object, 17.1%; (c) push, 14.4%; and (d) undetermined, 31.8%. Perpetrators were most likely to be family members or acquaintances.

The 1992–1997 NCVS analysis of self-report data revealed that elders sustained 36,290 injuries annually. Relatives/intimates injured 41%, and others known to the victims caused 59% of injuries (Klaus 2000). A different account indicates that genital injuries are exceptionally common among older sexual assault victims (age 55+) relative to younger assault victims (ages 18–54). Of the 53 women making up the older group in this study sample, 27 sustained genital injuries compared with 7 injuries among the 53 women in the younger group (Muram, Miller, and Cutler 1992). Another outcome for abused elders is a greater likelihood of death compared with nonabused elders, even though cause of death may not be directly traceable to injuries or ill health (Lachs et al. 1998). . . .

Searching for Patterns: Who Is Abused and Who Are the Abusers?

Elder abuse researchers have tried to classify types of elders who may be especially vulnerable to abuse and types of individuals who are most apt to abuse elders. They have examined issues of family relationship, gender, age, and race, as well as mental health and alcohol abuse. Kosberg and Nahmiash (1996) have developed a conceptual framework for categorizing characteristics of victims and abusers that includes the following factors: living arrangements, gender, SES, health, age, psychological factors, problem behaviors, dependence, isolation, financial problems, family violence, and lack of social support. Given definitional, sampling, and methodological limitations of available research, social scientists accept identified patterns as preliminary in nature.

Characteristics of Abused Elders

Research on elder abuse has revealed few consistent differences, if any, between victims and nonvictims. In their review of the literature, Brandl and Cook-Daniels (2002) were unable to uncover any standard victim profile. Compared with members of all other age and ethnic groups, an elderly White female is the least likely person to sustain a violent victimization (Klaus 2000). Chu's (2001) analysis of elder homicides revealed that risk factors for victimization are gender (male) and race (African American).

The American Bar Association's Commission on Legal Problems of the Elderly has outlined some risk factors, screening techniques, and remedies relevant to financial abuse of elders. Risk factors appear to be abuser dependency on elder or elder dependency on abuser, elder's physical frailty or impairment, social isolation, and substance abuse or psychiatric conditions of either abuser or elder victim (Stiegel 2001).

Age   Because not all researchers and organizations define the status of elder victims in the same way, the victim characteristic of age is difficult to pin down. Some state APS agencies typically serve all adults, without regard to age, whereas others serve only elders, defined as persons 60 or 65 years of age. The fastest-growing group of elders in the United States today is made up of individuals 80 years old and older, and these elders are targets of abuse and neglect significantly more often than others (NCEA 1998).

Gender   The data available concerning gender are somewhat contradictory. APS reports for the 2000 survey revealed that, of substantiated cases, more than half of elder abuse victims (56.0%) were female (Teaster 2003). In contrast, data from an older Boston self-report community survey indicated that more than half of the victims in that sample were male (52%). Even more important, the Boston study suggests that the victimization rate for men (5.1%) is double that for women (2.5%). One explanation for this finding is that 65% of the respondents were women. Equivalent numbers of male and female victims suggest that risk of victimization is greater for men (Pillemer and Finkelhor 1988). Chu's (2001) analysis of *SHR* data points to more intimate partner homicide victimization of males than of females. Of course, a large number of offender–victim relationships of murder victims are unknown.

Socioeconomic Status and Race   Some studies have found no racial disparities in rates of elder abuse (e.g., Pillemer and Finkelhor 1988), whereas others have (e.g., Klaus 2000). One investigation of the relationship between SES and elder abuse revealed that poor elders in the United States are no more likely to be abused than middle-class elders (Boudreau 1993). Another appraisal found that retired elders are at no greater risk than those still working (Bachman and Pillemer 1991). One team of researchers has suggested that members of various racial/ethnic groups may differ more in the behaviors they view as abusive than in actual frequency of abusive behaviors experienced (Moon and Williams 1993).

   Hudson and Carlson (1999) found the following abuse rates among 924 North Carolinians age 40+ years: African Americans, 9.2%; Whites, 7.7%; and Native Americans, 4.3%. One appraisal of 597 agency cases revealed that European Americans (Whites) were more likely to suffer from self-neglect, African Americans from neglect by others, and both races equally from physical or financial abuse (Longres 1992).

Other Factors   Studies suggest that there may be some relationship between living arrangements and elder abuse. Several researchers have found that significant numbers of abused elders live in the same homes as their abusers (e.g., Lachs et al. 1997; Vladescu et al. 1999). In a study of three model projects, staff rated "changes in living arrangements" as the most effective intervention strategy and "changes in the circumstances of the perpetrator" as the least effective. Of 266 cases for which data on resolutions were available, more than one-third judged the problem as "completely" resolved and another third believed that "some progress" in resolution had been made.

Victim receptivity to intervention was a key variable in successful resolution, and perpetrator lack of receptivity was pivotal in unresolved cases (Wolf and Pillemer 1989).

If elders become more isolated, however, they may become easier prey to other kinds of abuses, such as financial exploitation. Living arrangements possibly affect the likelihood of victimization in regard to gender. If elderly men are more likely to be living with someone, their rate of abuse may increase while women's decreases (see Paveza et al. 1992; Pillemer and Finkelhor 1988). An apparent ecological risk factor for elder abuse is the rate of reported child abuse in a community. Presumably, factors that affect child abuse rates, such as community resources and differing characteristics of caseworkers, may account for this correlation (Jogerst et al. 2000).

Older IPV victims often do not leave their abusers. A recent study identified three major reasons why abused elder women stay with their abusers: (a) pragmatic concerns, such as economic insufficiency; (b) belief systems common to their generation and inadequate societal assistance; and (c) aging and health issues (Zink et al. 2003). Because their plight is seldom recognized by professionals, they receive little assistance toward leaving. In addition, few shelter programs nationwide are prepared to meet the needs of older battered women (see AARP 1994; Boudreau 1993; McFall 2000; Vinton 1998; Vinton, Altholz, and Lobell 1997). Shelter eligibility requirements may restrict entry to IPV victims, so that elders victimized by adult children and grandchildren are not admitted. . . .

Characteristics of Elder Abusers

There are so many noncontinuities among research results that a high degree of uncertainty exists about the typical characteristics of elder/adult abusers. Customary risk factors for elder homicide perpetrators are gender (male) and race (African American) (Chu 2001). One might think, however, that women would be the most likely abusers because they provide most informal family caregiving for elders (Arber and Ginn 1999). Several variables may be descriptive of a subset of elder abusers: (a) cognitive impairments or mental illnesses (Collins and O'Connor 2000); (b) financial dependency on the abused elder (e.g., Bendik 1992); (c) substance abuse problems, arrest records, and poor employment records (see Greenberg, McKibben, and Raymond 1990); and (d) social isolation (Bendik 1992).

Age   With only 10 states reporting on this topic, the 2000 APS survey mentioned above determined ages of elder abuse perpetrators as follows: (a) under 18 years, 5.9%; (b) 18 to 35, 18.4%; (c) 36 to 50, 24.8%; (d) 51 to 65, 10.4%; (d) 65 +, 8.9%; and (e) not reported, 31.6% (Teaster 2003). Many abusive caretakers in Pillemer and Finkelhor's (1988) community survey were over age 50 (75%), and some were over 70 (20%). Abusers who are elders themselves may suffer from dementia or other problems that render them less able to care for dependent elders and more likely to abuse those elders. Although some neglect by such elders may be conscious and premeditated,

some may result from ignorance or incompetence. Accounting for intentionality of abuse in such cases is another important issue (Glendenning 1993).

Gender Even though women usually shoulder the major burden of elder care (Deitch 1993), they seem not to be the primary elder abusers. With only 17 states responding, the 2000 APS survey ascertained that with the exception of neglect, most abusers were male (52%) and a third (33%) were females, with the gender of the remainder (15%) unknown (Teaster 2003). A number of studies have found sons to be more abusive than daughters toward elderly parents (e.g., Crichton et al. 1998; Wolf and Pillemer 1997). One study, however, found opposite results when neglect was included as a category of abuse (Anetzberger 1998; Dunlop et al. 2000).

Relationship to Victim There has been considerable discussion about which group of family members or others is most likely to abuse elders/adults. Family members consist of spouses, parents, children, grandchildren, siblings, and other relatives. Many empirical data show that adult children are the primary offenders (e.g., Brownell, Berman, and Salamone 1999; Vladescu et al. 1999). The NEAIS-2000 survey of APS agencies, for instance, indicated that adult children are the largest category of abusers, 39% to 80% (NCEA 1998).

In contrast, several other comparisons have indicated that elder abuse is primarily "spouse abuse grown old," an extension of IPV into old age (Harris 1996). Several international evaluations have also found data congruent with the spouse abuse thesis. Grossman and Lundy (2003), for example, found notable discrepancies in accounts of victim–offender relationships arising from different service agencies. Although agencies serving domestic violence victims reported that husbands or ex-husbands perpetrated the largest proportion of abuse, APS organizations reported that adult children committed most of the abuse. In reality, available data cannot settle this debate with certitude. With so much ambiguity about definitions and types of reporters, not to mention underreporting biases and large gaps in data caused by non-responding organizations, there is much room for error.

Data from the APS 2000 survey, with 25 states reporting, indicated that the majority of confirmed elder/adult abusers (61.7%) were family members (Teaster 2003). Of family perpetrators, 30.2% were spouses or intimate partners, and 17.6% were adult children. Institutional staff committed 4.4% of abuses. A Canadian investigation of 128 elders 60+ years for whom services had been requested uncovered the following rates for abusers: spouse, 48%; adult child, 30%; and acquaintance, 22% (Lithwick et al. 1999). Although most of the abuse (87%) was psychological, spouses did perpetrate most physical abuse (31%).

In an examination of 1,855 substantiated elder abuse and neglect cases from January 1993 through June 1993, the Los Angeles County Department of Community and Senior Citizen Services (1994) determined that 66% of the suspected abusers were family members (35% offspring, 18% other relationships, and 14% spouses). Other suspects were care custodians (12%), no relationship (14%), unknown (4%), and health practitioners (3%).

Lithwick et al. (1999) ascertained that adult children carried out substantially more financial abuse (59%) and neglect (49%) than did spouses (financial abuse, 13%; neglect, 23%). Acquaintances, however, perpetrated the highest amount of financial abuse (75%), but less neglect (30%) and physical abuse (7%). In a small study of 28 cases of elder sexual assault, incestuous assaults were most frequent. These included 11 adult sons, 1 grandson, and 2 brothers. Spouses were perpetrators in 7 cases. The remainder were 1 boyfriend, 2 boarders, 1 friend, 1 distant relative, and 2 unrelated caretakers (Ramsey-Klawsnik 1991). . . .

Public Attitudes toward Abuse of Elders

Some members of society may have attitudes condoning violence against elders (Yan and Tang 2003). Emblematic of this problem is the concept of postmaturity, the idea that elders are living too long. Some believe that older people have had their "day in the sun" and now should just "fade away" (Ansello 1996). Kosberg and Garcia (1995) have formulated a list of six viewpoints that promote elder abuse: ageism, sexism, proviolence attitudes, reactions to abuse, negative attitudes toward people with disabilities, and family caregiving imperatives. When caregivers hold such attitudes, they are likely to miss signs of elder abuse (Fulmer et al. 1999).

Attitudes held by some members of the current elder cohort also have the effect of hiding abuse. Several anecdotal or qualitative reports have indicated that older women may feel humiliated to admit being abused by a family member. In fact, most abused elder women . . . do not seek help from anyone (Brandl et al. 2003; J. Mears 2003). The elderly women served by agencies tend to believe such mottos as "What goes on at home stays at home." They also have a strong ethic about "not being a burden" on their children. Such attitudes pose a challenge to agency personnel who wish to reach out to and help abused elders. In listening to older women's opinions, personnel at Project REACH in Maine learned to avoid using stigmatizing terms such as *domestic violence* and *battered woman* when placing advertisements about support groups. Using a trial-and-error procedure, they fashioned ads that used terminology suitable for attracting needy and isolated older women. They found that ads referring to the "concerns of older women," for example, were more palatable to their target audience than ads that mentioned the "abuse of older women" (see Brandl et al. 2003; London 2003; J. Mears 2003).

Various popular media tend to perpetuate stereotypes of older people, depicting them as primarily supportive of children and grandchildren or as cranky and laughable. The entertainment media include relatively few depictions of elders who lead rewarding lives (see London 2003). Although there is no adequate research on the topic, it probably is true that most Americans find it inappropriate for elders to be sexually active. Some nursing homes make it possible for elder residents to have privacy for sexual activities by providing door locks and keys, but others make such activities impossible by allowing residents no privacy.

Section Summary

Experts have advanced several theories to explain elder abuse. Learning theory accentuates the notion of the acquisition of abusive behaviors during childhood and their manifestation in adulthood, with the elder parent as victim. So little research has been conducted, however, that it is too early to evaluate this explanation.

Social exchange theory, as applied to elder abuse, posits that just as aging parents (or spouses) need more and more care, they are less and less able to offer rewards or benefits to those who care for them. This imbalance implies that caring for an elder "doesn't pay," so a caretaker might just as well neglect the elder. Social interactionism is related to social exchange theory but depends on elder abuse perpetrators' perceptions of an imbalance in the exchange.

A common theme in explanations of elder abuse is the situational stress of the caregiver. This model assumes that the dependency of an elder, brought about by impairments, raises the "costs" of elder care but not the benefits to the caregiver. Presumably, dependent elders' needs create such powerful feelings of stress in their caregivers that the caregivers may lose control and abuse the elders. For many middle-aged adult children caring for aging parents, the stress generated by this responsibility potentiates the stress from caring for their own children. Although most studies indicate little relationship between physical health indicators and abuse, a few have found that an elder's physical dependency clearly plays a role in vulnerability to abuse. Certainly, one might surmise that impairments of disabled persons make them vulnerable to abuse.

The individual differences (psychopathology of the abuser) theory presumes that elder abuse most likely results from the deviance and dependency of abusers. A large body of evidence demonstrates that perpetrators do tend to have far-ranging problems, such as alcohol abuse and emotional difficulties. The psychological status of abusers, in fact, may be a better predictor of elder abuse than characteristics of victims.

Given that all of these theories have limitations, it may be necessary to identify a configuration of related factors or to integrate theories. Situational stress, for example, in combination with particular personality types, might set the stage for elder mistreatment. Public attitudes toward elders, GLBT persons, and the disabled contribute to their abuse by intimates, acquaintances, and the entire health care system.

REFERENCES

AARP [American Association of Retired Persons]. 1994. "Survey of Services for Older Battered Women." Unpublished manuscript, Washington, DC.

Anetzberger, G. J. 1998. "Psychological Abuse and Neglect: A Cross-Cultural Concern to Older Americans." Pp. 141–51 in *Understanding and Combating Elder Abuse in Minority Communities,* edited by Archstone Foundation. Long Beach, CA: Archstone Foundation.

Ansello, E. F. 1996. "Understanding the Problem." Pp. 9–29 in *Abuse, Neglect, and Exploitation of Older Persons: Strategies for Assessment and Intervention,* edited by L. A. Baumhover and S. C. Beall. Baltimore: Health Professions Press.

Arber, S. and J. Ginn. 1999. "Gender Differences in Informal Caring." Pp. 321–39 in *The Sociology of the Family: A Reader,* edited by G. Allan. Oxford: Blackwell.

Bachman, R. and K. A. Pillemer. 1991. "Retirement: Does It Affect Marital Conflict and Violence?" *Journal of Elder Abuse and Neglect* 3 (2): 75–88.

Bendik, M. F. 1992. "Reaching the Breaking Point: Dangers of Mistreatment in Elder Caregiving Situations." *Journal of Elder Abuse and Neglect* 4 (3): 39–59.

Boudreau, F. A. 1993. "Elder Abuse." Pp. 142–58 in *Family Violence: Prevention and Treatment,* edited by R. L. Hampton, T. P. Gullotta, G. R. Adams, E. H. Potter III, and R. P. Weissberg. Newbury Park, CA: Sage.

Brandl, B. and L. Cook-Daniels. 2002. *Domestic Abuse in Later Life.* Washington, DC: National Resource Center on Domestic Violence.

Brandl, B., M. Herbert, J. Rozwadowski, and D. Spangler. 2003. "Feeling Safe, Feeling Strong: Support Groups for Older Abused Women." *Violence against Women* 9:1490–1503.

Brownell, P., J. Berman, and A. Salamone. 1999. "Mental Health and Criminal Justice Issues among Perpetrators of Elder Abuse." *Journal of Elder Abuse and Neglect* 11 (4): 81–94.

Cahill, S. and K. Smith. 2002. "Policy Issues Affecting Lesbian, Gay, Bisexual, and Transgender People in Retirement." *Generations* 26 (2): 49–54.

Calkins, P. 2003, July/August. "Cross-Discipline Gains in Indiana." *Victimization of the Elderly and Disabled* 6:17–18, 30.

Chu, L. D. 2001. "Homicide and Factors That Determine Fatality from Assault in the Elderly Population." UMI No. 3032861. *Dissertation Abstracts International* 62 (11): 5063B.

Cohen, D., M. Llorente, and C. Eisendorfer. 1998. "Homicide/Suicide in Older Persons." *American Journal of Psychiatry* 155:390–96.

Collins, P. G. and A. O'Connor. 2000. "Rape and Sexual Assault of the Elderly: An Exploratory Study of Ten Cases Referred to the Irish Forensic Psychiatry Service." *Irish Journal of Psychological Medicine* 17:128–31.

Cook-Daniels, L. 1999, May/June. "Interpreting the National Elder Abuse Incidence Study." *Victimization of the Elderly and Disabled* 2:1–2.

———. 2003, January/February. "2003 Is the Year Elder Abuse Hits the International Stage." *Victimization of the Elderly and Disabled* 5:65–66, 76.

Crichton, S. J., J. B. Bond, Jr., C. D. H. Harvey, and J. Ristok. 1998. "Elder Abuse: Feminist and Ageist Perspectives." *Journal of Elder Abuse and Neglect* 10 (3/4): 115–30.

Dawson, J. M. and P. A. Langan. 1994. *Murder in Families.* NCJ Publication No. 143498. Annapolis Junction, MD: U.S. Bureau of Justice Statistics.

Deitch, I. 1993, August. "Alone, Abandoned, Assaulted: Prevention and Intervention of Elder Abuse." Presented at the annual meeting of the American Psychological Association, Toronto.

Dunlop, B. D., M. B. Rothman, K. M. Condon, K. S. Hebert, and I. L. Martinez. 2000. "Elder Abuse: Risk Factors and Use of Case Data to Improve Policy and Practice." *Journal of Elder Abuse and Neglect* 12 (3/4): 95–122.

Dunn, P. F. 1995. "'Elder Abuse' as an Innovation to Australia: A Critical Overview." Pp. 13–30 in *Elder Abuse: International and Cross-Cultural Perspectives,* edited by J. I. Kosberg and J. L. Garcia. Binghamton, NY: Haworth.

Eckely, S. C. A. and P. A. C. Vilakazi. 1995. "Elder Abuse in South Africa." Pp. 171–82 in *Elder Abuse: International and Cross-Cultural Perspectives.* Binghamton, NY: Haworth.

Fulmer, T. T., M. Ramirez, S. Fairchild, D. Holmes, M. J. Koren, and J. Teresi. 1999. "Prevalence of Elder Mistreatment as Reported by Social Workers in a Probability Sample of Adult Day Health Care Clients." *Journal of Elder Abuse and Neglect* 11 (3): 25–36.

Glendenning, F. 1993. "What Is Elder Abuse and Neglect?" Pp. 1–34 in *The Mistreatment of Elderly People,* edited by P. Decalmer and F. Glendenning. London: Sage.

Greenberg, J. R., M. McKibben, and J. A. Raymond. 1990. "Dependent Adult Children and Elder Abuse." *Journal of Elder Abuse and Neglect* 2 (1/2): 73–86.

Grossman, S. E. and M. Lundy. 2003. "Use of Domestic Violence Services across Race and Ethnicity by Women Aged Fifty-Five and Older." *Violence against Women* 9:1442–52.

Harris, S. B. 1996. "For Better or for Worse: Spouse Abuse Grown Old." *Journal of Elder Abuse and Neglect* 8 (1): 1–33.

Horkan, E. M. 1995. "Elder Abuse in the Republic of Ireland." Pp. 119–37 in *Elder Abuse: International and Cross-Cultural Perspectives.* Binghamton, NY: Haworth.

Hudson, M. F. 1991. "Elder Mistreatment: A Taxonomy with Definitions by Delphi." *Journal of Elder Abuse and Neglect* 3 (2): 1–20.

Hudson, M. F., C. Beasley, R. H. Benedict, J. R. Carlson, B. F. Craig, and S. C. Mason. 2000. "Elder Abuse: Some Caucasian-American Views." *Journal of Elder Abuse and Neglect* 12 (1): 89–114.

Hudson, M. F. and J. R. Carlson. 1999. "Elder Abuse: Its Meaning to Caucasians, African Americans, and Native Americans." Pp. 187–204 in *Understanding Elder Abuse in Minority Populations,* edited by T. Tatara. Washington, DC: Taylor and Francis.

JCAHO [Joint Commission on Accreditation of Healthcare Organizations]. 2002. *How to Recognize Abuse and Neglect.* Oakbrook Terrace, IL: Author.

Jogerst, G. J., J. D. Dawson, A. J. Hartz, J. W. Ely, and L. A. Schweitzer. 2000. "Community Characteristics Associated with Elder Abuse." *Journal of the American Geriatric Society* 48:513–18.

Johns, S. and I. Hydle. 1995. "Norway: Weakness in Welfare." Pp. 139–56 in *Elder Abuse: International and Cross-Cultural Perspectives,* edited by J. I. Kosberg and J. L. Garcia. Binghamton, NY: Haworth.

Kershaw, S. 2003. "Elder Care Americanized." *Los Angeles Daily News,* October 20, p. 12.

Kivela, S. L. 1995. "Elder Abuse in Finland." Pp. 31–44 in *Elder Abuse: International and Cross-Cultural Perspectives,* edited by J. I. Kosberg and J. L. Garcia. Binghamton, NY: Haworth.

Klaus, P. A. 2000. *Crimes against Persons Age Sixty-Five or Older, 1992–97.* NCJ Publication No. 176352. Washington, DC: U.S. Department of Justice. Retrieved December 8, 2003 (http://www.ojp.usdoj.gov/bjs/pub/pdf/cpa6597.pdf).

Kosberg, J. I. and J. L. Garcia. 1995. "Introduction to the Book." Pp. 1–12 in *Elder Abuse: International and Cross-Cultural Perspectives,* edited by J. I. Kosberg and J. L. Garcia. Binghamton, NY: Haworth.

Kosberg, J. I. and D. Nahmiash. 1996. "Characteristics of Victims and Perpetrators and Milieus of Abuse and Neglect." Pp. 31–49 in *Abuse, Neglect, and Exploitation of Older Persons: Strategies of Assessment and Intervention,* edited by L. A. Baumhover and S. C. Beall. Baltimore: Health Professions Press.

Kurrle, S. E. and P. M. Sadler. 1993. "Australian Service Providers: Responses to Elder Abuse." *Journal of Elder Abuse and Neglect* 5 (1): 57–76.

Kwan, A. Y. 1995. "Elder Abuse in Hong Kong." Pp. 65–80 in *Elder Abuse: International and Cross-Cultural Perspectives,* edited by J. I. Kosberg and J. L. Garcia. Binghamton, NY: Haworth.

Lachs, M. S., C. Williams, S. O'Brien, L. Hurst, and R. Horwitz. 1997. "Risk Factors for Reported Elder Abuse and Neglect: A Nine-Year Observational Cohort Study." *Gerontologist* 37:469–74.

Lachs, M. S., C. Williams, S. O'Brien, K. A. Pillemer, and M. Charlson. 1998. "The Mortality of Elder Mistreatment." *Journal of the American Medical Association* 280:428–32.

Lithwick, M., M. Beaulieu, S. Gravel, and S. M. Straka. 1999. "The Mistreatment of Older Adults: Perpetrator–Victim Relationships and Interventions." *Journal of Elder Abuse and Neglect* 11 (4): 95–112.

London, M. 2003, May/June. "Crafting Support Services for Older Women." *Victimization of the Elderly and Disabled* 6:5–6.

Longres, J. F. 1992. "Race and Type of Maltreatment in an Elder Abuse System." *Journal of Elder Abuse and Neglect* 4 (3): 61–83.

Los Angeles County Department of Community and Senior Citizen Services. 1994. *Abuse by Others: 1/93 through 6/93.* Los Angeles: Author.

Lowenstein, A. 1995. "Elder Abuse in a Forming Society: Israel." Pp. 81–100 in *Elder Abuse: International and Cross-Cultural Perspectives,* edited by J. I. Kosberg and J. L. Garcia. Binghamton, NY: Haworth.

McFall, C. 2000, March/April. "Rainbow Services: A New Beginning for Older Battered Women." *Victimization of the Elderly and Disabled* 2:86.

Mears, J. 2003. "Survival Is Not Enough: Violence against Older Women in Australia." *Violence against Women* 9:1478–89.

Meddaugh, D. I. 1990. "Reactance: Understanding Aggressive Behavior in Long-Term Care." *Journal of Psychosocial Nursing and Mental Health Services* 28 (4): 28–33.

Moon, A. and D. Benton. 2000. "Tolerance of Elder Abuse and Attitudes toward Third-Party African American, Korean American, and White Elderly." *Journal of Multicultural Social Work* 8:283–303.

Moon, A. and O. J. Williams. 1993. "Perceptions of Elder Abuse and Help-Seeking Patterns among African American, Caucasian American, and Korean American Elderly Women." *Gerontologist* 33:386–95.

Mouton, C., S. Rovi, K. Furniss, and N. Lasser. 1999. "The Association between Health and Domestic Violence in Older Women: Results of a Pilot." *Journal of Women's Health and Gender-Based Medicine* 9:1173–79.

Muram, D., K. Miller, and A. Cutler. 1992. "Sexual Assault of the Elderly Victim." *Journal of Interpersonal Violence* 7:70–76.

National Center on Elder Abuse [NCEA]. 1998. *The National Elder Abuse Incidence Study: Final Report.* Madison, WI: Author.

Nelson, D. 2002. "Violence against Elderly People: A Neglected Problem." *Lancet* 360:1094.

Ockleford, E., Y. Barnes-Holmes, R. Morichelli, A. Moriaria, F. Scocchera, F. Furniss, et al. 2003. "Mistreatment of Older Women in Three European Countries." *Violence against Women* 9:1453–64.

Ogg, J. and G. C. J. Bennett. 1992. "Elder Abuse in Britain." *British Medical Journal* 305:998–99.

Otto, J. M. and K. Quinn. 1999, January/February. "The National Elder Abuse Incidence Study: An Evaluation by the National Association of Adult Protective Services Administrators." *Victimization of the Elderly and Disabled* 2:4.

Paveza, G. J., D. Cohen, C. Eisdorfer, S. Freels, T. Semla, J. W. Ashford, et al. 1992. "Severe Family Violence and Alzheimer's Disease: Prevalence and Risk Factors." *Gerontologist* 32:493–97.

Phillipson, C. 1992. "Confronting Elder Abuse: Fact and Fiction." *Generations Review* 2:3.

———. 1993. "Abuse of Older People: Sociological Perspectives." Pp. 88–101 in *The Mistreatment of Elderly People,* edited by P. Decalmer and F. Glendenning. London: Sage.

Pillemer, K. A. and D. Finkelhor. 1988. "The Prevalence of Elder Abuse: A Random Sample Survey." *Gerontologist* 28:51–57.

Pitsiou-Darrough, E. N. and C. D. Spinellis. 1995. "Mistreatment of the Elderly in Greece." Pp. 45–64 in *Elderly Abuse: International and Cross-Cultural Perspectives,* edited by J. I. Kosberg and J. L. Garcia. Binghamton, NY: Haworth.

Podnieks, E. 1992. "National Survey on Abuse of the Elderly in Canada." *Journal of Elder Abuse and Neglect* 4 (5): 5–58.

"Public Health and Aging: Nonfatal Physical Assault Related Injuries among Persons Aged > 60 Years Treated in Hospital Emergency Departments—United States, 2001." 2003. *Morbidity and Mortality Weekly Report* 52:812–16.

Ramsey-Klawsnik, H. 1991. "Elder Sexual Abuse: Preliminary Findings." *Journal of Elder Abuse and Neglect* 3 (3): 73–90.

Shah, G., R. Veedon, and S. Vasi. 1995. "Elder Abuse in India." Pp. 101–18 in *Elder Abuse: International and Cross-Cultural Perspectives.* Binghamton, NY: Haworth.

Social Services Inspectorate. 1992. *Confronting Elder Abuse: An SSI London Region Survey.* London: Her Majesty's Stationery Office.

Soos, J. N., Sr. 2000, September/October. "Gray Murders: Undetected Homicides of the Elderly Plus One Year." *Victimization of the Elderly and Disabled* 3:33–34, 42.

Stiegel, L. A. 2001. *Financial Abuse of the Elderly: Risk Factors, Screening Techniques, and Remedies.* Chicago: American Bar Association, Commission on Legal Problems of the Elderly. Retrieved December 8, 2003 (http://www.abanet.org/elderly/financial_abuse_of_the_elderly.doc).

———. 2003, July/August. "Washington Report." *Victimization of the Elderly and Disabled* 6:19–20.

Straus, M. A. 1979. "Measuring Intrafamily Conflict and Aggression: The Conflict Tactics Scale (CTS)." *Journal of Marriage and the Family* 41:75–88.

Sweeney, P. M. 2003, July/August. "Exploitation of Adults on the Internet." *Victimization of the Elderly and Disabled* 6:17, 29–30.

Teaster, P. B. 2003. *A Response to the Abuse of Vulnerable Adults: The 2000 Survey of State Adult Protective Services.* Washington, DC: National Center on Elder Abuse.

Tsukada, N., Y. Saito, and T. Tatara. 2001. "Japanese Older People's Perception of 'Elder Abuse.'" *Journal of Elder Abuse and Neglect* 13 (1): 71–89.

U.S. Bureau of the Census. 2000. *U.S. Population Estimates, by Age, Sex, Race, and Hispanic Origin.* Current Population Reports No. P25–1095. Retrieved December 8, 2003 (http://www.census.gov/population/estimates/nation/intfile2-1.txt).

Vinton, L. 1998. "A Nationwide Survey of Domestic Violence Shelters' Programming for Older Women." *Violence against Women* 4:559–71.

Vinton, L., J. A. Altholz, and T. Lobell. 1997. "A Five-Year Follow-Up Study of Domestic Violence Programming for Battered Older Women." *Journal of Women and Aging* 9:3–15.

Vladescu, D., K. Eveleigh, J. Ploeg, and C. Patterson. 1999. "An Evaluation of a Client-Centered Case Management Program for Elder Abuse." *Journal of Elder Abuse and Neglect* 11 (4): 5–22.

Wolf, R. S. and L. Donglin. 1999. "Factors Affecting the Rate of Elder Abuse Reporting to State Protective Services Programs." *Gerontologist* 39:222–28.

Wolf, R. S. and K. A. Pillemer. 1989. *Helping Elderly Victims: The Reality of Elder Abuse.* New York: Columbia University Press.

———. 1997. "The Older Battered Woman: Wives and Mothers Compared." *Journal of Mental Health and Aging* 3:325–36.

Yan, E. and C. S. Tang. 2001. "Prevalence of Psychological Impact of Elder Abuse." *Journal of Interpersonal Violence* 16:1158–74.

———. 2003. "Proclivity to Elder Abuse: A Community Study on Hong Kong Chinese." *Journal of Interpersonal Violence* 18:999–1017.

Zink, T., S. Regan, C. J. Jacobson Jr., and S. Pabst. 2003. "Cohort, Period, and Aging Effects: A Qualitative Study of Older Women's Reasons for Remaining in Abusive Relationships." *Violence against Women* 9:1429–41.

PART X

Families, Work, and Carework

45

THE WORK–HOME CRUNCH

KATHLEEN GERSON • JERRY A. JACOBS

More than a decade has passed since the release of *The Overworked American*, a prominent 1991 book about the decline in Americans' leisure time, and the work pace in the United States only seems to have increased. From sleep-deprived parents to professionals who believe they must put in long hours to succeed at the office, the demands of work are colliding with family responsibilities and placing a tremendous time squeeze on many Americans.

Yet beyond the apparent growth in the time that many Americans spend on the job lies a more complex story. While many Americans are working more than ever, many others are working less. What is more, finding a balance between work and other obligations seems increasingly elusive to many workers—whether or not they are actually putting in more time at work than workers in earlier generations. The increase in harried workers and hurried families is a problem that demands solutions. But before we can resolve this increasingly difficult time squeeze we must first understand its root causes.

Average Working Time and Beyond

"There aren't enough hours in the day" is an increasingly resonant refrain. To most observers, including many experts, the main culprit appears to be overwork—our jobs just take up too much of our time. Yet it is not clear that the average American is spending more time on the job. Although it may come as a surprise to those who feel overstressed, the average work week—that is, hours spent working for pay by the average employee—has hardly changed over the past 30 years. Census Bureau interviews show, for example, that the average male worked 43.5 hours a week in 1970 and 43.1 hours a week in 2000, while the average female worked 37.1 hours in 1970 and 37.0 hours in 2000.

Kathleen Gerson and Jerry A. Jacobs, "The Work–Home Crunch" from *Contexts* 3, no. 4 (Fall 2004): 29–37. Copyright © 2004 by the American Sociological Association. Reprinted with the permission of the authors and the University of California Press Journals.

Why, then, do more and more Americans feel so pressed for time? The answer is that averages can be misleading. Looking only at the average experience of American workers misses key parts of the story. From the perspective of individual workers, it turns out some Americans are working more than ever, while others are finding it harder to get as much work as they need or would like. To complicate matters further, American families are now more diverse than they were in the middle of the twentieth century, when male-breadwinner households predominated. Many more Americans now live in dual-earner or single-parent families where all the adults work.

These two trends—the growing split of the labor force and the transformation of family life—lie at the heart of the new time dilemmas facing an increasing number of Americans. But they have not affected all workers and all families in the same way. Instead, these changes have divided Americans into those who feel squeezed between their work and the rest of their life, and those who have more time away from work than they need or would like. No one trend fits both groups.

So, who are the time-squeezed, and how do they differ from those with fewer time pressures but who may also have less work than they may want or need? To distinguish and describe the two sets of Americans, we need to look at the experiences of both individual workers and whole families. A focus on workers shows that they are increasingly divided between those who put in very long work weeks and who are concentrated in the better-paying jobs, and those who put in comparatively short work weeks, who are more likely to have fewer educational credentials and are more likely to be concentrated in the lower-paying jobs.

But the experiences of individuals does not tell the whole story. When we shift our focus to the family, it becomes clear that time squeezes are linked to the total working hours of family members in households. For this reason, two-job families and single parents face heightened challenges. Moreover, women continue to assume the lion's share of home and child care responsibilities and are thus especially likely to be squeezed for time. Changes in jobs and changes in families are putting overworked Americans and underemployed Americans on distinct paths, are separating the two-earner and single-parent households from the more traditional households, and are creating different futures for parents (especially mothers) than for workers without children at home.

A Growing Divide in Individual Working Time

In 1970, almost half of all employed men and women reported working 40 hours a week. By 2000, just 2 in 5 worked these "average" hours. Instead, workers are now far more likely to put in either very long or fairly short work weeks. The share of working men putting in 50 hours or more rose from 21 percent in 1970 to almost 27 percent in 2000, while the share of working women putting in these long work weeks rose from 5 to 11 percent.

At the other end of the spectrum, more workers are also putting in shorter weeks. In 1970, for example, 5 percent of men were employed for 30 or fewer hours a week, while 9 percent worked these shortened weeks in 2000. The share of employed women spending 30 or fewer hours on the job also climbed from 16 percent to 20 percent (see Figure 1). In total, 13 million Americans in 2000 worked either shorter or longer work weeks than they would have if the 1970s pattern had continued.

These changes in working time are not evenly distributed across occupations. Instead, they are strongly related to the kinds of jobs people hold. Managers and professionals, as one might expect, tend to put in the longest work weeks. More than 1 in 3 men in this category now work 50 hours or more per week, compared to only 1 in 5 for men in other occupations. For women, 1 in 6 professionals and managers work these long weeks, compared to fewer than 1 in 14 for women in all other occupations. And because jobs are closely linked to education, the gap in working time between the college educated and those with fewer educational credentials has also grown since 1970.

Thus, time at work is growing most among those Americans who are most likely to read articles and buy books about overwork in America. They may not be typical, but they are indeed working more than their peers in earlier generations. If leisure time once signaled an elite lifestyle, that no longer appears to be the case. Working relatively few hours is now more likely to be concentrated among those with less education and less elite jobs.

Workers do not necessarily prefer these new schedules. On the contrary, when workers are asked about their ideal amount of time at work,

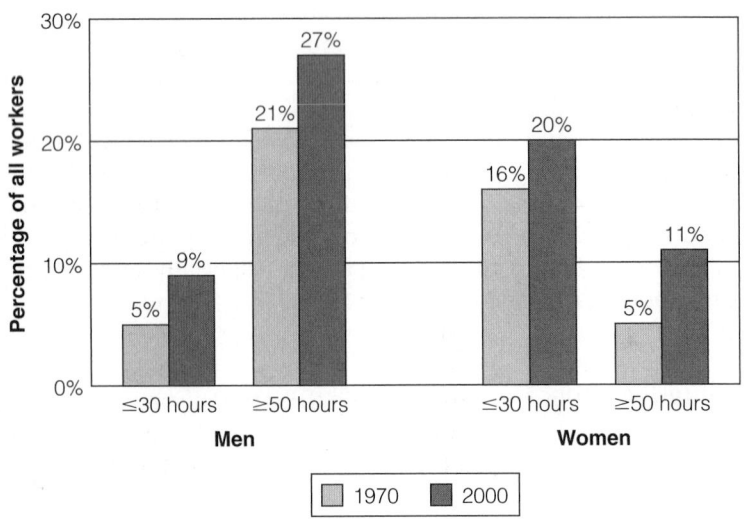

FIGURE 1   The Percentage of Men and Women Who Put in 30 or Fewer Hours and Who Put in 50 or More Hours a Week in 1970 and 2000

Source: March, 2000 Current Population Reports Surveys; nonfarm wage and salary workers.

a very different picture emerges. For example, in a 1997 survey of workers conducted by the Families and Work Institute, 60 percent of both men and women responded that they would like to work less while 19 percent of men and women said that they would like to work more. Most workers—both women and men—aspire to work between 30 and 40 hours per week. Men generally express a desire to work about 38 hours a week while women would like to work about 32 hours. The small difference in the ideal working time of men and women is less significant than the shared preferences among them. However, whether their jobs require very long or comparatively short work weeks, this shared ideal does stand in sharp contrast to their job realities. As some workers are pressured to put in more time at work and others less, finding the right balance between work and the rest of life has become increasingly elusive.

Overworked Individuals or Overworked Families?

Fundamental shifts in family life exacerbate this growing division between the over- and under-worked. While most analyses of working time focus on individual workers, time squeezes are typically experienced by families, not isolated individuals. A 60-hour work week for a father means something different depending on whether the mother stays at home or also works a 60-hour week. Even a 40-hour work week can seem too long if both members of a married couple are juggling job demands with family responsibilities. And when a family depends on a single parent, the conflicts between home and work can be even greater. Even if the length of the work week had not changed at all, the rise of families that depend on either two incomes or one parent would suffice to explain why Americans feel so pressed for time.

To understand how families experience time squeezes, we need to look at the combined working time of all family members. For example, how do married couples with two earners compare with those anchored by a sole, typically male, breadwinner? For all married couples, the work week has indeed increased from an average of about 53 hours in 1970 to 63 hours in 2000. Given that the average work week for individuals did not change, it may seem strange that the couples' family total grew so markedly. The explanation for this apparent paradox is both straightforward and crucial: married women are now far more likely to work. In 1970, half of all married-couple families had only male breadwinners. By 2000, this group had shrunk to one quarter (see Figure 2). In 1970, one-third of all married-couple families had two wage-earners, but three-fifths did in 2000. In fact, two-earner families are more common today than male-breadwinner families were 30 years ago.

Each type of family is also working a little more each week, but this change is relatively modest and certainly not large enough to account for the larger shift in total household working time. Two-earner families put in close to 82 working hours in 2000 compared with 78 hours in 1970.

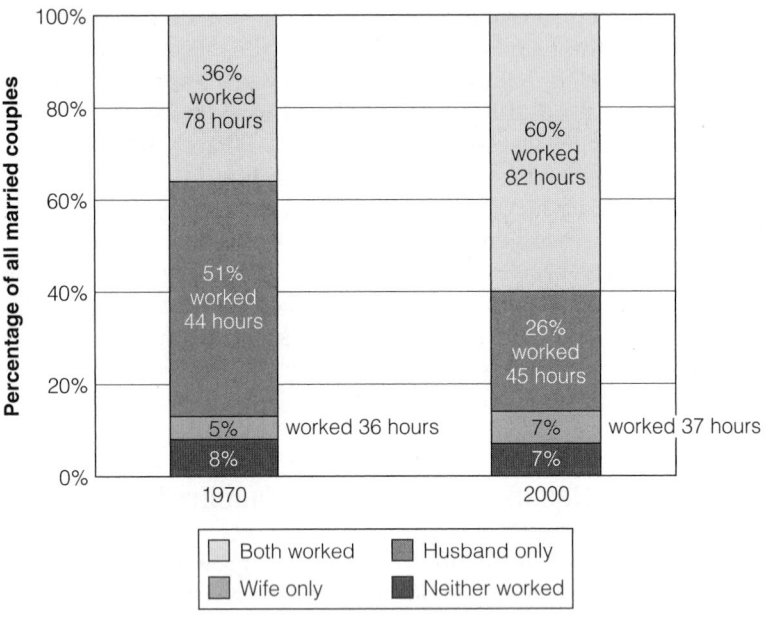

FIGURE 2   Total Hours of Work per Week for Married Couples, 1970 and 2000

Source: March, 2000 Current Population Reports Surveys; nonfarm married couples aged 18–64.

Male-breadwinner couples worked 44 hours on average in 1970 and 45 hours in 2000. The vast majority of the change in working time over the past 30 years can thus be traced to changes in the kinds of families we live in rather than to changes in how much we work. Two-earner couples work about as much today as they did 30 years ago, but there are many more of them because more wives are working.

Single parents, who are overwhelmingly mothers, are another group who are truly caught in a time squeeze. They need to work as much as possible to support their family, and they are less likely to be able to count on a partner's help in meeting their children's daily needs. Although these households are not displayed in Figure 2, Census Bureau data show that women headed one-fifth of all families in 2000, twice the share of female-headed households in 1970. Even though their average work week remained unchanged at 39 hours, the lack of childcare and other support services leaves them facing time squeezes at least as sharp. Single fathers remain a much smaller group, but their ranks have also grown rapidly. Single dads work almost as much as single moms—37 hours per week in 2000. Even though this represents a drop of two hours since 1970, single fathers face time dilemmas as great as those facing single mothers. Being a single parent has always posed daunting challenges, and now there are more mothers and fathers than ever in this situation.

At the heart of these shifts is American families' growing reliance on a woman's earnings—whether or not they depend on a man's earnings as well. Women's strengthened commitment to paid employment has provided more

economic resources to families and given couples more options for sharing the tasks of breadwinning and caretaking. Yet this revolution in women's work has not been complemented by an equal growth in the amount of time men spend away from the job or in the availability of organized childcare. This limited change at the workplace and in men's lives has intensified the time pressures facing women.

Dual-Earner Parents and Working Time

The expansion of working time is especially important for families with children, where work and family demands are most likely to conflict. Indeed, there is a persisting concern that in their desire for paid work, families with two earners are shortchanging their children in time and attention. A closer looks reveals that even though parents face increased time pressure, they cope with these dilemmas by cutting back on their combined joint working time when they have children at home. For example, U.S. Census data show that parents in two-income families worked 3.3 fewer hours per week than spouses in two-income families without children, a slightly wider difference than the 2.6 hours separating them in 1970. Working hours also decline as the number of children increases. Couples with one child under 18 jointly averaged 81 hours per week in 2000, while couples with three or more children averaged 78 hours. Rather than forsaking their children, employed parents are taking steps to adjust their work schedules to make more time for the rest of life.

However, it is mothers, not fathers, who are cutting back. Fathers actually work more hours when they have children at home, and their working hours increase with the number of children. Thus, the drop in joint working time among couples with children reflects less working time among mothers. Figure 3 shows that in 2000, mothers worked almost 4 fewer hours per week than married women without children. This gap is not substantially different than in 1970.

This pattern of mothers reducing their hours while fathers increase them creates a larger gender gap in work participation among couples with children compared to the gender gap for childless couples. However, these differences are much smaller than the once predominant pattern in which many women stopped working for pay altogether when they bore children. While the transition to raising children continues to have different consequences for women and men, the size of this difference is diminishing.

It is also important to remember that the rise in working time among couples is not concentrated among those with children at home. Though Americans continue to worry about the consequences for children when both parents go to work, the move toward more work involvement does not reflect neglect on the part of either mothers or fathers. On the contrary, employed mothers continue to spend less time at the workplace than their childless peers, while employed fathers today do not spend substantially more time at work than men who are not fathers.

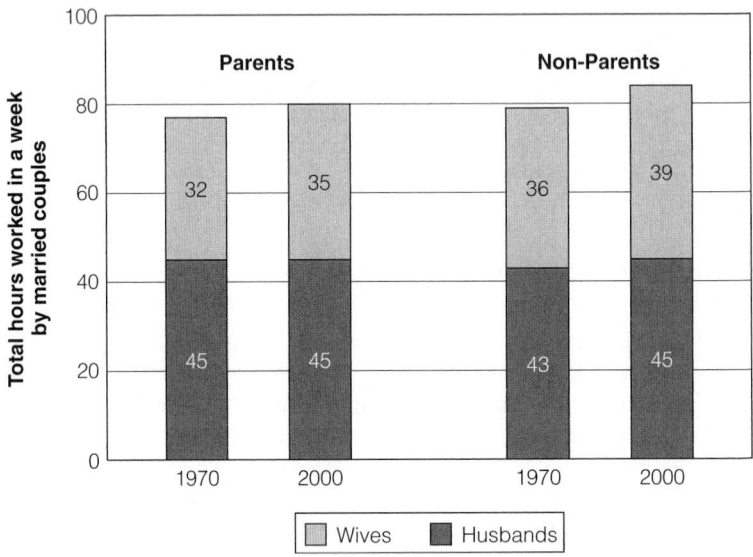

FIGURE 3 **Average Hours of Work per Week of Couples (parents and non-parents)**

Source: March, 2000 Current Population Reports Surveys; nonfarm married couples aged 18–64.

Solving the Time Pressure Puzzle

Even though changes in the average working time of American workers are modest, many American families have good reason to feel overworked and time-deprived. The last several decades have witnessed the emergence of a group of workers who face very long work weeks and live in families that depend on either two incomes or one parent. And while parents are putting in less time at work than their peers without children at home, they shoulder domestic responsibilities that leave them facing clashes between work demands and family needs.

The future of family well-being and gender equality will depend on developing policies to help workers resolve the time pressures created by the widespread and deeply rooted social changes discussed above. The first step toward developing effective policy responses requires accepting the social transformations that sent women into the workplace and left Americans wishing for a balance between work and family that is difficult to achieve. Unfortunately, these changes in the lives of women and men continue to evoke ambivalence.

For example, mothers continue to face strong pressures to devote intensive time and attention to child rearing. Indeed, generally they want to, despite the rising economic and social pressure to hold a paid job as well. Even though most contemporary mothers are counted on to help support their families financially, the United States has yet to develop the childcare services and flexible jobs that can help workers meet their families' needs. Whether or not mothers work outside the home, they face conflicting expectations that are difficult to meet. These social contradictions can be

seen in the political push to require poor, single mothers to work at a paid job while middle-class mothers continue to be chastised for spending too much time on their jobs and away from home.

To a lesser but still important extent, fathers also face intensifying and competing pressures. Despite American families' increasing reliance on women's earnings, men face significant barriers to family involvement. Resistance from employers and co-workers continues to greet individual fathers who would like to spend less time at work to care for their children. For all the concern and attention focused on employed mothers, social policies that would help bring men more fully into the work of parenting get limited notice or support. New time squeezes can thus be better understood by comparing the large changes in women's lives with the relative lack of changes in the situation for men. The family time bind is an unbalanced one.

Even as family time has become squeezed, workers are also contending with changes in the options and expectations they face at work. Competitive workplaces appear to be creating rising pressures for some workers, especially professionals and managers, to devote an excessive amount of time to their jobs, while not offering enough work to others. In contrast to these bifurcating options, American workers increasingly express a desire to balance the important work of earning a living and caring for a new generation.

Finding solutions to these new time dilemmas will depend on developing large scale policies that recognize and address the new needs of twenty-first-century workers and their families. As we suggest in our book, *The Time Divide*, these policies need to address the basic organization of American work and community institutions. This includes revising regulations on hours of work and providing benefit protections to more workers, moving toward the norm of a shorter work week, creating more family-supportive workplaces that offer both job flexibility and protections for employed parents, and developing a wider array of high-quality, affordable childcare options.

Extending protections, such as proportional benefits and overtime pay, to workers in a wider range of jobs and occupations would reduce the built-in incentives employers have to extract as much work as possible from professionals and managers while offering less work to other employees. If professionals and managers were given overtime pay for overtime work, which wage workers are now guaranteed under the Fair Labor Standards Act, the pressures on these employees to put in endless workdays might lessen. Yet, the Bush administration recently revised these rules to move more employees into the category of those ineligible for overtime pay. Similarly, if part-time workers were offered fringe benefits proportional to the hours they work (such as partial pensions), there would be fewer reasons for employers to create jobs with work weeks so short that they do not provide the economic security all families need.

Reducing the average work week to 35 hours would also reduce the pressures on workers and help them find a better work–family balance. While this goal may seem utopian, it is important to remember that the 40-hour standard also seemed unimaginably idealistic before it was adopted

in the early twentieth century. Other countries, most notably France, have adopted this standard without sacrificing economic well-being. A shorter work week still would allow for variation in work styles and commitments, but it would also create a new cultural standard that better reflects the needs and aspirations of most contemporary workers. It would also help single parents meet their dual obligations and allow couples to fashion greater equality in their work and caretaking responsibilities.

Time at work is clearly important, but it is not the whole story. The organization of the workplace and the structure of jobs also matters, especially for those whose jobs and occupations require intensive time at work. Among those putting in very long work weeks, we find that having job flexibility and autonomy helps ease the perceived strains and conflicts. The work environment, especially in the form of support from supervisors and co-workers, also makes a difference. In addition, we find that workers with access to such family-friendly options as flexible work schedules are likely to use them, while workers without such benefits would like to have them.

Flexibility and autonomy are useful only if workers feel able to use them. Women and men both express concern that making use of "family-friendly" policies, such as extended parental leaves or nonstandard working hours, may endanger their future work prospects. Social policies need to protect the rights of workers to be involved parents without incurring excessive penalties at the workplace. Most Americans spend a portion of their work lives simultaneously immersed in work for pay and in parenting. Providing greater flexibility at the workplace will help workers develop both short- and longer-term strategies for integrating work and family life. However, even basic changes in the organization of work will not suffice to meet the needs of twenty-first-century families. We also need to join the ranks of virtually all other industrialized nations by creating widely available, high-quality and affordable childcare. In a world where mothers and fathers are at the workplace to stay, we need an expanded network of support to care for the next generation of workers.

These changes will not be easy to achieve. But in one form or another, they have been effectively adopted in other societies throughout the modern world. While no one policy is a cure-all, taken together they offer a comprehensive approach for creating genuine resolutions to the time pressures that confront growing numbers of American workers and their families. Ultimately, these new time dilemmas cannot be resolved by chastising workers (and, most often, mothers) for working too much. Rather, the time has come to create more flexible, family-supportive, and gender-equal workplaces and communities that complement the twenty-first-century forms of work and family life.

RECOMMENDED RESOURCES

Bond, James T. 2003. *Highlights of the National Study of the Changing Workforce.* New York: Families and Work Institute. Bond reports findings from a major national survey of contemporary American workers, workplace conditions and work–family conflict.

Gornick, Janet and Marcia Meyers. 2003. *Families That Work: Policies for Reconciling Parenthood and Employment.* New York: Russell Sage Foundation. This important study compares family-supportive policies in Europe and the United States.

Hays, Sharon. 1997. *The Cultural Contradictions of Motherhood.* New Haven, CT: Yale University Press. Hays examines how American mothers continue to face pressure to practice intensive parenting even as they increase their commitment to paid work.

Heymann, Jody. 2000. *The Widening Gap: Why America's Working Families Are in Jeopardy and What Can Be Done about It.* New York: Basic Books. Drawing from a wide range of data, this study makes a compelling case for more flexible work structures.

Hochschild, Arlie Russell. 1997. *The Time Bind: When Home Becomes Work and Work Becomes Home.* New York: Metropolitan Books. This is a rich study of how employees in one company try to reconcile the tensions between spending time at work and caring for their families.

Jacobs, Jerry A. and Kathleen Gerson. 2004. *The Time Divide: Work, Family and Gender Inequality.* Cambridge, MA: Harvard University Press. An overview of trends in working time, our book shows why and how time pressures have emerged in America over the past three decades, how they are linked to gender inequality and family change, and what we can do to alleviate them.

Robinson, John P. and Geoffrey Godbey. 1999. *Time for Life: The Surprising Ways Americans Use Their Time.* University Park: Pennsylvania State University Press. Drawing on time diaries, Robinson and Godbey conclude that Americans' leisure time has increased.

Schor, Juliet. 1991. *The Overworked American: The Unexpected Decline of Leisure.* New York: Basic Books. This early and original analysis of how Americans are overworked sparked a national discussion on and concern for the problem.

46

FAST-TRACK WOMEN AND THE "CHOICE" TO STAY HOME

PAMELA STONE • MEG LOVEJOY

The phenomenon of women who leave professional careers to become so-called "stay-at-home moms" has generated considerable media attention and been the subject of numerous articles, editorials, on-air commentary (Stone 1998), and a best-selling novel, *I Don't Know How She Does It* (Pearson 2002). Recent high-profile examples include Bush administration staffers Karen Hughes and Victoria Clarke. Despite larger popular interest, there is little research on this phenomenon, a paucity noted by Ann Crittenden, author of *The Price of Motherhood* (2001), who characterized it as a "conspiracy of silence" borne of a "feminist and corporate taboo" (p. 30).

Whether or not Crittenden (2001) is correct in claiming a taboo, the specter of highly trained women who have made significant professional investments "stepping off the fast track" potentially undermines the arguments of feminist advocates for women's advancement and challenges the

rationale for, and/or effectiveness of, widely publicized corporate efforts to retain and promote women. Professional women's labor force departures to "stay home" are especially highly visible because many are still tokens in their fields and firms (Kanter 1977). When they quit, their actions can signal to supervisors and colleagues alike the perception that women are not committed to work, thereby setting in motion well-known processes of statistical discrimination.

The likelihood of deleterious stereotyping and ensuing discrimination is increased by what Joan Williams (2000) has called the "choice rhetoric" used to frame women's decisions to interrupt careers. Choice rhetoric attributes women's work status to their private and personal tastes and preferences and assumes that their decisions operate outside any system of constraints. A cover story in the *The New York Times Magazine* provides an especially vivid example of such an analysis. Titled "The Opt-Out Revolution," it asked "Why don't more women get to the top?" and answered "They choose not to" (Belkin 2003). In addition to Williams, a number of prominent analysts, including Susan Faludi (1991) and Rosalind Barnett (Barnett and Rivers 1996), have also challenged choice rhetoric, arguing that this portrayal of women's decisions about work and family is part of a broad backlash against feminism and gender egalitarianism.

Although the vast majority of women with professional degrees are working, they are out of the labor force at a rate roughly three times that of their male counterparts and overwhelmingly cite "family responsibilities" as the reason. In a 1993 national study of advanced-degree recipients ten years after graduation, 12.1 percent of women as compared to 4.0 percent of men in law were no longer in the labor force. Among MBAs, comparable figures were 7.8 versus 2.2 percent; and for those with an MD, the figures were 10.7 versus 3.7 percent (Baker 2002).

At the most elite echelons, there is anecdotal and accumulating evidence that these gender differentials may be even larger. Deloitte Touche, a leading professional services firm, for example, reported losing half the women in each incoming class during the five- to seven-year period from recruitment to partnership, a significantly higher rate than that seen for male recruits, until it took aggressive measures to stanch women's defections (McCracken 2000). Most of these women, moreover, were leaving the workforce, not the firm, findings echoed in studies of women graduates of leading business and professional schools. Swiss and Walker's (1993) study of the careers of women graduates of various Harvard professional schools found that about one-quarter were out of the labor force. The academy has long faced a "leaky pipeline" problem, with substantial numbers of women who have trained for scientific careers failing to pursue them (Preston 1994).

The costs of career interruption are significant (see Crittenden 2001 for an especially good summary of the research literature on this point). Individually, women bear them directly in the form of lost salary and blocked or slowed advancement. Cumulatively, interruptions account for as much as one-third of the gender gap in earnings and partly explain the relative absence of women in the upper reaches of most professions. The costs to

employers of replacing departing women professionals—high-priced talent in the so-called "talent wars"—are also considerable.

Married professional women, by virtue of the privileges their jobs confer as well as the demands they entail, are subject to numerous, competing pressures on their decision to quit jobs and exit the labor force. These pressures emanate from both the workplace (Jacobs and Gerson 1998) and from the home, where expectations about parenting are shaped by an ideology of intensive mothering (Hays 1996). The facile media depiction of these women's decisions as "choices" in favor of domesticity (Williams 2000) obscures our understanding of their actions and the complex decision making leading up to them. Nor does the limited information available from national surveys offer much insight. In this article, we seek to shed light on these issues by reporting the results of a qualitative study of professional women, married with children, who made the decision to quit their jobs and interrupt their careers—at least temporarily—by leaving the labor force. The goals of the article are threefold: (1) to develop a thematic analysis of the reasons behind professional women's decision to "go home" that is grounded in their experiences, (2) to explore the implications of our findings as they shed light on choice rhetoric, and (3) to inform the development of work–family (or as they are now more often called, work–life) policies and practices.

Data and Method

Study participants ($n = 43$) were women who were formally out of the labor force (neither at work nor actively looking for work) at the time of the interview. All were married, with at least one child younger than eighteen living at home, and all had formerly been employed in professional (which includes those in male-dominated professions such as law and medicine as well as female-dominated professions such as teaching) or managerial jobs. Participants resided in seven metropolitan areas throughout the United States and were recruited through referral or "snowball" sampling, primarily through alumnae networks of highly selective colleges. We confined the study to white women because cultural traditions vary significantly regarding work and family across different racial and ethnic groups.

Interviews were semistructured and conducted by the first author in the interviewee's home or a place of her choice and typically lasted about two hours. The interviews, which were audiotaped, explored women's work and family histories and elicited a detailed accounting of how and why these women made the decision to quit, including the work-family context in which this decision was made. To protect the identities of the women interviewed, we change their names and identifying information in the results presented here.

Women in the sample ranged in age from thirty-three to fifty-six, with a median age of forty-three. On average, they had worked thirteen years prior to dropping out and had been out of the labor force six years. Typically, they had two children, with just more than a third having preschoolers at

the time of interview. Across all women in the sample, the youngest child was three months and the oldest fourteen years. All but one woman in the sample had a college degree, and half had an advanced degree. Two-thirds worked in male-dominated fields such as law, business, medicine, or the sciences; approximately one-fifth worked in mixed or transitional fields such as publishing, public relations, and health and educational administration; and the remainder worked in traditionally female-dominated professions such as teaching. Their husbands also worked as professionals or managers, typically in law, medicine, or finance, or owned businesses. . . .

Results

In the rhetoric of choice often invoked to explain why successful professional women exit the workforce, women's decisions are largely seen as an expression of their unfettered individual preferences for home and hearth over career. Our findings largely contradict this view. Approximately 90 percent of women in our sample expressed a moderate to high degree of ambivalence about the decision to quit their jobs, and for many the decision was protracted and agonizing. Claire Lott, a manager at a public utilities company, took a leave of absence from her job before finally quitting, a period during which she vacillated constantly:

> *So at the end of that six months—I mean, it came down to literally the night before. What was again so hard was it was like a loss of identity. Ironically, that Sunday, after I made the decision, the sermon at church was "Loss of Identity because of Loss of Job or Loss of Spouse." That kind of clicked with me.*

Quitting to "go home" was weighed against women's solid sense of identification with their careers and the heavy investments they had made in them, which for many included not only extensive work experience but postgraduate education. Women also found it hard to leave their jobs because they took pride in their professional accomplishments and derived intrinsic pleasure from their work. Nancy Yearwood, senior editor at a publishing house, voiced the difficulty many women felt in making the decision and reflected on the variety of losses it entailed:

> *I would think about like well, "How could I do this?" I mean the financial was one aspect of it, but there are other aspects. Not to minimize that, but my whole identity was work. Yes, I was a mother and a wife and whatever, but this is who I was. And I would think like about the authors, and "Oh, my God, how can I leave this author?" And then the agents and these people I'd worked with for years and my books and the house and my colleagues. I mean just on and on and on. And I really thought long—I mean I just thought for a long time about it. And I would think like, "How could I do this?"*

For only five women (representing 16 percent of the sample) can the decision to step off the career track be viewed as a reflection of a relatively unconstrained choice or preference to become full-time, stay-at-home mothers.

Following Faludi (1991), we call these women "new traditionalists." Like the classic traditionalists, they give full-time mothering precedence over working; however, in contrast to their earlier counterparts, they had successful and even high-powered careers in fields such as publishing, marketing, banking, and health care before starting their families. Unlike most of the women studied, they indicated that they had always planned to become full-time mothers and experienced no indecision or ambivalence in making the decision to interrupt their careers, quit their jobs, or be at home with their children. Also, unlike many of the women studied (as we will report later in the context of reasons for quitting), they made no efforts to reduce their work hours or enhance schedule flexibility to maintain their careers.

The new traditionalists were further distinguished from the other women by the value that they, and often their husbands, placed on having a full-time mother in the home, seeing own-mother care as irreplaceable in their children's lives. They often rejected unequivocally any form of child care, especially in the early years of their child's development. Vita Cornwall, who quit her job as a nonprofit executive after the birth of her first child, exemplified this perspective:

> *The reason [I quit] is I want them to, for better or worse, interpret my values; our values, our moral system, speak in our cadence, with our grammatical errors or proper speech. I wanted them to be our children, and I don't think we would have been able to do that with me working full-time.*

As exceptions, the new traditionalists highlight the many constraints faced by the majority of women in our sample. Our analysis of women's reasons for interrupting their careers brings into focus the nature of these constraints and how they impinged on the women's "choice" to go home. The analysis revealed three major themes around which women's motivations for leaving the workforce revolved: (1) work, (2) children, and (3) husbands. Identification of major themes is based on both the frequency with which particular reasons were invoked and our assessment of the weight each one carried in the larger context of women's decision making. These themes are described below along with the processes by which they operated.

Work-Related Factors in the Decision to Quit

Work-related reasons were the most frequently cited reasons for quitting, figuring as important considerations for 86 percent of the sample. Managers and professionals are, paraphrasing Schor (1992), the most overworked Americans (Jacobs and Gerson 1998). The women in our study dwelled squarely in the world of sixty-hour workweeks and 24/7 accountability. The time bind (Hochschild 1997) was an almost taken-for-granted feature of their lives—and had been even before they had children. Typical was Nathalie Everett's description of the high-technology industry in which she had worked as a marketing manager: "The high-tech workweek is really sixty hours, not forty. Nobody works 9 to 5 anymore." Added to this, many women were employed in settings where the pace and expectations were

set by men with stay-at-home wives. Meg Romano, a trader at a large investment firm, was the only woman among a group of eleven men, men about whom she said, "Every single one, their wife stayed home . . . their wives handled everything."

The amount, pace, and inflexibility of work as well as the inadequacy of reduced-hour options led many women to quit. Economic restructuring played an important role in accelerating workplace demands but also operated in other ways to influence this outcome.

Workplace Inflexibility   Upon becoming mothers, about half of the women in our sample expressed a desire to cut back on their work hours and/or to increase the flexibility of their schedules. Their efforts met with mixed results, however, as almost one-third of the sample (and 62 percent of those who had actually gone part-time) cited workplace inflexibility as a major factor in their decision to interrupt their careers. Romano's experience is illustrative. Having worked both part- and full-time over a fifteen-year period with the same firm, she took a leave of absence to attend to her child's medical problem. Ready to return to work,

> I went back to talk to them about what was next, and a part-time situation presented itself in the sales area, and I got all gung-ho for that. I got all the child care arrangements in place, started interviewing people to watch the kids, and at the last minute the big boss wouldn't sign off on it. So I was like, "Alright, whatever."

Romano and others like her tried and failed, but a number who would have liked to work part-time or job share knew better than to ask. More than one-third characterized their work as "all or nothing" and viewed their options as being either working forty-plus hours per week or quitting. Maeve Turner, a federal attorney, said of workplace accommodation, "It just wasn't in their [her superiors'] realm of reality." Nancy Yearwood encountered the same phenomenon, as illustrated by her account of telling her boss that she was quitting her job in publishing after ten years with the firm:

> She was kind of shocked, and she said, "Is there anything [emphasis added] I can do to try to get you to stay?" I did bring up to her the fact that I thought about trying to get some kind of a part-time thing, but it's just not what they need. I know what they need. They need people who are there all the time, and working like dogs. And to work part-time in my business—I think you're going to end up working more than part-time. I wasn't willing to do that. I'd already been working time and a half. I raised it [part-time work] in this conversation, I guess, just to satisfy my curiousity about it. And she basically agreed with me.

Yearwood's belief that she would "end up working more than part-time" foreshadows the most frequent complaint among those who *were* able to arrange part-time work: for many, the nature of their jobs and the culture of their workplaces meant that they worked part-time in name only. Women spoke repeatedly about having full-time responsibilities on a part-time

schedule, of doing a "job and a half" when they were supposed to be doing half a job. Diane Childs, a nonprofit CFO, observed that "when you have young babies, they leave you alone for a while," but when the honeymoon period ended, she was asked to "take more responsibility, do more, manage more." Making it difficult to limit work hours was the fact that many of these women were the only ones in their immediate work environment who were working part-time. "[My colleagues were] putting in fifty to sixty hours a week and I was working thirty" was how Elena Toracelli, a management consultant, described her situation. Women's inability to limit their hours on a part-time schedule meant that they felt little relief from the spillover of work into their family lives. . . .

Mommy Tracking and the Maternal Wall Many of the women who worked part-time or job shared found themselves "mommy tracked," a career derailment that ultimately played a role in their decision to quit. Nancy Thomas, a marketing executive, used *Scarlet Letter*–like imagery to describe job sharing at her firm: "When you job share you have 'MOMMY' stamped in huge letters on your head." Reporting that "there were a dozen job sharers in the company and none were ever promoted," she recounted with triumph how she had finally succeeded in getting a promotion after a four-year campaign—a promotion, she observed somewhat incredulously, that "the chairman of the board of a six-thousand-person company had to approve."

Childs, the nonprofit executive, described the long-term prospects of continuing to work part-time, which eventually discouraged her from doing so:

> *And I'm never going to get anywhere—you have the feeling that you just plateaued professionally because you can't take on the extra projects; you can't travel at a moment's notice; you can't stay late; you're not flexible on the Friday thing because that could mean finding someone to take your kids. You really plateau for a much longer period of time than you ever realize when you first have a baby. It's like you're going to be plateaued for thirteen to fifteen years.*

Women were not only concerned about the loss of extrinsic rewards associated with the move to part-time but also bemoaned the loss of intrinsically interesting and engaging work. Toracelli, the management consultant, returned from maternity leave to a twenty-hour-a-week schedule, discovering when she did so that "I lost the vast majority of my interesting responsibilities and was really left with the more mundane modeling responsibilities that I wasn't nearly as interested in." Many felt marginalized. Paula Trottier, a marketing executive, described how her status and authority had been eroded when she went part-time, despite having considerable seniority, and how this played directly into her decision:

> *So I decided to quit, and this was a really, really big deal . . . because I never envisioned myself not working. I just felt like I would become a nobody if I quit. Well, I was sort of a nobody working too. So it was sort of, "Which nobody do you want to be?"*

Economic Restructuring   The women in our sample worked in fields such as finance, marketing, professional services, law, and technology. Since the 1970s, these fields have experienced both an influx of female professionals and an economic restructuring brought about by consolidation in mature industries (e.g., finance and publishing) and extraordinarily high rates of growth in newly emerging ones (e.g., biotechnology). Reflecting this, stories of reorganization, mergers, takeovers, and rapid expansion recurred throughout our interviews, figuring prominently in the career interruptions of just less than half (42 percent) of our sample.

Speedup and disruption. Restructuring influenced women's decisions in a number of ways, most importantly by creating tremendous turbulence and speedup in the work environment, which in turn disrupted the complicated and fragile articulation of work and family that women had been able to achieve. Consolidation and rapid growth dramatically increased the scope and demands of women's jobs. Nancy Taylor's experience as an executive with a company on an aggressive acquisition binge gives a flavor of what mergers meant for the people responsible for implementing them:

> *There are forty-nine hundred branches, fifteen thousand ATMs, and all of the myriad things associated with that—capital budget of maybe 260 million dollars, about seventy-five people. And only five of them were in [the same city]. And that's where everything got out of control. We were scattered to the four winds. What that meant was I was traveling. I had to travel before, but this was just on a scale like . . . [gesturing with her hands and making sounds to indicate a nuclear explosion].*

Women in high-growth industries such as biotechnology faced special challenges. Lynn Hamilton, an MD who was medical director of a start-up company, recalled continuously running fax machines and a grueling schedule of nonstop travel. She reflected on this life:

> *I think the punch line is, there's a reason why people that tend to be funded by venture capitalists are twenty and live on Doritos in their basement. Because the pressure's on you when you have a start-up company like this. With these kinds of guys [the venture capitalists] expecting results, it's tough to be forty, with two young children and a husband with his own job.*

Changes in corporate culture. Changes brought on by restructuring also prompted women to feel a growing disenchantment with their employers, often leading them to wonder aloud, "Why am I doing this?"—ultimately a question to which they had no answer. Restructuring was frequently linked to perceptions that the corporate culture was growing more hostile to women and more value divergent. "I think each of those changes [in ownership], it just became more and more corporate" was how Nancy Yearwood described what she observed as the publishing firm where she was an editor successively merged with others. Women frequently used the word *corporate* to connote a chill in the climate toward women as a result of restructuring. Edith Hortas, a Ph.D. scientist and biotechnology executive, recounted what

she called "a turning point" that occurred when her firm replaced its female CEO with a male CEO brought on to "grow" the company:

> *The company turned into a big corporation. And there were people there who became extremely corporate, who took a very hard-line financial view of things. And it became a much more male-run company. It was by no means a female-run company before, but it was a very inclusive kind of company.*

Manager turnover. Restructuring was often associated with rapid turnover in the managers to whom these women reported, resulting in the loss of mentors and the collapse of family-friendly work arrangements. In domino-like fashion, turnover at the top contributed to women's own turnover, which occurred via one of two processes, either by disrupting the work-family equilibrium that women had achieved or by diminishing their career prospects through the loss of an important mentor.

Because schedule flexibility and the pace of work are to some extent a function of managerial style, women often saw their work lives transformed by what they considered to be the rather arbitrary dictates of new bosses. Lisa Bernard, an executive in the health care field who worked under four senior managers in rapid succession, remarked of her last one,

> *This last person [who, she pointedly noted, had a wife, nanny, and mother-in-law at home] had a different approach to how to do certain things. I remember there was one time when he sent an e-mail to me on Sunday afternoon about a meeting that was 6:30 Monday morning and was just assuming that of course I would be reading my e-mail Sunday evening at home. . . .*

Children's Influence on the Decision to Quit

Seventy-two percent of the women we studied spoke of the pull of children as a factor in their decision to leave the workforce. Included among them are the five new traditionalist women in the sample. Three-quarters of women citing this reason quit when their children were in the baby or toddler years. Perhaps more surprising, a substantial number of women (32 percent)[1] who cited the pull of children were primarily compelled to leave the workforce by the needs of their older, school-aged children.

The Pull of Younger Children   Women who cited the pulls of their younger, preschool children as an important reason for taking a pause in their careers experienced these pulls in two ways.

Primacy of parental care. One-third cited their belief in the importance of one parent playing a primary caregiving role in the life of a young child. Melanie Irwin, formerly a marketing manager in a computer software company, put it this way: "I guess in my heart I didn't really want a kid raised by a nanny." Kristin Quinn, a former teacher, said, "It was hard thinking who could take care of my kid better than me." For these women, parental care in the early years was important in providing consistency and enrichment. Maeve Turner, the government attorney, reflecting on why she and her

husband decided that one of them (ultimately her) would be home after the birth of their first child, emphasized the constancy of parental care:

> The kids need especially—I think the kids need routine. They need a schedule. They need—I mean, not a schedule in the hourly sense, but they need a routine. They need to know that somebody is there connected to them who cares about them.

This theme more than any others cited by the women in the study reflects traditional notions of why women choose to stay home with their children rather than combining work and family. However, the new traditionalists and the nontraditionalists spoke about this issue in different ways. The nontraditionalists typically did not see full-time, mother-only care as the optimal or necessary solution, as the new traditionalists did. In fact, among nontraditionalists citing primacy of parental care, approximately one-third asked their employers if they could return to work on a reduced schedule but were denied this option.

The emotional pull of younger children. One-quarter of the women spoke of the emotional pull of younger children as a factor in their decision. For some women, this took the form of an intense feeling of attachment and bonding with their newborn baby or young child that made the return to a full-time work schedule difficult. Lauren Quattrone, formerly a lawyer, expressed it in this way: "I was just absolutely besotted with this baby. . . . I realized that I just couldn't bear to leave him." Regina Donofrio, a senior publicist for a large media corporation, decided to return to work full-time after the birth of her first child but described the anguish she felt in coping with her competing desire to be with her baby and to maintain a much-loved career:

> Then I began the nightmare of really never feeling like I was in the right place, ever. When I was at work, I should have been at home. When I was at home, I felt guilty because I had left work a little early to see the baby, and I had maybe left some things undone.

The pull of young children was also linked to their particular developmental phase and a desire not to "miss out" on it. Helena Norton, formerly an education administrator, commented, "I just don't want to miss this part because I know it does go by so fast." Three of the women who cited the emotional pull of younger children in their decision to leave work became first-time mothers in their early forties, and for these women, the desire to be fully present in the experience of motherhood was particularly keen since they did not expect to have any more children.

Among the nontraditionalist women who cited the emotional pull of young children, 40 percent tried to reduce their hours but were denied. Among this group, both Turner and Donofrio proposed job-sharing arrangements and left flourishing careers when their proposals were rejected.

The Pull of Older Children Older children were cited as having been a key factor in tipping the balance away from employment for one-quarter of our total sample and figured prominently for one-third of those who mentioned

children as a factor in their decision to leave. Nancy Taylor echoed the sentiments of many of these women when she remarked with surprise, "It's funny. I always expected as they got older it would be easier." Instead, an increase in both the scope and complexity of the perceived needs and demands of older children relative to younger ones, as well as growing doubts about the capacities of their paid caregivers, played a role in women's career interruption.

Increased demands. Bearing in mind that the oldest child among the women we interviewed was only fourteen, women were often surprised to learn that homework started young. Diane Childs expressed an amazement shared by many:

> *I don't know why this is happening, but elementary school kids get homework. These are children who can't read, who are in the first grade, and they have an assignment. And they'll be kind of sweet things, you know, "Use tally marks and count all of the pillows in your house." But if you come home from a frazzed-out day, . . . the last thing you want to do is find out that you have forty-two pillows in your house.*

After-school activities added to the stress of combining work and parenting. Childs noted that, like many professional women she knows who are now at home, a precipitating factor in her departure from work was an increasing awareness of her school-aged children's needs for extracurricular enrichment and the heightened demands that this placed on her as a parent, commenting dryly, "They can't drive themselves to piano lessons."

Lack of substitutability for own care. Women's perceptions about older children's increased demands were linked to their feelings that their children had "outgrown" their paid caregivers and that they themselves were increasingly needed at this point in their children's lives. Child care arrangements that had been regarded as highly successful were reevaluated as the more sophisticated needs of older children took precedence over the simpler, more straightforward "babysitting" needs of younger children. Elena Toracelli, the management consultant, expressed the satisfaction that most felt with their caregivers when children were younger:

> *I had great child care. In some ways, I think babies, if they're in a loving environment, other nonparents can fulfill their basic needs in a way that parents can too. And I liked that my kids got some tremendous socialization very early on in incredibly loving situations. And they are none the worse at all, if not the better for having been there.*

As their children started entering school, however, these high-achieving women begin to question their caregivers' capacities and suitability, often comparing themselves directly with them. The premium placed on education and values transmission at this point in their children's lives served to widen the gap between themselves and their less well-educated caregivers, most of whom were from very different class, race, and ethnic backgrounds.

Edith Hortas spoke of having "a sense that they were needing what I can provide and what the babysitter [her au pair] couldn't provide." Marina Isherwood, an HMO executive, elaborated this viewpoint:

> *There isn't a substitute, no matter how good the child care. When they're little, the fact that someone else is doing stuff with them is fine. It wasn't the part that I loved anyway. But when they start asking you questions about values, you don't want your babysitter telling them. . . . Our children come home and they have all this homework to do, and piano lessons and this and this, and it's all a complicated schedule. And, yes, you could get an au pair to do that, to balance it all, but they're not going to necessarily teach you how to think about math. Or help you come up with mnemonic devices to memorize all of the counties in Spain or whatever.*

Time and pleasure. For some women, watching their older children growing up created a heightened sense of urgency about quitting. These women saw childhood as a "little window" (as Nancy Yearwood put it) that was rapidly closing. Having worked a decade or more before quitting, many of them expressed a sense of "missing out" on their children's childhoods. Elena Toracelli described her feelings about the desirability of being home "when you sort of realize that time's running short. Paul's eight and tomorrow is going to be eighteen, and the same thing with Amanda. It's going to be over in a blink."

Complementing this sense of urgency, these women also found older children more *fun*, as Toracelli's observations convey:

> *I've realized within myself that I am much more stimulated by older children than I am by babies. I loved my children as babies, they were my own, . . . but I thrive more in the interaction with the level that they are at now than I did when they were infants and toddlers. They reason. They're funny. You can have conversations with them. You can plan and dream and do all kinds of great activities with them. They are much more fun now.*

Among this group whose children were older, 20 percent made efforts to navigate the demands of work and family by making part-time arrangements with their employers but had their requests refused.

Husbands' Role in the Decision to Quit

The majority of the women in this study, roughly two-thirds, discussed their husbands as one of the key influences on their decision to leave the labor force. That husbands' involvement was not cited universally indicates the degree to which women perceived the work–family decision to be theirs alone to shoulder. Husbands' influence on women's decisions to quit operated through multiple channels.

Lack of Husbands' Help with Parenting The women in our study were married to men who worked in professional jobs much like their own, entailing long hours and extensive travel. Husbands' high-octane careers effectively precluded their willingness or ability to provide help with child care or household chores. Often women did not explicitly mention their

husbands' lack of support, but it was clear from their narratives that their husbands were simply not around to share much if any of the "second shift" (Hochschild 1989) necessary to make their careers viable. Helena Norton, the educational administrator who characterized her husband as a "workaholic," described poignantly a scenario that many others took for granted:

> He was leaving early mornings; 6:00 or 6:30 before anyone was up, and then he was coming home late at night. So I felt this real emptiness, getting up in the morning to, not necessarily an empty house, because my children were there, but I did, I felt empty, and then going to bed, and he wasn't there.

Some women were more vocal in their estimation of how their husband's self-exemption from domestic labor affected their own career choices. Kristen Quinn observed about her husband, "He has always said to me, 'You can do whatever you want to do.' But he's not there to pick up any load."

Because these women had the resources to employ household help such as housekeepers, nannies, and babysitters, they rarely complained about "chore wars" occasioned by their husbands' failure to help with routine household tasks. Instead, the more profound impact of a husband's absence from the home was experienced by women in terms of his resulting inability to assist with the emotional labor of parenting. Many women were, like Helena Norton, the only parent available, and it fell to them to create a sense of family for their children. Leah Evans, a high-level medical administrator, highlighted this need when she described her decision to quit:

> So more than anything else it was just sort of what worked for the collective whole. Even though for Leah personally, I sort of feel like I'm the one who made the trade-off. Dick [her husband] certainly hasn't made any trade-off at this point and maybe eventually he will, but sort of realizing that it is a UNIT and you've got to do it [make your decision] based on what's best for the unit.

Toracelli found herself in a similar situation. Her husband's demanding career managing his own company in combination with her own near full-time work schedule meant that there was little time to create family:

> We had precious little family time, in part because, you know, here I am working like thirty hours. I have one day off, Friday, but my husband's not home Saturday and Sunday either. And so I am seven days a week, full-time, working with not too much of a break.

Another example of the "parenting vacuum" these women experienced as a result of their husbands' high-powered career came from Tricia Olsen, a former trader. Having herself once worked in the financial services industry, she was familiar with her husband's work world:

> My husband had taken a job three months earlier with a top investment bank, and we knew his life was going to go to hell because he was in the mergers and acquisitions department. So we knew that his life would be nonstop travel . . . and we decided that somebody should be home to be more attentive to the kids because now we had a second child. She was eighteen months old already, and

we found that she was requiring more and more attention just because she was a child. So I decided, knowing his life was going to go to hell, we figured that somebody should be home, and that somebody was me.

Secondary Income Despite the high-powered nature of their own careers, the majority of women in the study did not explicitly broach the idea of their husbands cutting back. Instead, they seemed to implicitly accept that their career was secondary. This perception was based to some extent on husbands' higher earnings. Approximately one-quarter of the women whose husbands played a role in their decision to quit perceived their own income, however high, as secondary to their husbands' and/or as unnecessary to family welfare. Typically, women were correct in their perceptions because they worked in lower-paying, female-dominated occupations like teaching or publishing and/or lower-paying sectors such as government; they were already working part-time at the time of their quitting; or their own high earnings were far outstripped by their husbands'. Diane Childs, who worked in the nonprofit sector, said that as a couple she and her husband did not even consider having him cut back on his career in finance, despite increasing family strains, since, as she put it, "There's too much money at stake at this point in time that I couldn't approach his earning power."

Because many of these women and their husbands are midcareer, about half mentioned promotions or other significant career achievements (such as making partner) that led to dramatic increases in their husbands' salaries during the period when they were considering the need to reorder their work lives. Marina Isherwood reported that her husband's income went up fivefold before she quit:

And mine wasn't going up fivefold, and so the amount of contribution I was making to our household dropped significantly. And then I thought, you know, [after] taxes, what are we really bringing in? So the economics changed.

Husband's Preference for Wife to Stay Home About one-quarter of the women whose husbands played a role in their decision to quit indicated that their husbands communicated to them, either explicitly or implicitly, that they expected their wife to be the one to sacrifice or modify her career to accommodate family responsibilities. A minority of husbands expressed this preference in traditionalist terms. For instance, Toracelli described the role her husband's attitude played in her decision to quit in the following way:

My husband grew up in a very traditional household. His mother was home all the time. It's an Italian household in a very traditional sense of the word where, you know, there's always sort of a warm plate of food waiting for you on the table when you get home, and he relished the idea of having that kind of person.

More often, husbands professed an egalitarian stance toward women's decisions about whether to cut back on their careers, captured in the frequent refrain, "It's your choice," while tacitly indicating discontent with their wives' working. Women seemed to take their husbands' overt statements at

face value, characterizing their husbands as "supportive" while recounting narratives that contradicted this assessment. For example, Bettina Mason described her husband in the following way: "He has always said do what I want. He would be supportive of whatever I chose." At another point in the interview, however, she admitted that part of her reason for quitting was that her husband, who was often out of town for weeks at a time, made it clear that he resented the fact that no one was around to "pick up the slack" when she worked full-time.

Some husbands simply refused to modify their careers in the face of mounting pressure on the home front. Lynn Hamilton, the MD turned medical director, described both herself and her husband as working "these killer jobs," a situation that was creating huge stress on their marriage and family life. They earned similar incomes and had similar credentials, and he was "admiring and supportive" of her work. When Hamilton repeatedly raised the need for them to "reconfigure" their work lives, however, he was nonresponsive, and she finally realized that "he wasn't going to."

Significantly, about one-third of the women who described their husbands' implicit or explicit preference for a stay-at-home wife as a factor in their quitting were earning comparable incomes or outearning their husbands at the time of their job departure. Thus, economics was not the only factor at play in these couples' perceptions that the wife's career was secondary.

Deference to Husband's Career Under the duress of a dual-career lifestyle, some women's decisions to quit were influenced by a perception that their husbands' careers were more important or prestigious than their own or by an unspoken agreement with their husbands that husbands' careers took precedence. Two women accommodated their husbands' careers by deciding to step off the career track when their husbands' jobs required a geographical relocation. Feeling the mounting stress of juggling family and two careers—their own and their husbands'—some women simply weighed their own careers against their husbands' and decided that theirs were more dispensable. Moira Franklin, a former engineer whose husband was in the same field as her, describes her decision to quit as influenced by her perception that her own educational credentials were less than those of her husband and that her career was not as prestigious:

> I think if I had gone to get a Ph.D., then it would have been harder to quit. But master's was kind of a half-way, you're qualified, but you're not a hotshot yet. So it's not as if I was the faculty member . . . so I think it was easier for me to quit than stick it out and torture myself a little longer.

Future Work

While this [reading] is concerned with the forces impinging on and reasons behind the decision to interrupt careers, in the larger study of which it is a part, we also asked women about their plans to return to work in the future. Two-thirds responded that they desired to reenter the workforce and

discussed their intention to return with varying degrees of specificity. Significantly, the majority of women who desired to return to work said they would prefer to do so on a part-time basis that would accommodate their ongoing family responsibilities. Despite the difficulty many had encountered in arranging a part-time schedule in their former jobs, most women who expressed interest in returning to work cited workplace flexibility as a critical feature of any future job. In fact, some women planned to switch into traditionally female-dominated fields such as teaching, in part because they perceived them to offer more flexibility than the "all-or-nothing" style of the male-dominated careers they had left behind.

ENDNOTE

[1] The percentages add up to slightly more than 100 percent here since there was some overlap between the categories of younger and older children. Specifically, one woman left the workforce when her youngest child was a preschooler and her oldest child was school aged and cited both types of reasons (the pull of younger and older children) as factors in her decision to quit.

REFERENCES

Baker, Joe G. 2002. "The Influx of Women into Legal Professions: An Economic Analysis." *Monthly Labor Review* 125:14–24.

Barnett, Rosalind C. and Caryl Rivers. 1996. *She Works/He Works*. New York: HarperCollins.

Belkin, Lisa. 2003. "The Opt-Out Revolution." *The New York Times Magazine*, October 26, pp. 42–47, 58, 85–86.

Crittenden, Ann. 2001. *The Price of Motherhood*. New York: Metropolitan Books.

Faludi, Susan. 1991. *Backlash: The Undeclared War against American Women*. New York: Crown.

Hays, Sharon. 1996. *The Cultural Contradictions of Motherhood*. New Haven, CT: Yale University Press.

Hochschild, Arlie. 1989. *The Second Shift*. New York: Viking.

———. 1997. *Time Bind*. New York: Metropolitan Books.

Jacobs, Jerry A. and Kathleen Gerson. 1998. "Who Are the Overworked Americans?" *Review of Social Economy* 56:442–59.

Kanter, Rosabeth Moss. 1977. *Men and Women of the Corporation*. New York: Basic Books.

McCracken, Douglas M. 2000. "Winning the Talent War for Women: Sometimes It Takes a Revolution." *Harvard Business Review* 78 (6): 159.

Pearson, Allison. 2002. *I Don't Know How She Does It*. New York: Knopf.

Preston, Anne E. 1994. "Where Have All the Women Gone? A Study of Exits of Women from the Science and Engineering Professions." *American Economic Review* 84:1446–62.

Schor, Juliet B. 1992. *The Overworked American*. New York: Basic Books.

Stone, Pamela. 1998. "Media Myths about Labor Force Dropout among Professional and Managerial Women: Bringing Some Facts Back In." Presented at the annual meetings of the Eastern Sociological Society, Philadelphia, March.

Swiss, Deborah J. and Judith P. Walker. 1993. *Women and the Work/Family Dilemma: How Today's Professional Women Are Confronting the Maternal Wall*. New York: John Wiley.

Williams, Joan. 2000. *Unbending Gender*. New York: Oxford University Press.

47

NEGOTIATING WORK AND PARENTING OVER THE LIFE COURSE
Mexican Family Dynamics in a Binational Context

JOANNA DREBY

Every year, more than 500,000 Mexicans migrate to the United States (Pew Hispanic Center 2007). Tens of thousands leave children behind in Mexico when they do.[1] These migrants make an unusual, but common, parenting decision. Taking advantage of the economic disparities between the United States and Mexico, parents move to places, where they can earn more for their human labor, while their children remain in hometowns in Mexico, where the cost of living is low. In this sense, migration is a gamble; by leaving children behind, migrant parents hope to better provide for their children. Their migration represents a sacrifice of the present for the future.

In some ways, Mexican migrant parents' strategy is not so different from those of other working parents in the United States. Like many American working parents, Mexican migrants put in long hours on the job and entrust the care of their children to others.[2] They expect that through continued labor force participation, they will be able to enhance their children's opportunities. They feel conflicted about their decisions over how to balance work and home life. Yet transnational parents work thousands of miles away from their children. Unable to see their children at the end of every day, these parents make an enormous sacrifice in their work–family life balance.

This [reading] describes how Mexican migrants, both mothers and fathers, reconcile the demands of their work life with those of parenting their children from a distance. In what follows, I briefly review the differences between the sacrifices made by mothers and fathers. I then consider how social conditions, changes in family composition over time, and the sharing of parental roles with children's caregivers affect parents' relationships with their children and the gendered expectations of parents' migrations. In doing so, I focus on how migrant men and women seek to achieve a work–family life balance over time, in accordance with their—and their children's—changing needs.

Past Patterns

Mexican fathers' decisions to migrate without their children are not new. What scholars previously termed "split-family migration" was common a century ago for, among others, Chinese, Polish, Jewish, and Italian immigrants to the United States. From 1870 to 1920, more than two-thirds of Italian migrants were men; the majority supported wives and children in Italy with remittances (Gabaccia 2001). Male Chinese immigrants outnumbered women 18 to 1 in 1860 and 26 to 1 in 1890, and more than half left wives at home in China (Nakano Glenn 1983). Many men gradually brought their family members to the United States when possible, although return migration rates were also high; between 1900 and 1920, more than a third of immigrants to the United States returned home (Foner 2000:172).

Unlike Chinese and Italian immigrants, at the turn of the twentieth century Mexican families generally migrated together. Indeed, for most of the nineteenth century—even after the Mexican American War (1846–48), when the United States took more than 500,000 square miles of land previously belonging to Mexico—the U.S.–Mexican border was much more porous than it is today. In fact, family migration grew considerably during the upheaval of the Mexican Revolution (1913–20). Yet with the economic turmoil of the Great Depression of the 1930s, entire families were sent back to Mexico during deportation campaigns (Sanchez 1993). By 1940, the Mexican American population was just half what it had been only ten years earlier (Hondagneu-Sotelo 1994).

Not until the mid-twentieth century did typical Mexican migrants begin to look more like those from Europe and Asia years earlier. After labor shortages during World War II, the United States instituted the Bracero Program (1942–64), which allowed Mexican men, but not women, to migrate on temporary labor contracts.[3] Unlike immigrants from other countries, who generally settled in the cities, *braceros* worked in agriculture, returning to Mexico at the end of the growing season. The Bracero Program was instrumental in establishing an entrenched pattern of male-led temporary migration between Mexico and the United States. Ever since, many Mexican communities—and families—have come to depend on some of their members seeking employment north of the border (Massey et al. 1987).

The migration pattern in which men worked abroad and women stayed in the home community and tended to children conforms, in many ways, to the gender division of labor in families. Such a balance between work and family was not without problems. The women and men in these families were divided between what William I. Thomas and Florian Znaniecki (1927) described as "old" and "new world" values. Ensuing conflicts between women and men led, they suggested, to wider levels of social disorganization in both the communities of origin where women lived and urban immigrant communities in the United States, which were mostly inhabited by men. Particularly during the early twentieth century, social workers and other reformers in the United States defined the problem of immigration as one of "family disorganization" (Gordon 1988; Irving 2000; Sanchez 1993). Although

Mexican men's migration patterns were typically more circular than those of European immigrants, fathers' periodic absences did not go unnoted. These absent fathers were often criticized, as the popular expression goes, for being "padres de cheque no mas" [fathers only by virtue of a check].[4]

New Patterns: Migrant Mothers

Today, a new migration pattern in which mothers leave their children to work abroad marks a major shift in the ways families balance work and family via migration. Pierrette Hondagneu-Sotelo and Ernestine Avila (1997) have labeled this phenomenon "transnational motherhood." Although some migrant mothers left their children behind in earlier periods, such cases appear to have been unusual.[5] A study of family separation among U.S. immigrants in 1910 found that only 7 percent of immigrant women across ethnic groups had left their children in their home country when they came to the United States (Robles and Watkins 1993). By the end of the twentieth century, transnational mothering spanned the globe, from Turkish women in Germany to Colombians in Spain and Filipinas in Canada, Hong Kong, and Italy.[6] The growing presence of women in migration streams and the increased frequency of female-led migration suggest that contemporary families are meeting productive and consumptive needs through migration in distinctly different ways than in times past, when men were the primary movers in families. When mothers from poorer countries such as Mexico migrate to more industrialized nations, they fill what Barbara Ehrenreich and Arlie Hochschild (2002) call the "care deficit" that emerges when women enter the workforce in wealthier nations. In effect, they pass on the "care deficit" to the children they leave behind, reproducing global inequalities within their families (p. 8).

Although rates of male migration still outpace those of females among Mexicans, in the past ten to twenty years, many characteristics of Mexican migration have changed. For one, the destinations of Mexican migrants have become increasingly diversified. Labor demands throughout the forty-eight continental United States have meant that Mexicans now seek work outside of the Southwest in rural, urban, and suburban areas that have not seen sizable immigrant populations in the past. Moreover, since the debt crisis in the mid-1980s, migration to the United States has become common throughout Mexico. Today, nearly every Mexican state has a significant number of migrants in the United States; they leave both rural and urban areas and come from areas where indigenous languages, not Spanish, are spoken (Cornelius 1991; Stephen 2007). More importantly, the past twenty years have seen a marked increase in female migration rates. Not only are men of all socioeconomic backgrounds migrating from all areas of Mexico as never before, but so are their wives and children (Cornelius 1991; Donato 1993). A considerable number of single women, including many divorced and widowed mothers, have begun to seek employment in the United States as a means for survival. Estimates suggest that 38 percent of Mexican fathers and 15 percent of Mexican mothers living in the United States have left children back in Mexico (Dreby forthcoming).

The increasingly diverse Mexican migrant population confronts an ever more hostile environment in the United States. Since the early 1990s, many policies restricting immigration to the United States have been implemented.[7] Such measures, aimed at reducing unregulated Mexican migration, have had a number of unintended consequences. The undocumented crossing of the U.S.–Mexican border has become more dangerous—especially for women—and death rates have soared (Cornelius 2001). The costs of migration have also risen considerably. Consequently, Mexicans are more likely than in times past to settle in new destinations further away from the border. As it has become ever more difficult for migrants to move back and forth between their homes in Mexico and their workplaces in the United States, they are staying longer (Massey 2006). In other words, Mexican families continue to depend on U.S. employment as a labor strategy, but they must endure longer family separations to do so. Immigration policy has created the conditions under which Mexicans working in the United States, and particularly mothers, must remain apart from their children.

Today's Mexican migrant mothers, as well as fathers, face a series of strains and stressors that, though they at times echo concerns voiced by reformers in the early twentieth century, are unique to their generation of migrants.[8] Transnational parents are caught in an increasingly complex web of migratory laws in both "sending" and "receiving" nations. Legal statuses within migrant families often vary, with some siblings having U.S. citizenship rights while others remain undocumented (Passel 2006). Moreover, new technologies facilitate more frequent contact between family members abroad and those back home (Mahler 2001). Parents can speak to their children on the phone and often do on a daily basis (Dreby 2006). Money is easily sent to Mexico, and parents can travel back home rather quickly in response to any immediate crisis, such as when a child is ill. More immediate and frequent means of communicating with children back at home may make mothers more willing to leave them when they migrate. Yet prolonged separation is accompanied by a new set of problems, particularly for women. When mothers migrate, expectations of women's roles at home lag behind their contributions as family wage-earners (Dreby 2006; Salazar Parreñas 2005). Mothers often feel guiltier than fathers about having left their children behind. Families lament that love becomes a commodity when it is only expressed through gifts parents send back home to their children. In summary, the balance between work and family in a transnational context is complicated by both changing gendered expectations in the family and by Mexicans' social status as migrant workers in the United States.

Methodology

The analysis in this [reading] draws on a *multi-sited ethnography* (Marcus 1998) in the United States and Mexico. Between 2003 and 2006 I conducted participant observation as well as interviews with 142 members of Mexican

transnational families residing in and around a new destination of Mexican migration in central New Jersey and in south-central Mexico.

In a city in central New Jersey, I interviewed forty-five migrant parents (twenty-two mothers and twenty-three fathers) between 2003 and 2004 and conducted participant observation in the Mexican immigrant community.[9] The migrant mothers I interviewed generally worked in local fast-food restaurants and factories, the fathers in landscaping, construction, and private restaurants. All but three of the men and women interviewed were undocumented, and nearly all came from the three-state region of Oaxaca, Guerrero, and Puebla. In Mexico, the men had been farmers (eight), government administrators (three), electricians (two), a police officer, and an accountant. Most mothers had not been regularly employed outside of the home in Mexico. I used various personal contacts to identify parents for the interviews. Indeed, the fact that my young son's father is a Mexican immigrant and part of the city's Mexican immigrant community helped pave the way for informal conversations and observations.

In south-central Mexico, between 2004 and 2005, I interviewed sixty children of migrant parents, ages five through nineteen, as well as thirty-seven of their caregivers, mostly grandmothers. Most of the people interviewed lived in a community in the lower Mixtec region of Oaxaca, which I call San Angel. (All personal names used in the [reading] are also pseudonyms.) Because I spent seven months in San Angel, I was also able to observe, at close range, how migration permeated everyday experiences. Surveys I carried out at the local middle school made clear how common it was for children to have close relatives in the United States: 65 percent of the students had members of their nuclear family (parents and/or siblings) in the United States and 28 percent had one or both parents there. Four of the families I focused on in San Angel were closely related to parents I had previously interviewed in New Jersey; I also made trips to other parts of the region to interview children and their caregivers in eight families whose parents had been part of the study in New Jersey.

Parent–Child Relationships

When Mexican parents and children live apart, three aspects of migrants' experiences shape how they manage the balance between work and family life and, ultimately, relationships with their children. First, parents' experiences as low-wage, undocumented workers in the United States influence their ability to fulfill parental obligations from a distance and often lengthen family separations. Second, events related to parents' changing relations with their family members, especially marital conflicts and the birth of children in the United States, cause tensions in relationships with children back at home. Third, parental struggles to negotiate their roles with children's caregivers, particularly in terms of feelings of jealousy and exerting authority over their children, affect their experiences as transnational parents.

Undocumented, Low-Wage Workers

Parents often did not anticipate the difficulties they would face when they decided to leave home. In San Angel, for example, return migrants sported fancy clothes, brought nice gifts for their relatives, and invited friends and others to parties during the holiday season. Not having lived as minority immigrant workers in the United States, few of San Angel's residents understood the psychological importance for return migrants of saving enough money to be able to show off their economic prosperity. Those in San Angel believed that anyone who works hard in *el norte* can be successful. Migrants who did not send money home regularly were considered lazy or suspected of spending money on vices such as alcohol or drugs. One migrant father in New Jersey said:

> I would say 75 percent of the people come fooled by this country. They are fooled by us immigrants who go back. We get a nice pair of shoes, good clothes and we say, "I earn so much and I have a car." . . . Everyone thinks that by coming they will make money quickly. They think coming here is living well.

Migrants arriving in New Jersey faced a stark reality. Work was not always easy to obtain; most migrants initially used temporary employment agencies that offered irregular jobs and deducted fees for their services, including transportation, from workers' salaries (Ortega 2006). Even when they were better established and able to obtain jobs directly from employers, migrants were frequently unemployed. Many Mexican women worked in factories that depended on a floating labor force and provided them no benefits or job security. One mother I interviewed had held a steady job for more than two years at a factory but was fired when she took time off to care for a family member diagnosed with AIDS. Ever since, she has moved from job to job, part of the temporary workforce. Work is irregular in construction and landscaping, common jobs for Mexican men in central New Jersey. While jobs may be plentiful during the summer, and some men I interviewed at times worked up to sixty hours a week at ten to fifteen dollars per hour, when it rained and during the winter they did not work at all.

Mexican workers also did not expect that health problems, coupled with lack of health insurance, would affect their ability to work. One mother, for example, had to leave her job when she underwent an emergency kidney stone operation. Others stopped working during and after pregnancies. A father, Armando, had health problems when he first arrived in the United States and landed a job in landscaping with his brothers. He told me:

> I didn't think it would be so hard here. My brother gave me the impression that there was money to be made everywhere. . . . I first worked mowing lawns. But I didn't last because my health wasn't good when I got here. . . . I couldn't last at that job. Instead, I went to work in a factory.

Because factory work pays less than landscaping, the move meant a lower salary than Armando had originally anticipated. Work-related accidents were also a problem for the fathers I interviewed. Mexican men are employed in

some of the most dangerous workplaces in the United States (Pritchard 2004). Even though workplace accidents are covered under worker's compensation (regardless of immigrant status), they affected migrants' ability to save money and send funds home.

Given these problems, migrants generally found they had to adjust their economic goals. José, who had worked steadily at a pizzeria for over three years, explained, *"My plan initially was to stay here for two, maybe three, years in order to save enough money just to fix up my house. I calculated pretty carefully that it would take me this long to earn the money I needed."* When I expressed surprise that he knew how much he would make before coming to the United States, José said, *"Well, [I didn't know] exactly* (pause). *But based on what they told me people earn, I thought I would work approximately this many hours a week at this salary and I thought it would take me two years to reach my goal."* José was already past the two-year mark when I first met him and was not sure when he would be able to go back to Mexico. He had made little progress toward his original goals.

One option was to simply return to Mexico. Some parents did. When I met Armando, he was frustrated by the difficulties he faced after his marriage fell apart (in New Jersey) and planned to go back to his three children in Mexico. *"I was going to leave now, but my siblings convinced me to stay to December and save up some more money before leaving."* True to plan, he returned home that Christmas. Such a return home requires parents to work long enough in the United States to pay off the debts accrued from their migration or, as in Armando's case, accrued at home during their absence. The result is that a return home is often delayed much longer than desired.

Many parents adjusted their economic strategies by sending for their children—although, like so much in the migrants' lives, bringing children to the United States is fraught with complications related to undocumented status. Generally, it took years to arrange, since it is considerably more dangerous and costly for unaccompanied children to cross the border than for adults (Marizco 2004; Nazario 2006). One mother, for example, decided to send for her teenage son after he dropped out of the university, but she had to wait until her boyfriend went back for a vacation and could accompany her son across the border. José eventually decided to bring his eighteen-year-old son (who was twelve when he first left) to New Jersey, but for the past three years has been figuring out how to do this.

I found that many children—particularly young children—resisted parents' efforts to send for them and preferred to stay in Mexico (Dreby 2007). In the face of such resistance—as well as the difficulty of meeting their economic goals in the United States—parents often resigned themselves to making family separation a more permanent arrangement than they had originally planned. At times, parents dealt with prolonged separation by returning to visit their children whenever possible. Return visits were again complicated by parents' legal status. A return visit required saving up significant money for the trip, making arrangements for the return passage to the United States, and securing time off or new employment upon their return.

Migrant mothers and fathers had different attitudes about these lengthy separations. Fathers were more likely to prefer that their children remain in Mexico. As one father said, *"I am not the kind of person who likes this life for my children. Here there is too much freedom for them. It is not really a safe environment. I prefer that they stay in Mexico where they can receive a good education."* Mothers hoped to be reunited with their children more quickly. Their return visits were generally motivated by the thought that if they saw their children in person, they could convince the children to migrate. Such visits were infrequent, however. Undocumented crossing is particularly perilous for women (Amnesty International 1998; Chavez 1992). In fact, I only interviewed three mothers who had been home to visit their children. One of these mothers, Zelia, explained how women manage the crossing:

> You know what we do? We look for someone from town to go with. So then when you are going to wash up, you say to them, watch out for us, and they say, oh sure, and since they know us, they watch out for us. . . . Alone, I wouldn't come.

Although fathers also described the undocumented crossing as dangerous, particularly as compared to years past, this did not prevent them from going home to visit their families. Indeed, thirteen of the twenty-three fathers I interviewed had made a return trip multiple times.

No matter how parents adjusted their economic goals after they came to the United States, the end result was almost always a longer separation from children than originally planned. Social status as low-wage, undocumented workers in the United States put parents in a bind. Once having left their children behind, reunification was almost always more difficult and costly than parents anticipated.

The Changing Composition of Families

Transnational parents not only face challenges at work, they also must deal with shifting family dynamics that may lead to strains. Changing relations with marital partners often lead to tensions with children in Mexico. Marital discord frequently arises in immigrant families as couples find they must adjust their relationships to the U.S. context.[10]

For men who migrated without wives, accusations of infidelity affected relationships with children in Mexico (Dreby 2008; Menjívar and Agadjanian 2007). One migrant father said his relationship with his oldest daughter was damaged by false rumors that he had had a baby with his sister-in-law. When this daughter migrated as a young adult, she refused to live with him; he complained that to this day she does not trust or respect his fatherly advice. A father of four teens told me that his wife suspected he had another wife in the United States. When he last went home, *"My two older boys came to me together and they said: 'Dad, if you have another wife, we don't want you here. You can leave.'"* At times such accusations were based on rumors; at other times men I interviewed did have new partners in the United States, although they still maintained ties to their wives and children in Mexico.

For women who migrated on their own, communication with children could be problematic when they had to deal with difficult ex-husbands. One mother, for example, left home when she found out her husband was living with another woman. For three years she had little contact with her three boys; she only occasionally spoke to the oldest when a neighbor helped arrange it. Another was unable to talk to her two children living with her ex-husband, who was remarried. He would not even accept the gifts that she sent the children. She was infuriated when she learned that the children were selling candy. *"When I was there, we were poor, but at least they weren't out on the streets."*

It was fairly common for divorced or widowed migrant mothers who came on their own to remarry once in the United States. Relationships with step-fathers could be very difficult for children in Mexico to accept (Chinchilla and Zentgraf 2007). Moreover, new partners did not always recognize the women's children back in Mexico as part of their new family. Occasionally, I heard criticism of mothers who had lost touch with their children in Mexico (although there were very few such mothers in my sample). I was told that they had remarried and that the new husband was unwilling to provide for children from a former partner. One woman I interviewed praised her new husband for not being like others; he had accepted her two daughters back home as his own. *"My girls even call him* papi.*"*

Couples migrating together were not immune from marital problems (Hirsch 2003; Smith 2006). Many divorced or separated once in the United States—and gendered expectations of mothers and fathers affected their relationships with children back home. . . .

It is also hard for children in Mexico to share their parents, particularly their mothers, with step-siblings born abroad. A consistent theme in interviews with parents and children was how the birth of children in the United States threatened parents' relationships with children left behind. One father, for example, wondered whether his two children in Mexico would accept his newborn son, but then decided *"they are young enough to grow attached to him."* Another explained that his daughters in Mexico are jealous of his U.S.-born child: *"Once one of the girls asked me to go home because [she worries that] if I don't, I am going to love the one that was born here more than them."* A mother who joined her husband two years earlier left two daughters with her sister-in-law and subsequently had a baby boy in the United States. She complained that on the phone *"the girls reproach me. They are jealous, extremely jealous, the younger one more than the older one."*

Children in Mexico described U.S.-born children as a potential threat. Younger children, in particular, feared that U.S.-born siblings or half-siblings would compete more successfully for their parents' love and attention since they lived with the parents. Fatima's mother, for example, had a baby in New York City, brought the baby back to Mexico to live with Fatima and her grandmother in San Angel, and then returned north. Fatima—age eleven at the time—said, *"Sometimes I think my mom loves my little sister more because she was born there with her. I feel like she gives her more love. When she arrived I didn't like her."* A sixteen-year-old whose father had a U.S.-born child told

me, *"I don't understand—it is so ignorant. If he cannot make it with us, how can he with another one."* In effect, U.S.-born children not only compete with children in Mexico for scarce parental resources, they also undermine parents' statements that migration to the United States was undertaken for the sake of their children back in Mexico.

Children's fears were not entirely unfounded. For mothers, the pain of separation was so great that having a new child in the United States made them feel better. According to one mother, who had a daughter in Mexico and two U.S.-born children, *"It is like you carry the weight of all the love that you have been holding in and then you put it on them [U.S.-born children]."* Fathers were often much more involved with the care of U.S.-born children than they had been with children in Mexico; when both partners work in the United States, they tend to share child-care, and many men migrated while their Mexican-born children were still infants or sometimes before they were born (Levitt 2001). A father who returned to San Angel with his U.S.-born daughter and his wife to be reunited with the couple's oldest son, said his son is not close to him and thinks that he loves his daughter more. The father insisted he loves his son, but he admitted that it is not the same. *"I also feel different [toward them]. I raised my daughter since she was born. I bathed her, I changed her diapers, I prepared her bottles. I never did that for my son because I was away working in the north when he was little."*

Of course, conflicts related to step-parents and step-siblings are common in the general American population. Yet in many American families, the passage of time helps parents and children adjust to the changes in family composition and eventually accept new routines and new family members (Furstenberg and Cherlin 1994). In contrast, for Mexican transnational families, parents and children have few, if any, opportunities to work out their differences in daily interactions. Over time, the likelihood of marital conflict, new partners, and U.S.-born children increases. The strains that the changes in family composition cause are likely to intensify or remain unresolved in the transnational context. . . .

Gendered Expectations

In some ways, the transnational context presents similar challenges to both women and men who parent children from afar. Mexican mothers and fathers working in the United States face legal constraints owing to their immigration status; it is estimated that 80 to 85 percent of Mexicans arriving in the United States between 1995 and 2005 were undocumented (Passel 2006). The migrant mothers and fathers I interviewed lived apart from their children mainly because financial and legal constraints prevented the family from migrating together. Nonetheless, Mexican mothers' and fathers' experiences differ in important ways that highlight the gendered expectations involved in parenting. They also underscore how gender inequality plays a critical role in the way men and women negotiate a work–family life balance during international migration.

In general, women faced greater difficulties visiting their children in Mexico than men did. They felt more at risk crossing the border to go home for visits. Their work patterns also played a role. Although migrant women often experienced spells of unemployment, they had greater job stability than the men I interviewed. Many men worked in seasonal occupations, like landscaping and construction, so that there was a regular time of the year when they had fewer obligations in the United States and could easily contemplate a visit home. Women, in contrast, worked year-round, for lower wages than men. Their regular labor-force participation was important to the family income. Among couples living together, many men depended on their wives' employment during the winter months to pay the bills—and wives, as a result, had less freedom to return home to see their children.

Fathers' visits home were often as unpredictable as their employment was volatile, which was not always a positive experience for their children. Some children had spent most of their childhood in Mexico living without fathers. Many in San Angel described their fathers as popping in and out of their lives; fathers' departures were a source of anxiety. One twenty-five-year-old looked back on her father's perpetual absences: *"I felt like the U.S. robbed my father from me."*

Mothers planned their separations more carefully than fathers did and, at least initially, anticipated being reunited with their children quickly. Although they visited Mexico less frequently than fathers, the mothers I interviewed averaged fewer years apart from their children. During separation, the migrant mothers felt more distraught than did fathers about maintaining communication with children whom they rarely saw. More so than fathers, their goal in saving money was to be reunited with their children. Although many mothers hoped to retire to Mexico, the burden of living apart from their children often became too much to bear. Many ended up reuniting with their children in the United States. Referring to her children's imminent arrival in New York City, Nicandra explained, *"This was not my plan. . . . I always thought I would work until I could go back there. But now I guess that all of us will end up here."* Fathers' separations from their children, in contrast, were often more longstanding.

Changes in family composition in the United States also shaped mothers' and fathers' relationships with children in different ways. Because fathers were evaluated as family providers, the fathers' new partners or children in the United States only became problematic for children in Mexico when fathers' economic resources were strained as a result. While fathers' economic support was enough to demonstrate love, children expected mothers to express greater concern and devotion. Fifteen-year-old Brian, for example, was quite resentful of his mother for divorcing his father in New Jersey and moving in with another man. He said he didn't feel like he loved his mother or that she loved him. *"Because if she loved us really, she would call. Or not even, that she doesn't send (money), because that doesn't matter. But at least she has to call."* In contrast, Brian said he loves his father, who also had remarried in New Jersey. Children were likely to question the devotion of their mothers when they became involved with new partners and had new children abroad.

The gendered double standard during migration is also evident in parents' conflicting emotions at being separated from their children. Both mothers and fathers worried about children's loyalties and were frustrated when children did not acknowledge them or their authority. Yet fathers described such tensions as unavoidable side-effects of the migratory experience, something they just had to deal with. They generally minimized the emotional costs of family separation—perhaps owing to men's efforts to distance themselves from "direct manifestations of sadness" (Riessman 1990:155). Mothers, in contrast, expressed great remorse over the decision to work in the United States. Fourteen mothers said that they cried for months upon arrival in the United States, lacked appetite, and became physically ill, and a number said they were severely depressed. One mother told me, "*I cried for two months when I first arrived. . . . I was nervous all the time and made lots of mistakes when I first started to work.*" Another complained that before her husband went back for her son, "*I didn't work well. I didn't sleep well. I didn't eat well.*" A mother in San Angel told me she returned to Mexico because "*I suffered a lot . . . without my son, especially when we had first arrived. When we would go out to the stores and I saw the children with their parents, I would start to cry.*"

Fathers rarely said they felt guilty about having left their children in Mexico. For example, a father of three, who called and sent money weekly to his children in Mexico, explained: "*No, [I don't feel guilty]. I think I would feel bad if I knew the children were suffering, and that they wouldn't suffer if I was there with them. But they aren't, so I don't.*" He considered his responsibility to be for his children's economic well-being. His children suffered less economically because he worked abroad and sent money home regularly, thereby making his sacrifice guilt-free.

In contrast, mothers often said they felt guilty about leaving their children behind (Dreby 2006). Nicandra, whose teenage sons lived in Mexico, told me, "*I often feel guilty. When things aren't going well I feel guilty. When my son wasn't doing well, it was like I wasn't on top of things. I mean, one feels guilty for not giving them the attention they need.*" Like many other migrant women, Nicandra felt that her children's emotional well-being was her responsibility. Even though the children's father (her ex-husband) lived near them in Mexico, Nicandra felt that because she was unable to meet her son's emotional needs from abroad she was failing to live up to her role as a mother.

Changing Dynamics over Time

Today's Mexican families are achieving a work–family life balance in new ways. Women are now joining men and using international migration without their children as a means to better provide for their children's future. In a number of ways, women's and men's experiences are similar. As low-wage, undocumented workers, mothers and fathers find they are unable to meet their migration goals as quickly as they originally anticipated. A combination of constraints related to their legal and labor statuses tends to prolong

separation from their children. While in the United States, events like the birth of a new child or marital conflict affect the types of relationships both mothers and fathers are able to maintain with children back in Mexico. Mothers and fathers struggle to exert their authority from a distance over children who are dubious and at times resentful of their parents' decisions to migrate. Mothers as well as fathers often feel jealous of their children's primary caregivers in Mexico.

Yet women and men ultimately have different experiences as transnational parents. Mothers cannot visit their children as easily as fathers. Mothers' absences are seen as more upsetting to children and the "family order" than those of fathers; mothers' attentions towards new family members in the United States are considered more disruptive to relationships with children in Mexico. Mothers also feel guiltier than fathers about their difficulties in parenting from a distance. In the end, what these differences make clear is that gendered expectations are of great significance in the transnational context. Comparing the experiences of Mexican mothers and fathers reveals that mothers' sacrifices are viewed more harshly, both by children and mothers themselves, than those of fathers.

Mexican mothers' and fathers' own evaluations of their sacrifices are also shaped by their children's reactions to separation. Because parents care about their children, they are generally responsive to their children's needs. When children refuse to migrate, for example, parents attempt to persuade them otherwise through return trips home. Children's reactions also make both mothers and fathers feel badly about being away. Parents, especially mothers, may reconsider their migration decisions, and even alter the family migration strategy, based on their children's reactions to separation. It may well be that American working parents are as influenced by children's emotions as the Mexican migrants I interviewed (see Galinsky 1999). Yet when parents and children live together, they interact frequently and more readily adjust to each other's changing needs. Children's influence over parents' work life is perhaps more evident in the transnational context, when physical separation heightens parents', and particularly mothers', sense of sacrifice as a result of employment.

The uncertainty inherent in managing relationships as intimate as those between parents and children from a distance means that intergenerational dynamics in many migrant families have distinctive features. When parents and children do not live in the same country, share in the same routines, or experience similar opportunities and constraints, intergenerational relationships are constantly in flux. During periods of separation, parents and children must constantly adapt to each other's changing needs. They do so based on the little information they can glean through weekly phone conversations, second-hand accounts from caregivers, and neighbors' gossip. Lack of contact increases insecurity and intensifies emotions. The effects of changes in family composition are harder to adjust to. And, over time, the work and legal conditions that both shape and restrict parents' choices about how to manage work and family life make the sacrifice inherent in international migration all the more difficult.

ENDNOTES

[1] A Pew Hispanic Center survey of immigrants at Mexican consulates throughout the United States found that 18 percent of all immigrants surveyed and more than one in four parents had one or more children in Mexico. Most were fathers, but a significant proportion of mothers also had children in Mexico. See Suro 2005.

[2] Of the nearly 10 million working mothers in the United States, 79 percent leave children with someone besides a parent while they are at work. See Johnson 2005.

[3] Today we know that return migration rates were also high among earlier immigrants and that many Mexicans outstayed their bracero visas and settled in the United States. However, the specific regulations of the Bracero Program, and the proximity of Mexico to the United States, meant Mexicans' migrations were generally much more temporary in nature than those of people traveling from Europe or Asia.

[4] For more on the lives of Mexican women whose husbands have migrated, see Hondagneu-Sotelo 1994.

[5] West Indian women, for example, have been leaving children with grandmothers to work in New York City since the 1920s. Wet nurses in eighteenth-century Spain left their infants with their husbands to work in the city of Madrid. See Sarasüa 2001; Watkins-Owens 2001.

[6] Chang 2000; Ehrenreich and Hochschild 2002; and Salazar Parreñas 2001.

[7] After an amnesty program in 1986, efforts were redoubled to restrict undocumented migration. Border enforcement was heightened and, more importantly, concentrated in areas considered to be the "main gates" of illegal entry on the U.S.–Mexican border, making crossing the border increasingly dangerous. Immigration reform in 1996 implemented greater penalties for the undocumented who had illegally crossed the border (read: Mexicans), and social benefits to the families of immigrants were curtailed under the Welfare Reform Act of the same year. See Chang 2000; Cornelius 2001.

[8] Echoing complaints waged nearly one hundred years earlier, today many journalists and social workers have pointed out the deleterious effects of migration on children left behind by their mothers. According to Salazar Parreñas (2005), who has studied Filipino transnational families extensively: "Much academic and newspaper writing on transnational families assumes that children growing up in the Philippines without their parents, particularly their mothers, are prone to delinquency and declining moral values, particularly materialism" (p. 39).

[9] In this city of about 50,000 residents, the Mexican immigrant population went from 1.3 percent in 1990 to 12.6 percent in 2000 (U.S. Census Bureau n.d.). I should note that I lived in this city for ten years starting in 1997 and had previously worked in four different social service agencies, including as an ESL teacher, where I came to know many Mexican families.

[10] Reanne Frank (2005) has shown rates of marital dissolution to be higher among Mexican migrants than their nonmigrant counterparts.

REFERENCES

Amnesty International. 1998. "Human Rights Concerns in the Border Region with Mexico" (AMR 51/03/98 May 20). Washington, DC: Amnesty International. Accessed September 16, 2005, at http://web.amnesty.org/library/Index/engAMR510031998.

Chang, Grace. 2000. *Disposable Domestics: Immigrant Women Workers in the Global Economy.* Cambridge, MA: South End Press.

Chavez, Leo R. 1992. *Shadowed Lives: Undocumented Immigrants in American Society.* Case Studies in Cultural Anthropology. Fort Worth, TX: Harcourt Brace Jovanovich.

Chinchilla, Norma and Kristine Zentgraf. 2007. "Immigrant Children's Views of Family Separation and Reunification." Presented at the Latin American Studies Conference in Montreal, September.

Cohen, Jeffrey H. 2004. *The Culture of Migration in Southern Mexico.* Austin: University of Texas Press.

Cornelius, Wayne. 1991. "Los Migrantes de la Crisis: The Changing Profile of Mexican Migration to the United States." Pp. 155–94 in *Social Responses to Mexico's Economic Crisis of the 1980s,* edited by M. Gonzalez de la Rocha and A. Escobar Latapi. San Diego: University of California, Center for U.S. Mexican Studies.

———. 2001. "Death at the Border: Efficacy and Unintended Consequences of U.S. Immigration Control Policy." *Population and Development Review* 27:661–85.

Donato, Katharine M. 1993. "Current Trends and Patterns of Female Migration: Evidence from Mexico." *International Migration Review* 27:748–68.

Dreby, Joanna. 2006. "Honor and Virtue: Mexican Parenting in the Transnational Context." *Gender & Society* 20:32–59.

———. 2007 "Children and Power in Mexican Transnational Families." *Journal of Marriage and Family* 69:1050–64.

———. 2008. "Gender and Transnational Gossip." *Qualitative Sociology* 32:1–20.

———. Forthcoming. *Divided by Borders: Mexican Migrants and Their Children.* Berkeley: University of California Press.

Ehrenreich, Barbara and Arlie R. Hochschild. 2002. *Global Woman: Nannies, Maids and Sex Workers in the New Economy.* New York: Metropolitan/Owl Books.

Esteinou, Rosario. 2004. "Parenting in Mexican Society." *Marriage and Family Review* 36:7–29.

Foner, Nancy. 2000. *From Ellis Island to JFK: New York's Two Great Waves of Immigration.* New Haven, CT: Yale University Press.

Frank, Reanne. 2005. "The Grass Widows of Mexico: Migration and Union Dissolution in a Binational Context." *Social Forces* 83:919–47.

Furstenberg, Frank F. and Andrew Cherlin. 1994. *Divided Families: What Happens to Children When Parents Part.* Cambridge: Harvard University Press.

Gabaccia, Donna. 2001. "When the Migrants Are Men: Italy's Women and Transnationalism as a Working Class Way of Life." Pp. 190–208 in *Women, Gender and Labour Migration: Historical and Global Perspectives,* edited by P. Sharpe. London: Routledge.

Galinsky, Ellen. 1999. *Ask the Children: What America's Children Really Think about Working Parents.* New York: William Morrow.

Gordon, Linda. 1988. *Heroes of Their Own Lives: The History and Politics of Family Violence.* New York: Penguin Books.

Hirsch, Jennifer S. 2003. *A Courtship after Marriage: Sexuality and Love in Mexican Transnational Families.* Berkeley: University of California Press.

Hondagneu-Sotelo, Pierrette. 1994. *Gendered Transitions: Mexican Experiences of Immigration.* Berkeley: University of California Press.

Hondagneu-Sotelo, Pierrette and Ernestine Avila. 1997. "'I'm Here But I'm There': The Meanings of Latina Transnational Motherhood." *Gender & Society* 11:548–60.

Irving, Katrina. 2000. *Immigrant Mothers: Narratives of Race and Maternity, 1890–1925.* Urbana: University of Illinois Press.

Johnson, Julia Overturf. 2005. *Who's Minding the Kids? Child Care Arrangements: Winter 2002.* Washington, DC: U.S. Census Bureau. Accessed August 28, 2005, at http://www.census.gov/prod/2005pubs/p70-101.pdf.

Levitt, Peggy. 2001. *The Transnational Villagers.* Berkeley: University of California Press.

Mahler, Sarah. 2001. "Transnational Relationships: The Struggle to Communicate across Borders." *Identities* 7:583–619.

Marcus, George E. 1998. *Ethnography through Thick and Thin.* Princeton: Princeton University Press.

Marizco, Michael. 2004. "Smuggling Children." *Arizona Daily Star,* November 21. Accessed November 4, 2005, at http://www.azstarnet.com/sn/border/49066.

Massey, Douglas. 2006. "Borderline Madness." *Chronicle of Higher Education,* June 30, p. B11.

Massey, Douglas, Rafael Alarcón, Jorge Durand, and Humberto González. 1987. *Return to Aztlan: The Social Process of International Migration from Western Mexico.* Berkeley: University of California Press.

Menjívar, Cecilia and Victor Agadjanian. 2007. "Men's Migration and Women's Lives: Views from Rural Armenia and Guatemala." *Social Science Quarterly* 88:1243–62.

Nakano Glenn, E. 1983. "Split Household, Small Producer and Dual Wage Earner: An Analysis of Chinese-American Family Strategies." *Journal of Marriage and the Family* 45:35–46.

Nazario, Sonia. 2006. *La Travesía de Enrique.* New York: Random House.

Ortega, Ralph R. 2006. "No Papers? No Problem." *Newark Star Ledger,* July 23.

Passel, Jeffrey. 2005. "Unauthorized Migrants: Size and Characteristics." Pew Hispanic Center, Washington, DC. Accessed August 8, 2005, at http://pewhispanic.org/files/reports/44.pdf.

———. 2006. "The Size and Characteristics of the Unauthorized Migrant Population in the US." Pew Hispanic Center, Washington, DC. Accessed April 7, 2006, at http://pewhispanic.org/files/reports/61.pdf.

Pew Hispanic Center. 2007. *Factsheet: Indicators of Recent Migration Flows from Mexico.* Washington, DC, May 30. Accessed August 28, 2007, at http://pewhispanic.org/files/factsheets/33.pdf.

Pritchard, Justin. 2004. "One Mexican Worker Dying a Day." *Associated Press,* March 13. Accessed March 23, 2006, at http://fmmac2.mm.ap.org/polk_awards_dying_to_work_html/DyingtoWork.html.

Riessman, Catherine Kohler. 1990. *Divorce Talk: Women and Men Make Sense of Personal Relationships.* New Brunswick, NJ: Rutgers University Press.

Robles, Arodys and Susan Cott Watkins. 1993. "Immigration and Family Separation in the U.S. at the Turn of the Twentieth Century." *Journal of Family History* 18:191–211.

Salazar Parreñas, Rhacel. 2001. *Servants of Globalization: Women, Migration and Domestic Work.* Stanford, CA: Stanford University Press.

———. 2005. *Children of Global Migration: Transnational Families and Gender Woes.* Stanford, CA: Stanford University Press.

Sanchez, George J. 1993. *Becoming Mexican American: Ethnicity, Culture and Identity in Chicano Los Angeles, 1900–1945.* New York: Oxford University Press.

Sarasüa, Carmen. 2001. "Leaving Home to Help the Family? Male and Female Temporary Migrants in Eighteenth- and Nineteenth-Century Spain." Pp. 29–59 in *Women, Gender and Labour Migration: Historical and Global Perspectives,* edited by P. Sharpe. London: Routledge.

Smith, Robert C. 2006. *Mexican New York: Transnational Lives of New Immigrants.* Berkeley: University of California Press.

Stephen, Lynn. 2007. *Transborder Lives: Indigenous Oaxacans in Mexico, California, and Oregon.* Durham, NC: Duke University Press.

Suro, Roberto. 2005. "Survey of Mexican Migrants Part 1: Attitudes about Immigration and Major Demographic Characteristics." Washington, DC, Pew Hispanic Center. Accessed February 5, 2007, at http://pewhispanic.org/files/reports/41.pdf.

Thomas, William I. and Florian Znaniecki. 1927. *The Polish Peasant in Europe and America.* New York: Alfred A. Knopf.

U.S. Census Bureau. n.d. *2000 Census of Population and Housing Summary File 3.* Accessed May 2, 2005, at http://www.factfinder.census.gov.

Watkins-Owens, Irma. 2001. "Early Twentieth Century Caribbean Women: Migration and Social Networks in New York City." Pp. 25–51 in *Islands in the City: West Indian Migration to New York,* edited by Nancy Foner. Berkeley: University of California Press.

48

GENDERED BARGAIN
Why Wives Cannot Trade Their Money for Housework

VERONICA JARIS TICHENOR

This [reading] examines the straightforward bargain implied by the conventional marital contract—that income is exchanged for domestic labor. While we know that employed wives have had little success trading their incomes for a reduction in their domestic labor burden, it is tempting to think that wives with substantially greater incomes could use their resources to negotiate a better deal. As the primary breadwinners, they

may be able to buy out of a greater proportion of housework than can wives who are secondary earners.

The data presented here are based on reports by husbands and wives from the questionnaires and the interviews. Spouses do not always agree in their reports of who does what and how often. Typically, they give themselves more credit than they give their spouses, which is common for research on domestic labor (Coltrane 2000; Cowan and Cowan 1992; Deutsch, Lozy, and Saxon 1993; Vannoy-Hiller and Philliber 1989). In a few instances, what respondents report on their questionnaires differs from the picture they paint in the interviews. All this makes it difficult to arrive at a precise number of hours spent by each spouse on domestic labor and child rearing. Therefore, I report differences in rough proportions to assess the equity of the arrangements. In cases in which spouses disagree over their relative contributions, I give more weight to the wives' responses, since husbands have been found to overreport their participation in domestic labor at a greater rate than do their wives (Press and Townsley 1998; Wright et al. 1992). Also, since husbands perform so little domestic labor on average, they are likely to underestimate the amount of labor required to run a household, as well as the amount of work their wives perform on a regular basis.

Employed Wives and the Conventional Marital Contract

We saw in [earlier research] how the gender structure sets up the bargain between spouses in the conventional marital contract. Husbands trade their income for the domestic labor and child care that wives provide. The bargain is simple and straightforward when husbands are the sole providers but has become more complex as women have moved into the workforce. Under the rules of the contract, as wives begin to share the activity of providing with their husbands, fairness dictates that husbands should respond by performing more domestic labor. This would be a simple and reasonable adaptation of the bargain; however, it does not seem to be happening.

Some of the research on domestic labor argues that men have taken on a greater share of the household burden as their wives moved into paid employment. However, this increased labor amounts to only a few hours per week. More importantly, this increase in men's contributions does not necessarily mean that men are providing their wives with substantial help or relief. Rather, these shifts in numbers suggest that employed women are no longer able to do as much around the house as they have in the past; in short, it looks like men are doing more because women, unable to do it all, are doing less. Therefore, these changes for men seem to reflect only a proportional increase in men's share of domestic labor rather than a substantial increase in real hours (Benokraitis 1985; Berk 1985; Bianchi et al. 2000; Coltrane 2000; Hochschild 1989; Nickols and Metzen 1982; Pleck 1985; Whyte 1990).

These small increases in the contribution of men notwithstanding, the bulk of the literature on the division of domestic labor has made clear

that wives have simply added paid employment to their duties as wives and mothers (see, for example, Berk 1985; Coltrane 2000; Hartmann 1981; Peterson and Gerson 1992; Sexton and Perlman 1989; South and Spitze 1994. These results hold cross-culturally as well: see Lewis, Izraeli, and Hootsman 1992). That is, the big story is that even when women are employed outside the home, they still bear the prime responsibility for their homes and children. This combined load of paid and domestic labor means that women work longer days and weeks than do their husbands—or, as Hochschild (1989) put it, women work an extra month of twenty-four-hour days each year. Women with children feel this burden even more acutely. Having a child increases not only the amount of household labor required, but also the inequity in the division of that labor. Men's participation in housework decreases with the birth of the first child, even among couples who shared household labor equitably before the arrival of children (Cowan and Cowan 1992; Rexroat and Shehan 1987).

Occupational disparities between spouses are often used to explain the continued inequities in domestic labor in dual-income households. Work-related variables such as relative earnings, occupational status, and time demands of spouses are thought to explain their relative contributions to household labor (Barnett and Baruch 1988; Mederer 1993; Perry-Jenkins and Folk 1994; Presser 1994; Shelton 1992; Wright et al. 1992). These results reinforce the logic of the conventional marital contract—if one spouse contributes more at work, she or he should contribute less at home. Since men typically earn more than do their wives and often work longer hours in pursuit of these higher incomes, their lesser contributions to housework and child care are seen as legitimate.

However, other research indicates that the division of domestic labor is not driven by the relative earnings or time demands of spouses (Brayfield 1992; Brines 1994; Greenstein 2000; Gupta 1999; Hochschild 1989). In fact, when wives earn more than their husbands do, men perform little or no domestic labor (Bittman et al. 2003; Brines 1994; Greenstein 2000; Hochschild 1989). In other words, the bargain seems to break down when women bring money to the table, because wives are unable to trade their income for domestic services from their husbands. This suggests that the bargain implied by the conventional marital contract is gendered—certain rights, obligations, or privileges are assigned by gender, rather than on the basis of role performance. Women seem obliged to perform nearly all the domestic labor even though their husbands are no longer providing the family's sole (or even major) financial support.

The "His" and "Hers" of Domestic Labor

The imperatives of the gender structure largely determine the division of domestic labor in households. Certain household chores are considered women's jobs, while others belong to men. Though there is some crossover in tasks, most couples still divide them largely on the basis of conventional

gender expectations. Men are more likely to handle the outdoors tasks and household repairs, while women are more likely to tend to the nurturing and physical care of the children, as well as the indoor activities required for daily living (food, laundry, cleaning, etc.). Women perform a greater variety of chores, and most of the domestic labor falls on their side of the marital ledger (see Coltrane 2000 for a review of this literature).

There are also distinct differences in the nature of the tasks that men and women perform. Men have more discretion in taking on household tasks, often choosing those they consider pleasant. For example, playing with the children is generally seen as a more enjoyable activity than scrubbing toilets, and when pushed to provide more help, men often choose the more agreeable tasks. Men also tend to perform chores that are more peripheral to the functioning of the household, rather than tasks that are crucial for daily living. This means that men are more often in a position to choose when they will perform these tasks, which gives them the freedom to postpone them. For example, changing the oil in the car or making a household repair can be put off—in some cases, indefinitely. The family is not likely to suffer if men do not perform these tasks immediately. On the other hand, it is difficult to tell a small child that you do not feel like making dinner or changing a soiled diaper right now. These tasks cannot be put off for a week—or even an hour. In short, men tend to do work that has clearly defined boundaries (mowing the lawn), has an element of discretion in timing (household repairs), and has a great leisure component (playing with the children) (Benokraitis 1985; Berk 1985; Berk and Berk 1979; Coleman 1991).

There are also differences in the way men and women view chores. Men seem to underestimate the work involved in ongoing household responsibilities. For example, one study found that 36 percent of the men interviewed regarded cooking as a "leisure activity," whereas only 14 percent of the wives described cooking in this way (Horna and Leipri 1987). Anyone who has tried to put a hot, nutritious meal on the table in between the after-school and evening activities of three or four people would not describe cooking as a "leisure activity." But viewing domestic labor as leisure, at least in part, may permit husbands to see some chores as discretionary, thus allowing them a sense of freedom from housework and child care that their wives do not share.

More fundamentally, much of the labor women perform at home is not viewed as work—it is "invisible" (Daniels 1987; Wright et al. 1992). This invisible work refers to the myriad details that women typically handle in the course of an average day or week and ranges from coordinating the schedules of family members to making sure someone is home to meet the cable repairer. It is the kind of work that family members do not notice unless the woman fails to do it. The very invisibility of this work further burdens wives, because men do not recognize the full measure of domestic labor their wives perform. This makes it easier for men to see themselves as contributing substantially to household chores when their contributions are, in fact, negligible (Mederer 1993).

Women, of course, feel the weight of this invisible work, as one of the wives in my sample made extremely clear. She filled out the initial questionnaire, which asked about only the most fundamental household chores, such as cooking, laundry, household cleaning, and basic child care, then added a written comment on the back of her questionnaire. Her response is a dramatic statement about the invisibility of women's work (as well as a critique of quantitative methods for studying domestic labor). I reproduce it here in its entirety:

> *The issue I think is missed here is that logistics, planning, contingency arrangements, etc.—all the prep work—usually fall completely to the mother. The mother secures daycare and backup daycare, evening baby-sitting, snow day school closing planning, etc. So while the father may have significant participation in doing any family tasks, the* planning *etc. is frequently all a mother's work.*
>
> *You don't highlight who calls the YWCA for the program schedule, who makes sure there is change each day for lunch money, who decides it is time for a dental checkup, who realizes last year's snow boots won't fit this year* before *this year's first snow, who arranges the* children's *social schedule, who plans the birthday parties, who communicates with the children's school (a real key activity in early elementary grades), who sells school fund-raising items at work, who sees that young children use the toilet before a trip in the car, who sets up the car pool for church, school, soccer, scouts, etc. All this—or most of this—is constant, continual* PLANNING. *The actual execution is a cakewalk by comparison!*

Clearly, the sheer number of tasks that women face in managing and caring for a family can be overwhelming, and the invisibility of this work only adds to the load that wives bear.

Power Struggles and Conflict in Dividing Domestic Labor

That men have not taken on domestic duties to balance their wives' economic contributions in dual-earner families suggests that housework is onerous or unpleasant—at the very least, something to be avoided. Couples often engage in open struggles over this issue; in fact, it is one of the leading causes of marital strife (Coltrane 2000; Hochschild 1989). The scenario is simple and familiar: Wives ask for help, while husbands resist or refuse. Men's ability to avoid domestic labor is seen as a reflection of their greater power in the relationship.

However, the struggle can be more subtle. We know that, in addition to performing the vast majority of household chores, wives maintain responsibility for these tasks regardless of who executes them. Wives keep track of all household details and know what needs to be done when, which sets wives up as the household experts. It also means that wives are often in the position of "supervising" their husbands as they perform household and childcare tasks. Spouses may have different ideas of what constitutes an adequate job on a particular task, and these differing expectations often lead to more

conflict. For example, women complain that their husbands do not clean to their standards, and that they must often redo tasks their husbands have undertaken. Differing timetables for the completion of chores is also a source of conflict between spouses. Women report that it is difficult to get husbands to complete chores on a timely basis, and wives find themselves nagging their husbands. Or men purposely drag their feet or feign helplessness as a kind of passive resistance through which they can avoid domestic labor without having to confront their wives directly (Hochschild 1989). These tactics often succeed. With all the extra effort required to get husbands to contribute more around the house, wives often conclude that it is easier to just do the task themselves and avoid the argument.

Carrying the domestic labor burden can have negative consequences for women. The continued gap between the number of hours spouses devote to household responsibilities means that wives pay higher personal costs to maintain the family than men do. For example, women have much less time than their husbands have to devote to leisure activities, which increases the level of stress wives experience and can be detrimental to their mental health (Berk 1985; Cockburn 1991; Geerken and Gove 1983; Pahl 1989; Pleck 1985; Shelton 1992). Perhaps most alarming is that women often try to meet the demands placed on them by sacrificing such basic necessities as exercise and adequate sleep (Hochschild 1989).

Carrying this load can also harm the marital relationship, as the symbolic issues associated with caring work come to the fore. If a husband refuses to help out at home, a wife may come to believe that he sees his time as more valuable than hers. Having to do it all can make a wife feel like a servant or slave rather than a partner or lover, as the burden she carries becomes a statement of her lesser worth in the relationship. The struggle over domestic labor can become a measure of her husband's affection— "If you really loved me, you'd help me." In short, wives may see their husbands' attempts to get out of housework as "not caring" about them or their needs (Erickson 1993).

However, other symbolic issues associated with domestic labor may undercut the potential conflict over housework. Since domestic labor is so tied to caring, wives who struggle with their husbands may see themselves as not caring about their families and consequently as bad wives and mothers (DeVault 1991; Finch and Groves 1983). This is especially true in the case of child care. What kind of mother fights over who has to put the children to bed or spend an afternoon with them? To be a good wife is to care for a husband, home, and children. A wife's desire to fulfill these caring obligations may discourage her from pushing for a greater household-labor contribution from her husband.

Wives may also avoid conflict over domestic labor to preserve marital harmony. Struggles over housework and child care can set an unpleasant tone for a marriage. Trying to share chores equally can mean rules, regulations, and schedules, in addition to conflict (Thompson 1991). Women may decide that a comfortable, companionate marriage is more important than equality in household labor (Bolak 1997; Branner and Moss 1987;

Foa et al. 1993). If this is the case, then domestic labor has as much to do with affirming one's sense of personal and marital well-being as it does with accomplishing the necessary tasks of daily living—particularly for women. In other words, the symbolic issues associated with household chores and child care may be more important than the actual division of that labor, and couples may be more willing to live with the inequities of the status quo than weather the storms that challenging the gender structure would certainly bring.

Couples with higher-earning wives organize their lives amid these same symbolic issues and power struggles. Like other employed wives, these women are burdened with the bulk of the domestic labor in their families. Like other employed wives, they often struggle to increase their husbands' participation. Like other employed wives, they feel the load they are carrying, and the stress takes its toll—on them and their relationships. In short, couples with higher-earning wives exhibit domestic labor patterns that are strikingly similar to those of other dual-income couples.

Continued Inequality for Higher-Earning Wives

Money does not drive the division of domestic labor in couples with higher-earning wives. That is, these women are not able to trade their substantial incomes for a corresponding reduction in their domestic labor burden. However, higher-earning wives get a little more relief than do comparison wives. This is especially true for the five wives in my sample who are the nearly sole breadwinners for their families. In each of these cases, the husband performs the majority of the household labor and child care. Of the seventeen remaining couples with higher-earning wives, only 41 percent of husbands perform a substantial portion of the domestic labor (from one-third to, in one case, nearly one-half). Among comparison couples, 25 percent of husbands contribute at this level. All remaining husbands in both groups contribute less than one-third of the domestic labor. This speaks for the ability of higher-earning wives to buy some additional relief from household labor, but the picture should not be painted too optimistically. These are women who earn a great deal more than their husbands, enjoy substantially higher status, or both. Yet, even in the best of circumstances, they are not able to trade these resources for a similarly substantial reduction in their burden of domestic labor. Surprisingly, few couples employed outside help with household chores. Only three couples with higher-earning wives and two comparison couples used paid housecleaners on a regular basis, and in all five cases, the wives performed most of the remaining household chores.

Higher-earning wives are more like than unlike other employed wives, in that they face the same inequities at home and carry most of the household-labor burden. Higher-earning wives also confront the familiar problems of trying to share domestic labor. First, they have to ask for help; their husbands do not tend to jump right into household chores. Second, these wives

struggle with differing standards of cleanliness, reporting that they have to redo chores that their husbands did not perform well enough. And finally, there are differing timetables for performing chores, with husbands frequently putting off tasks that their wives consider more urgent. All these issues can generate conflict in these marriages.

For example, Cindy is a higher-earning wife married to Don. They have three young sons and have lived in a variety of economic circumstances in their ten-year marriage. Each has supported the other through some schooling (she received her master's degree, he received his associate's degree), each has worked part-time at some point, and each has been the primary parent at home for a period of time. Now both spouses work full time. Cindy made the move back to full-time work this past year, and she and Don have had conversations about sharing the household chores more equitably. Don has made an effort to share more tasks, but Cindy says the plan works only because she has been willing to both praise her husband for his efforts and lower her standards:

> *Usually during the school year, he'll have two or three nights a week that he'll cook, I have two or three nights a week that I'll cook, and then the other nights are leftovers and that sort of thing. And we're pretty good about sticking to that. The only thing is, when he cooks, it means it's spaghetti, with maybe some French bread on the side. It's not like there's a fruit and a vegetable, you know? [She laughs.] But, if you're going to try and share things like this, you've also got to be willing to lower your standards somewhat; otherwise, it doesn't work out.*

Cindy also talks about her frustrations when it is Don's turn to do the laundry. The clothes are clean, but they rarely get folded and put away. Her sons have to go fishing through the laundry baskets to find outfits to wear, and they end up with wrinkled clothes. Cindy has tried talking to Don about this, but nothing has changed. She has decided that if it does not bother him that the boys have to go looking for clean clothes, she has to try not to let it bother her.

In addition, higher-earning wives are still primarily responsible for doing "the things that nobody sees," in the words of one husband. Some couples seem to be aware that the wives carry this extra load. Even if they think they work well together as a team, they recognize that there is something significant about what the wives do. For example, this husband with a higher-earning wife says:

> *To me, it doesn't make sense to say, "Who is more essential?" For us, we're both essential, and each would be sorely missed by the other. [Pause.] But Joyce could replace me with money—hire people to do what I do. I would have more trouble doing what she does because you can't replace it with money. It's the planning, looking for day-care programs for the girls, arranging outings on the weekends, buying their clothes, getting them into outfits on time, getting them into the shower, out of the shower, into bed without fighting—all of those things.*

That he could not "replace his wife with money" is a powerful statement about both the significance and the value of what women typically do at home. Women's work is so specialized, intimate, and all-encompassing that the average family could not pay someone to do it. On the other hand, that one cannot put a fair market price on these services often means that they are devalued or taken for granted. In fact, this work often becomes invisible—even to the women themselves, like the higher-earning wife quoted next. She claims that her husband is responsible for getting their two young daughters to day care every morning, but her description of what she and her husband do each morning tells a more complex story:

> *He does the basics, whereas I do the other little extra things, like laying their clothes out. I try to have everything ready for him in the morning 'cause he's not real good at functioning in the morning. I try to have everything laid out. The diaper bag's packed. Basically, really, all you would need to do is give the baby a bottle and change her diaper and put her clothes on. And it is still a lot, and I appreciate him doing that.*

It is striking that she places such value on his contributions and discounts her own. This demonstrates how much of what these wives do is still invisible and therefore not always recognized or defined as work; this means that women do not always get credit for performing it, which disadvantages them in the struggle for equity. This quote also highlights how tricky it can be to assess how domestic labor is divided in a particular household. I initially asked this wife, "Who is responsible for getting the children to day care?" She responded that her husband was, but this simple answer hides all the preparatory work she does to make the job easier for him. More importantly, it is quite probably her willingness to do all the background work that ensures his continued willingness to perform the task of taking their children to day care.

That higher-earning wives are working full time and shouldering the lion's share of labor and organizational responsibilities at home means that they carry the same heavy load that other employed wives do. Their lives exist in a "delicate balance," in the words of one wife. The woman quoted next is a physician with a complicated weekly schedule, including half days, long days, and one day off per week, to try to accommodate the needs of the house and her two young sons. Maintaining a balance between work and family is a constant challenge:

> *Right now I feel like things are in a pretty delicate balance between the family and the demands of work. And if something goes wrong, it's pretty stressful. I'd like to get a little more cushion in my life. [She laughs.] . . . It's very stressful when things are running late at work, and there's another patient to see, or a patient arrives late, and you know you have to be out at an exact time to pick your child up at nursery school. And if you're five minutes late to the nursery school, they get very upset with you and you feel terribly guilty. [She laughs.] And working on that kind of tight schedule is stressful.*

This tight scheduling and trying to do it all leaves little or no time for the women themselves. That is, higher-earning wives face the same leisure gap other employed women face. When asked if she enjoyed any leisure activities, one higher-earning wife speaks for many when she says:

> *Actually, no. At this point, I don't. I used to like to paint, but I don't have the time to paint anymore. I really don't feel like I have the time to do much of anything anymore. . . . [My husband's] got lots of hobbies. He's got plenty of time to do it all.*

For their part, most husbands with higher-earning wives recognize the inequities in their marriages. They are also aware that their wives would often like them to take on more responsibility. But like other husbands, they resist this pressure. They even talk about their "laziness" lightheartedly. The following is a typical justification for not doing more at home:

> *I look at a room and say, "Eh, it's not that dirty." [We laugh.] . . . One of my biggest vices is that I love to watch sports. And it just so happens that sports fall on the weekends, when you should be doing things around the house, like cutting the lawn and raking the leaves. But those doggone sports things are on. I get so wrapped up in those sometimes.*

Or, as this husband simply puts it: *"I could probably do more [around the house], but when it comes to the choice of doing laundry or watching VH1, VH1 wins."*

Wives do not express the same sense of humor when it comes to the inequities they face in housework and child care, but they are certainly aware of the ironies in their circumstances. This is evident in an anecdote relayed by one higher-earning wife, Joyce. She told me about a co-worker who got a call from her child-care provider one morning to say that she would be at work that day, but that she was going to be deported that night. The co-worker was understandably distraught and worried about what she would do with her children the following day. As her husband left for work that morning, he told his wife to "have a good day." Joyce says her co-worker *"went ballistic. 'Have a good day?' Child care is being deported tonight! How could those words come out of the man's mouth?"* Joyce and her friends try to laugh about the strains of working full time and being responsible for a family:

> *Right now, at this moment in your life, if you have multiple kids, you tend to have multiple child-care arrangements. If one person is gonna exit unannounced, it's gotta be the husband! [We laugh.] Because you can cry by yourself in your bed, and that's not a problem. But if a child care [worker] leaves unannounced, it's a major disruption in your life.*

And while this woman was laughing as she told me this story, she was not entirely joking. Because of the burdens they face, and their husbands' unwillingness to lighten this load, these wives may be starting to see their husbands as expendable.

Important Work

While higher-earning wives are not able to use their substantial incomes to negotiate equally substantial reductions in their household burden, in some cases their husbands contribute a larger portion (roughly 30 to 40 percent) of the domestic labor than do other husbands. Status and income differences do not explain this variability in patterns of sharing; earning more money does not automatically guarantee wives relief from domestic labor. Stated gender ideology, such as beliefs about a woman's right to pursue employment or a man's obligation to contribute to domestic labor when his wife works outside the home, also does not match actual sharing behavior in any systematic way. Similarly, relative time demands, as reflected in the number of hours spent at work, commuting, working overtime, and traveling, do not seem to drive the division of domestic labor for these couples. To assess the more subtle dynamics between spouses, I explored whether couples give one of their jobs priority over the other by examining the opportunities for advancement for each spouse, including the possibility of relocating for those opportunities; whether one spouse's work tends to define the family's daily schedule; whether spouses discuss each other's work; and how much respect each spouse seems to have for the other's work. Examining these issues revealed a subtle calculation that goes on within each relationship. Most couples seem to have a sense that one spouse's job is more important than the other's, and the spouse doing the important work is allowed to contribute less at home. In a few cases, spouses do not see either job as more important, and this situation also leads to more equitable sharing of domestic labor. . . .

Gendered Labor and Power

The results presented in this [reading] provide further evidence that resource and exchange models are inadequate to explain the division of domestic labor when wives earn more than their husbands do. Higher-earning wives are unable to trade their substantial incomes for equally substantial reductions in their domestic labor burden. These wives are performing the bulk of domestic labor in addition to bringing home the lion's share of the family income. . . .

However, while some higher-earning wives get more relief from domestic labor than do employed wives more generally, this was true for only half the women in this sample. And remember that, with the exception of the five wives who are nearly the sole earners in their families, these women are still performing more than half the household chores and child care. In other words, a wife's earning two-thirds of the family income in no case translated into a husband's performing two-thirds of the domestic labor. This means that the most important finding is the continued inequity at home, even for women with substantial income and occupational resources at their disposal.

These results demonstrate that all the patterns of sharing domestic labor among couples with higher-earning wives are still influenced by gender. First, the vast majority of wives continue to perform the bulk of household chores and child care, despite their substantial incomes. Second, while doing important work may lessen the load somewhat for wives, husbands still seem to benefit more from this calculation. Men doing important work have wives performing 80 to 90 percent of the domestic labor, whereas women doing important work get, at best, a 30 to 40 percent contribution from their husbands. In other words, wives still contribute much more, in terms of both income and domestic labor, no matter what their circumstances.

That men are able to evade housework and child care despite their lesser incomes demonstrates that the gender structure exerts an independent influence on the dynamics of these couples. Husbands' continued ability to limit their household-labor contributions means that they enjoy this privilege as *men*, rather than as *providers*. The cultural expectation that women are responsible for and perform domestic labor undercuts whatever power might be available in the greater incomes these wives earn. This explains why even higher-earning wives are unable to get a fair trade for their money.

REFERENCES

Barnett, Rosalind and Grace Baruch. 1988. "Correlates of Fathers' Participation in Family Work." In *Fatherhood Today: Men's Changing Role in the Family*, edited by Phyllis Bronstein and Carolyn Pape Cowan. New York: John Wiley.

Benokraitis, Nijole. 1985. "Fathers in the Dual-Earner Family." In *Dimensions of Fatherhood*, edited by Shirley Hanson and Frederick Bozett. Beverly Hills, CA: Sage.

Berk, Richard A. and Sarah Fenstermaker Berk. 1979. *Labor and Leisure at Home: Content and Organization of the Household Day*. Beverly Hills, CA: Sage.

Berk, Sarah Fenstermaker. 1985. *The Gender Factory: The Appointment of Work in American Households*. New York: Plenum Press.

Bianchi, Susan, Melissa Milkie, Liana Sayer, and John Robinson. 2000. "Is Anyone Doing the Housework? Trends in the Gender Division of Household Labor." *Social Forces* 79:191–228.

Bittman, Michael, Paula England, Liana Sayer, Nancy Folbre, and George Matheson. 2003. "When Does Gender Trump Money? Bargaining and Time in Household Work." *American Journal of Sociology* 109:186–214.

Bolak, Hale Cihan. 1997. "When Wives Are Major Providers: Culture, Gender, and Family Work." *Gender & Society* 11:409–33.

Branner, Julia and Peter Moss. 1987. "Father in Dual-Earner Households—Through Mother's Eyes." In *Reassessing Fatherhood: New Observations on Fathers and the Modern Family*, edited by Charlie Lewis and Margaret O'Brien. Beverly Hills, CA: Sage.

Brayfield, April A. 1992. "Employment Resources and Housework in Canada." *Journal of Marriage and the Family* 54:19–30.

Brines, Julie. 1994. "Economic Dependency, Gender, and the Division of Labor at Home." *American Journal of Sociology* 100:652–88.

Cockburn, Cynthia. 1991. *In the Way of Women: Men's Resistance to Sex Equality in Organizations*. Ithaca, NY: ILR Press.

Coleman, Marion T. 1991. "The Division of Household Labor: Suggestions for Future Empirical Consideration and Theoretical Development." In *Gender, Family, and Economy: The Triple Overlap*, edited by R. L. Blumberg. Beverly Hills, CA: Sage.

Coltrane, Scott. 2000. "Research on Household Labor: Modeling and Measuring the Social Embeddedness of Routine Family Work." *Journal of Marriage and the Family* 62:1208–33.

Cowan, Carolyn Pape and Philip A. Cowan. 1992. *When Partners Become Parents: The Big Life Change for Couples*. New York: Basic Books.

Daniels, Arlene Kaplan. 1987. "Invisible Work." *Social Problems* 34:403–15.

Deutsch, Francine, Jennifer Lozy, and Susan Saxon. 1993. "Taking Credit: Couples' Reports of Contributions to Child Care." *Journal of Family Issues* 14:421–37.

DeVault, Marjorie L. 1991. *Feeding the Family: The Social Organizing of Caring as Gendered Work.* Chicago: University of Chicago Press.

Erickson, Rebecca. 1993. "Reconceptualizing Family Work: The Effect of Emotion Work on Perceptions of Marital Quality." *Journal of Marriage and the Family* 55:888–900.

Finch, Janet and Dulcie Groves. 1983. *A Labour of Love: Women, Work, and Caring.* London: Routledge and Kegan Paul.

Foa, Uriel, John Converse Jr., Kjell Tornblom, and Edna Foa, eds. 1993. *Resource Theory Explorations and Applications.* San Diego: Academic Press.

Geerken, Michael and Walter R. Gove. 1983. *At Home and at Work: The Family's Allocation of Labor.* Beverly Hills, CA: Sage.

Greenstein, Theodore. 2000. "Economic Dependence, Gender, and the Division of Labor at Home: A Replication and Extension." *Journal of Marriage and the Family* 62:322–35.

Gupta, Sanjiv. 1999. "What Makes Men Change Their Housework Time?" Ph.D. dissertation, University of Michigan, Ann Arbor.

Hartmann, Heidi. 1981. "The Family as the Locus of Gender, Class, and Political Struggle: The Example of Housework." *Signs* 6:366–94.

Hochschild, Arlie. 1989. *The Second Shift.* New York: Viking.

Horna, Jamila and Eugen Leipri. 1987. "Father's Participation in Work, Family Life, and Leisure: A Canadian Experience." In *Reassessing Fatherhood: New Observations on Fathers and the Modern Family,* edited by Charlie Lewis and Margaret O'Brien. Beverly Hills, CA: Sage.

Lewis, Susan, Daffna Izraeli, and Helen Hootsman. 1992. *Dual-Earner Family: International Perspectives.* London: Sage.

Mederer, Helen. 1993. "Division of Labor in Two-Earner Homes: Task Accomplishment versus Household Management as Critical Variables in Perceptions about Family Work." *Journal of Marriage and the Family* 55:133–45.

Nickols, Sharon Y. and Edward J. Metzen. 1982. "Impact of Wife's Employment upon Husband's Housework." *Journal of Family Issues* 3:199–216.

Pahl, Jan. 1989. *Money and Marriage.* New York: St. Martin's Press.

Perry-Jenkins, Maureen and Karen Folk. 1994. "Class, Couples, and Conflict: Effects of the Division of Labor on Assessments of Marriage in Dual-Earner Families." *Journal of Marriage and the Family* 54:527–36.

Peterson, Richard R. and Kathleen Gerson. 1992. "Determinants of Responsibilities for Childcare among Dual-Earner Couples." *Journal of Marriage and the Family* 54:527–536.

Pleck, Robert. 1985. *Working Wives, Working Husbands.* Beverly Hills, CA: Sage.

Press, Julie and Eleanor Townsley. 1998. "Wives' and Husbands' Housework Reporting: Gender, Class, and Social Desirability." *Gender & Society* 12:188–218.

Presser, Harriet. 1994. "Employment Schedules among Dual-Earner Spouses and the Division of Household Labor by Gender." *American Sociological Review* 59:348–64.

Rexroat, Cynthia and Constance Shehan. 1987. "The Family Life Cycle and Spouses' Time in Housework." *Journal of Marriage and the Family* 49:737–750.

Sexton, Christine and Daniel Perlman. 1989. "Couple's Career Orientation, Gender Role Orientation, and Perceived Equity as Determinants of Marital Power." *Journal of Marriage and the Family* 51:933–41.

Shelton, Beth Anne. 1992. *Women, Men, and Time: Gender Differences in Paid Work, Housework, and Leisure.* New York: Greenwood Press.

South, Scott and Glenna Spitze. 1994. "Housework in Marital and Nonmarital Households." *American Sociological Review* 59:327–47.

Thompson, Linda. 1991. "Family Work: Women's Sense of Fairness." *Journal of Family Issues.* 12:181–96.

Vannoy-Hiller, Dana and William Philliber. 1989. *Equal Partners Successful Women in Marriage.* Newbury Park, CA: Sage.

Whyte, Martin King. 1990. *Dating, Mating, and Marriage.* New York: Aldine de Gruyter.

Wright, Erik Olin, Karen Shire, Shu-Ling Hwang, Maureen Dolan, and Janeen Baxter. 1992. "The Non-effects of Class on the Gender Division of Labor in the Home: A Comparative Study of Sweden and the U.S." *Gender & Society* 6:252–81.

49
_____

NO PLACE LIKE HOME
The Division of Domestic Labor in Lesbigay Families

CHRISTOPHER CARRINGTON

Sterling never cleaned toilets, he still doesn't clean toilets; he intends to clean the toilets, but right about the time when he gets to it, I have already cleaned the toilets.

—WAYNE OSMUNDSEN, 35-YEAR-OLD SOCIAL WORKER

The common metaphorical use of laundry, as in the phrase "to air their dirty laundry in public," connotes several things about actual laundry, most notably a common expectation that dirty laundry should remain hidden. This [reading] violates that common expectation, in both a metaphorical and in a literal sense.

Stigmatized and oppressed communities often struggle with the menacing question of how to deal with "dirty laundry." Many lesbian and gay authors feel the need to present ourselves, and our communities, to the dominant culture in ideal terms, a feeling that I have often shared. These portrayals, as opposed to the empirical realities, often reflect the efforts of lesbigay people to provide a respectable image of ourselves in a society often bent on devaluing and marginalizing us. Undoubtedly, the observations made here regarding the division of domestic work in lesbigay families violate the expectation that dirty laundry remain closeted.

The public portrayals and presentations of egalitarianism among lesbigay families do not cohere with the household realities that prevail among them. Two components of the research strategy used here expose the gap between public portrayals and empirical realities. First, the use of back-to-back interviews instead of joint interviews produces discrepancies in answers to the most routine of questions about domesticity. As Aquilino (1993) reveals, interviews often produce much higher estimates of spousal contributions to domestic work when the spouse is present than when he or she is not. Second, the fieldwork component of this research offers behavioral observations that reveal significant gaps between what participants say in interviews and what participants do in everyday life. The commitment to the ideology of familial egalitarianism within the lesbian and gay community, and among

the subset of lesbigay families, is palpable. Yet, the empirical reality for many of these families is something quite different, something much more akin to patterns among heterosexual families (Gerson 1985, 1993). Moreover, when a particular family achieves something close to parity in the distribution of domestic activities, this almost always occurs under unique social conditions: great affluence, relative impoverishment, or among a distinct minority of couples with significantly diminished senses of themselves as family. In this [reading] I examine each of these exceptions and what motivates lesbigay people to portray their relationships in ideal terms both to themselves and to the outside world. I will also consider what factors seem to most significantly influence the actual division of domestic labor among lesbigay families.

The Egalitarian Myth

There exists among the lesbigay families studied here a prevalent and persistent commitment to viewing both one's own relationship and those of other lesbians and gays as egalitarian. Most participants in this study, when asked to describe in general terms how they divide up household responsibilities in their relationship, relied upon the language of egalitarianism. Typical responses included: "Oh I would say it's fifty-fifty around here," or "we pretty much share all of the responsibilities," or "everyone does their fair share," or "it's pretty even." These perceptions persist even in the face of obvious empirical observations to the contrary. Many lesbigay family members fail to make much of a distinction between what they consider equal and what they consider fair. The blurring of these two quite distinct matters is necessary to maintaining the myth of egalitarianism. . . .

Consequently, one must remain aware of the distinct possibility that intense pressures exist upon a participant's answers to questions about the division of domesticity. I think these pressures go a long way in explaining why lesbigay families, when asked about domestic activities, particularly in public settings, often joke about the matter. The humor masks the awkward feelings such questions produce. And after a few humorous exchanges, and possibly a little dig or two, the families make a concerted effort to reestablish the perception of equality. The research of Hochschild (1989) indicates that heterosexual families do exactly the same; they construct myths of egalitarianism. But there is more to the story among lesbigay families than meets the eye. . . .

The Management of Gender Identity and Domesticity

Gender looms as a significant matter in the portrayal as well as the organization of domesticity in lesbigay families. Like many other scholars of gender, I find that domestic work results not only in the creation of goods and services but also in the creation of gender (Berk 1985; Brines 1994; Coltrane 1989; DeVault 1991; Ferree 1990; Hochschild 1989; Petuchek 1992; West and Zimmerman 1987). The potential for domesticity resulting in the construction of gender identity means different things to lesbian women and gay

men. For lesbians, the capacity of domesticity to construct gender carries important consequences for partners whose paid-work obligations prevent them from engaging in much domesticity. Examples abound. Many of the lesbian women employed in time- and energy-consuming occupations expressed guilt about, and made much humor of their inattentiveness to and lack of participation in, domesticity. Their partners often provide cover for them, assigning credit for domestic tasks that they really did not do, or emphasizing some femininity-producing activity that compensates. . . .

The Invisibility of Domesticity and the Egalitarian Myth

Much of domesticity is invisible. Many of the forms of domestic labor rest upon a foundation of unobserved efforts that consume an individual's time and energy. Monitoring the house for cleanliness, monitoring the calendar for birthdays, monitoring the catalog for appropriate gifts, monitoring the cupboard for low supplies, monitoring the moods of one's spouse, and monitoring the family finances all are expressions of domesticity, and all are mostly invisible. The vast stores of accumulated knowledge about domestic things go unobserved by most: the knowledge of a family member's food tastes, dietary requirements, clothing size, the last gift one bought for them, work schedule, and the last time the cat received a rabies shot are all forms of domesticity and are hidden in the heads of those who hold responsibility for doing these things.

This invisibility, even to those who do it, sometimes produces seemingly inexplicable feelings of anger and resentment. Domestic work often becomes the site of enduring conflict between partners in relationships. Joe McFarland and Richard Neibuhr have been together for just under four years. Their relationship is "on the rocks," as Richard puts it. They reluctantly agreed to an interview. The family recently bought a house together, using money from Joe's inheritance from his previous lover, who died in the late 1980s. Both Richard and Joe conceive of their domestic relationship in strongly egalitarian terms despite what to me resembles a clear pattern of specialization with Richard doing much of the domestic labor in the family—not just much of the invisible work, but the visible work as well. Richard is not happy about the situation, although he has difficulty finding the words:

> *I think things are pretty equal in the relationship, although I wish Joe would appreciate my contributions more, and maybe be a little more helpful. It's hard to describe, but I feel like I do a lot of stuff to make our life better, but he doesn't really care about that. I think he thinks I'm just nagging him. If I ask him to do certain things, like, for instance, I asked him to call someone about going out to a movie on Friday night. He got annoyed. He says that if I want to go out to a movie with someone, then I should call. He thinks that's my interest. It's funny, though, because if I don't do it, he will ask how come we're not doing anything, and complain that we don't really have many friends. I get sort of frustrated about it, but I don't push it too much. He feels like I am dominating his space, imposing on his free time too much, not respecting his boundaries. He's very big on boundaries, he gets that from his therapist, who thinks that he needs to keep his own space.*

A similar conversation took place with Joe. Notice how the advice of the therapist actually influences the division of domesticity:

CC: *Tell me about continuing discussions/points of conflict or unresolved feelings with your spouse over these kinds of cleaning tasks.*

Joe: *My therapist is of the opinion that Richard lacks empathy for me, and/ or maybe empathy for people in general, and doesn't understand that for me, time down and time alone is a chance for me to think my own thoughts, feel my feelings, expand my emotional life through reading or television. Richard doesn't have any appreciation for that. Consequently, the therapist thinks he lacks empathy. He asks me to do things that are his interests, and that's not fair to me.*

CC: *What kind of things?*

Joe: *Well, like stuff for the house. I mean, I paid for the house, or at least mostly, and I don't really care that much how the house looks. I mean, I want it clean, but a little messy is not a big deal. If he wants it a certain way, he can do it. I need my space.*

Richard feels frustration because Joe won't help with domesticity. If Richard expresses those sentiments, they actually become illegitimate because they are understood as an imposition of Richard's "interests" upon Joe. Both Richard and Joe conceive of their relationship as egalitarian with the differences over domesticity actually reflecting different individual "interests." The advice of the therapist, or at least the way it gets understood and deployed in the relationship, legitimates Joe's claim to private time and relaxation, and delegitimates Richard's desire for help.

Several months after these interviews I ran into Richard at the gym. He had just joined, and we talked for a while. He told me he was coming back to the gym to "get in shape, and get a man." He then reported that he and Joe had broken up, and that I was part of the reason. He said he wanted to thank me for helping him to get out of his relationship. I felt perplexed, guilty, mortified. Here is my rough approximation, scribbled on the back on my workout card, of what transpired that day at the gym:

CC: *I am very sorry; I certainly didn't intend any harm.*

Richard: *Oh, it's okay, it's not really about you, but what you helped me learn about myself.*

CC: *What do you mean?*

Richard: *Well, that interview helped me to realize just how much I actually do, and did for that jerk.*

CC: *Like what are you thinking of?*

Richard: *Well, like all those questions about going out and buying things for the house. You know, I did all of that. And I did it because I wanted us to have a nice home, to be a family. But, being a family, he thinks, is all about me and my needs. He says I am codependent. He just couldn't appreciate what I was doing for us. The interview made it so clear just how much I had*

taken for granted. I actually sat down and wrote a list up, thinking of the things that you asked about. Then I realized, I confronted him with it, but he basically thinks those things are my interests, and if I want to do them, that's all about me. Well, I knew I had to get out, and find someone else who appreciates me more.

The sociologist as homewrecker was not quite what I envisioned for myself. But this situation led me to wonder about why so much of domesticity is hidden from those who do it through discourses about individual "interests" and in narrow conceptions of what domesticity actually is. Families hide much of domesticity, closet it, and drape the door with the ideological veneer of egalitarianism for quite practical reasons. First, as previously suggested, they do it to avoid the stigma associated with violating gender expectations. Second, and perhaps more significantly, they do it to avoid conflicts and to preserve relationships existing in a broader socioeconomic context that does not enable families to actually produce much equality. When thinking about Joe and Richard and the demise of that relationship I can see the dilemma that many relationships face. . . .

The Egalitarian Pattern

A minority of lesbigay families do achieve a rough equivalence in the distribution of domestic work, even using a broad and inclusive conception of domesticity. Roughly 25 percent (thirteen) of the families I studied approach this rough parity. The participants in these families appear to take responsibility for, as well as spend similar amounts of time on domestic matters. Interview data and field observations reveal patterns of specialization among many of these families, although they still approach equity. For instance, in several families, one person pursues much of the feeding work while another manages housework and kin work. Some families go to great lengths to achieve this parity. For example, three families use quite extensive "chore wheels." Chore wheels list many of the major housework items—and in one family much of the feeding work was listed as well—but none of them listed consumption, kin work, or status work-related chores. These families share a number of distinct sociological characteristics explaining much of the parity in the division of domesticity, and to those characteristics I will now turn.

Egalitarianism: Reliance on the Service Economy

Wealthier lesbigay families often purchase much domesticity in the marketplace, therein enhancing the egalitarianism within the relationship. In contrast to working/service-class and middle-class lesbigay families, these affluent families rely extensively on the service economy, or upon an army of low-paid workers without fringe benefits who provide much of the domestic labor. This pattern closely resembles one detected by Hertz (1986) in a study of upper-middle-class, dual-career heterosexual families

who achieved greater equity in their relationships through reliance on service workers. Eight of the ten wealthiest families in this study hire someone to do housework for them. Four of those eight hire Latina women who work for an hourly rate without benefits. No family earning less than the study's median income hires someone to clean. Seven of the wealthiest ten families frequently either rely on laundry services or include laundry as a responsibility of the domestic workers who come to clean. Two families earning below the median income take laundry on a consistent basis to a laundry service. Six of the wealthiest twenty families hire someone to care for their lawns or gardens. Four families, all earning above the median income, hire someone to walk their dogs during the day. As mentioned in [my book], one in five lesbigay families eat at least four meals per week in a restaurant. Sixteen of those twenty-one families earn above the median income.

A very clear picture emerges here. Some lesbigay families achieve partial equity in their relationships through reliance on the labors of mostly working-poor people. One can see some of these workers behind the counters of taquerias, laundries, pasta shops, coffee shops, and delis in lesbigay neighborhoods, although many others one cannot see because their labors are more hidden (domestics, gardeners, laundry workers, daycare providers). These workers are for the most part Latino, Asian, and African American women, and young gay men and lesbians. Their labors contribute much to the achievement of egalitarianism within the families of the affluent.

Egalitarianism and Female-Identified Professional Occupations

The egalitarian pattern emerges with notable strength among those families where both individuals, regardless of gender, work in traditionally female-identified professional occupations: primary/secondary teaching, social work, healthcare assessment (nurses, dietitians, occupational therapy), librarians, school counseling, social work, and public-sector human resources jobs. A disproportionate number of lesbians and gay men in this study work in these professions. It remains an open question whether this pattern reflects the broader population of lesbigay people (Badgett and King 1997). Popular mythology holds that lesbigay people are everywhere, and perhaps they are, but lesbigay people in long-term relationships don't seem to be. It may well be the case that these forms of employment actually nourish longer-term relationships, providing at least one, and in the case of some egalitarian families, all family members the opportunity to pursue family matters more readily. When the primary partners in relationships work in these fields they establish a greater degree of equality between them in the distribution of domesticity. Why?

These forms of employment often feature *real* forty-hour work weeks, and they often offer paid vacation, paid holidays, more holidays, family leave, paid sick days, flex-time, flex-place, as well as employee assistance

programs offering services to families facing alcohol, drug, and domestic violence concerns. All of these family-friendly policies create a somewhat more conducive environment for doing family work. In contrast, lesbigay people working in other professional occupational categories infrequently receive such benefits, or they seem reluctant to take advantage of them, even if offered. Moreover, very few people in these professions report working more than forty hours per week for wages. This is not to say that these forms of employment are all dandy. In fact, they often feature short career ladders, glass ceilings, lower wages, and less control over the content of one's work than do male-dominated professional jobs (Glazer 1991; Preston 1995). In a sense, discrimination relegates lesbigay professionals into the female-dominated professions and enables them to do more domesticity. When looking at lesbigay professionals in the male-dominated occupations, including the engineers, physicians, attorneys, and middle-level managers, a starkly different pattern emerges, one encouraging a clear division of labor within the relationship. Moreover, most of the female-dominated professions do not require one to use one's residence in order to serve clients, or to entertain them very much. This reduces the amount of housework, feeding work, consumption work, and kin work within such households.

Egalitarianism and Downsizing the Family

There is one other form of the truly egalitarian family: the downsized family. These families, mostly composed of male couples, engage in relatively little domesticity. Similar to the affluent egalitarians, these families also rely on the service economy to provide domesticity, although they rely on it much less extensively. These families often live in urban environments, usually sharing a living space with multiple adults. These guys, mostly in their late twenties or early thirties, are often in their first relationship. They spend very little time in the places where they live, instead hanging out in cafés, bars, restaurants, gyms, and dance clubs. They don't put much effort into feeding work, eating out at cheap taquerias and hamburger joints throughout much of the week, or eating instant ramen noodles or microwaved frozen dinners. If they engage in body building, as many seem to, they eat simple meals of vegetables, bread, and pasta when they eat at home. They don't do much consumption work, although they do make joint purchases of CDs, linens and towels, and some used furniture. These joint purchases often become emblematic of their relationships. These couples do very little kin work, calling biolegal relatives mostly, but usually on major holidays or at Mother's Day, with each person responsible for his or her own biolegal relations. Even in these austere circumstances, domesticity often comes to play a crucial role in the creation of the relationship. For instance, several of these young-male couples understood the time they spent together doing laundry at laundromats as expressions of their relational identity, particularly when they mixed clothing items together for washing and drying.

The Specialization Pattern

One person specializes in domesticity in roughly three of four (thirty-eight) of the lesbigay families studied. This pattern actually parallels Blumstein and Schwartz's finding that longer-term families frequently consist of one person who places more emphasis on domesticity and one who places the emphasis on paid work (1983:172). In this study, the longer the family has been together, the more pronounced the specialization becomes. For instance, only among families together longer than nine years (twenty-one families), and mostly earning higher incomes, do I find someone working part-time by choice in order to handle domestic activities (seven families), or someone engaging in homemaking full-time (three families). Interestingly, these highly special-ized, longer-term lesbigay families conceive of their circumstances as *equal,* although I suspect they really mean *fair.* They consider things fair in light of a whole series of spoken and unspoken matters ranging from the num-ber of hours someone works for wages to the pleasures one garners from domesticity. Let me now turn to some of the central factors encouraging spe-cialization in domesticity or in paid work within lesbigay families.

Paid employment exerts the greatest influence upon the division of domesticity in most lesbigay families. The number of hours paid work requires, where the work takes place, the length of the commute to work, the pay, the prestige, and difficulty of the work all conflate to encourage a pat-tern of specialization. The relative resources that each person brings to the relationship from paid work influences the division of labor. In most cases the person with less earning potential, or with less occupational prestige, picks up a disproportionate share of domestic labor. This finding parallels the "relative resource" model put forward to explain the division of domes-tic labor among heterosexual families (Blood and Wolfe 1960; Brines 1994). The pursuit of such resources (money, benefits, stock options, prestige, and networks) also takes time, usually leaving the pursuant with little time left to handle domesticity. In this sense, my findings parallel the "time availabil-ity" explanation (Acock and Demo 1994; Coverman 1985; Hiller 1984) of the division of domestic labor. However, unlike some resource theory, my analy-sis does not conceive of domesticity as a great unpleasantness that the per-son with more resources (e.g., income, prestige, and education) forces onto the person with fewer. Such a view reduces domesticity to its unpleasant aspects and conceals its attractive ones, therein leaving us with no convinc-ing explanation of why some people prefer, and orient themselves toward, domesticity (Ferree 1976, 1980). Rather, I detect a pattern of family members attempting to maximize the quality of their household lives both through providing income and through providing domesticity. Among the affluent participants, each family member pursues income, and the family purchases meals, laundry, housecleaning, and so on in the service economy. Most lesbi-gay families can't afford this, even with both working full-time, and therein, they must pursue a different strategy. Longer-term families recognize the importance of domesticity to relational and family stability, and many of them pursue a strategy to attain both domesticity and financial well-being.

The most obvious strategy consists of encouraging the family member with the greatest economic opportunity to pursue paid work vigorously. This has its limits, but the pattern occurs in the majority of households, and becomes stronger over time.

Gravitating toward Domesticity

Practical economic concerns and occupational characteristics play the largest role in determining who gravitates toward domestic involvement. In a few instances those who gravitate toward domesticity "choose" employment that complements their family commitments. In most instances the character of one's paid employment facilitated participation in domesticity, with very little "choice" or much reflection on the matter. Some people appear to make conscious choices about domesticity, but the choices are constrained by economic and occupational realities. For instance, only among affluent families does the choice exist to work part-time for wages, devoting the remaining time to personal and/or family life. Similarly, those in professional careers frequently find it easier to merge work and family concerns together. Recall the professionals making phone calls to friends and family from work, as well as arranging their work schedule to pursue domestic matters. Working- and service-class lesbigay families don't have these options. I want to emphasize the importance of context to the question of "choice" here. Some participants choose to ensconce themselves in domesticity, but few really possess that option. Some participants choose to take on a disproportionate share of domestic labor, but most simply find themselves doing the work without much sense of choice. That doesn't necessarily mean they feel unhappy or conceive of things as unfair—some do, and some don't. Rather, they often simply adjust in light of the expectations and opportunities associated with their own paid work and the paid work of other family members.

Family-Friendly Careers and Jobs

Many of the women and men in these specialized families are employed within traditional female-identified occupations (teaching, nursing, and so on). They take on a disproportionate share of domesticity, especially when they are in relationships with individuals in professional, managerial, or executive positions. The pattern is quite apparent among school teachers. The summer recess, holiday breaks, the capacity to do schoolwork at home, and lower salaries all conflate to encourage teachers to pick up a disproportionate share of domestic life. Few of the teachers anticipated this state of affairs at the beginning of their relationships. . . . [Third-grade teacher] Andrew's experience is actually quite common among lesbigay families. Andrew did not really choose to become domestically oriented; rather, over time, he gravitated in that direction. Andrew's explanations of why he prepares evening meals, meets service and delivery people at the house, and does much of the consumption work all point to paid work, either the relative flexibility of his own career, or the inflexibility of his partner's career.

In Andrew's case the pull toward domestic involvement began early in his work experience, and in some ways this left him less cognizant of the ways that work influences family life. For others, the pull came later, and they have a much stronger sense of how work influences family life.

Fanny Gomez, now forty-four and in her second long-term relationship as well as her second career, recently finished school and began working as a social worker. In her first relationship she did very little in terms of domesticity. She worked sixty hours per week as an accountant for a large commercial real estate firm. After her first relationship broke up she decided she wanted to make a lot of changes in her life. Mostly she wanted to pursue a career that made her happier, and one that would "make some contribution to improving other people's lives." When she and her new partner, Melinda Rodriquez, moved in together, she realized that neither of them was particularly adept at domestic tasks. They wanted to eat meals together at home, but "the meals didn't seem that satisfying." Fanny decided to spend some time learning how to cook. She bought some cookbooks and attended a cooking course on Saturdays, something she "would not have had the energy to do when she was working at the real estate firm." Her new job, doing social work with elderly Latinos as part of a city-funded program, is stressful but it has more limits. Fanny says she works thirty-eight hours a week and "not an hour more," unlike her old job, where they knew no limits, where "my whole life was about that firm." She also receives more holiday time and more vacation time. She doesn't earn as much as she used to, but she's happier. Fanny noticed that her new job, and her new relationship with Melinda, a midlevel sales manager for a computer technology firm, brought new responsibilities on the home front:

> Fanny: *We've had some fights about housecleaning over the past couple of years. She says she doesn't have time to do the stuff, and I sort of understand that, but I don't think it's fair that I have to do it. But, I think I realized that if I didn't, then nobody would. And I am here more often than she is. I get home earlier, and I leave for work later. Because I get home earlier, it's easier for me to cook, and to stop by the store and stuff.*
>
> CC: *How is this different from your first relationship?*
>
> Fanny: *I never would have done that sort of thing in my first relationship. In fact, I've sort of gone through a transition. I had no interest in cooking when I was with Janet. But in this relationship, it seems more important to me. I guess I missed the meal time that I had with Janet, and I wanted to have that again with Melinda, but Melinda wasn't into doing it, so I sort of picked it up. I think Melinda appreciates it though.*

On the one hand, Fanny contributed to her new involvement in domestic life through choices she made about work. On the other hand, Fanny's work and the work of her new lover, Melinda, changed Fanny. Fanny's search for more fulfillment in her career brought her into an occupational context that facilitated more domestic involvement.

Fanny, a social worker, and Andrew, the teacher, are not alone. Of the twenty-eight professionals that work as nurses, primary/secondary-school teachers, counselors, social workers, librarians, and community college instructors, eighteen are more domestically involved than their partners while six appear equally involved and four of those six are in relationships with partners in similar occupations.

In addition to the female-identified professional career tracks that seem to encourage domestic involvement, those individuals who work at home as artisans, writers/editors, or independent service contractors, as well as those who are students, retired, or underemployed, also bear a disproportionate share of domesticity. Twenty-four participants do much of their paid work at home—work ranging from accounting services to daycare to running a bed and breakfast to book editing to building furniture. Of these twenty-four participants, eighteen carry a greater share of the domesticity. These participants often weave their paid work with their family work. . . .

In sum, many participants gravitate toward domesticity not out of choice, or because of a strong interest in domestic pursuits, or even because they possess certain skills. Rather, they gravitate toward domesticity because the character of their paid work and that of other family members encourages their involvement. . . .

Domestic by Choice

Few individuals actually choose, in a particularly conscious manner, to become more involved in family and domestic affairs. However, some do, and for a variety of reasons—reasons often reflecting growing disenchantment with paid work, or concern about maintaining an endangered relationship, or simply a love of domestic life. However, the nature of these choices varies dramatically across social class. The two men who conceive of themselves as homemakers are notable examples of choosing domestic involvement, as well as one woman, Virginia Kirbo, who works ten hours per week. All three made conscious choices to forgo paid employment in favor of concentrating on family and community life. All three are in relationships with highly successful, well-paid individuals. These families dwell in exquisite yet labor-intensive homes. I found the daily schedules of all three quite stunning, for not only do they maintain homes thick in domesticity, but also these three people expend great energy volunteering in the nonprofit sector. . . .

Hindered Work Opportunities

While some of the more affluent participants became disillusioned with their careers and "chose" to emphasize domestic life instead, many other participants found themselves unable to get onto career or promotional tracks or ran into glass ceilings and consequently shifted to a domestic focus. The lack of job/career opportunities resulted in a greater emphasis on domesticity for at least eleven of the families I studied. Five of these families came to San Francisco due to an employment opportunity for one member of the family.

These families migrated with hopes of finding suitable employment for both partners, but this didn't always happen. Carey Becker, forty-three years old and working part-time as a radiology technician, shares her life with Angela DiVincenzo, a special education teacher. Five years ago they moved to San Francisco from New Jersey. A suburban Bay Area school district offered Angela a position creating a new curriculum and program for special education. Carey, who worked as a full-time radiologist back East, discovered that she lacked the proper credentials for employment in California, and that few employment opportunities existed. Carey took a part-time position with hopes of finding something full-time. She never did. Initially, Carey picked up a larger share of the domesticity:

> CC: *Describe the impact of significant job changes on your relationship.*
>
> Carey: *The move to San Francisco had a major impact, and I think it still does. I am still trying to get into the kind of work I would like to do. Although, I don't know if it's possible now. The market for radiology techs is not very hot. I have thought about what else I could do. Angela just wants me to be happy, and she hasn't put any pressure on me to find something else. The part-time position actually is thirty hours, and now that Angela's school district offers domestic partnership, I don't need to worry about going without insurance.*
>
> CC: *Did the move change what you do in the relationship?*
>
> Carey: *In some ways, it did. I do a lot more of the housework and stuff now. I don't really mind it too much. Angela works pretty hard, and I try to contribute what I can to our relationship. . . .*

In a similar fashion, some lesbians and gay men ran into the proverbial glass ceiling at work and consequently reconceived of their careers as jobs, set limits on how much work could encroach on family life, and developed a new interest in domesticity. This pattern emerged with marked strength among lesbigay professionals and managers working in predominantly heterosexual contexts. . . .

Unsuccessful efforts to enter or progress in paid work, whether due to lack of credentials, discrimination, or too short career ladders, created disenchantment with notions of meritocracy and undivided commitment to work. As a result, the affected individuals shifted focus and infused greater effort and meaning into family matters.

Preserving Relationships

Finally, another dynamic bolstering active participation in domesticity springs from efforts to preserve a cherished relationship. At some point in their life together, several lesbigay families faced hard choices of maintaining two careers or maintaining the relationship. In most cases, these longer-term lesbigay families struck a deal. Sometimes the deal included someone turning down a promotion; in other cases the deal included a diminution of work involvement for one while the other put more into paid work. Narvin Wong and Lawrence Shoong, together for just over five years, faced just such a crisis about a year before I interviewed them. Narvin, a healthcare consultant,

made the decision to do independent consulting. He saw a lucrative economic opportunity and the chance to exert greater influence over his work, and he decided to take it. The decision also meant a great increase in the number of hours that he would work. Meanwhile, Lawrence had taken a promotion to a nursing position with a large, well-funded research project. The position entailed a pay increase and was much more prestigious, given that the project was associated with a major medical research center. The position required Lawrence to work many evenings with research subjects, and diminished the amount of time he could spend at home and with Narvin. About six months into their new work situations conflict began to develop at home. The conflicts initially circled around housework, but eventually expanded to questions about emotional availability, and the energy available for sexual interaction. Lawrence reflects on a question about the impact of work on his family life:

CC: *Describe the impact of significant job changes on family/relationship.*

Lawrence: *Narvin's choice to go into independent consulting created some big changes, changes in his attitude, and changes in our life together. He has very high expectations for himself. He went to an Ivy League business school, and I think he puts lots of pressures on himself to succeed. The problem was that I felt left out, sort of abandoned. I took the position at the medical center, and suddenly I wasn't around in the evenings, and I felt like our relationship just went into a spiral. I loved working at the medical center. I got to work with really great people, and the work was interesting, and I was putting in quite a few hours, more than I used to at Marin General. But after a while I began to feel like I no longer had a life with Narvin. We talked about it, and I asked him about working less on weekends, and maybe trying to have a little more energy for us being together. He was pretty stubborn, though.*

CC: *What was he stubborn about?*

Lawrence: *His career and his consulting work. He just felt so strong about trying to make it go.*

CC: *So, what did you guys do?*

Lawrence: *Well, I gave up the job at the lab. I mean, we talked about it, and I realized that I still wanted a relationship with him. He was in a tough place. It wasn't like he could easily go back to the hospital where he was; not at that level, you don't really go back. After a few months Narvin was making decent money, and I just decided I would rather be here at night. So I applied for a day shift position at St. Stephens, and they took me. They were a little surprised that I was leaving the medical center, but the woman who hired me was pretty understanding. I mean, I told her that I needed more time for my relationship. Once I got back onto the day shift, things really improved. I was able to come home at a decent hour, and keep things going around here, and be with Narvin, even if he spends most of his time in his office, I can still go in there and talk to him, and we can have dinner together. . . .*

Lawrence and Narvin preserved their relationship, but not without Lawrence's willingness to place more emphasis on family life. Both of them

view the choices made as practical, and both anticipate a financial gain from Narvin's commitment to his consulting business.

On the whole, those individuals who gravitate toward greater domestic involvement than their partners often share common socioeconomic characteristics. Frequently they share their lives with partners who earn more, have greater career opportunities, work more hours, and work outside the home. In addition, more domestically involved participants often work in occupations that offer real forty-hour work weeks, more flexible work schedules, the ability to work at home, more holiday and vacation time, and affiliation with colleagues who also share family obligations. Domestically involved participants seldom recognize the confluence of factors encouraging their domesticity. Instead, they rely on the vocabulary of individual choice, psychological disposition, and "interests," ignoring the social context in which such dispositions and interests develop. . . .

Pragmatic Choices and the Sense of Fairness

I have seen a practicality in the ways that lesbigay families sort and arrange domesticity, whether the family is egalitarian or specialized. Such practicality does not create equality, however. True equality, measured with a plumb line, eludes many of these families, but that has little to do with the families per se, and much more to do with the character and quality of employment opportunities that avail themselves to these families. If the reality is that only one member of the family can make money in a fulfilling way, then lesbigay families adjust to that reality.

Many lesbigay relationships don't survive, for a wide variety of reasons. I would add to that list the dilemmas of domesticity—not just the conflicts over who does what but the often overlooked fact that the opportunity to pursue domestic things is not available to everyone. If all of the family must toil at unpleasant and poorly compensating work in order to make ends meet, they do, and they try to fit domesticity in where they can. Of course, these are the families that often don't make it, and that should not be so surprising because without the resources, time, and energy to create family, it withers.

REFERENCES

Acock, A. and D. Demo. 1994. *Family Diversity and Well-Being*. Thousand Oaks, CA: Sage.
Aquilino, W. S. 1993. "Effects of Spouse Presence during the Interview on Survey Responses Concerning Marriage." *Public Opinion Quarterly* 55 (3): 358–76.
Badgett, L. and M. King. 1997. "Lesbian and Gay Occupational Strategies." In *Homo Economics: Capitalism, Community, and Lesbian and Gay Life*, edited by A. Gluckman and B. Reed. New York: Routledge.
Berk, S. F. 1985. *The Gender Factory: The Apportionment of Work in American Households*. New York: Plenum Press.
Blood, R. and D. Wolfe. 1960. *Husbands and Wives*. Glencoe, IL: Free Press.
Blumstein, P. and P. Schwartz. 1983. *American Couples*. New York: Morrow.
Brines, J. 1994. "Economic Dependency, Gender, and the Division of Labor at Home." *American Journal of Sociology* 100:652–88.

Coltrane, S. 1989. "Household Labor and the Routine Production of Gender." *Social Problems* 36 (5): 473–90.

Coverman, S. 1985. "Explaining Husband's Contribution in Domestic Labor." *Sociological Quarterly* 26:81–97.

DeVault, M. 1991. *Feeding the Family: The Social Organization of Caring as Gendered Work.* Chicago: University of Chicago Press.

Ferree, M. 1976. "Working-Class Jobs: Housework and Paid Work as Sources of Satisfaction." *Social Problems* 23:431–41.

———. 1980. "Satisfaction with Housework: The Social Context." In *Women and Household Labor,* edited by S. F. Berk. Beverly Hills, CA: Sage.

———. 1990. "Beyond Separate Spheres: Feminism and Family Research." *Journal of Marriage and the Family* 52:866–84.

Gerson, K. 1985. *Hard Choices.* Berkeley: University of California Press.

———. 1993. *No Man's Land: Men's Changing Commitments to Family and Work.* New York: Basic Books.

Glazer, N. 1991. "Between a Rock and a Hard Place: Women's Professional Organizations in Nursing and Class, Racial, and Ethnic Inequalities." *Gender & Society* 5 (3): 351–72.

Hertz, R. 1986. *More Equal than Others.* Berkeley: University of California Press.

Hiller, D. 1984. "Power Dependence and Division of Family Work." *Sex Roles* 10:1003–19.

Hochschild, A., with A. Machung. 1989. *The Second Shift: Working Parents and the Revolution at Home.* New York: Viking.

Petuchek, J. L. 1992. "Employed Wives' Orientation to Breadwinning: A Gender Theory Analysis." *Journal of Marriage and the Family* 54:548–58.

Preston, J. 1995. "Gender and the Formation of a Woman's Profession." In *Gender Inequality at Work,* edited by J. Jacobs. Mountain View, CA: Sage.

West, C. and D. Zimmerman. 1987. "Doing Gender." *Gender & Society* 1 (2): 125–51.

50

CREATING A CARING SOCIETY

EVELYN NAKANO GLENN

Why is it important to achieve a society that values caring and caring relationships? The answer might appear obvious: It seems inherent in the definition of a good society that those who cannot care for themselves are cared for; that those who can care for themselves can trust that, should they become dependent, they will be cared for; and that people will be supported in their efforts to care for those they care about. But even more is at stake. Currently we are caught in a nasty circle. To the extent that caring is devalued, invisible, underpaid, and penalized, it is relegated to those who lack economic, political, and social power and status. And to the extent that those who engage in caring are drawn disproportionately from among disadvantaged groups (women, people of color, and immigrants), their activity—that of caring—is further degraded.

In short, the devaluing of caring contributes to the marginalization, exploitation, and dependency of caregivers. Conversely, valuing and recognizing caring would raise the status and rewards of those who engage in it and also increase the incentives for other groups to engage in caring. Thus, a society that values care and caring relationships would be not only nicer and kinder, but also more egalitarian and just.

In addressing the question of how to create a society in which caring is valued, I first give a brief account of the contemporary "crisis" in care which stems from its being defined as a privatized, feminized, and therefore devalued domain. In the next section I review recent feminist attempts to rethink the concept of care in ways that open it up to critical analysis. I then define some desirable goals for a society that values care. In the final section I outline four major directions for change in social citizenship rights, family responsibility, organization of paid care, and employment policies and practices.

The Contemporary Problem of Care

A spate of popular books and articles in the last decade has sounded an alarm about a new "crisis in care," a crisis occasioned by the exodus of women from the home into the work force. The need for care of children, the elderly, and the chronically ill and disabled has not diminished, and may have grown because of increased longevity and medical advances that keep people with serious injuries or illnesses alive. Yet traditional caretakers—stay-at-home wives and mothers—are now less available to provide care on a full-time basis.

Dual-worker families—and more concretely, employed women—are said to be increasingly overburdened and strained by the need to meet both earning and care responsibilities. At the same time, most families don't have the economic means to purchase care, and state services are grossly inadequate. As Mona Harrington (1999) says in a recent popular treatment, "we have patchwork systems, but we have come nowhere near replacing the hours or quality of care that the at home women of previous generations provided for the country" (p. 17). The question of how care is to get done without substantial numbers of nonemployed women to do it has become the subject of research and policy initiatives. For example, the Alfred P. Sloan Foundation has funded several university research centers on work and family life, including one at my campus devoted to "Cultures of Care."

The "crisis in care" is just one impetus for recent critical examinations of the concept and organization of care in modern political democracies. Feminist theorists and researchers for some time have been examining care in its gendered dimensions. Their work makes it clear that the current crisis is a product of a privatized and gendered caring regime in which families, rather than the larger society, are responsible for caring and in which women (and other subordinate groups) are assigned primary responsibility for care giving.

The relegation of care to the private sphere and to women has had two further corollaries: the devaluation of caring work and caring relationships,

and the exclusion of both from the arena of equality and rights. As feminist critics of liberal political philosophy have explained, the very concept of citizenship (i.e., full membership in the community, including reciprocal rights and responsibilities) has been premised on two conceptual dichotomies. First has been a split between the public and private, with the private realm of concrete relations of care defined not only as separate from, but also in opposition to citizenship. The private realm encompasses emotion, particularity, subjectivity, and the meeting of bodily needs, while the public arena of citizenship is ruled by thought, universality, objectivity, and the ability to act on abstract principles. Those relegated to the private sphere and associated with its values—women, servants, and children—were long excluded from full citizenship. Second has been a dichotomy between independence and dependence, with the ideal citizen defined as an autonomous individual who can make choices freely in the market and in the political realm. Within the liberal polity, citizenship supposedly created a realm of equality in which independent individuals had identical rights and responsibilities, regardless of differences in economic standing and other attributes. Those deemed dependent, whether categorically (as in the case of women, slaves, and children) or by reason of condition (as in the case of mental or physical disability) lacked standing and therefore were defined as outside the realm of equality (Okin 1979; Pateman 1988).[1] The fiction of liberal philosophy that independent and autonomous actors exist also obscures the actual interdependence among people and the need for care that even "independent" people have.

Historically, then, in the United States caring work within the family has not been recognized as a public societal contribution comparable to paid employment. As Judith Shklar (1991) has pointed out, earning has always been seen as a responsibility of citizenship because it is the basis for independence. In this view, earners fulfill citizenship responsibilities and therefore deserve certain entitlements, such as old age pensions, unemployment insurance, and health and safety protection. In contrast, unpaid family caregivers perform strictly private responsibilities and do not fulfill broader citizenship responsibilities. Hence, they are not accorded entitlements comparable to those of wage earners.

Moreover, the dominant family model assumes that support for dependents and care givers comes from the male breadwinner. Historically, the United States has provided little support for care giving, compared to other Western nations where paid parental leave, family allowances, child care services, housing subsidies, and health care coverage have been common (Fraser and Gordon 1993). During the World War I era, Progressive reformers pushed though maternalist programs, such as the Mothers' Pension program, to allow widowed women to keep their children rather than sending them to orphanages. But pensions were so low that single mothers were forced to work as well as care for their children. The Mothers' Pension was quickly phased out. New Deal–era social welfare policies institutionalized a two-tier system based on a male breadwinner-female caregiver model. The upper tier consisted of safety net entitlements for male breadwinners, which

provided relatively generous, non-means-tested benefits such as unemployment insurance, social security retirement, and disability payments. Dependents of male breadwinners, including female caregivers, received indirect benefits through their relationship to a male earner, via provisions such as social security survivor benefits. The lower tier for women without connections to male breadwinners provided relatively ungenerous, means-tested "welfare" as in the original Aid to Dependent Children (ADC) and in the later Aid to Families with Dependent Children (AFDC). These benefits were considered a response to the neediness of children, not as an entitlement for mothers' caring labor (Abramowitz 1996; Gordon 1994; Nelson 1990). These programs were not only gendered, they were also raced. Black single mothers in the South and Mexican single mothers in the Southwest were routinely denied relief on the grounds that they were "employable." Thus, these women were not seen as "dependent" caregivers in the same way that white women were (Mink 1994).

Yet despite the prevailing ideology of the family as the realm of care, the growing need for care has generated a demand for paid care giving as an alternative or supplement to unpaid family care. Some of the demand has been met by institutions and services administered by the state and non-profit organizations. The greatest growth, however, has been in institutions and services organized by for-profit corporate entities formed to take advantage of payments available through (industry-backed) government medical insurance. Overall, then, there has been a shift of some portion of caring to publicly organized settings, whether administered by state, nonprofit, or for-profit entities.

In these settings, the actual work of caring is done by "strangers"—paid workers, sometimes supplemented by unpaid volunteer workers. When caring is done as paid work, it not only remains gendered, it also becomes conspicuously racialized. In institutional settings such as hospitals, nursing homes, and group homes, nursing aides and other workers who actually do the day-to-day work of caring are overwhelmingly women of color, many of them recent immigrants. Home care workers also are drawn disproportionately from the ranks of women of color (Glenn 1992).

When care work is done by people who are accorded little status and respect in the society by reason of race, class, or immigrant status, it further reinforces the view of caring as low-skilled "dirty" work. This dual devaluation—of care work and care workers—rationalizes the low wages and lack of benefits that characterize care work. From her analysis of national wage data, Paula England (1992) concluded that "being in a job requiring nurturing carries a net wage penalty of between \$.24/hour and \$1.70/hour" (p. 182). Taking into account such factors as workers' education, service jobs involving caregiving paid less than comparable jobs not involving caregiving. Thus child care workers earned less than manicurists; nursing aides and orderlies earned less than janitors; and psychiatric aides earned less than elevator operators. One ironic result is that those who care for others usually have to give up caring for their own dependents, yet cannot afford to pay anyone to care for them. Caring work is considered

low-skilled and largely physical in nature, despite the importance of emotional and psychological aspects of caring.

Care in institutional settings is compromised by a combination of factors: pressures to cut costs, government regulations, medicalization, and bureaucratization (Foner 1994). Deborah Stone (1999) notes that cost-containment pressures affect both private for-profit care and public nonprofit and taxpayer-supported facilities. Efforts to reduce or control costs have resulted in inadequate training and chronic understaffing. Government regulations, reflected in institutional procedures, also require caregivers to spend time on extensive paper work. As workers are stretched thin, they experience stress and frustration, leading to burnout and high turnover. Bureaucratic structures and regulations, which are designed to both keep down costs and protect care receivers, nonetheless often restrict the caring activities of caregivers. For example, because of Medicare regulations, health care institutions try to limit staff to performing strictly medical and medical-related tasks such as changing dressings, and not getting involved in social and emotional caregiving.[2] All of these pressures directly affect the care relationship. Caregivers complain about the lack of time and autonomy to respond to individual needs. Care receivers may be subject to controls that maintain "order" under conditions of understaffing (e.g., through use of sedation or physical restraints). Care receivers may not receive the kind of individualized and time-consuming care that would allow them maximum dignity and autonomy.

Rethinking Care

To develop alternatives to the present situation, we need to rethink the concept of care. Because care is so closely associated with womanhood, feminist philosophers and social theorists have subjected care to close analysis. My reading of several theorists of care, including Joan Tronto (1993), Diemut Bubeck (1995), Emily Abel and Margaret Nelson (1990), and Sara Ruddick (1998), suggests the usefulness of defining care as a practice that encompasses an ethic (caring about) and an activity (caring for). "Caring about" engages both thought and feeling, including awareness and attentiveness, concern about and feelings of responsibility for meeting another's needs. "Caring for" refers to the varied activities of providing for the needs or well-being of another person.[3] These activities include physical care (e.g., bathing, feeding), emotional care (e.g., reassuring, sympathetic listening), and direct services (e.g., driving a person to the doctor, running errands). The definition is not free of ambiguity, but it does establish some boundaries. For example, defining caring in terms of direct meeting of needs differentiates caring from other activities that may foster survival. Thus, economic provision would not be included, even though it may help support care giving. Men are often said to be "taking care of their family" when they earn and bring money into the household. Despite the use of the term *care* in this phrase, breadwinning would not be considered "caring." In fact, economic support has historically

been seen as men's contribution in lieu of actual caregiving; simultaneously, caregiving has been viewed as women's responsibility, an exchange for being supported by the primary breadwinner.

Within this definition of care as a practice, three features are important. First, this definition recognizes that everyone needs care, not just those we consider incapable of caring for themselves. Often only children, the elderly, the disabled, or the chronically ill are seen as requiring care, while the need for care and receiving of care by so-called independent adults is suppressed or denied. As Sara Ruddick (1998) notes, "most recipients of care are only partially 'dependent' and often becoming less so; most of their 'needs,' even those clearly physical, cannot be separated from more elusive emotional requirements for respect, affection, and cheer" (p. 11). At the same time, even those we see as fully independent—that is, able to care for themselves in terms of "activities of daily living"—may for reasons of time or energy or temporary condition need care to maintain their physical, psychological, and emotional well-being. They may turn to a family member, friends, a servant, or a service provider for hot meals, physical touch, or a sympathetic ear. The difference is that "independent adults" may preserve their sense of independence if they have sufficient resources, economic or social, to "command" care from others, rather than being beholden to relatives or charity.

A second aspect of defining care as practice is that care is seen as creating a relationship; as Ruddick (1998) puts it, "[caring] work is constituted in and through the relationship of those who give and receive care" (p. 14). The relationship is one of interdependence. Generally we think of the caregiver as having the power in the relationship; but the care receiver, even if subordinate or dependent, also has agency/power in the relationship. Focusing on relationships brings into relief the influence of the recipients of care on caring work. Tronto (1993) notes that for the work of care to be successful, its recipients have to respond appropriately—e.g., a screaming child betokens failure. In some situations where the care receiver employs the caregiver or has social authority (e.g., due to the norm of respect toward elders), the care receiver may have more power than the caregiver.

Third, the definition of care as practice recognizes that caring can be organized in a myriad of ways. The paradigmatic care relationship is the mother–child dyad, which often serves as the template for thinking about caring. In this model, caring (mothering) is viewed as natural and instinctive—women's natural vocation. However, this idealized model is deceptive in that it ignores the actual diversity in the ways mothering/caring is actually carried out within and across cultures. Caring can take place in the household or in publicly organized institutions, and can be carried out individually or collectively and as paid or unpaid labor. Much caring takes place in the family, usually as the unpaid work of women, but it is also done as paid work (e.g., by babysitters, home health aides, and the like). It also takes place in the community as unpaid volunteer work, as in the case of church or charitable organizations that run day care or senior activity centers. It also takes place in institutions organized by the state, corporations, or individuals as commodified services using paid caregivers.

Care can also be "fragmented," divided among several caregivers and between "private" and "public" settings. Thus, a parent may take ultimate responsibility for ensuring that a child has care after school but delegate the actual work of caregiving to a babysitter, a relative, a paid home care worker, and/or an after-school program. Barrie Thorne (1999) found in her study of childhoods in an urban multicultural community that parents often have to patch together several of these arrangements.

What Should Our Goals Be?

To achieve a society in which caring is valued in all spheres of social life, all of the elements—the work of caregiving and the people involved (care receivers and caregivers)—would have to be recognized and valued. Hence, a society in which caring is valued would be one in which:

- ▼ Caring is recognized as "real work" and as a social contribution on a par with other activities that are valued, such as working, military service, or community service, regardless of whether caring takes place in the family or elsewhere or as paid or unpaid labor.
- ▼ Those who need care (including children, the elderly, disabled, and chronically ill) are recognized as full members of the society and accorded corresponding rights, social standing, and the voice of citizens. This would mean that care receivers are empowered to have influence over the type of care, the setting, and the caregivers, and that they have access to sufficient material resources to obtain adequate care.
- ▼ Those who do caring work are accorded social recognition and entitlements for their efforts similar to those who contribute through paid employment or military service. These entitlements include working conditions and supports that enable them to do their work well and an appropriate level of economic return, whether in wages or social entitlements.

For each of these ideals to be achieved, additional specific conditions would have to be fulfilled; these conditions are also desirable for reasons of equity and social justice.

- ▼ Caring is legitimated as a collective (public) responsibility rather than purely a family or private responsibility.
- ▼ Access to care is relatively equally distributed and not dependent on economic or social status. Ultimately, the ideal would be a society in which there is an adequate amount and quality of care for all who need it—i.e., care that is individualized, culturally appropriate, and responsive to the preferences of those who are cared for.
- ▼ The responsibility and actual work of caring is shared equitably so that the burden of care does not fall disproportionately, as it now does, on disadvantaged groups—women, racialized minorities, and immigrants.

Some Directions for Change

Rethinking Social Citizenship

One important step is to redefine social citizenship to make care central to the rights and entitlements of citizens. This would involve a radical reversal of the present situation, in which care is defined as a private responsibility and therefore outside the realm of citizenship. Making care central to citizenship would entail three elements: establishing a right to care as a core right of citizens; establishing caregiving as a public social responsibility; and according caregivers recognition for carrying out a public social responsibility. These three elements are interrelated. If citizens have a right to care, then there is a corresponding responsibility on the part of the community to ensure that those who need care get it. Further, if caregiving is a public social responsibility, then those who do caregiving fulfill an obligation of citizenship and thus are entitled to societal benefits comparable to those accorded for those fulfilling the obligation to earn—for example, social security, seniority, and retirement benefits.

Additionally, a constraint that is specific to caring (in contrast to earning) and that needs to be addressed is what Kittay (1995) has called the "secondary dependence" of the caregiver. By taking on the care of a dependent and foregoing earning, unpaid caregivers become dependent on a third party—a breadwinner or the state—for resources to sustain both those they care for (primary dependents) and themselves (secondary dependents). Historically, U.S. welfare policy has been premised on the assumption that support for care giving belonged to the male breadwinner, and that the state should assume responsibility for support of caring only in the absence of a male breadwinner. Sometimes, as in the case of black single mothers, the lack of a male breadwinner was not seen as adequate grounds for the state to step in. Instead, black single mothers were deemed to be "employable mothers" who should support themselves and their dependents. In a step backward from recognizing caregivers' need for support, the U.S. Congress passed the Personal Responsibility Act in 1996, which abolished AFDC, devolved welfare back to individual states, and restricted the amount of lifetime benefits; most states have mandated stringent "workfare" to get single mothers off welfare.

In contrast to the U.S. welfare system, European welfare states have all provided some forms of family allowance for citizens with children. Most countries have supported caregivers with child allowances, and some even give small pensions to those who engage in unpaid care work. In conservative welfare regimes, such as France and Germany, the rationale for maternal allowances typically has been framed in terms of child welfare and promoting natalism, to ensure the size and well-being of the future population, rather than in terms of the value of caring and social citizenship rights and responsibilities in caring. Nonetheless, the allowances have been designed as universal entitlements not tied to income or means testing, unlike U.S. welfare programs. In more progressive social democratic welfare regimes, support for caregiving is extensive, including allowances,

subsidies, and direct services, such as child care and home aides (Pederson 1993; Sainsbury 1996).

Transforming citizenship in the United States to make care central to rights and entitlements would require us to challenge the linked ideologies of individual independence and family responsibility that I have described above. The United States for the most part has not even recognized mothering/parenting as a contribution to the national welfare, nor has it assumed a larger societal responsibility for supporting caregivers. As with previous historic changes in the boundaries and meanings of citizenship, it would require concerted struggle. Political citizenship, in the form of suffrage, was gradually extended to include previously excluded groups: nonpropertied white men in the early nineteenth century, black men after the Civil War, and, finally, women in 1920. The democratization of the vote was achieved only after concerted struggles by each of the groups in the course of over 100 years. Social citizenship rights of the welfare state, including social security, unemployment relief, minimum wage, and job creation were responses to the political mobilization of millions of Americans displaced by the Great Depression.[4] In the second half of the twentieth century, the second civil rights movement and second-wave feminism impelled legal, political, and social changes that dramatically expanded employment, education, and legal rights for racial minorities and women.

An important recent example of expanding citizenship is the success of the disability rights movement in establishing federal laws and policies that require schools and universities, employers, and public programs to provide facilities and activities that enable differently abled citizens to work, study, travel, and otherwise participate in the social and cultural life of the society. The latter movement comes closest to addressing the issues central to caring and social citizenship. It addresses the rights of citizens who have physical and mental conditions that limit their physical and economic independence to receive services and accommodations that allow them to achieve social and political independence.[5] There is thus a precedent for claiming the right to care as essential for meaningful citizenship.

Rethinking the Family as the Primary Site of Care

The previous discussion about state policies on social citizenship and care has assumed that most care takes place within the family and is carried out as part of unpaid labor of family members. However, if we take seriously the notion that caring is a public social responsibility, we also need to examine critically the conception of the family as the institution of first resort for caring. Indeed, one can argue that keeping the family as the "natural" unit for caring relationships helps anchor the gender division of caring labor. Seeing family and women's caring as "natural" disguises the material relationships of dependence that undergird the arrangement. But as those who care for others know, love is not enough: Care requires material resources. We need therefore to consider "defamilializing" care in order to relieve women

of disproportionate responsibility for caregiving and also to free both care receivers and caregivers from economic dependence on a male breadwinner.

Utopian societies in the past, ranging from communes to the Kibbutz movement, have attempted to transform care, especially infant and child care, into a public or communal responsibility by collectivizing child care. Theoretically, communal arrangements in which child care is treated as a form of "public" labor equal to other forms of labor free those who engage in caring from dependence on a breadwinner and also free children from dependence on (and therefore subordination to) biological parents. In practice, collectivized care has not eliminated the gendered division of caring labor, since it was still women who were the principal caregivers in publicly organized child care. Moreover, collectivized care generally has arisen in homogeneous religious and socialist communities where members shared fundamental cultural and political values. Completely collectivized care would be unlikely and perhaps undesirable in large-scale multicultural societies in which people maintain divergent cultural and political values. Family remains the main institutional nexus for anchoring distinctive cultural and social identities.

Thus, for both practical and ideological reasons it seems likely that families (broadly defined) will continue to value caring, and that family members will feel responsible for caring for children and, to a lesser extent, elderly and disabled members and will choose to do so. This does not mean that the family should be defined in the traditional way as the conjugal heterosexual household or that it should be the first resort for care in all cases. The states' and employers' care policies currently recognize dependency and caring relationships in rather traditional terms of parents and children (whether biological or adoptive) and spouses (defined through legal marriage). However, there are many other types of family relations that generate relationships of care, including cohabiting couples, gay and lesbian couples, extended kin such as grandparents and siblings, and sometimes "fictive kin" who participate in mutual support. As Carol Stack and Linda Burton (1994) point out in relation to their study of African American families, men, women, and children may be "kinscripted" to care for the children of siblings, grandparents, grandchildren, aunts, and uncles when there is no one else able to do so. To the extent that caring in the "family" is valued, the notion of "family" must be extended to encompass diverse kin relations, including "voluntary" or "fictive" relationships.

Regarding the knotty question of the primacy of family vs. the larger community in caregiving: In a survey conducted in England by Janet Finch (1996), respondents affirmed the importance of kin ties; they indicated that "rallying around in times of crisis" was what defined a functional family. The actual degree of responsibility that respondents felt in particular situations and toward particular relatives varied, however, depending on prior relationship and current circumstances. (I would also add that in a diverse society, there is considerable cultural difference in degree of obligation and in who is included in the net of obligation.) In general, Finch's respondents emphasized that relatives should not expect or take for granted assistance

from other family members. Another British researcher, Jenny Morris, found that, in turn, people requiring care often prefer not to rely on family. Many of the disabled adult women Morris interviewed said they preferred paid helpers or helpers provided by social service to help from family members, because it allowed them more independence (cited in Cancian and Oliker 2000:99).

Finch (1996) argues that the moral reasoning of people in her survey suggests the principle that people should have the right *not* to have to rely on their families for help: "To point in another way, the family should not be seen as the option of first resort for giving assistance to its adult members, either financial or practical" (p. 207).

Finch (1996) is careful to say that her point is not to deprecate generosity, care, and support within families, but only to see these as "optional, voluntary, freely given" (p. 207).

Taken together, the findings from Finch's and Morris' studies support the case that the community, as represented by the state, has primary responsibility for care of its citizens, and that citizens in turn have the right to nonfamily care. Public policy would thus be that all persons are entitled to publicly organized care or to allowances or vouchers to pay for care, regardless of whether or not family members are available to provide it.

Rethinking Paid Care

As noted in the introduction, the sheer demand for care, the inability of families to provide all care, and economic incentives to commodify care have brought about significant shift of caring to paid caregivers. This is especially the case for those needing physically demanding, round-the-clock care, such as children or adults with severe mental and physical disabilities, and elderly with dementia or Alzheimer's. Much of the latter care takes place in institutional settings, nursing homes, hospitals, and residential facilities, where the intensive face-to-face caring is done by nursing aides and other nonprofessional workers under the supervision and authority of administrators and medical and nursing professionals.

Thus, any scheme to create a society in which caring is valued in all spheres must address the growing commodification and defamilization of care. We need to think about the changes that occur when caring is made into a public rather than private function, when "strangers" rather than family members provide care, when caregiving is paid rather than unpaid, and most importantly when caring is regulated and controlled by bureaucratic rules and hierarchy.

Transferring caring from private household into publicly organized settings inserts "third parties" into the caring relationship. Both caregivers and care receivers are hemmed in by rules and regulations about time spent and kinds of care that are covered (e.g., shopping). Foner (1994) and others have argued that the "iron cage" of bureaucracy that constrains people in organizations creates fundamental dilemmas for care workers who are caught

between conflicting ideals. Whereas bureaucracies operate according to principles of standardization, impersonal rules, and efficiency, care relationships encourage individual treatment, personal ties, and patience.

Bureaucratic rules and control were instituted because of publicity about widespread abuse and neglect of patients. Having done an ethnographic study of a nursing home in New York, Foner (1994) agrees that bureaucratic rules and oversight are necessary to protect elderly patients, and that nursing aides, who do the actual physical care, feeding, cleaning, bathing, and so on, cannot be allowed to act autonomously. However, the rules and the way they are administered emphasize "efficiency" in getting physical care tasks done, meeting time deadlines, and maintaining records. Yet, as Tim Diamond (1988) found in his ethnography of a nursing home, emotional care is essential to the nursing aide's job: "holding someone trying to gasp for breath" or talking to residents to "help them hold on to memories of their past" (p. 48). Diamond observed that these kinds of emotional support were not listed in the aides' job descriptions, nor were the aides rewarded for these activities. In the nursing home she studied, Foner found that Ana, a nursing aide who regularly took time to talk to patients, and comfort or reassure them while bathing them or changing them, was constantly reprimanded for being inefficient, while Ms. James, an aide who never spoke to patients and handled them roughly to get them through their routines, was praised by supervisors as a model aide.

Deborah Stone (2000) found that home care workers also faced a conflict between bureaucratic rules and principles and their own ethic of care. Thus, they often stretched or evaded rules and supervisors to provide personal care, or spent off-work time or money to provide extra services.

The various ethnographic studies reveal that many care workers do provide quality emotional care, but they do so "around the fringes" so that their skills and effort are unrecognized or they do so in direct defiance of the rules. These studies point to the existence of "oppositional cultures" in which workers cooperate to provide the kind of care that the bureaucratic structure does not recognize or disallows. One case study of a psychiatric hospital (Lundgren and Browner 1990) found the quality of care was excellent because psychiatric technicians who did the daily care carved out areas of autonomy in which they could act in accordance with an ethos of care. Because the psychiatric technicians had opportunities to interact freely when residents were in classes, they developed camaraderie. Workers supported one another to go beyond the policies they considered unreasonable or against the interests of the residents. They developed customs, such as "time out" to leave the unit when they were about to lose control. These kinds of practices that workers themselves develop could be incorporated into organizational practices. Encouraging a team approach in which workers model and support each other for sensitive caring would be one such salutary practice. Procedures could also be reformed to build in more opportunity and recognition for aides who show kindness and go out of their way for patients. Organizations could offer more regular training in sensitivity and emotional aspects of care, include emotional caring work in job descriptions

and worker evaluations, and provide a reward system for caregivers who go beyond the call of duty to help patients.

At the professional level, the bureaucratic and chart-keeping imperatives of caring institutions could be harnessed to build in accountability for the social and emotional well-being of care receivers. Foner (1994) notes that one reform that has been adopted in many institutions is the psychosocial model of care, which pays attention to the emotional and social as well as the physical aspects of caring. The psychosocial model involves a case management approach that includes both health and social service needs of care receivers. Cancian and Oliker (2000) describe a "Clinical Practice Model" of nursing that Bonnie Wesorick has developed and introduced in several hospitals. This model challenges the medical model by emphasizing "holistic caring." It does so by such methods as keeping a record on each patient that includes personal histories, religious orientation, family situation, and individual concerns. Importantly, it calls for writing a plan of care that documents the patient's needs, concerns, and problems and an individualized approach to reach desired outcomes.

Encouraging caregivers to focus on social and emotional aspects of care may be salutary in some respects. Yet there is an inherent pitfall to empowering caregivers: It may exacerbate the already unequal relationship between caregivers and care receivers. Caregivers may feel that they understand the needs of care receivers and that they are acting in their best interests. However, care receivers might have different values and priorities. To the extent that care receivers depend emotionally and physically on their caregivers, they may feel they have no choice but to defer to the caregiver's judgment.

Thus, an additional concern should be to ensure that care receivers are given voice and influence over their care. In the case of mentally competent adults requiring home care assistance, for example, it would be preferable for them to be given grants or vouchers to hire their own caregivers rather than being assigned a helper by a social service agency. Several of the 50 disabled women interviewed by Jenny Morris in England said they especially valued helpers they hired and paid for themselves rather than those sent by government social services, because they had greater control. One woman said that only when she started employing her own helper did she feel she could pay attention to her own appearance. She had her paid helper assist her with clothing and makeup, which she felt justified in doing because "they need to be patient and I'm paying for that patience so I feel OK about expecting it" (quoted in Cancian and Oliker 2000:99). One group already has direct access to government funds for paid care. The Department of Veterans' Affairs has a program for Universal Aid and Attendance Allowance that gives direct unrestricted cash payments to 220,000 veterans to pay for homeworkers or attendants (Cancian and Oliker 2000:155). The right of veterans to state-supported paid care is acknowledged because of their "service to the country." What is needed is a more universal approach that extends entitlements to nonfamilial paid care to all citizens.

In short, both paid caregivers and receivers of paid care need to be empowered. Sometimes, when the interests of caregivers and care

receivers intersect, it makes sense for them to organize together. For example, when social service agency budgets are cut and home care and other services are reduced, caregivers may be forced to serve more clients less well and clients don't get the care they need. During the 1980s and '90s, coalitions of home health care workers, care receivers, and community leaders have formed to improve wages and benefits for care workers. Since services are paid from Medicaid or other public funds, care receivers will support wage increases for care workers, especially if it means that their caregivers will continue rather than leaving for higher-paying jobs in other fields (Cobble 1996; SEIU 1999).

Rethinking Employment Practices

Changes in employment practices are also needed to make it possible for people to integrate work and care and so that caregiving is not penalized. A small proportion of citizens currently benefit from private-sector initiatives by corporations that recognize the caring responsibilities of their employees. Some of these corporate employers provide child care and unpaid leaves to care for children or elderly relatives. Model programs include those by CitiBank, Stride Rite, and Campbell's Soups, which provide child care on or near their premises. Bristol Myers-Squibb has a family leave policy for employees that covers care for elderly relatives (Cancian and Oliker 2000:75, 155).

The passage of the 1993 Family and Medical Leave Act marked a first step in developing a national policy that supports combining work and care. The act recognizes care responsibilities for those engaged in paid work and accepts public responsibility so that dependents can receive adequate care. As in many European countries, the stated goal of the legislation was the development of children and promotion of the family unit rather than recognition of caregiving as a social responsibility. The preamble to the Act recognizes job security and parenting as important for citizens' well-being and acknowledges the role of the state in supporting both. However, coverage is extremely limited. By mandating only unpaid leave, the government accommodates care rather than fully supporting it, since few parents can afford to use the unpaid leave. Moreover, by exempting employers with fewer than 50 employees, the law leaves an estimated half of the workforce uncovered—56 percent of women and 48 percent of men, according to Spalter-Roth and Hartmann (1990). Ultimately, when employer interests are at stake, employer needs are allowed to trump care needs. Finally, the Act recognizes dependency only within traditional conjugal family relationships—spouse, children, and parents (Kittay 1995). It thereby "refamilizes" care by excluding other types of voluntary relations of dependency and care.

Besides parental and caregiving leave and child care, employment policy must consider the sheer number of hours needed for care. A national survey of a representative sample of 1509 English-speaking households

found an average of 17.9 hours of caregiving per week per household, while several other specialized surveys found a much higher number of unpaid caregiver hours in households with persons having specific medical conditions or disabilities (Arno, Levine, and Memmott 1999). At the same time, work hours of employed Americans have become the longest of those in all industrialized nations, according to a 1997 United Nations survey. The survey found that U.S. workers averaged 40 percent more hours than Norwegians and 25 percent more than the French (calculated from figures in the *San Francisco Chronicle,* September 6, 1999).

In combination with lack of state support for nonemployed caregivers, long work hours increase the strain on U.S. workers who have care responsibilities. Comparisons of worker productivity suggest that the longer hours of U.S. workers have not produced comparable increases in productivity. Thus reduction of work hours can be justified on economic as well as social welfare grounds. The 40-hour week was the goal of labor movements starting after the Civil War, but it was only when organized labor acquired sufficient political power in the 1930s that it became the standard. It involved the recognition of workers' rights for a life apart from the job. It is now time to recognize the reality of workers' multiple responsibilities for earning and caring by reducing work hours through a combination of reducing the standard for "full-time work" and increasing vacation and leave time.

Closing Thoughts

I have focused on specific ideological and structural constructions of caring. But ideas about and structures of caring are tied to other ideologies and structures that they support and are supported by. Achieving the kinds of changes needed to create a society that values caring will require transforming the ways we think about ourselves, our relationships with others, the family, civil society, the state, and the political economy. Ultimately, the transformation of caring must be linked to major changes in political–economic structures and relationships. Perhaps most fundamentally, the liberal concept of "society" as made up of discrete, independent, and freely choosing individuals will have to be discarded in favor of notions of interdependence among not wholly autonomous members of a society.

ENDNOTES

[1] Kittay (1995) has extended the critique to argue that dependence and relations of dependence are simply not accommodated in liberal theories of justice, which are premised on a model of autonomous individuals who can make choices in their own best interests.

[2] Thus, visiting nurses or health care coordinators may be allowed to make a single home visit to give discharged patients instructions on medical self-care, but not to take longer to provide social and emotional support to help them adjust to their new limitations.

[3] For the purposes of this essay, I am deliberately limiting the meaning of care to that of caring for people, even though for the other purposes, one might conceptualize care as encompassing caring for objects, animals, and the environment. For example, political theorist Joan Tronto (1993) defines caring as "a species activity that includes everything that we do to

maintain, continue, and repair our 'world' so that we can live as well as possible. That world includes our bodies, our selves, and our environment, all of which we seek to interweave in a complex, life-sustaining web" (p. 103). At the same time, I am adopting a somewhat broader definition than one that restricts caring only to meeting the needs of those who cannot care for themselves—e.g., Diemut Bubeck's (1995) definition of "caring for" as "the meeting of the needs of one person by another person where face-to-face interaction between carer and cared for is a crucial element of the overall activity and where the need is of such a nature that it cannot possibly be met by the person in need herself" (p. 129).

[4] Similarly, veterans' benefits, the G.I. Bill, hospitalization, and other social welfare benefits came about partly because of veterans' political organizing efforts.

[5] There has been a recent movement to franchise citizens with mental illness.

REFERENCES

Abel, Emily and Margaret Nelson, eds. 1990. *Circles of Care.* Albany: State University of New York Press.

Abramovitz, Mimi. 1996. *Under Attack: Fighting Back.* New York: Monthly Review Press.

Arno, Peter S., Carol Levine, and Margaret M. Memmott. 1999. "The Economic Value of Informal Caregiving." *Health Affairs* 18 (2): 182–87.

Bubeck, Diemut Elisabet. 1995. *Care, Gender, and Justice.* Oxford: Clarendon Press.

Cancian, Francesca M. and Stacey J. Oliker. 2000. *Caring and Gender.* Thousand Oaks, CA: Pine Forge Press.

Cobble, Dorothy Sue. 1996. "The Prospects for Unionization in a Service Economy." Pp. 333–58 in *Working in a Service Economy,* edited by Cameron MacDonald and Carmen Siriani. Philadelphia: Temple University Press.

Diamond, Timothy. 1988. "Social Policy and Everyday Life in Nursing Homes: A Critical Ethnography." Pp. 39–55 in *The Worth of Women's Work: A Qualitative Synthesis,* edited by Anne Statham, Eleanor M. Miller, and Hans O. Mauksch. Albany: State University of New York Press.

England, Paula. 1992. *Comparable Worth: Theories and Evidence.* Hawthorne, NY: Aldine de Gruyter.

Finch, Janet. 1996. "Family Rights and Responsibilities." Pp. 193–208 in *Citizenship Today: The Contemporary Relevance of T. H. Marshall,* edited by Martin Bulmer and Anthony M. Rees. London: UCL Press.

Foner, Nancy. 1994. *The Caregiving Dilemma: Work in the American Nursing Home.* Berkeley: University of California Press.

Fraser, Nancy and Linda Gordon. 1993. "Contract versus Charity: Why Is There No Social Citizenship in the United States?" *Socialist Review* 212 (3): 45–68.

Glenn, Evelyn Nakano. 1992. "From Servitude to Service Work: Historical Continuities in the Racial Division of Paid Reproductive Labor." *Signs* 18:1–43.

Gordon, Linda. 1994. *Pitied but Not Entitled: Single Mothers and the History of Welfare 1890–1935.* New York: Free Press.

Harrington, Mona. 1999. *Care and Equality: Inventing a New Family Politics.* New York: Knopf.

Kittay, Eva Feder. 1995. "Taking Dependence Seriously: The Family and Medical Leave Act Considered in Light of the Social Organization of Dependency Work and Gender Equality." *Hypatia* 10:8–29.

Lundgren, Rebecka Inga and Carole H. Browner. 1990. "Caring for the Institutionalized Mentally Retarded: Work Culture and Work-Based Social Supports." Pp. 150–72 in *Circles of Care,* edited by Emily Abel and Margaret Nelson. Albany: State University of New York Press.

Mink, Gwendolyn. 1994. *The Wages of Motherhood.* Ithaca, NY: Cornell University Press.

Nelson, Barbara. 1990. "The Origins of the Two-Channel Welfare State: Workmen's Compensation and Mothers' Aid." Pp. 123–51 in *Women, the State, and Welfare,* edited by Linda Gordon. Madison: University of Wisconsin Press.

Okin, Susan. 1979. *Women in Western Political Thought.* Princeton, NJ: Princeton University Press.

Pateman, Carole. 1988. *The Sexual Contract.* Stanford, CA: Stanford University Press.

Pedersen, Susan. 1993. *Family, Dependence, and the Origins of the Welfare State: Britain and France, 1914–1945.* Cambridge: Cambridge University Press.

Ruddick, Sara. 1998. "Care as Labor and Relationship." Pp. 3–25 in *Norms and Values: Essays on the Work of Virginia Held,* edited by Joram G. Haber and Mark S. Halfon. Lanham, MD: Rowman & Littlefield.

Sainsbury, Diane. 1996. *Gender, Equality and Welfare States.* Cambridge: Cambridge University Press.

San Francisco Chronicle. 1999. "UN Says Americans Are the Hardest Workers." September 6, p. 3.

Service Employees' International Union (SEIU). 1999. "Drive to Improve L.A. Homecare Takes Big Step Forward." Press Release.

Shklar, Judith. 1991. *American Citizenship: The Quest for Inclusion.* Cambridge, MA: Harvard University Press.

Spalter-Roth, Roberta M. and Heidi I. Hartmann. 1990. *Unnecessary Losses: Cost to Americans of the Lack of Family and Medical Leave.* Washington, DC: Institute for Women's Policy Research.

Stack, Carol and Linda Burton. 1994. "Kinscripts: Reflections on Family, Generation, and Culture." Pp. 33–44 in *Mothering: Ideology, Experience and Agency,* edited by Evelyn Nakano Glenn, Grace Chang, and Linda Forcey. New York: Routledge.

Stone, Deborah. 1999. "Care and Trembling." *The American Prospect* 43 (March–April): 61–67.

———. 2000. "Care as We Give It, Work as We Know It." In *Care Work: Gender, Labor and the Welfare State,* edited by Madonna Harrington-Meyer. New York: Routledge.

Thorne, Barrie. 1999. "Pick-Up Time at Oakdale Elementary School: Work and Family from the Vantage Points of Children." Working Paper No. 2, Center for Working Families, University of California, Berkeley.

Tronto, Joan. 1993. *Moral Boundaries: A Political Argument for an Ethic of Care.* New York: Routledge.

PART XI

Families and Poverty

51

AS AMERICAN AS APPLE PIE
Poverty and Welfare

MARK R. RANK

For many Americans, the words poverty and welfare conjure images of people on the fringes of society: unwed mothers raising several children, inner-city black men, high school dropouts, the homeless, and so on. The media, political rhetoric, and often even the research of social scientists depict the poor as alien and often undeserving of help. In short, being poor and using welfare are perceived as outside the American mainstream.

Yet, poverty and welfare use are as American as apple pie. Most of us will experience poverty during our lives. Even more surprising, most Americans will turn to public assistance at least once during adulthood. Rather than poverty and welfare use being an issue of *them*, it is more an issue of *us*.

The Risk of Poverty and Drawing on Welfare

Our understanding about the extent of poverty comes mostly from annual surveys conducted by the Census Bureau. Over the past three decades, between 11 and 15 percent of Americans have lived below the poverty line in any given year. Some people are at greater risk than others, depending on age, race, gender, family structure, community of residence, education, work skills and physical disabilities.

Studies that follow particular families over time—in particular, the Panel Study of Income Dynamics (PSID), the National Longitudinal Survey (NLS), and the Survey of Income and Program Participation (SIPP)—have given us a further understanding of year-to-year changes in poverty. They show that most people are poor for only a short time. Typically, households are impoverished for one, two, or three years, then manage to get above the poverty line. They may stay above the line for a while, only to fall into poverty again later. Events triggering these spells of poverty frequently involve the loss of a job and its pay, family changes such as divorce, or both.

There is, however, an alternative way to estimate the scope of poverty. Specifically, how many Americans experience poverty at some point during adulthood? Counting the number of people who are ever touched by poverty, rather than those who are poor in any given year, gives us a better sense of the scope of the problem. Put another way, to what extent is poverty a "normal" part of the life cycle?

My colleague Tom Hirschl and I have constructed a series of "life tables" built from PSID data following families for over 25 years. The life table is a technique for counting how often specific events occur in specific periods of time, and is frequently used by demographers and medical researchers to assess risk, say, the risk of contracting breast cancer after menopause. It allows us to estimate the percentage of the American population that will experience poverty at some point during adulthood. We also calculated the percentage of the population that will use a social safety net program—programs such as food stamps or Aid to Families with Dependent Children (AFDC, now replaced by the Temporary Assistance for Needy Families [TANF] program)—sometime during adulthood. Our results suggest that a serious reconsideration of who experiences poverty is in order.

Figure 1 shows the percentage of Americans spending at least one year living below the official poverty line during adulthood. It also graphs the

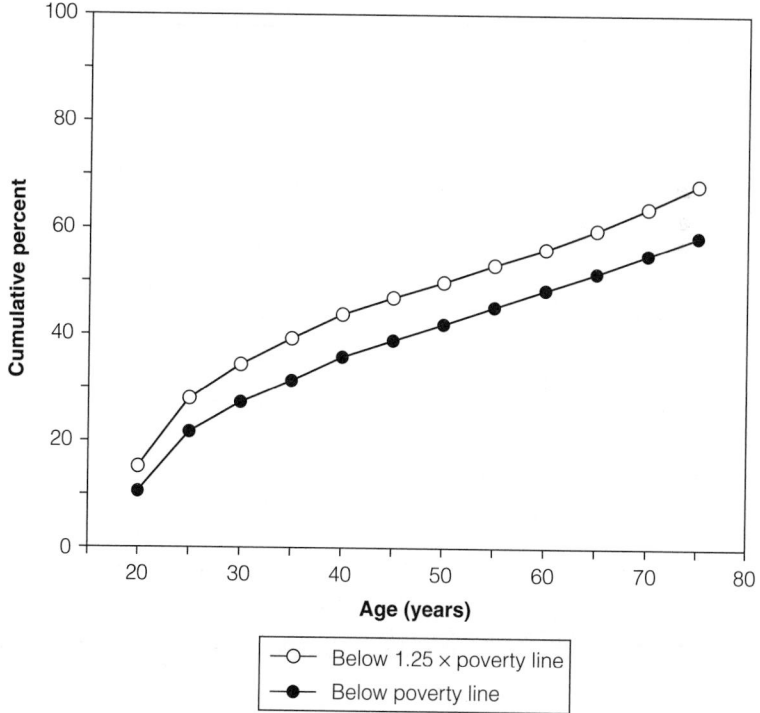

FIGURE 1 Cumulative Percent of Americans Who Have Experienced Poverty
Source: Panel Study of Income Dynamics.

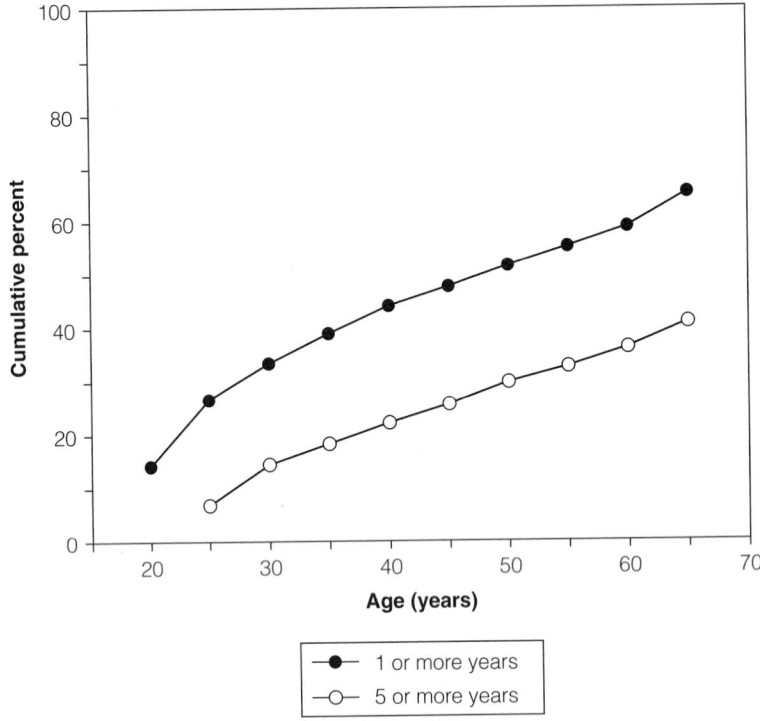

FIGURE 2   Cumulative Percent of Americans Who Have Received Welfare

Source: Panel Study of Income Dynamics.

percentage who have lived between the poverty line and just 25 percent above it—what scholars consider "near poverty."

By the age of 30, 27 percent of Americans will have experienced at least one year in poverty and 34 percent will have fallen below the near-poverty line. By the age of 50, the percentages will have risen to 42 and 50 percent, respectively. And, finally, by the time Americans have reached the age of 75, 59 percent will have spent at least a year below the poverty line during their adulthood, while 68 percent will have faced at least a year in near poverty.

If we included experiences of poverty in childhood, these percentages would be even higher. Rather than an isolated event that occurs only among the so-called "underclass," poverty is a reality that a clear majority of Americans will experience during their lifetimes.

Measuring impoverishment as the use of social safety net programs produces even more startling results. Figure 2 draws on the same PSID survey to show the proportion of people between the ages of 20 and 65 who will use one of the major need-based welfare programs in the United States, including food stamps, Medicaid, AFDC, Supplemental Security Income, and other cash subsidies such as general assistance. By the time Americans reach the age of 65, approximately two-thirds will have, as adults, received assistance

for at least a year, while 40 percent will have used a welfare program in at least five separate years. (Again, adding childhood experiences would only raise the rates.) Contrary to stereotypes, relying on America's social safety net is widespread and far-reaching.

Of course, people with disadvantages such as single parents or those with fewer skills will have even higher cumulative rates of poverty and welfare use than those shown in Figures 1 and 2. Yet to portray poverty as an issue affecting only marginalized groups is clearly a mistake.

Why Is the Risk of Poverty So High?

Time　First, most discussions of poverty look at single years, or five or ten years at a stretch. The life table techniques employed in Figures 1 and 2 are based upon assessing the risk of poverty across a lifetime, more than 50 years. Over so many years, individuals face many unanticipated events—households split up, workers lose their jobs, family members become sick, and so on—that become financial emergencies. The familiar saying of being "one paycheck away from poverty" is particularly apt. For example, it is estimated that families with average incomes have enough assets to maintain their standards of living for just over one month.

The Safety Net　A second reason poverty rates are so high is that there is little government help to tide households over during financial emergencies. Although most Americans will eventually rely on need-based government aid (as shown in Figure 2), that assistance often fails to save them from poverty. Contrary to the rhetoric about vast sums being spent on public assistance, the American welfare system can be more accurately described as minimal. Compared to other Western industrialized countries, the United States devotes far fewer resources to assisting the economically vulnerable.

Most European countries provide a wide range of social and insurance programs that effectively keep families from falling into poverty. These include substantial cash payments to families with children. Unemployment assistance is far more generous in these countries than in the United States, often providing support for more than a year following the loss of a job. Furthermore, universal health coverage is routinely provided along with considerable support for child care.

These social policies substantially reduce the risk of poverty in Europe and Canada, while U.S. social policies—aside from programs specifically directed to aid the elderly—have reduced poverty modestly at best. As economist Rebecca Blank notes in *It Takes a Nation*, "the national choice in the United States to provide relatively less generous transfers to low-income families has meant higher relative poverty rates in the country. While low-income families in the United States work more than in many other countries, they are not able to make up for lower governmental income support relative to their European counterparts" (pp. 141–42).

Scholars who have used the Luxembourg Income Study (LIS), an international collection of economic surveys, have documented the inability of the American safety net to reduce the risk of poverty. For example, Finnish social scientist Veli-Matti Ritakallio has examined the extent to which cash assistance reduces poverty across eight European countries, Canada, and the United States. European and Canadian programs reduce rates of poverty by an average of 79 percent from what they would have been absent the assistance. Finland, for instance, reduced the percentage of its residents who would have been poor from 33 percent down to 4 percent. In contrast, the United States was only able to reduce its percentage in poverty at any given time from 29 percent to 18 percent. As a result, the current rates of U.S. poverty are among the highest in the industrialized world.

The Labor Market   A third factor elevating the risk of American poverty across the life course is the failure of the labor market to provide enough jobs that pay well enough. During the past 30 years, the U.S. economy has produced increasing numbers of low-paying jobs, part-time jobs, and jobs without benefits. For example, the Census Bureau estimated that the median earnings of workers who were paid hourly wages in 2000 was $9.91. At the same time, approximately 3 million Americans were working part-time because of a shortage of full-time jobs. As journalist Barbara Ehrenreich and others have shown, these jobs simply do not support a family.

A higher percentage of the U.S. workforce falls into this low-wage sector than is true in comparable developed countries. For example, economist Timothy Smeeding and his colleagues have found that 25 percent of all American full-time workers could be classified as being in low-wage work (defined as earning less than 65 percent of the national median for full-time jobs). This was by far the highest percentage of the countries analyzed, with the overall average of non-U.S. countries falling at 12 percent.

In addition, there are simply not enough jobs to go around. Labor economist Timothy Bartik used several different approaches to estimate the number of jobs that would be needed to significantly reduce poverty in the United States. Even in the booming economy of the late 1990s, between 5 and 9 million more jobs were needed in order to meet the needs of the poor and disadvantaged.

To use an analogy, the demand for labor versus the supply of decent paying jobs might be thought of as an ongoing game of musical chairs. That is, the number of workers in the labor market is far greater than the number of jobs that pay a living wage. Using SIPP data for 1999, I estimated this imbalance as ranging between 9 percent and 33 percent, depending upon how poverty and labor market participation were defined. Consequently, between 9 and 33 percent of American household heads were either in non-living-wage jobs or looking for work. The very structure of the labor market ensures that some families will lose out at this musical chairs game and consequently will run a significant risk of poverty.

Some may point out that U.S. rates of unemployment are fairly low when compared to European levels. Yet Bruce Western and Katherine Beckett

demonstrate that these lower rates are largely a result of extremely high rates of incarceration. By removing large numbers of American men from the labor force and placing them into the penal system (thus out of our musical chairs analogy altogether), unemployment rates are kept artificially low. When this factor is taken into account and adjusted for, U.S. unemployment rates fall more into line with those of Europe.

Changing the Poverty Paradigm

A life course perspective shows us that Americans are highly susceptible to experiencing poverty first-hand. Understanding the normality of poverty requires us to rethink several of our most enduring myths. Assuming that most Americans would rather avoid such an experience, it becomes in our enlightened self-interest to ensure that we reduce poverty and establish an effective safety net. This risk-sharing argument has been articulated most notably by the philosopher John Rawls. As well as being charitable, improving the plight of those in poverty is an issue of common concern.

We are also beginning to recognize that, as a nation, we pay a high price for our excessive rates of poverty. Research shows that poverty impairs the nation's health, the quality of its workforce, race relations, and, of course, its future generations. Understanding the commonality of poverty shifts how we choose to think about the issue—from a distant concept of *them*, to an active reality of *us*. In addition, much of the public's resistance to assisting the poor and particularly those on welfare is the perception that the poor are often undeserving of assistance, that their poverty arises from a lack of motivation, questionable morals, and so on. Yet my analysis suggests that, given its pervasiveness, poverty appears systemic to our economic structure. In short, we have met the enemy, and they are us. C. Wright Mills made a similar point about unemployment:

> When, in a city of 100,000, only one man is unemployed, that is his personal trouble, and for its relief we properly look to the character of the man, his skills, and his immediate opportunities. But when in a nation of 50 million employees, 15 million men are unemployed, that is an issue, and we may not hope to find its solution within the range of opportunities open to any one individual. The very structure of opportunities has collapsed. Both the correct statement of the problem and the range of possible solutions require us to consider the economic and political institutions of the society, and not merely the personal situation and character of a scatter of individuals.

So too with poverty. That America has the highest poverty rates in the Western industrialized world and that most Americans will experience poverty during their lifetimes has little to do with individual motivation or attitudes. Rather, it has much to do with a labor market that fails to produce enough decent paying jobs, and social policies that are unable to pull individuals and families out of poverty when unforeseen events occur. The

United States has the means to alleviate poverty, and a range of models from other countries to borrow from. Allowing our policies to be mired in self-righteous moralism while millions of citizens suffer is unconscionable. It is time to shift the debate from one of blame, to one of justice and common concern.

RECOMMENDED RESOURCES

Bartik, Timothy H. 2002. "Poverty, Jobs, and Subsidized Employment." *Challenge* 45 (3): 100–11. An argument for the importance of labor demand policies that encourage job growth and improved wages for low-income workers.

Blank, Rebecca. 1997. *It Takes a Nation: A New Agenda for Fighting Poverty.* New York: Russell Sage Foundation. A review of the characteristics, nature, and current strategies for addressing American poverty.

Ehrenreich, Barbara. 2001. *Nickel and Dimed: On (Not) Getting By in America.* New York: Henry Holt and Company. A first-hand account of trying to survive on low-wage work in three different settings.

O'Connor, Alice. 2001. *Poverty Knowledge: Social Science, Social Policy, and the Poor in Twentieth-Century U.S. History.* Princeton, NJ: Princeton University Press. O'Connor critiques the dominant social science emphasis in the past 40 years on analyzing individual attributes as the primary cause of poverty.

Patterson, James T. 2000. *America's Struggle against Poverty in the Twentieth Century.* Cambridge, MA: Harvard University Press. A historical overview of American social policy directed at the alleviation of poverty.

Rank, Mark R. 2004. *One Nation, Underprivileged: How American Poverty Affects Us All.* New York: Oxford University Press. A new perspective on understanding and addressing U.S. poverty.

Rank, Mark R. and Thomas A. Hirschl. 2001. "Rags or Riches? Estimating the Probabilities of Poverty and Affluence across the Adult American Life Span." *Social Science Quarterly* 82 (4): 651–69. An examination of the likelihood that Americans will experience poverty or affluence at some point during their adulthood, which suggests a new conceptualization of social stratification.

Ritakallio, Veli-Matti. 2001. "Trends of Poverty and Income Inequality in Cross-National Comparison." Luxembourg Income Study Working (Paper) No. 272, Maxwell School of Citizenship and Public Affairs, Syracuse University, Syracuse, New York. Ritakallio uses the Luxembourg Income Study to assess the effectiveness of government policy in reducing poverty among nine developed countries.

Smeeding, Timothy M., Lee Rainwater, and Gary Burtless. 2001. "U.S. Poverty in a Cross-National Context." Pp. 162–89 in *Understanding Poverty,* edited by Sheldon H. Danziger and Robert H. Haveman. Cambridge, MA: Harvard University Press. The authors compare the extent of poverty in the United States and other developed countries.

Western, Bruce and Katherine Beckett. 1999. "How Unregulated Is the U.S. Market? The Penal System as a Labor Market Institution." *American Journal of Sociology* 104 (January): 1030–60. This study shows the role that incarceration plays in lowering overall U.S. unemployment rates.

52

FLAT BROKE WITH CHILDREN
The Ground-Level Results of Welfare Reform

SHARON HAYS

It's hard to date it precisely, but I think my severe case of cognitive dissonance set in on a summer evening in 1999. As part of my research on welfare reform, I'd spent the afternoon playing on the floor with Sammy, the four-year-old son of a welfare recipient. I was struck by his intelligence and creativity and imagined that if his mom were middle-class, she'd soon be having him tested and charting the gifted and talented programs he'd attend.

But Sammy's mom, Celia, had other things on her mind. Cradling her infant daughter, she told me that she had been recently diagnosed with cancer. Her doctor wanted her to start treatments immediately. Although she'd been working at a local Fotomart for three months, the welfare office still helped her with the costs of child care—costs she couldn't otherwise manage on her $6 per hour pay. When she asked her boss about flexible hours to manage the cancer treatments, he told her she was just too easily replaced. She'd also checked with her welfare caseworkers; they told her that if she lost her job she'd have to quickly find another or risk being cut off the welfare rolls. I talked to her about the Social Security Disability program, even though I knew that she had only a slim chance of getting help there. Celia had an eighth-grade education, no financial assets, few job skills, and no extended family members with sufficient resources to see her through. And she needed those cancer treatments now.

Under the old welfare system, she could have simply returned to full welfare benefits. Yet, knowing what I did from my research into the worlds of low-wage work, welfare, and disability, I was sure there was now virtually nowhere for her to turn, save all those local charities that were already incredibly overburdened. I didn't have the heart to tell her.

When I went home that night, the local television news was interviewing a smiling former welfare mother recently employed at a supermarket chain. It was a story of redemption—the triumph of individual willpower and American know-how—and the newscaster cheerfully pronounced it a marker of the "success" of welfare reform. That's when the dissonance set in. I've been suffering from it ever since.

Sharon Hays, "Flat Broke with Children: The Ground Level Results of Welfare Reform" from *Dissent* (Fall 2003). Reprinted with the permission of the Foundation for the Study of Independent Social Ideas.

From one point of view, it makes perfect sense that so many have celebrated the results of the 1996 Personal Responsibility Act. The welfare rolls have been cut by more than half—from twelve million recipients in 1996 to five million today. Among those who have left welfare, the majority (60 percent to 65 percent) are employed. Add to this the fact that public opinion polls show that almost no one liked the old system of welfare and most people (including most welfare recipients) agree that the principles behind reform—independence, self-sufficiency, strong families, a concern for the common good—are worthy ideals.

The problem is that there is a wide gap between the more worthy goals behind reform and the ground-level realities I found in the welfare office. There is also a tremendous amount of diversity hidden in those large-scale statistical accountings of the results of reform—and much of it is a great deal more disheartening than it first appears. After three years of ethnographic research inside two (distant and distinct) welfare offices, after interviewing more than 50 caseworkers and about 130 welfare mothers, and after five years of poring over policy reports on reform, it is clear to me that the majority of the nation's most desperately poor citizens are in worse shape now than they would have been had the Personal Responsibility Act never been passed.

Between Success and Failure

Political speeches, policy reports, and the popular media all cite the declining rolls and the employment of former recipients as the central evidence of the success of welfare reform. By these standards, Celia and her children would count as a success.

Of course there are genuine success stories. Take Sally. With a good job at the phone company, medical benefits, sick leave and vacation leave, a nine-to-five schedule, possibilities for advancement, and enough income to place her and her two kids above the poverty line, she was better off than she'd ever been on welfare benefits or in any of the (many) low-wage, no-benefit jobs she'd had in the past. And there was no question that the supportive services that came with reform had helped her to achieve that success. She got her job through a welfare-sponsored training program offered by the phone company. Welfare caseworkers had helped her out with clothing for work, bus vouchers, and a child care subsidy that got her through the training. "I think welfare's better now," she told me. "They've got programs there to help you. They're actually giving you an opportunity. I'm working and I feel like I can make it on my own."

Monique was also helped by reform. A messy divorce with an abusive (and stalker) husband had cost her her job as a nursing assistant. With two young sons to worry about, she sought help from the welfare office. Fortunately, she lived in one of the few states with a welfare policy that exempted domestic-violence victims from the immediate demand to find work. Using special funds made available by reform, welfare caseworkers not only provided her with a welfare check, but also helped her to manage car repairs

and the down payment on an apartment. Once she and her children were settled, her boss planned to hire her again. If Monique could remain hidden from her ex-husband, things would work out just fine. Like Sally, she was grateful for the help she'd received from the welfare office.

About one-half of the welfare mothers I met experienced at least temporary successes like these. Yet under the terms of reform, the long-term outlook for the majority is not so positive. And in many cases it is difficult to distinguish the successes from the failures.

Proponents of reform would mark Andrea, for instance, as "successful." When I met her, she was earning $5.75 an hour, working thirty-five hours a week at a Sunbelt City convenience store. After paying rent, utility bills, and food costs for her family of three, she was left with $50 a month to cover the costs of child care, transportation, clothing, medical bills, laundry, school costs, furniture, appliances, and cleaning supplies. Just four months off the welfare rolls, Andrea was already in trouble. Her phone had been turned off the month before, and she was unsure how she'd pay this month's rent. Her oldest daughter was asking for new school clothes, her youngest had a birthday coming soon, and Andrea couldn't take her mind off the upcoming winter utility bills. If she were single, she told me, she would manage somehow. But with children to worry about, she knew she couldn't make it much longer.

National-level accountings of reform would also place Teresa and her three children in the plus column. When I met her, she had a temporary (three-month) job at a collection agency. Thanks to public housing and the time-limited child care subsidy offered by the welfare office, she was making ends meet. Teresa was smart and capable, but had only a high school diploma and almost no work experience. She'd spent more of her adult life outside the mainstream economy—first married to a drug dealer, then working as a street-level prostitute, and finally, drug free, on welfare. As much as Teresa thought she was doing better than ever and spoke of how happy she was to be getting dressed up every morning and going out to work, she was still concerned about the future. The child care costs for her three kids would amount to nearly three-quarters of her paycheck if she had to cover them herself. And her job, like that child care subsidy, was only temporary. Given her résumé, I wondered just what career ladder she might find to offer her sufficient income and stability to stay off the welfare rolls and successfully juggle her duties as both primary caregiver and sole breadwinner for those three kids.

The cycle of work and welfare implied by these cases is the most common pattern among the welfare-level poor. It is a cycle of moving from welfare to low-wage jobs to mounting debts and problems with child care, husbands, boyfriends, employers, landlords, overdue utility bills, broken-down cars, inadequate public transportation, unstable living arrangements, job layoffs, sick children, disabled parents, and the innumerable everyday contingencies of low-income life—any and all of which can lead a poor family back to the welfare office to repeat the cycle again. Most of the people caught up in this cycle face a number of social disadvantages from the start. Welfare

recipients are overwhelmingly mothers (90 percent), they are disproportionately non-white (38 percent are black, 25 percent Latino, and 30 percent white), nearly half are without high-school diplomas (47 percent), the majority have experience in only unskilled jobs, about half suffer from physical or mental health disabilities, almost as many have a history of domestic violence, and all have children to care for. At the same time, most welfare recipients have work experience (83 percent), and most want to work. This was true long before welfare reform. Yet given their circumstances, and given the structure of low-wage work, it is not surprising that many have found it difficult to achieve long-term financial and familial stability.

Of those who have left the rolls since reform, a full 40 percent are without work or welfare at any given time. Of the 60 percent who do have jobs, their average wage is approximately $7 per hour. But most former recipients do not find full-time or year-round work, leaving their average annual wage estimated at just over $10,000 a year. Following this same pattern, about three-quarters of the families who left welfare are in jobs without medical insurance, retirement benefits, sick days, or vacation leave; and one-quarter work night or evening shifts. It is true that their average annual wages amount to more income than welfare, food stamps, and Medicaid combined. Yet, as Kathryn Edin and Laura Lein demonstrated in *Making Ends Meet,* taking into account the additional costs associated with employment (such as child care, transportation, clothing), working poor families like these actually suffer more material hardship than their counterparts on welfare.

The reality behind the declining welfare rolls is millions of former welfare families moving in and out of low-wage jobs. Some achieve success, most do not. Approximately one-third have found themselves back on welfare at least once since reform. Overall, two-thirds of those who have left welfare are either unemployed or working for wages that do not lift their families out of poverty. And there are still millions of families on welfare, coming in anew, coming back again, or as yet unable to find a way off the rolls.

The Personal Responsibility Act itself produced two primary changes in the lives of the working/welfare poor. On the one hand, welfare reform offered sufficient positive employment supports to allow poor families to leave welfare more quickly, and in some cases it offered just the boost that was needed to allow those families to achieve genuine long-term financial stability. On the other hand, welfare reform instituted a system of rules, punishments, and time limits that has effectively pressured the poor to steer clear of the welfare office.

A central result of welfare reform, in other words, is that a large proportion of desperately poor mothers and children are now too discouraged, too angry, too ashamed, or too exhausted to go to the welfare office. Nationwide, as the welfare rolls were declining by more than half, the rate of dire (welfare-level) poverty declined by only 15 percent. To put it another way: whereas the vast majority of desperately poor families received welfare support prior to reform (84 percent), today less than half of them do. Why are

all these mothers and children now avoiding welfare? To make sense of this part of the story, one needs to understand the complicated changes that have taken place inside welfare offices across the nation. I can here offer only a glimpse.

Punishment and the Push to Work

Upon arrival at the Arbordale welfare office, the first thing one sees is a large red sign, two feet high, twelve feet long, inquiring, "HOW MANY MONTHS DO YOU HAVE LEFT?" This message is driven home by caseworkers' incessant reminders of the "ticking clock," in the ubiquity of employment brochures and job postings, and, above all, by a carefully sequenced set of demanding rules and regulations.

The pressure is intense. It includes the job search that all new clients must start immediately (forty verifiable job contacts in thirty days), the "job readiness" and "lifeskills" workshops they are required to attend, the (time-consuming and difficult) child support enforcement process in which they must agree to participate, and the constant monitoring of their eligibility for welfare and their progress toward employment. Welfare mothers who are not employed within a specified period (thirty days in Arbordale, forty-five in Sunbelt City) are required to enroll in full-time training programs or take full-time unpaid workfare placements until they can find a job. Throughout, these working, training, and job-searching welfare mothers are expected to find somewhere to place their children. Although welfare recipients are all technically eligible for federal child care subsidies, only about one-third receive them. With only a $350 welfare check (the average monthly benefit for a family of three), child care arrangements can be very difficult to manage.

In Sunbelt City the pressure to get off the welfare rolls is introduced even more directly and forcefully. As is true in about half the states nationwide, Sunbelt City has a "diversionary" program designed to keep poor mothers and children from applying for welfare in the first place. Before they even begin the application process, potential welfare clients are required to attend the diversion workshop. The three workshops I went to all focused on the importance of "self sufficiency," the demanding nature of welfare require-ments, and the advantages of work—and left most of the poor mothers in attendance weary and confused.

For those who persisted through the application process, their com-pliance to the rules of reform was ensured not just by the long-term threat of time limits, but by the more immediate threat of sanctions. Any welfare mother who fails to follow through with her job search, workfare placement, training program, child support proceedings, reporting requirements, or the myriad of other regulations of the welfare office is sanctioned. To be sanc-tioned means that all or part of a family's welfare benefits are cut, while the "clock" keeps ticking toward that lifetime limit. National statistics suggest

that about one-quarter of welfare recipients lose their benefits as a result of sanctions.

Inside the welfare offices of Arbordale and Sunbelt City many of the women I met became so disheartened that they simply gave up and left the rolls. This included women who made it through some portion of the job search, or the employment workshops, or even took a workfare placement, but just couldn't manage the pressure. Some were sanctioned, others left on their own. Connected to these, but harder to count, were all those poor mothers who gave up before they got started. Eligibility workers in Arbordale estimated that as many as one-quarter of those who started the application process did not complete it. Caseworkers in Sunbelt City guessed that about one-third of the mothers who attended their diversion workshops were ("successfully") diverted from applying for benefits. In Arbordale, about one-quarter gave up before completing the application process.

Sarah was one example of a "diverted" potential welfare client. She was the full-time caregiver for her grandchild on a lung machine, her terminally ill father, and her own two young children. She'd been managing with the help of her father's Social Security checks and her boyfriend's help. But her boyfriend had left her, and medical bills were eating up all her father's income. Sarah discovered at her initial Arbordale welfare interview that in order to receive benefits she would need to begin a job search immediately. Because no one else was available to care for her father or grandchild, she said, it just didn't make sense for her to get a job. I met her as she conveyed this story to her friends in the Arbordale waiting room, fluctuating between tones of anger and sadness. "I have to swallow my pride, and come in here, and these people just don't want to help you no more," she told us. Leaving the office, she vowed never to return. As was true of so many others, it was unclear to me what she would do.

Sonya was one example of the many sanctioned welfare clients I met, though her case was more dramatic than most. She was so quiet and shy that I wondered if anyone would notice how she'd been affected by reform. Twenty years old, with a tenth-grade education and two children, she'd been on welfare most of the time since she gave birth to her oldest son at age thirteen. She'd had only one job in her lifetime, and that lasted for just four months. In the hours I spent with her, it became clear to me that she suffered from serious mental health problems—matching clinical definitions of depression and obsessive-compulsive disorder. She rarely left her apartment and lived in fear that she would catch a cold, or pneumonia, or worse. When I commented on her spotlessly clean and carefully decorated apartment, she told me that she completely rearranged it at least once a month and sometimes once a week. I watched her feed lunch to her son: every can, jar, plate, and utensil in her kitchen was precisely ordered, and she was unable to continue our conversation until all the dishes were washed and dried and the counters disinfected, twice, for good measure. When we talked about the possibilities for employment, she explained that she found it necessary to take four showers a day, and worried that she couldn't handle this with a full-time job, especially, she said, since buses don't always run on schedule.

In responding to my question about the men in her life she let me know, quietly, that her father had sexually abused her as a child. (She did not volunteer and I did not ask if her pregnancy at age twelve was the result of that abuse.) Sonya had been sanctioned for failing to carry out her job search. Without welfare income, she had no idea what she would do. I worried, a lot, about how she and her kids would get by.

Kendra might be included among those who found themselves too ashamed, discouraged, or exhausted to return to the welfare office when she needed help. One of the first welfare clients I met, Kendra was much loved by the caseworkers who knew her. She was sweet, quietly charming, and deeply earnest. Twenty-six years old, with two daughters aged six and eight, she had a history of working only part-time, on and off, in unskilled jobs. She'd finally landed a secure and meaningful job, she thought, working at a homeless shelter run by the Salvation Army. Even though it was the night shift and the pay was low, she felt good about helping out the homeless, and was grateful for the mentoring and support she'd received from the welfare office. She still didn't make enough money to get by without child care help and an income supplement from welfare, but was hoping for a raise, studying for her high school equivalency exam, and thinking about taking a second job. She was cheerful when last I saw her. Six months later her caseworkers told me how quickly Kendra's life had unraveled. In a heated argument, one of Kendra's brothers had shot and killed her other brother. One brother was dead, the other on his way to prison. Kendra fell apart emotionally, lost her job, and left the welfare rolls. Two caseworkers spent a day off trying to find her (an extremely rare undertaking), but no one knew where she had gone.

All these women and their children have contributed to the decline of the welfare rolls. They are a central basis for the celebration of reform. They are also a central basis for my case of cognitive dissonance.

The Costs

In focusing on the hardships wrought by reform, I do not mean to suggest that the successes of welfare reform are trivial or inconsequential. Those successes matter. I also don't mean to imply that all welfare mothers are saints and victims. They aren't. But there are many other issues at stake in the reform of welfare.

Reading the daily news these days, one can't help but notice that the topic of poverty has lost its prominence, especially relative to the early days of reform. One reason for this neglect, it seems to me, has been the highly effective campaign pronouncing the triumph of the Personal Responsibility Act. Like all the information that was invisible in popular accounts of the invasion of Iraq, the ground-level hardship and human costs of reform are largely hidden from view. Yet the price tag on welfare reform is real.

By 2002, the National Governors' Association found itself begging Congress not to follow through on plans to increase the pressure on welfare

offices and welfare recipients across the nation—the costs, they explained, would be far too high for already stretched state budgets to bear. The U.S. Conference of Mayors found itself pleading with the Bush administration for more financial help to manage the rising populations of the hungry and homeless in American cities. Food banks were running short on food, homeless shelters were closing their doors to new customers, and local charities were raising their eligibility requirements to contend with rising numbers of people in need. The Medicaid system was in crisis, and large numbers of poor families were no longer receiving the food stamps for which they were eligible. Half of the families who left welfare had no money to buy food; one-third have had to cut the size of meals, and nearly half have had trouble paying their rent or utility bills.

In the meantime, only a fraction of welfare families have actually hit their federal lifetime limits on welfare benefits: just 120,000 welfare mothers and children had reached their limits by 2001. Given the work/welfare cycling process, and given that many families can survive at least temporarily on below-poverty wages and pieced-together alternative resources, it will take many more years for the full impact of reform to emerge. But, over the long haul, we can expect to see rising rates of hunger, homelessness, drug abuse, and crime. More children will wind up in foster care, in substandard child care, or left to fend for themselves. More disabled family members will be left without caregivers. Mental health facilities and domestic violence shelters will also feel the impact of this law, as will all the poor men who are called upon to provide additional support for their children.

Of course, this story is not apocalyptic. The poor will manage as they have always managed, magically and mysteriously, to make do on far less than poverty-level income. Many of the most desperate among them will simply disappear, off the radar screen, off to places unknown.

In any case, assessing the results of welfare reform is not just a question of its impact on the poor. It is also a question of what this law says about our collective willingness to support the nation's most disadvantaged and about the extent to which welfare reform actually lives up to the more worthy goals it purports to champion.

RECOMMENDED RESOURCES

Hays, Sharon, 2003. *Flat Broke with Children: Women in the Age of Welfare Reform.* New York: Oxford University Press.

53

UNMARRIED WITH CHILDREN

KATHRYN EDIN • MARIA KEFALAS

J en Burke, a white tenth-grade dropout who is 17 years old, lives with her stepmother, her sister, and her 16-month-old son in a cramped but tidy row home in Philadelphia's beleaguered Kensington neighborhood. She is broke, on welfare, and struggling to complete her GED. Wouldn't she and her son have been better off if she had finished high school, found a job, and married her son's father first?

In 1950, when Jen's grandmother came of age, only 1 in 20 American children was born to an unmarried mother. Today, that rate is 1 in 3—and they are usually born to those least likely to be able to support a child on their own. In our book, *Promises I Can Keep: Why Poor Women Put Motherhood Before Marriage*, we discuss the lives of 162 white, African American, and Puerto Rican low-income single mothers living in eight destitute neighborhoods across Philadelphia and its poorest industrial suburb, Camden. We spent five years chatting over kitchen tables and on front stoops, giving mothers like Jen the opportunity to speak to the question so many affluent Americans ask about them: Why do they have children while still young and unmarried when they will face such an uphill struggle to support them?

Romance at Lightning Speed

Jen started having sex with her 20-year-old boyfriend Rick just before her 15th birthday. A month and a half later, she was pregnant. "I didn't want to get pregnant," she claims. "*He* wanted me to get pregnant. As soon as he met me, he wanted to have a kid with me," she explains. Though Jen's college-bound suburban peers would be appalled by such a declaration, on the streets of Jen's neighborhood, it is something of a badge of honor. "All those other girls he was with, he didn't want to have a baby with any of them," Jen boasts. "I asked him, 'Why did you choose me to have a kid when you could have a kid with any one of them?' He was like, 'I want to have a kid with *you*.'" Looking back, Jen says she now believes that the reason "he wanted me to have a kid that early is so that I didn't leave him."

In inner-city neighborhoods like Kensington, where childbearing within marriage has become rare, romantic relationships like Jen and Rick's proceed

at lightning speed. A young man's avowal, "I want to have a baby by you," is often part of the courtship ritual from the beginning. This is more than idle talk, as their first child is typically conceived within a year from the time a couple begins "kicking it." Yet while poor couples' pillow talk often revolves around dreams of shared children, the news of a pregnancy—the first indelible sign of the huge changes to come—puts these still-new relationships into overdrive. Suddenly, the would-be mother begins to scrutinize her mate as never before, wondering whether he can "get himself together"—find a job, settle down, and become a family man—in time. Jen began pestering Rick to get a real job instead of picking up day-labor jobs at nearby construction sites. She also wanted him to stop hanging out with his ne'er-do-well friends, who had been getting him into serious trouble for more than a decade. Most of all, she wanted Rick to shed what she calls his "kiddie mentality"—his habit of spending money on alcohol and drugs rather than recognizing his growing financial obligations at home.

Rick did not try to deny paternity, as many would-be fathers do. Nor did he abandon or mistreat Jen, at least intentionally. But Rick, who had been in and out of juvenile detention since he was 8 years old for everything from stealing cars to selling drugs, proved unable to stay away from his unsavory friends. At the beginning of her seventh month of pregnancy, an escapade that began as a drunken lark landed Rick in jail on a carjacking charge. Jen moved back home with her stepmother, applied for welfare, and spent the last two-and-a-half months of her pregnancy without Rick.

Rick sent penitent letters from jail. "I thought he changed by the letters he wrote me. I thought he changed a lot," she says. "He used to tell me that he loved me when he was in jail. . . . It was always gonna be me and him and the baby when he got out." Thus, when Rick's alleged victim failed to appear to testify and he was released just days before Colin's birth, the couple's reunion was a happy one. Often, the magic moment of childbirth calms the troubled waters of such relationships. New parents typically make amends and resolve to stay together for the sake of their child. When surveyed just after a child's birth, eight in ten unmarried parents say they are still together, and most plan to stay together and raise the child.

Promoting marriage among the poor has become the new war on poverty, Bush style. And it is true that the correlation between marital status and child poverty is strong. But poor single mothers already believe in marriage. Jen insists that she will walk down the aisle one day, though she admits it might not be with Rick. And demographers still project that more than seven in ten women who had a child outside of marriage will eventually wed someone. First, though, Jen wants to get a good job, finish school, and get her son out of Kensington.

Most poor, unmarried mothers and fathers readily admit that bearing children while poor and unmarried is not the ideal way to do things. Jen believes the best time to become a mother is "after you're out of school and you got a job, at least, when you're like 21. . . . When you're ready to have kids, you should have everything ready, have your house, have a job, so when that baby comes, the baby can have its own room." Yet, given their

already limited economic prospects, the poor have little motivation to time their births as precisely as their middle-class counterparts do. The dreams of young people like Jen and Rick center on children at a time of life when their more affluent peers plan for college and careers. Poor girls coming of age in the inner city value children highly, anticipate them eagerly, and believe strongly that they are up to the job of mothering—even in difficult circumstances. Jen, for example, tells us, "People outside the neighborhood, they're like, 'You're 15! You're pregnant?' I'm like, it's none of their business. I'm gonna be able to take care of my kid. They have nothing to worry about." Jen says she has concluded that "some people . . . are better at having kids at a younger age. . . . I think it's better for some people to have kids younger."

When I Became a Mom

When we asked mothers like Jen what their lives would be like if they had not had children, we expected them to express regret over foregone opportunities for school and careers. Instead, most believe their children "saved" them. They describe their lives as spinning out of control before becoming pregnant—struggles with parents and peers, "wild," risky behavior, depression, and school failure. Jen speaks to this poignantly. "I was just real bad. I hung with a real bad crowd. I was doing pills. I was really depressed. . . . I was drinking. That was before I was pregnant. I think," she reflects, "if I never had a baby or anything, . . . I would still be doing the things I was doing. I would probably still be doing drugs. I'd probably still be drinking." Jen admits that when she first became pregnant, she was angry that she "couldn't be out no more. Couldn't be out with my friends. Couldn't do nothing." Now, though, she says, "I'm glad I have a son . . . because I would still be doing all that stuff."

Children offer poor youth like Jen a compelling sense of purpose. Jen paints a before-and-after picture of her life that was common among the mothers we interviewed. "Before, I didn't have nobody to take care of. I didn't have nothing left to go home for. . . . Now I have my son to take care of. I have him to go home for. . . . I don't have to go buy weed or drugs with my money. I could buy my son stuff with my money! . . . I have something to look up to now." Children also are a crucial source of relational intimacy, a self-made community of care. After a nasty fight with Rick, Jen recalls, "I was crying. My son came in the room. He was hugging me. He's 16 months and he was hugging me with his little arms. He was really cute and happy, so I got happy. That's one of the good things. When you're sad, the baby's always gonna be there for you no matter what." Lately she has been thinking a lot about what her life was like back then, before the baby. "I thought about the stuff before I became a mom, what my life was like back then. I used to see pictures of me, and I would hide in every picture. This baby did so much for me. My son did a lot for me. He helped me a lot. I'm thankful that I had my baby."

Around the time of the birth, most unmarried parents claim they plan to get married eventually. Rick did not propose marriage when Jen's first child

was born, but when she conceived a second time, at 17, Rick informed his dad, "It's time for me to get married. It's time for me to straighten up. This is the one I wanna be with. I had a baby with her, I'm gonna have another baby with her." Yet despite their intentions, few of these couples actually marry. Indeed, most break up well before their child enters preschool.

I'd Like to Get Married, But . . .

The sharp decline in marriage in impoverished urban areas has led some to charge that the poor have abandoned the marriage norm. Yet we found few who had given up on the idea of marriage. But like their elite counterparts, disadvantaged women set a high financial bar for marriage. For the poor, marriage has become an elusive goal—one they feel ought to be reserved for those who can support a "white picket fence" lifestyle: a mortgage on a modest row home, a car and some furniture, some savings in the bank, and enough money left over to pay for a "decent" wedding. Jen's views on marriage provide a perfect case in point. "If I was gonna get married, I would want to be married like my Aunt Nancy and my Uncle Pat. They live in the mountains. She has a job. My Uncle Pat is a state trooper; he has lots of money. They live in the [Poconos]. It's real nice out there. Her kids go to Catholic school. . . . That's the kind of life I would want to have. If I get married, I would have a life like [theirs]." She adds, "And I would wanna have a big wedding, a real nice wedding."

Unlike the women of their mothers' and grandmothers' generations, young women like Jen are not merely content to rely on a man's earnings. Instead, they insist on being economically "set" in their own right before taking marriage vows. This is partly because they want a partnership of equals, and they believe money buys say-so in a relationship. Jen explains, "I'm not gonna just get into marrying him and not have my own house! Not have a job! I still wanna do a lot of things before I get married. He [already] tells me I can't do nothing. I can't go out. What's gonna happen when I marry him? He's gonna say he owns me!"

Economic independence is also insurance against a marriage gone bad. Jen explains, "I want to have everything ready, in case something goes wrong. . . . If we got a divorce, that would be my house. I bought that house, he can't kick me out or he can't take my kids from me." "That's what I want in case that ever happens. I know a lot of people that happened to. I don't want it to happen to me." These statements reveal that despite her desire to marry, Rick's role in the family's future is provisional at best. "We get along, but we fight a lot. If he's there, he's there, but if he's not, that's why I want a job . . . a job with computers . . . so I could afford my kids, could afford the house. . . . I don't want to be living off him. I want my kids to be living off me."

Why is Jen, who describes Rick as "the love of my life," so insistent on planning an exit strategy before she is willing to take the vows she firmly believes ought to last "forever"? If love is so sure, why does mistrust seem

so palpable and strong? In relationships among poor couples like Jen and Rick, mistrust is often spawned by chronic violence and infidelity, drug and alcohol abuse, criminal activity, and the threat of imprisonment. In these tarnished corners of urban America, the stigma of a failed marriage is far worse than an out-of-wedlock birth. New mothers like Jen feel they must test the relationship over three, four, even five years' time. This is the only way, they believe, to ensure that their marriages will last.

Trust has been an enormous issue in Jen's relationship with Rick. "My son was born December 23rd, and [Rick] started cheating on me again . . . in March. He started cheating on me with some girl—Amanda. . . . Then it was another girl, another girl, another girl after. I didn't wanna believe it. My friends would come up to me and be like, 'Oh yeah, your boyfriend's cheating on you with this person.' I wouldn't believe it. . . . I would see him with them. He used to have hickies. He used to make up some excuse that he was drunk—that was always his excuse for everything." Things finally came to a head when Rick got another girl pregnant. "For a while, I forgave him for everything. Now, I don't forgive him for nothing." Now we begin to understand the source of Jen's hesitancy. "He wants me to marry him, [but] I'm not really sure. . . . If I can't trust him, I can't marry him, 'cause we would get a divorce. If you're gonna get married, you're supposed to be faithful!" she insists. To Jen and her peers, the worst thing that could happen is "to get married just to get divorced."

Given the economic challenges and often perilously low quality of the romantic relationships among unmarried parents, poor women may be right to be cautious about marriage. Five years after we first spoke with her, we met with Jen again. We learned that Jen's second pregnancy ended in a miscarriage. We also learned that Rick was out of the picture—apparently for good. "You know that bar [down the street?] It happened in that bar. . . . They were in the bar, and this guy was like badmouthing [Rick's friend] Mikey, talking stuff to him or whatever. So Rick had to go get involved in it and start with this guy. . . . Then he goes outside and fights the guy [and] the guy dies of head trauma. They were all on drugs, they were all drinking, and things just got out of control, and that's what happened. He got fourteen to thirty years."

These Are Cards I Dealt Myself

Jen stuck with Rick for the first two and a half years of his prison sentence, but when another girl's name replaced her own on the visitors' list, Jen decided she was finished with him once and for all. Readers might be asking what Jen ever saw in a man like Rick. But Jen and Rick operate in a partner market where the better-off men go to the better-off women. The only way for someone like Jen to forge a satisfying relationship with a man is to find a diamond in the rough or improve her own economic position so that she can realistically compete for more upwardly mobile partners, which is what Jen is trying to do now. "There's this kid, Donny, he works at my job. He

works on C shift. He's a supervisor! He's funny, three years older, and he's not a geek or anything, but he's not a real preppy good boy either. But he's not [a player like Rick] and them. He has a job, you know, so that's good. He doesn't do drugs or anything. And he asked my dad if he could take me out!"

These days, there is a new air of determination, even pride, about Jen. The aimless high school dropout pulls ten-hour shifts entering data at a warehouse distribution center Monday through Thursday. She has held the job for three years, and her aptitude and hard work have earned her a series of raises. Her current salary is higher than anyone in her household commands—$10.25 per hour, and she now gets two weeks of paid vacation, four personal days, 60 hours of sick time, and medical benefits. She has saved up the necessary $400 in tuition for a high school completion program that offers evening and weekend classes. Now all that stands between her and a diploma is a passing grade in mathematics, her least favorite subject. "My plan is to start college in January. [This month] I take my math test . . . so I can get my diploma," she confides.

Jen clearly sees how her life has improved since Rick's dramatic exit from the scene. "That's when I really started [to get better] because I didn't have to worry about what *he* was doing, didn't have to worry about him cheating on me, all this stuff. [It was] then I realized that I had to do what I had to do to take care of my son. . . . When he was there, I think that my whole life revolved around him, you know, so I always messed up somehow because I was so busy worrying about what *he* was doing. Like I would leave the [GED] programs I was in just to go home and see what he was doing. My mind was never concentrating." Now, she says, "a lot of people in my family look up to me now, because all my sisters dropped out from school, you know, nobody went back to school. I went back to school, you know? . . . I went back to school, and I plan to go to college, and a lot of people look up to me for that, you know? So that makes me happy . . . because five years ago nobody looked up to me. I was just like everybody else."

Yet the journey has not been easy. "Being a young mom, being 15, it's hard, hard, hard, you know." She says, "I have no life. . . . I work from 6:30 in the morning until 5:00 at night. I leave here at 5:30 in the morning. I don't get home until about 6:00 at night." Yet she measures her worth as a mother by the fact that she has managed to provide for her son largely on her own. "I don't depend on nobody. I might live with my dad and them, but I don't depend on them, you know." She continues, "There [used to] be days when I'd be so stressed out, like, 'I can't do this!' And I would just cry and cry and cry. . . . Then I look at Colin, and he'll be sleeping, and I'll just look at him and think I don't have no [reason to feel sorry for myself]. The cards I have I've dealt myself so I have to deal with it now. I'm older. I can't change anything. He's my responsibility—he's nobody else's but mine—so I have to deal with that."

Becoming a mother transformed Jen's point of view on just about everything. She says, "I thought hanging on the corner drinking, getting high—I thought that was a good life, and I thought I could live that way for

eternity, like sitting out with my friends. But it's not as fun once you have your own kid. . . . I think it changes [you]. I think, 'Would I want Colin to do that? Would I want my son to be like that?' It was fun to me but it's not fun anymore. Half the people I hung with are either. . . . Some have died from drug overdoses, some are in jail, and some people are just out there living the same life that they always lived, and they don't look really good. They look really bad." In the end, Jen believes, Colin's birth has brought far more good into her life than bad. "I know I could have waited [to have a child], but in a way I think Colin's the best thing that could have happened to me. . . . So I think I had my son for a purpose because I think Colin changed my life. He *saved* my life, really. My whole life revolves around Colin!"

Promises I Can Keep

There are unique themes in Jen's story—most fathers are only one or two, not five years older than the mothers of their children, and few fathers have as many glaring problems as Rick—but we heard most of these themes repeatedly in the stories of the 161 other poor, single mothers we came to know. Notably, poor women do not reject marriage; they revere it. Indeed, it is the conviction that marriage is forever that makes them think that divorce is worse than having a baby outside of marriage. Their children, far from being liabilities, provide crucial social-psychological resources—a strong sense of purpose and a profound source of intimacy. Jen and the other mothers we came to know are coming of age in an America that is profoundly unequal— where the gap between rich and poor continues to grow. This economic reality has convinced them that they have little to lose and, perhaps, something to gain by a seemingly "ill-timed" birth.

The lesson one draws from stories like Jen's is quite simple: Until poor young women have more access to jobs that lead to financial independence— until there is reason to hope for the rewarding life pathways that their privileged peers pursue—the poor will continue to have children far sooner than most Americans think they should, while still deferring marriage. Marital standards have risen for all Americans, and the poor want the same things that everyone now wants out of marriage. The poor want to marry too, but they insist on marrying well. This, in their view, is the only way to avoid an almost certain divorce. Like Jen, they are simply not willing to make promises they are not sure they can keep.

RECOMMENDED RESOURCES

Edin, Kathryn and Maria Kefalas. 2005. *Promises I Can Keep: Why Poor Women Put Motherhood before Marriage.* University of California Press.

Gibson, Christina, Kathryn Edin, and Sara McLanahan. 2004. "High Hopes but Even Higher Expectations: A Qualitative and Quantitative Analysis of the Marriage Plans of Unmarried Couples Who Are New Parents." Working Paper 03-06-FF, Center for Research on Child Well-being, Princeton University. Online at http://crcw.princeton.edu/workingpapers/WP03-06-FF-Gibson.pdf.

Hays, Sharon. 2003. *Flat Broke with Children: Women in the Age of Welfare Reform.* New York: Oxford University Press.

Lareau, Annette. 2003. *Unequal Childhoods: Class, Race, and Family Life.* Berkeley: University of California Press.

Nelson, Timothy J., Susan Clampet-Lundquist, and Kathryn Edin. 2002. "Fragile Fatherhood: How Low-Income, Non-custodial Fathers in Philadelphia Talk about Their Families." In *The Handbook of Father Involvement: Multidisciplinary Perspectives,* edited by Catherine Tamis-LeMonda and Natasha Cabrera. Mahwah, NJ: Lawrence Erlbaum Associates.

54

IS THERE HOPE FOR AMERICA'S LOW-INCOME CHILDREN?

LEE RAINWATER • TIMOTHY M. SMEEDING

Despite high rates of economic growth and improvements in the standard of living in industrialized nations throughout the twentieth century, a significant percentage of American children are still living in families so poor that normal health and growth are at risk (Duncan et al. 1998; Duncan and Brooks-Gunn 1997a, 1997b). The previous [research has] shown that it does not have to be this way: In many other countries child poverty afflicts only one-half to one-quarter as many children as in the United States.

These numbers are startling and worrisome. For more affluent nations, child poverty is not a matter of affordability—it is a matter of priority. This country made a commitment nearly sixty years ago to deal with old-age poverty, and that effort has been fairly successful (Burtless and Smeeding 2001). When we found ourselves discussing the large federal and state budget surpluses at the beginning of the twenty-first century, that was a period when we could have made a serious commitment to reduce child poverty in the United States. This opportunity was missed. Even [in 2003], with the economy in a brief recession, making a commitment to spend the modest amount of money it would take to bring about a large reduction in child poverty is well within our grasp. Of course, such a policy would need to conform to American values (market work and self-reliance), utilize American social institutions (such as the income tax system), and continue the successful antipoverty efforts of the 1990s, such as the Earned Income Tax Credit.

Consider tax policy for a moment. There are progressive substitutes for the recent 2001–2002 regressive federal income tax reductions that would shore up income support for the working poor. For instance, as part of an expanded tax reduction plan, we could make the child tax credit refundable for working families with no federal income tax obligations; these families do pay Social Security and Medicare taxes, of course. Similarly, we could expand the Earned Income Tax Credit and link it to the child tax credit (Sawicky and Cherry 2001). These modest measures would be relatively inexpensive and effective first steps in the process of further reducing child poverty for the working poor.

While such changes are meant to be suggestive, our study underlines the need for a comprehensive policy to reduce child poverty rates and improve the well-being of children. Policymakers committed to reducing child poverty must address each of the six problem areas (employment, parental leave, child care, child-related tax policy, child support, and education) identified in this [reading]. And they must also consider the much smaller number of children living in families with no parent who can work.

Employment

The most important step in reducing poverty among children is to ensure that at least one parent is employed. In particular, the labor market position of mothers needs to be improved, as their earnings are crucial for maintaining an adequate standard of living in a society where two-income families dominate. Obviously, this is doubly true for single parents, where subsidized child care is an absolute necessity for employment.

In low-wage, high-employment societies such as the United States, employment is both a virtue and a challenge. Working mothers feel better about themselves when they are employed, and children feel better about their parents when they are employed (Chase-Lansdale et al. 2003). However, low-skill employment is almost always low-paying, sometimes requires working nonstandard hours, can involve long commutes, and is vulnerable to layoffs when the economy turns down. Thus, while employment is important, it needs to be supported by flexibility in work schedules and other public support services (Haveman 2003). For two-parent families, some mixture of these policies will suffice. For single parents who must act as both provider and caretaker, employment must be coordinated with their children's needs. To be successfully employed, parents, especially mothers, need state support to facilitate that employment. The evidence is that low-income American single mothers work more hours than single mothers in any other nation (Osberg 2002). The evidence is also clear that American single mothers receive the least income support of any nation's low-income mothers (Smeeding 2003). American policymakers therefore must find a better mix of income support and work that makes all working single parents nonpoor (see also Gornick and Meyers 2003).

Parental Leave, Child Care Subsidy, and Child Support

In many cases, parents—particularly mothers—need state support to enable them to work and to adequately take care of their children. The development of parental leave programs, guarantees for child support not paid by absent parents, and affordable child care are important conditions for keeping mothers in the full-time workforce and preventing poverty among their children. Child support enforcement measures are important and have become more successful over the past decade. But their potential for reducing child poverty is limited, since many of the parents who fail to pay child support are low earners themselves. The policy design issue is to find a public way to ensure child support, while not reducing the efforts that absent parents make to support their children.

The United States has lagged in these areas in all dimensions: our family leave is not universal and is, in fact, relatively short and unsubsidized; we have no child support insurance to protect single mothers from absent fathers who do not pay their obligated child support; and our child care support system helps the rich more than it helps the poor, despite many recent welfare reform–related efforts to expand child care subsidies for low-income parents (Gornick and Meyers 2003; Ross 1999).

According to the evidence presented [in other research], Sweden has low child poverty rates not only because of unique cultural characteristics but because as a society it has integrated women—mothers in general and single mothers in particular—into its labor force. In its configuration of welfare state policies, Sweden has traditionally stressed the importance of women's continued attachment to the labor market and supported them as wage earners by providing child care, a good parental leave program, and a comprehensive system of child care support.

Adequate parental leave programs and child care provisions are clearly important conditions for keeping mothers in full-time employment. For instance, the increased availability in the United Kingdom of child care, maternity leave, and more family-friendly corporate policies has increased the employment continuity of British women around the time of childbirth and thus reduced the indirect cost of children to their parents (Davies and Joshi 2001). It is also reported that British women can increasingly afford to make use of child care services. However, the direct cost of child care services still proves to be too high for women with smaller earnings potential. This is one of the main reasons why British women with low earnings potential, as well as those with middle earnings potential and more than one child, are more likely to stay home (see, for example, Meyers et al. 2001).

Child Care

Clearly, the introduction of comprehensive child care provisions should be complemented by measures that would make it possible for women with lower earnings potential to make use of these services. The greater the cost

of child care services relative to the mother's wage potential, the less likely it is that she will seek employment. It is therefore important to expand public support for child care services that reduces the direct cost of those services, with direct subsidies and also with indirect support through refundable child care tax credits, which would (partially) compensate low-income families' remaining expenditures for this type of service.

In 1989 the European Commission published a "Communication from the Commission on Family Policies" that underlined the importance of affordable, accessible, and high-quality child care arrangements to member states' efforts to increase the labor participation of women (European Commission 1989; Kamerman and Kahn 2001). The British government's 1998 green paper "Meeting the Childcare Challenge" (United Kingdom 1998) contains several proposals for improving access to child care in Britain that are now being implemented. Clearly, the lack of affordable child care support is not a uniquely American problem, but it does cripple efforts by single parents in this country to find steady employment and make work economically viable.

Many governments seem to have understood the need for such measures. According to Sheila Kamerman and Alfred Kahn (2001), child care services continued to increase in supply during the 1990s in most nations, including the United States. Many governments have extended existing parental leave policies, and these policies were even introduced for the first time in a few other countries. In 1998 President Clinton pushed an initiative to improve child care for working families that would have made child care more affordable in various ways and doubled the number of children receiving child care subsidies to more than two million by the year 2003. Unfortunately, most elements of the proposal were not enacted into law. The expansion of affordable child care services was still on the political agenda in 2003, but the recession from 2001 to 2003 forced many state governments to cut back on child care services and subsidies in the face of rising state government deficits. While child care subsidies continued, even during the recession, for many single parents who were leaving welfare, support was more generally needed for parents in families who had already left welfare and become independent of the welfare system.

Parental Leave

Parental leave policy is another area where much could be done. In 2000, Canada instituted paid family leave as a national policy, and Australia did the same in 2003. In the United States, where unpaid family leave is very short and still unpaid, California has made a first step by instituting a paid family leave policy for some workers. Other states are likely to follow suit. The actions of these states may pave the way toward a more effective and expansive federal policy in the near future (Gornick and Meyers 2003; Ross 1999).

Parental leave programs and comprehensive and affordable child care services represent, of course, only some of the policy measures needed to

integrate mothers into the workforce. Improving the skills of low-skilled workers (often women), job counseling, the removal of various structural obstacles (such as unemployment traps), and transportation assistance are also important initiatives that would make it easier for mothers to work full-time.

Child Support

The provision of steady, reliable child support is another important element of the semiprivate safety net in the United States and elsewhere. It is a widely held value that parents should support their children. The problem in doing so is often that absent fathers cannot or do not pay, owing to weak enforcement of child care laws or low earnings capacity. While significant progress has been made in upgrading child support enforcement for divorced mothers, much still remains to be accomplished for unmarried mothers (Ellwood and Blank 2001). Enforcement is uneven across states, paternity establishment by unwed mothers varies greatly across states, and often the fathers of the children of unwed mothers do not earn enough to support themselves, much less their children.

In Europe a different set of values prevails. The well-being of the child and the mother is usually the foremost value, and the absent father's willingness and ability to pay are of secondary concern. In these countries full child support is guaranteed by governments when absent fathers cannot or will not pay (Skevik 1998). While universal guaranteed child support on the European level would not fit American values, a more modest system might be achievable. When the custodial mother has established paternity and the absent father is deemed unable to pay (owing to imprisonment, unemployment, or low wages), a modest level of guaranteed child support—say, $2,000 per year for a first child and $1,500 for a second—could be a very important source of steady support for a single mother who is not otherwise receiving such aid. Similarly, states could increase the dollar amount of child support allowed to "pass through" to mothers receiving Temporary Assistance to Needy Families (TANF) without penalty, a measure that would increase the monthly amount received by the mother to $150 or $250, rather than only the first $50, which is the norm.

Child-Related Income Tax Policy

The minimum wage is insufficient to meet the income needs of working families with children. Full-time work at the current minimum wage leaves a family of three far below the poverty line, and the Earned Income Tax Credit does not fully close the gap. If we continue to pursue this policy line, additional child-related tax benefits are necessary to ensure that working families with children are not poor. Making families headed by parents with low earnings potential more dependent on market income is not sufficient

to end child poverty in a period of increased earnings inequality and slack labor markets (Haveman 2003). Earnings are often not sufficient to protect households with children from poverty, and although children living in two-parent dual-earner families are far less likely to be poor, poverty rates among children living in working single-parent families remain very high in the United States.

In recent years several countries have introduced or increased minimum wages, but these often remain insufficient to keep households with children out of poverty. Governments are reluctant to further increase the minimum-wage levels in their countries because they risk aggravating the unemployment problem faced by low-skilled workers. The "living wage" laws, which pay hourly wages of seven to nine dollars per hour to governmental contractors in some parts of the United States, are rarely applied to the private sector for this same reason—many fewer employees will be hired at this level of labor cost. Since the expansion of low-wage work might improve the job prospects of less-educated workers and make it easier for single-earner households to acquire a second income, we do not advocate significantly higher minimum wages, and certainly not "living wages" for all U.S. workers. It is clear, however, that many governments should do more to support the working poor when wages are insufficient to keep a family from becoming poor. The United States EITC is one important way to supplement earnings and help working families meet their financial responsibilities. However, it does not always guarantee that a family will avoid poverty (Moffitt 2002).

There is evidence of an increasing role for refundable tax credits in the support given to low-income working-age households in other nations as well. Many OECD countries offer social tax breaks and allowances to replace cash benefits, although they tend to be less important in countries with relatively high direct tax levies, such as Denmark, Finland, the Netherlands, and Sweden. In Germany, the value of tax allowances for the cost incurred in raising children alone amounted to almost 0.6 percent of the German GDP in 1993 (Adema and Einerhand 1998). Both the Netherlands and the United Kingdom have specific tax subsidies for single-parent families, and, as we mentioned before, many countries also use tax credits to compensate these families for expenditures such as child care costs. Yet we must emphasize that such measures have less effect on the incomes of families with earnings that are too low to fully benefit from them. It is therefore important that tax credits for child care and similar measures aimed at families with low earnings be made refundable.

In addition to the EITC, the American income tax system contains a set of tax credits that are partially refundable, but not to low-income parents who do not make enough to pay federal income tax. The several plans that have been proposed to integrate these two programs would produce a single family tax credit with more benefit adequacy and lower work disincentives than in the phase-down regime of the EITC (Cherry and Sawicky 2000; Sawicky and Cherry 2001). Adoption of these programs would give a well-targeted boost to the incomes of working poor parents.

Investment in a Socially-Oriented Education Policy

Central to the promotion of employment in a knowledge-based society is quality education for all children, regardless of their financial situation or their health. Such policies could reduce the likelihood that child poverty is passed on from generation to generation (Gregg and Machin 2001; Büchel et al. 2001). A special effort needs to be made to target education resources to the areas where they can do the most good for poor children in bad schools and to prepare low-income children for elementary school more generally. It is the responsibility of every democracy to provide an equal opportunity from birth for every child. We sorely need to give increased attention to the quality of schooling in low-income areas and develop better and more widespread preschool programs in low-income areas if we are to increase the chances of reducing adult poverty among the next generation of children. Making schools more accountable may be a partial answer to this need, but the legislation entitled "Leave No Child Behind" is insufficient by itself to reach this goal (Smeeding 2002).

An American Income Support Package for Families with Children

The previous six policy arenas can be drawn together into a benefit or "income" package that includes a role for the state, for the family, and for work, and a package that conforms to American values. Clearly, work alone is not enough to guarantee escape from poverty for low-income working families, especially single parents (Haveman 2003). The EITC is a good step, but it is not enough by itself to reach the goal. Additional refundable tax credits, subsidized child care, guaranteed child support (for those who meet specified criteria), and paid family leave must also be woven into the policy mix. This combination of work and benefits should increase the incomes and well-being of children whose mothers work. And both low-income students and their schools need to be better prepared to advance and thrive.

Policy efforts must be redoubled to meet the needs of mothers who cannot work and of households with no workers. Perhaps the answer lies in disability policy—for example, through the Supplemental Security Income (SSI) program. We will not delve into these issues here, except to say that the remaining TANF caseload (about two million households as of early 2003) is a manageable issue that could be tackled by a reauthorization of welfare reform targeted not only at removing these last welfare recipients from the rolls but at meeting their divergent and serious human needs.

Finding the Will Is Finding the Way

The findings [of our research] underline the need for a comprehensive policy to reduce child poverty rates and improve the well-being of children.

Human capital concerns in industrialized countries offer an overwhelming and very practical case for adequate investment in succeeding generations. Especially in the affluent economies of the industrialized world, there are no valid economic excuses for high child poverty rates. We can all afford low child poverty rates.

But no two countries can fight poverty in exactly the same way. Each nation's policies must fit its own national culture and values. Thus, the policy suggestions made here must be hewn together into a system of child poverty reduction that will work in the United States. Moreover, these policies cannot simply be taken off the shelf and plugged in. It takes political leadership to make such policies national priorities and to make programs mesh in a supportive fashion.

In recent years Prime Minister Tony Blair of the United Kingdom has shown that when a nation makes a commitment to reduce child poverty, much can be accomplished (see, for example, Bradshaw 2001; Walker and Wiseman 2001). Since 1997 the Blair government has spent an additional 0.9 percent of GDP (about $1,900 per family) on poor families with children (Hills 2002). An equivalent degree of effort in the United States would cost $90 billion. The high poverty rates of the late 1990s in the United Kingdom are now being gradually reduced (Bradshaw 2001; Hills 2002). Unfortunately, not all countries share this priority, particularly not the United States (Danziger 2001; Smeeding 2002).

The American social assistance system has now achieved a primary goal: increasing work and reducing welfare dependence for low-income mothers. Fewer than five million persons (two million cases) remain dependent on TANF benefits. The "welfare problem" is no longer. However, as welfare rolls have been trimmed, corresponding decreases in child poverty have not been achieved because market income alone is not enough to bring about serious reductions in child poverty. The United States needs to make this goal a top priority for its political agenda. Even a commitment of $45 billion—half the effort of the Blair government—could at least partially fund most of the policy options listed in this [reading]. The integrity of our democratic values will be ensured and the cultural and economic fabric of our society enriched when we can say that many fewer children grow up poor in America.

REFERENCES

Adema, William and Marcel Einerhand. 1998. "The Growing Role of Private Social Benefits." Labor Market and Social Policy Occasional Paper No. 32. Paris: Organization for Economic Cooperation and Development, April 17.

Bradshaw, Jonathon. 2001. "Child Poverty under Labour." In *An End in Sight?: Tackling Child Poverty in the United Kingdom,* edited by Geoff Fimister. London: Child Poverty Action Group.

Büchel, Felix, Joachim R. Frick, Peter Krause, and Gert G. Wagner. 2001. "The Impact of Poverty on Children's School Attendance: Evidence from West Germany." In *Child Well-Being, Child Poverty, and Child Policy in Modern Nations: What Do We Know?,* edited by Koen Vleminckx and Timothy M. Smeeding. Bristol, England: Policy Press.

Burtless, Gary and Timothy M. Smeeding. 2001. "The Level, Trend, and Composition of Poverty." In *Understanding Poverty,* edited by Sheldon H. Danziger and Robert G. Haveman. New York and Cambridge, MA: Russell Sage Foundation and Harvard University Press.

Chase-Lansdale, P. Lindsay, Robert A. Moffitt, Brenda J. Lohman, Andrew J. Cherlin, Rebekah Levine Coley, Laura D. Pittman, Jennifer Roff, and Elizabeth Votruba-Drzal. 2003. "Mothers' Transitions from Welfare to Work and the Well-Being of Preschoolers and Adolescents." *Science* 299 (March): 1548–52.

Cherry, Robert and Max B. Sawicky. 2000. "Giving Tax Credit Where Credit Is Due: A 'Universal Unified Child Credit' That Expands the EITC and Cuts Taxes for Working Families." Briefing Paper. Washington, DC: Economic Policy Institute (April). Available at www.cpinet.org/briefingpapers/EITC_BP.pdf.

Danziger, Sheldon H. 2001. "After Welfare Reform and an Economic Boom: Why Is Child Poverty Still So Much Higher in the United States than in Europe?" Presented to the Eighth Foundation for International Studies on Social Security (FISS) Conference on Support for Children and Their Parents: Why's, Ways, Effects, and Policy. Sigtuna, Sweden (June).

Davies, Hugh and Heather Joshi. 2001. "Who Has Borne the Cost of Britain's Children in the 1990s?" In *Child Well-Being, Child Poverty, and Child Policy in Modern Nations: What Do We Know?*, edited by Koen Vleminckx and Timothy M. Smeeding. Bristol, England: Policy Press.

Duncan, Greg J. and Jeanne Brooks-Gunn, eds. 1997a. *The Consequences of Growing Up Poor.* New York: Russell Sage Foundation.

———. 1997b. "Income Effects across the Life Span: Integration and Interpretation." In *The Consequences of Growing Up Poor,* edited by Greg J. Duncan and Jeanne Brooks-Gunn. New York: Russell Sage Foundation.

Duncan, Greg J., Wei-Jun J. Yeung, Jeanne Brooks-Gunn, and Judith Smith. 1998. "How Much Does Childhood Poverty Affect the Life Chances of Children?" *American Sociological Review* 63 (3, June): 406–23.

Ellwood, David and Rebecca Blank. 2001. "The Clinton Legacy for America's Poor." Research Working Paper No. RWP01-028. Cambridge, MA: Harvard University, Kennedy School of Government (July).

European Commission. 1989. "Communication from the Commission on Family Policies (COM [89] 363 final)." *Social Europe: Official Journal of the European Communities* 1 (94): 121–29.

Gornick, Janet and Marcia K. Meyers. 2003. *Families That Work: Policies for Reconciling Parenthood and Employment.* New York: Russell Sage Foundation.

Gregg, Paul and Stephen Machin. 2001. "Child Experiences, Educational Attainment, and Adult Labor Market Performance." In *Child Well-Being, Child Poverty, and Child Policy in Modern Nations: What Do We Know?*, edited by Koen Vleminckx and Timothy M. Smeeding. Bristol, England: Policy Press.

Haveman, Robert. 2003. "When Work Alone Is Not Enough." *LaFollette Policy Report* 13 (2): 1–15.

Hills, John. 2002. "The Blair Government and Child Poverty: An Extra One Percent for Children in the United Kingdom." London School of Economics. Unpublished paper.

Kamerman, Sheila B. and Alfred J. Kahn. 2001. "Child and Family Policies in an Era of Social Policy Retrenchment and Restructuring." In *Child Well-Being, Child Poverty, and Child Policy in Modern Nations: What Do We Know?*, edited by Koen Vleminckx and Timothy M. Smeeding. Bristol, England: Policy Press.

Meyers, Marcia K., Janet C. Gornick, Laura R. Peck, and Amanda J. Lockshin. 2001. "Public Policies That Support Families with Young Children: Variation across U.S. States." In *Child Well-Being, Child Poverty, and Child Policy in Modern Nations: What Do We Know?*, edited by Koen Vleminckx and Timothy M. Smeeding. Bristol, England: Policy Press.

Moffitt, Robert. 2002. "From Welfare to Work: What the Evidence Shows." Welfare Reform and Beyond 13. Washington, DC: Brookings Institution (January).

Osberg, Lars. 2002. "Time, Money, and Inequality in International Perspective." Luxembourg Income Study Working Paper No. 334. Syracuse, NY: Syracuse University, Maxwell School of Citizenship and Public Affairs, Center for Policy Research (November).

Ross, Katherin. 1999. "Labor Pains: Maternity Leave Policy and the Labor Supply and Economic Vulnerability of Recent Mothers." Ph.D. dissertation, Syracuse University.

Sawicky, Max B. and Robert Cherry. 2001. "Making Work Pay with Tax Reform." Issue Brief No. 173. Washington, DC: Economic Policy Institute (December 21). Available at www.epinet.org/Issuebriefs/ib173/ib173.pdf.

Skevik, Anne. 1998. "The State–Parent–Child Relationship after Family Break-Ups: Child Maintenance in Norway and Great Britain." In *The State of Social Welfare, 1997: International Studies on Social Insurance and Retirement, Employment, Family Policy, and Health Care,* edited by Peter Flora, Philip R. de Jong, Julian Le Grand, and Jun-Young Kim. London: Ashgate.

Smeeding, Timothy M. 2002. "No Child Left Behind?" *Indicators* 1 (3): 6–30, 67.

———. 2003. "Real Standards of Living and Public Support for Children: A Cross-National Comparison." Presented at the Bocconi Workshop on Income Distribution and Welfare, Milan, Italy, May 30, 2002. Revised January 2003.

United Kingdom. Department for Education and Skills. 1998. "Meeting the Child Care Challenge." National Child Care Strategy Green Paper. London: Department for Education and Skills (May). Available at www.dfes.gov.uk/childcare.

Walker, Robert and Michael Wiseman. 2001. "The House That Jack Built." *Milken Institute Review* (Fourth Quarter): 52–62.